# WORLD POLITICS

From the war on terror to the global financial crisis, traditional concepts of world politics are being challenged on a daily basis. In these uncertain times, the study of international relations and the forces that shape them have never been more important. Written specifically for students who are approaching this subject for the first time, *World Politics* is the most accessible, coherent and up-to-date account of the field available. It covers the historical backdrop to today's political situations, the complex interactions of states and non-state actors, the role of political economy, human security in all its forms, and the ways in which culture, religion and identity influence events. *World Politics* takes a new approach that challenges traditional interpretations, and will equip students with the knowledge and the confidence needed to tackle the big issues.

**Professor Jeffrey Haynes** is Associate Head of Department, Research and Postgraduate Studies, and Director of the Centre for the Study of Religion, Conflict and Cooperation, London Metropolitan University. He is the author of twenty-six books, including *Religion and Democratisations* (Routledge, 2010) and *An Introduction to International Politics and Religion* (Longman, 2007).

**Dr Peter Hough** is a Senior Lecturer in International Relations based at Middlesex University, where he is the head of subject. His previous publications include *The Global Politics of Pesticides* (Earthscan, 1998) and *Understanding Global Security* (Routledge, 2008).

**Dr Shahin Malik** is a Senior Lecturer in International Relations based at London Metropolitan University. His core research and teaching interests are in International Relations theory and international security and his publications include *Peacekeeping and the United Nations* (Dartmouth, 1996) and *Deconstructing and Reconstructing the Cold War* (Ashgate, 1999).

**Professor Lloyd Pettiford** is Associate Dean of the School of Arts and Humanities, Nottingham Trent University. His research interests lie in International Relations theory, and he is the co-author of *An Introduction to International Relations Theory* (Longman, 2010).

# WORLD POLITICS

**Jeffrey Haynes**
London Metropolitan University

**Peter Hough**
Middlesex University

**Shahin Malik**
London Metropolitan University

**Lloyd Pettiford**
Nottingham Trent University

**Longman**
is an imprint of

**PEARSON**

Harlow, England • London • New York • Boston • San Francisco • Toronto
Sydney • Tokyo • Singapore • Hong Kong • Seoul • Taipei • New Delhi
Cape Town • Madrid • Mexico City • Amsterdam • Munich • Paris • Milan

**Pearson Education Limited**
Edinburgh Gate
Harlow
Essex CM20 2JE
England

and Associated Companies throughout the world

*Visit us on the World Wide Web at:*
www.pearsoned.co.uk

First published 2011

ISBN: 978-1-4082-0492-4

**British Library Cataloguing-in-Publication Data**
A catalogue record for this book is available from the British Library

**Library of Congress Cataloging-in-Publication Data**
World politics : international relations and globalisation in the 21st century /
Jeffrey Haynes . . . [et al.]. – 1st ed.
    p.   cm.
  ISBN 978-1-4082-0492-4 (pbk.)
  1. International relations.   2. World politics–21st century.   I. Haynes, Jeffrey.
  JZ1242.W695   2011
                                                                    2010034351

10  9  8  7  6  5  4  3  2  1
14  13  12  11

Typeset in 10/14pt Minion by 35
Printed and bound by Graficas Estella, Spain

# Brief Contents

# Contents

## Supporting resources

Visit **www.pearsoned.co.uk/Haynes** to find valuable online resources

- **Video case studies**: Analyse recent world events by watching streaming video from major news providers
- **Current events quiz**: Master the headlines in this review of the week's most important news
- **Simulations**: Play the role of an IR decision-maker and experience how IR concepts work in practice
- **Mapping exercises**: Interactive maps examine important world events and test your knowledge
- **Flashcard glossaries**: Check your understanding of the key terms
- **PowerPoints (for lecturers)**: Key information from the book for classroom use

**Also**: The Companion Website provides the following features:

- Search tool to help locate specific items of content
- E-mail results and profile tools to send results of quizzes to instructors
- Online help and support to assist with website usage and troubleshooting

For more information please contact your local Pearson Education sales representative or visit **www.pearsoned.co.uk/Haynes**

# List of boxes and case studies

# List of tables

# Guided tour

**Learning outcomes** outline the aims and objectives of each chapter.

**Box features** provide interesting asides and point the way to opportunities for further study.

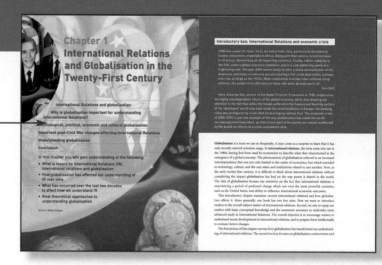

**Case studies** apply IR concepts to real-world events and encourage you to reflect on what you've learned so far.

**End-of-chapter questions** challenge you to reflect on what you've learned and develop your knowledge.

**Further reading** guides recommend the books that can help you achieve a better grade.

## Visit www.pearsoned.co.uk/haynes to access the following resources*:

**Video cases** provided by major news organisations analyse important world events.

**Financial Times** news feeds provide up-to-date coverage, ensuring that you're never behind with the latest developments.

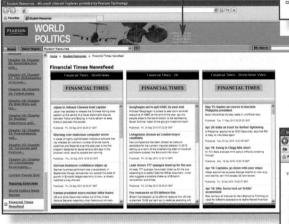

**Interactive simulations** put you in the role of an IR decision-maker and help you to understand how theory relates to practice.

**The current events quiz**, updated regularly, will help you master the headlines.

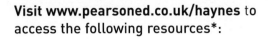

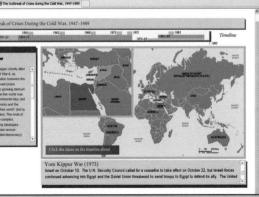

**Mapping exercises** don't just test your knowledge of geography – they're also interactive tools that illustrate the historical forces that have shaped our world.

**\* You will need to register using the access card packaged with this book**

# Preface

Any study of the world is fraught with complications and global politics is characterised by a high degree of confusion and complexity. Any textbook dealing with the international system has to be accessible, but it also has to be detailed enough to enable students from a wide variety of backgrounds and interests to draw on it for information. It was with these two objectives in mind that we began this mammoth project and now, as we reach its final stages, we strongly believe that these goals have been achieved. This book has been written with you – the student of World Politics – in mind, and it has been designed to make your life easier as you pursue your educational goals – whatever they may be.

There are nearly two hundred **sovereign** states in the world, and their governments and representatives interact with each other in a variety of ways. Into this mix we must also include countless institutions – governmental and non-governmental – thereby complicating the international environment even further. Presidents, prime ministers, foreign ministers, trade ministers and diplomats regularly communicate, co-operate and come into conflict with counterparts in other states on various issues, some of which we see in the media and many we do not. This situation has, of course, existed for centuries and questions of commerce, conquest and war have long been the concerns of governing elites and the people directly involved. This formal, **intergovernmental**, politics is complex enough but it is far from the whole picture. Through the phenomenon of **globalisation**, whereby sovereign states are increasingly interlinked by communications advances and common economic and political interests, intergovernmental interactions have multiplied and, at the same time, informal international economic, political and social interactions between 'ordinary people' (the non-governmental aspects) have increased.

Given the immense importance of globalisation, the book begins by providing an overview of this phenomenon. The opening chapters will equip you with the conceptual knowledge necessary to understand the nature of contemporary globalisation and its relationship to international relations. Part 2 then provides a set of historical chapters which highlight the key events and profound changes which occurred in the international system during the twentieth century. Chapter 5, for example, analyses the dramatic changes which occurred after the end of the Cold War in 1989 and shows how globalisation has been closely connected to the events since then. Making sense of the complexity of world politics requires the development of theories to explain and account for the behaviour of the actors (whether they be states or non-state actors such as international organisations). However, there is far more to international relations than avidly reading the news or knowing the names of Presidents (it is a constant source of irritation to us when people think this is all we do!) and that is where theory comes in. This is the theme of Part 3.

As well as increasing the prominence of the perennial concerns of IR, globalisation has brought on to the agenda of world politics issues previously not thought of as the stuff of foreign policy and diplomacy. Government ministers dealing with their country's financial, agricultural, environmental or legal administration have to do so with increasing reference to what is happening elsewhere in the world. One manifestation of this is the rise of intergovernmental organisations (such as the European Union or the United Nations), a theme which receives attention in Part 4 of this book. Globalisation has made topics such as human rights, land use and poverty the stuff of World Politics as well as domestic concerns, as government interests coincide or clash and non-government actors (such as pressure groups) propel them onto the international political agenda. These global issues are explored in Part 5. The discipline of International Relations covers a vast array of topics, but at its core we always find the issue of security and, although questions relating to war and peace are as old as humanity, they are complicated by globalisation. This element is the basis of the chapters in Part 6, where you will see that defining security as 'protection' is insufficient and that we must ask additional questions such as security from what, security for whom, how is that security to be provided and who is responsible for providing it? Finally, the theme of the concluding chapter is where globalisation may take world politics in the future.

The purpose of this book is to facilitate your studies, and we suggest you use it as follows:

- There are many chapters on topics which are likely to be covered on your course. There's no need to read the book from cover to cover.
- The index and a glossary will help you to gather specific information; this book may come in handy when you are doing other reading.
- Take a look at the website or at some of the other sources recommended.
- Do not worry if what you read here is not exactly the same as you find in other books or in your lectures. Understanding the world is no simple matter, and international relations is characterised by confusion and complexity.
- Ultimately, talking about what you read will be crucial to developing your own specific view of international relations.

There is no magic bullet to help in the understanding of international relations. However, to the extent that this book can provide a safety blanket, we hope it will be many students' first text and thereafter a reference point of value at all levels of study.

Jeff Haynes, Peter Hough, Shahin Malik, Lloyd Pettiford

# Acknowledgements

## Authors' acknowledgements

Writing this book has not been easy and it would be impossible to list all of those who have suffered in any way as our moods have been affected by deadlines and feedback. However, we should thank all those at Pearson – whether we have met them or not – for the backing they have given to this project. Paul Stevens has been foremost among these people and can stand as representative for all those affected by the writing of the book and all at Pearson. His line by line reading of the text has undoubtedly improved it immeasurably; any perceived errors and omissions remain, of course, the fault of the authors. We should also thank the anonymous reviewers who have performed a similar task, although unlike Paul, they have not had to deal with our initially grumpy responses.

In offering a list of others to thank, we run the risk of missing people out. Accordingly, with apologies to any such people, specific personal thanks are offered as follows (alphabetical order): Kate Ahl, Caroline Arnold, Tunc Aybak, James Booth, Angela Brown, Heather Deegan, Thomas Diez, Emma Foster, Fiona Gannon, Lisa Hough, Daisy Hough, Rosie Hough, Dave Humphreys, Malika Lakbiach, Phillip Langeskov, Rashmi Patel, Jill Steans and Paul Stevens.

## Publisher's acknowledgements

We are grateful to the following for permission to reproduce copyright material:

**Maps**
Map on page xxviii from Asia-Pacific Economic Cooperation; Maps on pages xxvi, xxix, xxx, xxxi, xxxiii, xxxiv, xxxvi and xxxvii from www.maps.com; Map on page xxviii from The global north and south, http://www.nationsonline.org/bilder/third_world_map.jpg, Nations Online Project.

**Tables**
Table 15.1 from European and regional integration (Christiansen, T.), *The Globalization of World Politics: An Introduction to International Relations*, pp. 495–518 (Baylis, J. and Smith, S. (eds) 2001), by permission of Oxford University Press; Table 18.1 from Human Development Report, 2007/08, http://hdr.undp.org/en/, published 2007, reproduced with permission of Palgrave Macmillan.

**Text**
Box 3.2 from The World War I Document Archive, http://wwi.lib.byu.edu/index.php/President_Wilson%27s_Fourteen_Points, World War I Document Archive online, courtesy Brigham Young University Library; Newspaper headline on page 531 from UK role in torture of British citizens in Pakistan condemned, *The Guardian*, 24/11/2009 (Cobain, I.), copyright Guardian News & Media Ltd 2009.

In some instances we have been unable to trace the owners of copyright material, and we would appreciate any information that would enable us to do so.

## Picture Credits

The publisher would like to thank the following for their kind permission to reproduce their photographs:

(Key: b-bottom; c-centre; l-left; r-right; t-top)

**Alamy Images:** Caro 100; **Bridgeman Art Library Ltd:** National Gallery, London 28, Private Collection 81tc, 118; **Corbis:** 122, Bettman 221, Sygma 660, Wally McNamee 138; **International Court of Justice:** Jeroen Bouman – Courtesy of the ICJ 248; **Detroitderek Photography:** 183; **Getty Images:** 2–3, 4, 10, 15, 26, 112–113, 114, 132, 152, 172, 190, 212, 268, 318–319, 320, 342, 360, 378, 382, 400, 416, 420, 421, 442, 466, 505, 515, 581, 628, 636, AFP 145, 193, 205, 226, 284, 299, 307, 345, 443, 533, 574, 680–681, 682, AFP 145, 193, 205, 226, 284, 299, 307, 345, 443, 533, 574, 680–681, 682, Altrendo 164, Barcroft Media 494, Bridgeman Art Library 54, Daisy Gildardini 484, De Agnosti Picture Library 521, Eddie Gerald 394, Gallo Images 46–47, 48, 68, 90, Hulton Archive 653, Lambert 615, Matt Cardy 356, Peter Dazeley 337, Somos / Veer 232–233, 234, 254, 274, 296, Time & Life Pictures 60, 70, 177, 327; **Kobal Collection Ltd:** UMBRELLA / ROSENBLUM / VIRGIN FILMS 543; **Panos Pictures:** Chris Stowers 490–491, 492, 512, 530, 550, 572, 592, 610, 634, 658; **Press Association Images:** Binod Joshi / AP 460, Jane Mingay 674, Jerome Delay 427, Karel Prinsloo / AP 606, Mohammed Seeneen / AP 468; **Reuters:** David Mercado 389, Goran Tomasevic 362, Jim Young 437, Kamal Kishore 556, Luke MacGregor 407, Mike Segar 256, Sean Adir 93; **Rex Features:** Andrew Testa 235, Pete Lawson 685, Sipa Press 38; **RIA Novosti Photo Library:** Lenin Library, Moscow 155

All other images © Pearson Education

Every effort has been made to trace the copyright holders and we apologise in advance for any unintentional omissions. We would be pleased to insert the appropriate acknowledgement in any subsequent edition of this publication.

# Abbreviations

| | |
|---|---|
| ABMT | Anti-Ballistic Missile Treaty |
| ALC | African Liberation Committee |
| AKP | Adalet ve Kalkınma Partisi (Justice and Development Party Turkey) |
| APEC | Asia-Pacific Economic Cooperation |
| APRM | Africa Peer Review Mechanism |
| ASEAN | Association of South East Asian Nations |
| AU | African Union |
| BWS | Bretton Woods System |
| CAFOD | Catholic Agency For Overseas Development |
| CANFWZ | Central Asian Nuclear Free Weapon Zone |
| CEDAW | Convention on the Elimination of Discrimination Against Women |
| CERD | Committee on the Elimination of Racial Discrimination |
| CIS | Commonwealth of Independent States |
| COMCEC | Committee for Economic and Trade Cooperation |
| COMECON | Council for Mutual Economic Assistance |
| COMIAC | Committee for Information and Cultural Affairs |
| COMSTECH | Committee for Scientific and Technological Cooperation |
| CSS | Critical Security Studies |
| CSTO | Collective Security Treaty Organisation |
| DRC | Democratic Republic of Congo |
| EAM | National Liberation Front |
| EC | European Commission |
| ECHR | European Court of Human Rights |
| ECOWAS | Economic Community of West African States |
| ECSC | European Coal and Steel Community |
| EEC | European Economic Community |
| EFTA | European Free Trade Association |
| EMU | economic and monetary union |
| EO | Executive Outcomes |
| EPZ | export processing zones |
| EU | European Union |
| EURATOM | European Atomic Energy Community |
| FAO | Food and Agriculture Organisation |
| FARC | Revolutionary Armed Forces of Colombia |
| FDI | foreign direct investment |
| FLM | Free Lebanon Militia |
| FNLA | Frente Nacional de Libertação de Angola (National Front for the Liberation of Angola) |
| FTAA | Free Trade Area of the Americas |
| FTAAP | Free Trade Area of the Asia-Pacific |
| GATT | General Agreement on Tariffs and Trade |
| GCPF | Global Crop Protection Federation |
| GDP | Gross Domestic Product |
| HDI | Human Development Index |
| HST | Hegemonic Stability Theory |
| IAEA | International Atomic Energy Agency |
| IBRD | International Bank for Reconstruction and Development |
| ICBMs | Intercontinental Ballistic Missiles |
| ICC | International Criminal Court |
| ICFM | Islamic Conference of Foreign Ministers |
| ICISS | International Commission on Intervention and State Sovereignty |
| ICJ | International Court of Justice |
| IGO | intergovernmental organisation |
| ILC | International Law Commission |
| ILGA | International Lesbian, Gay, Bisexual, Trans and Intersex Association |
| ILO | International Labour Organisation |
| IMF | International Monetary Fund |
| INFT | Intermediate-Range Nuclear Forces Treaty |
| INGO | international non-governmental organisation |
| INPFL | Independent National Patriotic Front of Liberia |
| INTERFET | International Force for East Timor |
| IPE | International Political Economy |
| IR | International Relations |
| IRA | Irish Republican Army |
| ISPO | Institute for Social and Political Opinion |
| ITU | International Telegraph Union |
| ITUC | International Trade Union Confederation |
| IUCN | International Union for the conservation of Nature |
| IWC | International Whaling Commission |
| KFOR | Kosovo Force |
| KLA | Kosovo Liberation Army |

| | | | | |
|---|---|---|---|---|
| **LDC** | Less Developed Country | | **SALT** | Strategic Arms Limitation Talks |
| **LIEO** | Liberal International Economic Order | | **SAPs** | structural adjustment programmes |
| **LRA** | Lord's Resistance Army | | **SARS** | Severe Acute Respiratory Syndrome |
| **LURD** | Liberians United for Reconciliation and Democracy | | **SDI** | Strategic Defense Initiative |
| | | | **SDR** | Special Drawing Right |
| **MAD** | mutual assured destruction | | **SEA** | Single European Act |
| **MDGs** | Millennium Development Goals | | **SEATO** | South East Asian Treaty Organisation |
| **MERCOSUR** | El Mercado Común del Sur: Southern Common Market | | **SEM** | Single European Market |
| | | | **SLA** | South Lebanese Army |
| **MNCs** | multinational corporations | | **SLBM** | Submarine Launched Ballistic Missile Systems |
| **MODEL** | Movement for Democracy in Liberia | | | |
| **MPLA** | Movemento Popular de Libertação de Angola-Partido de Trabalho (Popular Movement for the Liberation of Angola) | | **SPLM/A** | Sudan People's Liberation Movement/Army |
| | | | **START** | Strategic Arms Reduction Treaty |
| **MR** | Massive Retaliation | | **TCG** | transnational citizen group |
| **NAAEC** | North American Agreement on Environmental Cooperation | | **TCS** | transnational civil society |
| | | | **TNC** | transnational corporation |
| **NAALC** | North American Agreement on Labor Cooperation | | **TWRA** | Third World Relief Agency |
| | | | **UN** | United Nations |
| **NAFTA** | North American Free Trade Agreement | | **UNAMIR** | United Nations Assistance Mission for Rwanda |
| **NAM** | Non-Aligned Movement | | | |
| **NATO** | North Atlantic Treaty Organisation | | **UNCTAD** | United Nations Conference on Trade and Development |
| **NEPAD** | New Partnership for Africa's Development | | | |
| | | | **UNDP** | United Nations Development Programme |
| **NIC** | Newly Industrialised Country | | **UNEF** | United Nations Emergency Force |
| **NIEO** | New International Economic Order | | **UNFPA** | United Nations Fund for Population Activities |
| **NLI** | Neo-Liberal Institutionism | | | |
| **NNPT** | Nuclear Non-Proliferation Treaty | | **UNGA** | United Nations General Assembly |
| **NPFL** | National Patriotic Front of Liberia | | **UNESCO** | United Nations Educational, Scientific and Cultural Organisation |
| **NWFP** | North-West Frontier Province | | | |
| **NSC** | National Security Council | | **UNITA** | União Nacional para a Independência Total de Angola (National Union for the Total Independence of Angola) |
| **NWFZ** | Nuclear Weapon Free Zones | | | |
| **NWO** | New World Order | | | |
| **OAS** | Organisation of American States | | **UNITAF** | United Task Force |
| **OAU** | Organisation of African Unity | | **UNODC** | United Nations Office on Drugs and Crime |
| **OECD** | Organisation for Economic Cooperation and Development | | **UNOSOM** | United Nations Mission in Somalia |
| | | | **UNSC** | United Nations Security Council |
| **OIC** | Organisation of the Islamic Conference | | **UPU** | Universal Postal Union |
| **OPEC** | Organisation of Petroleum Exporting Countries | | **US/USA** | United States of America |
| | | | **USSR** | Union of Soviet Socialist Republics |
| **PECC** | Pacific Economic Cooperation Council | | **WAD** | Women and Development |
| **PKK** | Kurdistan Workers Party | | **WAND** | Women's Action for Nuclear Disarmament |
| **PLO** | Palestine Liberation Organisation | | **WHO** | World Health Organisation |
| **PMC/PSC** | Private Military Companies/Private Security Companies | | **WID** | Women in Development |
| | | | **WIPO** | World Intellectual Property Organisation |
| **PRC** | People's Republic of China | | **WSSD** | World Summit on Sustainable Development |
| **PRI** | Institutional Revolutionary Party (Mexico) | | | |
| **R&D** | research and development | | **WST** | World Systems Theory |
| **RUF** | Revolutionary United Front | | **WTO** | World Trade Organisation |

# Maps

## World States and Territories

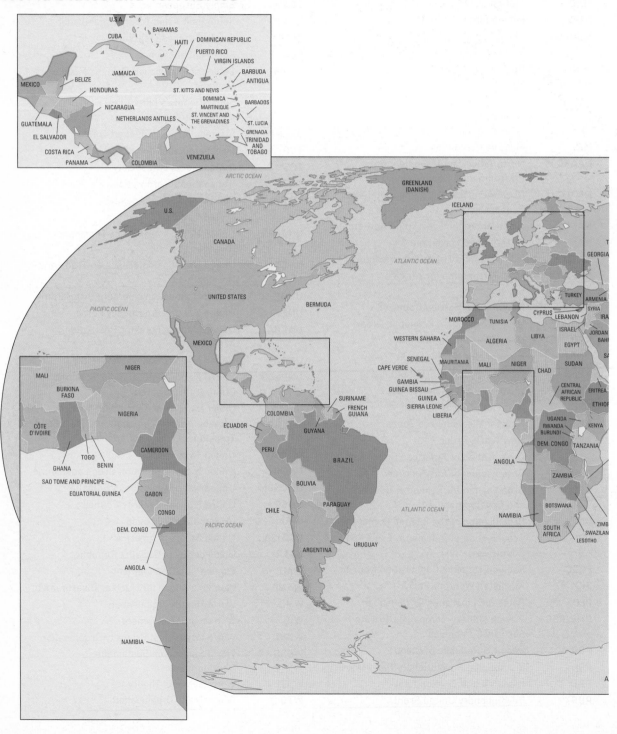

# The Global North and South

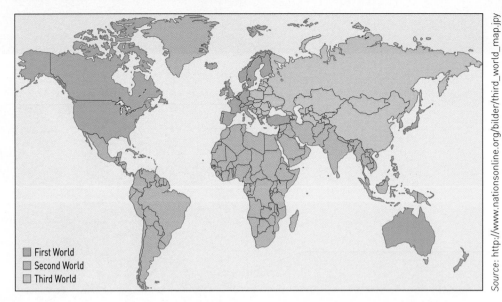

- First World
- Second World
- Third World

*Source:* http://www.nationsonline.org/bilder/third_world_map.jpy

# APEC

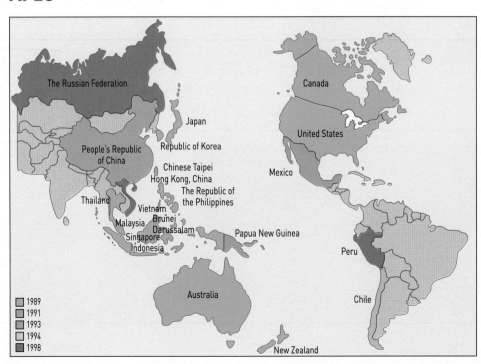

The Russian Federation

Japan

People's Republic
of China

Republic of Korea

Chinese Taipei
Hong Kong, China

The Republic of
the Philippines

Thailand

Vietnam
Brunei
Malaysia    Darussalam
Singapore
Indonesia

Papua New Guinea

Australia

Canada

United States

Mexico

Peru

Chile

New Zealand

- 1989
- 1991
- 1993
- 1994
- 1998

# North America

# Central America and the Caribbean

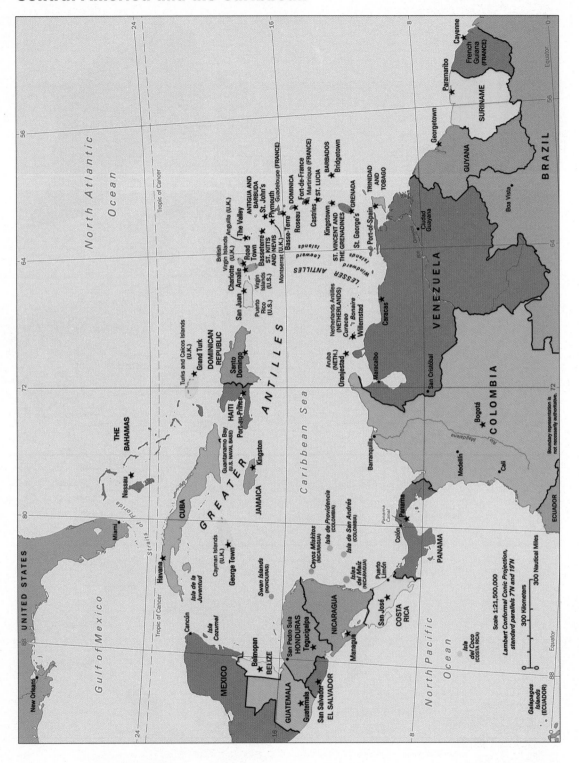

# South America

Caribbean Sea

Guadeloupe (FRANCE)
DOMINICA
Martinique (FRANCE)
ST. LUCIA
ST. VINCENT AND
THE GRENADINES
BARBADOS
GRENADA
Port-of-Spain
TRINIDAD AND
TOBAGO

North Atlantic Ocean

HONDURAS
Puerto Lempira
Tegucigalpa
Puerto Cabezas
NICARAGUA
Isla de San Andrés (COLOMBIA)
Managua
Liberia
San José
Colón
Panama
COSTA RICA
David
PANAMA

Barranquilla
Maracaibo
Caracas
Ciudad Guayana

San Cristóbal
VENEZUELA
Georgetown
Paramaribo
French Guiana (FRANCE)
Cayenne
GUYANA
SURINAME

Medellín
Río Magdalena
Bogotá
COLOMBIA
Cali
Boa Vista
Río Orinoco

Isla de Malpelo (COLOMBIA)

Mitú
Macapá

Equator

Quito
ECUADOR
Guayaquil
Río Negro
Fonte Boa
Amazon
Manaus
Santarém
Belém
São Luís

Iquitos
Río Napo
Río Marañón
Río Juruá
Amazon
Río Xingu
Río Tocantins
Fortaleza

Piura
Teresina
Natal

Trujillo
Río Branco
Pôrto Velho
BRAZIL
Recife

Huánuco
Palmas
Aracaju

PERU
Cusco
Lima
Ica
Lago Titicaca
Trinidad
Salvador

South Pacific Ocean

Arequipa
BOLIVIA
Cuiabá
Goiânia
Brasília

Arica
La Paz
Cochabamba
Santa Cruz
Sucre
Potosí
Belo Horizonte

Vitória

Antofagasta
PARAGUAY
Río Paraná
Rio de Janeiro
São Paulo

Tropic of Capricorn

Isla San Félix (CHILE)
Isla San Ambrosio (CHILE)
San Miguel de Tucumán
Asunción
Curitiba

Resistencia
Florianópolis

Pôrto Alegre

CHILE
Córdoba
Salto
South Atlantic Ocean

Archipiélago Juan Fernández (CHILE)
Valparaíso
Mendoza
Rosario
URUGUAY

Santiago
Río Paraná
Buenos Aires
Montevideo

Concepción
ARGENTINA
Bahía Blanca
Mar del Plata

Comodoro Rivadavia

Scale 1:35,000,000

Azimuthal Equal-Area Projection

San Carlos de Bariloche
Puerto Montt

0    250   500 Kilometers
0    250   500 Nautical Miles

Boundary representation is
not necessarily authoritative.

Strait of Magellan
Punta Arenas
Ushuaia

Stanley
Falkland Islands (Islas Malvinas)
(administered by U.K., claimed by Argentina)

South Georgia and the
South Sandwich Islands
(administered by U.K., claimed by Argentina)

# Organisation of the Islamic conference

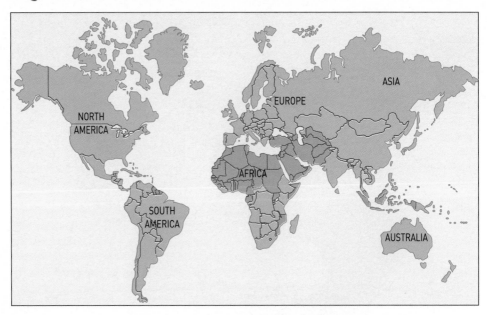

NORTH AMERICA

SOUTH AMERICA

EUROPE

ASIA

AFRICA

AUSTRALIA

# West Coast of Africa

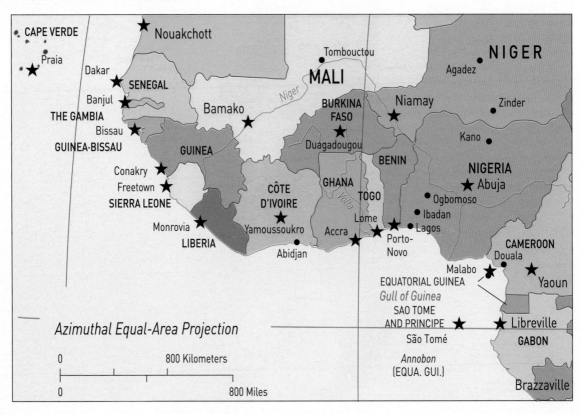

CAPE VERDE

Praia

Nouakchott

Dakar

SENEGAL

Banjul

THE GAMBIA

Bissau

GUINEA-BISSAU

GUINEA

Bamako

Conakry

Freetown

SIERRA LEONE

Monrovia

LIBERIA

CÔTE D'IVOIRE

Yamoussoukro

Abidjan

Tombouctou

MALI

Niger

BURKINA FASO

Duagadougou

GHANA

Volta

Accra

TOGO

Lome

Porto-Novo

BENIN

Niamay

NIGER

Agadez

Zinder

Kano

NIGERIA

Abuja

Ogbomoso

Ibadan

Lagos

CAMEROON

Douala

Yaoun

Malabo

EQUATORIAL GUINEA

Gull of Guinea

SAO TOME AND PRINCIPE

São Tomé

Annobon (EQUA. GUI.)

Libreville

GABON

Brazzaville

Azimuthal Equal-Area Projection

| 0 | 800 Kilometers |
| 0 | 800 Miles |

# Africa

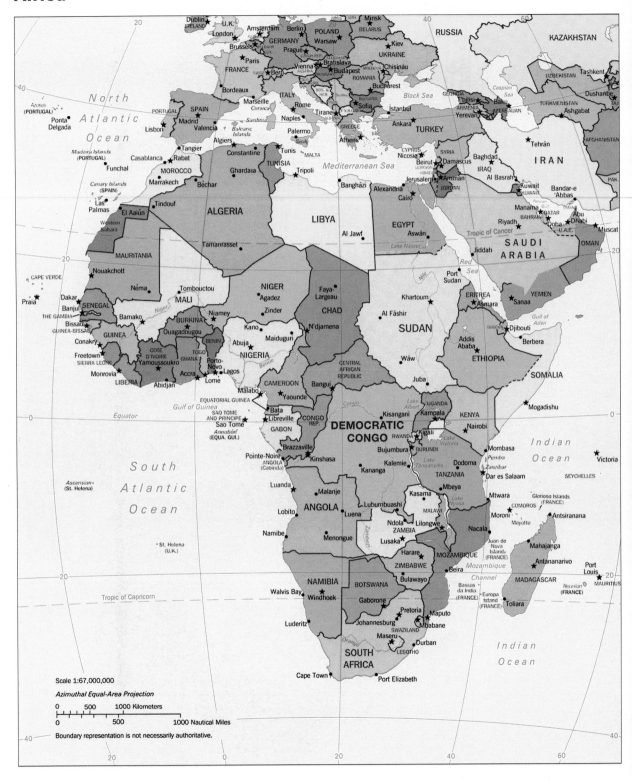

Scale 1:67,000,000

*Azimuthal Equal-Area Projection*

| 0 | 500 | 1000 Kilometers |
| 0 | 500 | 1000 Nautical Miles |

Boundary representation is not necessarily authoritative.

# Northern Africa and the Middle East

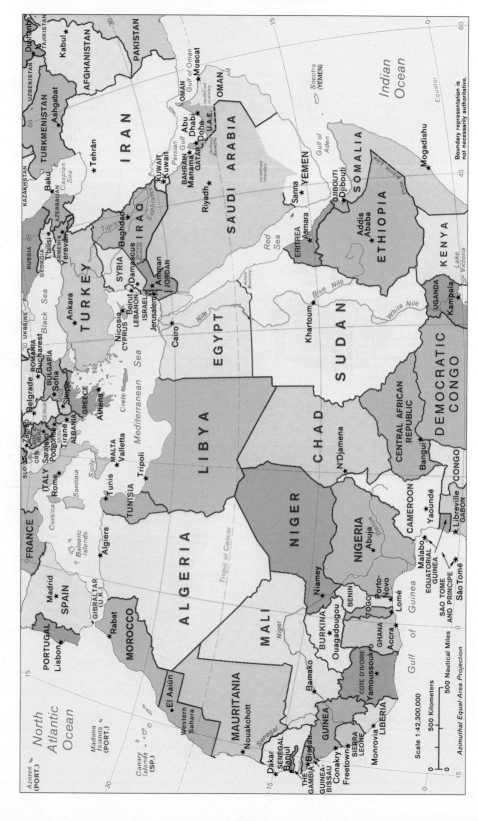

# Europe

# Asia

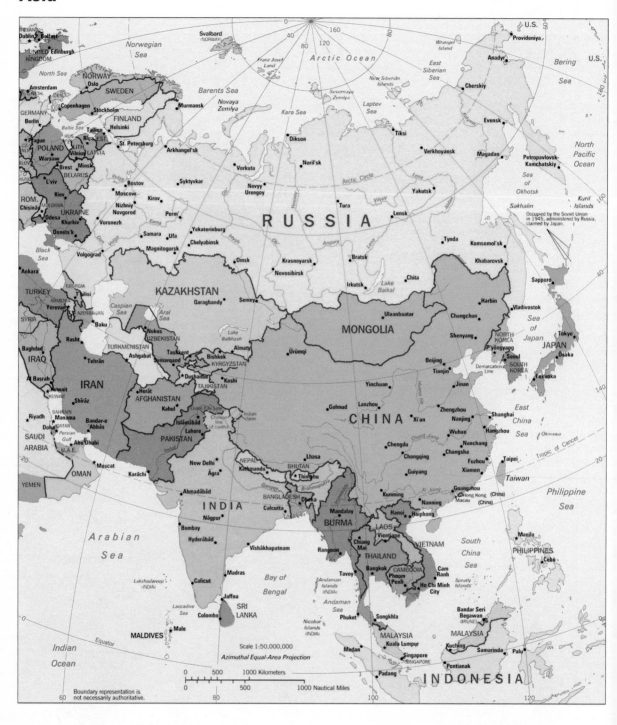

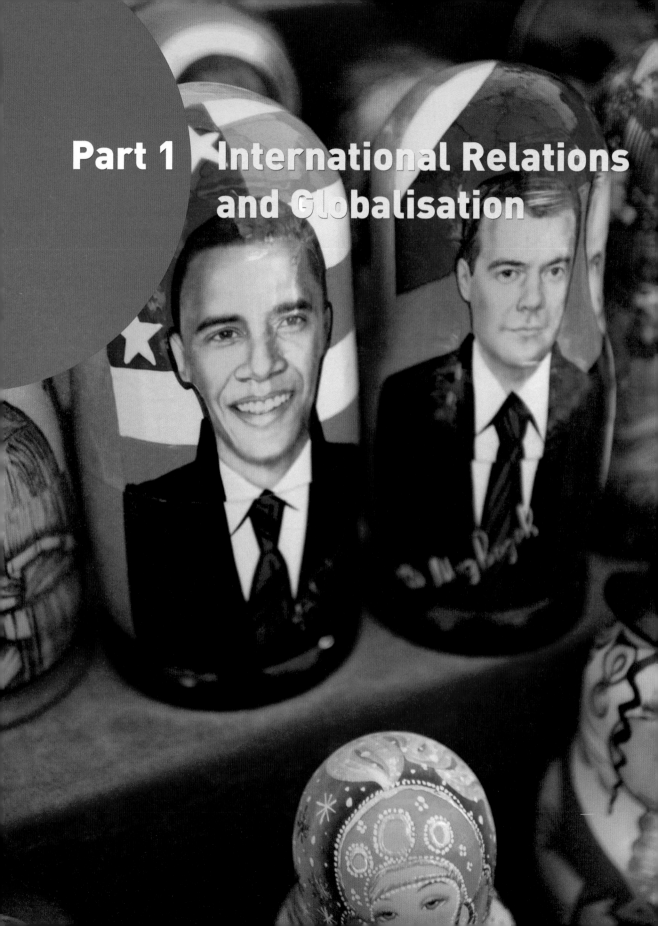

# Part 1 International Relations and Globalisation

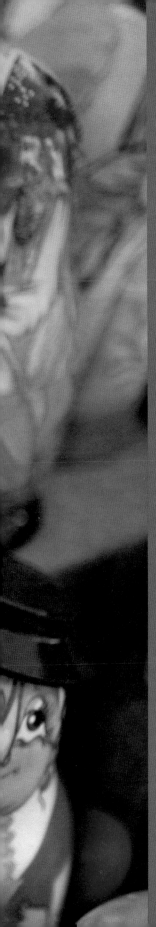

# 1 International Relations and Globalisation in the Twenty-First Century

# 2 International Order, International Society and Globalisation

The opening part of the book provides a focus on globalisation, enabling us to understand and use the concept in relation to current international relations. First, we examine several key terms: What is meant by *International Relations* and how it differs from *international relations*, and where globalisation fits in in our understanding of these terms. We also find out how globalisation has affected our understanding of international relations over time, why events since the 1980s have fundamentally affected how we understand international relations and, finally, how various theoretical approaches seek to incorporate globalisation into their worldviews.

Of course, we are now very accustomed to the idea of globalisation. It may come as a surprise to learn that 'globalisation' only entered common usage in international relations quite recently, in the 1980s. It was used a few years earlier by some economists, trying to understand what was happening in what they thought of as an emerging *global* economy. Now, however, at the end of the first decade of the twenty-first century, the contemporary significance of globalisation is both wide-ranging and immense. This encourages us to think of it in various ways in relation to many outcomes in international relations.

Not least, globalisation focuses our attention on the fact that international relations is experiencing a period of profound change – some might even say, transformation. This suggests various far-reaching processes of change, for example, the upheaval in the global economy (2008–2010), which saw even the most powerful countries, such as the United States, lose ability to influence international economic outcomes.

Chapter 1 examines current international relations and how globalisation affects it. The purpose of this is, first, to introduce readers to the overall subject matter of current international relations. Second, we want to equip our readers with basic conceptual knowledge and the awareness necessary to undertake more advanced study in international relations. The overall objective of this first part of the book is to facilitate readers' understanding of recent developments in international relations, and to prepare them intellectually to evaluate future changes.

In Chapter 2, we turn to an evaluation of the complexity of current international relations. Not least, the subject matter of international relations has expanded from the study of what states do to an awareness that there are also a great number of 'non-state actors', such as the United Nations, the European Union and al-Qaeda. This has occurred in the context of rapid technological change, political transformations, industrialisation, the emergence from colonial domination of the 'developing world' after the Second World War, the rise and fall of ideological conflict between the USA and the (now defunct) Soviet Union during the Cold War which followed the Second World War and, most recently, the impact of the multifaceted processes of globalisation.

In order to understand how international relations has developed over time and what factors have played a key role in its development, Chapter 2 examines the relationship between international order, international society and globalisation. Its overall purpose is fourfold, to explain: (1) Fundamental aspects of international relations after the Peace of Westphalia in 1648; (2) Conceptions of international order; (3) Conceptions of international society; and (4) the impact of globalisation on international order and international society.

*Source*: Getty Images

# Chapter 1
# International Relations and Globalisation in the Twenty-First Century

International Relations and globalisation

Why is globalisation important for understanding International Relations?

Technological, political, economic and cultural globalisation

Important post-Cold War changes affecting International Relations

Understanding globalisation

Conclusion

In this chapter you will gain understanding of the following:

- What is meant by International Relations (IR), international relations and globalisation
- How globalisation has affected our understanding of IR over time
- What has occurred over the last two decades to affect how we understand IR
- Rival theoretical approaches to understanding globalisation

*Source*: Getty Images

## Introductory box: International Relations and economic crisis

2008 was a year of crises. First, we had a food crisis, particularly threatening to poor consumers, especially in Africa. Along with that came a record increase in oil prices, threatening all oil-importing countries. Finally, rather suddenly in the Fall, came a global economic downturn, and it is now gathering speed at a frightening rate. The year 2009 seems likely to offer a sharp intensification of the downturn, and many economists are anticipating a full-scale depression, perhaps even one as large as the 1930s. While substantial fortunes have suffered steep declines, the people most affected are those who were already worst off.

(Sen 2009)

Here, Amartya Sen, winner of the Nobel Prize for Economics in 1998, emphasises the highly interdependent nature of the global economy, while also drawing our attention to the fact that while the losses suffered in the finance and banking sectors of the 'developed' world may have made the most headlines in Europe, the banking crisis was prefigured by crises that hit developing nations first. The economic crisis of 2008–2010 is just one example of the way globalisation has made the world increasingly interdependent, so that no one part of the world can remain unaffected by the knock-on effects of a crisis somewhere else.

**Globalisation** is a term we use so frequently, it may come as a surprise to learn that it has only recently entered common usage. In **international relations**, the term came into use in the 1980s, having first been used by economists to describe what they characterised as the emergence of a *global* economy. The phenomenon of globalisation referred to an increased interdependency that was not only limited to the realm of economics, but which extended to technology, culture, and the way states and institutions related to one another. Now, in the early twenty-first century, it is difficult to think about international relations without considering the impact globalisation has had on the way power is shared in the world. The idea of globalisation focuses our attention on the fact that international relations is experiencing a period of profound change which saw even the most powerful countries, such as the United States, lose ability to influence international economic outcomes.

This introductory chapter examines current international relations and how globalisation affects it. More generally, our book has two key aims. First we want to introduce readers to the overall subject matter of international relations. Second, we aim to equip our readers with basic conceptual knowledge and the awareness necessary to undertake more advanced study in International Relations. The overall objective is to encourage readers to understand recent developments in international relations, and to prepare them intellectually to evaluate future changes.

The first section of this chapter surveys how globalisation has transformed our understanding of international relations. The second section focuses on globalisation controversies and explains how they affect our understanding of international relations. Following your reading of this chapter, you should understand the nature of important recent changes in international relations, including the impact of globalisation.

## International Relations and globalisation

**Box 1.1  The emergence of International Relations as an academic discipline**

The academic discipline of International Relations has existed for nearly a hundred years, since soon after the end of the First World War. Over that time the world has changed in many ways, as have the ways in which we have theorised world politics. Globalisation represents one of the most profound changes to world political systems in the past century, and has had significant effects on how we understand power, identity, economics, and security, among other things.

The first thing to do is to introduce and explain the book's key term: '*international relations*'. It is important to note that 'international relations' has two distinct, yet interrelated, meanings. First, when spelt with a capital 'I' and capital 'R' (**International Relations**), it refers to an academic discipline which evolved in recent decades from the subject area called 'Politics'. Because it has its roots in the study of politics, the discipline of International Relations (or **IR**) is sometimes referred to as 'International Politics' or 'World Politics'. Whatever term we use, we are referring to essentially the same discipline, the aim of which is to explain and predict the behaviour of important entities whose actions have a bearing on the lives of people all around the world. These entities might be individual states and governments, whose actions undoubtedly have a direct effect on their citizens and neighbouring states – but they may just as easily be groups of states, international organisations, or businesses that operate worldwide. The aim of International Relations is to examine how these various types of bodies interact with one another, for what purposes, and to what ends. In sum, as an academic discipline, International Relations studies: (1) how and why states engage with each other, and (2) the international activities of various important 'non-state actors'.

Because of the nature of its area of enquiry, it will come as no surprise that the academic discipline of IR is multidisciplinary. This means it employs insights from various academic areas, including: politics, economics, history, law, and sociology. We can trace the start of the academic discipline of International Relations to a precise time. It started soon after the First World War ended in 1918, with the founding of a chair – that is, a professorship – at the University of Wales, Aberystwyth, in 1919. The chair was established for an explicit and understandable reason: to try to discover the causes of international conflict and thereby improve the chances for global peace, lessening the likelihood of international war. Initially then, IR was concerned primarily with international conflict and its causes. Over time, when it became clear that the causes of conflict are wide-reaching and complex, the discipline's subject matter expanded. Over time, it came to include:

- **international political economy** – often referred to as **IPE** – which studies the political effects of international economic interactions

- international organisation (how and why regional and international bodies form and interact)
- foreign policy-making (what governments do to try and achieve their goals beyond their domestic environments)
- **Strategic** (or **Security**) **Studies** (how governments seek to protect their citizens from external threats)
- peace research (how we can maintain peace and seek peaceful solutions to conflict).

All of these areas of concern fall under the general heading, and provide the subject matter, of the discipline of International Relations.

As already noted, when we refer to the academic discipline of International Relations we use a capital 'I' and capital 'R'. When we use a small 'i' and a small 'r' (**international relations**) we are referring to the totality of significant international interactions involving states and important non-state actors. Because this is theoretically a limitless endeavour, in practice our emphasis is on states (or governments: the terms are often used interchangeably) and a range of important non-state actors, including: **multinational corporations (MNCs)** (such as Microsoft, Shell, and Starbucks), **international non-governmental organisations (INGOs)** (such as Amnesty International, Greenpeace, and Friends of the Earth), and **inter governmental organisations (IGOs)** (such as the United Nations, European Union and the Organisation of the Islamic Conference). All such non-state actors play important roles in international relations and we shall examine them in future chapters.

Turning to globalisation we can note that, although only recently in common usage, it is not a new concept. The origins of current globalisation can be seen in the work of various nineteenth- and early twentieth-century intellectuals, including the theoretician of communism, the German intellectual Karl Marx (1818–83). Along with another German, Fredrich Engels (1820–95), Marx is widely acknowledged as a key figure in the development of communism, the ideology that animated the Soviet Union and its international relations for nearly a century following the Bolshevik Revolution in Russia in 1917. In the mid-nineteenth century, Marx and Engels had recognised that capitalism was both integrating and shaping the development of international relations, especially in the way that it was leading to a capitalist global economy. Marx and Engels turned out to be right: by the early twentieth century, there was a global capitalist economy.

The progress of both globalisation and of a capitalist global economy was temporarily disrupted by the First World War and the subsequent decades. The 1920s and, especially, the 1930s were characterised not by advancing economic globalisation but by **economic protectionism** and **economic nationalism** – that is to say, a shrinking rather than an expansion of international economic activity. The Second World War followed in 1939, and the Cold War came fast on the heels of the end of the Second World War in 1945.

The Cold War was a forty-year conflict which dominated International Relations with the fluctuating relationship between the USA and the USSR – and its significant global effects. The USA and the USSR were known as the 'superpowers', because of their possession of large quantities of nuclear weapons and their global foreign policies. Their conflict centred on vastly different ideological interpretations of what were desirable outcomes in international relations. Because their conflict did not involve 'hot' war – that is, actual face-to-face fighting – it is known as a 'cold' war between two ideologically opposed adversaries. While the USA wished to see the international spread of **liberal democracy** and **capitalism**, the USSR wanted to see the advance of revolutionary **communism**, with the goal of dramatically changing the international order. When the Cold War abruptly and unexpectedly ended in the late 1980s, it not only marked the end of the ideological division between the USA and the USSR, and the demise of international communism and its ideological challenge to liberal democracy and capitalism, but also signified the return to centrality of globalisation for our understanding of IR.

The end of the Cold War in the late 1980s coincided with the onset of a dynamic phase of globalisation. Our understanding of international relations was affected in various ways. First, the end of the Cold War threw the study of international relations into a state of still unresolved uncertainty and flux, as we considered how to move away from the serious ideological tension of the Cold War to increased international cooperation, now that the ideological division had ceased. Soon after the Cold War ended, there was talk of a 'new international order'. This reflected the fact that the end of the Cold War initially brought widespread optimism that there could now be improved international cooperation, with fresh commitment to strengthening the role of key international organisations, especially the United Nations. The goal was to achieve various aims, including: better, more equitable development; the reduction of gender inequalities; defusion of armed conflicts; the lessening of human rights abuses, and action to tackle environmental degradation and destruction. In short, to manage multiple global interdependencies it would be necessary greatly to improve processes of bargaining, negotiation and consensus-seeking, involving both states and various non-state actors, including the UN.

It soon became clear, however, there was a lack of workable ideas as to how the desired international improvements would be effected. During the 1990s, there were serious outbreaks of international conflict. Many were religious, ethnic or nationalist conflicts; many began within countries but often then spilled over into neighbouring states, creating regional and international crises. Examples include conflicts in Burundi, Haiti, Iraq, Rwanda, Somalia, and the former Yugoslavia – all of which led to serious, and in many cases still unresolved, humanitarian crises which required external intervention to try to resolve them. These new conflicts emphasised how difficult it was to move away from the problems of the old international order that had characterised the Cold War to a new era that, it had been hoped, would be marked by international peace, prosperity and cooperation.

The conflicts, which all attracted external interventions, emphasised how interconnected the world had become. In the past international relations was often interpreted as primarily involving the interaction of autonomous states. Their involvement with each other was primarily at the international level. It did not routinely involve domestic issues. Now, however, globalisation emphasised that both domestic and international issues were intimately connected, with significant effects on our understanding of international relations.

## Why is globalisation important for understanding International Relations?

Globalisation has become particularly important over the last two decades or so, a period which saw the emergence of a global economy and a communications revolution. It was also a time that saw the end of a fundamental ideological division centrally affecting International Relations, which involved both the USA and a multinational entity known as the Soviet Union or USSR, whose core state was Russia. As already noted, the end of the Cold War in the late 1980s coincided with increased globalisation. The post-Cold War period – roughly the last twenty years – was a time of rapidly expanding globalisation, involving increased technological, political, economic and cultural interdependence. The result was fundamentally to question orthodox thinking about International Relations. This is because a study of IR had long presumed strict separation between internal and external affairs, the domestic and international arenas, the national and the global. Now, in this newly interdependent world after the Cold War, events abroad often affect what happens at home, while developments within a country may well have knock-on effects internationally.

How best to understand the current impact of globalisation on international relations? To answer this question we need first to ascertain what globalisation is. Ulrich Beck, an influential sociologist who has written a lot about globalisation, supplies a useful definition. Globalisation can be understood as a name for collective 'processes through which sovereign national states are criss-crossed and undermined by transnational actors with varying prospects of power, orientations, identities and networks' (Beck 2000: 10). Conceptualised like this, globalisation has the potential to undermine a key idea in International Relations. That is, that states are all-important (a belief particularly central to the ideas of **Realists** and **neo-Realists**, discussed in Chapter 6). This view is undermined because, as Beck's definition indicates, globalisation involves various kinds of cross-border or, as he terms them, 'transnational' non-state 'actors'. For Beck (2000), the process of globalisation is characterised by:

- the geographical expansion and ever greater density of international trade, as well as the global networking of finance markets and the growing power of transnational corporations
- the ongoing evolution of information and communications technology
- the universal demands for human rights – the (lip service paid to the) principle of democracy
- the stream of images from global culture industries
- the emergence of a post-national, polycentric world politics, in which transnational actors (corporations, non-governmental organisations, United Nations) are growing in power and number alongside governments

*Source: Getty Images*

**Starbucks in the Forbidden City: is globalisation just another word for 'Westernisation'?**

- the question of world poverty
- the issue of global environmental destruction
- trans-cultural conflicts in one and the same place.

We can see that, conceptualised in this way, globalisation is characterised by intensification of global interconnectedness between both states and non-state actors. It is a multidimensional process involving technological, political, economic and cultural issues. It implies lessening of the significance of territorial boundaries and, theoretically, of government-directed political and economic structures and processes. In sum, globalisation is characterised by

1. rapid integration of the world economy,
2. innovations and growth in international electronic communications, and
3. increasing 'political and cultural awareness of the global interdependency of humanity' (Warburg 2001).

Four aspects of globalisation – technological, political, economic, and cultural globalisation – are of particular importance for understanding current international relations (Haynes 2005). Next we examine why this is the case.

## Technological, political, economic and cultural globalisation

### Technological globalisation

The technological revolution is a [key] aspect of globalisation, describing the effect of new electronic communication which permits firms and other actors to operate globally with much less regard for location, distance, and border.

(Woods 2001: 290)

The impact of what Woods refers to as a 'technological revolution' is apparent in relation to key areas of globalisation. These include economic and political globalisation in relation, for example, to the recent global spread of both democracy and international **terrorism**. In both cases the Internet and email, in particular, facilitate the spread of ideas, knowledge and finance that collectively can encourage networks devoted to such outcomes to spread. There were, however, limits to what technological globalisation could facilitate – if governments were able and willing to control its effects. For example, what is known as 'the third wave of democracy', which lasted for thirty years from the mid-1970s, was a widespread but not unlimited process. Some governments, including those of China, Iran and Saudi Arabia, were able to control the impact of technological globalisation – and especially the impact of the communications revolution – on their societies. Specifically, such governments were able to use their ability to control communications technology, for example by limiting access to various websites, in order to control what their people could access. Their intention was to maintain their people's isolation from 'wider international currents' (Clark 1997: 21). On the other hand various aspects of globalisation, including the trend towards democracy noted, were widely facilitated by increased ability to communicate, principally via electronic media, enabling ideas, money and strategies speedily to be transmitted from place to place. In addition, the ability of international terrorist groups, most egregiously al-Qaeda, to proselytise and organise was also linked to the technological globalisation encapsulated by the recent communications revolution.

### Political globalisation

Political globalisation can be thought of in two main ways: (1) a widespread process of democratisation, called the 'third wave of democracy', that began in the mid-1970s and peaked in the 1980s and 1990s, and (2) the growth in numbers and significance of politically significant intergovernmental organisations (IGOs) and international non-governmental organisations (INGOs).

First, we note the impact of the third wave of democracy. The sudden, spectacular collapse of the Soviet Union and its regional communist allies, leading to the end of the Cold War in the late 1980s, encouraged many people around the world living under non-democratic rule to demand democracy. During the Cold War, the effects of globalisation were muted by the ideological division between the USA and the USSR. During this time there was what was known as a bipolar division – that is, there were two 'poles' of influence in international relations, each dominated by one of the superpowers. Both had a key concern: increasing their influence and authority in relation to their key rival, the other superpower. As a result, there was little overt or consistent pressure from Western governments, including that of the USA, to seek to facilitate the spread of democracy around the globe. Instead, in the name of fighting communism, the USA and other Western countries tended to turn a blind eye to their allies' often poor democratic records. But once Soviet-style communism in Europe collapsed, the demand for democracy quickly became a key demand for many people living under non-democratic governments.

During both the 1980s and 1990s, the demand for democracy was a key component of political globalisation. It implied a growing global preference for democracy over non-democratic forms of rule. According to Mittelman (1994: 429), political globalisation was an 'emerging worldwide preference for democracy'. This was made clear following the end of the Cold War in the late 1980s, with many countries moving from non-democratic to democratically elected governments. This reflected growing demands from within many countries but also the impact of various external actors in encouraging democracy. Both Western governments and various international organisations, such as the European Union, not only proclaimed a general and theoretical commitment to encourage democracy around the world but also, in some cases, were able to back up their rhetoric with hard cash. That is, they promoted democracy in many formerly non-democratic parts of the world, including Central and European Europe, Asia and Africa, via strategies of political and economic conditionality. These policies implied that they would only provide significant economic assistance when recipient governments showed serious intent in democratising (Yilmaz 2002; Gillespie and Youngs 2002).

The second way that political globalisation is manifested in current international relations is via the influence of IGOs and INGOs. In this sense, political globalisation refers to the increasing number and power of human associations which influence political outcomes in international relations.

The first thing to note, as shown in Table 1.1, is that there is a large number of politically significant state and non-state actors. The huge numbers of actors represented in the table both create and reflect dense cross-border connections and are instrumental in creating more complex patterns of governance within countries.

### Intergovernmental organisations (IGOs)

Only internationally recognised states can be members of IGOs. Most were founded after 1945 although some functional bodies were established earlier, for example, the International Telecommunications Union was established nearly a century earlier in 1865. Several IGOs inaugurated after the Second World War – for example, the United Nations (UN), North Atlantic Treaty Organisation (NATO), EU, and the Organisation of the Islamic Conference (OIC) – have multiple tasks, including security, welfare and human rights goals.

Willetts (2001: 357) notes that there are about 250 IGOs. Conceptually, members of an IGO will aim to preserve their formal autonomy while being bound in certain policy-making options as a consequence of their IGO commitments. Precisely how IGO membership can

**Table 1.1** Types and numbers of international actors

| Actor | Number | Examples |
|---|---|---|
| States | 192 (members of the UN) | Brazil, India, Nigeria, United Kingdom |
| Intergovernmental organisations | c. 250–350 | European Union, North Atlantic Treaty Organisation, Organisation of the Islamic Conference, United Nations |
| Multinational business corporations | c. 60,000 | Coca-Cola, Ford, Microsoft, Nestlé, Shell |
| Single country non-governmental organisations | c. 10,000 | Freedom House, Médecins sans Frontières |
| International non-governmental organisations | c. 25,000* | Amnesty International, Greenpeace International, Oxfam, Red Crescent |

*Source*: Adapted from Willetts (2001: 357) and Anheier and Themudo (2002: 195).

* These are 'active' INGOs, although Anheier and Themudo (2002: 195) note another 22,000 they characterise as 'dead, inactive, and unconfirmed'.

impact upon countries' domestic politics depends on: (1) the extent to which countries are enmeshed in IGO networks, and (2) their domestic political arrangements.

## International non-governmental organisations (INGOs)

The number of active INGOs has grown more than tenfold in the last three decades – from around 2,000 in the early 1970s to over 25,000 now (Willetts 2001: 357; Anheier and Themudo 2002: 195). INGOs are cross-border bodies, such as Amnesty International, Greenpeace International and the Roman Catholic Church, whose members are individuals or private groups drawn from more than one country. The chief theoretical assumptions concerning INGOs are that: (1) states are not the only important cross-border actors in international relations and (2) INGOs can be politically significant. This can be noted in the case of 'failed' or 'collapsed' states – that is, countries where state authority no longer exists; current examples include Somalia, Zimbabwe and the Democratic Republic of Congo. Such countries are very reliant on aid provided by INGOs 'for basic supplies and services' (Hague and Harrop 2001: 47). INGOs can also be executors of policy stemming from various international organisations, including the UN and the EU.

Some INGOs also seek to change state policy more proactively in a variety of political, social or economic areas. The influence of such actors is not assured but depends on two main factors: (1) how skilful they are in infiltrating national policy-making processes, and (2) the extent to which a targeted government is receptive to them. Their effectiveness may be augmented when groups of transnational actors link up – for example, in pursuit of political, religious, gender-orientated or developmental goals – to encourage popular pressure for domestic change. This can lead to the development of transnational citizen groups (TCGs).

Partly a function of the global communications revolution, the chief consequence of TCGs is regional or global spread and interchange of ideas and information. To understand the social dynamics of TCGs it is useful to perceive the international system as an agglomeration of various issue areas – for example, religious, environmental, human rights, political, gender and development concerns – organised under the rubric of 'social transnationalism'. This is facilitated by multiple linkages between individuals and groups interested in the same goals but separated by large physical distances. Cross-border exchanges of experiences and information and shift of funds not only facilitate development of TCG strategies but can add to national, regional and/or global campaigns. This underlines that social transnationalism

> is not just a matter of individuals and masses who feel conscious of being primary international subjects as they are entitled to civil, political, economic, social and cultural rights by positive international law. In the world system these subjects form the international social layer which claims primacy over the diplomatic layer. Today the chances of social transnationalism reside in INGOs whose members cross states and assert 'pan-human' interests such as the promotion of human rights, environmental ecology, [and] international development co-operation.
>
> (Attina 1989: 350–1)

Collectively, the agglomeration of TCGs comprises transnational civil society (TCS). Unlike domestic civil society, TCS is not territorially fixed. Instead, according to Lipschutz (1992: 390), TCS is 'the self-conscious constructions of networks of knowledge and action, by decentred, local actors, that cross the reified boundaries of space as though they were not there'. Many component parts of TCS work towards normatively 'progressive' goals, including improved standards of governance, by encouraging popular, cross-border coalitions to challenge government decisions on a variety of issues. TCS effectiveness may be increased when influential organisations – such as Amnesty International, Human Rights Watch, and Freedom House – play a leading role (Risse and Ropp 1999: 238). Such INGOs were influential in getting various human rights issues on to international conference agendas, such as a UN-sponsored human rights conference, held in Vienna in 1992, and one on gender issues in Beijing in 1995.

## Economic globalisation

Economic globalisation involves the ability of both capital and capitalists to cross borders relatively freely. During early 2009, for example, there was a serious 'credit crunch' when it became very difficult to borrow money to finance a mortgage because of many banks' fears of bad debts. For many people, this implied clear evidence of economic globalisation, whereby what happened in one economy – the credit crunch spread from the USA to Europe and elsewhere – affected many others around the world.

But how geographically extensive is economic globalisation? Hirst and Thompson (1999) argue that economic globalisation is not global but a triangular phenomenon, of most importance to North America, Western Europe and Japan. In their view, as a consequence economically more marginal regions, such as sub-Saharan Africa and Central Asia, are comparatively little affected by economic globalisation.

Economic globalisation was encouraged by the collapse of the Soviet Union and its associated communist ideology from the late 1980s. Whereas the USSR developed from the late 1940s a non-capitalist, state-dominated economic system, its demise favoured the movement of capital, labour and goods across national boundaries while increasing international economic competition. Economic changes were also reflected in transformation of production systems and labour markets, characterised by general weakening of the

*Source: Getty Images*

One result of globalisation has been that many states struggle to engage with development concerns, including the reduction of inequalities.

power of organised labour to pressurise governments to enforce labour standards, such as minimum wage legislation. Many analysts agree, in addition, that the already weak economic position of many poor people has worsened as a result of economic globalisation, because it has increased the ability of the rich to benefit from new opportunities (Held and McGrew 2002; Haynes 2005).

## Case study: Economic globalisation and outcomes for the poor

Around the world, poverty is a huge problem. Of the world's more than six billion people, around half live on less than US$2 a day and over a billion on less than US$1 a day. One in twelve children do not live to be five years old. Ten per cent of boys and 14 per cent of girls who become old enough to go to school, do not get there, usually because their parents are too poor to send them. When adult, poor people tend to have less political power and voice than wealthier men and women. They are also often very vulnerable to ill health, economic dislocation, personal violence, and natural disasters. This already problematic situation was made worse by the global economic crisis of 2008–2010.

Why is this the case? First, there are said to be links between economic globalisation, reflecting an increasingly interdependent global economy, and these development failures. Economic globalisation is said not only to undermine state capacity to pursue independent macroeconomic and development strategies but also to make worse existing inequalities between and within countries. The historic process of economic globalisation is said both to have broadened and deepened since the 1970s and 1980s. This was a phase of world history characterised by the end of European colonial rule, diminution of the USA's hitherto dominant economic position, and significant growth in the internationalisation of productive capital and of finance. Together, these developments have led to powerful global changes – to the extent that even the most powerful industrialised states are said to have declining options in relation to economic policy, including welfare procedures and development outcomes. Second, as a result all states – rich or poor, weak or strong, large or small – are exposed to networks of economic forces and relations that range both in and through them. A significant consequence is to reduce significantly their governments' ability to pursue autonomous national economic and developmental policies. The result is that many struggle to engage meaningfully with development concerns, including the

reduction of inequalities. Monetary and fiscal policies of all states, especially in the developing world, must take cognisance of the influence of globally orientated economic actors, including Western-dominated international institutions, such as the World Bank and the International Monetary Fund (IMF).

Chief among the presumed culprits in this regard are the ubiquitous economic reform programmes in the developing world, known as **structural adjustment programmes** (SAPs). SAPs were adopted in the 1980s and 1990s following sustained pressure from the World Bank and its sister organisation, the IMF. However, a common outcome of SAPs was reduced welfare programmes that significantly disadvantaged the poor (Haynes 2008). As a result of their involvement in SAPs, both the IMF and the World Bank acquired increased economic and developmental influence in numerous developing countries.

Critics of SAPs allege that the reform programmes typically failed to kick-start economic development and recent research – from the World Bank, the United Nations Development Project, and various academic sources – backs this up. Research shows that: (1) poverty has actually grown in recent years, (2) most economic 'progress' has occurred in a small number of states (some of them with large populations and unusual appeal for foreign investors), and (3) even in successful cases many people are actually no better off, and may actually be poorer, than they were previously. Finally, SAPs were often judged to be seriously flawed development strategies. This in turn often led to political dissent and demands for governmental change. In sum, a vast and growing literature points to what many see as declining state control of national economies – and subsequent effects on national political arrangements – in many such states.

 **Would poor people be better off without economic globalisation?**

## Cultural globalisation

Some people regard cultural globalisation simply as a synonym for **Americanisation** or more generally **Westernisation**. There is said to be considerable pressure on people to adopt 'Western lifestyles', including the purchase of identical consumer goods and associated dissemination of American-style consumer culture. American-style consumerism is said to erode non-Western cultures and values, replacing them with a uniform culture of Disney, McDonald's, Coca-Cola, Microsoft and Starbucks. Spread by predominantly US-based multinational business corporations, this cultural globalisation is believed to subvert many non-Western, local cultures by encouraging people not only to buy Western goods and services but also to adopt what are sometimes perceived as Western political norms, including liberal democracy and individualistic conceptions of human rights. Some East Asian and Muslim countries have sought to meet this perceived onslaught by articulating defiantly anti-individualistic, anti-Western worldviews and cultures. They have focused upon non-Western cultural manifestations, including 'Asian values', **Islamism** and **Islamic fundamentalism**. Taken together – as they sometimes are (Huntington 1996) – Asian values and radical Islamism represent a challenge to Western-style cultural globalisation.

In sum, technological, political, economic, and cultural globalisation processes and relationships collectively amount to something qualitatively different compared to what existed before, with significant impacts on how we theorise and understand international relations. Next we look at some of the key manifestations of post-Cold War changes in international relations, all of which are linked to the increased impact of globalisation. After that we examine the case for and against globalisation.

## Important post-Cold War changes affecting International Relations

One of the consequences of globalisation is that *all* countries, rich and poor, large and small, are now significantly affected by global economic and information systems. In addition, many states, especially in the developing world, are also experiencing various political and/or cultural challenges, including those stemming from ethnic, religious or national forces. As a result, governments around the world face key – economic, technological, ecological and cultural – challenges which many find difficult to deal with.

Three key developments noted above – the end of the Cold War, increased desire for improved global cooperation, and emergence of new conflicts, including the spread of international terrorism – are all explicitly connected to the recent increased salience of globalisation. Later chapters will reflect this development in both theoretical and empirical ways. For now, however, we need to identify and briefly examine specific examples in order to emphasise the increased importance of globalisation for understanding international relations. We can identify seven interlinked post-Cold War changes in international relations, all of which are linked to globalisation and which require us to rethink how we understand international relations:

1. increased numbers of states
2. growing numbers of 'failed' states
3. new forms of international conflict
4. third wave of democracy
5. global importance of capitalism
6. development of transnational civil society
7. many examples of regional integration.

There are now more states than ever before and, second, there are growing numbers of 'failing' or 'failed' states. The term, 'state', is used in International Relations in two, more or less, discrete ways. The state is a community of people who interact in the same domestic political system and who have some common values. The state is also an entity enjoying exclusive recognition under **international law.**

The number of states has been growing for some time. In 1945 there were just over fifty states recognised by the UN, today there are nearly two hundred, almost four times as many. After the Second World War, most new states have emerged as a result of **decolonisation**, although recently the collapse of existing states – including the USSR, Yugoslavia, Ethiopia and Somalia – led to new ones. Sometimes, in addition, countries have seen their system of government collapse. These are what are called 'failed' states. Failed states – including Liberia, Sierra Leone, Afghanistan, Somalia, Iraq and Yemen – effectively 'implode', with governmental disintegration, and become key sources of domestic failure and international instability. This source of instability was often linked to the fourth important change after the Cold War: new sources of international conflict, involving religious, ethnic and national conflicts, which usually began within countries but then often spread across international borders to affect neighbouring countries and regions.

The last thirty years have seen the spread of democracy from Southern Europe to Latin America and East Asia, by way of Eastern Europe, sub-Saharan Africa, and South Asia. This phenomenon was called 'the third wave of democracy', following two earlier periods of democratic expansion, with the initial one occurring in the nineteenth century and the second one taking place after the Second World War.

 **Box 1.2 Three waves of democracy**

What is democracy? The first thing to bear in mind is that not everyone agrees what it is. Yet most people would probably agree that for any political system to be called 'democratic' it must have two features. First, all members of society must have equal access to power. Second, everyone enjoys universally recognised freedoms and liberties.

The first wave of democracy began in the early nineteenth century when the vote was granted to the majority of white males in the USA. At its peak, the first wave saw twenty-nine democracies, mainly in Europe. The first wave continued until 1922 when the fascist dictator, Benito Mussolini, gained power in Italy. The next twenty years – until 1942 – saw a drop in the number of democracies around the world, down to twelve. The second wave began following the Allied victory in the Second World War, proceeding over the next fifteen years until 1962, with the number of democracies rising to thirty-six. Then, there was a dip – with the number of democracies decreasing to thirty – until the mid-1970s. The third wave of democracy began in 1974, with democratisation in Greece, Portugal and Spain, followed by dozens more states democratising in many parts of the world.

As noted above in our brief survey of economic globalisation, there was the apparently inexorable international spread of capitalism after the end of the Cold War. This increased the international significance of powerful international non-state actors, including multi-national business corporations and international financial institutions, such as the World Trade Organisation, the International Monetary Fund and the World Bank. The spread of capitalism and the significance of international organisations created to police and govern it were influential in encouraging the 'alter-globalisation movement' to organise. This movement was in turn a manifestation of the sixth development: transnational civil society (TCS). What unites TCS is concern that globalisation is simply an expanded form of international capitalism which makes the rich richer and the poor poorer.

There is enhanced regional integration, now involving dozens of states in various parts of the world. Examples include not only well-established entities like the European Union (EU), but also newer regional blocs, such as: the North American Free Trade Agreement (NAFTA), Latin America's MERCOSUR (El Mercado Común del Sur; Southern Common Market), a revitalised Association of South East Asian Nations (ASEAN) and the African Union (AU), successor to the Organisation of African Unity. What all such regional organisations have in common is the desire for closer relations among neighbouring states, especially closer economic relations. The EU is the best current example of the importance of cross-border actors for regional political and economic outcomes. All EU member states *must* have democratic systems, characterised by (near) universal suffrage, and regular 'free and fair' elections. But beyond this, as Hay et al. (2002) note, there is also a 'collective ethos' among member states characterised by 'dynamic relationships between transnational, international and domestic processes and practices'. This means that in the EU political and economic outcomes are consistently affected by cross-border interactions involving a variety of actors. As a result, the EU is the world's most regionally integrated political and economic environment. Among member states, political and economic outcomes are informed by regular inputs not only from a supranational institution – the Commission – but also from various transnational and international actors.

The importance of cross-border actors for EU member states is exemplified in the accession processes of the new members – including Cyprus, the Czech Republic, Estonia, Hungary, Latvia, Lithuania, Malta, and Poland which joined the Union in May 2004, and Romania and Bulgaria, which joined in January 2007. All of these states had to be both democracies *and* have 'market' – that is, capitalist – economies in order to be eligible to join the EU. To explain the provenance of the necessary political and economic reforms, especially in the many former communist states that now belong to the EU, analysts often refer to the necessity of conforming to the regional body's *norms* and *values* (Pridham 2000); and in this regard, cross-border actors of various kinds are significant.

Together, these seven developments – numerous new states; significant numbers of failed states; widespread democratisation; global spread of capitalism; transnational civil society; new forms of international conflict and increased regional integration – collectively challenge two long-held assumptions in international relations:

- the separateness of domestic and international realms
- the autonomous nation-state is invariably the key actor.

## Understanding globalisation

To complete this brief survey of the impact of recent globalisation on international relations, it is useful to highlight the highly controversial nature of globalisation. Since the late 1990s, globalisation has become the source of intense political disputes at both domestic and international levels. Hundreds of thousands have protested on the streets against the impact of globalisation throughout the world while numerous non-governmental organisations and campaign groups have lobbied for change. As such, the claims made for and against globalisation are numerous, complex and sometimes highly technical. To summarise fully is impossible. The arguments offered below are largely indicative but provide a good sense of the main issues. Note that we shall examine in sufficient detail in later chapters key issues merely noted below. Also bear in mind that the views noted below – 'globalist', 'alter-globalist' and 'globalisation sceptic' – may be linked more to explicit positions taken by activists than reflect an academic view embedded in the International Relations literature.

Whether we think of globalisation in terms of an academic view or an activist's judgement, both would probably concur that globalisation is a continuing means by which the world is more and more characterised by common activity, in many highly important aspects of life – such as trade, politics, conflict, culture, religion, and crime. Certainly, as Ulrich Beck noted above, such factors are globally interrelated in many ways that seem significant for our understanding of international relations. In addition, globalisation is also a matter of a change in consciousness, with 'actors' from various spheres, including business, religion, sport, politics and many other activities, increasingly thinking and acting in the context of what is an increasingly 'globalised' world. For example, 'territoriality' – a term signifying a close connection or limitation with reference to a particular geographic area or state – now has less significance for many analysts of international relations than it once did.

Note, however, that in the study of globalisation no single account has managed to acquire the status of orthodoxy. Various theories vie with each other for best explanatory power and there is much continuing debate. Is globalisation 'good' or 'bad'? Is it a myth? Seeking to cut through this complexity, we can identify three distinct sets of arguments. First, there is the claim that globalisation is a real and profoundly transformative process; and sometimes it involves allegedly beneficial outcomes – such as improved democracy or human rights more generally. This is the 'globalist' view. Second, there is the 'alter-globalist' perspective. Proponents agree with the globalist view that globalisation is an important and influential development. They differ in this regard: at least potentially, globalists see globalisation as a progressive force; alter-globalists, on the other hand, see globalisation as leading overwhelmingly to unwelcome developments, especially for the 'have-nots'. Third, the 'globalisation sceptic' view sees globalisation as essentially a myth, a misplaced focus that distracts us from confronting the real forces shaping societies and political choices today.

Also note, however, that a three-way split is rather crude and simplistic, as it refers to what are called ideal-type constructions. Ideal types are heuristic devices (that is, they help us find something out) to order a field of inquiry and clarify primary lines of argument and, thus, establish fundamental points of disagreement. Ideal types provide an accessible way into the melee of voices – but they are starting points, not end points, for making sense of the great globalisation debate.

## Globalists

Globalists reject the assertion that globalisation is a synonym for Americanisation or Westernisation. While it is not denied that the discourse of globalisation may well serve the interests of powerful economic and social forces in the West, 'the globalist account emphasizes that globalization is an expression of deeper structural changes in the scale of modern social organization' (Held and McGrew 2002). Such changes are evident in, among other developments, the sustained growth in numbers and influence of **transnational corporations** (TNCs), world financial markets, and diffusion of popular culture (Willetts 2008).

Central to the globalist conception is an emphasis on the *spatial* attributes of globalisation, that is, a concern with space and territory. In seeking to differentiate global networks and systems from those operating at other spatial scales, such as the local or the national, the globalist analysis identifies globalisation primarily with activities and relations which crystallise on an interregional or intercontinental scale. This leads to more precise analytical distinctions between processes of globalisation and processes of regionalisation and localisation, that is, the nexus of relations between states that are geographically close to each other and the clustering of social relations within states, respectively. In this account, the relationship between globalisation and these other scales of social organisation is not typically conceived of in hierarchical, or mutually exclusive, terms. On the contrary, the interrelations between these different scales are considered to be both fluid and dynamic (Held and McGrew 2002)

Globalist attempts to establish a systematic specification of the concept of globalisation is further complemented by the significance attached to history. This involves locating contemporary globalisation within what the French historian Fernand Braudel refers to as the perspective of the 'longue durée' – that is, very long-term patterns of historical change. As, for example, the existence of pre-modern world religions confirms (Buddhism, Christianity, Hinduism, Islam, Judaism, etc.), globalisation is not only a phenomenon of the modern age. Making sense of contemporary globalisation requires placing it in the context of secular trends of world historical development. That development, as the globalist account also recognises, is punctuated by distinctive phases. For example, at times it seemed to intensify: for example, during the era of 'world discovery' from the fifteenth and sixteenth centuries – setting in train European colonisation of vast areas of the world – to the so-called *belle époque* (French, 'beautiful era') of the late nineteenth and early twentieth centuries. This is often considered a 'golden age', characterised by peace between Europe's major states, new technologies improving people's lives, and developments in art and culture. However, between the First World War (1914–18) and the Second World War (1939–45) – the interwar period – the pace of globalisation seemed to speed up, slow down or even to go into reverse. Thus, to understand contemporary globalisation involves drawing on knowledge of what differentiates these discrete phases, including how such systems and patterns of global interconnectedness are organised and reproduced, their different geographies, and the changing configuration of power relations. Accordingly, the globalist account stretches the concept of globalisation to embrace the idea of its distinctive historical forms. This requires an examination of how patterns of globalisation vary over time and thus what is distinctive about it now.

## Alter-globalists

**Alter-globalists** do not deny the transformative qualities of globalisation. But they have a wholly pessimistic view of it. And, as their name suggests, they want to 'alter' its outcomes to include better justice and equality for the world's poorest people. They see it as 'a force for oppression, exploitation and injustice' (Cook 2001). Unwelcome consequences of globalisation are said to include: restructuring of global trade, production and finance to disadvantage the poor; migratory and refugee movements, especially in the developing world and the former Eastern European communist bloc; increasing international terrorism; burgeoning ethnic and/or religious clashes especially within and between many **Third World** states; and the recent rise or resurgence of right-wing populists in Western Europe, in, for example, Austria, France, Germany and the Netherlands.

Such politicians seek to exploit some local people's fears of an 'influx' of foreigners – as a perceived result of economic globalisation – for their own political purposes. While they might be prepared to admit that global free trade theoretically has a good side – lower taxes and cheaper goods – for them this does not outweigh a less desirable outcome. This is a free(r) labour market with associated immigration, the consequence, they claim, of massive uncontrollable population movements from the poor world – for example, North and West Africa and Central and Eastern Europe – to the rich Western European world. (Whether such a movement of labour would actually be beneficial for European economies is rarely discussed.) Notable among the ranks of the alter-globalists are many conservative politicians and their media allies who claim that such population transfers result in often serious 'conflicts between immigrant and established communities in formerly tight-knit neighbourhoods' (Mittelman 1994: 429). Such concerns frequently inform xenophobic populist propaganda, for example, during Germany's recent presidential and legislative elections. In sum, while globalists see economic globalisation as a key to greater national and international stability and security, alter-globalists see the opposite outcome.

## Globalisation sceptics

For the **globalisation sceptics** the very concept of globalisation is rather unsatisfactory. What, they ask, is 'global' about globalisation? If the global cannot be interpreted literally, as a universal phenomenon, then the concept of globalisation seems to be little more than a synonym for Westernisation or Americanisation.

Examining the concept of globalisation, sceptics want to ascertain what would be a conclusive empirical test of the claims of the globalisation thesis. One way to do this is to seek to compare today's globalisation trends with those noted in the past. For example, is there 'more' globalisation today – with overall greater impact – than there was, say, during what economic historians have averred was the *belle époque* of international interdependence: the late nineteenth century to the First World War (1914–18). For the sceptics, such analyses invite the conclusion that what we are witnessing is not globalisation, but a process of 'internationalisation' – more and more significant interactions between what are fundamentally autonomous *national* economies or societies – and 'regionalisation' or 'triadisation', referring to geographically focused, cross-border, economic and social exchanges.

Other sceptics go further, highlighting the importance not of globalisation but of 'fragmentation', implying economic, political and cultural 'implosion'. For example, this view highlights that in recent years empires – for example, that of the Soviet Union, with its former 'imperial' control over vassal states in Central and Eastern Europe – have fragmented into many nation states, while on the other hand growing numbers of poor people in, for example, Africa are excluded from the benefits of economic development. Overall, the sceptic argument highlights the continued salience of what globalists say has declined in importance in the contemporary world order: continued pre-eminence of territory, borders, place and national governments in relation to distribution and location of power, production and wealth. In short, the sceptic view highlights a major divergence between a key understanding of globalisation theory – increased interdependence and declining importance of state boundaries – and what the sceptics see as a world that, for the most part, shows most people's everyday lives dominated primarily by local and national, not global, factors.

## Conclusion

We began this chapter with a key presumption: the world has significantly changed since the 1980s, characterised by the end of the Cold War in the late 1980s, the consequential demise of the Soviet bloc, and global emphasis on economic liberalisation, democratisation and the spread of 'Americanisation' or 'Western' values. Various aspects of globalisation, driven by a technologically sophisticated communications revolution, have collectively impacted upon domestic political outcomes in states around the world. This is because, as Webber and Smith (2002: 6) put it: 'all states [have] in some way . . . been touched by the consequences of the growth of post-war interdependence and by the end of the Cold War'.

## Resource section

### Questions

1. Identify and assess *three* characteristics of globalisation that are important for an understanding of global politics.

2. Is it possible to be objective about globalisation? Examine and comment on globalist, alter-globalist and globalisation sceptic views.

3. Does economic globalisation lead to greater inequality?

4. Thinking of conflict in international relations, did 9/11 change anything?

5. Does globalisation make regionalisation an attractive option for many states?

6. To what extent is 'transnational civil society' linked to globalisation?

7. Are there any 'universal human rights'? If so, how does globalisation encourage their development?

8. How has the concept and practice of security changed as a result of globalisation?

### Recommended reading

**Dicken, P. (2007)** *Global Shift. Mapping the Changing Contours of the World Economy* **(5th edn, Sage)**
A standard work on globalisation, this fifth edition provides a comprehensive and up-to-date coverage of economic globalisation. The book is a clear guide to how the global economy is transformed by transnational corporations, states and interest groups, and technology; a detailed literature review that explains different theories of economic globalisation in the larger context of a descriptive account of newly industrialising economies; sectoral case studies – with a new case study on agro-food industries – which illustrate diverse processes of globalisation; and new material on social movements, governance, environment, and alternative economic systems.

**Haynes, J. (2005)** *Comparative Politics in a Globalizing World* **(website with sample chapter: http://wip.polity.co.uk/haynes/) (Polity)**
This book offers an accessible and broadly conceived examination of the impact of globalisation, primarily on comparative politics and secondarily on international relations. At the centre of the book is a focus on forces and processes of globalisation and how they impact on domestic outcomes in various kinds of states. The book poses and answers two key questions: How do various aspects of globalisation affect outcomes within states? What are the implications of globalisation for our understanding of comparative politics? By focusing on three kinds of states – established democracies, transitional democracies, and non-democracies – Haynes explores how domestic outcomes are affected by contemporary globalisation.

**Held, D. and McGrew, A. (2007)** *Globalization/Anti-Globalization: Beyond the Great Divide* **(Polity)**
This short book provides a key to understanding one of the most important intellectual and political debates of our times. The authors interrogate the evidence about globalisation and assess global trends, in relation to: governance, culture, the economy, patterns of inequality and global ethics. All are examined in relation to contending claims and counterclaims from within the globalisation debate. The authors reflect on the central questions of political life posed by the

great globalisation debate, namely: who rules, in whose interests, to what ends, and by what means? They conclude by proposing a new political agenda for the twenty-first century – a global covenant of cosmopolitan social democracy.

**Held, D. and McGrew, A. (eds) (2007)** *Globalization Theory: Approaches and Controversies* **(Polity)**
This book focuses on explaining leading theoretical approaches to understanding and explaining globalisation, in both its current form and potential future shapes. It is divided into two parts: the first examines competing explanatory theories of globalisation in its contemporary form, and the second looks at competing prescriptions for the future of globalisation.

**Scholte, J.A. (2005)** *Globalization. A Critical Introduction* **(2nd edn, Palgrave Macmillan)**
A systematically revised and updated new edition of a book first published in 2000. The second edition takes a broader perspective giving increased coverage of other dimensions of globalisation alongside its core focus on the rise of supraterritoriality which, the author argues, is globalisation's most distinctive feature.

**Stiglitz, J. (2007)** *Making Globalization Work: The Next Steps to Global Justice* **(Penguin)**
Why doesn't globalisation benefit as many people as it might do? Stiglitz, a former chief economist at the World Bank, argues that things can change and that a world can exist where globalisation really does work for the many or most people.

## Useful websites

**Understanding Globalisation**

**http://www.etu.org.za/toolbox/docs/development/globalisation.html**
The aim of this guide is to provide an understanding of globalisation. When people talk about 'globalisation' or 'globalization' they are usually referring to technological, political, economic and cultural changes which they believe make the world function in a different way from the way it did twenty or thirty years ago. Different opinions exist about origins, driving forces and implications of globalisation. This useful website examines some of them.

# Chapter 2
# International Order, International Society and Globalisation

Fundamental aspects of international relations following the Peace of Westphalia (1648)

International order and international society after the Cold War

Globalisation, international order and international society

Conclusion

After reading this chapter you will be able to:

- Understand what is meant by international order
- Understand what is meant by international society
- See how international order and international society have evolved over time
- Understand rival theoretical approaches to understanding international order and international society
- Explain how current globalisation affects our understanding of international order and international society

*Source:* Getty Images

## Introductory box: International order and international society

**International order** can usefully be thought of as an arrangement or *regime* based on general acceptance of common values, norms – including the body of international law – and institutions that enforce it. In international relations a regime is a set 'of implicit or explicit principles, norms, rules, and decision making procedures around which actors' expectations converge in a given area of international relations' (Krasner 1983: 2). Such areas include: human rights, human and social development, and democratisation and democracy.

In international relations, a combination of actors, rules, mechanisms and understandings works to manage states' coexistence and interdependence. There are challenges to current international order in international relations. For example, what is the effect on international order of including extremist Islamist organisations, such as al-Qaeda and Lashkar-e-Taiba? What is the impact of increased international involvement and significance of various countries, including China, which highlight non-Western views of the world, such as **Asian Values**, which appear potentially to highlight different conceptions of international order?

The idea of **international society** is that states form a community shaped by shared ideas, values, identities and norms that are – to a significant extent – common to all. In this chapter we shall see that the 'English School' of international relations theory maintains that there is a 'society of states' at the international level, despite the condition of 'anarchy' (literally the lack of a ruler or world state).

Many International Relations scholars agree that the 'modern' state system dates from the Peace of Westphalia (1648), an agreement which ended the wars of religion that had plagued Europe for decades. This led eventually to the emergence of numerous states uniformly characterised by a centralisation of political power and a dramatic reduction in the influence of religion in politics. Since then, the process of what is usually referred to as 'modernisation' has accelerated enormously. Not least, international relations has expanded to include greater numbers to include a wide variety of state and non-state actors, while the levels of economic development among states has varied considerably. Further, there are now many more states (nearly 200), as well as numerous and important non-state actors, such as the United Nations, the European Union and al-Qaeda. All this has occurred in the context of rapid technological change, political transformations, industrialisation, the emergence from colonial domination of the developing world after the Second World War, the rise and fall of ideological conflict between the USA and the (now defunct) Soviet Union during the Cold War which followed the Second World War and, most recently, the impact of the multifaceted processes of globalisation.

In order to understand how international relations has developed over time and what factors have played a key role in its development, this chapter examines the relationship between international order, international society and globalisation.

## Fundamental aspects of international relations following the Peace of Westphalia (1648)

Most International Relations scholars would agree that the modern international system dates from the Peace of Westphalia in 1648. The Peace of Westphalia marked off the mediaeval from the modern period in international relations. Following the Peace, growing numbers of independent states – initially in Europe then, via colonisation, in the rest of the world – became the key components of international relations.

The Peace of Westphalia ended the last and most devastating of the great wars of religion, fought between armies of Roman Catholics and Protestants, that had by the

*Source:* The Bridgeman Art Library Ltd/National Gallery, London

**The Peace of Westphalia was the starting point for our modern international system.**

mid seventeenth century raged across much of Europe for thirty years (known as the Thirty Years War). Although the causes of the religious conflict were complex, the devastating outcome it led to was clear: across mainland Europe, there were millions of civilian casualties, with between one-third and one-half of the populations in many areas dying. There was also massive and widespread destruction of property, food shortages, and rampant disease. Because of this destruction and chaos, the impact of the war on Europe was similar to that inflicted centuries later by the First World War (1914–18) and the Second World War (1939–45): wholesale reorganisation of international relations with a view to lessening conflict between states.

The Peace of Westphalia, which ended the Thirty Years War (1618–48), is actually a collective term which includes two separate peace treaties, Osnabrück (May 1648) and Münster (October 1648). The Peace involved the following countries and leaders: the kingdoms of France, Spain and Sweden, the Dutch Republic, and the Holy Roman Emperor, Ferdinand III. The Holy Roman Emperor is a term used by historians to denote a ruler in the Middle Ages, who received the title of 'Emperor of the Romans' from the Pope of the Holy Roman Church, now widely known as the Roman Catholic Church. From the sixteenth century, the Holy Roman Emperor was also a monarch governing the Holy Roman Empire, a Central European union of territories which existed at this time.

The Peace of Westphalia resulted from the first modern diplomatic congress in 1648, which had the effect of starting a new political order in Europe, based upon what was then a new and innovative concept: a sovereign – that is, an autonomous or independent – state governed by an individual leader. From this we can see that the chaos of the Thirty Years War was instrumental in galvanising a revolutionary change in the way that European states sought to order their mutual relations. From this time, they wanted to create and develop a new form of international relations based on interactions between sovereign states with little or no input from either the Holy Roman Emperor or the Pope. In this way, the Peace of Westphalia helped create the basis for a new, decentralised system of legally sovereign and equal states. Henceforward, there was no idea that any one figure would be the leader of Europe. From now on, power was scattered among separate sovereign states, the main way of organising international relations. The result was a fragmentation of authority, with individual rulers enjoying absolute domestic authority and interacting as equals in international relations.

Once the principle of equality of states was established, there evolved an informal arrangement to minimise conflict and maximise cooperation in international relations, known as the **balance of power**. Over the next 140 years – that is, from the Peace of Westphalia (1648) until the French Revolution (1789) – there developed what is known to international historians as the 'golden age of the balance of power'. It is characterised in this way as it was a lengthy period, by and large, without significant international wars. There were still conflicts between states but they tended to be localised and limited, with civilian populations relatively unaffected. In other words, there were no widespread international wars from the mid seventeenth century until the end of the eighteenth century; it was a period of relative international tranquillity, ended by the French Revolution in 1789.

## Box 2.1 The French Revolution

Historians agree unanimously that the French Revolution was a watershed event that fundamentally changed Europe, following in the footsteps of the American Revolution, which had occurred just a decade earlier in 1776. The French Revolution is widely regarded as marking the emergence of the modern political world. This is because it amounted to a definitive shift in the ways we think about, discuss and 'do' politics. The French Revolution, which began in 1789 and lasted for a decade until 1799, violently transformed France. The country shifted from being a country led by a king with a rigid social hierarchy into a modern nation. This means not only that the social structure was loosened but also that political power

was more and more in the hands of middle class (bourgeois) people. Feudalism – a social system that had developed in Europe since the eighth century, where people of low social status (vassals) were protected by lords who they had to serve in war – was now dead. The Revolution unified France and enhanced the national state's power. Wars followed the Revolution – known as the Revolutionary and Napoleonic Wars – which served to demolish the ancient structure of Europe, hastened the advent of nationalism, and inaugurated the era of modern, total warfare: that is, conflict fought for unlimited ends with unlimited means. Overall, the French Revolution had an extraordinary influence on the making of the modern world.

One reason for this period of relative international tranquillity was the existence of a shared outlook – today, we would use the term 'ideology' – among Europe's rulers. This is a reference to the fact that Europe's leaders agreed that the status quo was desirable and that challenges to Europe's equilibrium were unwelcome. This is a way of saying that Europe's rulers had much more in common politically and culturally with each other than they did with the mass of 'ordinary' people living under their rule. But this elite unity did not eventually prevent a political challenge to this form of rule in France, in the form of the French Revolution in 1789. The Revolution highlighted that although there was elite unity among Europe's rulers there were also pronounced class divisions, with European countries characterised by a tiny elite of rich people and a huge mass of poor and underprivileged people. Over time, this led in France to that country's revolution in 1789. While the French Revolution was most obviously a profound challenge to the existing political order in France, its significance was also felt beyond that country. The 'have-nots' of France had a rallying cry: 'Liberty, Equality, Fraternity'. This reflected a desire for fundamental political and economic changes shared by millions of ordinary French men and women.

Beyond France the impact of the Revolution was, first, dramatically to destabilise Europe's status quo and, second, to highlight the importance of international order for peaceful and cooperative international relations. Three aspects of international order were of particular importance: the balance of power, international law, and diplomacy. They were important not only because they provided important bases of international order but also because they encouraged the development of international society, shaped by ideas, values, identities and norms that are – to a lesser or greater extent – common to all. This is the idea, held by the '**English School**' of International Relations theory, that there is a 'society of states' at the international level, despite the condition of 'anarchy' (literally the lack of a ruler or world state).

# The balance of power

To explain the importance of the balance of power for the development of international order we need briefly to go back in time again, before the French Revolution. This is because the decades between the Peace of Westphalia (1648) and the French Revolution (1789) were decades of relative international peace. Why was this? To explain what happened, many International Relations scholars point to the importance of the balance of power. The notion of the balance of power is a simple one, although it has many meanings. I am using it here in the sense of an arrangement whereby governments temporarily agree to work together to thwart a perceived threat to international order, emanating from another state. The balance of power first came into play in the early eighteenth century, when the states of Europe collaborated in a defensive war against King Louis IV of France, who was thought to have designs on the creation of a French-dominated super-state incorporating both France and Spain. Britain, the Dutch Republic, Austria and Prussia united against France in what was called the War of Spanish Succession (1702–1713), a conflict that ended in exhaustion of all warring parties and a temporary settlement, signed at Utrecht. Later examples of the balance of power in operation included a defensive coalition, featuring Britain and Prussia, which emerged to thwart the French leader, Napoleon Bonaparte, in the early nineteenth century, following the French Revolution and associated revolutionary conflicts. Napoleon's aggression resulted in the formation of a protective alliance – involving, among others, Britain and Prussia (the forerunner of Germany) – to defeat his bid for international domination. Later, during the Second World War (1939–45), the balance of power was invoked again, with Britain and later the USA leading a coalition to deal with Germany's Adolf Hitler and the Nazis and their dream of 1,000 years of German domination.

The balance of power – that is, an arrangement whereby governments temporarily agree to work together to thwart a perceived threat to international order, emanating from another state – needs four conditions to work successfully:

- enough states to work together to thwart the designs of a country seemingly intent on systemic domination
- states with relatively equal power – so that no single country can realistically dominate international relations
- continuous but controlled competition for scarce resources, including: territory, trade, and international influence
- agreement that the status quo benefits all.

The bullet points above indicate, however, that the balance of power is more than a series of pacts – it is in addition an arrangement which has wider ramifications for how power is distributed in international relations. It is important to note that such defensive coalitions were short-term alliances that almost inevitably fragmented following elimination of the aggressive threat from, for example, Louis IV, Napoleon or Hitler. This emphasises that the key characteristic of a coalition of states to defend the balance of power is its temporary nature: short-lived unity to defeat a common aggressor. The balance of power was not intended to prevent all international conflicts; it was not an institutionalised, formal mechanism to ensure long-term systemic stability and peace. There were no serious attempts to create such a mechanism until after the First World War ended in 1918, when the League of Nations was created. In summary, a balance of power exists when there is relative equilibrium between the leading countries in international relations. If a country tries to upset this equilibrium – like Louis IV in the early eighteenth century, Napoleon Bonaparte in the early nineteenth century and Hitler in the mid twentieth century, then a short-term defensive coalition forms in order to deal with the threat and defend the existing balance of power.

In sum, in international relations, a balance of power exists when competing forces are 'balanced'. It expresses a doctrine that was intended to prevent any one state from becoming sufficiently strong so as to enable it to enforce its will upon the rest.

## International law

The balance of power was not the only means developed from the seventeenth century to try to maintain peace in international relations. Over time, in addition, a body of **international law** developed, intended to cover many forms of international interactions. A key starting point for development of international law was publication in 1625 of a famous book, *Law of War and Peace* written by a Dutch student of law, Hugo Grotius. *Law of War and Peace* was significant because Grotius tackled a key issue in international relations: when is fighting war morally justified? He argued that all governments should follow specific rules of conduct when dealing with each other – even when their relations break down and war results. Over time, the idea developed that there should be universal rules covering war fighting, resulting in internationally agreed rules of conduct during times of conflict: for example, only civilians should not be ill-treated. Grotius developed his argument by identifying similarities between how individuals and states behave. He noted that while there was international anarchy – in the sense that there was no universal government – there was a variety of ways that states were linked with each other (for example, via religion, culture, customs) which could help significantly to regulate their conduct.

Grotius was pointing to the emergence and development of international order – regulated by international law – to form an international society of states. This term implies existence of a group of similar political entities – states – which regulate their mutual relations through broadly comparable domestic institutions – governments – and which use various international tools to reduce conflict and increase cooperation. Over time, European states began to accept that warfare should only be used for purposes of self-defence, righting an injury, or for upholding the fundamental outlines of international relations, including its norms and laws. A historian, Geoffrey Best (1982), has called the sixty-year period prior to the start of the First World War in 1914 as the law of war's 'epoch of highest repute'. This is because, during this time, states established a positive or legislative – that is, written – foundation which superseded earlier, more informal arrangements rooted in religion, chivalry and customs. Best's observations are also rooted in the fact that from the mid nineteenth century there developed a series of international conferences – for example, the Congress of Berlin in 1884–85 to carve up Africa among European states – emerging as the principle forum for debate and hopefully agreement between governments, a key way to recognise and promote international agreements between countries.

## Diplomacy

**Diplomacy** is the third factor to take into account when thinking about the development of international order. Diplomacy can be defined as the art or practice of conducting international relations, as in negotiating alliances, treaties, and agreements. Yet diplomacy was not new in the period after the Peace of Westphalia in 1648. By that time, official contacts between governments had been practised for hundreds of years, involving not only European states but also many farther afield, including China, Egypt, India, and the Ottoman Empire led by Turkey. The result was that over time diplomacy developed: a system of international interaction involving delivery of messages and warnings, pleading of causes, and the giving and receiving of gifts and/or tribute.

A new phase of diplomacy developed from the eighteenth century reflecting the growth and development of international relations. It was an important component facilitating development and extension of the norms, values and rules that underpin international relations, and which characterise international society. Country representatives became negotiators on behalf of their governments, not merely messengers. A permanent, institutionalised system of diplomatic interaction was established, developing into a cornerstone of international relations, reflective of a widespread desire for order and stability. Diplomats became agents of the state sent abroad for negotiation, reporting and intelligence work. They reported regularly to their home government. In sum, development of a diplomatic system underlined that all governments need regular contact with others and rules to govern such interaction, in order to ensure stability, order and development of mutually acceptable international norms and values.

## Summary

Three cornerstones of international relations – the balance of power, international law, and diplomacy – developed following the Peace of Westphalia in 1648. They were mutually reinforcing, fundamental aspects of the development of international order, serving to lay foundations for the international relations of today. This is a global network involving the world's nearly two hundred states and thousands of important non-state actors, such as multinational corporations, global civil society, international organisations and transnational religious organisations.

# International order and international society after the Cold War

In this chapter we have looked at three cornerstones of the development of international relations from the mid seventeenth century: the balance of power, and the development of international law and diplomacy. We have seen how this took place in the context of development of international order. International order can usefully be thought of as an arrangement based on the more or less consensual acceptance of common values, norms – including the body of international law – and institutions that enforce it. This combination – of actors, rules, mechanisms and understandings – works to manage the coexistence and interdependence of states and leads to the existence of an international society.

International Relations emerged as an academic discipline after the First World War, as a conscious attempt to discover the causes of international conflict and arrive at ways of eradicating it. Many interpretations of its subject matter and concerns emanated from an influential worldview known as Realism. Realism has three fundamental premises:

- State foreign policies seek to achieve greater power. Note, however, there are two forms of power: 'hard' power (the power provided by military and economic clout) and 'soft' power (the power to persuade).
- All states share similar international motivations and goals, for example, they all want as much power and influence as possible.
- The international system is a chaotic, self-help system, characterised by competition, conflict and cooperation.

In Britain, an important centre of international relations enquiry, there emerged from the 1950s what became known as the '**English School**' of international relations, a reaction against and an alternative to Realism. The English School focuses on states' shared norms and values and how they may regulate international relations. Examples of such norms include diplomacy and international law. The English School's focus was on what its proponents believe is the most important post-Second World War development in international relations: creation, evolution and operation of 'international society' and the norms and values that underpin it.

## Box 2.2 The English School of international relations

The English School acquired its name because most of its key figures, while not necessarily English by birth, worked in English universities including the London School of Economics and Political Science, and Oxford and Cambridge universities. Key names associated with the English School include: Hedley Bull, Barry Buzan, Tim Dunne, Robert Jackson, James Mayall, R.J. Vincent, Nicholas J. Wheeler, and Martin Wight. The English School can be thought of as an established body of both theoretical and empirical work. The English School's approach is characterised by a concern with both morality and culture in international relations, and a focus on problems of coexistence, cooperation and conflict.

The English School analysis of international society focuses primarily on states. Conceptually, the idea of 'international society' involves a network of 'autonomous political communities' – that is, states – that are free of control from any higher authority. For Hedley Bull, an International Relations scholar who, although an Australian, was a founder of the English School, the 'starting point of international relations is the existence of states, or independent political communities, each of which possesses a government and asserts sovereignty in relation to a particular portion of the earth's surface and a particular segment of the human population' (Bull 1977: 8). Thus for Bull, the main focus of study of International Relations is the 'world of states' not sub-state entities – such as nations, ethnic groups or religious communities – or claimed universal categories, such as 'humanity'. These various entities do feature in other analytical frameworks in International Relations, such as liberalism, as we shall see in later chapters.

In summary, it is a key premise of the English School approach that when states interact regularly and systematically they do not merely form an international *system* – that is, a purely functional arrangement for mutual benefit – but comprise an international *society*. An international society differs from an international system in a key way: an international society is an arrangement whereby members of the system accept that they have things in common – such as the pursuit of peace or good trade relations – which leads them to behave in certain ways, involving responsibilities towards one another and to the society as a whole. As we have already seen, in international relations over time, key ways to develop these shared norms and ways of behaving were developed in various ways, including international law and diplomacy.

Adherents of the English School approach to international relations would contend that international order is maintained by a shared conception of international society. This is the idea that the world's states form an international society – not 'just' an international system – whose constituent parts interact and are bound together by the pursuit and protection of common interests, values, rules, and institutions. The consequence is that the English School's distinctive approach to the study of international relations emphasises problems of coexistence, cooperation and conflict, especially in relations between sovereign states, the main focus of the approach.

## Globalisation, international order and international society

A cursory reading of what we have covered in this chapter so far would come to the conclusion that for international order and an international society to develop, it is necessary to have all constituent entities agreeing to certain kinds of conduct, which will come about through shared acceptance of certain ways of behaving. We have seen that from the time of the Peace of Westphalia, international relations was dominated by European states and their associated norms and values focused in the balance of power, international law and diplomacy.

How has international order and international society developed in recent years, specifically since the end of the **Cold War** two decades ago? The collapse of the Soviet

Union and its allied communist state systems – in Poland, Czechoslovakia, Bulgaria, Romania, East Germany and Hungary – came about soon after the Cold War ended. As we saw in Chapter 1, the Cold War was a defining feature of international politics for forty years, from the late 1940s until the late 1980s. The conflict centrally involved the USA and the Soviet Union. Because both sides had massive quantities of nuclear weapons and could count on other countries as allies, the conflict between them was widely agreed to be the most serious global crisis. The end of the Cold War was sudden and unexpected – followed by the swift collapse of all communist state systems in Europe a few years later. This amounted to a fundamental change in international relations – a watershed separating one era from another.

Initially there was widespread optimism that a 'new world order' (a term much used by, among others, President George H.W. Bush in 1991–92) would now develop, characterised by the spread of shared norms and values – including liberal democracy – with regular elections, many political parties, and improved **human rights**. Collectively, this would amount to a new regime – in effect, a new international order with a renewed and cohesive international society – that would hopefully spread to previously non-democratic countries, including the former European communist countries noted above. An American political scientist, Giovanni Sartori, summed up the changed international mood at the 1990 American Political Science Association meeting in San Francisco. After the Cold War, he claimed, liberal democracy 'now found itself without enemies or viable alternatives', a view also championed by the influential American commentator Francis Fukuyama, in his book *The End of History and the Last Man* (1992).

Feelings of optimism were, however, generally short-lived: many soon realised that Western political control of world events and dangers was *diminishing* rather than *increasing* in the post-Cold War era. In particular, the 1990–91 Gulf War (fought by the United Nations and led by the USA to oust Iraq from Kuwait, which it had invaded) made it clear that, despite the demise of the Soviet Union, there were, arguably, new challenges to the status quo – such as religious nationalism, as exemplified by Saddam Hussein's attacks on Israel at this time – which would require Western vigilance and solidarity. However, no sooner had the challenge of Iraq's invasion of Kuwait been thwarted than serious civil conflicts emerged in Haiti, Somalia, Yugoslavia and the former Soviet Union itself; outcomes of such conflicts very often seemed to be beyond the West's control. Optimism that a peaceful, cooperative post-Cold War order, stimulated by the spread of liberal democracy and improved human rights to Eastern Europe and the developing world, would underpin both international order and international society, faded significantly from the early 1990s. Instead, older concerns resurfaced. These included a burgeoning number – often of increasing intensity – of conflicts within countries, many of which spilled over into neighbouring territories: such as those in the former Yugoslavia and Somalia. Such conflicts and their regional and international ramifications made it plain that one of the more widespread, albeit less expected and unwelcome, outcomes of the end of the Cold War was an array of nationalist, religious, and ethnic conflicts – especially in many developing and former communist countries, which sprang up once the ideological straitjacket of the Cold War disappeared.

## Box 2.3 Globalisation and international society

Globalisation is significant for an understanding of international society for two main reasons. First, globalisation facilitates the transmission of both material and non-material factors: for example, funds and personnel, on the one hand, and ideas and ideologies, on the other. And both states and various non-state actors may seek to use available opportunities that globalisation provides to try to spread such factors. Second, under conditions of globalisation, state policy makers must attempt to cope with the demands both of domestic political actors, while simultaneously dealing with external developments that can influence domestic outcomes. As a result of globalisation, all states – both 'weak' and 'strong' – experience increasing 'porousness' of national borders. This leads to increased complexity requiring policy makers routinely to deal with external inputs when making and executing policy at both home and abroad. In sum, thinking about the idea of international society we must take into account how globalisation potentially affects both its viability and the bases of its existence.

With hindsight, it is easy to see that the optimistic scenarios of analysts like Sartori and Fukuyama were both simplistic and wrong. They were simplistic because it was no more than wishful thinking that the apparent demise of communism in Central and Eastern Europe would herald a new global liberal democratic dawn; they were wrong because it proved impossible to plant and cultivate the norms and institutions of liberal democracy and improved human rights into many previously undemocratic countries.

In order to see post-1989 changes in perspective it is necessary to place them in historical context. The end of the eighteenth century was marked by a transformation of the political and social order courtesy of the French, American and Industrial Revolutions. The end of the nineteenth century was characterised by industrialisation and the emergence of socialist and social democratic parties in the West. The last years of the twentieth century were notable for simultaneous political, economic, and technological revolutions, with the end of the Cold War and the demise of the Central and Eastern European communist states especially significant.

It is now reasonably clear that global changes associated with globalisation are having an impact on three issue areas of importance to international relations. First, *economic relations*, with particular impact on both manufacturing and employment, a result of the relentless globalisation of the world economy; second, in *scientific discovery*, with important advances in communications technology of particular significance. Third, there are political changes; rather than an 'end of history' as Francis Fukuyama prophesied, what we are seeing is an apparent *return* to history, with a common revival of *older forms of politics*, notable for the construction or reconstruction of ethnic and religious anxieties and expectations – serving, in dozens of countries around the globe, to reopen conflicts for long thought to be a thing of their 'traditional' pasts.

Globalisation is, as we noted in Chapter 1, a multidimensional process. Globalisation is significantly changing technological, economic, political and cultural arrangements and configurations both *within* and *between* countries. Many analysts believe that the result is a significant erosion of what was previously understood to be the nation-state's impenetrable

*Source*: Rex Features/Sipa Press

**Immigrant workers in Dubai: globalisation has erased nation states' 'hard' boundaries and led to significant changes in economic relations.**

'hard' boundaries and a consequent diminution of governments' ability to control both their domestic and international environments. That is, globalisation is said to reduce the power of governments to make definitive decisions regarding their state's and citizens' future; for example, the 2008–2009 international economic crisis demonstrated how hard it is for governments, even those which preside over strong economies, consistently to make and implement policies which take little or no cognisance of wider global developments.

The 'globalisation thesis' – a view which highlights the ability of globalisation to impact upon state policies in various ways and with a variety of outcomes – is, however, at odds with key assumptions of international relations analysis, notably those associated with Realism. For Realists, the world comprises: (1) confined political territories governed by sovereign – that is, independent – states; (2) nation states; and (3) national economies. For Realists, these are the fundamentals, the building blocks, of international relations. The globalisation thesis implies, however, that these long-standing arrangements are in the process of being overtaken by new developments involving the reduction in importance of states and the rise of various kinds of non-state actors: including various international and regional bodies, such as the United Nations and the European Union; and multinational corporations, such as Nike, Google and Apple. Globalisation not only poses a significant challenge to the dominance of state-centric international relations but also highlights various kinds of transnational networks for understanding international relations today.

In short, globalisation not only undermines the concept of international society as traditionally understood but also questions the bases of international order.

The issue of how to maintain and strengthen international order has received much attention, especially since the end of the Cold War in the late 1980s. Some analysts contend that a key impact of globalisation on international relations is to undermine the international state system, so that it is now in decline (Held and McGrew 2002). This is characterised by: withdrawal of the state or at least a reduction in its authority in various issue areas, including economic concerns, and the emergence of new realms with only minimal state involvement (such as, cyberspace and the Internet), as well as 'the rise of non-state actors showing signs of successfully influencing states' policies, and taking over subject areas that the state largely ignored or mishandled' (Mendelsohn 2005: 50). Despite such concerns, however, there is no consensus on the extent to which such issues collectively

## Case study: Lashkar-e-Taiba and the bombing of the Taj Hotel in November 2008

Attacks by Lashkar-e-Taiba on India's largest city, Mumbai, took place from 26–29 November 2008. They are known collectively as India's 9/11. The attacks involved more than ten coordinated shooting and bombing attacks. They were carried out by Islamist terrorists from Pakistan. In the attacks, more than 170 people were killed and over 300 were wounded. Following a siege of the Taj Hotel where many of the Islamists were holed up, India's National Security Guards stormed the hotel, in an action officially named 'Operation Black Tornado', which ended all fighting in the attacks. Ajmal Kasab, the only attacker captured alive by Indian security personnel, admitted that the attackers were members of Lashkar-e-Taiba (Army of the Pure), a Pakistan-based radical Islamist organisation, considered a terrorist entity by the governments of India, the United States and the United Kingdom.

On 7 January 2009, after more than a month of denying the nationality of the attackers, Pakistan's Information Minister, Sherry Rehman, officially accepted Ajmal Kasab's nationality as Pakistani. On 12 February 2009, Pakistan's Interior Minister Rehman Malik, in a televised news briefing, confirmed that parts of the attack had been planned in Pakistan and said that six people, including the alleged mastermind, were being held in connection with the attacks.

A man who identified himself as a former Lashkar militant now working with its charity arm, claimed in late 2009 that the organisation's aims in the Mumbai attacks – as well as more generally – was to wage 'war on the enemies of Islam' (Rosenberg 2009). But it is not clear what this means. Who, exactly, do

Lashkar-e-Taiba, and similar organisations like al-Qaeda, perceive as the 'enemies of Islam'? Such Islamist groups have two sets of linked enemies: the 'West' and their own domestic rulers, who they regard as 'non-Islamic' and 'pro-Western'. These politically organised, radical Muslims are not a new phenomenon, rather they are a well-established tradition in the Muslim world. They are people who characterise themselves as the 'just' involved in struggle against the 'unjust'. The division between 'just' and 'unjust' in the promotion of social change throughout Islamic history parallels the historic tension in the West between 'state' and 'civil society'. In Islam, the 'unjust' rule the state while the 'just' look in from the outside, aching to reform the corrupt system. This is the goal of militant groups like Lashkar-e-Taiba and al-Qaeda: to create a pan-Islamic state, which will, in the process, exclude Western influence from their regions and overthrow their own rulers. They do not imagine that such a state would be ruled via Western interpretations of democracy, where sovereignty resides with the people. This is because they see such a system as one that negates God's own sovereignty.

But the rise of groups like Lashkar-e-Taiba and al-Qaeda are not restricted to one or two countries. They are in many Muslim countries of the Middle East. Their existence reflects much popular disillusionment with decades of disappointing economic and political progress.

 **To what extent are groups like Laskhar-e-Taiba a threat to international order?**

represent a new and significant threat to international order. On the one hand, many important, non-state transnational actors accept the desirability of international order, albeit one normatively characterised by, for example, better human rights, more democracy and greater justice. For example, various Christian churches, including the Roman Catholic Church, the world's largest, have pursued such agendas in recent years. They are a key component of a global coalition of forces – both religious and secular (such as Amnesty International) – which work towards the aim of developing an international society based on liberal values (Thomas 2005). Serious challenges to such a conception of international order come from various terrorist groups, including Islamist terrorist organisations such as al-Qaeda and Lashkar-e-Taiba. Not as well known as al-Qaeda, Lashkar-e-Taiba is a Pakistan-based Islamist terrrorist group which was responsible for a dramatic hotel bombing in Mumbai in late 2008 with the loss of many lives (Tankel 2009). Such terrorist groups emphatically do not accept the legitimacy of the existing international order and the foundations on which international society is based. Instead, they try to advance an alternative order, based on quite different laws, norms and values.

Over time, the principle of state **sovereignty** in international society has been sustained by two important conditions: first, the absence of transnational – that is, cross-border – ideologies that fundamentally compete with nation states for people's political loyalties; and second, by the existence of a common set of values held by governments that engenders an element of respect for other rulers and regimes. Involvement of religious terrorist groups in international relations, such as al-Qaeda and Lashkar-e-Taiba, seriously weakens these two 'pillars' of the Westphalian system. This is because their challenge is bolstered by the development of new – or newly significant – transnational allegiances that challenge popular allegiances to the state by focusing on politically significant alternative, and often incompatible, beliefs and values – in this case radical Islamist values. As a result, they do not sit well alongside established Westphalian principles of international order. This is especially the case if these beliefs and values reject and hence undermine the basic rules on which post-Westphalian international order was founded and the institutions that seek to maintain it. This is expressed in four ways:

1. Such challenges can manifest themselves in the rejection of the state as the main political unit in international relations – the rejection of the principle that leaders of states have the right and duty to deal with other leaders in international relations.
2. Negation of the principle that states are the sole actors that can legitimately use force is significant, as rejection of restrictions on the use of force (for example, in international law civilians cannot legally be targets of war; terrorists, on the other hand, may explicitly target civilians as a key war-fighting technique).
3. Violent non-state terrorist actors also challenge values of international society in a third way: they undermine state–society relations by weakening the ability of governments to carry out a basic governmental responsibility to their citizens: general security. It is very difficult for governments to protect citizens against random terror attacks, as seen on 9/11 in the USA and in Mumbai in November 2008.

4. Violent non-state terrorist actors can also undermine international society by provoking an overreaction by the internationally dominant power, such as the USA, which invaded both Afghanistan (2001) and Iraq (2003) following 9/11. This has the effect of undermining the accepted code of conduct which decrees that states' sovereignty is normally inviolable.

One of the impacts of recent globalisation on international relations is to highlight the importance of various entities in international relations which do not share the norms and values of international society, including transnational terrorist Islamist organisations such as al-Qaeda and Lashkar-e-Taiba (Haynes 2007). These groups' activities highlight an important theoretical and practical question in international relations: Are international order and international society, based on shared norms and values, now possible in the multicultural, multinational, multi-religious international environment we inhabit? For the International Relations theorist, Chris Brown, it makes sense to think of the idea of international society as 'an occasionally idealized conceptualisation of the norms of the old, pre-1914 European states system' (Brown 2005: 51). What he means by this is that, in order to be relevant, international society must be built on consensual – or at least widely shared – norms and values among the members of the society. If Brown is right, can such a conception of international society be a satisfactory starting point when we bear in mind that most existing states are now *not* European? The Council of Europe has forty-seven member states. The Council of Europe was established in 1949 with the goal of working towards European integration, focusing on regional legal standards, human rights, development of democratic rule, the rule of law, and cultural cooperation. On the other hand, over three-quarters of the one hundred and ninety-two members of the United Nations are not European countries.

Brown is also referring to the fact that the pre-1914 international order functioned relatively well – in the sense that there were no significant international conflicts between the end of the Napoleonic Wars in 1815 and the First World War, a century later. Could this, however, have been the result of a high level of cultural homogeneity among the then members of international society which now no longer exists? At the time, most Europeans had a common history informed not only by cultural origins in the ancient Greek and Roman civilisations but also by their Christian faith. The latter did not, however, necessarily imply peaceful relations: historical relationships between European states were often marked by competition or conflict between, for example, followers of the (Greek) Orthodox and (Roman) Catholic churches or between Protestant and Catholic interpretations of Christianity, as in the Thirty Years War (1618–48). How much more likely is it now in our multicultural international system that the potential for competition and perhaps conflict is increased, given that the earlier normative basis for international society is said to be based on shared European religious and cultural underpinnings?

In recent years, some have suggested increased potential for international conflict linked to what is referred to as a 'clash of civilisations'. An American academic, Samuel Huntington, coined the term 'clash of civilisations' in the mid-1990s. Huntington claims there is a developing conflict between 'the West' and 'Islam', an important source of inter-national rivalry, antagonism and, potentially, conflict. Huntington's views have been regarded with interest by many within the International Relations scholarly community. Some at least accept the view that Islamic fundamentalism has now replaced communism as the main threat facing not only the United States (Halper and Clarke 2004; Dolan 2005) but also the West more generally. In addition, Willy Claes, a former secretary-general of the North Atlantic Treaty Organisation, an intergovernmental military alliance based on the North Atlantic Treaty signed on April 4, 1949, has stated that

> Muslim fundamentalism is at least as dangerous as communism once was. . . .
> Please do not underestimate this risk . . . at the conclusion of this age it is a serious
> threat, because it represents terrorism, religious fanaticism and exploitation of
> social and economic justice. . . . NATO is much more than a military alliance. It
> has committed itself to defending basic principles of civilisation that bind North
> America and Western Europe'.

(Claes 1995)

Such arguments, as expressed separately by Claes and Huntington, point to the new significance of what are known generically as *cultural* factors in international relations. According to an International Relations commentator, Simon Murden, the cultural dimen-sion to international relations 'appeared to be reaffirmed amid the reorganization of world politics that followed the end of the cold war and the release of new waves of globalization' (Murden 2005: 539).

In addition to the challenge to international order emanating from radical Islamism, there is also a differing interpretation of international order expressed in the worldview known as Asian Values, found in various countries in East and South East Asia – a region with religious, economic, historical and political diversity. In recent years, there has been a debate between two viewpoints involving what are the most politically and culturally important characteristics of the region's countries. One view maintains that the region's various forms of non-democratic rule – found in, for example, Burma, China and Vietnam – are 'culturally appropriate'. The other maintains that various non-democratic rulers in the region merely turn to old stereotypes as a way of denying democracy in their countries (Barr 2002).

Some analysts have argued that Asian Values do exist, linked to some of the region's religious traditions, such as Confucianism, a 'value system most congruent with Oriental authoritarianism' (King 1993: 141). The American International Relations scholar, Francis Fukuyama, claims that Confucianism is both 'hierarchical and inegalitarian' and character-istic of 'the community-orientedness of Asian cultures' (Fukuyama 1992: 217). His overall concern is that, according to the proponents of a distinctive 'Asian culture', including the prominent Chinese intellectual, Jiang Qing, liberal democracy – a centrepiece of the values of current international society – is actually 'culturally alien' to South East and East Asia (Ommerborn n/d). This is because the region's countries are said to have political cultures and histories that, while differing from country to country in precise details, nevertheless reflect an important factor: a societal emphasis on the collective or group, not the individual as in the West. The collective focus also emphasises 'harmony', 'consensus', 'unity' and 'community' – all cornerstone values of Confucianism – that are said to differ significantly from 'Western culture' and its liberal, individualistic, self-seeking values. Such values are central to Western-focused views of international society and it appears that articulation of Asian Values highlights the potential for a competing set of norms and values to make their mark in international relations.

## Conclusion

In this chapter, we examined how international relations has developed over time in relation to international order, international society and globalisation. We looked at the balance of power, international law and diplomacy as key components of the development of international order following the Peace of Westphalia in 1648. We also focused upon international society, a form of international community which over time developed according to the values and norms of behaviour championed by Western countries. Finally, we turned to the issue of how post-Cold War globalisation had the effect of bringing to the fore non-Western challenges to international order, especially those from Islamist terrorist groups and governments espousing non-liberal 'Asian Values'.

## Resource section

### Questions

1. What was the balance of power and why was it important for the development of international order?

2. How did the Peace of Westphalia help build international society?

3. What are the main characteristics of the English School of international relations?

4. Do you agree that current International Relations reflects Western ideas of international order?

5. Is there still an international society or do radical challenges undermine it significantly?

### Recommended reading

Brown, C. (2002) *Sovereignty, Rights and Justice. International Political Theory Today* (Polity)
This book surveys the relationship between International Relations theory and political theory, showing the way in which the two, for long considered separate, now overlap. In the first part of

the book, Brown presents an historical overview of international political theory from the Peace of Westphalia to now, with brief accounts of the law of nations, and the notion of an 'international society'.

**Bull, H. (1977)** *The Anarchical Society. A Study of Order in World Politics* (Macmillan)
Bull explores three main questions: 'What is the nature of order in world politics?'; 'How is it maintained in the contemporary state system?'; and 'What alternative paths to world order are feasible and desirable?'. According to Bull, the system of sovereign states is not in decline and far from being an obstacle to world order is actually its essential foundation.

**Buzan, B. (2004)** *From International to World Society?: English School Theory and the Social Structure of Globalisation* (Cambridge University Press)
Buzan offers a bracing critique and reappraisal of the English School approach. He begins with the often neglected concept of world society, focusing on the international society tradition and constructivism. He then develops a new theoretical framework that can be used to address globalisation as a complex political interplay among state and non-state actors.

**Orend, B. (2001)** *War and International Justice* (Wilfrid Laurier University Press)
Brian Orend contends in this book that Immanuel Kant's theory of international justice not only accommodates just war's traditional understanding of the morality of war, but improves it. The main strengths of Orend's book lie in its clear writing, theoretical analysis, and insightful interpretation of Kant's theory of international justice as well as his views on the morality of war.

**Walzer, M. (1977)** *Just and Unjust War* (Perseus Books)
This classic work examines not only the issues surrounding military theory, war crimes, and the spoils of war from the Athenian attack on Melos to the My Lai massacre, but also a variety of conflicts in order to understand exactly why, according to Walzer, 'the argument about war and justice is still a political and moral necessity'.

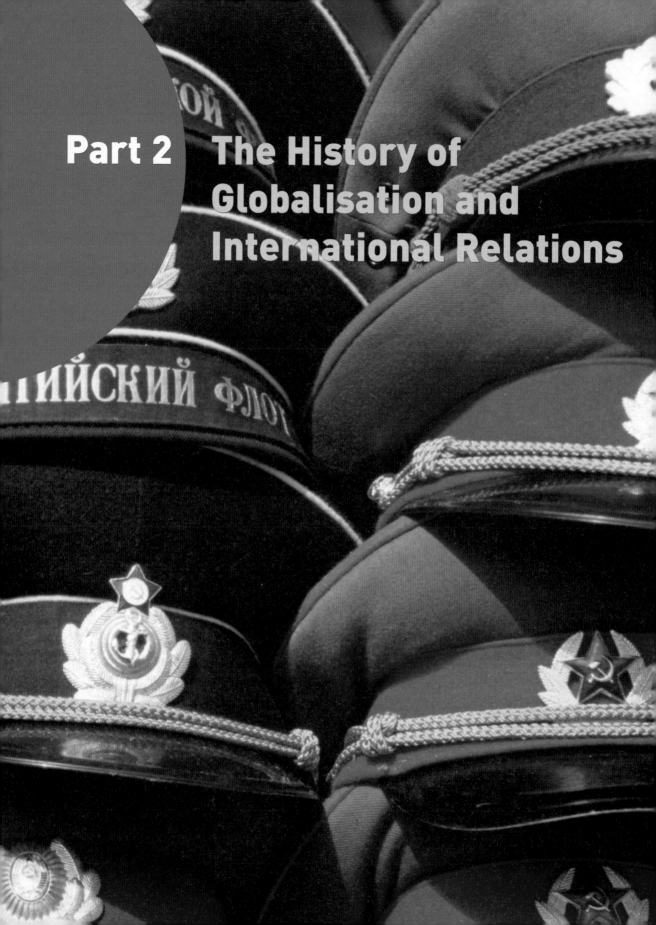

# Part 2　The History of Globalisation and International Relations

## 3. International Relations from the Early Nineteenth Century to the Second World War

## 4. International Relations after the Second World War

## 5. After the Cold War: International Relations in a Globalised World

This part focuses on the history of globalisation and international relations in the twentieth century. Chapter 3 looks at the first half of the century, until the end of the Second World War in 1945. It examines how the international system expanded over time, with a focus on four key events: European colonisation of the developing world in the early twentieth century; the First World War which lasted from 1914–1918; the inception and demise of the League of Nations (1918–1945), and the economic and ideological polarisation of the 1920s and 1930s, which paved the way for the outbreak of the Second World War in 1939.

Chapter 4 focuses on the period between 1945, when the Second World War ended, and the late 1980s, when the Cold War, between the USA and the Soviet Union (or USSR), finished. We look at: the formation and development of the United Nations from 1945; regionalisation in the 1950s and 1960s in the context of the Cold War between the USA and the Soviet Union, and finally, the impact of decolonisation and the subsequent emergence and development of the Non-Aligned Movement, a large group of developing countries with a focus on international relations.

Chapter 5 looks at the period following the end of the Cold War in the late 1980s and the subsequent collapse of the Soviet Union in 1991. Initially, there was a wave of optimism that the end of the Cold War would lead to greater international cooperation to deal with pressing international concerns, such as: profound economic and social injustices; armed conflicts, both between and within states; widespread human rights abuses; and worsening environmental degradation and destruction. There was hope that international efforts would be channelled through various international organisations, especially the United Nations.

In short, international relations significantly changed after the Cold War. Not only did the great communist monolith, the Soviet Union, collapse, to be replaced by Russia and a host of smaller, post-communist states in Eastern and Central Europe. In addition, there was widespread economic liberalisation, democratisation, and the spread of individualistic 'American' and 'Western values'. Globalisation was intimately connected to all these developments: it was the main way of spreading these ideas. Various aspects of globalisation – for example, pressures for more and better human rights, better protection of the natural environment and encouragement for 'ordinary' people to participate in politics – collectively impacted upon how we understand international relations. The chapter illustrates how, following the Cold War, *all* states – rich and poor, big or small – were significantly affected by the consequences of the spread of globalisation, with political, economic and cultural effects. One of the key consequences of globalisation was the spread of various *trans*national – that is, cross-border – actors and forces. While some, such as multinational corporations (MNCs; sometimes called transnational corporations, or TNCs) were widely seen as intimately connected to Western-style globalisation, others, such as non-Western, non-individualistic, 'Asian Values' and self-proclaimed champions of Islam, such as Osama bin Laden, defined themselves in opposition to Western-led globalisation. This is because they saw it as a malign, Americanised process, seeking to undermine or destroy, non-Western ways of life.

*Source*: Getty Images/Gallo Images

# Chapter 3
# International Relations from the Early Nineteenth Century to the Second World War

European nationalism and imperialism

The First World War and International Relations

The League of Nations: an attempt to build an international organisation to maintain collective security

The legacy of the League of Nations

Conclusion

After reading this chapter you will be able to:

- Chart how international relations expanded from Europe to the rest of the world via European imperialism
- Explain the impact of the First World War on international relations
- See how the League of Nations was created in 1919 in order to bring more security to international relations
- Understand why the League of Nations did not prevent the outbreak of the Second World War in 1939

*Source*: Getty Images/Gallo Images

## Introductory box: European imperialism and the creation of a global states system

European **imperialism** from the seventeenth century created the global states system. This political unification of the world emerged directly from a European, Christianity-oriented civilisation centring on the then emerging nation states of Western Europe. These states differed from their predecessors in a number of crucial respects, making the unification of the globe possible and ensuring that it followed certain patterns and took certain forms. Technology was also important in this process: European imperialist states possessed an unprecedented range of power, reflecting a comparative advantage in naval and military technology. They also drew strength from their statehood itself, providing them (1) with the means to mobilise and concentrate their power and (2) a form of ideology with which to support it and motivate their citizens. In addition, there was the ability and willingness to use large-scale violence, based on technological supremacy. Finally, there was an assumed cultural supremacy often translated into political and social institutions.

The power of independent statehood, combined with the force of nationalism, provided the basis on which the great maritime European colonial empires, which lasted in some cases from the seventeenth to the twentieth century, were founded and consolidated. To an extent the world was also politically unified as a result of this process, with colonial countries eventually adopting European forms of state, administration and economy.

Essentially, the global domination of the Europeans rested not only upon their multiple strengths – political, economic, and technological – but also relied on their organisational skills and institutions. These were crucial factors when it came to the translation of potential advantage into actual domination. Note, however, that the processes, practices and structures of imperial rule may have (superficially and temporarily) unified the globe politically under Western domination, yet they also helped to create divisions and tensions that became especially notable after decolonisation during the twentieth century.

Most International Relations experts would agree that the 'modern' international state system dates from two specific events that took place in what is now Germany in 1648: the signing of the Peace of Westphalia. Since then, the international state system has grown considerably in size, to encompass the globe. Now everywhere, except for Antarctica, is controlled by governments. There are now nearly two hundred states – nearly ten times more than in 1648, when there were less than two dozen. There are also tens of thousands of important non-state actors – including multinational corporations, international organisations and regional bodies such as the European Union – as well as a wide variety of levels of economic development among countries. All these developments have occurred during widespread technological, political and industrial changes affecting all countries. The international system has also experienced the emergence of a specific bloc of countries after the Second World War: the 'developing' or Third World, as well as the rise and fall of divisive ideological conflict between the USA and the (now defunct) Soviet Union, which was the leading country in the communist group of countries, known as the Second World. The United States, the USSR's chief rival, was the key state in the First World, made up of a number of countries which espoused both liberal democratic and capitalist norms and values. In addition, international relations has witnessed in recent years an intensification of globalisation, with often profound economic, political, cultural and technological impacts (see Chapter 1).

Overall, these events and developments have profoundly affected international relations. Yet, despite undoubtedly significant changes over time, the international system is still founded upon a key principle: state sovereignty or autonomy. This principle centres on the idea that the state is supreme within its own territory, acknowledging no higher authority. In this chapter we examine two fundamental questions: How did things change over time to change the course of international relations after the Peace of Westphalia in 1648? (For further coverage of the Peace of Westphalia, see Chapter 2, where we look at the development over time of international order and international society.)

This chapter examines three crucial developments for the understanding of current international relations:

- European imperialism from the early nineteenth century
- The First World War
- Formation and development of the League of Nations, devised to ensure increased international security and peace after the traumas of the First World War.

By the end of the chapter, you should understand why and how international relations developed over time, between the early nineteenth century and the outbreak of the Second World War in 1939. You should also have specific knowledge of important structures and processes, including: European imperialism, nationalism, and the first international organisation dedicated to collective security and peace – the League of Nations.

Following the French Revolution and associated wars in the late eighteenth and early nineteenth centuries, international relations over the next century was strongly influenced by two interlinked developments: nationalism and imperialism. Both were heavily implicated in the causes of the First World War, a conflict of such severity and consequence that a new collective security formal mechanism – the League of Nations – was founded in order to try to deliver 'collective security'. **Collective security** in international relations encompasses the idea that states will join together when necessary to take cooperative action to try to thwart an aggressor, for example Napoleon Bonaparte after the French Revolution in 1789 and Adolf Hitler and the Nazis during the Second World War.

## European nationalism and imperialism

European nationalism and imperialism from the late eighteenth century were important developments, of central significance to our understanding of international relations. They are important because they helped to spread key political and economic norms and arrangements from Europe to the rest of the world.

## Nationalism

The term, nationalism, is usually understood as both dogma – that is, a doctrine or code of beliefs accepted as authoritative, such as: 'she believed all the Marxist dogma' – and as an idea that can encourage people to act politically, as in the large number of nationalist movements that emerged and developed around the world over the last two hundred years. The idea of nationalism is to emphasise that a nation – understood here as a group of people of indeterminate but normally considerable size who believe themselves linked by intense feelings of community and, as a result, 'deserve' to have a state of their own – has a right to constitute an independent, sovereign political community. They believe this because of what they understand to be their shared history, informed by a perceived common national destiny. For nationalists, it is only right and proper that state borders should match, as precisely as possible, the boundaries of the nation. In extreme cases, such as that demonstrated in the ideology of Nazi Germany developed by Adolf Hitler in the 1920s and 1930s, and that of Fascist Italy under the dictator Benito Mussolini (1883–1945), the state regards nationalism as *the* supreme facet of a person's and a people's identity.

Some prominent scholars of nationalism, such as Ernest Gellner (1983) and Eric Hobsbawm (1990), highlight the importance of various historical and economic factors in the growth of nationalism. Increasingly, however, scholars of nationalism recognise that to develop a complete understanding of the development of nationalism over time, as it affected both developed countries such as Britain and developing countries such as India, we need in addition to take into account the direct and indirect influence of religion on the development and practice of nationalism (Reiffer 2003). Certainly, in the case of European nationalism and its close corollary, imperialism, the proclaimed desire to spread 'Christian values' to non-Christian parts of the world was an important motivation for European expansionism from the early nineteenth century, especially to Africa, the main focus of European imperialist attentions in the century prior to the First World War (1914–18).

A scholar of nationalism, Anthony D. Smith, is a key authority concerning links between religion and European nationalism. Smith claims that 'perhaps more detrimental than anything to our understanding . . . has been the general trend to dismiss the role of religion and tradition in a globalizing world and to downplay the persistence of nationalism in a 'post-national' global order' (Smith 2003: ix). Smith's 2003 book, *Chosen Peoples: Sacred Sources of National Identity*, is a persuasive account of the historical relationship of religion and nationhood, necessary for a complete understanding of the development of international relations in the nineteenth and twentieth centuries.

## Box 3.1  Religious nationalism

When there is a close or even synonymous relationship between religion and nationalism, we use the term 'religious nationalism'. Religious nationalism is an important component of present-day international life, defining many nations – such as Israel (Judaism), Saudi Arabia (Sunni Islam), the USA (Christianity) and India (Hinduism) – in terms of the religion followed by most people in those countries; in addition, it may also be connected to other components of identity, including culture, ethnicity, and language. Religious nationalism is identified in various contexts, leading to different outcomes. When the state, as in present-day Iran or Saudi Arabia or in Afghanistan under the Taliban (1996–2001), derives its political legitimacy primarily from public adherence to religious not secular doctrines, then what we have is a theocracy: the state is dominated by officials who believe themselves, or are widely thought to be, divinely guided. Overall, there are several ways in which religion and nationalism interact, identifying a number of degrees of influence which religion has on nationalism. In the first category, *religious nationalism*, religion and nationalism are inseparable. In other national movements, on the other hand, religion plays a less dominant role, 'merely assisting the more prominent nationalist movement as a cohesive element' (Reiffer 2003: 215).

Many examples of primarily ethnic and cultural nationalism, especially in the developing world, also include important religious aspects. However, they are a variable marker of group identity, not necessarily a *fundamental* impetus for nationalist claims. In other words, religion does not *necessarily* occupy an influential or central position in a nationalist movement. It may be that the secular goal of a nation state is the primary concern, but this does not imply that religion is utterly irrelevant to such a movement, rather that it can become significant as a supporting element that can help bring together a community in pursuit of a nation state. Reiffer calls this 'instrumental pious nationalism' (Reiffer 2003: 229). Examples are often noted among current Muslim-led liberation movements – for example, the Palestinians, Chechens, Filipino Moros and Kashmiris – as well as India's Sikhs (Reiffer 2003: 225–6).

The term 'religious nationalism' is widely used in literature concerned with the rise from the late nineteenth century and early twentieth century of anti-colonial nationalism in the Middle East, Asia and Africa (Engels and Marks 1994; Furedi 1994; Haynes 1993). During European imperial rule, as in British rule in India or French rule in Algeria, these Western powers sought to introduce and embed secular regimes which, however, in many cases, including the two countries just noted, India and Algeria, led to increasingly significant anti-colonial, religion-inspired, indigenous opposition campaigns which, in both cases, eventually led to the ousting of colonial rule – in India in 1947 and in Algeria a few years later, in 1964. More generally, Hinduism, Islam and Buddhism all underwent periods of intense political activity in various colonial countries during the late nineteenth and twentieth centuries. For example, East and West Pakistan (now Bangladesh and Pakistan respectively) was explicitly founded as a *Muslim* state in 1947, religiously and culturally distinct from *Hindu*-dominated India, following the withdrawal of British imperial rule. In addition, Buddhism was of great political importance in various South East and East Asian countries, including Burma and Vietnam, in the context of their struggle for liberation from British and French colonial rule respectively, from the 1940s. Prior to that, immediately after the First World War ended in 1918, the rise of Arab nationalism had been intimately associated with Islam in almost all such countries, an integral aspect of anti-European opposition ideology (Haynes 1993; Khan 2006).

Turning to the relationship between European nationalism and imperialism in Africa during the colonial era – that is, from the early nineteenth century until the 1960s – there was typically close affinity between Christian missionaries and European colonial administrators. This did not rest only on their shared Christianity but was also bolstered by the fact that they were all Europeans, striving to spread associated norms and values linked to what they regarded as European civilisation, including the rule of law, improved human rights, and improved gender equality. While Christian missionaries and religious figures may, on occasion, have been unhappy with certain aspects of colonial policy – such as European settlers' confiscation of Africans' land in Kenya's White Highlands without compensation, which incurred the wrath of the British-run Anglican Church – there were many points of agreement between Christian leaders and colonial administrators. This is because both religious and secular figures were pursuing the same broad aims, as they saw it: to bring the benefits of European civilisation, including the Christian God, to 'benighted 'Africa (Haynes 1996).

A second factor to unite European religious and non-religious figures was the challenge of Islam. By the early nineteenth century Islam was a highly significant religion in west, east and, to an extent, central Africa. Initially, during the early phase of European colonialism in the early nineteenth century there were frequent conflicts between Muslims and Europeans in many parts of Africa. However, over time, both Muslim leaders and colonial administrators had by and large arrived at ways of working together. The normal arrangement was that the former would guarantee their communities' acquiescence to European rule in exchange for personal financial rewards and for a large measure of religious and social autonomy. Christian missionaries had no choice but to accept the fait accompli; in some places, for example Muslim-dominated northern Nigeria, they were not even allowed to proselytise, that is, attempt to get people to convert to Christianity (Haynes 1996).

Of course Europeans did not bring only Christianity to Africa and other parts of what we would now call the developing world. They also brought with them many other aspects of Western-style modernisation, including: the money economy, urbanisation, Western education and centralised government. In doing so, Europeans helped to mould and develop Africans' changing responses to European colonialism. From an initial welcome, a groundswell of demands for autonomy and then independence gathered pace. By the early 1950s African nationalist leaders, encouraged by the success of India and Ceylon (now Sri Lanka) in achieving independence from colonial rule in 1947, were demanding the same for themselves and their followers. Many leading nationalists were Christians educated in schools and colleges founded by European Christian organisations. By the early 1970s, just twenty-five years after significant agitation for independence began, nearly all African countries had thrown off European imperial rule.

*Source: Getty Images/Bridgeman Art Gallery*

European
imperialism
created the
global states
system.

## Imperialism

The term, imperialism, refers to interlinked – political, social and economic – forces, including nationalism and religion, which significantly shaped international relations from the early nineteenth century until the withdrawal of a European imperial presence from Africa and elsewhere in the decades after the Second World War. Initially regarded by most Europeans as a desirable and acceptable way of spreading their civilisational values and norms, including Christianity, imperialism became increasingly contentious following the publication in 1902 of *Imperialism: A Study*, written by a British economic historian, John Hobson (2005). Hobson contended that the imperialistic rivalries of this time, involving the major European powers, was a dangerous source of friction which would lead inevitably to sustained and serious international conflict. Hobson's view – supported by the Russian Communist theoretician, activist and politician, Vladimir Ilych Lenin – was that imperialism was a key cause of the First World War in 1914. Hobson also argued that the Europeans' competition was not only contoured by competing nationalism but also by the desire for colonial territory, not only to demonstrate national 'greatness' but also to extend pursuit of economic goals to overseas contexts. For example, Britain's imperial activities in India sought both to acquire territory for the sake of British nationalist aggrandisement but also because India provided significant scope for selling goods produced in Britain to a growing number of Indian consumers.

Apart from territorial and commercial interests, European imperialism was also important in another way for our understanding of international relations. Imperialism helped to spread and embed European political and economic models which eventually developed during the twentieth century into a truly global system of international relations. What became a political and economic political unification of the world stemmed directly from a European, Christianity-orientated, state system. Centralised European states, developing from the seventeenth century after the Peace of Westphalia, differed from their predecessors in a number of crucial respects: most importantly, however, in making the centralisation of political power in a national government a fundamental aspect of their 'stateness' – as opposed to other forms of political power, as found for example in the Ottoman Empire organised from Istanbul (capital of present-day Turkey), which was far more decentralised. This helped make the unification of the globe possible by ensuring that territories in the developing world taken over by the Europeans during their imperialist phase (1880–1914) followed similar administrative and governmental patterns and took particular, European-derived forms – such as, for example, the government of India which emerged after Britain's imperial withdrawal from that country in 1947.

Technological developments were also highly important in this wide-ranging process of global Europeanisation. European imperialist states possessed an unprecedented range of power, reflecting a comparative advantage in both naval and military technology. They also drew strength from their statehood itself. That is, nationalism provided them (1) with the means to mobilise and concentrate their power, and (2) enabled them to unearth a form of collective ideology that helped support their imperialistic endeavours not least by motivating their citizens in support. In addition, there was a European ability and willingness to use large-scale violence, based on technological supremacy. This was apparent in any of the European wars of imperial acquisition from the early nineteenth century – from Morocco in the west to Indonesia in the east – which in all cases succeeded ultimately because the Europeans could rely upon sophisticated and technologically advanced 'weapons of mass destruction', such as the machine gun, artillery and bomber aeroplanes.

Finally, there was an assumed European cultural supremacy manifested in political, social and economic institutions, introduced and consolidated during imperialist control in many parts of the developing world. For example, every imperial takeover by European powers was followed by the introduction of European-style administrative, political and economic institutions, with the aim of turning the controlled territories into European-style polities. In sum, European imperialism, fused with the power of both nationalism and religious belief, provided the basis on which the European imperialists managed to spread and consolidate their international influence from the early nineteenth until the second half of the twentieth century. During this time, nearly all parts of the globe became increasingly interdependent, laying the foundations for today's technologically driven globalisation.

The imperialism of the Europeans led directly to a huge growth in the number of states making up the international system, as a result of the demise of the Europeans' imperialism after the Second World War. Note, however, that the decolonisation process actually began much earlier in the first years of the nineteenth century, which saw independence for former Spanish and Portuguese colonies in Latin America, including Brazil, Chile, and Mexico. The post-colonial independence of more than twenty countries in Latin America and the Caribbean in the first half of the nineteenth century came in the wake not only of two successful revolutions, the American (1776) and the French (1789), but also after a major international conflict – the Napoleonic Wars – which involved France, Britain, Prussia and many other countries.

The Napoleonic Wars took place during 1803–1815. They were a series of conflicts, all of which involved not only the French Empire led by Napoleon Bonaparte (1769–1821) but also various groups of European allies and opposing coalitions. They can be regarded as a series of conflicts with roots in the French Revolution (1789). Their impact was dramatic, involving widespread conflicts that for the first time employed mass conscription of troops, which in turn helped to revolutionise armies across Europe. Initially the French were triumphant, managing to control vast areas of Europe, although they found they were overstretched in Russia following invasion of that country in 1812. Eventually, in 1815, Napoleon suffered emphatic military defeat, leading to the return of the Bourbon monarchy in France. During the conflicts, Spain's empire fragmented as a result of French occupation of Spain, which served to weaken Spain's hold over its colonies in Latin America and enabled nationalist revolutions throughout much of the region. In short, the independence of many Latin American and Caribbean countries was facilitated by their isolation from the Spanish and Portuguese empires as a result of Napoleon's successes in the Peninsular War (1807–1814). A century later, after the First World War (1914–18), the demise of the Turkish Ottoman Empire was a catalyst for the independence of a number of countries in the Middle East and North Africa, including North Yemen (1919), Egypt (1922) and Iraq and Oman (both 1932).

However, the greatest catalyst for the creation of new countries in the developing world was the Second World War (1939–45). As a result of economic weakness caused by these years of often intense war, as well as a declining popular belief in the ethical and moral desirability of imperialism, the leading colonial powers – Britain and France – relinquished nearly all their colonies in a few decades after 1945. As a result, dozens of new countries, mainly in Africa, Asia, the Caribbean and the Middle East, were created. The Second World War was an important catalyst for the end of colonial rule, especially in Africa and South and East Asia. In South Asia nationalist politicians succeeded in gaining the exit of the British by the late 1940s, while the French were persuaded to leave Vietnam as a result of civil war. In Africa, nationalist politicians were increasingly influential, gaining widespread popular support for a policy of **decolonisation**. By the mid-1960s Africa's freedom from colonial rule was well advanced. It was not, however, solely domestic pressures which persuaded the colonial powers to quit.

There was an influential international anti-colonial lobby which played a major role in decolonisation. After the Second World War, there was growth of an international climate of anti-imperialism which served, in tandem with the nationalist struggles, to open the floodgates of decolonisation in the 1950s and 1960s. The emergent superpowers, the USA and the Soviet Union, despite their profound ideological differences, were united after the Second World War in their opposition to European imperialism. Their main argument was that because the Second World War had been fought by many European countries, including Britain and France against racist and totalitarian regimes in Germany, Japan and Italy, then it was quite inappropriate to return to the situation which had prevailed before the war where large portions of the globe were ruled by European imperialists. In the case of the United States in particular, another reason for the government's anti-colonial stance was that it was anxious to remove the colonial powers' economic control of their colonies so as to facilitate access for the USA's emergent multinational business corporations that were now anxious to expand their trading links beyond their borders in pursuit of increased profits.

In sum, after the Second World War the international environment was, in several ways, conducive to the success of anti-imperialism. This was augmented by domestic concerns promoting enfranchisement of racial and ethnic minorities in many Western states, including the USA. The reason for this was that after the Second World War, the principle of equality became much more pronounced than in the pre-war period. For example, this led in the United States to the enfranchisement of the offspring of black slaves who, for the first time, were able to vote in local and national elections. In addition, one of the key international manifestations of equality between nations – self-determination – was institutionalised as a primary international value in the Charter of the United Nations (UN), the leading international security organisation which emerged immediately after the Second World War. The General Assembly of the UN – comprising nearly all the world's states – was often to articulate this doctrine in later years, applying it in various Declarations and Resolutions.

A fourth wave of decolonisation, involving the creation of several new states, came at the end of the Cold War after 1989. At that time, Yugoslavia fell apart and several new countries were created, including: Croatia, Serbia, Slovenia and Bosnia-Herzegovina. The demise of the Soviet Union in 1991 also saw the founding of many new states, including: Estonia, Lithuania, Latvia, Armenia, Estonia, Georgia, Tajikistan and Uzbekistan. In sub-Saharan Africa, Namibia, Eritrea and Somaliland also emerged as new states following the Cold War.

To summarise, there have been four main waves of new state creation. They followed the Napoleonic Wars (new states in Latin America and the Caribbean), the First World War (the Middle East), the Second World War (Asia, Africa, the Middle East), and the Cold War (Africa, the Balkans, former Soviet Union). As a result, the number of states grew from less than fifty in 1945 to nearly two hundred now. The result is that over two-thirds of the total number of states today are in the developing world, and nearly all came about following periods of European imperial rule. There was an especially concentrated period of decolonisation during the 1950s and 1960s, when more than forty developing countries, mostly in Africa and Asia, gained their independence from colonial rule.

Following the Second World War, three factors were especially important in encouraging the demise of the principle that it was desirable for European countries to retain administrative control of territories in other parts of the world:

- an international climate that no longer regarded imperialism as appropriate
- the post-war weakness of the leading imperial powers, Britain and France
- increasingly vociferous and effective demands for independence expressed by nationalist politicians in many parts of the developing world.

A large number of developing countries – most of which were in Asia – achieved independence in the immediate post-Second World War period, that is, during 1945–50: including, Bhutan, Burma (Myanmar), Ceylon (Sri Lanka), East Pakistan (now Bangladesh), India, Indonesia, Israel, Korea, Laos, Lebanon, Nepal, the Philippines and West Pakistan (now Pakistan). This was important for international relations as it signified that, for the colonial powers, the game was up: the imperial dream was over. The greater the number of states gaining their independence, the swifter and more vociferous the demands for freedom from colonial rule from remaining colonies became.

In summary, by the time of the First World War, the near-global European dominance of international relations rested not only upon the Europeans' multifaceted strengths but also in the power and authority of their administrative organisations and institutions, a crucial factor when it came to translating potential into actual domination via imperial rule. The processes, practices and structures of imperial rule consolidated European domination of much of the globe for a lengthy period. In addition, they laid the foundations for future international divisions and tensions that became clear following decolonisation after the Second World War.

## The First World War and International Relations

It is important to understand that the First World War was one of the most important conflicts in human history. It was a rare watershed event that ended one era in international relations and ushered in a new one. It was the first general European war in more than two hundred and fifty years, like the religious wars of the seventeenth century in terms of the scale and impact of the conflict. As such, it marked both the triumph and the collapse of the balance of power policies that had been developed to such a high degree during the seventeenth and eighteenth centuries. The balance of power triumphed in the fact that the alliance commitments of various European powers were honoured: Russia honoured Serbia, as it had pledged to do, in the face of an ultimatum against the Balkan republic by Austria-Hungary; Germany thereby honoured its commitment in the Dual Alliance by supporting

Austria; France and ultimately Britain joined Russia, their ally in the Triple Entente, in the fight against the central powers. As a result, the First World War broke out.

Yet that is not at all the way balance of power politics was intended to work, and thus the general outbreak of war also signalled the failure of those policies. An ominous prelude had been sounded in 1907 when British statesmen felt compelled to abandon their traditional aloofness in the political rivalries of continental Europe – a posture that had permitted them to play the role of balancer and peace keeper throughout the nineteenth century – by aligning Britain with France and Russia in opposition to the growing militarism of Kaiser Wilhelm II, the leader of Germany. As a result, when war broke out, the conflict spread quickly. In the absence of an effective balancer, the logic of counterbalancing power with power had become perverse. The conditions were *too* evenly matched now, and neither could be intimidated into forsaking the battlefield by the threat of overwhelming opposing force. The honouring of commitments had the effect of emphatically closing off other avenues of choice and states played out their roles to the bitter end: global conflagration.

## Case study: Why the First World War (1914–18) was an important change in international relations

How do we know when an important change has taken place in international relations? In this case study, we look at the First World War and see why it represents an important shift from one era to another in international relations.

From the signing of the Peace of Westphalia in 1648 until the Napoleonic Wars in the early nineteenth century (a conflict involving France, Britain and Prussia) there was relative international peace. During the middle of the nineteenth century, peace broke down again, leading to the Crimean War which began in 1854 and involved Russia, France and Britain. Overall, however, the nineteenth century is known as a 'century of peace', which was maintained by a relatively stable distribution of power in the international system, known as the 'balance of power'. This enabled the leading European countries – including Britain, France, Prussia and Russia, collectively known as the 'great powers' – to enjoy relatively peaceful coexistence. This broke down in the Crimean War and again sixty years later when the First World War broke out.

Such wars signified the failure of the great powers to preside over an international system which would be peaceful. Because of its massive destruction of property and loss of life, the First World War indicated conclusively that the international system could no longer be maintained peacefully by an informal arrangement. Something more was needed: a formal organisation to try to ensure peace and cooperation. This was because international conflict was now both global and unprecedentedly destructive: over twenty million people died in the First World War. The period from 1918 (the end of the First World War) to 1939 (when the Second World War started) was a time of trying to build international order and stability under the auspices of an international organisation: the League of Nations, something which had never been tried before.

In addition, there was a second major change at this time: international relations was no longer an environment dominated by European powers. New, non-European powers, especially the United States and the Soviet Union (which included not only Russia but also great swathes of territory in Asia following the Bolshevik Revolution of 1917) were flexing their muscles and seeking to increase their international influence.

However, the factors disposing the international system towards instability and ultimately toward conflict were not dealt with by founding the League of Nations system. War broke out again just two decades after the First World War finished. So, while the First World War was an important period of change in international relations, the League of Nations did not signify a fundamentally different approach to the perennial approach of war and peace, mainly because states were not willing enough to put their trust in an international organisation to deal with their security problems after the First World War.

● **To what extent did the First World War represent a fundamental change in international relations?**

*Source: Getty Images/Time & Life Pictures*

The First World War (1914–18) showed that the world could no longer be maintained peacefully by informal arrangements.

## The League of Nations: an attempt to build an international organisation to maintain collective security

### The origins of the League of Nations

The League of Nations owed its origins to the First World War and the devastation with which it was associated. The revolutionary advances in military technology (for example, aerial bombing, submarines, tanks and 'mustard gas', so-called because it smelled to many people of mustard) used during the war led many people to question the notion that war could be a useful tool of state policy as it had routinely been for centuries. The war also highlighted the contradiction between national defence and national security. That is, while governments could provide national defence – albeit at huge financial cost – the war made it clear that this did not necessarily mean increased security. This realisation underpinned a move towards developing a collective security regime involving an international organisation – the League of Nations – with wide-ranging powers.

The American president, Woodrow Wilson, suggested such a move to the upper house of government in the USA, the Senate, in a speech in January 1917. This was three months before the US entered the war on the allies' side against Germany. Wilson argued that what the world needed was not a 'balance of power, but a community of power, not organized rivalries, but an organized common peace'. A year later, in 1918, Wilson elaborated on this in the announcement of his famous 14 Points. Beginning with a commitment to open diplomacy and a disavowal of secret treaties (which had become the norm in the second part of the nineteenth and the early years of the twentieth centuries), Wilson went on to include the removal of economic barriers ('free trade'), the limitations of armaments procurements ('no more arms races'), the admission of the right of national self-determination (although this was limited to Europe and not meant to include Europe's colonies) and the establishment of a mechanism and structure to ensure all this happened: the League of Nations.

## Box 3.2  President Woodrow Wilson's 14 Points

1. Open covenants of peace, openly arrived at, after which there shall be no private international understandings of any kind but diplomacy shall proceed always frankly and in the public view.

2. Absolute freedom of navigation upon the seas, outside territorial waters, alike in peace and in war, except as the seas may be closed in whole or in part by international action for the enforcement of international covenants.

3. The removal, so far as possible, of all economic barriers and the establishment of an equality of trade conditions among all the nations consenting to the peace and associating themselves for its maintenance.

4. Adequate guarantees given and taken that national armaments will be reduced to the lowest point consistent with domestic safety.

5. A free, open-minded, and absolutely impartial adjustment of all colonial claims, based upon a strict observance of the principle that in determining all such questions of sovereignty the interests of the populations concerned must have equal weight with the equitable claims of the government whose title is to be determined.

6. The evacuation of all Russian territory and such a settlement of all questions affecting Russia as will secure the best and freest cooperation of the other nations of the world in obtaining for her an unhampered and unembarrassed opportunity for the independent determination of her own political development and national policy and assure her of a sincere welcome into the society of free nations under institutions of her own choosing; and, more than a welcome, assistance also of every kind that she may need and may herself desire. The treatment accorded Russia by her sister nations in the months to come will be the acid test of their good will, of their comprehension of her needs as distinguished from their own interests, and of their intelligent and unselfish sympathy.

7. Belgium, the whole world will agree, must be evacuated and restored, without any attempt to limit the sovereignty which she enjoys in common with all other free nations. No other single act will serve as this will serve to restore confidence among the nations in the laws which they have themselves set and determined for the government of their relations with one another. Without this healing act the whole structure and validity of international law is forever impaired.

8. All French territory should be freed and the invaded portions restored, and the wrong done to France by Prussia in 1871 in the matter of Alsace-Lorraine, which has unsettled the peace of the world for nearly fifty years, should be righted, in order that peace may once more be made secure in the interest of all.

9. A readjustment of the frontiers of Italy should be effected along clearly recognizable lines of nationality.

10. The peoples of Austria-Hungary, whose place among the nations we wish to see safeguarded and assured, should be accorded the freest opportunity to autonomous development.

11. Rumania, Serbia, and Montenegro should be evacuated; occupied territories restored; Serbia accorded free and secure access to the sea; and the relations of the several Balkan states to one another determined by friendly counsel along historically established lines of allegiance and

▶

## Box 3.2 (*Continued*)

nationality; and international guarantees of the political and economic independence and territorial integrity of the several Balkan states should be entered into.

12. The Turkish portion of the present Ottoman Empire should be assured a secure sovereignty, but the other nationalities which are now under Turkish rule should be assured an undoubted security of life and an absolutely unmolested opportunity of autonomous development, and the Dardanelles should be permanently opened as a free passage to the ships and commerce of all nations under international guarantees.

13. An independent Polish state should be erected which should include the territories inhabited by indisputably Polish populations, which should be assured a free and secure access to the sea, and whose political and economic independence and territorial integrity should be guaranteed by international covenant.

14. A general association of nations must be formed under specific covenants for the purpose of affording mutual guarantees of political independence and territorial integrity to great and small states alike.

*Source*: http://wwi.lib.byu.edu/index.php/
President_Wilson's_Fourteen_Points

The League of Nations, established by a multilateral treaty at the end of the First World War, was founded in order to preserve peace and security and to promote economic and social cooperation among its members. Ultimately, sixty-three countries accepted membership, although the US Senate – despite President Woodrow Wilson's leading role in creating the League of Nations – refused to ratify the initiative, reflecting US fears of being told what to do by external forces. Setting itself against the secret practices of traditional European statecraft, the League of Nations represented an aspiration for 'a new and more wholesome diplomacy' (Wilson). The League sought to build on a nineteenth century innovation – the **Concert of Europe** (1815–56), which was actually an informal cooperative mechanism, not an institutionalised structure, like the League.

## Box 3.3 The Concert of Europe

The Concert of Europe was the name given to the balance of power that existed in Europe from the fall of Napoleon in 1815 to the start of the First World War a century later. The Concert's founding members were Britain, Austria, Russia and Prussia. All had been members of the Sixth Coalition (also known as the Quadruple Alliance) which had been the force that defeated Napoleon. After Napoleon's downfall, France became established as a fifth member of the Concert.

The Concert of Europe was also known as the 'Congress System'. This was because the members used to gather at periodic congresses – opportunities for what we would now call a summit meeting – where governments could meet face-to-face to plan a solution by mutual agreement (hence the use of the

word 'concert') whenever a significant problem emerged threatening the stability of Europe. Over time, the Concert became a formal institution although, unlike the League of Nations which came into being after the First World War, the Concert never had a permanent meeting place, bureaucracy or budget.

During the early years, the Concert met regularly (the Congress of Vienna [1814–15], Aix-la-Chapelle [1818], Carlsbad [1819], Verona [1822] and London [1830, 1832, and 1838–9]). However, as time went on and European rivalries developed – for example, in relation to imperialistic acquisitions – meetings of the Concert became less frequent until eventually they ceased altogether.

The League system envisaged regular conferences not ad hoc ones, as in the Concert system, triggered only by the eruption of international crises. The League aim was also to build a permanent leadership and bureaucracy to run the organisation, as well as a system of conciliation and arbitration involving a judicial body (the Permanent Court of International Justice) and, finally, a system of guarantees to the post-First World War status quo. Underpinning these innovations was a desire to establish a community of like-minded nation states cooperating fully with each other and settling their differences like reasonable bodies, enjoying a peace under a law which, if they needed, they would pool their resources to enforce. It is important to stress how radical a project this was, especially in light of what we learnt above about centralised states answering to no higher authority in the post-1648 period.

Although the League of Nations fostered an infrastructure of international organisation which could justifiably claim to be of enduring significance, its aspirations were dashed and its fate sealed, in the view of many commentators, by the growing international tensions of the 1930s and the eventual outbreak of international war in 1939. There is much evidence to suggest that few states, particularly among the most powerful, were willing to surrender one of the most integral elements of the idea of sovereignty: the freedom to define friend or foe and to pursue what they regarded as the most suitable policies towards them. For example, the Japanese invasion of Manchuria in 1931, a part of China, was not dealt with by the League with clear condemnation and willingness to act to reverse the invasion. This was because Japan was both feared and respected: a major source of power in international relations. In addition, the League's systems of discussion, arbitration and guarantees were at too great a distance from the realities of power politics.

## The structures and weaknesses of the League of Nations

The League of Nations was a tangible organisation with an Assembly of all member states, a Council of between four and six permanent members (Britain, France, Italy, Japan, later joined by Germany until 1933 and the Soviet Union, 1934–39), and between four and eleven floating, non-permanent members. It also featured a permanent Secretariat under a secretary-general based in Geneva in neutral Switzerland. All members of the Council and Assembly had one vote each, and the unanimity of all representatives present was required for all political decisions which were to have League of Nations endorsement including the most contentious: those to do with security issues. This turned out to be a recipe for paralysis in crisis, as every great power was able to rely upon several votes from their allies among the less powerful states. The outcome was that the required consensus was in fact impossible to achieve on any international question in which the great powers had a stake, for example the Italian invasion of Abyssinia (now Ethiopia) in 1935.

The origin of the League of Nations in the post-war settlement was symbolically expressed in the fact that the first 26 articles of its Covenant were identical to those of the post-war peace treaties (Article 10 made the League the defender of the territorial status quo). The two foundations that underpinned this status quo were the military disarming of Germany

## Box 3.4 Why did the League of Nations fail?

The League of Nations enjoyed some success in resolving conflicts between minor powers in the 1920s. These included conflicts between Italy and Greece over the island of Corfu (1923), Iraq and Turkey over the River Mosul (1924), and Bulgaria and Greece over boundary issues (1925). Yet, it failed to prevent or halt aggression by major powers: Japan (Manchuria 1931, China 1937), Italy (Ethiopia, 1935–6), Germany (after 1935).

In sum, there were three main reasons why the League of Nations failed to act when large powers were involved:

- Anglo-French disagreement at the highest policy-making level
- constitutionally, the Covenant of the League of Nations did not prevent the use of war by member-states in all circumstances; thus, if any country wished to use war as a diplomatic tool, all it had to do was claim that the conflict was for 'defensive' purposes
- the discrepancy between the distribution of power in the League of Nations and in the wider world.

The League's structure was predominantly European in a period when the international environment was no longer dominated by Europe. The USA did not join because of Congressional opposition while the USSR was only allowed to join in 1934 when it was no longer apparently 'exporting' revolution. It left in 1939, following its invasion of Finland. Although only 10 of the original 31 members were European, it was these countries – and especially Britain and France with their self-interested policies – that were most prominent. By 1939 when the League effectively collapsed as the Second World War began, of a maximum membership of 58 – achieved between September 1934 and February 1935 – a quarter (14) had left, including significant powers such as Japan (1932), Germany (1933), and Italy (1937). In addition, two countries had been annexed (Abyssinia by Italy and Austria by Germany) and one expelled from the League (the USSR after its attack on Finland in September 1939).

and the principle of **national self-determination**. Yet, from the outset, these were interpreted differently by the two leading powers in the League of Nations, Britain and France. (For the full League of Nations Covenant, go to: http://avalon.law.yale.edu/20th_century/leagcov.asp.)

France looked to the League to maintain its military preponderance while Britain saw the organisation more as a convenient forum to sort out its problems. Britain was also prepared to countenance Germany's return as a great power, within limits, not only in the interests of a general restoration of a balance of power in Europe but also as a prospective foil to Bolshevik Russia (the Russian Revolution, leading to the founding of the Soviet Union, had occurred a few years earlier, in October 1917). Over time, the conflict between French and British interests, perceptions and policies, led to a creeping paralysis of the League.

## The legacy of the League of Nations

Despite collectivist aspirations and attempts to introduce new norms of international behaviour, eventually they had to give way to the re-emergence of traditional balance of power devices. Nevertheless, the League of Nations does represent the first attempt to formalise the organisation of international order and develop a collective security mechanism in international relations.

Despite its failure in preventing inter-state conflict and the Second World War, the League created the template for later international organisation, giving rise to international institutions that survived its own demise – most notably the International Court of Justice at the Hague (to arbitrate in disputes between states) and the International Labour Organisation (ILO) established in 1933. Both are still functioning today and will be covered in later chapters.

Second, despite its failure, the Covenant of the League constituted a chart, an initial road map, for discovering and strengthening patterns of behaviour supporting a developing ideal of a world community, which reached something like fruition after the Second World War in the United Nations Organisation – once again the brainchild of a US president, this time Franklin D. Roosevelt.

## Conclusion

'Modern' international relations can be said to date from the time of the Peace of Westphalia in 1648. Over time, the international system grew in size, albeit with wide variations in economic development among states. There are now many more states (nearly two hundred), and many important non-state actors. Europeans were pivotal to the expansion of international relations from the late eighteenth century via imperialism and the spread of nationalism. Over time, however, this led to a backlash from the colonised countries, with European domination gradually being undermined – starting in Latin America in the early nineteenth century – before European imperialism came to an end in the decades after the Second World War.

Before the anti-colonial backlash, however, clashing European imperialisms and nationalism had been highly significant causes of the outbreak of the First World War in 1914. The immediate aftermath of the war saw a concerted attempt to found an international organisation, the League of Nations, in order to advance the cause of collective security. Although this attempt was ultimately unsuccessful, the League did provide the foundations of its successor, the United Nations, founded in 1945. These developments occurred in the context of rapid technological change, political transformations, industrialisation, emergence of the 'developing world', and rise and fall of ideological conflict between the USA and the (now defunct) Soviet Union during the Cold War.

## Resource section

## Questions

1. What is imperialism and why was it important for the spread of international relations from the early nineteenth century until the First World War a century later?

2. What were the links between religion and nationalism in European domination of areas of the developing world, such as Africa?

3. Why was the First World War such an important source of change in international relations?

4. Why was the League of Nations such an innovative idea?

5. Why did the League of Nations fail to prevent the Second World War?

## Recommended reading

**Henig, R. (2010)** *The League of Nations* **(Haus Publications)**
The League of Nations convened for the first time ninety years ago hoping to settle international disputes by diplomacy not war. Henig examines: (1) how the League was shaped and the multifaceted body which emerged, and (2) how it was used in ensuing years to counter territorial ambitions and restrict armaments, as well as its role in human rights and refugee issues. She also examines the failure of the League to prevent the Second World War.

**Porter, A.N. (1994)** *European Imperialism, 1860–1914* **(Palgrave)**
Porter surveys the growth of European intervention outside Europe between 1860 and 1914. For Porter, 'imperialism' is seen as a process of increasing contact, influence and control between Europeans and non-Europeans, rather than as the nature and consequences of colonial rule. The problems of defining 'imperialism' are discussed, as are various analytical approaches to the term. The book also criticises particular explanations of European imperialism, and introduces readers to some of the new directions in research and inquiry currently being explored by historians.

**Stephenson, D. (2005)** *1914–1918: The History of the First World War* **(Penguin)**
The book is a thorough and engrossing account of the war, why it happened and what it led to for international relations.

## Useful websites

The League of Nations and the United Nations

**http://www.bbc.co.uk/history/worldwars/wwone/league_nations_01.shtml**

League of Nations timeline

**http://worldatwar.net/timeline/other/league18-46.html**

European Imperialism in the 19th Century

**http://www2.sunysuffolk.edu/westn/imperialism.html**

# Chapter 4
# International Relations after the Second World War

After reading this chapter you will have gained an understanding of:

- The United Nations and collective security
- The Cold War and nuclear weapons
- The Non-Aligned Movement and the international relations of the developing world

## Introductory box: The Cold War and nuclear weapons

All governments must confront a key question: How can they provide their people with genuine security for themselves – without threatening others with unacceptable destruction?

During the Cold War the nuclear weapons policies of the superpowers – the United States of America and the Soviet Union (also referred to as the USSR) – led the world deeper and deeper into a serious, prolonged crisis that very nearly led to nuclear war in 1962. What happened in 1962 was that the USSR tried to base nuclear weapons on the Caribbean island of Cuba, at the time a strong ideological ally. But that policy choice led to a direct US response and ultimatum: if you put nuclear weapons on Cuba we will be forced to confront you on the issue, perhaps leading to a nuclear exchange between us. In the event, the USSR backed down and for over a decade a more congenial relationship developed between the superpowers. This did not mean that they stopped finding each other threatening but it did imply that they found it easier to live together than they had done before.

## International relations after the Second World War

We saw in Chapter 3 that the League of Nations failed to prevent the outbreak of the Second World War. The League foundered, first, on the principle of sovereignty: major countries were not willing to give up some of their freedom of action in order to give the League the necessary authority and legitimacy to succeed. Second, the League failed to demonstrate that an international agreement to provide security was workable in the 1930s: a period of increasingly serious economic, political and ideological tensions. But this was not the end of the matter (Henig 2010). The huge impact of the Second World War – during which tens of millions of people were killed, injured or displaced – made it plain to many national leaders, senior politicians and ordinary people that the organisation of international relations must change in order to avoid future catastrophes of this kind. Founded in 1945, the United Nations (UN) was the attempt to develop an authoritative **international security organisation** (Taylor and Curtis 2008).

Not that the attempt to create the UN was unproblematic. The UN soon found itself undermined by a lack of cohesion and purpose. This was manifested in two main ways: ideological division and the issue of decolonisation. First, ideological division followed the outbreak of the Cold War in the late 1940s, which primarily involved the liberal democratic/capitalist USA and the communist Soviet Union. Second, there was a period of intense

Following the Second World War (1939–45), states were forced to examine how they could provide security for their own citizens.

Source: Getty Images/Time & Life Pictures

decolonisation after 1945 which saw a new entity emerge in international relations: the developing world, which soon acquired its own international organisation, the Non-Aligned Movement.

In addition, the Cold War refocused international concerns on force and threats to use force. This was mainly because both the USA and the USSR began to collect considerable stocks of nuclear weapons. The introduction of nuclear weapons into international relations from 1945 meant that for the first time in human history it was no longer possible rationally for the possessors of nuclear weapons to use their biggest and 'best' weapons in a conflict. This is because if one side were to use its nuclear weapons against a rival who also has nuclear weapons, the rival would be highly likely to retaliate and use their nuclear weapons. This is known as **mutual assured destruction** with the comical yet chilling acronym: MAD. The paradox of nuclear weapons was, and is, that if only a tiny proportion of the existing nuclear arsenal was used in fighting a war, those involved – 'victors' and 'vanquished' alike – would suffer completely unacceptable damage (Howlett 2008). Consequently, other ways had to be devised to keep the peace between the main nuclear weapons' possessors, the USA and USSR. (Over time, other countries also officially acquired nuclear weapons: Britain, France and China, while others, including Israel, also got them but did not officially admit it.) In sum, post-Second World War international relations was significantly affected both by the founding of the United Nations and by the Cold War, which included the issue of the superpowers' nuclear weapons.

## Box 4.1 Decolonisation and international relations

The Second World War destabilised colonial rule in much of the developing world, by leading many nationalist politicians to question as never before its legitimacy. Why, they asked, should the colonial powers have the moral right to rule over us when they don't have the ability to work together in a peaceful and cooperative way? The result was that over the next two decades there was a fundamental process whereby dozens of former colonies in Africa, Asia, the Middle East and the Caribbean achieved freedom from colonial rule.

Decolonisation was also the result of a major structural change in international relations: the main colonial powers, Britain and France, were seriously weakened by the Second World War, which affected their ability to continue as colonial powers.

Decolonisation led to the creation of what we now refer to as the 'developing world' or the 'Third World'. Creation of this grouping of developing countries led to a transformation of the global political structure. Whereas in 1945 a relatively small number of countries – less than fifty – comprised the international state system, decolonisation led to large numbers of new countries. Many were – and still are – small and weak, with uncertain economic prospects. In sum, the international system was transformed by this influx of new countries, which helped to change the concerns of international relations from a limited number and range of issues – including trade, diplomacy and military security – to a new agenda involving, among others, economic development and human rights concerns.

Covering the 1945–89 period, the rest of this chapter is devoted to an examination of three key developments in international relations: the United Nations; the Cold War and nuclear weapons; and the developing world and international relations, focusing on the Non-Aligned Movement.

## Box 4.2 Timeline of international relations, 1945–89

| | |
|---|---|
| 1945 | United States gets nuclear weapons |
| 1945 | United Nations founded |
| Late 1940s | Cold War starts |
| 1949 | USSR gets nuclear weapons |
| 1955 | Non-Aligned Movement founded |
| 1962 | Cuban Missile Crisis |
| Early 1970s | Call for New International Economic Order |
| November 1989 | End of Cold War, marked by the fall of the Berlin Wall, separating East and West Berlin |

## The United Nations

The First World War led to an acknowledgment from the international community that **global governance** would have to improve considerably if the most extreme forms of violence against humanity were to be outlawed, and the growing interconnectedness and interdependence of nations recognised. The post-war attempt to develop an international security organisation, the League of Nations, soon foundered, however, as the major countries were without exception unwilling to give up any elements of sovereignty in order to give the League the authority and legitimacy it required. In other words, the subject matter, scope and the very sources of international regulation, particularly the conception of international law, were all called into question after the First World War.

The League of Nations emerged as a result of the cataclysm of the First World War. Although there had been much talk over the years about establishing an international organisation to deal with security issues, it was not until an international peace conference was held in Paris in 1919 that an agreement was finally reached to create a universal organisation. It would aim to settle disputes between nations and prevent the outbreak of war. Surprising as it may seem, the League's failure to prevent the Second World War did not destroy faith in the idea that a universal organisation charged with finding ways to deliver peaceful international relations was a good idea. Instead, the League's failure actually created more determination among many national leaders to learn from the mistakes of the past. This time, more effort would be made to create and develop a new global body – the United Nations (UN) – devoted to international peace and cooperation. There were several key differences between the League of Nations and the UN. First, they differed in the circumstances of their creation. The League's Covenant was drawn up soon after the First World War finished, while the UN's Charter began to be worked out while the Second World War was still being fought. Second, the UN had more comprehensive powers than the League. This reflected the understanding that the circumstances that make war possible are often both deep-rooted and wide-ranging, to be found in a lack of political and economic cooperation and an unequal distribution of power. Third, the agreement to establish the Covenant was undertaken by a small group of powerful states – France, Italy, Japan, Britain and the USA – which consulted a handful of other less powerful, friendly nations. The drawing up of the final text of the UN Charter was quite different. It was done in the open. It involved over fifty countries at an international meeting in San Francisco in 1945. As a result the Charter was seen to be more consensual, taking into account the views of smaller countries, including a concern that the new organisation should be entrusted with responsibility for helping both to promote economic and social cooperation and to champion independence from colonial rule. One of the key drivers of the Charter was the then US president, Franklin D. Roosevelt.

## Box 4.3  Franklin D. Roosevelt

Franklin D. Roosevelt (1882–1945) took the lead in establishing the UN although he died before it formally began its operations in late 1945. Roosevelt understood that collective security is an arrangement whereby all governments agree to work together in pursuit of agreed aims. If necessary, they will use force to do this. For Roosevelt, collective security was essentially a compromise, a kind of halfway house between, on the one hand, the concept of world government and, on the other, a balance of power system based on the nation state. Whereas the latter, Roosevelt believed, was either to be destructive or at best just not good enough to safeguard international peace, world government was not currently deemed achievable. On the other hand, Roosevelt believed that world peace depended on the relations between the USA and USSR. Consequently, although physically ailing, he devoted much time to the planning of the UN, through whose operations, he hoped, international difficulties could be successfully addressed.

But as the Second World War came to an end, Roosevelt's health took a turn for the worse. He died on 12 April 1945, in Warm Springs, Georgia, USA, of a cerebral haemorrhage.

After the Second World War, international law began to cover not only states but also individuals, in part because of the myriad war crimes committed by particular people, such as Germany's leader during the Second World War, Adolf Hitler. Henceforward, both single persons and groups became recognised as subjects of international law. The new focus was captured in various documents including: the Charters of the Nuremberg and Tokyo War Crimes Tribunals (1945), the Universal Declaration of Human Rights (1948), the European Convention on Human Rights (1950) and the Covenant on Civil and Political Rights (1966). During this time, public opinion also moved against the idea that international law should only – or even primarily – be about states' political and strategic affairs. Instead, it was now perceived that international law was in fact concerned progressively with orchestrating and regulating a variety of collective international concerns, including economic, social and environmental matters.

After the Second World War, there was also a growing number of significant non-state actors in international relations. For example, there was the UN itself, as well as various specialist agencies connected to it including: the UN Economic and Social Council, the International Bank for Reconstruction and Development (known as the World Bank), the International Monetary Fund (IMF), the International Whaling Commission, the Food and Agriculture Organisation and the World Health Organisation (WHO). Two key developments stimulated the growth of such organisations after the Second World War:

- the realisation that to build cooperation and 'collective security' was a much wider task than 'merely' deterring aggressors in traditional attacks on international order, as it also involved finding ways of agreeing international policy in a variety of areas
- the increasing of the coverage of international law to include new foci, including, human rights, social justice and the natural environment.

The overall result of these developments was that, after the Second World War, the development of the UN system took place within the context of the growth and expansion of international law. Consequently, international relations became less concerned with states' freedoms alone, and more interested in general welfare concerns including those affecting various non-state actors, such as pressure groups of various kinds, not least those demanding freedom from colonial rule.

## The UN Charter

After the Second World War a new model of international law and accountability was adopted, focused in the Charter of the United Nations. As already noted, the post-Second World War international environment became generally more conducive to a more sustained focus on international law for various reasons. In addition, there was a new yet important commitment among leading states – including the USA and USSR – to the principle of developing countries' freedom from colonial rule, which helped encourage decolonisation. As we shall see later in the chapter, one of the leading ideas coming from these concerns – national self-determination in colonial territories – was set out as a primary international value in the Charter of the UN. To focus attention on these new international concerns, the UN's New York based General Assembly – which functions as the organisation's 'parliament', as it comprises nearly all the world's governments – was concerned with the Charter's fundamental principles. Over the years, the General Assembly has sought to apply them in various Declarations and Resolutions.

However, the main image of international regulation projected by the Charter was one of states, linked together in a myriad of international relations, but still fiercely protective of their independence. On the other hand, following the Second World War, encouraged both by a shift in public opinion in many countries as a result partly of growing numbers of democratically elected governments – for example, in (West) Germany, Japan and Italy – many governments came under strong popular pressure to resolve international disagreements, such as the Korean War which began in 1950, by peaceful means and according to legal criteria. In addition, states were now also subject – in principle – to tight restrictions on when they could make use of force to settle disputes, as well as increasingly obliged to observe certain standards with regard to the treatment of all persons on their territory, both their own and foreign citizens. Table 4.1 shows the eight key areas of concerns focused upon in the UN Charter (for the Charter in full, go to: www.un.org/en/documents/charter/).

**Table 4.1** The UN Charter's key concerns

| Principles of the UN Charter | |
|---|---|
| 1. | The world community consists of sovereign states connected through a dense network of relations; states, individuals and groups are regarded as legitimate actors in international relations |
| 2. | Decolonisation. The UN's aim was to encourage a process of fundamental withdrawal of Western rule in the developing world |
| 3. | Restrictions are placed on the resort to force, including unwarranted economic force. This means that states should accept standards and values that don't depend on force or the threat of force. Such violations of given international rules – e.g. Iraq's invasion of Kuwait in 1990 – are not, in theory, regarded as legitimate by the UN |
| 4. | New rules, procedures and institutions designed to aid law making and law enforcement in international affairs were created |
| 5. | Legal principles delimiting the form and scope of the conduct of all members of the international community, providing a set of guidelines for the structuring of international rules |
| 6. | Fundamental concern with individual rights |
| 7. | The preservation of peace, advancement of human rights and the establishment of greater social justice |
| 8. | Systematic inequalities among people and state are recognised and new rules established to create ways of governing the distribution, appropriation and exploitation of territory, property and natural resources |

*Source*: UN Charter, available at www.un.org/aboutun/charter/

## The UN Security Council

Almost all the world's nearly two hundred states are represented in the UN General Assembly. They are all obliged to observe the UN Charter and a battery of associated human rights conventions. Yet it would be wrong to conclude that the era of the UN Charter model has fundamentally displaced the earlier logic of international governance, with its built-in hierarchy of power. In fact, the Charter framework represents primarily an extension of the pre-existing inter-state system rather than its replacement.

This becomes clear when we focus attention on the post-1945 balance of power. This arrangement privileged the most powerful states and their individual concerns. The hierarchy was formalised in the organisational structure of the UN and explicitly built into the Charter. After 1945, the most influential governments occupied the seats of the five Permanent Members of the UN Security Council (Britain, China,[1] France, the Soviet Union, and the USA). However, the downside was that, like the League of Nations had also often been, the UN often found itself immobilised as an autonomous actor on many pressing issues during the Cold War, due to the Security Council members' differing interests and concerns. Privileging the permanent members of the Security Council was most obviously manifested in their individual special veto powers, which only they enjoy. This privileged political status adds both authority and legitimacy to the major powers; for although they are barred in principle from the use of force on terms contrary to the Charter, they are protected against censure and sanctions in the event of unilateral action – that is, undertaken by one state acting alone – in the form of their veto. This means that they can veto – that is, prevent from happening – a UN course of action to which they are individually opposed, even if all the other UN members want it. In addition, the Charter gave renewed credence to unilateral strategic state initiatives if they were necessary in 'self-defence', since there was no agreed meaning of this phrase.

The Charter obliges states to settle disputes peacefully and lays down certain procedures for passing judgement on claimed acts of self-defence. For example, Israel's periodic invasions of Lebanon from the early 1980s are said to be in self-defence in order to deal with ongoing and existent threats from guerrillas – including rockets and suicide bombers. Some UN members such as the USA agree with Israel that this is justified self-defence while others, such as Libya and Syria, do not agree. Problems attached to such issues has meant in practice that although there is a possibility of mobilising the collective coercive measures envisaged in the Charter against illegitimate state action, these are only rarely used – as in the controversial case of the US-led invasion of Iraq in March 2003. In sum, the UN Charter model, despite its good intentions, has failed to generate effectively a new principle of organisation in international relations after the Second World War. Although the international community's commitment to the UN has not really wavered it is not always clear why this is the case, given that the UN has been a relatively weak actor in international relations.

---

[1] Until 1972, the 'China' seat in the Security Council was occupied by the island of Taiwan, as the People's Republic of China was excluded from the Council due to its pariah status in international relations.

It is widely agreed by most of the world's governments that it remains necessary to pursue cooperation in order to achieve desirable collective goals – including better human rights, development outcomes and environmental protection – but this does not mean to say that the UN has been able consistently to generate and develop useful mechanisms of coordination in order to become a really influential actor. On the other hand, it is also important to stress the innovative and often influential aspects of the UN. First, the UN provides an international forum, the General Assembly, in which all states are in certain respects equal, a forum of particular value to many developing countries that are conventionally weak. It also provides – at least in theory – a forum for seeking for 'consensus' solutions to international problems. Third, it provides a key framework both for decolonisation and for the pursuit of the reform of international institutions. Finally, the UN offers a vision of a new kind of collectively orientated world order based upon governments meeting regularly under appropriate circumstances.

## The Cold War and nuclear weapons

What the UN could not deal adequately with was the very question which had led to its creation in the first place: How was collective security for all the world's countries to be delivered? After the Second World War, the issue of collective security was of primary importance in relation to the emerging ideological conflict between the USA and the Soviet Union, which led to a period of prolonged international tension: the Cold War. The Cold War led the world into the most profound problem of international relations that humanity had until then had to face. Cold War tensions found their main outlet in a nuclear arms race between the USA and the USSR which centred on each country's acquisition and development of such weapons (Gaddis 2007).

This section of the chapter examines the Cold War and the relationship between the USA and the Soviet Union. First, it looks at the 1945–89 period as a time of global tension, centring on the competition for predominance between America and the USSR. Second, it examines the role of nuclear weapons in their relationship. The Cold War was a period of global competition for domination, focusing on ideology, territory and resources. Both countries were very suspicious of each other, with continued and serious hostility between them (Isaacs and Downing 2008).

### Understanding and interpreting the Cold War

To understand the impact of the Cold War on international relations we need to place it in context. The world wars of the last century (1914–18 and 1939–45) were central to an intense period of upheaval that began with the end of the traditional balance of power structure in the mid nineteenth century and ended in the emergence of two superpowers – the USA and the Soviet Union, often referred to as the USSR – after the Second World War. The three decades between 1914 and 1945 were characterised by immense reordering and change which saw the decline of existing great powers: Austria-Hungary, Britain, France, Germany, Italy and Russia (which before the communist revolution of 1917 was led by a Tsar, that is, a monarch). After 1945, a new term – superpower – was coined to refer to the USA and the USSR. This was because they had much more power than other states, with major capabilities and influence around the world, including nuclear weapons capabilities (Calvocoressi 2008).

How to understand and interpret the Cold War? We can note three different interpretations. The first focuses upon the political dimensions of the Cold War. In this view, the confrontation between the superpowers reflected a traditional form of rivalry between contending powers, each of which desired to be the most powerful. The two-way conflict during the Cold War between the superpowers involved each state's multiple resources – economic, ideological, geographic and military. Both sides sought to try to gain unchallenged pre-eminence over the other (Gaddis 2007; Isaacs and Downing 2008).

A second explanation stresses the 'functionality' of the Cold War. This focuses upon the instrumental role of the conflict in helping to entrench the dominance of each of the superpowers in their respective spheres of influence. This was starkly illustrated in what was known as the 'Brezhnev doctrine' of limited sovereignty, named after a former leader of the Soviet Union, Leonid Brezhnev. When, in 1968, Czechoslovakia[2] attempted to assert its independence from the USSR and develop an independent foreign policy, Brezhnev sent in overwhelming military force to crush the revolt. Seen from this perspective, a primary purpose of the Cold War conflict was to help maintain internal order within the superpowers' respective spheres of influence. Note that the USSR was made up of various countries led by Russia and including: Poland, (East) Germany,[3] Czechoslovakia and Hungary, Bulgaria and Romania (Keylor 2006).

A third view attaches a high degree of importance to the ideological dimension of the Cold War. In this view, the conflict between the superpowers – on the one hand, liberal democratic/capitalist USA and, on the other, communist Soviet Union – was mainly about their ideological competition. In this view the order-maintaining function of the Cold War, noted above, is placed in a wider context; that is, international order is not equated simply with the superpowers' ability to control or coerce. It is linked with a wider issue: the stability and continuity of a particular system characterised by competing ideologies: liberal democracy and capitalism, on the one hand, and communism, on the other. Each side's ideology was inseparable from the virtues which each believed marked out the superiority of their system from the vices and inadequacies of that of their rival. In sum, each of these interpretations highlights different aspects of the Cold War and attaches different weights to particular factors. However, all three reflect to varying degrees certain common themes: the globalisation of the superpowers' rivalry; interconnectedness of political, economic and military spheres; and blurring of dividing lines between domestic and foreign policies (Halliday 1986).

---

[2] Czechoslovakia was divided into two states, the Czech Republic and Slovakia, on 1 January 1993.

[3] Germany was divided after the Second World War between Western-leaning West Germany and Soviet-dominated East Germany. The country was reunified in 1990.

## Nuclear weapons and the Cold War

Reflecting in 1946 upon the atomic bombings of the Japanese cities of Hiroshima and Nagasaki which had occurred the previous year, Bernard Brodie (1946), a distinguished American military strategist, noted: '[t]hus far the chief purpose of our military establishment has been to win wars. From now on its chief purpose must be to avert them. It can have almost no other useful purpose.'

Brodie's words capture the essence of the nuclear weapons revolution in international relations. It transformed the traditional relationship between politics and war (once widely regarded as 'the continuation of diplomacy by other means', a saying attributed to the early nineteenth century Prussian military strategist, Carl von Clausewitz). However, as Brodie pointed out, the advent of nuclear weapons made the pursuit of (nuclear) war for purposes of domination quite simply unthinkable. This is because their use would almost certainly bring about the mutual annihilation of the warring parties. As the US president, Harry Truman (1884–1972) observed, soon after his decision to use nuclear weapons against Japan in 1945: 'If we do not abolish war on this earth, then surely one day war will abolish us from the earth.'

Truman's remarks emphasise that the development of nuclear weapons not only made war between the USA and the USSR rationally unimaginable but also more generally transformed assumptions upon which international relations had hitherto been based. In the past to go to war was a recognised strategy to achieve political goals. Now, nuclear weapons challenged the very utility of military force to achieve political goals in international relations. In contrast to their nineteenth century predecessors who were able to plan for war by including all weapons at their disposal, post-Second World War policy makers in both the USA and the USSR had to pursue their interests without relying on the most powerful and destructive weapons at their disposal: nuclear weapons. Moreover, their permanent preparation for war, consistently evident in the tense and competitive relationship between the superpowers during the Cold War, necessarily demanded close relations between industry, science and the state in order to harness the most relevant up-to-date and sophisticated technology for military purposes. Thus, during the Cold War, constant preparation for war, rather than war itself, became one of the most visible realities shaping politics between the superpowers. However, it is often argued that during the Cold War MAD (see Box 4.4) kept the superpowers from entering into 'hot war' – that is, armed, open conflict. In evidence, we can note the huge ideological gulf between the two states during the period and the enormous extent to which their interests clashed. In previous periods in history, prior to the creation of nuclear weapons, we could envisage such things would have made war between great powers so diametrically opposed to each other inevitable.

MAD, which the superpowers practised during the Cold War period, is sometimes held up as the supreme form of war prevention. Some have even argued that if nuclear weapons spread into all regional power balances, creating a series of little nuclear balances, then the special deterrence measures involved would create a largely peaceful world. The knowledge that the other side could inflict massive nuclear destruction upon it would prevent another

## Box 4.4 Mutual Assured Destruction (MAD)

Mutual assured destruction is a doctrine of military strategy. It involves the idea that an all-out use of nuclear weapons by two opposing sides would lead to the destruction of both attacker and defender. It is based on a simple idea, the theory of **deterrence**. This is where the deployment of powerful – typically, nuclear – weapons is judged to be necessary in order to threaten the enemy to such an extent that they will not use theirs. In other words, when MAD is in operation, both sides adopt a strategy aimed at avoiding the worst possible outcome: mutual nuclear destruction.

In short, MAD is a simple idea: if you use your nuclear weapons against a rival who also has nuclear weapons, they are highly likely to retaliate and use their nuclear weapons against you. This is mutual assured destruction, with the comical yet chilling acronym: MAD. MAD clearly shows up the paradox of nuclear weapons: if only a tiny proportion of those existing was used in fighting a war, those involved – 'victors' and 'vanquished' alike – would suffer completely unacceptable damage. Consequently, other ways had to be devised to keep the peace between the main nuclear weapons' possessors, the USA and USSR. (Over time, other countries also officially acquired nuclear weapons: Britain, France, and China, while others, including Israel, also got them but did not officially admit they had.) In sum, post-Second World War international relations was significantly affected both by the founding of the United Nations and by the Cold War, which included the issue of the superpowers' nuclear weapons.

nuclear weapon state from embarking upon a war, no matter how many reasons it might have for wishing to do so.

However, there are serious problems with such an argument. Perhaps the most obvious is that serious differences in ideologies and interests, as manifested by the diametrically opposed ideologies and philosophies of the superpowers during the Cold War, do not imply that states will *inevitably* go to war with each other unless MAD is in operation. For example, there has been no 'hot' war between the USA and other major ideological-political rivals – such as Iran and Libya, though neither has nuclear weapons. This observation would appear to undermine the argument that MAD was 'proved' to work during the Cold War. We should bear in mind that both the economic and human cost to the Soviet Union of the Second World War was enormous. More than 25 million Soviet citizens – more than one-tenth of the country's then nearly two hundred million people – were killed during the war. The war set back the country's economy very significantly. Given that this cataclysmic memory remained strong throughout the Cold War, both at elite and popular levels, then it would not be unreasonable to conclude that the USSR had no real interest in engaging in another massive war – whether nuclear or non-nuclear – *unless* it felt itself forced into that course of action by an external attack from the USA. For its part, as long as the USSR did not attack the USA or one of its European allies, then it is very difficult to envisage why the USA would wish to engage directly in war with the USSR. This was a country that during the Second World War, despite a potentially crushing loss of people, had consistently shown itself able to continue as a formidable fighting force.

## Box 4.5 The Cuban Missile Crisis of 1962

The USA used nuclear weapons for the first and only time at Hiroshima and Nagasaki in Japan in 1945. Two decades later, the USA had managed to get far ahead of the Soviet Union in terms of its nuclear weapons capabilities. The USSR had made great progress, but it was still only capable of delivering nuclear missiles to Europe, whereas the USA had the ability to strike the entire Soviet Union. As a way of trying to get the USA to understand the threat that the Soviet Union believed it was facing, in April 1962 the Soviet government planned to site medium-range missiles in Cuba – that is, missiles that could then reach the USA. This, the Soviet authorities believed, would not only double the Soviet strategic arsenal but would also serve as a clear deterrent to the USA not to attack the USSR.

At the same time, the Cuban leader Fidel Castro, who headed Cuba's communist government, was seeking a way to defend his island from an anticipated US attack. Since a failed US-led attack in 1961 – known as the Bay of Pigs invasion after the place in Cuba where it took place – Castro believed that a second US-led attack was inevitable. As a result, he was willing to countenance the proposal from the

Soviet leader, Nikita Khrushchev, to locate nuclear missiles on Cuba. During the summer of 1962, the USSR began to implement the plan.

Nuclear war was never closer than in October 1962 during a confrontation between the superpowers of the USA and the USSR, known as the Cuban Missile Crisis. Such was the seriousness of the crisis that the United States' armed forces were at their highest ever state of war readiness. For their part, Russian field commanders in Cuba, fearing a US invasion, were apparently prepared to use battlefield nuclear weapons – designed to be used on a battlefield in military situations – to defend the island if necessary. Sometimes known as tactical nuclear weapons, battlefield nuclear weapons are different from strategic nuclear weapons. The latter are designed to threaten large populations, with the purpose of seriously damaging the enemy's ability to fight.

In the end, however, nuclear conflict was averted over the issue of Cuba because of the willingness of the two countries' leaders – President John F. Kennedy (USA) and Premier Nikita Khrushchev (USSR) – to talk and prevent the crisis.

In conclusion, our discussion highlights that it might well have been the simple fact that neither superpower wanted war with each other that prevented nuclear conflict between them. The fact that they engaged in a nuclear arms race could be seen simply to be a consequence of their desire to guarantee the best defence and deterrence possible in a climate of serious mutual distrust, rather than signifying any intention on the part of either side to try and manoeuvre itself into a position where it could successfully wage an aggressive war. Both had a clear reason to support the status quo because they dominated it; so the Cold War can usefully be interpreted as a time of mutually assured domination which was able to deliver a high degree of stability to the international system for four decades.

## The international relations of the developing countries

So far in this chapter, we have briefly outlined the emergence and development of both the United Nations and the Cold War after the Second World War. We have noted their impact on our understanding of international relations. While the United Nations developed in the

*Source: The Bridgeman Art Library/Private Collection*

By the 1960s, European states were finding it difficult to hold on to their far-flung empires.

context of attempts to construct a viable system of international law which would include both states and significant non-state actors within its purview, the Cold War demonstrated that despite such efforts the course of international relations at this time was just as significantly affected by the polarisation of relations between the USA and the USSR: nuclear-weapons-possessing superpowers with very different ideological and philosophical systems of rule.

## Case study: Decolonisation and the Third World

The decolonisation process took off after 1945, started by the independence of various countries in Asia, including Indonesia, India and Ceylon (now Sri Lanka), before spreading to Africa in the mid-1950s with the independence of Sudan (1956) and Ghana (1957). Decolonisation was a result of a dual process involving both international and domestic factors. Internationally, there was widespread acceptance that colonisation was unacceptable and national self-determination was both necessary and legitimate. The situation was compounded by the evident weakness of the war-weary colonial powers, notably Britain and France, who began to question the desirability of retaining colonies in the developing world. Domestically, nationalist politicians were gaining increasing confidence and demanding freedom for their countries. Beginning with a trickle in the 1940s and 1950s, the pace of decolonisation picked up in the 1960s. By the 1980s there were very few colonies left.

The states which emerged from the colonial period in the developing world were often qualitatively different from those created in an earlier epoch in Europe. In Europe the nation usually created the state. This is a way of saying that people had a shared sense of being part of a nation – as for example in England, France and Spain – which gradually developed into a nation state with the founding of centralised and authoritative government from the seventeenth century. In the post-colonial developing world the situation was different. There new states sought to try to forge nations from often disparate people: a difficult, sometimes seemingly impossible task, as for example in Iraq, Afghanistan and Somalia. As a result, many governments in the developing world became authoritarian, justifying this by the imperative of nation-building after colonialism.

What did such countries have in common following the withdrawal of colonial powers? After the Second World War many observers broadly lumped them all together as 'Third World' countries. Historically, the notion of Third World had two main meanings: (1) the host of decolonising African and Asian states in the 1950s and 1960s that joined the already independent, older countries of Latin America to form a large bloc of the world's poorest countries; (2) the Third World was a political alternative to that presented by Washington and Moscow, leaders respectively of what were know as the First World (that is, the West) and the Second World (that is, the former communist countries of Eastern Europe). Over time, the Third World's identification with difficult social and economic circumstances, a bloc of countries in an unequal relationship with the 'developed' world, helped determine and define what decolonisation had resulted in.

We should note, however, that from the beginning of its usage in the 1950s the term Third World included nations with very different cultures, societies and economies. The Third World embraced and grouped together regions and individual countries of Africa, Asia, the Caribbean, Latin America and the Middle East under the assumption that they shared a common predicament: directly or indirectly they suffered the after-effects of colonisation and they came late – and on disadvantageous terms – into the competitive world economy. However, this interpretation was not directly applicable to the oil-rich Arab states.

 **Was decolonisation a good or bad thing for the developing/Third World?**

Growing numbers of decolonised countries emerged in the developing world and they sought to link themselves into a block with international clout. Western political scientists found themselves increasingly challenged to develop frameworks for understanding and predicting the politics of the new countries. Alfred Sauvy, a French economist and demographer, is usually credited as the first person to use the term **Third World**, in an article published in 1952. Its use caught on, and by the late 1950s the term was in widespread use. For Sauvy and others, the Third World referred not only to the then decolonising countries but also to the economically weak countries of Latin America, many of which had been independent since the early nineteenth century (Haynes 2008).

More than 90 per cent of today's 'Third World' or 'developing' countries were, at one time or another, colonial possessions of a handful of Western powers, including: Belgium, Britain,

France, Germany, Italy, Japan, the Netherlands, Portugal, Spain and the USA. Decolonisation came in two main waves, separated by more than a century. The first occurred in the early nineteenth century, resulting in the independence of eighteen Latin American and Caribbean countries, including: Argentina, Brazil and Chile. The second occurred in the decades after the Second World War, following the weakening of European powers and growing demands for national recognition in Africa, Asia and the Caribbean. Over the next thirty years, around ninety colonies achieved freedom from foreign rule. Decolonisation was virtually complete by 1990, marked by the independence of Namibia in that year (see Hadjor 1993: 73–8, for a complete list of former colonies in the developing world).

The term, Third World, had two separate yet linked senses during the Cold War. It was used to refer to certain countries: first that were economically 'underdeveloped', that is, they had agriculture-based economies and relatively little industrialisation; and second, had a relatively unimportant place in international politics. Developmentally, the term sought to capture the notion of a particular type of country: post-colonial and economically weak, compared to the rich countries of the First World. Regarding international relations, a bloc of post-colonial countries emerged and formed an alliance: the **Non-Aligned Movement (NAM)**, whose member countries claimed to be followers of neither the USA nor the USSR. While individually most developing countries played relatively minor roles in international relations during the Cold War, their collective voice focused in the NAM was relatively loud and, at irregular intervals, influential. In sum, the term, the 'Third World', had a dual meaning. On the one hand, it referred to a large group of economically underdeveloped, developmentally weak African, Asian, Middle Eastern and Latin American countries. On the other hand, it connoted the proclaimed neutrality of a large bloc of mostly post-colonial, developing countries, organised in the NAM (Arnold 2007).

## The rise and decline of the Non-Aligned Movement (NAM)

Inaugurated at Bandung, Indonesia in 1955, the NAM was formally launched in 1961 at a founding conference in Belgrade, Yugoslavia. Its general objective was to increase the

### Box 4.6 First, Second and Third Worlds

The concept of the Third World has an important meaning for understanding international relations during the Cold War. It reflected the fact that by the 1960s the world was divided into three ideologically defined blocs. There was the First World – that is, the industrialised democracies of Europe and North America (plus Australia, New Zealand and Japan). The Second World comprised the communist countries of Eastern Europe. In addition, some analysts would also include in this category the Soviet Union's ideological allies in Asia (North Korea, China) and Latin America (Cuba), as well as the neutral but certainly communist, Albania. Finally, there was the Third World, also known as the developing world, comprising dozens of mainly former colonial countries in Africa, Asia, Latin America and the Caribbean, and the Middle East. Many such countries organised themselves into the Non-Aligned Movement, an international governmental organisation whose purpose was to carve out a position of neutrality, equally opposed to both the USA and the USSR.

weight of the developing world during the Cold War. By the early 1960s the NAM was not only proclaiming its neutrality from both the USA and USSR but was also railing against western colonialism and military installations, issues announced at its conference in Cairo in 1964 attended by 47 developing countries.

The bloc of developing countries constructed the NAM as a vehicle to pursue its objectives. From the 1960s, for the next three decades, the NAM was the most important expression of the developing countries' alternative conception of the world. It was an important manifestation of the desire to project an alternative, less ideologically polarised, international relations. This was characterised by collective striving for international justice and fairness rather than the ideological polarisation demonstrated by the Cold War standoff between the superpowers. In short, the NAM was the chief manifestation of the developing world's conscious and collective challenge to the dominant international order. It was the main way through which developing countries could articulate demands and mobilise resources in response to developments involving the superpowers. However, the NAM did not initially act as a uniform platform for all developing countries: with the exception of Cuba, few Latin American countries were early members of the NAM. However, in 2010, the NAM comprised 118 members from all parts of the developing world.

Over the years, the NAM pursued, at varying times, three main goals:

- seeking to end colonial rule in the developing world (largely accomplished by the 1980s)
- developing countries' neutrality in international relations, especially from entanglements with the superpowers (developed but not achieved during the Cold War), global nuclear disarmament (not achieved), strengthening of global and regional mechanisms, such as the UN and the African Union, to deal with conflicts (partially achieved)
- a **New International Economic Order** collectively to benefit the developing countries, which felt that the existing order disadvantaged them economically and developmentally (not achieved).

Over time, the NAM developed to become an ambitious permanent vehicle for cooperation, bringing together dozens of developing countries. The members claimed to share the aim of fundamentally redrawing the economic and political contours of the international system. The NAM's later decline into near irrelevance reflected the impact of the end of the Cold War and globalisation processes, especially the widening of economic positions among developing countries; some such as China and India experienced swift economic development, while others, such as Zambia and Kenya, did not.

In sum, the NAM was founded at the height of the Cold War, the institutionalised expression of ideological conflict between liberal democracy and communism. After the Cold War ended in the late 1980s, the NAM declined into international irrelevance, mainly because the ideological polarisation of the Cold War years, which had sustained the NAM's neutral position in international relations, ended. This development was a metaphor for the crumbling of the long-held notion that the developing countries shared common aims which they could best pursue by working collectively. To some extent the NAM's decline and fragmentation reflected the impact of globalisation on the mass of developing countries, which included increased incorporation into the global capitalist economy and the diminishing of their previous solidarity based on neutrality between the superpowers. The post-Cold War history of the NAM is an example of how, among developing countries, globalisation stimulated the decline of both political and economic solidarity. These developments amounted to a serious decline in the collective orientation of the developing world and reflected how its economic and political trajectories are closely linked to global developments (Haynes 2002: 43–7).

## The Non-Aligned Movement: changing priorities

The economic successes of China and India were outweighed by economic disappointments for many developing countries clustered in, but not limited to, Africa. They saw their economic positions go from bad to worse from the 1970s. The NAM's collective institutionalised framework was, as a result, diminished. Fragmentation of the bloc of developing countries was also encouraged by another factor: divide and rule tactics employed by successive US governments, including those led by presidents Ronald Reagan (1981–89) and George Bush Snr (1989–93). These presidents viewed the NAM as an annoying distraction to the administration's goal of restoring American global influence. Under American leadership, Western governments sought to decrease NAM's influence by its established negotiating channels at the United Nations, replacing this form of interaction with one-to-one talks in the capital cities of important developing countries, such as Kenya and India.

 **Box 4.7 Demands in the 1970s for a New International Economic Order led by the Non-Aligned Movement**

By the 1970s, there were few remaining colonies in the developed world. A key goal of both the United Nations and the NAM was thus achieved: freedom for the developing world from European colonial control. At this time, the NAM's focus changed to focus upon demands for international economic reforms, centring on what was known as a New International Economic Order (NIEO). Calls for a NIEO were based on the idea that the world capitalist economy was structured in order to privilege the wealthy countries and discriminate against the poorer countries in the developing world. To pursue the NIEO, the NAM sought a thoroughgoing restructuring of the world economy. At this time there was an implicit assumption that nearly all developing countries shared similar economic characteristics and, consequently, were comprehensively and collectively disadvantaged by the prevailing capitalist international economic order.

Their campaign for the NIEO did not succeed; the world economic system stayed as it was. This failure reflected, on the one hand, the collective lack of influence of the developing countries and the collective clout of the much smaller number of rich, capitalist countries that were happy with the way things were. On the other hand, it also demonstrated that, by the 1970s, economic progress among developing countries was variable and that they no longer inevitably shared the same concerns. For example some developing countries, such as the oil-producing countries including Saudi Arabia, Venezuela and Nigeria, were doing fine out of the old international economic order as a result of rising oil prices. This was mainly because a number of oil producing and exporting developing countries organised themselves in the Organisation of Petroleum Exporting Countries (OPEC) and could raise their revenues significantly by virtue of coordinated actions. Others, however, were doing less well; for example, raw materials exporting countries in Africa, Asia and Latin America. They were not only forced to pay more for their oil imports but were also unable to register increased economic gains from their export proceeds which had limited demand. In other words, some developing countries were doing fine without reform of the existing international economic order.

This is not to suggest that the NAM did not try to move with the times. After the Cold War, it sought to refocus its efforts on the impact of globalisation and on a more just distribution of global economic resources. The new agenda was made plain at the 1989 NAM conference held in Belgrade, Yugoslavia. There, it was proclaimed that the NAM's main aim would continue to be to promote a 'transition from the old world order based on domination to a new order based on freedom, equality, and social justice and the well-being of all' (http://www.namegypt.org/Relevant%20Documents/01st%20Summit%20of%20the%20N on-Aligned%20Movement%20-%20Final%20Document%20(Belgrade_Declaration).pdf). Indonesia, chair of the NAM in the late 1990s, stated that under its leadership the goal was to address the new concerns of the world – environment and development, human rights and democratisation, refugees and massive migration.

Despite the attempt by the NAM to define for itself a new role after the Cold War, the NAM failed to achieve success. By the end of the Cold War it was clear that the NAM was a product of that conflict, an attendant phenomenon of the international division which had now ended. Without the Cold War divisions, the NAM no longer had a clear reason to exist. This is not to suggest that the NAM had no lasting achievements to its credit. On the contrary, it not only led the global condemnation of apartheid in South Africa and support for the liberation of the southern African countries of Rhodesia (now Zimbabwe) in 1980 and Namibia (formerly South West Africa) a decade later. In addition, it was also instrumental in helping keep public attention focused on the ethical concern against the doctrine of nuclear deterrence. Ultimately, however, the NAM's effort to reshape the prevailing international order was seriously constrained, not least because of its poor record in international conflict-resolution. While focusing on the larger issues of global disarmament and superpower rivalry, it was unable to develop institutions and mechanisms for addressing local and regional conflicts such as those in the Persian Gulf, Lebanon, Cambodia, Afghanistan and Southern Africa. In short, with the end of the Cold War, NAM faced distinct risks of further marginalisation in global peace and security affairs.

Its second main strand – development issues – led the NAM to call for meetings between the developed and developing countries to discuss debt relief, reduced trade barriers, increased aid for development, and increased cash flow. During the 1990s, NAM summit conferences were regularly held. The most recent (mid-2009) was held in Sharm el-Sheikh, Egypt, with 98 of the organisation's 118 members present. But very little real progress was recorded in spreading around more equitably the fruits of developments.

In conclusion, while the NAM continues officially to exist and meets periodically to pass resolutions about, for example, the continued desirability of a NIEO and the peaceful settlement of international disputes, its significance is now very limited. The NAM's decline into near irrelevance was not only a result of the end of the Cold War but also reflected the fact that while its membership grew, serious political and economic differences became increasingly clear, particularly between developing countries that enjoyed sustained economic growth – such as India and China – and those that did not. Secondly, the NAM proved itself unable to solve conflicts between its own members, a development not facilitated by the fact that members met only during its periodic summits. Finally, the NAM's institutional weakness was not aided by the fact that, over the years, the organisation lacked crucial institutions, such as a budget, staff or headquarters.

## Conclusion

This chapter has looked at the post-Second World War period, with a focus on three developments: the United Nations; the Cold War and nuclear weapons; and the international relations of the developing countries. The collective significance of these three developments is that they exemplify key changes in international relations in the four decades after the Second World War. First, the Cold War and nuclear weapons are important because, on the one hand, the Cold War signified the embedding of the international system centring on the two superpowers, the United States and the Soviet Union. For the first time, power was focused in international relations among just two countries. On the other hand, the Cold War period was also unusual in international relations as, for the first time, the two most powerful countries could not rationally use their most powerful weapons because of the impact of mutual assured destruction.

Second, the United Nations was the post-Second World War attempt by the international community, supported by both superpowers, to create a more significant and effective collective security organisation than the League of Nations. The League had shown itself to be incapable of preventing the Second World War. However, despite the UN's lofty ambitions it showed itself only patchily effective in dealing with key international problems after the Second World War, not least because the Cold War and the associated dual domination by the superpowers meant that the authority of the UN was limited, and that their relationship and concerns took centre stage in international relations. One area that the UN could point to as a success story was that of the decolonisation of much of the developing world from European control.

After the Second World War, the decolonisation process was swift – started in 1947 by the independence of India from British rule and that of Indonesia from Dutch domination. Numerous new countries swiftly emerged in the developing world, in Asia, Africa, and the Caribbean. The significance for international relations was not, however, restricted to a large number of new countries; it was also linked to the third development upon which we focused: entry into international relations of a new ideologically motivated, bloc of countries. This was the Non-Aligned Movement, an intergovernmental organisation with some influence during the Cold War, not least because the NAM focused international concerns about neutrality and the nuclear arms race.

## Resource section

### Questions

1.  Why was the Cold War an innovative period in international relations?

2.  In what ways were nuclear weapons so significant for the relationship between the USA and the Soviet Union?

3.  Would you classify the United Nations as a 'success' or 'failure'? On what grounds would you base your decision?

4.  Did the United Nations preside over greater collective security compared to the League of Nations? If so, how would we judge?

5.  During the Cold War, was the Non-Aligned Movement (NAM) an influential actor in international relations?

6.  Does the NAM still have a role in international relations?

### Recommended reading

**Arnold, G. (2007)** *Historical Dictionary of the Non-Aligned Movement and Third World* (Scarecrow)
Arnold examines the rise of the Non-Aligned Movement in the twin contexts of the post-colonial emergence of the developing world and the Cold War.

**Black, M. (2008)** *The No-Nonsense Guide to the United Nations* (New Internationalist)
Black explains clearly how the UN works while identifying and explaining its successes and failures.

**Gaddis, J.L. (2007)** *The Cold War* (Penguin)
An interesting and comprehensive history of the Cold War with interesting quotations from the key players and helpful assessments of US and Soviet political leaders.

**Hanhimäki, J. (2008)** *The United Nations: A Very Short Introduction* (OUP USA)
A brief and accessible introduction to the United Nations, which usefully provides both an historical overview and an account of the organisation's current and likely future directions.

**Isaacs, J. and Downing, T. (2008)** *Cold War: For Forty-five Years the World Held Its Breath* (Abacus)
Interesting and engaging history of the Cold War that takes the reader through the momentous events clearly and with insight.

## Useful websites

Cold War and nuclear weapons

http://www.nuclearfiles.org/menu/key-issues/nuclear-weapons/history/index.htm

United Nations

www.un.org/

Non-Aligned Movement Resource Site

http://www.nam.gov.za/

# Chapter 5
# After the Cold War: International Relations in a Globalised World

After reading this chapter you will be able to understand:

- What has changed in international relations since the end of the Cold War
- What has remained the same over the last twenty years
- How our understanding of international relations has been modified as a result

*Source*: Getty Images/ Gallo Images

## Introductory box: Globalisation and a changing world of international relations

International relations significantly changed after the Cold War, marked by (1) the fall of the Berlin Wall in November 1989, (2) the consequential demise of the Soviet bloc in 1991, and (3) widespread economic liberalisation, democratisation, and the spread of individualistic 'American' and 'Western values'. Globalisation was intimately connected to all these developments; it was the main means of spreading these ideas. Various aspects of globalisation – for example, pressures for more and better human rights, better protection of the natural environment and encouragement for 'ordinary' people to participate in politics – collectively impacted upon how we understand international relations. As a result, we can claim with confidence that following the Cold War, *all* states – rich and poor, big or small – were significantly affected by the consequences of the spread of globalisation, with political, economic and cultural effects. One of the key consequences of globalisation was the spread of various transnational – that is, cross-border – actors and forces. While some, such as multinational corporations (MNCs; sometimes called transnational corporations, or TNCs) were widely seen as intimately connected to Western-style globalisation, others, such as non-Western, non-individualistic, 'Asian Values' and self-proclaimed champions of Islam, such as Osama bin-Laden, defined themselves in opposition to Western-led globalisation. This is because they saw it as a malign, Americanised process, seeking to undermine or destroy non-Western ways of life.

## Introduction

### Box 5.1 Timeline of important international developments since the end of the Cold War

| | |
|---|---|
| 1989 | End of Cold War |
| 1990–91 | Iraq–Kuwait war |
| 1991 | Dissolution of Soviet Union |
| 1991 | New world order discussed by key international leaders |
| 1990s | Expansion of US foreign policy goals to include democratisation of non-democratic countries in the developing world |
| Mid-1990s | Economic rise of China and India |
| September 11, 2001 | Al-Qaeda attacks on the USA |
| 2001 | US-led invasion of Afghanistan |
| 2003 | US-led invasion of Iraq |
| 2004 and 2007 | Expansion of the European Union to 24 and then 27 countries |

When the Cold War ended – marked by the falling apart of the Soviet Union in 1991 – there was widespread optimism that there would now be increased and sustained international co-operation (Schrecker 2006). It was hoped there would be improved commitment to strengthening the role of international organisations, such as the United Nations, in order to achieve enhanced international security, stability and development. However, the end of the Cold War coincided with the First Gulf War between Iraq and Kuwait (1990–91) and the collapse of the Soviet Union (1991). These events were destabilising for international relations. They suggested that the end of the Cold War might not be followed by an unproblematic period of improved international cooperation. It did appear, however, that we were entering a new phase of international relations. To understand what happened requires a focus not only on sources of enhanced cooperation but also on those encouraging increased instability and insecurity. We will focus upon both cooperation and instability/insecurity in international relations over the last twenty years to explain how things have changed (Lechner and Boli 2007).

First, we need to understand the general impact that the end of the Cold War had on international relations (Held and McGrew 2003). The Cold War was a sustained period of inter-state competition, tension and conflict primarily involving the USA and the Union of Soviet Socialist Republics (USSR). Soon after the end of the Second World War in

## Box 5.2 Al-Qaeda and the 'clash of civilisations'

The attack on New York's 'twin towers' on 11 September 2001 ('9/11'), as well as many subsequent terrorist outrages, were perpetrated by al-Qaeda or its followers; they all involved extremist Muslims who wanted to cause destruction and loss of life against 'Western' targets but nevertheless often led to considerable loss of life among Muslims, for example in Istanbul and Casablanca. The US response – the Bush administration's 'War on Terror' – targeted Muslims, some believe rather indiscriminately, in Afghanistan, Iraq and elsewhere. Some have claimed that these events marked the start of a 'clash of civilisations' between Islam and the West. In such views, the 9/11 attacks and the US response suggested that the prophecy about clashing civilisations was now less abstract and more plausible than when first articulated in the early 1990s. Others contend, however, that 9/11 was not the start of the clash of civilisations – rather the last gasp of Islamic radicalism that had

seen significant setbacks in Algeria and Egypt in the mid-1990s. We can also note, however, that 9/11 not only had major effects on both the USA and international relations but also contributed to a surge of Islamic radicalism in Saudi Arabia. This was mainly a result of the presence of US troops in the kingdom, as highlighted by al-Qaeda's leader, Osama bin Laden.

It is, however, difficult to impossible to be sure about the actual level of support for bin Laden and al-Qaeda in the Muslim world, although there *is* a high degree of anti-US resentment and a widespread belief among many Muslims that the West is anti-Islam. Such a perception was fuelled by what is seen throughout much of the Muslim world as often uncritical American and European support for the government of Israel, the US-led invasions of Afghanistan and Iraq, and the subsequent slow speed of rebuilding viable and legitimate administrations in both countries.

*Source:* Reuters/Sean Adir

**To what extent did the events of September 11, 2001 change our understanding of international relations?**

1945, the Soviet Union and the USA became universally recognised as the only two global superpowers. This meant that they were the only states with the capacity and resources to dominate the international agenda in many ways, including: economic policy, foreign policy, military operations, cultural exchanges, scientific advancements (including the pioneering of space exploration), and sports (including the Olympic Games and various world championships). Things changed dramatically between November 1989 – the fall of the 'Berlin Wall' (see Box 5.3) – and the dissolution of the USSR in late 1991. From 1991, there were no longer two superpowers, but one: the USA. The main successor state to the Soviet Union – Russia – did not enjoy superpower status. This was because it did not enjoy the wide-ranging attributes that its predecessor state, the USSR had. This had enabled the Soviet Union to play a leading role in international relations during the Cold War (Clark 1997).

## Box 5.3 What was the Soviet Union and why did it fall apart?

The Soviet Union (also known as the USSR) was a multinational state comprising Russia and 15 dependent or 'satellite' territories. The Soviet Union existed for seven decades, from 1922 until 1991. (A soviet is a council, the theoretical basis for the socialist society of the USSR.) The USSR was a union of several Soviet republics. The Soviet Union initially comprised just four Soviet Socialist Republics (SSRs). Over time, the number grew to 15 SSRs: Armenian, Azerbaijan, Byelorussian, Estonian, Georgian, Kazakh, Kirghiz, Latvian, Lithuanian, Moldavian, Russian Federation, Tajik, Turkmen, Ukrainian, and Uzbek.

The USSR was the largest and oldest constitutional **Communist** state. It became the main model for a number of ideologically close states during the Cold War, such as East Germany, Hungary and Czechoslovakia. The Soviet Union was created out of the Russia Empire, following the Russian Revolution of 1917 and a subsequent civil war (1918–21). The geographic boundaries of the USSR varied with time but, after the last major territorial annexations of the Baltic states (Estonia, Lithuania, and Latvia), eastern Poland, Bessarabia, and certain other territories during the Second World War, from 1945 until dissolution the boundaries approximately corresponded to those of the former Imperial Russia, with the notable exclusions of Poland and Finland.

The Soviet Union began to collapse in the mid-1980s. This was the result of several factors, including a weak economy and the Soviet Union's war in Afghanistan against Islamist rebels which collectively fuelled domestic discontent. The last Soviet leader, Mikhail Gorbachev, instituted significant political and social freedoms but this did not stem the rising sense of crisis. In addition, a notable fall in the world oil price in 1985–86 dramatically affected the Soviet Union's foreign exchange position. (The Soviet Union was the world's biggest oil producer.) The overall result was that several SSRs, including Estonia, Latvia and Lithuania, began overtly to resist central control, leading demands for greater democracy. These, in turn, undermined still further the hold on power of the central government. The USSR finally collapsed in 1991 when a politician called Boris Yeltsin seized power following a failed coup d'état that sought to remove the reform-minded Gorbachev.

The Russian Federation is the successor state to the USSR. Russia is the leading member of the Commonwealth of Independent States, recognised as a global power (although not a superpower). Russia inherited its foreign representatives and much of its military from the former Soviet Union.

The end of the Cold War and the subsequent collapse of the Soviet Union in 1991 was an important dividing line between two eras: the first was the **bipolar** international system characterised by ideological division between the two global superpowers – the USA and the Soviet Union – from the late 1940s to 1991; the second was the post-1991 era which has been characterised by both increased cooperation, on the one hand, and significant instability and insecurity on the other. Cooperation was characterised, for example, by increased regional integration (see Chapter 14) and a collective international commitment to improved develop-ment outcomes. Instability and insecurity were, on the other hand, reflected in various ways including: widening economic and social injustices, especially in the developing world; armed conflicts, mainly within states; widespread human rights abuses; and significant and increasing environmental degradation (Schirato and Webb 2003) (see Chapters 22–27).

## International relations after the Cold War: the impact of globalisation

Informed by globalisation, five key developments provided the context for post-Cold War international relations.

First, **globalisation** was significantly responsible for the collapse of the Soviet Union, as it served to end the USSR's self-imposed isolation from the Western world (Haynes 2005). During the Cold War, the Soviet Union-led Communist system worked in isolation from the Western world, one that was increasingly informed by close economic, political and cultural links. After the Cold War, the former Soviet Union was swiftly integrated into a new 'globalised' world, characterised by its 'Western' dimensions including democracy and economies that functioned with declining state control. This is a reference to what occurred in the 1980s and 1990s: increasingly widely available methods of interpersonal commu-nications, such as the telephone, the Internet, email and fax. The result was that we now live in an increasingly globalised social reality, one in which previously effective barriers to communication no longer exist. Development of both domestic and transnational religious communities, many with political/social/economic concerns, was greatly enhanced by the rapid increase in interpersonal and inter-group communications. It facilitated the ability of transnational networks to spread their messages, to link up with like-minded groups, with geographical distance no longer an insuperable barrier. In this context, pro-democracy groups in the USSR were able to link up with like-minded networks from Western Europe, the USA and elsewhere.

Second, the two decades since the end of the Cold War have seen *23 new countries created*. There are also growing numbers of countries called 'failed' or 'collapsed' states (see Chapter 28). While in 1945 there were just over 50 countries which belonged to the United Nations, there are now 192, nearly four times as many. In the three decades after the Second World War ended in 1945, most new countries emerged as a result of decolonisation. After 1989, 21 new countries have emerged, mainly following the break-up of the Soviet Union and Yugoslavia.

## Box 5.4 Non-members of the United Nations

Only three states are *not* members of the United Nations – Kosovo, Taiwan and Vatican City:

- Kosovo declared independence from Serbia on 17 February 2008 but has not gained complete international recognition to allow it to become a member of the United Nations.
- Following China's civil war in 1949, two states claimed to be 'China': the island of Taiwan and mainland China, known as the People's Republic of China (PRC). Taiwan had the 'China' seat in the United Nations until 1971 when the PRC replaced it, following an accord between the USA and the PRC. Since then, Taiwan has not had a seat in the United Nations and the PRC continues to claim the island as an integral part of China.
- The independent papal state of Vatican City – situated in Rome, Italy – is by far the smallest in the world, comprising less than 800 people. Vatican City was created in 1929. Since its founding the state has not joined any international organisation.

More recently, however, it was the fragmentation of existing states that led to the emergence of new ones. From the early 1990s in particular, many new countries emerged from the disintegration of existing multinational states, notably the Soviet Union and the Federal Republic of Yugoslavia. A few new countries were created by divisions of existing countries in Africa: Ethiopia/Eritrea, Somalia/Somaliland. In addition, some states effectively collapsed: these are known as 'failed states'. While the causes of failed states vary, their impact on international relations is to become new sources of both domestic and international political instability (Haynes 2005: 236–42).

Third, from the mid-1970s, **democratisation** spread: first, to Southern Europe and then to Latin America and East Asia, by way of Eastern Europe, sub-Saharan Africa, and South Asia – thus ending numerous dictatorships and other forms of non-democratic rule. This was the famous 'third wave' of democratisation, analysed by the American academic, Samuel Huntington. Often, however, such countries – suddenly released from the grip of non-democratic rule – found themselves confronted not with a smooth passage to democracy and democratic consolidation but instead to frequently serious outbursts of religious, ethnic and/or nationalist conflict. Examples in this regard include: Somalia, Pakistan and Nigeria.

Fourth, there was the spread of **capitalism**, an integral part of the wider process of globalisation. The spread of capitalism, to include previously

## Box 5.5 23 new countries since 1989

- Armenia
- Azerbaijan
- Bosnia and Herzegovina
- Croatia
- Czech Republic
- Eritrea
- Estonia
- Georgia
- Kazakhstan
- Kosovo (not yet widely recognised)
- Kyrgyzstan
- Latvia
- Lithuania
- Montenegro
- Moldova
- Serbia
- Slovakia
- Slovenia
- Somaliland (not yet widely recognised)
- Tajikistan
- Timor Leste
- Turkmenistan
- Uzbekistan

non-capitalist countries such as Russia, encouraged a renewed focus on the economic and political power of powerful cross-border actors, including transnational corporations such as Microsoft, McDonald's, Shell and Nestlé, and international financial institutions, including the International Monetary Fund and the World Bank (Woods 2000; Stiglitz 2006).

Fifth, there were more examples of attempts to create regional organisations. Some, for example the African Union, were modelled explicitly on the European Union (see Chapter 15), regarded as a major success story, as it had led at the regional level to both greater prosperity and more peace in a previously unstable and insecure region: Europe. Subsequent to the end of the Cold War, greater regional cooperation was exemplified in, for example, the North American Free Trade Association (NAFTA) and Latin America's MERCOSUR (El Mercado Común del Sur). In the EU and NAFTA, and to a lesser degree in MERCOSUR, increased economic, political, social and cultural links across regional countries were relevant for both domestic political and economic outcomes. However, the EU provides the best current example of the importance of cross-border actors for regional political and economic outcomes (see Chapter 15).

In sum, these observations enable us to identify a key attribute of international relations after the Cold War: various aspects of globalisation are significant in helping explain post-Cold War developments in international relations.

## New World Order: more cooperation, less conflict?

Mikhail Gorbachev, president of the USSR from 1985–91 and winner of the Nobel peace prize in 1990, was the first world leader to speak publicly of a 'new world order'. In his address to the United Nations on 7 December 1988, Gorbachev stated that: 'Further global progress is now possible only through a quest for universal consensus in the movement towards a new world order.' In addition, George H. W. Bush, US president from 1989–93, spoke on numerous occasions about the desirability of a post-Cold War 'new world order'. (George H.W. Bush is the father of George W. Bush, president of the United States, 2001–2009.) From the summer of 1990 to March 1991, he used the term 'new world order' forty-three times. Among contemporary politicians, he was the person who most referred to the need for a new world order after the Cold War. (See http://www.youtube.com/watch?v=7a9Syi12RJo for a 107 second video clip of George H.W. Bush outlining his ideas about new world order. Have a look at http://www.infoplease.com/ipa/A0900156.html for George H.W. Bush's State of the Union Address, 'Envisioning One Thousand Points of Light', delivered on Tuesday, 29 January 1991.) What did Presidents Gorbachev and Bush have in mind when they referred to new world order?

The end of the Cold War in 1991 was followed by a few short years of international optimism, a period known as the 'New World Order'. This era was *new* because it appeared to reflect radically different international circumstances after the Cold War. In addition, it was a changed set of circumstances with potentially *world*wide ramifications. It was also, moreover, a time when the old bipolar order (the existing order with two main poles of influence: the United States and the Soviet Union) looked set to be replaced by a new and different *order*, no longer dominated by the superpowers and their long-running ideological conflict. There was widespread optimism, especially in the West, that there would now be significant improvements in human rights and increased liberal democracy – that is, a political system characterised by regular elections, individual freedoms, political pluralism, and a free press. It was hoped that democracy would now spread to numerous countries, especially in Eastern Europe and the developing world.

One consequence of this (mainly) Western optimism was that some believed that, after the Cold War, liberal democracy now found itself without enemies or viable alternatives. This was a view held by an influential American commentator, Francis Fukuyama (1992). He called the end of the Cold War 'the end of history', that is, there would no longer be significant ideological challenges to the core Western values of liberal democracy and capitalism. Initially, Fukuyama's claim was widely accepted. This is because it seemed to dovetail well with the idea and ethos of a New World Order, which would be dependent on consensual international goals for its fulfilment. However, by the mid-1990s, it became clear that there were problems with the end of history thesis: in particular, new and unexpected conflicts were breaking out, including genocides in the African countries of Rwanda and Burundi, as well as civil wars in the former Yugoslavia, involving Serbs, Croats and Bosnians. Some believed that what was occurring was not so much 'the end of history' but 'a return to history', with a revival of traditional sources of tension and conflict in international relations.

Despite these setbacks, the post-Cold War spread of improved liberal democratic and human rights buoyed the New World Order optimists. There was also confident hope – if not expectation – that we might soon be witnessing substantial improvements in how international relations worked: for whom and for what goals. There appeared to be the enticing prospect of a new, consensual post-Cold War framework of international order, characterised by both increased security and enhanced stability, based on the widespread – maybe global – dissemination of Western values and norms.

While there was imprecision about precisely what a New World Order would entail, the following topics and issues were often mentioned:

1. An important role in the new global order should be played by the *United Nations* – reformed and adapted to the new world balance of power, and to new challenges and threats. The New World Order must be equipped with an effective instrument in the form of an international military force. That force must constitute a reliable deterrent to any potential aggressor who might think of using his army as a tool for pursuing political objectives.

2. The New World Order would also mean an improved, more significant role for *diplomacy and diplomatic techniques of international conflict resolution*. It implied shifting the emphasis from military to diplomatic methods. Arms reduction would also continue to comprise an important component of the New World Order agenda.

3. It was widely although by no means universally accepted that the most effective way of ensuring world peace and stability was by the universal introduction and embedding of *liberal free-market capitalism*. President H.W. Bush often stressed the importance of the International Monetary Fund and the World Bank in shaping the new global order.

4. The New World Order was widely seen as a way of providing the world with improved *stability and security*. Yet democratisation and the growing struggle for sovereignty in various parts of the world appeared in many countries to be contributing more to a rise of tension and conflicts, more often internal than international (as in Yugoslavia, the former Soviet Union and Africa), than to a stabilisation of the situation.

5. The aim of an improved global security system under the auspices of the United Nations was often noted to be desirable yet problematic, given how the United Nations had struggled to establish its pre-eminence. As a result, some suggested that it was more plausible to look to *regional security systems* as a key component in the attempt to produce better security. At present, we only have one effective Euro-Atlantic security system, based on the North Atlantic Treaty Organisation (NATO). But that system does not even cover all of Europe. Regions such as Asia, Africa and Latin America, which are less stable than Europe, have not established any regional security structures. The establishment of regional security and cooperation systems remains a desirable yet problematic mid-term objective.

Collectively, these five New World Order goals underline the hope that order, security and stability would be increased by the combined efforts of states and non-state organisations, such as the United Nations, working together to try to achieve them. Soon, however, one of the key proponents of New World Order, Mikhail Gorbachev, was out of power, following the fracturing of the Soviet Union in 1991. Gorbachev failed to win election as Russia's president; instead Boris Yeltsin got the job. Henceforward, encouragement towards a New World Order was led mainly by the USA, the sole remaining superpower. The task – proclaimed by President George H.W. Bush and supported by his successor, Bill Clinton (US president, 1993–2001) – was that the USA should lead efforts towards a New World Order.

However, when President George H. W. Bush's son, George W. Bush, came to power in 2001, the US focus had shifted from the desirability of a multilateral effort to develop a consensual international order led by the USA. The foreign policy experiences of America in the post-Cold War 1990s – such as conflict in Somalia, from which it came off second best, and the failure to achieve a viable democracy in Haiti – led to a perception among US policy makers that America needed to go it alone if necessary in order to achieve key US foreign policy goals: liberal democracy, improved human rights and a capitalist development model. These were crucial, the US government believed, in order to achieve increased enhanced human development, prosperity and progress. If necessary, it was argued, the USA must try to build and maintain an international order on its own hegemonic terms, via its own unilateral efforts in order to deliver a qualitatively *better* world order.

## Competing norms and values in international relations after the Cold War

After the Cold War ended in 1991, the then US president, George H.W. Bush believed that the world could enter a New World Order. It would feature a strengthening of international order and the pursuit of normatively desirable goals, including: more democracy, improved human rights and better development outcomes. The alternative was to see a world which Henry Kissinger, a former US Secretary of State, described as being 'in a state of revolutionary disarray' (Pastusiak 2004).

Two decades on, no one any longer talks about New World Order as it is clear that we have not seen it achieved. Why not? Part of the blame can be laid at the door of contemporary politicians who were apparently so preoccupied with resolving current tensions and conflicts that they ignored or were unable to focus consistently on the necessarily collective effort required to achieve a qualitatively improved world order.

We should not, however, blame the politicians exclusively. Evidence for this comes from what occurred following the ends of earlier, major international conflicts. Earlier attempts to establish 'new world orders' were made following major wars that affected huge

*Source: Alamy Images/Caro*

**The post-Cold War world suggested a new, consensual framework of international order, based on the widespread dissemination of Western values and norms.**

geographical areas. These included the Treaty of Westphalia (1648) after the Thirty Years War; the Congress of Vienna (1815) after the Napoleonic Wars; the Treaty of Versailles (1919) after the First World War; and international agreements signed at Yalta and Potsdam after the Second World War (1945). Keeping in step with this history, it was entirely consistent that expressions of a desire to establish a new world order after the Cold War were made. In other words, the notion of new world order is not new.

Another problem is that the concept of new world order is usually rather abstract and there is typically controversy about what exactly it should comprise and how it might be delivered. A key question is: who should lead the efforts towards new world order? We have already noted that some US commentators and politicians believed that creation of new world order should be the task of the sole remaining superpower. Yet, under the democratic principles that formally govern international relations, that task should be assumed by all players on the world political stage even if it is obvious that the qualitative weight of individual states differs greatly.

The United States is the only superpower, and has been for twenty years. This is because only America possesses sufficient assets to justify this claim. It has the largest economy, the most formidable military, the greatest technological and financial potential, as well as the strongest political, ideological and cultural influence, although this attribute – sometimes known as its **soft power** – is said to have waned in recent years, an outcome linked for many people to the USA's ill-judged attempts to impose its political will in Afghanistan and Iraq. On the other hand, even now no country other than the United States can bring such a combination of so-called 'hard' (political, economic, and military) and 'soft' (diplomatic, ideological, and cultural) power to international relations (Scholte 2005).

After the Cold War there were various challenges to US domination (or 'hegemony' as it is sometimes called). These challenges came from both state and non-state actors. What they had in common was that they were entities which did not share America's proclaimed norms and values. Overall, these challenges amounted to a significant test to the US-led attempt to build a New World Order on its own terms, in pursuit of its proclaimed norms and values. For example, the 1990–91 Gulf War made it clear that, despite the demise of the Soviet Union, there were new challenges to the status quo. The First Gulf War came

## Box 5.6 Challenges to US power in the 1990s

President George H.W. Bush's own optimism about the creation of a New World Order appeared to decline during the 1990s. Part of the reason may have been that the USA had serious foreign policy problems during that decade, especially in the first half of it. They were linked to the USA's attempts to install both political stability and enhanced security in various countries, including Somalia, Haiti and former Yugoslavia. Beyond the USA's own foreign policy setbacks there were also more general causes of decline in new world order optimism. While it would be over-simplifying things to say that new world order optimism gave way emphatically to new world order pessimism, it was the case that during the 1990s there developed what many saw as increased instability, more security challenges and growing sources of international conflict.

about as a result of the aggression of Iraq against its neighbour, Kuwait. Iraq appeared to be taking advantage of the smokescreen provided by the gradual fragmentation of the Soviet Union to seek not only to extend its regional influence by grabbing Kuwait territory but also to try to acquire Kuwait's oil resources for its own use. To deal with this challenge, the USA was willing to apply overwhelming military force in order to reverse Iraq's aggression. However, the First Gulf War made it clear that the USA could not now rest on its laurels, but would need to show vigilance and willingness to act in order to demonstrate that it was both willing *and* able to continue to play a pivotal role in international relations. However, soon after the challenge to the status quo from Iraq's invasion of Kuwait had been overcome, serious civil conflicts erupted in three African countries – Burundi, Rwanda, and Somalia – as well as in the Caribbean country of Haiti, former Yugoslavia and the former USSR (Haynes 2005). In no case was the United States able to offer assertive leadership and to deal with the problems, typically of a humanitarian and security nature, which followed in each country.

Rarely did these *intra*state conflicts reach clear-cut resolution. (An intrastate conflict is a conflict that occurs within a country.) Instead they tended to drag on for years or even decades, contributing to the phenomenon of 'failed states', that is, countries whose ability to develop both stability and security is dramatically undermined by ethnic, nationalist and/or religious conflicts. Partly as a result of these enduring conflicts, optimism that a peaceful, cooperative post-Cold War order, stimulated by the spread of liberal democracy and improved human rights to formerly communist Eastern Europe and the developing world, ebbed in the 1990s, just a handful of years after expressions of New World Order optimism. In addition, new, urgent issues emerged at this time, posing questions without easy or simple answers, particularly in relation to regional and global stability and security. In sum, in the 1990s growing numbers of *intra*national conflicts – that is, wars fought within countries – underlined that one of the less expected and most unwelcome results of the end of the Cold War was an array of nationalist, religious, and ethnic conflicts, especially in the developing world, springing up as the ideological straitjacket of the Cold War disappeared. Part of the context for these developments is provided by globalisation. We have seen in earlier chapters that the dynamic transfer of people, information, capital and goods is progressing on a worldwide scale. Globalisation and the huge expansion of information technology in recent years has stimulated significant changes in international relations. While in this global era people from numerous countries and civilisations are for the first time able to work and play together, globalisation has also encouraged other, darker developments in international relations.

## Trends in post-Cold War international relations: security, economy, ideology and development

There were four key changes in international relations following the end of the Cold War: new challenges to international security; globalisation of the world economy; ideological fragmentation; and highly variable development outcomes in the developing world.

## New challenges to international security

International security comprises all the measures taken by both states and non-governmental organisations, such as the United Nations, in order to try to ensure mutual survival and safety. They include military action and diplomatic agreements such as treaties and conventions. International and national security is nearly always linked. We can see this for example in the phenomenon of failed states where the intrastate conflicts that stimulate such 'failure' very often attract regional or international attention to try to resolve them. This is because such conflicts often threaten peace and stability beyond the national borders of the country where the conflict is taking place.

During the Cold War, the most prominent international security issue was that of the nuclear weapons relationship between the superpowers: the USA and the USSR. Following the dissolution of the Soviet Union in 1991, there was an apparent decline in the significance of strategic nuclear weapons. As a result, from the early 1990s the world appeared to enter at the global level a transition stage from nuclear to conventional – that is, non-nuclear – deterrence. During the Cold War, the key attribute – or 'strategic pillar' as it was called – of the nuclear relationship between the USA and the USSR was known as mutual assured destruction (MAD). This was the belief that if either the USA or USSR launched a nuclear strike against the other then the attacked state would retaliate and, despite being damaged by the nuclear strike, they would retain sufficient undamaged nuclear weapons to launch their own strike and inflict unacceptable damage against the aggressor. The overall significance of MAD was that for both the USA and USSR it made conquest difficult and expansion futile. For both countries, MAD implied the necessity of developing a relationship which would minimise the likelihood of nuclear conflict between the superpowers. In addition, MAD was important for international security for two more key reasons: first, due to the futility of 'overkill', it was possible for the superpowers to reach a weapons parity, and thus equilibrium, bringing stability to the system; and second, ever fearful of the massive destructive might of nuclear weapons, each superpower had a powerful incentive to constrain its allies: not to do so would – albeit unwillingly – create conditions whereby what is known as a 'proxy war' could break out, with potentially calamitous results. (A proxy war is one that results when two powers use third parties as substitutes for fighting each other directly.) (Held and McGrew 2007.)

On the one hand, since the end of the Cold War, the danger of thermonuclear warfare appears to have diminished. On the other hand, it is not clear whether the world is now more peaceful in comparison to the Cold War period. For example, not only have several new states – including North Korea and Pakistan – acquired nuclear weapons in a desire to achieve greater regional security, but also we have seen the widespread, not always peaceful, rise of nationalism, religious fundamentalism and ethno-nationalist disputes in many parts of the world, including Europe, Asia and Africa. Together, these developments pose a significant and continuing threat to international peace and the integrity of nations. The point here is that the acquisition of nuclear weapons is a security threat made worse by heightened religious-nationalist disputes in which antagonists might be inclined to use them.

## Globalisation of the world economy

The 'world' or 'global' economy refers to the increasing integration of fragmented national markets for goods and services into a single global market. In such an environment, businesses may get natural resources from one country, conduct research and development (R&D) in another country, take orders in a third country, and sell wherever demand exists regardless of the customer's nationality. Kenichi Ohmae (2008), a Japanese consultant, calls this the *borderless world*. Ohmae is not, however, claiming that national borders are completely unimportant; 'only' that certain influences have caused the globe to become smaller and smaller. These include technological advances in global communication and transportation (Hirst and Thompson 1999; Woods 2000).

In the post-Cold War international economy, there is a clear and continuing trend toward 'tripolarity' (that is, three poles of major significance), involving: the European Union, the USA, and the Asia-Pacific region. Each country/region accounts for approximately a quarter of the world's gross national product (GNP). Since the end of the Cold War, the importance of economic factors in defining international relationships has grown in relative importance. Consequently, one of the major economic challenges facing the world today is the possibility of increased friction among these three major economic poles. In particular, the development of this tripolar economic arrangement suggests the following questions: Will the transatlantic security partnership run into trouble? Will transpacific trade friction intensify? Can regionalism and interdependence coexist in such a way as to maintain an open trading system despite, or perhaps facilitated by, the tripolar economic arrangement?

The Asia-Pacific region is undergoing extensive and unprecedented change and the trend is towards greater integration and deregulation. Market forces have become the instruments of change and transformation in international relations, nowhere more so than in the Asia-Pacific region where the trend is towards greater integration and deregulation. The forces for global change are economic in origin, but they operate within particular political systems and deeply rooted cultures that will modify and condition their effect. The impact of global change upon the many disparate cultures and political systems of the Asia-Pacific region is one of the most important issues of international relations today. Is globalisation a set of processes dominated by Western countries to their own advantage? It is not easy to answer, but the implication is that globalisation refers to a complex of changes rather than a single one. No single country, or group of countries, controls any one of them. It is often asserted that until now, economic globalisation has been and is shaped by US foreign and domestic policy. Globalisation will not have the same effect in the Asia-Pacific region as in North America or Europe, and it would be senseless to imagine that the impact would be similar, or that the results of globalisation would be uniform and comparable, for all regions and cultures.

Over time, Asian states have proved increasingly assertive and resilient vis-à-vis Western influence. Beyond their rising self-confidence, Asian states' policies in relation to China appear highly suggestive of a realignment of power in the region. As China is readying resources to substantiate its aspirations toward regional hegemony, most states of South East Asia are directing their attention toward Beijing. Will China – hailed as the greatest potential single market by economists – also supplant the Western powers in the global pecking order in the near future? (Scholte 2005).

## Case study: China

China now has the world's biggest economy. In recent years it has grown very swiftly, around 10 per cent a year, enabling China to leave its Western competitors behind in the race to emerge from the global recession. It did this by consistently increasing export revenues, primarily from sales to foreign countries of manufactured goods. In short, China has emerged in recent years as an especially dynamic regional and global economic power.

In recent years, China's foreign currency reserves – a measure of an economy's fundamental strength – have grown to more than US$2 trillion. To put this into perspective, China's currency accumulation is twice the size of its nearest competitor: Japan. One of the main reasons for China's notable increase in reserves was the result of the country receiving major increases in foreign investment.

China's recent emergence on to the global economic scene reflects the fact that it enjoys several key advantages: (1) relatively low wages and salaries, (2) a currency pegged to the US dollar, and (3) relatively few effective environmental and healthcare requirements of the kind that Western firms must be concerned about due to legislation. In particular, the value of the Chinese currency (the yuan) has long been a divisive issue, with China frequently accused of undervaluing its yuan to make its exports cheaper. Some say that the yuan is undervalued by up to 50 per cent, allowing big retailers and manufacturers to produce goods in China at artificially low prices and sell them for greater profit in the United States. In recent years, the US trade deficit with China has been in the region of $13 billion a year. In presidential election campaigns in 2004 and 2008, the loss of manufacturing jobs in the USA to China was an issue of major political significance – not least because many of the regions affected were crucial swing states, that is, American states whose backing for presidential candidates fluctuates between the Democrats and Republicans from election to election.

An early contender for the Democratic nomination in 2004, Richard Gephardt, backed by the United Steelworkers, stressed his long-time opposition of free-trade agreements with China. During President Obama's election campaign in 2008 he accused China of currency manipulation. Following his elevation to president in January 2009, however, the US Treasury Department has expressed 'serious concerns' about the 'flexibility' of China's currency. Later that year, Washington slapped tariffs on tyre and steel imports from China. China retaliated with a tariff of its own, and has also launched probes of US imports of chicken and auto parts. Some warn the measures could trigger a trade war. Others say they represent more normal trade relations.

 **Which country needs the other more: the USA or China?**

China's recent emergence as a globally important economic power means that it is now central to a new dimension in the development debate. Earlier, in the 1980s and 1990s, events in former Communist Central and Eastern Europe were widely understood as confirming the then conventional wisdom: there is no viable alternative to the market economy and the neo-liberal perspective on development. However, things have turned out to be much more complicated than originally believed, as both economic and political transitions in many former Communist Central and Eastern Europe countries have proved to be both complex and problematic. Politically, China has shown few if any signs that it is developing characteristics of a democratic country, while the state's headlong rush to develop the economy has led to a growing polarisation of wealth in the country.

In sum, the hopes of the early 1990s that growing international economic interdependence would provide the basis for a peaceful world order have not come to fruition. Instead, international economic relations continue to be highly complex, characterised by continuous change and a pervading sense of insecurity.

## Ideological fragmentation

During the twentieth century, **ideology** transformed international relationships. Earlier centuries had been influenced by various kinds of wars: dynastic, national, civil and imperial. Over time, diplomacy developed to try to advance various goals, including: national security, national expansion or to promote mutual advantages and general peace. During the twentieth century, however, international relations were significantly affected by ideology in various ways, such as: how wars were fought (including the Second World War between the forces of fascism and those of liberal democracy), how alliances were made, and how treaties were signed. The Cold War was a balance of power between the superpowers that was fundamentally informed by ideological polarisation: the Communist bloc confronted the West, with its liberal democratic and capitalist ideology. In addition, after the Second World War, the decolonising developing world demonstrated a nationalist, anti-colonialist ideology in a search for identity and modernity. Over time, however, the developing world threw off colonial control and the often strident ideology of earlier decades gave way to a focused search for improved development.

When the Cold War came to an end it appeared also to finish that particular ideological focus in international relations. The Soviet-dominated Communist bloc was no more and the liberal democratic and capitalist ideology of the West appeared to have triumphed. The collapse of Soviet-style Communism left the USA and its allies as the pre-eminent voices in intellectual, policy and scholarly discourse: most of the values that the Soviet Union held dear had been comprehensively discredited and generally rejected. State-controlled economies and many other elements of Communism were in disrepute; market principles, private property and competition were now widely regarded as essentials of economic health. Politically and socially, the Communist Party's monopoly of power and extensive and intrusive state bureaucracies were also fundamentally rejected; from now on, free and fair elections, democratic governments and influential, citizen-dominated civil societies were held up as hallmarks of good governance.

All this meant that the break-up of the Soviet Union in 1991 was a major shock for international relations. Suddenly, the forces of contending, polarised ideologies that had dominated our understanding of international relations for at least half a century were no more and a new international system of indeterminate ideological form was created. The United States was apparently at the height of its international stature, and core US values, such as liberalism and democracy, spread around the globe. American businesses were leading efforts to build a new global economy. US military forces were active in the international struggle to provide enhanced global stability. Yet, at the very time when US power seemed at its most dominant, power was actually becoming more diffuse, and thus the US ability to shape the global agenda had actually decreased. In the absence of a compelling nuclear logic of MAD, which as noted above was central to the Cold War, American and, by implication, Western dominance of international relations would come under increasing pressure. As we saw above, various events – included widespread hostility to the US-led invasion of Iraq in 2003 – have led to widespread hostility toward the only superpower.

## Highly variable development outcomes in the developing world

**Development** first emerged as a subject area in the second half of the twentieth century. After the Second World War, scholars and practitioners sought to study the causes of poverty and so-called 'underdevelopment' in a more systematic and sustained way. These days, the substance of development studies – especially in relation to the developing world – focuses mainly on poverty reduction and improving 'human development'. It is a dynamic field whose importance cannot be understated as the gap between rich and poor grows seemingly ever wider.

Inevitably, the topic of development is focused upon in the twin contexts of the end of the Cold War and globalisation. We have already noted that globalisation has increased in importance in international relations since the end of the Cold War. Initially, there were widespread hopes for: first, enhanced international cooperation between peoples and countries; and second, fresh commitment to strengthen the role of international organisations, especially the United Nations and its dedicated agencies, in pursuit of peace and development. This would lead, it was hoped, to renewed efforts to address and deal with a range of perennial global problems, including: economic, social and political injustices; war; human rights abuses; and environmental degradation and destruction. Various matters, however, emerged to make the issue of how to improve development outcomes in the developing world more complex than originally envisaged. First, there was realisation that globalisation could have both 'positive' and 'negative' effects. Second, globalisation affected the ability of developing countries to organise at the international level, as the previously expressed solidarity – via, for example, the Non-Aligned Movement (see Chapter 4) – declined as countries often sought to go it alone to achieve their developmental goals.

Put simply, however, the problem with globalisation today is the uneven distribution of development goods which it encourages. As already mentioned, many states of the former Soviet bloc in Central and Eastern Europe struggled to digest the shock of trying to make the transition from a state-led 'command' economy to a **free-market economy**; for many developing countries in Africa, Asia, and Latin America, the ostensible boon of globalisation did not clearly or consistently take place – that is, globalisation became associated with growing polarisation of wealth with many among the poor seeing their living standards decline. In short, globalisation often proved to be a source of widening of the global division between the haves and the have-nots.

Globalisation, no doubt, brings us into contact with one another, but it also strengthens profound divisions and fractures in terms of societies and income, and most importantly in our capacity to generate and utilise knowledge. The huge income gap between rich and poor is now being exacerbated by a North–South 'digital divide' between those who have access to computers and the Internet and those who do not. Although there have been tremendous advances in science and technology over the last few decades, the developing world is still far behind in the technological race. The world has seen a revolution, the third industrial revolution in technological know-how during the last thirty years, which has raised people's expectations to new levels. This revolution based on the information age and the rapid introduction of new technology into all facets of human life, is changing the world into a global one.

## International relations in the twenty-first century

The period between 1991 and today has brought much change to the international political and economic orders and can therefore appropriately be referred to as a 'formative decade' during which we have witnessed the transition from the Cold War world into the globalised world of the early twenty-first century. This chapter has sought to examine important developments in international relations following the end of the Cold War two decades ago. We can conclude by noting that without doubt the last twenty years has seen the world change faster and more profoundly than in the entire period from 1945 to 1991. Today we know that the old world order has broken down and is disappearing, and that if a new world order is beginning to emerge, it is doing so very slowly.

At the beginning of this chapter we highlighted three areas and issues for discussion:

- What has changed?
- What has remained the same?
- How does our understanding of international relations change as a result?

On the first question, we saw that the end of the Cold War and globalisation have led to major changes in international relations. We also saw that the end of the Cold War eroded the globalisation of security arrangements – while intensifying the globalisation of world economic processes.

It became clear that the pervasiveness of economic globalisation can be measured both in terms of its *extensiveness* and its *intensity*. In particular, we now have three poles of economic power – the USA, Europe and Asia-Pacific. This is an arrangement that might or might not lead to new conflicts in the future. The significance of economic globalisation is even greater when linked to the steady opening to the international market of many developing countries' economies, a process that has occurred since the 1980s.

However, it is more on the basis of the current *intensity* of globalisation that most claims for economic globalisation rest. The trends in this direction are now so entrenched and irreversible that they have raised questions about the relevance – and effectiveness – of individual countries as meaningful aggregations in terms of what to think about, much less manage, economic activity. Not only is the growth of economic globalisation said to be without precedent, but it is also claimed that it follows its own technical and economic logic. Even those who offer a more balanced account of what is happening concede that in the absence of a clearly defined security agenda, economic integration has a momentum of its own. The manifestations of this intensification of globalisation are deemed to lie in the global mobility of capital, the growth of foreign direct investment (FDI), and the role of transnational corporations.

As we have seen, however, the argument about the significance of globalisation for international relations extends beyond economic factors alone, even if they remain for many the most powerful cluster of arguments. More generally, the processes of globalisation are also thought to be expressed through the changed imagery of post-Cold War international relations. Here the emphasis is on New World Order and broadening security issues. Such images are not new – but they have intensified since the end of the Cold War after first capturing public attention in the early 1970s via the work of International Relations scholars, such as Robert Keohane and Joseph Nye. The most conspicuous feature of the new international situation is the emergence of issues that transcend national frontiers. It is argued that the limits on national autonomy imposed by the 'balance of nuclear terror' during the Cold War have now been supplemented by a much subtler, more structural form of erosion caused by the processes of environmental, social and economic globalisation.

The second question is: What has remained the same in international relations following the end of the Cold War and greater globalisation? It is clear that we haven't seen the birth of a New World Order. Instead, there is the continuation of an order fragmented on North–South lines. There is not a single world order, some argue, but rather a liberal democratic order on the one hand and, on the other, a non-democratic world *dis*order. Put another way, there are said to be two zones: the first, containing most of the world's power wherein no country faces substantial or significant military danger to its autonomy; the second, where 85 per cent of the world's population live, is a zone of turmoil.

This division touches also upon the extent of a globalised democracy and human rights order. It might have been thought that the end of the Cold War ushered in conditions favourable to a new respect for universally recognised human rights, and the emphasis on such rights in the new world order rhetoric of the early 1990s reinforced this impression. Moreover, since the superpowers had, for Cold War reasons, often been supporters of regimes that notoriously violated their own citizens' rights – such as in the case of the USA's support of Chile under the authoritarian rule of General Pinochet (1973–90) – then the removal of this structural condition appeared favourable to a general improvement in this realm. In addition, the new determination of the international community to implement war crime tribunals, following the wars in Iraq, Rwanda, Sierra Leone, and the former Yugoslavia, was symptomatic of the rediscovered universalism that had first been encouraged by the Second World War. Yet further evidence of the move in this direction was the greater emphasis that came to be placed on democracy and human rights issues in North–South relations – not only was liberal democracy triumphant in the Cold Wars competition but it became increasingly assertive in demanding change in political behaviour in the developing world. It is appropriate, unfortunately, to be sceptical about how pervasive – and universal – is an improved human rights regime. The wish to punish alleged war criminals has often proved stronger than the international community's ability to do so. There is little to indicate that the gulf between different conceptions of human rights is narrowing and much to suggest that these conceptions have become part of the substance of international relations, a continuation of political intercourse by other means.

Finally, there is the third question: How does our understanding of international relations change as a result of the end of the Cold War and enhanced globalisation? The first thing to note in this regard is that international relations has become more complicated. Globalisation has been accompanied by resurgence of what is sometimes known as 'fragmentationist' tendencies, that is, ethnic, national and religious challenges to the status quo. One argument sees the fragmentation of the international system to be the direct consequence of the loss of Cold War structures of control, likely to lead to a much more unruly world, perhaps illustrated by the events surrounding 9/11. In the most extreme, and ethnocentric, version of the argument it was claimed that a world without US primacy would be a world with more violence and disorder. As regards the developing world, the effects of this were early recognised to be ambiguous. If hitherto, superpower competition had resulted in attempts to control regional conflicts – to ensure that they would not draw in their superpower patrons – then the end of the Cold War was a form of liberation. This new freedom came, however, at a price because the removal of the restraining hands of the Cold War could be interpreted as the decline of any real interest in the developing world. In short, one aspect of the new fragmentation was a renewed regionalisation of international security and a disjunction between potential regional conflicts and the ordering mechanisms of the great powers.

However, it may be too simplistic to regard all manifestations of fragmentation as the mere by-product of the end of the Cold War, and the issue becomes particularly significant in the analysis of the apparent resurgence of ethno-nationalism and religion as powerful political forces in the international system. One line of argument might suggest that the political fragmentation of the globe is less the consequence of the loosening of superpower security controls than a side effect of the removal of the universalist ideological parameters which the Cold War had kept in place. Within the confines of the Cold War, the key issue of identity was with one or the other of the two rival systems – and for the developing world membership of a movement that renounced both while selectively engaging with each other. The removal of this ideological overlay has allowed questions of national and religious identity once again to come to the fore.

## Conclusions

The aim of this chapter was to enable you to understand important developments in international relations after the end of the Cold War. We addressed three key issues in this chapter:

- What has changed in international relations since the end of the Cold War
- What has remained the same over the last twenty years
- How our understanding of international relations has been modified as a result

We saw that despite the key changes that have occurred over the last two decades – increase in importance of globalisation, collapse of the Soviet Union, economic rise of China – much has remained the same, with the leading states, such as the USA, still able to wield considerable influence on outcomes in many contexts. On the other hand, it is the case that international relations has significantly changed in recent decades, marked by: the fall of the Berlin Wall in November 1989; the consequential demise of the Soviet bloc in 1991; and widespread economic liberalisation, democratisation, and the spread of individualistic 'American' and 'Western values'. Globalisation was intimately connected to all these developments: it was the main means of spreading these ideas.

## Resource section

## Questions

**1.** To what extent is international order enhanced by globalisation?

**2.** What were the main consequences of globalisation for international relations in the post-Cold War era?

**3.** How did the balance of power in international relations change after the Cold War?

## Recommended reading

Rusciano, F. (2006) *Global Rage after the Cold War* (Macmillan)
The aim of this book is to highlight new forms of domestic and international conflict after the Cold War. Rusciano seeks to explain the rise of ethnic and religious conflict by way of what he claims is people's need to assert their identity in changing local and global contexts, as a result of globalisation.

Schrecker, E. (ed.) (2006) *Cold War Triumphalism: The Misuse of History after the Fall of Communism* (The New Press)
In 2002, President George W. Bush declared, 'The great struggles of the twentieth century between liberty and totalitarianism ended with a decisive victory for the forces of freedom – and a single sustainable model for national success: freedom, democracy and free enterprise'. *Cold War Triumphalism* exposes the ideological roots of such unabashed triumphalist accounts, and counters the current attempt to rewrite the history of the Cold War struggle.

## Useful website

United States relations with Russia timeline: after the Cold War

**http://www.state.gov/r/pa/ho/pubs/fs/85965.htm**
This is the US Department of State website – motto 'Diplomacy in Action' – which usefully traces the development of US–Russia relations since the end of the Cold War.

# Part 3 International Relations Theories

Many students tend not to be instantly drawn to theory; many of them try to avoid it at all costs. You might wonder why we bother with theory at all. Why not just tell people about current affairs and allow their pre-existing moral and political dispositions to make sense of them?

Theories are attempts to make the complex intelligible or explicable. They seek to engage us with questions of what we should study and how we can build up knowledge about it. In a simple way we can compare theories to maps; they cannot include everything or they become unwieldy, but if they leave too much out then they will be unable to guide us.

Sometimes we need many different maps. For example, a hiker might want a map of footpaths, a weather map *and* a geological map for a hazardous expedition. None of these are incorrect because they explain different things. In IR, we can think about how each theory adds to our understanding of the whole.

To use another analogy, it is important to remember that theory is a language that must be learned. There are no native speakers. Learning a theory is not easy, and for some it can be difficult. One must start with the basics. Once you can 'say' a few things, you can begin to learn contextually and even through making mistakes. Our experience is that once students have simple ideas to hang on to, they have the confidence to go out and learn for themselves.

These chapters tell the story of IR theory, and they provide a foundation for further study. They cannot explain absolutely everything, and they are not intended to be a substitute for further reading. We must also make a couple of essential points before we begin. First, sometimes things come out of order, so that we only need to mention them once. For example, you might expect to see the 'neo-neo debate' between Realism and Liberalism in one of the early chapters. However, given the narrowness of that debate, we consider it later on in the book in terms of how it has been critiqued in more recent approaches. Similarly, taken out of context, the chapter on Marxism would seem too limited, even in an abbreviated history. However, you will see that developments in Marxian thought are considered in subsequent chapters where we felt they were relevant.

Finally, if theory is a hard slog for you, we don't just sympathise, we empathise. But like many difficult things, getting through them can bring a great sense of, not only just relief, but also satisfaction. Beyond such feelings, engagement with theory is likely to lead to better grades for your assignments; that might well be your initial motivation in turning the next few pages but we hope they also enhance your understanding of the rest of the book, and international relations in general.

*Source*: Getty Images

# Chapter 6
# Realism and Neo-Realism

Context

The 'back-story' to Realism

Realism in International Relations

Key assumptions

Key concepts

Conclusions and criticisms

After reading this chapter you will be able to:

- Describe the history of Realism as an approach, including the key assumptions it makes about the world

- Update the history of Realism in terms of contemporary politics

- Demonstrate the strengths of the approach as well as its weaknesses

- Recognise both the commonalities in, but also differences between, variants of Realism such as neo-Realism

- Evaluate Realism's historical, current and future contributions to the discipline of IR in both practice and theory

*Source*: Getty Images

## Introductory box: The decline of Realism?

Carl von Clausewitz is most famous for the words 'war is merely a continuation of politics by other means'. He is one of many influences on Realism in international relations. Realism is a theory of International Relations which accepts war as a perfectly normal (if regrettable) part of the relationships between states. War is said to be not just normal but inevitable such that theories which do not accept its inevitability are unrealistic, and by not preparing us for the worst, actually dangerous. Realism's dominance of IR theory is one reason that many textbooks start with it; and even if other theories might now claim to be intellectually or morally superior, Realists would still argue that they have the ear of many states-people.

Nonetheless, there are a number of reasons for its relative decline in recent years. One might be considered the terrifying consequences of applying Clausewitz's simple and elegant phrase (especially the word 'merely') to the nuclear era. *Threads* was a terrifying and influential TV drama about the possibility of nuclear war and the horrors of nuclear winter. Unlike some such dramas this one doesn't end with the explosive terror of a nuclear explosion but takes us thirteen years beyond to a society and population stunted and hideously mutated both physically and mentally. Originally transmitted in 1984 its capacity to induce nightmares is hardly possible to convey in a few dozen words.

**Realism** is a theoretical approach to international relations which suggests that countries are the most important players (as opposed to companies or individuals for instance). Realism suggests that the most important processes taking place in global politics involve violent conflict between countries (as opposed to cooperation or environmental degradation for instance). These simple ideas dominated International Relations, at least for a time, in a way that no other approach has managed to. Realism often seems to tell us much about the motivation of those who act in the name of the state. Realism describes itself as 'the essence of IR' and as 'elegantly simplistic'. For these reasons Realism both merits our attention and tends to be a theoretical approach which students feel comfortable with right away.

As with all the chapters here on theoretical approaches, the point is not to encourage you to adopt one as 'your' theory, but rather to regard all theories as *potentially* adding insight and to help you see which insights Realism helps with – and which it does not. In your other reading you should bear in mind that academic authors can be very good at selecting evidence. You should recognise that theories cannot be vindicated by every partial explanation or piece of evidence which seems to fit them.

## Box 6.1 Unnecessary wars

Realism's dominance in IR theory after the Second World War is largely to do with it being able to say 'we told you so' about the pre-war period. Non-Realists had hoped that the First World War was the 'war to end all wars' but Realists argued that relying on the League of Nations and a policy of 'appeasement' towards aggressive powers, was just inviting failure and another war because essentially international relations would always be competitive and underpinned by threatened or actual violence. Despite being right in the context of the Second World War (which happened despite Realist warnings), critics argue that Realists end up with a view of the world which is distorted and dangerous and causes *unnecessary* wars. For instance, in South East Asia in the 1960s the US government was determined not to appease the Communist powers the way the Nazis had been. Accordingly, in attempting to avoid a communist takeover in Vietnam it became embroiled in a pointless, unwinnable war, arguably confusing Nazi *expansionist* aims with the legitimate post-colonial nationalism of the Vietnamese.

## Context

Although we should not necessarily succumb to the charms of simplicity, where a theory is both simple *and* seems backed by plenty of evidence, it is easy to see why it could come to dominate a discipline. So, from the perspective of today it is easy to point out that Realism fails to acknowledge major sociological features of world politics, such as the position of women. Also from the perspective of today it is easy to see that Realism misses major aspects of economic life that play themselves out in all sorts of ways in Africa, Latin America, and Asia. However, we should at least try to understand Realism in context; it is a context (emerging in the 1930s and then after the Second World War) where personal morality and the demands of international politics were seen by its proponents to be divorced from each other – the economic troubles of individuals and nations were viewed as subordinate to issues of war and violence.

## Box 6.2 A moral perspective?

Realists do not deny the existence of inequality and injustice in the world. However, they argue that they are not relevant for the purposes of managing inter-state rivalries and conflicts nor for studying international relations. Is this position morally defensible?

Oddly perhaps, as an already simple theory (concentrating as it does on states and violence), Realism is the easiest to *oversimplify* and it is easy to see why this might be the case. Although Realism can lead to heated debate over nuance and interpretation, it deliberately curtails the size of the international arena we are dealing with. Furthermore, it then looks at this arena with a limited number of assumptions about actors, issues and human nature. For this reason scholars tend to either embrace Realism as clear or despise it for oversimplification.

Finally, we should say something about the 'label' for this particular approach. Rightly or wrongly, many other approaches have names which, to some people, imply negative connotations. To be an idealist, or a Liberal or a feminist can lead to knee-jerk critique from certain quarters; but rarely has someone been attacked for being *too* realistic. Realism implies sensibleness or commonsense. It therefore *suggests* a theory which cuts through the confusion and takes us to the heart of the matter. With such a powerful semantic weapon at its disposal it is important for us to re-emphasise here that Realism describes a set of assumptions about international relations which may, or may not, be realistic. Just as a person may feel they are 'realistic' but are actually blunderingly insensitive, we should not read too much into the label 'Realism'.

## The 'back-story' to Realism

If Realism's theoretical dominance is a relatively recent phenomenon, it nonetheless claims a historical lineage going back thousands of years. When Realism is able to point to thinkers such as Thucydides in ancient Greece (around 2400 years ago) and beyond to the ancient China of Sun Tzu (a hundred years before that), it is able to argue for strong philosophical roots; that it provides *timeless* wisdom.

Sun Tzu was a general in the Chinese army of around 500 BC and he recounts his wisdom (which he regards as universally applicable) in a treatise called *The Art of War*. The book is a philosophy of war and military strategy. Less important for our purposes is the precise content of the book and more the fact that it supports Realist contentions that history is cyclical in the sense that patterns of peace and violence tend to repeat themselves and the notion of military preparedness therefore remains paramount. Thucydides wrote on the Peloponnesian wars, between the Greek city states of Athens and Sparta, using the war to demonstrate how the logic of power politics characterised inter-state relations. Thucydides' studies showed, in essence, that the powerful did what they were able to and that the less powerful just had to accept it. Appeals to higher principles such as those by the people of Melos (that their neutrality should be respected or that their Athenian adversary should show mercy) met with the same iron fist which has been the fate of so many powerless peoples throughout recent centuries.

Somewhat nearer to the present day Niccolo Machiavelli, a sixteenth-century Italian political thinker, and the seventeenth-century English philosopher Thomas Hobbes, are also part of Realism's heritage in justifying 'political expediency' over 'moral principle'. Machiavelli is famous for the practical advice he offered to statesmen by which they could maximise their power (Machiavelli 1988). His advice included the instruction that promises must be broken when there is an interest to do so. This is one of many reasons why Machiavelli is often accused of being an immoral thinker. The term 'Machiavellian' is used to denote cynical and unprincipled behaviour, or used to describe people who act in a cunning and subtle manner, unscrupulously manipulating situations to their own advantage. Although Machiavelli was not explicitly concerned with ethics or justice, it is clear that he regarded moral principles or justice as simply the stated preferences of the already powerful. There is no doubt that Machiavelli held an extremely dim view of human nature. Realists continue to argue there is no place for trust or sentiment in politics and point to Machiavelli's wisdom in elucidating this point.

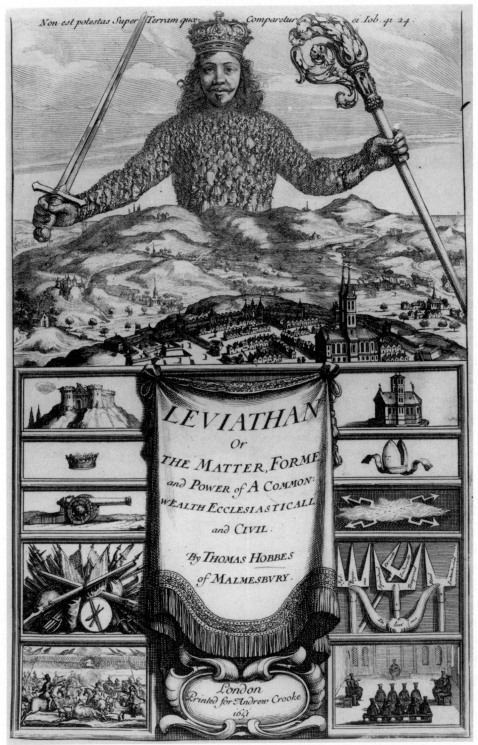

**Political expediency over moral principle: Thomas Hobbes'** *Leviathan* **played an influential role in developing Realism.**

The work of Thomas Hobbes has also been a key influence on Realist thinkers. Hobbes is influential because he was among the first political thinkers to undertake a sustained discussion on the nature of secular (non-religious) power and authority. Living at a time of great social change and political instability, among Hobbes' major preoccupations were the nature of political power, the basis of political order and, particularly, the origins of the state as the central, sovereign power. In order to explain the reasons and justification for the state and government, Hobbes posited the existence of a 'state of nature' in which all enjoyed freedom from restraint but in which, in consequence, life was 'nasty, brutish and short'. The conditions of life were unpleasant because he claimed it was man's nature to try and dominate and oppress others. Only mutual vulnerability and the desire for self-preservation allowed the setting up of a sovereign body that would secure the conditions necessary for civilised life. However, while men might be persuaded to give up their natural liberty for the protection of the sovereign, the international realm would remain a war of all against all, since the conditions which forced men to give up their natural liberty in the 'state of nature' for security could never be realised in an international context and states needed to remain ever vigilant. Hobbes' classic work *Leviathan* remains one of the most influential writings on the nature of sovereignty and international anarchy (Hobbes 1904). Indeed, international relations is sometimes likened to a 'state of nature'.

At times, Hobbes appears to evoke images which suggest religious influence and sympathies – inherent evil or wickedness for example. However, his beliefs about the essentially selfish impulses of human beings were actually rooted in what he understood to be the insights of modern science. The extent to which we can discern scientific laws which help us to explain individual or social behaviour is debatable. So is drawing a parallel between the individual in a state of nature and the state in the international realm. However, together, these two central assumptions provide Realists with support for their argument about the need for states to behave selfishly in international relations. Such a view suggests that states are unified (internally), purposive and a rational actor in international relations, somewhat in the way that individuals are when seeking survival in a state of nature.

The next section will talk about Realism emerging in the 1920s and 1930s as a challenger to previous ideas which had emphasised both cooperation and the possibilities inherent in human nature. However, the foregoing indicates that in many senses this is the re-emergence (or rebranding) of ideas, rather than the emergence of a distinctively new understanding of human nature and inter-state dynamics.

## Realism in International Relations

Although students and scholars of the discipline should not be fooled by the name Realism, it is neither an accidental nor a fortunate name. It is given the name for a deliberate reason; that being to associate it with realistic attributes as held by individuals. Realism as it began to emerge in the 1920s and 1930s is explicitly saying 'this is a realistic way to think of international affairs' and it is saying this in comparison to the Utopianism or Idealism dealt with in Chapter 7. Utopianism and Idealism are labels attached to a particular type of Liberal perspective which came to the fore between the First World War and the Second World War; it was associated with notions of disarmament, the power of human reason and cooperation to avoid violence.

Such Liberal/Utopian ideas emerged from the First World War with great force as people demanded that the mindless and miserable slaughter not be allowed to happen again. These ideas were based on a positive conception of human nature and a related belief in human progress. Although arguments can support such a view, Realists were saying that we could not simply eradicate war by force of will; the best we could do was try to control it, regulate it, minimise it. They argued that it was dangerous to attempt otherwise because peace and disarmament could always be exploited by the unscrupulous. When the Second World War broke out – bringing different, more terrifying, horrors – they seemed to have been proved correct, were not slow to say so, and did not expect to be challenged. It is for these reasons that Realism is often presented first in IR courses, the foundation stone that all other theories must chip away at and the only theory of IR to have dominated, alone, for any length of time.

Realism has become known as a 'tradition of pessimism'. Its pessimism is based, primarily, upon two things. First of all because of its negative view of underlying human nature; this does not deny altruistic and caring impulses but suggests humans tend to act selfishly. But a factor overlaying the *individual* level concerns the *systemic* level. The international system of states is said to be characterised by **anarchy** and this fact is the most important in understanding international relations. Although this word has several meanings, for Realists it is taken literally to mean 'absence of government', in the sense that there is no authority above the state. If two states have a disagreement there is no higher authority to which they can turn; their relationship takes place, therefore, not necessarily in an absence of rules (accepted norms of behaviour such as regarding the treatment of prisoners) but certainly in an absence of world government. The title of one famous work in IR *The Anarchical Society* (Bull 1977) suggests a more complex picture where 'rules' are still important despite the lack of authority.

## Box 6.3 Edward Hallett (E.H.) Carr (1892–1982)

The reaction against Idealism produced a number of very influential works in International Relations which mark the emergence of Realism as the dominant worldview in the post-Second World War period. One such work was E.H. Carr's *The Twenty Years' Crisis*, first published in 1939 (Carr 1946). Carr is a central figure in the history of IR, whose continuing importance has been highlighted by recent attempts to (re)interpret this central work in the cause of (re)claiming Carr as a Liberal, Marxist, English School scholar and as a Critical Theorist. However, for a long period, Carr has been identified with Realism because he produced a powerful critique of the core assumptions of Idealism, arguing that the tragic events of the 1930s (as the world descended once more into war) bore witness to the fragility of international institutions, the realities of the underlying struggle for power among states and the fallacy of a world public opinion supporting pacifism. Carr also rejected the normative underpinnings of Idealism (a concern with questions of law, morality and justice) arguing instead for a 'science of international politics'.

Realists (both academics and states-people) argued strongly against the League of Nations which others hoped would play the role of an ultimate world authority after the First World War. Realists suggested that states would only obey the League when it was in their interests to do so; as protection from attack the League was thus useless and, regrettable though it might be, if states wanted peace they should prepare for war. Although it is a position ameliorated by (shifting) alliances, the bottom line for Realists is that states can only rely on themselves. Treaties, alliances and international institutions may have roles to play, but one of those roles is not substituting for self-reliance. The Second World War seemed to even more firmly underscore Realism's practical, 'commonsense' pessimism.

## Case study: The League of Nations

Prior to the First World War countries adhered to the view that governments were the legitimate representatives of sovereign states and that all sovereign states had the right to judge their own best interests and pursue these through an independently formulated foreign policy and, when necessary, through military action. The view prevailed that the 'national interest' and security concerns demanded that diplomatic relations be conducted in secret and foreign policy be guarded from public scrutiny and criticism. The horrors of the First World War brought about a far-reaching change in attitudes among both political elites and influential sections of the public across the European continent. Even before the end of the war, the principle of sovereignty was being subjected to critical challenges. A League of Nations Society was formed in London in 1915 and similar bodies sprang up in a number of European countries. In Britain the idea of forming a League of Nations won backing from across the political spectrum, as leaders joined together to argue for the formation of a new international system which would secure the peace, if necessary by the collective efforts of the 'peace loving' powers.

The League of Nations was formed at the end of the First World War. Its aims were to provide a system of collective security and to deter aggressor states from pursuing their 'national interests' at the expense of their smaller, weaker, neighbours. The basic idea underpinning collective security was that if any one member state fell victim to the aggression of a powerful neighbour, all members of the Organisation would collectively join together to deter or repel the aggressor. The idea was to make violence illegitimate as an option for states, and for other states to combine and oppose any state which used violence as a means of resolving its disputes in international relations. While it was recognised that this might ultimately require armed force, it was widely believed that 'world public opinion' would, in itself, prove to be a powerful deterrent to any would-be belligerent

power. It was also recognised that if the League was to be a success, the United States of America (USA) would need to end its period of 'isolation' and play a leading role in world affairs. Unfortunately, this was not to be. Although the US President Woodrow Wilson played a prominent role in the original conception and planning of the League, the US Senate refused to ratify the Covenant of the League of Nations, thus preventing US membership. However, the League gradually expanded its role in world affairs, setting up, among other things, a Permanent Court of International Justice to arbitrate international disputes.

Although the existence of the League was, in itself, a powerful challenge to the view that states were exempt from public debate and criticism in their relations with other states, major powers were reluctant to refer their own disputes to the League. Similarly, action to achieve general disarmament was not successful. By the late 1930s events in world politics had served to undermine the wave of optimism on which the League was born, as the behaviour of some states failed to live up to Idealist/Liberal expectations (see Chapter 7). In 1931 Japan attacked China and the latter appealed to the League under Article 11. The League sent commissions and issued condemnations, but Japanese aggression was not punished. Italy invaded Abyssinia (Ethiopia) in an attempt to establish Italy as one of the great European imperial powers. This led to economic sanctions and protest by the League, but without the backing of military sanctions these were ineffective. In Germany, Hitler sent troops into the demilitarised zone of the Rhineland in 1936 but referrals to the League, rather than resulting in resolute action, allowed Hitler to get away with a huge military and political gamble. Power politics appeared to be very much the order of the day and by the end of the decade, the world was at war once again.

**Does the failure of the League prove Realism to be correct?**

Source: Corbis

**The rise of Nazi Germany is regarded as one of the League of Nations' gravest failures. Does the emergence of such a regime underline Realism's essential 'truth'?**

Emerging from the Second World War Realists were strengthened in their belief that the pursuit of power and national interest were the major forces driving world politics. Focusing on these important forces, Realists revealed that leaders had far less freedom to organise the world, and solve its problems, than proponents of Idealism had originally suggested (see also Chapter 7). Although Realists accepted that laws and morality were a limited part of the workings of world politics, respect for law would only be achieved if it were backed by the threat of force. Realists also insisted that a state's primary obligation should be to itself, not to a rather abstract 'international community'.

The onset of the Cold War so soon after the Second World War simply reinforced Realism's dominance. Although since that time alternative theories have emerged to challenge Realism in various ways, it is still the modus operandi for states-people. While future chapters will move to explain alternative theories it is important to re-emphasise two points at this stage. First, that much state behaviour can be seen to support the view taken by Realists. Second, we cannot accept this apparent correlation as proof that the theory is universally valid.

## Box 6.4 Martin Wight [1913–1972]

Martin Wight might be considered a good example of the tradition of pessimism. His work concentrates on the regrettable continuities of international relations (war and conflict) rather than on elements of change (progress and cooperation). As the cover to the 1985 edition of his classic *Power Politics* (1979) suggests he is 'concentrating not on the ephemera of current events but on the features of international politics that are fundamental and enduring'. As far as authors such as Wight are concerned, things as they 'are' must be divorced from how we would like them to be and from our personal morality. Wight is known for having had a strong religious morality, but that faith could not overcome the pessimism associated with Realism's tradition of despair. As a founding father of specifically *British* International Relations, whose work has recently been re-examined, Wight is worth further investigation.

## Key assumptions

So far this chapter has given a sense of where Realism is coming from; its history, pessimism and its political pragmatism. It is now time to make some of the key points of Realism explicit and to outline the foundational assumptions of a realist perspective. In brief Realism is a perspective in IR which concentrates overwhelmingly on the interaction of states. It suggests that as far as relationships between states go, 'politics ends at the water's edge' or border; what this means is that whatever different political systems states have *internally*, their *external* behaviour will be motivated by similar concerns. These concerns are for power, with power being the means to an end; namely protecting the national interest. Since Realists regard the absence of a central authority (anarchy) as the defining characteristic of international relations, protecting the national interest is difficult. The possibility of conflict is ever present; unlike individuals, the state never sleeps and must be eternally vigilant. Realists think the best that can be done is to 'manage' this inevitable situation through shifting alliances, and that international law has a place only if backed by effective sanction.

Assumptions are important because they can actually affect what we see. The other day I looked out of my office window and saw a leaf by a door. How did I know it was a leaf? What I actually saw was a small brown object lying on the floor, somewhat in the distance. But since it was in a small courtyard, infrequently visited by people and with many trees in it, I assumed it was a leaf. My assumptions radically altered when it jumped! I discovered it to be a frog, but since there are no ponds nearby, I can only assume it hopped by for the moment when I needed a good example like this. The point is that, although Realism is claiming to be realistic, it may be that its assumptions are actually shaping what it 'sees'. What and how Realism sees the world is expanded upon in the next section, but for now we need to look at the assumptions which provide it with a 'lens' on the world in the first place.

The first key Realist assumption is of human selfishness. This is assumed not only to be in the dark heart of humanity but to be reflected in the behaviour of leaders of states who act in a self-interested manner. Second, states are assumed to be the central actors for

## Box 6.5 The stag–hare analogy

Originally developed in the ideas of Rousseau, this 'tragic' explanation of international affairs is sometimes known as the 'security dilemma' and can be illustrated using a variety of stories. Perhaps the most famous analogy involves a group of primitive hunters isolated on an island. They have a strong motive to cooperate since they agree that if they can kill a stag they will have enough to feed all of them, but that to do this will require all of their efforts to entrap and kill the animal. Accordingly they set off to hunt the stag, but shortly afterwards one of the hunters sees a hare. A hare would certainly be enough to satisfy the hunger of an individual and in breaking off from the stag hunt to capture the hare the hunter ensures that he will satisfy his need for food. However, in so doing he effectively allows the stag to escape and the rest of the group are condemned to hunger. Cooperation among all the hunters could have led to an optimal solution where all were fed. However, the hunter faced a dilemma because he could not be sure that the group would catch the stag. Furthermore, and perhaps more to the point, he could not be sure that another member of the group would not break ranks in pursuit of the hare if he did not, in which case *he* would have gone hungry for his loyalty to the group. In the context of this uncertainty, it was, therefore, rational to behave in a self-interested manner.

The point of the stag–hare analogy is to illustrate that under conditions of uncertainty (that is anarchy) it is rational to act in a self-interested way. Following Realist logic, the tragedy of international relations is, therefore, that under conditions of anarchy even mutual interest does not guarantee cooperation and hence mutual gain.

purposes of study; international relations is therefore about how these selfish entities interact. Third, states are sovereign; that is they have the right and ability to act in international affairs, which encourages their leaders to pursue their own national interests through the maximisation of their power. With all states acting selfishly as sovereign entities, a fourth assumption concerns the inherently conflictual nature of international relations. Realists tend to differ as to whether the inevitability of conflict should be explained primarily by reference to human nature, the state as an institution, or the 'tragedy' of an anarchic system which 'encourages' selfish behaviour.

The point, perhaps, is that if you are looking for a leaf you might see a leaf – if my 'leaf' had not jumped it would have continued to be a leaf as far as I was concerned. Likewise, if you are expecting to see selfishness and conflict, what chance is there that you will look for and find the possibilities of cooperation or progress? And if you regard things as unchanging, what chance will you see, let alone take action, in terms of things which ought to be changed? We leave these points to be answered in future chapters; for now we look at the differences in assumption between traditional or classical Realists and a group known as neo-Realists.

## Realism v. neo-Realism

Realist approaches share some basic assumptions but there are differences. An obvious difference is between Realism and neo-Realism. At the most basic level, what we might now call 'classical Realism' is an attempt to understand the world from the point of view of the statesman, stateswoman or diplomat who is forced to operate in an uncertain and dangerous world. Realism provides a guide to action based on guiding principles of realpolitik

(Realism about what is possible and a preparedness to use force where necessary). Thus Realism focuses on states as actors and analyses international politics in terms of states and violence. On the other hand, neo-Realism places more emphasis on the importance of what is described as the 'anarchic international system' as well as considering the rise of economic issues in importance after the 1950s. These are, in fact, two sides of the same coin and the difference is one of *emphasis*. To draw an analogy it is like trying to analyse and explain a football match; one could look at the motivations, tasks and skills of individual players (their agency) or on the other hand look at the constraints (rules/structure) under which they must operate, but in either case there is agreement on the game that is being analysed. The rest of this section looks at these two sides of a coin. (See also agency/structure debate in Chapter 11 and Box 6.6 on Waltz below.)

Classical Realism's dominance in International Relations, especially after the Second World War, came at the end of around a hundred years of shifting alliances which finished with two world wars and appeared, therefore, to teach particular lessons about what the world was really like. Waltz is important in highlighting the relationships between structure and agency (see Box 6.6), but this is only part of a neo-Realist response to a changing world. Neo-Realists tried to cope with the fact that the world was not going to war and that a third world war did not look very likely. And while the Cold War seemed to inhibit conflict, many states also seemed to be acting together for mutual (primarily economic) benefits through regional and international institutions.

Neo-Realists have used the idea of a dominant state (a **hegemon**) as part of their answer. Accordingly, British dominance in the nineteenth century helps explain a long period of peace. But the argument is more used in terms of United States' dominance after the Second World War and the institutions they helped set up, such as the International Monetary Fund (IMF) and the United Nations (UN). When conditions of **hegemony** prevail, they have argued, there is a much better chance that institutions will be established and/or function effectively. The hegemon is able to offer other member states positive inducements to cooperate, or conversely might impose certain sanctions on states that refuse to engage with other states cooperatively. It follows that in the absence of hegemony, institutions will be more fragile and less effective. Neo-Realists have found the concept of hegemony useful in explaining how a liberal international economy (that is a world of trading states based on fundamentally Liberal principles and Liberal economic practices such as free trade) could be secured in a world in which political authority was vested in nation states with competing interests and possibly mercantilist (selfish, wealth-maximising, economic) impulses (see Chapter 7 for a discussion of Liberalism and its principles). Neo-Realists believe that states aim to maximise wealth and that this is best achieved by securing a broadly Liberal, free-market international economy.

Attempts to fuse an analysis of the growth and expansion of a Liberal international economy with an analysis of where power lies in the international state system, gave rise to a theory of Hegemonic Stability. The idea of Hegemonic Stability was originally advanced by Charles Kindleberger (1910–2003) to explain the collapse of the international monetary order in the early twentieth century and the Great Depression that ensued from this

(Kindleberger 1973). Hegemonic Stability Theory (HST) holds that there is always a proclivity towards instability in the international system, but this can be avoided if the dominant state assumes a leadership or hegemonic role. This role involves creating and upholding a system of rules which provide a secure basis for international order and cooperation under conditions of anarchy. In this way Liberal values and norms could be fostered and upheld. Hegemonic powers are able to control finance, trade, and so on. The Bretton Woods System which was established in 1944 and comprised the General Agreement on Tariffs and Trade (GATT), the International Bank for Reconstruction and Development (World Bank) and the International Monetary Fund (IMF) is an example of international order founded upon US hegemony. It provided a system of rules, values and norms, based broadly on Liberal economic principles which largely served the interests of the USA, although many other states were consenting partners in forging the post-Second World War international order.

Robert Gilpin, who is arguably the pre-eminent contemporary neo-Realist scholar of something called International Political Economy (IPE; see Chapter 16), developed an analysis of US hegemony which rested on the premise that there was a direct relationship between US power and the stability of the international economic order (1987). The Bretton Woods System (see Chapter 7) eventually experienced serious operational difficulty, it is argued, because of a decline in the power and influence of the USA, a decline reflected in the switch to a regime of floating exchange rates from 1971. The USA could no longer maintain its currency at a high rate relative to its economic competitors. Gilpin argued that

## Box 6.6 Kenneth Waltz [1924– ]

Perhaps the most famous neo-Realist author is Kenneth Waltz. His 1959 classic *Man, the State and War* deals with what is, in effect, a 'level of analysis' issue head-on (that is, do we study at the level of individuals/states or the system?). His *Theory of International Politics* (1979) was an even more influential intervention. In this book Waltz argues that traditional Realism contained significant deficiencies, notably when arguing that states constituted the main agents and units of analysis. Waltz's chief argument was that any theory of International Relations should be able to tell us something about both the units – states – and the system as a whole. While unit level theories focused on agents such as individuals – or in the case of Realism, states – system level theories focused on the overall structure or system in which action took place. The international order was said to be unique in that while domestic orders were centralised and hierarchic, the international system was a realm of coordination and self help. Moreover, while the units in domestic orders (citizens, for example) were subjected to law,

the units in the international order (states) were at best interdependent, autonomous entities.

Waltz argued that although the system level had been neglected in IR theory, it was clearly important in exerting pressures upon states from outside. Since we could potentially differentiate between externally generated and internally generated pressures, it would then be possible to identify the level at which crucial change occurs. It was possible that changes at unit level could affect the system as a whole, or conversely, changes at systems level could affect the unit (state) level. An example of a unit level change affecting the system might be the collapse of the Soviet Union which profoundly affected the global power structure. A change at the system level might occur if an alliance system collapses (in the absence of a clearly defined enemy), which in turn impacts on individual states. Although criticised in many quarters, Waltz's work has been highly influential because of how it opens up debate concerning the appropriate level of analysis in IR.

economic realities would eventually bring about an adjustment in the system and so the USA would eventually retreat from its commitment to the multilateralism of the Bretton Woods System as US foreign policy adjusted to harsh economic realities. This had obvious implications for the stability of the international economic and political order. As with British decline in the later part of the nineteenth century we are only talking about a decline in relative terms; the United States is still the pre-eminent power in world politics.

## Key concepts

Having outlined some of the key ideas in Realist thought and how these have played out in terms of their more recent application, it is now time to look at how these are then applied to some of the key concepts of international relations.

## Power

Most scholars of International Relations will readily agree that power is a central concept. However, behind this simple statement is a concept over which there is much disagreement and complexity. In this disagreement, however, Realism once again sees things as much simpler than some of the theoretical perspectives we shall come to. For Realists having power means being able to defend oneself militarily, although, as world politics demonstrates time and again, being able to 'defend' oneself can easily be interpreted as meaning having the power to launch pre-emptive strikes and win (that is, attacking someone now because you believe they would attack you later). This can mean, in actuality, something akin to unprovoked attack.

Authors such as Hans Morgenthau have specified those factors which contribute to national power such as geography, topography, resources, population and size (Morgenthau 1973: Chapter 9). Each can add to a state's power capability. While the strong frequently do impose their will on the weak (as Thucydides suggests), the problems with this approach are numerous. First, it may only be by testing relative power that we can see which state *is* most powerful; that is, we need a war to see who is most powerful. Second, sometimes a war is won by the state which seems obviously weaker such as North Vietnam against the United States (see Box 6.1). Here our answer lies in a whole range of intangible factors. Morale and willingness to sacrifice would be examples of intangible factors. But even the factors listed by Realists can be double-edged swords. Mountainous terrain may be very useful for defending, but an impediment to economic development. A large population can mean a large army, but it can also mean a large number of starving people in certain circumstances.

## Conflict

The view of power held by Realists suggests immediately a particular military approach to conflict which is dismissive of conflicts which might be described as social, economic or gender-based. We will see that conflict may be interpreted in many ways (in later chapters), but for Realists the phenomenon is something visible and violent. Even if we define conflict simply as disagreement which parties seek to resolve satisfactorily, once again Realism is somewhat narrow in its understanding of conflict as primarily war.

So, Realists limit their interest for the most part to the causes and nature of wars. There are differences of opinion as to where the focus should lie if we are talking about general rather than specific causes. One argument is for a concentration on the nature of human beings; another suggests a focus on states themselves; or one could prefer to pin the blame for conflict on the workings of the international system as a whole and the behaviour it forces on states.

## Security

Although the word security has a number of meanings, for realists in IR, security pertains to the state and a state is more or less secure to the extent that it can ensure its survival in the international system (by having power and engaging in conflicts as necessary). For those states, the majority, unable to guarantee their own safety through their own military forces, the balance of power represents a reasonable hope of being able to feel secure in international relations. Realists argue that unlike domestic politics (where governments are responsible for enforcing laws), in world politics there is no government to enforce laws and, as a result, each state has to provide for its own security. Self-preservation under such conditions demands that a state be able to protect itself, because it cannot rely upon help coming from other states. Policy makers, conclude Realists, must therefore seek power for their country. To do otherwise, it is argued, would invite war and defeat, as another state or states would take advantage of this misjudgement. Realists argue that creating institutions, such as the League of Nations, that presuppose states have an interest in cooperation, was foolish and therefore bound to fail.

### Box 6.7 The balance of power

A simple definition of the balance of power is that it is a mechanism which operates to prevent the dominance of any one state in the international system. The balance of power is sometimes viewed as a naturally occurring phenomenon, or a situation that comes about fortuitously. At other times it is suggested that it is a strategy consciously pursued by states. States engineer such balances to counter threats from powerful states and so ensure their own survival. As we would expect, the balance of power is frequently measured in terms of military strength. For Realists, the primary aim of the 'balance of power' is not to preserve peace but to preserve the security of (major) states, if necessary by means of war. The balance of power is about the closest Realists ever come to outlining the conditions for a peaceful international order, in so far as peace is defined negatively as an absence of war.

In nineteenth-century Europe the balance of power situation was characterised by the existence of five or six roughly equal powers. These states were quite successful at avoiding war, either by making alliances or because the most powerful state, Great Britain, would side one way or the other to act as a 'balancer'. Although the balance was seen as a good and beneficial thing, unfortunately, the system of alliances which became 'set' in the early twentieth century saw Europe ultimately embroiled in the First World War. The bipolar Cold War is another example of a balance of power (see also Chapter 4) but this time involving just two superpowers.

## Inequality and justice

Realists argue that we should accept what we cannot change. For instance, they see great dangers for the international system in emphasising or prioritising social justice or human rights, because such a concern will simply increase instability by generating conflict. Realists therefore emphasise the principle of sovereignty as the cornerstone of the international system. For this reason, Realists also argue that states have no grounds to comment on, or criticise, the domestic political, social or economic order of other states. If all such issues were taken up by all states, that is if internal sovereignty were not accepted, great instability might well result as states meddled in each others' affairs. Put another way, turning a blind eye is the lesser of evils, and this helps to explain why states-people are much slower to condemn apparent abuses in other countries than are NGOs and the media.

Although Realists are not unaware of issues of social and economic inequality and injustice, in a sense they are irrelevant to them. Realists believe that certain proposals for the eradication of poverty by means of world government, for instance, hold within them the seeds of disaster or are simply impossible. It is important to note that very often theories can look internally consistent and convincing; but if we want to discuss their usefulness to students we need to know what they do not say or include as well as what they do. Theoretical positions imply choices about what it is important to study and how to study it; we need to understand such choices in evaluating a theory.

## Conclusions and criticisms

In summary the real strength of Realism is that it is not theory at a high level of abstraction or complexity and, in whichever form, seems to give us ways of understanding foreign policy which correlate strongly with reality. If we think of theories as 'maps' we can see that while maps are useful simplifications, if they simplify too much they start to become less useful, or even useless. Some critics argue that Realism does precisely this; it takes so much off the map of IR that we are left with something profoundly unsatisfying in terms of explaining and understanding the world. However, the criticism is not a neutral one. It is suggesting that this 'simple' theory is actually prohibiting a focus on what is important, particularly issues of inequality and injustice in the world. By presenting the world order as natural, Realism in a sense permits and encourages it to remain unchanged. Realism is not the only approach to represent reality in a way which seems to benefit particular, powerful groups as we shall see in Chapter 7 on Liberalism in IR.

## Resource section

## Questions

(If you find these questions difficult now, you are likely to have more developed answers if you return to them after looking at other theory chapters.)

1.  To what extent do you agree with Realism's claim to 'elegant simplicity'? (Or does it make 'the map of IR' too simple?)

2.  Is Realist thinking *necessary* for states-people? Or has Realist thinking among states-people actually prevented them from seeking cooperation or compromise?

3.  Is there a sense in which the serious moral dilemmas posed by the use of nuclear weapons (and therefore the fact that they have been rarely used) invalidate some of Realism's assumptions about the inevitability of violent conflict?

4.  Realism is able to cite plenty of evidence to support its view. However, it fails to explain positive developments, for instance the development of a strong European Union between previously warring powers. Are Realists able to provide an adequate view of 'change' or 'progress' in international relations?

5.  Discuss the contention that Realism's understanding of 'power' is flawed on many levels?

6.  What Realism tells us about international relations is more important than the things it doesn't tell us. To what extent do you agree with this statement?

7.  Is the Balance of Power a confused or enlightening idea in seeking to understand international relations?

8.  Hegemonic Stability Theory emerges primarily from US theorists. Is this fact significant? Does your answer have any implications for all theory? Can theory ever be 'neutral/scientific' or is it always for someone and some purpose?

## Recommended reading

**Carr, E.H.** (1946) *The Twenty Years' Crisis 1919–1939: An Introduction to the Study of International Relations* (London: Macmillan)
Along with Morgenthau – below – this is sometimes cited as an influential text within the classical realist tradition, although Carr has also been read as, among other things, a member of the English School, a Critical Theorist and even a proto-Critical Realist (see Chapter 9).

**Gilpin, R.** (1987) *Political Economy of International Relations* (Princeton: Princeton University Press)
Sets out the neo-Realist approach to International Political Economy – note both the similarities and differences between how Waltz and Gilpin conceptualise 'hegemony'.

**Hobbes, T.** (1985) *Leviathan* (London: Penguin)
First published in 1651.

**Keohane, R.** (1986) *Neorealism and its Critics* (New York: Columbia University Press)
A collection of papers that in various ways critique the assumptions of neo-Realism.

**Morgenthau, H. (1973)** *Politics Among Nations: The Struggle for Power and Peace* (5th edn, New York: Knopf)
First published in 1948. A highly influential text not only within the academic discipline of IR, but among policy makers in the United States in the post-Second World War period.

**Waltz, K. (1979)** *Theory of International Politics* (Reading, MA: Addison-Wesley)
Possibly, *the* major work on neo-Realism in IR.

**Wight, M. (1979)** *Power Politics* (Leicester: Leicester University Press [and simultaneously in Pelican edition])
A fine example of Realism as concentrating on the enduring features of international relations rather than ephemera.

# Chapter 7
# Liberalism

After reading this chapter you will be able to:

- Describe the basic characteristics of Liberalism (including key assumptions), understand why these are different from Realism, and evaluate what this offers the discipline of IR in both theory and practice

- Distinguish between different sorts of Liberalism (including Idealism) and appreciate the importance of the differences

- Understand clearly why Liberalism and Realism actually have many things in common despite their superficial differences

- Appreciate why subsequent chapters critique both Liberalism and Realism, which together dominated the discipline for at least seventy years

*Source*: Getty Images

## Introductory box: Defining Liberalism

The word Liberal frequently goes hand in hand with the word 'democracy'. At the level of generalisation the Liberal democracies of the world are those countries in which we (the target market for this book) would like to live; countries like Sweden or France or Australia rather than states struggling to establish anything like democracy, such as Sierra Leone or Haiti or Honduras or non/less democratic states such as North Korea, Myanmar or Iran. As well as its association with democracy, the word liberal when taken in isolation can refer to a person who is tolerant and open. Liberalism, said to be the dominant ideology of globalisation, is about freedom and opportunity and the protection of human rights. All of the above is open to question, but even if you take it at face value, the world is one in which tolerance and openness are far from universal; freedom is often the freedom to struggle; opportunity is constrained in various ways; and human rights are infringed. Does Liberalism offer a universal vision to which we can all aspire and which might one day be achievable? Or does it help justify injustices which might otherwise be unacceptable? This chapter and the next provide different answers to these questions.

**Liberalism** in International Relations is associated with theories which emphasise the importance of several (a plurality of) actors, including **non-state actors** (such as institutions and NGOs), issues other than war and violence (such as economics) and processes other than conflict (that is, also cooperation). Liberalism as a political idea is particularly concerned with *individual* rights and freedoms, both political and economic. As a term 'Liberal Pluralism' gives a good sense of how International Relations theory has combined both Liberal ideology and a belief in a complex 'cobweb' of relations in which a plurality of actors play their part on the world stage.

As you can see, Liberalism in International Relations is apparently very different from Realism and a little more complicated, even at first glance. Liberal theories of international relations feel that Realism is too simple and too pessimistic and are optimistic that human rationality can lead to progress, rather than the inevitable, cyclical, repetition of historical patterns of violence.

Liberalism can be described as a political and economic philosophy or ideology. This chapter aims to give a sense of the complexity inherent within it.

As with all the chapters here on theoretical approaches, the point is not to encourage you to adopt one as 'your' theory, but rather to regard all theories as *potentially* adding insight and to help you see which insights, in this case Liberalism, helps with, and which it does not. In your other reading you should bear in mind that academic authors can be very good at selecting evidence. You should recognise that theories cannot be vindicated by every partial explanation or piece of evidence which seems to fit them.

## Context

The simplicity which adherents of **Realism** claim as a virtue (see Chapter 6), provides a starting point for criticism of it. We should not see Liberalism as existing simply as a critique of Realism, but their competition to explain the world, over many decades, dominates the history of the discipline. As with Realism, a long tradition of thought is associated with Liberalism. In the eighteenth and nineteenth centuries, Liberal philosophers and political thinkers debated problems associated with establishing just, orderly and peaceful relations between peoples. One of the most systematic and influential accounts of the problems of world peace was Immanuel Kant's 1795 essay *Perpetual Peace* (Kant 1991, see below).

The First World War gave philosophical speculation added impetus as Liberal thinking offered hope that the senseless waste of life which characterised that conflict could be avoided by the application of human reason. Following the 'war to end all wars' (as it was hopefully known) a new generation of International Relations scholars wanted to help promote cooperative relations among states and allow the realisation of a just order. These people were termed Idealists and their beliefs were founded on the notion that since people in general had no interest in prosecuting wars and suffered greatly in consequence of war, all that was needed to end war was respect for the rule of law and stable institutions which could provide a semblance of international order conducive to peace and security. The widespread anti-war sentiment which existed at the time, seemed to provide the necessary widespread public support for such an enterprise to succeed.

As suggested in Chapter 6, in the 1930s and the lead up to the Second World War, Idealism began to fall out of favour as it did not seem to account for the power politics (or put another way 'might is right') characteristic of that period, such as Japanese aggression in Manchuria and the Italian takeover of Abyssinia. However, Idealism did dominate the academic study of International Relations between the First and Second World Wars with an optimistic promise of the rule of law, democracy and human rights, and it continues to be influential within Liberal IR theory today. But while Idealism was the first Liberal theory in contemporary IR there have been many other distinctive strands, notably 'interdependence', 'transnationalism', 'Liberal internationalism', 'Liberal peace theory', 'neo-Liberal institutionalism' and 'world society' approaches.

After the Second World War, Realism dominated theoretical approaches to international relations and the uneasy balance of power between the superpowers of the United States of America (USA) and the Soviet Union (USSR) provided plenty of evidence that states needed to be on their guard and prepare militarily. At the same time, and particularly in the West, the world economy grew and the importance of international economics was increasingly recognised as the period of peace between the superpowers looked to be prolonged, even if also precarious. In the 1970s a Liberal literature on transnational relations and world society

## Box 7.1  Who are the Liberals?

In trying to calm inevitable anxiety about theory, we cannot deny that Liberalism is very varied. Liberals have views about the economic organisation of society, for instance, but it is divided between those on the political 'right' and 'left'. The former believe that individual liberty must extend into the economic realm; people must be free to buy and sell their labour and skills (as well as goods and services) in a free market which is subjected to minimal regulation. On the other hand, 'left' leaning Liberals recognise that the principles of *political* liberty and equality can actually be *threatened* by the concentration of economic power and wealth. This school of Liberalism supports a much more interventionist role for the state in the regulation of the economy, in the interests of providing for basic human needs and extending opportunities to the less privileged. We try to navigate these differences as clearly as possible, but you need to reflect upon them for yourself.

developed. So-called 'Liberal pluralists' pointed to the growing importance of **multinational corporations (MNCs)**, **non-governmental organisations (NGOs)** and pressure groups, as evidence that states were no longer the only significant actors in international relations. Liberal pluralists believed that power and influence in world politics were now exercised by a range of actors and Liberal-Pluralism became an important part of the inter-paradigm debate which emerged explicitly in the 1980s (see Banks, 1985 and also the summary of IR's debates in Chapter 11, Table 11.1) pitting Realism, Liberalism and Marxism/structuralism against each other. Liberal Pluralists were not simply rehashing the Idealist belief that Liberal views *could* end war; they were also saying that the Realist world was changing and changed. Violent conflict was said not to be such a major process in international relations, and cooperation – in pursuit of mutual interests – became a prominent feature of world politics.

Notwithstanding the discussion in Box 7.1, Liberalism is presented here as a more or less uniform worldview. Our justification for this, despite differences, is that Liberalism is an approach to politics and economics, it is a social theory and a philosophy. Liberalism is an all-embracing ideology. It has something to say about all aspects of the human life. It is a philosophy based on a belief in the ultimate value of individual liberty and the possibility of human progress. Liberalism speaks the language of rationality, moral autonomy, human rights, democracy, opportunity and choice, and is founded upon a commitment to principles of liberty and equality, justified in the name of individuality and rationality. Politically this translates into support for limited government (though with big arguments about *how* limited) and political pluralism. In other words, Liberals find plenty to argue about, but these are pretty much family arguments.

## The 'back-story' to Liberalism

Like Realism, Liberalism has a significant 'back-story' and in this section the aim is to point to some of the biggest historical influences on Liberal IR such as Immanuel Kant, John Stuart Mill, Jeremy Bentham, Adam Smith and David Ricardo. We divide Liberalism here into political and economic strands; this is an artificial divide but useful in getting to grips with what is important about Liberalism. The aim here is not to specify precise linkages in every case, but to show the foundations of Liberalism, a doctrine which has gradually evolved over hundreds of years.

In the political realm the German philosopher Immanuel Kant (1724–1804), like Hobbes (see Chapter 6), used the idea of a 'state of nature' in his work. Starting from the premise that the international system was something akin to an international 'state of nature' or 'war of all against all' Kant argued that perpetual peace cannot be realised in an unjust world. The only way that this state of affairs could be overcome would be for states to found a 'state of peace'. Kant did not envisage the founding of a world government, or even the pooling of sovereignty, but, rather, a looser federation of free states governed by the rule of law.

Kant saw this state of affairs coming about neither fortuitously, nor quickly. While the application of Kantian thought to international relations has been dismissed as utopian (unrealistic in thinking an ideal society possible), it is important to note that Kant recognised that in order to achieve a just world order, certain conditions were necessary, including the establishment of republics (as opposed to monarchies or dictatorships) and, perhaps, a near-universal commitment to Liberal democracy. Kant held that only civilised countries, those countries which were already governed by a system of law and in which people were free citizens rather than subjects, would be able to leave the state of lawlessness that characterised the international state of nature.

There is debate about how Kant saw the relationship between republics and other forms of political organisation. However, Kant is frequently interpreted as suggesting that countries where people were not free citizens, but rather subjected to the rule of a monarch, perhaps, or a dictator, were much more likely to be belligerent and warlike. If this was the case, logically it followed that a world federation would only be achieved when all states were republics and that this would take time.

 **Box 7.2 What is rational?**

For Realists 'rationality' is concerned with acting in the national interest in terms of what must be done, rather than adhering to any moral yardstick. For Kantian Liberals, the essence of reason/rationality is seen to be the ability of all human beings to understand moral principles and act accordingly.

Type and extent of government are both key issues for Liberals. One of the most celebrated Liberal thinkers of the nineteenth century, John Stuart Mill, argued that government was a *necessary* evil. That is to say, government was necessary in order to protect the liberty of individuals, but could become oppressive and tyrannical if its power was unchecked (if it were not limited). For these reasons, Liberals generally argue for a 'separation of powers' and 'checks and balances' which ensure that no one political leader or arm of government can become dominant.

This basic idea is the origin of political pluralism, which means the distribution or diffusion of power across a range of institutions or among a number of 'actors'.

**Economic Liberalism** is rooted in an intellectual tradition stretching back particularly to the works of Adam Smith (see Chapter 16 on International Political Economy) and David

### Box 7.3  David Ricardo (1772–1823)

David Ricardo argued that individual countries had a comparative advantage in the production of certain kinds of goods and services. For reasons to do with their natural resource base or climate, perhaps, or because of the particular composition and skills of the workforce, some countries would always be able to produce certain types of goods more cheaply and efficiently than others. Ricardo argued that for this reason it made sense for countries to specialise in the production of certain goods and services and engage in trade with each other. Trade was to be positively encouraged because even though not all individuals, groups and countries benefited equally, it was beneficial to everybody's overall welfare.

Ricardo (see Box 7.3). The key assumption of nineteenth-century classical Liberalism is that it is, in the long run, beneficial to all if markets are allowed to operate freely without state intervention and if countries are able to trade openly and freely with each other. This is because the market is seen as the most efficient means of organising human production and exchange, operating almost as if 'an invisible hand' were guiding and coordinating economic activity. That is, everyone is acting self-interestedly but the overall result is a match-up between consumers and producers/supply and demand.

Liberals assume that human beings act rationally in the economic sphere. In this usage, 'rationality' is evidenced by a person's ability to weigh up carefully the costs and benefits of any course of action. According to 'utilitarian' thinkers like Jeremy Bentham (1748–1832), people who are behaving rationally will always act to maximise their own 'utility' or interest. If at first sight this appears to be entirely selfish behaviour rooted in a pessimistic view of human nature (akin to Realism, see Chapter 6), Liberals offer a moral justification for allowing such a state of affairs to continue. While individuals are essentially self-interested, collectively this type of behaviour is held to produce beneficial outcomes. According to Bentham we should base our judgements on what is 'right' or 'wrong', or 'good' or 'bad' on how far any action works to ensure the greatest happiness of the greatest number.

This does not mean that Liberals see no role for the state in the economy. Liberals like Adam Smith accepted that the market would not necessarily produce much needed 'public goods' (for example, clean air or aspects of infrastructure like roads or drainage systems) and that governments would need to provide them. States were also necessary, because they provided a regulatory framework – a legal system – to, among other things, enforce contracts and protect against corruption and unfair competition. However, classical Liberalism held that it is in the best interests of all people, in the long term, if state intervention is kept to a minimum.

According to Liberals, the advantages of an unfettered free market are not only confined to the domestic economy. **Free market economics** generates a need for 'inputs', such as raw materials, into the production process and some of these have to be imported from abroad. Enterprises are also constantly seeking new markets for their goods and services. In this way, trade between states is encouraged. Liberals believe the advantages of trade are numerous. This is, of course, a very strong argument against economic protectionism

*Source: Corbis/Wally McNamee*

**Comparative advantage illustrated: what are the determining factors that lead us to associate certain goods and services with particular countries?**

(imposing taxes on goods from elsewhere), which, from a Liberal perspective, is a consequence of states acting according to short-sighted and perverse conceptions of the national interest. Left alone, trade would prove to be mutually beneficial by, for example, bringing about interdependence among states and generating wealth, both of which would reduce the likelihood of conflict.

## Liberalism in contemporary International Relations

Liberalism has developed as a complex and overlapping set of ideas. Partly this is because Liberalism values individual freedom and there can be quite large differences as to what extent this needs to be 'enforced' by states. It is also because Liberalism is about politics (freedom of expression, to vote, to associate, to move) *and* economics (freedom to buy, to sell, to exchange).

Liberalism is a complex and overlapping set of ideas because of trade-offs. For instance, if someone has absolute political freedom but is also starving, this is not a good outcome. On the other hand, someone might have the economic essentials of life, only because the political system controls the various means of production and distribution to an intolerable degree. Different Liberals thus argue about how to balance different individual freedoms. It is important for us to reflect on political and economic freedoms; which we feel are more important, in what contexts, and why.

Liberal political ideas on International Relations, building on Kant, are evident in the more recent work of Michael Doyle on **Democratic Peace Theory**. The theory's basic hypothesis is that as states become more democratic they become more peacefully inclined. The theory is based on a research project called the *Michigan Project* and on David Singer's work which documented in detail the incidence of wars since 1816. Researchers sought first to establish empirically how many wars had been fought by Liberal states and against whom. On the basis of this they claimed to identify a trend: Liberal states fought wars, but not with each other. Thus, they concluded, Liberal states do not fight wars with each other. The implications of such a finding were that there existed in world politics a Liberal 'zone of peace' and that democratisation (see Chapter 21) along Liberal lines was a recipe for peace. The prescriptive implication was that foreign policies should include democratisation and human rights as central planks. Democratic Peace Theory is sometimes held to be the closest IR has come to establishing a 'scientific law' of international relations.

**Box 7.4 Democratic Peace Theory**

Despite its superficial appeal Democratic Peace Theory has been much criticised. The sample included republics as well as democracies. In some cases 30 per cent male suffrage was deemed enough to qualify as a 'democracy'. Certain types of wars, like civil wars, were excluded. Many states that are not democracies are *also* at peace with one another.

Kant's commitment to the pursuit of peace and the establishment of a just international order where states' actions are regulated by international law is widespread among Liberals today. One of the most celebrated works on the end of the Cold War, Francis Fukuyama's *The End of History and the Last Man* (1992) contained much which would have been familiar to Kant. Fukuyama argues that human history has been driven by conflict and struggle over value systems and different ways to organise human societies. The driving force behind the Cold War was the ideological struggle between East and West, communism and capitalism. According to Fukuyama, the end of the Cold War saw the ultimate triumph of Western capitalism and Liberal democracy. Liberal values are now widely accepted – if not widely practiced – across the world, and, since communism is seemingly discredited, there is no longer a credible alternative form of social, political and economic organisation.

While it was noted above that nineteenth-century Liberal economic theorists were against state intervention and regulation of the economy, for much of the twentieth century, Liberals have been less hostile to state intervention. Indeed the economic order which emerged in the aftermath of the Second World War, in Western economies at least, saw the state playing a greater role in directing the economic activity of private individuals and firms, and providing welfare support for citizens – the so-called 'welfare state'. This order was influenced by Keynesian economic theory (after the British economist John Maynard Keynes 1883–1946), which supported interventionist government policies to regulate what were basically free market economies.

Keynesian theory thus formed the basis of the ideas which underpinned many Western economies after the Second World War through the establishment of the **Bretton Woods System**. This consisted of an International Bank for Reconstruction and Development (IBRD), the International Monetary Fund (IMF) and later the General Agreement on Tariffs and Trade (GATT) and aimed to facilitate economic growth, development and trade by providing a stable framework for international economic activity. After the Second World War, prevailing wisdom suggested its cause had been economic collapse and world recession in the 1930s which had created an unstable climate allowing extreme nationalism to flourish. It was believed that when the economic climate was harsh, states immediately took action to protect their own economies. Typically, this involved measures to protect domestic markets, such as increasing tariffs. The knock-on effects of such 'selfish' behaviour were a slow down in world trade and, eventually, international recession. The Bretton Woods System was designed to create a framework in which it would be difficult for states to act in a self-interested way when the going got tough, by – at the same time – both discouraging protectionism *and* providing a helping hand to countries in temporary economic difficulties.

It was envisaged that the IBRD, more commonly known as the World Bank, would play an important role in distributing aid to the devastated economies of Western Europe. In more recent history, the World Bank has served as a source of investment, aid and loans to the developing world. The International Monetary Fund was designed to ensure liquidity in the international economy. This means that, in effect, countries experiencing short-term balance of trade difficulties (spending more than they are earning) can borrow money and so continue to trade effectively. In the longer term, if any individual country has an enduring – or 'structural' – balance of payment deficit, the IMF can insist upon changes in domestic economic policy, including the devaluation of the currency, in return for fresh loans. The General Agreement on Tariffs and Trade (since superseded by the World Trade Organisation) was designed to bring about a gradual reduction in trade barriers around the world.

These institutions all played an important role in regulating the world economy. However, the linchpin of the system was the US dollar. The US dollar served as the major world trading currency. The relative value of other world currencies was fixed in relation to the US dollar. Since, in the post-war period, the US economy was easily the largest and most powerful economy in the world, it was believed that pegging all currencies to the US dollar would ensure confidence in the international economic system.

The dollar-based Bretton Woods System has been described as an economic order in which the broad principles of Liberalism were 'embedded'. The system of multilateral institutions, fixed exchange rates, capital controls and trade regulation, aimed to encourage the progressive liberalisation of trade among countries and to promote the principles of free market economics internationally. However, none of these institutions or rules was incompatible with state intervention and the management of the *domestic* economy. This meant that even while encouraging a large degree of free trade and open competition *internationally*, states could pursue 'liberal welfare' or 'social democratic' goals, such as full employment and the provision of welfare goods at home.

In more recent years, classic economic theory, described above, has been highly influential in the theory and practice of development in countries of the so-called Third World. The belief that the unfettered market ensures the most efficient allocation of resources, the best distribution of rewards, and the most effective means to foster economic growth continues to be widely held among elites at the International Monetary Fund, the World Bank and in many government overseas development agencies. Such theory has been used to justify structural adjustment programmes (SAPs) in the developing world, even though the social consequences may be very harsh indeed.

Structural adjustment programmes have been widely 'recommended' to Third World states by the IMF and the World Bank as an effective means of dealing with the related problems of poverty and indebtedness. The idea is that indebted states should try to export their way out of debt. As well as generating much-needed foreign currency to service foreign debt, export-led growth strategies are held to encourage economic competitiveness, dynamism and growth which will eventually 'trickle down' to all sectors of society. At the same time, developing countries are encouraged to cut back on welfare spending by the state, effectively privatising the provision of health and education services. It is argued that ultimately this will make economies more efficient. In the short term, however, 'spend less' means sacking government employees and slashing welfare budgets rather than buying medicines and building schools. Meanwhile 'earn more' can lead to wage reduction, chopping down forests, selling off assets to foreign firms at cut price rates and so on. In recent years SAPs have been heavily criticised, by NGOs and also former employees of the World Bank. Consequently SAPs now often include some notional safety net beyond which basic services and welfare goods should not be cut.

## Key assumptions

Having outlined some of the key ideas in Liberal thought and how these have played out in terms of their more recent application, it is useful here to try to summarise and condense Liberal assumptions, before looking at how these are then applied to some of the key concepts of international relations. Liberals believe that all human beings are rational, meaning both that they have the ability to articulate and pursue their own interests and are able to understand moral principles and live according to the rule of law. Liberals value individual liberty above all else and have a positive (optimistic?) view of human nature, believing that it is possible to achieve positive changes in international relations.

In distinctive ways, Liberalism challenges the distinction between the domestic and the international realm. For a start it is a universalist doctrine and so is committed to some notion of a universal community of humankind which transcends identification with, and membership of, the nation-state community. Furthermore Liberal ideas on interdependence and world society suggest that in the contemporary world the boundaries between states are becoming increasingly permeable. Cooperation is a central feature of all human relations, including international relations. Government is necessary, but the centralisation of power is inherently bad, and individual liberty is of supreme political importance. There is more we could deduce or infer from the above, but we move here to look at how the central assumptions of Liberalism affect its view of key terms for IR.

## Key concepts

### Peace

Liberalism is a doctrine which has a faith in the capacity of human beings to solve seemingly intractable problems through political action. The notion that human beings understand moral principles, suggests that it is possible to transcend 'power politics' and govern relations between people (and indeed peoples) on the basis of legal norms, moral principles and according to what is 'right' and 'just'. However, Liberalism should not be confused with pacifism. While some Liberals might indeed be pacifists, it does not necessarily follow that a commitment to the peaceful resolution of disputes entails the rejection of the use of force whatever the circumstances. Clearly, even 'peace loving' peoples and states could not be expected to forgo the right to use force in order to defend themselves from hostile aggression or, perhaps, if there was no other way to right a wrong.

Contemporary Liberals have developed a distinctive Democratic Peace Theory (see Box 7.4). Liberal peace theory returns to a familiar Liberal theme that the people have no interest in war, in the sense that war is not in their interests. It follows from this that wars are frequently the result of aggression on the part of belligerent leaders or states pursuing a particular interest. Many Liberal peace theorists are of the view that it is only when an end is put to tyranny around the globe and when universal Liberal democracy and respect for human rights exist that international peace will prevail. In so far as democracy will also check the power of leaders and states, wars are likely to become less prevalent when, and if, democracy flourishes throughout the world. Therefore, a peaceful world order is also likely to be one in which human rights are respected and upheld.

**Box 7.5 Leader of the free world**

The USA uses 'peace-loving' rhetoric. Investigate how many wars and violent interventions it was involved with during the twentieth century and the declared good intentions behind these. Are these best explained by its commitment to Liberalism or to the darker realities of international relations, such as the need to control resources?

In addition to the 'political' strand of Liberal thought, 'economic Liberalism' has similarly made a contribution to our understanding of peace. Along with the stress on moral reason and the capacity for good in human beings, after the First World War, Liberals were also advancing a notion of a 'harmony of interests' which would have been familiar to Adam Smith and David Ricardo. This was based on the idea of a harmony of interests between the states and peoples of the world and, in good part, these mutual interests are rooted in the mutual benefits which arise from trade. However, just as Smith recognised the need for certain 'public goods', Liberals acknowledge that in order to have peace it is necessary to establish international institutions which can overcome the problem of anarchy and facilitate cooperation.

## Security

Peace and security are intertwined in Liberal thought (though not in all theoretical approaches). The League of Nations (see Case Study in Chapter 6) was supposed to guarantee the security of states through a system which identified threats to 'peace and security' and allowed collective action to be taken against aggressive states, to deter or stop them. Clearly, since insecurity was itself a possible cause of war, a system of collective security would strengthen the international order and make peace more likely. The League of Nations also had an International Court to arbitrate disputes and so provide a peaceful means to resolve conflicts. Although the League of Nations foundered, the idea that an international organisation was needed to provide some sort of system of collective defence, and a court of arbitration, lived on in the United Nations, set up after the Second World War.

### Case study: The United Nations

The United Nations was set up after the Dumbarton Oaks conference in 1944, in order to 'save successive generations from the scourge of war'. The conference was attended by only the United States and its wartime allies, including Britain and France, the Soviet Union, and China, but despite this limited representation, nearly all of the basic features of the new organisation were agreed at that meeting. The United Nations remained close to the spirit of the League of Nations in its stated objective of maintaining peace and security through the peaceful settlement of disputes and the promotion of trade and economic and social cooperation. The UN also added economic and social development and the promotion of human rights to its stated aims. However, while similar to the League in many respects, it was recognised that the founders of the United Nations must pay due regard to its failures in order to ensure that the organisation did not duplicate its shortcomings and weaknesses. Above all, the new organisation had to be as universal as possible, and must include the membership of both the Soviet Union and the United States. It also needed to be able to take effective action, rather than rely upon the force of world opinion.

The two organisations were similar in structure. Like the League, the United Nations had an assembly, the General Assembly, which acted largely as a consultative body; a Court of Justice, located in The Hague (Netherlands); and a council (the Security Council), which formed the executive arm of the organisation. The United Nations also had a Secretariat headed by a Secretary General, whose role included identifying and alerting the Security Council to 'threats to peace and security'.

Despite differences in ideology, the United States and Soviet Union were able to agree on most substantive issues to do with the structure and operation of the new organisation. However, they disagreed sharply over the structure and precise role of the Security Council. Eventually, these differences were resolved when it was agreed that the so-called big five (the USA, the Soviet Union, China, France and the United Kingdom) would enjoy permanent representation on the Security Council and would have the right of veto over Security Council actions.

Do you agree with the view that permanent representation of the 'big five' was a concession to the realities of power politics which effectively paralysed the Security Council, preventing it from taking any effective action throughout the Cold War period?

## Power

For Realists the need for (military) power to achieve peace and security is straightforward; for Liberals the relationship is more complex. Liberals within IR (sometimes referred to as Liberal Pluralists) argue that it is impossible to quantify power simply in military terms. The economic wealth of countries such as Japan or many multinational corporations (MNCs) – such as Shell, IBM, Nissan and so on – is clearly a factor in understanding where power lies in international relations. The money of MNCs for instance has great influence on people's lives, and governments are keen to attract their investment.

Furthermore, 'actors' might also have more or less power depending on the issue area under consideration. For example, Norway is a relatively small country and does not play a particularly prominent role in organisations like the UN. However, Norway has tremendous influence in negotiations over the international ban on whaling as one of the major whaling states. Indeed, analysing the world according to different issue areas gives a very different, and perhaps comforting, impression of how power is distributed compared to approaches such as Realism. For example, in international negotiations over the dumping of toxic waste, developing countries – primarily the target for such waste – have been able significantly to affect negotiations and achieve global regulation of such activity (see Chapter 23).

## Order

One of the ways in which Liberalism has contributed to our understanding of international relations is through various works on the nature of institutions and world order. The themes of cooperation and complex interdependence are strongly suggestive of how Liberals see the regulatory and facilitating role played by institutions in international relations. In more recent years, Liberals have developed a fairly sophisticated analysis of the nature of world order and the crucial role played by institutions and various regimes in regulating relations between states. This section discusses Liberal ideas that have emerged in this context. First we need to consider briefly an earlier school of thought which, while not strictly speaking Liberal, anticipated many arguments about the nature of interdependence and the need for institutions.

Like other ideas in International Relations (see later theory chapters), functionalism had its origins in another branch of the social sciences – Sociology. However, as the idea began to influence IR, its meaning changed somewhat. Functionalists argued that inter-action among states in various spheres created problems which required cooperation to resolve; the most obvious examples being areas like telecommunications and postal services. The positive benefits and mutual confidence which arose from cooperation in any one area would be likely to spill over, encouraging cooperation in other more significant areas such as trade. Functionalists argued that integration was necessary because states were unable to cope with the effects of modernisation. International institutions were thought to be increasingly necessary as a complement to states whose individual capabilities to deal with problems generated by new technologies were decreasing. Also, functionalists believed that as the level of cooperation and integration increased, it would be more and more

*Source: Getty Images/98474314*

**The role played by institutions and regimes in regulating interactions between states is an important subject of Liberal analysis**

difficult for states to withdraw from the commitments they had entered into since their people would be aware of the benefits achieved by cooperation. Such functional interaction would, in turn, have effects on international society, enhancing peace and making war so disruptive and costly that it would no longer be considered a rational means for states to realise their aims and interests.

In the 1970s, Liberal Pluralist perspectives began to contribute to our understanding of institutions and world order in international relations. It was clear that states were becoming more interdependent – more sensitive to, or even affected by, the actions of other 'actors'. In any given issue area in world politics the interaction of states and other actors was in need of, and in many cases subjected to, regulation according to a system of rules and practices (norms). This notion of interdependence continues to have resonance today. For example, many states and non-state actors have an input into the global debate over deforestation through conferences and other regular meetings. In Liberal Pluralist interdependence theory, politics is presented as a mutually beneficial process in which many actors seek to resolve problems in international relations. Furthermore, we are now living in a world where there are multiple linkages between not only governments but also societies. NGOs and elite groups are increasingly involved in forging links with like-minded individuals and groups in other countries, which bypass, or perhaps even subvert, state control. In addition, advances in technologies have made the boundaries of states increasingly permeable. For example, the development of nuclear weapons had profound implications for the security of state boundaries which could not be protected with conventional armed forces. Periodic international recessions demonstrate the growing interconnected nature of economic activity across the globe, while, in more recent years, the growth of satellite television and the Internet have demonstrated how quickly ideas and cultural artefacts can travel around the world.

In contemporary IR, Liberals continue to argue that interdependence compels states to cooperate much more extensively than they had done before. As we will see below there is now an extensive Liberal literature on the nature and functions of regimes and institutions in international relations. Moreover, modern states are incapable of meeting the complex and diverse needs of their citizens *without* cooperating with other states. International institutions and regimes become necessary to coordinate the ever more powerful forces of interdependence. Large and small states, developed or not, are members of some or all of these institutions and all are said to benefit to some degree from cooperation. Although conflict is always present, institutions or regimes provide the forums for states to settle their differences without resorting to war.

In summary, for Liberals, cooperation is possible because the nature of twentieth-century science, technology and economics has produced interdependence between states and other actors. In some cases, interdependence has forced states to give up some of their sovereignty and independence to international institutions, like the UN and EU. Increasingly, states are being required or compelled to engage in more intensive forms of cooperation which frequently give rise to regimes to regulate behaviour over a range of issues areas.

The term **regime** has a particular meaning in IR going beyond a way of describing a government as in 'the North Korean regime' for instance. In contemporary IR, regime is most frequently used to refer to a set of rules and procedures concerning a given issue area which govern the behaviour of a particular group of actors – who are said to make up the regime which then makes decisions on the basis of this consensus. The International Whaling Commission (IWC) is thus an example of an international environmental regime – though not an effective one. There is a more coherent international trade regime expressed in the World Trade Organisation. There is no doubt that the number of regimes, treaties and institutions *has* multiplied rapidly in the past two decades. Furthermore, security considerations, defined as military defence, are consequently superseded by considerations of well-being or welfare.

## Inequality and justice

Traditionally Liberals have concentrated on the importance of formal equality among people and equal rights. Idealists insisted that the rule of law and questions of justice and rights were absolutely central to international relations. Liberals have been extremely active in promoting human rights regimes through the United Nations. The UN has been particularly important in promoting human rights as a *legal* obligation of states (even if not always lived up to), clearly recognising that such rights should not be confined within national borders and establishing a range of international standards.

The original UN Charter talks of 'the principle of equal rights and self-determination of peoples' and 'human rights and fundamental freedoms for all without distinction' (Articles 1 and 55). By late 1948 a UN Universal Declaration on Human Rights had been signed after much wrangling by communist states such as the USSR, religious states such as Saudi Arabia, and by other states such as South Africa, who feared that they would be accused of violating the human rights of some of their people. However, despite some initial resistance, the signing proved to be simply the beginning of a lengthy and ongoing process. Liberals stress the importance of civil and political rights. However, as more developing countries have become member states of the UN, the General Assembly has become more important in the development of human rights. In the 1960s, for instance, there were further declarations on civil and political rights and on economic, social and cultural rights. In more recent years, there have been significant conventions which cover the rights of minorities and indigenous peoples, the rights of the child, and the elimination of discrimination against women.

Some commentators argue that the gradual expansion of human rights provisions has resulted in a situation where we now have a global consensus on human rights. However, it is important to note that many states have refused to ratify certain conventions and treaties. Moreover, the abuse of human rights is still widespread throughout the world despite the significant advances which have been made in international law.

## Identity

At first sight Liberalism appears to have very little to say about identity. After all, Liberalism places emphasis on the individual rather than the group. However, contemporary Liberalism does recognise the importance of issues of identity in International Relations.

In the first place, of course, Liberals have offered a conception of community and identity which spans the entire planet and which defies the usual boundaries of state, nation, race, ethnicity, culture, class and gender. This is the community of humankind, possessing inalienable human rights by virtue of the universal capacity for reasoned thought. Liberal Pluralists have long expressed commitment towards a global society as a means by which the sovereign state system is transcended and more inclusive forms of community are realised. 'Global society' can be viewed in terms of a normative consensus bonding people together. In this view, people owe obligations to the 'people of the world' rather than simply to their fellow citizens. Some commentators argue that forms of complex interdependence have resulted in the global spread of universal values; for example, human rights and democracy.

The growing significance of transnational politics and social movements in world politics also raises issues of identity and community. Transnationalism implies that people engage in numerous social interactions which tie people together across state boundaries. In this view, technological innovations and increasing 'flows' such as media communications, technology and finance, bring in their wake the disintegration of previous forms of identity and attachment. The growing importance of transnational relationships has been noted by Liberals like Ferguson and Mansbach (1997) who argue that human beings identify themselves in a variety of ways, are enmeshed in a multitude of networks and have loyalties to a variety of authorities. Some Liberals see an open and participatory politics emerging from transnational linkages across societies, which transcend the state.

Many contemporary Liberals concede that not only individuals but specific communities might also have rights which need to be recognised and protected. The rights of indigenous peoples to continue to enjoy a traditional way of life and the rights of certain ethnic or religious minorities in societies across the world, to celebrate their own unique expressions of identity and community, are now both enshrined in international law, even if not always respected in practice. The dilemma for Liberals is not in accepting the concept of difference or the right to be different, but in what to do when certain cultural practices or religious beliefs conflict directly with the individual's right to choose.

As an example of such conflicts, we would expect Liberals to support the right of a woman to defy customs and practices rooted in traditional or religious belief systems – in relation to say marriage or the family – if this was her choice. However, frequently, the position and role of women is absolutely crucial to the expression of group identity. In such circumstances, group rights and the rights of the individual might be in tension. Liberal human rights scholars like Jack Donnelly have tried to find a way out of this dilemma by accepting a weak cultural relativist position, arguing that rights are universal, but different cultures may provide for rights through different means and so some variation in the way rights are implemented might be allowed. The notion of universal rights is retained, but some concessions are made to particular cultural differences which will affect the interpretation and implementation of the universal principles.

## Conclusions and criticisms

Some of the most heated arguments take place between people quite similar in terms of their basic position. Socialists are famed for the ferocity of arguments among themselves, and the complex, diffuse ideology of Liberalism makes such arguments entirely possible within Liberalism too. Liberalism has many overlapping ideas and contradictions about which individual freedoms to prioritise. This point can be summarised as follows.

Liberal thought has a long intellectual tradition. Early Liberal thinking on international politics and peace was particularly influenced by eighteenth-century German philosopher Immanuel Kant. In terms of economics, Liberal theories of the market are particularly associated with Adam Smith, David Ricardo and John Maynard Keynes. There have been a number of distinctive ways in which Liberal thought has been applied to IR, for example, Liberal Pluralism, world society, interdependence and neo-Liberal institutionalism, as well as the related schools of Functionalism and Idealism. Liberals are optimistic about human nature, because they believe that behaviour is largely the product of various interactions with our social environment; because of this, Liberals have faith in the possibilities of education, human progress and the establishment of fair and just institutions. Liberals believe that the central characteristic of all human beings is rationality. This gives rise to notions of the intrinsic value of human life, the moral worth of the individual and the existence of inalienable human rights. Liberals believe that the role of government should be limited, although there is some disagreement about just how far and to what ends the state should intervene in civil society. In the international realm, Liberals have faith in the possibility of cooperation, and suggest that all states can achieve their aims if they abandon the notion of self-help. Liberals believe that not only states, but also NGOs, multinational corporations and institutions are important 'actors' in IR.

In terms of the above summary, one obvious criticism concerns the fundamental contradiction between economic and political liberty. It can be argued that the operation of free markets and the private ownership of property and resources leads to the progressive concentration of wealth in fewer and fewer hands. This inevitably leads to a concentration of power among the wealthy, which in turn impinges greatly upon the liberty and meaningful choices available to poorer groups. Despite this, some Liberals justify the continuing operation of the free market on the grounds that it increases the overall level of wealth in society which then 'trickles down' to the poor, even though there is little empirical evidence to support this contention. This has been criticised both within and outside Liberal circles.

Despite Liberalism being apparently quite different to Realism, the Liberal view can be reasonably criticised as simply providing a justification of the way things are; the way things are being of benefit to a very narrow section of humanity. For example, Liberal Pluralists generally provide a benevolent view of international institutions, MNCs and the whole Liberal free-trade ethos which dominates today's international political economy. Early Idealists were concerned with avoiding war between the major powers, rather than things such as ending world poverty. Liberalism can end up being a status quo orientated view of international relations, even if it explains that status quo differently. This is one main similarity that Liberalism has with Realism and is one of the reasons why it has been attacked by the theories we discuss in subsequent chapters.

It has been argued that the characteristics held to be essentially human are actually specific to a particular group of people at a particular period in history. So-called universalism actually expresses the particular experience of dominant groups in the West, so the argument goes. Liberalism gives us a linear view of human progress and development. Again, this is because Liberalism tends to universalise Western experience. In development theory, for example, Liberals have suggested that poorer states are further 'behind' in the development process, but essentially on the same road and travelling in the same direction as richer, more developed countries.

The Liberal Pluralist view of international relations as a series of complex interactions between an enormous variety of actors is, at first sight, less contentious. However, it is disputed by Realists who, as we have seen, argue for the continued primacy or dominance of the state in IR, and Marxists, who argue that a pluralist view misses the fundamental issue which is inequality between various groups or *classes* at the international level.

## Resource section

## Questions

1. Is a Liberal view of human nature best described as positive, optimistic or simply as recognising the potential in human beings?

2. Barbara Goodwin notes in her introductory text *Using Political Ideas* (1982) that 'In Britain we imbibe Liberal ideas effortlessly from an early age, with the result that Liberalism appears as a necessary truth'. Do you feel this a fair assessment?

3. One way of viewing a Liberal worldview is that it is somewhat like a complex cobweb, with different types of overlapping relationships. Does this imply that all actors are considered equally important?

4. Realism and Liberalism are better at pointing out the flaws in each other than they are at explaining the world. Is this a fair statement?

5. Is cooperation the opposite of conflict? Since the answer to this question is 'no' the key question is 'why not'?

6. To what extent is a Liberal view one which promotes particular outcomes, or rather one which is concerned with providing a framework within which human beings could create a multitude of possibilities?

7. To what extent is the Liberal Utopia an unattainable myth which works to the advantage of the already powerful?

## Recommended reading

Claude, I. (1956) *Swords into Plowshares: The Problems and Progress of International Organisation* (New York: Random House)
An early Liberal work that envisages a more peaceful, cooperative world.

Donnelly, J. (2006) *International Human Rights* (3rd edn, Boulder, CO: Westview Press)
An excellent example of Liberal thinking in IR on a core Liberal concept.

Doyle, M. (1986) 'Liberalism and World Politics', *American Political Science Review*, 80 (4): 1151–69
Sets out the relationship between Liberalism, peace and international order.

Fukuyama, F. (1992) *The End of History and the Last Man* (New York: Free Press)
At the time of publication, a highly influential text that presented a Liberal vision of the post-Cold War international order.

Keohane, R. (1984) *After Hegemony: Cooperation and Discord in the World Political Economy* (Princeton: Princeton University Press)
Regarded as a key work in the development of what would eventually be called 'neo-Liberal institutionalism'.

# Chapter 8
# Marxism and Neo-Marxism

Context

The ideas of Marx

The ideas of Lenin

Dependency Theory

World Systems Theory

Key concepts

Conclusions and criticisms

After reading this chapter you will be able to:

- Gain clarity on the insights of Marxism which have informed neo-Marxist contributions to the inter-paradigm debate

- Provide an analysis of what neo-Marxism has to say about IR and what its weaknesses are

- Use neo-Marxism as a critique of both Realism and Liberalism

- See how neo-Marxism provided a catalyst to a huge variety of subsequent critical interventions in IR theory

*Source*: Getty Images

## Introductory box: Marxism today

Karl Marx was influenced at first at a human level and then in terms of his writing by the conditions of the working class in the nineteenth century. He experienced this first in Paris and then in Victorian England. The experience of the working class was of poverty, to a lesser or greater extent. It was about poorly paid, back-breaking and insecure labour often in appalling and unsafe conditions. Unemployment was an ever-present threat as were disease, disablement and death. The working classes lived in poor and overcrowded housing. Although Marxism has never dominated British politics, always being at best an influential critique, much action has been taken over the years to address these conditions. Legislation has led to social security, free health services, employment legislation and aspirations of all governments that all its citizens should enjoy a reasonable standard of living. As students of international relations what might be most significant is how many of the descriptions of life in Victorian England could now be said to apply to life in present day Sierra Leone or Bangladesh or Haiti or parts of the former Soviet Union – and many other countries or regions within them. This is one reason why we should start with the idea that, even after the end of the Cold War (the struggle between capitalism and communism, between the USA and the USSR, that occurred between roughly 1950 and 1990), Marxism still has relevance to students of international relations today.

Both explicitly and implicitly the work of Marx has been a point of departure for the vast majority of thinkers who understand that there are many things wrong with the world and the point is to change them. Marx was a prolific writer whose ideas changed significantly over his life time; those ideas have been subject to even more prolific interpretation and reinterpretation, not to mention mis-interpretation since. Ironically, as Eastern European socialist experiments (for which Marx is often wrongly blamed) lost the Cold War in 1989, Marxist-inspired ideas were simultaneously gaining significant influence and transforming the discipline of International Relations. While this is exemplified in many of the succeeding chapters, this chapter deals primarily with Marxism's initial incorporation into the discipline, which in contrast to either Realism or Liberalism wanted to put poverty and suffering at the centre of our analysis. This work is directly inspired by Marx, whereas for future chapters we might describe Marx as the point of departure.

Marxism is not a theory of International Relations but *has* informed a variety of approaches to IR theory. Marxism regards classes, not states, as key actors and regards class conflict, not war or economic competition, as the main form of conflict. Marxism has directly influenced a variety of approaches which have something to say about international relations, including Structuralism, Dependency Theory, neo-Marxism and World Systems Theory. In this chapter, we use the term 'neo-Marxism' to refer to them as a whole, although some IR texts prefer 'Structuralism'. Both are shorthand for a range of theories directly influenced by core Marxist ideas on class, the importance of economics and the nature of conflict. This chapter aims to introduce them.

Structuralism was actually the third viewpoint in the so-called inter-paradigm debate of IR in the 1980s (see summary of IR debates in Chapter 11). Rather than introduce unnecessary confusion it is probably best to regard the word paradigm as meaning a perspective/approach with its own assumptions. Therefore an inter-paradigm debate is the competition between different perspectives with different assumptions. IR's inter-paradigm debate was between Realism, Liberal Pluralism and Structuralism (for us, neo-Marxism).

## Context

This chapter deals with neo-Marxism specifically as it was involved in the inter-paradigm debate. However, the inter-paradigm debate was fleeting, and it is important to note that what we term here neo-Marxism has probably turned out much less important than the post-Marxism we move to discuss in later chapters. In this sense what we present here could be considered dated, but it is an important part of IR's story because it begins to move IR away from establishment-orientated theorising concerned primarily with the major powers.

### Box 8.1 Karl Marx (1818–83)

Born in Trier, Marx was also educated in Bonn, Berlin (where his mentor exposed him to atheism) and Jena. After his PhD he worked as a newspaper editor in Cologne where he encountered socialist ideas. Fearing arrest for his radicalism he moved to Paris, there linking up with a variety of radicals most notably the Russian anarchist Mikhail Bakunin (1814–76) and fellow German Friedrich Engels (1820–95). Marx here encountered the shocking living conditions and comradeship of the working class and began to openly attack capitalism and to write about its alienating qualities. He also commenced his formidable writing partnership with Engels. As the son of a wealthy industrialist Engels helped to support Marx, much of whose work was not published in his lifetime. But *The Communist Manifesto* was published and commenced with the line: 'The history of all hitherto existing society is the history of class struggles.' (Marx and Engels 1965). Marx's views saw him expelled from Belgium, France and Germany and he ultimately ended up in London. Marx spent some time in poverty eking out a living between journalism and handouts from Engels, all the time convinced of

the inevitability of revolution. Through it all Marx continued to write, publishing the first volume of perhaps his most famous work *Das Kapital* in 1867. Following the death of his wife and eldest daughter, his often tragic and difficult life came to an end in 1883.

Marx's published works, with date of publication are:

- *Critique of Hegel's Philosophy of Right*, 1843
- *On the Jewish Question*, 1843
- *The German Ideology*, 1845
- *The Poverty of Philosophy*, 1847
- *Wage-Labor and Capital*, 1847
- *Manifesto of the Communist Party*, 1848
- *The Eighteenth Brumaire of Louis Napoleon*, 1852
- *Grundrisse*, 1857
- *A Contribution to the Critique of Political Economy*, 1859
- *Capital*, Volume I (Das Kapital), 1867
- *Capital*, Volume II, 1885
- *Capital*, Volume III, 1894

The last two were published posthumously by Friedrich Engels.

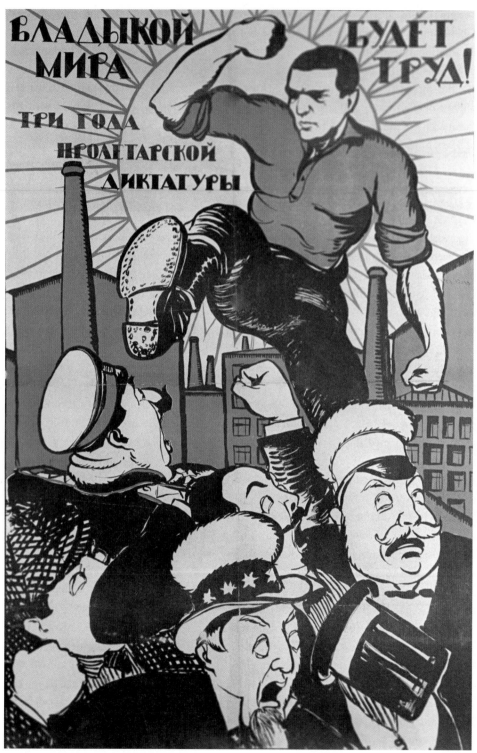

*Source*: RIA Novosti Photo Library/Lenin Library, Moscow

**Marxism regards economic classes, not states, as the principal actors in world politics.**

Superficially, however, neo-Marxism shares common ground with both Realism and Liberalism. It resembles Realism because both emphasise conflict as a central process in International Relations and also shares common ground with Liberal Pluralist approaches in emphasising the profoundly interconnected nature of international economic relations and the importance of non-state actors. However, neo-Marxists stress the conflictual nature of the global economy and structural relations of domination and dependence, rather than the anarchy of the state system, or complex-interdependence. We need to look at the ideas of Marx himself as context for this different view of conflict and economic relations.

## The ideas of Marx

The work of Marx is central to neo-Marxism but Marx's guiding ideas were modified as they were applied to Dependency theory and World Systems theory which are examples of neo-Marxist thought. This means that the contributions of neo-Marxist authors such as Prebisch, Gunder Frank, Cardoso and Faletto should be regarded as important in their own right and not as mere adjuncts or restatements of Marx. Also, the work discussed in this chapter actually owes more to the later works of Marx, produced after 1857, in close collaboration with Engels (a German social scientist). Finally, it is worth restating that Marx has had significant influence on some of the post-Marxist theories discussed in subsequent chapters.

Marx's later work paid close attention to the nature of economic relationships in capitalist societies. Marx argued that the organisation of the economy and economic relationships formed the material base of society. Capitalism is built upon the principles of private ownership of property and the pursuit of profit. Most people go to work every weekday in shops, factories or offices, producing goods and services for the 'boss' (be it a single entrepreneur or huge multinational), which are subsequently sold for a profit in the 'market'. People do not own the goods and services which they produce but instead are paid a wage for their labour. Collectively, the ways in which goods and services are produced (the division of labour, factory production and so on) and the conditions under which they are produced (wage labour) constitute the 'economic base' or 'mode of production'.

In a series of influential essays, Marx developed a 'labour theory of value', which suggests that the 'exchange value' of any good or service (what in capitalist economies is called the 'price') is really made up of congealed human labour. Marx argued that capitalists paid workers considerably less than the true value of what they produced, which in Marx's time (and still in many parts of the world) would perhaps cover only bare subsistence. Marx called the difference between what workers actually produced and what they were paid, surplus value. What we commonly call 'profit' is the surplus value extracted from labour and 'expropriated' by capitalists. Marx argued that capitalism was driven by the accumulation of surplus value.

The accumulation of surplus value could be achieved in one of three ways: capitalists could search out new markets for the products of labour; they could constantly drive down wages in order to extract more from their workers; or they could replace people with machines. Marx believed that to some extent these strategies were pursued simultaneously and that sooner or later capitalism would collapse, as workers were rendered too poor to provide a market for the goods produced and as new markets were exhausted. Capitalism was then an exploitative system, riddled with tensions, conflicts and inherent contradictions which would ultimately cause it to collapse.

Marx believed that the economic 'base' supports a range of other political and social institutions, such as the state, the law courts, the church, the family, the education system, and what we now call the mass media. This 'superstructure' is intimately connected with, but conceptually distinct from, the economic base. Marx devoted a great deal of time to trying to elucidate the relationship between the economic 'base' and the political, social and legal 'superstructure'. He believed that ultimately economic forces drove (determined) social and political change, and much of his work was concerned with explaining how and why such change occurred. The relationship between base and superstructure has been much debated within Marxism and developed particularly by Antonio Gramsci (see Chapter 9).

By combining some of Marx's ideas on the historical and changing nature of human societies – known as 'historical materialism' – with Marxist economic analysis, it is possible to construct a coherent analysis of the overall structure of capitalist societies which can then be used to inform our understanding of the individual 'parts'. To simplify, Marx claimed that human societies were made up of various institutions and forms of social organisation which fulfilled a particular function or role in terms of the overall social system. He believed that as societies changed over time, so too did forms of social organisation, practices and institutions.

Marx believed that the dynamic force propelling change of this kind was economic, rooted in the particular 'modes of production' of society. Productive forces developed over time as humanity developed more knowledge of/mastery over nature. As modes of production advanced and changed, the superstructure of society also changed. So, at different periods in history we find different modes of production and a corresponding system of legal and political forms of organisation and social relationships. Marx argued that social relations could be characterised in different ways – feudal, bourgeois and so forth.

Marx argued that all forms of social and economic organisation, to date, were based on forms of oppression and exploitation and contained inherent contradictions which eventually brought about their downfall – usually through violence. During periods of transition, emerging classes struggled for ascendancy over the old ruling order and established their own dominance over the rest of society. From a Marxist perspective, the French Revolution and the subsequent period of social turmoil/political upheaval, were illustrative of a process by which an emerging social class (the bourgeoisie) rose up and displaced the established ruling class (the aristocracy). Marxists continue to view classes in terms of their relationship to society's mode of production; contemporary capitalism is characterised by a ruling class (bourgeoisie) which owns/controls the means of production and the working class (proletariat) who must sell their labour to survive.

Marx was interested in the dynamism of capitalism and the ways it was radically transforming the economic, social and political landscape across Europe. He believed that while the crisis/collapse of capitalism would occur in a relatively advanced industrial economy, the ramifications would be felt in other countries across the European continent. Marx was a committed member of the Communist International, an organisation dedicated to the task of raising awareness of transnational working-class interests, uniting the working class across Europe and stressing the need for solidarity with the poor and oppressed across the world.

Marx's ideas must be taken in context which means they contain important omissions if one attempts to apply them to contemporary world politics and there are certain caveats we must make on their behalf. First, Marx did not develop a sustained analysis of the state system. Second, it is not clear that Marx was always sensitive to non-European peoples and certainly not to other forms of oppression other than class-based ones (for example, those based on gender or ethnicity). Third, although often dismissed as ideological, Marx made claims on a scientific basis. He was sometimes wrong, of course, but he was actually trying to suggest that what was happening was based on certain *observable*, inevitable processes. History was 'determined' in the sense that capitalists could not prevent their own demise and workers were destined to inherit the world and build a better and brighter future. In terms of all three points, what is more important than Marx's ideas is how later theorists (below and in subsequent chapters) have either developed or responded.

## The ideas of Lenin

The work of Lenin (1870–1924) is an important stepping stone between Marx's analysis of industrialised capitalist countries in Northern Europe and an analysis of international capitalist expansion and inter-state conflict. Lenin's ideas also draw from the English economist/historian J.A. Hobson (1858–1940). We suggested above that Marx believed capitalism would eventually collapse as workers became more impoverished and new

### Box 8.2 Vladimir Ilyich Lenin (1870–1924)

Born in Simbirsk, Russia, Lenin was introduced to the ideas of Marx by his brother who was executed in 1887 for his part in attempting to assassinate the Tsar. After a period in education he helped found the Union of Struggle for the Emancipation of the Working Class in 1895 and was soon after sentenced to three years in exile in Siberia. Here he developed his ideas and continued to do so in collaboration or contestation with others and at various points around Europe in the opening years of the twentieth century. It is a complicated and bloody story, but the First World War ultimately opened the way to a revolution in Russia with Lenin as the leading figure. Although much of the notoriety which accompanies the Soviet experiment concerns events after his death, Lenin undoubtedly started down that path himself.

markets became exhausted. Hobson, and later Lenin, did not necessarily disagree with Marx's basic ideas; however, they believed that Marx seriously underestimated the ability of the capitalist system to survive (in the short/medium term) in the face of periodic crises. The nature of capitalism, it was argued, was such that it needed to expand in order to find new markets and secure new sources of raw materials and labour.

At the same time, industrialisation furnished the elites of developed European states with the means to undertake campaigns of colonial expansion across the globe. Hobson believed that these campaigns were designed to ensure that rich elites in European states had captive markets and was a form of exploitation. Lenin took this basic idea of expansionism and, using guiding ideas on the nature of capitalism provided by Marx and Engels, developed a sustained analysis of imperialism as 'the highest stage of capitalism' in that it would bring about the total exhaustion of new markets in accordance with Marx's predictions. However, Lenin believed that long before that occurred, capitalism would collapse because the search for captive markets and sources of raw materials was already generating conflicts between imperialist powers. Lenin believed that the First World War was the result of such squabbles and that, along with the working class of industrialised countries, subjugated peoples across the world would eventually rise up, throwing off the yoke of imperialist domination as the world descended into vicious war.

Lenin's ideas about the end of capitalism were popular among intellectuals between the two World Wars but in Liberalism's 'golden years' (the economic boom after the Second World War) such ideas quickly became unfashionable and Marxist ideas did not play a significant role in the early development of International Relations. However, that changed in the 1960s and 1970s, partly because of the problems faced by newly independent (formerly colonial) states, and partly because of increasing economic instability. Accordingly, IR scholars became more interested in the relationship between international economics and international politics. Neo-Marxism gradually increased its influence in IR through ideas such as Dependency Theory and World Systems Theory.

## Dependency Theory

**Dependency Theory** first came to prominence in the 1960s. It developed as a critique of liberal modernisation theory which suggested (in an ironic echo of Marx) that poorer countries would pass through various inevitable stages of wealth creation on their way to 'take off' (that is, development and prosperity). However, for many countries the physical evidence of this seemed not to exist, and the economic and political climate of the late 1960s and early 1970s meant that such countries tended to be receptive to critiques of Western-led development models. Modernisation theory rejected/ignored the possibility that deep *structural* factors might prevent economic progress, and more importantly, that the nature of the international system itself might be an obstacle to development. Accordingly, Dependency Theory developed a critique of modernisation theory which emphasised the structural constraints to development.

Liberal economic theory suggests that successful modernisation depends to some extent upon the growth of an indigenous entrepreneurial class. Accordingly, development strategies frequently targeted resources at a 'modernising elite', believing that as countries underwent industrialisation and economic growth, wealth would 'trickle down' from this elite to the masses. They also believed that this elite would imbue Liberal social and political values and these would gradually spread from the 'advanced' middle classes to the rest of society. Dependency theorists contended, to the contrary, that while elites did indeed benefit from their particular position in the system, the promised 'trickle down' did not materialise and was unlikely to do so. In fact, as a country ostensibly 'advanced', the masses became progressively more impoverished (and inequality increased) as the wealth generated was used by elites to mimic their well-off counterparts in other countries.

Dependency authors (the first of whom were from Latin America) undertook a detailed historical analysis of the pattern of economic growth and development in Latin America and claimed to find that it actually achieved its most impressive performance at times when there was a slow down in world trade and trading links with developed countries were disrupted. Taking this observation as a starting point, they suggested this was because the basic structure of the global economy worked to further the interests of the already rich, developed economies and progressively to impoverish already poor countries. This basic structure (the trading regimes that existed, the nature of the markets for basic commodities and so on) was said to make inevitable the development trajectory of individual countries. Therefore, even as large parts of the world emerged from imperialism and colonialism, the former masters continued to dominate – hence the terms *neo*-imperialism and *neo*-colonialism. At international level this mirrors Marx's insight that the prosperity of the few is dependent on the misery of the majority (masses).

Dependency theorists recognise that transnational elites share some common interests, but they also argue that to some extent the workers in developed countries, while relatively impoverished and exploited, have actually benefited to some degree from the exploitation of the developing world. They have shown how the bourgeoisie in the rich countries can exploit the poorer countries and use the profits to dampen demands from its proletariat, for instance by offering slightly better working conditions including wages. In this way, Dependency theorists suggested that through such cooption of the masses there might well be obstacles to international worker solidarity. They have questioned (and complicated) Marx's notion of a simple divergence of interests between the proletariat (all workers) and the bourgeoisie (all owners).

## World Systems Theory

World Systems Theory (hereafter WST) is an idea associated with US sociologist Immanuel Wallerstein and suggests that different elements of the international economy cannot be understood in isolation. Many centuries ago, we could conceive of all societies as mini-systems – self-contained economic, political and social units with a single culture and isolated from each other. Such societies were characterised by a simple division of labour and all members had a specific, clearly defined role – hunter, farmer, carer and so on. Today, there are very few examples of these kinds of societies left in the world. Over time they have been swallowed up by larger systems of social, economic and political organisation. A world system is the largest and most complex of all and comes in two types – world empire and world economy. According to Wallerstein, prior to the birth and expansion of capitalism, there were examples of world *empires* based on the conquest and subordination of peoples across the world – the so-called 'great civilisations' of pre-modern times in China, Egypt and Rome.

In about 1500 a world economy emerged in Europe and gradually expanded across the globe. New transportation technology allowed far-flung markets to be obtained and maintained especially when combined with Western military technology to dictate and enforce favourable terms of trade. As this capitalism spread throughout the globe, there developed a 'core', composed of well-developed towns, flourishing manufacturing, technologically progressive agriculture, skilled and relatively well-paid labour, and high investment, and – on the other hand – a 'periphery', from which raw materials necessary for expansion and certain key primary goods were extracted. In such a system, the periphery stagnated, its towns withered, and those with money, technology and skills moved to the core. At first, the differences between the core and the periphery were small. Gradually, however, the gap widened as increasingly the core countries concentrated on the production of manufactured goods while the periphery produced only primary products and basic commodities. Accordingly, uneven development across the world – and the existence of rich and poor areas – is not a consequence of historical lag or a technical hitch to sort out, but actually a consequence of the capitalist world system.

The idea of 'core–periphery' is also used by Dependency theory but WST also posits the existence of a semi-periphery – intermediary societies which play an important role in the functioning of the world system as a whole. When applied to International Relations, what this effectively boils down to is an argument that lower levels (states, communities, individuals) matter, but that the highest level (the world system) constrains behaviour in all sorts of ways. Therefore, it makes no sense to start from the premise that the state is the basic unit of analysis in IR, or posit that states are autonomous 'actors'.

## Key concepts

With other theoretical approaches (Realism and Liberalism for instance) it is easy to discuss different philosophers and authors who have influenced them and to then go on to describe how this is played out within the discipline. However, in this case it is difficult. As already alluded to, this is because Marxism has been a starting point for many other theories than those dealt with in this chapter. Nonetheless, the above gives a sense of how later, economic Marxism influenced IR. Below we expand upon and clarify how it did this for specific concepts.

## Inequality

To Marxist theories inequality is fundamental and enduring because the international system is divided between the 'haves' and the 'have-nots'. The 'haves' live mostly in rich countries, predominantly in the northern hemisphere. Marxists argue that the capitalist elites of such countries, along with smaller local Third World elites, constitute a strong centre or core in the world economic and political order, or world system. The 'have-nots' are the downtrodden classes; they are the weak, powerless and live mostly in what is known as the periphery. The geography of this situation is quite fluid in the sense that pockets of poverty exist in richer countries, while ostentatious affluence can be encountered in very poor countries. For this reason terms which attempt to divide the rich and poor up on a state basis hold within them this difficulty. Third World, for instance, developed as a term associated with the marginalised and, in terms of levels of development, those states not part of the affluent West (First World) or the Communist East of the Cold War (Second World). Although Third World still has some emotional power as symbolising those without, or those marginalised, a number of other terms are now used and preferred in different contexts. In your reading you may therefore come across different ways of talking about the marginalised, excluded and poorer areas of the world such as the South, Developing World or Majority World. Economists sometimes use terms like LDC for Less Developed Country or underdevelopment, but these both share the pejorative undertones of Third World.

By focusing on structures of the international system and world economy neo-Marxist theories put the plight of developing states at the centre of our concerns, rejecting the blasé optimism of liberal modernisation theories. Indeed neo-Marxist theories reinterpret a number of liberal conventions. The end of colonialism (where Third World countries were ruled as colonies of other states such as Britain) for instance, cannot be seen as signalling the end of exploitation of the Third World states by rich, industrialised nations. Instead, the 'end' of colonialism simply changes the nature of colonialism from a direct type, based on military occupation, to an indirect type based on economic structures (that is, neo-colonialism).

To neo-Marxist viewpoints, developing country interaction with the financial and commercial centres of the rich states of the First World is undertaken on unequal terms; the rich countries have used their previously existing position of economic dominance in order to structure the international economy to serve their interests and maintain their dominance. Majority World states which have tried to 'opt out' of the system have not fared well economically and so, however unfair the existing situation, most developing states are dependent upon it – and trapped by it. This dependency has left most developing states unable to define effectively their own development goals, or to advance the welfare concerns of their populations, because their economies are set up and organised to serve the interests of the industrialised states.

## Case study: Rogue states

States such as Cuba and North Korea are (to lesser or greater extent) isolated from the world economy being the only notable non-members of the IMF (see Box 17.1). This is for a variety of reasons; some voluntary (to maintain internal political control) and others involuntary (such as economic blockade or ostracism because of their political system). As a result, these states have faced extremely difficult problems in terms of being able to ensure adequate supplies of basics such as food to their populations. While it is true that isolation from the vagaries of the market has allowed such states political control through control of distribution, life is generally hard for a tightly controlled population. In Cuba (unless people have relatives in Miami who send US dollars or have somehow got a car/taxi licence) people shop at government-run stores (peso stores); these shops offer very little variety or are actually empty. Ingredients for traditional Cuban cuisine such as pork, fish and garlic, are difficult to find. Cubans get a very limited monthly ration of food and can have to spend plenty of time queuing up for that which they do get. Maintaining control in such a situation requires some subtle and some not so subtle methods of repression but is summed up by the following Cuban joke. A man at a public meeting asks why the chocolate in Cuba is so poor. The government official says he does not know but will look into it and answer at the next meeting. At the next meeting another man stands up to ask a question. 'I suppose you want to know about the chocolate?' says the official. 'No', says the man, 'I want to know where the man is who asked about it last time'.

Jokes about North Korea on the other hand are rare, information hard to come by and (the regime's propaganda notwithstanding) life almost certainly harsher than in Cuba for the majority. According to a recent UN report, the people of North Korea are subjected to intolerable suffering, including starvation, torture and almost universal spying. Elsewhere, life has been described as about lies and potatoes (for those lucky enough to get potatoes).

The case against both states is easily made. However, looking at Cuba (for which information is more readily available) we can find contradictory evidence. The Human Development Index (HDI) of the United Nations Development Programme (UNDP) measures a range of indicators to give an HDI ranking. These indicators are a long and healthy life, knowledge (education) and standard of living. Cuba is ranked 51 of 182 countries (2009) which, despite recent economic austerity, is higher than a few years ago (55 in the year 2000). Costa Rica held up by many as the democratic success story of Central America is at 54; European Romania is at 63; powerful Brazil is at 75; fellow Caribbean island Jamaica is 100 and so on. In other words, according to some basic indicators, there are many countries in the world in which one would not want to live before Cuba. It is important, therefore, to remember the politics involved in both criticising and defending a socialist experiment less than a hundred miles from the United States.

> **What is the truth of the joke that the only thing worse than being exploited by the global economy is not being exploited by the global economy?**

Dependence describes a type of relationship between rich and poor which ensures that money and resources are increasingly concentrated with the former because of the way the world economy is structured. For instance poorer countries might export raw materials such as bauxite and foodstuffs like coffee beans and bananas, whereas richer countries export manufactured goods, such as cars, fridges and so on. Statistical evidence supports the contention that over the long term the prices of raw materials and food – primary products – tend to decline *relative* to the price of manufactured goods and that many countries are, therefore, destined to be poorer because of the way they are incorporated into the global economy.

Despite a contemporary rhetoric of free trade, richer countries actually control prices, and the situation described above, by trade restrictions. Furthermore, technical innovation keeps pushing the development of better products, which have ever higher levels of

Source: Getty Images/Altrendo

**How does Cuba's relatively high HDI rating affect our understanding of the 'rogue state' label?**

'value-added'. Of course, some people (plantation owners in Guatemala for instance) can be very rich despite the overall poverty which may exist in their country; this ensures that the system is kept going since there is a commonality of interest between the rich of the core and the rich of the periphery.

Neo-Marxist theories, such as World Systems Theory, inherit from Marxism a belief that sooner or later the contradictions of such an unequal system will bring about its demise. They are not always optimistic about what this will mean, predicting for instance socialism (felt to be positive) or barbarism (where everyone conflicts with everyone else). Periodic stock market crashes and the overall effects of things such as eroded consumer confidence alert us to the interconnectedness of the global economy – and perhaps to its fragility.

## The state

The state is a central concept in neo-Marxist theories, but is viewed in a different way from Realist or Liberal approaches. The difference concerns the level of importance attached to states. Some writers in the Marxist tradition argue that international political and economic analysis would be better focused on social classes and the nature of transnational alliances among elites. However, even those who prefer such a class-based analysis recognise the actual political division of the world into states, and the role that these states play in helping to maintain class-based inequalities.

Rather than seeing the state as a sovereign power representing the interests of the nation in international relations, Marxist theorists hold that the state reflects the interests of dominant social classes. There is, however, disagreement as to whether the state is dominated by elite social classes, or whether it exercises a degree of autonomy. In classical Marxism and early neo-Marxist work, the state was seen as a coercive, repressive apparatus supporting an exploitative social and economic order and reflecting the interests of dominant classes. Marx famously described the state as the 'executive committee of the bourgeoisie'. Some neo-Marxists point to the way in which the institutions of the state – the law courts, the police, the military, the economic system – work to protect the interests of the already powerful.

Others hold that the state can have a degree of autonomy from the dominant class. Although not seen as a 'neutral arbiter', the state is considered to be relatively independent of specific interests. States clearly do make choices when formulating policies. Moreover, these same choices are sometimes bound to affect adversely some sections of capital. States might even struggle for more autonomy from dominant classes, in response to democratic pressures. However, even if we accept that the state has a degree of autonomy, the state is, nonetheless, compelled to deal with the political and economic contradictions inherent in capitalism and so is never able completely to escape the constraints imposed by the global capitalist system. In order to formulate autonomous policies the state requires resources, including financial resources which it raises through taxation. Arguably then, the state relies largely on the capitalist class to bring about an acceptable level of economic activity, which it needs to maintain support.

In terms of the overarching global economy as a constraining/determining factor in state behaviour, neo-Marxists have made a distinction between 'core' and 'peripheral' states, arguing that in the core, the state is relatively strong, but functions to advance the interests of the bourgeoisie by preventing other states erecting political barriers to the profitability of their activities. Core states, then, shape the world market in ways that advance the interests of some entrepreneurs against those of other groups. Core states cooperate to extend and deepen the capitalist world system. The most powerful states, for example, the United States of America, Japan and Germany work together (and through their influence in international financial organisations like the OECD, the World Bank or IMF) to ensure the survival of an international capitalist economy, which benefits elite classes across the globe. It follows from this that while neo-Marxists believe that states are of central importance, the study of international relations must also extend to a range of other 'actors' like the World Bank, International Monetary Fund, and multinational corporations.

## Power

Power to neo-Marxists is not about relational 'trials of strength' (for example who wins the war) but something much more subtle. Power is embedded in social relations; that is, it is a part of the structure. Power thus involves the inequalities of capitalist class relations and core–periphery relations. It also involves less tangible ideas such as persuasion or influence and may be 'invisible'. One person or group may have power over others not only through threats and coercion but via ideology and manipulation. In this way, power relations may come to be seen as such a 'natural' order of things that no one is consciously aware that power is, in fact, being exercised.

Accordingly, the operation of the global capitalist economy might not always appear conflictual, oppressive or exploitative because the relationships of power are often not overt or obvious. The factory worker may be happy with life. Many factory workers may get the trappings of a rather comfortable lifestyle; a car and other consumer goods, health care, holidays and so on. However, it is probably the case that this 'good fortune' is contingent upon the poverty of other workers in poorer countries. The analysis of power, oppression, marginalisation and 'otherness' is greatly developed in IR beyond neo-Marxism (see later theory chapters).

## Order

Neo-Marxists conceive of world order as a capitalist system of interconnected sets of social, economic and political relations which collectively constitute a structure. From such a perspective, modern capitalism has expanded to become a global system; local, national and regional economies now form part of a much larger interconnected economic system and are conditioned by that system. Similarly, the conditions of life for individuals, social groups and even states, are determined by their place in the overall, global capitalist system.

In essence, neo-Marxists see the global capitalist system as being structured along both a vertical and horizontal axis. Relations between states are structured hierarchically between those which are wealthy and powerful – the core – and those which are poor and without much influence – the periphery. There is also a horizontal structure of class relationships, namely the relationship which exists between elites in both core and periphery countries. Elites in both the rich 'North' and poor 'South', share fundamental interests in supporting this system because they actually benefit from the exploitation of other social groups.

The economies of Asia, Africa and Latin America are on the margins of the global economic system and dependent on the capitalist countries of Western Europe and North America at the centre. Trade relations and capital flows between the core and periphery of the global economy are asymmetrical, shifting the economic surplus to the core and undermining the resource base of the periphery. Broadly speaking, countries in the periphery produce primary products like raw materials – cotton or coffee beans – not manufactured goods like motor vehicles or electronic goods. This degree of 'specialisation' or division of labour perpetuates inequalities. Surplus flows out of the periphery to the core. Peripheral countries (the South or Third World) are not 'catching up' with the core because of their dependence on, and exploitation by, the core (West or North) of the international capitalist economy. Economic growth and development in the periphery is sluggish due to a lack of technology and investment, which again is a consequence of their dependence on the core.

Starting from the central premise that economics and politics are intimately connected allows neo-Marxists to make various points about the nature and role of states and institutions in international relations, in 'managing' world order. Neo-Marxists argue that capitalism is maintained and perpetuated by a range of institutions and practices and by dominant ideologies or belief systems which legitimise the current world order. The fundamental economic inequality which exists between core and periphery determines the nature of the state – put simply, core states are powerful and peripheral states are weak. States in the periphery have little autonomy in relation to the global economy in which they are embedded, because ruling classes in peripheral countries are tied by economic interest to international capital and play a managerial or intermediary role within their own countries. Neo-Marxists believe that major institutions like the UN, the World Bank and IMF, and trading blocs like NAFTA are dominated by elite groups and/or hegemonic states. Thus we cannot take statements of the World Bank and IMF about their role in poverty alleviation at face value; these organisations have a role in the capitalist structure which helps to maintain current injustices, even if it can point to specific instances of ameliorating the worst excesses of the system.

## Identity

Initially neo-Marxists writers failed to pay significant attention to identity issues unless they fitted within the broad framework of a global capitalist order and notions of class struggle. Although nationalism was highly significant, as both an ideology and political force in nineteenth-century Europe, Marx devoted most of his time and energies to exploring the theme of *class* consciousness, *class* interests and *class* struggle. Some Marxist authors can therefore be accused of acting as if nationalism, religious belief, cultural and ethnic identification and so on are simply manifestations of 'false consciousness'; in effect, a distraction from the real class-based structures of politics.

Despite this neglect the 1960s saw the emergence of national liberation movements in parts of Africa and Latin America which were leaning to the left, or pro-Marxist-Leninist; for this reason, it became necessary to develop an account of nationalist struggle which was not dismissive of identity other than class based. In Wallerstein's account of the modern world system, we find attention given to nationalism as a powerful source of political identification. Wallerstein argues that the increasing definition of state structures has led to the shaping, reshaping, creation and destruction, and revival of the idea of 'peoples'. He believes that these peoples come to see themselves (and are seen by others) as controlling state structures. Through this identification of peoples with the state, 'nations' are created. On the other hand, within the boundaries of the nation state, there are significant groups who are not identified as having rights to control state structures or exercise political power directly. These people come to be seen by 'nationals' as 'minorities'. However, it is important to realise that Wallerstein does not regard national identity as rooted in some real shared ethnic heritage or history. Nations are 'solidarity groupings' whose boundaries are constantly constructed, defined and redefined; and nationalism is a device which is used to strengthen and consolidate the power of the state.

World Systems Theory incorporates an analysis of those forces which work against the system as well as dominant, class-based, structures. Thus, it is possible to identify a number of oppositional or 'anti-systemic' forces at work in world politics. Nationalism is not all of one kind. Some forms of nationalism certainly work to consolidate capitalism and disguise the exploitative nature of the capitalist world system. However, some national liberation movements are clearly anti-systemic. Various groups have an interest in supporting and opposing particular definitions of the 'nation state' and so, according to Wallerstein, 'nationalism' must be seen as both a mechanism of imperialism/integration *and* of resistance/liberation. Clearly, here we have an analysis of nationalism which is influenced by the underlying theory of class politics.

Neo-Marxists have also endeavoured to give some account of racism and sexism in the world system. According to Wallerstein racism is a belief system which functions to justify the inclusion of certain groups in the workforce and the political system at a level of reward and status sharply inferior to that of some larger group. Sexism has the same objective, although it is reached via a different path. By restricting women to certain modes of producing income and by defining such modes as 'non-work' (through the concept of the 'housewife'), sexism works to reduce wage levels in large sectors of the world economy. However, for those theories covered by this chapter, despite attempts to offer some account of identity, forms of solidarity and types of community (including anti-systemic movements), it is fair to say that analysis has been influenced by the primacy of social class and class struggle. Much post-Marxist work covered in subsequent chapters is far more explicit about identifying other forms of identification, and its relationship to patterns of power and oppression.

## Violence

For neo-Marxists, global economic relations are conflict ridden because of tendencies inherent in capitalism. Conflicts between social groups, and states, are generated by the nature of the system itself. In terms of direct physical violence, like war, the link between capitalism and conflict can be seen in terms of imperialism and the violent subjugation of those peoples who opposed it. It has been claimed, by Lenin for example, that capitalist competition leads to inter-state war. What is evident is that some conflicts appear to have, at least partly, capitalist economic motivations. For example, Indonesia's invasion of East Timor was followed by a treaty with Australia on oil exploitation off the Timorese coast. Many observers suggest that US/UN action in the Gulf in 1991 and again in 2003 was motivated more by economic considerations than for reasons of protecting democracy.

Another way of looking at violence is as something indirect or structural. Johan Galtung is particularly known for his work on structural violence, which has made an important contribution to Peace Studies. One can suffer great harm, both physical and psychological, if deprived of social and economic security. In this view violence is something which pervades the structures of society and which oppresses the working class and other marginalised groups. The economic structure of capitalism works to damage subordinated

## Box 8.3 Looking elsewhere

Despite the Anglo-American dominance of International Relations, to some extent reflected in the way these theory chapters are presented, much of the most ground-breaking, provocative and progressive ideas have come from elsewhere; from countries such as the Scandinavian countries, the Netherlands, Finland and beyond Europe. Peace Studies is an example of theory tangential to the mainstream of IR that you may find useful to explore. In later chapters you will come across the **Copenhagen School** of Critical Security Studies. It is always useful to reflect upon the source of work and how this might be influencing the presentation of ideas.

groups in many and varied ways; they get less education, poorer health care and so on, leading to shorter life expectancies. Feminists have gone beyond the class-based analysis of Galtung's original work to suggest that structures in society also tend to impact negatively on the lives of women.

## Conclusions and criticisms

This chapter has discussed a number of theories which draw upon a Marxist legacy, but are also influenced by other ideas. Probably the best known variants of neo-Marxism are Dependency theory and World Systems theory. From a neo-Marxist perspective, the contemporary world order is constituted by a global capitalist system and a corresponding inter-state system. A fundamental feature of this order is inequality. Capitalism is based on the exploitation of the poor by the rich. In pursuing their (class) interests, the rich (people and states) are able to maintain their position by their exploitation of the poor.

In line with Marx, many neo-Marxists see class groupings as the dominant actors in IR, despite the importance of the state, but they have not neglected the role of the state system. Neo-Marxists have developed an analysis of the state as either an instrument used to perpetuate the rule of dominant classes – a conduit for class oppression – or as a relatively autonomous entity which, nevertheless, plays an important role in facilitating capitalist expansion and supporting an unjust order. While the world is divided up into rich and poor countries, an accurate appraisal of IR needs to look at how classes promote their interests and how they use the state to help them. Various approaches which emphasise the role of economic structures look carefully at the role of institutional actors such as the World Bank and IMF, and how these help legitimise and maintain existing structures. Neo-Marxism suggests that processes of capital accumulation, the extraction of surplus value and exploitation can be measured objectively and we can understand processes of contradiction, crisis and change by reference to these same economic 'laws'.

One criticism of neo-Marxism concerns its level of determinism. This means that the theory suggests that the position of actors within the structure determines the way they behave. States are said to have little autonomy in the way they conduct themselves in terms of winning or losing within the international economy and this seems to dismiss as meaningless even noble, heroic and revolutionary struggles to overcome such constraints. Some authors, such as Wallerstein, have been slightly less deterministic in the sense that they give an account of when change might happen and when human agency can be more effective. However, these criticisms tend to forget that the whole point is to demonstrate the injustice of a situation where poorer states have very little possibility to improve their position.

Neo-Marxist theory can also be criticised as reductionist; that is, it reduces all phenomena – war, economic crisis, inequality, religion, culture, etc. – to the dynamic of capitalism and to social class and class struggle. What this means in practice is that neo-Marxists have failed to ask a whole range of questions about gender, ethnicity and identities of other sorts by reducing a highly complex situation to one which is explained by class. Subsequent chapters show how post-Marxist theorists have contended that patterns of oppression are multifaceted and overlapping.

Finally, theories such as these, emphasising the oppression of the working class in Marxist terms, implicitly suggest an end point to history. The end point is hopefully (for these theories) socialism, at which point a good life will be enjoyed by everyone. Quite apart from the fact that much of what Marx predicted as inevitable has not happened, this (teleological) position can be criticised because the explanation of what *is* happening (the dynamic of history and social change) is coloured by the assumption that a socialist society will eventually emerge – that is to say, the posited end point colours the explanation of past and present events. Moreover, not only does this suggest that the 'end point' influences the theory, but it also has implications for different cultures which might be seen as temporary stages or impediments, rather than as possessing of intrinsic value.

As we see in subsequent chapters, thought in a Marxian tradition has recognised and sought to address these criticisms. Overall, however, we should conclude by saying that the theories presented here have been useful to the development of IR, and can be useful to students in beginning to see the agenda of IR as much more than that presented by the debate between Realism and Liberalism. However, their weaknesses did not allow them a position of pre-eminence in IR and in the context of the Cold War such approaches were almost absent from the US version of the discipline. The Marxist *influenced* theories of Chapter 9 have, on the other hand, become highly significant in the discipline. Why this is so, and why they are different from neo-Marxism will be explained.

## Resource section

## Questions

**1.** Was Marx way ahead of his time in noting the internal contradictions of capitalism?

**2.** Do neo-Marxist theories fall into the trap of telling us what is wrong with the world, while forgetting the dangers inherent in trying to put them right?

**3.** What is the difference between 'free trade' and 'fair trade'? Can they ever be effectively the same?

## Recommended reading

**Arrighi, G. and Sliver, B.J. (2001) 'Capitalism and World (Dis)Order',** *Review of International Studies,* **27, Special Issue: 257–79**
Contemporary neo-Marxist analysis of change and future uncertainty.

**Baran, P. (1957),** *The Political Economy of Growth* **(New York: Monthly Review Press)**
On his death it was observed: 'His major work, *The Political Economy of Growth*, has been translated into eight languages and has sold well over 50,000 copies. Its ideas are known, admired and debated wherever economic growth is seriously studied.'

**Cardoso, F. and Faletto, E. (1979)** *Dependency and Development in Latin America* **(Berkeley: University of California Press)**
A sophisticated analysis of Latin American economic development arguing that its economic dependency stems not merely from the domination of the world market over internal national and 'enclave' economies, but also from the much more complex interaction of economic drives, political structures, social movements, and historically conditioned alliances.

**Galtung, J. (1971) 'A Structural Theory of Imperialism',** *The Journal of Peace Research,* **8 (1): 81–117**
Uses core–periphery analysis to explain the tremendous inequality in the world and the lack of change in this situation.

**Harvey, D. (2003)** *The New Imperialism* **(Oxford: Oxford University Press)**
A committed Marxist, Harvey analyses actions of the US Bush Administration to that point in light of a larger chain of events, stretching back to the transformation of the global political and economic order in the early 1970s.

**Rodney, W. (1972)** *How Europe Underdeveloped Africa* **(London: Bogle l'Ouverture)**
Ground breaking work arguing that Africa was deliberately exploited and underdeveloped by European colonial regimes, thus accounting for current problems and suggesting the way forward.

**Wallerstein, I. (1974, 1980, 1989)** *The Modern World-System, Volumes 1 to 3* **(San Diego, CA: Academy Press)**
His key ideas in just three volumes (1000+ pages) subtitled 'capitalist agriculture and the origins of the European world-economy in the sixteenth century', 'mercantilism and the consolidation of the European world-economy, 1600–1750' and 'the second era of great expansion of the capitalist world-economy, 1730–1840'.

# Chapter 9
# Critical Theory

**Context**

**Contemporary Critical Theory and IR**

**Key concepts**

**Conclusions**

After reading this chapter you will be able to:

- Describe what Critical Theory is, and how it emerged in, and relates to, International Relations

- Highlight the ways in which Critical Theory has used other 'non-IR' social theory to modify and expand the remit and insights of IR

- Reflect on the purpose of theory and the relative merits of simplicity and complexity

- Read with confidence the next, and connected, chapter which deals with so-called 'alternative theories' of IR

## Introductory box: Rethinking Marxism

Stalin and Mao are each responsible for millions of deaths. Pol Pot was guilty of genocide. Nicolae Ceausescu enjoyed luxury in Romania, a facade which hid the misery of the masses. Humanitarian organisations express frustration about a regime in North Korea which is more interested in hiding the terrible consequences of its rule than in those consequences themselves. Soviet tanks crushed rebellion in Hungary in 1956. When lists of injustices are drawn up they seem to include, perhaps disproportionately, the actions of states inspired by the ideas and thoughts of Marx. However, it seems a particularly harsh fate that his ideas be associated with some of history's most notorious tyrants given that he was personally committed to the cause of the downtrodden masses (see Chapter 8). It has been to reclaim the 'humanism' in Marx, and to steer us away from the practical and theoretical dangers of Marxism, that a range of critical theories have developed in IR and which seek to go beyond the neo-Marxism of Chapter 8.

**Critical Theory** draws upon the early work of Karl Marx and other social theorists like Max Weber. Contemporary Critical Theory also owes much to the work of a number of writers in the Frankfurt School tradition. While potentially a great many writers and thinkers could be included in this chapter, other than Marx arguably the Italian communist Antonio Gramsci and the German social theorist Jürgen Habermas have had most impact on the development of Critical Theory as applied in IR. These terms and why Critical Theory is not the same as Marxism/neo-Marxism will be explained in the course of this chapter.

In a sense this chapter could be considered the second half of the previous chapter; both start with Marx, but we have chosen to make the distinction, explained in the previous chapter, between neo-Marxism (Chapter 8) and 'Marx-influenced' theory covered here and in Chapter 10. The differences between these chapters also marks an important boundary between 'old' IR (based on the inter-paradigm debate) and 'new' IR (influenced by an increasing range of other social theories). This chapter begins to tell the story of how International Relations changed, and in what ways, over the last quarter of a century.

One criticism of parsimonious (that is, simple, bare) Realism, optimistic Liberalism or deterministic Marxism was that they omitted too much in coming to neat analyses of the world; in doing so they offered little insight or use beyond a certain limited point. If this allowed clarity in essay writing it led others to the conclusion that these theories were really saying very little of import. It might be argued that Critical Theory and those theories described in the next two chapters took International Relations into more complicated waters. At the same time, however, they have provided insights which many will find indispensable in understanding world politics. Furthermore, they go beyond an interest in explanation and understanding, hoping to cause reflection in the individual and change in the world around them.

### Box 9.1 Robert W. Cox (1926– )

In a lifetime spanning the dates of the Russian Revolution to the fall of the Berlin Wall it is perhaps appropriate that Cox argued against the idea of universal truths, however well-intentioned. A Canadian scholar of International Relations, his work provides an effective critique of the previous theory chapters. If you remember one thing from this chapter it ought to be his words that 'theory is always for someone and some purpose'.

In each of the theory chapters so far this note has appeared encouraging you to regard all theories as *potentially* adding insight, rather than being correct. It has gone on to add that authors are very good at being selective with evidence. *Within* a theory, however, adherents do often believe that the theory is correct and of universal relevance; this is true of Realism, Liberalism and Marxism. **Critical Theory** is attempting to dismantle much of what the theories covered so far hold to be self-evident, rather than assembling evidence to support a universal vision; whatever you think about the theories studied so far it would be advisable, therefore, to bear this fact in mind, reflect, and be prepared either to change your views or to work out how to defend the theory you currently find most convincing.

## Context

In contemporary IR the dominance of Realism is well and truly over. In the resulting confusion, the term 'Critical' has been applied to more or less any theory inspired by the social theory invasion described above. However, this chapter deals specifically with Critical Theory as a school of thought which has its intellectual roots in Marxism. Others such as post-structuralism, feminism, green theory or postmodernism are covered in Chapter 10.

Critical Theory in IR is, above all, an urging for us to be reflective about our everyday practices and the relationship between our 'theories' and the way that we act. This means a focus on such things as the role of ideas, culture and communication. It also means thinking about intersubjective negotiation and dialogue, which we will come to. For now it is enough to note that Critical Theory is about acknowledging an intimate connection between theories or ideas and actual social practices. So in Marx's time Liberal ideology legitimised economic and social relationships and practices that were inherently exploitative. The difference between the rhetoric of the dominant Liberal ideology and the lived experience of the working classes (and Marx's ideas on these) provides a starting point for looking at the origins of Critical Theories in IR.

### Marx

As a young man, Marx was particularly interested in how capitalist society affected the human person or subject, and particularly with problems of human alienation. He believed that people were, by nature, social beings and so needed to live in social groups. Humans were also creative beings, in the sense that human beings made and used tools which, in turn, helped them to create things. In a very real sense, human beings created their own social world. Yet, in capitalist societies human beings seemed to experience a sense of disaffection and remoteness from society, because of how it and its methods of production were organised. Marx's theory of human alienation thus suggested that disaffection and a sense of remoteness lay in the particular form of social organisation which existed under capitalism. It also implied that a major purpose of theory was to understand how human beings could overcome such conditions and, in so doing, achieve emancipation.

In capitalist society, the products of human labour – commodities – were no longer produced to satisfy human needs, but were produced in order to be sold on the market at a profit. The profit was kept by the factory owner, who accumulated wealth in this way. Human labour was no longer viewed as something physically and socially necessary for the survival and welfare of the community, but rather as an 'input' into the production process. Under capitalism people no longer owned the means of production, nor the product of their own labour. Rather, labour was expropriated – taken – by capitalists, who owned the means of production, paid wages and so claimed ownership of what was produced.

For this reason, society was not experienced as beneficial and necessary to most human beings, but as hierarchical and oppressive. The class system was deeply exploitative, allowing some people to benefit by taking advantage of others. Marx argued that not only did capitalists own the means of production, but they were also able to rule through the force of ideas or ideology. Marx believed that this was the reason why society/life were so awful for the vast majority of people. Human beings had lost their sense of themselves as inherently cooperative beings and experienced a sense of estrangement from others and ultimately themselves.

It seemed to Marx that Liberalism did not in any way represent a 'truth' about human nature and society, but merely reflected the point of view of the dominant class. Even so, Liberalism *had* established itself as a dominant understanding or explanation of the world – a kind of 'common sense' – which in itself was an important factor in consolidating support for the capitalist system. If this is the starting point, or inspiration, for Critical Theory, then clearly its concern with inequality and exploitation are shared by more 'orthodox' Marxists. But whereas the neo-Marxists of Chapter 8 were concentrating on the structures or mechanics of capitalism, post-Marxist Critical Theorists wanted to emphasise much more the importance of culture and ideology in perpetuating certain forms of social relationships – and, conversely, challenging them.

Another highly significant difference between these Marxist inspired approaches is that orthodox Marxist thought holds that society can be understood scientifically. Actual processes of exploitation and expropriation in capitalism are said to be observable and major inequalities in the distribution of wealth and income which emerge in consequence can be measured objectively. Furthermore, changes in economic organisation determine changes in the organisation of societies. Accordingly it is possible to understand the dynamic that drives historical change and to make predictions about what future social and economic order will emerge out of the ashes of the old one; so according to orthodox Marxism and neo-Marxism, some versions of 'the truth' are therefore better than others, because they are better able to grasp the exploitative nature of capitalism and the forces at work that will eventually lead to its collapse.

Critical Theorists, on the other hand, are not claiming scientific authenticity and do not hold such a rigid or deterministic view of the relationship between the economic and social systems, nor of the dynamic of historical change. In fact they suggest that *all* knowledge is ideological; intimately connected with social practice and the pursuit of interests, all theory is for someone and some purpose. Related to this is the argument that all theories about the world are so intimately connected with the practices which they support and perpetuate that it is meaningless to see theory and practice as distinctive realms of human activity; in a sense there is a feedback loop between our ideas about reality and the way we act in that context, which are inextricably linked.

## The Frankfurt School

In the twentieth century the so-called 'Frankfurt School' (see Box 9.2) continued to develop Marx's analysis of capitalism as a social and economic system with profound implications for what it meant to be human. Frankfurt School scholars combined Marx's interest in capitalism with processes of rationalisation characteristic of the modern world. The term 'modern' in this usage refers to interrelated historical developments such as the secularisation of the political authority in the form of the state, and the development of industrial capitalism. As Marx had observed, modern societies were characterised by a complex division of labour and a high degree of social differentiation; as opposed to traditional societies, people supposedly achieved their social status, and were increasingly identified, in terms of their occupation. People also increasingly saw themselves as individuals rather than, say, members of a particular family, community or religious group. Modernity not only changed the way in which people lived, but also the way in which people thought about themselves and their lives. The modern world was one in which people believed in progress – history was moving forward and they were 'going' somewhere.

## Box 9.2 The Frankfurt School

Critical Theory approaches to IR cover a wide spectrum of approaches all of which have in common a debt to the writings of the younger Marx and to the Frankfurt School, that is the Institute of Social Research at Frankfurt University established in 1923 and reconstituted in exile from Nazism in New York as the New School for Social Research after 1934. Critical Theory draws first of all on an epistemological critique – a vision of critical knowledge which is built from Marx's Eleventh Thesis on Feuerbach – philosophers have only sought to interpret the world [but] the point is to change it. That question, of how critical knowledge effectively understood could contribute directly to radical change, is at the heart of all critical theory in IR (and much postmodernism too). Critical theory in IPE and IR has also helped to create critical security studies, peace studies and provided a basis for much feminist work in the field.

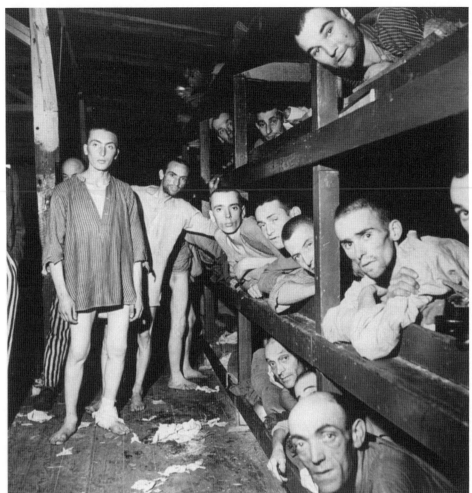

*Source: Getty Images/Time*

**Catastrophic events such as the Holocaust prompted many thinkers to evaluate modernity's basic premise that humanity was 'going forward'.**

It is not surprising to find that the first half of the twentieth century also produced a prodigious legacy of social and political thought, much of which was universalist, secular and anti-authoritarian, seeing the major sources of social evils in prejudice and intolerance. Enlightenment thinkers concentrated on the possibilities inherent in throwing off the dictates of custom and tradition, and organising society in a more rational way, in the interests of human progress and emancipation. In this respect Marxism is very much a modern discourse. Indeed, Frankfurt School thinkers recognised that modernity and the Enlightenment (see Box 9.3) represented a major step forward in the development of the human race, because for the first time people were able to imagine the possibility of change and progress and so, potentially, gain some control over their destinies. However, Frankfurt scholars also saw a 'dark side' of modernity (epitomised in the bureaucratisation/industrial process involved in the extermination of the Jews and other groups by the Nazis) and developed an

**Box 9.3 The Enlightenment**

The Enlightenment was a period in European history (more or less the eighteenth century) in which a scepticism towards traditional authority emerged in religion and politics and where a respect for reason became both the guiding principle and defining property of the human condition.

analysis of how the growth of large-scale economic and commercial enterprises, combined with the increasing reliance upon and deference towards scientific knowledge and technical expertise, was creating a situation in which a sort of instrumental 'means–ends' rationality dominated more and more areas of life.

In classical political thought, politics as an activity was seen to be directed towards realising the conditions in which it was possible to live the good life (meaning in this context, a life guided by principles of morality and justice, rather than in the material sense of a 'good standard of living'). However, in most modern societies politics had been reduced to managerialism and finding technical solutions to a range of human problems, rather than examining the root causes of those same problems. Similarly, human knowledge was not seen as something that should be used to advance the position of human beings generally, but as an instrument of control. In their everyday working lives, busy people were preoccupied with the task in hand, and spent little time reflecting on the ultimate purpose of life, or path to human happiness and satisfaction. In society at large, capitalism manufactured a desire for consumer goods, which meant that people were encouraged to buy into consumerism and seek fulfilment through the ownership of *things*. In such circumstances, the capacity of people to think critically and reflectively was eroded.

As we saw in Chapter 8, Marx believed that eventually capitalism would reach a major crisis and collapse. He also believed that the social conditions were emerging which would enable workers to develop a consciousness of their exploitation and, through the process of revolution, take control of their destiny. However, Frankfurt scholars began writing in the light of one major crisis of capitalism – the worldwide depression of the 1930s. In the 1930s, in some countries, rather than rallying to the socialist cause the working class had lent their support to right-wing populist, even fascist, movements. In addition, even where socialism *had* triumphed – in the Soviet Union, for example – it had proved to be a travesty of what Marx had envisaged. Rather than realising the conditions for the emancipation of working people, Stalinism was characterised by widespread repression.

Frankfurt School thinkers were forced to confront these unpleasant realities and to try to explain why working people had failed to revolt against capitalism. In trying to explain the continuation of capitalism despite crisis, they turned to the crucial role played by the education system and the mass media in consolidating support for capitalism, as well as organisations like the police that were used to put down strikes forcibly or other open displays of revolt against authority and private property. In this way, Critical Theorists came to understand that, while the economic organisation of society was important, other social institutions played a vital role in supporting capitalism. Through the education system and the mass media, for example, people were indoctrinated into accepting 'received truths' about the world which prevented them from understanding the true nature of the exploitation they suffered.

Frankfurt scholars also noted that changes associated with developments of the capitalist economy in the twentieth century had brought about schisms among workers – for example, a gulf between the regularly employed, casual labour and the unemployed. The introduction of labour-saving technologies produced mass unemployment in the 1930s, and the lives of the employed were better than those of the unemployed. The unemployed had very little to lose and so were more likely to take risks. However, these groups lacked organisation and consciousness. Class consciousness also diminished as tasks and knowledge became more and more fragmented, because people began to see themselves more in terms of their specialist role or job, rather than as simply 'workers'. Disillusioned with the lack of revolutionary potential in the working class, many Frankfurt School thinkers began to look for other sources of resistance and other possible agents of wide-scale social change.

## Contemporary Critical Theory and IR

The express purpose of Critical Theory in IR is to further the self-understanding of groups committed to transforming society. They believe that social theory (which includes IR) should be concerned with understanding the activity of the thinking person, and moments of reflection and self-understanding. Critical Theorists have, therefore, reminded scholars that understanding and explaining the international/global domain does not only simply involve identifying the structures and processes which will be the object of study, but also reflects critically upon what can be said to constitute knowledge of the world, and what our knowledge is for. Crucially, as a whole, Critical Theorists have recognised that forms of domination or oppression in capitalist societies go beyond 'class'. Accordingly, work in the 'critical' arena raises other important issues such as nationality, ethnic origin, race and gender in analysing multiple sources of oppression.

For example, in the post-Second World War period there was an explosion of nationalist discontent across areas of the world previously subjected to colonial rule. Later in the 1960s and 1970s, in the wake of a new wave of political radicalism sweeping across the Western world, a number of social movements emerged which organised themselves around everything from ecological issues, racism, human rights violations, civil liberties, sexuality and gender discrimination. Contemporary Critical Theorists similarly look beyond the industrial working class to such forces which frequently take the form of 'new' or 'critical' social movements and which engage in struggles to resist global capitalism and are potential agents of social change.

So as critical thinkers have become more circumspect about the possibility of progressive working class revolution they have become much more sensitive to the multiple oppressions inherent in capitalism. From a critical perspective, capitalism is transforming the world radically, but in the process it is generating major forms of inequality based on class, race, culture, ecology and gender. Capitalist enterprises are devouring more and more of the world's precious resources in order to promote mindless consumerism in the name of

### Box 9.4 Antonio Gramsci [1891–1937]

Gramsci's work on **hegemony** has been very important in critical International Relations theory, particularly in relation to the study of world order and institutions. Gramsci highlighted the central importance of ideology in maintaining class rule and in bringing about social change. Gramsci argued that ruling groups were able to legitimise their rule by persuading people that it was just and fair. He insisted that, in order to bring about change, it was necessary to not only win the battle 'on the ground', but also in the realm of ideas.

Counter-hegemony involved, therefore, not only social and political struggle against capitalism, but also the development of an alternative set of values and, crucially, an alternative set of concepts in order to think about and describe the current social 'reality' and possible alternatives. The application of some of Gramsci's ideas is described below in the section on key concepts, and, along with the neo-Gramscian application of his ideas, here is a theorist you are very likely to want to engage more with.

'freedom of choice'. Moreover, the search for markets is destroying traditional societies and the way of life of many of the world's peoples.

However, while this more nuanced analysis of the global impact of capitalism might have more explanatory power in looking at contemporary world politics, once the analysis of capitalism moves away from a central concern with class, what happens to the project of human emancipation? How can Critical Theorists develop a conception of a fair and just society, if it is no longer a question of getting rid of inequalities rooted in social class? Who will be the agents of radical change? Moreover, what does it mean to be 'emancipated'? We begin the process of answering these questions by looking at the ideas of a theorist who has been particularly useful in answering these difficult questions, the German Jürgen Habermas. Before that you might want to look at the ideas of Antonio Gramsci (see Box 9.4) who has been a significant influence on contemporary IR.

### Jürgen Habermas [1929– ]

Habermas (both linked to and critical of the Frankfurt School) has become an influential figure in critical thought because he seems to have an answer to many difficult questions. IR scholars have drawn upon some of his key concepts and ideas in developing a critical International Relations theory and in opening up a new research agenda within IR. Habermas provides an effective critique of approaches (for example, Realism and Liberalism) which generate knowledge in the service of social control (that is, tend to reinforce the status quo/existing power relations). Critical Theorists believe that knowledge about the social world should be sought in the interests of furthering human emancipation.

In one crucial respect Habermas's work represents a major departure from Marxist analysis. Although Marx was correct in stressing the inherently social nature of human beings, he limited himself to analysing the particular kinds of social organisation. He failed to pay adequate attention to the central importance of communication in shaping consciousness and developing understanding of one's self and one's relationship to others. The sociability of human beings is, of course, expressed through language. Habermas has argued that the role of language and communication had been neglected in critical thought. According to Habermas, communication – the use of language and the manipulation of symbols – allows a sort of collective learning process to take place. Through language and communication, human beings construct intersubjective knowledge about the world.

This emphasis on the importance of communication and human understanding led Habermas to advocate a process of open dialogue and democracy in the interests of furthering human emancipation. Habermas was a very modern thinker in the sense that he valued the modern achievement of being able to criticise, challenge and question authority, and existing duties and obligations. Habermas believed, however, that such criticism was only a prelude to developing a better understanding of what it meant to live in a moral society in which people were treated justly. He argued that the formation of self-understanding, self-identity and moral judgements concerning justice were intimately linked; we became aware of our own self and our own needs and desires by entering into dialogue with others and becoming aware of the needs, interests and desires of others. Habermas also moved away from orthodox Marxist thinking by arguing that social movements promoting feminism or green issues or indigenous peoples also resisted the extension of 'technical' or 'means–ends' rationality into all spheres of social life, promoted alternative values, and so could contribute to an emancipatory politics. However, this emancipatory politics was no longer rooted in the notion of labour free from alienation. Emancipation was about extending the realm of moral understanding and justice in human life. Habermas was committed to the democratic process because it fostered dialogue and this was necessary in order to further develop our moral codes and thinking about justice.

Of course, a process of genuinely open dialogue is difficult to achieve in a divided society where people have different – even opposing – interests. Habermas recognised this problem but insisted that it was, nevertheless, an ideal to be striven for. For this reason, much of his early work was concerned with the conditions under which it was possible to create an 'ideal speech situation'. In an ideal speech situation, all people would be able to participate in open dialogue – black or white, rich or poor, Christian or Muslim, male or female. In such a situation, people might be encouraged to consider the perspective of the 'other', rather than their own selfish interest alone.

## Key concepts

As Critical Theory is orientated towards the project of human emancipation, it follows that when Critical Theorists engage in the process of thinking about the forms of political, social and economic organisation that exist in the world, they are explicitly seeking to answer the question: how far do existing arrangements constrain or facilitate the project of human emancipation? In relation to the current 'world order', key questions for Critical

Theorists are: What is the state? Why did the state become the dominant form of political organisation globally? What kind of world order might there be in the future? What tendencies can we see in the existing order that point the way to future changes? Below we look at how Critical Theory has been applied to ideas with which you will be somewhat familiar. It is hoped in so doing that the foregoing might begin to appear more real or relevant. While the emancipatory aims of Critical Theory are clear, it is questioning a whole series of concepts used by traditional scholars of IR; the discussion that follows seeks to allow you to engage with such critique.

## The state

The state performs a number of vital roles for a capitalist economy, including the provision of a system of law to regulate contracts between individuals and companies, and a police force to ensure that society remains orderly. Orthodox Marxists hold that the state mediates (and therefore controls) conflict resulting from class struggle. In this way, the state legitimises and ensures continuing class rule. The state also maintains conditions conducive to economic growth. There are important differences between Critical Theory and orthodox Marxist views of the nature and role of the state. Critical Theorists pay much closer attention to the role of ideology in maintaining the rule of dominant groups.

## Hegemony

The concept of hegemony expresses the idea that dominant groups establish and legitimise their rule through the realm of culture and ideas. Hegemony rests on a broad measure of consent; nevertheless, it functions according to basic principles that ensure the continuing supremacy of leading social classes, within the state. The stronger the ruling group the less need it has to use force. Hegemony is the outcome of class struggle and serves to legitimise capitalist rule. Gramscians, following the Italian Marxist, Antonio Gramsci, use the term 'hegemonic project' to refer to the way in which classes present their particular interests as the interests of all people and, in this way, are able to maintain their power. Free trade and economic growth are often presented in this way for instance, although they tend to focus benefits and increase inequality, not to mention their negative impacts on the environment.

The degree to which counter-hegemonic groups achieve influence in this context varies over time. In the current period, the globalisation of capital has undermined the autonomy of the state and its ability to meet the demands of its citizens for economic and social welfare. The so-called 'rolling back of the state', which has been a phenomenon across the industrialised world during global restructuring, must be seen as a means of insulating economic policy from popular pressures, specifically from the demands of poor groups. At the same time, trade unions have been weakened and the position of capital in the production process significantly strengthened. Thus, in the contemporary world order capitalism is fairly securely embedded. Moreover, neo-Liberalism serves as a powerful ideology in furthering the hegemonic project of dominant states and social forces.

## Box 9.5  Can capitalism be dismantled?

The discussion of hegemony suggests that 'capitalism is fairly securely embedded'. As if to illustrate this, it is significant that when interlocking crises hit the global economy from 2008, very few commentators – beyond those who were already critiquing it – questioned the capitalist framework itself in looking for solutions. In other words, alternative frameworks were not explored, just ways of maintaining the system. Few asked if capitalism could be safely dismantled? Nor if it is more likely to collapse now? What might be the consequences of either possibility?

However, we can also identify 'counter-hegemonic' tendencies and social forces that struggle to achieve new ways of living. Examples include the Green movement and radical forms of feminism (see Chapter 10 and later chapters on environment and gender); both seek to reconstitute human societies and human relationships on the basis of radically different social and political values. Recent global crises have given a certain fresh impetus to those demanding a Green new deal, for instance, if not yet widespread support – given the vested interests lined up in opposition.

*Source: Detroitderek Photography*

**Disused auto plant, Detroit. Manufacturing throughout the western world is in steep decline. Is it still safe to assume that capitalism is safely embedded?**

## Power

For Critical Theorists it follows that power cannot be understood solely in terms of the military and/or economic might of the state. Clearly, power is exercised directly by states in some situations. In making the world safe for capitalism, the USA has intervened in conflicts all over the world in order to try to influence the outcome in ways which favour global capitalism. However, power is also exercised through a range of other social institutions, and works to support a particular kind of social order. The state supports a capitalist order and, in so doing, supports particular kinds of power relations that exist among social groups – the power of business and commerce over workers, the power of multinational corporations over local communities dependent upon the employment it generates, and the power of currency speculators, investors and traders in basic commodities to shape the global economy and the distribution of wealth throughout the world.

Power is also exercised more insidiously through the spread of certain ideas and beliefs in society which work to legitimise the existing order.

## Institutions

In an IR context, Critical Theory has made a major contribution to our understanding of world order and institutions. How, for instance, does it help us to understand the role of international institutions such as the International Monetary Fund and the World Bank? In the post-Second World War period the state has become 'internationalised' in the sense that it has become the dominant form of political organisation across the world. The state has become internationalised in a second sense; its traditional regulatory functions are now performed by different states and organisations. If we think about the state in terms of what it does, the control and regulation of capitalism, rather than as an entity or 'actor', we see that these functions are now dispersed among different states in the world and among a range of international institutions and regimes.

The Gramscian notion of transnational class alliances and hegemonic domination has been successfully applied to conceptions of world order. Critical Theorists adapted this idea to suggest that the dominant state in the world creates order on the basis of ideology. For example, the Bretton Woods System (BWS – see Chapters 7 and 16), would not have been possible without the support of a hegemonic state: the USA. The USA played a number of crucial roles in establishing the BWS and making it work effectively. Perhaps most important, the USA provided vital ideological support for the New World Order, arguing that free trade and monetary stability would allow freedom and democracy to flourish throughout the world.

However slowly, world orders do change and alternative political, economic and social arrangements can and do emerge. Critical Theorists are concerned with the nature of such change and the ways in which social forces and social structures enter periods of transition. The existing order is not 'fixed', because social structures comprise institutions and the prevailing socio-economic form of organisation and ideas. Although social action is constrained by structures, these can be transformed by collective action involving leading or subordinate groups in society. Counter-hegemonic forces, of a transnational nature, are challenging prevailing institutional and political arrangements. Intellectuals also have a role to play in generating change by developing a 'counter-hegemonic' set of concepts and concerns to deal with the problems of militarism, and economic and social inequalities.

In some respects, the expansion of the state system can be viewed as a positive development, because it extends the principles of self-determination and citizenship to more and more of the world's peoples. However, at the same time, the nation state embodies something of a moral contradiction, because it is at once both an inclusionary and exclusionary form of political community. The nation state is inclusionary, because it is founded on the idea that all citizens are equal. There are certain rights which flow from citizenship and these should be enjoyed by every member of the community. All citizens are, therefore, of equal moral worth. However, the nation state is by its very nature exclusionary. It discriminates against 'foreigners' on the grounds that they are different; the differences between 'insiders' and 'outsiders' are held to be morally relevant.

## Community and identity

The bounded community of the nation state excludes people whose 'difference' is deemed to threaten the state's distinctive identity. International law sets out just what obligations states owe to non-citizens temporarily residing within the boundaries of the state, including their protection from harm; in certain cases states might extend temporary rights of asylum to foreigners who fear persecution in their homeland. Nevertheless, while the state has a certain obligation to 'foreigners', these are clearly not the same as or equal to the obligations owed to 'nationals'. Moreover, the boundaries of national communities are constantly being policed to ensure against 'invasion' from outsiders – so much so that we regard 'foreigners' as a threat to the extent that we can even debate the morality of the use of nuclear weapons to deter outsiders from encroaching on our 'space'. The emancipatory project at the heart of Critical Theory necessarily raises questions about the limits of political community, how boundaries between self and other are constructed and the moral implications of doing so.

Critical Theorists are interested in how the boundaries of community change over time. So, historically, certain groups have been denied citizenship on the grounds that they are 'different' – less rational and not up to the demands of active participation in society. Women, for example, were held to be in need of strong moral guidance from their menfolk. Of course, women have made great strides in overcoming such prejudices and now enjoy rights of citizenship in most states around the world. Since the UN was established in 1945, there has been a gradual development of human rights law which recognises the equal moral worth of every human being. The widespread commitment to respect human rights seems to suggest that there exists among humankind a moral conviction that all individuals belong not only to sovereign states, but to a more inclusive community of humankind – even if, in practice, this has been denied to some groups and many people. Arguably, we might now be witnessing the eclipse of the sovereign state system in favour of more cosmopolitan forms of identity and community; given the increasingly globalised nature of social relations, expressions of loyalty and solidarity can be both sub-state and transnational. Social movements give expression to, or reflect, plural forms of identity, loyalty and solidarity.

## Justice and equality

While there are variations and nuances within different strands of Critical Theory, all share a fundamental commitment to human equality. In contemporary Critical Theory other forms of inequality and discrimination, such as sexism and racism, and the denial of human rights to some groups, are also recognised as highly significant. However, once the multiple sources of oppression are recognised, it raises the question of how a more equal and just world might be realised. Critical Theorists are sceptical of Liberal schemes because these grant formal equality to people and at the same time endorse a social and economic order that generates great inequalities in wealth and power. However, they also recognise that, while experiments in state socialism have been partially successful in creating a more equal society, this has often been at the cost of widespread oppression and tyranny. The great challenge for Critical Theorists is to realise an emancipatory politics, which is socially inclusive and democratic. The difficult question is whether in a world divided along lines of nationality, ethnicity, religion, culture, class, sexuality and gender such a project can be realised.

There have been a number of responses. One has been to draw upon Habermas' notion of dialogic politics, which appears to meet the needs of a world in which the nation state remains significant, but which is no longer the only site in which debates about equality and justice are taking place, and a time when Liberal and/or Western visions of equality and justice have been subject to criticism. It is recognised that it might not always be possible to reach agreement, especially in situations where societies have radically different forms of government and cultural preferences. Dialogue does not necessarily have to reach consensus of course and might simply reflect the heterogeneous quality of international society. However, the commitment to dialogue requires efforts to build wider communication channels. The universal communication community may be unobtainable, but it remains the ultimate standard of social criticism to which we should aspire.

From this perspective, human conflict is not rooted in the problem of anarchy per se, but in the nature of global capitalism. The Gramscian variant of Critical Theory accepts, with some qualifications and modifications, the more orthodox Marxist view that major wars this century have been caused by the search for raw materials and resources, and the forcible opening up of large areas of the world to capitalist expansion. On the other hand, many struggles for 'national' liberation have come about in response to forms of colonial or imperialist domination. Capitalism, by its very nature, generates conflict and violence. A second variant of Critical Theory influenced by Habermas has taken the notion of intersubjectivity, dialogue and negotiation as a starting point for understanding how peaceful change can be promoted.

A key concern of Critical Theory has been how to develop institutions and fora in international politics that facilitate negotiation, so that conflicts are settled by consensus rather than power – although Critical Theorists differ from, say, neo-Liberals as to how this might be achieved. We might argue that the 'next stage' in the development of IR was, in part, inspired by a desire to escape from Realist/neo-Realist despair and to challenge the idea that international politics would always be dominated by the pursuit of power and the instrumental and/or strategic interests of states.

## Conclusions

Critical Theory is centrally concerned with possibilities of human emancipation from oppressive forms of social relationships. However, this is a far from inevitable process and Critical Theorists acknowledge both the problems and possibilities of the existing system which places important constraints on the degree of change which can be generated by oppositional social groups and through the political process. Critical Theorists view society and the state as having a certain degree of autonomy, reflecting the complex configuration of forces at work in society. Critical Theorists believe that, while capitalism is an exploitative and oppressive system, it does generate certain opportunities for social change that oppositional groups can use to their advantage. So, for example, while critical of the Liberal ideology of so-called individual freedom and choice, Critical Theorists nevertheless see some value in working for change through the democratic process, and certainly in democratic values and practices more broadly defined.

Complex ideas and difficult terminology have been unavoidable in this chapter, and many potential arguments have been abridged or omitted, but we hope the foregoing provides enough clues to help you see why this approach is a different, but potentially exciting, offering compared to the theories described in the previous three chapters. The case study seeks to distil some key elements of Critical Theory; if this is all clear you will almost certainly want to investigate more closely the literature of Ashley, Rupert, Gill and Law, Linklater, Cox and others (see Bibliography). If this is not yet clear, as this book demonstrates, IR is not just theory and your success does not depend entirely on you grasping Habermas or Gramsci. That said, to be somewhat aware of these debates is likely to be important.

In conclusion, to Critical Theorists, the world should be understood primarily in terms of the major economic and social forces generated by capitalism, which are now international or global in scope. States and institutions should be understood primarily in terms of the functions they perform in supporting global capitalism. While a 'real' world exists, our understanding of the world is always mediated though ideas, concepts

## Case study: Critical Theory in a nutshell

Critical Theory was not developed in International Relations but became influential in IR from the 1980s onwards. Like neo-Marxism, Critical Theory is influenced by Marxism, though more by the early 'humanistic' Marx, in contrast to neo-Marxism which takes more inspiration from later 'economistic' and 'scientific' Marxism. Critical Theorists see an intimate relationship between theory and practice. Critical Theorists hold that knowledge is ideology, not truth, although some believe that it is possible to negotiate or agree upon propositions. As well as roots in Marx, Critical Theory has also evolved from the ideas of the Frankfurt School (particularly Jürgen Habermas) and Italian Marxist Antonio Gramsci. Critical Theory is very much a 'modern' project, because it aims to further human emancipation. However, Critical Theory acknowledges and seeks to overcome the 'dark side of modernity'. Many Critical Theorists recognise that class-based oppression is not the only form inherent in capitalist societies. Other oppressions include those on the basis of ethnicity, gender, culture/religion, nationality, sexuality and so on. Contemporary Gramscians see 'counter-hegemonic' forces (struggles to resist global

capitalism) in terms of new social movements (women and environmental for example) and look beyond the industrial working class as potential agents of social change. Habermas similarly believes that social movements are a radical force in international politics because they ascribe to value systems and advocate ways of living that challenge dominant (capitalist) forms of economic and social organisation. Critical Theory makes us aware of the historically contingent nature of certain features of human life and reminds us, therefore, that international relations are not fixed or immutable. Critical Theory makes claims in the name of all of humankind – it is universalistic. For this reason, it questions forms of exclusion or discrimination which make distinctions between different groups of people. This necessarily raises questions about how we define ourselves, and how we distinguish ourselves from others, leading to consideration of how boundaries between communities are drawn and the consequences of this.

 **Is Critical Theory's universalism sustainable?**

and theories which are a product of critical thought and reflection. All knowledge is ideological – it is a reflection of the values, ideas and, crucially, interests of particular social groups. Culture and ideology are, in themselves, an important and powerful force working to support or challenge the existing economic and social order. International relations (or politics) constitute a struggle between a variety of social groups and movements – or social forces – some of whom have an interest in supporting the status quo, while others struggle to change it. Through political action human beings can challenge existing structures and achieve freer forms of human existence. Theory should be directed towards uncovering impediments to change and identifying the emancipatory potential of certain social groups and forces. Knowledge should be directed towards the project of human emancipation/freedom.

Whether you are convinced or not by Critical Theory it is the universalistic aspirations of Critical Theory which have been most challenged by a whole range of what this book terms alternative theories. For example, postmodernists argue that it is impossible to establish what *is* morally right or just, even through the process of intersubjective dialogue, because there is no agreement about these issues across cultures. The most likely result of a (critical) project of this kind would, then, be a profoundly Western, middle-class and gendered conception of a 'good society', masquerading as a 'universal' point of view. It is to such alternative views that we turn presently.

## Resource section

## Questions

1. Does Critical Theory clarify or confuse the study of International Relations?

2. If you believe Critical Theory clarifies, what are its major contributions to understanding?

3. If you believe Critical Theory confuses our study, to what extent is this because theories have previously been open to the accusation of over-simplification?

## Recommended reading

Ashley, R.K. (1981) 'Political Realism and Human Interests', *International Studies Quarterly*, 25 (2): 204–36
A very early and still influential article on the need to develop a Critical Theory of IR.

Cox, R.W. (1986) 'Social forces, states and world order', *Millennium: Journal of International Studies*, 10, 2: 126–55; reprinted as 'Social forces, states and world orders: beyond international relations theory' in R. Keohane (ed.), *Neorealism and its Critics* (New York: Columbia University Press, pp. 204–54)
Another influential piece within the Critical IR literature, particularly useful in setting out the distinction between problem solving and Critical Theory.

Gramsci, A. (1971) *Selections from Prison Notebooks* (London: Lawrence and Wishart)
His key ideas in a chunky volume.

Habermas, J. (1972) *Knowledge and Human Interests* (London: Heinemann)

Hoffman, M. (1988) 'Conversations on critical international relations theory', *Millennium: Journal of International Studies*, 17 (1): 91–5
Along with Rengger (below) an important article in taking the debate about Critical Theory and IR forward.

Kracauer, S. (1947) *From Caligari to Hitler* (Princeton, NJ: Princeton University Press)
A major influence on how people relate films to history and society

Linklater, A. (1988) *The Transformation of Political Community* (Oxford: Polity Press)
An important work that applies Habermas' Critical Theory to IR.

Rengger, N.J. (1988) 'Going critical? A response to Hoffman', *Millennium: Journal of International Studies*, 17 (2): 81–9
A cautious response to Hoffman (above) that alerts us to some of the problems in using Critical Theory in an international/global context, inherent in its universalist claims.

Rupert, M. (1995) *Producing Hegemony* (Cambridge: Cambridge University Press)
Dealing with the politics of mass production and American global power in the twentieth century.

# Chapter 10
# Alternative Approaches

Theoretical context

Postmodernism

Feminism

Green Theory

Conclusions

After reading this chapter you will be able to:

- Understand what terms like postmodernism, feminism and ecological theory mean in the context of IR

- Explain the differences between the above terms as well as why, how and if they overlap

- Critique earlier chapters and read the next one in context. (We should also note that although feminism and Green Theory are dealt with briefly here as theoretical approaches in the discipline of International Relations, the material they deal with and its incorporation in world politics is covered in more detail in later chapters)

## Introductory box: Alternative theories

The word 'alternative' often indicates something peripheral or marginal
(a lesser alternative). On the other hand, in popular culture, the word is often
equated with something 'cool' or 'cult'. In this chapter, it is probably best to
think of 'alternative' in the sense of music or fashion. In these cases, adding the
description alternative does not necessarily imply lower quality; and whatever
is today's alternative may well become tomorrow's classic song or design.
That is not to say you should regard these theories as automatically superior
either; simply to note that their marginal position in this chapter says everything
about the development of the discipline of International Relations and not
necessarily anything about how useful or appealing you will find them. We deal
with them briefly here also because the extremely abstract nature of some of
this literature, combined with our specific focus of providing an accessible text,
make it sensible to offer only the broadest outline and key points. Saying that,
this chapter gives students interested in alternative approaches the tools to
engage in further study on the topic.

Notwithstanding the Introductory box, all the approaches covered here actually have a
good case for being regarded much more centrally. Feminists could quite rightly regard our
approach as appalling tokenism; taking issues which directly affect half the population and
indirectly the other half and reducing them to 'oh and another thing . . .'. Similarly, Greens
could suggest that issues of environment must become central to our endeavours unless the
planetary future is to be very bleak. And postmodernists could easily argue that their more
tentative approach to knowledge could set humanity on a different path; not wrong simply
because it is not easily grasped.

Realists assume a world where human nature and/or the structure of international
politics create conflict; they then find a world of never-ending, cyclical violence. Liberals
assume a world where the self-interested actions of individuals are leading to global
prosperity; what they find is a world of progress. In many aspects of life what we see,
and how we act, depends fundamentally on the assumptions we make. What the following alternative approaches have in common is their desire to make us reflect upon our
assumptions and upon the assumptions of traditional approaches to IR. They each argue
that our current assumptions missed something fundamental in global politics and thus
lead to misleading or wrong conclusions.

## Theoretical context

This chapter seeks to give a sense of why and how these sometimes very different approaches are a part of IR. Whether we are talking about the many currents of feminism or Green Theory or postmodernism, however, there is a very long story which could be told in each case of political, social, economic and philosophical thought which has informed them. In other words, this is a brief contextualisation. In terms of the discipline of IR the preceding four chapters plot much of the path that brings us to these alternatives. For some, IR is now a more theoretically sophisticated discipline (or at least it is catching up) because it has become a much more reflective enterprise inclusive of broader trends in social theory. For others, the inclusion of approaches such as those covered in this chapter has seen IR fall into a sticky morass in which it is difficult to make any definitive statements and, therefore, impossible to argue for policy relevance. One reason for this is that these approaches have not become central to the discipline, but have been incorporated substantially at the level of critique of the way the enterprise tends to be conducted.

## Postmodernism

**Postmodernism** is sometimes used to connote a cultural change and a difference from modernism. It challenges many of the ideas central to International Relations theory. The origins of postmodernism can be seen in the late 1960s' identification with a range of disaffected groups such as student protesters, feminists, environmentalists and the gay liberationists and a rejection of a narrow focus on 'class'. Many of this 'New Left' began to argue that in their attempt to generate the impetus for widespread social change, Marxists had 'universalised' the conditions of human emancipation, at the cost of marginalising and silencing large numbers of groups and peoples. Given that postmodernists express such incredulity towards 'meta-narratives' like Marxism – that is to say, postmodernist thinkers have difficulty believing all-encompassing theories or explanations – it would be somewhat surprising to find postmodernists subscribing to a coherent, comprehensive worldview or grand vision of International Relations. Rather than sketch out a perspective on international relations, therefore, postmodernists prefer to engage in a critique of such projects and concentrate instead on what is different, unique and defies grandiose forms of theorising, in order to open up space to think 'outside the box' and from different, often marginalised angles. Postmodernist thinkers welcome the proliferation of perspectives and approaches in IR during the past two decades. Far from seeing this as a weakening or undermining of IR as a distinctive 'discipline', postmodern thinkers argue that scepticism and uncertainty, combined with a plurality of worldviews, visions and voices, is an appropriate response to a highly complex world.

This is not to say that postmodernist scholars simply reject everything as bias, perverse or a reflection of the perspective of the powerful. Postmodernists are not necessarily cynics or nihilists. They are no different from people in general, in that they have certain values and may subscribe to a particular ethical or moral code. However, postmodernists are different from, say, Liberals or Critical Theorists, because they are more willing to admit that ultimately there might not be any solid grounds, or ultimate source of appeal, on which to establish the 'rightness' or 'wrongness' of particular value systems, beliefs, or worldviews. They certainly do not claim to have an insight into the 'truth' about the human condition, or the inherent virtue or wickedness of a particular action or event. Instead, they see it as the defining nature of politics that there is a choice between various 'truths'.

A cause of confusion is as follows: Since modernity and the Enlightenment (see Chapter 7) are built on a vision of hope for the future of the human race why do postmodernists (as the name suggests) subject these ideas to such intense criticism? In part, this criticism of the Enlightenment project is a consequence of the rise of fascism in the 1930s; the experience of a modern nation submitting willingly to the Führer in the interests of the glorification of the Aryan race (and associated wartime atrocities), seemed to defy the idea of history as progress and cast doubt on the West's claims to be advanced and civilised. In more recent years, the spectre of nuclear war, environmental degradation, and widespread feelings of alienation and hopelessness, which seem to be endemic to advanced capitalist societies, have added further to the criticism of the West as a bastion of progress.

*Source: Getty Images AFP*

**The French philosopher Michel Foucault, whose works on knowledge and power had a tremendous impact on postmodernist thought.**

## Box 10.1 Michel Foucault (1926–84)

Postmodernist thinkers have drawn heavily upon the work of this French philosopher. For Foucault, the discourses in which we engage are not controlled by us. Rather, they are powerful in themselves in that they generate a particular knowledge, including the core concepts and 'common sense', within which we operate and which we accept without questioning most of the time. This means that there are no undisputed 'truths' about human 'nature' or human life. Everything that we think we 'know' for sure is tied to our particular discursive contexts. We 'know' because we believe these things to be true. We believe these things to be true because we are taught in schools, or told by scientists, technical 'experts', bureaucrats and policy-making elites. While the most powerful people in society are in a much better position to have their views accepted as 'truth', and are able to dismiss or trivialise alternative views, they do not control discourses. Rather, the meaning of whatever they say makes sense itself, only against the background of a wider discursive context. This illustrates that power does not rest with individuals but within discourses. For example, many people have a commonsensical notion of what poverty is; however, if we interrogate the term we might find that poverty is actually not so easily defined. In other words, from a Western perspective poverty often relates to the amount of money people have to spend. However, this would mean that people who sustain themselves from small holdings in terms of food but do not earn a great deal of money would still be labelled impoverished, through dominant Western discourses, despite the fact they are providing for their immediate needs. Nonsensically, someone earning $1 a day and starving in an urban slum may be considered 'richer' than someone in a solid rural dwelling with adequate food and other needs met. Such a person may well not consider themselves impoverished in a context where money is largely irrelevant. This demonstrates that dominant discourses give meaning to the term poverty (as related to financial income) without questioning the term, thereby creating a truth. For the most appropriate work by Foucault that looks at dominant discourses and the construction of truth students should turn to Foucault's, *Power/Knowledge: Selected Interviews and Other Writings 1972–1977* (edited by Colin Gordon).

Postmodern thinkers have argued that all attempts to establish the universal conditions for human freedom and emancipation will inevitably be used in practice to subordinate and marginalise those who are deemed 'different'. This is because (following Foucault see Box 10.1) power/knowledge relations are always at work in social relationships. To illustrate this point, postmodernists point to the ways in which liberal ideas about rationality, civilisation and progress have also been used historically to divide up and categorise the world's people as 'advanced' or 'backward', 'civilised' or 'barbarian' according to what were actually European (or Western) social, political and cultural values of the time. They pointed out that the Enlightenment period was actually accompanied by the widespread oppression of many peoples in the cause of spreading the benefits of civilisation.

While postmodernist thinkers therefore share some common ground with Critical Theorists in the Marxist tradition, Critical Theorists hold that through dialogue aimed at consensus we might at least arrive at 'truths' of a kind – even if they are always open to refutation. Postmodernist thinkers, on the other hand, argue that such a project will only replace one orthodoxy with another. Postmodernism therefore is *a* critical theory in the sense that it problematises and undermines supposedly self-evident truths that carry with them power and domination. However, in contrast to the Critical Theory of Chapter 9 it does not accept any secure foundations for alternative truths, including the notion of 'social classes', and therefore also rejects the project of constructing alternative world orders as guidance for political action.

All of this does not mean that postmodernists would deny that there is a reality 'out there'. Of course there are states and there are wars, there is suffering and there is hunger. The point, however, is that we do not have direct access to this reality. Like Social Constructivists who we shall come to, postmodernists argue that the social reality is discursively constructed; that states, for instance, only exist because of particular discourses tied to particular historical developments. Furthermore, however, postmodernists also contend that we can never speak about any reality objectively; reality is not directly accessible to us, and our understanding of it is always mediated and informed by particular discourses.

## Box 10.2 Jean Baudrillard (1929–2007)

One author/philosopher who questioned the accessibility of reality and who is particularly relevant to IR is Jean Baudrillard. Baudrillard controversially argued that the 1990–91 Gulf War was not a reality in his book *The Gulf War Did Not Take Place* (1995). In this Baudrillard suggests that the media presented an image of war that was, in fact, not war but a symbolic representation of war. Partly, Baudrillard's position is drawn from the idea that the media, and television in particular, creates or constructs the reality of war. Reality and unreality become confused. This meant that most people experiencing the Gulf War did so in an abstract way while watching history unfold in real time through television screens before their eyes. In addition, Baudrillard concluded that the Gulf War did not take place because there were no victors or defeated parties at the end of the conflict. Unsurprisingly, scholars have been critical of Baudrillard's position, suggesting that he insensitively underplayed the conflict and therefore the deaths of real people.

## Box 10.3 Jacques Derrida (1930–2004) and post-structuralism

The terms postmodern and post-structural are sometimes used interchangeably. However, postmodernism is centrally concerned with the nature and consequences of modernity and develops a thoroughgoing critique of the Enlightenment project. To simplify somewhat, post-structuralism is more concerned with the nature, role and function of language and how social meaning is constructed through language. Jacques Derrida is a key figure here. He argued that much philosophical thought was metaphysical. That is, it was a belief system which depended ultimately upon an appeal to an ultimate truth, or a solid foundation: for example, the idea of God or the human subject. In so far as human language is used to convey these ideas, Derrida called this single 'truth' a transcendental signifier. That is, the definitive word which gives meaning to all others; in the final analysis, metaphysical belief systems are based on a fiction, but a whole hierarchy of meaning is then constructed upon this. Derrida pointed out that many philosophers, primarily Descartes, had used the opposition between nature/culture as a basis for theory.

The notions of archaic man living in a 'state of nature' and desiring to establish 'society' were alluded to in earlier chapters. The structure of the nature/culture dichotomy repeats itself in other binary oppositions: man/woman, national/international. The first term in each opposition constitutes the privileged entity, while the secondary term is always viewed as in some way inferior. Such binary oppositions are used to draw rigid boundaries between what is acceptable and what is not, between self and non-self, truth and falsity, sense and nonsense, reason and madness, central and marginal. It is from Derrida that we get the notion of deconstruction – a critical method of reading a text to expose the ways in which meaning is constructed. One of Derrida's most important early works that investigates dichotomies and deconstruction is *Of Grammatology* (1967).

Given that terms such as transcendental signifier are not instantly transparent, it is enough to note here that there *is* quite a lot of overlap between postmodernism and post-structuralism. It is more important at this stage to grasp the general critique of power relations, dominant forms of knowledge and social practices which arise from both post-structural and postmodern insights.

From a postmodernist perspective, the study of world politics investigates the ways in which power operates in the discourses and practices of world politics; it maps the many and varied ways that political space is constructed and utilised by individuals and groups; unpacks the complex processes involved in the construction of political identities; celebrates differences and diversity among people and across cultures; and encourages a proliferation of approaches and worldviews. This has the effect of displacing or undermining 'orthodox' or hegemonic forms of knowledge and power, and highlights issues or concerns frequently dismissed as trivial or insignificant, in order to give a voice to or empower people and groups who have been marginalised in the study of IR.

## Key assumptions and summary

According to postmodernists human 'nature' is not immutable. The human subject is 'open' and malleable, a product of practices of subordination and resistance. Human values, beliefs and actions vary according to the wider social and cultural context. There are no characteristics or values with universal applicability. The behaviour/actions of people and particular values can only be understood and judged in terms of specific cultural meanings and contexts. Similarly, we cannot outline any general theory which helps us to 'make sense' of the world, or prescribe a blueprint or scheme for universal human emancipation. There are no 'facts' about the world. All we have are interpretations and interpretations of other interpretations of 'reality'.

Postmodernism is not easy. It challenges many ideas central to International Relations. Postmodernism is not simply about the period of history following modernity, but provides ways of thinking about the consequences of modern thought and practice. Despite some leftist origins, postmodernism has been accused of profound conservatism. This is because postmodernists, due to their suspicion over truth claims and reality, tend to criticise IR rather than offer suggestions as to how to improve IR in theory and practice. Its questioning attitude is just one reason why it is difficult, if not impossible, politically to categorise. Postmodernism enquires into multiple power/knowledge relationships. Postmodernists have been concerned with drawing out hidden assumptions (making visible the invisible) by a process of critique. Postmodernism does not mean a person can have no values or should believe in nothing, more that they should be tentative about the grounds for the claims they make based upon these.

## Feminism

A feminist perspective employs gender as a central category of analysis. We would say that feminists look at IR through a gendered lens (see Chapter 19). Indeed, feminists regard gender as a particular kind of power relationship. One of the key facets of this power relationship is the separation in society, of men, who tend to engage in wage work and politics, and women, who tend to engage in domestic work and childcare. This is what feminists call the public/private division or dichotomy and it is arguably this division which has meant that women have not been considered very often in relation to IR. For feminists, gender is central to our understanding of IR. As such, these scholars trace the ways in which ideas about gender are, and have been, central to the functioning of major international institutions and how gender relations might be perpetuated or transformed through policies or laws emanating from international institutions. Overall, feminist IR scholars challenge dominant assumptions about what is significant or insignificant, or what is marginal or central, in the study of IR through the adoption of gender lenses which work to revise or 're-vision' the study (and potentially the practice) of IR.

Through reading you will discover that feminist work has contributed significantly to many debates in IR by, for instance: developing critiques of IR theory; interpreting ecological degradation; suggesting alternative visions of security and community; exploring questions of ethics and human rights; broadening understandings of violence and conflict; highlighting the significance of gendered identities and subjectivities in IR; documenting the gender dimension of globalisation; and developing knowledge of the working of international institutions. Meanwhile, feminists might be labelled, for instance, critical, standpoint, radical, Marxist, post-structuralist, postmodern, liberal or eco-. Inevitably, this short section glosses over some differences and there are many different authors under each label. In short, **feminism** will *require* further investigation (see also Table 10.1).

Feminism is thus extremely varied. However, in a limited sense we *can* talk about the development of a (single) 'Feminist perspective' in IR since the term perspective can be used to describe a way of looking at the world which prioritises certain features, issues or processes. Women and gender issues were ignored or marginalised in the study of International Relations until recently. So although when we hear various facts about the status or treatment of women we may be shocked, the rationale for ignoring this was that the position of women specifically fell outside the realm of the study of International Relations, because it was not relevant to relations between *states*. However, using the lens of gender has had an impact beyond feminism (in thinking about processes of marginalisation) and the view that gender was irrelevant to IR has been effectively challenged. So feminists ask what might the world of International Relations look like if we made women's concerns central?

Feminism can point to thinkers who, while not identifying themselves in this way, make intellectual contributions which have influenced contemporary feminist thinking. Some of the earliest contributions (in the modern period) were in a Liberal tradition, holding that women and men are basically alike and that perceived gender differences are simply the effects of discrimination. The political project of liberalism is largely confined to securing for women the rights and privileges already enjoyed by men; a good early example would be the work of Mary Wollstonecraft who was passionate about education for girls in the late eighteenth century. Although not self-defined as a feminist she suggested that men and women would have the tools to be equal if they were educated in the same way. Accordingly, Wollstonecraft's work *A Vindication of the Rights of Woman* (1792) was heavily influential on the first wave of feminism at the end of the nineteenth century which sought political equality (most importantly women's right to vote).

In the nineteenth century, Marxist work influenced and contributed to feminist thought by suggesting that the emergence of capitalism as a social and economic system brought

## Box 10.4 Sexual violence and women's rights in Afghanistan

According to a report in *The Independent* newspaper published on 10 July 2009, a law has been in the processes of being passed in Afghanistan's parliament which allows Afghan husbands to starve wives who will not have sex with them. This law, which was in fact an amendment to a wider law which legalised rape, was met with outrage from the international community and feminist/women's rights groups. This law, and other women's rights abuses, are put forward under the guise of cultural and religious expectations. In this case, it is via the Shia community in Afghanistan which also allows rapists to marry their victims in order for them to be pardoned of the rape; it also allows child marriage.

These problematic cultural practices that contravene women's rights are often met with resistance in Western countries. Indeed, both American President Barack Obama and former British Prime Minister Gordon Brown publically criticised the Afghan law, urging Afghanistan to re-write the legislation. However, it may well be important to note here Britain's response to this legislation in light of the fact that the UK did not recognise rape within marriage itself until as recently as 1991. This shows that gender inequality and women's rights are important across the globe and not just in war-torn and/or developing countries, as the media and politicians may sometimes suggest.

about a clear distinction between the public world of work and the private realm of the home and the family. According to feminists influenced by Marxist work, the advent and development of capitalist economies led to particular ideas about what constituted 'work' and 'production', and in this process 'women's work' came to be denigrated and undervalued. Women's labour was constructed as a labour of love which did not require financial reward. The male head of household was the 'breadwinner' who provided for *his* family. Marxist analysis showed how the home and the family had come to be viewed as 'private' areas of human life, clearly separate and distinct from the public realm. Here human relations were supposedly based on affection and particularism. A man's relationship with his wife and family was not then subject to the rather more abstract and universal principals of justice and equality that governed the public world. However, this idealised view of the family disguised the reality of power relations and inequality that permeated both the public and private realms. The construction of a public/private division effectively served to reduce women, and children, to the private property of men.

The construction of women as the gentler, weaker, nurturing sex reduced women's labour – cooking meals, washing, and clearing away the clutter – to a 'natural' extension of their caring role (primarily as mothers). However, in the 1960s, such idealistic notions of women's nature and family life were subject to profound and wide-ranging criticisms during the so-called second wave of feminism.

### Box 10.5 Betty Friedan [1921–2006]

Betty Friedan's *The Feminine Mystique* (2001) articulated the deeply unsatisfying and unfulfilling position of the middle class, educated American woman confined to the 'private' realm in her roles as housewife and mother.

Radical feminists took this insight into the nature and significance of the public/private division further, arguing that the 'personal' was, in fact, profoundly 'political'. That is to say that, for radical feminists, areas of life conventionally held to be characterised by particularism and affection, were actually characterised by processes of subordination and domination. From this perspective, women's liberation would only be achieved through a transformation in the most private and intimate spheres of human relationships. However, radical feminists also developed the concept of **patriarchy** to explain the institutionalisation of male domination over women, and so demonstrate that gender was not just a question of individual identity, or sexuality. Patriarchy is the word that explains a hierarchical system where men are at the top and women are at the bottom. In other words, patriarchy is shorthand for systems of male domination and consequent female subordination. Using the idea of patriarchy, radical feminists argued that the structure of gender relations in any given society was determined, in large part, by prevailing social institutions and practices like, for example, the institution of marriage, or the family, or the education system. These institutions served to reinforce relations of inequality and subordination.

Critical feminists have developed an approach within IR that draws upon some of the insights of radical and Marxist feminism, but also stresses the importance of ideas about gender in legitimising and perpetuating this form of social inequality. Critical feminists argue that gender is constructed as a socially relevant difference that is then used to justify differential treatment between men and women. Gender is both a facet of individual identity, but is also institutionalised in a whole set of social practices; thus gender can be seen in terms of the interweaving of personal life and social structures. Critical feminist analysis in IR concentrates on the construction of gender and gender relations rather than on women per se. However, politically, the project of critical feminism is to construct knowledge about IR (current institutions and practices) to serve an emancipatory interest in freeing women from oppressive relationships and expanding the realm of autonomy that women enjoy over their own lives.

A contemporary strand of feminism applied to IR is feminist postmodernism (often used by critical feminists). Feminist postmodernism is critical of feminist liberal, radical and Marxist strains of feminism. This is because feminist postmodernists, like the post-modernists reviewed in the last section, are concerned with how discourses work to construct realities, particularly the 'reality' of gender. As such, they are critical of other feminists for believing that there is a real world out there (not constructed by discourse) that they can understand. Also, feminist postmodernists such as Christine Sylvester are critical of radical feminists for considering women to be naturally different to men and for glorifying women's particular knowledge drawn from this biological difference. Feminist postmodernists are critical in these ways because they believe that gender categories (men and women) are discursively constructed. In other words they believe that gender categories are fictitious and have no meaning outside of language and culture. Therefore, in relation to IR, feminist postmodernists seek to deconstruct and criticise the ways in which these fictitious categories are employed within theory and practice.

Finally (and in some ways related to feminist postmodernism and critical feminism) is post-colonial Feminism. Post-colonial feminists, such as Cynthia Enloe, seek to highlight the complexities of gender relations as they are affected by other identity intersections such as ethnicity, geographical location and class. These feminists are concerned with the universalising character of feminism within 'Western' countries. Beyond gender, post-colonial Feminists recognise that racial stereotypes are also damaging and highlight the colonial legacy of considering those who reside in low-income countries (many of which are ex-colonies) to be somehow backward. These feminists seek to dispel such myths which work to legitimise the expansion of Western norms and values globally. For post-colonial feminism there needs to be recognition of the difference between women, whereby other identity intersections are taken into account.

## The feminist contribution to IR

One could argue that feminist theorising has largely been accepted within critical IR theory but has failed to convince the more traditional positivist theories. Positivist approaches to IR concentrate on establishing causal laws by formulating hypotheses that can be tested in the 'real world'. From such a perspective, feminist scholarship can contribute to IR, but only if feminists emulate existing 'scientific' approaches – hence the greater acceptance of feminist empiricism within mainstream IR. What this means in practice is that gender

**Table 10.1** Theoretical perspectives on feminism

| Feminist theoretical position | Primary focus/aim |
|---|---|
| Liberal feminism – drawn from liberal political theory | To promote women's rights to education, employment/income and political representation within the current political and economic system |
| Marxist feminism – drawn from Marxist political theory | To overcome capitalism and, therefore, the disadvantages associated with class and gender prevalent under the capitalist system |
| Radical feminism | To overcome patriarchy and subvert the system of male dominance so that female 'traits' (such as nurturing and caring) are given greater regard |
| Critical feminism – drawn from a mixture of Radical feminism and Marxist feminism | To overcome capitalism and patriarchy as both these structures/systems cause the undermining of women's status and problematic gender practices |
| Feminist postmodernism – drawn from postmodernist theory | To illuminate the fictitious and constructed character of the categories 'man' and 'woman' and to explain how the belief in these categories is problematic in society, the economy and the political world |
| Post-colonial feminism – drawn from post-colonial theory | To demonstrate the importance that constructed identity intersections – such as race, ethnicity and geographical location – have on how we experience our gender and dispel myths which universalise Western norms across the globe |

analysis can find a space in IR, but only if we regard gender as one of many 'variables' that might be relevant to understanding the causes (or impacts) of war, for example, or the nature and extent of global poverty perhaps.

However, most Feminist scholars regard themselves as post-positivists and argue that **positivist** or scientific analysis is problematic because it assumes that gender is a natural or essential, rather than constructed or learnt, feature of men and women respectively (hence the possibility of identifying a gender variable). The assumption that gender can be reduced to a variable is problematic because positivists are unreflective about how one is never outside gender. This assertion that one is never outside gender is really the key to grasping the insights that feminism brings to the study of IR. While the 'gender as a variable' approach might serve to expand the boundaries of existing IR, positivist scholars are ultimately asking the wrong kind of questions. Feminist IR is rather more ambitious, seeking to escape boundaries of mainstream discourse in IR. Some of the ways in which this feminist IR can be used are outlined below, but considerable engagement with a complex literature will bear much fruit in terms of shining new light on International Relations' theory and practice. Feminist theories are providing insights at a number of different levels.

'Bringing in' women is a first stage in developing feminist insights into the nature of the state. Looking at the world through a Liberal feminist 'lens' allows us to see that the world of International Relations is a man's world, in so far as the state's representatives are mainly men – politicians, soldiers, spies and so on. Women have historically been excluded from political power and today remain heavily under-represented in the 'high politics' of statecraft. From a feminist perspective, very few women are involved in the making of foreign or defence policy, so the 'national interest' is nearly always defined by men of statecraft. Liberal feminists recognise that, historically, the state has not been equal and impartial in its treatment of women. However, for liberal feminists, male domination is largely explained by historical circumstance and accident. Given opportunities, like the same level of education, women can prove that they are the equals of men. In this way, women can gradually overcome prejudices. A central question for liberal feminists is: Given that the state is the dominant form of political organisation around the world, to what degree can it be viewed as a vehicle for women's liberation? By enacting pro-woman legislation and outlawing discriminatory practices, the state can help to advance the status of women.

However, in many respects Liberal feminism falls into a trap which might be understandable if we view it as a development within white, Western, middle-class women. It certainly seems to simplify both the problem and the application of a solution. Historically the state has performed as a patriarchal site of power, but the state is not inherently patriarchal. That is to say, feminist organisations and women's groups have successfully lobbied to change government policies and interventions, often in ways that bring positive benefits to women. Critical feminists view the state both as a set of power relations and political processes in which patriarchy is both constructed and contested. From this perspective, feminists can work through the state to try to achieve positive changes for women.

Some of the most interesting feminist work in IR is being done in the general area of gender, sexuality and sexual identities (see Chapter 19). This is part of a much broader critical interest in sexualities and identities in contemporary International Relations, which is not exclusively feminist. Feminists have drawn upon some of this work in order to develop a critique of gender bias and the profoundly masculinised and feminised imagery which is employed in orthodox (Realist) IR discourse. Gender is also a central factor in understanding world orders, old and new. Given the emphasis on gender as a specific form of inequality which is supported and perpetuated by social institutions/practices and ideologies, critical feminism has much to say about world order and the nature and purpose of international institutions. What does the world order look like when viewed from a feminist perspective? How do the policies of international organisations and institutions like the UN, the World Bank and the International Monetary Fund affect gender relations in countries across the world? There is a growing critical feminist literature on gender relations, which is integrated into and informed by an analysis of the changing 'world order'. Of course, in Marxist terms, 'world order' is constituted by global capitalism and the states and institutions which provide a framework in which capitalist economic and social relations are 'managed'. 'Women's work' is frequently unpaid and so not deemed to be part of the activities of states, markets and international institutions which collectively constitute world order. However, not only is the contribution of women's labour highly significant in national terms, but increasingly so in global terms.

As is evident from the above discussion, issues of inequality and questions of justice have been central to feminist theory, and, from the eighteenth century onwards, feminists in the West have asserted the equal moral worth of women and men, and have demanded equal rights and justice for women. In so doing, liberal feminists have internationalised the issue and also encouraged an active debate on what should be recognised as a 'human right'. Rights discourse is increasingly being adopted by NGOs in a variety of countries and cultural contexts around the world. Many transnational women's NGOs believe that human rights discourse is politically useful to disempowered groups. Moreover, both the conception and substantive context of human rights has been expanded to incorporate the needs of many groups – including women – previously denied rights.

However, not all feminists favour a rights-based strategy to address gender inequalities. Some postmodern and post-colonial feminists argue that rights discourse is rooted in a Western tradition, grounded in an abstract 'universalism' and embedded in Western ideas about 'progress' and emancipation. Post-colonial feminist thinkers have argued that all too frequently, criticism of cultural practices is based on misunderstanding and misrepresentation. Women in the non-Western world are not passive and voiceless 'victims' of uncivilised societies and 'backward' cultural practices, but non-Western societies have been viewed through the eyes of Western social and political values and condemned for their ignorance and barbarity. Furthermore, where rights have been connected to the ownership of property – a traditional source of European Law exported through colonialism – the ramifications for women have been enormous, serving sometimes to displace women from land they had previously controlled or from other resources which confer a certain amount of social power on women. These historical examples illustrate, perhaps, the dangers inherent in advocating strategies to address inequality which have been developed in a specific historical context and which may not be appropriate in another.

## Summary

Feminism is a broad church with many different strands. There are important differences in feminist theories, but also commonalities. Contemporary feminist theory does not focus solely on the lives of women but is an analysis of the socially and culturally constructed category 'gender' (see Chapter 19). A great deal of feminist scholarship is concerned with practices of discrimination and exclusion. However, feminists do not regard women as 'victims'. Feminism is also concerned with uncovering and highlighting ways in which women are empowered to achieve positive changes in their social position. Contemporary feminism does not regard 'women' or, indeed 'men', as a single category but is sensitive to the nuances of gender identities along with other identities which intersect gender – such as race, class and sexuality. Given the great variety of women's experiences and those in gender relations, it is clear that oppression takes many forms. Feminism has gained influence in International Relations theory since the 1980s, though the scholarship which informs it has a much longer history. Feminist scholarship has made a valuable contribution to very many areas long held to be central to International Relations. Some (male) commentators argue that the gender 'variable' can be incorporated into mainstream IR research agendas. At the same time, feminism challenges conventional ideas about what is central or marginal, important or unimportant in IR; in effect what constitutes a 'mainstream agenda'. The central insight of feminism is, perhaps, the way in which the notion of a clear private/public distinction renders invisible a particular set of power relations. From a feminist perspective, the private is not only political, but increasingly international or global.

## Green Theory

The case for a section on **Green Theory** differs somewhat from the case of feminism. On the one hand it might be argued that 'the environment' is more of a contemporary news story or issue than 'gender'; Chapter 23 on the environment outlines some of the reasons as to why it has become significant. However, in terms of IR's theoretical approaches it might be argued that ecological thought is not generally considered a separate perspective in the way that feminism now probably is. Rather than get too involved with the question of why this should be so, this section seeks to look at some of the insights offered by Green Theory and philosophy. Although not everyone may be explicit about their ecological values it is important to start out by noting that all political and economic positions must have – even if only implicitly – a base in an ecological ethics. Similarly, any ecological position (a Green manifesto) must imply political decisions on the way to have them accepted and put into practice.

### Box 10.6 The potential political implications of sustainability

Is the sustainable society the perfect society? The paragraph above suggests that all politics/economics must imply an ecological position and vice versa. So for example, global capitalism based on liberal democratic practices (though rarely by explicitly saying so) employs an ecological ethics which is highly instrumental and anthropocentric. This means that the environment is valued primarily for what it can offer human beings, even if this is occasionally an aesthetic use. For those who regard this system as abhorrent for its inequity, destructiveness and so on, it is important to remember the 'vice versa' above. A sustainable society is simply one that can be sustained ecologically. Of course many Greens hope that this will lead to harmonious relations with nature *and* happy human beings living in societies where they are free and empowered in various ways. But we must not forget that this is not an automatic given. The desirable outcome of sustainability might be achieved through some highly undesirable methods and a Green leviathan. So for instance harmony with nature might be achieved through excessive controls on personal freedom, including such things as surveillance or high levels of incarceration. One could argue that the following is de facto the current situation, but the wealthy/powerful in totalitarian regimes might tread heavily on the resources of the planet only by limiting say the number and type of calories that the vast majority were permitted. It is important to remember that even if ecological balance is accepted as the end, the political and economic implementation (the means) could still be hugely problematical for humankind.

What we deal with briefly below in introducing the idea of Green Theory is, in reality, the insights which distinctly ecological, philosophical and ethical positions offer us in terms of current political and economic practices. Running alongside these insights it should be noted that the traditional approaches to IR have all found ways to include 'the environment' in their work. This has been necessary: Realists could hardly ignore the ecological/resource pressures leading to war and to a lesser extent the ecological effects of militarism in general; for Liberals, economic models have proved insufficient by regarding the environment as an externality, while analysis of regimes has offered some hope in terms of how selfish states might achieve joint outcomes through collective diplomacy; and neo-Marxists have been interested in the inequality of ecological impacts connected to global economic structures. However, what we deal with below is Green Theory as opposed to the 'greening' of existing theory.

Two words which crop up a lot in discussions of Green Theory and IR are *anthropocentric* and *eco-centric* (or variants such as bio-centric). Anthropocentric means human-centred and in terms of the environment it describes a worldview which sees environmental problems purely from the perspective of humanity and thinks that nature's value lies in the extent to which it can be useful to human beings. Eco-centric on the other hand means nature-centred. Strictly speaking it would be impossible for human beings not to be anthropocentric, but eco-centrism describes the attempts to prioritise and privilege nature in arriving at prescriptions for the ordering of societies and international relations. Eco-centrism is about humans having the power to put nature first and about ascribing intrinsic value to it. There is a long history of how anthropocentrism came to dominate modern thought and how environmental problems have since led ecological philosophers to discuss the need for an eco-centric reversal, or at least a more 'aware' anthropocentrism. Chapter 23 on the environment will give you a sense of why demands for ecological sensitivity have been raised.

It is worth emphasising what an eco-centric (also known as bio-centric or Deep Green) position entails in asking us to think differently, not so much about international relations but about the relationship between our species and the planet it inhabits. Green Theory demands radical changes in forms of sociopolitical organisation and respect for non-human species. As its proponents, such as Robyn Eckersley, have pointed out, a Deep Green position involves: a rejection/renegotiation of anthropocentric worldviews; the belief that human interference in the natural world is currently threatening the survival of both humankind and other species; an insistence on the need for fundamental changes in social, economic and technological structures and ideological/value systems; a distinction between vital and non-vital needs; a rejection of development strategies which encourage economic growth above quality of life; an ethics based on a 'green theory of value' which places an intrinsic value on non-human life; an active commitment towards implementing the changes necessary to achieve a genuinely green future, which includes promoting alternative lifestyles, values and a decentralisation of power.

One interesting way to look at the move away from unreflective anthropocentrism is to regard the previous position as *Promethean*. The word comes from Prometheus who in Greek mythology stole fire from the gods; in this context it is used to represent humanity's faith in its own ingenuity always to find solutions to problems. This view notes how humanity has found technical solutions to all kinds of environmental problems; it is an optimistic view of human material progress which need not even worry about the impossibility of infinite growth on a finite planet. Prometheanism was more or less 'natural' by the start of the twentieth century; humanity was used to progress and over-coming impediments to it through technology. In the second half of the twentieth century the number of problems with the environment was increasing and a number of technical solutions to impediments to progress (such as the pollutant DDT or CFCs) had had a kind of boomerang effect, coming back to cause problems.

It was because of this that a so-called 'Survivalist' discourse emerged, urging caution and arguing that a Promethean discourse was undermining humanity's long-term viability. In effect they were suggesting something similar to the idea that humans were funding prosperity by 'maxing out' the credit card which would sooner or later need to be repaid. Emblematic of the survivalist urging for caution was *The Limits to Growth* Report (1972). Researchers used computer modelling techniques to 'prove' their findings that environmental factors would soon place restrictions on growth and/or lead to disaster. Exponential economic growth and population growth were producing a set of interrelated crises

Source: Getty Images/AFP

**Many accept the need to work towards an environmentally sustainable world, but have we considered what the social and political implications might be?**

they said. The world was rapidly running out of resources to feed people or provide raw material for industry. Finally, the ability of the environment to absorb the waste products of human consumption and industrial output was being exhausted. Human society would collapse before 2100 they predicted.

Some aspects of the survivalist discourse have proved incorrect. For example, the survivalist Paul Ehrlich in his book *The Population Bomb* (1968) asserted that between 1970 and 1985 there would be mass famines due to increased population and, consequently, lack of food resources. However, this did not come to pass as Ehrlich had predicted and nowadays famine is linked to political and social instability rather than food scarcity. Nevertheless, survivalists still argue that we ought to take them seriously because ultimately the more optimistic Prometheans can only prove, rather than predict, 'trends' which can end abruptly. Accordingly, eco-centrism urges us to look at international relations with a related set of assumptions: an emphasis on the global over the international (for example, the importance of global community is recognised as well as the rights of local communities to control their own resources, in addition to the existence of bio-regional communities as the basic building blocks of the earth); an implicit understanding that current human practices are in some way or other 'out of sync' with the non-human world; a stress that modern practices, underpinned by anthropocentric philosophical belief systems, have been critical in causing the environmental crisis.

With these assumptions, eco-centric positions cast different light on some of the core business of IR. So, for instance, they suggest questions about the state: is the autonomy/ legitimacy of the state being undermined by the need for global responses to environmental problems? If sovereign power must be conceded to global institutions, does cooperation mean that we need to rethink the distribution of power among states and other actors? Is our notion of sovereignty changing? If the state is facing multiple challenges, is this necessarily a good thing? Then there are other questions, such as those about the relationship between environmental stress and violent conflict or social justice. These also lead on to questions of inter-generational justice. In fact, the questions posed are so varied and wide ranging that the hope here is simply that the seriousness of the issue (highlighted in Chapter 23) will inspire further investigation.

## Summary

Environmental issues have been taken up by IR scholars in varying degrees and so have shaped the discipline in various ways. 'Adding in' the environment has served to enrich many existing theoretical perspectives in International Relations and furthered our understanding of a range of areas and concerns such as the state, conflict, inequality, cooperation, institutions and governance. However, 'adding in' is a problem-solving approach to the environment based on an anthropocentric worldview. Contemporary environmental problems and disasters have shown the dangers inherent in adopting such an anthropocentric view. Environmental concern has developed as a result, especially since the 1960s. It is possible also to identify a distinctive tradition of 'Green Thought'. Drawing upon this it is possible to construct a distinctive Green position or Green perspective on IR. At the very heart of the Green perspective is a concern with the human–nature relationship. It emphasises the change from pre-modern to modern worldviews as crucial to our understanding of environmental problems. Whereas in pre-modern times people were deferential towards and/or fearful of nature, modern perceptions have emphasised humanity's ability to conquer nature. A Green perspective demands, then, a radical restructuring of the various facets of human organisation – from everyday practices like consumerism, to contemporary world order built on the exploitation of the natural world and the oppression or marginalisation of specific social groups. While we should be careful not to overstate the similarities, such a Green position shares some similarities with feminism and postmodernism. The problems of going beyond a Deep Green critique (that is, actually putting such suggestions into practice) should not be under-estimated. Nonetheless it provides a powerful rejection of the contemporary organisation of international society. Awareness not only of environmental problems but also of the philosophical underpinnings of how human beings relate to nature may be crucial to the future of the planet.

We started this section by noting a concern that environmental futures could easily be authoritarian even as they achieved harmony with nature. Similarly, eco-centrism in the present has been criticised for conservatism, or even authoritarianism, because of a concentration on the oppression of nature over other oppressions. This is because if the primary concern is the natural world, tackling unequal social relations becomes secondary creating a conservative politics in relation to things like human rights and equality. However, there is much misunderstanding surrounding 'deep ecology' and such accusations are refuted partly by arguing that humans dominating other humans is an effect of humans dominating nature. Moreover eco-feminism, for example, is a very influential strand of Green Thought, which seems to suggest that Greens are attuned to the complex forms of social oppression and exclusion which exist. Fundamentally, the impossibility of growth in a finite system and the lack of respect offered the non-human world by the human necessitates profound changes in *all* aspects of our social and political behaviour.

There are, though, some very practical problems for an ecocentric position. In the real world, wars may start over water; whales may be saved through the deliberations of an international regime; and children may die because of contaminated water supplies – arguably some of the more established IR perspectives such as Realism or neo-Marxism are more helpful in understanding the nature of these things. Furthermore, the dangers of actually attempting to dismantle current patterns of social, political and economic organisation are likely to be very great. To achieve such Deep Green futures is deeply problematical; it would require a complete reversal of the economic growth trajectory and a radically revised international system. In other words, deep ecological prescriptions frequently tend towards the unrealistic.

## Case study: The value of alternative approaches

Clearly, in some respects there are overlaps and similarities between the approaches outlined above. At the same time, they offer distinct ways of analysis. What they have in common, is that each goes beyond dominant or standard understandings, be these theoretical or otherwise. For instance, we might look at the war fought by the United States of America in Vietnam in the 1960s and 1970s. Notwithstanding the relatively recent efforts of Hollywood to capture for the American public a real sense of the cost of this conflict in films such as *Full Metal Jacket* and *Born on the Fourth of July*, standard explorations and/or explanations of this conflict tend to be fairly similar (see Box 6.1). The USA, it is argued, was acting in order to contain the global threat of communism; and as per the logic of Realism, preparedness to use military force was crucial to this.

Of course, the standard account has been questioned in many ways and by many people. Noam Chomsky, for instance, is one of many who have offered different and illuminating accounts of US motivations and actions. The theoretical approaches outlined in this chapter can add to our understanding of Vietnam, although none would claim to be offering as comprehensive and overarching a critique as does Chomsky.

In Box 10.2 Jean Baudrillard's views on the Gulf War are outlined in the context of postmodern thought on the 'accessibility of reality'. The Vietnam War – as probably the original 'TV war' – was a wholly mediated experience and Baudrillard's thoughts on the Gulf War can be applied here too.

Although Green Theory may not be useful in terms of explaining the causes of the war in Vietnam, environmental issues have had some bearing on a number of conflicts; water as an issue in the Palestinian/Israeli conflict would be one example and the prospect of environmentally induced migration provoking future conflicts is one taken seriously. Beyond this, however, Greens can point to the environmental cost of militaries in terms of their huge use of natural resources. In the specific context of Vietnam, studies have shown the incredible destructiveness of modern warfare both because of immediate explosive effects and the longer-term effects of using chemicals such as the infamous Agent Orange (see Westing 1986, for instance).

In Box 19.3 entitled 'Debates over women on the "frontline"' in Chapter 19, you will read about the gender stereotyping which goes on in this debate. Analysis of the Vietnam War from a feminist perspective can undoubtedly correct the impression that the absence of women in front-line combat is somehow natural. Women were absolutely vital to the military efforts of the Vietcong, and in the tunnel complexes of Cu Chi their smaller stature was crucial to effectiveness. Many a hapless GI, announced by the smell of his American perfumed soap, sadly failed to live to tell this story.

All in all then, alternative theories can offer us new lenses on international relations; new ways of viewing things. While to some people these enhancements might be seen as ornamental, for adherents of these theories the need to regard knowledge as tentative, to protect the planet on which we depend and to take seriously half the population of that planet are absolutely central.

**In light of this chapter, is the clear and limited nature of Realist analysis (see Chapter 6) a virtue or a dangerous oversimplification?**

## Conclusions

The major criticism of all this critique is that IR has become over self-indulgent. Rather than observing the real world, we cannot even talk of a real world anymore. Instead of being able to offer practical advice on concrete situations to pressured statespeople, we are interrogating our underlying assumptions. Whether you agree or not with these criticisms, IR has certainly become much more complex. It is also perfectly possible, more so than with other chapters, that you will find some of the foregoing extremely useful even as you reject other parts. Regardless, it all provides important context for IR's great compromise. Compromise can be good, but it can also mean falling between two stools. In any case, as we move to the next chapter, it is up to you to decide whether you feel Social Constructivism lives up to the promises it makes and helps IR to enjoy the best of all possible worlds.

## Resource section

## Questions

1.  How useful is postmodernism to the study and practice of IR?

2.  What are the feminist criticisms of mainstream IR? Do you think these criticisms are valid?

3.  To what extent, if at all, will environmental sustainability lead to a better society?

4.  What are mainstream IR theorists criticisms of alternative approaches?

## Recommended reading

### Postmodernism specific recommended reading

Der Derian, J. and Shapiro, M. (eds) (1989) *International/Intertextual Relations: Postmodern Readings of World Politics* (Lexington MA: Lexington Books)
At the forefront of 'pomo-IR'. A collection of essays which attempts to suggest what 'postmodern' IR theory might be like.

Edkins, J. (1999) *Poststructuralism and International Relations: Bringing the Political Back In* (Boulder CO: Lynne Rienner)
An introduction (so the book tells us) to the works of Foucault, Derrida, Lacan and Zizek (among others) suggesting that 'they provide the tools for the rearticulation of the question of the political'.

Walker, R.B.J. (1993) *Inside/Outside: International Relations as Political Theory* (Cambridge: Cambridge University Press)
Attempts both to deconstruct IR and provide it with alternative visions.

## Feminism specific recommended reading

Enloe, C. (1989) *Bananas, Beaches and Bases: Making Feminist Sense of International Relations* (London: Pandora)
Highlights the complexities of gender relations as they are affected by other identity intersections such as ethnicity, geographical location and class.

Marchand, M. and Runyan, A.S. (2000) *Gender and Global Restructuring: Sitings, Sites and Resistances* (London: Routledge)
An edited collection of leading feminist writers answering questions concerning how a gender lens can improve conventional accounts of globalisation, gender and global restructuring, gendered ideologies and relations changing in different national/regional contexts and more.

Steans, J. (1998) *Gender and International Relations* (Oxford: Polity Press)
Very popular in the USA where students are keenly aware of the link between books and credit points. Covers with clarity such topics as feminist theories; international relations theory; gender in the theory and practice of 'state-making'; feminist perspectives on war and peace; feminist approaches to security; the gender dimension of international political economy; gender and the politics of development; and women's human rights.

## Green specific recommended reading

Dryzek, J. (1997) *The Politics of the Earth: Environmental Discourses* (Oxford: Oxford University Press)
Looks at environmental discourses as a way into describing what is happening to the planet. Accessible and illuminating.

Laferriere, E. and Stoett, P. (1999) *International Relations Theory and Ecological Thought* (London, Routledge)
Might be described as dry in places, but a bold attempt to bring together IR theory and eco-philosophy, suggesting how the latter can make a much needed innovative contribution to the former.

O'Neill, K. (2009) *The Environment and International Relations* (Cambridge: Cambridge University Press)
Says the author: 'This exciting new textbook introduces students to the ways in which the theories and tools of International Relations can be used to analyse and address global environmental problems.' Well put.

Sachs, W. (1999) *Planet Dialectics* (London: Zed)
The book is actually subtitled 'explorations in environment and development'. Not an 'easy' read, but provocative, enlightening and always interesting.

# Chapter 11
# Social Constructivism

Social Constructivism as a bridge between the traditional theories

Agency and culture in IR

A Social Constructivist reappraisal of IR's key concepts

The empiricists strike back? Critiques of Social Constructivism

Conclusion

After reading this chapter you will be able to:

- Describe what Social Constructivism is, and how it emerged in and relates to International Relations

- Provide a central ground from which you might reflect further on the debate between rationalist and reflectivist approaches to IR theory

- Evaluate the significance of human agency and culture in IR

- Complete our comprehensive and introductory survey of IR theory such that you can engage with high-level theory in other books and the other non-theory chapters of this book

*Source*: Getty Images

## Introductory box: Germany and the European Union

The enthusiastic approach of successive German governments to European integration since the 1950s is not easily explained by mainstream theories of IR. Germany has had the biggest economy of any EC/EU member state from the start but has never sought to dominate the other countries in the **hegemonic** manner apparent in many inter-governmental organisations. In the 1990s Germany abandoned the mark as its currency in favour of the euro in spite of the fact that the mark was a hugely influential world currency and they have consistently paid far more into the EU coffers than they can hope to recoup in the form of agricultural or regional subsidies. Such a stance does not fit easily in a Realist or Liberal view of International Relations. The Germans do not appear to have viewed the EU as a vehicle to project their power and also do not appear to have chosen the path of cooperation purely for the economic pay-offs.

In contrast France can be seen to have ditched the franc for broadly the same reasons that they instigated European integration in the 1950s: the pragmatic realisation that they were no longer an independent global power and needed to embrace Europe in order to have a prominent role in the world. The British have stuck with their currency despite it having been less powerful than the mark for many years and have consistently approached European integration on the basis of a 'What's in it for us?' calculation, including insisting on an annual rebate from Brussels despite being far less of a net contributor to the EU budget than Germany. For many other members of the EU there are clear economic pay-offs for surrendering some control of their economies in order to reap the mutual benefits of free trade and/or claim redistributive subsidies. The gains of EU membership for Germany are less obvious, from a Realist power politics or Liberal cooperative perspective, than for any other member state but they have, nevertheless, consistently been among the most enthusiastic supporters of the integration process.

For Social Constructivists the German stance over the EU provides evidence that IR is not always comprehensible through the rationality of material 'gain' and 'who gets what'. Germany has embraced European integration because of the *idea* of European integration not because it automatically, always or directly serves their immediate material interests.

Social Constructivism attempts to find a practical answer to the challenge to scientific knowledge presented by critiques of IR, especially postmodernism, in order to be able to find a way forward in terms of conducting empirical and policy orientated research.

Social Constructivists analyse the interplay between *structure* and *agency* in international politics; are interested in the role of ideas, norms and institutions in foreign policy making; argue for the importance of identity and culture in international politics; do not deny the role of interests in policy making, but try to understand how these interests are *constructed*; accept that social science cannot operate like the natural sciences (because humans are not like electrons and can reflect upon what happens to them and use this to inform reasons for subsequent action), but nonetheless insist that it is possible to theorise and empirically analyse international politics as a reality.

## Social Constructivism as a bridge between the traditional theories

**Table 11.1** IR theory as a history of debates

| Debate | When it took place | Key battlegrounds |
| --- | --- | --- |
| Idealism (early liberal IR) v. Realism, inter-war debate, first great debate | 1920s and 1930s | The possibility of cooperation in international affairs and the inevitability, or otherwise, of military conflict |
| Consensus | 1940s and 1950s | Realism is seen by most as the way to approach international relations |
| Tradition (philosophy) v. behaviourism (science), second great debate | 1960s | Could international relations be studied using scientific methodology? Essentially a debate between Realists |
| Inter-paradigm debate* | Begins to grow in the 1970s, the term actually coined in 1985 | Not really a debate but a reference to the division of International Relations into three separate approaches. Namely those covered in Chapters 6, 7, and 8 |
| Neo-Neo debate*, also neo-neo synthesis | 1990s | A discussion about the relative importance of states seeking either relative or absolute gains in an anarchic world |
| Rationalist v. reflectivist* | 1990s ongoing | 'Dialogue of the deaf' between a belief that rational knowledge can be built and the need for metaphysical/overarching critique |
| Social Constructivism | 2000s ongoing | Not a debate but a broad church and approach in which many authors accept merit in both rationalist and reflectivist positions |

* All the debates marked with an asterisk could be called the third great debate. In reality the ongoing disagreements between rationalists and reflectivists have had the most long-term significance.

The story of Social Constructivism is told, in a sense, by the previous chapters. By this we mean that after 'traditional' theories were picked apart by an invasion of ideas from social theory, Social Constructivism tried to – in a sense – put the discipline back together again. Rather than rely on you having internalised all of those previous chapters, however, we shall introduce here material which you will possibly be expected to become familiar with, and that is the history of disciplinary IR told as a history of so-called 'great debates' (see Table 11.1). Although privileging these debates marginalises other work, it has become conventional to talk about these standard reference points. The first one was between Realism and Idealism (that is, the name given to the Liberalism of the 1920s). It essentially involved questions about the nature of international politics, and the inevitability of conflict or possibility of cooperation. It rested most fundamentally on questions of human nature and whether humans were inherently selfish, violent and prone to give in to passion and desire, or whether they were altruistic, peace loving and rational.

The second debate (which we have hardly touched upon thus far) was about how to *do* IR. The debate raged at the height of the Cold War and perhaps at the peak of Realism's dominance. What else *was* there to argue over than how best to do Realism? The argument was between *traditionalists* and *behaviouralists*. The latter wanted to turn IR into a science, and focus on the formulation of universally valid theories that explain outcomes in international politics on the basis of causal relationships between observable behaviour. Traditionalists, in contrast, argued that international politics cannot be studied like the natural sciences but needs to employ the methods of history and philosophy. One of its key adherents was named Hedley Bull who headed up what became known as the 'English School' (see also Chapter 6) grouping together a number of non-US scholars, who were very sceptical of the possibility of scientific method (Bull 1977).

The neo-neo debate was between neo-Realism and neo-Liberalism. This was a variation on an old theme, picking up on the first great debate (Idealism v. Realism) but in a new era. However, it is very narrow; both look at states but differ over whether they pursue absolute or relative gains. Both see power as a key interest of states but argue over the significance of military and economic power. The similarities are so clear that newly emerging critiques of the discipline tended to lump them together as *rationalist* theories, barely recognising their minor issues of disagreement.

These emerging critiques, covered in Chapters 9 and 10, attacked rationalism on many levels questioning the status of states and the assumption of rationality on the one hand while agreeing with the 'English School' in terms of the impossibility of scientific method. The critiques became styled as *reflectivists* and their approaches included reflecting on the basis for which we can have any knowledge about the world; they focused their research on the production of knowledge in IR and the consequences of constructing international politics in particular terms for the practice of international politics. Rationalism (Chapters 6, 7 and 8) versus Reflectivism (Chapters 9 and 10) is IR's fourth great debate. The Marxism of Chapter 8 belongs in the rationalist camp, but as you will have seen includes developments which lead into later chapters. Marxist-inspired social theory marks the crossover points between the two.

## Box 11.1  Constructing international politics

In the paragraph above you will have read 'the consequences of constructing international politics in particular terms for the practice of international politics'. What does this mean? For example, if we accept the Realist theoretical view of the world (that is, have a mental 'construct' of international politics which is Realist) we actually encourage statespeople to prepare for war, to accept war as inevitable and to regard problems of violent conflict as so vital that we may be less worried with injustices such as poverty, gender inequality and environmental degradation. That is, what happens in international relations is actually shaped by how we think about it (construct it) in the first place.

Arguing that the dominance of **rationalism** had served to make neo-Realism and neo-Liberalism barely distinguishable, the scholar and UN advisor John Ruggie coined the term 'neo-Utilitarianism' to describe a catch-all paradigm from which Social Constructivism was seeking to distance itself. The Realists and Liberals could still be distinguished by their assumptions about how actors in international relations operate, with Liberalism giving more credence to international organisations and other cooperative actions, but they both assumed that this was rational gain-driven behaviour. The neo-Utilitarians on both sides of the fence view international organisations as instrumental and a means to an end of material gain for states, whether through mutual gains or the opportunity to dominate others. The notion of actors choosing whether or not to cooperate on the basis of non-material factors such as norms, ideas and culture is not catered for in either approach (or, indeed, in Marxism).

> They share a view of the world of international relations in utilitarian terms; an atomistic universe of self-regarding units whose identity is assumed given and fixed, and who are responsive largely if not solely to material interests that are fixed by assumption.
>
> (Ruggie 1998: 3)

## Box 11.2  Methodology in IR

### Traditional - Realism v. Liberalism

Using rival philosophical/ideological perspectives to explain state behaviour based on assumptions of human nature as either selfish or cooperative.

### Behavioural/Positivist (post 1960s) - neo-Realism and neo-Liberalism

The 'behavioural revolution' ushers in the 'scientific method' of value-free (**Positivist**) study. Testing theories through empirical analysis comes to be seen as a more rigorous and valid means of enquiry.

### Post-Positivist (post 1990s) - Reflectivism and Social Constructivism

The rationality of the scientific method comes to be doubted when applied to human behaviour as does the notion of value-free enquiry.

The context for Social Constructivism's emergence then is the story of how the rationalist and reflectivist poles appear in the first place. How Social Constructivism seeks the middle ground is then the story of Social Constructivism in IR. As you might imagine, such an attempt to occupy the middle ground between very divergent poles produces a rather mixed bag of approaches. Indeed the 'church' of what passes as social constructivism is so broad that one sometimes wonders whether it is a coherent church at all: the range of 'followers' span from those merely integrating ideas into a materialist–rationalist framework to those who focus on the analysis of discourse and operate, both theoretically and methodologically, close to Reflectivism, and especially post-Structuralism. With such caveats in mind we nonetheless move on to make sense of a highly significant current in contemporary IR.

In a review of social constructivist work on European integration, Thomas Christiansen, Knud-Erik Jørgensen and Antje Wiener (Christiansen et al. 2001) have used the image of an arch between the poles of Rationalism and Reflectivism to symbolise the 'middle ground'. In doing so, they wanted to indicate that, while sharing a few central assumptions, Social Constructivists predominantly define themselves by distancing themselves from both poles to varying degrees. Some of the Social Constructivists who emerged in the 1990s were 'new kids on the block', particularly from outside the traditional US–UK 'power base' of the discipline (for instance, from Scandinavia). Many others, however, were established names who had experienced a partial conversion through reflecting on the methodological challenge that was sweeping IR. Among the most prominent IR scholars within this approach, John G. Ruggie, for example, can best be characterised as a Liberal-turned-Constructivist while Alexander Wendt is a neo-Realist who has come to project his state-focused power politics assumptions though a Social Constructivist lens. Scholars like Wendt and Ruggie have not abandoned sinking ships so much as sought to re-equip them for the modern age.

### Box 11.3 Differences in IR around the world

The discipline of International Relations was once dominated by scholars in the United Kingdom and the United States. Outside this core, thinking has tended to be more diverse and more influenced by currents in philosophy, culture and social theory. Within the core it is perhaps fair to say that the United States has been more conservative, eschewing for the most part any Marxist currents and more recent engagements with social theory. Social Constructivism, partly for being such a broad church, has allowed influences into US IR which were not there previously. Nonetheless some US scholars, committed to conventional Liberal or Realist positions tend to describe anything beyond their limited boundaries as constructivist and relativist; in so doing they lump together the many varieties of Constructivism in the same basket as postmodern approaches (themselves very diverse).

Investigating the differences between the way International Relations is studied around the world can be interesting; for those studying in the United States or Europe seeking out non-Western perspectives can be both rewarding and illuminating.

Part of the point of this chapter is to bring the chapters on theory to a close in a coherent and clear way. The fact that Social Constructivism is a 'best of all possible worlds' compromise in some ways makes this tidy aim possible. However, hopefully you have already picked up that the story of IR is not a tidy one – even where we have tried to make it so. Indeed attempts to make IR 'simple' can be considered deeply problematical; Realism and Liberalism are sometimes considered to have perpetuated elite-focused discourses, and efforts to give IR the certainty of natural sciences may be doomed to failure.

The above notwithstanding, the story of IR is not without a logical and clear narrative. The early influence of Idealism was created by the despair of the First World War and the optimism/necessity of thinking that such a horror could be avoided in the future. Realism dominated after the Second World War because pessimism seemed more appropriate in the face of another global conflagration and an emerging and perilous nuclear balance in the Cold War. Reflecting the discipline's Western bias when war seemed to have become something fought by others in far away places, there was room for more consideration of economics. Again economics comes with an optimistic Liberal variant and a more critical Marxist-inspired version.

In the last two chapters we have seen that the recent history of IR has not been tidy in some senses, except that it has been a sustained attempt to critique the whole enterprise. Adherents of traditional approaches have tried to defend themselves against these critiques and/or have carried on regardless. Interesting work has been done and the whole field has become enlivened (or for some confused) by an engagement with broader fields of social theory. As intimated in the last chapter, into this arena marches Social Constructivism (or sometimes just 'constructivism'): suggesting the construction of 'bridges' in IR; acknowledging the power of recent critiques but wanting to find a way to go beyond abstractions.

Social Constructivism is not so much a substantive theory of world politics but a social theory or approach, which rather than making predictions about what may or may not happen in international affairs, suggests how we should investigate world politics. It eschews the grand universalising visions of Realism, Liberalism and Marxism, but tends to accept the points being made by the critiques found in Chapters 9 and 10. At the same time, however, it feels that IR can be a more useful (that is, policy relevant) field of social theory if it does more than undermine its own foundations. In previous chapters we have encouraged you to regard all theories as *potentially* adding insight, rather than being correct. It is important to bear that in mind here too, and even to go further in saying that Social Constructivism – as an approach – accepts implicitly that other approaches might be important for generating different *kinds* of knowledge in different situations.

As alluded to above, the word 'constructivism' does not actually come from the fact that these theorists wish to build bridges between different strands of IR. Nor does it come from the fact that they have a practical way forward in terms of the impasse which had been created between what might be called the simple and complex wings of IR theory. Instead 'Constructivism' here means that its adherents do not accept any social features in life as given (that is natural/pre-existing), but rather as being constructed. Social Constructivists start from the notion that human beings are situated in particular contexts which inform their actions. Furthermore they reproduce (or construct) their 'world' through those actions. If that seems unclear, we might contrast this idea that we are creating the context in which we live with the 'givens' that inform Realist approaches to IR; for Realists, the basic features of the international system are universal, and have been operating in history as well as at present, in the ancient Greek system of city states as much as during the Cold War. For Constructivists, there is no denial of constraints on human behaviour (through material and ideational structures, that is the way things and ideas affect us) but neither is the system unchanging.

Social Constructivism can nowadays legitimately be seen as one of the mainstream approaches to International Relations but, unlike say Realism, Social Constructivism – as an approach – does not put forward a set of coherent hypotheses that would form a unified theory. However, in the sense that theory is used somewhat loosely, to denote abstract thinking, it is part of International Relations theory. In contrast to the neo-neo-debate, Social Constructivism is not specific to IR at all – instead, it is an approach that crosses the disciplinary divides in the social sciences, and so it might well be that you have come across its central assumptions elsewhere in a way in which you would not have encountered, say, neo-Realism in Sociology.

In terms of IR, one could argue that the approaches covered in the previous two chapters were not so much concerned with how to do IR, but more with demonstrating the philosophical poverty of those approaches which had constituted the inter-paradigm debate (Chapters 6–8). In some senses Social Constructivism is the next wave, after Chapters 9 and 10, of critical international theory in seeking to move such theory away from abstract philosophy. Crucially, in the Marx-averse academy of the United States, constructivism in its broadest sense has allowed the social, historical and normative to become central features of the discipline.

## Agency and culture in IR

From the above we can see that for Social Constructivists there is a role for human agency in shaping, and indeed changing, the world in which we live. Human beings can influence things, even if they cannot always determine specific outcomes. They are not powerless, held by fate nor facing an inevitable future even though structures in the world do limit possible and appropriate action and make desirable outcomes tricky. This is especially so given the existence of other actors with different interests. Finally, the process of construction is a 'social' process – it cannot be done by one person alone, but only in the engagement with others.

## Box 11.4 Agency–structure debate

Most students of social behaviour face a fundamental dilemma when they approach their subject: On the one hand, individuals act, they do something, and this has certain effects; this is known as *agency*. On the other hand, most of the time what individuals do is shaped by their environment, which in turn is influenced by what people do. As analysts, we need to start somewhere – but do we begin with the structures that influence the behaviour of individuals, or with the (more readily observable) acts of individuals or groups? Traditionally, most theories and approaches have focused on one side or the other of this structure–agency problem, often without explicitly reflecting on their own bias in this respect. A classic example is the explanation of underdevelopment: those who blame incompetent leaders focus on agency; those who explain underdevelopment on the effects of the colonial heritage or capitalism favour structure over agency. While most people will intuitively agree with Social Constructivism's project to overcome the structure/agency divide, this is much easier said than done when it comes to concrete empirical research.

IR has always drawn on other disciplines, most notably from Philosophy and History, but Social Constructivism owes a great deal to the increased attention paid to global phenomena by sociological enquiry. Sociologists have long studied the importance of culture in shaping human behaviour and advanced ideas like 'socialisation' which is concerned with how institutions influence individual actions and such insights have come to be employed in the study of 'global society'. The culture of particular states and other actors can inform the way that they act on the world stage and distort the rationality inherent in Liberal, Realist and Marxist assumptions about behaviour. Governments and people within particular countries may have a particular way of doing things and/or a particular perspective on their role in the world. In the introduction to this chapter the positive German attitude to European integration can partly be explained by the country's historical legacy. German governments and German people have wanted to move on from the Nazi era and make amends to their European neighbours by consciously avoiding dominating the continent.

Cultures on an international scale can also be seen to influence policy. Organisations like the EU develop their own culture and are often thought to socialise their member states (see Chapter 15). In less formalised settings, norms of behaviour between actors emerge over time as they increasingly interact with each other in given areas as globalisation advances. Most people accept that individual people do not always interact with other individuals in their societies in a way which is entirely about maximising their own wealth or status (whether through a selfish or cooperative strategy) because they also have the agency to act according to ideas. Human behaviour may often be self-serving but it can also at times be altruistic, moralistic or simply strange. Many now contend that, with much greater interaction with, and awareness of, others beyond our own borders, this logic should be applied to the study of International Relations. Hence we can see how Social Constructivists have built upon the idea of a 'society of states', first articulated by the English School from the 1970s, in which values (and not just self-interest) are thought to inform the norms of societal behaviour that emerge.

*Source: Corbis/Bettman*

If we accept that our attitudes and actions are motivated by social or historical forces, can the actions of African tyrants such as Idi Amin be explained by a legacy of European imperialism?

## A Social Constructivist reappraisal of IR's key concepts

The approach to concepts we have encountered so far might be characterised as, on the one hand, those where concepts are solid and rigidly understood such as the state for Realists or class for Marxists; on the other hand, we have theories where the certainty of concepts is subject to an overarching theoretical critique. Although Social Constructivism is a very broad-based approach it is an attempt, at least, to be able to make concrete progress in terms of knowledge production, while avoiding obvious generalisations, at the same time as not becoming simply a tool of the establishment or status quo. What is offered below, then, is simply a flavour of the kinds of insights Social Constructivism can offer in order to make this middle ground compromise seem like a realistic proposition in its own right rather than merely 'splitting the difference'.

### The state and sovereignty

For Social Constructivists, international politics is not adequately captured in an analysis of the international system, as it is for Realists. For Realists, the international system is composed of states which behave as they do because of the dynamics of timeless laws which apply to such bodies. However, for Social Constructivists, states behave in the way they do because they are *socialised* into the institutions of particular forms of international politics. It follows from this that international politics is not governed purely by power and interests. There are fundamental norms of behaviour in international politics, even though they might be such basic ones as state sovereignty and non-intervention. The balance of power, for instance, could then be seen not as a *law* of the international system, but as a norm that states come to accept over time and act in accordance with.

The fact that norms are broken, therefore, does not mean they do not exist but, paradoxically, proves they *do* exist. For instance, states have always broken the norm of non-intervention. At the same time, however, such invasions have regularly been condemned by other states, and sometimes justified military interventions to return to the status quo before the invasion. Even the governments of the invading states are often at pains to justify their violation of the norm of non-intervention – for instance, by making historical claims about the territory occupied, or by reference to security concerns. If the norm of non-intervention did not exist, there would be no need to go through the motions of justifying such an occupation. For instance, in 1990 Iraq invaded Kuwait, an act which ultimately led to the first Gulf War. It is widely believed that the motivations for this act were political in the sense of relieving pressures on the Iraqi regime, claiming that the Kuwaiti regime was unpopular, but more to the point economic. Kuwait's oil reserves were significant and Iraq also accused Kuwait of stealing its oil through slant drilling. However, to the international community, the invasion was largely justified in historical terms with the argument that Kuwait was a natural part of Iraq which had only been separated by British imperialism. A little earlier (in 1983) the United States invaded the tiny Commonwealth Caribbean island of Grenada in an operation code named Operation Urgent Fury. The invasion supported a military coup which ousted a brief revolutionary government on the island. Although successful, and justified in terms of keeping international communism at bay, many commentators questioned the US view of this action as a vital to its security.

Social Constructivists do not necessarily dispute the Realist premise that contemporary international society is **anarchical**, with no single, hierarchical government. However, while Realism tends to take this anarchy to be universally valid across different times and cultures, Social Constructivism suggests a more nuanced approach. It can point to a variety of evidence. The European Union (EU) stands out as a case in which a regional system of states is now governed in part by hierarchical relationships, where the set of rules and laws directly affect all member states. Many of these rules and laws are now decided by what is called 'qualified majority voting' such that a member state that is outvoted by this system will nonetheless have to follow and implement the agreed legislation. This has introduced a considerable degree of hierarchy within the EU, even if it is not yet the same kind of centralised government as found within the state. Over time sovereignty has come to be redefined by (at least some) EU member states through the gradual appreciation of the fact that in a globalised world it cannot mean what it once did.

## Box 11.5 Alexander Wendt [1958– ]

Alexander Wendt, one of the best known Social Constructivists, became well known for a series of articles in the late 1980s and early 1990s, the most famous of which is 'Anarchy is what states make of it', published in the journal *International Organization* in 1992. He argues that anarchy is a given, but is moulded over time through the behaviour of states. In his main book, *Social Theory of International Politics* (1999), Wendt argued that there are 'three cultures of anarchy', which he labels Hobbesian, Lockean and Kantian. The Hobbesian culture is closest to the Realist image of anarchy, in which power and interests dominate, whereas in the Lockean version states – although rivals – recognise each other's sovereignty and therefore submit to a minimum standard of common norms. In a Kantian system, the scope of shared norms is much more extensive, with states no longer seeing themselves primarily as rivals but as equal partners.

In short, anarchy is a very broad category, and although the Greek city-state system and the post-Cold War global international system might both be characterised as anarchical, there are indeed important differences between them. Anarchy is therefore context-specific, changing over time and according to region. Following the logic of structure and agency in a Social Constructivist view, states shape anarchy through their interactions, and the particular form of anarchy prevalent in any given historical and spatial context shapes the nature and behaviour of states.

Meanwhile, at a global level, international law, has gained more and more relevance in international relations. The UN Security Council has the power to legitimise the use of force against a state that has violated international law while the World Trade Organisation has been granted supranational authority by the most powerful states so that they can reap economic rewards not likely to be garnered in a system of anarchy. These may be isolated examples but they represent important qualifications to the notion of a condition of anarchy in the international system.

## National interest

As illustrated in the example of Germany at the start of this chapter, Social Constructivists contend that states do not always act in ways easily explained by Realist, Liberal or Marxist assumptions of how the political world works. The 'national interest' is frequently invoked to justify, and by Realist analysts to explain, policies and is often presented as somehow self-evident. Social Constructivism (and the other approaches in Chapters 9 and 10) offers a much more critical lens for looking at the idea of national interest. Not least this stems from recognising that the nation is not a unitary actor; it consists of many different groups and people who are likely to define what is in the national interest in different ways. Given the existence of international level norms and institutions, Social Constructivists tend to refer to an international 'society' rather than a system. A society is characterised by the existence of mutually agreed norms and common institutions, while a system can exist without any of these and operate solely according to mechanical laws.

For Realists, ideas about the state and anarchy are intrinsically linked to the notion of an objective national interest, but for Social Constructivists the national interest is not objective. They are particularly interested in the relationship between identity and interests, and how certain ideas shape interests and vice versa. Liberal states in a Kantian international culture will, therefore, pursue interests different from dictatorships in a Hobbesian international order (see Box 11.5). Similarly, particular ideas about economic development will, for instance, shape what is seen by developing countries to be in their interest. In all of this, Social Constructivists insist that the relationship between ideas, identities and interests is a complex one. Ideas do not *simply* determine interests. More to the point, one cannot talk about one without the other.

Neo-Liberals, collating behavioural evidence of foreign policy making from the 1960s, sought to qualify the Realist rational actor model of states doggedly pursuing their national interest by positing that, owing to the possibility of misperception and the necessity of taking decisions via the bureaucracies of the state, 'bounded rationality' is more often the result. Social Constructivists do not deny that states often act amorally and selfishly in their foreign policies nor that mistakes often occur in the policy-making process due to bureaucratic procedures but, again, contend that ideas and culture distort the logic of both models. Chinese Premier Zhou Enlai, when asked for his thoughts on the French Revolution nearly two centuries before, famously replied that 'it was too early to tell'. This could be dismissed as a nice sound bite from a leader noted for his rhetorical flourishes but also, perhaps, gives an insight into Chinese international political thinking. Foreign policy analysis gives some credence to the idea that China often takes a much more long-term perspective than most Western countries or as is assumed by either the rational actor or bureaucratic politics models of decision-making. In the West it was widely anticipated that, with the coming to an end of the Cold War, China would more strongly assert its sovereign claim over Taiwan given that the US motivation to defend the independence of the island would weaken. Does the fact that this has not happened suggest the Chinese are in no rush to act, safe in the knowledge that – in the long term – the province will inevitably be reabsorbed again?

## Identity

Social Constructivists argue that a particular identity will provide actors with a role in international relations, and that they will try to act in a way they see as appropriate to that role. Social Constructivists are interested in the *construction* of identities, and how they change (or are reconstructed). In a similar way to postmodernists, they refer to processes of 'othering' when they analyse the construction of identities. This is based on the insight that every identity requires an 'other' against which it is set. If there were no other, there would be no identity, as everything would be the same. In contrast to postmodernism, however, Social Constructivists do not derive this argument from linguistic philosophy, but from social psychology. Research into group behaviour has shown that groups tend to distinguish between insiders and outsiders, and gain their identity from this distinction. There are lots of examples of such identity constructions in international relations such as: the construction of British identity versus Europe, of European identity versus Turkey, or American identity versus first Communism and then terrorism. Some observers of EU integration have noted the phenomenon of a Eurocentric identity emerging in recent years. As people within the EU have come to enjoy the benefits of a single market, surveys suggest that tolerance of people from other EU states (at least among the longer standing members) has increased but, at the same time, tolerance of non-EU nationalities has *decreased* (Pettihome 2008). European identity is particularly difficult to define, given the long-established national identities held by its people, leading to it being increasingly constructed in terms of what it is widely held not to be. To some, this is not Islamic, which goes a long way to explaining the reluctance to admit Turkey to the European Union.

In terms of changing identities, Constructivists normally assume that identities are difficult but not impossible to change. A helpful way to understand them, therefore, is as 'sticky'. If they did change easily, they would be rather less useful as a category in understanding international politics. But how and why do they change at all? One straightforward answer is that states enter into new relationships, and become socialised in the process. Indeed, research on state identities and European integration has shown that identities on that level are rather stubborn, and that socialisation is a very long process. Greater tolerance of each other between EU nationals can be observed, but the embrace of symbols like the EU flag or anthem are limited and most EU citizens still identify themselves primarily with their nations (Pettihome 2008). For identities to be changed radically, there may have to be an 'external shock': something must happen that challenges them fundamentally. The Second World War was such an event for Europe and Japan; the terrorist attacks of 9/11 might prove to be so for the USA. Such events go to the heart of the self-understanding of a state, and its core norms. Eventually, these norms and self-understandings might well be strengthened as a result of the challenge. Alternatively, however, the perception of a misfit between them and the outside world is stronger, and they need to be adjusted.

## Violence

Social Constructivism has also reconfigured perhaps the quintessential debate of IR between Realism and Liberalism: about the causes of war and peace in the world. Realists contend that war is an inevitable feature of international relations but containable through respect for the **balance of power**. Liberals in contrast believe that war is avoidable since it is structurally determined by the existence of an antagonistic state system and undemocratic governments, and so can be averted by political integration and **democratisation**. Empirical evidence for democracies and partners in regional blocs not fighting each other is strong but, additionally, fighting over the idea/existence of democracy could be said to have been a factor in recent wars fought between democracies and undemocratic states such as those fought in Iraq, Afghanistan and Yugoslavia. Social Constructivists have highlighted the phenomenon of 'warlike democracies' to demonstrate how ideas and perception undermine the logic of democratic peace theory (see Chapter 7). '(D)emocracies to a large degree create their enemies and their friends – 'them' and 'us' – by inferring either aggressive or defensive motives from the domestic structures of their counterparts' (Risse 1995: 19–20).

## Security

We can see that Constructivists try to deal with concepts of the traditionalist camp but still draw concrete conclusions about these concepts rather than just performing a Reflectivist critique. This is true of security issues which Social Constructivists have looked at in a variety of ways, including the analysis of security communities. Security communities are said to exist when a group of states share a sense of community and develop institutions for a stable peace between them. On the far end of the spectrum, so-called 'amalgamated security communities' are essentially autonomous political communities of their own (Deutsch 1957). More common in international relations is the case of a pluralistic security community, where states retain their identities, but nonetheless also share a deep sense of (collective) identity. Social Constructivist research has centred on the themes explored above: how do the norms and institutions of security communities influence the security policies of a state that is part of such a community? How do states get socialised into a security community? How do these communities change?

Social Constructivists have also participated in debates about expanding the concept of security itself which until the 1980s in IR (and maybe earlier in sub-fields such as Peace Research) had been seen very much in terms of military power. In the early 1980s though,

Source: Getty Images/AFP

The 'soft power' practised by Nelson Mandela's administration proved that influence can come from subjective constructs like respect, trust and admiration.

various authors began to suggest that security was also economic and societal, with the latter pertaining to questions of identity. So-called Critical Security Studies aimed at changing the main reference point of security from the state to the individual, and developed the concept of human security which has also become very influential in policy making at the United Nations (see Chapters 24–27). Against this, traditionalists wanted to keep a narrow definition of security. Their main argument was that the concept would otherwise lose its analytical value and could no longer be distinguished from any kind of politics.

Together with his colleague Ole Wæver, from the late 1980s onwards Barry Buzan became the core of the so-called **Copenhagen School** of Security Studies. They proposed that security should not be defined substantially. Paraphrasing Wendt's argument about anarchy, one could summarise their argument as 'security is what actors make of it'. In other words, they argued that security is defined through discourse, and its meaning will depend on what in a particular societal and historical context is accepted as security. In their own definition they therefore focused on the formal criteria that turned something into a security object. They specified these criteria as the representation of something as an existential threat to a particular community, justifying measures that would otherwise not be seen as legitimate – war would be an extreme case (Buzan et al. 1998).

## Case study: South Africa and Nelson Mandela

South Africa did not become notably more economically or militarily powerful after undergoing revolution from white minority rule under the apartheid system to become a democratic multiracial state in 1994, but few would contest the idea that its government quickly became much more influential in the world. The new South Africa unilaterally disarmed itself of nuclear weapons and has not sought to coerce any of its neighbouring states militarily, unlike during the apartheid era when the government maintained colonial rule over Namibia – in violation of international law – and became embroiled in conflicts in Mozambique and Angola. Additionally, post-apartheid South Africa was beset with economic difficulties arising out of the problems experienced during the post-revolutionary transition, due to restructuring and the financial outflow of capital which accompanied the emigration of some of its wealthy white citizens.

In spite of such problems, support around most of the world for the revolutionaries and the personal charisma and celebrity status of their leader, President Nelson Mandela, transformed the diplomatic fortunes of the country. From being a pariah state in the late 1980s, cut adrift from the UN General Assembly, the Bretton Woods institutions and all meaningful international sporting events, South Africa quickly became a significant force in international affairs. It emerged as a regional power through playing a leadership role in the South African Development Community and African Union, and also become an important global player through the exercise of *soft power* – as evidenced by its role in the G20 grouping of the world's leading economies and becoming widely touted as a future permanent member of the UN Security Council. The 'Rainbow nation' also moved rapidly from being excluded from competing in international sport to become the first African country to host the football World Cup in 2010. Even the last apartheid President and one time adversary Frederik Willem De Klerk has admitted that: 'It is only thanks to Nelson Mandela's leadership, his tolerance, his remarkable lack of bitterness that South Africa is today peaceful and prosperous' (Binyon 2009).

What the new South Africa stands for in the eyes of the world has opened doors for them, serving to demonstrate that influence can come from purely subjective constructs that emerge from social interaction – like respect, trust and admiration.

## The empiricists strike back? Critiques of Social Constructivism

While Social Constructivism is certainly influential it has also put itself in a position where it is shot at by almost all sides, including those who find its compromise unhelpful in terms of its explanatory power. The rationalist critique focuses on the empirical evidence for the proposed arguments. They argue that most of the puzzles addressed by Social Constructivism can be adequately explained by interests and other 'material' factors, and that the impact of such things as norms accounts for, if anything, a very small portion of the variation in state behaviour. While Social Constructivists may have offered contributions to our understanding of political change, as in South Africa and the European Union, by highlighting the previously marginalised considerations of agency and culture, perhaps they have offered little in terms of explaining why such change occurs. Some also find the very notion of identity or norms as explanatory factors problematic, as they cannot be readily observed. This criticism is difficult to counter – in the end it boils down to the question of whether or not one accepts the critical–realist epistemological foundations of most Social Constructivist work.

Nonetheless, some major problems remain. One is that a lot of the concepts that Social Constructivists operate with are rather unclearly defined. Some analyses, for instance, talk about identity, culture, norms and institutions, and it can be rather difficult to separate them. Needless to say, this problem becomes more important the closer Social Constructivist work gets to the rationalist pole and does indeed want to explain. Similarly, nearly all attempts to distinguish empirically between different types of logic which lead to action have run into severe difficulties. The reason for this is that, while the differentiation, for instance between strategic and argumentative action, might make a lot of sense as an abstract ontological theorisation, unless we find a means to look into a policy maker's head, we cannot determine whether he or she does the things they do because they are motivated by interests, norms or the search for the best argument.

There are also several criticisms from the Reflectivist camp. Whether in the work of Hedley Bull or Alexander Wendt, in a lot of mainstream Social Constructivist work the state is taken as an unproblematic category and is treated as the central actor in international relations. Both Critical Theorists and postmodernists disagree with this, as should be clear from Chapters 9 and 10. Another common criticism, especially from postmodernists, is that Social Constructivists do not take language seriously. While they acknowledge the importance of discourse, their understanding of it remains shallow, and very few Social Constructivists recognise the power of language in its own right rather than as a transmitter of norms and a means of socialisation.

None of this should detract from the critical insights that Social Constructivism has provided us with since the 1990s. Also, perhaps one should also be grateful that Social Constructivists have not stayed in the corners of the fourth debate but opened up a space between the poles where dialogue is possible, if not necessarily always easy. IR was labelled the backward discipline by its critics precisely because it had spent too long not even considering questions which had for a long time been seen as essential starting points for other types of social theory. The criticism might be too harsh; as an Anglo-American enterprise growing up in the Cold War it may be considered hardly surprising that concrete policy advice won out over theoretical speculation, even if methodological rigour did become part of the disciplinary debate. However, once the can of worms was opened it did appear that some work faced the danger of excessive reflection.

There seem to have been four responses to this. First, to argue that we need to dispense with postmodernism; reject it as a fad and get back to the core business of providing policy advice to help beat the bad guys. This is understandable, if unsophisticated, and likely to lead to a repeat of mistakes made in the past. Second, that all this critique, far from being beyond what might be called a 'boundary of negativity' is essential; we must pay more attention to the reality spoken by different people and denaturalise disciplinary norms in IR.

Third then is Social Constructivism. Its merits are described above and it has been a success in terms of allowing disciplinary IR to be seen as some kind of whole, and complementary, working on different sides of the same coin perhaps. However, as noted on a number of occasions, the 'cake and eat it' approach is not always easy to sustain. Thus the so-called Copenhagen School of Constructivist Security Studies, for instance, is attacked by 'old School' IR theorists for its excessive reflection. However, for the other 'side' it is in danger of imposing a rigid, near positivist framework. In this context Social Constructivism can seem like a pragmatic move primarily; understandable but ultimately unsatisfactory. All in all Social Constructivism has moved International Relations theory away from being too simple and too complicated; although it is also a very broad church. Just as the idea of being 'left wing' can lead to serious arguments among those who would accept the label, Social Constructivism ultimately ends up replicating some of the same old arguments about how scientific our study can be, what the role of ideas is, and so on.

In his work *Social Theory of International Politics*, Alexander Wendt (1999) seeks what has been described as a philosophically principled middle way. According to Steve Smith 'against rationalist accounts of international relations Wendt wants to argue for both an idealist and a holist account; against more radical constructivists he wants to argue for a science of international relations' (Smith 2000). In the end, rather than Social Constructivism being the middle ground which unites IR theory it is rather the new battleground. There is so much difference within the approach, that like the old neo-neo battleground it may seem to those on the outside as fairly unified with only nuanced differences but in effect replicates some of the discipline's oldest disagreements. Except this time the argument is somewhat more sophisticated after the discipline's engagement with social theory more generally. So the fourth and final reaction is taken by those who adamantly support a *particular position* within Social Constructivism (such as hardline critical Realists) and reject its status as a compromise and broad church.

One key counter-argument to the Rationalist criticism is that it misunderstands the whole Social Constructivist project, which is not to explain outcomes through recourse to independent variables, but rather to show that there are no really independent variables in social relations, and that we need to approach international politics with the aim of understanding actors' behaviour from the 'inside'. Similarly, the criticism that Social Constructivism is not really a theory can be rebutted by pointing out that it does not want to be a theory in the universally applicable sense of, say, neo-Realism.

## Conclusion

Social Constructivism is not one single theory but is better characterised as a range of different approaches. These argue that our world is continuously reproduced in the interplay of structure and agency. In contrast to post-Structuralism, Social Constructivism does not question the possibility of knowledge. Therefore, Social Constructivism is often seen as constituting the middle ground in International Relations between rationalist and reflectivist theories. Social Constructivism draws on sociological theories and consequently stresses the societal aspect of international relations, as opposed to the mechanistic qualities of the international system. Social Constructivism has an affinity with the older so-called English School of International Relations but has taken their scepticism of Behaviouralism and actor rationality a step further. Social Constructivism focuses on the role of norms, institutions, identity and culture in international relations. This makes it different from interest-based theories such as neo-Realism and neo-Liberalism. Norms and institutions are crucial in the process of socialisation. Social Constructivists argue that, just like individual human beings, states become socialised into particular forms of international society. For Social Constructivists, the national interest is a category that needs to be explained, rather than being treated as an explanatory factor. They are interested in how interests, norms and institutions interact – for instance – in the making of foreign policy. Methodologically, a Social Constructivist approach normally stresses historical processes, because it is otherwise unable to demonstrate the interplay of structure and agency.

Social Constructivism is criticised by both the rationalist and the reflectivist end of the spectrum of the fourth debate for being either inconsistent or not radical enough. What we hope we have shown in this chapter is that Social Constructivism does add some valuable insights to the analysis of international politics.

## Resource section

## Questions

**1.** How significant a contribution to International Relations theory has been made by Social Constructivism?

**2.** To what extent does describing Social Constructivism as the 'middle ground' serve to conceal the great differences that exist within this school of thought?

**3.** 'Social Constructivists do not explain change in world politics, they merely describe how it occurs'. Discuss.

## Recommended reading

Adler, E. (1997) 'Seizing the middle ground: constructivism in world politics', *European Journal of International Relations*, 3(3): 319–63
This core article outlines Social Constructivism as the middle ground between Rationalism, Reflectivism and Structuralism.

Bull, H. (1977) *The Anarchical Society: A Study of Order in World Politics* (Basingstoke: Macmillan)
A core work of the English School, in which Bull sets out clearly the organising institutions and norms of international society.

Christiansen, T., Jørgensen, K.E. and Wiener, A. (eds) (2001) *The Social Construction of Europe* (London: Sage)
A very valuable and influential collection of essays from all parts of the Social Constructivist spectrum on European integration and governance.

Onuf, N.G. (1989) *World of Our Making: Rules and Rule in Social Theory and International Relations* (New York: Columbia University Press)
Onuf was one of the first Social Constructivists in International Relations. Many constructivists have been influenced by this book.

Risse, T., Ropp, S. and Sikkink, K. (eds) (1999) *The Power of Human Rights: International Norms and Domestic Change* (Cambridge: Cambridge University Press)
This has become a classic empirical work from a Social Constructivist perspective. The 'spiral model' of the impact of human rights on domestic change is outlined and applied to several case studies.

Wendt, A. (1999) *Social Theory of International Politics* (Cambridge: Cambridge University Press)
Wendt is widely regarded as the most influential Social Constructivist. In this book, he summarises his ideas about institutions, norms, culture and anarchy in international politics.

# Part 4 International and Regional Cooperation

In this part of the book we will provide a wide-ranging survey of international and regional actors. We shall explain what they do in international relations and why they do what they do. The previous three parts of the book have been designed to give you a comprehensive foundation for the study of contemporary international issues, by examining: international relations and globalisation; the history of globalisation and international relations; and International Relations theories.

As with the first three parts, this one has several aims. First, we want to give you an understanding of why international and regional organisations are often of importance for outcomes in international relations. We aim to show how and why they relate to some of the more important pressing problems which appear every day in the media headlines and which, directly and indirectly, affect the lives of each of us, including economic, political, social and environmental issues and outcomes. These issues are at the heart of globalisation, and they take a number of different forms.

The key questions we examine are: Why do nearly all states around the world now pursue international and regional cooperation? What does this imply for our understanding of international relations in the context of globalisation?

We shall see that most examples of international and regional cooperation are the result of new or newly understood challenges, which governments believe can be better met by means of inter-state cooperation than by relying on national strategies alone. By engaging in these forms of collaboration, states believe they can create or strengthen policy domains, providing them with new, improved instruments to deal with actors, situations and processes. This means that states expect international and regional cooperation to help them pursue various objectives in the context of 'new challenges', especially those emanating from globalisation. These forms of cooperation are regarded by states as both 'functionally efficient' and in line with the pursuit of national interests. Over time, the arrangements may lead to the development of new regional regimes, implying shared and agreed regulations, structures and processes governing interactions.

The picture that emerges from these chapters is that the process of globalisation is a highly complex one, with major disagreements existing about its significance and its impact. Some examples point to greater inter-state cooperation because of globalisation among international and regional actors while others underline the likelihood of increased levels of non-cooperation among states in the early twenty-first century.

*Source*: Getty Images/Somos/Veer

# Chapter 12
# Intergovernmental Organisations

After reading this chapter you will be able to:

- Understand what an intergovernmental organisation is and the variety of forms they take

- Appreciate how intergovernmental organisations have evolved in line with globalisation and other changes in the international political system

- Be able to evaluate the political significance of intergovernmental organisations from rival theoretical perspectives

*Source*: Getty Images/Somos/Veer

## Introductory box: The Kosovan War 1999

The North Atlantic Treaty Organisation (NATO) instigated the only war in their history against Yugoslavia in 1999 after its member states reached 'consensus' on the need to act against Serb violence being meted out against the Albanian population in their province of Kosovo. Massacres and displacements of the Kosovans had shocked much of the world, and public and political demands for an armed 'humanitarian intervention' by the international community had built up. When the United Nations could not get its membership to agree to act NATO stepped in. NATO consensus means the agreement of all members but it was well known that one of the membership, Greece, was not enthusiastic at the prospect of siding against their near neighbour and traditional ally. The Greeks were, however, persuaded to drop their objection and go along with the desires of the other states in the organisation. The Greek government being brought on board can be understood in two different ways which serve to illustrate the competing school of thought in IR on the influence of intergovernmental organisations.

1. The Greeks, as a relatively minor power within NATO, were bullied into towing the line in an exercise of power politics.
2. The Greeks were convinced of the need to act against their instincts for the good of international security and human rights through the discourse promoted by being part of an influential intergovernmental organisation.

Source: Rex Features/Andrew Testa

British and French troops in Kosovo. NATO's mission in the region shows the importance of intergovernmental cooperation.

## What is an intergovernmental organisation?

International Relations, traditionally, focuses on interactions between states conducted through their governments but, over time, has come also to focus on the role of *non-state actors* on the world stage. Non-state actor is a generic term covering any organisation other than a state with a role in international relations. There are two broad subcategories of non-state actors: intergovernmental organisations (IGOs) and international non-governmental organisations (INGOs). IGOs are non-state actors essentially comprising governments as members. INGOs, according to the UN, include 'any international organization which is not established by inter-governmental agreement' (United Nations 1950). Hence INGO can be seen as an umbrella term for all other non-state actors which are 'private', in that they do not include governments in their membership. In domestic politics the term 'non-governmental organisation' is usually used to denote a 'pressure group' or 'not-for-profit organisation' that is independent of government and representing citizens' interests in a given area. Such organisations, like Amnesty International or Oxfam, are also INGOs as they are prominent on the international stage, but the term non-governmental organisation in IR is wider than this application (see Box 12.1).

There is not always a clear distinction between IGOs and INGOs. IGOs increasingly involve pressure groups as observers alongside government representatives and some INGOs are not entirely 'private' and permit such a significant role for governments that they are sometimes considered to form a distinct category of non-state actor; a hybrid IGO/INGO. Examples of

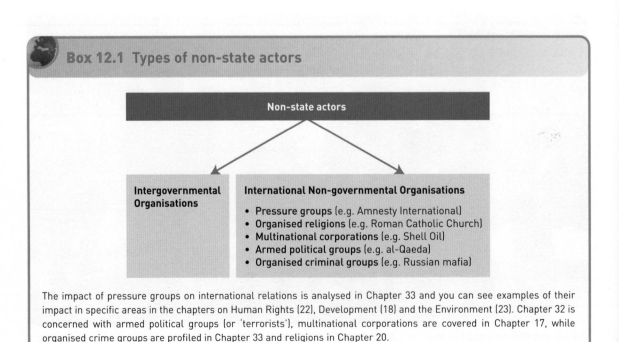

**Box 12.1  Types of non-state actors**

Non-state actors

**Intergovernmental Organisations**

**International Non-governmental Organisations**

- **Pressure groups** (e.g. Amnesty International)
- **Organised religions** (e.g. Roman Catholic Church)
- **Multinational corporations** (e.g. Shell Oil)
- **Armed political groups** (e.g. al-Qaeda)
- **Organised criminal groups** (e.g. Russian mafia)

The impact of pressure groups on international relations is analysed in Chapter 33 and you can see examples of their impact in specific areas in the chapters on Human Rights (22), Development (18) and the Environment (23). Chapter 32 is concerned with armed political groups (or 'terrorists'), multinational corporations are covered in Chapter 17, while organised crime groups are profiled in Chapter 33 and religions in Chapter 20.

such organisations include the World Conservation Union and the International Conference of the Red Cross and Red Crescent, which feature representatives of both governments and pressure groups as members with voting powers.

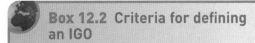

**Box 12.2 Criteria for defining an IGO**

- Two or more sovereign governments
- Permanent
- Regular meetings and a decision-making process

There is no precise or official definition of what constitutes an IGO but Box 12.2 gives the three generally agreed upon conditions that need to be met to distinguish such an entity from other forms of international cooperation.

Obviously, an IGO has to be international and involve more than one government. There is some disparity in view on this, however. The Union of International Associations only considers groupings of at least three states to count as an IGO while others consider that two is sufficient (Wallace and Singer 1970).

More crucially in terms of definitions, forms of association between governments that are one-off agreements or temporary arrangements are not considered to constitute an IGO. There are many examples of governments cooperating in *alliances* before and since the emergence of IGOs to achieve common foreign policy goals, particularly in fighting together against a common foe in wartime. Alliances, however, are generally not IGOs in that they are usually transient arrangements, intended only to achieve short-term objectives, such as winning a war. Alliances, also, are not usually institutionalised. The Allied and Axis governments worked together closely in the Second World War (particularly the former) but this was purely for the purpose of winning the war. After the war some of theses countries, most notably the USSR and its allies, quickly became estranged.

An IGO, additionally, is more than a case of intergovernmental cooperation resulting from the ratification of an international treaty. An IGO has a 'life of its own' in that it continues to produce new coordinated policies on a regularised basis. Accordingly, we can see that some alliances have become more than that and transformed themselves into IGOs. NATO was set up as a military alliance among North American and West European states to counter the threat posed by the USSR and operates on the basis of a founding treaty, but has evolved into more than this. Most notably NATO has outlived the Cold War it was set up in relation to, expanded its membership and also widened the remit of what it does in accordance with its decision-making procedures. Coming to the defence of people not within the organisation's membership, over Kosovo in 1999, was a clear instance of this.

A clear illustration of what distinguishes an IGO from lesser forms of intergovernmental cooperation comes from looking at the World Trade Organisation (WTO). The WTO was set up in 1995 to take over work previously carried out under the auspices of The General Agreement on Tariffs and Trade (GATT), established in 1947. GATT brought a steadily growing number of governments together in the cause of freeing up international trade and gradually took steps to implement its founding treaty through a series of 'Rounds', but was not an IGO. GATT was not institutionalised and not a political actor because it did not have a decision-making procedure or permanent staff to enable it to do any more than periodically implement the founding treaty. The WTO, in contrast, sought

## Box 12.3  Interpol – an example of IGO structure

Interpol, the organisation responsible for coordinating police work on an international scale, has:

- a General Assembly attended by representatives of all 187 member states which is the supreme decision-making body and meets once a year
- an Executive Committee comprising thirteen representatives elected by the General Assembly

which meets three times per year and is responsible for implementing General Assembly decisions and formulating new policy ideas

- a secretariat based at the headquarters in Lyon which works full time and is headed by a Secretary General, the lead figure of the organisation.

to strengthen the political compulsion on governments to fulfil the GATT treaty obligations, develop new rules to free up trade and authoritatively resolve trade disputes and so developed a permanent headquarters, staff and regularised decision-making structure.

IGOs vary considerably and there is no identikit of how they operate but a conventional structure includes:

1. **Legislature**   A plenary meeting of all members occurring infrequently (perhaps once a year) at which the overall strategy of the IGO and key issues arising are debated by government ministers or delegates representing their governments. Typically the admission of new member states or amendments to the founding treaty, possibly establishing new roles for the organisation, are decided in this way.
2. **Executive**   A body responsible for more regular decision-making and the implementation of policy, usually comprised of a subset of members elected by the legislature. The executive will usually be made up of delegates of the governments represented – that is by diplomats rather than members of the government.
3. **Secretariat**   The administrative body responsible for day-to-day work in support of the organisation at its headquarters. The secretariat will usually be staffed by full-time administrators who perform a role equivalent to the Civil Service in a given country. Heading up this body is often a Secretary General, who assumes the function of lead individual for the organisation in international diplomacy.

## The evolution and diversity of IGOs

Estimates of the number of IGOs in the world vary because of the definitional ambiguities previously described but, as is illustrated in Box 12.4, the general trend over the last two centuries has been one of near continual growth until a tailing off since the 1980s. The onset of globalisation has facilitated both the need for and the possibilities to create IGOs, as linkages between states and international trade have grown. Hence the growth of international trade in the late nineteenth century, fuelled by industrialisation, proved a spur for the first IGOs. Subsequently, the collapse of international trade in the 1930s' Great Depression saw this period of growth come to a halt until reactivated by the end of the Second World War and the onset of the second and present process of globalisation in the guise of the Bretton Woods System. As well as trade and globalisation, Box 12.4 clearly shows how IGO growth has been greatly influenced by the ending of major international wars. The years 1815, 1918 and 1945 were important watersheds in international relations since a widespread desire to avoid such bloodshed again prompted governments to seek ways to encourage greater international dialogue and provide fora for disputes to be resolved before they got out of hand. The Concert of Europe system initiated in 1815 did not spawn anything as advanced as the League of Nations or United Nations, which arose out of the twentieth century's two great international conflicts, but it did sow the seeds of such cooperation and the world's first IGO, the Central Commission for the Navigation of the Rhine.

An exception to this trend of IGOs flourishing in the optimism of a new world order after a major war ends can be seen with the end of the Cold War. In the last twenty years we have, perhaps paradoxically, seen IGO numbers fall despite the most peaceful inter-state relations witnessed since the nineteenth century and unprecedented globalisation. However, it is the end of the Cold War and the onset of globalisation that explain this phenomenon. On the one hand, by the 1990s many organisations whose memberships were defined on Cold War lines ceased to have any rationale to continue. NATO's metamorphosis into a post-Cold War peacekeeping organisation is a glaring exception to this but, from the other side of the Iron Curtain, the Soviet empire's military association the Warsaw Pact (World

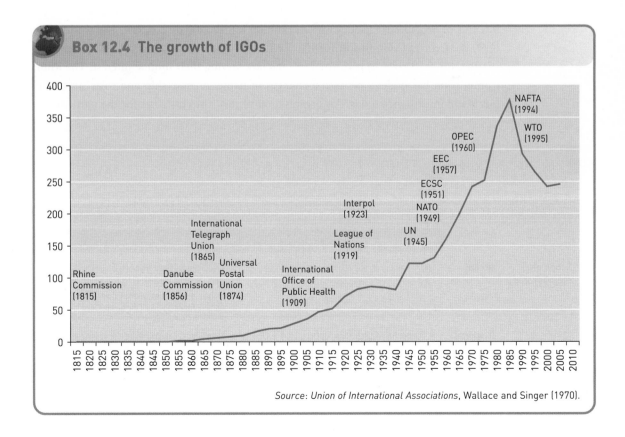

**Box 12.4 The growth of IGOs**

*Source: Union of International Associations,* Wallace and Singer (1970).

Treaty Organisation) and its economic equivalent COMECON met their demise alongside the Communist empire. On the other hand, over the last twenty years other regional organisations have been wound up as an increasingly politically and economically unified state system has rendered such groupings irrelevant and they have essentially been super-seded by wider organisations performing the same functions. The European Coal and Steel Community, for example, ceased to function in 2002 as its rules had come to be absorbed by the European Union which grew from it. The International Natural Rubber Organisation, set up in 1980 as a producers' cartel seeking to control the price of the commodity, ceased to operate in 1999 in the context of greater global trade liberalisation promoted by the WTO which had served to undermine its influence. Hence, the recent downturn in the number of IGOs is not a repeat of the 1930s and not indicative of a decline in intergovernmental cooperation. It is more a rationalisation of the process.

The two hundred and fifty or so IGOs in the world today differ greatly, both in their size and in what they do. In order to comprehend this diversity and also understand their evolution over the last two hundred years it is useful to construct a typology. Box 12.5 pre-sents a convenient way of breaking down the array of IGOs into four general categories according both to the range of their memberships and of what they do.

## Regional functional IGOs

The most basic and original IGOs emerged on utilitarian grounds in that they served the interests of neighbouring states with a common transboundary concern. The world's first IGO, the Central Commission for the Navigation of the Rhine, was set up by the states sharing this great river to perform a specific task serving their mutual interest. The Rhine Commission has undergone several changes of name, membership and roles since 1815 but is still in existence today. An organisation of this sort cuts costs for the participating

---

### Box 12.5  Typology of IGOs

| Scope of membership | | Scope of issues | |
|---|---|---|---|
| | | **Multi-purpose** | **Functional** |
| **Scope of membership** | **Global** | UN | • **UN Specialised agencies** (e.g. World Health Organisation) <br> • **Other specialist global bodies** (e.g. World Trade Organisation) |
| | **Regional** | • **Regional diplomatic actors** (e.g. EU) <br> • **Associations of former colonies** (e.g. The Commonwealth) | • **Resource Co-management IGOs** (e.g. Rhine Commission) <br> • **Trade Blocs** <br> • **Cartels** (e.g. Organisation of Petroleum Exporting Countries) <br> • **Military IGOs** (e.g. NATO) |

governments by putting in place a mechanism to co-manage a common resource and circumvent having to set up negotiations every time a policy issue on matters related to the resource arises, as they inevitably will. Hence a similar institution performing a comparable role for the states sharing Europe's other great international river, the Danube, was set up in 1856 to become the world's second IGO. Over time many of the world's major river systems have come to be regulated by IGOs, as have other forms of shared waterways such as seas. The Scheldt is co-managed by an international commission similar to that of its near neighbour the Rhine. The Sénégal, Niger and Gambia river basins in Africa; the Irtysh and Mekong in Asia; and the Uruguay in South America have also spawned intergovernmental authorities to regulate navigation, irrigation and pollution issues. Some IGOs have similarly emerged to co-manage common seas. Examples of this include the Lake Chad Commission, Barents Euro-Arctic Council and the Arctic Council.

Regional functional IGOs also proliferated on a utilitarian basis in the twentieth century in the economic sphere. The European Coal and Steel Commission (ECSC) was set up by the Paris Treaty of 1951 collectively to manage the coal and steel policies of six European countries (West Germany, France, Italy, Belgium, the Netherlands and Luxembourg) and was selected deliberately by leading advocates of a federal Europe to act as a catalyst for political 'spillover' into other sectors (see Chapter 15). The success of the ECSC kick-started the integration process that led to the European Union and also inspired the creation of other trade blocs; regional grouping of countries who open up commerce by fully or partially removing trade barriers such as tariffs (taxes on imports). Trade blocs have multiplied throughout the world since their inception in Europe in the 1950s with organisations like the North American Free Trade Agreement (NAFTA), the European Free trade Association (EFTA) and Economic Community of West African States (ECOWAS) among prominent examples.

A large number of economic IGOs are **cartels** in which countries who have significant export earnings from a particular product coordinate in an effort to control the world price of that commodity. Such groupings of countries will not necessarily be 'regional' in a geographic sense but, since they are exclusive clubs they can be considered regional for the purposes of the typology. Far and away the most influential cartel is the Organisation of Petroleum Exporting Countries (OPEC) set up in 1960 by the world's leading oil exporters (see Chapter 17). Other cartel IGOs have had less impact than OPEC since other products, like rubber, coffee and tin, though important, are less crucial to importers than oil and more easily substituted for other commodities.

As pointed out earlier, NATO is unusual in being a military alliance/IGO. Many other significant military alliances are not represented in an institutional form but are nonetheless politically important. The US's military cooperation with Japan and Israel are prominent examples. Some other Cold War IGOs like the Soviet's Warsaw Pact and the US's South East Asian Treaty Organisation (SEATO) were wound up with the end of the Cold War but NATO has survived and redefined itself. NATO's membership has expanded to include several former enemies from beyond the Iron Curtain and it is now committed to the maintenance of peace and security across Europe and beyond, rather than the deterrence of a particular enemy. So powerful was NATO that, come the end of the Cold War that defined the organisation, its members came to the conclusion that it would be a shame to see it go and it was, instead, redesigned for the post-Cold War geopolitical land-scape. The persistence of NATO presents a clear illustration of how IGOs can survive and evolve beyond their original purpose.

Some other regional military organisations have emerged in the post-Cold War era. The Commonwealth of Independent States (CIS) was established on the demise of the USSR to maintain diplomatic, security and economic links between the Soviet successor states but has been undermined by the subsequent Western orientation of many of those states (such as Georgia and Ukraine) and now military cooperation is coordinated through the Collective Security Treaty Organisation (CSTO) comprising the pro-Russian successor states (Russia, Armenia, Kazakhstan, Kyrgyzstan, Tajikistan and Belarus). The Gulf Cooperation Council was set up by the Arabian peninsular states in 1981, who quickly agreed upon a defence pact which was then brought into operation on the Iraqi invasion of Kuwait in 1990. That war led to a strengthening of defence cooperation and the establishment of a joint military committee in 1994.

## Global functional IGOs

The logic of states institutionalising their cooperation for utilitarian reasons, evident from the creation of the Rhine Commission, came also to be expressed at a wider, global level later in the nineteenth century as international trade blossomed like never before and a prelude to contemporary globalisation took hold. Advances in communications technology and the proliferation of global commerce provided the incentives for the creation of the world's first global IGO; the International Telegraph Union (ITU) in 1865 and then the Universal Postal Union (UPU) in 1874. Having agreed international standards for postal rates and for sending telegrams served to cut costs and make business easier for all. As with the Rhine Commission, the UPU and ITU have undergone changes of name, membership and function since the nineteenth century but still exist today as specialised agencies of the UN. The specialised agencies are autonomous IGOs, with their own budgets and memberships, but operate within the UN system. This arrangement, a replication of the League of Nations' successful system, is built on a symbiotic relationship whereby the global multi-purpose IGO draws on the expertise of the functional organisation and the functional organisation benefits from the exposure of being linked to the world's most prominent organisation.

Other global functional organisations have emerged outside the UN system as globalisation has brought more and more issues of common concern into focus. At one end of the scale is the World Trade Organisation, established in 1995 to free up and harmonise international trading standards, which has **supranational** powers to punish member states which violate its founding treaty. At the other end of the scale lie many obscure IGOs which have emerged over recent decades as governments have agreed to implement common rules in particular areas of trade or policy for their mutual convenience. Bodies like the International Maritime Satellite Organisation and the International Union for the Protection of New Varieties of Plants have arisen to provide arenas for achieving specific, technical goals requiring cross-border cooperation.

## Box 12.6 The specialised agencies of the United Nations

- **FAO (Food and Agriculture Organisation of the UN)**
  Works to improve agricultural productivity and food security
- **IAEA (International Atomic Energy Agency)**
  Works for the safe and peaceful uses of atomic energy
- **ICAO (International Civil Aviation Organisation)**
  Sets international standards for the safety, security and efficiency of air transport
- **IFAD (International Fund for Agricultural Development)**
  Mobilises financial resources to raise food production in developing countries
- **ILO (International Labour Organisation)**
  Formulates policies and programmes to improve working conditions and sets international labour standards
- **IMF (International Monetary Fund)**
  Facilitates international monetary cooperation and financial stability
- **IMO (International Maritime Satellite Organisation)**
  Works to improve international shipping safety and reduce marine pollution
- **ITU (International Telecommunication Union)**
  Fosters international cooperation to improve telecommunications and coordinates usage of radio and TV frequencies

- **UNESCO (UN Educational, Scientific and Cultural Organisation)**
  Promotes education for all and scientific and cultural cooperation
- **UNIDO (UN Industrial Development Organisation)**
  Promotes the industrial advancement of developing countries through technical assistance
- **UNWTO (UN World Tourism Organisation)**
  Serves as a global forum for tourism policy issues
- **UPU (Universal Postal Union)**
  Establishes international regulations for postal services
- **WHO (World Health Organisation)**
  Coordinates programmes aimed at solving international health problems
- **WIPO (World Intellectual Property Organisation)**
  Promotes the international protection of intellectual property
- **World Bank Group**
  Provides loans and technical assistance to developing countries to reduce poverty and advance sustainable economic growth
- **WMO (World Meteorological Organisation)**
  Promotes research on the Earth's climate and facilitates the global exchange of meteorological data

## Regional multi-purpose IGOs

The success of functional regional IGOs, as well as inspiring global equivalents to be set up, also served to inspire regional organisations to deepen their scope of issues. The ECSC's success in increasing coal and steel production and fostering peaceful cooperation between recent adversaries paved the way for the creation of the European Economic Community and EURATOM (fostering cooperation on atomic energy) six years later, so launching the 'European Communities' (of the three institutions) at the Treaty of Rome in 1957. Through the integrative process often explained by the theory of **neo-functionalism**, the European Communities have since continued to widen their membership and deepen their functions to become the world's most politically far-reaching IGO, the European Union. This phenomenon is explored in Chapter 15.

Other regional IGOs have followed the EU lead and sought to coordinate a range of political areas but without going down the same road towards supranationalism and a 'pooling' of sovereignty. The Common Market of the South (America) (MERCOSUR) and

Association of South East Asian Nations (ASEAN) have become more than the trade blocs they started off as, with the former developing organs to facilitate political cooperation in a range of areas and the latter including provisions for conducting peacekeeping operations in the region. The African Union, as its name implies, has long had aspirations to follow the European example but, while it serves to coordinate diplomacy in a range of political issues, it has not evolved beyond a purely intergovernmental forum for discussing a wide range of issues of common interest. The Organisation of the Islamic Conference, considered in Chapter 13, is cultural rather than economic and links together 57 predominantly Islamic countries across four continents to act as a voice for the Muslim world and, hence, is perhaps best described a 'global'.

Some other IGOs which provide arenas for discussing a wide remit of issues are relics of the imperial era. The UK, France and Portugal set up organisations to maintain political, cultural and economic relations between former colonies and their 'mother country'. Again, these organisations are only regional in a notional sense since their memberships are arrived at through historical rather than geographical circumstance. The Commonwealth links most of the former British Empire and even one country never ruled from London, Mozambique, which chose to join in 1995. This decision by the Mozambique government is indicative that the Commonwealth, despite its legacy of imperial domination, is viewed as a useful diplomatic forum for its members and is not without political significance. In particular this seemingly esoteric association took an influential diplomatic stance for human rights when it agreed to suspend the membership of Fiji in 1987 in response to a racist coup. Fiji was allowed to rejoin the organisation ten years later, but only after amending its constitution and renouncing racism. The Francaphonie and Community of Portuguese Speaking Countries have not had the same level of political impact as the Commonwealth and are more focused on the preservation of those European languages, however, they still serve as arenas for facilitating diplomatic exchanges on a range of international issues.

## Global multi-purpose IGOs

There are only two cases which come into the category of global multi-purpose IGOs; the League of Nations established in 1920 and its successor the United Nations, set up in 1945. The League and UN are also distinguishable from other IGOs in that they were/are, additionally, the centre points of systems linking together many global functional intergovernmental organisations.

The League of Nations was born of the Paris Peace Conference at the end of the First World War and was very much moulded in the spirit of Liberal Idealism which dominated international relations in this age. As with many IGOs, fostering international peace and commerce were the twin motives for the League. The unprecedented horrors of the First World War, and the feeling that this had been a conflict which could have been averted with greater international dialogue, gave political momentum to Liberal ideas like **collective security** and *open diplomacy*. Hence measures were enacted to ensure that diplomatic exchanges were made openly in conferences, rather than in closed private meetings, and that conflicts could be resolved through negotiation or in court. Where this was not sufficient to keep the peace, military action by the whole international community would punish those who had violated international law (collective security). The League established an Assembly at which all members could debate international issues of the day, a Security Committee of fifteen members to enact measures to uphold the peace and punish violations of its Charter, and a Permanent Court of International Justice to allow members to seek judicial remedies to disputes. The League also established an organ to implement a particular aim of promoting the independence of colonies seized from Germany, Italy and Turkey by the allied powers in the war, establishing the notion of **decolonisation** as an international norm.

The League is generally viewed as a failure because it demonstrably failed in its primary goal of maintaining world peace as it collapsed amidst the Second World War. The League, on several occasions, failed to punish blatant acts of aggression. The 1931 Japanese invasion of Manchuria, 1935 Italian invasion of Abyssinia (Ethiopia), and German military re-occupation of the Saar prompted some condemnations but no military response. Soviet, German and Italian interventions in the 1936–9 Spanish Civil War were similarly ignored and, although the USSR were expelled from the League in 1939 for the invasion of Finland, this was too little too late.

Ultimately, the League failed for two key reasons. First, it did not represent the whole international community. Secondly, its decision-making procedure was unworkable. The League of Nations was handicapped from the start by not being a truly global organisation. Much of the non-European world was still under imperial rule at this time and so not directly represented in the organisation. Most crucially, the emerging superpower of the USA never took up membership despite its then President Woodrow Wilson, at the Paris Peace Conference, having been its chief advocate. The US, instead, retreated into its shell after the First World War, fearful of being sucked into European squabbles, not to emerge until 1940 when the world had become a very different place. The other emerging superpower, the USSR, only joined the League in 1934, while Germany, Japan and Italy withdrew their membership in annoyance at the token criticism they had received for their military adventurism. Shorn of any involvement by the US and any real commitment to peace from Germany, Japan, Italy and the USSR, the League was left dominated by just two of the powerful states of the day: France and Great Britain. These two countries held permanent seats in the Council (as did the USSR during their membership) and represented the only serious military antidote to violations of the League's covenant. The French and British however, having recently emerged heavily indebted from the bloodiest war in their histories, did not have the stomach to become 'world policemen'. Hence the British and French governments went out of their way to ensure that condemnations of Japan for the horrific Manchurian invasion were not too severe and that economic sanctions levied against Italy for the seemingly motiveless annexation of Abyssinia were cosmetic. The Council's voting system rested on unanimity which meant that Britain and France could always veto any action, as could any of the other thirteen temporary member states during their stay in the spotlight. Unanimity in an international organisation, even among a sub-group of fifteen, is hard to find at the best of times and proved impossible in the polarising world of the 1930s.

Hence the United Nations, established at the San Francisco Conference of 1945, sought to learn from the failings of the League in the way it was set up. It took steps to ensure that it was genuinely global, including keeping the vanquished states from the Second World War on board. Germany and Japan thus became key players in the new system (albeit economically rather than militarily) rather than being dangerously ostracised as had been the case at the Paris Peace Conference. The active encouragement of decolonisation by the UN also served to ensure that it could become the very near universal organisation it is today with a membership of 192 states, with North Cyprus and Taiwan the only notable absentees from participating in the main debating chamber, the General Assembly (owing to the disputed nature of their statehood).

The UN was set up so that open diplomacy and international cooperation were again encouraged but, at the same time, Realist balance of power logic was grafted on to the Liberal-inspired structure, with five great powers – the USA, USSR, UK, France and China – entrusted to manage the system through the Security Council. The permanent five, together with ten other periodically elected members, are empowered to decide on action against states considered to have aggressively violated international law. This ensured the participation of these key players and made the application of force to uphold international order a more realistic possibility than under the League. The Security Council has been seriously hampered by the veto power ascribed to the five permanent members but has, on occasion, been able to get agreement for robust action to keep the peace beyond that achieved by the League. The UN's role in peacekeeping is analysed in Chapter 31.

### The UN and international law

One important function of IGOs is the role they can play in the development and implementation of Public International Law. Public International Law is a body of rules that has emerged over several centuries in order to regulate relations between states and also IGOs. It is distinct from domestic law and traditionally is not thought of as overlapping with sovereignty and states' own legal systems, although this is now increasingly challenged. Hence Public International Law is to be distinguished from Private International Law which is a means of settling disputes with a transboundary character (such as when a business merger between companies from different countries occurs) by deciding which state's law applies to the case. Public International Law is about finding settlements for international disputes not resolvable in this way, such as establishing whether a country has a right to claim a particular territory, or issues which are inherently global rather than national – such as with environmental change or human rights. It is not solely the product of IGO rulings, since customary practice between states is an acknowledged source of law, but the development of international law is closely linked to the UN system.

Some functional IGOs have facilitated the development of international law in their particular domains, such as human rights, the environment and international trade as is highlighted in Chapters 22, 23 and 17 respectively. This law is fundamentally different to domestic law in that, in the main, it applies only to those countries party to the relevant organisation or treaty and is hence constrained by sovereignty (although exceptions exist in a few areas such as torture and genocide considered to have universal application). By and large, however, the maxim that 'no one is above the law' does not apply to states and Public International Law.

Opinion on whether or not Public International Law should evolve beyond a purely intergovernmental body of rules *between* states to a supranational body of law *above* states is, essentially, divided into two camps. The 'Natural Law' perspective believes that international law should be informed by morality and proscribe what is right and wrong in the

## Case study: The International Court of Justice

The settlement of territorial disputes is chiefly the responsibility of the UN's court, the International Court of Justice (ICJ). The ICJ, sometimes referred to as the World Court, is a permanent IGO based at the Hague and is the successor to the League of Nations' Permanent Court of International Justice. The ICJ is made up of 15 judges of different nationalities elected by the General Assembly, subject to the approval of the Security Council. Hence, in an additional perk for the five permanent members of the Security Council, a judge of their nationality is always among the 15. Any state with a case up before the court is, however, entitled to have one of the 15 judges substituted by one of their own nationality if they are not already represented. The judges though, it should be pointed out, are not supposed to represent their governments but the international community at large.

Perhaps inevitably, however, sovereignty and national interest has hampered the ability of the ICJ to be a robust and independent global judiciary comparable to the highest court in a given land. Most significantly the ICJ is authorised only to adjudicate on cases in which both (or all) sides in a dispute agree to it (although some states have given the ICJ the automatic right of 'compulsory jurisdiction'). This, it could be said, is akin to your local court only having the right to try the man who burgled your house if he agreed to go before the judge. Certainly many international disputes have not found their way to the ICJ due to this sovereign restraint but that is not to say that the court has been a total irrelevance. While there is little prospect of major territorial conflicts – like India and Pakistan's dispute over Kashmir or the Arab–Israeli contention over Palestine – being resolved in the court, several lower level disputes have been sorted out in this way. Nigeria and Cameroon in 2002 allowed an ICJ verdict to decide on

a border dispute and several disagreements over the demarcation of territorial waters have been resolved at the Hague. While the ICJ falls short of being a global high court it has come to serve a useful role as a sort of arbitration panel open to states in dispute.

The limitations on the ICJ's role have led it to develop a secondary, unofficial function in addition to dispute settlement – that of offering 'advisory opinions'. In an illustration of how IGOs can develop new roles and evolve in unforseen directions, the ICJ has taken upon itself occasionally to make pronouncements on international controversies not referred to it. Hence in 1970 an ICJ Advisory Opinion declared the South African occupation of Namibia to be illegal and in 2004 stated that the Israeli government's construction of 'peace walls' to separate Jewish and Palestinian communities was unlawful. Such pronouncements carry no official legal weight but do, it is suggested, have some significance as statements of the acceptability of controversial international political practices which would, otherwise, be somewhat overlooked. South Africa did not leave Namibia after the ICJs Advisory Opinion but, twenty years later, they were compelled to pull out of Africa's last colony in the face of demonstrably hostile international opinion.

**Choose a recent international political news story with which you are familiar (perhaps read one from the international section of a newspaper) and consider:**

**1. Are any IGOs prominent in the story?**

**If so:**

**2. Do you think these IGOs are taking an independent position on the issue or just serving as mouthpieces for certain governments?**

*Source:* International Court of Justice/Jeroen Bouman – Courtesy of the ICJ

**Issues of sovereignty and national interest have hampered the ICJ's ability to be a robust and independent global judiciary.**

same way as national bodies of law do, irrespective of whether that infringes sovereignty. In contrast, the 'Positivists' contend that international law can and should only reflect customary practice in international relations and not some notion of universal morality. In this view it is useful to use past precedent as a guide on how to resolve the disputes which inevitably arise in international relations but sovereignty must be respected and **supranational** jurisdiction is inappropriate in a world of diverse states with their own culturally defined ideas of right and wrong. This division mirrors the classic IR debate between Liberals and Realists on IGOs to which we will now turn.

## IR theories and IGOs

While the growth of IGOs over the twentieth century is indisputable, the level of significance this phenomenon carries in terms of the nature of international relations is open to very different interpretations and is, perhaps, the central point of distinction between the theories of IR.

## (Classical) Realism

To a large extent, Realist theory in International Relations was built on the core assumption that international organisations serve little purpose in the pursuit of peace and order in the world. The failure of the League of Nations to prevent the world slipping into a second world war was considered by founding fathers of Realism, like Edward Carr and Hans Morgenthau, to demonstrate that organisations were not just irrelevant but also dangerous for international relations in giving a false sense of security. It was the employment of state force that was required to curb German, Italian and Japanese expansionism, not the open diplomacy of the **Idealists**. It came to be reasoned that had the allies acted sooner to restore the balance of power, rather than relying on dialogue and appeasement, the full horrors of the world's worst ever conflict could have been avoided.

Intergovernmental organisations flourished after the Second World War, while Realism was in the ascendancy; but they were, predictably, less Idealist than those that made up the League of Nations system. The United Nations maintained the League's commitment to open diplomacy and the promotion of functional organisations to promote international commerce and relief, but it was infused with a heavy element of Realism in its peacekeeping functions. **Balance of power** logic was built into the Security Council with five of the victorious great powers from the Second World War – the US, USSR, UK, France and China – given special privileges in exchange for acting as world policemen. This was a profound shift from the classic **collective security** on which the League was based (although never activated) in which all members had an equal responsibility to maintain international peace (see Chapter 31).

Intergovernmental organisations in Realist eyes can and should be no more than flags of convenience for states. They can serve state utilitarian interests by cutting the costs of having to arrange intergovernmental meetings on issues of common concern but should do no more than this. Such organisations should be strictly intergovernmental and not compromise sovereignty in the pursuit of illusory global interests. Hence, for Realists, the prolific growth of IGOs in the second half of the twentieth century is not considered to be evidence of their increased significance since these organisations are not more than the sum of their parts.

This classical Realist scepticism of IGOs was, to some extent, revived in the 1990s when the end of the Cold War seemed to many to offer opportunities for a revitalisation of the United Nations and other organisations. Notable among such sceptical voices was John Mearsheimer who echoed similar sentiments to predecessors like Morgenthau in rebuffing the new Idealists: 'institutions have minimal influence on state behaviour and thus hold little promise for promoting stability in the post Cold War world' (Mearsheimer 1994: 7).

## (Neo) Realism

The new breed of Realists who emerged alongside the onset of contemporary globalisation from the 1970s gave more credence to the significance of IGOs in International Relations, since their growth did appear to have made the political world seem more complex than that observed just by focusing on the state system. For writers like Gilpin (1981) and Waltz (1970), however, the significance of these new organisations did not lie in their capacity to erode state power and redefine state interests but quite the opposite. Neo-Realists noted how many IGOs set up after the Second World War actually served as a means of projecting US power and influence and reinforcing their **hegemony** of international affairs. The key elements of the new UN system were sited in the United States and they were designed in such a way that American dominance was ensured. This was most explicit in the sphere of international political economy, where the International Monetary Fund and World Bank were bankrolled by the US but also set up so that they could put 'their mouth where their money was' and use their wealth to control the new trading and monetary system (see Chapter 17). A similar phenomenon could be seen in the military domain with the emergence of NATO and other institutionalised regional alliances serving as vehicles for projecting US power. Far from moving us away from seeing IR as a state system governed by power, for neo-Realists the rise of IGOs served to reinforce this logic.

## Liberalism

On the other side of the 'classic IR debate' from the Realists, the Liberals see IGOs (and non-state actors in general) as challenging the notion of IR being determined by states and also welcome this change. Kant's route to 'Perpetual Peace' was a triumvirate of republican democracy, trade and international organisations and **Idealists** in the 1920s looked to put this philosophy into practice with the League of Nations system. The League's demise, however, prompted a similar demise in fortune for Liberalism in IR, with Realists assuming the ascendancy in the 1940s and 50s.

From the 1960s, however, Liberalism in IR re-emerged in the guise of *Pluralists*, like Rosenau, Burton, Keohane and Nye, who viewed IGOs not only in Idealist terms as a preferred path for IR, but also for the objective analytical reasoning that such organisations were demonstrably changing the nature of world politics. Keohane and Nye contended that the increased level of transactions between states had created conditions of 'complex interdependence' in the world which undermined the Realist model of international politics being determined by states pursuing their own interests irrespective of the interests of others. In addition, it was argued that 'transgovernmental relations' could now be observed in international politics due to increased cooperation between governments. This concept disposes not only with the notion of states representing no more than the interests of their governments but also with the idea that governments themselves are coherent entities (Keohane and Nye 1971). Due to the increased prominence of IGOs in international relations it came to be contended that many governments were becoming disaggregated, as ministers or subsets of one government came to form alliances with parts of other governments which might be at odds with their own governmental partners. In the EU, for example, the regular contact and increasingly common interests that link ministers of the members states have often seen them act as transgovernmental blocs in Brussels, able to fashion coordinated policy beyond that which would be likely to emerge from conventional intergovernmental diplomacy conducted by foreign ministers or the heads of government.

## Marxism/Critical Theory

Marxist IR theorists are sceptical about the impact of IGOs since they see wider economic structures, rather than actors, as determining international events. Within Critical Theory, however, neo-Gramscians share the neo-Realist view that IGOs have significance in terms of serving the interest of powerful actors: 'one mechanism through which the universal norms of a world hegemony are expressed is the international organization' (Cox 1994). In contrast to neo-Realists, though, this perspective considers that the hegemony concerned is that of the world's economic elite, a transnational class of people, rather than particular states. This position came to acquire greater resonance in international economic affairs from the 1970s when the US's pre-eminence started to diminish and yet economic organisations like the IMF and World Bank persisted and new ones like the World Trade Organisation emerged. Vested interests were behind such organisations but they were the interests of big business across the world rather than direct projections of US foreign policy it came to be reasoned.

## Social Constructivism

As highlighted in Chapter 11 Social Constructivists came to prominence by arguing that the importance of culture in international relations was ignored by the Realists, Liberals and Marxists. Sociologists have long reasoned that institutions moulded culture and the behaviour of individuals in a society through the process of *socialisation* and this came to influence IR thinking from the 1990s as globalisation brought international institutions more into focus. Hence IR thinkers like Ruggie came to reason that organisations develop their own culture which can come to socialise government representatives and redefine the interests of those administrations (Ruggie 1998). This view, then, reinforces the Liberal–Pluralist view that the very experience of regularised international diplomacy leads to compromises, horse trading and learning which make IGOs more than just the sum of their parts – unlike the view of Realists. Prime Minister Margaret Thatcher of the UK is known to have complained that Lord Cockfield, the Conservative politician she dispatched to Brussels as European Communities Commissioner to defend her strictly intergovernmental vision of European cooperation, had 'gone native' when he came to work closely with colleagues in the Commission and advance political integration in the form of the Single Market and associated reforms. Despite such concerns, Cockfield appears to have been successful in his aim since the UK government were brought on board the European integration train in a way not seen before and that did not seem likely at the time to most observers. For Social Constructivists, then, there is support for the notion that IGOs can develop a 'life of their own' and become far more than flags of convenience for states.

## Conclusions

The theoretical discourse on the importance of IGOs represents, perhaps, the quintessential debate of International Relations. IGOs have proliferated with globalisation but, as with globalisation itself, there are profound differences of opinion as to how significant this is in terms of understanding why international political events occur in the way that they do. Liberals see the evolution of IGOs as a natural phenomenon occurring as globalisation erodes sovereignty and the capability of states to function effectively as political entities and satisfy the needs of individual people. From this view, therefore, we are today in the early stages of a new era of global governance succeeding the Westphalian system of states which has been in operation for the past three and a half centuries (see Chapter 33 for a full discussion of this). For most Realists, though, it is too early to write off the state and we wish it away at our peril. Global governance left to IGOs risks ushering in the lawlessness of the pre-sovereign age referred to by Hedley Bull as a 'new mediaevalism' (Bull 1977: 254). Without a system of states, upheld by the notion of sovereignty, we would have a chaotic political world of unaccountable and overlapping organisations. A middle way between these two perspectives considers that the future of international relations need not be about one or the other forms of actor taking centre stage and may see IGOs and states coexist and both thrive in a symbiotic relationship. The Realist leaning Social Constructivist Wendt forecasts the inevitability of a 'world state', not through the gradual abandonment of the nation state but because many states will come rationally and self-servingly to redefine the idea of their sovereignty and accept a stronger role for international organisations to deal with the complexities of contemporary globalisation (Wendt 2003). This debate on the future of states and international organisations is explored in the final chapter of this book.

## Resource section

## Questions

1. With reference to rival theoretical perspectives, consider whether or not intergovernmental organisations are more than the sum of their parts.

2. For an IGO of your choice describe what it does and how it works; and also evaluate its impact in international politics.

3. Do you agree with Mearsheimer's assertion that 'institutions have minimal influence on state behaviour'?

## Recommended reading

Archer, C. (2001) *International Organizations* (3rd edn, Routledge)
A classic historical and theoretical overview of the growth of intergovernmental and non-governmental organisations.

Diehl, P. (ed.) (2005) *The Politics of Global Governance: International Organizations in an Inter-dependent World (3rd edn, Lynne Rienner)*
A multi-authored volume providing a strong analysis of the significance of IGOs in the contemporary international political system from a range of theoretical perspectives.

Pease, K.-K. (2009) *International Organizations. Perspectives on Global Governance (4th edn, Prentice Hall)*
An authoritative and thorough textbook describing and theorising about IGOs of all forms and offering some competing predictions for the future.

## Useful websites

Union of International Associations: http://www.uia.be/
Widely cited database of information on IGOs and other non-state actors.

United Nations: http://www.un.org/

All IGOs have their own websites, for example:

• NATO: http://www.nato.int/cps/en/natolive/index.htm
• Interpol: http://www.interpol.int/
• ICJ: http://www.icj-cij.org/

# Chapter 13
# Global Multi-Purpose IGOs: The United Nations and the Organisation of the Islamic Conference

Intergovernmental organisations and globalisation

The United Nations and international law

The UN Charter

The five permanent members of the UN Security Council: permanent privileges

Organisation of the Islamic Conference (OIC)

The OIC: history and development

The OIC as an international relations actor

Conclusion: comparing the UN and the OIC

In this chapter you will gain an understanding of:

- Structures and processes of the United Nations (UN)
- Structures and processes of the Organisation of the Islamic Conference (OIC)
- How the UN and the OIC are similar and different
- Growing accord between the UN and OIC in pursuit of shared goals

*Source*: Getty Images/Somos/Veer

## Introductory box: The Organisation of the Islamic Conference and Islamic terrorism

Why did radical Islam emerge? It's generally accepted that it was a response to decades of perceived Western hegemony and accompanying secular modernisation, encouraged by a small Westernised elite in many Muslims countries in the Middle East and elsewhere. What if anything did radical Islam have to do with the main international Islamic organisation, the Organisation of the Islamic Conference (OIC)? Evidence suggests that the rise of radical Islam was *not* in response to encouragement from the OIC or from individual countries, such as Iran (a leading member of the organisation). In recent years, the OIC has been concerned with the rise of radical Islam, as it affects the relationship with the West. In addition, the OIC has witnessed serious and sustained rivalry between leading Muslim countries, including Iran and Saudi Arabia – both of which have been accused of encouraging Islamic radicals, including terrorists. More generally, the issue of Iran – Saudi Arabia rivalry in the context of the OIC has been a key issue for the organisation since Iran's 1979 Islamic revolution.

Over the last few years, especially since 11 September 2001, the OIC has found itself in the forefront of the USA-directed 'War on Terror' and the Muslim world's responses to these developments. These concerns led to a pronounced focus in the December 2005 OIC summit, which declared its condemnation of all terrorism, while stressing the need to criminalise all its aspects, including financing. The OIC also took the opportunity to reject, in line with Islamic tenets, *any* claimed justification – for example from al-Qaeda, for the deliberate killing of innocent civilians. More recently, the OIC has repeatedly condemned 'extremism', while calling for the development of educational curricula in schools that 'strengthen the values of understanding, tolerance, dialogue and pluralism'. Finally, the OIC has stressed its encouragement to Iraq to complete its transitional political process and elect a full-term government under its new democratic constitution. In short, the OIC has been compelled to respond to the changing world environment since 9/11 by seeking to stand up to the USA and to highlight its anti-terrorism, anti-extremist stance by underlining its moderate, consensus-seeking credentials.

## Intergovernmental organisations and globalisation

There are today around two hundred and fifty **intergovernmental organisations** (IGOs). Only internationally recognised states can be members of IGOs. Membership of an IGO does not undermine a state's sovereignty but it does mean that members are bound legally by certain policy-making options as a consequence of their IGO commitments (Hanhimäki 2008).

Source: Reuters/Mike Segar

**Some in the west still associate the OIC with extremism. Here, Libyan leader Muammar Gaddafi takes a break during his controversial speech to the UN General Assembly in 2009.**

Most IGOs were founded after the Second World War, although some were established much earlier. The early IGOs tended to be ones that existed for a functional purpose, that is, their existence was seen to make life easier for everyone (Archer 2001). For example, the International Telecommunications Union – a functional IGO whose main job is to facilitate the global spread of mail – was established nearly one hundred and fifty years ago, in 1865. However, most IGOs have been founded over the last sixty years, with security, welfare and human rights concerns. Examples of such multi-purpose IGOs include: the United Nations (UN) and the Organisation of the Islamic Conference (OIC). This chapter looks at the UN and the OIC. It looks at the UN as it is by far the largest international organisation, which has had a major impact on international relations since its founding in 1945. It looks at the OIC partly because it is the second largest multi-purpose international organisation and partly because it is the only IGO whose members are linked by religion. How, if at all, does this affect how the OIC 'does' international relations?

We survey both the UN and the OIC as IGOs, seeking to understand what they do and what they hope to achieve in international relations in the current era of globalisation. We also take account of the fact that the organisations are increasingly close partners in the period following 11 September 2001, in the context of the 'War on Terror' and resulting international attempts, led by the USA, to establish a new international era of stability and security under American auspices. Since 9/11, there has also been a growing focus on what might be called the 'Islamic' dimension of international relations, with significant ramifications for international and collective security concerns.

## The United Nations and international law

As noted in Chapter 12, there are only two organisations which conventionally come into the category of global multipurpose IGOs: the League of Nations established in 1920 and its successor the United Nations (UN), set up in 1945. (Below, when we look at the OIC, we shall see that there is a case to be made for adding it to the shortlist of global multipurpose IGOs.) The First World War led to an acknowledgment that the nature and process of international governance would have to change if the most extreme forms of violence against humanity were to be outlawed, and the growing interconnectedness and interdependence of nations recognised. The attempt to develop an international security organisation, the League of Nations, however soon foundered. This was because the major countries at this time – such as Britain and France – were not willing to give up their ability to make decisions solely based on perceived national interest, which would have been necessary to give the League the required authority and legitimacy (Northedge 1986).

The League and UN are also distinguishable from other IGOs in that they were/are, additionally, the centre points of systems linking together many global functional intergovernmental organisations. The League was created following the Paris Peace Conference at the end of the First World War. It was moulded in the spirit of Liberal idealism which briefly dominated post-First World War international relations. The League's main goal – like, as we shall see, those of both the UN and the OIC – was to seek to encourage international peace and understanding. Consequently, measures were enacted to ensure diplomatic exchanges were made openly in conferences, rather than in closed private meetings, and that conflicts could be resolved through negotiation or in court. Where this was not sufficient to keep the peace, military action by the whole international community would punish those who had violated international law. The League established an Assembly at which all members could debate international issues of the day, a Security Committee of fifteen members to enact measures to uphold the peace and punish violations of its Charter, and a permanent Court of International Justice to allow for members to seek judicial remedies to disputes (Marburg 2009).

The League is generally viewed as a disappointment because it demonstrably failed in its primary goal of maintaining world peace: the League collapsed during the Second World War. The League, on several occasions, failed to punish blatant acts of aggression. The 1931 Japanese invasion of Manchuria, the 1935 Italian invasion of Abyssinia (Ethiopia) and German military reoccupation of the Saar prompted some condemnations, but no military response. Soviet, German and Italian interventions in the 1936–9 Spanish Civil War were similarly ignored and although the USSR was expelled from the League in 1939 because it invaded Finland, this was too little too late. Hence the UN established at a conference held in San Francisco, USA in 1945, sought in its organisation to learn from the League's failings. The UN sought to be genuinely global, not least by keeping the states that lost the war – in particular, Germany and Japan – as key players in the new order, rather than them being dangerously ostracised as had been the case at the Paris Peace Conference, when Germany's exclusion led, inexorably, to the rise of Hitler and Nazism. In addition, the UN actively encouraged **decolonisation** which over time saw membership grow to enable the organisation to be an IGO with nearly universal membership.

The UN was instituted in order to encourage both open diplomacy – that is, diplomatic interaction conducted in open meetings – and international cooperation. Yet, at the same time, the post-Second World War **Realist** balance of power logic, manifested most obviously in the Cold War, with two main *poles* of power – the USA and the Soviet Union – was grafted on to the UN's liberal-inspired structure. As a result, five great powers – USA, the Soviet Union, Britain, France and China – were able to get their dominance institutionalised through their exclusive permanent membership of the body at the apex of the UN structure: the Security Council. This ensured the participation of these key players and made the application of force to uphold international order a more realistic possibility than under the League. However, over time, the Security Council has been seriously hampered by the veto power ascribed to the five permanent members, for example in relation to the controversial US-led invasion of Iraq in 2003 when the USA could not find unanimity for its invasion plan. Nonetheless, on occasion, the members of the Security Council have been able to get agreement for robust action to keep the peace beyond that achieved by the League. The UN's role in peacekeeping is analysed in detail in Chapter 31.

Thus the Second World War (1939–45) led to a concerted attempt to develop the UN as a global multipurpose IGO whose main goal was to develop and consolidate collective security. The UN's task was pursued at a time when many people began to feel that international law should involve not *only* states but should also be concerned with what individuals did too, individuals such as Germany's Adolph Hitler. Henceforward, both single persons and groups became recognised as subjects of international law. It is now generally accepted, for example, that persons as individuals are subjects of international law on the basis of such documents as the Charters of the Nuremberg and Tokyo War Crimes Tribunals, the Universal Declaration of Human Rights (1948), the International Covenant on Civil and Political Rights (1966), and the European Convention on Human Rights (1950). It was now perceived that international law was in fact concerned progressively with orchestrating and regulating economic, social and environmental matters.

The post-war world was also notable for substantial growth in the number of international actors with a role in global politics. As well as the United Nations itself, there also emerged various international specialist agencies connected to the UN, including: the United Nations Economic and Social Council, the World Bank, the International Monetary Fund, the International Whaling Commission, the Food and Agriculture Organisation and the World Health Organisation. The growth of these entities reflected two key developments: (1) a realisation that the notion of 'collective security' was much wider than 'merely' deterring aggressors undermining international order, and (2) mounting public pressure to increase the scope of international law to include new areas, such as the natural environment and human rights. This was largely the result of democratisation after the Second World War when increasing numbers of people had a say in what policies their governments adopted in relation to a growing range of issues. The result was that, after the Second World War, the development of the UN system was characterised by the changing reach of international law. This was now concerned less with the freedom or liberty of states, and more with the general welfare of all those in the global system who are able to make their voices count, such as pressure groups of various kinds, not least those demanding freedom for colonies.

Today, a number of sources of international law jostle for recognition. These include the traditional sources such as international conventions or treaties which are recognised by states; international custom or practice which provides evidence of an accepted set of rules; and the underlying principles of law accepted by countries recognised as 'civilised nations'. These differ from each other in that custom was what states habitually did as a consequence of repetition, while international law was thought to reflect basic fundamental tenets of behaviour which all civilised nations, irrespective of religion or culture, would be expected to pursue. In addition, there is the 'will of the international community', expressed through the UN – most recently in relation to Iraq's alleged 'weapons of mass destruction' – which can assume the 'status of law' or which can become the 'basis of international legal obligation' under certain circumstances. The last represents a break in principle with the requirement of individual state consent in the making of international rules and responsibilities.

## The UN Charter

After the Second World War a new model of international law and accountability was widely advocated and accepted, culminating in the adoption of the UN Charter (Fassbender 2009). It is important to understand that the post-war international environment was, in several ways, conducive to changed circumstances of greater international cooperation, for example in relation to anti-colonial ideologies which, added to by domestic concerns, served overall to promote the enfranchisement of racial and ethnic minorities in Western states. One of the key emergent ideas, national self-determination, was institutionalised as a primary international value in the Charter of the UN. The General Assembly of the UN – comprising nearly all the world's states and acting as a kind of UN legislature, albeit one with weak executive powers – was often to articulate this doctrine in later years, applying it in various declarations and resolutions.

The main image of international regulation projected by the Charter was one of states, still jealously sovereign, but increasingly linked by various relations and interactions. This primarily reflected the general growth of interdependence between countries after 1945, a development which over time came to be known as globalisation. Moreover, following the Second World War, states with democratically elected governments and encouraged by public opinion, were under strong domestic and international pressure to resolve

## Box 13.1 Concerns of the UN Charter

- The world community consists of sovereign states connected through a dense network of relations; states, individuals and groups are regarded as legitimate actors in international relations.
- Decolonisation.
- Acceptance of standards and values which call into question the principle of effective power con- sequently, major violations of given international rules – e.g. Iraq's invasion of Kuwait in 1990 – are not in theory regarded as legitimate. Restrictions are placed on the resort to force, including unwar- ranted economic force.
- New rules, procedures and institutions designed to aid law making and law enforcement in inter- national affairs were created.

- Legal principles delimiting the form and scope of the conduct of all members of the international community, providing a set of guidelines for the structuring of international rules.
- Fundamental concern with individual rights.
- The preservation of peace, advancement of human rights and the establishment of greater social justice.
- Systematic inequalities among people and state are recognised and new rules established to create ways of governing the distribution, appropriation and exploitation of territory, property and natural resources.

The UN Charter is a bulky document.
The full version can be found at:
http://www.un.org/en/documents/charter/

disagreements by peaceful means and according to legal criteria. In addition they were not only subject – in principle – to tight restrictions on the resort to the use of force to settle disputes but also increasingly obliged to observe certain standards with regard to the treat- ment of all persons on their territory, including their own and foreign citizens. Of course, how restrictive the provisions of the Charter have been to states, and to what extent they have actually been operationalised, are controversial issues, generating much debate among International Relations scholars.

Partly as a consequence of the League's failures, the UN structure was drawn up to accommodate the international power structure, as it was understood in 1945. However, the shift in the structure of international regulation from the Westphalian to the UN Charter model raised fundamental questions about the nature and form of international law, questions which point to the possibility of a significant disjuncture between the law of states – of the states system – and of the wider international community. At the core of this shift lies a conflict between claims made on behalf of individual states and those made on behalf of an alternative organising principle of world affairs: a global, democratic community of states. Whatever their size or power attributes, all states have equal voting rights in the UN General Assembly, a forum where they can openly and collectively debate circumstances and developments in international life. However, while states are constrained to observe the UN Charter and observe a battery of human rights conventions, it would be quite misleading to conclude that the era of the UN Charter model simply displaced the Westphalian logic of international governance. The essential reason for this is that the Charter framework represents, in many respects, an extension of the inter-state system.

## The five permanent members of the UN Security Council: permanent privileges

The post-1945 balance of power, privileging the more powerful states – which comprised the five permanent members of the UN Security Council (USA, USSR, Britain, France, China), all with their distinctive sets of geopolitical interests – was built into the Charter at its inception. As a result, however, the UN was virtually immobilised as an autonomous actor on many pressing issues. One of the most obvious manifestations of this was the special veto power accorded to the five permanent members. This privileged political status added authority and legitimacy to the position of each of the major powers; for, although they were barred in principle from the use of force on terms contrary to the Charter, they were protected against censure and sanctions in the event of unilateral action in the form of their veto. Moreover, the Charter gave renewed credence to unilateral strategic state initiatives if they were necessary in 'self-defence', since there was no clear delimitation of the meaning of this phrase. Further, while the Charter placed new obligation on states to settle disputes peacefully, and laid down certain procedures for passing judgement on alleged acts of self-defence, these procedures have rarely been used and there has been no insistence on compliance with them. The possibility of mobilising the collective coercive measures envisaged in the Charter itself against illegitimate state action has, furthermore, never materialised and, as we shall see in Chapter 31, even the UN's peacekeeping missions have normally been restricted to areas in which the consent of the territorial state in question has first been given. The UN's susceptibility to the agendas of the most powerful states has been reinforced by its dependence on finance provided by its members. This position of vulnerability to state politics is underlined by the absence of any mechanism to confer some kind of direct UN status on non-state actors – such as, regional and transnational functional or cultural forces (agencies, groups or movements) – who might well have significant perspectives on international questions which would be worth considering. In sum, many argue that the UN Charter model, despite its good intentions, has failed effectively to generate a new principle of organisation in the international order – a principle which might break fundamentally with the logic of Westphalia and generate new democratic mechanisms of political coordination and change.

Nonetheless, it would be wrong simply to conclude that the UN has been a failure. Some of the deficiencies commonly attributed to the organisation can be better placed at the door of the states system itself. Indeed, the UN Charter system has been distinctively innovative and influential in a number of respects. It has provided an international forum in which all states are in certain respects equal, a forum of particular value to many developing countries and to those seeking a basis for 'consensus' solutions to international problems. It has also contributed a very useful framework for decolonisation, especially between the 1950s and the 1970s when most existing colonies gained their independence. Finally, the UN Charter has provided a vision, valuable in spite of all its limitations, of a kind of new world order based upon a meeting of governments and, under appropriate circumstances, of a supranational presence in world affairs championing human rights.

The theoretical discourse on the importance of IGOs in international relations represents, perhaps, the archetypal debate in the discipline. On the one hand, IGOs have proliferated with globalisation but on the other, as with globalisation itself, there are profound differences of opinion as to how significant this is in terms of understanding why international political events occur in the ways that they do. Liberals see the evolution of IGOs as a natural phenomenon occurring as globalisation erodes sovereignty and the capability of states to function effectively as political entities and satisfy the needs of individual people. From this view, therefore, we are today in the early stages of a new era of *global governance* succeeding the *Westphalian* system of states which has been in operation for nearly four centuries. For most Realists, though, it is too early to write off the state and we wish it away at our peril since global governance through IGOs risks ushering in a return to the lawlessness and chaos of the pre-1648 world, an era dominated by often savage inter- and intra-religious conflicts. A middle way between these two perspectives considers that the future of international relations need not be about one or the other forms of actor taking centre stage and may see IGOs and states coexist and both thrive in a symbiotic relationship. A leading International Relations academic, the Realist-leaning Social Constructivist, Alexander Wendt, forecasts the eventual inevitability of a 'world state'. He argues this, not as a likely consequence of a gradual abandonment of the idea of the nation state but through a process of evolution whereby governments will – rationally *and* self-servingly – begin to redefine the idea of their sovereignty and accept a stronger role for international organisations to deal with the complexities of contemporary globalisation (Wendt 2003). The debate on the future of states and international organisations is explored in Part 7 of this book.

## Organisation of the Islamic Conference (OIC)

Debate about IGOs and their roles in international relations was affected, like all other areas of the discipline, by the tragic events of 11 September 2001 (9/11). For many analysts and scholars, 9/11 marked the end of one era and the beginning of another. Some claimed that the unfolding of unprecedented acts of transnational terror on 11 September represented the key manifestation of a new era of 'civilisational', 'cultural' or 'religious' cleavages between the Muslim world and the West (Huntington 2002). Certainly, Islam as an international entity suddenly gained unanticipated prominence both in Western political concerns and in international relations after 9/11 (Haynes 2007). Often perceived from an ethnocentric or sensationalist viewpoint, how best can we understand Islam as a strategic entity in contemporary international relations? One important focus in this regard is the Organisation of the Islamic Conference, sometimes referred to as the 'Muslim United Nations' (Kalin 2006). This classification is partly the result of the OIC's widespread international involvement in attempts to settle various post-Cold War conflicts, including: the first Gulf War (1990–1); the continuing Palestine problem, involving Israel and the

Palestinians; the Balkan wars of the 1990s; the unresolved conflict between Russia and rebel Chechens; and the simmering nuclear competition in South Asia between Pakistan and India. Overall, the OIC has an agenda concerned with striving for unity and solidarity among Muslim peoples, fighting against terror and extremism of all kinds, and pursuing what it calls 'the middle path of moderation' (http://www.oic-oci.org).

## The OIC and Islam

As the OIC is an IGO whose main concern is the well-being of Muslims, it is appropriate to examine briefly what unites and divides the world's numerous Muslims. There are over one billion Muslims in the world, making Islam the second largest religion following Christianity. Muslims are found in probably every country in the world with major populations throughout the Middle East, North and Central Africa, South and South East Asia and in most European countries, including France, Germany and Britain.

## The OIC: history and development

The OIC is the second largest IGO in the world with fifty-seven member states, about one third of the size of the United Nations which has one hundred and ninety-two members. All OIC members are also members of the UN. The OIC has members spread over four continents: Africa, Asia, Europe and South America. It has a permanent delegation to the UN, and ties between the UN and the OIC are close and growing.

The OIC is sometimes classified as falling into a category of IGOs known as 'cultural, ethnic, linguistic, and religious organisations'. Examples include: the Commonwealth of Nations (mainly former British colonies), La Francophonie (French-speaking countries), Community of Portuguese Language Countries (Portuguese-speaking countries), Organisation of Ibero-American States (Spanish- and Portuguese-speaking European and American countries), the Latin Union (countries speaking a language derived from Latin), and the Arab League (Arab countries). However, the OIC, whose official languages are Arabic, English and French, is the *only* IGO whose membership comprises countries with a shared *religious* orientation: Islam. There are no other IGOs characterised by religious orientation: no 'Organisation of Christian States', 'Organisation of Buddhist Nations' or 'Organisation of Hindu Countries'. The OIC presents itself as the global collective voice of Muslims, which aims to ensure, safeguard and protect Muslims' interests in the spirit of promoting international peace and harmony among various people of the world. These wide-ranging concerns make it best to think of the OIC as a global multipurpose IGO.

The OIC was established following a decision taken at a summit meeting in Rabat, Morocco, in September 1969. The first OIC meeting was held in 1970, under the auspices of the Islamic Conference of Foreign Ministers (ICFM) in Jeddah, Saudi Arabia. Participants decided to establish a permanent secretariat in Jeddah headed by the OIC's secretary general.

## Box 13.2 The Charter of the OIC

1. Enhance and consolidate the bonds of fraternity and solidarity among the Member States.
2. Safeguard and protect the common interests and support the legitimate causes of the Member States and coordinate and unify the efforts of the Member States in view of the challenges faced by the Islamic world in particular and the international community in general.
3. Respect the right of self-determination and non-interference in the domestic affairs and to respect sovereignty, independence and territorial integrity of each Member State.
4. Ensure active participation of the Member States in the global political, economic and social decision-making processes to secure their common interests.
5. Reaffirm its support for the rights of peoples as stipulated in the UN Charter and international law.
6. Strengthen intra-Islamic economic and trade cooperation; in order to achieve economic integration leading to the establishment of an Islamic Common Market.
7. Exert efforts to achieve sustainable and comprehensive human development and economic well-being in Member States.
8. Protect and defend the true image of Islam, to combat defamation of Islam and encourage dialogue among civilisations and religions.
9. Enhance and develop science and technology and encourage research and cooperation among Member States in these fields.
10. In order to realise these objectives, Member States shall act, inter alia, in accordance with the following principles:
11. All Member States commit themselves to the purposes and principles of the United Nations Charter.
12. Member States are sovereign, independent and equal in rights and obligations.
13. All Member States shall settle their disputes through peaceful means and refrain from use or threat of use of force in their relations.
14. All Member States undertake to respect national sovereignty, independence and territorial integrity of other Member States and shall refrain from interfering in the internal affairs of others.
15. Member States shall uphold and promote, at the national and international levels, good governance, democracy, human rights and fundamental freedoms, and the rule of law.

The OIC's Charter is a lengthy document.
It is available in English at:
http://www.oic-oci.org/is11/english/Charter-en.pdf

Professor Ekmeleddin Ihsanoglu is the current Secretary General of the OIC. He took up his post in January 2005 after being elected by the 31st ICFM. Just over three years later, the current Charter of the OIC was adopted by the Eleventh Islamic Summit held in Dakar, Senegal, on 13–14 March 2008. The Charter laid down the objectives and principles of the organisation and fundamental purposes to strengthen the solidarity and cooperation among the member states.

The membership of the OIC has doubled in size over the last forty years: from thirty in 1970 to fifty seven in 2010 (see Table 13.1).

Like states everywhere, OIC members face many challenges in the early years of the twenty-first century. Seeking to address those challenges, the third extraordinary session of the Islamic Summit held in Mecca in December 2005 set out a Ten-Year Programme of Action. The Programme envisaged that the OIC would henceforward seek actively to promote tolerance and moderation, modernisation, extensive reforms in all spheres of activities including science and technology, education, trade enhancement, and good

**Table 13.1** OIC – member states and year of joining

| State | Year of Accession | State | Year of Accession |
|---|---|---|---|
| Afghanistan | 1969 | Malaysia | 1969 |
| Albania | 1992 | Maldives | 1976 |
| Algeria | 1969 | Mali | 1969 |
| Azerbaijan | 1991 | Mauritania | 1969 |
| Bahrain | 1970 | Morocco | 1969 |
| Bangladesh | 1974 | Mozambique | 1994 |
| Benin | 1982 | Niger | 1969 |
| Brunei Darussalam | 1984 | Nigeria | 1986 |
| Burkina Faso | 1975 | Oman | 1970 |
| Cameroon | 1975 | Pakistan | 1969 |
| Chad | 1969 | Palestine state (proposed) | 1969 |
| Comoros | 1976 | Qatar | 1970 |
| Côte d'Ivoire | 2001 | Saudi Arabia | 1969 |
| Djibouti | 1978 | Senegal | 1969 |
| Egypt | 1969 | Sierra Leone | 1972 |
| Gabon | 1974 | Somalia | 1969 |
| The Gambia | 1974 | Sudan | 1969 |
| Guinea | 1969 | Surinam | 1996 |
| Guinea-Bissau | 1974 | Syria | 1970 |
| Guyana | 1998 | Tajikistan | 1992 |
| Indonesia | 1969 | Togo | 1997 |
| Iran | 1969 | Tunisia | 1969 |
| Iraq | 1976 | Turkey | 1969 |
| Jordan | 1969 | Turkmenistan | 1992 |
| Kazakhstan | 1995 | Uganda | 1974 |
| Kuwait | 1969 | United Arab Emirates | 1970 |
| Kyrgyzstan | 1992 | Uzbekistan | 1995 |
| Lebanon | 1969 | Yemen | 1969 |
| Libya | 1969 | | |

**The OIC Observer States**

Bosnia and Herzegovina
Central African Republic
Thailand

*Source*: http://www.infoplease.com/spot/oicstates1.html

governance and promotion of human rights in the Muslim world – especially with regard to rights of children, women and the elderly and the family values enshrined by Islam.

The OIC has various institutions: the Islamic Summit, the Council of Foreign Ministers and the General Secretariat, whose functions are explained in Table 13.2. Further, in order to coordinate and boost its actions, align its viewpoints and pursue its objectives, the OIC seeks concrete results in various fields of cooperation: political, economic, cultural, social, spiritual and scientific areas. To these ends the OIC has created different committees, nearly all of which are at ministerial level and some are chaired by heads of state. The Al-Quds Committee (al-Quds is the Arabic name for Jerusalem; it is a key goal of the OIC to wrest

**Table 13.2** OIC – main bodies

| Body | What it is and what it does |
| --- | --- |
| Islamic Summit | Composed of kings and heads of state and government of member states, the Islamic Summit is the supreme authority of the OIC. It convenes once every three years to deliberate, take policy decisions and provide guidance on all issues pertaining to the realisation of the objectives, and to consider other issues of concern to the member states and, more generally, Muslims around the world. |
| Council of Foreign Ministers | The Council meets once a year and considers the means for the implementation of the general policy of the OIC. It does this in two main ways:<br>• Adopting decisions and resolutions on matters of common interest in the implementation of the objectives and the OIC's general policy;<br>• Reviewing progress of the implementation of the decisions and resolutions adopted at the previous Summits and Councils of Foreign Ministers. |
| General Secretariat | The General Secretariat is the executive organ of the OIC, entrusted with the implementation of the decisions of the two preceding bodies. |

from Israel control of the city known as Jerusalem by the Israelis and al-Quds by the Arabs), the standing Committee for Information and Cultural Affairs (COMIAC), the standing Committee for Economic and Trade Cooperation (COMCEC), and the standing Committee for Scientific and Technological Cooperation (COMSTECH) are the committees chaired by heads of state.

The OIC also has a Secretariat with Political, Cultural, Administrative, and Financial divisions, each headed by a deputy secretary general. Various other bodies have also been established within the OIC, including the International Islamic Press Agency (1972), the Islamic Development Bank (1974), the Islamic Broadcasting Organisation (1975), and the Islamic Solidarity Fund (1977). Finally, over the years the OIC has also established various ad hoc bodies with the aim of trying to help resolve specific international conflicts involving Muslims in various parts of the world. For example, there is an OIC 'contact group' on what is known as the Kashmir question (a conflict which began following India's independence from the British in 1947 and which centres on which country, India or Pakistan, would control Kashmir), as well as 'an assistance mobilisation group' charged with generating financial aid for the very poor, mainly the Muslim country of Bosnia-Herzegovina, located in the Balkans region of southern Europe (http://www.oic-oci.org/).

In sum, the number and types of secondary organs and institutions, working toward the achievement of the OIC objectives, have been steadily increasing. It now covers many areas of concern, including culture, science, economy, law, finance, sports, technology, education, and media. Depending on their degree of autonomy vis-à-vis the parent organisation, they are classified as either subsidiary organs or specialised or affiliated institutions.

## The OIC as an international relations actor

We have noted that the OIC has a wide range of concerns which comprehensively transcend the parameters of religion. In addition, the OIC has extensive consultative and cooperative relations with the UN and other intergovernmental organisations. Working with bodies like the UN, the OIC seeks to achieve two main goals: (1) to seek to protect the vital interests of Muslims, and (2) to work for the settlement of conflicts and disputes involving member states.

In this section we examine the OIC's general influence on international relations. Some people believe that *all* transnational Islamic organisations, including the OIC, want to overthrow the established international order and institute a global Islamic state (*khalifa*). Instead, since its establishment in 1969, the OIC has been a forum for senior Muslim figures to discuss not only religious but also political, economic, developmental, social and environmental issues, in the context of seeking to establish a path of moderation in international relations. Somewhat surprisingly, given its significance, the overall international role of the OIC has not been widely debated in the literature. There is, however, agreement that its influence in international relations is less than it might be given the large number of countries that make up the body and its far-reaching and ambitious goals (Kepel 2004; Roy 2004; Haynes 2007).

One key reason for the OIC's relative lack of importance is not necessarily because the OIC primarily – although not exclusively – pursues narrow cultural and religious goals. We should recall that the OIC professes to be the primary voice of the *ummah*, that is, the global

### Box 13.3 The OIC and international relations

What does the OIC aim to achieve in international relations? For Ziauddin Sardar (1985: 51–2), a London-based scholar, writer and cultural-critic who specialises in the future of Islam, the OIC has the

> ability to bring all the nations of the Muslim world, even those who have openly declared war on each other, under one roof, and to promote cooperation and communication between Muslim people that has not been possible in recent history. Moreover, it has the potential of becoming a powerful institution capable of articulating Muslim anger and aspiration with clarity and force. . . . The creation of the OIC . . . indicates that the movement of a return to Islamic roots is a transnational phenomenon.

From this, we can see that Sardar, someone who has written a lot about the role of Islam in international relations, is claiming that the main purpose of the OIC *should* be to promote Islamic solidarity and strengthen cooperation among member states in the social, cultural, scientific, political and economic fields. The OIC, an organisation of nearly sixty Muslim countries, sees itself as a supporter of the established international order. The organisation sees threats to international order as a threat to the international society of states and, as a result, it seeks to develop and sustain good relations with all states, including non-Muslim ones.

Muslim community. Yet, like the UN, the OIC has been dogged by various conflicts between organisational goals and member states' interests. For example, the OIC has been affected for decades by competition over leadership of the organisation between Egypt, Iran, Pakistan and Saudi Arabia. Overall, Dogan (2005) avers, the OIC has played a marginal role in the foreign policies of the member states. However, it is sometimes argued that the OIC could and should play a greater role in encouraging Muslim people and Islamic states to pull together for 'a unified ethical approach to such issues as international terrorism, international development, and democracy. This role of the organization is critical for both ending "clashes" between "civilizations" and bringing peace to the "Greater Middle East"' (Dogan 2005: 1).

In pursuit of concrete improvements, the UN and the OIC jointly organised an international conference in November 2008, entitled: 'Terrorism: Dimensions, Threats and CounterMeasures' in Tunis, capital of Tunisia. It indicated that the organisations stand together in rejecting forcefully and wholeheartedly any linkages between terrorism and Islam. In addition, OIC leaders have spoken out against those who seek to justify violence in the name of religion. These efforts helped to reinforce the UN's own steps to promote tolerance and understanding through its initiative, known as the Alliance of Civilisations (http://www.unaoc.org/).

*Source: Getty Images*

**Despite having over fifty member states, the OIC is perceived by many observers as little more than a vehicle for Iran's regional aspirations. Is this a fair accusation?**

## Case study: Iran and the OIC

While the OIC has been in existence since the late 1960s, it only began to attract much Western attention from the early 1980s, following the Islamic revolution in Iran. In 1979, the secular, pro-Western ruler of Iran was overthrown in a popular revolution led by Muslim clerics who proceeded to take over the institutions of the state. From that time the OIC has often been a battleground, a place to play out the rivalries of leading Muslim countries, including Saudi Arabia, Iran, Pakistan and Egypt. From the perspective of some Western observers, the OIC encourages a transnational 'Islamic fundamentalism' and, as a result, is a serious threat to Western security. Some have even appeared to believe that the OIC could develop into a coordinator of Islamist terror. An eminent American academic, the late Samuel Huntington (2002), claimed that after the Cold War many Muslim-majority countries were very dissatisfied with the existing international status quo and, as a result, are sliding into a period of conflict with the West. Over the last few years, successive United States governments collectively put much effort into combating Islamist terror around the world. This was because Islamic terrorist groups, such as al-Qaeda, work towards undermining governments in the Middle East friendly to the United States, including those of Egypt, Saudi Arabia and Pakistan. In response, American foreign policy has long been concerned to help protect such friendly governments. In addition, the US government has also long been concerned by the conduct of the Islamic Republic of Iran, especially in relation to its foreign policy, which has long been perceived by the West as expansionist and having the potential to radicalise already dissatisfied Muslim groups in many parts of the Middle East and elsewhere in the developing world. In short, successive US administrations have claimed that Iran's government is a dedicated sponsor of transnational religious terrorism (Hauser 2006) and might seek to use its leading position in the OIC as a vehicle for its aspirations. What this implies is that Iran might seek not only to hijack the OIC for its own foreign policy purposes but also to use the organisation as a cover for the extension of its support for Islamic terrorists in, for example, Afghanistan and Iraq. There is, however, a fundamental flaw in the perception that the OIC is an important *collective* sponsor of transnational Islamic terrorism: the leading members of the OIC are frequently at each other's throats and find it very difficult or impossible to agree on what the organisation should do.

 **To what extent is Iran a threat to international order because of its radical Islamic ideology?**

Over the last thirty years, much attention has been focused in and by the OIC on wars involving its members, including the Iran–Iraq war (1980–8), Iraq's invasion of Kuwait (1990–1), civil war in former Yugoslavia in the 1990s, and US invasions of Afghanistan (from 2001) and Iraq (from 2003). Yet such was the lack of concord between leading OIC members that the organisation's sixth summit – held in Dakar, Senegal, in December 1991 – was attended by less than half of the members' heads of state. This not only reflected the OIC's long-standing international ineffectiveness but also highlighted serious cleavages within the global Islamic community more generally. Discord between OIC members led to fears that the organisation would fade from the international political scene because of its failure to generate or focus real Islamic solidarity. This has not, however, been the case as in recent years the OIC has not only increased in size but, unlike the UN, has managed to become an important diplomatic actor in conflict zones, including Sudan and Somalia.

By the mid-1990s the OIC was concerned about the global image of Islam following the rise in Islamic terrorism. The 1994 summit sought to create a code of conduct regarding terrorism and religious extremism in order to try to deal with the 'misconceptions' that associated Islam with violence – especially among some Western governments and populations. As a result, in an attempt to bolster the OIC's credentials as an organisation committed to strengthening international order, members formally agreed not to allow their territories to be used for any terrorist activities. In addition, none would 'morally or financially' support Muslim 'terrorists' opposed to member governments. However, with states such as Iran and Sudan (both charged with supporting extremist Islamic groups in other nations) signing the OIC statement, it was possible to see the agreement as little more than a face-saving measure that sought to mask continuing deep divisions in the OIC on the issue.

The overall point is that the OIC has never managed to function as an organisation capable of achieving its goals of enhancing the global position of Muslims – largely because of divisions between its members. Some have sought to cultivate transnational links with radical Islamic groups, primarily as a means to further their own influence; but this is individualistic realpolitik not an institutional campaign coordinated by the OIC per se. In some respects, then, the OIC is very much like the UN: aspirations towards cooperation and achievement of collective goals are undermined by individual national interest concerns of leading countries. On the other hand, however, the OIC's shared religious and cultural focus has enabled it to carve out for itself a major role in international relations as a facilitator of mediation between conflicting Muslim groups, as in Somalia in the mid-2000s.

An International Relations scholar, Saad Khan (2001), has studied the international role of the OIC and its attempt to represent Islam globally and transnationally and the implications for international relations. He avers that the OIC is an important organisation in the Muslim world. Although it is not always considered to be very successful due to a lack of coordination, the OIC has been attempting to institutionalise and represent Islam at a global level and is a major interlocutor with the European Union. It is clear that the OIC can have a cooperative role in contemporary world politics. To achieve this objective, the OIC must attempt to improve its strategy of intra-organisational cooperation. As the international relations analyst, Arsalan Ghorbani notes, 'It is the responsibility of the OIC to show Islam is a religion protecting the interdependence image in world politics not a religion for hegemonic purposes' (Ghorbani 2005: 9). In the post-9/11 era, Muslim countries are heavily concerned with various security issues, and the OIC has sought to focus attention on the principles of building a global cooperative policy in this regard. To achieve this goal, however, will depend on the ability of the OIC to endorse rules and laws pertaining to both social life and international security, and to strive to present a 'realistic' nature of Islam that reflects its core concerns as a religion of moderation and empathy.

## Conclusion: comparing the UN and the OIC

The aim of this chapter was to examine the United Nations and the Organisation of the Islamic Conference as global multi-purpose intergovernmental organisations. We not only wanted to see what each of them does but also to understand how they do things in similar ways to pursue similar goals. What common criteria did we see them bringing to bear on international issues? On what basis could we make a comparative analysis? We saw that the OIC stresses territorial integrity and this can be compared to the approach the UN adopts (see Article 3 of the Charter), as well as the recent attempts to put into practice the 'Responsibility to Protect' (R2P), formalised in 2005, which focuses when the international community must intervene for human protection purposes. Similarly, the OIC Inter-Institutional Forum on Universal Shared Values: Challenges and New Paradigms shows a shared conviction that fundamental human rights can only be strengthened by all concerned working closer together. The United Nations and the Organisation of the Islamic Conference have much in common in this regard. In short, both organisations are similar in their wish to cooperate closely in their common search for solutions to global problems, such as questions relating to international peace and security, disarmament, self-determination, decolonisation, fundamental human rights, and economic and technical development. The UN seeks to encourage such activities through regional cooperation for the promotion of the purposes and principles of the United Nations, while the OIC aims to achieve them through collective, concerted effort on the part of all its fifty-seven member states.

The UN is often criticised for its apparent inability to resolve key international problems, while the OIC is sometimes regarded as spending too much time on the particular concerns of the Muslim world and not enough on global issues. Nonetheless, it would be wrong simply to leave the account of the UN here. Some of the deficiencies attributed to the organisation can be better placed at the door of the states system itself, a system which has shown itself relatively unwilling to hand responsibility to IGOs, including the UN. Further, the UN Charter system has shown itself to be both innovative and influential in a number of respects. First, it has provided an international forum in which all states are in certain respects equal, a forum of particular value to many developing countries and to those seeking a basis for 'consensus' solutions to international problems. Second, it has provided a robust and successful framework for decolonisation of much of the developing world and for the pursuit of the reform of international institutions, including the UN itself. Third, it has provided a vision, valuable in spite of all its limitations, of a kind of new world order based upon a meeting of governments and, under appropriate circumstances, of a supranational presence in world affairs championing human rights.

Turning to the OIC, it is clear that the period since 11 September 2001 has been a difficult time for the Islamic world. For several years the international community has been paying close attention to the events taking place in the member countries of OIC, from the situation in Iraq, the political crisis in Sudan, the consequences of the US-led invasion of

Afghanistan and the continued suffering in the occupied Palestinian territories, linked to the Israeli control not only of Jerusalem/al-Quds but also of much territory under Arab control until the 1967 Six-Day War between Israel and neighbouring Arab countries, including Egypt. Such concerns give the OIC a special international role and, as the most important and progressive organisation of the Islamic world, the OIC has a special legitimacy. Expressing the aspirations and concerns of over one-fifth of humanity, the OIC is the institutional voice of Muslims around the world. The OIC is a key partner of the United Nations in its efforts to promote international peace and cooperation.

Over time, links between the two organisations have strengthened. Both the OIC and the United Nations have now applied their collective efforts to many concerns: seeking to advance economic and social justice, improving human rights, promoting better understanding between cultures and religions – especially Islam and the West – and in trying to strengthen international peace and security.

Nevertheless, divisions within the global Muslim community, the *ummah*, continue to undermine the OIC's effectiveness as an international actor. Shared beliefs, relating especially to culture, sentiments and identity, link all Muslims yet at the same time Islam is significantly divided by various doctrinal issues, especially the schism between Sunni and Shia interpretations of the faith – an issue which has been played out in the OIC in relation to foreign policy rivalries between Iran and Saudi Arabia over which would lead the Muslim world. The post-9/11 focus on transnational religious extremism has tested the ability of the OIC to provide leadership to the *ummah* and the signs are that the organisation still lacks skill and political will to translate its frequent condemnations of terrorism and extremism into practical policies and programmes.

## Resource section

## Questions

1. What do the UN and OIC have in common and how are they different?

2. To what extent does the UN represent the aspirations of the 'international community'?

3. How does the OIC represent Muslims in international relations?

## Recommended reading

Akhtar, S. (2005) *The Organization of the Islamic Conference: Political and Economic Co-Operation (1974–1994)* (Islamabad: Research Society of Pakistan)
This is a useful survey of a twenty-year period during which the OIC grew in stature as an international organisation.

Hanhimäki, J. (2008) *The United Nations: A Very Short Introduction* (New York: Oxford University Press)
The United Nations has been called everything from 'the best hope of mankind' to 'irrelevant' and 'obsolete'. In this introduction to the UN, Jussi Hanhimäki examines the current debate over the organisation's effectiveness. He provides a clear understanding of how it was originally conceived, how it has come to its present form, and how it must confront new challenges in a rapidly changing world.

## Useful websites

The English-language United Nations website is at http://www.un.org/en/

The English-language OIC website is at http://www.oic-oci.org/home.asp

# Chapter 14
# Regional Organisations and Regionalisation: Theory and Practice

After reading this chapter you will have gained an understanding of:

- Why numerous states in many parts of the world now pursue regional cooperation
- What they get out of it
- How it is linked to globalisation

## Introductory box: Regional organisations and international relations

From the end of the Cold War in the late 1980s, there was a surge in growth and a renewed focus on regional organisations in international relations. During the next few years, old regional organisations – such as the Association of South East Asian Nations (ASEAN) – were revived and new organisations, such as the North American Free Trade Agreement (NAFTA) and Asia-Pacific Economic Cooperation (APEC), were formed. Overall, regionalisation (or as it is sometimes put, regionalism) and the call for strengthened regionalist arrangements became central to many of the debates about the nature of the post-Cold War international order.

One of the main reasons for the renewed interest in regional organisations was the fact that while international wars decreased in number following the Cold War, conflicts within countries – many of which spilled over to become regional concerns – increased. Over time, one of the main aims of any regional organisation was to try to provide increased security to regional countries afflicted by conflict. The premise was that a country that is at risk of conflict, or seeking to recover from it, has multiple needs that no one expert or organisation can provide. Humanitarian organisations, such as the Red Cross, work to address basic human needs for food, shelter and medicine; military or international organisations may have armed forces providing security; and governance experts may be helping local officials establish or improve legal frameworks and government agencies.

## Introduction

Regional organisations are a special kind of international organisation, organised on a geographical basis for various purposes. A regional organisation can be defined as a 'specific form of IGO [intergovernmental organisation] in which neighbouring countries join together for common purposes' (Hague and Harrop 2001: 50). The term, 'regionalisation' (sometimes the word, 'regionalism' is used instead), describes the tendency to form regions, or the process of doing so. Most regional organisations are recent creations, emerging over the last few decades. Since the 1980s and the onset of a deepening phase of globalisation (see Chapters 4 and 5), we have seen an increasing tendency towards regionalisation, leading to growing numbers of regional organisations. All regional organisations have an international membership, contoured by national boundaries and focused within a specific geographical area. Examples of regional organisations include: the African Union, the European Union (both of which are analysed in Chapter 15), the North American Free Trade Agreement, the Organisation of American States, the Association of South East Asian Nations, and Asia-Pacific Economic Cooperation.

This chapter focuses upon why numerous states around the world now pursue regional cooperation, with the aim of developing regional organisations. There are many regional organisations so to make our task manageable we shall look at two recently formed regional organisations in some detail: the North American Free Trade Agreement (NAFTA) and Asia-Pacific Economic Cooperation (APEC). We will compare and contrast their key institutions in order to draw conclusions about their differences and similarities. At the end of the chapter we shall be in a position to understand what roles these regional organisations play in international relations.

Why do countries around the world join regional organisations? As Table 14.1 shows, while some regional organisations – including the Arab League, the Commonwealth of Nations, and the North Atlantic Treaty Organisation – were formed many decades ago, most regional organisations were formed much more recently, in the 1980s or later. Put another way, nearly 70 per cent of existing regional organisations (13 out of 19) were formed in the last twenty-five years. In many cases, older regional organisations were created to try to deal with various important concerns at the time, including inter-state security in the context of the Cold War (North Atlantic Treaty Organisation, founded 1949), cultural solidarity after the Second World War (the Arab League, founded 1945), or coming to terms with colonial realities, especially development shortfalls (the Commonwealth of Nations, founded 1931). More recently formed regional organisations – for example, Asia-Pacific Economic Cooperation (1989), El Mercado Común del Sur (MERCOSUR; Spanish; Southern Common Market; English) (1991) and the North American Free Trade Agreement (1994) – were formed primarily to pursue economic and developmental goals in the context of deepening globalisation. Yet, despite differing reasons for formation, all regional organisations have in common a desire to try to 'reduce uncertainty about the behaviour of other nations, whether friends or adversaries' (Rittberger 1993, cited in Lowndes 2002: 102). This implies that states join regional organisations in order to establish, build and develop cooperation among member states for specific purposes, typically linked to security and economic development. Some regional organisations build dedicated institutions, others do not. In some cases, for example, the European Union (see Chapter 15), institutions are created for specific purposes of integration, covering a range of political and economic concerns.

## Regional cooperation and globalisation

As Table 14.1 indicates, regional organisations are a global phenomenon. Yet, wherever they are geographically located, they all reflect the fact that, as a consequence of globalisation, most countries are 'enmeshed in networks of important regional . . . political and economic institutions' (Smith 2000: 24). What then drives regional cooperation? While there is no simple answer to this question, we shall see that states generally pursue regional cooperation in order to help them pursue various objectives which they believe that they cannot easily achieve when acting alone. Increasingly, one of the main purposes of regional

**Table 14.1** Regional organisations

| Regional organisation | Date formed | Comments |
|---|---|---|
| Commonwealth of Nations | 1931 | Includes countries which are also members of: European Union, European Economic Area, African Union, Arab League, South Asian Association for Regional Cooperation, Union of South American Nations, and Association of South East Asian Nations |
| Arab League | 1945 | Includes countries which are also members of the African Union |
| North Atlantic Treaty Organisation | 1949 | |
| European Free Trade Association | 1960 | Includes countries which are also members of the European Economic Area |
| Organisation of Petroleum Exporting Countries | 1960 | |
| Association of South East Asian Nations | 1967 | |
| South Asian Association for Regional Cooperation | 1985 | Includes countries which are also members of the Economic Cooperation Organisation |
| Economic Cooperation Organisation | 1985 | Includes countries which are also members of the South Asian Association for Regional Cooperation |
| Asia-Pacific Economic Cooperation | 1989 | Includes countries which are also members of NAFTA, ASEAN |
| Commonwealth of Independent States | 1991 | |
| Mercado Común del Sur (MERCOSUR; Spanish; Southern Common Market; English) | 1991 | Includes countries which are also members of the Union of South American Nations, NAFTA |
| European Union | 1993 | Includes countries which are also members of NATO |
| Collective Security Treaty Organisation | 1994 | Includes countries which are also members of the Commonwealth of Independent States, Shanghai Cooperation Organisation |
| European Economic Area | 1994 | Includes countries which are also members of the European Union, European Free Trade Association, and Commonwealth of Nations |
| North American Free Trade Agreement | 1994 | Includes countries which are also members of MERCOSUR, Commonwealth of Nations |
| Eurasian Economic Community | 2001 | Includes countries which are also members of the Commonwealth of Independent States and Shanghai Cooperation Organisation |
| Shanghai Cooperation Organisation | 2001 | Includes countries which are also members of the CIS and Eurasian Economic Community |
| African Union | 2002 | Includes countries which are also members of the Arab League |
| Union of South American Nations | 2005 | Includes countries which are also members of the MERCOSUR |

cooperation is to enable member states to try to overcome challenges emanating from globalisation. In this respect, attempts at regional cooperation are both functionally efficient – that is, governments believe that they increase the probability that various problems can be resolved by dedicated policies and programmes. They also believe that such policies square with individual national interests, which invariably seek to ensure countries' security and stability. According to an International Relations scholar, Stefan Schirm,

> Regional cooperation results from new challenges, which governments believe can be better met by means of new regional regulations than by adhering to present national or regional strategies. Such new challenges make regional cooperation seem 'functionally efficient' and compatible with the 'national interest'. *By engaging in new regional cooperation, states create or strengthen a policy domain in which they receive new instruments for dealing with specific actors, situations and processes.*
>
> (emphasis added; Schirm 2002: 10)

Schirm is emphasising that over time, initiatives towards regional cooperation may lead to development of new regional 'regimes', with associated regulations, structures and processes. In a domestic context, a regime can be defined as the sum total of rules of behaviour that impact upon political decision-making and the values that underlie relationships between state and citizen. In international relations, regimes are 'sets of implicit or explicit principles, norms, rules, and decision making procedures around which actors' expectations converge in a given area' (Krasner 1983: 2). Such areas might include: the nature of a political system, human rights practices, and norms governing trade. Overall, regional organisations are important for an understanding of international relations for two main reasons. First, many regional organisations are primarily concerned with economic and developmental issues. Second, over time such issues may 'spill over' into a concern with other areas, including political integration and social policy. The European Union is the best example in this regard, as we shall in Chapter 15.

One of our main concerns in the current chapter is to understand why in recent years increasing numbers of countries, both rich and poor, have sought to adopt and implement cooperative policies with regional counterparts and, to this end, decided to join regional organisations. As already mentioned, for many states, regional economic cooperation in particular is a crucial mechanism to try to regulate the impact of their national economies and national interests in the context of deepening globalisation, especially: volatile global market trends and capital flows, activities of transnational corporations, and some states' protectionist policies (see Chapters 16 and 17 for further details) (Webber and Smith 2002; Hirst and Thompson 1999; Schirm 2002).

The direct link between economic globalisation and regional cooperation is that the latter is widely seen as both a 'shelter from' and 'an accelerator of' global processes (Christiansen 2001: 511). We can see this in relation to the developing countries of Africa, Asia and Latin America. It is sometimes suggested that developing countries objectively 'need' regional economic integration as a key means to increase their capacity to negotiate with 'hostile forces' associated with economic globalisation, which may result in loss of state control of national economies. Partly as a consequence of globalisation, such issues have been of great importance for developing countries since the 1980s and 1990s. During this time, developing countries in Africa, Asia and Latin America were collectively encouraged by Western governments, the International Monetary Fund and the World Bank to adopt economic reform programmes known as Structural Adjustment Programmes (SAPs). SAPs were designed to be a panacea for economic weaknesses in the developing world, but overall their impact on economic weaknesses and poor performance were limited, with in many cases unfortunate and unwelcome economic, social and political impacts. In many developing countries, for example Ghana, the measures were effective at trimming budget deficits but much less successful in reducing poverty. In addition, during the 1980s and 1990s, globalisation became a new and volatile issue which also affected developing countries' economies, presenting new challenges with which many governments struggled. A consequence of these two developments – externally-encouraged SAPs and deepening globalisation – was that many governments and observers believed that developing country governments could most likely produce better economic and developmental results by turning to regional cooperation and forming or rejuvenating regional organisations. We can note from Table 14.1 that several regional organisations involving developing countries date from this time, including Asia-Pacific Economic Cooperation, El Mercado Común del Sur/Southern Common Market, the North American Free Trade Agreement and the South Asian Association for Regional Cooperation.

This suggests a widespread willingness to pursue economic and developmental goals within the context of regional cooperation rather than rely solely on individual national policies. In other words, in the 1980s and 1990s it became widely accepted by many governments of developing countries that pursuing regional cooperation with neighbouring countries was a necessary means to try to improve development outcomes. This suggested that regionalisation would 'be the key to the success of globalisation in the years to come'. Without it, developing countries would experience a 'lack of stability and growth' that would push them 'further into the desperate margins of global society' (Roy 1999: 120). In short, it was widely accepted that developing countries 'should' develop regional cooperation as a vital step to enable them to 'adapt to the process of globalization without being excluded from it' (Heine 1999: 114).

## Old regionalisation and new regionalisation

The history of regional cooperation can conveniently be divided into two distinct historical periods. The first period covered the decades from the end of the Second World War in 1945 to the 1980s, a period of deepening globalisation. During this time, the main focal point of regional cooperation was Western Europe. The key international context at this time was the Cold War between the USA and the Soviet Union. After the Second World War, many governments – including those of internationally important countries such as the United States, France and (West) Germany – believed that it was crucial for international peace that European countries learn to cooperate and seek to reduce conflict between them. This was the region, we should not forget, where both world wars had begun. The proposed solution to the history of regional conflict was to form a regional cooperation organisation which, from its founding in the early 1950s, developed over the next few decades into the twenty-seven member, pan-European regional organisation we know today: the European Union (EU). But although the EU's creation was explicitly linked to the region's history of conflict which had destabilised international relations more widely, it is important to understand that its formation and development was moulded by the circumstances of the Cold War between the main global ideological rivals: the USA and the USSR.

When the Cold War ended in the 1980s, in the context of the deepening importance of globalisation for international relations, there was a consequential shift in the focus of regional cooperation. During this second phase of regionalisation, sometimes known as 'new regionalisation', regional cooperation moved from being primarily a European phenomenon to become a global phenomenon.

The new regionalisation differed from the old regionalisation in three key ways. First, as already explained, old regionalisation was rooted in the circumstances of the Cold War, a time when regional cooperation in Western Europe was directly and consistently affected by the circumstances of the Cold War. Reflecting these changes, the new regionalisation was concerned with a wide range of issues and processes, moving beyond the state-level ideological polarisation which characterised the Cold War and subsequent relations between the USA and the Soviet Union from the 1940s until the 1980s. In this context, the European Union was an important example to other aspiring regional organisations. The EU was widely seen as a success story: how to develop regional cooperation among previously hostile regional countries. The signing of the Maastricht Treaty (1992), which created the Single European Market (SEM), especially encouraged widespread interest in Europe's regional cooperation and attendant functional outcomes. The SEM focused attention on the success of the EU's decades-long economic cooperation and consequent long-term regional economic growth and prosperity.

Second, for many other regions the EU's economic and developmental successes stimulated a wider, extra-European 'urge to merge'. However, this was not only because the EU offered an example of a successful regional organisation; it was also because the SEM appeared to create or deepen competitive pressures for other regions, in competition with the EU for market share for exports. In other words, governments in regions of the world engaged in serious economic competition with Western Europe – such as, North America and Asia-Pacific – became increasingly concerned that facilitation of easier market access for member states within the EU itself would lead to trade diversion at the expense of their own exports. As a result, the linked emergence of what the international relations scholar, Thomas Christiansen (2001) calls, '"Fortress Europe"/SEM' provided a new impetus to encourage dynamic regional cooperation in regions outside Europe.

Third, the old regionalisation had focused primarily on state-level commitments. The new regionalisation, in contrast, shifted attention beyond governments to include various groups of non-state actors such as trade unions, business interests and women's groups.

These include: the European Platform of Women Scientists and Transnational Trade Union Rights. Scholars have characterised the change from state-centric regional cooperation to a new form, which also includes important groups of non-state actors, as a 'heterogeneous, comprehensive, multidimensional phenomenon . . . linked to global structural change'. What this is pointing to is a new focus on 'state, market and society actors and . . . economic, cultural, political, security and environmental aspects' (Schultz et al. 2001: 4, 7) of globalisation which have ramifications for regional cooperation and regional organisations. The issue is also contextualised by the fact that the end of the Cold War and deepening globalisation which characterised international relations from the 1980s had significant repercussions for regional cooperation, both within Europe and elsewhere. It led to new opportunities for states to cooperate in various areas, especially trade, economic cooperation and security. In addition, it also encouraged groups of important non-state actors to try to influence outcomes at the regional level via attempts to inform decision-making. This suggests that to be useful in a changed international context, studies of regional cooperation needed to move beyond a tight focus on formal regional structures led by states to include an additional concern with informal ones, including those involving important groups of non-state actors. Until recently, however, many studies of regional cooperation ignored or paid only scant attention to the role of non-state actors in encouraging regional cooperation and integration. Now, however, studies of the new regionalisation tend to emphasise 'contemporary forms of transnational cooperation and cross-border flows through comparative, historical, and multilevel perspectives' (Mittelman 1999, quoted in Schultz et al. 2001: 12). In other words, non-state actors active at the regional level search 'for relevant space for action' (Smouts 2001: 96). This directs our attention to both the geographical spread of regionalisation and the multiple dynamics at work in the process of regional cooperation, which involve both state and non-state actors.

Some regional environments – for example, Western Europe and North America – appear to be more conducive to building the influence of cross-border actors compared to some other regions, such as Asia-Pacific. The success of such actors – whether acting singly or in coalitions – may be linked to the extent to which they manage to develop highly cooperative and institutionalised relationships, both among themselves and with certain domestic actors. This suggests a point of wider relevance to our concerns in this chapter. It is that regional institutions can theoretically have substantial effects on member's domestic policies and programmes, both in terms of the policies themselves and in relation to the wider issue of interests and preferences. Put another way, national control over policies can be significantly influenced when states are members of regional organisations, such as the European Union (see Chapter 15).

To conclude this section, we can note a substantial increase in the 1980s and 1990s of regionally based attempts at cooperation in various parts of the world in the context of the end of the Cold War and increasing globalisation. This led observers to coin a novel phrase: the new regionalisation. According to the international relations scholar, Deborah Leslie (1997), this development reflected the impact of 'globalization, which transfers economic power from states to private sector entities (from politics to markets) . . . [and] seemingly stimulates the emergence of regional systems'. In addition, there was much concern in some parts of the world, for example, North America and Asia-Pacific, about the emergence of protectionism in Europe ('Fortress Europe') linked to the development of the Single European Market. This provided much of the impetus behind the dynamic development of regional organisations away from Europe. In the remainder of this chapter we shall look at these issues in relation to two specific regional organisations, the North American Free Trade Agreement and Asia-Pacific Economic Cooperation, both of which were created about the time as the inauguration of the Single European Market, in the late 1980s/early 1990s.

## The North American Free Trade Agreement

The North American Free Trade Agreement (NAFTA) is a regional cooperation organisation with just three members: Canada, Mexico, and the United States (Hufbauer and Schott 2005). The agreement creating NAFTA came into force on 1 January 1994. It followed an earlier agreement involving only Canada and the United States, the Canada–United States Free Trade Agreement, which dates from 1988. NAFTA has two supplements, the North American Agreement on Environmental Cooperation (NAAEC) and the North American Agreement on Labor Cooperation (NAALC). As their names suggest, they cover environmental and labour issues in the context of NAFTA.

In general, regional cooperation attempts away from Europe are in various stages of development. However NAFTA, founded less than twenty years ago, has made relatively swift progress towards increased regional cooperation involving the three member states. This may be in part because the three-country organisation, a much smaller regional grouping than the twenty-seven member EU, finds it relatively easy to get agreement among the three governments on policies and programmes. NAFTA is also significant as it is one of the few regional cooperation organisations with a North–South membership. According to Christiansen (2001: 513), NAFTA 'is the most far-reaching example of a regional cooperation project spanning the North–South divide'. NAFTA brings together two developed countries (Canada, the USA) and a developing nation (Mexico).

This is not to suggest that the members of NAFTA are equal in economic terms. Indeed, NAFTA is characterised by considerable asymmetry in the economic size and strength of its members (Hufbauer and Schott 2005). In addition, the economies of the members are very different: in particular, the USA economy features a relatively low level of state involvement while in Mexico the government has traditionally had an important voice and role. Canada falls somewhere between the two: it has a primarily market economy but with some significant state involvement.

### Box 14.1 The North American Free Trade Agreement (NAFTA)

NAFTA is the largest regional economic cooperation block in the world when measured in terms of its members 'purchasing power parity Gross Domestic Product (GDP)' and second largest by nominal GDP comparison. (A nation's GDP at purchasing power parity exchange rates is the sum value of all goods and services produced in the country valued at prices prevailing in the United States. This is the measure most economists prefer when looking at per capita welfare and when comparing living conditions or use of resources across countries.)

Differing economic features and different levels of economic development between the member states suggest that attempts at greater regional cooperation and creating a single free trade area, the main goal of NAFTA, would not be an easy or straightforward task. When NAFTA was inaugurated in 1994, the USA contributed nearly nine-tenths (88 per cent) of the Agreement's gross domestic product. Mexico contributed just one-twentieth (5 per cent) and Canada one-fourteenth (7 per cent). Given this asymmetrical relationship, it was appropriate for Schirm (2002: 137) to claim that 'the US market – [was] much more relevant to Canada and Mexico than its neighbouring markets are to the USA'. However, while NAFTA's overt *raison d'être* was both economic and financial (abolition of impediments between the three countries to trade in goods and services), the Agreement also had another consequence: it encouraged significant political changes in Mexico. This illustrates that although NAFTA was founded as an explicitly economic grouping, one of its side effects was to encourage Mexico to democratise.

In sum, the issue of NAFTA membership resulted in clear and sustained signs of democratisation and improved human rights in Mexico in the 1990s and 2000s. For example, in 1991, the then ruling Institutional Revolutionary Party (PRI) controlled 320 (out of 500) seats in the country's parliament, the Congress. By 1997, this had fallen by over a quarter, to 239 seats. Importantly, this meant that the PRI had lost its congressional majority for the first time since it first gained power decades earlier, in 1929. The electoral decline of the PRI was further underlined in December 2000, when an opposition candidate, Vicente

## Box 14.2 Mexico and NAFTA

What occurred in relation to Mexico's political development was not an isolated outcome of regional cooperation. The same effect but on a bigger scale has also been noted in relation to the development of the European Union. As we shall see in Chapter 15, during the 1990s and early 2000s many post-communist governments in Central and Eastern Europe wished to join the EU, as it was believed that EU membership was likely to be a fast-track route to economic development. However, one of the key criteria for EU membership is that candidates must have not only market economies but also recognisably democratic political regimes before they could be accepted as members. In other words, the desire to become an EU member was a key stimulus for many of Europe's post-communist countries both to democratise and to develop market economies.

We can note a similar cause and effect in relation to Mexico's wish to join NAFTA. As a result, Mexico's government embarked on a twin-track approach: significant political and economic reforms, in order to bring the country into line with what both the United States and Canada demanded in these regards. These efforts were instrumental in the government's attempts to 'dismantle Mexico's statist economy, which was essential to undermining the economic basis of Mexican [political] authoritarianism' (Delal Baer 2000). This emphasises how Mexico's government regarded the prospect of NAFTA membership in the early 1990s – as a crucially important means to help the country develop economically, primarily by attracting increased investment from the USA, the region's economic giant. In addition, this would not only contribute to the country's economic growth, but also increase its credibility more generally, both regionally and internationally. Second, NAFTA 'has contributed to greater decentralization of economic and political power, as Mexican states attempt to capture NAFTA-related investment'. Third, 'Mexican political and human rights practices came under greater international scrutiny as a result of the political battle to pass NAFTA in the U.S.' (Delal Baer 2000).

Source: Getty Images/AFP

**Mexico's economic and political troubles demonstrate that there are costs as well as benefits to maintaining regional organisations such as NAFTA.**

Fox, a vociferous supporter of NAFTA, won that year's presidential elections. Fox's victory led to improvements in both political rights and civil liberties, as Table 14.2 indicates.

Mexico's democratisation also resulted in greater openness in Mexican policy towards the involvement of various interest groups – for example, labour, business and women – in consultations on the Free Trade Area of the Americas (FTAA) process. The FTAA Treaty

**Table 14.2** Political rights and civil liberties in Mexico, 1972–2009

| Year | Political rights | Civil liberties | Status |
|------|-----------------|-----------------|--------|
| 1972 | 5 | 3 | Partly Free |
| 1980 | 3 | 4 | Partly Free |
| 1990 | 4 | 4 | Partly Free |
| 1995 | 4 | 4 | Partly Free |
| 1999 | 3 | 4 | Partly Free |
| 2003 | 2 | 2 | Free |
| 2009 | 2 | 3 | Free |

*Source*: http://www.freedomhouse.org/template.cfm?page=363&year=2005&country=6790

Note: Freedom House, an America non-government organisation, first compiled its data in 1972. 'Partly Free' implies that a country has some but not all democratic characteristics. 'Free' implies that a country has most necessary democratic characteristics. The best score is a '1' and the worst, a '7'. So, we can see from the table that Mexico's grading consistently improved from the early 1970s until 2003.

was signed in Quebec City in 2001. The intention was that from 2005 the FTAA would be a regional free trade agreement covering both the Americas and the Caribbean. However, the FTAA missed the targeted deadline of 2005. This was consequential to a long period of prevarication among regional governments about the FTAA, and what it would do and what it was for. Over time, however, some regional governments, for example Brazil, not wishing to lose the opportunity of hemispheric trade expansion, moved in the direction of establishing a series of bilateral trade deals with regional countries. The 'Fifth Summit of the Americas', which focused discussions on the FTAA, took place in Trinidad and Tobago in April 2009. So far, however, no definitive progress has been recorded towards establishing the proposed FTAA.

## NAFTA's coordinating institutions

NAFTA is less institutionally developed than the European Union. The three member states – Canada, Mexico, and the United States – maintain tight control over trade negotiations, both because of the centrality of trade to their national economic agendas and because of the perceived need for secrecy in negotiations. However, while the Agreement's administration largely relies on national ministers, it does have four coordinating institutions: the Free Trade Commission, 'Coordinators', Committees and Working Groups, and the Secretariat.

- **The Free Trade Commission.** This is the Agreement's central institution. It comprises cabinet-level representatives from the three member countries, Canada, Mexico and the USA. However, the Commission is not an institution in a key sense, as it only holds meetings when required. Its main work is to supervise implementation and further elaboration of the Agreement and to help resolve disputes that arise from its interpretation. The Commission oversees the work of the Committees and Working Groups, as well as other subsidiary bodies.
- **'Coordinators'.** These senior trade department officials are designated by each country both to carry out day-to-day management of the organisation's work programme and to seek to implement the Agreement more broadly.
- **Committees and Working Groups.** There are more than thirty of these bodies, helping to smooth implementation of the Agreement and to provide fora to explore ways of further liberalising trade between members. The Agreement envisages that further work will be required towards fulfilling the objectives of the FTA, in various areas. These include: trade in goods, rules of origin, customs, agricultural trade and subsidies, standards, government procurement, investment and services, cross-border movement of business people, and alternative dispute resolution.
- **The Secretariat.** Comprising national offices in each of the Canadian, US and Mexican capitals, the Secretariat is responsible for the administration of the dispute settlement provisions of the Agreement. Each national section maintains a court-like registry relating to panel, committee and tribunal proceedings. The NAFTA Secretariat maintains a 'trinational' website where current information on NAFTA is presented (www.nafta-sec-alena.org/).

## Interest group representation in NAFTA

As noted above, NAFTA institutions are relatively underdeveloped compared to those in the EU. As a result, regionally focused interest groups do not primarily focus upon such institutions to try to achieve their goals. Instead, various interest groups – including business and 'NAFTA-protest' groups – generally lobby domestically within the member states. What they manage to achieve will be related to the success they have in exploiting each country's opportunity structures for participation. Canada has a federal parliamentary system with multiple, cohesive political parties and relatively strong provincial authorities. As a result, lobbying efforts will be directed at both federal and provincial levels. Mexico has a highly centralised polity with a powerful national president. Interest groups focus their attentions at the national level because, while the country has a federal system, it has weak provincial authorities. The American political system is different again. It has a congressional system of divided powers and rather wide-ranging political parties, an arrangement offering much scope for 'individual political agendas', while allowing 'local and regional interests considerable opportunity for representation and influence at the national level' (Macdonald and Schwartz 2002: 138–9).

There are several sets of circumstances that NAFTA shares with the EU. First, interest groups in the former sharing common concerns – for example, jobs preservation and environmental protection – have not yet managed to develop an effective network of regional organisation, although the existence of English as a common language in both the USA and Canada might be expected to facilitate efforts over time. Consequently, victories on several labour and environment issues achieved by 'citizen politics', such as the campaign not to cut down historic redwood trees in California in the early 2000s, were achieved via domestic organisational efforts. The peculiarities of the USA congressional system were important, 'with its openness to district-level influences . . . to win support for bills, and the effective cooptation by US administrations of part of the environmental NGO coalition' (Macdonald and Schwartz 2002: 139).

Second, like in the EU, trade policy debates in NAFTA member states often focus upon bilateral issues rather than those affecting the region as a whole. Third, big business is widely regarded as having considerable ability to influence decision-making in NAFTA, just as in the EU. Leslie (1997) suggests that this is linked to the nature of these regional systems. He explains that regionalisation can assume different forms, and not all states are affected in exactly the same way. However, seeking to respond to globalisation, a strategy open to any regional grouping of national states is to remove barriers among themselves. The more fully integrated a regional economic environment – the most advanced is the EU followed by NAFTA – then the more facilitative it is both for creating multinational corporations (MNCs) and for enabling them to increase their regional influence. Focusing upon markets of hundreds of millions of people, as in both the EU and NAFTA, MNCs have opportunities both to specialise and to develop advanced technologies. This enables them to create or to exploit economic opportunities and can also lead to them becoming important political actors.

Within NAFTA, 'business interest groups' have been influential in various ways. In the absence of powerful regional institutions, their main focus is the member governments. For many US (and Canadian) business corporations, the opportunity to expand into Mexico's newly liberalised economy was an important motivating factor for action in the 1990s. The adoption of neo-Liberal concepts and policies in Mexico was strongly supported by transnational business networks, involving both Mexican and primarily American companies. One example of such a network is the 'Americas Society', based in New York. Its membership includes influential American entrepreneurs, such as David Rockefeller and John Reed (Citibank), and important Mexican businessmen, including Miguel Alemán and the head of a media conglomerate (Televisa), Emilio Azcárraga (Schirm 2002: 150).

## Case study: From NAFTA to FTAA?

Although business groups are influential, able to organise to take advantage of opportunities resulting from NAFTA's expansion to include Mexico, other non-state actors, such as labour interests, have had a relative lack of success in influencing outcomes in the regional organisation. On the other hand, as in the EU, NAFTA's member governments have been willing to include civil society groups in consultations around trade policy. One key area of current and future discussion is the scheduled expansion of NAFTA into the FTAA. These have focused upon – but not been restricted to – issues linked to the increasing politicisation of trade issues and consequent mobilisation of interest groups in the member countries. Like their counterparts in EU member states, such actors in NAFTA are primarily concerned with the impact of trade liberalisation on jobs, the environment and, increasingly, domestic systems of social regulation. But because NAFTA lacks the type of institutionalised fora that the EU has, notably the Commission and the Parliament, the regional impact of their campaigns has been patchy (Morales 2008).

Opponents of the FTAA – including some trade unions and environmental groups – claim that, despite repeated calls for the open and democratic development of trade policy, the expanded NAFTA will be a disaster. This is primarily because of fear of both extensive job losses and serious environmental damage, expected by critics to be a key result of the extension of free trade policies. Critics also claim that despite governmental assurances, the FTAA negotiations have been conducted substantively without citizen input. While the governments maintain that they want to hear citizens' views, opponents claim that this amounts to only a widely-denounced 'mailbox' mechanism, that is, an electronic 'suggestion box'. They assert that this is mere window dressing, not a substantive mechanism to incorporate the public's

concerns into the actual negotiations. At the same time, however, hundreds of corporate representatives are said to be advising FTAA negotiators, with advance access to the negotiating texts. As a result, the anti-FTAA campaign claimed that 'citizens are left in the dark, [and] corporations are helping to write the rules for the FTAA' (http://www.globalexchange.org/campaigns/ftaa/topten.html).

The issue of citizen access to FTAA negotiations came to a head at the 2001 FTAA Summit in Quebec City. Foreign and trade ministers from the Summit countries agreed to meet with sixty representatives from hemispheric NGOs inside the chain link fence that separated the dignitaries from the ordinary citizens. Outside, hundreds of representatives of NGOs demonstrated, and were sprayed with teargas for their pains. Critics contend that this indicates that the main aim of government policy is to sidetrack 'actions on issues such as the environment, gender, human rights, labor standards, and democracy to other forums', including institutions of the Organisation of American States (Macdonald and Schwartz 2002: 153). NGOs and citizen groups oppose this policy, arguing that it is not appropriate to try to divide trade and social issues which should be discussed together during the FTAA negotiations. So far, however, there are few signs that the FTAA Committee of Government Representatives – the key institution overseeing the negotiations – is willing to open up and extend the process in the ways that their critics would like to see. It may be that to find a way out of this impasse will require more open and transparent processes of consultation than have so far been adopted.

 **Is NAFTA soon likely to develop into the FTAA? What are the main constraints on this development?**

## NAFTA: Conclusion

Our brief examination of NAFTA suggests several conclusions. First, Mexico's recent democratisation appears to be linked to pressures emanating from the Agreement's founder members – the USA and Canada. This is significant for the issue of links between globalisation and comparative political analysis as it suggests that Mexico's rulers believed that membership of NAFTA was worth the price: economic liberalisation and democratisation (to the extent that the incumbent regime eventually lost power). In short, free trade helped break down rigid economic and political traditions in Mexico, leading to the institution of both democratic norms and economic liberalisation.

Second, what were initially seen as 'only' trade issues in NAFTA have gone beyond narrowly defined economic outcomes to affect a wide range of social and political issues, while informing discussions about its probable successor, the FTAA. In the NAFTA member states, trade issues are defined and underlined along sharply partisan lines. On the one hand are the proponents of free trade, notably the member states and big business. On the other hand are ranged what might be called 'the popular sector', with its concern with what it sees as the unwelcome social, environmental, economic and political results of regional trade liberalisation (Morales 2008).

Third, widespread involvement of various interest groups suggests that, while excessive optimism about the role of both domestic and transnational NGOs in trade talks would not be warranted, it is unlikely that what has been called the era of 'competitive elitism' will soon return. This is because opponents of regional trade agreements are very unlikely to accept passively trade agreements negotiated behind closed doors in meetings of elites. Instead, domestic and to some extent transnational coalitions of actors now mobilise around trade issues and have been successful in affecting popular perception of trade issues, including the free trade assumptions behind both NAFTA and FTAA. The issue has opened up the consultation process in countries in Latin America and the Caribbean in the context of FTAA discussion, where these issues were in the past normally determined by executive fiat. Macdonald and Schwartz (2002: 153) aver as a result of these developments that, although regional 'states . . . continue to control the trade agenda, we may nonetheless be seeing the first stages of a movement toward more participatory and consultative forms of trade agreements and a convergence between "globalization from above" and "globalization from below"'. However, this union is only likely to succeed if it manages to develop thinking 'about ways in which both party and NGO models of political representation, and both national and international politics, can be viewed as synergistically linked, rather than as diametrically opposed realities'.

## Asia-Pacific Economic Cooperation

In recent years, the Asia-Pacific region has consistently been the most economically dynamic region in the world (Beeson 2008). Since the Asia-Pacific Economic Cooperation (APEC) organisation was founded in 1989, the region's total trade has increased 395 per cent, a rate of growth which significantly outpaces the rest of the world. In the same period, GDP (in purchasing power parity terms) in the APEC region tripled. This compares favourably with GDP in the rest of the world which did not even manage to double during this period. APEC encompasses economies with a population of over two billion people with a combined GDP of over US$13 *trillion*. APEC's main purpose is to facilitate economic growth, cooperation, trade and investment among the 21 member states, referred to by the organisation as 'Member Economies'. Together, APEC's 21 members account for over 40 per cent of world population, more than 50 per cent of global GDP and in excess of 40 per cent of world trade.

Bob Hawke, then prime minister of Australia, first suggested the idea of APEC in January 1989. Later that year, governments of twelve Asia-Pacific countries got together in Canberra, the Australian capital, to discuss the idea. The outcome of the talks was the founding of APEC. As Table 14.3 shows, APEC's founding members were: Australia, Brunei Darussalam, Canada, Indonesia, Japan, Korea, Malaysia, New Zealand, the Philippines, Singapore, Thailand and the United States. In 1991, three more members joined the organisation, China, Hong Kong (now a province of China, Hong Kong was a British colony until 1997), and Taiwan. Two years later, in 1993, Mexico and Papua New Guinea also became members, followed by Chile a year later. Finally, in 1998, Peru, Russia and Vietnam gained membership, bringing the number of members to twenty-one. After that, a moratorium on new membership was announced, to run until the end of 2010, at which point APEC member economies will consider whether or not to lift the moratorium. A notable regional country, India, is lobbying for APEC membership.

**Table 14.3** Asia-Pacific Economic Cooperation members

| Asia-Pacific Economic Cooperation members | Date of joining |
| --- | --- |
| Australia | 1989 |
| Brunei Darussalam | 1989 |
| Canada | 1989 |
| Indonesia | 1989 |
| Japan | 1989 |
| Republic of Korea | 1989 |
| Malaysia | 1989 |
| New Zealand | 1989 |
| The Philippines | 1989 |
| Singapore | 1989 |
| Thailand | 1989 |
| The United States | 1989 |
| Hong Kong, China | 1991 |
| People's Republic of China | 1991 |
| Taiwan | 1991 |
| Mexico | 1993 |
| Papua New Guinea | 1993 |
| Chile | 1994 |
| Peru | 1998 |
| Russia | 1998 |
| Vietnam | 1998 |

Between 1989 and 1992, APEC met as an informal senior official and Ministerial level dialogue. In 1993, as the number of members increased, the then president of the USA, Bill Clinton, suggested the APEC Economic Leaders' Meeting, which henceforward became an annual event. From this time, there was enhanced cooperation at ministerial level to include regular meetings of members' finance ministers, trade ministers, environment ministers, and ministers responsible for small and medium enterprises.

APEC's initial aim was both to enhance members' economic growth and prosperity, and to strengthen the idea of Asia-Pacific community. From its inception, APEC has worked to reduce tariffs and other trade barriers across the Asia-Pacific region, sought to create efficient domestic economies and dramatically increase the region's exports. The main policy statement about what APEC seeks to achieve was presented in 1994. The 'Bogor Goals', as they became known, were adopted by APEC leaders at their 1994 meeting in Bogor, Indonesia. The Bogor Goals highlight the importance for the economic development and prosperity of APEC members of regionally free and open trade and investment. For APEC's industrialised economies – such as Australia, the United States, Canada, and Japan – the goal is to achieve these targets by 2010. For APEC's developing economies, including Indonesia, Papua New Guinea and Vietnam, the objective is to attain them by 2020 (Beeson 2008).

Like the EU and NAFTA, APEC leaders have an ideological commitment to free and open trade and investment. This is because they believe such policies are necessary to facilitate economic growth among members which, in turn, would create jobs and provide greater opportunities for international trade and investment. Protectionism, in contrast, is believed by APEC to lead to higher prices and inefficiencies in certain industries. In addition, it is averred, free and open trade helps to lower the costs of production and thus reduces the prices of goods and services. This is believed to be a direct benefit for all, rich and poor. In addition, again like both the EU and NAFTA, APEC 'works to create an environment for the safe and efficient movement of goods, services and people across borders in the region through policy alignment and economic and technical cooperation' (http://www.apec.org/apec/about_apec.html).

## APEC: coordinating institutions

APEC was founded in 1989, a few years before NAFTA's inauguration in 1994 (Morrison and Pedrosa 2007). These years were a time of dynamic globalisation which encouraged the formation and development of regional organisations in many parts of the world, as a means both to deal with the challenges of globalisation and to try to ensure enhanced prosperity and economic development. However, whereas NAFTA has four main coordinating institutions – the Free Trade Commission, 'Coordinators', Committees and Working Groups, and the Secretariat – APEC operates without such institutions. Instead, it prefers working on the basis of 'non-binding commitments, open dialogue and equal respect for the views of all participants'. In addition, unlike NAFTA members, APEC participants are not bound by any treaty obligations. Instead, 'decisions made within APEC are reached by consensus and commitments are undertaken on a voluntary basis'. An APEC Eminent Persons' Group

(EPG) Report published in 1994 characterised APEC as 'a like-minded group that aims to remove barriers to economic exchange among its members in the interests of all'. The report states that the term 'big family', translated directly from the Chinese original term, captures the concept and seeks to characterise APEC's activities.

APEC has no permanent institutional infrastructure. The organisation is serviced by a small secretariat of about twenty staff, located in Singapore. 'The secretariat of the longer-established Pacific Economic Cooperation Council (PECC), a research and networking forum with representatives of business, academia and government (but not labour) from most APEC member states as well as some other countries, also based in Singapore, has often served as institutional back-up to APEC by undertaking studies on its behalf.' (http://www.apec.org/apec/about_apec.html).

Although APEC does not have institutions of the kind that the EU or NAFTA have, it does have ten working groups, in the following areas:

- Trade and Investment Data
- Trade Promotion
- Industrial Science and Technology
- Human Resources Development
- Regional Energy Cooperation
- Marine Resource Conservation
- Telecommunications
- Transportation
- Tourism
- Fisheries.

These working groups operate in functional areas of mutual interest to APEC members. They 'concentrate on data standardization, collection and provision; exchange of missions between member economies; seminars and training courses; programmes to share information; and projects to facilitate sharing of experiences. There are two additional Committees, on trade and investment in the region and on economic trends and issues; two sub-committees on customs procedures and on standards and conformance; and a policy-level group on small and medium enterprises.' This is not, however, to suggest that APEC is unmindful of wider regional and global developments. It now focuses on: counter-terrorism (The Shanghai Statement, 2001, which involved creation of the Counter-Terrorism Task Force); human security (Health Working Group); emergency preparedness (Task Force for Emergency Pre-paredness); climate change, energy security and clean development (The Sydney Declaration in 2007); and the global financial crisis, focused upon in the Lima Statement in 2008.

By the early 2000s, after being in existence for more than a decade, APEC was still very much in the formative phase of institution building. This was because APEC had consciously followed a path involving both informal and looser forms of institutional organisation. APEC wished to avoid what it saw as the European model of economic integration which involved, it believed, legalism, formal agreements and binding contracts. In addition, APEC shied away from calling itself a community because it believed that it carried unwelcome overtones of inward-looking approaches which it associated with the EU and which for APEC carried negative connotations, making the idea of an Asia-Pacific *community* unwelcome. We can see from this that the underdeveloped state of APEC's institutions is entirely deliberate. In defining the organisation's vision, the APEC Eminent Persons Group explicitly cautioned against 'over-institutionalization and over-bureaucratization'. Consequently, we should understand the lack of APEC institutional development as part of a conscious policy to develop APEC as a 'voluntary, non-binding arrangement with emphasis on informality, consensus-building and ad hoc problem-solving' (Avila 2000: 1).

Yet, despite the lack of formal institutions, as already noted, APEC's activities have multiplied over the years (Morrison and Pedrosa 2007). The 'big family's' scope of activities has broadened to include more countries as members, with numbers increasing from 12 to 20 (plus a province of China, Hong Kong). Critics contend that its lack of institutional development is partly the reason for its failure to be an influential actor in international relations, in the Asia-Pacific region and beyond. The charge is that the low level of its institutional development makes it difficult for the organisation to keep pace with the demands and expectations placed on it. Consequently, critics charge, APEC's institutions and processes need to move forward, further and faster. To make sustained progress and increase its regional and international influence, it is suggested that APEC must try to advance towards a higher stage of institutional development to cope with demands it now encounters. However, APEC leaders are still distrustful of 'bureaucratic structures and contractual arrangements that prevent it from moving towards more definite rules and procedures' (Avila 2000: 1).

### Box 14.3  APEC – interest group representation

Like NAFTA, APEC is considering prospects and options for a regional free trade area. In APEC's case, the focal point is the proposed Free Trade Area of the Asia-Pacific (FTAAP). FTAAP would include all member economies of APEC. Over the last few years, APEC's Business Advisory Council has advanced the idea that a regional free trade area is the best potential way of bringing together member nations in pursuit of collectively satisfactory stable and speedy economic growth. As a result, the Business Advisory Council 'has lobbied for the creation of a high-level task force to study and develop a plan for a free trade area'. The aim is to create FTAAP as a dynamic free trade zone 'that would considerably expand commerce and economic growth in the most dynamic region in the world'.

'The lack of a social dimension in APEC contrasts greatly with the proposals and activities of trade unions in the APEC region'. Business interests are heavily represented in the organisation's Business Advisory Council and the latter's goal of a FTAAP is not endorsed by trade unions, who fear the social implications of FTAAP. In 1994, regional trade unions adopted a general set of principles covering what they saw as workers' rights, addressed to governments and employers in all states of the Asian and Pacific region. These principles covered such issues as: 'employment, wages and working conditions, vocational training and retraining, industrial relations, safety and health and the environment, women workers', transnational corporations activities and 'export processing zones (EPZs), migrant workers, social security and trade union development'. However, as APEC does not have institutions, the labour issues mentioned here have no obvious forum for airing and the only interest group which finds its concerns taken into account regularly in APEC are business interests, organised in the Business Advisory Council ('A Trade Union Perspective on the APEC Forum'; http://actrav. itcilo.org/actrav-english/telearn/global/ilo/clause/tuapec.htm).

## APEC: conclusion

APEC is an important political and economic entity. It is the principal forum for promotion of free market principles across the Asia-Pacific region. It remains to be seen, however, whether APEC can make progress in the medium- and long-term without attending to its institutional lack of capacity.

From its inauguration, APEC has emphasised the importance of 'informal consensus-building, ad hoc problem-solving diplomacy, confidence-building, elite-bonding, and peer pressure' (Avila 2000: 6; also see Higgott 1998 and Kahler 1995). Distrustful of the 'European model', with its developed, authoritative institutions, the APEC approach emphasises member states' dislike of bureaucratic structures – while stressing the importance of 'informality, non-interference in each other's internal affairs, and tacit postponement of conflict-prone issues'. Critics contend, however, that if APEC is ever to function as an effective regional organisation, it must strive 'to bring its institutions to organizational maturity' (Oxley 1999). This would however necessitate a thorough rethinking of the organisation's fundamental norms, principles and processes, from which it has not deviated since inception.

## Conclusion

We noted at the beginning of the chapter that a key aim of virtually all existing regional organisations is to expand trade among member countries in the context of globalisation. We have seen that when there are appropriate formal and/or informal institutions – which has happened to an extent in NAFTA although not yet in APEC – then political, social and/or developmental objectives, even when officially of no or minimal importance, can grow in significance in the context of trade talks. Yet, 'APEC is unlikely to transform itself into a trade negotiating body similar' to NAFTA or the EU. This is not only because of its perceived institutional inadequacies. Like many other regional organisations, APEC's membership overlaps with other regional organisations, including the older and more established Association of South East Asian Nations (ASEAN). ASEAN officials take the view that APEC should be supplementary to their activities, not seek to replace them. What this means is that APEC should remain 'a forum for consultations and constructive discussions on economic issues and that it "should proceed gradually and pragmatically, especially as regards its eventual institutional structure." In this sense, institution-building in APEC will only go so far as its members will allow' (Avila 2000).

## Resource section

## Questions

1. If regionalisation is a response to globalisation, how can we explain the existence of regional organisations *before* the current era of enhanced globalisation?

2. Explain why many regional organisations see globalisation as both a challenge and an opportunity.

3. Which is more successful: NAFTA or APEC? What criteria should we choose in order to make this judgement?

4. Do NAFTA policies simply reflect the domination of the USA in the organisation?

5. Why is APEC so unwilling to develop institutions?

## Recommended reading

Beeson, M. (2008) *Institutions of the Asia Pacific: ASEAN, APEC and Beyond* (London: Routledge)
The Asia-Pacific region is home to the world's largest economies and some of its most volatile strategic relationships. But for all its geopolitical importance, it has generally failed to develop the sorts of powerful and effective institutions that are found in Western Europe. This book explains why and considers the prospects for future institutional development in this pivotal region.

Hufbauer, G.C. and Schott, J.J. (2005) *NAFTA Revisited: Achievements and Challenges* (Washington DC: Institute for International Economics)
NAFTA was inaugurated in 1994 after a bitter Congressional debate in the USA. During its years of life, NAFTA in operation has also proved to be highly controversial. Both supporters and opponents of regional trade liberalisation have cited experience with the agreement to justify their positions. To provide a factual basis for this ongoing debate, the authors evaluate NAFTA's performance since its inception, comparing actual experience with both the objectives of the agreement's supporters and the charges of its critics.

Morales, I. (2008) *Post-NAFTA North America: Reshaping the Economic and Political Governance of a Changing Region* (New York and Basingstoke, UK: Palgrave Macmillan)
Since NAFTA was conceived in the early 1990s, it has been regarded as a mechanism of economic integration, drawing Canada, Mexico and the US into one single economic space. The author seeks to challenge this long-held assumption. He argues that in fact for the USA, NAFTA is not an integration mechanism, but rather a means of reinforcing 'export-enhancing' policies generated by Washington.

Morrison, C. and Pedrosa, E. (2007) *An APEC Trade Agenda?: The Political Economy of a Free Trade Area of the Asia-Pacific* (Singapore: Institute of South East Asian Studies)
The book explains that a proposal for an Asia-Pacific-wide free trade agreement is one of the oldest ideas for promoting mutually beneficial regional cooperation dating back to the mid-1960s. The authors assess the political feasibility of the Free Trade Area of the Asia-Pacific (FTAAP) proposal and look at alternative modalities for achieving free trade and investment in the Asia-Pacific.

**Tavares, R. (2009)** *Regional Security* (London: Routledge)
Regional organisations are a highly important component of international relations. Most countries are members of at least one regional or other intergovernmental organisation. In recent years, as the author explains, regional organisations in Europe, Africa, Asia, and the Americas, have increasingly become concerned with issues of peace and security. Despite suffering from important discrepancies in both their mandates and capacities, regional organisations, the author asserts, have become key actors that play a role from the outbreak of a crisis to the reconstruction efforts in the aftermath of a conflict.

## Useful websites

United States Institute of Peace comprehensive survey of current activities of regional organisations

**http://www.usip.org/issue-areas/international-and-regional-organizations**

Comprehensive list of regional organisations

**http://www.unescap.org/tid/publication/t&ipub2281_part2.pdf**

List of 'world and regional' organisations

**http://www.au.af.mil/au/awc/awcgate/awc-regn.htm#orgs**

# Chapter 15
# The European Union and the African Union

After reading this chapter you will have gained an understanding of the following:

- Structures and processes of the European Union
- Structures and processes of the African Union
- How the EU and the AU are similar and different

*Source*: Getty Images/Somos/Veer

The European Union (EU) has been in existence since 1992. Before that there was another, smaller, organisation called the European Economic Community (EEC), created in 1957. And prior to that there was the European Coal and Steel Community (ECSC), which was founded in 1952. The overall point is that a European-wide organisation has been in existence since soon after the end of the Second World War. Now, over fifty years on, many Europeans are not convinced that a European-wide entity of this kind is a good thing.

Euroscepticism is a general term used to describe various forms of (1) criticism of the EU, and (2) opposition to continued European integration – that is, the gradual coming together, both economically and politically, of the member states of the EU. One of the main complaints of the Eurosceptics is that integration weakens the nation state and undermines national identity. Other Eurosceptic concerns include the charge that the EU is undemocratic, a top-down organisation that pays little attention or concern to the problems and aspirations of ordinary people, or that it is too bureaucratic: dominated by unelected, over-paid civil servants. A periodic European-wide public opinion survey, known as the Eurobarometer, found that support for the EU was lowest in Hungary, Latvia, and Britain (http://ec.europa.eu/public_opinion/index_en.htm).

## Introduction

To what extent does a regional organisation manage to achieve their objectives? What more might it do to gain greater success? To what extent are member states prepared to allow regional organisations to act independently in international relations?

The main aim of this chapter is to examine what regional organisations do in international relations. There are numerous regional organisations of various types so to make our task manageable we shall look at two important regional organisations in some detail: the European Union (EU) and the African Union (AU). We will compare and contrast their key institutions in order to draw conclusions about their differences and similarities. At the end of the chapter we shall be in a position to:

1. understand what roles these regional organisations play in international relations
2. see how successful they are in dealing with the peace and security issues with which they are concerned.

Many international relations scholars would agree that, despite all the changes we've seen in the world in recent years, states are still the key actors in global politics. Many aspects of globalisation – including extensive economic interactions, expanding communications links, major environmental interactions and overlaps – collectively encourage individual governments to cooperate in order to try to achieve goals that, acting on their own, they may not believe they can achieve. The implication is that today no country is fully self-sufficient or capable of living in complete isolation from the rest of humanity. This state of affairs suggests that the very concept of national sovereignty (sometimes, called 'independence' or 'autonomy') is now much less certain than it once was. In some regions of the world, especially Europe, this realisation has led to highly structured attempts to promote cooperation across state boundaries, in the form of regional organisations. The most far-reaching of these efforts thus far has been the EU. In some regions, such as Sub-Saharan Africa, the successes of European integration efforts over the last six decades have led to copy-cat attempts at *regional integration*. Examples include Africa, which we examine in this chapter in comparison with Europe, as well as parts of Asia, Latin America and elsewhere.

The key issue we examine in this chapter is: Thinking about regional integration in recent years, how has Africa done compared to Europe?

## The European Union

## Background and history

What makes the EU distinctive in today's international relations? According to a British academic, Ben Rosamond, the EU is 'by some distance – the most developed project of regional integration in the world'. This is largely because it has a 'mature set of institutions' (Rosamond 2002: 498). The current advanced stage of EU institutional development is the culmination of more than five decades of integrative efforts involving growing numbers of countries, increasing from six to twenty-seven over the last six decades, since integrative attempts began in 1952 with the inauguration of the European Coal and Steel Community (see Box 15.1). Over the last sixty years, the EU has pursued multiple – economic, cultural, security, and political – goals, leading now to an advanced state of regional integration. It has been marked by stages of institutional development, with several key milestones. The most prominent are: the Treaty of Rome (1957) and the Single European Act (SEA) in 1986. The SEA was signed by the then twelve members of the European Community (see Box 15.1). The SEA was particularly important because it established a single European market (defined as an area without frontiers with free movement of goods, services, people and capital). It was the first major revision of the Treaty of Rome, signed three decades earlier. In addition, the SEA allowed for increased involvement of the European Parliament in the decision-making process, as well as qualified majority voting in the Council of Ministers for some policy areas. Finally, the Act included provisions covering collaboration in research and development and in environmental policy. The 1986 SEA was followed by the Maastricht, Amsterdam and Nice treaties (1992, 1997, and 2000, respectively) which deepened Europe's political integration. Major changes since 1945 in relation to the development of a European regional organisation are presented in Box 15.1.

*Source: Getty Images/AFP*

The EU: undemocratic and needlessly bureaucratic, or an increasingly relevant institution in a multi-polar world?

## Box 15.1 European Union timeline since 1945

| | | |
|---|---|---|
| 1945 | The Second World War ends |
| 1951 | Treaty of Paris |
| 1952 | European Coal and Steel Community (ECSC) |
| 1957 | Treaty of Rome |
| 1957 | European Economic Community (EEC) |
| 1963 | French president, Charles de Gaulle, vetoes British entry into the EEC |
| 1965 | European Atomic Energy Community (EURATOM) |
| 1967 | ECSC, EEC and EURATOM merged |
| 1973 | Britain, Denmark and Ireland join Community |
| 1979 | First direct elections to European Parliament |
| 1981 | Greece joins |
| 1985 | Greenland leaves Community |
| 1986 | Single European Act |
| 1986 | Portugal and Spain join |

| | |
|---|---|
| 1989 | End of Cold War, marked by fall of the Berlin Wall |
| 1992 | Maastricht Treaty, leading to European Union |
| 1993 | Copenhagen criteria defined for EU membership, centring on both political and economic conditions |
| 1995 | Austria, Finland and Sweden join |
| 1997 | Amsterdam Treaty |
| 2000 | Nice Treaty |
| 2002 | Euro replaces local currencies in twelve member states |
| 2004 | Ten more countries join EU |
| 2005 | France, Ireland and the Netherlands reject European Constitution |
| 2007 | Bulgaria and Romania join |
| 2007 | Lisbon Treaty signed |

**Table 15.1** Regional integration in Europe and elsewhere

| Parameters | Regional cooperation other than in the EU | Integration in the EU |
|---|---|---|
| Institutional characteristics | Reliance on purely intergovernmental forms of decision-making | Presence of autonomous **supranational** institutions that initiate and enforce common policies |
| Forms of decision-making | Consensual decision-making (i.e. states have veto over decisions) | Extensive use of qualified majority voting (i.e. states have no veto over decisions) |
| Degree of legal integration | Arbitration and dispute settlement of individual cases | Permanent court system developing a supranational legal order |
| Extent of political integration | Concentration on economic cooperation among states | Development of a political union with a system of economic, social, and political rights for citizens |
| Range of issues covered | Emphasis on trade, investment, and related economic issues | Expansion of competences into much wider areas (single currency environment, culture, etc.) |
| Presence of democratic procedures | Minimal, if any, involvement of parliaments | Establishment of a democratic process, based on a directly elected parliament |
| Foreign policy cooperation | Coordination of external relations limited to participation in multilateral trade negotiations | Development of a common foreign, security, and defence policy |

*Source*: Christiansen (2001: 515).

Table 15.1 highlights differences in institutional development between the European Union and other examples of regional cooperation in the world, including Africa, Asia and the Americas. What Table 15.1 shows is that, while some non-EU countries have also been involved in sometimes lengthy integration efforts – for example, the European Free Trade Agreement, the North American Free Trade Agreement, El Mercado Común del Sur (MERCOSUR in Spanish, Southern Common Market in English) and the African Union – none of these schemes has reached a level of institutional development which is anything close to comparable with the EU. This is a way of saying that one of the keys to understanding Europe's advanced integrative position is to highlight how important are regional institutions with power and authority. In the EU context, this includes the European Commission and the Council of Ministers, which we shall examine below.

The immediate forerunner of the EU, the European Economic Community (EEC), was created over half a century ago, in 1957, under the terms of the Treaty of Rome. The agreement initially involved just six states (Belgium, France, Italy, Luxembourg, the Netherlands and West Germany). Over the next five decades, membership expanded greatly, increasing to twenty-seven countries, drawn from west, central and eastern Europe, creating a pan-European grouping. The process of EU enlargement reflects above all a shared under-standing among member states that joining the EU is a sensible thing to do, as it is likely to increase their stability, prosperity and peace. These are, of course, goals that all govern-ments would like to achieve; they are by no means a solely European objective.

Until recently, the EU was exclusively a Western European regional grouping of established democracies. However, in May 2004, it expanded both numerically and geographically, to welcome ten new members: Cyprus, Czech Republic, Estonia, Hungary, Latvia, Lithuania, Malta, Poland, Slovakia and Slovenia. In 2007, two further countries joined: Bulgaria and Romania. The new, enlarged EU symbolised the final end to Europe's artificial division after the Second World War. During the Cold War (late 1940s–late 1980s), Europe was divided into 'West' and 'East'. The West comprised liberal democracies with market economies, while the East was the shorthand term for the communist countries under the leadership and domination of the Soviet Union.

It is safe to assume that an important draw of the EU for non-members was the expecta-tion that membership of the Union would likely lead to increased economic growth and consequential prosperity, compared to countries which were not members. We have already noted that the EU attaches strict political and economic criteria for membership: members must be both democracies and market economies. The draw of the EU means that the Union is able to exert considerable pressure on would-be members, strongly encourag-ing them both to democratise politically and to liberalise economically. Overall, the EU exerts considerable influence on aspirant applicant countries. They collectively amount to a com-bined 'carrot-and-stick approach', featuring both political and economic conditionality ('conditionality' means that for something to happen, certain conditions have to be fulfilled). The chief incentive for putative members was a 'clear timetable for quick accession to the EU' and 'generous aid, credit and direct investment flows from the member to the candidate countries' (Yilmaz 2002: 73).

Some observers claim in addition that for Europe's post-communist countries – such as the Czech Republic, Bulgaria and Slovenia – a main objective of joining the Union extends beyond expected greater economic prosperity to include a further objective: a sense of post-communist 'European-ness' or 'European-belonging'. This touches on a key issue of central importance to the EU and its future development, which also involves the issue of Turkey and its continuing application to join the Union. How do we understand the concept of Europe? Is Europe a territorial designation alone? Or does it also include the idea of Europe being a 'social construct', that is, an idea encompassing certain norms of behaviour, including democracy and well-developed human rights, and not just territory? This implies that Europeans collectively share certain norms and values which together comprise a fundamental

 **Box 15.2 What is civil society?**

Civil society is defined by Bjorn Hettne as a range of 'inclusive institutions that facilitate a societal dialogue over various social and cultural borders', while 'identities and loyalties are transferred from civil society to primary groups, competing with each other for territorial control, resources and security' Bjorn Hettne (2001: 40). A simpler way of expressing these ideas is to think of civil society as bringing together lots of groups of people with social and/or political goals which seek to gain their objectives by working collectively.

aspect of 'European-ness'. A Swedish social scientist, Bjorn Hettne, highlights the following norms and values as characteristic of 'European-ness': 'strong role for civil society, various institutionalized forms such as parliamentary decision making, and a democratic culture stressing above all individualism and human rights inherent in the individual human being' (Hettne 2001: 38–9).

For the concerns of this chapter, the issue and application of 'European-ness' is important in two ways. First, it focuses attention on the question of how Europe's former communist countries changed in order to fulfil the requirements of EU membership. Second, it also helps explain why the continuing attempts of Turkey to join the EU have been both protracted and problematic.

## Box 15.3 Turkey and the European Union

In his book, *The Crescent and the Star: Turkey between Two Worlds*, published in 2001, an American author, Stephen Kinzer, examines social and political tensions in Turkey over the last decade or so that collectively encouraged the country's political leaders to seek Turkey's membership of the EU. Kinzer examines the kind of state that modern Turkey's founder, Kemal Atatürk, created in the context of the country's historical background in Islam. According to Kinzer (2001), Turkey reached an important turning point on 17 August, 1999. On that day, more than 18,000 Turks were killed in a massive earthquake. The inadequacy of the state's response to the earthquake – thousands of people were left without suitable shelter or services for months – led millions of Turks to question the country's entire power structure. Popular concern was exacerbated when it became known that the authorities had allowed thousands of death trap buildings to be constructed, and then stood by impotently when there was no disaster plan to put into operation when many of them collapsed.

In addition, powerful forces of globalisation have affected Turkey's political culture over time, making it more secular and democratic. These two issues – the impact of globalisation and the decline in trust between state and society as a result of the 1999 earthquake – were present in the sustained, so far unresolved controversy, about Turkey's bid to join the EU. Coincidentally, in the same year as the traumatic earthquake, the EU announced that Turkey was an official candidate for membership. A wave of ecstatic self-congratulation washed over the country, accompanied by solemn newspaper commentaries declaring it the most important event since the founding of the Turkish Republic in 1923. The EU laid down strict con-

ditions under which Turkey could become a member. The country's rulers were dismayed by the conditions as they were very far reaching. To attain membership of the EU, the following reforms would be necessary:

1. repeal limits on free speech
2. grant every citizen the right to cultural expression, including Turkey's main minority people, the Kurds, whose aspirations had long been suppressed in pursuit of nation-building goals by successive Turkish governments
3. subject the military to emphatic and consistent civilian control
4. resolve social conflicts by conciliation
5. allow all citizens to practise their religion as they see fit.

Such was the overall magnitude of these putative changes that many among the ruling elite seriously questioned how desirable it would actually be to join the EU (Jenkins 2008: 174–9).

Thus, EU membership was the touted reward – *if* Turkey made profound progress towards an interlinked democratic and human rights regime which met the EU's stringent standards. To the surprise of some observers, over the next few years there were clear signs of progress. In 2007, eight years after Turkey's EU membership bid began, Turkey's political system was judged by Freedom House (2008) to be 'partly free'. The qualifying adjective ('partly') was awarded because the country was only slowly emerging from many decades of strong military involvement in politics. In other words, by 2007, Turkey's democratic and human rights credentials were significantly improving, although there was still some way to go to achieve a good European standard.

The American non-governmental organisation, Freedom House, reported in 2002 that 'Turkey [had] registered forward progress as a result of the loosening of restrictions on Kurdish culture. *Legislators made progress on an improved human rights framework, the product of Turkey's effort to integrate into European structures.* At the same time, political rights were enhanced as the country's military showed restraint in the aftermath of a free and fair election that saw the sweeping victory of a moderate Islamist opposition party' (emphasis added; Freedom House 2002: 12). In 2007, in addition, Turkey 'received an upward trend arrow for holding free and fair parliamentary elections' (Freedom House 2008). In a bid to encourage improved democracy and human rights, the EU has sought to apply both political and economic 'conditionality' on Turkey from the early 2000s. The EU sought to exert conditionality as a means to try to achieve particular reforms in Turkey: good governance, democratisation, better human rights, the rule of law, and economic liberalisation. (Conditionality is a concept used not only in international relations but also in international development and political economy. It refers to the use of conditions to encourage compliance by a country in relation to aid, a loan, debt or membership of an international organisation, such as the EU.)

There was, in addition, another important factor to note regarding EU–Turkey relations at this time. Following the terrorist attacks on the United States on 11 September 2001, it became clear that many EU governments believed that it was better to have 'Muslim' Turkey in the EU rather than, potentially, as a component of an 'anti-Western' grouping of Muslim countries. Partly as a consequence, in early 2003 the European commission recommended that foreign aid to Turkey should be doubled – from €0.5bn to €1.05bn – in 2004–6. This was a calculated attempt both to encourage the then newly elected Adalet ve Kalkınma Partisi (AKP; in English, the Justice and Development Party) government to refrain from military intervention in Iraq as well as to encourage continuation with domestic political and human rights reforms that would hopefully bring the country 'civilisationally' closer to Europe (Osborn 2003). Subsequently, during 2007–13, the EU's foreign aid programme to Turkey continues, with financial transfers scheduled to amount to nearly €800 million. While this was a significant fall, some 20 per cent, compared to 2004–6, it still represents a considerable sum at a time of European financial restraints, underlining the EU's continued commitment to support continued democratisation and human rights reforms in Turkey (Ayvaz 2008).

## Important institutions

For the EU to implement conditionality on Turkey or the post-communist new members, it is crucial that the organisation has a set of workable and robust institutions. In fact, the range of institutions that the EU has developed is extensive. All are concerned with governance of the organisation. The EU's main institutions are:

- **European Council of Ministers.** The Council is the predominant governing body of the EU. The ministers – all of whom are cabinet ministers in their respective countries – are chosen by member states to represent them. A president coordinates the Council's work, a rotating position changing every six months. The Council is both an executive and a legislative body, with the final word on most significant issues in the Union.

- **European Commission.** This is the executive body of the EU. It puts into effect decisions made both by the Council of Ministers and the European Parliament. It is made up of Commissioners, individually appointed by member states (although they do not represent their home countries, but are supposed to represent the EU only), and given areas of responsibility akin to those presided over by government ministers in domestic contexts. The Commission has a president, selected following a consensual decision by member states.
- **European Parliament.** This is the legislature of the EU. Its 626 members are chosen via the ballot box in each member state every five years. It is the only elected institution in the EU. The most recent elections were held in June 2009.
- **European Court of Justice.** The Court of Justice of the European Communities (often referred to simply as 'the Court') was set up in 1952 under the Treaty of Paris. Its job is to ensure that EU legislation (technically known as 'Community law') is interpreted and applied in the same way in each member state, so that it is always identical for all parties and in all circumstances. The Court has the power to settle legal disputes between member states, EU institutions, businesses and individuals. The Court is also important as it can legally settle disputes in the EU.
- **European Council.** This body comprises the heads of member governments. It meets a few times a year for discussions about various pressing issues.
- **European Central Bank.** This is a coordinating organisation. Its key function is to bring together the central banks of member states for policy-making in their areas of competence.

Politically, the EU is policed by the Commission, a body with **supranational** powers. ('Supranational' means that an authority has jurisdiction over national decision-making bodies.) The EU also has a Parliament and a Court to interpret EU laws. Over time, intervention in each other's internal affairs has become the norm for EU members. Prior to ten new members joining in May 2004, and two more in January 2007, most of the then fifteen members shared both a central bank and a single currency (the euro). Following the increase from fifteen to twenty-seven members between 2004 and 2007, there was a transition period during which the new members worked towards integrating their national banks and currencies within the EU.

The EU's governing bodies feature a mix of two governmental models. The first is **intergovernmental**, with national parties, legislatures, and governments functioning as key supports of EU governing bodies. The second is supranational, with the EU governing bodies such as the Commission, separate from and superior to national political institutions and organisations (Beetham and Lord 1998; Christiansen 2001; Hix 2003). It is sometimes observed that the first (intergovernmental) model has gained ground at the expense of the second (supranational) in recent years. That is, national governments have managed to retain their influence despite the developments of supranational institutions. However,

## Box 15.4 The euro

The euro is the single currency currently (mid-2010) shared by sixteen of the European Union's twenty-seven member states. The euro was introduced in 1999. Full economic and monetary union has been in effect since 1 January 2002, initially for twelve countries, with further members joining over time bringing the number up to sixteen. Together they make up the euro area. Adoption and use of the euro was a major step in European integration.

Many observers believe that the euro has been a success. Over 300 million EU citizens now use it as their currency and enjoy its benefits. This includes the obvious benefit of being able to travel across national borders among the sixteen states and continue to use the same currency as they do at home.

Adoption of the euro is a key focus of the wider goal of economic and monetary union (EMU). EMU was adopted in three stages:

1. coordinating economic policy
2. achieving economic convergence (that is, their economic cycles are broadly in step)
3. adoption of the euro.

The final stage for the sixteen member states was achieved in 2002. The other eleven members have not yet reached this stage of economic and monetary union, leading to fears of a two-tier EU involving, on the one hand, euro states, and on the other, non-euro states.

this does not really make a difference in terms of representation, because in the first model, relationships between ordinary people and the EU institutions are indirect; in the supranational model they are weak. Combining the two models is thus unlikely dramatically to increase EU institutional representation. However, the picture is by no means static. According to Etzioni-Halevy (2002: 205), 'European governing institutions are in constant flux, and suffer from excessive complexity, fuzziness, and ambiguity of procedures', characterised by 'euro-jargon' and the use of numerous technical terms and over thirteen hundred acronyms! She suggests, plausibly, that this situation is 'off-putting for citizens, and makes it difficult for them to understand what is really going on in these bodies, and what they need to do to link up with them'. We saw this expressed in the concept of Euroscepticism at the beginning of the chapter.

Both in theory and practice, the EU's governing institutions have important functions, but how do they measure up as representative bodies? That is, how democratically accountable are they? It is often noted that the EU suffers from what is referred to as a 'democratic deficit'. This refers to a real or perceived gap between the Union's lofty aspirations and what many say is the mundane reality. This concern stems from the fact that while some of the Union's governing institutions – including the Parliament and to some extent the Commission – have inbuilt provisions for regularised interactions with ordinary people, there are often said to be major problems in how these arrangements work in terms of their representativeness. This is not to suggest that things were designed like this, only to note that this is how they have turned out, 'due to factors beyond the control of anyone in particular' (Etzioni-Halevy 2002: 209). However, it is worth noting that the EU is often thought less problematic in this regard than several other important international governmental organisations, including the United Nations, the North Atlantic Treaty

Organisation and, as we shall see below, the African Union. In these organisations, no real provision exists for significant public interaction with power holders and senior policy makers (Hill and Smith 2005).

The issue of accountability was called into question in the context of the EU's attempt to introduce a constitution, which began in 2004. Three years earlier, in 2001, EU heads of government met at Laeken, Belgium, declaring that Europe's citizens were 'calling for a clear, open, effective, democratically controlled Community approach' (europa.eu.int/comm/laeken_council/index_en.htm). For this reason they established a convention to draw up proposals for a European constitution. Consequently, the EU heads of government sought to:

1. clarify where power resides, by defining powers of various EU institutions
2. identify the rights of citizens vis-à-vis the established powers
3. provide 'an indication of purpose, a rallying cry for the citizen' (Bogdanor 2003).

However, progress towards the proposed EU constitution has not been entirely smooth. Most EU member states had ratified their country's acceptance of the constitution by late 2009, including Ireland which had rejected the constitution when it first voted on the issue. By the end of 2009, the Lisbon Treaty had been enacted. This implied the following: first, there would now be qualified majority voting in the Council of Ministers, meaning that even if some countries rejected a measure it could still go through. Second, the European parliament had greater involvement in decision making, working more closely than before with the Council of Ministers. Third, creation of the post of President of the European Council (currently, mid-2010, a Belgian, Herman Van Rompuy) and that of High Representative of the Union for Foreign Affairs and Security Policy (currently, mid-2010, a Briton, Catherine Ashton) meant that the EU was able to present a more consistently united position on EU policies than it had in the past. Finally, the Lisbon Treaty made the Union's human rights charter – the Charter of Fundamental Rights – legally binding, much to the chagrin of many Eurosceptics.

## Conclusion

The EU is sometimes described as a 'post-sovereign' entity. This means that over time power has steadily moved away from individual member states to supranational EU institutions. As a result, the EU has established a new form of governance at an intermediate level – the regional – which is between the global and the state.

What makes the EU unique among existing regional organisations is that it has a mature set of institutions which make it the most developed project of regional integration in the world. The current advanced stage of EU development represents a complex process over five decades, since the early 1950s. This half century was a time when the Union developed a multifaceted agenda with economic, cultural, security and political goals, arrived at via a series of important treaties, in order for the EU to become a key player in today's international relations.

*Source: Getty Images/AFP*

**The African Union has played a crucial role in maintaining security on this troubled continent.**

## The African Union

### Background and history

> Conflicts, particularly violent conflicts between and within states in other parts of
> Africa, and in the world in general, are also a danger to our peace and tranquillity.
> Helping other peoples keep and maintain peace is also a way of defending our
> own peace.
>
> (Harsch 2003: 16)

These words were spoken in 2003 by Mozambique's president Joaquim Chissano, in the context of his government's efforts to build peace, prosperity and development following the country's long civil war (1977–92). However, while Mozambique experienced more than a decade of serious conflict, it was by no means unique in this regard among African countries. Many – including Burundi, Democratic Republic of Congo, Liberia, Rwanda, Sierra Leone and Somalia – have also recently experienced serious political violence and conflict. These examples highlight that in government policy making in Africa there is a key question to address: How can African governments build an environment where peace, stability and prosperity can be expected to develop?

## Box 15.5 Organisation of African Unity/African Union timeline

| | |
|---|---|
| 1961 | First Organisation of African Unity (OAU) summit meeting in the Ethiopian capital, Addis Ababa |
| 1963 | OAU founded as formal organisation |
| 2001 | Final OAU summit meeting in the Zambian capital, Lusaka |
| 2002 | OAU disbanded |
| 2002 | African Union replaces Organisation of African Unity |

| | |
|---|---|
| 2003 | The AU's first military intervention in a member state (Burundi) |
| 2007 | AU troops deployed in Sudan to help deal with Darfur issue when thousands of civilians were killed or injured by marauding 'militias' |
| 2008 | Sudan mission handed over to United Nations |

Like Europe, Africa is a region which has long sought to build and develop viable regional institutions. Following the founding of the European Coal and Steel Community in 1952, Europe seriously began to build its regional institutions in 1957, marked by the signing of the Treaty of Rome. Africa began its own attempt to build a regional organisation – the Organisation of African Unity (OAU) – six years later in 1963.

Unlike Europe, which has seen its own regional organisation go from strength to strength, Africa's attempts at regional integration have been less successful. Because of its perceived lack of success, the OAU was eventually disbanded and replaced in 2002 by the African Union (AU), a regional intergovernmental organisation modelled directly on the European Union.

## Box 15.6 Creation of the Organisation of African Unity

The Organisation of African Unity (OAU) was created at a time of decolonisation, in the late 1950s and early 1960s, when European colonial powers, including Britain, France and Belgium, were withdrawing from Africa. In international relations, this period was a time of pronounced ideological polarisation. On the one hand, there was the liberal democratic and pro-market USA and on the other hand there was the communist Soviet Union, which saw these issues very differently. Reflecting this ideological division in international relations, African leaders disagreed about what kind of organisation the OAU should be. Some, including Kwame Nkrumah, prime minister of Ghana, wanted to create a regional wide states' union, with a central government that would seek to unite all African countries under the authority of one leader. However, the plan was very problematic as very few African countries, most of which were only then emerging from colonial rule, would seriously countenance the idea of moving from colonial control by European countries to a new arrangement whereby one African leader – perhaps Nkrumah – would seek to dominate the OAU. As a result of such concerns, other African leaders, such as President Félix Houphouët-Boigny of Côte d'Ivoire, strongly opposed Nkrumah's idea. Eventually, Africa's leaders reached a compromise on this issue which directly related to the ability of the OAU to achieve its goals: the OAU was divided among factions, leaving it with little power to act on its own.

While over the years, the OAU did appear to help build links between African countries, mainly through the periodic meetings which took place under OAU auspices, it also faced many problems of disunity that ultimately meant that it was unable to achieve its goals of peace, prosperity, security and stability for the African region.

## Problems and issues

Reflecting its problematic origins, the OAU was troubled by disputes among member states throughout its existence. One of the earliest divisive issues was a civil war in Angola which started in 1975. The war was ostensibly fought on ideological grounds, between Soviet Union-supported communists grouped together in the Movemento Popular de Libertação de Angola-Partido de Trabalho (MPLA), on the one hand, and two competing pro-Western factions on the other, supported by the United States and other Western countries. These two other factions – the National Front for the Liberation of Angola (Frente Nacional de Libertação de Angola, or FNLA) and the National Union for the Total Independence of Angola (União Nacional para a Independência Total de Angola, or UNITA) – were also supported by the region's most powerful country, South Africa. The OAU held a vote in December 1975 to try to decide which of the groups to support. Half of the OAU members backed the MPLA, while the others backed either the FNLA or UNITA. During the later 1970s, the OAU was consistently divided on ideological grounds in a similar way to the situation over Angola. Conflicts afflicting Africa during this time included a civil war in Katanga Province, Zaire (now called the Democratic Republic of the Congo), Somalia's invasion of Ethiopia in 1978, and attempts at independence from Morocco fighters in the Western Sahara. Later, during the 1980s and 1990s, the OAU's ability to work collectively was further undermined by a serious and accelerating regional economic decline. Under these circumstances, African countries tended to be inward looking, seeking to resolve their problems by individual effort rather than looking to regional mechanisms and solutions.

## Successes and improvements

The OAU did record some successes. For example, in 1964 it successfully mediated a border dispute between Algeria and Morocco, and in 1968–70 it was able to resolve problems involving Somalia, Ethiopia and Kenya.

The OAU was also actively involved in assisting efforts by African countries to end colonial rule. This was a policy which did not divide its members in the same way that questions of leadership of the organisation or ideological direction did. Soon after its founding in 1963, the OAU formed its African Liberation Committee (ALC). The main goal of the ALC was to channel financial support to movements trying to defeat Portuguese colonial rule in Angola, Guinea-Bissau and Mozambique. Unlike Britain or France, which by this time were happy to relinquish their colonial possessions in Africa, the Portuguese government made no such commitment, vowing to maintain its African colonies. Portugal's resolve did not last long, however. In 1974, liberation movements in all three of its colonies were successful in overturning centuries of Portuguese domination.

On the other hand, during the 1970s and 1980s, the OAU engaged in several mediation efforts and even a couple of military missions (for example, in Chad and Zaire, now the Democratic Republic of Congo). The OAU was able to act in this way due to the acceptance of the actions by the government of the country affected. The main drawback, however, was that the OAU Charter's emphasis on 'national sovereignty' and a consequent prohibition against OAU involvement in the internal affairs of other member states made such initiatives quite difficult. The non-interference clause, in particular, was often invoked as an excuse for inaction.

The OAU also supported liberation movements against white minority rule in three southern African countries: Namibia, South Africa and Rhodesia (renamed Zimbabwe at independence in 1980). The white minority governments in each case managed to hang on longer than those in the Portuguese colonies, but not for that long: in 1994, South Africa threw out its white minority government, following Zimbabwe (1980) and Namibia (1990). The OAU received a boost when South Africa became a member in 1994; earlier, membership of the OAU had been denied to the country because of its white minority-led government. Following South Africa's admittance to the OAU in 1994, the organisation sought – albeit unsuccessfully – to redouble its efforts in pursuit of regional peace, democracy and swifter economic development.

By the early 1990s, as more conflicts broke out across the region, such notions began to change and, as a result, the idea of national sovereignty underwent reinterpretation in two main ways. First, it became less categorical – by considering massive human rights violations and population displacements resulting from domestic conflicts as regional security threats. Second, the concept of 'security' was broadened to include not just state security but also human security, including the idea that people had a right to expect food, shelter, and other aspects of a decent life. The result of these developments was to shift the emphasis on regional security concerns and make it more likely that multinational interventions would be undertaken in order to try to arrest anarchy, restore order and protect innocent civilians.

## From the OAU to the AU: new initiatives for regional progress

The development of the African Union (AU) from its predecessor organisation, the OAU, was widely regarded as an encouraging sign that Africa's governments were at last serious in seeking to tackle endemic problems of political violence, poor governance and developmental disappointments which had dogged the region for so long (Makinda and Wafula Okumu 2006). One of the key goals of the AU was to focus on regional conflict prevention, conflict management and conflict resolution. Unlike the charter of the OAU, that of the AU allowed the organisation the authority to 'intervene in cases of war crimes, genocide and crimes against humanity' (www.africa-union.org/). The AU created a new institution in 2002 to pursue these goals: the fifteen-member Peace and Security Council, which South Africa's then president, Thabo Mbeki, identified as 'a collective security and early-warning arrangement to facilitate timely and efficient responses to conflicts and crisis situations in Africa' (African Union 2002: 4).

## Case study: The AU and the International Criminal Court

The International Criminal Court (ICC) was founded in 2002. Many people hoped that those guilty of appalling crimes against humanity would now be brought to justice. But that was not all. In addition, there was also expectation that the behaviour of warlords and dictators – individuals with power who pay little or no regard to the well-being of ordinary people under their control – would henceforward see fit to change their behaviour and activities and seek to behave better in relation to the hundreds of millions whose lives they affect, increasing the security of many of the most vulnerable.

Less than a decade later, these hopes were badly undermined by the African Union's decision in July 2009 to withdraw cooperation with the ICC. Why would the AU see fit to do this? African leaders, meeting at the AU summit in Libya, made the decision that if indicted by the ICC, no African figure would be extradited to face trial. In fact they would not even be arrested. The reason for this decision was that some African governments had complained that the ICC, despite its professed universal focus, was actually a 'Western court' whose key purpose was unjustly to prosecute Africans.

Omar al-Bashir, the Sudanese president – indicted by the ICC over alleged war crimes and crimes against humanity by his country's armed forces in Darfur – was the first African to benefit from the AU's decision. The AU's resolution contained a demand that not only should no African government try and arrest al-Bashir if he happens to be in their country but also they should not allow the ICC to conduct investigations on their territory.

This decision was unexpected. While some African countries have rejected the remit of the ICC from the start, the July 2009 AU resolution also gained the agreement of those governments – a majority of African countries – who signed the Rome Treaty that established the ICC.

It appears that many African governments, formerly supportive of the ICC, had been persuaded by pressure from Sudan to change their position – pressure which only a month earlier they had resisted. A June 2009 meeting in Addis Ababa, capital of Ethiopia, had seen many such AU countries resisting pressure from Sudan and other staunch ICC opponents to change the AU position of willingness to work with the ICC.

On the other hand, some African critics of the July 2009 AU decision, including the governments of Botswana and Uganda, refused to drop their commitment to justice and human rights and maintained their support for the ICC. South Africa's position was particularly important. This was partly because the country played a leading role in setting up the ICC and partly because it is one of only three states in Africa to have incorporated the ICC statute's provisions into the law of the country. One outcome was that Sudan's president declined to attend the inauguration of South Africa's president, Jacob Zuma, in May 2009, fearing that he might be arrested if he set foot in South Africa.

It is worth noting that the ICC is a very new international organisation; it is important when necessary to critique it, for it may well be necessary for the growth of its maturity and capabilities. But this is not how the AU's July 2009 statement should be interpreted: it is hard not to conclude that African leaders – not all but most – were more inclined to protect one of their own than to stand up for the principles that most had officially signed up to.

The first African Secretary General of the United Nations, Kofi Annan, was in his post when the ICC came into existence. He is and remains a strong supporter of the organisation, not sharing the view of some African power holders that the ICC is primarily concerned with protecting Western interests and undermining those of Africans. Annan noted that the AU's July decision implied there is 'little hope of preventing the worst crimes known to mankind, or reassuring those who live in fear of their recurrence, if African leaders stop supporting justice for the most heinous crimes just because one of their own stands accused' (Annan 2009).

 **Has the ICC enough authority to become an important component of international law?**

The AU launched a flagship regional development strategy in 2002: the New Partnership for Africa's Development (NEPAD), which included an 'African Peer Review Mechanism' to check on progress within individual countries. This was designed to promote good governance within African countries, seen as one of the best ways to prevent domestic political conflicts from leading to coups, insurgency or civil war (www.nepad.org/).

NEPAD's key reforms included a focus on several desirable reforms in African countries: improved civil order and democracy; better conflict prevention and reduction; better human rights; enhanced human resources, especially in health and education sectors; greater economic diversification and increased trade with the rest of the world; and more effective policies in relation to combating various killer diseases, notably HIV/AIDS and malaria.

This list of reforms suggests that demands on African states would be considerable, notably the political measures adopted by the AU, underlining that human development *necessarily* accompanies both promotion of democracy and good governance. The consequence was that all AU states had to agree to develop political systems with the following characteristics:

- uphold the rule of law;
- adhere to a governmental separation of powers, including an independent judiciary and an effective legislature;
- promote the equality of all citizens before the law, including equality of opportunity for all;
- safeguard individual liberties and collective freedoms, including the right to form and join political parties and trades unions;
- acknowledge the inalienable right of the individual to participate, by means of free, credible and democratic processes, in periodically electing leaders for a fixed term of office;
- uphold probity in public life;
- combat and eradicate corruption;
- ensure free expression including media freedom;
- facilitate the development of vibrant civil society organisations;
- strengthen electoral commissions, administration and management.

One very important feature of NEPAD was the voluntary Africa Peer Review Mechanism (APRM), established in April 2003, designed to 'ensure that the policies and practices of participating states conform to the (mutually) agreed . . . values, codes and standards contained in NEPAD's Declaration on Democracy, Political, Economic and Corporate Governance'. The peer review process aims to spur African countries 'to consider seriously the impact of domestic policies, not only on internal political stability and economic growth, but also on neighbouring countries.' Any member of the AU can adopt APRM as a self-monitoring instrument. By early 2009, over thirty African governments had signed up to APRM. Operationally, APRM is directed and managed by a five to seven member Eminent Persons' Panel, whose members are appointed by the heads of states and government of the participating countries. They serve for a period of up to four years, retiring on rotation. Members of the panel must be Africans who have expertise in the areas of political governance, macro-economic and public financial management and corporate governance. There must also be 'broad regional balance, gender equity and cultural diversity' in the APRM make up.

There is no doubt that the AU's adoption not only of NEPAD but also the focus on conflict resolution, governance and reform are ambitious and potentially far-reaching developments that potentially usher in a new era for Africa's development prospects.

Critics, however, suggest that there is one fundamental problem – that of implementation. What might be the key obstacles in this regard? First, there is the basic issue of sovereignty and the extent to which African states will cede it to the AU. Second, there is the question of whether or not there is sufficient political will within African states for the relevant reforms to be implemented. Third, it is unclear what roles will be played by existing elites and political leaders, many of whom, it is suggested, are primarily motivated by goals of personal power and prosperity and may have relatively little concern for popular democratic legitimacy. In other words, how might the AU encourage many African political leaders to change how they rule, to improve governance and, in many cases, adopt more even-handed development policies that would benefit the majority of their people, rather than the few? Finally, as the AU acknowledges, the often-embryonic nature of civil society within many African states often significantly undermines public participation and engagement in polit-ical life. What the AU would like to see in relation to African citizens – a fundamental shift from being often passive subjects of authoritarian or dictatorial rule to become politically active citizens seeking consistently to hold their governments to account – does not as yet show many signs of developing in the region.

In sum, the AU's efforts have focused on attempts to try to deal with the region's most serious problems: regional instability and conflict; poor governance; and disappointing development outcomes. So far, however, outcomes have been relatively disappointing.

## The African Union: institutions

Following the example of the EU, the AU seeks to create a common African currency, foreign policy, defence structure and economic programme. The AU also wants to develop a pan-African parliament, an economic community, a central bank and a court of justice (Muthiri 2008). Overall, the AU's institutions are designed to accelerate the political and socio-economic integration of the continent; to promote and defend African common positions on issues of interest to the continent and its peoples; to achieve peace and security in Africa; and to promote democratic institutions, good governance and human rights:

- **Assembly of the African Union.** This body makes the most important decisions of the AU. The Assembly is the highest decision-making organ of the AU. Comprising heads of state and government of the fifty-three member states, the Assembly meets twice a year.
- **African Union Commission.** The AU's secretariat to the political structures is located in Addis Ababa, capital of Ethiopia. (A secretariat is an administrative unit responsible for maintaining records and other secretarial duties, especially for international organisa-tions such as the AU.) In February 2009, AU leaders decided that the African Union Commission would be henceforth known as the African Union Authority.
- **Pan-African Parliament.** The AU's representative body comprises 265 members elected by the national parliaments of the AU member countries.
- **Executive Council.** Other political institutions of the AU include this Council, which is constituted by member states' foreign ministers. The Executive Council prepares decisions for the Assembly.

- **Permanent Representatives Committee.** This body comprises the AU Member states' ambassadors.
- **Economic, Social and Cultural Council.** The Council is a civil society consultative body.

## Conclusion

[In February 2009] the Heads of State and governments of the various nations in Africa met in Addis Ababa, Ethiopia to discuss issues affecting the Continent. For five years such meetings have been taking place and after each meeting nothing happens to the numerous problems facing the continent. There is very little to show for all the millions of dollars of tax payers' money that has gone into such meetings. What has the AU achieved or got right in Africa since it replaced the toothless OAU (Organisation of Africa Unity)? How effective has the AU been in tackling the numerous problems facing the continent? Can the AU tell the people in the continent why it should be allowed to hold such meetings in the name of the people after five years of no results? Can the AU tell the people in Africa one single thing that it has got right since it changed its name from OAU to AU? What at all has the AU achieved in Africa that merits another waste of tax payers' money?

(Adusei 2009)

In July 2002, the Organisation of African Unity (OAU) was renamed and rebadged as the African Union (AU) during the OAU Summit in Durban, South Africa. The new treaty was used to formulate more exacting criteria for membership in the AU compared to the OAU. Article 30 of the treaty establishing the AU states explicitly: 'Governments which shall come to power through unconstitutional means shall not be allowed to participate in the activities of the Union'. However, any transparent procedures for the exclusion or suspension of member states on the basis of this article were absent – as condemnation of unconstitutional governments belongs only to the *guiding* principles of the treaty. A (military) intervention in the domestic affairs of an AU member state is only possible in the following cases: crimes against humanity, war crimes and genocide. So far, as we saw above in relation to the International Criminal Court, these have not been forthcoming.

Reflecting the AU's focus on both political and human security, African mediators, troops and civil society activists – whether acting within the context of the UN or acting alone – now play an increasingly active and central role in trying to resolve the numerous conflicts that still unfortunately afflict many parts of Africa. At the annual summit meeting of the AU, held in Maputo, Mozambique in July, 2003, Africa's heads of state jointly expressed their 'determination' through the AU 'to address the scourge of conflicts in Africa in a collective, comprehensive and decisive manner'. This expression of intent by African leaders to shoulder more of the burden of peacekeeping in Africa was not only a reflection of a shared regional determination that the means to deal with conflicts should be found from within regional resources. It was also a sign that non-African countries and organisations, such as the UN, were now very reluctant to undertake large-scale peacekeeping operations or to become directly entangled in African conflicts. This is because when they have done so, for example in Somalia, Sudan and Liberia, they have found it very difficult or impossible to make good progress. Currently, while several thousand European and US troops are engaged in peace missions in Africa – for example, there were hundreds of British troops stationed in Sierra Leone during the early 2000s, central to the successful efforts to end that country's civil war in 2002 – most of these personnel are in place as a result of ad hoc, often bilateral, arrangements for very specific assignments, not as part of UN peacekeeping operations.

According to the former UN Secretary General, Kofi Annan, the AU should now 'play a variety of important roles' in African peacekeeping. According to Annan, such initiatives can not only 'help ensure that regional peace efforts are closely integrated with the approach of a [UN] peace operation', they can also identify personnel for such operations and develop long-term peace-building strategies to stabilise African countries emerging from conflicts (Annan 2009). Adding weight to the opinion expressed by Kofi Annan, the then South African President Thabo Mbeki told the July 2003 summit that 'conflict resolution is a top priority for the [African] Union. As a consequence, conflicts that have been raging for many years are being tackled with increased determination and many African countries are committing their own resources to conflict prevention, management and resolution' (http://www.africa-union.org/Official_documents/Speeches_&_Statements/HE_Thabo_Mbiki/Opening_speech_Maputo_10%20July.htm)

## Conclusion

We noted at the beginning of this chapter that a key aim of virtually all existing regional organisations is to expand trade among member countries in the context of globalisation. We have seen that when there are appropriate formal institutions – as in the EU and, but not to the same extent, in the AU – then political, social and/or developmental objectives, even when officially of no or minimal importance can grow in significance in the context of trade talks. For example, the issue of EU enlargement was not only about the economic ramifications of regional augmentation, but also importantly concerned wider political, cultural and social issues subsumed under the heading of what constitutes 'European-ness'.

A further point is that states engaged in regional cooperation attempts, in effect, want both to have their cake and to eat it: that is, they 'attempt to gain the economic advantages of larger and more open markets without sacrificing their political sovereignty' (Hague and Harrop 2001: 52). However, we have seen that the history of the EU, the most developed regional organisation, indicates that advanced regional cooperation can have multiple – economic, political, security, and cultural – outcomes.

We saw that the AU shares Europe's aspirations but has so far failed to enjoy the kind of success that Europe has in relation to regional integration. Despite long-term calls for African unity, there has been in reality much less commitment to the ideals of regional integration on the part of African governments. Until this situation changes, we should expect to see a failure of Africa's regional efforts despite continuing rhetorical commitment to them on the part of the region's governments.

## Resource section

## Questions

1. Which is more successful: the EU or the AU? What criteria would you choose for making this judgement?

2. Explain why the EU grew in size in both 2004 and 2007.

3. Why is Turkey so keen to join the EU?

4. Can the AU fulfil its goal: 'Africa must unite'?

## Recommended reading

**Abass, A. (2004)** *Regional Organisations and the Development of Collective Security: Beyond Chapter VIII of the UN Charter* (London: Hart Publishing)
This book examines the development of collective security by regional organisations particularly after the Cold War. It analyses the various constitutional developments that have occurred within regional organisation, including the African Union. The book evaluates the impact of regional organisations' evolving powers to authorise enforcement action and determine when situations within member states warrant their intervention. The book also analyses the regime of complementarity between the UN and regional organisations.

**Hill, C. and Smith, M. (eds) (2005)** *International Relations and the EU* (Oxford: Oxford University Press)
The aim of this book is to locate the European Union in the context of International Relations theory and to explore the ways in which the EU seeks to undertake its international relations. Various chapters deal with three key themes: the EU as a sub-system of international relations; the EU and the processes of international relations; and the EU as a regional and international power.

**Makinda, S. and Wafula Okumu, F. (2006)** *The African Union: Challenges of Globalization, Security, and Governance* (London, Routledge)
This book is a comprehensive examination of the work of the African Union. The book's main special emphasis is on the AU's capacity to meet the challenges of building and sustaining governance institutions and security mechanisms.

**Muthiri, T. (2008)** *The African Union and Its Institutions* (New York: Femela)
This volume brings together the analysis and research of 17 mainly African scholars, policymakers, practitioners and civil society representatives. It presents a positive but realistic picture of the African Union, while diagnosing several key challenges that face the organisation. While the AU has established an array of institutions to deal with Africa's security and governance problems, the book makes it clear that there is still some way to go before we can conclude that institutional development is effective in terms of pursuing the organisation's goals.

## Useful websites

African Union

**www.africa-union.org/**

European Union

**http://europa.eu/**

International Criminal Court

**http://www.icc-cpi.int/Menus/ICC**

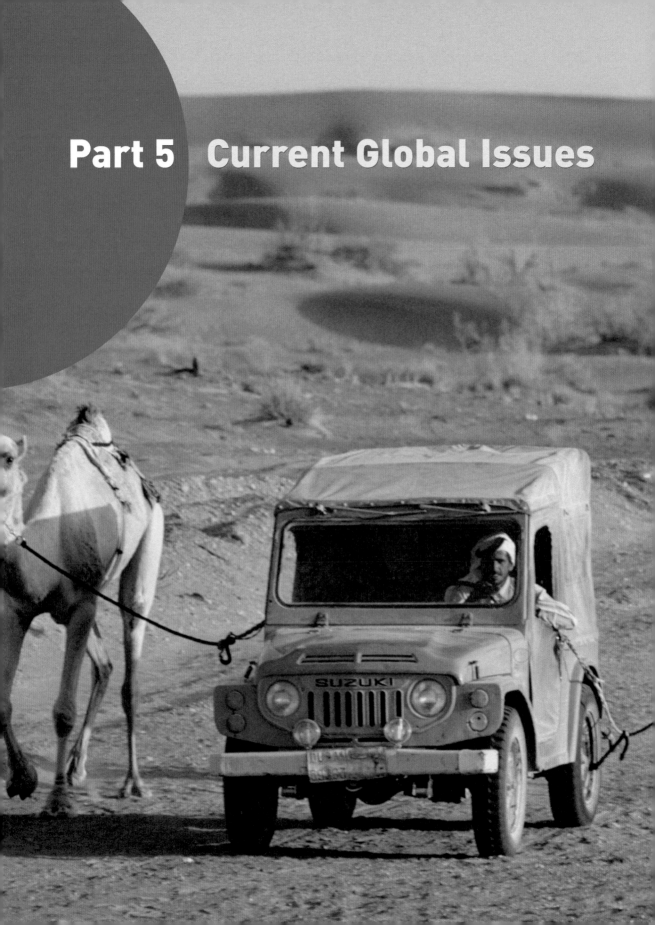

# Part 5  Current Global Issues

A key dimension of how globalisation has transformed International Relations in recent decades is the emergence of 'new' issues on the international political agenda to accompany the traditionally dominant concerns of peace and military security. These issues of human development, which are more concerned with the advancement of the individual than state interests, are not, in fact, 'new'. International trade has gone on for centuries as has the pursuit of economic development by relatively poor states. The notion of rights empowering and protecting all men and women and also societies to 'national self-determination' has been prominent in politics since the enlightenment of the eighteenth century. Political Ecology is genuinely new – dating from the 1960s – and has more rapidly found its way on to the international political agenda than the other issues of human development. The unprecedented technological advances that have swept the world since the Industrial Revolution have helped gradually to move the issues of human development from being on just the political agenda of some states to becoming the concerns of International Relations, as awareness of other countries has increased and ideas have been able to spread across borders. Most significant, however, has been the global political change produced by the ending of the Cold War.

The global ideological and power politics conflict between Communism and Capitalism tended to subsume all other issues in international relations between 1945 and 1990. The world economy could not globalise fully while such diametrically opposed views on the management of the world economy fought for mastery. Development was able to emerge as an international political issue during the Cold War but was distorted by the conflict reaching out into the Global South. Human rights were propelled onto the international political agenda by the horrors of the Second World War but progress was stifled by the Cold War as both sides consistently ignored the abuses of allies and perpetrated abuses of their own when it was seen to serve the national interest. National Self-Determination was well-established as a principle of international relations before the Second World War but was also suppressed or politicised by superpower interests during the Cold War. Environmental concerns spread through the developed capitalist world from the 1960s to the 1980s but could not be globalised while the Communist World and Less Developed Countries chose not to prioritise them.

Hence the study and practise of International Relations began to diversify in the 1990s and issues of human development were able to take a more prominent place as a 'New World Order' appeared to dawn. The international political agenda today remains far more diverse than during the Cold War, but many of the newly established issues are not always prioritised in the face of a resurgence of more traditional concerns as the 'War on Terror' has unfolded. In today's world the great powers still regularly claim that national security must trump human development.

*Source*: Getty Images

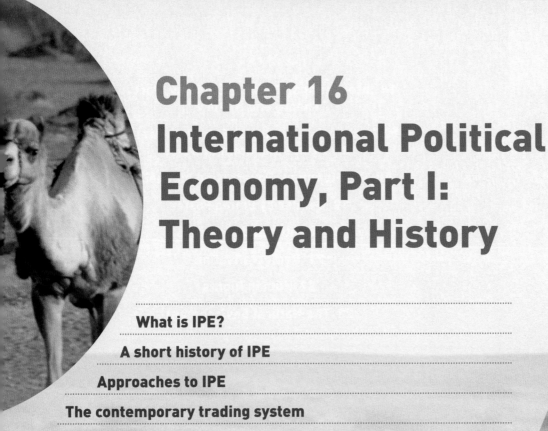

# Chapter 16
# International Political Economy, Part I: Theory and History

In this chapter you will gain understanding of the following;

- What is meant by International Political Economy
- How the global economy has evolved over time
- Rival theoretical approaches to understanding International Political Economy
- How trade is regulated in the contemporary world
- The political significance of increased transnational flows of money

*Source*: Getty Images

## Introductory box: Bra wars

In 2005 a trade dispute between China and the European Union occurred when the Europeans began to block the import of certain forms of Chinese clothing after seeing their domestic industries undermined by a sudden influx of much cheaper-produced garments from the Orient. The Chinese cried foul play at such politicised interference in commerce while European textile industries and Trades Unions defended the action, pointing out that they could hardly be expected to compete in price with clothes produced in the 'sweatshop' conditions of China.

A compromise solution ended the dispute but the incident highlighted how politics and economics are increasingly entwined in the contemporary world. That the world's leading Communist power could lecture the world's leading trading actor and epitome of Liberalism on free trade served to illustrate how economic globalisation has produced political contradictions, uncertainties and dilemmas for governments in their dealings with the international economy and for students in understanding IPE.

## What is IPE?

International Political Economy (IPE) is a sub-discipline of International Relations that arose in parallel with globalisation. From the 1970s it came to be broadly accepted across the theoretical approaches to IR that globalisation had blurred the distinctions between two traditional demarcations of the discipline: first, what is political and what is economic, and second, what is domestic and what is international? Hence Political Economy is the study of the intersection of politics and economics within a given country, while International Political Economy is the study of this at the international level.

As has been discussed in earlier chapters, globalisation is a contested term and there is no consensus on when it started, precisely what it is and how significant it is for International Relations. Nobody, however, seriously disputes that the flow of people, ideas, goods and money across state borders has greatly intensified over recent decades with implications for our understanding of both politics and economics. The volume of goods traded today is over twenty-seven times what it was in the late 1940s (WTO 2007) and foreign investment from businesses has grown tenfold in just the last two decades (Global Policy Forum 2009). While we have had periods of growth in the internationalisation of economic activities before this current phase of globalisation, none have been to this extent. Hence the study of IPE in academic circles and appreciation of it in governmental circles emerged from the 1970s as a number of key realisations became apparent which challenged previous assumptions about how to compartmentalise issues into the subjects of 'Economics', 'Politics' and 'International Relations':

● **Economic events in one country can have economic implications for other countries**
  For example, the global 'credit crunch' recession of 2008–10 originated in the collapse of the US housing market as numerous international banks began either to cease lending or collapse, with implications for businesses and individual borrowers throughout most of the world.

● **Political events in one country can have economic implications for other countries**
  For example, the reunification of Germany in 1990 was a key factor in the collapse of the UK pound in 1992. The Bundesbank had to raise German interest rates to pay for the absorption of their relatively poor neighbour, causing financial fluctuations in the European markets unused to such extravagance from the Continent's traditionally prudent economic leader.

● **Economic events in one country can have political implications for another country**
  It has long been observed that the political fortunes of a government are closely linked to the performance of the domestic economy. Increasingly, however, the performance of the domestic economy is as much dictated by international economic events as it is by how a government manages its fiscal (tax), monetary or industrial policy. Evidence for this can be found as far back as 1929 and the Wall Street stock market crash in the USA which precipitated the world's worst ever economic recession, and was then a contributory factor in the fall of many democratic governments and the rise of the ideologies of Fascism and Communism as alternative models of economic management.

● **Power in international relations can come from economic as well as military might**
  (West) Germany and Japan rose again as world powers in the 1950s and 60s not by rearming and invading neighbouring countries, as they had done in the 1930s and 40s, but by building their economies and trading their way to wealth and influence. During the oil crises of the 1970s countries like Saudi Arabia, Iran and Iraq suddenly became much more influential players on the world stage because of their possession of the world's most important commodity – oil.

● **International political structures reflect economics**
  Intergovernmental organisations set up to regulate the international economy after the Second World War, such as the International Monetary Fund and World Bank group, were from the start very much dominated in their decision making by one country: the United States. The USA in 1947 accounted for around half of all economic production in the world, a level of superiority never seen before and never repeated since. As a consequence these organisations, along with emergent trading rules established under the auspices of the General Agreement on Tariffs and Trade (GATT), were designed to further the US economic interest of promoting more trade opportunities and the

political interest of propping up the capitalist world against the threat of Communist expansion. Recognition of how international organisations and rules can both reflect and reinforce national economic power, rather than serve to diminish the importance of the state, gave new impetus to Realist thought in International Relations with the emergence of neo-Realism (see Chapter 6).

## A short history of IPE

Although it may not have been a recognised academic discipline, there was, of course, an 'international political economy' well before the 1970s. International trade has linked countries together since ancient times and, from the fifteenth and sixteenth centuries, it is possible to see such commercial exchanges as being clearly political as well as economic as the global market became more interlinked and more competitive in line with transportation advances and the idea of compartmentalising people into states. Box 16.1 gives an overview of how it is possible to understand the evolution of the international economy in terms of the internationalisation of political ideas on how governments should orientate themselves towards the rest of the world.

In the early modern world of the sixteenth and seventeenth centuries the economic policies of the great powers and the overall economic system are often referred to by the

---

### Box 16.1 Timeline of International Political Economy

**1500–1780: Age of Mercantilism**

**1780+: Industrial Revolution**

**1815–1873: Age of Liberalism**

| | |
|---|---|
| 1821 | Great Britain adopts the gold standard (ties its currency to a set value in gold) |
| 1834 | Zollverein – economic union between Germanic states which precipitated the creation of a unified Germany |
| 1846 | Repeal of the Corn Laws – landmark British act of Parliament which reduced protectionism |
| 1860 | Cobden–Chevalier Treaty – Franco-British agreement to free up bilateral trade |
| 1866 | Latin Monetary Union – short-lived currency union based on the French franc involving several south European countries |
| 1871 | Germany adopts the gold standard |

**1873–1945: Return of Mercantilism**

| | |
|---|---|
| 1873–96 | The Long Depression |
| 1929 | The Great Depression |
| 1930 | Smoot–Hawley Act – Highly protectionist law passed in the US |
| 1931 | Collapse of the Gold Standard |

**1944: International Liberal Economic Order**

| | |
|---|---|
| 1944 | Bretton Woods Conference |
| 1947 | GATT launched |
| 1971 | Collapse of the Bretton Woods monetary system |
| 1971–4 | Oil crisis |
| 1995 | World Trade Organisation founded |
| 1997–9 | East Asian Financial crisis |
| 2008–10 | Credit crunch global recession |

term 'Mercantilism'. Mercantilism is a term that can also be applied today to refer to certain government policies – as is explored later in the chapter – but, in the Age of Mercantilism it was really the only approach that was in operation. During this phase of history international economic relations were very much carried out within the context of imperialism. A small number of states controlled most of the world, both politically and economically. Hence these countries, such as Britain, France, Spain, Portugal, The Netherlands and Turkey, constructed their own international economic systems in which they imported what they needed from their colonies while also using those territories as markets for their own surplus exports. These imperial powers also traded with each other where it was necessary but, in general, saw other trading giants as commercial rivals rather than partners and looked to beat them to the acquisition of any remaining uncolonised territories while, at the same time, jealously guarding their own possessions from their covetous glances.

Mercantilism never disappeared, and persists today in less explicit forms. However, from the time of the Industrial Revolution and Age of Enlightenment, it faced for the first time a rival philosophy, Economic Liberalism. In the nineteenth century a significant precursor to contemporary globalisation took place in which there was a huge growth in the volume of trade, due to a rise in both the economic capacity and political willingness to engage in international commerce. A great leap in economic production occurred, due to the emergence of manufacturing industries, allied to an intellectual shift in favour of seeing other states more as partners than rivals in the international economy. In 1860, for example, that most bitter of regional and imperial great power rivalries, between Britain and France, entered a new era with the signing of a treaty – drafted by Liberal politicians on both sides of the Channel – which saw barriers to trade between the two countries significantly lowered. As a consequence of this a 200 per cent increase in trade across the Channel occurred over the next two decades with, most notably, a huge growth in French wine heading northwards and British textiles, from their booming newly mechanised industry, heading south.

This period, in which Economic Liberalism began to flourish and challenge the logic of Mercantilism, was aided by the peace and diplomatic cooperation which marked the nineteenth century **Concert of Europe** era and, hence, it started to unravel in line with the renewal of political conflicts on the European continent from the Franco-Prussian War of 1870–1. A growth in nationalist ideologies allied to an economic recession at the end of the nineteenth century saw governments look more inwardly again and renew their traditional focus on acquiring resources for themselves, through force if necessary, rather than looking to enjoy the mutual spoils from encouraging global trade. An economic downturn invariably encourages governments to be more cautious about trading and focus instead on holding on to what they have got. This, added to a political reluctance to trade with countries deemed to be rivals, saw international trade slow down after this first era of globalisation in the nineteenth century.

Mercantilism thus came back to the fore in the early twentieth century in the context of the global military conflicts and extremist ideologies that emerged in that era. A revival of cordial international relations between the great powers and of liberal thought occurred in the 1920s, in the wake of the horrors of the Great War, but a potential new era of economic and political globalisation came to a crashing halt with the world's worst-ever global economic recession – the Great Depression – which started in 1929. Illustrating the economic interconnectedness of the world well before the contemporary era of globalisation, the effects of the 'Wall Street Crash' quickly reverberated around much of the world and saw a massive downturn in international trade. A sudden stock market collapse occurred due to the bursting of a 'speculative bubble' of stocks and shares that had become over-priced on the back of a domestic economic boom. This caused banks and businesses to collapse as the US economy shrunk by a third. This domestic crisis quickly internationalised as the US government responded in a Mercantilist manner. Loans given to European allies indebted by the Great War were recalled and measures were enacted to cut imports in order to protect weakened US industries from being undercut by foreign competition. Between 1929 and 1933 the value of world trade fell from $35 billion to just $12 billion as countries, such as many in Latin America, suddenly saw their main market for exports dry up and many European countries followed the example of the USA and put up barriers to trade.

The world only came out of this economic depression as a consequence of the Second World War, which prompted renewed industrial growth and international trade in order to support a burgeoning arms industry. Recognising that relying on world wars to ensure economic growth was not a viable long-term strategy, leading capitalist governments at the close of the Second World War sought to take international political steps to ensure that another Great Depression, as well as another world war, could not happen again. At a 1944 Conference, held at Bretton Woods in the USA, the governments of the host country and the UK led discussions which created the institutional architecture of what would become known as the 'Bretton Woods System'. To support international capitalism both against Communism and another depression, it was decided that intergovernmental organisations were needed to provide stability to the international economy and prevent governments lurching towards Mercantilism when the going got tough.

Hence, at the close of the Second World War, the present era of International Political Economy – the Liberal International Economic Order – was initiated, based upon the Bretton Woods System of two institutions created within the newly established UN system and an international treaty:

- **The General Agreement on Tariffs and Trade (GATT)** – a Treaty establishing a regime intended to promote international trade and prevent governments resorting to Mercantilist measures
- **The International Monetary Fund (IMF)** – an organisation based in the USA, which would provide a source of money for governments facing economic problems
- **The International Bank for Reconstruction and Development (The World Bank)** – an organisation also based in the USA, which would lend to governments in order to develop their economies.

GATT is analysed later in this chapter while the roles and impact of the IMF and World Bank are explored in Chapter 17.

## Hegemony

A key means of understanding the progression of the global economy and illustrating the maxim that international political structures reflect economics comes from appreciating the importance of the role of a hegemon and the phenomenon of **hegemony** in IPE. A hegemon is a term used in IR to refer to a government with sufficient political power and motivation to dominate international affairs in ways that create rules and institutions which serve to further its interests. To a large extent, the emergence of IPE as a distinct discipline was built upon an appreciation of the significance of this concept which transcended rival IR theories. Neo-Realists like Robert Gilpin saw this as a new, more sophisticated way of understanding how states could exert power over others by using institutions and rules (Gilpin 1987). For Neo-Marxist or critical theories (particularly those known as 'Neo-Gramscian') hegemony provided a way of understanding how a dominant transnational economic class could exert power over a majority exploited global class of people (see Chapter 8). Some Liberal thought also embraced hegemony as a means of achieving the goal of free trade by getting over the *collective goods problem*. A dominant trading state is in a position to play an entrepreneurial role by creating and enforcing international rules which promote trade. Getting a group of equally powerful traders to set up such a system is more complicated since any one of them could break ranks for short-term gain and bring it down.

All three of these theoretical perspectives could see hegemony as a key explanation for the emergence of the Liberal International Economic Order. The USA's economic power at the close of the Second World War, allied to a desire to project it worldwide, allowed them to – from a neo-Realist perspective – mould the structures of international politics and commerce to their liking and/or – from an Economic Liberal perspective – take the lead in promoting and freeing up international trade. A government which enjoys a preponderant share of international trade will naturally be inclined to take steps to increase the overall volume of international trade, since they will gain most from this. However, there will be short-term costs incurred through taking the lead in terms of lowering restrictions on imports coming into their country and funding international initiatives to get other countries to do the same. In the period of nineteenth century liberalisation, Great Britain emerged as the world's leading economic power on the back of going through the world's first industrial revolution and because it had the largest empire. In 1860 the British were responsible for 20 per cent of all industrial production and 24 per cent of international trade. Fourteen years earlier the British government had taken the landmark and controversial decision to initiate opening up their agricultural industry with the Repeal of the Corn Laws Act. Additionally, the British took the lead in stabilising the international economy by devising the Gold Standard, in which most of the world's many national currencies agreed to tie their value to the price of gold. Other countries followed the British lead and reduced measures protecting their economies, a more stable international economy emerged and international trade flourished to the benefit of Britain and many other states.

Towards the end of the nineteenth century British hegemony diminished, not through their decline but as a result of others, like Germany and the USA, catching up and rivalling them. Under these conditions, allied to the political circumstances described earlier, it was harder to maintain the gold standard and prevent countries again resorting to Mercantilist policies and, hence, the liberalisation of the mid nineteenth century unravelled. By the 1920s, with the European powers economically weakened by the Great War, the USA was possibly strong enough to play the role of a new hegemon but, at this time, lacked the political will to lead the world. Becoming embroiled in the essentially European struggle that was the First World War had reinforced in American culture a preference for isolationist foreign and economic policies. The response of the US government to the 1929 Wall Street Crash was to look inwardly rather than outwardly and in 1930 the Smoot–Hawley Act imposed the highest ever US tariffs (taxes on imports). Other major powers followed suit and international trade collapsed.

By 1945, however, the USA was much more powerful than in 1929 (and more powerful than Britain had been in the mid nineteenth century), and far more inclined to move away from its traditional isolationism and involve itself in international affairs. Hence the USA bankrolled the Bretton Woods institutions and other international economic initiatives and took a strong lead in managing them, in spite of the significant costs of doing so.

*Source: Getty Images/Time & Life Pictures*

**Keynes and White. The Bretton Woods system would have a profound effect on international relations following the Second World War.**

## Box 16.2  Keynes and White

The USA and the UK were represented at the Bretton Woods conference by, respectively, the Treasury Department Official Harry Dexter White and the Liberal politician and economist John Maynard Keynes. The two men acted as co-chairs of the event, in line with the expectation that their two countries would be co-hegemons of the Liberal International Economic Order. The outcome of the conference very much favoured White's preferences for free trade and reducing government involvement in economics. This demonstrated that power in the world had shifted very quickly and that the USA was to act much more unilaterally than had been anticipated during the

Second World War when the planning for the international political and economic futures took place. Curiously, however, for the architects of modern capitalism, both men came to be associated with the political left of their respective countries. Keynes continues to be lauded by Social Democrats for his defence of using government expenditure to boost a flagging economy by creating jobs and demand for goods. White was, by US standards, a Liberal interventionist and even suffered persecution in the anti-Communist hysteria that swept the USA in the late 1940s on the suspicion that he had spied for the Soviet Union during the Second World War.

## Approaches to IPE

Three broad theoretical approaches are generally used to characterise the politics of the international economy, both in terms of understanding government policies vis-à-vis the global system and the functioning of the overall system itself. The previous section introduced Mercantilism and Economic Liberalism as government approaches and these are further explained in this section in addition to outlining a third broad theory of IPE: Marxism.

### Economic Liberalism

Economic Liberalism emerged in the era of industrialisation and the Enlightenment as a branch of the wider political and philosophical Liberal movement that had swept through Western Europe and North America (see Chapter 7). The approach is underpinned by the core Liberal tenet that people are naturally inclined to cooperate with each other and can be trusted by governments to control their own destiny without this producing disorder and problems in society. This logic applied to the economic sphere manifests itself in a belief in the following key principles:

- **Free trade**

  As already discussed, Economic Liberalism is at its fundament the belief in free trade. This is the minimisation of government involvement in the affairs of international trade so that businesses are not restricted from exporting their goods, while imports from other countries are not restricted by protectionist measures.

- **Invisible hand**

  Adam Smith illustrated his thesis that freeing up international trade benefited all with the metaphor of the 'invisible hand'. The invisible hand refers to what is more commonly today known as 'market forces', meaning the way business and trade operates

### Box 16.3  Adam Smith [1723–1790]

The eighteenth century Scottish Philosopher turned Economist, Adam Smith, is widely revered as the father of Economic Liberalism and, possibly, of the discipline of Economics itself. Smith's landmark work *The Wealth of Nations* developed an economic rationale for why free trade was a good thing and, ultimately, to the advantage of all. He reasoned that markets free from government interference were not chaotic and were more likely to achieve mutually beneficial cooperation through an efficient division of labour. A well-known illustration used in the book concerns the manufacture of pins. Ten people making pins in which they cooperated, by dividing up the tasks involved in the production between them and specialising in that, will make more pins than ten people making them independently. In the competitive and selfish arena of international commerce the less efficient method was operated to the detriment of everyone.

Published in 1776 *The Wealth of Nations* influenced British policy and also the founding fathers of the United States of America, who declared their country's independence that same year.

in the absence of governmental interference. In a direct riposte to Conservative (and Mercantilist) fears that an unregulated economy leads to anarchy and exploitation, as greedy individuals enrich themselves without regard to the suffering this may inflict on others, the invisible hand posits that society would be better off without government interference because it is this that distorts the natural inclination of people to work together, exchange goods and make money. Governmental interference in the economy, rather than protecting its citizens, actually serves to impoverish them by stifling their potential to enrich themselves and their fellow citizens. Cautious governments, reluctant to allow imports into their country for fear of exposing their domestic industries to cheaper competition and preferring to strive for self-sufficiency, serve to reduce the overall volume of international trade. As a consequence of this, citizens are left to pay more than they otherwise would for goods that were traded on the open world market and suffer from the overall amount of money that could be generated from commerce being artificially restricted. In an example of what is known as the **collective goods problem** self-serving governments, in the name of protecting their own citizens, actually disadvantage them with their caution (another example of the collective goods problem is the polluter's dilemma outlined in Chapter 23).

- ● **Comparative advantage**
The English protégé of Adam Smith, David Ricardo, built on his work by developing a further rebuttal to the Mercantilist approaches which had up until then dominated the policy of Britain and other great powers, commonly known as the theory of **comparative advantage**. The theory lends support to the notion of the invisible hand by offering an economic rationale for why free trade produces more trade and more wealth for all states. For reasons of climate, terrain and the abundance of natural resources, it stands to reason that some countries have an advantage over others in the growth of particular crops or production of particular goods. This advantage can be to the benefit of all if allowed to flourish and not stifled by government interference in commerce. In a system of unrestricted international trade, states can concentrate on what they are good at producing rather than trying to do a bit of everything since they can freely import goods that are produced more efficiently elsewhere. More particularly, comparative advantage ensures that even the relatively disadvantaged countries gain from specialisation. For example, in a situation in which the economies of two countries are based on the production of cars and corn but State A produces both more cheaply than State B, State B can, nonetheless, still prosper because the *relative* costs of producing the two goods will differ and give an incentive to trade. If State B, although less efficient in the production of both corn and cars than State A, produces corn more efficiently than it produces cars this will make it advantageous for both states to trade. Even though it appears cheaper for State A to produce its own corn and cars, it is cheaper still to produce more cars instead and trade for State B's corn. Ricardo's work was a major influence on the British government's decision to pass the Repeal of the Corn Laws Act and trade with countries producing goods cheaper than they were and so usher in an era of much freer trade.

- **Trade brings peace**

  In addition to the economic rationale for free trade, Economic Liberalism, in line with Liberal political thought, sees that there are political gains to be had from throwing off the shackles of government protectionism. Though it tends to be best known for its advocacy of democracy, the notion of Kantian peace also advocated tying states together through commerce and so giving an economic incentive for peace (see Chapter 25). A motivation for the British and French politicians who designed the 1860 Cobden–Chevalier Treaty, in addition to the opportunities for increased trade revenues, was to bind these two traditional political rivals together with mutually beneficial economic ties. Concerns had begun to rise of the possibility of another in a long line of wars between them due to rival interests in Italy. In more recent times, the Second World War was the catalyst for the binding together of Western European states into the economic bloc that has now evolved into the European Union.

## Mercantilism

**Mercantilism** refers to the traditional, and still significant, approach to International Political Economy to which Economic Liberalism emerged as a challenge. Although it reached its height in the late Middle Ages, as far back as in Ancient Greece Plato advocated a self-serving strategy of favouring exports over imports so that wealth could be accumulated. Since then the Romans and other empire builders have tried to put systems in place ensuring such an imbalanced pattern of trade – which, of course, cannot be pursued by all states.

The core tenets of Mercantilist thinking are as follows:

- **The government *should* interfere in international trade**

  In direct contrast to Economic Liberals, Mercantilists advocate that governments should involve themselves in matters of international commerce in order to protect the interests of the state and their citizens. Mercantilism in IPE shares the same Conservative logic as Realism that the world is anarchic and states are, by necessity, self-serving and inward-looking entities. If this mindset is adopted, you cannot trust other states to fulfil their part of the comparative advantage bargain since they could easily switch their trade to another country or take an opportunity to plunder your resources if it suited them. A state's economic resources are a key source of its power and should not be subjected to the vagaries of the international marketplace. A government should look to secure as many resources as it can and protect them. Hence Mercantilism advocates limiting imports to those absolutely necessary (important goods you cannot produce yourself) while exporting what you can in order to profit from it.

- **International economics is competitive not cooperative**

  Mercantilists reject the notion of comparative advantage due to their more pessimistic take on human nature and the behaviour of governments. In the fiercely competitive arena that is the international political system 'collective goods' will never be acquired and there will always be losers as well as winners. Governments thus should 'beggar thy neighbour' and concentrate on ensuring that they are not one of the losers. While the logic that free trade leads to more trade and more goods can scarcely be denied, it is far from certain that all participants in the global economy will gain from this increase. Some states risk seeing their domestic industries decimated by being undercut by cheaper imports, as in the 'bra wars' dispute highlighted at the beginning of this chapter. Weak states could be weakened further by not being able to compete with the 'big boys'; the big boys themselves could be weakened by finding themselves unable to compete with lower priced goods from poorer states, with lower wages and slacker working conditions. This sort of gamble is one that many governments will be unwilling to take. Telling recently laid-off steelworkers that importing cheaper steel from the other side of the world is better for the country and the world in the long run is unlikely to be a wise political move for a democratic government seeking re-election in the short term.

- **Self-sufficiency**
The pessimistic assumptions of human nature and state behaviour that underpin the thinking of Mercantilists also mean that they advocate governments hoarding what they have and trying to reduce reliance on other states. An extreme manifestation of self-sufficiency is the policy known as **autarky** which is the pursuit of total self-reliance. This would, of course, be straightforward for governments of countries blessed with all the natural resources they could want but, in practice, this has never been achieved. Attempts at achieving total self-reliance have thus tended to be associated with states driven by ultra-nationalist ideologies. On the one hand this can take the form of simply stealing resources from others. Hence Imperial conquests, the rise of Fascism and Nazism and Iraqi expansionist ambitions in the 1980s and 1990s can be seen in this context. On the other hand, autarky has occasionally been pursued by states through isolationist strategies in order to guard jealously their own resources. Burma and Albania in the second half of the twentieth century pursued such a strategy and North Korea has continued to do so, in the guise of their state ideology of *Juche* (which seeks development as a communist country but without reliance on external support). The poverty that accompanied such policies in these three states, however, is indicative of the poverty of such a strategy in the modern world. Hence, Mercantilist strategies today tend not to be as purist as autarky and aim, instead, for the accumulation of resources allied to the implementation of measures to protect domestic industries.

- **Protectionism**
The most prominent form of Mercantilism in the contemporary world is protectionism, which refers to a variety of economic policies employed by governments to insulate their domestic industries from foreign competition. The most common of such strategies are outlined in Box 16.4.

### Box 16.4  Forms of protectionism

- **Tariffs** – the taxing of imports
- **Currency devaluations** – changing the value of your currency so as to make exports cheaper and imports dearer
- **Quotas** – allowing in imports only up to a certain number (e.g. the EU stance which prompted the 'bra wars' with China)
- **Export subsidies** – giving government support to exporters to help them sell abroad

- **Government subsidising of industry** – giving hand-outs to struggling domestic industries so that they can be supported against foreign competition
- **Red tape** – using domestic laws unofficially to restrict foreign competition by insisting on particular product standards more likely to be achieved by domestic goods

The progression of the Liberal International Economic Order has been marked by political efforts to reduce or outlaw government recourse to these various measures, and is explored later in this chapter.

## Marxist approaches

Given the fall of the Soviet empire and the fact that Communist states which have persisted since the end of the Cold War, like China and Vietnam, have embraced capitalism in their international policies, one might be forgiven to conclude that Marxism was on the wane as an approach to International Political Economy. However, while very few states take a Marxist or Maoist approach in their dealings with other countries, Structuralist perspectives on the global economy as a whole have actually become more prominent in academia as the sorts of exploitative working conditions Marx wrote about in regard to industrialised countries have become more apparent at the global level. Concerns over sweatshop labour in the urban slums of nineteenth century Europe mirror the anxieties many express today about sweatshop labour in the industrialising world.

Marxist approaches to International Relations, explored in more depth in Chapter 8, assume that global economic structures are the chief determinants of international political behaviour and events and, hence, see IPE as being synonymous with IR, rather than a mere subset of the discipline. Marxists do agree with Mercantilists that capitalist economics is a zero-sum game of losers and winners rather than the Liberal's sum-sum game of comparative advantage. Hence **Dependency Theorists** have advocated that governments of the 'zero' (that is, loser) countries adopt protectionist measures to save themselves from exploitation. However, as Neo-Marxist approaches have evolved and economic globlalisation has intensified, the emphasis has shifted to seeing the competition in the global economy as not being between states but between transnational classes of 'haves' and 'have-nots'. Neo-Marxists see IPE as based on a global bourgeoisie systematically exploiting a global proletariat. Some of that bourgeoisie is composed of small elites in poorer states who operate in 'enclave economies', profiting from the proceeds of exporting their country's resources to wealthier people in the richer states. Some of the exploited transnational class reside in the richer states as underpaid workers or unemployed beggars, also short changed by the global system.

## The contemporary trading system

In an illustration of the difficulties inherent in steering governments away from Mercantilism, even with the scale of hegemony that the USA enjoyed in 1944 they could not secure agreement for a third institution of Bretton Woods, the International Trade Organisation. The Americans pulled the plug on their own idea owing to the number of governments who sought special exceptions to far-reaching plans to eradicate protectionist measures. In place of the International Trade Organisation, a lesser non-institutional arrangement was agreed based on the 1947 General Agreement on Tariffs and Trade (GATT) Treaty.

Central to GATT was the resurrection of an old idea for facilitating trade which the British had used in their nineteenth century hegemony and had periodically been employed between European powers as far back as the fifteenth century, the **Most Favoured Nation** principle. The Most Favoured Nation principle is an undertaking between two governments that, in granting trade concessions to each other (e.g. mutually reducing tariffs on certain goods), they also agree not to grant even greater concessions to another country. Hence if State A and State B have a Most Favoured Nation agreement, they are both committed not to then conclude a new deal with even greater concessions to States C or D, no matter how mutually beneficial it may be. The point of this principle is to give some order and openness to international trade and to avoid the otherwise likely endless series of undercutting deals and ensuing rows. Also, in terms of liberalising trade, if Most Favoured Nation agreements multiply between states, this will see tariffs start to be cut on a multilateral basis. Hence the early 'Rounds' of GATT – periodic phases of negotiation among parties to the Treaty – were dominated by the extension of Most Favoured Nation agreements before then moving on to get agreement on the phasing out of tariffs and other forms of government protectionism. The key features of the nine GATT Rounds are summarised in Table 16.1.

On the face of it GATT has been hugely successful in liberalising international trade. In 1947 the average tariff its members were imposing on industrial imports was 38 per cent but, by the end of the Uruguay Round, it was only 4 per cent and covered most countries in the world. During this period international trade grew twenty fold. By 1995 globalisation and the end of the Cold War prompted the International Trade Organisation idea, abandoned half a century earlier, to be revived in the guise of the World Trade Organisation (WTO). The WTO absorbed the 1947 GATT Treaty and regime and added to it measures, committing its members not to violate the rules and mechanisms to enforce decisions. Hence the WTO became widely referred to as 'GATT with teeth'. The ambition of the new institution was evident from the words of its first leader in a speech to the United Nations Conference on Trade and Development after the close of the Uruguay Round: '(the WTO) is no longer writing the rules of interaction among separate national economies. We are writing the constitution of a single global economy' (Renato Ruggiero 1996).

**Table 16.1** GATT/WTO Rounds

| Round | | Number of states | Key agreements |
|---|---|---|---|
| 1947 | Geneva | 23 | |
| 1949 | Annecy | 13 | Extension of the use of Most Favoured Nation |
| 1951 | Torquay | 38 | Agreements between parties. Tariff cuts between |
| 1956 | Geneva | 26 | some parties. |
| 1960–1 | Dillon | 26 | |
| 1964–7 | Kennedy | 62 | 35% average cut in industrial tariffs. |
| 1973–9 | Tokyo | 102 | 25% average cut in industrial tariffs. Principle of exempting Less Developed Countries from Most Favoured Nation obligations established. Rules on *Non-Tariff Barriers* introduced for the first time (on government subsidies). |
| 1986–93 | Uruguay | 123 | 40% average cut in industrial tariffs. Some (limited) measures to reduce agricultural protectionism introduced for the first time. Creation of the WTO. |
| 1999– | Doha | 153 | Impasse over liberalisation of agricultural trade. |

However, despite unprecedented international political efforts to liberalise international trade, the contemporary global system is far from being entirely free and government recourse to Mercantilist measures is still regularly seen. While progress on reducing industrial tariffs may be impressive the liberalisation of the trade in food and textiles is far more limited. In striking contrast to the figures for industrial protection, the tariffs imposed on agricultural imports are at an average of 30 per cent in the European Union and nearly 33 per cent in Japan (Josling and Hathaway 2004). Steps were taken to tackle agricultural protectionism in the Uruguay Round, with the Europeans agreeing to cut export subsidies (unpopular in the rest of the world for artificially reducing high EU prices so that their surpluses could be 'dumped' on the international market). Further liberalisation concessions could not be won, due to the political sensitivity attached to protecting farmers in some EU states – and particularly France – but the subject was now on the table and the principle of more significantly freeing up this area of commerce was agreed to for the next Round. The Doha Round has, however, proved more intractable than any of its predecessors and agricultural trade remains largely as unfree as it ever was, with particular implications for **Less Developed Countries** whose economies tend to be based on food rather than industrial exports.

In addition to the issue of agricultural protectionism, over the course of the GATT/WTO era there have emerged so many exceptions to the Most Favoured Nation principle that some posit that industrial trade is not as free as the tariff reduction figures would suggest. It was agreed in the 1947 Treaty that members forming trade blocs which freed up trade between them could be exempted from the Most Favoured Nation principle (that is, they could give greater concessions to their trade bloc partners than to their 'Most Favoured Nations'). At the time this was not particularly significant, since there were very few trade blocs, but the proliferation of these arrangements is such that today all WTO members bar Mongolia are in, or are negotiating to be in, a regional free trade area and most are simultaneously members of several. Whether this phenomenon is good or bad for the cause of freeing up international trade is hotly disputed. Some see trade blocs as a positive development for liberalisation since they are, after all, freeing up trade and so can be seen as stepping stones towards global free trade. Others, however, voice concern that trade blocs are detrimental to global free trade since they produce 'trade diversion' by increasing trade among their own members at the expense of trading with the rest of the world. The European Union, for example, has greatly facilitated flows of trade among its members but this has been accompanied by those states trading less with countries outside of the EU. Hence, although it is indisputable that there is more trade then ever in the world some contend that this is misleading since the logic of the invisible hand and comparative advantage are only really being applied at the regional rather than the global level.

A further exception to the Most Favoured Nation principle was established in the Tokyo Round by allowing Less Developed Countries preferential access to developed country markets. The intention of this was to help their infant economies grow by giving them some protection from competition with stronger economies but it has also sometimes proved controversial. During the 'banana wars' of the 1990s, for example, the US government complained that the EU was using this principle as a means of capturing the fruit exports of Caribbean ex-colonies.

An additional complication in regard to freeing up international trade is that there is more to protectionism than tariff-cutting but these 'Non-Tariff Barriers' are far more difficult to legislate for. Quotas and subsidies have come to be restricted by GATT but such measures tend to be harder to implement than restrictions on tariffs since they are less explicit and more easily disguised than a tax. Protectionism through creating red tape is harder still and governments have taken to ingenious measures to seek to protect domestic industries in this way. In the 1990s Japan's government defended unique national standards for the construction of skis on the basis that Japanese snow was different than that found in the rest of the world. Hence we see the central dilemma of achieving free international trade. Strong domestic pressures will often be exerted on governments to bail out or protect domestic jobs and industries from foreign imports, while the realisation of global collective goods is rarely prominent in the demands made by the public on the officials who represent them.

## The contemporary international monetary system

Political involvement in economic affairs centres on enacting measures to regulate the money supply, as well as the flow of trade. Money, essentially, was created to facilitate trade. It allowed people to buy goods rather than just exchange them by coming to a mutual agreement on the respective worth of those goods every time they are swapped (bartering). With the progress of international trade this also came to apply to international commerce, with many imports coming to be paid for in money rather than 'in kind'. Crucially, then, the value of money has to be agreed upon by the participants in a commercial transaction. Domestically this comes from the existence of a national currency as legal tender. The state, via its Central Bank, issues coins and notes and authorises other kind of monetary exchanges to an amount considered appropriate to maintain the value of the currency and facilitate business. This monetary policy amounts to expanding the national money supply (to boost businesses or create jobs) or contracting it to prevent inflation (the problem of an excess of money undermining the value of goods). Traditionally government monetary policy focuses on the raising or lowering of Central Bank interest rates or by the raising or lowering of taxes (fiscal policy). Lowering the tax rate gives people more money as their income while lowering the interest rate makes it easier for them to borrow money from banks. Raising either rate contracts the money supply by doing the reverse.

This crucial dimension of political economy has functioned within states since ancient times and control of the money supply is, alongside control of the use of force, the basis of sovereignty. With the rise of international trade, however, a problem emerged with monetary exchanges in that there was no international currency and the world's myriad national currencies had very different and fluctuating values. The 'exchange rate' between any two currencies is likely to vary on a regular basis and create uncertainties for traders. Hence the idea of the Gold Standard emerged with a value in gold – chosen as the amount of it in the world was broadly known – assigned to the national currency of each of the states partaking in international trade. The world's leading trading states agreed to have their currencies given a set value in reference to gold and so avoid competitive devaluations. The Gold Standard was a key feature of the trading system of the nineteenth century, upheld by Britain as hegemon, but this system collapsed as Mercantilism resurged in the twentieth century.

As with measures introduced to liberalise international trade at the Bretton Woods Conference, the method used to give order to the international monetary system revived a scheme from the nineteenth century but strengthened it through the creation of an intergovernmental organisation to uphold the new rules. The International Monetary Fund (IMF) would, on the one hand, provide an international pot of money from which countries could borrow in times of hardship and, on the other hand, be the centre of a new system of managed currencies. A significant variation on the Gold Standard was created, however, clearly reflecting the extent of US hegemony in the 1940s. The US dollar was made the unofficial currency of the capitalist world (not, of course for the Soviet Union and their allies) by establishing a monetary system in which other countries promised to keep the values of their currencies tied to the value of American money. Gold was still pivotal to the system, however, since the US dollar was tied to the price of that precious metal (at $35 per ounce). Hence Washington became the world's lender while not having to worry about exchange rates or balancing its own books. Hence the USA was able to run a trade surplus (export more than import) and so act in a Mercantilist manner while propping up a liberalising international economy.

The US economy, and the global economy, thrived under this monetary system through the 1950s and '60s but it all came unstuck in the 1970s. This era of US hegemony came to an abrupt halt amid the global economic recession of 1971–4. The sudden rise in oil prices, instigated by the Organisation of Petroleum Exporting Countries taking advantage of having secured political control of this crucial commodity from MNCs, allied to the spiralling costs of the Vietnam War, led to the US budget deficit (amount of debt acquired through borrowing) getting so large that bondholders and other governments began to lose faith in the dollar holding its value in relation to gold. Importantly, the revival of European economies and emergence of Japan as a major player in the international economy meant that the USA's hegemony was not what it had been and other currencies were emerging to rival the US dollar. While political factors undoubtedly hastened the collapse of the Bretton Woods monetary system, many have come to concur with the views of the Belgian economist Robert Triffin that any international monetary system based on any one country is doomed to fail, regardless of political circumstances (see Box 16.5).

## Box 16.5 The Triffin dilemma

The 'Triffin dilemma' posits that it is unsustainable for one country to act as the world's banker since, in time, it will eventually come to pass that more of that country's currency will be held outside of its own borders than within. History and common sense dictates that lending more than you own is a recipe for disaster. This is precisely what happened with the US dollar and, hence, in 1971 President Nixon pulled the plug on the Bretton Woods monetary system by revaluing the dollar and abandoning its conversion rate to gold.

Attempts were made to revive the Bretton Woods monetary regime through the early 1970s but, eventually, a system of fixed exchange rates was abandoned and the capitalist world entered a new era of floating exchange rates (that is, unregulated at the global level), one which persists to this day. The present monetary system is not a return to financial anarchy, however. Not all states do 'float' their currencies. Some continue to peg their currencies to the dollar and some to other powerful currencies. Ecuador and El Salvador have gone further and actually adopted the US dollar as their national currency in 2000 and 2001 respectively. Most European Union members have now adopted a new joint currency, the euro to give them strength through unity in the global financial system. A number of states, including the USA and UK, do float their currencies and have come to accept the consequent fluctuations in their exchange rates in the confidence that their standing in the financial world will keep their currencies and economies strong. A huge growth in the flow of money across the borders of countries has led to a situation

*Source: Getty Images/Peter Dazeley*

**The credit crunch: temporary setback, or evidence of an unsustainable global economic system?**

in which governments have come to have less control over their money supplies and have become more vulnerable to market forces. Around a third of the world's paper money is now held outside of the country where it is legal tender (Cohen 2003). Several Asian countries suffered a significant economic downturn between 1997 and 1999 when rapid financial outflows from Thailand occurred when the government decided to float the baht rather than peg it to the US dollar. The effects quickly spread to Japan and other states but the North American and European economies remained relatively unaffected and the fashion for floating currencies and liberalising capital markets (relaxing government rules on financial firms) persisted. After a decade of economic growth in Europe and North America, however, another sudden – and this time global – economic recession caused by financial turbulence threatened the remaining Bretton Woods edifice.

## Case study: The credit crunch recession

From 2008 a financial crisis spread through the world triggered by the collapse of the US housing market. Banks had been granting loans to people to buy houses much more readily than in the past and then selling on the money based on this debt to other financial companies to fund investments. These financial companies assumed these loans were 'secure' because mortgages have traditionally been viewed in this way (because the sum is seen as guaranteed by the fact that the banks have people's homes as collateral) and credit rating agencies in the city assured them that they were. House prices had been rising for several years, allowing this sort of lending to appear viable, but when this financial bubble inevitably burst it became apparent that it was not. The loans were not traditional mortgages and were not secure because the banks had been increasingly lending to, first, poor people unlikely to be able to make the repayments and, second, rich people who had bought property purely for investment purposes. Hence, when the poor borrowers started to default on repayments and rich borrowers responded to a fall in prices by simply handing back the house keys, the mortgage lenders were left owning property nowhere near the value of the sums of money they had lent. When it became obvious that banks had been lending sums far in excess of what they owned, businesses lost confidence in them and the whole financial system was plunged into chaos. Many major international banks collapsed, many others had to be bailed out with $ multi-trillion injections of government (i.e. taxpayers') money, and a slump in production occurred as businesses became starved of bank loans,

creating a huge growth in unemployment. Across the world around $4 trillion was lost (to put this in context global GDP or 'all the money in the world' is around $60 trillion) in the worst economic recession since the Great Depression of the 1930s.

From the perspective of the three positions on globalisation outlined in Chapter 2 this recession can variably be viewed in the following ways:

- For *Globalists* this is a temporary setback; the bursting of another economic bubble after which the market will correct itself and allow the normal pattern of economic growth – which has dominated the past sixty years – to resume.
- For *Alter-globalists* the recession represents a political failing; the failure of certain governments properly to control banks and the financial markets. By learning from this and putting reforms in place the global economy can be resurrected in a better, more regulated, form.
- For *Anti-globalists* the scale of the downturn provides damning evidence that capitalism is simply unsustainable as a global economic system.

Unlike the 1930s, however, the overall response governments has not been to 'beggar thy neighbour' and turn inwards but to look to cooperative international solutions to preserve the global economic system, while reforming the way its institutions operate. This is explored in Chapter 17.

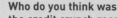 **Who do you think was to blame, if anyone, for the credit crunch recession?**

## Conclusions

Economic globalisation has brought the states of the world closer together than ever before into a single economic system. Those states, however, are still prone to act unilaterally in economic policy and where international cooperation has thrived it has tended to be at the regional rather than global level. Mercantilism, in the form of economic protectionist strategies, persists in the Liberal International Economic Order and remains a popular recourse for governments at times when the global economy does not appear to be delivering collective goods. Although beset by periodic downturns, the persistence of the Bretton Woods System and its apparent success in delivering unprecedented levels of global trade and economic growth, and in avoiding a repetition of the Great Depression, seemed to vindicate the international political architecture fashioned by the USA in 1944. The spectre of the 1930s economic catastrophe which loomed again with the financial crash of 2008, however, has challenged many assumptions and prompted a reappraisal of the nature of International Political Economy.

Prescriptions for the global economic system from the rival perspectives of International Relations, and the states that inhabit the world, have come to be broadly the same as for the other core aspirations of the discipline: peace and human rights. Realists, as always, put their faith in the state and advocate that governments should 'look after number one' and follow a Mercantilist agenda to ensure that they are not the losers in a competitive, anarchic marketplace. Marxists see the persistence of perennial poverty in the **Global South** and of the periodic poverty of economic boom and bust in the **Global North** as evidence of the need for systemic change rather than mere reform.

IR Liberals in this regard are not synonymous with Economic Liberals in that they propose greater political intervention rather than pure market solutions, through the promotion of global governance. In this view a single economic system needs to be regulated accordingly. That there are 176 currencies not fixed to the amount of gold or any other fixed variable, while financial flows cross borders in ever greater amounts and at increasing speeds, could be said to be a recipe for economic disorder – and even serve to undermine the meaning of money. Money was invented to facilitate trade but, to some extent, has become a commodity in its own right with the rise of financial speculators earning their living by betting on – and encouraging – currency and share collapses. In light of this, some Liberals have come to advocate the most far-reaching of all economic reforms in terms of its implications for state sovereignty: the creation of a single global currency. As radical a proposal as this might be, it is far from new. John Maynard Keynes at Bretton Woods advocated an 'international clearing union' in which state currencies would be fixed to a hard currency (that is, not for public use) held by a global central bank. All states would have what approximates to a bank account with the international clearing union and be charged for running an excessive trade surplus or deficit with the value of their currency automatically recalculated accordingly. In this way Keynes believed that global economic stability could be guaranteed, through all governments having to balance their books and currency speculation coming to an end.

Radical solutions, calling for a complete overhaul or overthrow of the Liberal International Economic Order, have emerged from the margins of the IPE debate due to the shock to the system presented by the 2008 downturn. The future of IPE is far from certain with very different predictions and prescriptions about how the role of the state will be affected by globalisation and the unprecedented complexities and dilemmas that it continues to produce for governments.

## Resource section

### Questions

1. How free is world trade today?

2. Contrast Liberal and Mercantilist theories of International Political Economy and consider which approach is most apparent in the contemporary world.

3. Is a hegemon an essential prerequisite for the construction of a Liberal World Economy?

### Recommended reading

O'Brien, R. and Williams, M. (2004) *Global Political Economy: Evolution and Dynamics* (Basingstoke, UK, New York: Palgrave)
A thorough yet accessible overview of IPE, particularly strong in terms of an historical overview but also covering rival theories and key contemporary issues. Helpful, concise case studies and data are presented throughout.

Ravenhill, J. (ed.) (2008) *Global Political Economy* (2nd edn, Oxford: Oxford University Press)
A well-presented textbook which is particularly strong in presenting the theoretical approaches to IPE and in defining key concepts.

### Useful websites

Global Policy Forum 'Globalization of the Economy'

http://www.globalpolicy.org/globalization/globalization-of-the-economy-2-1.html
An authoritative and well set out website (good for IR in general) providing overviews and data for all of the key themes in IPE as well as links to analytical essays.

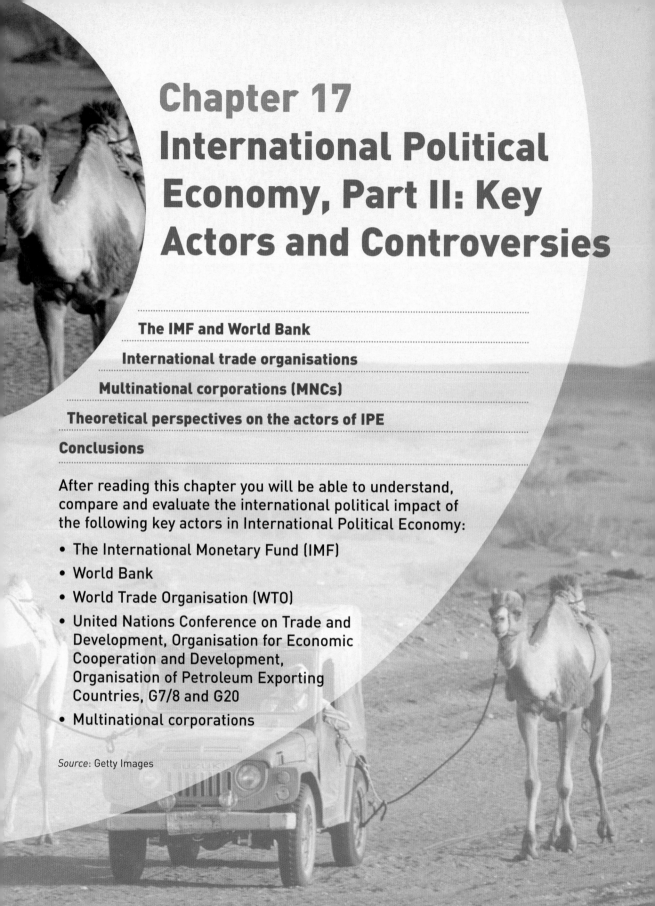

# Chapter 17
# International Political Economy, Part II: Key Actors and Controversies

After reading this chapter you will be able to understand, compare and evaluate the international political impact of the following key actors in International Political Economy:

- The International Monetary Fund (IMF)
- World Bank
- World Trade Organisation (WTO)
- United Nations Conference on Trade and Development, Organisation for Economic Cooperation and Development, Organisation of Petroleum Exporting Countries, G7/8 and G20
- Multinational corporations

*Source*: Getty Images

## Introductory box: Chavez's IMF walkout

In 2007 the colourful left wing President of oil-rich Venezuela, Hugo Chavez, announced that his country would be pulling out of the United Nations' twin economic organisations, stating, 'We will no longer have to go to Washington, nor to the IMF, nor to the World Bank, not to anyone'. The incident highlighted disillusionment with international economic organisations and the increasing power of some of the newly industrialising states. It also, however, served to signify the importance of international economic organisations in providing a platform for Global South leaders like Chavez and it is worth noting that, in spite of having paid off their debts, Venezuela has yet to follow up on their leader's promise and pull out of the two organisations.

## The IMF and World Bank

As highlighted in Chapter 16, the institutions set up at the 1944 Bretton Woods Conference were always intended to be sister organisations, providing support for the freeing up of international trade by offering help to governments in economic difficulties. In this way it was hoped that countries would be better able to resist putting up the barricades when the going got tough, as had happened in the Great Depression of the 1930s. In the early years of the Bretton Woods system both organisations were principally involved in the reconstruction of the economies' of developed countries crippled by the Second World War. From the 1950s, however, both organisations became more focused on the politics of development, although the IMF continued to play a role in bailing out developed countries who had got into financial difficulties. From 1989 both organisations also became key players in the politics of democratic transition as many Communist states restructured their economies to a capitalist model.

The names of the Bretton Woods siblings are misleading in that the IMF is more of a bank while the World Bank is more of a fund. Over time the IMF has come to be associated with providing shorter-term finance with strings attached, while the World Bank looks to help the most needy with longer-term loans. As an analogy with sources of personal finance, you could compare the World Bank to a government agency you would use for a loan to

## Box 17.1  Profile – the IMF in 2010

**Location:** Washington
**Member states:** 186 (Cuba and N. Korea are the only notable non-members)
**Head:** Managing Director is Dominique Strauss-Kahn (France)
**Key functions:** provides a source of funding for governments in economic difficulties and facilitates free trade by creating monetary stability
**Decision making:** overall steering by Board of Governors – an annual meeting of all member states' finance ministers. Lending decisions taken by an Executive Board of twenty-four Executive Directors with weighted voting rights according to the economic size of the members. Eight states represented individually (US 16.77%, Japan 6.02%, Germany 5.88%, UK 4.85%, France 4.85%, China 3.66%, S.Arabia 3.16%, Russia 2.69%). The rest of the membership are organised into loose geographical groups and represented by one of their members in turn, with their quotas combined (for example Nordic states represented by Sweden 3.44%).

study at university, in that the terms of the loan are relatively generous but would not be open to anyone who simply happened to want some money. Going to the IMF, in contrast, is more like re-mortgaging your home with a high street bank, in that it is a source of finance with less generous terms but available to anyone creditworthy and willing to meet the terms of the loan.

The IMF and World Bank are located very close to each other in the US capital and, in addition to their own meetings, they meet collectively under the auspices of the 'Development Committee'. By tradition, the IMF is headed by a European and the World Bank by an American (USA). This, added to the decision-making processes, explains how these organisations have long been seen to exemplify **hegemony** in International Relations, as explored in the previous chapter. In the early years of the Bretton Woods system this was very much a US hegemony but since the collapse of the US dollar-based exchange rate system in the early 1970s, it is more often characterised as a wider collective hegemony of the EU, Japan and the USA. Hence, the IMF's unit of account for its monetary reserves since then has been the Special Drawing Right (SDR), a 'basket currency' of the four leading national currencies (the US dollar, the Japanese yen, the euro and the UK pound) weighted according to their strength in the global economy. Sometimes referred to as 'paper gold', since they effectively came to replace the use of gold in the IMF, SDRs are, in fact, not directly comparable since they are a unit of account in the IMF (and some other IGOs) and not the basis for valuing national currencies. However, the SDR does provide a more stable form of liquidity (money for governments to balance their books) than relying on one national currency.

The World Bank is also a misleading name for the additional reason that it is not a single organisation but actually a cluster of institutions, better referred to as the 'World Bank Group'. Over time, as the focus of its work has shifted, the International Bank for Reconstruction and Development, set up at Bretton Woods, has been joined by three other partner organisations, exclusively focused on the financing of projects in the developing world.

*Source: Getty Images/AFP*

**Are institutions like the IMF and World Bank unfairly dominated by the Global North?**

As is explored in Chapter 18, the IMF and World Bank have become more distinct over time with the latter becoming more socially oriented and focused on development in a wider sense, rather than just economic growth. The World Bank is still, however, subject to criticisms similar to those targeted at the IMF, summarised in Box 17.3.

---

## Box 17.2 Profile – the World Bank Group in 2010

**Location:** Washington
**Member states:** 186 (same as IMF)
**Head:** President Robert Zoellick (USA)
**Key functions:** lends money for economic development projects

- *The International Bank for Reconstruction and Development* – gives loans to 'middle-income' states
- *International Development Association* – gives long-term interest-free credit to the poorest states
- *International Finance Corporation* – gives loans to private businesses to locate in Less Developed States

- *Multilateral Investment Guarantee Agreement* – provides insurance to investors in development projects

**Decision making:** steering by Board of Governors – annual meetings of ministers (finance or development) of all member states. Day-to-day decisions come from Boards of Directors of the four organs made up of twenty-four Directors organised in broadly the same manner as the IMF.

### Box 17.3 Debate – for and against the IMF

**Criticism**                                    **Defence**
*Unfairly dominated by the Global North*          *Those who pay the money should decide where it goes*

As can be seen in Box 17.1, the world's richest states far outweigh the rest in quotas allocated for decision making. Constitutional changes require an 85 per cent 'supermajority' giving the USA (or EU acting collectively) a veto. Defenders of the decision-making system, however, posit that this is fair since the weightings are in accord with how much money the states contribute to the IMF coffers.

*Conditions for loans are too harsh*             *Loans should be conditional*

The most prominent criticism of the IMF is that the conditionality attached to its loans exacerbates problems and poverty by insisting on 'Structural Adjustments' to cut government expenditure. It is widely held that the IMF worsened the 2001 financial crisis in Argentina by insisting on the privatisation of state utilities, which saw unemployment rise as foreign firms bought up local industries. In Less Developed Countries the effects of Structural Adjustment have been consistently controversial (see Chapter 18). Defenders of the IMF, however, observe that not insisting on measures to ensure governments do not waste or embezzle funds – as has been known to happen – would be irresponsible. Some governments – such as the 'Asian Tigers' (e.g. S. Korea) and post-Communist transition states of East Europe (e.g. Poland) – have successfully used IMF funds to kick-start rapid economic growth.

*Secretive and politicised decision making*      *Governments want a global monetary facility and need some secrecy*

IMF decision making is complex and far from transparent. As a consequence a lot of horse trading and arm twisting goes on behind the scenes, adding to concerns about poorer countries being dominated. Critics observe that decisions to lend money to countries are often made on a political, rather than strictly economic, rationale. An example sometimes cited is the 1999 agreement to give loans to Russia, which many felt ignored issues of financial prudence in order to improve strained relations between Moscow and the Western powers in the context of the war against Kosovo. However, nearly every state in the world is a member of the IMF and, even if flawed, most seem to accept the need for a global organisation to promote financial stability. Some observe that if the world did not have an IMF it would have to invent one and that, for all its flaws, the current model 'is better than nothing'.

On the face of it the World Bank can similarly be charged with a US or **Global North** bias, given its location, leadership and decision-making structure; but, beneath this, the staff and culture of the group have evolved in as clear as case of institutional change as you will see in international relations. As the remit of the World Bank shifted towards development in the **Global South**, so too did the personnel within the group and the way that it operated. Even under the stewardship of some highly conservative US-appointed presidents, the prominence of Development Studies and Social Policy specialists among its experts has ensured that the World Bank has acquired a social conscience in its operations and taken steps to ensure that development projects it sponsors do not benefit just a small sector of a country at the expense of others or harm the environment. Hence critics of the Bretton Woods system have tended to focus their attention on the 'ugly sister' of the pair. The IMF has undergone less of a transformation than the World Bank but, nonetheless, has given its name to the 'Post-Washington Consensus' of reformist measures in development politics – explored in Chapter 18 – and is coming to be increasingly influenced by voices outside of the traditional Western European/North American/Japanese powerbase, such as China and India.

## International trade organisations

As described in Chapter 16, the World Trade Organisation was born in 1995 as a reincarnation of the International Trade Organisation, stillborn at Bretton Woods half a century earlier. The emergence of this 'GATT with teeth' signified a new era of economic globalisation but has been, from the start, beset with controversy and difficulties both in terms of its functioning and its role in the world. It has not been able to oversee the successful completion of the Ninth GATT Round as new policy has been paralysed by the reluctance of many states to liberalise agricultural trade. Many developed countries have been unwilling to lessen measures protecting their farming industries from foreign competition, much of it from the Global South. The 1999 Seattle Summit (the Third Ministerial), intended to launch the Ninth Round, was abandoned amid scenes of rioting protestors and it was instead launched two years later at Doha in the desert of Qatar, inaccessible to all but the most intrepid members of the new anti-globalisation social movement. The next summit in 2003, at Cancun in Mexico, was most notable for a mass walkout of delegates from Less Developed Countries in protest at the failure of developed states to deliver on promises of agricultural liberalisation made at the Eighth GATT Round. In 2005, at the Fifth WTO Ministerial in Hong Kong, internal and external protests were less prominent but the impasse continued and the Doha Round could not be completed. Tellingly, what was supposed to be the Sixth Ministerial in 2007 never even took place since it was accepted that progress was impossible. A Seventh Ministerial was held, in 2009 at Geneva, but proved to be a low key affair effectively held only to restart the process and keep the Doha Round alive.

Within the WTO a lot of business and negotiation is done outside of the Ministerials and General Council meetings in caucus groups, whereby governments coordinate their positions with like-minded states in order to give themselves a chance of being heard in

## Box 17.4 Profile – the WTO in 2010

**Location:** Geneva
**Member states:** 153 (Russia, Iran and Ukraine are among non-members)
**Head:** Pascal Lamy (France)
**Key functions:** implement the General Agreement on Tariffs and Trade (see Chapter 16), resolve trade disputes and promote free trade

**Decision making:** overall steering by a biannual WTO Ministerial (meeting) of all member states. Regular decisions taken by the General Council (which also meets in the guise of the Trade Policy Review Council or the Dispute Settlement Body). All decisions are by 'consensus' – that is, they need to be accepted by all member states.

the inevitable noise and complexity of a 153-way debate. The most powerful of these loose, unofficial coalitions is 'the Quad', comprising the European Union (itself, of course, already a large grouping of states), the USA, Japan and Canada. If this grouping can reach common accord it greatly enhances the likelihood of achieving consensus. The Quad have held many formal and informal meetings prior and adjacent to WTO Ministerials allowing them, for example, to advance intellectual property rights (patents protection) on the agenda. Less Developed Country delegations at the WTO have coordinated their positions in three fluid and overlapping groupings. The most influential industrialising Less Developed States, such as Brazil, India and China, have operated in the grouping G20 at WTO Ministerials, pushing aggressively for agricultural liberalisation (confusingly, this is not the same 'G20' of leading industrialised states which later formed containing some of the same countries – this is highlighted later). G33 is a grouping of Less Developed States with a common interest in securing special exemptions for products that they are particularly dependent upon. Prominent members include Indonesia and Malaysia seeking exemptions to tariff cuts for products such as rice and rubber which are seen as critical for their economic well-being. G90 is a more residual grouping of the world's Less Developed States, banded together for strength but concentrating more on ensuring the protection of their infant industries, rather than taking on the 'big boys' in the way the G20 has done. The desire to open up the agricultural markets of some countries is not uniquely a concern of Less Developed Countries and, from the Uruguay Round, developed major food exporters like Australia, Argentina and Canada (in this instance switching allegiance from the Quad) have cooperated in a caucus known (after the Australian city in which they first met) as the Cairns Group.

The volatile short history of the WTO can be interpreted very differently. The riots, walkouts and overall political impasse can variably be seen as evidence of failure and disillusionment with the Liberal International Economic Order or as the inevitable consequence of having a robust global body which facilitates debate from all quarters. The mantra 'no deal is better than a bad deal', which has been adopted by some developing state delegations and sections of global civil society in relation to the Doha Round, can be read as either signifying the death knell of the WTO or, conversely, the fact that this is a forum in which the developing world is able to make itself heard and not be sidestepped.

Outside of and predating the WTO, a number of other intergovernmental organisations have served to coordinate the positions of groups of states in the International Political Economy.

● **OECD** – The Organisation for Economic Cooperation and Development was established in 1961 as a permanent intergovernmental organisation with headquarters in Paris to promote economic growth through the cooperation of its membership of the world's most advanced industrial states. It evolved from the Organisation for Economic Cooperation in Europe, set up in 1948 to coordinate Western European economies and administer the USA's 'Marshall Plan' of post-war reconstructive aid to that region. The OECD today

## Box 17.5 Debate – for and against the WTO

**Criticism**                                    **Defence**
*Dominated by the Global North*                  *Decisions are consensual*

As with the IMF and World Bank, a prominent criticism of the WTO is that it is another vehicle for hegemony and provides a post-colonial means for the states of the Global North to dominate those of the Global South by compelling them to open up their economies, providing the North with new markets and cheap labour forces. In defence it can be pointed out that the WTO's decision-making structure is egalitarian since, with no majority or weighted voting, any state is free to block a new proposal it disapproves of. In addition, many WTO decisions have ended restrictive trade practices in powerful Global North states. Critics respond by observing that consensus, far from empowering the weak, actually reinforces hegemony since the large WTO delegations of the Global North countries, having coordinated their own positions in caucus meetings outside of the formal decision-making structure, are able to lean on the small delegations of Global South countries and stifle opposition.

*Undermines state sovereignty*                   *Restraining governments is in the public interest*

In addition to concerns that the WTO favours rich countries over poor, many critics have also voiced fears that the organisation is fundamentally undemocratic, since its rules often overturn popular domestic laws. Perhaps the chief grievance of the whole anti-globalisation movement is the view that a **democratic deficit** has emerged in which global rules are being codified and enforced by a secretive and unaccountable body serving the interests of big business and over which ordinary people have no real influence. Defenders of the WTO, and globalisation in general, contend that freeing up trade is in the common human interest and, if we want to reap the benefits of this collective good, we need to have a global body powerful enough to stop governments acting in their own, rather than their citizens', best interests.

*Puts profit before people*                      *The WTO is about trade – it is up to governments to protect their citizens from exploitation*

Related to the previous two concerns, anti and alter-globalisation perspectives are concerned that the power of the WTO has served to undermine the security of workers in poorer states and damaged the environment the world over. Freer cross-border trade has led to a 'race to the bottom' in which multinational corporations from rich states take the opportunity to exploit low wages and lax safety standards in poor states and an exploitative global division of labour emerges. This problem is most pronounced in the Global South but, even in richer states, opposition has mounted to jobs being relocated to poorer states and environmental protection measures being eroded on the grounds that they are barriers to free trade. In defence, it is often suggested that the WTO cannot be held responsible for governments who fail to enact necessary domestic laws to protect their citizens. A middle-way (alter-globalisation) perspective is to suggest that the problem is not so much the WTO but its 'success' relative to other organisations and regimes. A global body freeing up trade is in the common good but the relative weakness of global governance in areas such as worker safety and the environment means that we have, to date, seen only a partial, economic globalisation and not a fully rounded globalisation in the full human interest. Hence, in this view, what is required is *better* globalisation rather than an unravelling of globalisation.

has a membership of thirty states and an annual budget of just over $500 million, based on subscriptions weighted according to the economic size of the participants. OECD meetings, which include annual Ministerials and a range of other fora, have produced non-binding 'soft law' agreements on issues, such as the 1976 Guidelines for Multi-National Enterprises setting out principles for businesses to observe in Less Developed Countries and the 1999 Anti-Bribery Convention.

- **UNCTAD** – The United Nations Conference on Trade and Development was set up in 1964 to focus on the development implications of international trade and particularly the GATT regime. Despite its name, UNCTAD is an organisation – a programme of the UN – with a permanent secretariat in Geneva. It was a focus of Third World radicalism in its early years but declined in influence in line with the decline of the Third World as a bloc in the 1980s (see Chapter 18); since then, it has come to be somewhat marginalised by the emergence of the WTO. While developed states have continued with their membership of UNCTAD, their interest in its meetings and research has become limited and it has occasionally been suggested that the acronym for the organisation should actually now stand for: 'under no circumstances take any decisions'.

- **G7/8** – the Group of Seven evolved from the Group of Five, formed in 1975 between the USA, UK, France, Germany and Japan which was later expanded to include Canada and Italy. Meetings now also usually include an eighth member, Russia, although the seven continue to meet without the Russians when dealing exclusively with financial matters. G5 was inspired by the oil crisis (see below) of the 1970s which focused minds in the world's wealthiest states on the need to keep the Liberal International Economic Order together and resist the challenge presented by the newly emboldened oil exporting states of the Middle East. G7/8 is not a formal intergovernmental organisation and has no headquarters or decision-making structure, but it has developed a model of working based on annual summits and other regular ministerial meetings, chaired and hosted by each member in turn in a rotating presidency. Tackling transnational organised crime and fraud has become an increasingly important focus for meetings, with the involvement of Russia particularly useful in this regard, given the international prominence of the Russian mafia.

- **OPEC** – As introduced in Chapter 12, there are a number of intergovernmental organisations that are **cartels**: groups acting to coordinate the pricing of a particular international commodity that they are prominent exporters of. Essentially this is the practice of coordinated price-fixing; although illegal for private businesses in most capitalist countries, it is performed by governments in international trade where there are no such restrictions. Price fixing is clearly against the free trade spirit of GATT/WTO but, such is the sensitivity of this subject, it has largely been ignored. Governments engaging in such practices are typically from the Global South and argue that they are not exploiting a monopoly but merely safeguarding their development through protecting a crucial export. The most influential cartel has been the Organisation of Petroleum Exporting Countries (OPEC), which was set up in 1960 and initially comprised five states: Saudi Arabia, Iran, Iraq, Kuwait and Venezuela. The OPEC countries today produce around 45 per cent of the world's crude oil and represent around 55 per cent of exports. The organisation shot to prominence in the early 1970s when its members began to take control of the North American and Western European multinational corporations which had been dominating their oil extraction and petroleum manufacturing industries, giving it the means to raise prices.

## Box 17.6 Profile – OPEC in 2010

**Location:** Vienna
**Member states:** 12 (Algeria, Angola, Ecuador, Iran, Iraq, Kuwait, Libya, Nigeria, Qatar, Saudi Arabia, United Arab Emirates, Venezuela)
**Head:** Secretary-General Abdalla Salem El-Badri (Libya)
**Key functions:** to coordinate the price of oil exports

**Decision making:** OPEC conference made up of government ministers meets twice per year and decides on membership applications and overall policy direction on the basis of unanimity. A Board of Governors, nominated by the members and approved by the Conference, implements policy and oversees regular day-to-day decision making.

Crucial to OPEC, as with many economic organisations, is the hegemonic role played by one of its members, Saudi Arabia. The Saudis' oil exports are three times that of the next biggest exporters, Iran and Venezuela, allowing it to call the shots. OPEC sets quotas for oil production among its members so that it can control the supply vis-à-vis the rest of the world's demand and so manipulate the price in their favour. The flaw in such a strategy is the temptation likely to present itself to any of the members to break ranks and exceed their quota in order to sell more and make a quick profit – an example of the **collective goods problem**. The Saudi government are in a position to sanction that by being able to flood the market with oil if any country does step out of line, an action they have taken on several occasions.

OPEC has continued to be an influential actor in IPE but has yet to relive its heyday in the 1970s, when it effectively held the Global North to ransom and many of its members underwent rapid economic growth on the back of burgeoning oil prices. From the 1980s the Global North countries coordinated their position as oil consumers, looked to alternative supplies, such as Mexico and Azerbaijan, and learned to be more efficient with their consumption, reducing OPEC's control of the oil supply.

However, OPEC is far from a spent force and it seems inevitable that it will rise again in prominence as the world's oil supply starts to shrink. There are alternatives at present for Northern consumers but OPEC controls around 80 per cent of proven oil reserves, which means it cannot be avoided in the medium to long term. Despite the emergence of alternative power sources in Europe, overall demand for oil is rising due to the economic development of control like China, India and Brazil. Additionally, OPEC have developed an increasingly close relationship with prominent non-member exporters Mexico and Russia, and would be likely to absorb any other state that happened to strike it lucky and start exporting oil.

## Multinational corporations (MNCs)

Multinational corporations are businesses with significant operations in more than one country. Like other international organisations, a small number of MNCs existed before the mid twentieth century (the Dutch East India Company which operated in the seventeenth and eighteenth centuries is sometimes considered the first) but it is over the last sixty years that they have significantly grown both in number and influence. There are currently around 77,000 MNCs operating in the global economy, carrying out roughly two-thirds of all of the exports in the world (Kegley and Raymond 2010: 164–5). If the oft quoted maxim 'money is power' is correct, then the presence of MNCs in today's world is huge. It is frequently asserted that the largest multinationals outstrip the resources of some poor states but this is, in fact, an understatement. The biggest MNCs surpass *all* developing countries and many developed countries in their assets. In 2009 the MNC with the world's biggest turnover was the oil giant Shell, whose estimated value of $458 billion put it just behind Saudi Arabia and ahead of Norway as the 24th richest actor in the world. US-based shopping retailer Wal-Mart is the world's 28th richest actor, ahead of Iran (Fortune 2009, World Bank 2009).

As with other non-state actors, not all IR analysts accept that the rise of MNCs is necessarily indicative of declining state power in a globalising world. Liberal pluralists from the 1960s saw the rise of MNC influence as contributing to interdependence and a diminished role for the state. As independent entities with significant economic clout MNCs can influence IPE in their own right. In the oil crisis of the early 1970s Western oil companies were often at odds with their home governments since they stood to gain from prices being forced up by their host governments. Similarly, when UN economic sanctions were imposed on the racist governments of South Africa and Rhodesia in the 1970s many Western-based MNCs acted against their governments and the international community by continuing to operate in those countries. In addition to acting contrary to the interests of their home governments, MNCs often greatly influence the framing of those interests as a result of their economic leverage. Oil industry lobbying was a factor in persuading the British and French governments to launch a controversial war against Egypt in 1956 as their government's nationalisation of the Suez Canal was seen as threatening business interests. More recently, oil MNC lobbyists helped to persuade the Bush government in the USA not to cooperate in international efforts to combat global warming because of the business costs.

However, on the other side of the debate and at much the same time as the Pluralists, neo-Realists began to see MNCs in the global economy as giving renewed vigour to a state-centric power politics approach to understanding the international political economy. In particular, neo-Realists pointed out that MNCs often serve as a means of projecting the power of their home country government. The US government, notably, had used American MNCs as an arm of their Cold War strategy of containing the USSR, by giving them incentives to set up in geopolitically significant states in Western Europe and Asia in order to prop up capitalism and gain military influence.

Since the Cold War the political debate on the role of MNCs has been principally focused on the politics of development and whether or not it is in the interests of Less Developed Countries to invite corporations in to boost their drive for economic growth. For Economic Liberals, MNCs are the key agents of development; for Marxists they are the agents of dependency. The key dimensions of this debate are summarised in Box 17.7.

## Box 17.7 Debate – for and against MNC investment

**Criticism**
*They syphon off resources to the home country*

**Defence**
*They bring financial and technical investment*

Critics of economic globalisation focus much of their anger on the role of MNCs in the Global South, arguing that they represent the key means by which the Global North can secure resources they cannot produce in their own countries – like bananas or cocoa. In opposition to this, those with a more benign view of economic globalisation see MNCs as the means by which crucial investment can be secured by developing countries; citing the likes of Singapore and South Korea, who successfully kick-started their development with the aid of US multinationals.

*They exploit workers in the host country*

*They bring employment to the host country*

MNCs are often accused of engaging in a 'race to the bottom' in which they seek out countries with the cheapest labour costs or most lax safety standards in order to maximise profits. The world's worst ever industrial accident, at Bhopal India in 1984, was at the plant of a subsidiary to the US chemical MNC Union Carbide, where standards were much lower than in the home country. In defence it could be said that disasters such as Bhopal, along with incidences of poorly paid labour, are the fault of inadequate governance in the host country rather than falling solely on the multinationals. In developing countries governments are keen to attract MNCs because they boost employment and people want to work for them because they usually pay better than domestic firms.

*They undermine local industries*

*They provide better value and choice for consumers*

Rather than giving a helping hand to local enterprise, critics point to cases of MNCs throttling industries in Global South host countries. In recent years Ghana's major cocoa industry has oriented itself so much towards exports that its domestic industry has collapsed and it now even imports chocolate products made by Northern MNCs from its beans. A more positive perspective on the impact of MNCs notes how consumers across the world have benefited from being able to shop in a global rather than just a national marketplace and from prices being forced down by greater competition.

*They produce cultural colonialism*

*They help bring people together*

Critics lament that MNCs contribute to the bland homogenisation of the world, undermining local cultures with Western fast food, clothing and entertainment. In defence globalists maintain that MNCs are a key element of a positive cultural interdependence, contributing to us all getting to know each other better through common cultural reference points and the sharing of each others foods and styles.

The influence of MNCs increasingly can be measured not only vis-à-vis their home or host country government but also at the global level. MNCs are powerful lobbyists within various elements of the UN system, at the WTO and at other IPE arenas – either directly or banded together into specially designed lobby groups. The Global Crop Protection Federation (GCPF), for example, represents a range of pesticide manufacturers, including major chemical corporations like Monsanto and Bayer, in fora in which international policy on the trade in these products is debated. The drive for wealthy MNCs to band together in this way was to counter the growing influence in international politics of pressure groups seeking to temper economic globalisation in the name of environmental or development interests. The creation of GCPF was a counter-response to the successful lobbying of pressure groups, banded together as the Pesticide Action Network, for the introduction of rules limiting the trade in potentially hazardous chemicals, which had gathered momentum in the wake of the Bhopal disaster. MNCs have not always been obstructive to global policy, however. The World Heath Organisation, for example, has actively courted the support of corporate philanthropy, such as from IT tycoon Bill Gates, to assist campaigns against diseases like HIV/AIDS and malaria.

Hence it is possible to envisage the global economy developing a form of politics somewhat akin to that which is already well-established in developed democracies, with businesses lobbying for influence alongside non-profit organisations representing consumer, environmental and worker interests. Pressure groups like Oxfam and CAFOD are influential lobbyists and have contributed to a burgeoning global civil society seeking to advance a humane counterbalance to global rules freeing up trade. This has manifested itself in movements like Jubilee 2000, which campaigned for the writing off of debt in the world's poorest countries and Make Poverty History, which has mobilised considerable public support for a restructuring of global trade laws to allow Less Developed Countries to export agricultural goods more freely to the developed world. Trades Unions have become more globally oriented. The International Trade Union Confederation (ITUC) was established in 2006 to provide a unified international voice for workers, previously represented on the global stage over past decades by disparate federations. The ITUC have, in particular, called for an empowerment of the UN's body dealing with this issue, the International Labour Organisation (ILO). The ILO actually pre-dates all of the IPE IGOs previously described, with its origins going back to the launch of the International Labour Office in 1901, set up to promote minimum global workplace standards in the age of industrialisation in the Global North. ILO standards today, however, have little influence compared to the WTO, IMF and World Bank – a fact often cited by alter-globalists as evidence of a skewed globalisation which has become driven purely by economic and not necessarily human interest.

Whether we are witnessing the emergence of an increasingly pluralistic international political economy, however, is open to debate, as is considered in the next section.

## Theoretical perspectives on the actors of IPE

The present and future significance in international relations of the various IGOs considered in this chapter can be viewed in very different ways, in line with the rival theories of IR/IPE.

- Realists/Mercantilists
  In line with the traditional **Realist** view that the significance of IGOs and of globalisation in general is exaggerated, some analysts have suggested that the IMF, World Bank, WTO and other IPE actors are not as influential as many suggest. With the WTO, the most common illustration of its impact and defence of its success is the unparalleled growth of international trade that has occurred under the watch of the GATT/WTO regime. However, could this be what is referred to in philosophy as a post-hoc fallacy? Does

it necessarily follow that the increase in trade must be *due* to the rules introduced by GATT/WTO or could this be coincidental? A much cited empirical study by the economist Andrew Rose observed that many states increased their volumes of trade while they were outside the GATT/WTO regime, as much as their members, and concluded that overall this was more the result of trade blocs and bilateral deals than global rules (Rose 2004). For the sceptics IPE is and will continue to be dictated by states and IGOs represent no more than convenient vehicles for the expression of state interests.

- **Marxists**

The anti-globalisation camp view the organisations of IPE as rotten expressions of a rotten system which needs to be completely replaced. Most contemporary **Marxist** analysts of IPE are not, however, advocating some form of global replication of centralised, state-centric Soviet Communism but the emergence of a much more devolved system in which power is localised again.

> The Socialism that seems most likely to emerge out of the global capitalist system is not going to come about as a result of a revolutionary seizure of state power (this method has failed miserably wherever it has been tried), but as a result of a successful period of social experimentation in which the hegemony of global capitalism is increasingly and effectively challenged by a combination of local and transnational democratic social movements.
>
> (Sklair 2002: 325)

In this vision 'localisation' should replace globalisation through re-empowering the state, or some other local political entity, over global organisations and rules through the increased use of protectionist measures and controls on foreign businesses and transnational capital flows (Hines 2000).

- **IPE (Economic) Liberals**

The pro-globalisation camp defend the record of the IMF, World Bank, WTO and multinationals, and point out that the current era of the Liberal International Economic Order is one that has witnessed the greatest increases in trade and overall prosperity the world has ever seen. The intergovernmental institutions are essential for propping up that system by providing safeguards against governments lurching back to economic nationalism, which history shows has happened when the global economy is unregulated. In the 1920s and 1930s states devalued their currencies and raised tariffs at will and such short-termist and short-sighted practices culminated in the Great Depression, followed by the Second World War. The IPE institutions both compel governments to desist from resorting to damaging acts of protectionism while also offering them a lifeline when the going gets tough.

- **IR Liberals ('alter-globalists')**

A growing middle ground perspective finds much fault in the global IPE actors but still believes that the world needs such organisations and focuses on the need for reform rather than abolition. Epitomising this worldview is former World Bank Chief Economist, Joseph Stiglitz (see Chapter 18, Box 18.5) who, in 2009, was put in charge of a UN Commission of economists, academics and politicians to come up with proposals for reforming global economic institutions so as to learn lessons from the 'Credit Crunch' depression. The 'Stiglitz Commission' report advocated significant reform in the governance of the global IPE actors, so as to involve developing states more, but did not advocate their abolition. Instead the report's main recommendation was to create a new, powerful institution 'The Global Economic Council' on a par with the UN Security Council. The Global Economic Council would be an inclusive and genuinely global forum for all IPE issues bringing together the IMF, World Bank and WTO, and allowing issues to be raised more effectively and equitably than currently exists with the myriad intergovernmental fora. The most appropriate overall steering mechanism for global economic governance, the Report argues, is not a G7 or G8 but a 'G192' (that is, all the UN member states) (UN 2009). In spite of a growing consensus in favour of institutional reform and more multilateral approaches in IPE, the future is more likely to be about making the corridors of power less exclusive but still far from globally inclusive.

*Source: Getty Images/Matt Cardy*

In the eyes of its critics, the G20 has failed to carry out reforms that would ensure social justice and economic equality.

## Case study: The rise of the G20

The hitherto obscure 'Group of 20 Finance Ministers and Central Bank Governors' suddenly emerged as a key actor in IPE against the backdrop of the 'Credit Crunch' global recession in 2008–10. This G20 was not the same as the G20 WTO caucus group of the most powerful developing states referred to earlier. It includes the following nineteen states: USA, Japan, UK, Germany, France, Canada, Italy, Spain, Russia, Australia, China, Brazil, India, South Africa, Mexico, Argentina, South Korea, Turkey, Indonesia and its twentieth member is the EU. G20 was set up by G7 in 1999 in response to the Asian financial crisis in order better to coordinate monetary planning, since key economies had been affected by the downturn (which spread to Latin America). Once the global economy began slumping in 2008, however, low-key annual meetings of finance ministers and the heads of the Central Banks became high profile, twice yearly summits inclusive of heads of government.

G20 is not an intergovernmental organisation – the meetings are chaired and hosted by its members in a rotational 'presidency' – and it has no formal criteria for membership. However, the fact that it contains members accountable for 85 per cent of global GDP and 80 per cent of global trade and that there is a recognised need for a more universal means of coordinating policy has thrust the group into the spotlight. G20 has emerged from relative obscurity to become an overall political steering mechanism for the global economic system. That this grouping, rather than just the G7, had come to be seen as necessary to consider measures to get the world out of recession

and debate the future of the Bretton Woods system was indicative of a significant shift in the balance of world economic power.

Key G20 proposals to have emerged from its recent summits include the following:

- Increased funds for the IMF and reformed decision making for the fund and the World Bank with greater input from newly emerging economies, particularly China
- An expansion, in role and membership, for the Financial Stability Forum – a little-known organisation set up in 1999 by the G7. China joined the forum in 2008 and its role was expanded in an effort to increase transparency and have more oversight of where risks exist in the global financial system
- Coordinated national policies to limit the level of bonuses paid by banks to financiers and the sums they are able to lend. A financial stability board was established to oversee this
- Coordinated sanctions to be imposed on tax havens that refuse to reveal bank details
- A commitment to complete the Doha Round of GATT/WTO trade liberalisation and the Millennium Development Goals (see Chapter 18).

**If you ruled the world would you**

1. **abolish,**
2. **radically reform, or**
3. **retain in broadly the same form the IMF, World Bank and WTO?**

## Conclusions

The arena of International Political Economy has become increasingly crowded over time as the actors have multiplied. Intergovernmental organisations have proliferated, hundreds of trade blocs of various shapes and sizes with overlapping membership have emerged (see Chapter 14) and thousands of non-state actors with financial muscle and access to the levers of global power have together created a complex system.

Central to IPE, however, are the three global IGOs of the Liberal International Economic Order (LIEO), the IMF, World Bank and the WTO. Although frequently attacked, the IMF and World Bank are close to universal in their membership, while the WTO has expanded its membership rapidly in its short history, with most non-members queuing to join its ranks. The Credit Crunch depression re-invigorated attacks on the LIEO trio but no serious prospect of abolition has emerged in the mainstream discourse of international diplomacy. The IMF was beefed up rather than slaughtered in response to the downturn, with greater say given to newly emerging economic powers in this organisation and the World Bank. The spectre of the 1930s Depression, exacerbated by government protectionism, has served to knock heads together and make the completion of the Doha Round more rather than less likely. Hence the shock of the 2008–9 depression has been the catalyst for evolution rather than revolution, with the major international organisations surviving but coming more to reflect the realities of the new economic balance of power. A system fashioned by US hegemony has started to evolve into a far more multilateral form with intergovernmental organisations and businesses from a growing band of developed countries managed by a widening concert of great economic powers.

## Resource section

## Questions

1. Is it fair to say that the world would be better off without the International Monetary Fund (IMF)?

2. Why have the World Bank and International Monetary Fund attracted controversy and how far have they modified their policies in response?

3. Why is the World Trade Organisation so often the focus of anti-globalisation sentiment and is such sentiment justified?

4. Assess the case for and against a developing country attracting multinational corporations (MNCs) in order to aid their economic growth.

## Recommended reading

**Peet, R. (2009)** *Unholy Trinity: The IMF, World Bank and WTO* (Zed)
A highly critical analysis of the three global IPE actors, citing evidence that they exist purely to serve the interests of big business and also that, with the rise of global discontent and economic crisis, their time may be nigh.

**Woods, N. (2006)** *The Globalizers: The IMF, The World Bank and Their Borrowers* (Ithaca NY, London: Cornell)
Woods presents an 'alter-globalisation' analysis of the Bretton Woods institutions that is critical but reformist rather than revolutionary.

## Useful websites

WTO website, http://www.wto.org/

IMF website, http://www.imf.org/

World Bank, http://www.worldbank.org/

OECD, www.oecd.org/

UNCTAD, www.unctad.org/

OPEC, http://www.opec.org/home/

Bretton Woods Project, http://www.brettonwoodsproject.org/
A site set up by activists and journalists from many prominent pressure groups and media sources which monitors the activities of the IMF and World Bank, producing regular critical articles, reports and data.

BBC, 'Beat the World Trade System', http://news.bbc.co.uk/1/hi/business/6183887.stm
Try your own hand at international trade negotiation with this online exercise.

# Chapter 18
# Development, Poverty and Inequality

**The persistence of global poverty**

**Approaches to development**

**The evolution of development policy**

**Conclusions**

After reading this chapter you will be able to:

- Comprehend the disparity of wealth in the contemporary world and appreciate rival explanations for this phenomenon

- Evaluate competing arguments for the causes of hunger and famine in the world

- Be able to evaluate, from a variety of theoretical perspectives, the progress of international policies designed to facilitate the development of poorer states over the past sixty years

*Source*: Getty Images

## Introductory box: The 2009 Kenyan food crisis

The chronic food shortages which afflicted Kenya between 2006 and 2009 prompted the government to declare a national emergency and international relief agencies to warn that a sudden escalation of deaths from starvation and ill-health related to malnutrition was imminent without significant political action. The causes of the crisis were manifold but among the contributory factors were the following:

- The previous five years had seen several droughts reduce water supplies well below normal levels and negatively affect crop yields.
- President Kibaki's government had been accused of being negligent – and possibly fraudulent – in distributing international aid. Concerns at corruption had prompted many international pressure groups not to give aid to the country.
- Internal conflict between tribes and political factions, triggered by a contentious 2007 presidential election, disrupted the sale of food within the country. Many farmers hoarded food supplies and increased tension emerged in terms of the allocation of this and dwindling water sources.
- The Kenyan economy had suffered as a consequence of an unprecedented rise in world food prices over recent years, augmented by the global financial collapse of 2008–9. Many see greed in wealthy countries as a factor behind the global food crisis with the supply of food in the world negatively affected by more agricultural land being converted to growing crops for biofuels used in cars, rather than food. Similarly, the global financial crisis was caused by greedy corporate practices in wealthy countries but its effects were felt everywhere and most acutely in Less Developed Countries like Kenya.

Hence this crisis could variably be chiefly explained by: first, poor governance, second, the misfortune of experiencing a natural disaster, or third, the exploitative nature of the global economy. The rival explanations for this particular episode essentially mirror the wider debate on the root causes of inequality, poverty and a lack of economic development in many parts of the world explored in this chapter.

## The persistence of global poverty

To paraphrase Rousseau via Orwell, all states are born equal but some are born more equal than others. The spread of sovereignty through the international system over the last five centuries has given us a world today in which the map has been redrawn from one dominated by a small number of vast international empires to a post-imperial mosaic of around two hundred independent states, each free to pursue their domestic affairs as they choose and conduct relations with fellow members of this 'sovereign club', protected by international law. That, of course, is the theory. The reality is quite different. Most

*Source*: Reuters/Goran Tomasevic

Contributing factors to the Kenyan food crisis were natural disaster, poor governance and the exploitative nature of the global economy.

ex-colonies have struggled to match their former colonial masters in economic or political terms, even with legal equality in place; and, leaving aside the legacy of history, it stands to reason that some states, whether through luck or political guile, will be richer and more influential than others.

Poverty, in general and in relation to international relations, can be expressed in two forms: relative and absolute.

## Relative poverty

Economic inequality in the world has always existed but is more pronounced today than it has ever been and there is little evidence that this trend is likely to be reversed in the foreseeable future. The 80:20 ratio is a well-known and effective means of expressing global inequality. Roughly 80 per cent of the world's people live in the '**Global South**' but only 20 per cent of the world's wealth is possessed by those same countries. Hence the reverse of this is that the '**Global North**' has 20 per cent of the world's people but 80 per cent of its resources. During the Cold War it was customary to subdivide the world into three groupings: the Global North comprised the developed capitalist First World and the Communist Second World, while the Third World was the less developed remainder of states principally in Latin America, Africa and South Asia. China could be said to span the Second and Third Worlds but, as a developing country, is categorised as in the South. This 'North' and 'South' are only loosely geographic and an increasing number of countries cannot easily be fitted into either camp. The development of oil rich Middle Eastern states and 'Asian Tigers', like South Korea and Singapore, made the distinction unclear even before the end of the Cold War. Nevertheless, the 80:20 statistic still gives us a useful snapshot of the 'haves' and 'have-nots' in today's world.

Just over one-quarter of the world's population – 1.4 billion people – live on or below an income equivalent to $1.25 per day (the more striking indicator of $1 per day was abandoned by the World Bank in 2005 due to the inevitable impact of inflation) (Ravallion and Chen 2008). Perhaps most striking is the fact that the disparity between the haves and have-nots has significantly widened over recent decades. The world's richest 20 per cent of people (not countries) had a combined wealth thirty times greater than the poorest 20 per cent in 1960 but by 1997 this ratio had widened to 74:1 (UNDP 1999: 36–8).

It is, however, an age old political debate as to whether such relative inequality – even if it is ever-increasing – necessarily constitutes a problem or is an indicator of political failure. Put very simply the political left consider that it is morally unacceptable that resources should be so unevenly allocated, while many Liberals and Conservatives would not necessarily agree that 'relative poverty' is a problem and a failing. For example, the Liberal philosopher John Rawls's test of justice for a political system contends that inequality in the distribution of social goods can be considered fair if the least advantaged, nonetheless, gain increased social goods over time and everyone has the opportunity to advance (Rawls 1971). In this view inequality can still be fair.

## Absolute poverty

While not everyone would accept that the existence of great and ever-widening disparities in wealth across the world represents a problem or a political failing, the persistence of absolute poverty, in the form of hunger and famine, must indisputably represent a problem and a political failing. Whether this amounts to a domestic or global political failure, however, is open to debate.

Eradicating absolute poverty has long been articulated as an important aim of international politics but today remains a problem of similar dimensions to that existing in 1963 when US President John F. Kennedy stated at the UN World Food Congress: 'We have the means; we have the capacity to wipe hunger and poverty from the face of the Earth in our lifetime. We need only the will'.

A famine is a sudden increase in mortality resulting from food shortages. The more precise causes of famines are frequently disputed by analysts and politicians. Most famines are the result of a combination of both natural and political factors, and disputes on causation centre on determining the relative weighting of these two dimensions. There are three fundamental explanations for any particular famine related to the balance between the supply and demand for food:

- A fall in the food supply
- An increase in the demand for food
- Disruptions to the normal distribution of food.

The third of these factors is most particularly influenced by politics and economics. As will be explored in the next section, if considered from a global perspective all famines can be attributed to disruptions to the normal distribution of food, since there is demonstrably sufficient food in the world for all people to be adequately fed. We do not live by effective global governance, however, and all three explanations can variously be applied to the situation in states where famines do occur. The food supply in countries can fall below the level sufficient to meet demand because of poor harvests or the population can grow at a rate that the food supply is unable to match. When famines occur, however, natural variations in supply and demand are frequently magnified by political factors. The famines that ravaged Ireland in 1845–7 and India on several occasions throughout the nineteenth century, for example, had natural causes but are generally considered to have been exacerbated by the political situation of the two countries. Droughts instigated the Indian famines and a potato blight the Irish disaster and, while their British rulers did not cause nor wish such suffering on their colonials, a political failing must be considered to have occurred given that these were food shortages occurring on the watch of the world's richest country. More recently, the 1990s North Korean famine had natural origins but was, undoubtedly, greatly worsened by the government's drive for economic self-sufficiency and a nuclear weapons capability, which had seen food imports reduced at the same time as the domestic food supply had dwindled.

The demand for food continues to increase in the Global South and natural disasters continue to blight many of the same countries, creating food shortages, but most contemporary analysts of famine emphasise distributive factors in their explanations of particular cases. Modern governments can insure against future crop shortages by stockpiling reserves of food and protecting the price of agricultural products. As a consequence of this it is possible to construe protecting people against famine as a political obligation of governments as has most notably been highlighted by the Nobel prize winning Indian Economist, Amartya Sen, in his 'entitlements thesis' (see Box 18.1).

Democratic governments are compelled to be responsive to the needs of ordinary people facing death by malnutrition, whether directly in elections or indirectly through pressure exerted by the media or other concerned citizens, in a way in which tyrannical dictators or neglectful colonialists are not. Hence Liberals believe that democracy saves people as well as empowers them and that democratisation in the world will help in the fight against famine. Food shortages will still occur from time to time but these can normally be planned for by governments and, when they cannot be dealt with, the international community can step in.

## Box 18.1 Amartya Sen's entitlements thesis

Sen's 'entitlements approach' argues that all individuals should by rights be able to expect to be protected from famine by their government, regardless of changes in food supply or population. Sen draws on extensive evidence to propose that:

> no substantial famine has ever occurred in any independent and democratic country with a relatively free press . . .

. . . Even the poorest democratic countries that have faced terrible droughts or floods or other natural disasters (such as India in 1973, or Zimbabwe and Botswana in the early 1980s) have been able to feed their people without experiencing a famine.

(Sen 1999: 6–7)

## Hunger

International political action, coordinated inter-governmentally by the UN's World Food Programme (WFP) and non-governmentally by pressure groups such as Oxfam, CAFOD and CARE, has in recent decades succeeded in curtailing the number of famines that occur. However, such groups are quick to point out that these periodic disasters are merely the tip of the global hunger 'iceberg'. Far more people in today's world die of starvation through plain poverty than as a result of short-term regional imbalances between the supply of and demand for food. The WFP claim that some 25,000 people die every day as a result of hunger and related ailments and that over one billion in the world suffer from malnutrition (World Food Programme 2009; malnutrition defined by the WFP as a daily intake of below 1,800 calories. 2,100 is the recommended intake). Some consider this a conservative estimate but this death toll undoubtedly outstrips more commonly prioritised threats to human existence, such as war and terrorism.

Why, then, does such a death toll persist in a world in which the food supply is sufficient to permit every person in the world at least the recommended 2,100 calories per day?

There are, essentially, three answers to this question in line with the general schools of thought concerning the equity of globalisation outlined in Chapter 2.

1. *Globalists* will tend to pin the blame for hunger on poor governance in the countries concerned. Corruption and/or a lack of democracy or a political reluctance to engage in international trade prevent people gaining the food they should be entitled to from their governments.

2. *Anti-globalists* tend not to blame the governments of malnourished peoples for their plight as they see them as essentially powerless in the face of global economic structures. Marxist analysis argues that global economics accounts for hunger and famines more than the inadequate political responses of particular governments to crop failures. Marx himself considered the famines of his era to be the product of capitalism. It is, indeed, striking that so many of the worst famines in history occurred in the late nineteenth century, an era of as-then unparalleled global economic liberalisation when the trade in foodstuffs greatly increased. On a global level the production and trade in food reached

new heights, but profound inequality in the world saw many colonies exporting food northwards while their own nationals went hungry.

Marxist explanations for the persistence of poverty-induced starvation hold that it is, like famine, actually caused by the global economy and more a case of wilful ignorance by the world's wealthy. In the 1960s Norwegian peace studies scholar Johan Galtung, using language deliberately designed to equate the issue of global poverty with the typically prioritised concern of war, coined the phrase 'structural violence' to encapsulate the nature of the phenomenon:

> . . . if people are starving when this is objectively avoidable, then violence is committed, regardless of whether there is a clear subject-action-object relation, as during a siege yesterday or no such clear relation, as in the way economic relations are organized today.

(Galtung 1969: 170)

3. *Alter-globalists* do not accept that hunger is inevitable in a capitalist world economy but argue that global political failings are still culpable for the persistence of poverty. Alleviating hunger is possible without abandoning global capitalism by reforming international institutions and encouraging governments to act less selfishly in international trade. The Make Poverty History campaign of the 2000s, for example, sought to increase

---

## Box 18.2 Timeline of development in international relations

**Liberal International Economic Order**

| | |
|---|---|
| 1944 | Bretton Woods Conference establishes World Bank and IMF |
| 1949 | US President Truman's Inaugural address promises help for 'underdeveloped areas' of the world |
| 1951 | UN publishes *Measures for Economic Development of Under-developed Countries* |
| 1955 | Non-Aligned Movement established |
| 1960 | 'UN Decade for Development' begins Rostow's *Stages of Economic Growth* published |
| 1961 | UN World Food Programme established |
| 1964 | United Nations Conference on Trade and Development (UNCTAD) established Group of 77 established |
| 1965 | United Nations Development Programme (UNDP) created |
| 1971–4 | Oil Crisis prompted by price rises engineered by Middle Eastern exporters |

**NIEO**

| | |
|---|---|
| 1974 | 'New International Economic Order' adopted by UN General Assembly |
| 1973–9 | Tokyo Round of GATT |
| 1980 | Brandt Report published |

**Washington Consensus**

| | |
|---|---|
| 1981 | Cancun Summit on International Development Issues |
| 1982 | Mexico payment defaults trigger debt crisis |
| 1985 | Live Aid concerts channel charitable aid to African famine relief |
| 1990 | UNDP's annual Development Reports initiated |
| 1992 | UN Conference on Environment and Development |
| 1995 | World Trade Organisation established |

**Post-Washington Consensus**

| | |
|---|---|
| 2000 | Millennium Development Goals adopted |
| 2003 | Mass walkout of Global South delegates at Cancun WTO Summit |
| 2005 | Make Poverty History campaign holds *Live 8* concerts |
| 2015 | Deadline for judging Millennium Development Goals |

public awareness of the daily death toll due to hunger and pressure governments into structural political actions to alleviate this tragedy. The agricultural industry in the Global North has managed to remain largely exempted from the international trade liberalisation of the last sixty years and, in many countries, enjoys heavy government subsidisation and protection. This undermines the capacity of the Global South countries to export their food produce to Northern markets. The losses resulting from this distortion of the free market – an estimated annual $100 billion – far exceeds the sums given to the Global South in aid (Watkins 2002). Hence 'trade not aid' became a mantra of the Make Poverty History campaign in contrast to the charity-focused Band Aid/Live Aid movement of the 1980s which had inspired it. Hence alter-globalists argue for a 'mixed economy' for the world in which more political intervention is required in some cases but, in other instances, the invisible hand of the free market should be allowed to do its work.

The logic of these three approaches applied to the wider theme of how poor countries can achieve development is expanded on in the next section.

## Approaches to development

### The orthodoxy

The orthodox position on poverty argues that it can be eradicated by those countries affected taking steps to replicate economic development of the kind experienced by Global North states. In this view, **Less Developed Countries** (LDCs) can best mimic Northern development by integrating themselves into the global economy to permit export-oriented industries to flourish and gain from the inward investment provided by multinational corporations (MNCs). The clearest articulation of this view came from the influential US Economic Historian Walt Rostow with his 'Stages of Growth' thesis in the 1960s. Rostow analysed the history of development in the North and concluded that all states pass through five similar stages of progression towards 'take off' and an end stage of a wealthy consumer-driven society (Rostow 1960) (see Box 18.3).

### Box 18.3 Rostow's five stages of economic growth (1960)

1. **Traditional society** – pre-industrial economy and pre-modern society, e.g. Europe in the Middle Ages.
2. **Preconditions for take off** – transition stage towards industrialisation and modernisation. Manufacturing industries emerge, banks emerge and the provision of education becomes more widespread, e.g. Western Europe in the late seventeenth and early eighteenth centuries.
3. **Take off** – the industrial revolution and the key watershed for development. Economic growth becomes the norm and service industries emerge to aid manufacturing industries, e.g. Britain in the late eighteenth century, France and US in the mid nineteenth century.
4. **Drive to maturity** – more national income is invested and the economy diversifies, e.g. Britain, France, USA, and Germany in the late nineteenth century.
5. **Age of high mass consumption** – a diverse economy based on consumer goods and services.

Rostow's thesis is part of the general belief that economic development is linked to *modernisation*, a generic term encompassing a combination of social and economic changes such as having smaller families, making transactions by money instead of bartering, secularisation, mass education, literacy and urbanisation. Encouraging foreign investment is seen as the key to being able to finance and learn how to embrace these changes. This then allows 'take off' to occur and permit export earnings to enrich producers and the wider society through the trickle-down effect of some of that money then being spent and invested in other sectors of the economy.

The failure of many LDCs to show any sign of such progression over the last fifty years has dented the viability of Rostow's thesis but the discourse on international economic relations is still dominated by variations on this orthodox position. In particular, the successful economic development in the 1980s and 90s of the Newly Industrialised Countries (NICs), such as the 'Asian Tigers' of Taiwan, South Korea, Hong Kong and Singapore, after opening themselves up to foreign investment and developing export-oriented manufacturing industries, served to reinforce the notion that a global route out of poverty is available for those states stuck in pre-modernity. The subsequent recent growth of 'Big Emerging Markets' like Brazil, China and India is seen as further evidence of this view of progress.

The new Liberal International Economic Order (LIEO) built from the 1944 Bretton Woods Conference was not, however, pure Economic Liberalism since the international development policy was founded on the notion that interventions from Global North states could and should stimulate economic growth in the South. The capitalist world had learned from the Great Depression of the 1930s that free markets do not always correct themselves when in a downturn and *Keynesian Economics* (named after the UK economist and politician John Maynard Keynes who was his country's head delegate at the Bretton Woods Conference) had become mainstream in domestic economic policy. Keynesian economics advocates government interventions and spending to combat unemployment and boost the demand for goods in order to kick-start a slumping economy. In line with this thinking, President Roosevelt had sought to regenerate the US economy in the 1930s by pumping money into the poorest areas of the country in his New Deal package (an approach not followed at the time in the UK). It was in this framework of thinking that the idea of a 'New Deal' for the capitalist world emerged in the mid 1940s with a US-led international drive to give foreign aid and developmental loans to the world's poorest countries and offering incentives for businesses to locate there in order to stimulate growth. This interventionist variant of Economic Liberalism thus became the orthodoxy of the emergent development policy and the Liberal International Economic Order.

## Radical challenges

The conventional notion that economic development was a stage that all states would eventually reach if they underwent social and economic 'modernisation' came to be challenged from the 1960s since much of the Global South had not experienced significant economic growth. 'Dependency theorists' led by Frank (1971) built upon the previous work of Structuralist economists like Paul Prebisch who advocated 'Import Substitution Industrialisation', which saw protectionism as the route to Global South development, rather than opening up trade with the Global North. From this perspective *developing* states are nothing of the sort; they are *dependent* states being systematically and deliberately exploited by their wealthy counterparts. The global economic system requires *underdeveloped* states in order to feed the voracious capitalist appetite for more wealth in the developed states. Hence, building on evidence that some Latin American states' economic fortunes improved rather than worsened when their principal trading partners were distracted in the Second World War, Frank and others advanced the notion that the poor states of the world would be better off cutting themselves off from the Global North and concentrating on developing their own resources (see Chapter 8).

Wallerstein's 'World Systems Analysis' is a less state-centric version of Structuralism which builds on the notion of a *core* of haves and a *periphery* of have-nots inevitably occurring in dependent countries, by applying this to the global level. In this view it is not so much the rich states of the world exploiting the poor states as a transnational wealthy class (including elites in less developed countries) exploiting a transnational class of the poor (including the poor in developed countries) (Wallerstein 1979; see also Chapter 8).

## Reformist challenges

A range of perspectives we will refer to as 'Reformist' do not reject the idea that all can progress in a capitalist world economy but believe that a more nuanced understanding of the process than that offered by the orthodoxy of the Liberal International Economic Order is required. Reformists contend that the drive for pursuing economic growth through industrialisation and modernisation needs to be compromised in a variety of ways:

- **Needs-oriented growth**

  In particular, the reformists came to challenge the notion that development was all about money and suggested that to observe economic growth was not necessarily to observe development. This approach to development contends that progress necessitates more than a growth of GDP per capita (total earnings of all citizens of a country divided by the number of people) since this might be just enriching a small elite in a country, in line with the core–periphery phenomenon outlined earlier. Instead, real development should be judged in terms of improvements in securing 'basic human needs' for the whole population. The greater provision of food, clothing, shelter, work and services like health care and education to the population of a state is considered a better indication of development than economic growth.

  To get over the limitations of judging development purely in economic terms, the United Nations Development Programme (UNDP) drew upon the expertise of academics like Amartya Sen, to devise a 'Human Development Index' to rank a country's progress (see Table 18.1). This figure combines income, life expectancy and educational attainment to give a more thorough picture of whether a state's wealth is being utilised to the benefit of its people.

**Table 18.1** HDI versus GDP

| Richest states – by GDP per capita ppp* (HDI rank in brackets) | Highest HDI rank compared to GDP (italicised) | Lowest HDI rank compared to GDP (italicised) | Poorest states (HDI in brackets) |
|---|---|---|---|
| 1. Luxembourg (18) | Cuba (51/*94*) | Botswana (124/*54*) | 173. Niger (174) |
| 2. USA (12) | Myanmar (132/*167*) | S. Africa (121/*56*) | 174. Tanzania (159) |
| 3. Norway (2) | Palestine (106/*139*) | Eq. Guinea (127/*73*) | 175. Congo DR (168) |
| 4. Ireland (5) | Tajikistan (122/*154*) | Namibia (125/*172*) | 176. Burundi (167) |
| 5. Iceland (1) | Albania (30/*98*) | Swaziland (141/*104*) | 177. Malawi (164) |

*purchasing power parity – factoring in the relative worth of a state's money (UNDP 2008)
http://hdr.undp.org/en/

Anomalies emerge from comparing income and HDI which demonstrate that there is more to development than money. Equatorial Guinea was Africa's richest country and ranked in the top 30 of the world by GDP per capita as recently as 2004 on the back of export earnings from oil production. Most of the country's citizens have not benefited from the oil rush, however, as it has been beset by corruption, poor governance and civil turmoil. Hence states which, for various reasons, do not utilise their resources for the benefit of all of their people are judged, by HDI, to be less developed than their GDP would suggest. Equally some countries, such as Cuba, under HDI can be understood as more developed than their income would suggest due to relatively good health and educational systems benefiting their citizens. At the same time, the most developed countries by GDP are rich but not necessarily the richest in terms of overall quality of life. The USA may be the world's second wealthiest state but the average life expectancy of its citizens has sometimes been surpassed by much poorer Cuba in recent years. However, the fact that Cuba and Myanmar (Burma) – two dictatorships where political opponents are regularly jailed – rank so highly does suggest that HDI scores do not encompass quality of life in terms of rights and freedom.

● **Gender-neutral growth**

In a clear illustration of how national economic growth may not be to the advantage of all, the Women in Development movement emerged in the 1970s to highlight the gendered effects of orthodox development thinking. A globalising women's social movement and an emerging feminist approach to Development Studies revealed how, often, modernisation and industrialisation may have produced economic growth but one that benefited only men. Industrialisation tends to favour male employment as the prevailing assumption across most of the world is that men are better suited to hard manual labour. This is the model developed countries followed in earlier ages and, therefore, assumed appropriate in development projects. In contrast, agricultural labour in much of the world has traditionally been shared more equally between men and women. Hence the growth of urban industries in many developing countries in the 1950s and 60s saw women's employment and income often decline in the face of overall economic 'progress'.

As the emphasis of global development policy shifted towards encouraging domestic reforms in the 1980s, the gendered implications of the interventions took a new form. The focus of Structural Adjustment Policies on cutting public expenditure in order to balance the books, while often harmful to men as well, tend to have a greater impact on women since they are more often the principal child-rearers and as such more vulnerable to the effects of a decline in the provision of schooling or health services.

- **Endogenous growth**
  While not going as far as the Dependency Theorists in advocating the outright severance of trade links with the developed world, many reformists came to argue for a measure of short-term economic nationalism to protect infant industries. Countries like Britain, the USA and Germany had not had to open up themselves to foreign competition in the early stages of their industrialisation and had employed protectionist measures, such as putting tariffs on foreign imports. Countries developing in the nineteenth century had been able to grow up until strong enough to find their way in the world and had not had to open themselves up to competition as rapidly as was being expected of their twentieth century equivalents, it came to be reasoned.

- **Sustainable growth**
  The globalisation of environmental politics saw the emergence of the notion that economic growth may need to be compromised if it was at the expense of the environment. This 'Limits to Growth' thesis was most unpalatable to those countries who had not yet got to 'grow' and so came to be succeeded in environmental political discourse by 'Sustainable Development'. This approach acknowledges that economic development has to be a priority for the Global South but that it should not be pursued without regard to its polluting consequences. Longer-term thinking was required if development could be sustainable in the long term and not be a quick dash for profit which saw future generations hampered by a depletion of resources and an increase in pollution (see Chapter 23).

## The evolution of development policy

## The 1950s and 1960s – Orthodoxy

The very new political landscape at the end of the Second World War was where the idea of development in international politics took hold. Harry Truman first used the term 'underdevelopment' in his inaugural US Presidential address of 1949. With Western Europe no longer the main source of political power in the world, the one thing the two new superpowers could agree on was that the former colonies of Britain, France, The Netherlands and Portugal should be free to pursue their own destiny and given a helping hand to make their way in the world. Of course, Cold War **realpolitik** as well as empathy was at work and the USA and USSR each saw the emergent Third World as an arena in which they could secure strategic allies in the context of the unfolding ideological conflict. Many parts of Latin America, Asia and Africa became the focus of superpower competition, most prominently in Korea, Vietnam and Cuba.

## The 1970s – New International Economic Order

The first systematic challenge to the orthodoxy which had directed development policy in the 1950s and 1960s was a package of reformist ideas which became known as the New International Economic Order (NIEO). Utilising the changed composition of the UN, which occurred due to the wave of **decolonisation** that had swept Asia and Africa, the Third World found its voice in the General Assembly and a challenge to the international economic orthodoxy was signalled with the creation of the United Nations Conference on Trade and Development in 1964, headed by the radical Argentine economist Paul Prebisch. That year also saw the launch of G77, a coalition of (initially seventy-seven) Third World states acting in unison to give themselves more leverage in international trade negotiations and advance the cause of development. The Non-Aligned Movement, set up in 1955 as an organisation of states declaring themselves to be aligned to neither Cold War superpower, also became a vehicle of Third World solidarity and announced an NIEO manifesto at its annual summit of 1973. This emergent Third World activism was then fuelled by the 1971–4 oil crisis that was already challenging the supremacy of the developed First World in global economic relations.

The list of reformist demands making up the NIEO was adopted by the General Assembly in 1974 by 120 votes to 6 (including among the dissenters the USA and UK). The NIEO sought to offer Global South states certain protections within the framework of the world's Liberal International Economic Order and promote a more endogenous form of economic growth. The key demands are summarised in Box 18.4.

As the 1974 General Assembly vote indicates, the NIEO was something broader than a wish list of the world's underprivileged. Many Global North governments and a burgeoning movement of humanitarian international pressure groups also took up the cause. Several

### Box 18.4 The New International Economic Order demands

- Full sovereign control of Northern MNCs operating in their territories
- Debt relief
- Reallocation of military expenditure in the developed world on Global South development
- Preferences in trading rules to allow LDCs to be able to compete with other countries and gain access to protected developed world markets

- Greater emphasis on 'technology transfers' from North to South in aid and development programmes
- Establishment of 'Common Funds' to stabilise the global price of primary products on which many Less Developed Countries are dependent
- Reform of the World Bank and IMF so that Less Developed Countries have a greater say in decision making and that the conditions for IMF loans are more favourable

NIEO themes were taken up by the Reports of the Independent Commission on International Development Issues (better known as the Brandt Reports) of the late 1970s and early 80s, a fairly conservative think-tank set up at the suggestion of the World Bank. The Brandt Reports upheld the virtues of liberalising trade but advocated greater international cooperation to cushion LDCs from the insecurities of free trade and help them to help themselves. Specifically on the question of hunger, the Brandt Reports advocated: greater food aid, the establishment of a global grain reserve, less agricultural protectionism and, more radically, land reform in LDCs to empower the poor (ICIDI 1980: 90–104).

None of the specific NIEO demands came to be transformed directly into international policy but, to varying extents, they did start to become addressed in the progress of development policy in the 1970s and early 1980s.

- **MNCs**

  Sovereign control over US and European corporations operating in oil exporting countries of the Global South was confirmed with the unfolding of the oil crisis of the 1970s, in which the likes of Saudi Arabia and Kuwait demonstrated they could and would manipulate the price of this key commodity. The Organisation of Petroleum Exporting Countries' (OPEC) actions ensured that MNCs would now be set up in countries at the consent of the host state and abide by their terms. In the biggest of all oil producing countries, the Saudi Arabian government through the 1970s gradually acquired full ownership of the chief company Aramco, originally controlled from the USA.

- **Debt**

  Debt escalated as a problem in the 1980s as a knock-on effect of the 1970s' oil crisis. The economic downturn of the 1970s saw private banks in the Global North, who were the principal creditors of Global South countries, increase their interest rates and so also the repayment rates for development loans. Led by Mexico in 1982 several countries began defaulting on their debt repayments, on the basis that they were crippling their economies, and the whole global financial system appeared to be in danger of meltdown. Private banks responded by devising schemes to reschedule the debt and the International Monetary Fund (IMF) and World Bank, mindful that developing states were turning to the banks because their conditions were seen as too tough, looked to set better lending terms and find debt relief solutions. One prominent solution that came to be employed was for debtor states to allow MNCs to take some of their industrial assets in exchange for writing off some of the debt. These 'debt for equity' swaps and other initiatives relieved the crisis, although debt repayments continue to represent a huge burden for many Global South countries today. It is important to recognise that the response of the Global North to the debt crisis was not driven purely by altruism; it was also an exercise in self-preservation. The Global North's banking system, as well as the economies of the Global South, appeared to be in danger of collapse due to the spiralling amount of debt that was building up.

- **Reduction of Military expenditure**

  This NIEO aspiration, predictably, had little tangible impact on international affairs in the 1970s and early 1980s, given the backdrop of the Cold War and unprecedented levels of arms expenditure. The end of the Cold War at the end of the 1980s, however, did appear to open up opportunities for a 'peace dividend' to be allocated to development.

- **Preferences**

  The principle of exempting developing countries from some of the commitment to free international trade being developed through the implementation of the General Agreement on Trade and Tariffs (GATT) was promoted by UNCTAD and established in the Tokyo GATT Round of 1973–79. Under the Generalised System of Preferences which emerged, developed countries could allow Less Developed Countries to export to them on terms preferable to those given to other GATT countries on the understanding that this was 'positive discrimination' intended to help those countries (see Chapter 16).

- **Technology transfers**

  One key concern with orthodox development policy was that it was too fixated with monetary loans rather than passing on skills to allow the developing country itself to get itself on its feet. The old maxim of 'Give a man a fish and he will feed for a day. Teach a man to fish and you feed him for a lifetime' was not being observed and a too short-termist view of economic progress was being employed. In response, in 1975 the UN General Assembly passed Resolution 3384 calling for reform of the Paris Convention on Intellectual Property to loosen standards seen as limiting the possibility for Less Developed Countries to mimic technological innovations subject to patents.

- **Common Funds**

  Common Funds also became a feature of some trading regimes established between North and South in the 1970s. For example, as part of its Lomé Convention with African, Caribbean and Pacific island states from 1975 the European Community introduced the STABEX and SYSMIN mechanisms under which Global South exporters could receive compensation for loss of earnings due to a fall in the price of a range of, respectively, certain agricultural products and minerals.

- **IMF/World Bank reform**

  Third World demands for voting reforms to the financial institutions was not responded to but the shifting tide in development politics and thinking did begin to have some impact on how they operated. The IMF did not deviate too much from its Economic Liberal path but the World Bank in the 1970s shifted to a Basic Needs approach to development which was more sceptical about the notion of 'trickle down' and sought to ensure that projects benefited the poorest sectors of developing countries. US conservative politician Robert McNamara did much to promote the Basic Needs approach in his tenure as President of the World Bank, which included setting up the Brandt Reports to develop these ideas further.

# 1980s and 90s – Washington Consensus

Following this period of reform, the 1980s witnessed a revival of the Economic Liberal orthodoxy in development politics, often encapsulated in the expression 'The Washington Consensus' (so named to highlight the importance of the US government and the IMF, based also in Washington). A decline in Global South influence and the marginalisation of the NIEO agenda occurred through this decade, which can largely be explained by four international political developments:

1. **The end of the Cold War**

   The gradual coming to an end of the Cold War in the late 1980s, although giving an opportunity for non-military issues to gain global attention, actually represented a setback for the Third World since there was no longer a First and Second World to play off against each other. In the 1970s many African, Asian and Latin American countries were able to compete for the attention of two superpowers who saw it as in their strategic interests to help them. The enthusiasm for development articulated by US Presidents, such as Truman and Kennedy, was undoubtedly influenced by their desire to steer African and Asian states away from the lure of Communism. This became evident when, with the ending of the Cold War, much of the focus of Western Europe and North America shifted to the transition of the former Communist countries and further marginalised the Global South.

2. **A breakdown of Third World solidarity**

   The very notion of a Third World was further undermined throughout the 1980s and beyond by the fact that, while it was always a diverse grouping of states, its 'membership' gradually became so disparate that they ceased pulling in the same direction. The OPEC countries had helped inspire Third World countries not fortunate enough to possess bountiful oil deposits but the economic growth of countries like Saudi Arabia and Kuwait saw them essentially join the First World. Similarly, the Asian Tigers or Newly Industrialised Countries, like Thailand, South Korea and Taiwan, had joined the developed world by taking them on at their own game and producing modern manufactured goods more cost-efficiently than them. At the other end of the scale, some of the Third World of the 1970s had made so little economic progress in the following decade that many commentators started to talk of a 'Fourth World', containing countries impoverished by war and/or famine – like Afghanistan, the Democratic Republic of Congo, Zambia and Ethiopia. In addition to this, political conflicts between elements of the Third World served to further undermine their cohesiveness as a coalition. The 1980–88 Iran–Iraq War disrupted Middle Eastern cooperation and the persistence of disputes in other parts of the developing world, such as between India and Pakistan, Ethiopia and Somalia, and Libya and Chad further diluted solidarity.

3. **A reassertion of First World power**

   In addition to international political changes serving to dilute the influence of the Third World, it is important to recognise that another factor serving to bring back the orthodoxy in development politics was that orthodox elements in the First World successfully fought back against the coalition of the South. Displays of Third World solidarity inspired the First World to follow suit and beat them at their own game. The shock of the challenge presented by OPEC prompted the major oil importing countries similarly to cooperate by forming a directly rival body, the International Energy Agency (IEA). The IEA is a **cartel** of consumers which seeks to coordinate the positions of First World countries vis-à-vis OPEC by negotiating as a bloc over prices and stockpiling reserve barrels of oil in a collective manner. Similarly, in another case of Goliath mimicking David, the impact of G77 prompted the world's richest countries to form G7 to further strengthen their positions in trade negotiations through unity.

4. **The rise of the New Right**

In addition to structural and political changes the Washington Consensus was also inspired by an intellectual sea change. A renaissance in classic Economic Liberal thinking occurred in the 1980s as a backlash against the apparent failings of 'Keynesian Economics' as a consequence of the economic downturn of the 1970s. Conservative politicians, most notably President Ronald Reagan in the USA and Prime Minister Margaret Thatcher in the UK, looked to nineteenth century Liberalism to revamp their ideology. Both were swept into power to carry out mandates at odds with four decades of cross-party political consensus in favour of a reformist 'mixed economy', combining free enterprise and a strong role for government in providing a welfare safety net for the poor and often baling out ailing industries.

Thatcher and Reagan's New Right philosophy was principally targeted at their domestic economies, seeing the privatisation of state-run industries and the scaling back of government ministries as a way of reviving the economic fortunes of the two countries, once they were voted into office in 1979 and 1980 respectively. The New Right philosophy also, however, spilled over into foreign policy and international development. At a major international development summit at Cancun in 1981, intended to push forward the Brandt Report agenda, the attending Reagan and Thatcher launched an assault on the NIEO – effectively bringing to an end this period of reformist international economic relations.

The New Right also took the fight to the UN. In 1984 the government delegations of the USA, UK and prominent Asian Tiger Singapore walked out of the United Nations Educational, Scientific and Cultural Organisation (UNESCO) in protest at what was claimed to be a wasteful global bureaucracy promoting left-wing propaganda. The following year the USA began defaulting on their budget contributions to the UN. This was a 'hardball' strategy designed to threaten the Third World with the possibility that the whole UN system, which had done much to give them a voice, could effectively be dismantled if they did not tow the new line.

The debt crisis of the 1980s provided an opportunity for New Right 'monetarist' economic policies to be put into practice on the international political stage. Faced with the prospect of countries defaulting on their loan repayments, the emphasis of the World Bank and IMF in bailing out Third World countries in economic crisis shifted from lending more money to 'Structural Adjustment Policies', which involved tying assistance to the enactment of measures to control inflation and to seek economic growth through private rather than state-led enterprises. Just as it was felt that poor citizens of the USA and UK could best be helped by allowing them to help themselves by becoming less dependent on state benefits, saving their money and becoming more entrepreneurial, the New Right felt poor states needed to keep their own finances in order and allow the invisible hand of market forces, rather than handouts, to fuel their development.

Hence the agenda of international development politics in the 1980s and early 1990s was once again chiefly informed by the Economic Liberal orthodoxy but a purer more 'fundamentalist' orthodoxy than that seen in the 1950s and 1960s. Most notably, Japanese and East Asian state-led industrialisation was marginalised from the new discourse through Japanese fears of provoking further hostility from the US and Western European governments who were already at loggerheads with them over levels of protectionism and the persistent running of a trade deficit (Payne 2005: 77). Of course, not all of the First World shared this purist position but the balance of ideological and economic power within the North had shifted towards Washington.

## 1990s and 2000s – Post-Washington Consensus

From the 1990s, however, we have witnessed the renaissance of an NIEO-like agenda and a *Post-Washington Consensus* emerge which, while still advocating economic development through modernisation, acknowledges structural failings in the contemporary global economic system. The New Right tide ebbed away in the 1990s as evidence of the limitations of purely free market solutions to poverty became apparent. The Asian Tigers had followed a broadly orthodox script (albeit with a stronger role for government than many Economic Liberals would favour) but many Global South countries found the prescription of opening up their economies to foreign competition a bitter medicine with no remedial effects. In Mozambique, for example, their once major cashew nut industry collapsed in the early 2000s when the government was compelled to stop subsidising the sector as a condition of World Bank loans. With more interventionist administrations coming into power in London and Washington civil society criticism of Structural Adjustment became more prominent and, as a consequence, the World Bank came to listen to different voices and further reorientated itself on a reformist and socially conscious path.

> The overall goal of development is therefore to increase the economic, political and civil rights of all people across gender, ethnic groups, religion, races, regions and countries.
>
> (World Bank 1991: 31)

**Box 18.5** Stiglitz, *Globalization and its Discontents* (2002)

US academic and government advisor Joseph Stiglitz was Chief Economist of the World Bank from 1997 to 2000 when he was forced out of his post for his outspoken criticism of 'free market fundamentalists' in his organisation and the IMF and WTO. He subsequently became the leading voice for the Post-Washington Consensus, setting out his vision most clearly in his work *Globalization and its Discontents*:

> Even if Smith's invisible hand were relevant for advanced industrialized countries the required conditions were not satisfied in developing countries. The market system requires clearly established property rights and the courts to enforce them.
>
> (Stiglitz 2002: 74)

Notwithstanding Stiglitz's exit, the World Bank has continued on a reformist path and is now generally accepted to be a much more socially oriented set of institutions than the IMF or other global economic fora like the World Trade Organisation set up in 1995. Even under the stewardship of some ultra-conservative US-appointed presidents, a reformist approach has persisted since Social Policy and Development Studies perspectives have become established among staff previously dominated by traditional economists and financiers. Hence loans for development projects are now only approved after carrying out an Environmental Impact Assessment and the implementation of 'gender mainstreaming' measures to ensure that the marginalisation of women does not occur.

The World Trade Organisation, while undoubtedly dominated in decision-making terms by the Global North, has nevertheless given a prominent platform for the Global South to again project its voice. Global civil society, with campaigns such as Make Poverty History has also played its part in giving momentum to an agenda for reform. Hence some of the NIEO demands, having been largely ignored in the 1980s, have come back to the fore and, to some extent, been acted upon.

In line with this Post-Washington Consensus, and in order to move international development policy beyond rhetoric and build a genuine consensus, a new global reformist agenda – the Millennium Development Goals (MDGs) – was adopted by the UN General Assembly in 2000. Importantly, unlike the NIEO, the MDGs were also adopted by the IMF, World Bank, Organisation for Economic Cooperation and Development and G7: institutions dominated by the Global North and with more political muscle than the UN's talking shop.

*Source:* Getty Images

**The Millennium Development Goals set pragmatic and verifiable targets by which the international community can be judged.**

## Case study: The Millennium Development Goals

Goal 1: Reduce extreme poverty and hunger by half
Goal 2: Achieve universal primary education
Goal 3: Promote gender equality and empower women
Goal 4: Reduce child mortality by two-thirds
Goal 5: Reduce maternal mortality by three-quarters
Goal 6: Reverse the spread of HIV/AIDS, malaria and other diseases
Goal 7: Ensure environmental sustainability
Goal 8: Develop a Global Partnership for Development (fair trade and more aid)

As can be seen the MDGs are far from a utopian wish list and represent an attempt to set pragmatic and verifiable targets by which the international community can be judged. The baselines for the calculations are the various indicators as of 1990 and the judgement on meeting the goals will be made in 2015.

Progress towards meeting the Millennium Development Goals in 2015 can best be described as 'mixed'. The proportion of the world living on less than $1.25 has fallen significantly but hunger levels have not improved. The World Food Programme estimates that the number of malnourished people in the world topped the 1 billion mark for the first time in 2009, significantly up on the 1990 level (WFP 2009). On unpicking these figures a general trend for all the goals emerges. Asia, Latin America and North Africa have seen significant progress, and are likely to meet many of the targets on a regional basis, but Sub-Saharan Africa is out of step

with this improvement. Universal primary education is close to a reality in Asia and Latin America but over a quarter of Sub-Saharan African children still do not attend school. More girls have come to be enrolled in schools across the Global South but gender equality in 2015 is not a likely prospect. Similarly, child and maternal mortality rates have fallen significantly in much of the Global South but have not improved (and have even deteriorated) in much of Sub-Saharan Africa. Although significant funds have been mobilised for international programmes combating AIDS, malaria and tuberculosis, these diseases show little sign of abating in the near future, with Sub-Saharan Africa again most afflicted. The goal of environmental sustainablity is, in itself, a mixed picture. The sub-aim of reducing by half the number of people without access to clean water is on target but indicators for deforestation, fish stocks and biodiversity have actually worsened. The notion of establishing a global partnership by 2015 has also made limited progress. By then it is likely only a small number of countries will be meeting the target of giving 0.7 per cent of their GDP in foreign aid. Freeing up agricultural trade has also proved a difficult concession to wrest from the Global North.

 **Would you support you and/or your country's citizens contributing more in taxes towards development in the Global South?**

Not everyone, of course, is subsumed within the Post-Washington Consensus, broad church though it is. To the left Structuralists still contend that development is impossible in a capitalist world and see salvation as only coming once globalisation eats itself and a socialist revolution follows. At the other end of the spectrum, Economic Liberal purists resent the dilution of their credo and – in a case of right meeting left – see Northern interventions in the South as merely reproducing dependency. From this perspective, market forces not handouts are the best way to encourage the poor to drag themselves out of the gutter. Hence economist Peter Bauer's assertion that: 'aid is a phenomenon whereby poor people in rich countries are taxed to support the life-styles of rich people in poor countries' (Bauer 1976: 115).

Some thinkers and activists have come to question development as a concept altogether. 'Post development theory' rejects the whole notion of development as has emerged in either the orthodox or reformist forms and its coalescence in the Post-Washington Consensus. Influenced by Critical Theory (see Chapter 9) some writers have, since the early 1990s, challenged the ontology (meaning) of 'development' as a Northern construct. Majid Rahnema, for example, has defined development as: 'an ideology that was born and refined in the North, mainly to meet the needs of the dominant powers in search of a more "appropriate" tool for their economic and geopolitical expansion' (Rahnema 1997: 379).

## Conclusions

Opponents of capitalism will, of course, continue to reject any agenda that is about the preservation of the Liberal International Economic Order, however socially oriented and reformist it may be. The rise of a powerful transnational social movement rallying against the inequities of globalisation over the past decade and the sudden downturn of the global economy in 2008, resulting from anarchic private banking practices, offer some hope for the radicals that capitalism is a doomed venture

The radicals, however, are increasingly on the margins of the discourse of international development policy. The Post-Washington Consensus is far more consensual than what preceded it and broad global agreement on a reformist Liberal path seems to be well-established. 'The principal achievement of the Post Washington Consensus was to head off opposition to the most fundamental principles of a liberal international economic order by coopting potentially challenging ideas, bringing them into the service of the neo-liberal mainstream and rendering their radicalism redundant' (Payne 2005: 89).

At the 2009 G20 Summit the world's leading economic powers (including countries like Brazil, China, South Africa, India and Mexico) – which had by now superseded the G7 in significance – reaffirmed their commitment to development in spite of the pressing concern to re-establish their own economic growth. Ideas like IMF reform were also re-aired and a commitment to the Millennium Development Goals re-stated, this time with Global North countries compelled to acquiesce to them.

Dependency Theory could be applied well to the experiences of countries like Mexico and Brazil in the 1940s but, in the twenty-first century, it is probably not a realistic prospect for any country to cut itself off from the global economy. North Korea's attempts at self-reliance (added to the pursuit of nuclear weapons technology) resulted in the 1990s famine which has killed hundreds of thousands. Development policies have sometimes been counter-productive and sometimes self-serving for the Global North but criticising past practice can be used constructively to improve future policy rather than just to pick holes in it (Ziai 2004).

Without doubt, the economic gap between the world's rich and poor continues to widen and many countries remain undeveloped and appear unlikely to develop in the foreseeable future. If we return to the Rawls test of gauging fairness in the distribution of resources, the onset of political globalisation from the mid twentieth century could be considered just since, in spite of the growing disparity between rich and poor, the quality of life has improved for nearly all the people of all countries. Across the board increases in life expectancy and, more latterly and indicatively, of Human Development Index (HDI) scores support this. Of all states in the world only Zambia recorded a lower HDI rating in 1999 compared to 1975 (Goklany 2002). A recent drop off in HDI of some states, however, largely due to a rising problem of disease, suggests that global governance is beginning to fail the Rawls test. Some sixteen Sub-Saharan African states experienced a decline in HDI between 1990 and 2007 (UNDP 2008). The overall trend is still upwards but a significant enough number of exceptions to the 'rule' have emerged – too many to be easily put down to chance or purely internal factors. The Post-Washington Consensus has put development more to the forefront of international politics than ever but the persistence of absolute poverty in a world of sufficient food and resources for all is indicative of a similarly persistent global political failing.

## Resource section

## Questions

1.  Evaluate the past and present impact of the Global South on global economic policy.

2.  Why has the traditional approach to understanding economic development been challenged and how far has this challenge succeeded?

3.  Is the achievement of economic development by the 'Newly Industrialised Countries' in recent decades proof that this is also possible for the rest of the Global South?

## Recommended reading

**Payne, A. (2005)** *The Politics of Unequal Development* **(Basingstoke UK and New York: Palgrave)**
A well-researched study chronicling the progress of international policy and theory on development issues since the end of the Second World War. An insightful study of how and why different prevailing schools of thought on development have emerged over time.

**Regan, C. (ed.) (2006)** *80:20. Development in an Unequal World* **(5th edn, Educating and Acting for a Better World)**
A glossy and accessible volume, designed partly to appeal to sixth formers, but still an authoritative introduction to the various themes of development and global poverty suitable for university study.

## Useful websites

**Human Development Report, http://hdr.undp.org/en/**
See the annually collated data and analysis broken down into sub-categories and individually for most countries of the world

**Millennium Development Goals, http://www.undp.org/mdg/**
See the targets and sub-targets in full and regularly updated analysis of progress towards meeting them.

**World Food Programme, http://www.wfp.org/**

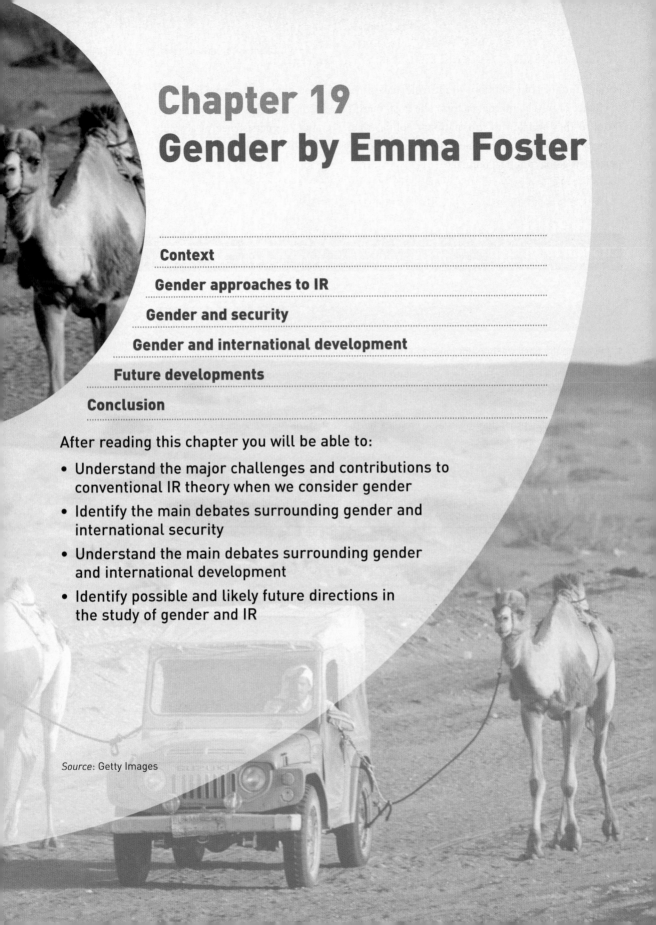

# Chapter 19
# Gender by Emma Foster

After reading this chapter you will be able to:

- Understand the major challenges and contributions to conventional IR theory when we consider gender

- Identify the main debates surrounding gender and international security

- Understand the main debates surrounding gender and international development

- Identify possible and likely future directions in the study of gender and IR

*Source*: Getty Images

## Introductory box: Gender inequality on a global scale

Although women are the 'cornerstones of economic life' (Steans 2006: 99) labouring as farmers, workers and carers, their work is undervalued across the globe, often dismissed as 'women's work' and receiving lower pay or no financial remuneration at all. Women make up the majority of workers in many export processing zones (EPZs) that are crucial to global market chains. For instance in Bangladesh women make up 85 per cent of the workers in EPZs and in Nicaragua they make up 90 per cent. This work is almost always low paid and low status yet is crucial to international trade. Women, on average, are paid 17 per cent less than men for the same work. Similarly, in terms of political equality, women are still very much under-represented. Although the number of women in national assemblies has increased by 8 per cent in the last decade, reaching 18.4 per cent in 2008, this is far from reaching the goal of gender parity whereby neither men nor women hold more than 60 per cent of the seats. In fact, at the current rate it is unlikely that developing countries will achieve parity until 2045 (UNIFEM 2009).

Beyond economic and political inequality more drastic forms of gender inequality can be recognised globally. For example there is what, economist and development theorist, Amartya Sen calls 'natality inequality' (2001: 35) which refers to the use of sex-selective abortion, whereby female fetuses are aborted due to the preference for boy children in **patriarchal** countries and regions. This has had an impact on female to male population ratios in states such as China, South Korea and India and elsewhere in South and East Asia. For example, in India in 2001 the ratio of boys to girls aged 0 to 6 years was 927 girls to every 1,000 boys, a ratio gap that has increased since 1981 when the figures were 962 girls to 1,000 boys. This difference in sex ratios is considered to be, in part, an outcome of prenatal sex determination – through ultrasound scanning which is widely available in India even in rural areas – and the decision then to terminate unborn females (Jha et al. 2006: 211). The favouring of boy children over girls is an issue of international relevance and is an extreme manifestation of gender inequality.

Until fairly recently the field of International Relations has been completely dominated by men and has, therefore, been open to the charge of ignoring the situations of women described above. However, some feminists have sought to rectify what they refer to as the 'invisibilty' of women in IR by highlighting the crucial part(s) women play – and therefore the importance of gender – in IR. Above all, studying gender and IR highlights the inequalities between men and women; or in other words, outlines unequal gender relations internationally.

## Context

Gender is a complex term that refers to masculinity and femininity and how this is acquired or learned by people. Gender works as a framework that allows people to categorise or interpret bodies. In other words, gender is a way of 'understanding' oneself, as either a man or a woman, and for 'understanding' others, as either men or women. Moreover, through this 'understanding' a variety of (gendered) relationships can be organised. Often, as feminists have sought to point out, these gendered relationships are characterised through unequal systems of power which subordinate women to men. Historically gender has been considered as 'naturally' linked to a body's biological sex whereby, femininity or feminine behaviour belongs to female bodies and masculinity or masculine behaviour belongs to male bodies. In turn, this has worked to justify the subordination of women to men as natural and, therefore, correct. Moreover, this 'naturalisation' of gender, by this rationale, has also worked to fix people's identities. What this means is that historically people born male who acted in ways that were considered feminine (and vice versa) have been considered to be unnatural or abnormal.

The idea that if you are born male it is 'natural' for you to act in a masculine way and if you are born female it is 'natural' for you to act in a feminine way has shaped International Relations in a number of ways. Common understanding is that those born female are considered to be passive, nurturing, caring, dependent and in need of protection (largely legitimised by their potential reproductive roles as mothers) and that those born male are considered to be aggressive, strong, independent and protective. This has shaped IR practice considerably. First, it is this stereotyping which has arguably led to the absence of women in IR. For example, women have not been considered suited to lead states or militaries or even to fight in war, as they are 'naturally' not built for this.

However, many feminists and gender theorists who work in the field of IR contend that women have and do play a part in IR and that the problem has been that women have previously been written out; their roles as army wives, the producers of export goods, symbols of nation and so on have been ignored offering a distorted narrative in IR scholarship. Moreover, gender relations have also been written out and the masculine perspective that has been offered by IR scholars and actors has been considered the objective and complete one.

## Gender approaches to IR

Traditionally, like many other academic disciplines, IR has been male dominated resulting in a gender bias in the subject. Moreover, in terms of IR practice, women have been and are under-represented at national and international level politics. This is made clear by the focus on the few women who have made it to positions of formal institutional power such as Margaret Thatcher (Prime Minister of Britain 1979–90) or Hillary Clinton (who has had a long running political career in the USA). Politics and International Relations scholars, as well as the media, have over-focused on these women as curiosities. This demonstrates how they are exceptions to the masculine norm of national and world politics. As the IR feminist scholar Christine Sylvester notes, this focus is a marker of the fascination with women who are 'out of line, out of place, out of their minds' (1996: 255). The fact that these women in positions of power are given much consideration shows that they are the exception rather than the rule. Accordingly, feminist scholarship has worked to position gender more visibly within the academic discipline of IR (for more details of feminism and feminist IR see Chapter 10). In addition, in terms of IR practice, it seems that decision-making processes are becoming increasingly 'gendered', that is taking gender into account as policy is created and implemented. It is becoming acknowledged that policy decisions affect men and women differently. This is true in terms of international security and international development, the two areas we will focus on in the following sections.

## Box 19.1 Key readings in gender and IR

There was little reference to gender or feminism within the discipline of IR until the very latter stages of the twentieth century. Saying that, there were a few related literatures published prior to 1985 that are considered to be housed within the realms of International Development and Political Economy; the most seminal of these being the classic feminist work of Esther Boserup, namely, *Women's Role in Economic Development* published in 1970. In this study, Boserup documented the role that women of the 'developing' world played in terms of production, particularly in relation to agriculture. Other works prior to the late 1980s that could be considered to fall into International Political Economy and Development studies and which have been influenced by feminist or gender insights are those of the dependency theory feminists. One example of this would be June Nash and Maria Patricia Fernandez Kelly's 1983 edited collection entitled *Women, Men and the International Division of Labour.* This collection of articles sought to expose how the gendered divisions of labour worked to sustain (and were a microcosm of) unequal international economic systems.

Apart from International Political Economy and Development Studies, feminist and female scholars and political activists have been committed to what one may term 'peace studies' before the late 1980s. For example, Helen Caldicott founded the Women's Action for Nuclear Disarmament (WAND) in 1982 after the 1978 publication of her groundbreaking work *Nuclear Madness.* During this era there were a number of female activists campaigning for peace (such as the protests at Greenham Common in the early

1980s) whereby women sought to demand a withdrawal from what they saw as masculine-driven militarism. Political activism that allied women with peace corresponded to an increasing academic literature on feminist peace ethics.

However, it was not until 1988, with a special issue of the International Relations journal *Millennium* that gender began to be explicitly linked to the discipline of IR itself (Steans 2006: 1–2). This special issue was centered on the question: *'where are the women in International Relations?'.* A year later the seminal text by Cynthia Enloe (1989) entitled *Bananas, Beaches and Bases* was published. This work directly applies feminism to IR by convincingly attempting to write women into the practices of international relations through a series of stories that increase the visibility of women as producers (similar to the work done on international development and gender) or involved in security issues (similar to some of the work associated with feminist peace studies). Arguably this work has had such an impact on IR that the position of men and masculinities has/is also beginning to take shape with increasing momentum. Authors, such as Sandra Whitworth (2004), Marysia Zalewski and Jane Parpart (1998), and Parpart and Zalewski (2008) are interrogating the position of men and masculinities within IR. In fact Zalewski and Parpart have asked and re-asked the 'man question' in two insightful edited collections; namely *The Man Question in International Relations* (1998) and *Rethinking the Man Question* (2008). Within and outwith IR there is a significant feminist literature to investigate.

## Gender and security

### Widening notions of (in)security

An important area of IR that has received a great deal of feminist and gender based scholarship and activism is the area of security studies. Traditionally in IR, it has been the state's security which has been a focal point (see Chapter 5). A secure state is one where national boundaries can be upheld through its economic and military capabilities. However, feminist scholars, in line with critical security scholars (see Chapter 26), have effectively worked to redefine notions of security. They see security to be multidimensional and multifaceted, going beyond just the security or insecurity of a state. For these feminists, such as J. Ann Tickner, security threats include 'domestic violence, rape, poverty, gender subordination, ecological destruction' (Tickner and Sjoberg 2007: 194) as well as war; as with IR more generally, feminists have broadened the meaning of security. In fact, as security becomes such a broad term encompassing state, community and individual or personal security, some feminist scholars have demonstrated that by securing one of these elements (for example the state) another may be rendered insecure (for example marginalised women).

Tickner (1992) contends that IR is built on masculinist notions of human nature which perpetuate insecurity. She argues that IR is built on the premise of a Hobbesian state of nature, a war of all against all, which is played out repeatedly. This creates a circular problem whereby when one state heightens their security another state recognises this as a threat, steps up its own military preparations and so heightens tensions and the possibility of conflict. This prevailing threat increases insecurity for all. She argues that economic

### Box 19.2 Gender/security literature

The widened view of insecurity and the notion of gendered lenses has influenced feminist scholarship in international security. For example, Katherine Moon (1997) has written a convincing account of the impact of international security issues on women's lives in her study of US military bases in South Korea. In this piece she notes how prostitution around these military bases was 'cleaned up'. She details that women working as prostitutes became the subject of increasing monitoring and health checks, in order to create an 'improved' situation for US troops who were looking to withdraw from the area. This study identifies how increasing national security (by encouraging the US troops to stay) worked to undermine the personal or individual security of some women. Furthermore, there is contemporary scholarship on gender and security that focuses at length on International, or more specifically United Nations, responses to insecurity. For example, Sandra Whitworth's *Men, Militarism and UN Peacekeeping* (2004) which, as the title suggests, focuses on men and masculinities and questions the notion of masculinised warriors and military success. There is also work by Laura J. Shepherd, *Gender, Violence and Security* (2008) which investigates UN security policy by focusing on gender. Shepherd outlines the way in which gendered assumptions and notions of gendered violence underpin these security discourses, shaping the implementation of such policy and, in turn, contributing to policy failure.

hardship is also a form of insecurity. She notes that the international political economy is based on the liberal rational man and has, therefore, ignored that women and men are differently affected by economic transformations. In saying this she contends that gender and IPE/IR scholars have failed to recognise the wealth of information exposed by women/gender and development scholars (which shall be detailed more thoroughly in the next section). Tickner concludes that we should adopt a 'non-gendered global security' whereby one remains vigilant and reflexive about how insecurities are constructed through gendered 'lenses'.

## Gender dynamics and combat

Returning to perhaps the most tangible expression of insecurity, namely war, it seems that women have been written out of these historical narratives (arguably because they are less likely to be soldiers, prominent politicians or heads of state – direct actors in the exercise of war). However, this narrative ignores the fact that women are affected by wars. More so than ever before, women are more likely to be 'officially' involved in combat (Steans 2006: 49) despite controversies over the issue. These controversies include the notion that women are less inclined to kill due to their maternal instincts and that women in the armed forces are a distraction to their male counterparts. The latter part of the argument infers that men will be distracted from their 'duty' by women as they may feel the need to protect women soldiers and also because women are seen as a sexual temptation.

There is something about women fighting in war that is seen as 'unnatural'. This unnaturalness is a by-product of ideas on gender which suggest that women are naturally passive, peaceful and in need of protection while men are aggressive and built to protect (women, children and nation), making them suited to war situations. Despite the increased number of women taking part in active combat, the response to those positions in the military exemplifies gender ideologies. In all, women in the military are still met with much resistance. This is due to wider gender ideologies and the notion that women act as a distraction to their male counterparts. These ideologies are powerful myths in societies and are not based in biological fact. Nevertheless the power of these myths works to shape war scenarios by sustaining the masculinism traditionally tied to it and also the idea that women (and children) are those that ought to be protected while men are the protectors.

Traditionally as they are more likely to be involved in direct combat men have made up the main casualties of war. However, in recent times women and children have been more likely to be affected as civilian casualties have dramatically risen from about 10 per cent at the beginning of the twentieth century to around 90 per cent by the end (Tickner and Sjoberg 2007: 193). Apart from those caught in the crossfire, women are affected by war in a number of other ways. For example, women are arguably particularly hard hit by the economic consequences of war. This is because in many societies women are the primary caregivers in the family so problems caused by conflict regarding access to resources, such as food, water and clothing, is especially problematic for women looking after a family.

## Box 19.3 Debates over women on the 'frontline'

In 2001, the British Chief of Defence Staff, Admiral Sir Michael Boyce stated that he had no more problem with women 'being killed on the battlefield, shot down or being mutilated' than men. He argued that if women meet the training (physical and mental requirements) for fighting in direct frontline combat then there should be no restrictions. However, a review in 2002 on women serving in 'close combat' concluded that women should continue to be excluded from various types of combat. Currently women cannot be considered for 33 per cent of posts in the army, 29 per cent in the Navy and 4 per cent in the RAF. Moreover, women are not allowed to serve as Royal Marines, in the Household Cavalry, or any of the infantry regiments.

Although the 1975 Sex Discrimination Act sought to rectify inequalities between men and women in the workplace a sub-clause of the act states that women can be excluded from military posts if they are seen to have a negative impact on military effectiveness. This sub-clause was upheld in the European Court of Human Justice in 1999. This leads one to question the possible negative impacts of women serving in the military. Often these justifications are heavily linked to gender ideologies, stereotypes and myths. For example, one justification is that women are less aggressive, need more provocation to become aggressive and are more likely to fear the consequences of aggressive behaviour. A second justification for the exclusion of women is that they are distracting to their male counterparts and inhibit group cohesion necessary for war situations. Moreover, there is a wider societal view that mothers in particular should not undertake dangerous occupations due to their responsibilities at home.

Arguably, these views are more to do with gender stereotypes or discourses than biological fact. Many points of contention could be raised in response to the justifications for women's exclusion in close combat. For example, are all women less aggressive and likely to fear the consequences of their aggressive behaviour? Secondly, are male soldiers easily distracted because women represent sex and sexuality and/or the need for protection? Finally, why are soldiers who are mothers considered to be behaving negligently when their male (father) counterparts are not held up to the same scrutiny? Looking at the history of women's experience in Vietnam, including the Vietnam War but also pre-dating it by at least 2,000 years, is in itself enough to dispel these as particular constructions rather than biologically rooted (see Block 2009: 65–78).

Another issue of concern to gender theorists in international security is the direct targeting of women, particularly by rape. During military conflict rape is often used as a tool to achieve military gains. It goes largely under-reported as the victims of rape may be ashamed or may not have the ability to report incidents for various reasons, such as ineffective judicial systems. Nevertheless, it is known that sexual abuse and rape is rife in some war-torn states. For example, in the Democratic Republic of Congo (DRC) and in Darfur rape is a huge problem with typically many hundreds of reported incidents per month in areas such as North Kivu. Similarly, in Sierra Leone (50 per cent) and in parts of Liberia (90 per cent) a high percentage of all women and girls have experienced sexual violence of some kind during times of conflict (Refugee Council Report 2009).

Rape in times of conflict can be considered a symbolic act primarily affecting women. As mothers of the nation, the next generation of people, women are symbolic of maintaining the social order. Women's bodies are in turn targeted by aggressors to disturb the social order of a nation or race of people. Practically, rape works to displace people and destroy communities in areas that are being fought over as people and communities wish to escape violence. It is used as an 'informal' way to gain victory in conflicts. A report for

*Source: Reuters/David Mercado*

**Can society's reluctance to see women on the frontline be explained by constructed gender ideologies or simple biological fact?**

the United Nations Development Fund for Women (UNIFEM) noted that rape, '[l]ong seen as the collateral damage of conflict . . . has become a means of achieving military ends. Rape under orders is not merely an aggressive manifestation of sexuality, but a sexual manifestation of aggression' (UNIFEM 2009).

### Box 19.4 Sexual violence and rape in DRC

One country where sexual violence towards women is a particular problem is the Democratic Republic of Congo. According to the World Health Organisation (WHO) there were at least 40,000 cases of rape or sexual violence in the five years following the DRC's most recent outbreak of conflict in 1998. This is even more concerning considering that rape often remains unreported, which means that the figure of 40,000 is likely to be a modest estimate. In Western societies rape is considered to be a demonstration of power of one person over another. However, rape in conflict is often a demonstration of one faction or country's power over another. In light of this, the UN, focusing on sexual violence in DRC, have pledged to put into practice procedures which not only help the survivors of sexual violence but also assist in healing the community of the wider socio-economic repercussions of rape as a tool of conflict.

## Gender and international development

### The dawn of gender and international development

International development and issues of production are perhaps the first to have been considered through gender analysis or influenced by feminist theory in a way that has impacted both policy and academia. The empiricist feminist or liberal feminist approach, which argued that liberal economic approaches to development are correct but that women should be included on an equal basis to men, has had an impact relating to gender and international development (and, therefore, gender and IR) both in theory and practice.

These early gender and development scholars, like Esther Boserup, noticed and problematised the fact that women were not considered in terms of development practices, suggesting as early as 1970 that women should be considered (added in) and have equal access to the opportunities that come with international development and modernisation. These feminist scholars pointed out that previous reference to women and development, by development organisations and practitioners, perceived women's economic activity to be in the realm of the household or domestic (private) sphere and relating primarily to reproduction. In other words, that women's involvement in the economy was seen as largely informal and related to their domestic roles as mothers and wives. Development agendas that were directed at women before the 1970s tended to be connected to 'women's issues' or what Caroline Moser (1989) has termed 'welfare approaches'. These approaches basically included population control, maternal and child health and nutrition (Momsen 2004). Accordingly, although women had been recognised in terms of their reproductive capacities during this time, their roles in production were largely ignored. For example, women's roles in agricultural production were not considered by development organisations.

Boserup offered an important empiricist/liberal feminist challenge to the way that development had been previously played out. She argued that encouraging gender equality worked to boost economic efficiency, to ensure that women as well as men in the developing world could reap the benefits of modernisation. In fact, some scholars (see Momsen 2004) suggest that it was Boserup's work that inspired or initiated the UN decade for women (1976–85). The UN decade for women was a set time period, recommended by the Commission on the Status of Women (CSW), to address the needs of women globally in relation to equality, peace and development. Furthermore, Boserup and her contemporaries, through highlighting the particular contribution which women made to economic development and also the effects of economic development processes on women, influenced the international policy agenda – an influence which still carries a great deal of weight today (Rai 2005).

Throughout the 1970s Boserup's work contributed to policy formulation, inspiring an approach to international development called Women in Development (WID) which by the mid 1970s was institutionalised – that is, promoted within international development policy. WID became a legitimate and respected area of study in academia (particularly sociology and anthropology), making it a focus of both development practice and theory.

Indeed, the lobby activities of WID proponents did work to raise the profile of women in relation to international development by highlighting the effects that development had on women and women's interests more widely. During the United Nations (UN) decade for women (1976–85) WID was very influential. The major outcome of this decade was the creation of a plan of action entitled the 'Forward Looking Strategies' (FLS). The principles of the Forward Looking Strategies were to create equality between the sexes, for women to be fully integrated into the mainstream of economic development, and for women to be offered equal access to education and resources. These strategies currently remain resonant with the gender and development aims of the UN.

## WID and the Millennium Development Goals (MDGs)

Due to the criticisms outlined below, the WID approach is seen as quite unfashionable in contemporary scholarship. However, in terms of policy the liberal feminist emphasis remains largely intact (Rai 2005). A good example of this can be seen if we look at the Millennium Development Goals (MDGs). The MDGs represent a global partnership that has grown from the commitments and targets established at the world summits of the 1990s. Responding to the world's main development challenges and to the calls of civil society, the MDGs promote poverty reduction, education, maternal health, gender equality, and aim at combating child mortality, AIDS and other diseases. Set for the year 2015, the MDGs are an agreed set of goals that can be achieved if all actors work together and do their part. Poor countries have pledged to govern better, and invest in their people through healthcare and education. Rich countries have pledged to support them, through aid, debt relief, and fairer trade (UNDP 2009).

The third MDG (MDG3) specifically focuses on gender – or, more accurately, gender equality. This focus is strongly influenced by liberal feminist principles. For example, the targets for this development goal which seeks to create gender equality and empowerment for women are: to eliminate the unequal access between girls and boys in terms of primary and secondary education; to increase the number of women in wage labour that is non-agricultural; to increase the proportion of seats that women share in national parliaments.

These targets, then, are looking to integrate women into the system but not to overturn it. Moreover, it is looking at production in relation to wage labour but not reproduction. Overall, it is seeking to improve women's education and skills so that they can compete more readily with men in the labour market. Indeed, with regard to the MDG education targets, girls' education has been expanding all over the world. However, this expansion has not been occurring fast enough to ensure a basic education for the millions of girls still out of school. The prospect of some countries failing to meet the MDG by the target year of 2015 is extremely likely. About two-thirds of countries and territories reached gender parity in primary education by the target year of 2005, but in many other countries, especially in Sub-Saharan Africa, girls are still disadvantaged. Indeed, there are important regional differences. The largest gender gaps in terms of primary level schooling are in Africa, the Middle East and South Asia. Moreover, gender disparities are greatest in rural

### Box 19.5 Criticisms of WID

The main criticisms of the WID approach include:

- This is an 'add women and stir' approach to international development which does not seek to transform the traditional (socio-economic) systems which are the root of women's oppression
- Integrating women into the mainstream does not allow for women to choose the type of development they want
- This approach assumes that women of the 'developing' world want a 'Western' model of development, which is in itself patriarchal. In

other words, these women swap one type of male domination (cultural patriarchy) for another (Western patriarchy)

- This approach universalises the aims and objectives of all women globally – that is, to participate in the labour market on an equal basis to men
- This approach, by not disrupting the system, emulates men in a male-biased environment. It focuses on the importance of production in male terms and, in so doing, ignores the importance of the reproductive side of women's lives

areas and among poor households in these areas. So, although successful in some regions, MDG3 has yet to be realised, with a third of countries unlikely to reach the 2015 goals. This potential failure may, in part, be due to some of the theoretical problems with WID approaches to development outlined in Box 19.5.

Due to WID's emphasis on modernisation theory and their liberal feminist positioning, the WID approach came up against much criticism from Marxist feminist influenced development theorists. Perhaps the most interesting of these was the criticism that it followed a liberal feminist agenda of 'bringing women in' or 'women as addendum' vis-à-vis development issues. Due to its liberal motivation, the WID subfield of development studies went only as far as calling for equity between 'men' and 'women', but by no means did it question the fundamental assumptions and Western stereotypes regarding gender (Marchand and Parpart 1995: 13). The approach treated women as homogenous and disregarded other identity intersections they may have (race, class, culture, etc.). In other words, it supposed all women were after the same goals – that is, to be active participants in accessing economic wealth. This universalises a Western women's perspective across the globe, suggesting all women – despite class, ethnicity, age, geographical location, etc. – have the same wants and needs.

In response to these types of criticisms the latter part of the 1970s saw the more radical Women and Development (WAD) approach influencing development dialogues. Gender and Development scholar Janet Momsen notes that the WAD approach proposed '[t]he alternative vision put forward, of development *with* women, demanded not just a bigger piece of someone else's pie, but a whole new dish, prepared, baked and distributed equally' (2004: 11). WAD, unlike WID, sought to reorganise the structure of development. The main focus of the WAD approach is a direct critique of the liberal emphasis within the WID approach. They argued that women have always been part of development processes and, therefore, the idea of integrating women into development processes was a myth. Rather they suggest that what should be considered is the relationship between *women and development* processes. So the WAD perspective looks at how the integration of women in development sustains the existing international structures of inequality – namely, the exploitation of cheap labour and resources from the 'developing world', the ex-colonies and women.

With its roots in Marxist feminism, however, it is arguable that the WAD approach fails to analyse the problems particular to women since both sexes are seen as disadvantaged by the structure of global capitalism and class oppression. WAD did not draw strong enough links between patriarchy, differing modes of production and the subordination/oppression/exploitation of women in particular. WAD was criticised for not theorising gender and class sufficiently. Moreover, like WID, WAD failed to account for women's reproductive roles as it was preoccupied with their productive roles. And finally, again like WID, WAD concentrates on women as its sole focus rather than gender as a relationship more generally, so is theoretically problematic. For Marxist feminist orientated WAD theorists, gender is also an observable and significant factor in the current global division of labour. Since the 1970s and 1980s, across the world, employers have sought to undermine trade unions in order to achieve maximum labour flexibility. Some employers have relocated abroad in order to enjoy the benefits of cheap labour. Frequently this labour force is made up of women. Women are paid less, because women's work is constructed as bringing in a second wage. This has been at a time when the number of female headed households is actually rising. The impact of neo-liberal development strategies such as structural adjustment is one example of how international institutions both reflect and perpetuate gender inequalities.

 **Box 19.6 The gender problems associated with SAPs**

Structural Adjustment Programmes (SAPs) are loans which are provided by the World Bank and IMF to nation states considered to be in economic difficulties. These loans were given out, largely in the 1980s, to stabilise the economies of poor countries. However, the loans came with conditions, founded on neo-liberal principles, whereby the recipient country should reduce the role of the state in favour of market principles. It was assumed that reducing state intervention would create a pathway towards accelerated economic development. However, SAPs did not target women or recognise the importance of gender. As such SAPs in relation to gender have been criticised in two main ways. First, as the state was reduced due to the conditionality of the loan agreement, so were government run welfare strategies. This meant that the most vulnerable groups in society, which includes women and children, were more at risk from deteriorating welfare standards. Secondly, due to the existing sociocultural beliefs surrounding gender, for example the idea that women's place is in the home and not in wage work, the benefits of economic growth through SAPs benefited men more than women as men were the ones working in the growing economies. It is argued that SAPs, although appearing gender neutral, were in fact biased because they focused on areas of employment and efficiency that were male orientated and ignored the position and work done by women, which is traditionally more domestically based.

Throughout the 1980s a new approach was sought to rectify problems regarding gender and development. Backgrounded by the UN Decade for Women (1976–85), the critical feminist and to some extent post-colonial feminist (see Chapter 10) approach to 'women's' development was accompanied by the increased involvement of Southern perspectives. This worked to move the debate around what has been entitled the Gender and Development (GAD) approach. Here, due to the underpinnings of a more theoretically robust critical/post-colonial feminism and the input from Southern women, the intersection of race, class and gender became visible and central to development dialogues. Therefore, the GAD approach offers a holistic perspective and aims to investigate all areas of women's lives.

This approach tends to look at gender relations, rather than just women, and to highlight the contribution women make in relation to the public arena of wage work/ production and the private arena of domestic work (reproduction and non-commodity production). Moreover, it questions the basis of assigning different roles to different sexes. GAD represents an insightful shift in women/gender and development discourses as it is rooted in the notions of constructivism (see Chapter 11). Although there is often a recognition of a 'real' biological sex, a great deal of emphasis is placed on the social construction of gender (and gender relations) intersected with issues of class, race and ethnicity.

*Source: Getty Images/Eddie Gerald*

**Is this female oppression, or is it a symbol of identity and community?**

## Case study: The *hijab* – an IR and gender perspective

*Hijab*, meaning to cover, refers to the clothing worn by Islamic women such as the veil and a modest dress code. In Islamic culture this type of dress represents purity, privacy and morality and is a symbol of Islamic consciousness. Wearing the *hijab* is symbolic of Islamic culture and in this instance (as is often the case) women are the carriers or demonstrators of such culture.

Many academic debates, as well as policy and legislative activities, have been brought to the fore through the controversies of wearing the *hijab*. For example, to some scholars and commentators (feminist and otherwise) the *hijab* represents a form of female oppression tied to constraining Muslim women's freedom and sexuality, and exemplifying their subordinate status within Islamic communities. On the other hand, counter arguments from scholars of gender, race and ethnicity, such as some post-colonial feminists, suggest that the *hijab* offers a sense of identity and community for women. The wearing of the *hijab*, in this sense, is arguably enabling for Muslim women in order for them to signify their religion to other Muslims and to negotiate their identity within or in contrast to Western culture.

Internationally the wearing of the *hijab* is a particularly salient issue as it relates to matters of immigration and multiculturalism, also alluding to the relationship between nations. In some Western countries such as France and parts of Germany the wearing of the *hijab* has been banned in public educational and government spaces on the grounds that the state does not promote religious beliefs. For example in 2004, with the ethos of consolidating a secular state (separating the state from religion), the French Government banned the wearing of the *hijab*, along with any other religious symbols, in schools. This subsequently caused an international backlash

as pro-*hijab* Muslims, many of whom were women, protested outside French embassies in a number of countries including the UK. Moreover, the proponents of the hijab sought to lobby the European parliament to get the ban repealed.

Some Islamic countries, such as Egypt and Morocco, have also tried to distance themselves from the *hijab* as they see it as demonstrative of extreme Islamic fundamentalist beliefs. However, other Islamic countries, such as Iran, are trying to encourage the wearing of the *hijab* and are concerned about the growing numbers of women (named by the Iranian authorities as 'Western Dolls') who are choosing to dress in more 'Western' type clothing. This supposed spread of Western culture has become such a threat to the authorities in Iran that they have tried to impose traditional dress for women by force. For example, a woman can be imprisoned for up to two years for not covering her head and for dressing immodestly. However, given that these strong arm tactics were largely ineffective, some Iranians are beginning to attempt a compromise by redesigning the traditional clothes with a little more style and less of a uniform feel.

Overall, the wearing of the *hijab* has become, at least symbolically, an issue of international relations. Carried on women's bodies, it is arguably an expression of difference between Islamic culture and non-Islamic cultures in a post-9/11 era, whereby Islam has been *constructed* as synonymous with terrorist threat (see Chapter 11 for a discussion of the idea of 'construction').

 **In what ways does the controversy over the *hijab* highlight the inconsistencies between women's rights and cultural rights?**

## Future developments

## Men and masculinities

The future of gender and IR can be characterised by a movement away from focusing of women and towards looking at gender relations more holistically. This has meant that more scholars, rather than merely outlining the hardships that women face, are now interrogating the impact men and masculinities has in relation to IR theory and practice.

Men and masculinities is a relatively new topic of academic attention across the social sciences. The focus on masculinities highlights that not all men reap equal rewards under patriarchal systems or from just being men. Some men, due to their class, race or other identity intersections, receive more benefits than others. Some men are more powerful than others and this creates the idea of dominant masculinity which is also known as hegemonic masculinity. Hegemonic masculinity is the highest ranked form of masculinity in a given sociopolitical context and works to subordinate other forms of masculinity (such as homosexual masculinities) as well as women. It is this acknowledgement of a hierarchy of masculinities which is beginning to have an influence on the discipline of IR.

Arguably, this work on men and masculinities is a corrective to the focus on women in feminist IR. The focus on masculinities in IR highlights how an idea of dominant masculinity, as synonymous with authority, violence and power, has shaped and continues to shape IR practice. For example, gender/IR scholars Jane Parpart and Marysia Zalewski (2008: 4–6) point out that 9/11 worked to construct a new international arena based around potentially dangerous constructions of masculinity. They argue that this event wounded masculine pride in America as subordinated, Islamic and 'othered' masculinities humiliated America through the attacks on the World Trade Center. This wounded pride has led to a backlash which has fuelled the War on Terror and has further global ramifications based on masculinist heroism. However, the masculine hero versus the masculine enemy could be ultimately catastrophic with regard to global security.

## Queer Theory

Queer Theory is related to postmodern strands of feminism and gay and lesbian studies. It is based on the premise that stable sex, gender and sexuality categories do not exist. For example, just because you are born with female genitalia does not mean that you will/should act in feminine ways or that you will/should be attracted to masculine characteristics. In other words, Queer Theorists recognise identities – especially gender identities – as mythic and, therefore, potentially fluid. Also, Queer Theorists are critical of the system that makes heterosexuality seem natural and homosexuality appear inferior or abnormal in relation to it. Queer Theorists call this system heteronormativity.

Although it seems that Queer Theory is more about personal relationships and individual identities, numbers of scholars are using Queer Theory as a conceptual framework with global political implications. For example, in relation to international law Queer Theory can be used as a justification to extend existing legal frameworks to include the universal prohibition of homophobic abuse or the universal right to homosexual marriage. However, Queering international law, as well as other types of international relations subfields such as development, environment and security, means to be critical of the heterosexual assumptions that international legislation and policy are based upon. Moreover, it suggests that policy and legislation should be grounded in the idea that identities and relationships are Queer and therefore fluid, rather than rigidly heteronormative.

As an example of the above, Queer Theorists would argue that policies and legislation concerned with population are based on an idea of assumed and natural heterosexuality. In other words, policy makers and legislators, when dealing with issues of population reduction, inheritance law, taxation and welfare/social security, organise their policy and legislation around the framework of heterosexual kinships – namely married couples and their biological children. The knock-on effect of this presumed heterosexuality is to reinforce such relations as correct and superior to other forms of association. Therefore, to undermine the privileging of heterosexuality, more fluid and mobile forms of association need to underpin future policy and legislation.

## Conclusion

Sub-disciplines of IR, such as international development and peace studies, have increasingly been influenced and critiqued by feminists and gender scholars since the 1970s. Gender scholars in both security studies and international development began by pointing out that women have been rendered invisible or ignored while, in a practical sense, women and gender ideologies have always been crucial to both security and development. In terms of security, women have always been victims of war. For example, rape is often used as a tool of warfare as a symbolic act (of penetrating a nation through the mothers of the nation) and, as a practice to disturb the social order. Furthermore, women are increasingly involved in 'formal' combat as members of the armed forces. Similarly with development, feminists and gender scholars have sought to make women's role in economic development visible. For example, women produce export and subsistence products, reproduce the next generation of workers and are consumers. As such, feminist and gender scholars have sought to render women's roles in security and development visible.

Beyond looking at issues of security and development, contemporary gender scholars in the field of IR are further challenging IR theory and practice through men and masculinity studies and Queer Theory. Men and masculinity studies offers a corrective vision for IR whereby masculinities can be theorised and interrogated. Perhaps more ground-breaking is the addition of Queer Theory to perspectives on IR. Queer Theory, beyond challenging gendered assumptions and highlighting gender inequalities, challenges the notion of a natural and superior heterosexuality which is used in international policy and legislation formation.

Despite these successes, international development and security studies, along with IR generally, are still resistant to the contributions and challenges made by feminists, gender analysts and Queer Theorists. Moreover, complex gender inequalities are still very prevalent globally. As Sen notes: '[t]he afflicted world in which we live is characterized by a deeply unequal sharing of the burden of adversities between men and women' (2001: 35). As such, beyond presenting academic critiques that challenge mainstream or traditional IR scholars, feminist and gender-based scholarship remains extremely necessary in the contemporary world.

## Resource section

### Questions

1.  What are the feminist criticisms of mainstream/traditional IR?

2.  In what ways is the study of gender important to international security studies?

3.  In what ways is the study of gender important to international development studies?

4.  Is the study of gender still as important to IR as it was twenty years ago? Why/Why not?

### Recommended reading

**Momsen, J.H. (2004)** *Gender and Development* **(London: Routledge)**
This book gives a very user friendly, but in-depth, discussion of gender and development theory and practice.

**Parpart, J. and Zalewski, M. (eds) (2008)** *Rethinking the Man Question: Sex, Gender and Violence in International Relations* **(London: Zed Books)**
This edited collection offers a number of gender perspectives focusing on men and masculinities within international politics generally and international security more specifically.

**Steans, J. (2006)** *Gender and International Relations* **(Cambridge: Polity Press)**
This is a great textbook which focuses completely, in a sustained way, on gender and IR theory and practice.

# Chapter 20
# Identity and Identities

After reading this chapter you will be able to:

- See how questions of national identity manifest themselves in the form of nationalism

- Understand why identities are frequently multifaceted and more complicated than simply questions of nationality

- Understand how religions have resurged in significance in International Relations

- Explain how different theoretical perspectives on International Relations address the issue of identity

*Source*: Getty Images

## Introductory box: National self-determination for Quebec

The predominantly French-speaking province of Quebec has long had a prominent secessionist movement and its people have twice been polled (in 1980 and 1995) on the question of independence from Canada. Both referenda failed to endorse the idea of a sovereign Quebecois state but the second vote was very close and the secessionist movement remains strong. Fifty per cent of the vote for the Quebecois nationalists in a future referendum is a strong possibility and would give them a democratic mandate to launch a new nation state able to take up its place in international society alongside many others formed by secession over the last two hundred years.

However, while such a development would continue the trend of national self-determination seen in decolonisation and the break up of multinational socialist states, many have come to question whether such a development would be practical or just. In the run up to the 1980 vote Canadian Prime Minister Pierre Trudeau warned the secessionists that; 'if Canada is divisible, Quebec must also be divisible' and it has become evident that Inuit and Native American Crees within the province are strongly opposed to independence. Under the logics of national self-determination and democracy should these nations not also have the right to secede from Quebec? Should other non-French speaking Quebec citizens have the right to have a new national border redrawn so that they can remain within Canada? Should the rest of Canada have a say in the dissection of their highly prosperous country? In the modern world, drawing neat territorial lines around national groups is increasingly difficult (and it was never straightforward). The desire to give political expression to identities fuels many contemporary political issues but, with the onset of globalisation, such desires are becoming harder and harder to accommodate satisfactorily.

One of the clearest international political changes to have accompanied globalisation and the end of the Cold War has been the revival of conflict based more on nationalist and religious lines than ideological or state-to-state power rivalries. It is now obvious with hindsight that the Cold War kept a lid on many identity-based rivalries as Soviet–US domination of the globe subdued localised conflicts or else transformed them into superpower *proxy wars*. Hence in the 1980s Afghanistan was the focal point of Soviet–US hostility but in the 2000s it became the frontline of Western/Islamic fundamentalist hostility. Yugoslavia in the 1990s, shorn of the bonds provided by its own brand of socialism, revisited old nationalist squabbles thought by the rest of the world to be consigned to history.

In addition to the opportunities provided by the end of the Cold War for localised concerns to re-emerge, the changes brought by globalisation have further enhanced the significance of identity in IR. Identities are forged by people constructing 'in' and 'out' groups in relation to other people. Identifying yourself with or against others is, hence, related to how regularly you encounter others in order to make such a differentiation. In today's world, where transnational movements of people and information about people have increased far beyond anything previously experienced, identities are more readily formed than ever and, as a result, more often politicised and fought over. It is important to remember that the international political system we have is a long way from mirroring the identities held by the people of the world. The world map today may be more representative of differences than in the Imperial age but, as IR scholar Chris Brown notes, 'the core institutions and practises of the international community, the sovereign state, diplomacy and international law, are the product of one particular part of the world, one particular cultural heritage' (Brown and Ainley 2009: 200).

## Forms of identity

### National

Before reading any further, it is probably best to spend some time thinking about basic state-based identity and nationalism. Even a cursory glance around the world at different nationalisms gives one the sense that these must be very different concepts, based upon very different things and invoked by different experiences and perhaps changing over time. In any case, the issue is complicated and not susceptible to pseudoscientific generalisation. To get a sense of the complexity of nationalism you might think of the factors involved in at least the following nationalisms: Jewish, American, Indian, Japanese. And to think about how nationalism is not fixed either through time and space, you might think of different ideas of British, English, Welsh, Scottish and/or Irish nationalism and how these are evolving in the face of devolution, regionalism, the European Union and demands for independence.

National identity is highly subjective. The bases for defining who are and are not members of any given national group vary from case to case and over time. Box 20.1 lists a number of criteria commonly considered to be the basis of nationhood.

All of these criteria (and others) can be seen as a central basis for some national identities but, equally, none are universal and all are irrelevant to some nations. For many people national identity is synonymous with their political identity, particularly statehood. British, American or French national identity has come to be equated with being a citizen of the UK, USA or France. Hence all three are socially diverse countries with multi-ethnic and – at least in the cases of the UK and USA – multilingual populations whose make up changes all the time as migrants come to acquire citizenship and, with it, nationality. This equating of nationality with citizenship is not the same across the world, however. There are many 'stateless nations';

### Box 20.1  Criteria for a nation

- Distinct political identity
- Particular geographical region
- Racial/ethnic ties
- Common language
- Common religion
- Common history
- Common culture
- Economic ties

groups of people with a common sense of identity who do not have a state to represent them on the world stage. The Kurds, the Tamils, the Tibetans, the Basques and the Chechens are some examples of this phenomenon. Indeed, not all the citizens of the UK, USA and France buy into the notion of conflating citizenship and nationality, as the existence of cultural and political movements based on the Corse, Scots, Welsh, Irish and Native Americans testifies. Most states in the world are multinational to some extent and there is no neat match up between the nations and the sovereign states of the world.

For many stateless nations it is, nonetheless, still possible to point to them on a map and have a spatial, geographic conception of them. The examples listed are people who have inhabited particular regions and have cultures influenced by that, even if they do not completely control their own political destinies. The Poles persisted as a nation in Central Europe despite not having a state of their own for long periods of history. Most people today have an idea of what it means to be Tibetan, Scottish or Native American even though these are not state-based identities. However, if you attempted to draw a map of the world's nations – including stateless ones – you would soon run into difficulties. *Diaspora nationalities*, for example, defy geographical definition. The Jewish and Armenian national identities persisted for centuries without any state or common homeland and, while both now do have a nation state to call their own, most Jews and Armenians do not live there. Today ex-pat communities of people whose national identity persists far from their 'homeland' are commonplace, and in the case of the Roma (gypsies) we can see a national identity that persists without any particular 'home'.

Ethnicity, also, is an important basis to nationality in some cases but not in others. In Germany, Switzerland or Japan it is unusual for migrants to gain citizenship of the country if they are not considered ethnically German, Swiss or Japanese but this does not apply in countries with a tradition of multiracial citizenship, such as France, the UK and USA. Nations were once often thought of as 'extended families' or sub-groups of wider races, but few ethnographers subscribe to such a view today. Centuries of migration and re-drawing 'national' borders, added to increased genetic evidence that all humanity descends from common stock, have eroded the idea of any biological basis to nationhood. Where ethnicity is stressed in national identity it is in cases where defining the nation is cultural as well as political. Unlike the French, the Americans, the English or the British, whose national identity emerged from the formation of their states, Germans existed long before there was a Germany. Hence non-German-speaking migrants from outside Central Europe, such as Turks, have tended not to be thought of as German nor granted citizenship.

Language and religion are among cultural characteristics frequently considered to form the basis of national identity. Hence the unification of Germany in 1870 was based on the idea of uniting German speakers. In contrast, religion was not important in German identity with its people split fairly evenly between Catholics and Protestants. In Switzerland, by contrast, language is unimportant in terms of national identity with its people speaking German, Italian or French depending on where they are in the country. In addition, it becomes evident on enquiry that languages are usually more political than cultural. Norwegian, for example, was effectively invented in the late nineteenth century by nationalists keen to assert their distinctiveness from Swedes and Danes. Similarly, while religion represents an important means of defining nationality in some cases – for example, the Irish (Catholic) or Tamil (Buddhist) or Serb (Orthodox) cases – most nations are multi-faith.

The idea of nations being defined on the basis of common historical bonds or unique cultural traditions is frequently asserted but rarely stands up to much scrutiny. Great battles and leaders that brought independence or glory are revered in most national cultures but this is invariably more about government/nationalist-led socialisation than representing any kind of natural bond among peoples. Again the shifting of people and borders over time ensures that links with the past are often exaggerated, as are the battles and leaders in the construction of 'national histories'. Similarly, while national characteristics undoubtedly can be found, assertions of uniquely national cultural characteristics are usually designed for the political ends of 'nation-building'. Tartan and bagpipes did not originate in Scotland; St George, the patron saint of England, was from the Middle East.

A less frequently asserted dimension of nationhood that seems to have become more significant in recent years is common economic interest. When the people of the Ukraine voted on independence from the Soviet Union in a referendum in 1991, most Russians residing in the republic (as well as nearly all Ukrainians) voted in favour for reasons of economic rather than national self-determination. Elsewhere, the Northern League political party have asserted the cultural distinctiveness of North Italy in their campaign for independence but few would dispute that their support is based on the fact that many in places like Lombardy and Piedmont believe they would be better off not having to subsidise their poorer southern counterparts. Such cases lend support to the notion that cultural characteristics of nationhood tend to rise or fall according to political and economic circumstances.

Nations, then, are abstract and subjective social constructions (see Chapter 11). Famously described by Benedict Anderson as 'imagined communities' (Anderson 1991), nations defy simple, objective definition yet have been for the last two hundred years the most significant basis of conflict in international politics, through assertions of nationalism. Nationalism is a very broad ideology. Acting politically on behalf of your nation (which can be distinguished from the *patriotism* of simply expressing a fondness for your nation) can encompass pretty much the full range of political ideas and practices. Nazi genocide was an expression of nationalism but so was Gandhi's peaceful opposition to British rule in India. Nationalism thus is multifaceted. In terms of method it can be sometimes repressive and at other times emancipatory. In terms of type it can be subdivided into distinct forms in terms of how the nation at stake is being acted upon politically. In particular, this is to do with the relationship between nation and state. Nationalism can be exhibited by nations seeking to become states (such as the Quebecois) or by *nation states* in the cause of internal or external political aims.

## Liberal nationalism

National self-determination was proclaimed as a right of all at the Paris Peace Conference that followed the First World War and partly put into practice with the break up of the multinational Ottoman (Turkish) and Hapsburg (Austrian/Hungarian) Empires. This confirmed the trend established in nineteenth century Europe for legitimacy to separatist uprisings on the basis that nations had a right to statehood and also that conferring this was a route to peace. The reasoning for this was: if all nations ruled themselves, there would be a lot less left to fight about. Hence the cause of independence for nations like the Serbs, Greeks and Bulgarians received moral and armed support from many European governments and also individuals, such as the English poet Lord Byron who died in Greece preparing to fight the Turks. In nineteenth and early twentieth century Europe nationalism had little of the negativity it would later come to be associated with and was widely viewed as an expression of Liberalism since it seemed to embrace modernity, democracy and republicanism.

## Integral nationalism

Within a decade of the Paris Peace Conference in 1919, however, nationalism had come to be viewed in much more negative terms due to the emergence of Fascism, Nazism and other strands of chauvinistic politics. What was subsequently witnessed in the expansionism and brutality of the regimes that emerged in Germany, Italy, Japan and elsewhere was nationalism based not on the nation as a political idea, but on the projection of one's *own* nation in domestic and international politics – and hence often referred to as 'Integral nationalism'. Given the ethnic/cultural basis of nationhood in Germany, Italy and Japan this nationalism took on forms of chauvinism and racism, but Integral nationalism is not unique to countries that embraced Fascism and related forms of right-wing dictatorship at this period of history. Over a century earlier post-Revolutionary France entered an era first of internal authoritarianism under the Jacobins where regional, religious or class dissent was crushed in the 'reign of terror' and then external militarism under Bonaparte, in which much of Europe was conquered. Integral nationalism itself is a broad phenomenon which can be understood to include internal authoritarianism and external expansionism common to the Second World War axis powers, the Soviet Union, contemporary dictators and all imperialist powers.

In the contemporary world we can see both Liberal and Integral forms of nationalism exhibited, but the distinction is not as straightforward as contrasting democratic and autocratic politics. The break up of the Soviet Union, its East European 'Empire' and Yugoslavia can easily be seen as a renaissance of Liberal nationalism, as can the collapse of apartheid in South Africa. Armed secessionist campaigns widely viewed as terrorist, such as those waged by the Tamil Tigers in Sri Lanka or Basque separatists in Spain, can also be seen as part of the same phenomenon but would not fit many people's understanding of Liberal today. The Integral nationalist logic of 'my country right or wrong' has been most clearly witnessed in the campaigns of Saddam Hussein in Iraq and Slobodan Milosevic in Yugoslavia but can also be applied to the policies of many states, both democratic and otherwise, in advancing the 'national interest' in domestic and foreign policy. The tightening of migration controls, the sanctioning of illiberal counter-terrorist strategies and unlawful military adventurism seen in the 'War on Terror' are cases in point.

## Religious identity

Religion has become increasingly important in both the study and practice of International Relations. When told that the Roman Catholic Church had been critical of his suppression of Christianity, Soviet leader Joseph Stalin famously retorted, 'How many divisions has the Pope?'. Over the last three decades, however, we have undoubtedly witnessed the rise in profile of religions and religious identity as a factor in international relations. Indeed, with the inspirational role played by Pope John Paul II in the Polish revolution of 1989 (in which the church supported the Solidarity trade union movement which overthrew the government of the Polish United Workers Party) it could be said that Catholicism ultimately did triumph against the divisions of Communism.

Religious identity predates national identity by many centuries and was the chief cause of political conflict within and between the rudimentary states of the pre-Westphalian era, aside from the age-old and perennial motive of straight territorial gain. The 1648 Treaty of Westphalia marked the end of the Thirty Years War between Catholicism and Protestantism, and also the end of an era of religious domination over the kingdoms of Europe. From 1648 the sovereignty of kingly states began to supersede the supranationality of the Pope and the loyalty and identity of citizens shifted accordingly from their religion to their monarch and nation. In subsequent centuries the Westphalian system spread beyond Europe to the rest of the world but nations have never entirely replaced religions as a social identity for which individuals are prepared to kill and be killed. In many cases, national identity succeeded rather than superseded religious identity and provided a framework for pre-Westphalian conflicts of faith to persist in a sovereign, secular age. The Wars of the Reformation (which culminated in the Thirty Years War) were still being fought in Northern Ireland in the 1990s, although by then this was very much about national self-determination rather than Papal authority. There can be an overlap between religious and national identity, as discussed in the previous section, but conflicts such as those over the status of Northern Ireland, the break up of Yugoslavia or Tamil independence are best understood as nationalist struggles in which the nation is defined on the basis of religious identity rather than religious conflicts per se.

Secular, Westphalian states today have come to be wary of the alternative lure religious identity may hold for their citizens with the radicalisation (or politicisation) of many religions in the last quarter century. Religious **fundamentalism** first came to the attention of the international community in 1979 when an absolute monarchy was transformed into a Shiia Muslim semi-theocracy in Iran. For Iranians Shiia Muslim clerics, who had always been their spiritual leaders, would now be their political leaders also. Revolutions in other countries have always made governments nervous of their own citizens following suit and, just like the French and Russian Revolutions in earlier eras, the Iranian revolt prompted copycat uprisings in other societies and pre-emptive strikes against this possibility by other governments.

The rise of Islamic fundamentalism prompted US Realist Samuel Huntington to warn of an upcoming 'Clash of Civilizations' between the Islamic and Western worlds

(Huntington 1993). For some this prophecy seemed to be vindicated by the emergence of the 'War on Terror' but, for others, this was a speculative and sensationalist theory not supported by conclusive evidence. Liberals have noted that there is no higher incidence of conflict between Western and Islamic states than any other kinds of states (Russet and Oneal 2001) and, while the Iraqi and Afghan Wars may seem to represent such civilisational struggles, Muslims are actually on both sides of these conflicts. Additionally, in the 1990 Gulf War and 1999 Kosovan War the 'West' explicitly fought for the freedom of Muslim nations. It is important to remember that Islamic fundamentalism in its various forms represents a politicised interpretation of the Qur'an rejected by most of that faith and that more Muslims have been killed by the fundamentalists than people of any other religion or culture. In Sunni Muslim states such as Egypt, Algeria and Uzbekistan, the undisputed national religion, in fundamentalist form, has come to be seen as a threat to the government, prompting civil war and societal fissures. The enemy of Islamic fundamentalism is secularism and Western influence in Islamic states rather than the West per se.

While many dispute the clash of civilisations thesis, there is little doubt that religious identity has risen in significance as something around which disaffected groups can rally. Given the transnational nature of most religions and the fact that, in radicalised forms, they serve to challenge the secular sovereign foundations of the Westphalian order, this has become an issue of great importance in international relations. The notion of a trans-national brotherhood of Muslims (encapsulated in the term *Ummah*) has prompted some of that faith to take up arms in support of perceived injustices against their brethren in places

*Source*: Reuters/Luke MacGregor

Religious fundamentalism isn't just a matter of faith – there is a complicated political dimension that also needs to be understood.

like Palestine, Iraq and Afghanistan. The clash of loyalties this can invoke was illustrated starkly with the revelation that the perpetrators of the 2005 London bombings which killed fifty-two public transport users were all British citizens. While Islamic fundamentalism has attracted most concern in terms of the renaissance and radicalisation of religion, most of the world's great faiths have similarly spawned militant, anti-secular sects which have come to play a role in international relations. Christian fundamentalists, The Lord's Resistance Army, have fought a long-running and particularly brutal armed campaign from Southern Sudan which aims to establish a theocratic state based on the Ten Commandments in Uganda. Jewish and Hindu fundamentalist groups have played a role in the context of the Arab-Israeli and Indo-Pakistani territorial disputes which are now far more than the state-based conflicts they once were.

## Case study: What makes a British Muslim fundamentalist?

MI5, the intelligence arm of the UK government concerned with internal security, in 2008 produced an internal classified report – *Understanding Radicalization and Violent Extremism in the UK* (uncovered by the *Guardian* newspaper) – which collated evidence drawn from an extensive profiling of 'several hundred individuals known to be involved in, or closely associated with, violent extremist activity'. Perhaps contrary to what most people would envisage, the report concluded that the sample was a: 'diverse collection of individuals fitting no single demographic profile, nor do they all follow a typical pathway to violent extremism'. The following were typical characteristics:

- Mostly British
- Most not overtly religious
- Not 'mad and bad'
- Ethnically diverse
- Mainly male
- Mainly young
- Not 'loners'
- Educationally 'normal'

Very few Islamic fundamentalist terrorists or 'potential terrorists' were illegal immigrants and around half were British born. Possibly the most interesting finding of the study was that the profile group tended not to be from overtly religious families. There were a higher than societally average number of converts to Islam and many did not practice the faith on a regular basis, with some even leading culturally un-Islamic lives in which they drank alcohol, took narcotic drugs and frequented prostitutes. In light of this, it may be that the widely held view, supported by the UK

government, that the 'normal' Islamic community could play a key role in reining in the extremist fringe does not stand up to scrutiny. For these people Islam appears to be important for political rather than spiritual reasons and the findings support the idea that fundamentalism is not simply a more militant interpretation of the faith.

The sample also did not have any higher proportion of mental instability or pathological personality traits than the general UK population. Ethnically, Islamic fundamentalists appear to be as diverse as the general UK Muslim population with no concentration among Arabs or Pakistanis and also a few white people among the cohort. More predictably, most of the sample were male and in their twenties but there were also many older men and some women. Socially, the sample did not fit the 'loner' profile typical of serial killers. Those men over thirty were usually married and those in their twenties had steady girlfriends, exposing as a myth the sometimes held notion that Islamic fundamentalist terrorism appeals to sexually frustrated young men attracted by the promise of beautiful virgins in the afterlife. The educational profile of the sample group was also unexceptional with no pattern of gullible unintelligent individuals lured into terrorism and some (but no more than societally average) degree-educated recruits (Travis 2008).

**In view of the above, should we always be careful when making assumptions about people, whether in relation to their identity formation or behaviour in light of this?**

Globalisation, in its different guises, is the backdrop to the revival of religious identity in international relations. The cultural globalisation of *Westernisation* or modernisation has been an important spur to religious fundamentalism and the common thread that runs through the radicalised versions of all faiths – that is, a desire to go back to basics and revolt against contemporary liberal norms. In Iran in 1979 the revolution that overthrew the Shah was, in fact, more than a religious uprising and included many other disaffected groups; but they coalesced around the belief that their country had become a US stooge and should return to more traditional values. Further back in history, the roots of contemporary Islamic fundamentalism can be traced back to the Muslim Brotherhood in the 1920s who started out as anti-colonialists fighting British rule in Egypt but quickly internationalised and evolved from seeking to remove formal Western control in the Arab world to ensuring that independent Arab governments abandon secularism and put the Qur'an at the centre of politics. While the rise of religion can be viewed in terms of a backlash against globalisation it has also been aided by technological dimensions of that phenomenon. The opportunities presented by global media and information technology have been seized upon by those seeking to 'spread the word', ranging from Christian TV evangelists in the USA to al-Qaeda's recruitment of *jihadists* and their public online execution of opponents. In this regard the information revolution has been a great leveller, prompting US diplomat Richard Holbrooke, in reference to al-Qaeda leader Osama Bin Laden, to exclaim with despair: 'how can a man in a cave out-communicate the greatest communications society on earth?' (Holbrooke 2001).

## Gender

As can be seen in Chapters 10 and 19 some of the most interesting feminist work in IR is being done in the general area of gender, sexuality and sexual identities. This is part of a much broader critical interest in sexualities and identities in contemporary International Relations which is not exclusively feminist. Increased appreciation of gender in International Relations has highlighted, for example, how women can be disproportionally affected by political change such as that brought about by economic development or transition and how female subjugation in patriarchal family structures can be exacerbated by sovereignty.

Similarly, there are often gender consequences of identity politics based on nationalism and religion. In the West and more recently in many post-colonial countries, the struggle for popular sovereignty and national independence has stimulated demands for citizenship rights, and women have often benefited from this. Moreover, it is clear that women, like men, frequently have a very strong sense of identification with the nation. However, adopting a feminist perspective on state-building projects around the world reveals that, even while granting women formal rights, nationalism and economic development can work to institutionalise male privilege and so impinge upon women's citizenship. Ideas about gender and women's roles are often a central and powerful part of the 'story' told about the nation, its history and its distinctive identity. The idea of the nation is constructed out of an invented, inward-looking history: a 'cult of origins'. Women are often held to be the guardians of national culture, indigenous religion and traditions. This serves to keep women within boundaries prescribed by male elites. Women's behaviour is often policed and controlled in the interests of demarcating identities. The incidences of rape in armed conflicts (that frequently accompany independence struggles) have to be seen as political acts through which the aggressor attacks the honour of other men. Moreover, if women challenge their ascribed duties and roles they can find themselves accused of betraying the nation, its values, culture and ideals. In struggles based on religious fundamentalism the role of women is almost always more circumscribed, rather than enhanced, due to the emphasis on a return to traditional pre-modern social relations and values.

## Class

For Marxists International Relations is all about class, and its perspectives on this and other identities is examined later in the chapter (see also Chapter 8). Short of adopting a full neo-Marxist approach to IR, however, it is possible to note how globalisation has in some cases heightened transnational class consciousness. Reformists as well as revolutionaries now regularly voice concerns over how economic globalisation can contribute to worker exploitation. A globalised division of labour is becoming more evident and is reflected in the increasingly international outlook of trades unions and also the increasingly collectivist lobbying of multinational corporations on the world stage. In some ways 'class' seems less and less the issue, not least because of how people were manipulated and controlled under East European communism and the perceptions this led to. Even so, it is still an important category for analysis.

## Theorising identity

Traditional approaches to International Relations have tended to reduce issues of identity to a more or less stable and uniform identification of peoples with the nation state. In this reading identity becomes, if not unimportant, such a stable factor/variable that we can almost dismiss it in our analysis of the real essence (see Chapter 6). However, even within Realism it is unusual to find identity completely ignored, and many Realists pay attention to identity not only as the foundation of state identity but also in challenging order within states.

As we have already seen, however, we do not need to look very hard to find cases where primary identification might not be with the state or where experience has radically altered senses of identity. Religious identity has always been important to many people, but in contemporary Afghanistan we might argue that for significant portions of the population religious identity has become paramount and a driving force for resistance in a land where several distinct nationalities inhabit a state that is more a colonial relic than a coherent social entity. Similarly, we cannot deal with state-based identities as if they are all the same and all equally important. We might suspect that the people of affluent Tunbridge Wells in the UK consider themselves, in the majority, to be primarily British. The meaning attached to this state-based identity is likely also to be different from those seeking Palestinian state-hood or the Britishness felt by Falkland Islanders. In the case of Palestinian demands for a homeland we should also consider how decades of struggling for this goal seem also to have shaped the political and religious identity of many of those concerned. It is not difficult to think of areas of the globe, and the peoples who inhabit them, and find senses of identity at odds with the simple assumptions of early International Relations. People identify themselves not only by nationality but by religion, region, ethnicity, cause (for example environmentalism), class, politics, sex and sexuality, and so on. Given the multilayered and diverse nature of patterns of allegiance *within* the state the discipline of International Relations has had little choice but to move towards a more nuanced theoretical position.

## A Realist lens

As part of the traditional core of the discipline, Realism has, as alluded to above, not paid significant interest to issues of identity believing them fixed, stable and based around the state; beyond the boundaries of the nation state lies the realm of international anarchy where 'might makes right'. Identity politics is much less important than this, and than the law-like generalisations which stem from it, giving us a handle on the essence of inter-state dynamics.

There is a strong sense in Realist writings that national security issues, particularly in times of war, offer a sense of shared political purpose. Therefore, it is meaningful to speak of an underlying national interest which governs state behaviour particularly in relations with 'foreigners'. The state must, of necessity, be concerned first and foremost with national security and the well-being of its own citizens. For this reason, Realists anticipate that migration and asylum seekers are likely to generate feelings of unease if not of outright hostility and nationalism among citizens and nationals of existing states. This is not because Realists are personally indifferent to the plight of displaced people, but because they see fear of the 'foreign' as a core element of the insecurity inherent in international relations. Realists do not, however, endeavour to unpack the processes and practices involved in the construction of such identity groups and communities but rather take the nation as dominant identity and community as a given in IR.

Realism is often accused of helping to create what it suggests the world is like. By assuming the primacy of military power, an aggressive human nature and the need for prudence and suspicion in dealing with the outside world, it is said to help create that world. Thinking here about identity it is worth noting that when states find themselves at war it is at that point that some people find themselves prepared to subvert other identities in service of the nation; but it is also in such times that the state itself tends more freely to repress other identities than allow them to flourish.

## A Liberal lens

Liberalism places primary emphasis on the individual rather than the group but does recognise the importance of issues of identity and community and their relevance to

International Relations. In one sense Liberals offer a conception of community and identity which spans the entire planet and which defies the usual boundaries of state, nation, race, ethnicity, culture, class, gender and so on. This is the community of humankind, who possess inalienable human rights by virtue of the universal capacity for reasoned thought. Liberal pluralists have long expressed commitment towards a global society as a means by which the sovereign state system can be transcended and more inclusive forms of community achieved. 'Global society' can be viewed in terms of a normative consensus bonding people together. In this view, people owe obligations to the 'people of the world' rather than simply to their fellow citizens. Some commentators argue that forms of complex interdependence have resulted in the global spread of 'universal' values; for example, human rights and democracy. Hence Liberals are cosmopolitanists rather than communitarians. **Communitarians** say that ethical ideas are rooted in specific communities and arguments about justice are only convincing within community boundaries. Cosmopolitan thinkers, on the other hand, get around this problem by extending the notion of community to the entire human race.

The growing significance of transnational politics and social movements in world politics (under processes of globalisation) also raises issues of identity and community. **Transnationalism** implies that people engage in numerous social interactions which tie people together across state boundaries. An alternative way of conceptualising global society is as a series of network-type, transnational relationships. In this view, technological innovations and increasing 'flows' such as media communications, technology and finance, bring in their wake the disintegration of previous forms of identity and attachment. Liberals have noted the growing importance of transnational 'legitimised relationships' arguing that human beings increasingly identify themselves in a variety of politically relevant ways, are enmeshed in a multitude of authoritative networks and have loyalties to a variety of authorities. Indeed, some Liberals see an open and participatory politics emerging from transnational linkages across societies, which transcend the state (Ferguson and Mansbach 2007).

## A Marxist lens

Recognition of the significance of gender and racial discrimination was fairly central to the 'post-Marxist' turn which occurred in the late 1960s and early 1970s in much social theory. However, generally speaking neither early Marxist nor later structuralist writers in IR paid much attention to aspects of identity and community that did not easily fit within the broad framework of a global capitalist order and notions of class struggle. Despite the importance of nationalism, as both an ideology and political force in nineteenth century Europe, Marx devoted most of his time and energies to exploring the theme of class consciousness, class interests and class struggle.

Given the national and ethnic diversity which existed in the Soviet Union, it is somewhat surprising, perhaps, to find that none of the leading Bolshevik revolutionaries – including Lenin and Trotsky – gave sustained attention to the ideology of nationalism. Moreover, the intellectual and political climate of the USSR during the first half of the twentieth century was such that there were no serious challenges to Stalin's rather simplistic view of the world 'community' as being fundamentally divided into two opposing blocs or 'camps'. Throughout the nineteenth and early twentieth century Marxists tended to regard nationalism, or indeed any other form of identification – religious, cultural, ethnic, and so on – as some kind of 'false consciousness' diverting people from the predominant class issue. This view continues to find echoes in some contemporary Marxist work.

That said, in the 1960s there emerged many national liberation movements and guerrillas in parts of Africa and Latin America which were left-leaning or pro-Marxist-Leninist and, for this reason, it became necessary to develop an account of nationalist struggle which was neither dismissive (as in the notion of false consciousness) nor incompatible with the basic assumptions of Marxist thought. Thus, in Immanuel Wallerstein's account of the modern world system, we find some attention being given to nationalism as a powerful source of political identification.

Wallerstein's **World Systems Theory** incorporates an analysis of those forces which work against the system as well as dominant, class-based structures. Thus, it is possible to identify a number of oppositional or 'anti-systemic' forces at work in world politics. Nationalism is not all of one kind. Some forms of nationalism certainly work to consolidate capitalism and so disguise the exploitative nature of the capitalist world system. However, some national liberation movements are clearly anti-systemic. Various groups have an interest in supporting and opposing particular definitions of the 'nation state' and so, according to Wallerstein, 'nationalism' must be seen as both a mechanism of imperialism/integration *and* of resistance/liberation (Wallerstein 1984).

Clearly, here we have an analysis of nationalism which is influenced by the underlying theory of class politics. Indeed, Wallerstein goes on to say that anti-systemic movements are organised in two main forms around two main themes: social movements around class and the national movements around 'nations' or peoples. Anti-systemic (or revolutionary) movements first emerged in organised form in the nineteenth century to promote human equality and so were, by definition, incompatible with the functioning of the capitalist

 **Box 20.2 Wallerstein's idea of 'peoples' and nationhood**

Wallerstein argues that the increasing definition of state structures has led to the shaping, reshaping, creation and destruction, and revival of the idea of 'peoples'. He believes that these 'peoples' come to see themselves (and are seen by others) as controlling state structures. Through this identification of 'peoples' with the state, 'nations' are created. On the other hand, within the boundaries of the 'nation state' there are significant groups who are not identified as having rights to control state structures or exercise political power directly. These people come to be seen by 'nationals' as 'minorities'. However, it is important to realise that Wallerstein does not regard national identity as rooted in some real shared ethnic heritage or history. Nations are 'solidarity groupings' whose boundaries are constantly constructed, defined and redefined, and nationalism is a device which is used to strengthen and consolidate the power of the state (Wallerstein 1984).

world economy. It was the political structure of the capitalist world economy – a series of sovereign states – which compelled movements to seek the transformation of the world system via the achievement of political power within separate states. However, because the capitalist world system is based fundamentally on class division and exploitation, which is transnational or global in nature, the organisation of anti-systemic movements at the state level necessarily has contradictory effects. Nationalism counterposes the logical and ideological necessity of worldwide struggle against the immediate political need of achieving power within one state. Whatever the tactic of a given social movement, it achieves power in a state structure and is then constrained by the logic of the inter-state system.

Marxists have also endeavoured to give some account of racism and sexism in the world system. According to Wallerstein, racism is a belief system which functions to justify the inclusion of certain groups in the workforce and the political system at a level of reward and status sharply inferior to that of some larger group (Wallerstein 1984). Sexism has the same objective, although it is reached via a different path. By restricting women to certain modes of producing income and by defining such modes as 'non-work' (through the concept of the 'housewife'), sexism works to reduce wage levels in large sectors of the world economy. According to Maria Mies, in the contemporary global economy the coercion of women as 'housewives' remains essential for a system which allowed male workers to be free citizens (Mies 1986).

However, while Marxists have attempted to give some account of identity, forms of solidarity and types of community (such as nation states and anti-systemic movements), it is fair to say that this analysis has been profoundly coloured by their basic beliefs about the primacy of social class and class struggle. Indeed, overall Marxists have tended to emphasise class as the coming together of identity and interests.

## A Critical lens

Enlightenment thinkers believed that the modern state created the conditions in which it was possible to live under the rule of law and according to principles of justice. Furthermore people (or at least some people), enjoyed the status of active citizens, playing a role in deciding the politics of their country in the public sphere where issues of law, justice and morality were debated openly, rather than that of subjects who simply obeyed the monarch. In so far as 'emancipation' was closely connected with a sense of autonomy and control over one's life, this was a major step forward for human beings.

The rise of nationalism as a powerful ideology in the eighteenth and nineteenth centuries strengthened the claims of the state to be the sole legitimate representative of citizens, in the first place by extending citizenship rights and, secondly, by inculcating a feeling of emotional attachment to the nation state. In the twentieth century, nationalist sentiment has worked to challenge the authority and legitimacy of existing state boundaries. However, radical and secessionist national movements, acting under the banner of the rights of people to self-determination, only strengthened the attachment between the individual and the 'national homeland' and thus consolidated, rather than weakened, the state system.

In some respects, the expansion of the state system can be viewed as a positive development, because it extends the principles of self-determination and citizenship to more and more of the world's peoples. However, at the same time, the nation state embodies something of a moral contradiction, because it is at once both an inclusionary and exclusionary form of political community. The nation state is inclusionary because it is founded on the idea that all citizens are equal. There are certain rights which flow from citizenship and these should be enjoyed by every member of the community. All citizens are, therefore, of equal moral worth. However, the nation state is by its very nature exclusionary. It discriminates against 'foreigners' on the grounds that they are different. The differences between 'insiders' and 'outsiders' are held to be morally relevant.

The bounded community of the nation state excludes people whose 'difference' is deemed to threaten the state's distinctive identity. International law sets out just what obligations states owe to non-citizens temporarily residing within the boundaries of the state; among other things, they must be protected from harm. In certain cases states might extend temporary rights of asylum to foreigners who fear persecution in their homeland. Nevertheless, while the states have a certain obligation to 'foreigners', these are clearly not the same as or equal to the obligations owed to 'nationals'. Moreover, the boundaries of the communities are constantly being policed to ensure against 'invasion' from outsiders, so much so that we regard 'foreigners' as a threat to the extent that we can even debate the morality of the use of nuclear weapons to deter outsiders from encroaching on our 'space'. The emancipatory project at the heart of Critical Theory necessarily raises questions about the limits of political community, how boundaries between self and other are constructed, and the moral implications of this.

Critical Theorists are interested in how the boundaries of community change over time. So historically certain groups, such as women and working-class men, have been denied citizenship on the grounds that they are 'different' – less rational and not up to the demands of active citizenship. Women, for example, were held to be in need of strong moral guidance from their men-folk. Of course, working class men and women have made great strides in overcoming such prejudices and now enjoy rights of citizenship in most states around the world, although significant forms of discrimination still exist.

Since the UN was established in 1945, there has been a gradual development of human rights law which recognises the equal moral worth of every human being. The widespread commitment to respect human rights seems to suggest that there exists among humankind a moral conviction that all individuals belong not only to sovereign states, but to a more inclusive community of humankind even if, in practice, this has been denied to some groups. Arguably, we might now be witnessing the eclipse of the sovereign state system in favour of more cosmopolitan forms of identity and community; given the increasingly globalised nature of social relations, expressions of loyalty and solidarity can be both sub-state and transnational. Social movements give expression to, or reflect, the plural forms of identity, loyalty and solidarity which exist.

As well as understanding the dynamics of social exclusion, however, it is also important to recognise the way in which those practices are being challenged, by groups involved in both national and transnational political action. Moreover, there are many arenas in which people have expressed significant political commitment, and in which people think about and debate moral and political issues. Drawing upon Habermasian ideas about the importance of communication and dialogue in achieving an emancipatory politics (see Chapter 9), Andrew Linklater highlights the multiple 'public spheres' in which these kinds of debate take place. He claims that political communities are already being transformed by, for example, struggles over equality, rights, claims to resources and notions of obligations to others, and how they might change more radically in the future (Linklater 2007).

## A Postmodern lens

Postmodern scholars accept that the nation state is an important expression of political community. However, they point out that it is certainly not the only significant expression of identity or community. The problem is that, when we study international relations, we necessarily privilege citizenship over and above other expressions of identity and community. Dominant ideas of identity/political community are confined to identification with the nation state as a consequence of the way in which the creation of state boundaries in Europe was linked with the rise of nationalism as a powerful discourse and political force, and war as a frequent expression of this. However, if we focus solely or mainly on the nation state, we may well miss other significant expressions of community and identity. State-centric

*Source: Getty Images*

**Does the concept of hybridity make nationalist movements redundant?**

models of International Relations marginalise the political significance of social movements, which identify on the basis of class or gender or are organised around specific issues, such as the environment.

Postmodern scholars embrace the idea of globalisation, not because it necessarily captures real material processes or developments, but because it represents a powerful challenge to state-centrism in IR. In the manner of Foucault (see Chapter 10), postmodernists are also sensitive to the power relations that underpin discourses of globalisation – that is to say, globalisation is itself a contested term for a contested process or project. It is important to realise, therefore, that postmodernists see value in any idea or perspective which encourages us to think about the world differently but are, as always, alert to the discursive contexts in which claims about the world are made. Nevertheless, 'globalisation' might be encouraging new forms of identification and expressions of identity and solidarity which cut across state boundaries. Therefore, the concept of globalisation opens up possibilities for revisiting thinking on identity.

Postmodernists are interested in social movements because they see them engaging in a politics that challenges the rigid inside/outside boundaries of state-centric analysis. Innovative new technologies are being used by a wide variety of social movements to network, campaign and articulate dissent and resistance. All of this political activity is being carried out in a particular 'space' – cyberspace – which is outside the jurisdiction and control of individual states though, ironically enough, vulnerable to hacking and virusing by individual people. Accordingly, postmodern scholars argue, we need radically to rethink our conceptions of global political space.

## Box 20.3 Hybridity

The notion of hybridity implies the mixing of different elements of identity to form something new. The concept of hybridity is particularly associated with the ideas of Homi Bhabba (Bhabba 1994). In order to flesh out the concept of hybrid identities, it is helpful to consider further the ways in which globalisation is relevant to the study of identity. Globalisation implies increased travel, the growth of media and communication and a generally 'smaller' world. In a globalised world, therefore, cultural encounters and mixings are likely to become the norm. For example, while most people may still be the same nationality as both their parents and live in the country of all their births, it is entirely possible (given processes of globalisation) that someone 'out there' has a Malaysian father and a Bolivian mother, was born in Dubai, lives in Nigeria and attends an English speaking school. If this person exists, the only people to share her particular mix of identities are likely to be her siblings – who even then will be unique, perhaps, owing to gender, sexuality and so on. This simply gives an idea of how it is possible for identity to be much more complex in the contemporary world.

It is also interesting to speculate on what all this means. Perhaps hybridity, the mixing and transmission of ideas mean more than anything else that stereotypes are increasingly hard to 'hold on to'. Are the reinforcement of ideas such as the 'American Dream', or attempts to deny or frustrate global trends by 'protecting' the French language from Anglicisation, worthwhile projects or discourses of the powerful, whose power is dependent on these discourses?

## A Social Constructivist approach

To a large extent Social Constructivism as a theory is built on the premise that identity and culture are crucial variables in International Relations and are given insufficient consideration by the traditional approaches to the discipline. To Social Constructivists, the national interest is not objectively given; attention is given particularly to the relationship between identity and interests, and how certain ideas shape interests and vice versa. Liberal states in a Kantian international culture will, therefore, pursue interests different from dictatorships in a Hobbesian international order (see also Chapter 11). Being a member of an international organisation, and being socialised into the norms and institutions of such an organisation, makes a difference to a state's formulation of its national interest. Similarly, particular ideas about economic development will, for instance, shape what is seen by developing countries to be in their interest. In all of this, Social Constructivists insist that the relationship between ideas, identities and interests is a complex one. Ideas do not simply determine interests. More to the point, one cannot talk about one without the other.

Social Constructivists argue that identities in themselves matter for policy making – and not only through the definition of interests. This is a consequence of assuming the logic of appropriateness: an identity will provide actors with a particular role in international relations, and they will try to act in a way they see as appropriate to that role. As we saw in Chapter 11 the belief in European integration in post-war Germany, and the self-definition of Germany as a European state, has led to policies that are very different from the much more trans-Atlantic self-definition of Britain or the social democratic nationalism of Denmark.

### Box 20.4 Normative entrapment

Because identity is such a core concept to Social Constructivists, they are also interested in the construction of identities and how they change. One of the core processes in the interplay between norms and interests is what one might call 'normative entrapment'. This refers to situations in which actors make promises which it seems opportune or in their interest at the time to make, but which they never actually intend to keep. These promises come back to haunt them at a later time, when those to whom promises were made eventually call them in. From a Realist perspective, there is no obligation to fulfil the promises at a later stage. Yet, even a closer inspection within a Rationalist framework makes the choice appear rather more difficult. The state that made the promises might not want to be seen as lying,

especially if it wants something from the state to which the promises had been made, or if there is a good possibility that it might want something in the future. The promises made might also lead other actors to put increasing pressure on the 'promising' actor, whose initial stance might eventually become untenable. From a Social Constructivist perspective, however, we also need to take into account the logic of appropriateness. States will fulfil at least some promises because they see it as appropriate to do so. They might not initially have thought that they would ever have to keep their promises but, especially if the promises have become part of the self-understanding of a state (or other international actors), it would require a significant challenge to the state's identity not to do so.

## Conclusions

People's identities, other than that with their state, are not easily accommodated in either the practice or study of International Relations. The simple Realist view of identity as primarily being a national thing – bound up with statehood – is clearly challenged by a number of different perspectives within International Relations. The nature of a globalising world is such that identities become increasingly cross cutting and, although identities are relatively stable (sticky), they are increasingly challenged. For some, this mixing and increasing hybridity is a cause of celebration. However, for others, challenges to traditional cultural norms are a cause of resistance. The interplay of these two tendencies is likely to be crucial to the future of International Relations and your study of the discipline.

## Resource section

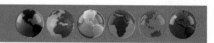

## Questions

1. With the use of contemporary examples to illustrate, describe and explain how nationalism is a multifaceted phenomenon.

2. Describe and explain the rise to prominence of religion in International Relations over the last thirty years.

3. Compare and contrast how issues of identity are dealt with by rival International Relations approaches.

## Recommended reading

Alter, P. (1994) *Nationalism* (London: Hodder Arnold)
Academic treatments of Nationalism tend to lack consistency in the use of terminology and can hence prove unsatisfactory for students new to the subject but this book stands out for its clarity and logical approach to explaining and subdviding this complex phenomenon into types.

Haynes, J. (2007) *An Introduction to International Relations and Religion* (London: Pearson)
A comprehensive and accessible analysis of how religion and religious identity has come to manifest itself again in international affairs.

Huntington, S.P. (1993) 'The Clash of Civilizations?' *Foreign Affairs* 72(3): 22–49
He did not coin the term but probably made it famous; makes the argument (to counter other fashionable arguments of the time) that people's cultural and religious identities would cause significant conflict even after the Cold War.

Krause, N. and Renwick, J. (eds) (1997) *Identities in International Relations* (London: St Martin's)
Multi-authored volume that explores national, religious, gender and other identities from a range of theoretical perspectives.

# Chapter 21
# Democratisation

After reading this chapter you will be able to:

- Explain what a democratic political system is and the different forms they take

- Understand how and why the idea of democracy has spread internationally through the process of *democratisation*

- Argue different views on why democracy sometimes fails to take hold in states and yet, in other cases, becomes (apparently) permanent

- Debate whether democracy can be imposed by force in a process of 'nation building'

- Understand why some see democratisation as crucial for justice, human rights and world peace but others dispute this

*Source*: Getty Images

In 2000 Cuban Communist dictator Fidel Castro responded to confusion that surrounded the US presidential elections by offering to send a team of 'electoral advisors' to teach the Americans about democracy. George Bush had defeated Al Gore despite polling fewer votes across the country, since he had won in a majority of states. However, in the state of Florida, upon which the result ultimately rested, Bush's victory was disputed by many due to polling irregularities.

There is a long history of antipathy between the USA and its island neighbour dating back to the 1950s when Castro had masterminded a left wing revolution on the island and overthrown a US-backed dictatorship. In 1961 the USA responded by backing an ultimately unsuccessful invasion (the Bay of Pigs) to overthrow Castro and have imposed economic sanctions on the regime ever since.

In the light of this back-story Castro was, of course, opportunistically riling his old foe but the episode did serve to highlight the ambiguous and contested nature of democracy. Could Cuba actually claim to be more democratic than the US? Why is democracy 'claimed' by states with such differing political systems? Why is democracy used in international relations by states seeking to defend themselves from criticism or in order to criticise others?

## What is democracy?

Democracy is an old idea, originating in Ancient Greece, yet today its precise meaning is still contested and the best means of putting it into practice is not agreed upon. The word means 'rule by the people' combining the ancient Greek words *demos* (the people) and a derivation of *kratos* (rule by). In Ancient Greece, Athenian Democracy sought to put this into practice by initiating mass meetings of all eligible citizens to make political decisions. Opinion at the time was divided as to the appropriateness of this method of decision making. The leading statesman of his day, Pericles, was a key architect of the system and drew praise from the likes of the renowned historian Thucydides for his stewardship of a government constrained by regular popular votes. The Philosophers Socrates, Aristotle and Plato, however, were more sceptical of this democratic experiment, fearing that 'mob rule' might not be in the best interests of society. This debate persists today and is revisited later in this chapter.

There is no agreed understanding of what 'rule by the people' actually means but a good starting point is the oft-quoted phrase used by US President Abraham Lincoln in his famous 'Gettysburg Address' of 1863: 'government of the people, by the people, for the people'. This phrase is useful for reminding us that there is more to democracy than voting as it has increasingly come to be portrayed. Democracy was pretty much forgotten for several centuries after Ancient Greece as monarchical rule dominated most of the world. It re-emerged in its modern form with the rise of Liberal political thought in the eighteenth century and, while it is debateable whether modern democracies are more democratic than Pericles' Athens, the 'of the people' element has certainly advanced since the time of Lincoln. Only around 40,000 of the 250,000 or so Ancient Athenians were actually citizens and thus entitled to vote. In particular, women and the large slave population were not involved in the political process. By contemporary standards this seems 'undemocratic' since the extension of the franchise (that is, the right to vote) through the twentieth century generally saw women and all adult 'citizens' (usually barring prisoners) given the vote in modern 'democracies'. Ancient Athens, however, can lay claim to be more democratic than most contemporary democracies in that its government was more clearly 'by the people' since over one-sixth of them were effectively in the government. This could be said to have empowered people more than in the contemporary USA where less than half of those who voted got the President they wanted in 2000 and only 51 per cent of the eligible adult citizens voted at all.

In recent history balancing the 'of the people' and 'by the people' dimensions of democracy has become the key difficulty in applying the concept. Liberal Democracy from the eighteenth century has focused more on the former and come to see legitimate government as being not so much by the masses but by the consent of the masses, demonstrated through elections. Hence Liberal Democracy is usually distinguished from the Classic Democracy of Ancient Athens in that it is more about having a government accountable to the people than one which is directly 'of them' (which, with population growth, could also be argued to have become impractical).

Within contemporary Liberal Democracies, however, there is still a balance to be established on how much 'by the people' you can or would want to have. At one end of the contemporary spectrum is 'participatory' or 'popular' democracy in which all citizens have a regular, direct input in decision making in a kind of modern version of Athenian Democracy. In Switzerland, either as a whole or within its constituent cantons, most significant political decisions are subject to a referendum of all eligible citizens. There is a central Swiss government but it has limited powers compared to most state executives. At the other end of the Liberal Democratic spectrum is Representative Democracy where the emphasis is more on elections than referenda or any other means of directly involving the public in decision making. In this form of Liberal Democracy the justification for limiting the 'by the people' element is 'Burke's principle' – named after the conservative Irish/British politician and thinker – that too much popular democracy undermines the role of elections and elected officials. According to this principle politicians should be trusted to act on behalf of their citizens once they have been elected and be more than just delegates of them. They should look after their constituents' interests but be prepared to act according to their conscience and expertise and not simply articulate the opinion of the majority of the people they represent. In this view we should elect politicians to run the country on our behalf, accepting that we have voted them in because they are better equipped than us to evaluate the political complexities and priorities of the day. All Liberal Democracies lie somewhere on a continuum between representative and popular democracy with none entirely one or the other. The UK, where referenda are rare, is a good example of a state towards the former end of the scale.

Representative democracy, then, limits the 'by the people' element of the concept in the hope that this better serves the third element of Lincoln's maxim and leads to decisions taken that are better 'for the people'. Plato's 'mob rule' argument is revived through concerns that 'the people' may take decisions not in the interest of 'the people'. Nineteenth century Liberals, like Alexis de Toqueville and John Stuart Mill revived this concern with the 'tyranny of the majority' argument that a popular vote should not be allowed to undermine individual liberty. Popular support for imprisoning or slaughtering people for their beliefs could not make such policies legitimate and truly 'democratic'.

The 'for the people' element of democracy is, of course, more subjective than the other two and can lead to the concept being stretched well beyond the confines of Liberal Democracy. Unelected Communist governments have frequently claimed to be 'people's democracies' in that they represent and act on behalf of 'the people', rather than the minority elite interests catered for in previous monarchical or dictatorial regimes. Liberal Democracies may be accepted by Marxists to be an advance on such systems but can they really claim to be 'for the people' when, as Lenin observed of Britain, they are 'a democracy for one second every five years' (that is, when casting a General Election vote)? Mao went as far as describing his one party authoritarian Chinese government as a 'people's democratic dictatorship'. While it is probably fair to say that much policy produced in Marxist/Maoist regimes, such as full employment and universal health and education, was 'for the people', the fact that Mao, Lenin, Stalin, Pol Pot and others slaughtered millions of their own people makes it hard to rank such characters alongside Pericles, Lincoln, Mill and Nelson Mandela in the ranks of history's notable democrats.

Democracy is more than just free and fair elections, something dismissed by critics as mere 'electoralism' (Karl 1995). It is now widely accepted that full or 'substantive democracy' (Grugel 2002: 65–6) also necessitates elements of pluralism or what US political scientist Robert Dahl (1971) has referred to as 'polyarchy' (rule by many), in which ordinary citizens can influence the political process in a variety of ways other than through elections (see Box 21.1). This notion of 'active citizenship' is, however, difficult to measure with any exactitude and free and fair elections remain the most straightforward and unambiguous indicator of democracy in today's world, if not an entirely satisfactory one.

> **Box 21.1 Dahl's seven criteria for a democracy**
>
> 1. Control over politicians after election
> 2. Free and fair elections
> 3. Universal adult suffrage
> 4. Right to run for public office
> 5. Freedom of expression
> 6. Access to non-governmental sources of information
> 7. Freedom of association

## The three waves of democratisation

As introduced in Chapter 1, US academic Samuel Huntington popularised the idea of democratisation as having occurred in three broad waves over the last three centuries, interspersed by two counter-waves when anti-democratic authoritarianism has resurged

(Huntington 1991). Critics have opined that Huntington's definition of democracy is limited by electoralism and reflects a Western and, in particular, a US bias (Grugel 2002: 34–5; Pettiford 2004: 37–8) but the notion of ebbs and flows within the general progression of global democratisation is widely accepted as a broadly accurate analysis of the phenomenon. Box 21.2 bears this out.

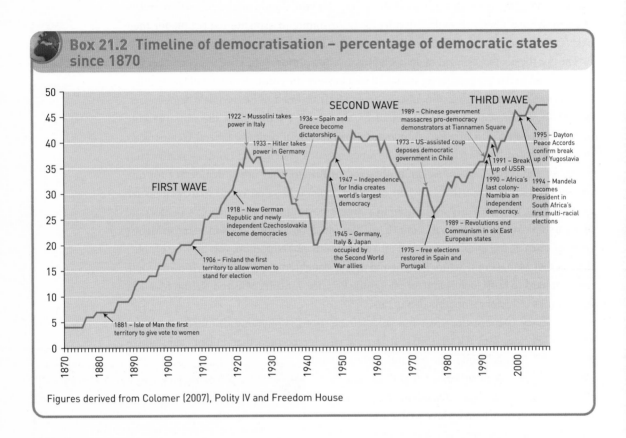

**Box 21.2 Timeline of democratisation – percentage of democratic states since 1870**

Figures derived from Colomer (2007), Polity IV and Freedom House

## The first wave

The influential French political writer Alexis de Tocqueville, while conducting research on the US political system in 1835, prophesised that the embryonic American democracy he had come to admire would soon be copied throughout the world in a global revolution (see Box 21.3). Though the idea of democracy has developed and spread since then, it has proved more evolutionary than revolutionary. A 'long wave' of progress from the birth of Liberalism grew when many Western European and North American states underwent industrialisation. The governments of these states were then compelled to respond to the demands of a new working class and initiated reforms that empowered the masses. However, the first of what were to be two interregnums in global democratisation came sometime in the 1920s and 1930s. Both the starting and ending points of this first wave of democratisation are debateable. Huntington suggests it began in the USA in the time

## Box 21.3 Alexis de Tocqueville, *Democracy in America*

Published in two volumes, in 1835 and 1840, after de Tocqueville had been despatched by the French government to study the penal system in the United States, *Democracy in America* is revered on both sides of the Atlantic both as a classic social and political history of the age and as a prophetic treatise on the future of democracy and democratisation. De Tocqueville was so taken by the USA that his research expanded well beyond studying the prison system and he produced a wide, comparative study of the political system, economy and society he felt was a model for France and for the world. A strong independent judiciary, checks on government power, a free press and involving people in public affairs (such as through jury service and local government) were highlighted as essential both to the establishment of democracy and for avoiding purely self-serving individualism from undermining democratic rule through 'the tyranny of the majority'. With such institutions in place de Tocqueville prophesied that democracy would soon spread around the world in a process that would be 'irresistible and universal' (de Tocqueville 1863).

of de Tocquville in the late 1820s. Dahl considers that it can be traced back further to the birth of Liberalism and Republicanism (the abandonment of monarchical rule) in the late eighteenth century (Dahl 1971). Grugel, however, contends that it is more appropriate to see the starting point of democratisation as in the 1870s, by when the expansion of the franchise had come to include most of the 'demos', or adult citizenship, in some European countries, North America and British colonial states (Grugel 2002: 37).

The First World War weakened many countries, both politically and economically, and this was furthered by the onset of the Great Depression from 1929. Discontent with the Western economic and political model manifested itself in the rise to popularity of radical socialism, prompting the response of a right wing authoritarian backlash from elites in many states. In the 1920s and 1930s the political systems of Germany, Poland, Portugal, Spain and Italy moved in an authoritarian direction and, by the outbreak of the Second World War, Britain and the states of Benelux and Scandinavia were the only substantive democracies remaining in Europe (Switzerland is excluded from this categorisation on the basis that the right to vote and stand in national elections was not extended to women until 1971). Even those beacons of democracy, France, Britain and the USA, experienced severe social discontent in the inter-war years as people began to feel disillusioned with capitalism and party politics, and become attracted to authoritarian alternatives of both the right and left. In France a prolonged period of political crisis saw thirty-six different governments take office in the twenty-one inter-war years. With the rise in popularity of Fascism and Marxism, the first wave of democratisation receded and showed little sign of being succeeded by a second at the outbreak of the Second World War in 1939.

## The second wave

The allied triumph over Nazism, Fascism and Japanese monarchical ultra-nationalism in the Second World War boosted democracy (though also Communism) and prompted a second wave, but the clash that ensued between 'The West' and The Communist world ensured that this wave was far shorter in duration than the first wave had been. West Germany, Japan and Italy were democratised by force and, as decolonisation redrew the word map, many newly independent countries, like India and Israel, embraced democracy at their birth. This proved to be a short wave, however, since the prioritisation of the West was resisting the spread of Communism rather than promoting Liberal Democracy, and Cold War geopolitics saw right wing authoritarian governments hostile to Communism propped up by the USA and her allies. It is pertinent to remember that the Cold War was more of a struggle between Communism and Capitalism than between authoritarianism and democracy, as it is sometimes painted in the West. The Western alliance was sometimes happy to undermine democracy in the cause of deterring Communism. An elected Iranian government was deposed by the British and Americans in 1953 after nationalising the Anglo-Iranian Oil Company (a predecessor of British Petroleum) in order to ensure Western control of the Persian Gulf oilfields. Similarly, US support helped snuff out democracy in Guatemala in 1954 and in Chile in 1973, when elections delivered leftist governments on the US doorstep. Armed border disputes between newly independent India and Pakistan saw the US backing the Pakistani dictatorship over the fledgling democracy which received the support of the Soviets.

Additionally, many of the democracies that emerged from the wave of decolonisation that swept large swathes of the world after 1945 proved to be weak and saw countries like Nigeria and Cameroon drift towards authoritarianism as the key groups which had secured independence, and particularly the 'strongmen' who had assumed presidency, also sought to secure their long-term political dominance. Even the beacon of Third World democracy, India, briefly flirted with authoritarian rule when Indira Gandhi introduced emergency rule in 1975 in response to internal unrest following allegations of electoral corruption. In 1960 nine of the ten Latin South American states had competitive electoral systems but by 1973 only Venezuela and Colombia had not reverted to military government. Indeed, in 1971 there were only twenty-five democratic governments in the world, all of which were in Western Europe or former Western European colonies with the isolated exception of Japan. Hence the second wave of democratisation had come to an end by the early 1970s.

## The third wave

A third wave of democratisation began to emerge in the mid 1970s when Spain and Portugal abandoned military dictatorship and a lessening of repression in the Soviet bloc sowed the seeds of the post-Communist transition that occurred across most of Eastern Europe over a decade later. The ending of the Cold War between 1989 and 1991 served to accelerate the progress of democratisation on both sides of the Iron Curtain. The 1989 revolutions which swept through the six 'Eastern Bloc' Soviet satellite states took the world by surprise and heralded a major retreat from Communism and a rejuvenation of Liberal Democracy as people 'voted with their feet' for a Western European model of rule.

The USSR's subsequent transformation has been less complete, with states like Russia and Georgia only partly embracing democracy and others such as Belarus remaining firmly autocratic, but several successor states have also become fully fledged democracies. Communist Yugoslavia broke up later in the 1990s in similar, though much bloodier, fashion and has gradually spawned five new democracies.

---

**Box 21.4  Francis Fukuyama, *The End of History and the Last Man***

US academic Fukuyama epitomised the optimism of the New World Order in the early 1990s with his prophecy that the end of the Cold War marked the 'end of history'. Fukuyama reasoned that the ideological triumph of Liberalism over Communism was an ultimate victory that had set the world on a course for a new future, in which Liberal Democracy had established itself as the final form of government. For sure the end of democratisation had not yet come but no other serious challenges to the ascendancy of this form of government now existed and its full globalisation was assured – and with it world peace since democracies conduct their relations with each other in peace (Fukuyama 1992).

*Source: Press Association Images/Jerome Delay*

At the end of the Cold War, Francis Fukuyama declared that Liberal Democracy's victory marked the 'end of history'. Was his optimism premature?

## The current state of play with democratisation

Despite three waves of democratisation advancing the idea further than ever before, a majority of the world's countries still live under undemocratic political systems. Even among 'transition states', such as Russia, some question whether substantive democracy will be the end point of the process. It has been suggested that only around a fifth of the countries undergoing democratic transition in the twenty-first century were clearly set to stabilise as fully fledged liberal democracies (Carothers 2002). It seems that the end of history is not yet with us. China, home to one-sixth of the world's people, has modernised and embraced global capitalism but shows little likelihood of abandoning its one-party system. Similarly Cuba, Vietnam, North Korea and Belarus are ruled in much the same way as they were during the Cold War. Absolutist monarchical rule remains in Saudi Arabia and Swaziland, and a military dictatorship persists in Burma, while Libya and Syria also have non-democratic systems. Additionally, a number of African third wave 'democracies', such as Zimbabwe and Algeria have gone backwards and reverted to more authoritarian and elitist forms of governance in a similar fashion to the reversals of the 1960s elsewhere on the African continent. Governance of any sort – let alone democracy – is elusive in 'failed states' like Sierra Leone, Congo, Sudan and Somalia which have emerged as such over the last two decades due to persistent civil wars and a lack of international interest (see Chapter 28).

Contemporary Russia has properly structured general elections and a range of political parties but is considered by many not to be a democracy since its electoral process is manipulated by a small elite (for example, by only ever allowing government election broadcasts to be televised) who often appear to run the country more for the convenience of a handful of oligarchs (powerful businessmen) than 'the people'. More charitably Russia could be described as a 'semi-democracy', as could the political systems of Malaysia, Singapore, Egypt and Tunisia, where regular elections are held but the same party inevitably wins through stifling opposition voices. It is worth noting, however, that Vladimir Putin's authoritarianism, while criticised by some, is not altogether unpopular with the Russian demos who have no popular collective memory of democracy and many instead observe how their lives and their country's influence in the world have diminished in the period since elections and a party system were introduced. Russians, after all, have more political freedom than they and their parents had under the Communists but they also have less job security and can barely conceive that their country was once ahead of the USA in the 'space race'.

Many have come to contend that, far from coming to an end, history is repeating itself with another anti-democratic tide emerging against the third wave of democratisation. This may even be something of a coordinated response with countries irritated at their marginalisation and interference in their affairs from democratic states finding common ground and banding together in diplomatic and economic coalitions. Russia and China, whose relations were frosty even while on the same side of the Cold War – owing to their differing interpretations of Marxist doctrine – have increasingly turned to each other for economic and diplomatic support since 1991. The two have developed cooperative strategies through the Shanghai Cooperation Organisation and also sought the support of international pariah states like Iran, Belarus and Zimbabwe (Diamond 2008: 86).

## What can make democracy permanent?

Democracy, then, can unravel and it is far from certain that a country which has introduced competitive elections will continue on this path. Explanations for how democracy can become entrenched as a political system are varied, and differ from case to case, but a number of key factors are most frequently cited:

- **Military defeat**

  Military defeat is likely to undermine a military-based government since the armed forces will have been weakened, as will any legitimacy they may have with the general public as guarantors of their security. Greece's defeat by Turkey over Cyprus in 1974 and Argentina's by the UK over the Falklands eight years later marked the beginning of the end of military rule in those countries and a return to democracy which has, thus far, been sustained. The inability of Portugal's Salazar regime to suppress colonial uprisings in Angola, Mozambique and Equatorial Guinea similarly undermined that system's 'strong man' credibility and made democracy unstoppable.

- **Consensus on the need for a new start**

  Democracy can unravel if, when the going gets tough, people's faith in the system weakens and they either desire a return to the certainties of the old order or, at least, are not inclined to do much to prevent the old elites from assuming control again. The commitment of ordinary Russians to Liberal Democracy has been less than many of their Slavic neighbours and, while a return to the old Communist order has been resisted by the elites, the country has reverted to a more authoritarian form of rule. In contrast, the 1989 anti-Communist revolutions in East Europe set six countries (Poland, East Germany, Hungary, Czechoslovakia, Romania and Bulgaria) with little Liberal tradition on what now seems an irreversible democratic path, because there was such widespread support for change. Even when change made life more difficult for many, as transition produced higher levels of unemployment and poverty, there was insufficient support for a return to a centrally planned economy and one-party rule.

- **A good standard of living**

  A number of works on democratisation have emphasised a correlation between economic development and the stabilisation of democratic rule. Industrialisation brings greater wealth to a country and with it social change as a large proportion of the population abandon peasantry or subsistence farming for work in new industries vital to the government and national economy (Lipset 1959; Przeworski et al. 2000). This link is, to some extent, indisputable. Most developed states are democracies and most non-democracies are relatively poor states. Democratisation did accompany the Industrial Revolution in many states during the first wave, as a working class emerged to fuel industrialisation and then become empowered as a result. Over time, however, the correlation between economic growth and democracy has become less clear. Germany and Italy did not follow the examples of the USA, UK and France in the early twentieth century and evolve into substantive democracies while, later, India democratised well before it industrialised. The Soviet Union achieved an economic miracle under brutal authoritarian rule and China later followed suit by embracing capitalism but not democracy. Oil rich Gulf states, like Kuwait and Saudi Arabia, have similarly seen their people enriched but not significantly empowered.

While it is evident that a good standard of living does seem to help facilitate democracy, modern industrialised living may even serve to undermine democratic rule. Some analysts and political voices have come to suggest that the lobbying power of big business can create a new elite that distorts the link between the demos and the government, undermining the notion of polyarchy discussed earlier. Prominent US government adviser Robert Reich has even gone as far as to assert that 'capitalism is killing democracy' (Reich 2007).

● **A diverse economy**

A significant exception to the norm of democracy accompanying industrialisation can be seen with states whose authoritarian rule is actually strengthened with economic growth due to the 'resource curse theory'. Economic development based on a particular, abundant natural resource can inhibit democracy since control over this sector of the economy becomes more important to the elites for maintaining control than popular support (Acemoglu and Robinson 2006). Hence a number of major oil exporters – such as Libya, Saudi Arabia and Equatorial Guinea – have continued to grow economically in recent decades without any commensurate empowerment of their populaces. Similarly, in a more complex manner, Russian political elites have needed to pay more attention to keeping the support of the handful of 'oligarchs' who bought up control of state industries that were rapidly privatised in the 1990s, than to that of the general public.

● **Civil society**

Some analysts of democracy take a more sociological approach to explaining the establishment of this form of rule. As discussed earlier, there is more to democracy than elections and it is increasingly acknowledged that involving a significant proportion of society in public life through polyarchy is integral to permanent democratisation. De Tocqueville, early in the history of Liberal Democracy, noted the importance of individuals cooperating in 'associations' in sustaining American democracy. Central to polyarchy is the notion of a civil society defined by British democracy specialist David Held as:

> areas of social life – the domestic world, the economic sphere, cultural
> activities and political interaction – which are organized by private or
> voluntary arrangements between individuals and groups outside of the
> direct control of the state

(Held 1987: 281)

Civil society provides crucial links between government and the demos, and can keep a check on the executive, ensuring that it is not allowed to slide back towards authoritarianism. Pressure groups in Turkey advanced democracy in that country by exposing the failings of the democratically elected government in acting 'for the people' in their lack of preparation for the devastating earthquakes of 1999. Turkey had not reverted to military rule since 1983 but was not a substantive democracy since civilians had little connection with public life and the military remained the dominant influence on government. In the wake of the earthquakes, however, several small voluntary groups stepped in to provide relief and, in doing so, were empowered by being able to expose government weakness and convince ordinary Turks of their entitlement to safeguards from earthquake damage, safeguards of the sort enjoyed in other countries (Keyman and Icduygu 2003).

Civil society depends on communication so this, too, is a key driver of democratisation. Closed societies can inhibit democratic challenges to governing elites. The paranoid Ceausescu regime in 1970s and 1980s Romania went as far as banning photocopiers since this seemingly innocent form of office technology is a key means of producing protest leaflets. Such methods of restricting protest, allied to far more heavy-handed forms of suppression, appeared to have successfully stifled any opposition to Ceausescu but, in late December 1989, his regime was quickly toppled in line with the revolutions in the neighbouring Eastern bloc states. The unfolding of these nearby revolutions was not reported in the Romanian media but many Romanians had learned of the events by accessing relatively free uncensored broadcasts from Yugoslavia. These broadcasts were also able to reveal to Romanians the full horrors of a recent government massacre of peaceful protestors and, consequently, many were moved to action.

In a similar vein, the 1992 Thai 'cell phone revolution' occurred when pro-democracy activists were able to respond to the military government's attempt to suppress a popular uprising by cutting down telephone lines, by using their mobile phones instead. After seventeen coups in sixty years the military's grip on the reins of power in Thailand was significantly weakened (though not removed altogether). Another example of communications technology advancing democracy can be seen in the 1998 overthrow of the Suharto regime in Indonesia after thirty-two years of sometimes brutal rule. In the main, the overthrow was achieved through a peaceful democratic revolution focused on the Internet and other forms of mass media (Hill and Sen 2000). In 2009 the world witnessed the latest variant of IT-based political revolt when the – ultimately unsuccessful – 'Twitter Revolution' challenged the authenticity of President Ahmadinejad's electoral victory in Iran. Iranian authorities had acted to suppress opposition expressed on websites and more traditional media but the multifaceted nature of the online blogging system (accessible via emails or phones and constructed in a way to withstand hacking) made it much harder to contain. Hence messages calling on Iranians to march in opposition to the government and informing the rest of the world of their struggle proved impossible to contain.

Social activism can bring down governments but also needs to be evident after a democratic revolution if democracy is to be sustained, which is not always the case. British political scientist Richard Rose considers that a key factor behind many 'third' wave democracies' failing to complete the process is that they have 'democratized backwards' compared to 'first wave democracies'. In establishing competitive elections before other democratic norms which check the power of government – such as a constitution and permitting private non-governmental organisations to flourish – countries like Russia have not followed the model of most of the world's mature democracies which became modern states with an active citizenship before the full extension of the franchise (Rose and Shin 2001).

- **Force of example**

The democratic waves metaphor is supported by the tendency for neighbouring states often to follow suit in undergoing democratic revolution or reform in a process referred to by Huntington as 'snowballing' (Huntington 1991: 100–106). Spain and Portugal moved from right wing dictatorships to democracy almost simultaneously between 1974 and 1977. Ten Latin American states democratised in the six years that followed the 1979 revolution in Ecuador. Even more dramatically, democracy was ushered in in East Germany, Poland, Romania, Czechoslovakia, Hungary, Bulgaria and Romania within the space of the latter six months of 1989. Pro-democracy activists can be inspired by successes from like-minded groups in neighbouring countries and, equally, authoritarian governments can be persuaded that the 'game is up' by observing similar regimes lose legitimacy and topple. The Czechoslovak 'Velvet Revolution' of 1989 was so named as it proved to be a bloodless transition to democracy in which the ruling Communist Party simply stood aside in the face of mass public protest and the recent fall of the communist parties in Poland and Hungary.

- **Help from established democracies**

Long-standing members of the democratic club of nations can play a key role in ensuring that new entrants remain within their ranks by providing incentives to both join and stay in the club. With the end of the Cold War, US foreign policy in the 1990s shifted from the 'Truman Doctrine' of supporting any anti-Communist regime to the 'Clinton Doctrine' of encouraging democratic change in some Global South countries through gentle diplomatic pressure and by linking this to the amount of development aid being allocated. This shift was actually a furthering of a similar, short-lived initiative in the late 1970s in the aftermath of the 1975 Helsinki Accords (see Chapter 22) when propping up right wing dictatorships came to appear hypocritical in the context of pushing for human rights reform in the Communist world. For example, the Carter administration in 1977 initiated the annual production of a State Department report on the state of human rights in all countries of the world and approved the creation of the Inter-American Court of Human Rights (see Chapter 22). **Realpolitik** returned to US foreign policy in the 1980s, however, as the second Cold War took shape and again in the aftermath of the 11 September 2001 attacks when dictators suppressing Islamic fundamentalism, such as former Soviet Communist Karimov of Uzbekistan, came to be viewed in a similar perspective to those suppressing Marxist revolutionaries in the 1950s and 60s.

A clearer and more consistent case of democratic promotion has come from the European integration process since the 1950s. The EC/EU has greatly advanced European democratisation in two localised waves by opening its doors first to the fledgling democracies of Spain, Portugal and Greece in the 1980s and, secondly, in the first decade of the twenty-first century, to ten former Communist states. These countries have seen their living standards improve by a combination of being part of the world's biggest and richest trading bloc and by being in receipt of redistributed funds from the richer members. NATO have followed suit since the end of the Cold War in opening their doors only to states with impeccable democratic and human rights credentials. This had not been a precondition in earlier times when Greece, Turkey and Portugal had been recruited while under military rule.

Some consider that the successes of the EU/NATO model of democratisation demonstrate that the carrot is better than the stick and the longer game of establishing 'linkages' with new democracies is a more fruitful policy than the 'leverage' of relying on diplomatic pressure or intervention to create permanent change (Levitsky and Way 2005). The use of the 'big stick' of full scale military intervention has of late been employed to promote democracy and is assessed in the next section.

## Democratisation by force – 'nation building'

A core contemporary debate on how democracy can be made permanent has emerged in light of the post-Cold War UN operations in Bosnia and Kosovo, and US-led interventions in Iraq and Afghanistan – and, more particularly, the processes of supervised 'nation building' which have followed the initial military campaigns. Although often viewed as a contemporary phenomenon, some strong historical precedence for attempts at democratisation by force can be seen with the post-Second World War allied occupations of Germany, Italy and Japan. As the Iraqi and Afghan occupations have unfolded, attempts have been made to see what can be learned from these past successes and applied to their contemporary equivalents (see Case study).

The scale of the breakdown of governance in Afghanistan and Iraq was not anticipated in advance of the conflicts. In particular, the collapse of law and order has posed a particularly acute problem for the occupiers, most notably with the vacuum created with the dismantling of Saddam's police force. The successes of the post-Second World War nation building exercises stand in stark contrast to their post-Cold War equivalents. West Germany, Italy and Japan, as developed states with some experience of democratic reform, were more easily 'built' than Iraq and Afghanistan. It could be added that the Second World War axis powers had also been more clearly militarily defeated and pacified. It is still worth noting, however, that colossal time, expense and effort were expended by the USA and their allies in the nation building exercises in Germany, Japan and Italy. In relative terms the USA was far richer in 1945 than in 2001 and also driven by a fear of Communism that was far greater, even, than the fear of terrorism produced by the 11 September 2001 strikes (at least

## Case study: Can you build a democratic nation?

The prominent US international affairs think tank, the RAND Corporation, have been at the forefront of research on nation building and, drawing on historical precedent for such ventures, have reached the following conclusions (Dobbins et al. 2003):

- Prior democratic experience, economic development and national homogeneity facilitate nation building but the crucial factor is the level of effort given to the process
- Multilateral nation building is more complex than unilateral but more realistic in terms of sharing the burden and cost
- Multilateral nation building is more likely to produce lasting change and regional reconciliation than unilateral
- The more troops that are committed the fewer the casualties that will be suffered
- The support of neighbouring states is important and should be sought
- Providing reconciliation for past injustices is important but may be too difficult to achieve
- Nation building takes a long time – at least five years.

RAND has built up a strong body of research on this theme of externally enforced nation building as the occupations of Iraq and Afghanistan have evolved and become more contentious (Dobbins et al. 2007). While accepting that such endeavours must inevitably be costly and long term, RAND nonetheless remains positive and reason that it is possible to democratise by force. Many others have come to disagree and consider that the quagmires faced by the USA and their allies in occupying Afghanistan and Iraq, after initial military successes, is testimony to the fact that democratisation by force can, perhaps, only be possible in exceptional circumstances. Additionally, it could be argued that imposing a particular form of political system on another country is fundamentally undemocratic.

### How will history judge the occupation of Iraq?

The occupation of Iraq has proved to be extremely controversial and, some would say, even counterproductive since it has intensified radical Islamist groups' opposition to Western imperialism around the world. Some defenders of the occupation, however, have suggested that history may come to view the 'nation building' exercise in a more positive light. In, say, fifty years' time if Iraq is a stable Liberal Democracy with cordial relations with its neighbouring states and a strong economy built on oil exports, might the turmoil, expense and bloodshed of the past decade actually be viewed as having been worth it in the long run?

 **What do you think of this proposition?**

in the government), prompting an unparalleled level of finance for the foreign policy aims of the Truman Doctrine. Troops, sometimes topping one and a half million in Germany and over a third of a million in Japan, were stationed for several generations. Many are still there today.

Set against this the operations in Iraq and Afghanistan have been comparatively small-scale and yet, at the same time, are trying to build a nation from a more divided and hostile population lacking any of the democracy-enabling characteristics listed in the previous section. To make more contemporary comparisons, UN-led nation building in the post-Yugoslav states of Kosovo and Bosnia-Herzegovina and in facilitating East Timor's secession from Indonesia have also been smoother since a majority (or at least a large proportion in Bosnia) see the occupiers as liberators and have welcomed democratic change. Even in these 'successes', however, the process has been far from straightforward and, possibly, not yet completed. Law and order has deteriorated during the occupations in Bosnia and particularly Kosovo, with organised crime flourishing and spilling over into the rest of Europe. An exit strategy for the West is still problematic since Serb nationalism and Russian power politics see independent and Western-oriented Bosnian and Kosovan states as counter to their own national interests. The full handover of power to the local population has proved more difficult than anticipated with critics suggesting that these states, instead of independent democracies, had become European 'Raj's (as with Indian regions under British colonial rule) ruled as Western puppet states with only the trappings of local empowerment (Knaus and Martin 2003).

Ultimately, however, comparisons between the post 1945 and post 2001 nation building exercises are misleading since the *nations* in Germany, Japan and Italy were already built. In the post 1945 situations, these were actually cases of '*state*-building'; a reconstruction of political institutions and the economy in a Western, democratic manner. Though they have come frequently to be used interchangeably, the terms *nation* and *state* are not the same thing and the significance of this is beyond a matter of academic semantics. While a state is a legally definable concept – a territory with people, ruled by a single government – a nation defies such an objective definition. A nation is a subjective and social construct; a group of people sharing common social characteristics they feel distinguish them from other groups of people (see Chapter 20). Despite periods of brutal rule, the vast majority of the native populations in the allied occupied territories after 1945 were Germans, Japanese and Italians unified by language, ethnicity and cultural norms which distinquished them from other nations. The same is broadly true of Kosovans and East Timorians (though not of the more divided Bosnians). Iraq and Afghanistan, in contrast, are not, never have been and probably never will be 'nations'. Iraq was artificially carved out of the Turkish Ottoman Empire by Western powers at the end of the First World War and was always an uneasy hotch-potch of Sunni Arabs, Shia Arabs and Kurds held together only by repressive government. Afghanistan, similarly, is an artificial relic of the British Empire; an ethnically diverse land only ever united historically in resisting foreign occupations. While there are precedents for externally supervised state reconstruction and democratisation, there are none for doing this in addition to 'nation building'.

## Is democratisation important for international relations?

Even among democrats, opinion on whether the active promotion of democratisation should form part of a state's foreign policy is divided. Is democracy something that should be promoted diplomatically or, even, forcibly? What significance do liberal democratic political systems have for international relations?

- **Liberals**
  Liberalism as an ideology is most closely associated with democracy and Liberal approaches to IR tend to view the active promotion of Liberal Democracy as making sense both in moral and security terms. Democracy enhances **human security** since democratically accountable governments are compelled to respond to people's needs and demands, when they may have reason not to do so, out of a sense of duty and

responsibility. Human rights can be enshrined in constitutional systems limiting the power of government over their citizens and avoiding the tyranny of the majority dilemma. Governments can also be held to account by democracy in terms of delivering basic entitlements to their people, such as food and welfare (see entitlements thesis, Chapter 18).

Liberals also see the promotion of democracy as a basis for achieving peaceful and ordered international relations through the firmly held conviction that 'democracies do not go to war with each other'. This proposition is well-supported empirically, so the fact that more and more states in the world have embraced democracy in recent years has given scope for optimism in the realisation of Kant's vision, expressed in *Perpetual Peace* in the eighteenth century. Kant, in fact, proposed that it was the trinity of democracy, trade and international cooperation which were the basis for a peaceful world and these three factors are all more prominent today than at any point in history. Over two centuries after its promulgation, the Kantian peace proposition has been rigorously tested by Liberal Pluralists for its applicability to the contemporary global political system. Russett and Oneal's *Triangulating Peace*, for example, draws on over a decade of statistical analysis with each of these three corners of the 'peace triangle' examined in turn to show how they mutually reinforce each other over time in 'virtuous circles' (Russett and Oneal 2001). Democracies trade with each other more and form common organisations more, both of which are phenomena also demonstrably contributing to pacific relations. Democracies in dealing with other democracies more easily find non-military means to resolve inevitable clashes of interest that arise in their relations and increasingly realise that their interests are not served by violent confrontations. Democratic peace is a political theory with uncharacteristically solid empirical foundations if we consider that: '(e)stablished democracies fought no wars against each other during the entire twentieth century' (Russett and Starr 1996: 173). If we also consider that the number of democratic states in the world has increased in recent years, the future prospects for perpetual peace look good also. Both of these sets of figures are challengeable, but the overall trends they indicate are not. This democratic peace thesis is explored in more detail in Chapter 25.

## Box 21.5 The 'neo-Cons' and democratisation

It is possible to see democratisation by force as a manifestation of Liberal foreign policy even though much Liberal political opinion was opposed to the Iraq War and occupation. Liberalism in IR is not always synonymous with Liberalism as an ideology. The 'neo-Conservative' thinkers, who were the key advocates of the US nation building exercises in Iraq and Afghanistan are, as their name implies, located on the right of US politics but their belief in forcibly planting seeds of democracy in the Middle East is not conventionally Realist in that it is a morally driven foreign policy and, as such, *Idealist* (see Chapter 7).

*Source: Reuters/Jim Young*

**George W. Bush's administration (2001–2009) was heavily influenced by neo-conservative thought. Were their nation-building exercises in Iraq and Afghanistan actually manifestations of Liberal foreign policy?**

- **(Classical) Realists**

  Realists are likely to be democrats since it is a school of thought closely associated with conservative politics in the Western world but IR traditionalists – in contrast to neo-Conservatives – tend to see democracy as largely irrelevant to the achievement of peace. From a Realist perspective, conflicts of national interest inevitably occur in relations between countries, be they democratic or not, and the best means of managing this is to pay respect to the balance of power and not the promotion of ideas and ideals (the term *Idealism* was coined by Realists intending to denigrate Liberalism in international relations as unrealistic). Imposing values on others is only likely to fuel resentment. Sovereignty should be respected and it should be left up to others to decide if they want to have a democratic political system or not.

- **(Neo) Realists**

  A key reason for the metamorphosis of most Realist thought to Neo-Realism from the 1970s was the belief that the international political system was no longer entirely anarchic but becoming a 'society of states' in which values could and should play some role. Neo-Realists remain far more protective of sovereignty than Liberals and continue to see peace, as being more about maintaining the balance of power than democratic peace, but those of the '**English School**' variant see a society of mature democratic states as the best means of advancing human rights and governance in the human interest (Dunne and Wheeler 2002). Democratisation represents the best way of ensuring that politics in a globalising world is 'for the people', rather than moving towards forms of global governance advocated by Liberals which Neo-Realists see as undermining both sovereignty and democracy (see Chapter 33).

- **Marxists**

As referred to earlier in the chapter, Marxists consider themselves to be democrats but, for them, the achievement of global peace and justice is not about Liberal Democracy. For Marxists a 'people's democratisation' of the world could only be achieved through global structural change: the abandonment of capitalism.

- **Social Constructivists**

Social Constructivism is less associated with any particular ideology than the other IR approaches so does not have such a clear position on whether promoting democracy is a good idea or not. However, this school of thought's particular emphasis on the importance of culture in the conduct of international relations does lead many of its advocates to be sceptical of democratic peace since the culture of democratic promotion, rather than pacifying the world, can push some countries into war. Hence in this view, the post-Cold War nation building exercises have been the result of cultural clashes with 'warlike democracies' feeling righteously driven to confront non-believers in a modern form of crusade (Risse 1995). From this perspective, then, democratisation could actually be a source of conflict rather than peace.

## Conclusions

The meaning of democracy and its significance in International Relations is disputed and the progress of democratisation is also open to different interpretations. Two decades on from the end of the Cold War we are still not at the 'end of history' but Liberal Democracy does appear to be the world's most popular form of government. In spite of notable reversals, the general long-term trend is for countries to continue on a democratic trajectory. Perhaps, as Churchill famously opined, 'democracy is the worst form of government except for all those other forms that have been tried from time to time' (Churchill 1947).

A reversion to authoritarianism for the world's established democracies seems unlikely in the contemporary climate and, while it may take a long time to become established, democracy tends not to go away completely in countries where it has been tried but then abandoned. 'Attempts at democratization, even when they fail or only partially succeed, form part of the collective memory of communities' (Grugel 2002: 247). However, while a democratising trend is apparent, it is also far from inevitable that this will globalise and that current authoritarian regimes will democratise. Countries like China and Saudi Arabia have no collective memory of democracy, have achieved economic growth without democracy and are sufficiently influential in the world to be subjected to only gentle external pressure to reform through fear of causing offence.

Nevertheless, even in some of the world's least open societies, where democracy has never been tried out, people are slowly becoming more aware of what they have not got. The Chinese government crushed the pro-democracy protests of 1989 but democracy's proliferation elsewhere that year and the global exposure of this tyranny ensure that the movement for democracy in China lives on. A movement demanding greater rights for women has emerged in Saudi Arabia over the last decade despite profound difficulties in accessing or voicing feminist ideas in such a highly patriarchal and censorial country. In a move which epitomised the democratising potential of globalisation and information technology, activists in 2008 posted a video on the Internet of a Saudi woman driving a car, a practice illegal in the country. The idea of democracy has globalised beyond its practice and, in an era of increasingly global mass communication, this makes it harder and harder for authoritarian governments to resist its waves.

## Resource section

## Questions

1. Describe and explain the phenomenon of democratisation.

2. 'History shows us that it is possible to democratise countries successfully through foreign occupation'. Do you agree or disagree with this assertion in the light of the Afghan and Iraqi occupations since 2001?

3. Why do IR theories differ in terms of the level of significance they attach to democratisation?

4. Are you a representative or popular democrat (if a democrat at all)? List any issues which in your country you imagine could command popular support in a referendum but which you personally would not support (for example, on whether or not to impose the death penalty for murder). Would you: (a) accept these decisions being implemented for your country despite them being against your own views or (b) consider that some issues cannot be accepted as legitimate, even if they do have popular support because they are not in the interests of 'the people'. If you have answered (a) you appear to support popular democracy. If you have answered (b) you appear to prefer representative forms of democracy (or, possibly, do not support democracy at all).

## Recommended reading

**Diamond, L. (2008)** *The Spirit of Democracy: The Struggle to Build Free Societies Throughout the World* **(New York: Times Books)**
A comprehensive analysis of democratisation using case studies of countries that have recently slid back from democracy to puncture the optimism of Fukuyama's 'End of History' thesis. Ultimately, however, this is not a pessimistic dismissal of Liberal support for democratisation but the views of a more cautionary proponent of democratic promotion who sees the process as being more complex and long term than most other analysts.

**Grugel, J. (2002)** *Democratization. A Critical Introduction* **(Basingstoke, UK: Palgrave)**
In an impressive academic critique of the democratisation literature, which is broad and often incoherent, Grugel thinks clearly about what democracy actually is and about how democratisation can occur.

*The Journal of Democracy*
This pre-eminent journal is an invaluable source of research in this area, having published many seminal articles on case studies and the theory of democratisation.

*Democratization*
This highly-regarded journal is another very valuable source of scholarship in the area. Established nearly two decades ago, it has published important contributions on both the theory and practice of democratisation.

## Useful websites

**Freedom House:** http://www.freedomhouse.org/template.cfm?page=1
Well-known US pressure group who produce an annual 'Freedom in the World' report which gives a democratic rating and assessment for all countries.

**Polity IV:** http://www.systemicpeace.org/polity/polity4.htm
An extensive academic database containing widely cited statistics, graphs and analysis on democratisation and other related aspects of international politics.

# Chapter 22
# Human Rights

After reading this chapter you will be able to:

- Understand the meaning and rise of the concept of human rights in international affairs

- Identify the roles played by the United Nations and civil society in advancing human rights by promoting the implementation of existing legal instruments and developing further ones

- Explain why there is resistance to this development of human rights (from quarters other than human rights abusers themselves!)

*Source*: Getty Images

## Introductory box: Should the international community intervene in Darfur?

A humanitarian tragedy has unfolded in this Western province of Sudan since 2003 when long-running ethnic tensions between some Arab and Black groups escalated dramatically. Human rights pressure groups suggest that at least 300,000 people have been killed in this time, although the government – which is Arab – denies that it is anywhere near this level. Systematic massacres of principally Black Darfurians by an Arab non-state armed group, the Janjaweed, with the apparent support of the Sudanese government, have shocked the world and brought calls for an armed intervention to end the suffering.

But, would such a response end the suffering?

Liberal opinion (though not exclusively) contends that, when faced with such a humanitarian catastrophe, traditional notions of sovereignty should be set aside and 'something should be done'. Many Realists, however, contend that such well-intentioned action would be wrong, arguing that history suggests it is best not to interfere in other countries' affairs since it is only likely to inflame matters.

Would you support your country's troops being despatched to fight for an end to this conflict or do you feel that they should only be expected to put their lives at risk in defence of their own citizens?

*Source: Getty Images/AFP*

**Do you think the international community should have intervened in Darfur? Your answer will probably be determined by whether you position yourself as a Liberal or a Realist.**

## The evolution of the idea of human rights

### The early history of human rights

**Box 22.1  Early development in human rights law**

1815    Slave trade declared immoral at Congress of Vienna and Treaty of Ghent
1864    1st Geneva Convention sets out rules of war
1890    Brussels Convention on Slavery
1901    International Labour Office established to set global standards for workers
1926    Slavery Convention
1946    United Nations Commission on Human Rights established
1948    Universal Declaration of Human Rights adopted

The idea that all individuals have certain inalienable rights which should be enshrined in national law has, in some countries, been advanced from ancient times but most notably started to become established from the late eighteenth century when the political philosophy of Liberalism took hold in some countries. The notion of governments taking legal or political steps to protect individuals other than their own nationals/citizens is, however, a relatively recent one in international affairs and still a long way from being firmly established in international law. The cooperative diplomatic environment of the nineteenth century 'Concert of Europe' – when the major powers of the continent, shocked by the devastation of the Napoleonic Wars resolved to work together to ensure peace – prompted the first significant attempts to enshrine human rights in international law. At the Congress of Vienna in 1815 the great European powers of France, Great Britain, Russia, Austria-Hungary and Prussia agreed to work towards ending the slave trade throughout the world, declaring it to be 'repugnant to the principles of humanity'. A similar declaration was made earlier in that year by the British and US governments at the Treaty of Ghent. It was not until the 1890 Brussels Convention on Slavery, however, that the slave trade was actually made illegal under international law and not until the 1926 Slavery Convention that slavery itself (in addition to slave trading) was outlawed.

From the 1870s unprecedented European diplomatic coordination dissolved into unprecedented conflict and nationalism as the continent split into two armed camps and became the focus of two world wars. Against this backdrop human rights predictably did not progress greatly in the first half of the twentieth century. The League of Nations did not develop any global bill of rights, despite a US–British initiative to incorporate this into the Covenant (the founding Treaty upon which the organisation was built). The British dropped the proposal after the Japanese government requested an article on racial equality be included, since this would have proved embarrassing given the 'White Australia' policy in operation in its colony which discriminated against potential non-white migrants. The League, nonetheless, did give birth to some important human rights initiatives. It made guaranteeing the right of national minorities a condition of membership for states newly established from the break up of the Austro-Hungarian and Turkish Ottoman empires (such as Iraq) and its Permanent Court of International Justice condemned state discrimination against minorities in the 1935 *Minority Schools in Albania* case and other Advisory Opinions. Most significantly the League pioneered the idea of a right of **asylum** for individuals fleeing political persecution

## Box 22.2 From where does the idea of human rights originate?

There is, of course, no definitive answer to this question. Inevitably, different countries lay claim to being the home of human rights. The French Revolution of 1789 justified deposing a monarchical political system as advancing the 'rights of man' and in doing so was influenced by similar claims of individual empowerment advanced in the US Declaration of Independence issued after the overthrow of British imperial rule thirteen years earlier. The British themselves point to *Magna Carta*, of 1215, which began the process of limiting the powers of their monarch and developing the idea of certain legal rights pertaining to all people.

Much earlier still than Magna Carta, however, was a fifth century BC proclamation by a Persian king announcing measures to safeguard members of non-Persian religious and ethnic groups in his empire from persecution. The 'Cyrus Cylinder', today housed in the British Museum, sets out these rights. Contrary to most Western expectations, might Iran (modern day Persia) be the true home of human rights?[1]

from their own government or fellow countrymen by emigrating. The Nansen Passport, named after the legendary Norwegian Polar explorer turned League High Commissioner for Refugees, guaranteed asylum in fifty-two of the organisation's member states. The League also helped promote the notion of universal workers' rights by incorporating, within its system of Specialised Agencies, the International Labour Organisation (ILO), which as far back as 1901 had initiated resolutions seeking to ensure fair standards in terms of issues like working hours, maternity rights and unemployment benefits for all people.

## What are human rights?

Precisely what does and does not constitute an inalienable right of all people in the world is disputed. Countries differ in the rights – if any – they confer on their citizens and there is no clear consensus on where the line is drawn between an indisputable right of all regardless of circumstances and a wish list of preferences only achievable if the economic and security situation permits it.

Conventionally it is suggested that there are three broad categories of human rights:

- **civil and political** rights are most associated with Liberalism and the 'Western' world of the European and North American democracies. Magna Carta, the US Declaration of Independence and the reforms of the French Revolution are in this tradition of setting out measures to safeguard individuals from the possibility of tyranny meted out by their governments. Hence civil and political rights include ideas associated with Liberal Democracy, such as free speech, the right to vote for your government, and guarantees against being arrested without good reason.

---

[1] It should be noted that many historians dispute that the Cyrus Cylinder is any sort of declaration of human rights and argue that this was largely invented by the Shah of Iran in the 1970s for nationalistic purposes and then acknowledged by the UN in order to curry non-Western support for human rights law. M. Schulz, 'UN Treasure Honours Persian Despot', *Spiegel Online International* 15/7/08 http://www.spiegel.de/international/world/0,1518,566027,00.html (accessed 30.9.08).

- **economic and social** rights are concerned with an individual's *entitlements from* the state – such as health care and an education – rather than protection against it. This idea of rights was originally most associated with socialist political thought but began to be more generally recognised in the twentieth century after the emergence of civil and political rights in the Western world. To a Marxist the idea of an individual needing rights against their government is illogical since they consider the (socialist) state to be the embodiment of the people. Economic and social rights are not, however, the preserve of countries with histories of Communist or even Social Democratic rule. Western Liberal Democracies and liberal political philosophy in the twentieth century came to embrace the idea of state welfare and social protection as a consensus among Liberal, Conservative and Socialist political parties (hence the International Labour Organisation had begun drafting global worker standards from 1901).

- **collective** rights were most associated with what was once known as the 'Third World'. African and particularly East Asian political philosophy is often considered to be less preoccupied with individuals and more focused on the rights of societies. This, like economic and social rights, is most associated with twentieth century international politics though has deeper roots. The notion of national self-determination as a right swept through Europe and Latin America in the nineteenth century with political activists from one country often lending their support to separatists from other countries in a wave of 'Liberal nationalism'. British poet Lord Byron, for example, met his death preparing to fight for Greek independence from the Turkish Ottoman Empire. After the First World War this phenomenon globalised as **Idealists** (see Chapter 7) embraced decolonisation as part of a new, more moral world order. The League of Nations thus devised the mandate system under which colonies of Germany and Turkey seized by the British, French and their allies in the Great War, rather than simply being conquered as the spoils of war, were groomed for independence. This right to independence was more clearly still enshrined in international affairs when the UN emerged after the Second World War with many newly decolonised Asian and African states among its ranks.

## The United Nations and the codification of human rights

The horrors of the Second World War prompted the first systematic and sustained attempt to enshrine human rights into international law as part of the UN system. Mandated by Article 68 of the UN Charter, a Commission on Human Rights, comprising top lawyers, was established to work on drafting a bill of rights for the world. This became known as the Universal Declaration of Human Rights. The Declaration is made up of thirty short articles of mainly civil and political rights and was adopted by the General Assembly on 10 December 1948 (Human Rights Day). No member state voted against the Declaration but there were abstentions from the Soviet Union and their East European allies, South Africa and Saudi Arabia. Apartheid era South Africa could hardly have been expected to support ethnic equality and Saudi Arabia objected to the notion of religious freedom.

Stalin's Soviet Union was an even less likely enthusiast for human rights but they based their objections on the Western bias of the Declaration and argued for economic and social rights to be included. It is also often considered that many countries who did vote in favour probably had little idea that the resolution would ever have any real significance.

The Declaration was just that – a statement without any legal commitment on the states – and from 1948 the Commission on Human Rights turned their attention to developing legal instruments to codify the themes of the articles and other rights. In line with the Soviet objections and the increased acceptance of a widened notion of rights in Western Europe, the legal instruments devised were twin Covenants on Civil and Political Rights and also on Economic and Social Rights (see Table 22.1). Against the backdrop of the Cold War it took nearly twenty years to get these covenants ratified but by 1976 they had finally entered into international law. By 2010 their application was impressively universal with – of the 192 UN members – 165 having ratified the Civil and Political Covenant and 160 the Economic and Social Covenant.

**Table 22.1** The UN twin covenants

| Civil and Political Rights | Economic and Social Rights |
| --- | --- |
| a) Right to life, liberty and property | Right to: |
| b) Right to marry (reproductive rights) | a) Work for just reward |
| c) Right to fair trial | b) Form and join trade unions |
| d) Freedom from slavery, torture and arbitrary arrest | c) Rest and holidays with pay |
| e) Freedom of movement and to seek asylum | d) Standard of living adequate to health |
| f) Right to a nationality | e) Social security |
| g) Freedom of thought and religion | f) Education |
| h) Freedom of opinion | g) Participation in cultural life of the community |
| i) Freedom of assembly and association | |
| j) Right to free elections, universal suffrage | |

The Covenant on Civil and Political Rights also has two optional protocols allowing parties additionally to commit themselves to the abolition of the death penalty (except in times of war) and permitting their citizens to make individual petitions to the UN if they feel their government has violated their rights.[2]

Collective rights were not awarded a distinct covenant but the right to self-determination is written into the first article of both covenants and was incorporated into Chapter XI of the UN Charter. In fact it could be argued that collective rights are the most fully implemented of the three types since the UN has succeeded in completing the League of Nation's mandate system work and nearly all colonies desiring independence have achieved this under its watch.

---

[2] By 2010 113 states were party to the individual petition protocol and 72 to the death penalty protocol.

The 1993 World Conference on Human Rights at Vienna in its Programme for Action, adopted by 171 states, confirmed that the three categories all made up the notion of human rights. A consensus had been arrived at that governments had a duty to grant their own citizens both freedoms and core entitlements as well as respecting other people's rights, both individually and collectively. These various obligations should be understood as: 'universal, indivisible and interdependent and interrelated' (World Conference on Human Rights, 1993, I, 3).

In addition to codifying the twin covenants, the Commission has sought to further the development of human rights by developing a series of more specific instruments, seeking to protect specifically vulnerable groups of people summarised in this section.

## Genocide

The first major achievement of the UN Commission of Human Rights after drafting the Declaration was to formulate the 1948 Convention on the Prevention and Punishment of Genocide. The convention proscribes acts which aim to 'destroy in whole or in part a national, ethnic, racial or religious group'. Commission member Raphael Lemkin, a Jewish International Law lecturer at Yale University who had fled Nazi persecution in Poland, both coined the term 'genocide' and played a leading role in the formulation of the 'Genocide Convention'. The word, which combines the Greek *genos* (meaning race/family) with the Latin *cide* (to kill), had particular resonance to him since forty-nine members of his family and six million of his fellow nationals had been murdered in what Winston Churchill called the 'crime without a name'.

Though the word did not exist at the time, the first systematic international political response to an act of genocide occurred during the First World War when a declaration was made by the allied powers of France, Russia and Great Britain about the widespread massacres of Armenians which had occurred in the Turkish Ottoman Empire. Hundreds of thousands of Armenians were systematically killed in an episode which was noted in Hitler's *Mein Kampf* and possibly inspired his 'Final Solution' for Europe's Jews. No real justice for the estimated 1.5 million slaughtered Armenians was ever achieved, however. The 'Young Turk' revolution of 1922, which replaced the Ottoman monarchy with a more Western-oriented secular Republic, brought about a reconciliation between the allied powers and the Turks, and absolved the new government of responsibility for pursuing crimes committed in the Ottoman era (Schabas 2000: 14–22).

In 1951 the UN's International Court of Justice declared that, since the 1948 convention was so widely ratified, genocide came into the category of 'customary international law', making it a crime anywhere in the world. The precedent for the universal jurisdiction of the Genocide Convention was established by the 1962 Eichmann case when Israeli secret agents kidnapped the former Nazi general and tried him in Israel for anti-Jewish genocide.[3] This means that genocide can be understood as a rare case of **Public International Law**

---

[3] *Attorney General of Israel* v. *Eichmann*, 36 International. Law Report 277.

functioning as 'proper' law. Countries which have not ratified the convention are not excluded from its jurisdictional reach and there is a duty on all states which have ratified to prosecute those guilty of the crime where they can. Hence, while the Rwandan genocide of 1994 represented a crime against over 800,000 Tutsis committed by their Hutu murderers, it was also a crime that the international community neglected to come to their aid. Some Hutus have since been prosecuted for the crime by a specially established UN court, but there have been no recriminations for the UN member states who lacked the desire or incentive to intervene in the carnage beyond rescuing some of their own nationals. While there can be no doubt that the rapid scale of ethnic killing in Rwanda amounted to genocide, determining when racial or religious killings come into this category is a moot point and in situations such as the Darfur crisis there is a marked caution by governments to user the 'g word' since this would entail an obligation to act.

## Torture

The 1984 Convention against Torture followed up Article 5 of the UN Declaration to criminalise state torture under any circumstances (including the theoretical 'ticking bomb' scenario – where an apprehended terrorist refuses to reveal the whereabouts of a weapon primed to inflict mass casualties imminently – frequently offered as a defence of such tactics). The Torture Convention is considered part of customary international law but has seen its rules bent even by Western Liberal Democracies. The US government's approval for 'torture lite' techniques, such as sleep deprivation and 'water boarding'[4] at its Guantanamo Bay camp on the island of Cuba, holding prisoners of the Iraq and Afghan Wars, was a clear case of this.

## Refugees and migrants

The 1951 Geneva Refugee Convention continued with the League of Nations' refugee regime by declaring it illegal for a receiving state to deport a person fleeing persecution to a country where they are likely to be imperilled. The Geneva regime at the time was largely seen as a 'mopping up' operation for living victims of Nazi oppression in the same way that the League's regime was aimed at re-settling people uprooted by the Russian Civil War after the First World War, but it has become much more than that. By 1967 it was clear that long-running conflicts, such as in Palestine and the Congo, were making refugees far more than a temporary phenomenon and a Protocol to the convention removed geographical and time limits from its scope and effectively universalised and made permanent its core provisions. By 2010, 147 states were covered by these provisions.

   In recent years, however, the permanence and universality of the Refugee Convention has started to come into question. Countries have always differed in how readily they will grant asylum to a refugee but some governments have begun to question whether they

---

[4] A procedure in which the prisoner has water poured into their mouth so that they imagine they are drowning.

should continue to be bound to give refuge at all. This is largely the result of the unforeseen rise in numbers of refugees. In 2008 there were an estimated 16 million refugees and asylum seekers in the world, up from around 3 million in the early 1970s (UNHCR 2008). The increased prevalence and persistence of civil wars is a major factor behind this. People in many democratic countries have pressurised their governments for action to curb the numbers of asylum seekers through the belief that many are really economic migrants using political unrest in their countries as a pretext for moving. As a result of this, many governments – such as in Australia and the UK – have made the process of applying for asylum more rigorous and even resorted to incarcerating asylum seekers until their applications have been processed.

## Other – non-universal – human rights treaties

- Racial

  For ethnically based abuses short of genocide (that is, not systematically seeking to eliminate a whole national group) the International Convention on the Elimination of All Forms of Racial Discrimination (ICERD) came into force in 1969, outlawing racial or national discrimination and holding the ratifying states accountable for societal as well as governmental violations. Since it is near universally and unreservedly ratified, CERD is significant enough to amount to 'an international law against systemic racism' (Robertson 2000: 94). Many Liberal democracies have followed the lead of CERD in framing domestic race relations laws and criminalising the incitement of racial hatred. The CERD regime also permits individuals to take up cases against governments. Set against this, however, countries with the most serious ethnic tensions have systematically failed to report to the CERD committee which implements the regime.

- Women

  The 1981 Convention on the Elimination of All Forms of Discrimination Against Women (CEDAW) is a bill of rights for the women of the world outlawing sexual discrimination. CEDAW appears impressively universal, having amassed some 186 ratifications by 2010 (Iran, Sudan, Somalia and the USA have not ratified due to the power of religious conservatism in these countries). Robertson, however, argues that CEDAW is far less influential than its close relation CERD owing to the number and nature of reservations to its provisions lodged by the ratifying parties (Robertson 2000: 94). The most frequently derogated are from Articles 5 and 16 which deal with, respectively, the role of women in relation to customs/culture and the family. Since these two factors are those that most threaten the rights of women this is a serious limitation on the Convention's effectiveness.

- Children

  The Convention on the Rights of the Child is centred on ensuring that 'the best interests of the child' are respected in legal matters, such as in guaranteeing a relationship with both parents in the event of their separation or legal measures taken against them. The use of the death penalty against anyone under 18 is also proscribed. All UN members bar Somalia and the USA have ratified the Convention. The US government have justified their non-participation as necessary to protect 'family rights', although the execution of children in Texas is an additional barrier to their ratification.

- **Economic migrants**

  The 1990 Convention on the Rights of all Migrant Workers and Members of their Families seeks to protect economic migrants from exploitation. The Migrant Workers Convention came into force in 2003 but it is as yet ineffectual, since its parties are overwhelmingly countries of emigration with recipient states reluctant to commit to measures ensuring they treat non-nationals equally to their own nationals.

- **The disabled**

  Around 650 million people, or one tenth of the world's population, are restricted by mental, physical or sensory impairment but, until recently, were not specifically covered by international human rights legislation. Following a campaign led by pressure groups cooperating in the International Disabilities Alliance, a Convention on the Rights of Persons With Disabilities was adopted unanimously by the UN General Assembly in 2006 and entered into force in 2008. The articles of the Convention, in general, look to ensure a better quality of life for the disabled through fuller participation in society with economic and social rights such as employment and a right to an education to the fore, accompanied by civil liberties such as reproductive rights.

## Forms of human rights abuse not specifically covered by global human rights regimes

- **Homosexuals**

  Many people have been abused and continue to be abused purely on the grounds that they practice consensual sexual activities with other people of the same sex. Domestic legal restrictions on homosexuality have greatly lessened in most of the developed world over recent decades but in 2009 there were still eighty states legally prohibiting same-sex relationships and five which retained the death penalty for homosexuality (Iran, Mauritania, Sudan, Saudi Arabia and Yemen). In many of these states illegality is a technicality which does not necessarily lead to prosecution but several Iranians have been hanged in recent years for consensual, adult homosexuality (ILGA 2009).

  Even more clearly than with women's rights, the difficulties of overcoming cultural differences in establishing global standards are apparent when considering the rights of homosexuals and other minority sexualities. The UN has been unable to reach a consensus to give the same status to sexual freedom as religious or political freedom in international human rights law. The right to have same-sex relationships is not covered in the UN Declaration or Covenants and the extermination of people on grounds of their sexual practices – which occurred in the Nazi holocaust – is not included in the 1948 Genocide Convention.

- **Politicide**

  Strikingly absent from the UN definition of genocide is the mass, systematic killing of political and/or social opponents by governments or non-governmental forces. Since the targets of such action are not necessarily national, ethnic or religious minorities the distinct category sometimes referred to as *politicide* is necessary for a complete understanding of this form of human rights abuse (Harff and Gurr 1988). The omission of politicide from the UN Convention is the result of the predictable opposition of the USSR to classifying their extermination of opponents alongside that of the Nazis. The Soviet regime represented at the UN drafting of the Convention on Genocide can claim the dubious distinction of being history's most brutal ever with an estimated 62 million political opponents killed during the three-quarter century lifespan of the USSR (Rummel website). Politicide and other non-specified forms of human rights abuse are, however, increasingly accepted as coming within the residual category of '**crimes against humanity**' covered in the UN Charter and previously referred to in the actions initially taken against the Turkish government for the Armenian genocide since that word and crime had yet to be defined.

## Implementing human rights

Codifying law is only part of the process of developing human rights. Implementing international law is always a more difficult task than with domestic law because of the barrier presented by the notion of sovereignty. This is especially so when a law is focused on individuals, traditionally considered the preserve of governments and domestic courts.

### United Nations

There are UN mechanisms for implementing human rights but they have been limited and uneven in their impact. The UN Commission on Human Rights' record on encouraging the implementation of the Declaration and Covenants it crafted is, according to the esteemed human rights lawyer Geoffrey Robertson, 'woeful' (Robertson 2000: 45). The Commission, restrained by intergovernmental politicking, failed even to condemn the horrific politicides/ genocides in Cambodia and Uganda in the late 1970s. In Uganda, dictator Idi Amin had massacred political opponents and expelled thousands of ethnic minorities from his country; in Cambodia, Pol Pot's reign of terror in the 1970s had seen up to a million of his own citizens slaughtered for the ideological mission of returning his country to 'year zero'. The Commission was beefed up in the 1990s, with the appointment of a full-time Commissioner at its head, but still lacked any enforcement powers beyond 'naming and shaming'. Hence, in 2006 the General Assembly approved the creation of a new body to take over from the Commission, the Human Rights Council (HRC). The HRC meets three times per year (the Commission met only once per year) and comprises representatives of forty-seven states elected by the General Assembly. Concerns that the voting procedure would continue the trend established under the Commission of electing members from countries with poor rights records and that its actions may be politicised was cited by Israel to explain their non-involvement in the organ.

Also contributing to the implementation of human rights standards are committees established with some of the covenants and conventions that have entered into force. The Human Rights Committee was set up to monitor the implementation of the Covenant on Civil and Political Rights. However, only a small number of admissible cases had been lodged with the HRC by this time and many governments – including of the USA, UK and China – have shown no inclination to be committed to the procedure.

The Committee on the Elimination of Racial Discrimination (CERD) and the Committee on the Elimination of Discrimination Against Women (CEDAW) have the capacity to take up individual cases for states that permit this. CEDAW has on occasion been cited in defence of women in domestic legal cases. The Constitution of Brazil, for example, has been amended to bring it into line with the provisions (IFUW 1999). Within the Children's Rights regime a UN Committee on the Rights of the Child examines parties' progress in implementing the convention and has made some progress in embarrassing some governments into implementing legal changes, such as separating juvenile from adult war criminal suspects detained in Rwanda.

The HRC and implementing committees have had some successes in informing legal cases but these instances are few and far between. In addition, of course, the countries concerned are not the ones where the most serious human rights violations are occurring, which are invariably – though not exclusively – undemocratic states.

## Civil society

Pressure groups have played a big role in facilitating the implementation of international law on human rights by forming a key partnership with the United Nations. Amnesty International – which has grown from a one-man campaign, launched by British journalist Peter Benenson in 1961, to a multi-million pound operation with over two million members in over 150 countries – works on highlighting non-compliance with the UN Covenant on Civil and Political Rights and have a particular focus on judicial rights (for example, fair trials). As well as helping implement existing legislation, Amnesty has taken the lead in promoting the development of new law to be taken on by the UN, such as with the Torture Convention. The US-based group Human Rights Watch, while also working in conjunction with the UN, has focused on facilitating the implementation of the Helsinki Accords, established during the Cold War to improve human rights in the context of East–West relations, and most of its activities serve to highlight violations of free expression. Over two hundred other pressure groups perform similar functions in the world today, mainly in the area of civil and political rights.

## National courts

Since genocide, torture and 'crimes against humanity' are part of customary international law some national courts have come to assume the right to pass verdicts on crimes committed on individuals other than their own citizens. In the 1990s new impetus was given to the politics of human rights by the end of the Cold War but the world also witnessed the spectre of genocide revived in Rwanda and Yugoslavia. This prompted successful cases brought in Germany and Belgium for such crimes committed in Bosnia and Rwanda.[5] The 1999 *Pinochet Case* in the UK also proved to be a key test case in international human rights law. The British courts rejected a Spanish request to arrest the former Chilean dictator General Augusto Pinochet (on the grounds of ill health) but, at the same time, made it clear that his crimes (of politicide and torture) did amount to 'crimes against humanity' against which sovereignty was no defence. The UK verdict also indicated that diplomatic immunity (Pinochet claimed this as a former president and 'life senator') was no protection against such crimes.

A setback to the development of this method of implementing global human rights came with a 2002 verdict by the UN's court, The International Court of Justice, which ruled that Belgium was not entitled to try a Government Minister of the Congo, Ndombasi, for his role in a massacre of Tutsis in Kinshasa.[6] Belgian authorities were instructed that they had no right to strip Ndombasi of diplomatic protection, even in view of the gravity of the offences of which he was being accused. This development was to the relief of some in the Belgian government who had become alarmed at the likely diplomatic fallout from their country vainly seeking to bring a long list of recent tyrants to justice in Brussels. The ICJ verdict brought dismay to human rights activists for setting back the cause of universality in human rights law but, ultimately, the case may help strengthen the arguments in favour of global justice. The prospect of dozens of states around the world simultaneously pursuing various individuals in the name of international law could also be said to demonstrate the necessity of a global judiciary less vulnerable to criticisms of partisanship and more likely to be able to meet success in pursuing individuals traditionally protected by sovereignty. The International Criminal Court (ICC), considered in the next section, could yet fulfil this function.

## Global courts

The idea of an international court to try individuals, alongside the International Court of Justice dealing with state-to-state conflicts, was around at the birth of the United Nations but, like many other global aspirations, was frozen in time by the Cold War. An international criminal court had earlier been proposed during the time of the League of Nations in relation to a stillborn 1937 convention dealing with terrorism. An early draft of the Genocide Convention floated the idea of a court to enforce its provisions but this was soon shelved as too radical a notion to put to the bifurcating international community (Schabas 2000: 8). Instead Article VI of the convention provides for justice to be dispensed either in the courts of the country where the crimes occurred or in a specially convened international tribunal. This was the case with the Nuremberg and Tokyo trials, which

---

[5]  *Public Prosecutor* v. *Djajic*, No. 20/96 (Sup. Ct. Bavaria 23 May 1997).

[6]  *Democratic Republic of the Congo* v. *Belgium*, ICJ verdict 14 February 2002. General List no. 121.

prosecuted Nazi and Japanese war criminals in the 1940s, and the ad hoc tribunals established by the Security Council to try individuals for genocide and war crimes in Yugoslavia and Rwanda in the 1990s.

The idea of the ICC did not perish during the Cold War years and, when the opportunity then presented itself at the close of the 1980s, the UN's International Law Commission (ILC), a body responsible for the codification of international law, revived the plan. In 1992 the General Assembly gave the go ahead to the ILC to draft a blueprint for the ICC, paving the way for the 1998 Rome Conference, at which the statute for the court was agreed upon and opened for signature. By 2002 the statute had received enough ratifications to enter into force and the court was born. Only seven states opposed the court at the Rome Conference (USA, Israel, China, Iraq, Sudan, Yemen and Libya) and, by 2010, it had 110 parties. The USA declined to ratify the Rome Convention that underpins the ICC largely on the grounds that it would be unconstitutional to permit a US citizen to be tried outside of the US legal system for an alleged US-based crime and that, as the world's only superpower, it would be more likely to have cases brought against it than other states, whether through the fact that the USA is more prominent in UN military operations than most or due to trumped-up charges based on anti-Americanism.

How influential the ICC can become remains to be seen (by 2010 it had only taken up cases in four countries) but it could eventually give real meaning to international human rights law by exercising the sort of **supranational** authority witnessed only sporadically and selectively to date. A key difference between the ICC and previous ad hoc human rights courts is that it does not have to get approval to act from the 'Big 5' in the UN Security Council, and so will be less vulnerable to criticism of partiality to the Great Powers and of only ever being an arbiter of 'victor's justice'. In 2005, a significant boost to the credibility of the court was given by an agreement by the UN Security Council to refer to it the Darfur (Sudan) genocide case, despite the initial hostilities of the USA to involving a body it does not support and the fact that Sudan is not a party to the Rome Convention. In time, the court could also potentially widen the grounds upon which it can launch a prosecution beyond the current remit of genocide, war crimes and crimes against humanity since Article 10 of its Treaty refers to the evolution of its statutes in line with customary international law.

## Regional courts

● **European Convention on Human Rights**

The regime centred on the Council of Europe, an older and wider body than the European Union, is undoubtedly the most extensive international human rights system in the world. Established in 1950, it now covers forty-seven states (essentially all of Europe – including Turkey and Russia – barring Belarus, the continent's last dictatorship). Individual petitions by citizens is the main channel for taking up cases, although some cases taken up by one government against another have also occurred.

The Convention originally sought to implement the UN Declaration in Western Europe but has evolved into something much more extensive than anything within the

UN system. The European Court of Human Rights (ECHR) has gradually assumed the right to be 'creative' in interpreting the articles of the convention, thereby allowing it to pass verdicts – binding on all government parties – that go well beyond the most blatant forms of human right abuses. The ECHR, for example, has interpreted Article 8 of the European Convention on Human Rights, which upholds 'Respect for Private and Family Life', originally intended to give protection against forced sterilisations, to include gay rights. As a result of this huge advances in gay rights have occurred in Europe, including the decriminalisation of homosexuality in Northern Ireland (1981), the Republic of Ireland (1988) and Cyprus (1993).

- **Organisation of American States**
  The OAS's Declaration on the Rights and Duties of Man actually pre-dates the UN Declaration (by seven months) but the Western hemisphere's human rights regime lags well behind its European counterpart. There is a similar institutional set up with an Inter-American Convention Commission to take up cases from individuals as well as states and a Court, but the system has had very little influence. Gross human rights violations in most of its twenty-six parties throughout much of its history have under-mined the regime's credibility, as has the non-participation in the court of two of its potentially most influential members: Canada and the United States.

- **Africa**
  The African Union's (AU's) African Charter on Human and People's Rights (Banjul Charter) of 1981 covers nearly all of Africa and features a Commission that promotes human rights but there is, as yet, no implementing body. A 1998 protocol did set up a court but it has yet to function. The Economic Community of West African States (ECOWAS) does, however, have a functioning court and in 2008 passed a landmark verdict against the government of Niger for failing to protect a girl from being sold to slavery.[7]

## Foreign policy

The 1990s saw something of a rise in 'ethical foreign policy' with countries declaring that human rights would be allowed to enter the calculations of foreign policy objectives long dominated by the geopolitics of Cold War. In the UK Robin Cook was explicit in stating this on becoming foreign minister of the Labour government in 1997 and, in the USA, the '**Clinton doctrine**' emerged with greater emphasis on the diplomatic encouragement of democracy and human rights than had been seen since the Wilson government of the 1920s. In fact, however, the starting point of this development can be traced back to the **Détente** era of the Cold War in the 1970s when it appeared that the conflict was coming to an end with a significant thaw in East–West relations. The Helsinki Accords of 1975 was the high point of détente: a wide-ranging diplomatic/human rights treaty which saw the West agree not to interfere in the affairs of the Eastern Bloc in exchange for the Soviets improving human rights in their empire. A notable improvement in political persecution

---

[7] *Hadijatou Mani Koraou* v. *Niger*, 2008.

in the USSR did occur after this and also in the West, since the USA was now vulnerable to charges of hypocrisy if they persisted in propping up oppressive military dictatorships who took an anti-communist line. An ethical foreign policy is always a hostage to fortune, however, and numerous claims of hypocrisy have been levelled at the USA, UK and other countries when lurches back to following the 'national interest' have occurred.

On a more consistent level human rights have been clearly stated as an objective of Dutch and Norwegian foreign policy since the early 1970s. Norway and the Netherlands together with Sweden and Canada came to be known as the 'Like Minded Countries' for their generous foreign aid budgets and particularly for linking this to the human rights record of recipient countries. The governments of Norway and Canada have subsequently played the lead roles in launching the Human Security Network: an alliance which advocates the development of global policies focused on the human interest, whether or not these happen to coincide with state interests. By 2010 the network had expanded to include eleven other states, both geographically and politically diverse (Austria, Chile, Costa Rica, Greece, Republic of Ireland, Jordan, Mali, the Netherlands, Slovenia, Switzerland and Thailand). Cynics have suggested that this sort of strategy is just a tactical move by less powerful governments to raise their diplomatic profile through populist moves and that it is easier to take the moral high ground when you can more easily avoid the tough politics of the 'low ground'. IR human rights specialist Jack Donnelly, for example, comments that 'small states rarely have to choose between human rights and other foreign policy goals' (Donnelly 2007: 135). The USA and UK have used such arguments in defending something of a return to Cold War **realpolitik** in controversial actions taken in the 'War on Terror' since 2001, such as the prolonged British derogation from Article 5 of the European Convention (covering rights on arrest), to allow for legal principles in place since Magna Carta to be suspended for arresting terrorist suspects.

## Humanitarian intervention

The most significant foreign policy initiative to implement human rights that can be taken is to use force in order to end humanitarian suffering. The case study below presents a

 **Box 22.3  Craig Murray**

Craig Murray was UK ambassador to Uzbekistan, an important ally in the 'War on Terror', from 2002 to 2004 when he was withdrawn by the Foreign Office after attracting much controversy and media interest during his tenure. Murray had felt compelled to speak out about human rights abuses perpetrated by the Uzbek government against Islamic insurgents (which notoriously included the boiling of suspects to extract confessions), corroborated by several human rights pressure groups (Human Rights Watch 2004). The UK government were keen not to offend the Uzbek government, and charges of improper conduct used to justify Murray's withdrawal were widely seen as a smokescreen for an exercise in realpolitik.

 Do you think Murray was right to speak out or – as a Civil Servant rather than a politician – should he have respected his employer's wishes and put national interest before human rights?

chronology of military interventions since the end of the Second World War which have purported to have been inspired, at least partially, by the motivation of relieving the suffering of nationals distinct from the interveners. Such interventions are most associated with the modern age but their origins can be traced back to the nineteenth century Concert of Europe era. Concert powers occasionally enforced their agreement to abolish the slave trade by intercepting Arab slave ships returning from Africa and sent troops to lend support in several parts of the Ottoman Empire prompted by Turkish massacres.

## Case study: Notable 'humanitarian interventions' in the UN era

| Date | Intervention | Interveners | Humanitarian spur |
|------|-------------|-------------|-------------------|
| 1960–4 | Congo | 1. Belgium   2. UN 3. Belgium and USA | Civil war and massacres following independence (from Belgium) |
| 1965 | Domincan Republic | USA | Protect foreign citizens from new military dictatorship |
| 1971 | East Pakistan | India | Pakistani genocide against breakaway region (Bangladesh) |
| 1978 | Zaire | France and Belgium | Massacres of civilians by anti-government guerillas |
| 1978 | Cambodia | Vietnam | Politicide of various sections of own people by Khmer Rouge government |
| 1979 | Uganda | Tanzania | Expulsions, massacres and human rights abuses against ethnic minorities and opponents |
| 1979 | Central African Republic | France | Overthrow of Bohasia government responsible for massacres of civilians |
| 1983 | Grenada | USA and Organisation of East Caribbean States | Protect foreign citizens after military coup |
| 1989 | Panama | USA | Protect foreign citizens in civil unrest |
| 1990–7 | Liberia | 1. Nigeria   2. ECOWAS | Restore order amid Civil War |
| 1991 | Iraq | UN | Protect Kurds in North and 'Marsh Arabs' in South from government massacres |
| 1992 | Yugoslavia | UN | Protect Bosnian Muslims from Serb massacres |
| 1992–3 | Somalia | UN | Restore order amid Civil War |
| 1994–7 | Haiti | UN | Restore democracy and order following military coup |
| 1997 | Sierra Leone | ECOWAS | Restore order amid Civil War |
| 1999 | Kosovo (Yugoslavia) | NATO | Protect Kosovar Albanians from Serb massacres |
| 1999 | East Timor (Indonesia) | INTERFET (Australia, UK, Thailand, Philippines and others) | Maintain order in transition to independence |

All of the above listed 'humanitarian interventions' have been contentious. Go through the table and list any non-humanitarian motives you suspect or know to be applicable for the intervention concerned.

Differentiating between a humanitarian military action and one motivated by more traditional goals of gain, self-defence or ideology is a difficult judgement. In all of the cases listed in the case study one or more of these more familiar reasons to take up arms have been claimed by some observers to be the real cause of war.

The legal basis for humanitarian intervention is a moot point and it has been in and out of fashion in international affairs over the last three centuries. Dutch jurist and father of International Law, Hugo Grotius, in the seventeenth century considered rescuing imperilled non-nationals to come into the category of just war but it was not until the Concert of Europe era in the nineteenth century that the concept was first put into practice, albeit sporadically. Humanitarian intervention fell out of favour amid the amoral realism of twentieth-century state practice but rose to prominence again in the '**New World Order**' that was heralded by the demise of the Cold War in 1990. Despite more frequent recourse to it in recent years, humanitarian intervention remains a highly contentious concept in international relations since it challenges that fundamental underpinning of the **Westphalian system**, state sovereignty. International Law is ambiguous on the issue, with the UN Charter appearing both to proscribe and prescribe the practice. Articles 2.4 and 2.7 uphold the importance of sovereignty and the convention of non-interference in another state's affairs but Chapter VII suggests that extreme humanitarian abuses can constitute a 'threat to peace', legitimising intervention.

## Are human rights 'right'?

Although it is entirely predictable that a tyrannical government will oppose calls for it to improve its human rights record, many Realists also voice concern over the notion of a global bill of rights on principle. The main arguments against implementing and further developing human rights in international relations can be summarised as follows:

- **The humanitarian figleaf**

  When human rights abuses in a given country are alleged, and particularly when action to remedy this is called for, the suspicion of the accused and many onlookers is often that this is merely an excuse by the accuser to advance more basic self-interests. One man's humanitarian intervention is always another person's imperialist or power-inspired venture. All of the interventions listed in the case study were opposed by some states, unconvinced by moral claims of the intervener. In all cases other motivations for intervention can easily be found. NATO's 1999 action in Yugoslavia, ultimately, was 'sold' to the general public of the intervening countries more on the grounds of maintaining European order than on averting humanitarian catastrophe. Some measure of self-interest, alongside compassion for others, appeared to be necessary to justify going to war. The notion of humanitarian war was more clearly undermined when the USA and UK, unable to justify the 2003 Iraq War on legal or self-defence grounds when no Weapons of Mass Destruction (WMD) could be found, switched instead to a justification of regime change on humanitarian grounds.

- **Inconsistency in application**

  It is quickly obvious from looking at the Case Study that humanitarian interventions have not been consistently applied in the event of widespread human rights abuses. The willingness of NATO to act in defence of the Kosovar Albanians and the UN's 1991 initiatives in Iraq stood in stark contrast to the lack of repsonse to the far greater horrors which occurred in Rwanda's genocidal implosion of 1994. Central Africa in the post-Cold War landscape lacked the strategic importance to the major powers of the Middle East or Eastern Europe. Equally, humanitarian intervention is always more likely to be considered an option where the target state is not going to be too tough a military opponent. Power politics dictates that the Chinese suppression of Tibetan rights or Russian massacres of Chechen seperatists were/are never likely to be awarded the same response as Serb or Iraqi atrocities. In general diplomacy, ethical foreign policies have frequently been relaxed when – as in the Uzbekistan case referred to earlier – the trump card of national interests is played. Many claim selective justice undermines the credibility of asserting human rights in international relations.

- **Meddling is likely to worsen the situation**

  Even where a clear case of tyranny can be established, there is the concern that a diplomatic or military intervention may not be the answer to the problem in that it may

Source: Press Association Images/Binod Joshi/AP

**Despite strong rhetoric from the Global North, humanitarian intervention is inconsistently applied in the face of widespread human rights abuses.**

well inflame the situation. At one level some question whether the aggressive response of a humanitarian intervention can ever be a legitimate way to punish acts of aggression. On another level, many Realists contended that NATO's action in defence of the Kosovar Albanians led to an escalation of the Serb campaign against them. US military historian Edward Luttwak, for example, has called upon the international community to let conflicts run their natural course and 'Give War a Chance'.

> Policy elites should actively resist the emotional impulse to intervene in other peoples' wars – not because they are indifferent to human suffering but precisely because they care about it and want to facilitate the advent of peace.
>
> (Luttwak 1999: 44)

In this view international interference in local disputes tends only temporarily to dampen the conflict which will then inevitably resurface once the interveners have gone. In view of this, some contend that it may be better to let the dispute run its course and reach a natural conclusion.

### • Rights are relative

The chief moral objection to the universal application of human rights is the position commonly known as cultural relativism. Cultural relativism argues that the world's cultural diversity means that any attempt to apply rights universally is, at best, difficult and, at worst, an immoral imposition of dominant cultural traits. Judging a country as being a danger to its own citizens is likely to be prejudicial since such judgements are likely to be made by the dominant power of the day and so, in effect, represent a hegemonic imposition of a particular ideology. Recent humanitarian interventions have been dominated by the USA, a country which has otherwise sometimes shown a disinterest in furthering the implementation of human rights, such as by not partaking in the ICC.

The Foreign Minister of Singapore, Wong Kan Seng at the Vienna Conference in 1993, voiced the view of several Asian governments who had met earlier that year to release the 'Bangkok Declaration', that the extent and exercise of human rights 'varies greatly from one culture or political community to another' and 'are the products of the historical experiences of particular peoples' (Seng 1993). This statement in support of cultural relativism came forty-five years after the first major articulation of this viewpoint in international politics in the run up to the 1948 Universal Declaration of Human Rights. Concerns at the notion of a global bill of rights riding roughshod over the minority cultures of the world prompted leading anthropologists, including Melville Herskovits and Ruth Benedict, to petition the UN Commission for Human Rights.

In Benedict's view, and that of most traditional anthropologists, the notion of what is morally right can only equate to what is customary within a given society (Benedict 1934). Hence the notion of rights pertaining to all humankind is not 'natural'. Rights are the rules of mutual give and take which develop over time within a society in order for it to function peacefully and survive. Rights here are seen as being implicit agreements arrived at purely within societies.

## The Universalist response

Universalists suggest that a fundamental weakness with Realist and relativist arguments in regard to human rights is that they presuppose that governments can be relied upon to secure the rights of their individual constituents and that the states they govern equate to the national cultures we should respect. Nations and states, however, do not match up. There are numerous stateless nations: like the Kurds or the Basques – and numerous multinational states: like the UK, Russia or Nigeria. Multinationalism, whether arrived at through migration or historical accident (such as in the partitioning of Africa), is the norm in the modern state system. If the states of the world mirrored its distinct 'cultures' cultural relativism could perhaps stand as a realistic alternative to universalism in protecting human rights. In the real world, however, how are the rights of cultural minorities within states to be fully safeguarded? The fact that national or religious minorities are frequently imperilled rather than protected by states cannot be questioned. The Kurds in Saddam's Iraq, the Jews in Hitler's Germany, the Tutsis in mid 1990s Rwanda or the Darfurians in contemporary Sudan were massacred because they were perceived by their governments to be alien to the national culture. Women, the disabled, homosexuals and people linked by any other form of collective identity stand little chance of having their 'cultural differences' respected when they overlap with far more influential 'cultures'. Entrusting states to be the arbiters of human rights frequently leads to the imposition of dominant cultural norms on minority cultures in precisely the fashion that relativism purports to prevent. In the same way that no countries tolerate criminal 'cultures' within their societies, Liberal Universalists hold that the global society of humanity should not tolerate acts of barbarity – like genocide and torture – which are outside the basic norms of human behaviour and mutual interest that link us all.

## Conclusions

Human rights have advanced significantly over the last sixty years and the individual has started to emerge as an entity in international law and international affairs alongside states and non-state actors, challenging the sovereign underpinnings of the **Westphalian system** in operation for nearly five hundred years. Liberals support this development and wish it to continue arguing that human rights are 'natural law', and can and should inform international law and politics. Many neo-Realists, particularly of the English School variant, respond by complaining that states should not all be tarred with the same brush and that the tyranny that has marked the rule of many brutal governments in history is not an inevitable feature of the state system. From this perspective the best way to advance protection for all individuals comes not from relying on arbitrarily defined and implemented global standards of justice but from allowing 'particular states to seek as wide a consensus as possible and on this basis to act as agents of a world common good' (Alderson and Hurrel 2000: 233). While most of the world accepts the notion that people have rights of some sort, the question of what those rights are and how they can best be safeguarded is still hotly disputed.

## Resource section

## Questions

1. Describe and evaluate the United Nation's record in advancing human rights law.

2. Why, when global standards exist, do human rights continue to be abused in the contemporary world?

3. Why has enforcing a global set of human rights standards proved such a difficult task?

4. To what extent do global human rights instruments safeguard the liberty of all of the world's people?

5. In the US TV series *24* an Islamic Fundamentalist suicide bomber is held by government agents while a nuclear device he has left in an urban area is primed to detonate. Fearless for his own life, the agents decide to threaten to kill the terrorist's family members to get him to reveal the bomb's location. Two or three innocent lives may have to be sacrificed in order to save thousands of innocent lives it is concluded. Could such an extreme measure be acceptable?[8]

6. Are values universal or cultural? List any values you consider as applicable to all people in the world (for example, free speech, equality for women). The shorter your list the more of a relativist and less of a universalist you are.

## Recommended reading

Donnelly, J. (2007) *International Human Rights* (3rd edn, Cambridge, MA: Westview)
A classic IR text on human rights which explores the relativism–universalism debate.

Robertson, G. (2007) *Crimes Against Humanity. The Struggle for Global Justice* (3rd edn, London: Penguin)
A thorough insider's guide to the politics of human rights from a prominent lawyer. Robertson pulls no punches in giving his expert assessments of international instruments and the record of governments in ratifying and observing them.

Schabas, W. (2000) *Genocide in International Law. The Crime of Crimes* (Cambridge: Cambridge University Press)
This book provides an authoritative history of the genocide convention and analyses the contemporary legal significance of this obligation to act in the face of humanitarian horrors.

Smith, R. (2007) *Textbook on International Human Rights* (3rd edn, Oxford: Oxford University Press)
A comprehensive and systematic legal overview of global and regional human rights regimes.

---

[8] In the show the full extent of this moral dilemma is circumvented by the Agents actually faking the murder of the bomber's children.

## Useful websites

Amnesty International: http://www.amnesty.org/

Columbia University, Human Rights and Humanitarian Affairs Information Resources: http://www.columbia.edu/cu/lweb/indiv/lehman/guides/human.html

Genocidewatch: http://www.genocidewatch.org/

Human Rights Watch: http://www.hrw.org/

International Criminal Court: http://www.icccpi.int/php/show.php?id=home&l=EN

Rummel, R. Freedom, Democracy, Peace; Power, Democide and War: http://www.hawaii.edu/powerkills/welcome.html

United Nations, Human Rights: http://www.un.org/rights/

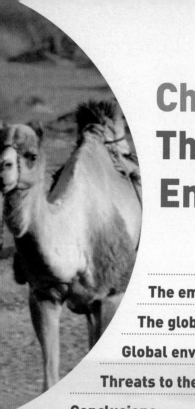

# Chapter 23
# The Natural Environment

The emergence of political ecology

The globalisation of political ecology

Global environmental policy and human security

Threats to the global consensus on environmental policy

Conclusions

After reading this chapter you will be able to:

- Explain the emergence of environmental politics and political ecology

- Understand how and why environmental politics has globalised

- See why achieving global consensus for political action on environmental issues has proved difficult

- Understand how, in spite of such difficulties, a consensus on global political action on the environment has emerged, persisted and survived US-led resistance

*Source*: Getty Images

## Introductory box: Undersea politics

In 2009 the government of the Maldive Islands held a cabinet meeting below the sea at which ministers donned sub-aqua swimming gear and discussed policy around a submerged cabinet table. This was, of course, a publicity stunt to highlight concerns at rising sea levels rather than an act of political necessity since the low lying islands had yet to be reduced to the status of sand banks in the Indian Ocean. However, this remains a likely future scenario. The country's highest point is just 2.4 metres above current sea level and 80 per cent of the archipelago lies below 1 metre above sea level. Forecasts of the United Nations' International Panel on Climate Change suggest a sea level rise of between 25 and 58 centimetres by the end of the present century. It is widely accepted that this is an eventuality which could be averted by global political action to limit global warming (which is melting the world's glaciers and ice sheets and so raising global sea levels), but the prospects of this happening seem – by 2010 – to be remote. In other parts of the world the impacts of global warming appear less stark and the incentives to enact costly measures to limit them – such as curbing carbon dioxide emissions from vehicles and industry – are less obvious, leading to the intransigence which prompted the Maldive government's stunt. The government, indeed, seem to recognise that getting the world to act to save their country – and other low lying territories – is likely to be in vain and have simultaneously been pursuing a political 'Plan B': buying a new homeland in India or Sri Lanka for their entire 300,000 population to relocate to as environmental refugees.

The Maldives incident highlights why environmental issues tend to polarise opinion in International Relations. To some, issues like global warming, overpopulation and ozone depletion are the most pressing of all items on the international political agenda, since they imperil all human and other life forms on earth. To others such issues are minor concerns relative to the threats posed by war and terrorism and, possibly, do not represent any sort of threat at all.

This chapter will explore how and why environmental issues have become more prominent in International Relations but still tend not to be afforded the same level of political significance at the global level as military or economic matters.

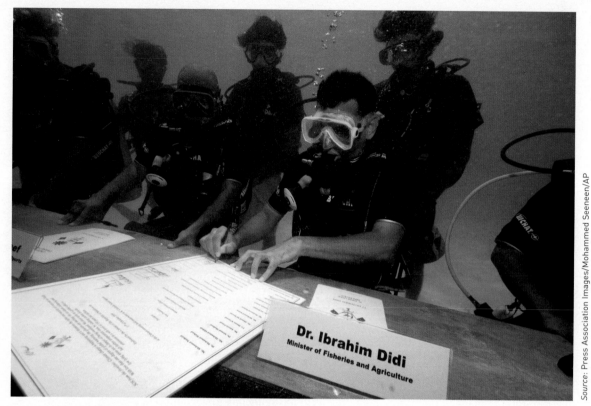

*Source:* Press Association Images/Mohammed Seeneen/AP

The Maldives Islands underwater cabinet meeting highlighted concerns about the impact of rising sea levels.

## The emergence of political ecology

Issues relating to the natural environment are comparatively 'new' to politics and have only been on the agenda of International Relations since the late 1960s. That is not to say, however, that problems of environmental change are in any way new. The extinction of certain animal species due to human recklessness and the decline of woodland areas through over-exploitation are centuries old phenomena. The dodo, moa, and passenger Pigeon, for example, were hunted to extinction before the twentieth century. Other notable changes to the natural environment have occurred entirely independent of human action. The 'Cretaceous/Tertiary Impact' – caused by either a comet or an asteroid which created the 250km wide Chicxulub crater in the Gulf of Mexico – is widely held to be responsible for the extinction of the dinosaurs and other life forms long before the dawn of humanity. In addition, the temperature of the earth has periodically naturally warmed and cooled throughout human and pre-human history with various effects on the natural environment.

## Box 23.1 Timeline of environmental politics

**Emergence of the science of ecology**

1864  US scientist George Perkins Marsh's *Man and Nature* (Marsh 1965) released – arguably the first book to prove human activities can harm the environment

1866  German biologist Ernst Haeckel (1866) coins the term *ecology*

**Emergence of conservation policies**

1872  Yellowstone National Park, USA becomes world's first major nature conservation scheme

1889  Royal Society for the Protection of Birds in Great Britain becomes world's first conservation pressure group

1889  First ever international policy on non-human life form agreed – combating the spread of the disease *phylloxera* in wine grapes

1892  Sierra Club conservation pressure group founded in the USA

1902  Convention on the Protection of Birds Useful to Agriculture becomes the first international policy on animal conservation

1946  International Whaling Commission established

1948  International Union for the Preservation of Nature founded by pressure groups and the UN (later became International Union for the Conservation of Nature)

**Emergence of political ecology**

1962  US marine biologist Rachel Carson's book *Silent Spring* (1962) quickly prompts political action in the USA and much of the West to restrict the use of industrial chemicals because of their effects on wildlife

1967  *Torrey Canyon* oil tanker disaster

**Development of international environmental policy**

1968  UN Biosphere Conference

1969  UN Population Fund established

1972  UN Conference on the Human Environment in Stockholm

1973  UN Conference on the Law of the Sea initiates process leading to ratification of the UN Convention in 1994

1973  First International Convention for the Protection of Pollution from Ships (MARPOL)

1973  Convention on the International Trade in Endangered Species (CITES)

1974  First UN Population Conference in Bucharest

1979  Long-Range Transboundary Air Pollution (LRTAP) agreement

1985  Vienna Convention on Protection of the Ozone Layer

1987  Montreal Protocol to the Vienna Convention

1987  World Commission on Environment and Development set up by UN

1992  UN Conference on the Environment and Development (Rio Earth Summit)

1992  International Framework Convention on Climate Change (IFCCC)

1993  UN Convention on Biological Diversity

1994  Convention to Combat Desertification

1997  Kyoto Protocol to the IFCCC

2001  Stockholm Conference on Persistent Organic Pollutants

2002  UN's World Summit on Sustainable Development in Johannesburg

Conservation policies, driven by the aesthetics of loving the countryside or nationalism of preserving rural lifestyles, permeated the domestic politics of some developed countries in the early twentieth century (including, even, the Nazis who linked natural and racial German purity in the slogan 'blood and soil', and whose agriculture minister enacted policies in line with this, such as the 1935 Reich Law for the Protection of Nature). However, the emergence of truly environmental rather than human-focused policies – that is *ecocentric* rather than *anthropocentric* policies – did not occur until around a century after the birth of the science of ecology in the 1960s. The *phylloxera* and bird protection policies of 1889 and 1902 in Box 23.1 dealt with a non-human species but for purely human (economic) interests. A major factor in this development was the publication of Rachel Carson's hugely influential pollution polemic *Silent Spring* in 1962. *Silent Spring* most notably highlighted the polluting effects of the insecticide dichlorodiphenyltrichloroethane (DDT) on wild animals, vegetation and rivers. The book quickly influenced US policy, with the government enacting legislation restricting DDT use in 1969 and then outlawing its use altogether in 1972.

## Biodiversity

**Biodiversity** first emerged as a term as recently as 1986, during a 'National Forum on Biodiversity in the US', but the idea of seeking to maintain the variety of life forms on Earth pre-dates the age of international policy on the environment and even the emergence of political ecology that followed in the wake of *Silent Spring*. The Royal Society for the Protection of Birds in the UK (RSPB) was prompted into action in the nineteenth century through fears that the grebe was in danger of becoming extinct due to the fashion of using its feathers for hats. Grebes and other animals are, of course, not confined by state frontiers and so, after the Second World War, the RSPB, Sierra Club and other groups came to orientate their campaigns through the United Nations. Several groups, principally from the UK and USA, worked with the newly established United Nations Educational, Scientific and Cultural Organisation (UNESCO) to found the body that became The International Union for the Conservation of Nature (IUCN), and this became a focus of international information exchange on endangered species based on the compilation of 'Red Lists' of flora and fauna close to extinction throughout the world (Adams 2004: 43–62). The IUCN then took the lead in drafting the first international policy on biodiversity when their research revealed that the cross-border trading in certain species was a key factor in them becoming endangered. The 1973 Convention on the International Trade in Endangered Species (CITES) restricts the trading of goods derived from flora or fauna identified as being at risk of extinction, such as ivory and certain furs. Eighty states became party to this Convention when it came into force in 1975 and by 2010 it had 175 parties – including all major industrialised states – and featured laws criminalising the trade in around 30,000 species.

A regime specific to the conservation of whales can also be dated back to the 1940s but, similarly, did not become legally significant until several decades later. The International Whaling Commission (IWC) was set up in 1946, through concerns at the likely extinction of certain species due to hunting, but was very much anthropocentric as it was guided by the desire of whaling states to continue their practices in a sustainable manner. From the 1970s, however, the nature of the IWC was swept by the ecocentric tide as many states abandoned whaling in the face of concerted pressure group campaigning. Hence in 1986 the IWC framed a moratorium which outlawed the hunting of all whale species apart from for scientific purposes. However, Norway and Iceland have not signed up to the moratorium and have continued commercial whaling activities, while Japan's claims that they are continuing the practice for purely scientific purposes are widely challenged by environmental pressure groups.

## Transboundary pollution

Soon after the upsurge of political interest in environmentalism prompted by *Silent Spring* it became apparent that, like biodiversity, pollution had international ramifications and could not be dealt with by domestic policy alone. Most notably, the phenomenon of *acid rain* came to be understood and older issues such as oil pollution by tankards came to command far greater prominence.

Acid rain became a contentious issue in the 1960s, not only through the emergence of evidence that rainwater could become contaminated and had consequential effects on ground water and wildlife, but also because it was a problem in some states which could not be resolved by that state's government. Sulphur dioxide and other emissions from the burning of fossil fuels (coal, oil and natural gas) which accumulate in the Earth's atmosphere, can return to the surface as precipitation hundreds of miles from where they departed as waste fumes. Hence countries particularly suffering from this phenomenon, such as Sweden, Norway and Canada, found that they could not resolve the problem since the root cause of it lay in other sovereign states. This form of transboundary pollution most graphically demonstrated the need for international cooperation to resolve certain environmental issues, which was already obvious in the case of states sharing rivers and other forms of water.

### Box 23.2 Acid rain

Sulphur dioxide & nitrogen dioxide released

Carried on the wind

Gasses dissolve in water vapour forming sulphuric or nitric acid which then falls to earth as rain or snow

In 1979 the Long-Range Transboundary Air Pollution (LRTAP) agreement was signed up to by the USA, Canada and most Western European states, establishing cuts across the board in sulphur dioxide and other industrial emissions. That it was not until over a decade since the problem had become apparent that this modest agreement between friendly states emerged is testimony to the challenges presented by environmental problems to those traditional determinants of government policy: sovereignty, self-sufficiency, the national interest and economic growth. The 1970s also saw the rise of international cooperation on curbing pollution between states sharing common stretches of water. A series of 'Regional Sea Programmes' emerged, such as the Mediterranean Action Plan and North Sea Convention.

The 1967 *Torrey Canyon* disaster, when an oil tanker was wrecked and spilled its load off the coast of the UK's Scilly Isles, was also influential in stimulating awareness of – and an international political response to – oil pollution. This was far from being the first such disaster but it was the biggest to date and received huge media attention, with telegenic

## Case study: The polluter's dilemma

Four states share a common sea and for many decades have deposited waste materials in the sea without political restriction. However, pollution levels in the sea have now reached levels that are affecting fish stocks and tourism on the coast so the four governments convene a conference to discuss the possibility of a coordinated response.

The costs of pollution to each state's income and the costs of enacting restrictions on pollution are represented below.

| State | Cost of pollution | Cost of curbing pollution |
|-------|-------------------|---------------------------|
| A | $2 million per year | $1 million |
| B | $2 million per year | $3 million |
| C | $4 million per year | $12 million |
| D | $5 million per year | $10 million |

### What policy is in the best interest of each state?

For State A the decision is clear. Curbing pollution makes economic sense with a net benefit arising within a year of action. For State B, also, a net benefit is likely soon enough for this to make political sense. Such gains are, however, contingent on *all* states enacting the reforms, so States A and B must also rely on

States C and D following suit. For these two states, and particularly State C, the costs of curbing pollution outweigh the costs incurred for several years and possibly beyond the lifespan of their government's term in office. Although there is a gain to be made in the long term the decision is more difficult because, as well as imposing short-term and unpopular costs, there is the nagging fear that acting on this might not even work since another state may fail to implement the required cuts. States A and B also share this dilemma – the polluter's dilemma – since, although their cost–benefit analyses are more straightforward, their fear of State C or D not acting is higher. Any one of the states may conclude that it is worth carrying on polluting and enjoy the benefits of an overall reduction in pollution through relying on the others to enact cuts – the *free-rider problem*.

Ultimately, coordinated action is in the interests of all but short-termism and a lack of trust in other states makes it difficult to guarantee that states will choose this option – *the collective goods problem*.

Many criticised the US Bush administration's position on environmental policies such as global warming but it is also worth reflecting on the fact that reducing $CO_2$ emissions (the key international policy in this area) would, in many ways, be an unpopular move domestically. What sort of pressures *not* to act do you imagine any US president would face?

images of blackened birds and beaches fuelling the mood of public protest that was transforming domestic politics in Europe and North America. International political action soon followed and in 1973 the first International Convention for the Prevention of Pollution from Ships (MARPOL) was drafted, which for the first time set standards aiming to prevent accidents and criminalise the deliberate discharge of oil and other pollutants from ships on the high seas, which had been a recognised problem for several years. It took a spate of further tanker accidents in the late 1970s, however, for MARPOL eventually to receive enough ratifications to enter into force in 1983.

## Resource depletion

A global version of the collective goods problem emerged in the late 1960s with the crystallisation of the notion that sovereign control over the common 'goods' of water, air and natural resources was unsustainable. In 1968 the ecologist Garret Hardin used as a parable a warning first aired in the nineteenth century by the economist William Foster-Lloyd on the finite quality of shared resources, known as the 'Tragedy of the Commons'. Foster-Lloyd described how the traditional English village green, conventionally open to all villagers, had become endangered because of an abuse of privilege by the villagers in overgrazing their cattle. As the practice had gone on for centuries it had been assumed that it always could but it had emerged that an increase in the number of cattle above an optimum level was eroding the land and ruining the common resource for all. Hardin argued that the village green was analogous to **global commons** such as clean air, freshwater and high seas fish stocks, endangered by states continuing to exploit or pollute them oblivious to the fact that the cumulative effect of this would eventually be their depletion. 'Ruin is the destination toward which all men rush, each pursuing his own best interest in a society that believes in the freedom of the commons' (Hardin 1968: 1244). Hardin's solution to the problem was population control. 'The only way we can preserve and nurture other and more precious freedoms is by relinquishing the freedom to breed' (Hardin 1968: 1248).

Global population control became a major international political concern in the late 1960s and early 1970s, more through anthropocentric fear in the North than compassion for the South or ecocentrism. Another analogy which later came to be popularised by Hardin, likened global overpopulation to a situation where there are insufficient lifeboats in the sea after a shipping disaster. Hardin's thesis argued for the application of 'lifeboat ethics' to combat this, which essentially posited that international action to tackle famine was folly as wealthy countries would risk sinking their own 'lifeboats' in doing so. Better to let the overcrowded 'lifeboats' of the Third World sink than ensuring everyone drowns (Hardin 1996).

Such apocalyptic views of the global implications of overpopulation were nothing new and can actually be traced back as far as the eighteenth century and the works of British economist Thomas Malthus, who warned that the earth's food resources were likely to soon be insufficient to support its population. Malthus' doomsday scenario never came to pass since the Industrial Revolution increased humanity's capacity to utilise resources and feed itself. The fears of *neo-Malthusians* – like Hardin – were also somewhat averted by the Green Revolution which greatly increased food production in the Global South through the utilisation of intensive agricultural technology and techniques (such as the use of organochlorine pesticides). The demand for food has continued to rise in the less developed world and natural disasters continue to blight many of the same countries, creating food shortages, but most contemporary analysts of famine emphasise distributive factors in their explanations of particular cases. Modern governments can insure against future crop shortages by stockpiling reserves of food and protecting the price of agricultural products (Sen 1981).

The UN established a programme specifically to encourage population control in 1969, the Fund for Population Activities (UNFPA), and the first in a series of UN inter-governmental conferences on population took place in Bucharest in 1974. International political action on population control lessened in prominence from the 1980s, however, when it had become apparent to some Northern governments that growth in the South did not greatly affect their countries. There were also concerns in civil society and some governments that promoting birth control in Global South countries could have human rights implications by encouraging abortions, sterilisations and compromising women's reproductive freedom. To some the neo-Malthusians, and environmentalists in general, came to be seen as overly pessimistic doomsayers who failed to appreciate humanity's ingenuity in surmounting problems. The *Cornucopians*, led by US economist Julian Simon, reasoned that technical innovation had already improved the food supply, allowing it to meet a rising demand, but also that such a supply and demand rationale was outdated. Rather than a drain on resources, people in a modern service and consumer based economy were actually a resource themselves (Simon 1981).

A separate strand of neo-Malthusian thinking associated with the Tragedy of the Commons that emerged in the 1970s was the popularisation of the 'Limits to Growth' thesis, which argued that increases in industrial production and economic growth in developed countries would have to be checked. A major report commissioned in 1972 by the Club of Rome, a think tank of scientists, businessmen and politicians, warned that '. . . the limits to growth on this planet will be reached sometime within the next one hundred years' (Meadows et al. 1972: 23). This warning gathered credence with the recognition that oil supplies were finite and greatly influenced political developments over the following decade. While anxieties over population growth generally receded in international politics, concerns over the depletion of certain key resources have persisted ever since.

## The emergence of international environmental policy

The arrival of environmental politics on the international stage was confirmed by the con-vening of the 'Biosphere Conference', focusing on resource conservation, by UNESCO in 1968. Representatives of sixty states were present at the conference in Paris, including delegates of Cold War adversaries the USA and Soviet Union. Although a barely remembered footnote in diplomatic history, the Biosphere Conference initiated two phenomena central to the progress of international environmental politics since then. First; the event was organised through collaboration between several groups from within the UN system and civil society. Representatives of the UN's World Health Organisation (WHO) and Food and Agricultural Organisation (FAO) attended alongside UNESCO staff, and the event was chaired and hosted by the International Union for the Conservation of Nature and attended by several pressure groups and prominent individual activists. This UN–civil society collaboration has been a central feature of the International Relations of the environment ever since. A second and related legacy of the Biosphere Conference was the idea of improving understanding of complex environmental problems by building a transnational network of experts, an **epistemic community**, who can share information and seek to reach a consensus. Given the lack of scientific certainty on many environmental issues, trying to get some sort of consensus is necessary to prevent governments using maverick scientific opinions to support non-action and take the easy option in the polluter's dilemma.

## The Stockholm Conference

The Biosphere Conference's most important legacy was to pave the way for a bigger UN summit four years later: the 1972 Conference on the Human Environment (UNCHE) at Stockholm. The Conference was boycotted by the USSR and its Eastern Bloc allies, over a row about the failure of Western states to recognise East Germany, but was attended by representatives of 113 states from across the world. The Stockholm Conference did not produce a new body of international law at a stroke but served to build consensus by getting agreement on several key principles of environmental governance which challenged conventional notions of state sovereignty. Among the Stockholm Conference's most significant legacies were the following outcomes:

- 'Principle 21' confirmed that states retained full sovereign authority over resources located in their own territory but charged them with the responsibility to exploit them with due regard to the environmental effect of this on other states.
- The concept of a *common heritage of mankind* was agreed whereby resources located outside of territorial borders (such as minerals on the bed of the high seas) should be considered as belonging to the international community collectively.
- The United Nations Environmental Programme (UNEP) was created, to nurture and institutionalise epistemic communities.
- Establishing environmental questions firmly on the political agenda by prompting many governments to create new ministers and departments of the environment, and greatly deepening and widening a global network of environmental pressure groups.

UNEP became an important focus for epistemic communities on a range of environmental issues and assumed responsibility for the stewardship of regimes for common seas, such as the Mediterranean and the North Sea. The common heritage of mankind principle became more established, at least in the Western world, but did not fully displace the notion of sovereign control over resources. In political practice both sides of Principle 21 have been enacted and two very different solutions to the Tragedy of the Commons parable have been attempted. First, you can have a Liberal solution: informed collective management to regulate use of the 'village green' for the benefit of all. Secondly, in a more Realist solution, you can abandon the idea of common land and divide the 'green' up into individual holdings in the expectation that each plot holder would graze sustainably. Both types of solutions are evident in the development in the 1970 and 1980s of international law for a 'commons' already subject to many centuries of contention, the high seas (seas outside of any state's jurisdiction). The Third United Nations Conference on the Law of the Sea (UNCLOS III), which concluded in 1982, included an agreement that minerals on the bed of the high seas would be the property of a new International Seabed Authority. This form of collective management to sustain collective goods can, however, be contrasted with the encroach-ment on the tradition of the 'freedom of the seas' by the huge growth of waters claimed by states in the legitimisation at UNCLOS III of 200 mile 'Exclusive Economic Zones (EEZs)'. An EEZ does not denote the full sovereign control of *territorial waters* (12 miles from the coast) but gives the state concerned primary rights over fishing and mineral exploitation in the zone. The rationale offered for the creation of EEZs was that fish stocks and other resources would be utilised more sustainably if under sovereign jurisdiction rather than subject to a 'free for all'. A tension between the 'freedom of the seas' and sovereign management persists and looks set to become more acute in forthcoming years as a number of states look to extend the EEZ principle to continental shelves beyond 200 miles of their coastlines. The recent spate of claims over the Arctic Ocean, where oil and mineral prospecting has become more practical due to the declining ice sheet, by Russia, Canada, Norway and Denmark, is a case in point.

## The globalisation of political ecology

Throughout the 1970s and early 1980s international environmental policy deepened but did not significantly widen. States, principally from the developed capitalist world, became party to numerous new **international regimes** as well as developing existing legal instruments in the areas of conservation, pollution and resource management. Changes in both the physical and political climate, however, came to bring the First, Second and Third Worlds closer together and globalise environmental politics from the 1980s.

Although transboundary pollution and the management of the global commons were, by the 1980s, firmly on the international political agenda, the majority of the harmful effects of environmental change were viewed as localised problems and as such were of little concern to the wider international community. Domestic legislation in the developed world had banned the use of notoriously polluting chemicals like DDT and curbed the excesses of industrial emissions and waste disposal, leading to visible improvements in atmospheric quality and animal conservation. However, the emergence of evidence that seemingly remote problems, experienced primarily in the Global South, had wider repercussions served to reframe some environmental issues and bring others to global political prominence.

Deforestation – the progressive decline in tree numbers – seen for a number of years as a problem for forest-dwellers, human and otherwise, came to be cast in new light by the discovery in the 1980s of the 'carbon-sink effect', the fact that trees absorb atmospheric carbon dioxide. Carbon dioxide in the atmosphere contributes to global warming and above a certain level is poisonous to man. It has been estimated that the loss of trees in the world contributes more to global warming than the more frequently cited impact of transport (Stern 2006). The realisation that the net loss of tropical rainforest could, ultimately, harm North American and European urban residents as well as Amazonian Amerindians helped bring this issue to the global political agenda. Additionally, the increased economic globalisation of the world can bring external environmental problems into the domestic arena. Harmful organochlorine insecticides may have been virtually eliminated from use in developed countries by the 1980s but their continued use, promoted by multinational corporations (MNCs) from the Global North deprived of a domestic market, was seeing them return to their places of origin in imported foodstuffs in a 'circle of poison' effect (Weir and Schapiro 1981).

As well as seeing some environmental issues from a wider perspective, in the 1980s it began to become apparent that globalisation in general was transforming all environmental issues. The vast majority of environmental problems are related in some way to the processes of economic development and growth, which have dominated how governments frame their policies, both domestically and in the global marketplace. Industrialisation and urbanisation, the classic ingredients of development, put extra strain on a country's resources, while changing its pattern of land use and altering the balance between the human and natural environment. Increased industrial and agricultural production invariably brings more pollution as well as more raw materials, food and wealth. At the Stockholm Conference Indian premier Indira Gandhi signalled that the Global South would not compromise economic development for the sake of the environment since 'poverty is the worst pollution'. The fundamental paradox of how to reconcile economic growth with environmental concerns was apparent at Stockholm but, by the 1980s, could no longer be ignored. By then it had become clear that global environmental policy was being stymied because, although the developed world was coming to terms (albeit partially) with the need to put some limits on industrial 'progress', the Global South would not compromise economic development since the stakes were so much higher.

## Sustainable development

In an effort to get around the economic–environmental paradox, the UN General Assembly in 1987 authorised the establishment of a World Commission on Environment and Development (WCED). Chaired by Norwegian Prime Minister Gro Harlem Brundtland, the WCED produced the report *Our Common Future*, identifying *sustainable development* as the solution. Sustainable development reconciled environmental and economic interests by framing them as interdependent. The Global North would have to take the lead in implementing costly anti-pollution measures and recognise that the South would need more time to follow suit. To the South this was only fair since the North was responsible for most global pollution and had been able to develop without constraints being put on their industrialisation. To the North this was a price worth paying as it was the only way to win support from developing countries like China and India, who would eventually come to be major global polluters also.

Sustainable development is less pessimistic than the 'Limits to Growth' thesis, which was prominent in environmental thinking in the 1970s, in that it does not consider economic growth to be anathema to avoiding pollution and the depletion of the Earth's resources. Economic growth, even for wealthy states, can be acceptable so long as it is at a level that can be sustained in the long run and not at the cost of degrading the environment. Hence sustainable development is less obviously contradictory to the national interest instinct as it merely calls upon governments to be more rationally long-termist in their economic policy. The message is that rapid economic growth today may enrich the present generation but risk impoverishing or endangering future generations if resources are not utilised in a sustainable and responsible manner.

### The Rio Summit

The *Our Common Future* report prompted the UN General Assembly in 1989 to approve a conference as a twenty year follow up to Stockholm to flesh out the concept of sustainable development. As the title indicates, the 1992 UN Conference on the Environment and Development (UNCED), held in Rio de Janeiro, recognised the need to couple together the two issue areas and was a much larger and more diverse gathering than in 1972. One hundred and seventy states were represented, most at some stage by their head of government, and some 1,400 pressure groups were also present at the myriad formal and informal meetings that characterised the Conference. In contrast, at Stockholm only two heads of government and 134 pressure groups had attended. Although decision-making authority was reserved for government delegates, the pressure groups at Rio played a pivotal role in organising the event and in the extensive lobbying of the decision makers.

Among twenty-seven general principles agreed to in the 'Rio Declaration' at the summit were two particularly important points of consensus which served to clarify the meaning of sustainable development.

- **Principle 7** identified the 'common but differentiated responsibilities' of developed and less-developed states in environmental protection. The Global South were to be part of the process but the North would have to take the lead and incur most of the initial costs.
- **Principle 15** acknowledged the legitimacy of the 'precautionary principle' in developing environmental policy. This proposes that a lack of absolute scientific certainty over the harmful side-effects of some form of economic activity widely believed to be environmentally damaging, should not be used as an excuse to continue with it. This was an important agreement because issues of environmental change tend to be complex and subject to some level of scientific disagreement. In the face of this, excuses can more readily be found for ignoring environmental demands and choosing the short-term option in polluter's dilemma scenarios.

Like Stockholm, the Rio Summit did not instantly create international law but, unlike its predecessor, it did explicitly set the signatory governments on a legislatory path. 'Agenda 21' of UNCED set out a programme of action for implementing sustainable development across a range of environmental issues, including issues debated in recent years but not yet subject to conventions, such as biodiversity, global warming, deforestation and desertification. A Commission for Sustainable Development was established regularly to review progress towards establishing and implementing the conventions that were to follow. In addition, a crucial tenet of sustainable development was realised in the creation of the Global Environmental Facility, a fund subsidised by developed countries, from which Less Developed Countries could draw in order to be able to implement agreements. Four specific regimes were initiated at Rio:

- **The UN Convention on Biological Diversity (CBD)** entered into force in 1993 and went far beyond the previous most significant regime in this area, the Convention on the International Trade in Endangered Species, by committing the parties to biannual conferences at which their progress in conserving biological diversity in their countries is opened to scrutiny.
- **The Forest Principles** agreement emerged when negotiations to establish a deforestation convention failed due to the reluctance of states with prominent logging industries, like Brazil and Malaysia, to sanction significant restraints on their trade. In its place what emerged instead was a weak, non-legally binding regime which, while proclaiming the virtues of sustainable forestry management, in effect gives the green light to states to continue deforesting by asserting that forests are sovereign resources. A short-termist and selfish response to the collective goods problem had occurred. Effectively regulating deforestation was too much of an economic burden for most prolific 'logging' states to countenance and, despite knowledge of the 'carbon sink effect', this was still not seen as sufficiently threatening to the Global North for their governments to push harder for action.
- **The Convention to Combat Desertification** was a response to the most visible manifestation of the 'tragedy of the commons' effect in the world over recent years, whereby deserts have grown in size at the expense of fertile lands surrounding them. Once land becomes arid in this way it is effectively lost forever in terms of its productive value, and so can have food security implications for the local population and, to a limited extent, humanity at large. The convention, established in 1994, sets out a code of practice for the management of semi-arid lands. The convention was unusual in global environmental politics in that it was prompted by developing rather than the industrialised states. It was principally African states, affected by the spread of the Sahara and Kalahari deserts, who championed the inclusion of this issue in Article 21. The regime has evolved slowly since 1994 and, although it is now virtually global in scope, it lacks any of the legal rigour of other environmental regimes that have subsequently emerged. The effects of desertification remain more localised than global and the level of political commitment has followed suit.

● **The UN Framework Convention on Climate Change (UNFCCC)** emerged following a build up of concern at the implications of worldwide rises in temperature. An **epistemic community** had for a few years been voicing fears that global warming was not natural and a potential danger but without any conclusive scientific certainty. However, in the spirit of the precautionary principle, the UNFCCC was signed at Rio and entered into force two years later. The Convention at this stage, however, was also a limited, non-binding agreement without any explicit commitments imposed on states.

## Global environmental policy and human security

Sustainable development and the end of the Cold War brought the world more together intellectually and politically and served to globalise environmental politics, but it was a reactivation of anthropocentric values from the mid 1980s that did most to push some of those environmental issues further up the international political agenda – 'securitising' them – through the fear that certain aspects of environmental change could be life-threatening. Environmental changes which have human health implications are much more likely to invoke international political action.

### Ozone depletion

Hard epistemic community evidence was able to prompt perhaps the most successful international policy on the environment some five years before the Rio Summit. In 1985 the British Antarctic Survey were able to prove conclusively what had been suspected by scientists for at least a decade, that the Earth's ozone layer had a hole in it. The ozone layer is a protective gaseous shell in the upper atmosphere which absorbs ultraviolet rays from the sun before they reach the Earth's surface; this is a vital function since such radiation can kill in the form of skin cancer and other ailments.

The clear danger posed by the loss of this defensive shield prompted an unusually rapid international response. Within a few months of the British Antarctic Survey discovery the Vienna Convention on Protection of the Ozone Layer established a framework treaty, fleshed out two years later in the 1987 Montreal Protocol on Substances that Deplete the Ozone Layer. The 1987 Montreal Protocol saw twenty-four industrialised states bind themselves to an agreement for major cuts in the future use and emission of chlorofluorocarbons (CFCs) and some other chemicals known to be agents of ozone depletion. In the years since 1987 the regime has been strengthened in a series of amendments deepening the cuts to be made by states and widening its application to most of the world. This was achieved by the application of key sustainable development principles agreed on at Rio with developing countries allowed to take a slower track towards phasing out CFCs than the developed states and a multilateral fund created to overcome the costs of implementing the agreements. The success of the regime can be proven by evidence that, within twenty years, the ozone layer had begun to repair itself (WMO/UNEP 2006).

# Climate change

The clearest case of how environmental change can become an issue of human security is in the threat posed by global warming. The Earth's average temperature has risen consistently over the last century and it is now almost universally accepted that this is more than a natural development and likely to accelerate if not dealt with. The central cause of global warming is an exacerbation of the natural phenomenon of the 'greenhouse effect', caused by increased industrial emissions. Increased releases of carbon dioxide and methane over the years, principally through the burning of fossil fuels, have served to exaggerate the natural tendency of the atmosphere to trap a certain amount of infrared sunlight after it is reflected from the Earth's surface. There are numerous implications arising from this phenomenon, summarised in Box 23.3.

A rise in appreciation of such threats, and recognition that the UNFCCC was inadequate as a means of countering them, prompted a significant revamp of the convention in the form of the 1997 Kyoto Protocol. The Kyoto Protocol enacted the principle of common but differentiated responsibilities by requiring developed countries to cut emissions of greenhouse gases by 5.2 per cent from 1990 levels by 2012 without any initial commitment from developing countries. Penalties for non-compliance are also included in the regime, along with an imaginative means of meeting overall targets through 'carbon trading'. This idea, initiated in the USA in the 1970s, as part of the Long Range Transboundary Air Pollution (LRTAP) regime, provides a market mechanism to get round the collective goods problem. Countries exceeding their emissions target can pay countries below their target to acquire their 'carbon credits'.

Although scientific uncertainties inevitably still exist over an issue as complex as climate change, a definitive epistemic consensus has gradually emerged from the UN's Intergovernmental Panel on Climate Change, since its establishment in 1988. By its fourth report in 2007 this substantial grouping of the world's top climatologists was able to pronounce, in the cautious words of science, that it was between 90 and 95 per cent certain that global warming was caused by human action (IPCC 2007). Climate change presents the quintessential polluter's dilemma with significant costs inherent in political action but with potentially the most

## Box 23.3 Human security threats from climate change

The implications of climate change are various but include increased desertification and a raising of sea levels due to the polar ice caps melting, both carrying significant threats to human life in the following forms:

- More frequent and lengthy heat waves
- More frequent droughts
- Coastal flooding due to sea level rises
- Reduced crop yields due to reduced rainfall

- Spread of tropical diseases north and south
- Increased rate of water-borne diseases in flooded areas
- Ocean acidification due to carbon dioxide, affecting fish stocks
- More frequent and stronger riverine flooding in wet seasons due to glaciers melting/reduced water supply in dry season
- Increased incidences of wildfires
- More frequent and stronger windstorms

profound of consequences of inaction. Costing such an issue must inevitably be somewhat sketchy but the 2006 'Stern Review', compiled by a British economist on behalf of the UK government, calculated the cost of non-action on climate change as amounting to at the very least 5 per cent of global GDP for evermore. Set against this, the costs of effective action to curb climate change would cost around 1 per cent of global GDP per year (Stern 2006).

Global warming is a global problem, in both cause and effect, but the scale of human security threat is not equal across the globe. As illustrated in the opening box, for low-lying island states the prospect of a rise in the level of the oceans is a threat of the utmost gravity. For other states the threat is seen as far more remote – both geographically and chronologically – and the urgency to act, which is generally needed for governments to ratify costly environmental agreements, is not there. Indeed, it should be noted that the Stern Review was very much a cost–benefit analysis and, while noting that globally the balance is undoubtedly weighted in favour of the former, it makes clear that some parts of the world could experience net gains from fewer cold related deaths, the increased revenue from tourism and improved agricultural fertility. It is also apparent that some of the threats associated with global warming could be averted by human adaptation to a changing landscape (for example, by migration), a point Cornucopians like Julian Simon have made in the face of another prophecy of environmental catastrophe like overpopulation in the 1960s and 1970s (Simon 1999).

The threat posed by global warming, however, is increasingly thought not just to be a theoretical future scenario. The human cost is already significant and is not confined solely to the developing world, where other factors can more easily be employed to explain mortality figures. The World Health Organisation has estimated an annual death toll of 150,000 due to global warming since the 1970s (McMichael et al. 2004). Most of these casualties are from the Global South but the North has been rocked by events such as the 2003 heatwave in Western Europe which killed up to 35,000 people and Hurricane Katrina, the following year, which claimed around 1,200 lives and caused an estimated $200 billion worth of damage in the USA. While proving categorically whether such single events are attributable to global warming is impossible, the changes associated with climate change are already occurring and a dwindling few believe that this overall trend can be put down to chance.

## Box 23.4 Bjorn Lomborg, *The Sceptical Environmentalist*

Lomborg's 2001 work, *The Sceptical Environmentalist*, attracted great interest (and great derision from ecologists) for questioning whether implementing international policy on global warming made any rational sense. The Danish academic claims that he was converted to a sceptical view of the Kyoto Protocol and other international environmental policies he had previously supported by an exercise in one of his classes at the University of Aarhus in which he asked his students to consider the most efficient way to allocate money to solve the most pressing global problems. The students' results and Lomborg's subsequent research suggested that, when set against other global problems, the costs of acting to curb global warming exceeded the gains. Lomborg did not deny that global warming was a human-caused problem but suggested that it is not as significant a threat as it had been painted and that the expenditure to be allocated to tackling the problem would be better spent on addressing global poverty (Lomborg 2001).

# Persistent Organic Pollutants (POPs)

The 1992 Rio Summit was also the catalyst for significant global political action in the area of human health-threatening atmospheric pollution. UNEP's Governing Council in 1997 endorsed the opinion of the Intergovernmental Forum on Chemical Safety, which had been established at the Rio Summit, that a binding treaty be set up to phase out the production and use of thirteen POPs (initially a 'dirty dozen') including DDT and several other organochlorine pesticides across the world (see Table 23.1). The Treaty was signed by 127 governments at a Diplomatic Conference in Stockholm in 2001, initiating a regime that will continue to consider adding new chemicals to the original thirteen through a Review Committee. The production and use of the thirteen outlawed chemicals had long ceased in most developed countries but their properties ensured that they remained a domestic hazard to those populations. The listed chemicals are all highly persistent, have a propensity to travel globally in the atmosphere through a continual process of evaporation and deposition, and frequently end up in human foodstuffs through the process of bioaccumulation. Hence, sterility, neural disorders and cancer in peoples of the developed world can be attributed to the use of POPs in other parts of the planet. The political significance of this is such that even President George W. Bush, already known in some quarters as the 'Toxic Texan' for his administration's lack of enthusiasm for environmental concerns, declared the USA to be a firm supporter of international political action on POPs.

**Table 23.1** Chemicals subject to the Stockholm Convention

| Intentionally produced | | |
|---|---|---|
| Aldrin | Pesticide | *Use and production banned apart from for laboratory-scale research* |
| Chlordane | Pesticide | |
| Dieldrin | Pesticide | |
| Endrin | Pesticide | |
| Heptachlor | Pesticide | |
| Hexachlorobenzene (HCB) | Pesticide | |
| Mirex | Pesticide | |
| Toxaphene | Pesticide | |
| Polychlorinated Biphenyls (PCBs) | Industrial chemical | |
| Dichlorodiphenyltrichloroethane (DDT) | Pesticide | *Use restricted to disease vector control* |
| **Unintentionally produced** | | |
| Polychlorinated dibenzo-p-dioxins and dibenzofurans (PCDD 'dioxins'/PCDF 'furans') | | *Use and production minimised with aim of elimination* |
| Hexachlorobenzene (HCB) | Pesticide | |
| Polychlorinated Biphenyls (PCBs) | Industrial chemical | |

Aside from the POPs 'dirty dozen', pollution in general still represents a major threat to human life. It has been estimated that between a quarter and a third of all deaths in the world by disease have environmental causes, such as air and water pollution (Smith et al. 1999: 573). Developed countries have long been aware of the human cost of pollution, as can be evidenced by the UK Clean Air Act of 1956 that followed in the wake of the Great Smog four years previously, a Smog which had claimed the lives of around 4,000 Londoners. Over time, however, recognition has grown that national actions alone are not enough.

## Natural disasters

Natural disasters are often caused by human-induced environmental change. Deforestation exacerbates global warming and can be seen as a causal factor behind natural disasters such as mudslides down once naturally secure hillsides (Humphreys 2006: 1). Human vulnerability to natural hazards has increased in recent years due principally to population growth and movement in the Global South. Natural disasters also often occur for rational, natural reasons related to environmental change. Tropical cyclones, for example, can be understood as 'safety valves' which dissipate the build-up of excessive heat in the ocean or atmosphere. This has led some climatologists to suggest that the increased prominence of

*Source: Getty Images/Daisy Gildardini*

The polluter's dilemma: environmental policy in the twenty-first century is at a crossroads, as individual states threaten to pursue their own national interest.

the El Niño effect in the 1990s, associated with more frequent cyclones and other extreme weather phenomena, could be linked to global warming (Mazza 1998; Trenberth 1998). The 2003 European heatwave, unprecedented in history, provided even clearer evidence of a correlation between global warming and natural disasters.

## Biodiversity

Other issues of environmental change have come to be framed in more human security terms. In 2008 The Economics of Ecosystems and Biodiversity (TEEB), a think tank funded by the EU and German government, replicated the Stern Report on a classically ecocentric issue somewhat put in the shade by the politics of climate change. The TEEB review posited that global GDP would be likely to decline by 7 per cent by 2050 if greater commitment to preserving fish stocks, forests and other species needed by humanity was not given (Sukhdev 2008). Released against a backdrop of unprecedented rises in global food and energy prices this seemed a particularly pertinent warning.

## Threats to the global consensus on environmental policy

The widening and deepening of international environmental policy in the 1980s and 1990s hit something of a crossroads in the new millennium with some erosion of the global consensus that had been carefully forged. The First and Third Worlds had been reconciled by the concept of sustainable development, and the First and Second Worlds merged together by changing political circumstances; however, it was a division within the ranks of the First World that came to threaten global solidarity. The United States under George W. Bush charted a new course in relation to global environmental policy, marked by a return to a more individualistic foreign policy with a non-collective strategy towards polluter's dilemma situations.

The US from 2001 backtracked on several commitments to principles and policies accepted by the Clinton administration at Rio. Most notably the Bush government broke ranks and failed to ratify the Kyoto Protocol despite the USA having signed the framework treaty under Clinton. The US government sidestepped the precautionary principle and common but differentiated responsibilities concept by citing the lack of scientific certainty over human-induced global warming and concerns over the lesser constraints imposed on developing countries. In addition, they admitted that the treaty was simply not in their 'national interest' because of the economic cost. Similarly, the US delegation at the negotiations of the Stockholm POPS Convention fought hard to ensure that the term 'precautionary principle' did not appear in the final text and it was eventually replaced with the more ambiguous compromise phrase 'precautionary approach', which the industrialists hoped would open the door to less expansive 'scientific' toxicity assessments for future chemicals to be subject to the regime (Olsen 2003: 99–100). The significance of such semantics is clear from considering the Bush administration's pronouncements on the principle accepted by the US government at UNCED: 'the US government supports precautionary approaches to risk management but we do not recognize any precautionary principle' (Graham 2002). By 2010 the USA had still not ratified Stockholm with their initial enthusiasm curbed by the inclusion of chemicals on the 'POPs list' still used extensively by the US chlorine industry.

The exasperation of the international community at the new US strategy became evident at the ten year follow-up to Rio, the World Summit on Sustainable Development (WSSD) in Johannesburg in 2002. The conference is best remembered for the widespread booing and heckling which greeted the addresses of US Secretary of State Colin Powell, who had been sent to Johannesburg in place of his president, mindful of the hostile reception he would receive. Johannesburg represented the third environmental 'mega-conference' but was more low-key than its predecessor. It was also noticeably more anthropocentric and more focused on development than the environment. Little progress was made in advancing the agenda on biodiversity established at Rio and, although global warming policy was kept alive, it was not developed in any significant way. New proposals to set a framework for phasing in the use of renewable energy sources and improving Global South access to developed world food markets were sidestepped but some new goals were set in line with the recently agreed upon Millennium Development Goals (MDGs) (see Chapter 18). The target date of 2015 was set for the realisation of two new human security aims: halving the number of people who lack access to clean water and achieving sustainability in global fishing.

Despite US obstruction global environmental politics in the twenty-first century has continued to evolve and served to demonstrate the limitations of hegemonic power politics in the contemporary world. Fellow recalcitrant states, like Russia and Australia, were gradually converted to the Kyoto Protocol through pressure by the society of states and non-state actors. Epistemic consensus and global civil society have given such momentum to global environmental politics that it can survive being pushed off the international agenda by displays of national interest against the common good. That the USA were out of step with the world became clear when their spokesmen were again booed and, most noticeably, yelled at to 'get out of the way' by the delegation of Papua New Guinea at a 2007 UN Climate Change conference in Bali.

By 2009 and under a new president, the USA had been brought partly back into the fold and at a Copenhagen Summit (the 15th Conference of the Parties of the International Framework Convention on Climate Change) signalled acceptance of both the precautionary and common but differentiated responsibilities principles by agreeing to carbon dioxide cuts and contributing to a global fund for assisting developing states to follow suit.

## Conclusions

Global political action on the natural environment has seen many issues politicised and put on the international agenda but only a few securitised at the top of that agenda. Myriad international regimes have emerged since the high water mark of environmental politics at Rio in 1992, but global policy today stands in stark contrast to domestic environmental laws in Western European and North American states which are marked by precautionary consumer standards and ecocentric measures. Where successful international environmental regimes have emerged, it has usually been where a clear and unambiguous human health threat is apparent. It is far rarer for the value of environmental protection to be prioritised at the global level than it is at the domestic level. Internationally, governments are still prone to taking blinkered decisions informed by short-term economic interest in the face of epistemic consensus and longer-term utilitarian calculations of 'national interest', as has most clearly been seen in the USA's stance on climate change under the Bush government. From the perspective of governments worrying about an apparently imminent terrorist threat, economic downturn or their next election global environmental issues often do not get placed near the top of their political 'in trays'.

In the face of this the short-term and easier response is to play the polluter in the polluter's dilemma. The scale of the threat posed by environmental change is difficult to quantify but it is undoubtedly significant and, to a large extent, avoidable given the political will. Probably the highest profile issues of environmental change, at different times over the past forty years, have been: resource scarcity due to population growth, ozone depletion, and global warming. The fact that the first of these 'crises' never really materialised and the second one was partially averted by reasonably effective global political action has served to reinforce the notion that contemporary threats posed by environmental change, such as global warming, are potential rather than actual threats and perhaps exaggerated. As a result, despite gradually becoming more of a feature on the global political agenda, environmental issues still struggle to be treated as a political priority. The unprecedented scale of the threats posed by global warming and the increased appreciation of environmental principles among ordinary people around the world, however, may yet see this change.

## Resource section

## Questions

1.  Analyse and account for the increased international political concern that has been given to environmental issues over the last forty years.

2.  Why has environmental policy at the global level generally proved harder to attain than it has domestically in most developed states?

3.  Why do some people (and states) consider global warming to be an issue of critical importance while others do not?

4.  Explain what is meant by sustainable development and account for the rise of this concept in international politics.

5.  How green are you? Are there any environmental issues that concern you? What is it about these issues that concerns you? Do you support action for economic or personal health reasons or are your concerns intrinsically about the natural environment?

## Recommended reading

Kutting, G. (ed.) (2010) *The Environment and International Relations* (Abingdon: Routledge)
A thorough overview of contemporary global environmental politics across all the major issues by bringing together several leading writers in an authoritative but accessible reader.

Lomborg, B. (2007) *Cool It – The Sceptical Environmentalist's Guide to Global Warming* (London: Cyan & Marshall Cavendish)
In this follow up to the influential and controversial *Sceptical Environmentalist* Lomborg develops his controversial thesis – that expenditure allocated to reducing greenhouse gases would be better allocated to global health issues instead – with the support of the 'Copenhagen Consensus' of prominent economists.

Stern, N. (2006) *The Economics of Climate Change – the Stern Review* (Cambridge: Cambridge University Press)
An economist's call to arms on global warming which clearly sets out the costs and benefits of climate change, concluding that action to curb further temperature rises would be cost effective as well as in the human interest.

## Useful websites

Stern Report: http://www.hm-treasury.gov.uk/independent_reviews/stern_review_economics_climate_change/stern_review_report.cfm

United Nations Environment Programme: http://www.unep.org/

World Summit on Sustainable Development (Johannesburg 2002): http://www.johannesburgsummit.org/

# Part 6 War and Peace

Even though the discipline of International Relations covers a very wide range of topics – many of which have been covered in this book – the issue of security has always been at its core. We have, therefore, devoted an entire part to looking at a number of factors which are centrally concerned with security. As with all the parts of this book, there are a number of objectives. The first is to encourage you to reflect on the complexity surrounding the concept of security itself. As you will notice, once you begin reading the opening chapters, it is not sufficient merely to define security as 'protection'. This in itself raises many questions; namely, security from what? Security for whom? How is that security to be provided and who is responsible for providing it?

These questions appear simple on the surface but as you begin to delve into the subject matter you will see that even asking the question 'What is security?' is loaded with complications. As the very first chapter in this part will show, there is a serious schism among academics (and politicians) over whether we should be concerned with the security of the state or that of the individual. Consequently, we have suggested that the best way of evaluating the nature of the concept is to use a variety of International Relations theories, such as realism, feminism, liberalism and critical theory, given that these provide us with alternative lenses through which we can view and address the greatest problems facing not only states but also us as humans.

Following the conceptual chapters, therefore, we turn our attention to a number of seemingly intractable problems facing the international community. In this list you will find the remarkably brutal consequences of state failure where civilians suffer at the hand of criminal networks, insurgency groups and private mercenaries that begin to emerge as state structures are eroded. We also introduce you to the consequences of nuclear proliferation whereby numerous states now have the potential to cause death and destruction at an unprecedented level. Conflicts in many parts of the world in the post-Cold War era have raised questions regarding the ability of the international community to solve these issues. As the pre-eminent international organisation, the United Nations, has effectively failed in its primary goal of maintaining international peace and security and we seek to explain why this is so. No one will forget the horrific impact of the terrorist attacks of 11 September 2001 on the World Trade Center in New York and, although terrorism did exist prior to these attacks, it has since then acquired unprecedented importance. The invasions of Afghanistan and Iraq, the Taliban insurgency in Pakistan and Afghanistan, the bomb blasts in London, Madrid, Bali and elsewhere all testify to the terrible spectre haunting our world. As the various chapters will show, there are many problems facing us each of which must be solved by means of a different set of policies, but the one thing they all have in common is that they are all a function of security.

*Source*: Panos Pictures/Chris Stowers

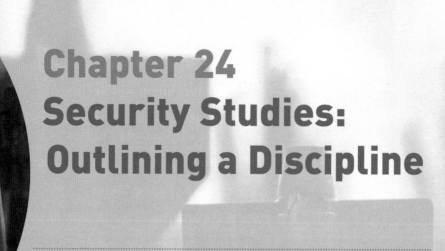

# Chapter 24
# Security Studies: Outlining a Discipline

Defining security and outlining the categories

Defining security – framing the debate

The debates in Security Studies

Conclusions

After reading this chapter you will be able to:

- Account for some of the links between Security Studies and key historical events

- Understand what is meant by the *referent object*

- Trace the development of Security Studies as a discipline and provide an account of some of the categories

- Use the various perspectives within the discipline to define 'security' as a concept

- Assess whether military force remains central to global politics

*Source*: Panos Pictures/Chris Stowers

## Introductory box: Referent object? What referent object?

Human security does not supplant national security. A human security perspective asserts that the security of the state is not an end in itself. Rather it is a means of ensuring security for its people.

(Lloyd Axworthy: Former Canadian Foreign Minister, Ottawa 1999)

Pakistan conducted nuclear tests in May 1998, thereby joining the exclusive handful of nuclear weapons states (the others being the United States, Russia, China, Britain, France, India and Israel). Ask yourself, from the point of view of security, is it better for a poor state like Pakistan to spend its scarce resources on acquiring expensive nuclear weapons, or should it spend its limited money on reducing poverty, improving health and increasing education levels for its citizens? The issue of 'focus', in other words, is should those seeking to provide security for Pakistan be concerned with the security of the *state* itself or that of the *individuals* residing within the state? To use the vocabulary of academics – should the *referent object* be the state or the individual? This question is one of the most important in Security Studies and has been the subject of much debate. The only way we can resolve this issue is by analysing the various opinions which exist within the discipline.

## Defining security and outlining the categories

This chapter, and the next few, are essentially concerned with the concept of *security*. This is one of the most important areas of study in global politics and 'security' is the central concept of a discipline known as Security Studies. 'Security' generally implies a sense of protection, safety from harm or indeed even survival in the face of some kind of threat. Obviously then, it is a necessity which is of immense value to us as individuals and to the many states of the world, and it is understandable that governments across the globe expend a lot of resources in making themselves and their territories safe. This explanation of the concept of 'security' may seem obvious, and indeed we would argue that it is perhaps a little too simple. Academics who have written about security issues have done so on a very wide variety of topics, ranging from the causes of conflict between states – civil wars, deterrence, arms control, disarmament and nuclear proliferation – to topics such as the deterioration in the global climate, the role of international institutions in maintaining peace and security, upholding human rights, the effects of population growth, mass migration and refugee flows, concern over women's rights in the international system, and even poverty. This is quite a disparate group of issues, but the one thing that connects them is that they can all be a function of security. In the face of so much complexity one may be

*Source: Getty Images/Barcroft Media*

The traditionalist, narrow view of Security Studies argues that states themselves are the referent object for analysis.

tempted to ask how any discipline can be concerned with so much and yet remain coherent. Herein lies the problem with Security Studies, since academics cannot agree on a focus for the discipline. This chapter, therefore, provides a simple route through the minefield surrounding the concept of security and broadly speaking there are four categories which need to be explained.

## Category 1: The traditionalist narrow view

This view argues that Security Studies should have a narrow military focus, where the greatest threat perceived is to the territorial integrity of states during times of conflict. Generally known as the *traditionalist view*, the focus for this category is on states themselves as the *referent object* and the basic premise of the approach is that the only way for states to protect themselves is to maximise their military power.

## Category 2: The concept of security – the broad view

This view belongs to those who argue that the threats faced by states do not necessarily emanate from other states during times of conflict but that states can be threatened by a 'broader' category of threats, such as economic threats, environmental threats or political threats. The state, however, remains the main object for concern in this category, though some views have begun to highlight the threats faced by 'societies' which exist at a level below the state. These subdivisions will be highlighted later.

## Category 3: Shifting the focus away from the state as referent object – deepening the concept

The third category is quite broad, but shares one crucial feature – an intense dissatisfaction with the narrow military focus of the traditional views of security. The basis for this view was established in Chapter 9 and we suggest you read that alongside this one. Among the various approaches in this category we will need to discuss Critical Security Studies which, in its criticism of traditionalist views, argues that it is necessary to move away from a military focus of state action to focus on other referent objects such as individuals and communities.

Another view under the general heading of Critical Security Studies stresses that individual humans should be the ultimate referent object and that the only way in which individuals can achieve true security is through a process referred to as '**emancipation**'. Emancipation has often been interpreted as achieving 'freedom' and to be secure in this sense means the 'freeing of people from those physical and human constraints which stop them carrying out what they would freely choose to do' (Booth 1991: 319). Critical Security Studies, then, generally provides alternatives to mainstream Security Studies in the sense of focusing on substitutes to the state as ultimate referent object.

Feminist critiques of traditional Security Studies form another group in this category, and the argument here essentially claims that women have been ignored for too long in traditional Security Studies and that the views expressed by the discipline are too state-centred and too masculine. Feminists claim that since most of the casualties during times of conflict are civilians, including women and children, Security Studies should focus on them rather than on the security of the state.

## Category 4: Human security

During the 1990s the United Nations was instrumental in encouraging the development of **human security** – a view which continues along the theme of regarding the human as the key referent object. Since then human security literature has addressed a broad range of issues which make people insecure. These factors encompass not only physical violence against humans but also developmental concerns such as poor access to society's resources (for example, health, education and general welfare).

## Defining security – framing the debate

Each of these general categories needs further elaboration but already we can see that it is not easy for students of security to focus on a specific starting point. Arguments over what the referent object should be, whether military force is central to achieving security or not, who should be responsible for providing security and, ultimately, what Security Studies as a discipline should consider as its subject matter; these all make for a very complex series of questions and understandably confuse students of security. Our goal in these chapters is to simplify the route through this minefield.

## Box 24.1  The concept of security – what should we be concerned with?

The categories above lead to one overwhelming observation, namely that security is an ambiguous concept and defining it is likely to be difficult. Consider the following list of examples and write down your initial thoughts in terms of which of the above categories appears to be the most applicable.

1. On 2 August 1990 Iraq's armed forces invaded neighbouring Kuwait. During the subsequent seven-month-long occupation the then President of Iraq (Saddam Hussein) announced that the state of Kuwait no longer existed and that its territory was now part of Iraq.
2. On 11 September 2001 nineteen al-Qaeda terrorists hijacked four planes and intentionally crashed two of them into the Twin Towers of the World Trade Center in New York City. Over three thousand innocent civilians were killed in this attack.

Put yourself in the place of those who witnessed at first hand the destruction of these famous landmarks.

3. During the final stages of the Second World War the United States dropped atomic bombs on two Japanese cities. These were Hiroshima on 6 August 1945 and Nagasaki three days later on 9 August. Think about the survivors of these attacks.
4. Human trafficking is the transport and sale of humans for the purpose of profit. It is seen as a modern form of slavery and those people who are trafficked often end up working for the profit of others through activities such as begging or prostitution. Human trafficking is the fastest growing crime in the world. The United Nations estimates that more than 2.5 million people are being trafficked and revenues from their sale are estimated to be up to $9 billion a year.

Security is ultimately about the absence of threats to life, property, the freedom of individuals or core values (however one defines those values). The examples in Box 24.1 demonstrate an important point, namely that the security of some entity (the *referent object*) is being threatened. This referent object could be the state – as in the case of the annexation of Kuwait by Iraq – or it could be humans as shown by the example of human trafficking. However, it is important to remember that the categories are not clear-cut given that dropping an atomic bomb on a city not only affects the security of humans but also threatens the security of the state. The examples do, nevertheless, demonstrate the potential for disagreement over the definition of security, namely whether it is the state that needs to be secured or the individual human.

One of the reasons for these different viewpoints is that, after the Second World War, the concept became closely associated with the military and ideological dynamics of the Cold War. During this time the main threat to the territorial integrity of states stemmed from the possibility that war could break out at any time. The focus for academics and policy makers during these years, therefore, was on the relationship between the two superpowers, the United States and the Soviet Union, both of whom sought to maximise their security by engaging in an arms race. It was in this context, therefore, that the concept of security became synonymous with military power during the Cold War and the prevailing view was that the more military power a state had, the more secure it was. Furthermore, International Relations explained the intense competition between the two superpowers during the Cold War by reference to its main theoretical tradition, that of Realism, which was introduced in

Chapter 6. As highlighted there, this approach attempts to persuade us that its view of international affairs is realistic and that we must, therefore, look at the relationship between states and ultimately the concept of security in that context. Realism is based on the premise that the anarchic conditions of the international system led to states having to seek survival either through the maximisation of their own military might or via alliances with more powerful states.

It was this intense narrowing of the field which led to many calls for security to be reconceptualised, since it was soon recognised that military threats were not the only perils faced by states. For instance, in an interesting article entitled 'A New Security Paradigm', Gregory Foster argues that it is now necessary to elevate the threats posed to states, societies and individuals by a deterioration in the world's climate to a level where they feature in the strategic calculations of states (Foster 2005: 35–46). By the same token it could be argued that AIDS, poverty, drug abuse, domestic violence and so on could also be considered as legitimate security concerns. The end of the Cold War and the collapse of the Soviet Union, in particular, led to calls to reconsider both the nature of order in the international system and the various threats. It was, therefore, inevitable that the debates over the concept of security would intensify, indeed it is now widely recognised that 'security' is an *essentially contested* concept. In other words, there may be widespread agreement over its core principles, but it remains subject to continuous debate over its proper use (Gallie 1956: 169). The remainder of this chapter, therefore, will introduce you to the various debates over the concept and the state of Security Studies as a discipline.

## The debates in Security Studies

## Category 1: The traditionalist view

A number of features stand out in an analysis of the traditionalist view, namely:

- The state is the referent object and therefore it is the state that seeks to achieve security
- War and other forms of military conflict between states are the main cause of insecurity for states
- The only certain way for states to achieve security is by maximising their military power which sends a signal to other states and potential aggressors that any attempt at conquest would be futile and met with deadly force
- The views in this category are heavily influenced by Realist theory

You will have read about the central features of Realist theory in Chapter 6 of this book, but a quick summary here will enable you to further grasp the basic connection between the traditionalist view and Realist theory. After the Second World War Realism became the main theoretical tool used by analysts to explain state behaviour in the international system. It claims to view the world as it really is and its core beliefs revolve around the notion that 'the best description of world politics is a state of war – not a continuous war or constant war but the constant possibility of war among all states' (Doyle and Ikenberry 1997: 10). This means that states are obliged to follow *realpolitik* and need to remain self-interested, continuously preparing for conflict and always being mindful of their relative military strength vis-à-vis other states. Realists also argue that all individuals must 'accept the national interest as an ideal, as the one true guide to the formulation of the public policy of states . . . [and] failing to follow the national interest . . . is a prescription for national disaster' (Doyle and Ikenberry 1997: 11).

Furthermore, for Realists, anarchy is a central feature of international relations. As Chapter 6 explains, an anarchic international system essentially refers to the perception that 'there is no world government analogous to the national government of states, which can maintain the law, administer justice, and prevent large-scale outbreaks of violence' (Sheehan 2005: 8). This means that states exist in a system characterised by the notion of *'self-help'*, defined as a condition where 'the structure of the system does not permit friendship, trust, and honour; only a perennial condition of uncertainty generated by the absence of a global government' (Dunne 1997: 119). If this is the true nature of the international system, it is no wonder that states continuously calculate their military strength in relation to other states. This is as a result of the fear that they may be attacked at any time and therefore, from this perspective, maximising the strength of its armed forces becomes an essential feature of the security and survival of the state.

Realism provided a powerful theoretical basis for the traditionalist view of security. This view relied heavily on the central role of the state as the primary actor in the international system and anarchy as the dominant feature of that system. In an environment dominated by beasts roaming a jungle, survival is only likely to be achieved by the strongest and fittest. But we must also look at the historical context, since the study of security emerged immediately after the Second World War and that the impetus for the discipline 'came from the twin revolutions in American foreign policy and military technology caused by the emergence of the Cold War and the development of atomic weapons' (Nye and Lynn-Jones 1988: 8). The use of atomic bombs by the United States on Japanese cities – Hiroshima and Nagasaki (6 and 9 August 1945 respectively) – may have persuaded the Japanese to surrender but they also signalled to the world that the US was at this stage the most powerful of all states. However, the US nuclear monopoly was short-lived since the Soviet Union tested its own atomic bomb in 1949. This was soon followed by the Soviet launch of the *Sputnik I* Satellite which introduced intercontinental ballistic missiles to the arms race between the two superpowers. The Soviet Union was now able to use nuclear weapons to strike directly, if it so wished, anywhere on the globe – including the United States. These events fuelled ever-growing levels of suspicion and mistrust, ultimately resulting in the major arms race between the two superpowers.

Such events encouraged analysts to consider the role played by force in relations between states, and security became synonymous with strategy where 'strategy' was defined as 'the art of distributing and applying military means to fulfil ends of policy' (Liddell Hart 1967: 335). The study of strategy came to be known as Strategic Studies and the development of the discipline was heavily influenced by the Cold War, the nuclear revolution and the

## Box 24.2 Strategic Studies and Security Studies – a clarification

### Strategic Studies

During the Cold War the main challenge facing the West was how to confront the perceived threat from the Soviet Union. Strategists conceptualised security in excessively narrow military terms, largely due to the arms race with the Soviet Union and the pressures exerted by the development of nuclear weapons and the rapid improvement in military technology.

### Security Studies

By the 1980s an increasing number of academics and politicians held the belief that war was disappearing as an option among a large number of states – particularly those of Western Europe, North America and Japan. When the Cold War came to an end in 1989, it was assumed that the Soviet Union could also now be included in this 'no war' camp. Given that war was now unlikely among these states, Realist assumptions about military security appeared increasingly archaic. A large number of academics began to call for the concept of security to be broadened beyond the narrow confines of the Realist tradition and so, by the end of the 1980s, elements of a broader discipline – Security Studies – began to emerge.

dominance of Realist theory. With Realism highlighting the importance of military power in achieving security for the state and the Soviet Union increasingly seen as a military threat to the United States and its allies, it is easy to understand why the focus for the discipline became the study of the use of military force to achieve security for the state. The innovative use of military power (including land and air-based weapons and forces), tactics on the battlefield, nuclear and conventional force postures of the Western military alliance (NATO), and the impact of technology on warfare, were just some of the areas considered by strategists (Klein 1994; Baylis et al. 2007; Mahnken and Maiolo 2008).

Events between 1945 and 1950 show the Cold War unfolding, leading to the ensuing reliance on military power to ensure state security. The first step was the gradual Soviet takeover of states liberated by their army after the Second World War, whereby Czechoslovakia, Romania, Bulgaria and Hungary succumbed to communist rule between 1945 and 1948. Secondly, in 1947, both Greece and Turkey were still holding out against a takeover by Soviet-inspired communist insurgents. However, when Britain announced that it would no longer be supporting their governments financially, the Americans stepped in to provide the necessary support resulting in the famous Truman Doctrine (see Box 24.3). The immediate concern for President Harry Truman was for Congress to agree to a $400 million package of economic and military assistance for both Turkey and Greece. The longer-term effect of this, however, was equally significant since it signalled an American willingness to assist groups or governments across the world in resisting Soviet influence (Spellman 2006: 27–9).

A third element was the Marshall Plan, an ambitious American strategy for rebuilding war-torn Europe. Named after the then US Secretary of State George Marshall, once it was approved the United States channelled almost $13 billion into European reconstruction between 1948 and 1951 (Ferrell 1999: 120). Many explanations have been put forward as

### Box 24.3 The Truman Doctrine and containment policy

Announced in a speech to Congress by US President Harry S. Truman on 12 March 1947, the Truman Doctrine pledged American support for 'free peoples who are resisting attempted subjugation by armed minorities or by outside pressures'. The first test of the Doctrine was to provide aid to Greece in its fight against communism, but the wider aims of Truman's plan were to provide military and economic advisors to states perceived to be under threat from the Soviet Union. Containing the Soviet Union was also implied in Truman's Doctrine, and in essence it attempted to limit and prevent further Soviet expansion. George Kennan – a US diplomat in the Soviet Union after the Second World War – presented the basis for containment policy as an attempt to confront the Soviet Union whenever it sought to expand its influence. He saw Soviet communism as a 'fluid stream which moves constantly, wherever it is permitted to move, toward a given goal. Its main concern is to make sure that it has filled every nook and cranny available to it in the basin of world power' (Kennan 1947).

motives for the financial support the Americans gave to Europe, most notably humanitarian, political and economic reasons. However, as argued by John Gimbel the plan was also 'referred to as a corollary to the Truman Doctrine' (see Box 24.3) 'a program to stop communism, to frustrate socialists and leftists, to attract the Soviet Union's satellites [Eastern European states] and to contain or roll back the Russians' (Gimbel 1976: 1). The Soviet Union refused to participate in the American plan and, given that Eastern European states were now under its control, the Soviet Union also refused to allow the American aid to reach them.

Finally, in 1947 the US National Security Act created the Joint Chiefs of Staff and the CIA, as well as the Departments of Defense and the National Security Council (NSC). One of the first acts of the National Security Council was to undertake a study into US foreign policy objectives in response to the various events which had contributed to the inevitable decline into the Cold War. Among these was the Soviet testing of an atomic bomb mentioned earlier, but there was also a belief that the Soviet Union would proceed with its research into nuclear technology and ultimately develop the hydrogen bomb – a weapon of far greater destructive power than the earlier fission bomb. Principally written by Paul Nitze (Director of Policy Planning for the State Department – 1950–53), NSC-68 became a blueprint for US foreign policy during the Cold War, with the aim of preparing the United States to use its economic and, in particular, its military capability to contain the Soviet Union. As can be seen from Box 24.4, the drafters of the document believed that the Soviet Union intended to use its own military and economic strength to expand its system of communist rule wherever possible, a form of governance which was hostile to the free liberal democracy of the United States and its allies. It, therefore, recommended a huge expansion in US military development which included a massive increase in funding for the armed forces and for the rapid development and deployment of the hydrogen bomb – the next phase of nuclear technology.

**Box 24.4 Key statement from NSC-68 – United States Objectives and Programs for National Security, April 14, 1950**

Thus unwillingly our free society finds itself mortally challenged by the Soviet system. No other value system is so wholly irreconcilable with ours, so implacable in its purpose to destroy ours, so capable of turning to its own uses the most dangerous and divisive trends in our own society, no other so skilfully and powerfully evokes the elements of irrationality in human nature everywhere, and no other has the support of a great and growing center of military power.

Strategic Studies, then, was overwhelmingly geared towards analysing the possibility of a clash between the two superpowers, and the danger that nuclear weapons could be used added a sense of urgency to this military stand-off. While the United States had the monopoly on nuclear weapons (until 1949) they were just another weapon in their arsenal. After the Soviet test in 1949 and the arrival of intercontinental ballistic missiles, the danger to mainland USA and the rest of the Western alliance became obvious, as did the rationale for Strategic Studies. Military threats and the use of military power to defend the state were crucial, although it was this very focus which was later criticised for being intensely narrow and increasingly irrelevant to issues concerning security. Attention now turns, therefore, to the second category and those who sought to broaden the concept of security.

## Category 2: Broadening the concept of security

As shown, the early literature on the concept of security employed a rather narrow definition of politics. The field of Strategic Studies tended to ignore the non-military sources of international tension and to focus solely on military balances. It was this restricted focus that led to calls for a reassessment of the range of threats facing states and a broadening of the concept of security. The primary driving forces behind this attempt to redefine security were important developments in global politics such as the increasing realisation that the deteriorating global climate was beginning to threaten the security of states, as was the rapid increase in global population levels. The Oil Crisis of 1973, during which the world saw a four-fold increase in the price of oil, demonstrated how political events in the Middle East could threaten the economic security of states. The 1990s increasingly demanded a redefinition of what constituted security and two elements were crucial here: the first was that the 'new' types of threats were of a non-military nature and the second was that armed force was not deemed to be an appropriate response to them. Factors such as excessive population growth, the damage being done to the global climate and the increasing inability to match available resources to the increasing numbers of people on the planet showed that the narrow Realist basis of security was no longer appropriate.

### Box 24.5  Richard Ullman, 'Redefining Security'

One writer who was instrumental in calling for a broader view of security is worthy of mention here. Ullman showed his dissatisfaction with traditionalist Security Studies as far back as the early 1980s when he stated that, since the beginning of the Cold War 'every administration in Washington ha[d] defined American national security in excessively narrow and excessively military terms'. In a key article (Ullman 1983) he showed that concentrating exclusively on the military sector led to us ignoring the many non-military threats facing nations. For instance he compared natural disasters such as earthquakes with nuclear conflict, arguing that the former can be equally devastating. Think about the earthquake that struck Haiti's capital, Port Au Prince, on 12 January 2010 where countless people lost their lives and the capital city itself was largely destroyed. Ask yourself whether the narrow definitions imposed by Realism could be relevant in the case of Haiti.

These types of studies encouraged others to think about the limitations imposed by traditional ideas of security; however, the work of Barry Buzan, most notably his analysis of the concept of national security in a famous book entitled *People, States and Fear* (1991) is of particular importance. Here Buzan supported the developing view that the state faced a multiple range of threats of which the military element was just one. He, therefore, encouraged us to consider political, economic, societal and environmental threats to the state, in addition to the traditional military aspect.

In addition to introducing us to these sectors, Buzan's analysis was also important because he highlighted questions relating to the appropriate level at which security should be assessed, whether individual, national or international (Sheehan 2005: 47). In this sense Buzan does consider the individual but he refused at this stage to consider the possibility of moving away from the state as the ultimate referent object. His reasons revolved around the

### Box 24.6  Barry Buzan's non-military sectors

As a well-established academic in the field of International Relations, Barry Buzan has been instrumental in influencing the evolution of the concept of security. Currently a professor at the London School of Economics, Buzan succeeded in persuading the academic community that states were faced by threats which were distinctly non-military in nature. These included:

1. Political security: the organisational stability of states, systems of government and the ideologies that give them legitimacy.
2. Economic security: access to the resources, finance and markets necessary to sustain acceptable levels of welfare and state power.
3. Societal security: the sustainability, within acceptable conditions for evolution, of traditional patterns of language, culture and religions, and national identity and customs.
4. Environmental security: the maintenance of the local and the planetary biosphere as the essential support system on which all other human enterprises depend.

*Source*: Barry Buzan (1991) *People, States and Fear:
An Agenda for International Security Studies
in the Post-Cold War Era*: 19–20.

premise that it was the state that had to cope with threats that occurred at the sub-state level as well as at the international level.

As you will recall from the section on the traditionalist view, the hostile relationship between the two superpowers during the Cold War encouraged them to seek security based largely on maximising their military power. In this scenario, therefore, the state was the ultimate referent object seeking security. This emphasis seemed increasingly out of place once the Cold War came to an end in 1989, particularly when Eastern European states such as Romania, Hungary and Poland took the dramatic step of replacing their communist systems with elected governments. By 1991 the Soviet Union itself had dissolved into its various republics and the Realist emphasis on state security seemed increasingly misplaced. The easing of tensions between East and West at the end of the Cold War meant that state security appeared assured, and as a result the search for alternative referent objects became more earnest. Buzan himself found it increasingly difficult to uphold his opinion that the state was the ultimate referent for security and he therefore shifted his attention to 'societal' security. Whereas the essence of security for the state is its continued survival in the face of military threats from other states, the central components for societal security were seen by Buzan as being 'the ability of a society to maintain its traditional patterns of language, culture, religious and national identity and customs' (Smith 2002: 2). As Smith claims, Buzan now recognised that societal security had to be given greater attention because 'societal security issues were becoming far more relevant to the debates of the 1990s . . . [and] prominent among these were issues such as migration which simply could not be fitted into the state security debate' (Smith 2002: 2).

In light of his work on societal security, Buzan was to join forces with other academics, namely Ole Wæver and Jaap de Wilde, and together they formed the famous Copenhagen School of Security Studies. The essence of their work was to continue to argue in favour of broadening the concept of security beyond the traditional view. One of the ways of achieving this was to analyse the 'process' that led to certain threats being considered serious enough to devote resources to reducing their impact. This process was labelled by the Copenhagen School as 'securitisation' and they claim that 'something is designated as an international security issue because it can be argued that this issue is more important than other issues and should take absolute priority' (Buzan et al. 1997: 24). Just as during the Cold War there was constant reference to the threat posed by the Soviet Union, in the post-Cold War era the variety of perceived threats to security have expanded significantly. Indeed Wæver and others have gone so far as to claim that all it takes to create a perceived threat is for someone at a high enough level to highlight the danger. The ultimate aim of the Copenhagen School, therefore, is to analyse why certain issues are considered to be threats, who considers them as threats, and which referent object is threatened (Smith 2002: 3).

Buzan's work on societal security has had a major impact on the debates over the concept of security. He has simultaneously moved us away from thinking about security in the purely narrow militarist sense and forced us to acknowledge the existence of alternative referent objects, thereby succeeding in broadening the concept. However, even though he managed to reject these two central pillars of Strategic Studies, as Mutimer writes,

> Buzan's work did not move very far from the conventional understanding of security. Buzan continued to accept that anarchy, as generally understood in realist [terms], placed formidable constraints on security [namely that states remained the] principal referent object of security because they are both the framework of order and the highest source of governing authority.
>
> (Mutimer 1999: 80–81)

Despite being criticised for generally remaining within the fold of conventional ideas on security, Buzan's work nevertheless persuaded others that the concept of security could be developed further.

## Category 3: Shifting the focus away from the state as referent object – deepening the concept

Buzan's influence is apparent in the work of those who have sought to deepen the concept of security further. Although the members of this group are numerous and their opinions varied, this is a brief introduction to the affiliated areas of Critical Security Studies, Feminist Security and Human Security. The one common element shared by this group is the fierce opposition to the narrow state-centric emphasis on military security. Those who want to deepen the concept further seek to construct definitions of security that permit individuals to be the referent objects. In the traditional sense of the concept, security for individuals could only be achieved once the state was secure. The emphasis, therefore, was on the state and the threats to the state came primarily from the armed forces of other states. The prevailing condition within which states exist – anarchy – meant that there was no higher body that could be seen as safeguarding states from aggressors. They, therefore, had to manage their security themselves – predominantly through the maximisation of their own military potential. Those who have sought to shift the focus of security away from the state to the individual have questioned whether this method of seeking security is truly adequate and have highlighted that it is often states themselves which threaten the security of individuals. The examples in Box 24.7 illustrate this point further.

---

 **Box 24.7 States as threats to individuals**

- Saddam Hussein's use of chemical weapons against his own Kurdish population during a clampdown in March 1988.
- The establishment of a Security Zone in Southern Lebanon by Israel may provide security to its own citizens but what about the citizens of Lebanon?
- Robert Mugabe's use of terror tactics against his own citizens in Zimbabwe to ensure his re-election

in June 2008. The rape of women and the murder of opposition members were documented in the press.
- Following the terrorist attacks on the World Trade Center on 11 September 2001 many states, including the United States and Britain, have taken steps to curtail civil liberties, citing that it is necessary if citizens are to be secure.

*Source: Getty Images*

**Shifting the focus of Security Studies has led some to note that it's often states *themselves* which threaten the security of individuals.**

These are simple examples which illustrate this school of thought's dissatisfaction with perceptions of security based largely on the state. The primary exponents of this view were Keith Krause and Michael Williams, who developed the idea of Critical Security Studies. Their goal was to highlight and draw together the many different critiques of traditional perceptions of security under the umbrella term '*critical*' in order to stimulate deeper debate by including, as Smith explains, 'many different perspectives, all of which are outside the mainstream, but which together do not add up to one view' (Smith 2000: 89). In other words their intention was not to create a single theoretical framework which stood in opposition to traditionalist Strategic Studies, but rather to show that many disparate views and theories opposed the narrow views held during the Cold War. One of the most important effects of this was the questioning of the main assumptions of traditionalist views, whereby the state as ultimate referent object and the reliance on military security came under intense scrutiny. However, perhaps their most important contribution has been the attention which literature is now devoting to the individual (Krause and Williams 1997: 33–59).

The work by Ken Booth and the so-called Welsh School is a variation on the themes highlighted by Critical Security Studies. As a critical theorist, Booth certainly highlights the individual as the ultimate referent object, but he goes further by arguing that not only is it important to oppose the narrow traditionalist state and military-centric views but also, it is necessary to offer a clear alternative by re-conceptualising the discipline of Security Studies, by developing ideas relating to the **emancipation** of humans. Emancipation for Booth is the only way of achieving true security, and in his 1991 article 'Security and Emancipation' he provided this definition:

> the freeing of people (as individuals and groups) from those physical and human
> constraints which stop them carrying out what they would freely choose to do.
> War and the threat of war is one of those constraints, together with poverty,
> poor education, [and] political oppression.

> (Booth 1991: 319)

In developing his ideas relating to emancipation Booth not only advocated a shift of referent object from the state to the individual but also stressed that the state merely needed to be the means of achieving security, rather than an end in itself. Booth was instrumental in encouraging us to resist the narrow views expressed by Realists and he argued that people everywhere were made insecure by a mixture of threats and processes including poor governance, political oppression, civil conflict, corruption, human rights abuses, gender violence as well as environmental destruction. Unlike Krause and Williams, who sought to provide a wide base for the critique of traditionalist ideas, however, Booth's Welsh School is more definitive and seeks to re-conceptualise the discipline by offering a clear alternative to the state as referent object, namely the emancipated human individual. Ken Booth's ideas are further developed in Chapter 26.

Similarly, feminist perceptions of security are 'critical' in that they oppose and criticise the narrow Realist-orientated views associated with Strategic Studies. Feminist literature sees the world of global politics as dominated by men, and the process of achieving security as based on a strongly masculine worldview. The military and foreign policy making are the least appropriate arenas for women and one of the intentions of feminist literature, therefore, is to show how the discipline of Strategic Studies has ignored the role and place of women in global politics. They claim that even the broadened perceptions of security as advocated by the likes of Buzan present only an incomplete view and need to be strengthened by a consideration of the concerns that are specific to women as a group. Furthermore, feminist literature seeks to deepen the concept of security by supporting other marginalised groups affected by non-military threats such as a degrading environment, poverty, social exclusion, and even diseases such as HIV/AIDS.

One of the main accusations levelled against traditionalist perceptions of security by feminists is its tendency towards an overly masculinist basis. As you will have read in Chapter 6, Realism claims to see the world 'as it is' where states and the possibility of war are central, but feminists claim that traditional Realist accounts of security are far too limiting and exclude a significant portion of what really happens in global politics. Writing in 1992, a comment by Ann Tickner (a leading feminist writer) is notable:

> As a scholar and teacher of international relations, I have frequently asked myself
> the following questions: Why are there so few women in my discipline? If I teach

the field as it is conventionally defined, why are there so few readings by women to assign to my students? Why is the subject matter of my discipline so distant from women's lived experiences? Why have women been conspicuous only by their absence in the worlds of diplomacy and military and foreign policy-making?

(Tickner 1992: ix)

Tickner's goal then is to understand the masculinist perspective which has been applied to the field and also to 'examine what the discipline might look like if the central realities of women's day-to-day lives were included in the subject matter' (Tickner 1992: xi). Cynthia Enloe is another important feminist writer and her work on militarism is particularly interesting in that she has attempted to show that, rather than being marginal, women are in fact central. However, rather than occupying positions of power the roles they fulfil are important for the functioning of male-dominated institutions, such as being prostitutes around military bases or the wives of diplomats (Enloe 1990). Kennedy-Pipe sees Enloe's work as being important because it succeeds in explaining why 'even though women have over the last forty years been integrated into many institutions of the state, the military and the issue of combat have remained predominantly the province of the male' (Kennedy-Pipe 2007: 81).

Others have attempted to steer us towards thinking about issues which are of particular concern to women. For instance, Terriff et al. draw our attention to physical violence perpetrated against women, 'especially in the form of rape [which] is an obvious direct breach of their security'. They further refer to rape in warfare as being 'recognised as an international security concern by the Geneva Convention' (Terriff et al. 2001: 87). When they also remind us that at least 20,000 women were housed in 'rape camps' during the recent conflict in Bosnia we begin to see the obvious and horrifying security implications. Their analysis then shifts to domestic violence against women, pornography, the objectification of women and even the threats posed by pro-life campaigns that oppose abortion – all of which limit the choices available to women, thereby diminishing their security (Terriff et al. 2001).

The impact of feminist writings on security has been significant. They have undermined the narrow traditionalist position at an intellectual level and highlighted the shortcomings of even those who seek to broaden the concept of security by demonstrating that they have not gone far enough. Feminist perceptions show us that certain forms of security, such as state security, have been privileged over others, and that this state-centric logic operates on strictly masculinist terms where women are seen as objects of men in need of protection against the armed forces of other states. The feminist attempt to reorientate the focus of Security Studies away from these narrow boundaries is beneficial, since it makes us aware that if marginalised groups like women feel insecure at a domestic level, this has an impact on the state itself. Rather than seeing feminist literature as totally dismissive of traditionalist perceptions, perhaps we should see the goal of the feminist project as opening up discussion on how to make the concept of security more all-inclusive, given that it is not just the state that is in search of security.

## Category 4: Human Security

Before ending this chapter we would like to introduce one more category which has also sought to develop a people-centred approach to security – that of **Human Security**. As shown, the various approaches under the general heading of Critical Security Studies such as Ken Booth's **Welsh School** and feminism have also favoured shifting the referent object away from the state to humans. There does appear, therefore, to be a considerable overlap between Critical Security Studies and Human Security and this has led to a high degree of confusion and ambiguity surrounding the concept of security. Nevertheless, there is considerable literature on Critical Security Studies as well as on Human Security and we have, therefore, devoted separate chapters to each of these categories (see Chapters 26 and 27). By way of introduction, the concept of Human Security was initiated primarily by the United Nations Development Programme in the *Human Development Report*, an important document published in 1994. As in the case of Critical Security Studies, the main thrust of this report was to encourage governments to promote the security of people by protecting them from a wide range of threats. Alongside Critical Security Studies, the literature on Human Security has also sought to show the inadequacy of the traditionalist state-centric framework. Given these crucial similarities, therefore, the obvious question is, what then are the essential differences between the two categories?

The differences between the two will become clearer in subsequent chapters, but here we can introduce a few key components. To begin with, Critical Security Studies is a broad category which also challenges Realist orthodoxy, albeit from a much more theoretically sophisticated standpoint than is found in Human Security literature. Critical Security Studies is a subset of International Relations and the label 'critical' is applicable to both disciplines – since in both cases critical approaches seek to provide a wide base for the critique of traditionalist Realist ideas. In the case of International Relations the approach is known as Critical Theory and its closest relative in Security Studies is the Welsh School, of which Ken Booth is a key proponent. We dealt with Critical Theory in Chapter 9 of this book and you should read that alongside this one. Both Critical Theory and the Welsh School have their roots in the Frankfurt School which outlines the premise that theory does not just exist for the purpose of understanding the world but also, crucially, that it should lead to processes that bring about change in peoples' lives, often referred to as emancipation.

As shown in Chapter 9 and later in Chapter 26, a key contribution made by Robert Cox was the attempt to distinguish between Critical Theory and traditional approaches to security or 'problem-solving' theory as he called it. This is particularly relevant in helping us to establish the differences between critical approaches to security and Human Security. According to Cox, problem-solving theories accept the world as it is and their aim is to work alongside existing state institutions to create solutions. Problem-solving theories, therefore, do not question the nature of the prevailing order, or whether that order is fair or not. Critical views on security, however, stand apart from the prevailing order and seek to question where that order came from and whether its essential purpose is to transform unfair global and domestic realities. In this sense Robert Cox saw Critical Theory as superior to problem-solving theories because of its emancipatory concerns, which echoes the emphasis placed by Ken Booth on the notion of emancipation.

Human Security has not been treated seriously within the debates among Critical Theorists such as Ken Booth, and this may appear surprising given that both schools of thought argue that security can only be achieved if individual humans are seen as the key referent object. Advocated by the United Nations, Human Security has been adopted by governments such as Japan, Norway and Canada (see Chapter 27) and, although Human Security may seek to challenge the state, it is equally willing to work alongside it to find solutions. Critical scholars, however, are immediately suspicious of this, given that they see the state as complicit in creating insecurity for its citizens. Indeed, Booth sees Human Security as allowing states to 'tick the good international citizen box of foreign policy, but without significantly changing their behaviour' (Booth 2007: 323). It is in this context, therefore, that we find the main difference between critical approaches to security and Human Security. The policy orientation of Human Security has meant that the approach fails to question whether the prevailing global structures and processes are fair or not. Rather critical scholars label it as a problem-solving approach given that it seeks merely to enact solutions to problems of insecurity rather than posing a genuine challenge to the prevailing order that created the insecurity in the first place.

From this brief comparison we can see that Human Security scholars have sought to remain relevant to the policy-making processes of states and are reluctant to explore the theoretical issues pursued by critical security advocates. Therefore, Human Security has prioritised human progress and development rather than dealing with the theoretical basis of complex concepts such as emancipation. It is in this context that Human Security appears deliberately protective, has a strong practical basis, and recognises that people and communities everywhere are threatened by events over which they have no control. As stated in the UN Report, 'The world can never be at peace unless people have security in their daily lives. Future conflicts may often be within nations rather than between them – with their origins buried deep in growing socio-economic deprivation and disparities. The search for security in such a milieu lies in development, not in arms' (UNDP 1994). This practical attempt to find solutions to problems of insecurity faced by humans is at the heart of this approach and is far removed from the essence of critical approaches such as that advocated by Ken Booth. Let us not forget, however, that the impact of the UNDP report has been significant and ideas relating to Human Security are now firmly entrenched in Security Studies literature. The concept may be vague given that it is so multidimensional, but it remains a useful addition to the literature since it provides us with a mechanism through which we can analyse factors which affect economic, physical and social threats to human survival.

## Case study: The concept of security – a variety of views

In this case study we present a number of quotes relating to the concept of security and we want you to discuss them in the context of the various categories outlined in this chapter.

- National security must be defined as integrity of the national territory and its institutions (Morgenthau 1960).
- Security, in an objective sense, measures the absence of threats to acquired values, in a subjective sense, the absence of fear that such values will be attacked (Wolfers 1952).
- The concept of security must change from an exclusive stress on national security to a much greater stress on people's security, from security through armaments to security through human development, from territorial security to food, employment and environmental security (UNDP 1994).
- Gender inequality is itself a form of violence which contributes to the insecurity of all individuals (Tickner 1995).
- States are, or at least can be, a means for providing security, but ultimately it is only with reference to individuals that the notion of security has any

meaning: it is illogical therefore to privilege the security of the means as opposed to the security of the ends (Booth 1991).
- Security and emancipation are two sides of the same coin. Emancipation, not power or order, produces true security. Emancipation, theoretically, is security (Booth 1991).
- Something is designated as an international security issue because it can be argued that this issue is more important than other issues and should take absolute priority (Buzan et al. 1997).
- For most people, a feeling of insecurity arises more from worries about daily life than from the dread of a cataclysmic world event. Will they and their families have enough to eat? Will they lose their jobs? Will their streets and neighbourhoods be safe from crime? Will they be tortured by a repressive state? Will they become a victim of violence because of their gender? Will their religion or ethnic origin target them for persecution? (UNDP 1994).

**What are the pitfalls of expanding the concept of security excessively?**

## Conclusions

This chapter has been framed around the concept of 'security' for good reason. Whether we seek security for the state as the traditionalists advise us to, or for marginalised groups such as women as advocated by feminists, or recommend that the emancipation of humans should be the ultimate goal, or even advocate the practical underpinning of Human Security, one thing is certain: any analysis which concerns itself with security will require an examination of the various definitions of the concept. It is not for us to advise you to choose any particular category of definitions over another, but we can assure you that someone else will dispute whatever you choose. As this chapter has shown, any examination of the concept has to take into account a number of factors, and perhaps the most important of these is what the referent object should be. We have identified the state, society, groups and the individual as the most obvious candidates, but this list is not exhaustive, and you might be able to include other referent objects.

Equally important is the nature of Security Studies as a discipline today, which is directly linked to its ambiguous central concept – *security*. The issue you will examine is whether it is a good idea to include so much in a single concept. Given that there is already so much disagreement over the meaning of security and the referent object, are we not in danger of seriously overloading Security Studies as a discipline if we continue to argue in favour of expanding the concept? Stephen Walt (a traditionalist academic) once stated, 'by this logic, issues such as pollution, disease, child abuse, or economic recession could all be viewed as threats to security. Defining the field in this way would destroy its intellectual coherence and make it more difficult to devise solutions to any of these important problems' (Walt 1991: 213). Walt, therefore, pleaded for the focus of the field to be restricted to the 'study of the threat, use and control of military force' (Walt 1991: 212). Ultimately, however, if we were to restrict its scope, where would we discuss and design solutions to the myriad of non-military problems that face us as humans?

## Resource section

## Questions

1. What are the key differences between Strategic Studies and Security Studies?

2. Why do you think critical thinkers have a problem with the notion of Human Security?

3. What do critical scholars mean by the concept of emancipation?

4. Compare and contrast the various categories dealing with the concept of security.

5. Do you think military force remains central to world politics?

## Recommended reading

**Booth, K. (ed.) (2005)** *Critical Security Studies and World Politics* **(Boulder, CO: Lynne Rienner Publishers)**
As an important advocate of the Frankfurt School tradition, Booth has written extensively on the notion of emancipation as security while at the same time trying to undermine the narrow state-centric vision of traditional Realist approaches. This book is Booth's latest defence of emancipation.

**Buzan, B. (1991)** *People, States and Fear: An Agenda for International Security Studies in the Post-Cold War Era* **(2nd edn, London: Harvester Wheatsheaf)**
The impact of this book on the debates over the concept of security should not be under-estimated. One could go as far as to argue that perhaps this is the book that started it all off.

**Smith, S. (2000)** 'Conceptualizing security in the last 20 years', in S. Croft and T. Terriff (eds) *Critical Reflections on Security and Change* **(London: Frank Cass)**
Steve Smith is a leading professor of International Relations and this chapter in this important book is an excellent survey of the young field of Security Studies.

**Walt, S. (1991)** 'The renaissance of Security Studies', *International Studies Quarterly*, 35 (2) June
As a traditionalist, Stephen Walt has often pleaded for the field of Security Studies to remain narrowly concerned with military power and state security. He makes a powerful argument in defence of traditionalism in this article based around the notion that loading the concept of security excessively will destroy the intellectual coherence of the field of Security Studies.

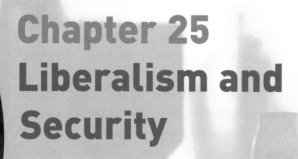

# Chapter 25
# Liberalism and Security

Introduction

Categorising Liberal strands

Analysing the strands

Conclusions

After reading this chapter you will be able to:

- Highlight the key links between Liberalism and Security Studies

- Consider the differences between some liberal approaches and their relationship to security

- Understand Liberal criticisms of Realist approaches to security

- Gain an understanding of the *liberal peace thesis*

- Consider the importance of institutions in fostering cooperation between states

*Source*: Panos Pictures/Chris Stowers

## Introductory box: The peaceful intentions of liberal democracies

On 8 June 1982 Ronald Reagan (US President: 1981–89) gave a speech before the British Parliament in which he expressed an opinion long held by a large number of academics – the notion that liberal states do not easily resort to war and that they exercise restraint in dealing with other states of the world. In contrast to the peaceful intentions of Western Liberal democracies, he accused totalitarian states – which was how the Soviet Union was perceived in the West – of being hostile and stressed that they sought to encourage conflict in the world. Here are some excerpts from that speech:

> Historians looking back at our time will note the consistent restraint and peaceful intentions of the West. They will note that it was the democracies who refused to use the threat of their nuclear monopoly in the forties and early fifties for territorial or imperial gain. Had that nuclear monopoly been in the hands of the Communist world, the map of Europe – indeed, the world – would look very different today. And certainly they will note it was not the democracies that invaded Afghanistan or suppressed Polish Solidarity or used chemical and toxin warfare in Afghanistan and Southeast Asia. . . .
>
> If history teaches anything it teaches self-delusion in the face of unpleasant facts is folly. We see around us today the marks of our terrible dilemma – predictions of doomsday, anti-nuclear demonstrations, an arms race in which the West must, for its own protection, be an unwilling participant. At the same time we see totalitarian forces in the world who seek subversion and conflict around the globe to further their barbarous assault on the human spirit. What, then, is our course? Must civilization perish in a hail of fiery atoms? Must freedom wither in a quiet, deadening accommodation with totalitarian evil?

## Introduction

In his June speech President Reagan built on a long-held belief that liberal democracies are inherently peaceful and that they do not resort to war easily. However, you will be struck immediately by the seeming inaccuracy of this statement given that liberal democracies have waged war against other states throughout the twentieth century and more recently in Iraq and Afghanistan. Perhaps, therefore, the statement needs to be changed to reflect the premise that liberal democracies do not go to war with *each other* and that they have succeeded in establishing a *separate peace* among themselves. In Chapter 24 we introduced you to the discipline of Security Studies and also to the concept of *security*. You will have read not only that there is a wide range of definitions for this concept but also that there is no agreement over which definition is the most appropriate. You were, therefore, urged to consider the concept through a variety of theoretical and conceptual lenses such as Realism, Feminism and Human Security. One of our key arguments in Chapter 24 was that the *traditionalist* framework, with its heavy reliance on Realist theory, might be inadequate to define security. In this chapter we intend to introduce you to the Liberal strand which, alongside Realism, has had a tremendous impact on the debates surrounding the concept of security. You should be aware from the outset that there is no single liberal theory. Rather, there are a number of liberal approaches, all of which have significantly distinct features, although they are all connected by a series of core assumptions, with the *liberal peace thesis* introduced above being one important example.

Despite the problems associated with defining security, it has been an overriding concern for the discipline of Security Studies. The theoretical approaches highlighted in Chapter 24 compete with one another not only as regards their preference for a particular referent object and the threats that it may face, but also in regard to the means of safeguarding the referent object from those threats. Liberal approaches to security are no different in this respect, since they also refer to the need to identify a recipient for security and indicate how this security may be achieved. A complication arises, however, when we begin to unravel Liberalism itself, since it is so wide-ranging that it can give rise to a degree of confusion. In order to avoid this, we recommend that you first read Chapter 7 on Liberalism. This will provide a firm foundation for your understanding of the connections between liberal approaches and security issues dealt with below.

There is no clear definition of Liberalism. Rather, liberalist approaches are a family within which each strand shares particular key characteristics. These include individual rights to private property, democratically elected government, and a commitment to freedom for the individual. As one of the main traditions of the European Enlightenment, Liberalism stressed political freedom, democracy, and constitutionally guaranteed rights; at the same time, it sought to further the liberty of the individual and equal treatment before the law. This positive view of human nature is the hallmark of most liberal theories, as is a belief that humans are capable of progress and have an ability to 'reason' which can be translated into cooperation in all fields of human endeavour, including at the international level. In this sense, therefore, conflict is not inevitable and, when people use their reason, cooperation within and between states can be achieved.

Liberalism, therefore, identifies the individual as being of key importance since it is the freedom and dignity of the *individual* which needs to be respected. However, once individuals are accorded due respect, this has the effect of releasing the potential of the individual. In other words, since individuals possess the ability to reason and a capacity for virtue, they are free to develop their talents and hold the potential for social progress. Consequently, liberals of all persuasions believe that the search for security need not be surrounded by a high level of fear and pessimism. Security threats for liberals are not necessarily fixed and there is a belief that they can be reduced, managed or even overcome by establishing certain conditions (which vary according to the strand of Liberalism). The first great liberal experiment for dealing with man's perennial tendency to resort to conflict came immediately

*Source: Getty Images*

**Liberalism holds that the individual is an important object of analysis.**

after the First World War, when the League of Nations was formed on the basis of liberal idealist principles. Founded under the Treaty of Versailles, the League's main objective was to prevent the outbreak of war through a variety of mechanisms which included *collective security* (see Box 25.1), negotiation, disarmament and diplomacy. However, problems with the League's structures and a lack of political will on the part of the member states led to its inevitable failure to prevent a number of conflicts during the 1930s, including the Second World War. Liberal idealists had thus failed in their endeavour to bring peace and security to the international system and this encouraged Realist thinkers such as Edward Carr to accuse them of utopian wishful thinking, which refused to see the international system as it really was. Alongside Hans Morgenthau's book, *Politics Among Nations* (1960), Carr's attack on inter-war Liberal Idealism paved the way for political Realism to become established as a powerful explanation for global politics. Its emphasis on the premise that all states are compelled to compete with each other in order to fulfil key interests, most specifically state security, made its view of international relations seem realistic. Since the international system was anarchic, this approach portrayed survival as an overriding concern for states, achieved either through a maximisation of their own military might or through alliances with other states. The liberal tradition did not end here, however, and liberal thinkers have continued to debate the strength of their principles in explaining the nature of the international system, including the search for peace under conditions of anarchy. An attempt at categorisation will, therefore, be useful at this stage.

## Categorising Liberal strands

Since the eighteenth century, liberal thought in one guise or another has sought to explain how states can increase the possibility of peace among themselves. Today there are many liberal strands, each of which provides an assessment of the problems leading to conflict and the possible ways of avoiding it. Among the most important are Liberal Idealism, the Liberal Peace Thesis and neo-Liberal Institutionalism.

- **Liberal Idealism** is the term used for the study of global order and is largely, though not exclusively, based on the views of US President Woodrow Wilson, who claimed that there was a need to restructure international society along democratic principles and establish an international organisation that would provide for a system of **collective security**. Collective security can be defined as the principle enshrined in the League of Nations Covenant, namely that the collective strength of all members would be summoned in the face of aggression.
- **Liberal Peace Thesis** One overriding premise of liberal theories is that the domestic structures of a state will have a direct impact on the way in which it behaves in the international sphere. Among the most prominent and influential advocates of this view was Immanuel Kant, whose 1795 essay '*Perpetual Peace*' laid the foundations for the view that states with democratic political systems do not resort to war with one another.
- **Neo-Liberal Institutionalism** emerged in the early 1980s to challenge the Realist tradition's claims that international institutions such as the European Union or the United Nations are of little consequence in facilitating the possibility of cooperation under the conditions of anarchy prevalent in the international system. Among the most important proponents of this strand of Liberalism are Robert Keohane who developed this perspective in response to the claims made by the neo-Realist tradition that the possibility of cooperation under anarchy was minimal at best.

## Analysing the strands

### Liberal Idealism

This strand was particularly influential during the period between the two world wars (1919–1939). Following the carnage of the First World War, Idealism formed the basis of the League of Nations. As one of the most vocal proponents of Idealist views, and a figure whose idealism had a major impact on the nature of the international system during the early part of the twentieth century, US President Woodrow Wilson (1913–1921) outlined his vision for an international system within which states could live in peace with one another. It is worth remembering that the world Wilson inherited at the beginning of his presidency was highly polarised and in many ways traditional, and this was clearly manifest in the way that the balance of power mechanism still dominated relations between states. In order to maintain or restore this balance, states often resorted to conflict and any attempts to regulate relations through legal mechanisms were also geared towards a desire to maintain the balance (Tucker 2004: 93).

However, the onset of the First World War and the horrors committed by the warring sides showed that, even in the twentieth century, humanity was capable of catastrophic levels of death and destruction and the mechanism suffered a serious setback. As David Steigerwald (a historian) stated:

> The destruction unleashed violated all previous measures of civilized
> behaviour, rendered absurd the claim that nations recognised natural restraints,
> and confirmed prevalent doubts about humanity's rationality. The carnage
> reached from Russia to France and turned large sections of the Western Front
> into swampy craters. The great battles of the attrition period, the Somme, Verdun,
> Ypres, were almost wars in themselves, so great was their scope and duration.
>
> (Steigerwald 1994: 7)

The First World War began soon after Wilson came to power, and at first he worked hard to keep the United States isolationist and therefore out of the war, but increasing German belligerence – manifested through attacks on neutral merchant shipping (including American ships) – eventually persuaded him to make a case for a declaration of war against Germany, a step which Congress took in April 1917. Wilson went to great lengths to explain that the war was not against the German people but their autocratic leaders. These sentiments reflected the idealism expressed by Wilson, which was built upon reason, individual liberty and social openness, but which also referred to domestic politics. Wilson contended that citizens in all nations did not want war but that wars occurred because of the narrow selfish interests of autocratic leaders. The dominance of the international system by undemocratic and imperial systems stifled debate and openness and, therefore, it was necessary for the natural will of the people to emerge. According to Wilson, people naturally wanted democracy and if the dominance by autocrats could be ended, it would be possible for people themselves to create the conditions for peace.

Wilson's domestic analogy was based on the view that if states themselves were able to form laws and enforcement powers in order to extend peace within the domestic realm, this could be replicated at the international level. The League of Nations would therefore be able to function as a provider of the security that nations had attempted, according to Chris Brown, 'unsuccessfully, to find under the old, balance of power system'. He goes on to state that the League would provide public assurances of security backed by the collective will of all nations to resort to expedients such as military alliances or the balance of power (Brown 2001: 23). In other words collective security and international law would replace war as the underlying basis of the international system.

## Box 25.1 Collective security and the League Covenant

Inis Claude associates the term *collective security* with the period immediately after the First World War and defines it as the attempt by the international community to establish a system for 'the maintenance of international peace [and] . . . intended as a replacement for the system commonly known as the balance of power' (Claude 1984: 247). However, as an idea, collective security is much older than the twentieth century. Established in 1815, the Concert of Europe was an early attempt to establish an international society designed to maintain peace between the member states. The Quadruple Alliance made up of Austria, Britain, Prussia and Russia sought to protect their governments and maintain the status quo by establishing a balance of power among them. However, the mechanism envisaged by Woodrow Wilson was a departure from the traditional reliance on balance of power as a way of maintaining peace. The collective security system of the League of Nations (and subsequently the United Nations) worked on the principle that all members would not only agree not to attack one another, but also collectively to defend each other if one of them was attacked. In order for the system to work, member states would have to agree to abide by the principles of the League and surrender some of their sovereignty, thereby enhancing the degree of interdependence between all member states. Collective security, therefore, is the attempt to institutionalise the use of force by the international community so that it can defend itself against an aggressor.

Article 10 of the League's Covenant empowered the Council to advise on the type of action to be taken in the event of aggression by a state:

> The Members of the League undertake to respect and preserve us against external aggression, the territorial integrity and existing political independence of all Members of the League. In case of any such aggression or in case of any threat or danger of such aggression the Council shall advise upon the means by which this obligation shall be fulfilled.

Article 11 specified that any breach of the peace would be the concern of all the members of the League:

> Any war or threat of war, whether immediately affecting any of the Members of the League or not, is hereby declared a matter of concern to the whole League, and the League shall take any action that may be deemed wise and effectual to safeguard the peace of nations. In case any such emergency should arise the Secretary General shall on the request of any Member of the League forthwith summon a meeting of the Council.

Article 16 established the premise that if one member attacked another it would be deemed to have committed an act of war against all other members. It also instructed all members to cut financial and trade ties with the aggressor, giving the League Council the right to instruct all member states to provide relevant military, naval and air contributions to be used for the protection of the Covenant's obligations.

Inter-war Idealism, therefore, rested on a variety of elements such as a dedication to collective security, a commitment to international organisation, and the establishment of an international police force with greater reliance on codified international law. Although, as highlighted, this early idealism was criticised by academics such as Carr and Morgenthau for being too utopian and unrealistic, the strand has continued to attract thinkers. More recently, academics have pointed to greater economic interdependence through increased trade and a belief in the value of public opinion. Even an international court of justice has featured prominently within the field. In a highly influential study, Charles Kegley, for instance, encouraged us to return our focus to the ideas expressed by Woodrow Wilson in the wake of the First World War. He pointed to events such as the end of the Cold War in 1989, during which revolutions in central and eastern Europe resulted in the end of Soviet rule in states such as Poland, Hungary, Bulgaria, East Germany and Czechoslovakia. These remarkable and historic events also signalled the end of the Soviet Union itself, and gave rise to the belief that greater cooperation between states was possible.

In Kegley's view, therefore, war was not inevitable and international anarchy, regarded as central by Realists, could be eliminated by adopting a range of mechanisms akin to the views expressed by President Wilson seventy-five years earlier. Like Wilson, Kegley was also concerned with bad forms of organisation and argued that if people could communicate with one another it would be possible to identify common standards. He insisted that people were capable of moral action and that societies themselves could be improved if it were only possible to engage populations in increased communication. Indeed, in an article published in 1993 Kegley questioned whether conditions had emerged with the end of the Cold War which transcended 'the realpolitik that ha[d] dominated discussion of international affairs for the past five decades' (Kegley 1993: 132). These events undoubtedly had a major impact on the perceptions of Kegley himself and of other academics, who drew on Wilsonian Idealism to argue that humans were essentially good and that it was actually poor institutions that led to conflict and immoral human behaviour. He further contended that events such as wars and other international problems needed a multilateral approach to solve, which would be achieved through the pursuit of common interests such as peace and justice: 'The post-Cold War world no longer has ideological fissures and an unrestrained arms race to preoccupy its attention and encourage a fixation on power politics. The vacuum has opened a window that exposes a view of world politics which realism largely ignores' (Kegley 1993: 134). In the post-Cold War world Kegley saw the possibility of the emergence of a 'new system in which the questions realism ask[ed]' became 'increasingly less relevant'. It was a world in which politics was to be 'remarkably consistent with that portrayed by Woodrow Wilson' (Kegley 1993: 134).

## The Liberal Peace Thesis

The **Liberal Peace Thesis** has been highly influential in recent years, with many academics within the liberal tradition arguing that the best way of maintaining security in the international system is by increasing the number of liberal-democratic states. The premise that democracies do not fight one another has been the subject of much debate, with numerous analysts attempting to '*prove*' this contention statistically. The idea itself is an old one, however, with Immanuel Kant (dealt with later) being the classical source. More recently, Dean Babst attempted to demonstrate that democracies do not fight one another (Babst 1972: 55). This was followed by the sustained efforts of others such as Rudolph Rummel, who became particularly interested in seeking solutions to war and other forms of collective violence such as genocide. Rummel showed that despite attempts to reduce conflict through treaties or schemes for multilateral institutions such as the United Nations, international violence has continued to dominate global politics. Writing in 1997, he argued that alongside the mass deaths resulting from inter-state conflicts, we continue to experience civil violence within states where 'bloody riots, revolutions, guerrilla war, civil war, lethal coups d'états, terrorism, and the like, have also claimed millions of victims' (Rummel 1997: 2). He

## Box 25.2 Mass killings are the stuff of history

- **The Mongol invasions** of Eastern Europe, China and other parts of Asia between the twelfth and thirteenth centuries under Mongol leaders such as Genghis Khan resulted in the establishment of one of the greatest empires the world has seen, all of which was built on conquest and mass slaughter.

- **The Thirty Years War** began in 1618 and continued until 1648. Predominantly fought within the German states, what initially began as a religious war between Protestants and Catholics soon descended into a general conflict involving most of the European powers. The one defining feature of the conflict was the high level of destruction of entire regions, including a significant number of deaths.

- **The Napoleonic Wars** (1803–1815) between Napoleon Bonaparte's French Empire and various European powers including Britain, Austria, Russia and Spain, revolutionised warfare – changing it from being the sport of kings, and moving towards the notion of *total war*, one feature of which was mass conscription.

- **The Crusades** began in 1095 and lasted nearly two hundred years. Though they were not exclusively directed against the Muslims of the Middle East, they are generally characterised as attempts by Christian European states to recapture holy lands such as Jerusalem from the advancing Muslim armies.

- **The Taiping Rebellion** (1851–64) led by Hong Xiuquan was directed against China's Qing Dynasty which the rebels felt had failed to relieve the poor conditions in which people in the southern parts of China were living. Seeing himself as the Son of God, Xiuquan succeeded in mobilising thousands of followers to rebel, but by 1864 the rebellion had failed. Estimates of the people killed as a result of conflict, famine and starvation range from a staggering 30 to 40 million.

- **The First and Second World Wars** (1914–18 and 1939–45 respectively). Little detail needs to be given about the two most horrific wars of the twentieth century; suffice it to say that between them they were responsible for the deaths of almost a hundred million people – mostly civilians.

*Source*: Rummel 1997: 2

also argues that attempts to end these types of conflict have been 'no less creative and varied' ranging from eliminating poverty, promoting understanding, teaching human values to decentralising government, emphasising minority self-determination and initiating conflict resolution and yet, as he goes on to state, 'we still have bloody conflict in Russia, Rwanda, Burundi, Sudan, Somalia, Angola, Afghanistan, Bosnia, Sri Lanka, Myanmar, Iraq, Turkey, and a dozen or more other nations' (Rummel 1997: 2).

Box 25.2 lists events from history famous for significant levels of death and destruction. These and many other events have influenced thinkers to seek solutions to the problem of war and conflict, and one name in particular – Immanuel Kant – has had a tremendous impact on recent developments in the liberal peace thesis. Kant philosophised on ethics as well as on the nature of the 'good state' in international relations. In an essay written in 1795 – 'Perpetual Peace' – he insisted that only *republican government* could behave in a peaceful manner within the international system. The essence of Kant's argument was that, since decision makers in republican states were elected, this made them accountable to the electorate who had given them their power. He then took this a step further by assuming that, since citizens were generally unwilling to risk their lives and property, they would be unwilling to see their nation embroiled in conflict. These risk-averse sentiments are easier to express in a state where the officials themselves have been elected.

**Immanuel Kant philosophised on the nature of the 'good state' in international relations and is considered a major influence on the Liberal tradition.**

## Box 25.3  Republican states – Immanuel Kant's vision

A republican state is deemed to have a representative government which acts in the name of all subjects. In addition, the powers of government are divided between the legislature and the executive arms. The state's main function is the protection of the rights of the individual citizens, including their property rights.

However, Kant argued that adopting a republican constitution was not sufficient in itself and that it was necessary for republican states to establish laws at an international level if true peace was to be achieved. These laws would enable states to regulate their relations with each other. It was important, therefore, for republican states to be liberal not merely within their domestic context, but also to establish liberal relations at the international level. Kant was particularly critical of the balance of power that states continuously sought to establish between themselves. Increasingly accepted as a way of keeping peace between states, Kant saw the balance of power mechanism as unworkable, since the continuous need for a state to calculate its own power relative to other states led to continuous confrontation, rather than peace. Kant argued, however, that peace between states could only be established through reasoning (of which humans were capable) and political will on the part of politicians, and it is in this context that he outlined his peace programme: first the 'preliminary articles', the initial conditions which had to be established to create perpetual peace and, secondly, the three 'definitive articles' which went further towards establishing a lasting peace (see Box 25.4).

By laying down these articles Kant stressed that certain provisions were necessary to ensure perpetual peace. The 'preliminary articles' refer specifically to the prevention or cessation of hostilities, but for peace to endure, Kant specified three further 'definitive articles'. The purpose of the initial articles was to stabilise relations between states in an attempt to reduce levels of mistrust and thereby pave the way for a more permanent peace. The

## Box 25.4  Immanuel Kant's *Perpetual Peace*

### Preliminary Articles

1. No treaty of peace shall be held as valid in which there is a tacitly reserved matter for future war.
2. No independent states, large or small, shall come under the dominion of another state by inheritance, exchange, purchase or donation.
3. Standing armies shall in time be totally abolished *given that they* 'incessantly menace other states by their readiness to appear at all times prepared for war'.
4. National debts shall not be contracted with a view to the external friction of states.
5. No state shall by force interfere with the constitution or government of another state.

6. No state shall, during war, permit such acts of hostility which would make mutual confidence in the subsequent peace impossible, such as the employment of assassins and making use of treachery.

### Definitive Articles

1. The civil constitution of each state shall be republican.
2. The law of nations shall be founded on a federation of free states.
3. The rights of men, as citizens of the world, shall be limited to the conditions of universal hospitality.

definitive articles went significantly further by arguing in favour of a republican state which would represent the wishes and opinions of its citizens. Any resort to conflict by the state had to be in accordance with the consent of the citizens of that state and if that consent was not forthcoming, the government had no right to enter into a condition of war. Kant was also insistent that, just as laws govern relations between citizens within a state, they should also govern relations between states themselves. The second article, therefore, advocated the establishment of a federal contract between states in order to abolish war. In the final article Kant argues that all citizens of states – governed in accordance with republican principles – have the right to expect universal hospitality wherever they travel, especially when visiting other similarly governed states. This article hints at Kant's belief that it would be possible to establish a global community of like-minded states.

A number of additional factors become apparent when we further analyse Kant's perceptions of how to achieve perpetual peace. The first is that Kant saw war, rather than peace, as the natural condition of the international system. In his opinion, therefore, peace had to be constructed between states in the same way that republican states had managed to construct peace within them. A key aspect of this constructed peace was man's innate ability to reason – as mentioned earlier. In this sense, Kant did not blame man's warlike tendencies for the onset of war – but rather his abandonment of reliance on reason when the likelihood of war arose. His objective of establishing a global community of states connected by their obedience to universal laws has not only encouraged the liberal peace thesis to become highly influential in recent years, but also undoubtedly had an impact on Woodrow Wilson's Idealism (discussed earlier). Although the League of Nations may not have been exactly what Kant envisaged, the idealists were heavily influenced by him in recognising that peace was not a natural condition but one that had to be constructed.

Among contemporary liberal peace theorists, Michael Doyle is perhaps one of the most prominent. In 1983 he wrote an influential article entitled 'Kant, Liberal Legacies and Foreign Affairs', where he stressed that the idea of a liberal peace was not unique and that Kant had established it over two hundred years ago. Since publishing this article Doyle has convincingly argued that democratic states are peaceful and have successfully established a 'separate peace' among themselves. Democracies, according to Doyle, respect individual rights such as free speech, private property and other civil liberties. These characteristics are further strengthened by the basis of democratic representation, and as Doyle states:

> When citizens who bear the burdens of war elect their governments, wars become impossible. Furthermore, citizens appreciate that the benefits of trade can be enjoyed only under conditions of peace. Thus the very existence of liberal states, such as the United States, the European Union and others makes for peace.
>
> (Doyle 2004)

A comparably influential book was written in 1998 by Spencer Weart who makes similar claims after conducting an exhaustive survey of military conflict throughout human history. In *Never at War: Why Democracies Will Not Fight One Another*, Weart attempts to show that well-established liberal states have never resorted to war with one another.

### Box 25.5  Democracies waging war in the twenty-first century

The invasion of Afghanistan began in October 2001 when the United States, with support from Britain, launched an attack on the Taliban regime. Under the operational name – *Operation Enduring Freedom* – the invasion was a response to the regime's refusal to hand over Osama Bin Laden, leader of al-Qaeda, the group responsible for the attacks on the World Trade Center on 11 September 2001. The objective of the war was to destroy al-Qaeda, remove the Taliban from power, and capture Bin Laden. The war continues at the time of writing, with none of the objectives except the second having been fulfilled.

In March 2003 the United States, alongside other democracies, namely Britain, Poland, Denmark and Australia, launched an invasion of Iraq. Both the United States and Britain attempted to convince other states in the international system that their reasons for attacking Iraq were based on the belief that the latter was developing weapons of mass destruction and supporting terrorism. This war also continues to this day.

However, there is another issue that needs some elaboration: namely, that in addition to not waging war against one another, the belief is that democracies are more generally peaceful within the international system. Thinkers such as Kant have provided much support for contemporary academics such as Doyle who remain firmly committed to the liberal peace thesis. However, although Doyle states that 'Constitutionally secure liberal states have yet to engage in war with one another' (Doyle 1983: 213), the twentieth century has shown repeatedly that democracies engage in wars with illiberal states, the most recent examples of which are the wars in Afghanistan and Iraq (see Box 25.5).

These two are recent examples which dispute the notion that liberal democracies are more peaceful generally in their international conduct. Indeed, in Afghanistan and in Iraq, both the USA and Britain have been singled out by human rights NGOs for failing to protect civilian populations, for carrying out acts of abuse and torture on prisoners, and for conducting their operations in an aggressive and often brutal manner. The conduct of US troops in Abu Ghraib prison (Baghdad) came to light in 2004 with accounts of rape, torture, murder, and other forms of physical and psychological abuse being carried out frequently.

Before ending this section we will revisit the original thesis once more and encourage you to analyse it in more depth. Despite the overwhelming support for the liberal peace thesis, there are those who have, since the end of the Cold War, referred to examples where democracies themselves have fought one another. Knutsen and Moses, for instance, begin their 1996 article by analysing the war between two democracies – Peru and Ecuador – in 1995. They argue that the war should have come as no surprise since the two states had contested the border region for a long time. Furthermore, with diminishing popularity at home, the leaders of both states sought to use the 'conflict to bolster their domestic approval rating'. They cite further examples of leaders using external conflicts to gain popularity at home – for instance, 'in the new democracies which . . . emerged from the former USSR' (see Box 25.6) (Knutsen and Moses 1996: 1). In light of these examples, they suggest that we should remain sceptical of the democratic peace thesis. Over two hundred years

**Box 25.6  Recent democracies waging war – Russia–Georgia – August 2008**

Georgia gained independence following the break up of the Soviet Union in 1991 and soon adopted the constitution of a representative democracy. The task of transforming Russia (the largest of the former soviet states) into a democracy has been a long and arduous process. It could be argued, however, that both states claimed to be democracies in August 2008 when they went to war over the breakaway South Ossetian region of Georgia. Increasing tensions in 2008 encouraged Georgia to launch an attack against South Ossetia in an attempt to regain control of the territory and this led to Russia launching military strikes deep into Georgia in support of the Ossetians.

ago Kant predicted that liberal states would manage to establish a zone of peace among themselves. Perhaps the older established democracies, such as those in Western Europe and North America, have already done so, but the brief examples above of the wars between the 'newer democracies' should encourage us to question whether the thesis could be universally applicable to all democracies – old and new.

## Neo-Liberal Institutionalism

Although there are further strands to Liberalism, we would like briefly to discuss one other view which has had a significant impact on the notion of security, namely, Neo-Liberal Institutionalism (NLI). The essence of this approach is that it sees international institutions as playing an important role in fostering cooperation between states, thereby enhancing the prospects for peace and stability. To understand this approach, however, we must understand its relationship to Neo-Realism (see Chapter 6) since it is in this context that it has had the greatest impact on the question of security.

Neo-Realism was outlined primarily by Kenneth Waltz who used the term 'structure' to specify the ways in which the units (in our case 'states') in a system were arranged. He argued that structures could be either hierarchical (as in domestic political systems) or anarchical (as in the international political system). He further claimed that since there was no authority above that of the state, it was the present *anarchical structure* which explained the self-help nature of state behaviour. Of particular importance in our context is the conclusion that Waltz reached on the issue of *cooperation* in such an anarchical system. Since the international system lacks a central authority, states become primarily interested in their own security and in such an environment the chances of cooperation are entirely dependent upon states calculating their positions relative to other states. The neo-Realist position is that states are unlikely to seek cooperation because of the fear that the other states could gain more as a result. This is in sharp contrast to the view expressed by Neo-Liberal Institutionalists, who concentrate much more on absolute rather than relative gains, and accuse the Neo-Realists of overstating the potential for conflict in the international system. They suggest, therefore, that institutions and other interactions between states increase the possibility for cooperation.

## Case study: The separate peace among liberal democracies – the European Union

Western Europe was at the centre of two major wars during the twentieth century: the First and Second World Wars. In both cases numerous European states, including France and Germany, were engaged in conflict with one another. Today, liberal peace theorists claim that war between these two states is all but impossible. Some of the numerous reasons for this have been outlined in this chapter and are briefly summarised below:

1. Most prominent is the view expressed by Immanuel Kant, highlighted in this chapter, that the leaders of states with democratic systems of rule are especially responsive to the wishes of the general public. Furthermore, it is assumed that citizens would prefer not to risk their own lives in war and, since the leaders of democratic states are elected into office, the political costs of ignoring the wishes of the electorate are likely to be high.
2. A second view expresses the value of democratic norms, which emphasise respect for human rights and individual freedom, as well as the peaceful resolution of conflict. The perception here is that because these characteristics have become embedded in the very identity of democracies, their peaceful internal nature is also manifest at the international level. This means that states with similar democratic norms have been able effectively to eliminate war between them.
3. Finally, liberal peace theorists also highlight the premise that liberal democracies are subject to a system of checks and balances which constrain whatever aggressive desires they may have.

The question we must ask ourselves is whether any of these three key characteristics are apparent in the case of France and Germany. In France, for instance, the government is determined by the French Constitution which upholds secular and democratic principles. The checks and balances are provided for by a separation of powers specified in the Constitution itself and, consequently, power is divided between the executive, the legislative and the judicial branches, thereby ensuring that no one branch acquires supremacy over the others. As a founding member of the European Union, it has transferred part of its sovereignty to European Institutions and is therefore obliged to abide by EU regulations and treaties.

Germany was also a founding member of the EU and is, therefore, bound by many of its laws. It is a federal state and a parliamentary representative democratic republic. The Chancellor is the head of the government, but power is devolved between the three arms of government – the executive, the judiciary and the legislative branches. Like France, it too has a constitution which catalogues in detail the protection of individual liberty and human rights.

Given that both states are members of the European Union and liberal democracies with written constitutions upholding democratic values and individual freedom, is it conceivable that they will ever resort to conflict with one another?

 **Why do you think liberal democracies are intolerant of non-liberal states?**

## Conclusions

As shown in this chapter, liberal strands appear to be far more optimistic regarding the possibility of achieving peace and security than Realist approaches. To begin with, we presented Woodrow Wilson's Liberal Idealism as a way of studying the problem of anarchy at the international level. His beliefs stressed that if states were able to enact laws to maintain peace in the domestic environment, it should be possible to replicate this at the international level. It is in this context that Liberal Idealists encouraged the creation of the League of Nations, based on principles of democratic openness, collective security and international law. We also analysed elements of a related strand – the liberal peace thesis –

which has had a tremendous impact because of its controversial claims. On the one hand, proponents of this thesis have claimed that liberal democracies do not go to war with one another while, on the other, the thesis stresses that these democracies are also more generally peaceful in the international system. However, we encouraged you to question both claims and in particular presented examples that demonstrate the aggressive nature of democracies in times of conflict, showing that they have often waged war – the Iraq and Afghanistan wars being the most recent examples.

Finally, cooperation between states features strongly in the case of Neo-Liberal Institutionalism. As the chapter has shown, Neo-Liberal Institutionalists criticise the Realists for failing to recognise the potential of institutions for facilitating cooperation between states. In the case of NLIs, states are much more interested in how much they gain in absolute terms than in what other states may be gaining. This gives the impression that liberals are much more open to the possibility of trust being fostered in the international system than Neo-Realists and consequently this opens the way for increased instances of cooperation, thereby reducing the prevalence of anarchy in the international system.

Despite the broad nature of Liberalism, however, it is possible to tease out a number of key features – the most obvious of these is its treatment of conflict and security. Like the Realists, Liberals recognise that conflict is widespread in the international system. However, unlike the pessimism of Realism, the liberal approaches we have analysed adopt a much more optimistic outlook on the possibility of reducing conflict among states, and they see the possibility of a better life for everyone. The optimism of the Classical Liberals is at its clearest in Kant's belief that men are essentially good and that peaceful relations among them are likely given man's ability to reason. The Idealists of the inter-war period also highlighted the moral nature of man and advocated that war should be outlawed, once again demonstrating the liberal belief that peace lay within the grasp of men. Modern liberals such as Neo-Liberal Institutionalists and liberal peace theorists see the chances of cooperation among states as significant. All of this contrasts sharply with the world of the Realist, within which self-interested states exist in an anarchic setting characterised by the continuous possibility of conflict, with the balance of power mechanism providing the only method for ensuring stability. It is an environment in which states continuously calculate their strength relative to each other and rely heavily on military power to safeguard their position. The Realist claim that the best description of world politics as an environment within which war could break out at any time is, therefore, significantly different from the optimism expressed by Liberals of all shades and persuasions.

## Resource section

## Questions

1. Compare and contrast liberal and realist approaches to security.

2. What are the essential features of the liberal peace thesis and, in your opinion, how realistic are its objectives?

3. What role do institutions play in the international system?

4. What are the central features which unite liberal approaches?

5. Why do you think inter-war Wilsonian idealism was labelled as being 'utopian'?

## Recommended reading

Baldwin, D.A. (ed.) (1993) *Neorealism and Neoliberalism: the Contemporary Debate* (New York: Columbia University Press)
This is a comprehensive book which covers much ground in the debate between Neo-Realists and Neo-Liberals over the nature of international anarchy and the potential for cooperation between states.

Doyle, M. (1983) 'Kant, liberal legacies, and foreign affairs, Part I', *Philosophy and Public Affairs*, 12
There has been a resurgence of interest in Kant's philosophy that republican states with written constitutions are not likely to resort to war with one another. Among the theorists most vividly caught up in this resurgence is Michael Doyle who presents a convincing argument in this article.

Kegley, C. (1993) 'The neo-idealist moment in international studies? Realist myths and the new international realities', *International Studies Quarterly*, 37
In this important article Kegley encourages us to revisit the ideas expressed by US President Woodrow Wilson over seventy-five years ago as a way of taking advantage of the potential for peace and stability offered at the end of the Cold War.

Weart, S. (1998) *Never at War: Why Democracies Will Not Fight One Another* (New Haven: Yale University Press)
Weart is another supporter of the liberal peace thesis and in this book he presents a survey of military conflicts in an attempt to show that liberal democracies do not fight one another.

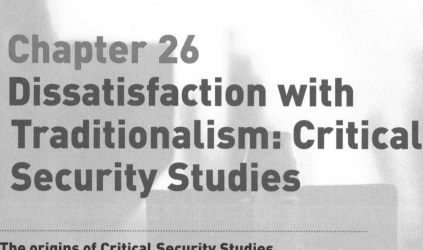

# Chapter 26
# Dissatisfaction with Traditionalism: Critical Security Studies

The origins of Critical Security Studies

Feminist perceptions of security

Critical International Relations Theory: Ken Booth and the Welsh School

The Copenhagen School

Conclusions

After reading this chapter you will be able to:

- Understand why critical approaches advocate a shift to the individual
- Understand the impact of the earlier studies conducted by the likes of Barry Buzan and Ole Wæver on the concept of security and ultimately on Critical Security Studies
- Reflect on the differences between the various critical approaches
- Account for some of the contributions made to Security Studies by feminist approaches
- Consider some of the practical implications of the shift in emphasis to humans

*Source*: Panos Pictures/Chris Stowers

## The origins of Critical Security Studies

Some of the most exciting and challenging approaches in Security Studies are 'critical' in nature. In Chapters 24 and 25 we showed that two approaches in particular have dominated the landscape when it comes to security – Realism and Liberalism. Both of these approaches have long been in competition over identifying solutions to the recurring problem of conflict in the international system and their essence is that the security of the state is of paramount importance. But what about the security of people living within states? This is where **Critical Security Studies** (CSS) comes in and academics of this persuasion have encouraged us to think about instances when the security of the state comes at the expense of its citizens, when the state actively oppresses its own people or when it ignores the security of some of its people.

Critical Security Studies has much in common with Critical International Relations Theory (see Chapter 9) and some of these connections will be highlighted later. The one crucial feature, however, is that CSS fervently disputes the state-centric, narrow and largely military focus of traditional Realist definitions of security. Indeed, it advocates the need for us to shift focus away from the state and highlight the human as the key referent object. CSS incorporates a number of different views including Feminist perceptions of security, the

'Copenhagen School' and the 'Welsh School' headed by academics such as Ken Booth (mentioned in Chapter 24). Despite the dominance of state-centric approaches such as Realism, the impact of critical approaches in the context of security issues means that a detailed study of them is equally important. Trying to grasp the essence of critical approaches to security and the connections between Critical Security Studies and International Relations can be quite overwhelming. Critical Theory has been discussed elsewhere in this book and we suggest you read Chapter 9 alongside this one. In order to make this challenging field relevant to Security Studies and for the sake of simplifying the concepts, first take a look at Box 26.1 and then keep in mind some of the issues raised there.

### Box 26.1 State collusion in diminishing the security of individuals

In addition to those given in Chapter 24, the examples below vividly demonstrate how states themselves or state institutions can brutalise their own citizens.

- **Saloth Sar and the Cambodian Killing Fields.** Better known as Pol Pot, Sar was the leader of the Khmer Rouge (Cambodian Communist Movement) during the 1970s. As Prime Minister of Kampuchea (1976–79) he enacted policies which abolished money, religion, private property and even education. Countless Cambodian citizens were taken from their homes and forced to work on massive collectivised farms which proved to be unworkable. Estimates of the number of deaths from slave labour, lack of medical care and the execution of dissenters range from one to two million people – almost a third of the Cambodian population.
- **Augusto Pinochet** – Chilean President (1974–90). Prior to appointing himself as president, Pinochet was an army general, but in 1973 he led a coup d'état which resulted in the overthrow of the democratically appointed government. From the outset, Pinochet refused to brook any opposition to his rule and in order to facilitate this he suspended all civil liberties. This naturally resulted in a massive violation of the human rights of innocent Chilean citizens with thousands of opponents killed and countless more tortured.
- **Faith based laws – Pakistan and the Hudood Ordinance.** Enacted in 1979 as a drive towards the Islamisation of Pakistani society by General Muhammad Zia-ul-Haq (military ruler of Pakistan 1977–88) the laws were finally repealed in 2006, but only after coming under severe criticism for their violation of human rights. Their purpose was

to force through the implementation of Islamic law as set down in the Qur'an (the Islamic holy text), and in particular related to the 'crimes' of theft, the consumption of alcohol and extramarital sex. It is in the case of extramarital sex where the unjust nature of these laws was particularly felt, since more often than not it was women who suffered. Under Islamic law the punishment for this act is the stoning to death of the individuals, but under cases where women had been raped the victim had to present (according to Islamic law) four male witnesses who could prove that she had in fact been raped. In most cases of rape in Pakistan the women are unable to produce this number of witnesses, with the subsequent effect that they themselves were accused of adultery. Women who were raped therefore had no incentive to report their ordeal to the authorities since they could not prove their case, and the state became a party to violating countless women's lives. It is important to realise that these laws have been applied not only in Pakistan, but also in other Islamic nations such as Bangladesh, Nigeria and Afghanistan.
- **Human rights violations in Iran.** In February 1979 the Iranian constitutional monarchy was overthrown and the name of the state changed to the Islamic Republic of Iran. Since then it has been ruled by a non-elected supreme religious authority referred to as Ayatollah. In contrast to the Iranian president, the Ayatollah wields unlimited power. Free speech is outlawed, human rights activists are often arrested and tortured and those who convert from Islam to any other faith often face execution for apostasy, with religious minorities often subjected to persecution.

Source: Getty Images/AFP

**Iranian security forces clash with reformers. Should we be concerned with the security of the state, or the security of the individual?**

## Establishing Critical Security Studies: Keith Krause and Michael Williams

The examples in Box 26.1 highlight one important feature, namely, that states themselves are often a threat to their own citizens. If this type of insecurity was limited to a few states and was rare in occurrence, then we could perhaps make a strong case for retaining our emphasis on traditionalist perceptions of security and downgrading the value of critical approaches. However, the examples above are a tiny fraction of the abuse that many states around the world bring to bear upon their own citizens. Traditional approaches such as Realism fail to focus on such abuse and this is one of the reasons why critical approaches are having such an impact on the disciplines of International Relations and Security Studies. One of the most important steps towards establishing the field of Critical Security Studies was taken by Keith Krause and Michael Williams in an important book entitled *Critical Security Studies: Concepts and Strategies* (published in 1997). Their purpose was not to develop a single unified critical theory; rather, they began their project in response to the concerns levelled against the narrowness of the traditional conceptions of security. Their main concern was to question the referent object of security and ask who or what should be secured. It is in this light, therefore, that they sought to bring together the many different critiques of traditional perceptions of security under the umbrella term, *'critical'*. Their aim was not to create a single theoretical framework but rather to stimulate debate among the many views which opposed the mainstream perceptions of security. Ultimately their goal was to provide a platform upon which views opposing the state as main referent object – with its monopoly on controlling violence – could be expressed and to prevent the establishment of a straitjacket imposed by traditionalist concepts of security. They had no desire to engage in a lengthy debate over a definition of 'critical'; indeed, they regarded such a debate as unnecessary.

It is largely as a result of their efforts that the many disparate views that came under the general heading of 'critical' could now be grouped. Consequently the variety of critical approaches, including feminist literature on security, the Welsh School headed by Ken Booth and the so-called Copenhagen School (of which Barry Buzan is a key academic) have made significant strides in disputing the narrow traditionalist views of security advocated by Realists. We will begin by looking at some feminist ideas on security.

## Feminist perceptions of security

It must be stated at the outset that feminist approaches to security have been marginalised in the face of the dominance of more traditionalist perceptions. Conventional ideas of conflict, such as those promoted by Realists, argue that states continuously engage in a struggle for power, and make the broad assumption that at the most basic level they are driven by national interests. The vital components of the Realist conceptualisation of the national interest are the preservation by states of their political autonomy and of their territorial integrity. The national interest is defined in terms of power and – although 'power' is a broad concept which can be defined in economic, political, diplomatic or even cultural terms – for many Realists it is primarily the fear of the military power of other states that persuades all states that the best way of achieving security is through the accumulation of their own military power. This simple framework gives the impression that the international system is populated by battlefields, soldiers, military strategies, generals, diplomats and politicians, isolated from the civilian population and engaged in a dangerous game in order to safeguard the security of their own states against others.

In this environment security comes to be seen in terms of the experiences and perceptions of the actors themselves and when the actors are predominantly soldiers, diplomats, generals and their political masters, it is easy to see why the concept is perceived in this narrow fashion. However, as this chapter has shown, the debates over the nature of security and the referent object have become firmly established and as a result many academics have begun to identify issues that are not traditionally seen as legitimate matters of security. Despite their continued marginalisation, feminist perceptions of security have also become firmly entrenched within the literature, with the result that the boundaries of Security Studies have been broadened significantly. Feminist opposition to traditionalism stems from the latter's narrow focus and its inability to view security from any perception other than that of the state. This state-centric view of security works according to masculinist logic which sees women as a group that need to be protected against the aggressive desires of other states. By placing women and other 'vulnerable' groups within this protective shield, traditionalist perceptions effectively diminish their value as independent agents and end up ignoring the security concerns of the groups themselves.

Feminist writers have, therefore, attempted to draw our attention to this serious short-coming within International Relations and Security Studies literature by showing us what the disciplines might look like if the concerns of women and other vulnerable groups were brought in from the margins and made central. In Chapter 24 we referred to Ann Tickner, who sought to address the issue of why the discipline of International Relations has traditionally attracted so few women writers and why the subject matter itself appears so distant from the way in which women as a group experience life in the international system (Tickner 1992: ix). This theme of exclusion is apparent amongst other feminists such as Lene Hansen who, writing in 2000, referred to women's exclusion from international politics as 'security as silence' which 'occurs when insecurity cannot be voiced [and] when raising something as a security problem is impossible or might even aggravate the threat being faced' (Hansen 2000: 287).

One important assumption made by traditionalists is that during times of conflict, men and women (indeed all civilians) are affected in the same way and that there is, therefore, no need to consider the impact of the violence on specific groups such as women – in other words there is no need to 'gender' the analysis. Feminist writers on security, however, dispute this narrow view and argue that not only are women and girls affected in different ways from men and boys during violent conflicts, but also that the traditionalist, state-centric conceptualisation of security itself creates vulnerabilities by failing to acknowledge these differences. The failure to recognise women as a separate group with legitimate security concerns is directly related to the perception that they are part of a wider collective based on nationality or religion, rather than having a separate identity of their own. It becomes

### Box 26.2 The theme of 'exclusion' – reflecting on the public and private realms

The public realm is often seen as the state or a city where people come together to enact laws, to participate in establishing principles of community and ideas relating to social conduct. The private realm is defined as the home where one seeks comfort and love. These two realms come with particular inhabitants; the public realm has traditionally been dominated by the male and the private realm belongs to the wife, the mother or sister. Ask yourself why this is so and place your thoughts into the context of 'exclusion'. Exclusion simply refers to the idea of omitting something or someone from participating in an act or process. By relegating them to the private realm of the home, feminists claim that women are prevented from participating fully in what society has to offer. They are denied access to resources and consequently are powerless to make choices as free individuals and citizens of the state.

easy, therefore, to exclude women from the possibility of acquiring the status of referent object.

Women's exclusion is also highlighted in the many writings of Cynthia Enloe who has over the last two decades analysed the notion of militarism. Among the issues she raises is the view that militarism is a 'package of ideas' that seeks to indoctrinate us into thinking that the world is a dangerous place and that there are those who must be protected within this environment as well as those who must provide the protection. Enloe sees the distinction between the two in terms of the masculine (protectors) and feminine (the protected) and she argues that militarism requires that every government must have a military in order to protect its civilians (Enloe 2004: 219). What this framework ignores, however, is the premise that in providing protection, as defined by the state, it ensures the omission of group-specific security and therefore the insecurities experienced by women remain marginalised.

Traditionalists see the protection of the 'feminine' as a natural and core component of the 'masculine' state. During times of conflict, therefore, even when the women of a particular national group become victims of rape, it is the men of that grouping that are often portrayed as the real victims. This stems from the premise that if the protection of their women is seen as central to the masculinity of the men of a particular state, then the rape of their women is a tool with which to punish the men and by extension their state. In her analysis of female Palestinian prisoners, for instance, Elham Bayour argues 'Although sexual abuse is designed to dehumanise and disempower women, this practice is also targeted at Palestinian men, for whom the protection and control of women are a core part of their . . . masculinity' (Bayour 2005: 207). Abuse of the women, therefore, demonstrates how weak they are without their men, but it also effeminises the men by showing them how incapable they are of protecting their women. As Terriff et al. (2001) remind us, up to a staggering 20,000 women were housed in rape camps during the conflict in Bosnia.

As discussed in Chapter 1, although globalisation's increased level of interconnectivity has led to many opportunities for states to generate wealth and opportunities, it has also resulted in the increased vulnerability of groups already weakened by poverty, conflict and poor access to resources. Feminists have increasingly argued that today's world is largely a patriarchal one and, as Enloe notes, 'Patriarchal societies are notable for marginalizing the feminine' through processes that lead to the exclusion of women from positions of power (Enloe 2004: 5). One experience of global interconnectivity in the post-Cold War era has been the rise of religious fundamentalism, and when this is connected to the high levels of patriarchy that exist globally, the exclusion of the feminine becomes even more pronounced. Religious fundamentalism has strengthened patriarchal notions of the roles that women should fulfil both inside and outside the home. Religion successfully completes the marginalisation of women by increasingly confining them to the private realm of the home. This has the effect of weakening them in that it denies them the choice of whether to gain employment in the public realm in contrast to their male counterparts.

An additional feature associated with the post-Cold War era has been the discernible shift towards conflicts between different groups within states as opposed to wars between states themselves. Many of the civil conflicts in Africa, for instance, are characterised by conflicts between different ethnic groups within the same state. We have provided numerous examples in Box 26.3, but Somalia in 1992, Rwanda in 1994, and the wars which accompanied the break up of the former Yugoslavia during the early 1990s are only some examples of the most brutal conflicts of the post-Cold War period. These conflicts were not only characterised by a deliberate targeting of civilians, thereby resulting in a high level of casualties, but were also civil conflicts. The higher incidence of these types of wars has meant that academics and policy makers have increasingly had to consider the impact of conflict on the groups, communities and individuals within the civil society of a state itself. Mary Kaldor provides us with an important interpretation of this phenomenon, which she attributes to the rapid globalisation that has occurred in the post-Cold War era. She labels the emerging conflicts as 'new wars' and characterises them in terms of an increased blurring between three features of the international system, namely, traditional war (defined as violence between states), transnational organised crime (defined as violence undertaken by privately organised groups generally for financial gain), and the massive violation of human rights (Kaldor 2006: 2).

The wars in Somalia, former Yugoslavia and Rwanda should be seen as wars against the very societies of those states, where the targets were the civilian population and the tools employed by the warring parties were geared towards the intimidation of the opposing sides. In Bosnia, for instance, the rape of women was used as a mechanism not only to terrorise the population, but also to carry out ethnic cleansing and force certain groups to flee their homes and communities. Even in cases where the United States has invaded other states – as in the case of Afghanistan immediately after 9/11 and Iraq in 2003 – they have increasingly acquired the characteristics of being complicated and multilevelled civil conflicts. In both these cases, outside forces such as the United States and Britain have supported competing national and religious groupings with the result that both states have been converted into battlegrounds within which external actors attempt to further their own interests.

Kaldor and others are absolutely right in encouraging us to think about the nature of new wars because the impact of these types of conflict on the civilian population cannot be underestimated. In all cases, civilian deaths are very high; in fact, generally more civilians than soldiers are killed. In many of the civil wars in Africa, for instance, countless children are abducted by rival groups and forced into becoming soldiers, with the inevitable result that they end up losing their childhood and find readjusting to normal life difficult once the war has ended. In addition to this, as demonstrated by the examples below, these civil conflicts are always accompanied by the displacement of people, deaths from disease as societal infrastructures break down, torture, murder and of course rape. Indeed, in the case of many conflicts such as the one in the Republic of Congo (see Box 26.3) extreme and brutal forms of rape have become a weapon in themselves.

Kathryn Farr's research has shown that large numbers of women are raped in times of civil conflict: up to 250,000 women were raped in Sierra Leone, 50,000 women were raped during the four-year Bosnian war, 35,000 Haitian women were sexually assaulted following the US/Canadian intervention in 2006, during the Serbian-Kosovan war between 23,000 and 45,000 women were raped, and three-quarters of women involved in post-conflict demobilisation programmes in Liberia claim to have been sexually abused during that particular war. Also, as Farr reports, 'According to Algerian women's rights activists, at least 5,000 Algerian women were raped by armed combatant groups between 1995 and 1998'. She also states: 'To be sure, war is brutal, and some wars are more brutal than others. Yet the pervasive sexual violence against women in today's civil armed conflicts has included some of the most vicious raping and torturing ever witnessed' (Farr 2007).

---

## Box 26.3  Civil conflicts – the impact on civilians

- Civil War began in **Sierra Leone** in 1991 and officially ended in January 2002. Up to one-third of the population (two million people) became displaced, and tens of thousands were killed. During the conflict the Revolutionary United Front (RUF) mutilated over 20,000 civilians, with these attacks ranging from amputating limbs to cutting their lips and ears off with machetes and axes. The conflict also had a serious regional impact, as surrounding countries had to cope with the influx of refugees. British troops were deployed in 2000 under Operation Palliser and succeeded in stabilising the situation, eventually leading to a ceasefire in 2002.

- **Liberia's** fourteen-year civil war ended in 2003 but left over 10,000 children who had been forced into the role of combatants (some of whom were as young as eight years old). Having spent their childhood at war most find it difficult to adjust to 'normal' life.

- The twenty-year civil war between **Uganda's** government troops and the Lord's Resistance Army (LRA) resulted in around 20,000 children being recruited to fight and over a million internally displaced people. As part of one of Africa's longest running wars, the LRA has been accused of mass rapes, murder, sexual enslavement and other serious violations of human rights. (*Source*: 'Uganda's Northern War', BBC News Online, http://news.bbc.co.uk/2/hi/africa/3514473.stm. Accessed 23 March 2009.)

- In **Sri Lanka** civil war broke out in 1983 and continued into the twenty-first century. Over 70,000 people lost their lives in the fighting between the Tamil Tigers and government forces.

- Civil War in **Nepal** began in 1996 between government troops and Maoist rebels who sought the overthrow of the monarchy. The war, which lasted for ten years, resulted in the killing of over 10,000 people and the displacement of over 150,000. The war also forced many Nepalese to leave their country and look for work elsewhere. (*Source*: P. Bouckaert (2004) 'The brutal trap of Nepal's civil war', *The International Herald Tribune*, 22 October.)

- As a 2000 report in the online edition of the *New York Times* stated, '**Congo** and the nine nations around it sit on what may be the richest patch of this planet: there are diamonds, oil, uranium, gold, plentiful water, fertile land and exquisite wildlife. It is now also one of the biggest battlefields in Africa's history' (see source below). The Republic of Congo has experienced civil war almost continuously since 1996 and is often regarded as one of the widest-ranging wars in modern African history. It has involved many foreign actors not only from within the region, but also some based much further away. This has complicated the scenario and made reaching a peace agreement significantly more difficult. Estimates of the death toll have ranged up to five million people, entire communities have been destroyed and their people killed or displaced, with women brutally raped. A *Guardian* report in 2008 claimed that, even though the war was to 'officially end in 2002, malaria, diarrhoea, pneumonia and malnutrition' are claiming up to 45,000 lives a month (Chris McGreal, *The Guardian*, 23 January 2008). (*Source*: I. Fisher et al. (2000) 'Armies ravage a rich land, creating Africa's "First World War"' *The New York Times on the Web*, 6 February. http://www.nytimes.com/library/world/africa/020600africal-congo.html. Accessed 23 March 2009.)

- Over 800,000 humans were massacred in **Rwanda** between April and June 1994 in one of the worst genocides of the twentieth century.

These few examples hint at the conditions that prevail during such conflicts. Combatants are generally numerous in number and the weapons available are diverse and widely available. All civil conflicts are also characterised by a very large number of civilian deaths, and people who are not killed often end up being uprooted from their homes and communities, emerging as refugees elsewhere. Women and children remain vulnerable throughout the conflict, with women being murdered, raped or abused in other ways. Their ordeal does not end even when they reach the supposed safety of refugee camps. Indeed, it is well documented that countless women continue to be abused at the hands of the very soldiers and officials tasked with protecting them. Reports have shown that even UN peacekeepers have raped women and demanded sexual favours in exchange for food in the refugee camps surrounding many of the war zones of Africa (Milmo 2004).

Realists have generally remained committed to state security and have skirted such issues, putting them down to the anarchic nature of international relations. However, feminists refuse to accept such limited concern for vulnerable groups such as women and children and call for the prevailing structures that reinforce such brutal practices to be dismantled. Feminism, however, is a rather broad approach and it is not easy to identify a single and universally accepted feminist perspective on security. There are significant differences among feminists with regard to the nature of the security threats facing women and the possible solutions to them. Liberal feminists, for instance, seek emancipation for women through the achievement of equality in the public sphere, and focus on the extent to which women remain underrepresented in state institutions – both within the domestic environment and in the international realm. In contrast, radical feminists refuse to acknowledge that the liberal approach to achieving security is the route to true emancipation, claiming instead that the institutions themselves are depriving women of resources. They stress that as long as existing patriarchal power structures remain in place, society will not be transformed in any meaningful and emancipatory way. For this reason, radical feminists focus not on equality, but rather on the differences between men and women and argue that it is through being different that women can bring a fresh perspective to security issues, one that is more in line with the nurturing and pacific nature of women – as opposed to the aggressive and militaristic tendencies of men.

These branches of feminism are only two among many which you can read about in Chapter 19 of this book. Regardless of the differences between the perspectives, they do share a number of important features, including the premise that women as a group have been marginalised and are in a subordinate position compared to men. Acknowledging that marginal position is not sufficient, however, and therefore most feminist literature seeks to identify the sources that contribute to their subordination. Finally, there is a strong activist tendency amongst feminists in that they seek to devise ways of bringing inequality to an end. These characteristics show that feminists are generally 'critical' in that they stand in opposition to the narrow traditionalist views of approaches such as Realism and are not content with merely identifying the inequalities which lead women to experience insecurity, but also seek emancipation from them.

## Critical International Relations Theory: Ken Booth and the Welsh School

A second variant under Critical Security Studies is that of the **Welsh School**, of which Ken Booth is a key proponent. The Welsh School has close connections to Critical International Relations Theory, which was discussed in Chapter 9. Indeed both approaches have their roots in Marxism and the Frankfurt School tradition and remain human-centric, as demonstrated by the importance that both place on the emancipation of individuals. Karl Marx in particular must be credited for his inspiring and extensive work on the notion of emancipation. Although it is not possible to provide a simple account of his ideas, Chapter 8 of this book will have shown you that Marx saw human history as being characterised by class struggle between different socio-economic groups, particularly during the capitalist phase. Marx's concern with capitalism stemmed from its competitive and exploitative nature, characterised by the unequal relationship between the poorer working class and the rich industrialists – the so-called 'owners of the means of production'. He believed that class-based tensions within capitalism would ultimately contribute to its downfall as the proletariat became aware of their mediocre position in capitalist society and rose up to overthrow the exploitative system through organised action – *revolution*. After a period of extensive central control over all means of production (socialism), the state itself would wither away giving rise to communism – a classless society characterised by equality, abundance and freedom.

Marx was also concerned with analysing how the powerful ideology of Liberalism successfully explained the freedoms enjoyed by the richer segments of capitalist society. The contradiction, however, emerged in the context of the poorer working class where liberal values failed to explain the less than adequate conditions of their lives. As Steans and Pettiford state 'from the point of view of the emerging bourgeois class, Liberalism did, indeed, seem to describe the reality of their lives', whereas the impoverished working class saw 'themselves as having few choices and little opportunity to exercise any control'. They go on to highlight the important premise that Liberalism itself appeared to legitimise 'economic and social relationships and practices that were inherently exploitative' (Steans and Pettiford 2005: 103). In challenging the class-based inequalities of capitalism, Marxism therefore became committed to *normative* goals (that is, how things ought to be) and this emancipatory vision has led to the development of many perceptions, not least those held by the critical theorists of the Frankfurt School tradition.

This tradition brought together a varied group of theorists who had become disillusioned with the possibility of working class revolutions taking hold in Western Europe during the 1930s. Marxist ideas in particular provided a significant basis for them to reflect on the prevailing social conditions at the time. Numerous events during the first half of the twentieth century are often used to question why Marxist revolutions failed to occur across Western Europe, the most prominent being the Great Depression of the 1930s. This was a major worldwide economic recession which had a devastating effect on developed and developing states alike. Indeed, one could argue that conditions were ripe for the working classes in the capitalist states of Europe to rise up and revolt against the bourgeoisie. Marxist revolutions did not take hold, however, and in some states the working class even supported right wing nationalist movements such as that of Adolf Hitler in Germany, thereby establishing further grounds for the outbreak of the Second World War in 1939. Furthermore, as Steans and Pettiford state, 'even where socialism *had* triumphed – in the Soviet Union for example – it proved to be a travesty of what Marx had envisaged. Stalinism was characterised by widespread repression and tyranny' (Steans and Pettiford 2005: 111) – see the Case study: Brutal humans – genocide at the end of this chapter.

The horrific examples of human brutality highlighted in the case study are the kinds of events which the Frankfurt School thinkers had to consider. Not only did they have to explain why Marxist inspired revolutions were failing to occur, they also had to analyse the processes which might lead to human emancipation in the midst of these types of brutal occurrences. Consequently, the question uppermost in the minds of the Frankfurt School theorists was why mankind, rather than entering a truly enlightened existence, was beginning to experience these new forms of barbarism. Although Critical Theory is a challenging approach, it revolves around a number of key features including the process of 'criticism' which, put simply, is the application of judgement to something in order to bring about some type of change. Marx believed that humans collectively were capable of bringing about change in their lives, but in order to do so they had to think critically and act practically to create better conditions for themselves. This suggestion by Marx has been adapted by the critical theorists of the twentieth century, as demonstrated by a famous quote from Robert Cox (one of the most important thinkers in Marxist inspired Critical Theory): 'theory is always for someone and for some purpose' (Cox 1981: 128). This outlines the premise that theory should not just exist for the purpose of understanding the world but also, crucially, that it should enable processes that bring about change in peoples' lives, often referred to as **emancipation**.

One of Cox's most important contributions to the process of theorising was to create a distinction between Critical Theory and traditional theory (such as Realism or Liberalism) or 'problem-solving theory' as he called it. In his view, problem-solving theories accept the world as it is and their aim, when confronted with problems affecting security, is to work alongside existing state or global institutions to enact solutions. In this context problem-solving theories do not question the nature of the prevailing order, nor do they question whether the existing order and its institutions are fundamentally fair or not. Rather, they seek to enable the existing institutions to operate smoothly when dealing with problems that fall within their remit. Critical Theory on the other hand departs significantly from this rather limited view and is 'critical in the sense that it stands apart from the prevailing order of the world and asks how that order came about' (Cox 1981: 129). Importantly, Cox does not oppose the goals of problem-solving theories, but regards Critical Theory as superior given its emancipatory concerns. Critical Theory is not only concerned with the process of understanding and explaining the nature of prevailing domestic and global realities, but also seeks to transform them.

What then is the relevance of Marxist inspired Critical Theory to Security Studies? The easiest way in which to answer this question is to compare some of the central features of Critical Theory with those of traditionalist (problem-solving) approaches such as Realism. Two features stand out in particular: the emancipatory basis of Critical Theory and its choice of referent object. In thinking about these features we now need to analyse the extent to which critical thinking in Security Studies considers emancipation as central to its values. We have already established that Critical Theory is centrally concerned with emancipation and that critical theorists consider traditionalist approaches as merely confirming the status quo, with the result that traditionalist approaches – especially Realism – have come to dominate the field to such an extent that other views have been in danger of becoming excluded from consideration.

By referring to George Orwell's influential book, *Nineteen Eighty-Four*, Anthony Burke (an academic in the field of International Relations) has provided us with a useful means of considering the influence of Realism on International Relations and ultimately on the concept of security. In earlier chapters we have established that Realism Regards the state as the crucial unit of the international system, and that any conceptualisation of security must take this aspect into account. In this state-centric world the referent object is the state itself and when one combines this feature of Realism with its dominance of the field, it is understandable that other non state-centric views become relegated.

The word 'Orwellian' is often used to depict a society in which all facets of human life are dominated by a powerful, totalitarian state. Through the eyes of Winston Smith (the main character of *Nineteen Eighty-Four*), Orwell warns us of a future in which the state uses extensive, constant and all-embracing surveillance to control the actions and thoughts of its population. This theme is developed by Anthony Burke, who refers to Orwell's visualisation of the future where the state's 'Party was to reduce the scope for human thought and action by removing concepts from the language until English disappeared in favour of *Newspeak*' (Burke 2007: 13). Interestingly, Burke then questions 'whether the concept of security itself ha[d] not become a form of *Newspeak* whose hold on people's minds drives away other possibilities of conceiving and enabling human existence on this planet' (Burke 2007: 13).

Here Burke is, of course, referring to the influence that the dominant Realist conceptualisations of security have had on our thoughts and actions. Critical theories, on the other hand, have launched a challenge to this dominance, and by doing so have expanded the disciplinary boundaries of International Relations (as well as those of its sub-discipline Security Studies) considerably. The challenge has largely centred around the notion that continuing to regard the state as the ultimate referent object is too short-sighted and that by doing so, traditionalist approaches continue to accept the prevailing order, failing to question its moral and ethical basis. A powerful counter argument could be made that humans can only be secure when the state is secure. However, what happens when states themselves become a threat to the security of their own citizens? See Box 26.1.

## Box 26.4 Explaining *Newspeak*

*Newspeak* was an imaginary language developed by George Orwell in his famous novel *Nineteen Eighty-Four*. In contrast to 'normal' English (referred to by Orwell as *Oldspeak*), the essence of *Newspeak* was to diminish important meanings in the English language by reducing and simplifying the vocabulary. So while someone can 'love' a partner, a family member or even animals, in *Newspeak* the meaning would become restricted to a love only of the Party. This enabled the state's only political party to reinforce totalitarian forms of rule and its dominance over the citizens, turning society into one in which any form of independent thought and action was a crime.

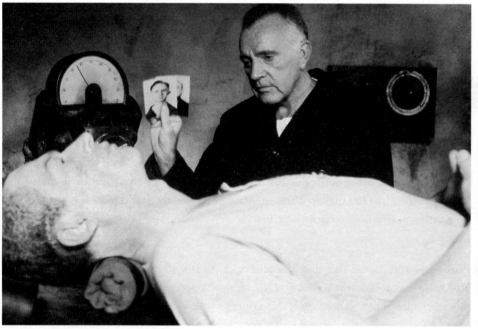

*Source: Kobal Collection Ltd/UMBRELLA/ROSENBLUM/VIRGIN FILMS*

**For Anthony Burke, Critical Theory challenges the dominance of Realism, which constitutes a form of *Newspeak* in International Relations.**

Just as the Frankfurt School theorists of the inter-war period had to contend with the horrors of genocide and other forms of human brutality, the Critical Theorists of today have to deal with the continuing horrors perpetrated by humans upon each other. The first explicit reference to 'Critical Security Studies' was made by Ken Booth in an important article published in 1991 – 'Security and Emancipation' – in which he called for a significant redefinition of security. More specifically, as a descendent of the Frankfurt School, Booth's views have shown the military-focused and state-centric grasp of security to be short-sighted and he therefore called for a critical project that sought to place emancipation at the centre. Booth defined emancipation as the 'absence of threats' and as the

> freeing of people (as individuals and groups) from those physical and human constraints which stop them carrying out what they would freely choose to do. War and threat of war is one of those constraints, together with poverty, poor education, political oppression and so on. Security and emancipation are two sides of the same coin. Emancipation, not power or order, produces true security.
>
> (Booth 1991: 319)

The commitment to the 'security as emancipation' perspective by the so-called Welsh School headed by Ken Booth has definitively broken with the problem-solving basis of traditionalist state-centric approaches such as Realism. The most obvious point of departure is the way in which Booth treats the state. Whereas established, traditional conceptualisations adopt a state-centric perspective, Booth has sought to establish that states are actually the means to achieving security for other referent objects such as individuals and that they should not, therefore, be seen as the recipients of security. Indeed, Booth regarded it as illogical to empower the means to security (states) as opposed to the ends (individuals). Although he accepted that states were obviously important in world politics, he saw it as illogical to label them as the primary referent object. To further explain his point Booth drew an analogy with a house and its inhabitants:

> A house requires upkeep, but it is illogical to spend excessive amounts of money and effort to protect the house against flood, dry rot and burglars if this is at the cost of the well-being of the inhabitants. There is obviously a relationship between the well-being of the sheltered and the state of the shelter, but can there be any question as to whose security is primary?
>
> (Booth 1991: 320)

If we agree with Booth that it is indeed illogical to label the state as the primary referent object, we have to ask why so many academics and politicians have been preoccupied with this particular entity. Indeed, it is this concern with the security of the state which has stunted the growth of alternative conceptualisations. The premise that the state is the primary unit for organising humans into political communities is widely accepted, and humans themselves have chosen this particular unit to represent them in their relations with other national groups. As a consequence, no other institution has commanded as much commitment and loyalty from the national population. The state is also generally perceived as having a monopoly on the tools of legitimate violence: namely, the police force and the armed forces, combined with the recognition that the state will be responsible for the protection of its territory.

Realists argue that since it is the state that provides security, its own security needs to be given primacy. However, it is this type of narrow rigidity that proponents of critical thinking find objectionable. Not only have states themselves been implicated in causing harm to individuals (see Box 26.1) but, privileging their security inevitably comes at a heavy price – the near exclusion of all other possible referent objects such as individuals or the environment. Thinkers such as Booth therefore claim that it is necessary for the concept of security to be expanded to take into account the possibility of multiple referent objects. In making the case for the emancipation of individuals Booth, writing in 1991 (soon after the end of the Cold War), argued that the timing was perfect given that the twentieth century

> has seen the struggle for freedom of the colonial world, women, youth, the proletariat, appetites of all sorts, homosexuals, consumers, and thought. The struggle for emancipation goes on in many places. Some groups have done and are doing better than others. For the moment there is a spirit of liberty abroad. In the struggle against political oppression, one striking feature of recent years has been the remarkable success of non-violent 'people-power' in many countries, ranging from Poland to the Philippines.

(Booth 1991: 321)

Booth further argued that it was by placing emphasis on notions of emancipation that we could break the hold of the Realist tradition. He does not diminish the importance of a Realist understanding of world politics, but rather argues that in order to make better sense of the world it is necessary to go beyond its narrow range of options. For Booth, Critical Theory assists us in this aim because it highlights the idea that politics should be ethical and human-centric – an important premise which Realism ignores.

## The Copenhagen School

As shown, both the Welsh School and feminism have thrown down a major challenge to the narrow state-centric vision of security put forward by the traditionalists. The story of critical approaches to security does not end with these two, however, and in this section we would like to develop a theme briefly introduced in Chapter 24 – that of the **Copenhagen School**. The ideas expressed by academics within this tradition are worthy of mention since they have had a tremendous impact on rejecting the traditionalist insistence on the state as the key recipient of security. Their conceptualisation of the key referent object of security, however, is fundamentally different from both the Welsh School and feminism. Whereas the Welsh School and feminists stress the emancipation of individuals as paramount, the Copenhagen School has put forward the notion of 'securitisation'.

Securitisation is a challenging concept and cannot be understood simply. It is perhaps best defined as the *process* which leads to the elevation of a particular entity to a position where it acquires the status of being regarded as the key referent object. To clarify further, we must reflect on the procedure which ultimately results in this elevated status. Imagine a situation where the politicians of a state regularly appear on television talking about 'everyday' issues. As citizens of that state, we may or may not be interested in what is, for all intents and purposes, 'normal' everyday politics. Imagine, however, that suddenly a key politician begins to concentrate on one specific issue (terrorism for instance) and that one issue begins to acquire both increasing media as well as political attention. Bombarded by continuous references to that single issue we, as citizens, become conditioned into accepting that it is now of paramount importance. In other words it has become *securitised*. As stated by Ole Wæver (an academic within the Copenhagen tradition):

> What then is security? With the help of language theory, we can regard security as a speech act. In this usage, security is not of interest as a sign that refers to something more real; the utterance itself is the act. By saying it, something is done (as in betting, giving a promise, naming a ship). By uttering 'security' a state representative moves a particular development into a specific area, and thereby claims a special right to use whatever means are necessary to block it.
>
> (Wæver 1995: 55)

## Case study: Brutal humans – genocide

In this chapter we referred to some of the central concerns of the academics in the Frankfurt School tradition that has had a tremendous impact on contemporary Critical Theorists such as Ken Booth. The following two case studies demonstrate the value of this tradition's central concern with emancipation.

### Joseph Stalin, repression in the Soviet Union, and the failure of the state to 'wither away'

Marx predicted that once revolution took hold, the state would temporarily become the guardian both of the ideals of the revolution and of all the resources of the nation, and that once conditions permitted, the state itself would disappear, giving way to the establishment of classless communism. Revolution may have occurred in 1917 resulting in the establishment of the Soviet State, but Marx's vision of emancipation was never achieved; right until the disintegration of the Soviet Union in 1991, the state never disappeared. Indeed, the system of rule in the Soviet Union was often characterised as that of a totalitarian state. Joseph Stalin, for instance, came to power in 1924 and ruled until 1953, but rather than working towards the emancipation of Soviet citizens, his rule became associated with cruelty and oppression. The purpose of his 'five-year plans', for example, was to industrialise the Soviet Union rapidly and collectivise the peasantry, but a key feature of both objectives became the murder and oppression of opponents on a massive scale. In *The Harvest of Sorrow*, Robert Conquest (1987) shows how Stalin's policies contributed to the onset of a famine which resulted in the deaths of up to seven million people in the Ukraine alone. By forcing the peasantry to increase the amount of grain they had to surrender

to the state by a massive amount, Stalin prepared the way for what has recently been recognised as one of the most destructive genocides of the twentieth century (Conquest 1987: 144–55).

In order to further consolidate his rule, Stalin began the 'Great Purges' between 1937 and 1938 during which time he removed people he believed were a threat to him. So-called 'enemies of the state' were imprisoned or killed, ethnic minorities were deported, peasants were repressed and the police carried out mass surveillance of ordinary citizens. No Soviet institution was left unscrutinised and the purge included individuals from the Army and even the Communist Party of the Soviet Union. Estimates of the number of victims range up to a staggering two million.

### The Holocaust

Up to six million European Jews were exterminated during the Second World War by the Nazis as part of their 'Final Solution' to rid Germany of all races and ethnic minorities that were regarded as a threat to the 'purity' of the German nation. By the end of the War in 1945, up to six million Jews had been murdered in what came to be known as 'death camps'. Locations such as Auschwitz, Belzec, Chelmno, Dachau (among many others) became associated with the concentration, transportation and subsequent torture and murder of countless humans. Although Jews were the primary target of the Nazis, other alleged 'inferiors' were also condemned to torture and death including mentally and physically disabled patients, as well as up to three million Soviet prisoners of war (Gilbert 1986).

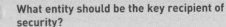
**What entity should be the key recipient of security?**

Here Wæver highlights the importance of language – specifically the 'speech act' in constructing the threat to security. Consequently, this becomes a component of a specific social process by which threats become recognised as such and Wæver further hints at the placing of the issue into a 'specific area'. In other words the threat is elevated to a position beyond normal everyday politics and once it acquires this status, it has the right to demand whatever societal resources may be necessary to deal with it. We cannot underestimate the impact of securitisation theory, particularly on the debates over what the referent object should be. It has increasingly become recognised that *any* referent object can be placed at the centre of concern for a state, be it the individual, the environment, a particular group or any other entity. The only proviso is that the security issue needs to be highlighted by a key politician engaging in what the Copenhagen School has referred to as the 'speech act' and this act then begins the process by which the threat is subsequently constructed.

## Conclusions

Having reached the end of this chapter, we need to assess the contribution that critical approaches have made to security studies. As outlined, these various approaches have one overriding concern, namely their rejection of the narrow focus of Realist perceptions of security. Realism's dominance of the discipline is also a cause for concern for these newer approaches in that it has prevented alternative referent objects and definitions of security from featuring as key aspects of the discipline. The effect, according to critical analysis, has been the exclusion of a significant amount of what is actually central to Security Studies.

Approaches such as Realism have not only dominated the field but have also contributed to its slow development in theoretical terms. New perspectives such as Critical Theory enable us to expand the boundaries of the discipline considerably by opening up space for discussion and debate. By drawing our attention to the premise that world politics is characterised by much more than the military-centric world of Realist power politics, ultimately Critical Security Studies has forced us to consider referent objects other than the state. The Copenhagen School's emphasis on the 'speech act' as a basis for 'securitisation' may not have an emancipatory basis, but it at least allows for the inclusion of a variety of referent objects other than the state. The only condition is that the process of securitisation is carried out by a figure in authority – such as a leading politician. This analysis has undoubtedly fed into the emancipatory and human-centric essence of Critical Security Studies. Indeed, Booth argues that security can only be achieved for humans once they are free from threats to their core values. Similarly, despite the broad nature of feminism, there is a common emancipatory basis to its gender-based analysis. Feminists have attempted to draw our attention to the vulnerabilities that women (and other vulnerable groups) suffer as a result of prevailing unjust power structures, wherever they occur. Some of the most insightful analyses by feminists have demonstrated the extent of the brutality that humans are capable of inflicting upon each other and on vulnerable groups such as women.

## Resource section

## Questions

1. What do critical thinkers mean by the notion of emancipation?

2. Why is feminism often referred to as a critical approach?

3. Explain Robert Cox's distinction between Critical Theory and problem-solving theories.

4. Why is Critical Security Studies such a broad area of study?

5. What is the value of the Copenhagen School and how does it differ from other critical approaches?

## Recommended reading

Booth, K. (1991) 'Security and emancipation', *Review of International Studies*, 17 (4): October
Closely associated with the Welsh School, Ken Booth is a fervent critic of orthodox Realism and this article is one of the most important statements of his support for the notion of emancipation.

Buzan, B., Wæver, O. and de Wilde, J. (1998) *Security: A New Framework for Analysis* (Boulder, CO: Lynne Rienner Publishers)
The Copenhagen School has had a major impact on how we think about the concept of security and the referent object. This book was one of the first to deal with the tradition's theory of securitisation.

Enloe, C. (1990) *Bananas, Beaches and Bases: Making Feminist Sense of International Politics* (London, Pandora Press)
As a well-known feminist, Enloe has written extensively on the disempowerment of women and their exclusion from politics. This is one of the most famous books written on the topic.

Krause, K. and Williams, M. (1997) *Critical Security Studies: Concepts and Strategies* (London, Routledge)
This is the first book you should read on critical approaches to security as it was this text which helped to bring together a large number of disparate views, all united by their goal of furthering the cause of critical thinking.

Tickner, A. (1992) *Gender in International Relations: Feminist Perspectives on Achieving Global Security* (New York, Columbia University Press)
Tickner is required reading for all students of International Relations. In this book she takes us through a large number of major issues in world politics from a feminist viewpoint. This book is particularly important for us given that many of the issues she considers are central to Security Studies, for example economic, ecological and global security.

# Chapter 27
# The Globalisation of Human Security

The dimensions of human security

The broad view of human security – freedom from want

The impact of globalisation

Problems with the broad view and attempts to narrow the concept

Conclusions

After reading this chapter you will be able to:

- Define human security

- Account for the *narrow* and *broad* views of the concept

- Analyse the connections between human security and globalisation

- Locate the study of human security within the broader field of Critical Security Studies (as outlined in Chapter 26)

- Understand the connections between the foreign policies of specific states (Canada and Japan) and human security

*Source*: Panos Pictures/Chris Stowers

## Introductory box: It isn't just about military force and state security

**Natural Disasters:** It is not possible to say with any great certainty how many natural disasters have occurred since the year 2000. Many pass by unnoticed by the media but some attract great attention. An earthquake in the Indian Ocean on 26 December 2004 resulted in a tsunami of such force that over 230,000 people were killed with Indonesia, Sri Lanka, India and Thailand the worst hit. The earthquake in Haiti on 13 January 2010 caused over 200,000 deaths and devastated the capital Port au Prince. Some commentators are claiming that it will take decades for Haiti to recover.

**Trafficking of Women and Children:** It may come as a surprise to some, but slavery *does* exist in the twenty-first century and is mostly manifested in the form of trafficking of women and children from poorer states. An expanding commercial sex industry, for instance, demands an increasing number of sex workers and the preferences are for younger women and girls.

**Poverty** exists globally but is more prevalent in some states than others. Africa, for example, includes some of the poorest countries in the world. Adverse environmental conditions in regions such as Sub-Saharan Africa further exacerbate poverty. Dry barren lands, the lack of adequate rainfall and the overuse of fertile lands are leading to desertification in states increasingly prone to famines and droughts. States such as Ethiopia, Somalia, Sudan and Mali regularly experience famines.

**Acid Attacks against Women:** The following excerpt is from *The Independent* newspaper: She lay still, pretending to be asleep. He sat at the foot of the bed, shook her foot and called her name. 'What do you want?' she replied, sitting up. He grasped her hair, holding her head rigid, and emptied a bottle of liquid of some sort over her head and torso. Fakhra looked down and saw her clothes melting into her skin and tried to scream – but her lips were stuck together. The concentrated acid that Bilal Khar sluiced over Fakhra Yunus fused her lips, burned off her hair, melted her breasts and one ear, closed one eye and gave what remained of the skin of her face and upper body the look of melted rubber.' (*Source*: Peter Popham, 'Pakistan horrified by feudal husband's acid attack on beauty', *The Independent*, 2 September 2001). Pakistan may have been horrified by this particular attack back in 2001 – but such attacks remain widespread and it is not just in this particular state that such brutality occurs, since many cases are also documented elsewhere. State authorities often turn a blind eye.

## The dimensions of human security

After reading the above examples – ask yourself the question – who is responsible for protecting these vulnerable humans when the responsible states are often powerless to help or do not even care? One factor appears certain, namely, that traditional Realist conceptions of security (outlined in Chapter 24) are wholly inappropriate and it is largely because of their narrow concerns that critical approaches sought to shift attention from the state to the human. **Human security** is the latest field within Security Studies that has encouraged us to go beyond thinking purely in terms of the military defence of state territory and interests. In this sense the concept shares ground with critical approaches such as Feminism and Critical Theory. Although the term appeared for the first time in the 1980s as a counter to the concept of 'national security' it wasn't until the United Nations Development Programme (UNDP) based its *Human Development Report* on it in 1994 that the concept became widely used. In this report the UNDP maintained that it was necessary to recognise that humans the world over were vulnerable and that we must ask ourselves how they could be protected.

The attempt to secure international cooperation for the myriad of problems facing individuals in different regions of the world has become a key feature of the UN's interaction with states and international institutions. Indeed certain states, such as Canada and Japan, have adopted features of the UN proposals on human security by incorporating them into their foreign policy agendas and the results have often been impressive. The establishment of the International Criminal Court, the UN Small Arms Conference and the ban on anti-personnel mines have been some notable successes as a result of this interaction. The essence of human security is that for most people a sense of insecurity arises not from a tragic global event (such as a war) but rather from everyday occurrences revolving around a wide range of issues. These can be as varied as job or environmental security, concern about crime or even health, ensuring access to food or political rights and safeguarding cultural and personal security. In the cases of most of the examples given above, traditional Realist conceptions of security are inappropriate and, like critical approaches to security (dealt with in Chapter 26), human security also calls for a major shift in thinking about the key referent object.

In order to understand the practical value of human security we must analyse the concept itself, which is not as straightforward as it might seem. Fen Hampson (a professor of International Affairs) identifies three distinct conceptualisations of human security including, first, the notion of *natural rights* applicable to all humans. To understand these rights a distinction can be made between these and *legal rights* which are the rights given to humans by the political entity within which they reside. Natural rights, on the other hand, are not dependent upon the laws of any particular society but rather are universally applicable to all humans. They are, as Hampson argues 'anchored in the fundamental liberal assumption of basic individual rights to life, liberty and the pursuit of happiness'. In other words natural rights are those which are conferred upon humans at the point at which they enter society and no government should deny them. The *right to life* is perhaps one of the most important examples of a natural right. The key to understanding human security is that the international community has an obligation to protect and promote these rights, and it is in this context that the attempts to strengthen international law, particularly in relation to genocide and war crimes, form a second view of human security. According to Hampson, this is the basis for humanitarian intervention and can be seen in attempts to improve the lives of displaced people and refugees. The third view is far broader than the other two and has at its core a powerful connection to social justice and human dignity. In Hampson's words, 'the state of the global economy, the forces of globalisation, and the health of the environment . . . are all legitimate subjects of concern in terms of how they affect the security of the individual' (Hampson 2008: 231).

Hampson's categorisation is useful in that it enables us to identify two views which have featured prominently in discussions on human security. The first, the *broad view*, has been advocated by the UNDP itself, and seeks to take into account not only the impact of conflict and war, but the *whole range* of threats facing humans. Often referred to as *freedom from want*, this view encourages us to recognise that humans can be threatened by everyday occurrences such as the loss of earnings, crime or lack of access to key resources such as health. The second, the *narrow view* criticises the broad one for being too expansive and all-inclusive and advocates imposing limits on what can be achieved. Often referred to as *freedom from fear*, this view argues that protecting humans during times of conflict should be the primary objective. The main difference between the narrow view and the broad view, therefore, is that the narrow view has a very limited focus, whereas the broad view encompasses all aspects of human security, even incorporating the narrow view itself.

## The broad view of human security – freedom from want

Advocated by the UNDP in its 1994 report, one of the most important features of the broad view is the premise that, rather than being alarmed by dramatic global events such as war, most people around the globe are more concerned with everyday occurrences. To quote from the report itself:

> For most people, a feeling of insecurity arises more from worries about daily life than from the dread of a cataclysmic world event. Will they and their families have enough to eat? Will they lose their jobs? Will their streets and neighbourhoods be safe from crime? Will they be tortured by a repressive state? Will they become a victim of violence because of their gender? Will their religion or ethnic origin target them for persecution?
>
> (UNDP 1994: 22)

The report therefore identified a range of threats to human security such as economic, food, health, environmental, personal, community and political. Four further dimensions were then identified, beginning with the premise that human security had to be *universally applicable* in that it was relevant to everyone everywhere. Second, it was deemed to be

### Box 27.1  UNDP Human Development Report, 1994

In the final analysis, human security is a child who did not die, a disease that did not spread, a job that was not cut, an ethnic tension that did not explode in violence, a dissident who was not silenced. Human security is not a concern with weapons – it is a concern with human life and dignity (UNDP 1994: 23).

The concept of human security stresses that people should be able to take care of themselves: all people should have the opportunity to meet their most essential needs and to earn their own living. This will set them free and help ensure that they can make a full contribution to development – their own development and that of their communities, their countries and the world. Human security is a critical ingredient of participatory development (UNDP 1994: 24).

It is embedded in a notion of solidarity among people. It cannot be brought about through force, with armies standing against armies. It can happen only if we agree that development must involve all people (UNDP 1994: 24).

*interdependent* since 'famine, disease, pollution, drug trafficking, terrorism, ethnic disputes and social disintegration were no longer isolated events, confined within national borders', but rather their consequences were globally felt (UNDP 1994: 22). The report also recommended *pre-emption* to maximise the potential for achieving human security in that it is less costly to meet the threats earlier than through later intervention. Finally, it stressed that human security had to be *people-centred* in that it was 'concerned with how people live and breathe in a society, how freely they exercise their many choices, how much access they have to market and social opportunities – and whether they live in conflict or in peace' (UNDP 1994: 22–3).

A continuing commitment to the *freedom from want* vision of the United Nations was further established by its 2001 Millennium Development Goals (MDGs). In recognition of the links between the development of human societies and human security, the goals were particularly geared towards eight objectives, namely: eradicating extreme poverty, achieving global primary education, empowering women, reducing child mortality, reducing the mortality rate of mothers, combating diseases such as HIV/AIDS, malaria and other major diseases, ensuring environmental sustainability and developing a global partnership for development (United Nations 2005: 8–9). Human security as envisaged by the broad school therefore, is integrative in the sense that it combines the myriad challenges facing individuals and communities, and at the same time stresses the close connections between the security of humans, the development of their societies and the protection of their human rights.

This all-inclusive approach makes the individual human being the centre of analysis and, in doing so, stresses that the key to achieving human security lies in tackling such diverse threats as hunger, disease, environmental disasters and poverty. According to those advocating the broad view of human security these are legitimate concerns because combined, they kill far more people across the globe than war or terrorism. The features already highlighted demonstrate the strong practical basis for human security in that its central concern is to persuade governments and other relevant actors such as non-governmental organisations (NGOs) to cooperate in the design and implementation of policies geared towards the

**Box 27.2 Kofi Annan, former Secretary General of the United Nations, 1997–2007**

Human security, in its broadest sense, embraces far more than the absence of violent conflict. It encompasses human rights, good governance, access to education and health care and ensuring that each individual has opportunities and choices to fulfill his or her potential. Every step in this direction is also a step towards reducing poverty, achieving economic growth and preventing conflict. Freedom from want, freedom from fear, and the freedom of future generations to inherit a healthy natural environment – these are the interrelated building blocks of human – and therefore national – security.

*Source*: 'Secretary-General Salutes International Workshop on Human Security in Mongolia', Two-Day Session in Ulaanbaatar, May 8–10, 2000. Press Release SG/SM/7382.

protection of individuals. In addition to this, as shown by the UNDP Report and the subsequent UN Millennium Development Goals, human security has become most obviously equated with the United Nations itself. Even though it wasn't until the 1994 Report that the UN explicitly referred to the notion of human security, much of what the Organisation has been doing since its inception, from advocating the protection of human rights to peacekeeping and managing refugees during times of conflict, is central to the human security framework.

The UN's involvement with human security, therefore, is longstanding, as demonstrated not only by the types of roles it has fulfilled in the past but also by the pressure it has brought to bear on states to shift some of their attention and resources to enhancing the lives of individuals. The various reports by the UNDP since 1994, for instance, have all stressed the importance of human security with its 2000 report, *Human Rights and Human Development*, stressing the link between human security and development (UNDP 2000). Kofi Annan (see Box 27.2) also appeared to take a strong interest in publicising the concept and pushing its agenda onto the world stage.

Poverty features strongly in this broad view and the United Nations has been at the forefront of bringing this to the attention of states. While acknowledging that states across the world, most notably India and China, have managed to bring a significant proportion of their populations out of extreme poverty, there remain many states and regions which have become poorer and have failed to share in the wealth generating benefits of globalisation. To quote from a 2005 United Nations General Assembly (UNGA) Report entitled *In Larger Freedom*:

> Today, more than a billion people . . . still live on less than a dollar a day, lacking the means to stay alive in the face of chronic hunger, disease and environmental hazards. In other words this is a poverty that kills. A single bite from a malaria-bearing mosquito is enough to end a child's life for want of a bed net or $1 treatment. A drought or pest that destroys a harvest turns subsistence into starvation. A world in which every year 11 million children die before their fifth birthday and three million people die of AIDS is not a world of larger freedom.

(UNGA 2005)

The report goes on to criticise commonly held beliefs that for centuries this level of poverty was a 'sad but inescapable aspect of the human condition' and it stresses that adhering to this view today is no longer intellectually or morally defensible and that states now need to work towards eradicating poverty and freeing humans from want. The United Nations, therefore, has been particularly supportive of a shift to human security and highly critical of the tendency of states to overlook the millions of people who have lost their lives at the hands of states themselves. In this sense, those who advocate human security share ground with critical thinkers (see Chapter 26), in that both groups claim that preserving the security of the state has often been used as an excuse for policies that undermine the security of people. By connecting developmental and humanitarian issues to security, therefore, those who promote human security have encouraged many to alter their conceptualisation of security away from the narrow confines imposed by the Cold War.

## The impact of globalisation

Chapter 26 showed that the post-Cold War era has been characterised by intense debate over the choice of referent object, with human security being a central component in the discussions. This concept has offered academics and policy makers an alternative to the narrow and largely gloomy offerings of the Realists. With its emphasis on human welfare, human security has not only criticised the Cold War's obsession with interstate conflict, but

Human security is about more than military force and state security, as the UN's World Water day illustrates.

*Source: Reuters/Kamal Kishore*

has also sought to shift attention to the impact of globalisation on the security of humans, and in this context there are two overarching views to consider. The first relates to the premise that this phenomenon has had a positive impact on the international system and that it is leading to the opening up of economies and increased trade thereby generating wealth for all countries. An alternative view sees globalisation as central to countless problems that relate to increased levels of poverty, the underdevelopment of vulnerable societies, and increased levels of insecurity for millions of people in the developing world. It has also been implicated in moral decline, drug trafficking, a loss of faith in institutions, population pressures and even the spread of diseases such as AIDS. Closely linked to these is the view that the rapid growth of unregulated capitalist markets has brought untold misery and inequality to vulnerable human societies in many regions of the world. Although globalisation is not a new phenomenon, its impact has been felt particularly during recent decades, following the emergence of a highly interconnected global economy intertwined with significant advances in communications. Those who criticise globalisation argue that threats such as these need to be viewed in terms of global trends which are beginning to affect individuals everywhere to a lesser or greater degree. In this light it is understandable that the UN Development Programme was among the first of the world's institutions to draw human security to our attention.

As has been discussed elsewhere in this book (Chapter 24), one of the main contentions of the Realist tradition has been that states are the main actors in the international system. Indeed, Realists have gone even further in their assessment of world politics by distinguishing between the international environment and the domestic realm. Neo-Realists (see Chapter 6), for instance, distinguish between the two in terms of the manner in which they are organised, with the international environment being characterised as *anarchic* (i.e. lacking in any overarching ruler or government). On the other hand, the domestic realm is defined as being *hierarchical*, where the state or government can rule legitimately with the help of laws and coercive powers (such as the police) over society. Furthermore, Realists argue that it is the anarchic nature of the international system which compels states to see their security in terms of the acquisition of power relative to other states, because ultimately it is only the most powerful states that can ensure their own survival.

## Box 27.3 The United Nations Development Programme (UNDP)

As the UN's key development institution, the UNDP focuses primarily on the following goals:

- Supporting democratic governance by providing advice and technical support.
- Helping states to develop policies and strategies that lead to a reduction in poverty.
- Being centrally involved in activities designed to prevent the outbreak of violence and working towards helping to rebuild those societies when they occur. This activity also extends to enabling societies recover after natural disasters.
- Treating sustainable development as a core function especially geared towards the developing world, given that it is disproportionately affected by climate change, lack of access to resources such as clear water and reliable sanitation and energy.
- Working towards reducing the impact of the spread of HIV/AIDS.

This traditional perception of security, therefore, claims that states direct their attention towards the international system *and* other states in their search for security. Apart from criticising this view for being too narrow and simplistic, those who advocate human security stress that many of the threats that confront humans the world over are actually internal to the state. Indeed, the insecurity experienced by individuals, such as job losses, poor health facilities, disease, hunger, environmental disaster or poverty often seem to lie within the confines of states. However, given the high levels of interconnectivity created by globalisation, it is no longer possible to separate the two realms – as Realists claim. Globalisation has meant that the two levels, the domestic realm and the international environment, are closely interlinked, and this has had significant implications for human security, since security problems in weak regions of the world (such as Africa) have implications for stable areas (such as Europe or the United States). As Held and others have explained:

> That computer programmers in India now deliver services in real time to their employers in Europe and the USA, while the cultivation of poppies in Burma can be linked to drug abuse in Berlin or Belfast, illustrate the ways in which contemporary globalisation connects communities in one region of the world to developments in another continent.

> (Held et al. 1999: 4)

In addition to highlighting such linkages, globalists also claim that states are no longer the only actors of any significance in the international system, and that borders are becoming increasingly permeable as the connections between societies, institutions, cultures and individuals intensify. Globalisation has not only implied a shrinking of distances but also a reduction in the time needed to cross those distances; thereby giving the impression that the world is a smaller place where economics, politics and security begin to interconnect at a deeper level and in more locations than previously (Clarke 1997: 15). One of the consequences of this increased interaction is the impression that the ability of states to act independently has diminished. Indeed, globalists go so far as to argue that globalisation represents a new period of human history in which states are no longer the only significant actors in the international system. For many, globalisation is predominantly an economic phenomenon, leading to a global economy which is not only becoming increasingly interconnected but is also one in which states themselves have little control. Importantly, for our purposes, one view is that economic globalisation is leading to the further entrenchment of the divisions between the wealthier regions of the world and the poorer, thereby exacerbating already deep levels of poverty in certain regions. As highlighted, attempts to alleviate poverty have been central to the human security agenda.

While it is possible to argue that globalisation may have contributed to increasing levels of poverty – thereby increasing levels of insecurity – in the developing world, we should not forget that its impact on the richer parts of the world is not necessarily regarded as entirely beneficial either. A rather xenophobic view, for instance, sees globalisation not only as contributing to the loss of European jobs to the 'poor masses' of the developing world, but also sees the erosion of an indigenous European culture due to the influx of people who have a different culture, religion and way of life.

**Box 27.4 Quotes from the press – the perceived Islamic threat to European culture and society**

Italy's Northern League, allies of centre-right Prime Minister Silvio Berlusconi, want to limit the growth of Islam in the centre of world Catholicism by blocking the construction of mosques through strict new regulations. Muslim immigrants using Italy as a route into Europe already get a foretaste of the mistrust with which many Europeans view their religion, with many projects for mosques and prayer halls already blocked by the opposition of local Italian residents.

*Source:* Stephen Brown, 'Italy's right to curb Islam with mosque law', 16 September 2008, http://www.reuters.com

Close to half of Flemish voters have an extremely negative opinion of Islam and Muslims. 46% think that Islam has nothing to contribute to European culture . . . Yet more voters (48%) think that Islamic values are a threat for Europe and 37% think that most Muslims have no respect for European culture and way of life [and] The harshest statement – Islamic history and culture are more violent than other cultures was accepted by almost 42% of interviewees. Study conducted by ISPO (Institute for Social and Political Opinion)

Research of Katholieke Universiteit – Leuven.

*Source:* 'Belgium: Flemings afraid of Islam', Islam in Europe: News and Opinions about the Islamic Community in Europe, 25 January 2009, http://islamineurope.blogspot.com

The riots that consumed the French suburbs last November, and now the uproar over the Danish cartoons of the Prophet Mohammed, have underlined for all to see that the ongoing struggle with radical Islamism . . . is if anything more of a problem for Europe than it is for America. For the United States, with a Muslim population of less than 1 percent, radical Islam is an issue to be dealt with 'over there', in dysfunctional areas of the Middle East like Pakistan and Saudi Arabia. For Europe, however, it is a much more immediate and threatening crisis because it is domestic . . . Many of the organisers of recent terrorist incidents – including Mohammed Atta, the Sept. 11 ringleader; the March 7 Madrid bombers; Mohammed Bouyeri, assassin of the Dutch filmmaker Theo van Gogh; and the July 7 bombers – were radicalised not in the Middle East, but in Western Europe.

*Source:* Francis Fukuyama 'Europe vs Radical Islam', 27 February 2006, http://www.slate.com/id/2136964

Whether the impact of globalisation is positive or otherwise may be a matter of debate, but it has certainly had an impact on the debates surrounding human security. As shown, institutions such as the UNDP have not only highlighted some of the negative effects of globalisation, but have also argued that human security reflects the growing vulnerability within states in light of increasing levels of interconnectivity. From the point of view of the United Nations, security perceptions associated with the Cold War were insufficient for addressing the challenges brought about as a result of globalisation. We must, therefore, view the UNDP's commitment to human security as a way of dealing with these new challenges. Kofi Annan's commitment to human security when he was the Secretary General of the UN is well documented. Similarly, Sadako Ogata, the UN High Commissioner for Refugees (1991–2000), was very well known for her support for human security. Throughout the 1990s, she had to deal with situations relating to refugees and internally displaced persons in conflict-ridden regions such as the former Yugoslavia, the Kurdish refugees in Northern Iraq, the great lakes region in Africa, as well as addressing the continuing tragedies inflicted on Afghan people following years of war. Her claim was that 'there was not a single humanitarian case that could be solved without addressing the underlying political, social and economic causes'. Furthermore, she recognised that, although the end of the Cold War brought with it a sense of optimism, it led to the emergence of significant sources of danger in the form of conflicts *within* states.

Importantly, she also recognised that globalisation had further added to the range of threats to people everywhere since 'while creating wealth, opportunities for work, and a better life for many, it has impacted adversely on some vulnerable strata of society' (Ogata 2001: 10). She, like Kofi Annan, saw human security as an important way of addressing the new range of threats facing people in the post-Cold War era. The broad (*freedom from want*) approach to human security, therefore, has drawn on the definitions provided by the UNDP itself and has been instrumental in highlighting the links between globalisation and the new set of challenges facing states and, more especially people in the post-Cold War era. In this broad view of the security of humans, the key focus is on the protection of the individual whatever the nature of the threat. In this sense, human security represents a major departure from the traditional Cold War view of security, but perhaps most importantly it brings to centre stage the connection between human development and the security of people, in whatever circumstances they find themselves. This association with developmental issues has led to the United Nations giving significant support to human security and seeking to adopt it into many of its post-Cold War functions.

## Problems with the broad view and attempts to narrow the concept

It is precisely because this view is so broad, however, that it has attracted a great deal of criticism. Furthermore, there appears to be no consensus over how human security should be approached and in the context of the broad view, making everything a priority diminishes the value of each element. Roland Paris (an ardent critic of human security) makes the point that the main problem with the concept is that it lacks a precise definition.

> Existing definitions of human security tend to be extraordinarily expansive and vague, encompassing everything from physical security to psychological well-being, which provides policy makers with little guidance in the prioritisation of competing policy-goals and academics with little sense of what, exactly, is to be studied.
>
> (Paris 2001: 88)

For Paris the concept is too broad and vague to be meaningful. Its ambiguity arises because it has come to entail such a wide range of threats, and its association with development issues has not only led to increasing this ambiguity, but also contributed to considerable conceptual overstretch. Indeed, it is easy to see that conflating the concept with a wide range of other issues such as development, poverty, health and disease effectively discounts the possibility of any simple and straightforward meaning. This undoubtedly makes it difficult for both the UN and interested states to design policies that seek to fulfil key human security objectives. Another problem relates to the concept's central concern with morality, in the sense that it seeks to address human suffering wherever it occurs. This ethical basis obviously brings the concept into competition with the traditionalist view which concentrates on securing the strategic interests of states. This contradiction between the two visions and the high degree of ambiguity surrounding human security has meant that neither policy-makers nor many academics have been encouraged to accept the concept. One important element of the UNDP's broad view was its reference to enabling humans to live both in *'freedom from fear'* and in *'freedom from want'*. However, it is precisely because of the all-inclusive nature of the UNDP's perceptions that some academics have sought to narrow the concept, in the hope that this may make human security more useful not only as a concept, but also as a policy option. In this sense, advocates of human security have begun to distinguish between the two perspectives, concentrating on either freedom from want or freedom from fear.

## State interest in human security

Clearly, then, considerable ambiguity surrounds the concept of human security and, as has been shown, this confusion over meanings has led to a split even amongst advocates of the concept, between those for whom a broad view is a necessary framework and those who insist on narrowing the concept considerably to a focus on the effects of actual physical violence. Despite the continuing debate between the narrow and broad views of human security over what the concept should entail, there is, nevertheless, agreement between the two schools that it is the human that needs to be protected. Furthermore, it must be recognised that despite the problems of ambiguity, those who have adopted the broad view's framework have achieved considerable success. We referred to Roland Paris earlier as one of the foremost objectors to the way in which human security is being conceptualised, but even he has acknowledged its successes. In fact he states, 'The political coalition that now uses human security as a rallying cry has chalked up significant accomplishments, including the signing of an anti-personnel land mines convention and the . . . creation of an international criminal court' (Paris 2001: 88).

One key element we have yet to consider in the context of some of these successes is the role that states themselves have played in these and other achievements. The incorporation of either the broad (freedom from want) or narrower (freedom from fear) view has begun to feature in the foreign policy objectives of a number of states, including Japan and Canada. A consideration of Japan's support for human security must begin with a brief analysis of its role during the Second World War, during which time it was one of the Axis Powers (the others being Germany and Italy). Because it lacked many of the raw materials needed to sustain its industrial development, Japan turned its attention to South East Asia where, rather than increasing trade, it decided to begin hostilities in order to secure access to key resources. The only force capable of preventing Japanese goals of expanding its territories was the American Pacific Fleet at Pearl Harbour, which was effectively destroyed by Japan during the infamous attack on 7 December 1941. Similarly, destroying the

American bases in the Philippines was necessary in order to ensure that the supply lines back to Japan were unhindered. Ultimately Japan's aggression led to it establishing control over Burma, Malaya, Singapore and the Dutch East Indies in quick succession and by the beginning of 1942 the Japanese controlled much of South East Asia.

The Japanese were finally forced to surrender after the United States dropped atomic bombs on two Japanese cities, Hiroshima on 6 August 1945 and Nagasaki on 9 August 1945. Japan's role during the Second World War, the devastation it suffered and the pressure from the victorious powers led to elements of Japan's new post-war constitution being decidedly pacifist in nature. For instance, Chapter 2 of its constitution is entitled 'Renunciation of War' and states 'Aspiring sincerely to an international peace based on justice and order, the Japanese people forever renounce war as a sovereign right of the nations and the threat or use of force as a means of settling international disputes'. What is the significance of this? Given the brutal treatment suffered by South East Asian nations at the hands of the Japanese, it is understandable that many of the states view it with a degree of suspicion. Its pacifist constitution undoubtedly helps to allay fears amongst the various states of the region, and some commentators such as Lam Peng Er believe that Japan has deliberately sought to avoid 'a hard security approach towards the region' and that 'Instead a human security [approach] allows Japan to fulfil its desire to play a larger role beyond economics in Southeast Asia without upsetting its general public and neighbours' (Peng Er 2006: 143).

Peng Er goes on to argue that the prevailing image of Japan as merely an economic giant is not accurate and that it has, since the UNDP Report of 1994, adopted human security as one of the main pillars of its foreign policy, fulfilling this objective most particularly in South East Asia. Japan's involvement in various crises, whether financial, political or catastrophic, in which human lives have been threatened, has been significant. To quote from Peng Er, aid has ranged from:

> . . . providing massive financial assistance and currency swap arrangements in the aftermath of the 1997–98 Asian financial crisis to stabilize the regional economies and strengthen social and political stability, engaging in peacemaking in Cambodia and Aceh, peacebuilding in East Timor, Ache and Mindano, offering financial and medical assistance when East Asia was hit by the SARS . . . epidemic, and deploying the largest contingent of Japanese troops since the end of World War 2 for humanitarian assistance to tsunami-striken Aceh in early 2005.
>
> (Peng Er 2006: 143)

Japan is a significant donor of foreign assistance and when this is combined with the restrictions on its constitution, its inherent pacifism and the tendency of its neighbours to be suspicious of its motives, it is easy to understand why it has adhered to a more development-oriented approach to human security. Japan also founded the Commission on Human Security in January 2001, whose mandate was to stress recognition of the adverse effects of globalisation and to make recommendations that would provide guidelines for concrete action. The Commission presented its Final Report to the then Prime Minister of Japan (Junichiro Koizumi) in February 2003 and it was subsequently submitted to UN Secretary General Kofi Annan in May of the same year. Its final proposals not only confirmed Japan's acceptance of the developmental component of human security (as stressed by the earlier UNDP Report of 1994), but also highlighted the importance of protecting humans during times of violent conflict and providing funds and facilities to aid their recovery following the end of hostilities.

Finally, in cooperation with the United Nations Secretariat, Japan launched the Trust Fund for Human Security which amounted to $227 million, in 1999. As the largest fund of its type within the UN system, it was earmarked particularly for supporting activities related to human security. Clearly then, Japan's perception of human security is not only geared towards developmental issues but is also centrally concerned with enhancing prospects for protecting people during times of conflict.

As far as Canada is concerned, there are two views that explain how it has sought to incorporate human security into its foreign policy. The first appears to suggest that Canada has enthusiastically and wholeheartedly absorbed crucial elements of a broad understanding of human security. There is no doubt that Canada was also influenced by the UNDP Report of 1994 and for a while was fully in accord with it. Canada's foreign minister between 1996 and 2000, Lloyd Axworthy, for instance, was particularly supportive of attempts to shift the focus of security from the state to the human. The Human Security Network, established by Canada and a number of other states, including Norway, in 1988, is one example of this commitment to human security. The purpose of this network was to establish political and legal mechanisms that would enable non-governmental organisations and states to enhance the human security agenda. Through the Network Canada has succeeded in persuading many other states to adopt the Ottawa Treaty, or as it is sometimes called, the Mine Ban Treaty, which aims to put to an end the suffering caused by anti-personnel mines by persuading states to give up their stockpiles and to undertake de-mining activities. As of February

---

### Box 27.5 Summary of the Commission on Human Security Final Report to the UN Secretary General, 1 May 2003

The report of the Commission proposes that in the world today in which globalisation is progressing, given the reality that there are many cases where states are unable to ensure the security of their citizens adequately, various comprehensive measures should be taken in response to both conflict and development. Specifically, focusing on individuals and communities, it emphasises the necessity of protecting and empowering individuals.

#### Main proposals

1. Protecting people in violent conflict
2. Protecting people from the proliferation of arms
3. Supporting the security of people on the move
4. Establishing human security transition funds for post-conflict situations

5. Encouraging fair trade and markets to benefit the extreme poor
6. Working to provide minimum living standards everywhere
7. According higher priority to ensuring universal access to basic health care
8. Developing an efficient and equitable global system for patent rights
9. Empowering all people with universal basic education
10. Clarifying the need for a global human identity while respecting the freedom of individuals to have diverse identities and affiliations.

*Source*: Japan Ministry of Foreign Affairs
http://www.mofa.go.jp/policy/human_secu/
commission/report0305.html

2009 almost one hundred and fifty-eight states had signed up to it. Canada has also, again through Axworthy's efforts, been at the forefront of establishing the International Criminal Court, the purpose of which is to provide a permanent forum for the prosecution of individuals accused of inciting genocide and other crimes against humanity.

This first view, therefore, seems to suggest that there has been a definitive change in Canadian foreign policy since the end of the Cold War. Mark Neufeld, for instance, accounts for important and influential elements within Canadian civil society which sought to identify alternatives to the traditional Realist orientation of Canada's foreign policy during the Cold War. He claims that 'security was Recast to signify radical progressive change in terms of disarmament, economic development and wealth redistribution, environmental policy and democratisation of the foreign policy-making process' (Neufeld 2004: 113). A nationwide public enquiry in 1992, entitled *Transformation Moment: A Canadian Vision of Common Security*, highlighted the security concerns of ordinary Canadians which are encapsulated on the very first page of the report: 'Canada should set an example of social and environmental responsibility . . . take the initiative on debt relief and take a leadership role in efforts . . . to forge a new, more just and sustainable international economic order' (Canadian Peace Alliance 1992). Amongst other factors, Lloyd Axworthy's commitment to human security, the establishment of the Human Security Network, and the pressure exerted by the UN system have led to human security becoming a significant aspect of Canada's foreign policy objectives.

However, a second narrower view claims that the traditional grasp of security remains the strongest feature of Canadian foreign policy. Although it acknowledges Canada's interest in human security, it also demonstrates its criticism of the UNDP's all-inclusive approach. This perception, therefore, argues that the *freedom from fear* component of human security is far more applicable to the way in which Canada pursues its foreign policy. Here again we can refer to Lloyd Axworthy, who is often credited with recognising that Canada's limited military capability meant that it could not play a major role in world affairs and that it therefore had to find a role more suited to its position as a middle power. Axworthy took note of the problems confronting the international system in the post-Cold War era and came to the conclusion that Canada could carve out an international role for itself as a leading contender for peacekeeping missions.

Cross-border terrorism, pollution, mass refugee movements and genocide are just some of the problems which have confronted states in the post-Cold War period. Alongside these is the realisation that many of the conflicts in recent years have predominantly occurred *within* states themselves and, as a consequence, have been particularly brutal since they have impacted directly upon ordinary civilians. Recent conflicts, for example, have resulted in extensive population displacements, serious psychological damage, the destruction of entire communities and countless civilian deaths. This trend encouraged many within the UN system to increase the organisation's involvement in crises which were primarily defined in terms of their humanitarian impact. Often referred to as **humanitarian intervention**, the UN and many states sought ways in which to protect civilians who found themselves in the midst of brutal ethnic conflicts. Many interventions of this kind have occurred during the 1990s and some are listed with brief descriptions in Box 27.6.

**Box 27.6  Humanitarian interventions during the 1990s**

- **Operation Provide Comfort (Iraq 1991):** On 2 August 1990 Saddam Hussein (the then President of Iraq) invaded and occupied Iraq's neighbour, Kuwait. The United States, under the auspices of the United Nations, successfully established a coalition of states which were authorised by the UN Security Council to use force against Iraq and expel it from Kuwait. The war, known as Desert Storm, ended on 28 February 1991 and resulted in Iraq's expulsion from Kuwait. However, because of their support for the coalition forces during the war, Saddam Hussein turned his attention towards Iraq's indigenous Kurdish population. Reprisals by his forces led to almost the entire Kurdish population attempting to flee from Iraq and hundreds of Kurdish civilians began to die weekly in the ensuing humanitarian crisis. This persuaded the United States to deploy a Joint Force tasked with saving lives threatened by both the harsh conditions and Saddam's forces. Led by the US, Operation Provide Comfort created demilitarised zones (known as Safe Havens) in Northern Iraq within which the fleeing Kurds could find safety.

- **Unified Task Force (Somalia 5 December 1992–4 May 1993):** The humanitarian crisis in Somalia which began in 1992 was the result of a combination of civil war and famine. The establishment of UNOSOM 1 (United Nations Mission in Somalia) in April 1992 failed to stabilise the situation as the various warring factions remained unprepared to allow humanitarian aid to be delivered to those in need. The US came under intense pressure from aid agencies and Boutros Boutros-Ghali (the then UN Secretary General) to help stabilise Somalia. The result was a 37,000 strong Unified Task Force (UNITAF) which was authorised by the UN Security Council to 'use all necessary means to establish as soon as possible a secure environment for humanitarian relief operations in Somalia' (UNSC Resolution 794).

- **Operation Restore (Uphold) Democracy (Haiti 19 September 1994–31 March 1995):** A military coup on 30 September 1991 led by Lieutenant General Raoul Cédras resulted in the removal of elected President Jean-Bertrand Aristide. The United States refused to accept the new military junta, and the then US President (George Bush Snr) began a process (continued under Bill Clinton) of intense

diplomatic pressure along with economic sanctions as well as threats of full-scale invasion in an attempt to restore Aristide. The junta's refusal persuaded Clinton to authorise an invasion force and, faced with this prospect, the junta finally stepped down even before the troops arrived.

- **United Nations Assistance Mission for Rwanda (1994):** Over 800,000 humans were massacred in Rwanda between April and June 1994, in one of the worst genocides of the twentieth century. The historical relationship between the two main ethnic groups in Rwanda, the Tutsis and the Hutus, is a complicated one, and the genocide of 1994 has its basis in many years of inter-ethnic rivalry and violence. The Arusha Peace Agreement signed by the two sides on 4 August 1993 led to the establishment of the United Nations Assistance Mission for Rwanda (UNAMIR) later that year in October. UNAMIR's mandate had been to assist in the security of Kigali (the capital), aid in mine clearance, establish and expand a demilitarised zone, and assist in the provision of humanitarian aid. The key event which triggered the genocide was the assassination of Rwandan President Juvénal Habyarimana, a Hutu, on 6 April 1994. The Hutus blamed the Tutsis for the killing thus signalling the start of a systematic campaign of slaughter of Tutsis and moderate Hutus over the next three months. In light of this renewed fighting UNAMIR's mission was expanded to enable it to protect refugees in secure humanitarian zones. However, given the scale of the slaughter, and UNAMIR's rather limited mandate and inadequate resources the mission is deemed to have been a major failure.

- **The Kosovo War and the NATO bombing of Serbia (1999):** The NATO air strikes against Serbia in 1999 occurred against a background of almost ten years of conflict within the former Yugoslavia. Prior to 1991 Yugoslavia consisted of six republics, namely Slovenia, Croatia, Bosnia Herzegovina, Montenegro, Macedonia and Serbia, which was further split into autonomous regions, namely Kosovo and Vojvodina. The disintegration of Yugoslavia began in 1991 when Slovenia declared independence from the federation and broke away following a short war. This was immediately followed by the Croatian, Krajina and Bosnian Wars, all of which involved the military forces of the Yugoslav government. During the

▶

**Box 27.6 (Continued)**

decade of war in the other republics, Kosovo remained firmly under the control of the Serbian government in Belgrade even though the Kosovar Albanians sought greater autonomy. The international community failed to do anything about the gross human rights violations being perpetrated by the Serbs, and this persuaded the Kosovo Liberation Army (KLA) to step up its own operations against the Serb forces, although it too was criticised for gross violations of the rights of Serbs and even Albanians suspected of cooperating with them. The ongoing conflict and the failure of peace negotiations strengthened the international community's resolve to bring the war to an end. This began with NATO forces starting to bomb Serbia on 22 March and ended on 11 June 1999. It was immediately followed by the arrival of the Kosovo Force (KFOR) mandated with securing Kosovo, deterring renewed hostilities and importantly, providing support for organisations tasked with bringing humanitarian aid to civilians.

As the examples show, there are now many instances where the international community has been involved in providing some kind of support to protect human lives during times of conflict and war. This role has major implications for our understanding of the concept of human security, in that the humanitarian intervention carried out by the international community has further reinforced the distinction between the broad and narrow views of the concept. States such as Canada and Japan have both been longstanding advocates of human security and have built their foreign policies around that concept, but they differ quite significantly over key issues of definition. Canadian foreign policy, in particular, has sought to define human security in the context of a narrower commitment to helping humans live in freedom from fear, whereas Japan has sought to remain broadly in line with the view expressed by the UN.

Canadian support for measures to protect human lives during times of conflict and war came about in response to a controversial speech made by UN Secretary-General Kofi Annan to the UN General Assembly in 1999. In this speech he criticised the international community's record on addressing man-made humanitarian disasters and stressed the need for a new approach to dealing with massive human rights violations and the many violations of international humanitarian law. Humanitarian intervention (as shown above) had been one of the defining characteristics of the 1990s, but as Annan noted, and as shown in the cases above, the record of the international community in committing itself to saving human lives had been rather mixed. Canada established the International Commission on Intervention and State Sovereignty (ICISS) in September 2000 in response to Annan's speech, with the purpose of conducting a yearlong consultation in order to develop a consensus over the notion of the 'responsibility to protect'. This referred to the problem of intervening in the internal affairs of sovereign states and when it was appropriate to do so. For this reason, humanitarian intervention, when it is carried out (as in the case of Kosovo in 1999) is as controversial as when the international community fails to intervene to protect innocent lives – as in the case of the genocide in Rwanda in 1994 (see Box 27.6). As Annan stated:

If humanitarian intervention is, indeed, an unacceptable assault on sovereignty, how should we respond to a Rwanda, to a Srebrenica – to gross and systematic violations of human rights that offend every precept of our common humanity? But surely no legal principle – not even sovereignty – can ever shield crimes against humanity. Armed intervention must always remain the option of last resort, but in the face of mass murder, it is an option that cannot be relinquished.

(Annan 1999)

For this reason, the role played by Canada in supporting this component of human security has been an important one even though, ultimately, Canada has been as reluctant as other states to wholeheartedly commit itself when the need for intervention has arisen. An apparent trend has been the gradual decrease in enthusiasm amongst Canadian policy makers for human security. Although the Human Security Network remains in existence, the Mine Ban Treaty has been a resounding success, the International Criminal Court has been established, and the notion of 'responsibility to protect' is now firmly part of the debate on human security, there has, since NATO's intervention in Kosovo, been a definitive shift in Canadian attitudes away from the UN's vision. There are a number of reasons for this, one of which is the ambiguity surrounding the concept of human security, which has meant that policy makers have found it difficult to adapt the visions expressed by academics and the UNDP into actual policy. Problems of deciding who is to be protected, from which of the very wide range of threats they should be protected, and what instruments should be utilised are just some of the problems confronting the advocates of the human security agenda. A second issue concerns the impact of 9/11 in that interest in a wider conception of human security has diminished significantly since this horrendous event. Indeed, as Hataley and Nossal have shown in their analysis of Canada's response to the crisis in East Timor in 1999, Canadian enthusiasm was beginning to diminish even before 11 September 2001:

 **Box 27.7 Humanitarian intervention and the sovereignty principle**

There is a general reluctance on the part of states to intervene in what are generally considered to be the internal affairs of other states – even when serious human rights violations are taking place. This is largely due to the principle of sovereignty which is enshrined in the United Nations Charter. As stated in Article 2:

Nothing contained in the present Charter shall authorize the United Nations to intervene in matters which are essentially within the domestic jurisdiction of any state or shall require the Members to submit such matters to settlement under the present Charter; but this principle shall not prejudice the application of enforcement measures under Chapter VII.

The principle of non-interference in affairs that are within the domestic jurisdiction of states is the anchor to state sovereignty within the system of international relations. However, since the end of the Cold War, there have been concrete challenges to the principle of sovereignty, and humanitarian intervention has been one of them. Nevertheless, the contradiction between the two principles has led to a great deal of controversy.

We conclude that there was a significant gap between the rhetoric of the human security agenda and the Canadian government's actual policy in East Timor. While the Canadian government did eventually respond to the outbreak of violence in Timor by contributing troops to the International Force for East Timor (INTERFET), we show that Ottawa's response was slow, cautious, and minimalist. There was neither the willingness nor the capacity to be at the forefront of the efforts to interpose a robust force in East Timor once the Indonesian government had given its consent.

(Hataley and Nossal 2004: 7)

The consequence of this has been a withdrawal of support for the broad visions of human security as expressed by the UNDP and states such as Japan in favour of a narrower view as expressed by Canada.

## Case study: The drugs trade in West Africa and the implications for human security

Government agencies have increased their efforts at monitoring drug traffickers within the borders of Europe and at the same time there has been a rising number of crackdowns on drug suppliers in the Americas. The combined effect of these processes has been to encourage drug barons to alter their strategies, and consequently they have begun to look for alternative routes into their markets (such as Europe). There is growing evidence that international drug smuggling groups have penetrated many West African states such as Senegal, Ghana, Mauritania, Togo, Nigeria, Guinea and Guinea Bissau. The region's attractiveness for drug traffickers is down to a number of factors such as close geographical proximity to Europe, the latter's high demand for narcotics, the long unprotected West African coastlines and porous land borders. Furthermore, the states listed here are well known to be weak and therefore prone to high levels of poverty, under-development, corrupt governance and civil conflict. It is not surprising, therefore, that the states devote few of their resources to tackling drug related crime.

The consequences for human security in these states are immense and most clearly manifest in the increased levels of violent organised crime and political instability. The increasing levels of crime are chasing away foreign investors and this is leading to increasing levels of unemployment with the resulting problems. The United Nations Office on Drugs and Crime (UNODC) recently acknowledged that drug trafficking was transforming Africa as a whole (and particularly West Africa) into a major crime hub with increasing links between drug smuggling, crime and even terrorism becoming apparent. It has further claimed that the collapse of Somalia in East Africa had further facilitated the flow of drugs across the continent, with West African states rapidly becoming a hub for trafficking (*Source*: http://news.bbc.co.uk/1/hi/8402820.stm). UNODC has stressed that this type of transnational crime is one of the major threats to human security and that it is lowering the ability of the states to safeguard the welfare of their citizens. In addition to the factors highlighted above, one of the most destructive effects of the increasing drugs trade in this region has been the accompanying rise in the numbers of small arms, which has been recognised as one of the main causes for political instability across large parts of Africa – including West Africa. This has even contributed to rising levels of human smuggling, money laundering and corruption. The consequence of these activities is to diminish development prospects in West Africa, thereby diminishing levels of human security.

 **Is it necessary for Human Security to incorporate notions of human development? What is the difference between the two?**

## Conclusions

Even though the UNDP report was published over a decade ago and numerous academics have since attempted to provide definitions of human security, there is still no consensus on a meaning for this concept. We must, however, recognise that the field is in its early stages, and as a result, a significant portion of the literature since the report has been concerned with establishing definitions and boundaries. Despite the failure to achieve common ground most analysts appear to identify human security with the welfare and well being of ordinary people, wherever they live. We have tried to clarify some of the confusion surrounding human security by categorising it in broad and narrow terms. Undoubtedly, there remain considerable definitional problems with the broad version in that it seeks to be deliberately protective of humans and their communities in the whole range of threats that are not of their making. In this sense, then, any issue that harms humans can be seen to be a threat, be it an infectious disease, a financial crisis, poor investment in health, a violent conflict or indeed a terrorist attack.

The expansive nature of the UNDP's view of human security has led some academics (including Roland Paris, as mentioned) to argue that the concept is of little value to Security Studies. These academics (and indeed policy makers) argue that its all-inclusive nature renders it unworkable, given that it becomes difficult to prioritise the different aspects of the human security agenda. This in turn means that it is immensely difficult for policy makers to allocate resources and this may be one reason why states such as Canada, though broadly supportive of the notion of human security, have sought to limit their understanding of it to instances where human lives are protected from actual physical violence such as during times of conflict and war. Whatever value we place on human security as a concept, we can be certain that the debate will continue and that it is unlikely to disappear from either the academic world or the world of policy making.

## Resource section

## Questions

1. What are the essential differences between the broad and narrow views of Human Security?

2. Is there any value to basing state policy on principles of Human Security?

3. Why do you think the United Nations has been at the forefront of advocating the concept of Human Security?

4. Should the principle of sovereignty be discarded when states commit human rights atrocities against their own citizens?

5. What are the essential features of Human Security?

## Recommended reading

**Alkire, S. (2003)** *A Conceptual Framework for Human Security*, **Working Paper 2, Centre for Research on Inequality, Human Security and Ethnicity (CRISE, University of Oxford)**
This is a comprehensive attempt to define human security, identify the conceptual pitfalls and offer a framework for incorporating it into state policies.

**Kaldor, M. (2006)** *New and Old Wars: Organised Violence in a Global Era* **(2nd edn, Oxford: Polity)**
This volume is a particularly important one which has fundamentally influenced the way in which we think about contemporary conflict. In distinguishing recent conflicts from those of previous eras, Kaldor has successfully made the all-important link with the phenomenon of globalisation. This second edition is an excellent analysis of the 'new wars' thesis in the context of the post-9/11 era.

**MacFarlane, S.N. and Khong, Yuen Foong (2006)** *Human Security and the UN: A Critical History* **(Bloomington, Indiana University Press)**
This book raises a number of important questions, such as how the human became the focus for contemporary thinking on security and the role that the United Nations in particular has played in furthering that process.

**Paris, R. (2001)** 'Human security: paradigm shift or hot air?' *International Security*, **26 (2): Autumn**
Critics of the concept of human security have argued that the concept is unhelpful given that it is so expansive and ambiguous. In this important article Paris established himself as an ardent critic and presented a detailed analysis of why, in his opinion, significant academic research is required to refine the concept.

**United Nations Development Programme (1994)** *New Dimensions of Security*, **Human Development Report. http://hdr.undp.org/en/reports/global/hdr1994/chapters**
It was this report by the UNDP which started the process of analysing the concept of human security and led to states such as Japan and Canada seriously considering incorporating it into their policy frameworks. This report was also instrumental in establishing the UN at the forefront of human security efforts.

# Chapter 28
# Failed States

- September 11 and state failure
- Why 'failed states' matter
- The rise of non-state groups
- Political violence and failed states in Africa and Europe
- Conclusion

After reading this chapter you will have gained an understanding of the following:

- 11 September 2001 and increased focus on state failure

- What failed states are and why they matter for an understanding of international relations

- The contribution of globalisation to state failure in the developing world

- How non-state groups – characterised by their willingness to use violence to achieve their goals – contribute to and exacerbate state failure

- What the international community has done to try to improve failed states in Africa and Europe

*Source*: Panos Pictures/Chris Stowers

## Introductory box: Somali pirates and state failure

Small groups of Somali men regularly get into their small wooden boats and set off with a key purpose in mind. Many of them will be armed, perhaps with a Kalashnikov rifle and other weapons. They will leave their home villages and enter the waters of the Gulf of Aden. They are hunters aiming to catch their prey in order to get a pay off. In the waters of the Gulf of Aden, they may attack a commercial ship. They will seek to capture the ship and then demand a ransom from the owners for safe return of the vessel and its crew. How should we characterise such men? Often they are referred to by an old name: pirates. It might be said that they are opportunistic pirates; that is, they are not regularly professionals in this line of work. Formerly, they may have been farmers or goat herders. But they see piracy as a more efficient way of gaining money, compared with struggling to grow crops or raise goats in Somalia's hot, dry climate.

The often desperate position of such people is exacerbated by the fact that Somalia – afflicted by war for two decades and without a functioning government for much of that time – is a prime example of a failed state. It is estimated that US$80 million was raised in ransoms by this type of piracy in 2008. In fact, in 2008 and 2009 piracy was booming off the Somali coast. During 2008 alone there were a recorded one hundred and eleven attacks on ships and forty-two were hijacked successfully (International Maritime Bureau's Piracy Reporting Centre; http://www.icc-ccs.org/index.php?option=com_fabrik&view=visualization&controller= visualization.googlemap&Itemid=219). Overall, in the year to 20 October 2009, there were one hundred and seventy-four attacks. At this time, twelve or so vessels were being held hostage off Somalia, with more than two hundred foreign sailors, including a British yachting couple, Paul and Rachel Chandler (Rice 2009).

What to do about the burgeoning problem of piracy, both in Somalia and elsewhere? Many world leaders accept that the problem requires more than just a few warships and airdrops of food aid to a starving, well-armed, and desperate nation. Moreover, to capture the foot soldiers would probably do little or nothing to deal with the bigger problem. That is, if you can pick up the small fry you would simply find that their place would be taken by others: poor and desperate Somalis ready to fill the gap their arrest would create. In fact, the Somalis actually undertaking the piracy are at the lowest level in a criminal network. Above them are a network of corrupt port officials, politicians, and investors from Europe, Asia, and America. Thus, even if a big ransom is received – some ransoms raise US$2 million or more – the money does not stay with the immediate perpetrators who may 'only' each receive US$10,000–20,000. Note, however, that in a country like Somalia, devastated by two decades of war, where the average income is US$500 a year and tens of thousands of people are in serious risk of dying of starvation, $20,000 is a huge sum of money, for which some ordinary Somalis would be prepared to take drastic actions (Baldauf 2009).

In recent years, there is one issue that seems to unite many views: there should be much greater international efforts to try to deal with the widespread problem of failing states. Failing states are a problem for various reasons. For those concerned with development failure, they are places which highlight sometimes desperate suffering, often for millions of people, while for strategists, these states are places where terrorists could step into the vacuum produced by non-functioning governance.

States that lose their ability to act purposefully in international relations are known as failed states. Failed states present a major problem for the international community. This is because of their inability to control their internal environment which inevitably creates serious insecurities for both communities within the country and for neighbouring states and perhaps for others further afield. Often failed states are characterised by military challenges to the state. Since the end of the Cold War over 20 years ago, there have been increasing numbers of failed states. Many but not all are in Sub-Saharan Africa. The top twenty failed states in 2009 featured eleven from Africa, three from the Middle East and the remainder from Asia, with the exception of Haiti, the only state in the Americas to appear in the top twenty. (http://www.foreignpolicy.com/articles/2009/06/22/2009_failed_states_index_interactive_map_and_rankings)

Source: Getty Images/AFP

Failed states like Somalia have lost their ability to control their inner environments, and present a major problem to the international community.

## September 11 and state failure

> One of the principal lessons of the events of September 11 is that failed states matter – for national security as well as for humanitarian reasons. If left to their own devices, such states can become sanctuaries not only for terrorist networks, organized crime and drug traffickers as well as posing grave humanitarian challenges and threats to regional stability.
>
> (Commission on Post-Conflict Reconstruction 2003: 4)

> On traditional grounds of national interest, Afghanistan should be one of the least important places in the world for U.S. foreign policy – and until the Soviet invasion of 1979, and again after the collapse of the Soviet Union in 1991 until September 11, the United States all but ignored it. Yet in October 2001 it became the theater of war.
>
> (Keohane 2002: 35)

The US government responded to the attacks of September 11 2001 ('9/11') with an assault in 2001–2 on both the Taliban regime and al-Qaeda bases in Afghanistan (Hoffman 2006). At that time, the Taliban government controlled much of Afghanistan, a 'failed state' with a shattered social and political structure. Following more than two decades of constant warfare, the country was a nation in ruins, with numerous towns and cities reduced to rubble, and with its social and political structure destroyed by years of unremitting conflict. These circumstances allowed al-Qaeda to set up bases, with the explicit or implicit agreement of the Taliban regime. According to international legal expert, Daniel Thürer (1999: 731), failed states like that of Afghanistan, 'are invariably the product of a collapse of the power structures providing political support for law and order, a process generally triggered and accompanied by anarchic forms of internal violence'. In short, failed states are characterised by total or substantial collapse of both institutions and law and order, the consequence of serious and prolonged conflict. Former UN Secretary-General, Boutros Boutros-Ghali (1995: 9) described the situation as follows:

> A feature of such conflicts is the collapse of state institutions, especially the police and judiciary, with resulting paralysis of governance, a breakdown of law and order, and general banditry and chaos. Not only are the functions of government suspended, but its assets are destroyed or looted and experienced officials are killed or flee the country. This is rarely the case in inter-state wars. It means that international intervention must extend beyond military and humanitarian tasks and must include the promotion of international reconciliation and the re-establishment of effective government.

Currently existing 'failed states' are affected by three geopolitical factors:

- *End of the Cold War.* During the Cold War (late 1940s to late 1980s), the two superpowers, the United States of America and the Soviet Union, often helped to maintain illegitimate or unrepresentative governments in power. The purpose was to preserve them as potential or actual allies. The superpowers usually supplied such governments with military equipment. When the Cold War ended, US and Soviet interest in propping up allies declined almost instantly. This exposed many dictators, such as President Mobutu in Zaire (now Democratic Republic of Congo (DRC)) who lost US support, to popular opposition forces for the first time. In many cases, as in DRC, the dictators were no longer able to rule effectively with the result that state failure became apparent.

- *Heritage of colonial regimes.* Nearly all currently failed states are in the developing world. Typically, colonial administrations were in power for sufficient time to destroy or seriously undermine traditional social structures, as was the case typically in Africa, swiftly colonised by, among others, Britain and France from the 1880s. But in most cases this was at the cost of not replacing them with working constitutional structures and/or effective state identity. The consequence was that, in many cases of state failure, necessary foundations for state strength and stability were not in place when colonialism came to an end.

- *Processes of modernisation.* Modernisation served to encourage people in the colonised areas both to move around – often in search of work – and to engage with educational processes, often for the first time, as a means to acquire better jobs. On the other hand, such modernisation processes were only rarely matched by nation-building processes that led to the placing of a post-colonial state on firm foundations.

From the political and legal point of view, the phenomenon of the 'failed state' is characterised by geographical and territorial, political, and functional factors:

- *Geographical and territorial.* Failed states are inherently associated with both internal and endogenous problems, even though these may incidentally have cross-border impacts. Thus a failed state is characterised by an *implosion* rather than an *explosion* of the structures of power and authority, with a wholesale disintegration and destructuring of the institutions of political authority.

- *Political.* The key political dimension is a collapse of law and order, and the structures that normally guarantee it, rather than the kind of fragmentation of state authority characteristic of civil wars. (In the latter circumstances, 'clearly identified military or paramilitary rebels fight either to strengthen their own position within the State or to break away from it'.)

- *Functional.* This state of affairs is associated with the 'absence of bodies capable, on the one hand, of representing the State at the international level and, on the other, of being influenced by the outside world'.

(Thürer 1999: 731)

Failed states are invariably non-democracies and the absence of political opportunity structures facilitates state breakdown, failures of political and social stability, degeneration into civil war and, in some cases, the establishment of terrorist organisations, whether domestically or internationally focused.

The US focus upon terrorism in Afghanistan was later extended to another 'failed state': the regime of Saddam Hussein in Iraq. Note that this implies another meaning of the term 'failed state': that is, an 'aggressive, arbitrary, tyrannical or totalitarian' state, said to have *failed* according to the norms and standards of current international law (Thürer 1999: 731). Alleged links between Saddam's regime and al-Qaeda was a stated reason for the US-led invasion of Iraq in March 2003 and of Saddam's subsequent arrest in December 2003.

Sometimes, however, an external intervention aiming to rebuild a state's authority and capacity fails, such as the US-led intervention in Afghanistan following the al-Qaeda attacks on the United States on 11 September 2001 ('9/11'). While the phenomenon of failed states was already present in international relations, the al-Qaeda terrorist attacks produced a unique sense of urgency (Ghani and Lockhart 2008). The events of 9/11 made it clear that, in addition to the myriad of other problems posed by state failure – including the desperate suffering experienced by large swathes of the population – they can also function as breeding grounds for growth and development of terrorist groups, posing a significant threat to international security and stability. Connections between the Taliban government in Afghanistan and al-Qaeda are well documented and it is these links which led to the US-led invasion on 7 October 2001, less than four weeks after 9/11. Known as Operation Enduring Freedom, the official reason for the US-led invasion of Afghanistan was the destruction of al-Qaeda as well as the Taliban regime, widely accused of harbouring the organisation and its leaders, including its chief, Osama bin Laden. Beyond Afghanistan, 9/11 also acted as a catalyst for persuading the US (and other states) to look at two other states – Iraq and Somalia – as possible safe havens for terrorist groups. Regarding Iraq, it turned out that there were not groups of international terrorists active in the country. However, this did not prevent the country undergoing a prolonged process of state failure following the US-led invasion of March 2003. Turning to Somalia, since civil war broke out in 1991, the country has not had a government with much legitimacy or capacity. Increasingly, Somalia has been classified as a failed state and several attempts since then to establish transitional national governments have failed. By the end of the 2000s, the outlook for the country was still very poor, with Somalia immersed in a prolonged, yet inconclusive Islamist insurgency (International Crisis Group 2008).

Major international concern over Somalia stemmed not only from the possibility that Islamist groups such as al-Shabaab (an Arabic word meaning 'The Youth') and the Popular Resistance Movement in the Land of the Two Migrations, are seeking to establish control of the country but also because of its long coastline which has helped to give rise to many instances of piracy. As noted above, piracy off of the coast of Somalia increased significantly in 2008 with over sixty ships attacked and held for multi-million dollar ransoms. As the piracy expert, Roger Middleton (2008: 3) states: 'Piracy off the coast of Somalia is growing at an alarming rate and threatens to drastically disrupt international trade. It provides funds that feed the vicious war in Somalia and could potentially become a weapon of international terrorism or a cause of environmental disaster'. Middleton also notes the connection between the growth of Somali based piracy and the lack of effectiveness of the Somali state, and argues that:

The only period during which piracy virtually vanished around Somalia was during the six months of rule by the Islamic Courts Union in the second half of 2006. This indicates that a functioning government in Somalia is capable of controlling piracy. After the removal of the courts piracy re-emerged. With little functioning government, long, isolated, sandy beaches and a population that is both desperate and used to war, Somalia is a perfect environment for piracy to thrive.

(Middleton 2008: 3)

## Why 'failed states' matter

Although failed states differ from each other in many ways, they share a key characteristic: low and diminishing state capacity to put into effect government policies and protect citizens. States are often classified according to how successful they are at fulfilling the basic functions and responsibilities of a sovereign government. In the post-Cold War era, increasing numbers of countries have been classified – whether temporarily or permanently – according to the degree to which they exhibit a systematic breakdown of political authority, that is, where government loses control over significant swathes of territory (Ghani and Lockhart 2008).

Since the late 1980s, nearly all failed states have experienced serious *intra*-state conflicts. Intra-state conflicts are those that occur *within* a state, while *inter*-state conflicts are those that take place *between* countries. For instance, many of the criteria highlighted above can be applied not only to Afghanistan and Somalia but also to numerous other countries, mainly in Africa and Asia. For example, the wars in Somalia and Rwanda during the early 1990s brought about the complete disintegration of central state structures and, even today, Somalia ranks top of the list of states most likely to fail according to the Failed States Index published by the journal *Foreign Policy* (Foreign Policy 2009).[1] Sudan at number two, Chad, at number four, and Democratic Republic of Congo, at number five, all experienced recent or current civil wars. Many failed states have shown themselves to be particularly prone to failure in the face of challenges from armed groups.

Since the Cold War ended over 20 years ago, governments in various African countries, including: Cote d'Ivoire, Democratic Republic of Congo, Liberia, Rwanda, Sierra Leone, Somalia, and Sudan, have, for varying lengths of time, lost control of much of their territory and those states have, as a consequence, experienced brutal and protracted civil wars. Note, however, that it is possible to repair state failure: although Côte d'Ivoire (no. 11), DRC (no. 6), Somalia (no. 1) and Sudan (no. 3) were all in the top 20 failed states in 2009, Liberia, Rwanda, Sierra Leone were not, having improved their level of 'failed-ness' in recent years, with the help of external agencies, including the African Union. (http://www.foreignpolicy.com/articles/2009/06/22/2009_failed_states_index_interactive_map_and_rankings)

This is not to claim that all well known cases of state failure are the result of pronounced intra-state conflict or civil war. A major impact of the 11 September attacks was that they

---

[1] The Failed States Index is updated annually.

focused the international community's attention on lawless regions of the world and although Afghanistan featured prominently at the time because of the presence of al-Qaeda on Afghan soil, the United States and other Western countries such as Britain also started to pay more attention to states such as Pakistan, ranked as the tenth most failed state in the 2009 Failed State Index.

## Case study: Pakistan – creeping state failure without an end in sight

In recent years, the government of the United States has paid increasing attention to Pakistan for the following reasons:

1. Pakistan's acquisition of nuclear weapons in the late 1990s, increasing tensions with its regional neighbour and rival, India;
2. The Pakistan government's apparent inability to govern authoritatively the tribal regions bordering Afghanistan, a place where the renegade al-Qaeda leader, Osama bin Laden is thought to be holed up;
3. Increasing Islamist militancy, characterised by growing violence and confrontation with the governments, and a growing Islamist threat to the state;
4. Killings of prominent politicians (including in December 2007, the prime minister Benazir Bhutto);
5. Rising ethnic tensions;
6. Growing political instability;
7. Large numbers of internally displaced civilians; and
8. A devastating earthquake in October 2005.

A US Central Intelligence Agency report, entitled *Mapping the Global Future* (declassified in December 2004), painted a grim picture of the possibility of nuclear weapons falling into the hands of militant Islamists, and stated:

> With advances in the design of simplified nuclear weapons, terrorists will continue to seek to acquire fissile material in order to construct a nuclear weapon. Concurrently, they can be expected to continue attempting to purchase or steal a weapon, particularly in Russia or Pakistan. Given the possibility that terrorists could acquire nuclear weapons, the use of such weapons by extremists before 2020 cannot be ruled out.
>
> (National Intelligence Council 2004: 95)

Indeed, the Islamist threat to the state has recently increased significantly, as Afghanistan's still extant Taliban consolidated their hold on regions of Pakistan's North West Frontier Province (NWFP). By April 2009, this had brought the Taliban forces to within 100 kilometres of the national capital, Islamabad. The Taliban advance prompted the United States government to accuse Pakistan of capitulating to the Taliban. It also led Hillary Clinton (US Secretary of State) to claim that the Taliban were now in a position to pose an 'existential threat' to Pakistan and by extension a 'mortal threat' to the world, given the possibility that its nuclear weapons could fall into the hands of the Islamist militants. Later in 2009, the Pakistan army launched a campaign against the Taliban in the NWFP, but progress was slow and uncertain and by the end of the year, the Taliban was not definitively defeated.

In Pakistan, over time, widespread violations of economic and social rights have provided a fertile ground for strengthening various militant groups. While the continuing fight against terrorism is both legitimate and necessary in Pakistan, the sometimes illegal practices deployed frequently have led to violent responses and, more generally, have prevented the strengthening of democratic practices and the rule of law. The situation is aggravated by: anti-terrorist laws and courts; by practices systematised by the 'War on Terror', particularly since September 11, 2001; and forced disappearances, torture and inhuman and degrading treatment. According to an international human rights organisation, the International Federation for Human Rights, illegal detention and ill-treatment in prison in Pakistan are common, perpetrated by state personnel, including army, police, intelligence services, and prison officers (http://www.fidh.org/A-long-march-for-democracy-and-the).

It is sometimes asserted that Pakistan's problems are caused mainly by long periods of military rule. However, this is at best only a partial explanation for growing state failure. The most recent presidential elections, held in September 2008, saw the return to power of the Pakistan People's Party, led by Benazir Bhutto's widower, Asif Ali Zardari, who won the presidential poll in a landslide. Since then, however, there have been very few signs of the ability of the government to reverse the process of state failure in Pakistan.

 **To what extent is Pakistan a failed state? On what basis can we make such a judgement?**

Finally, we can note that, in each case, state failure in Afghanistan, Somalia and Pakistan is linked to the impact of **globalisation**. The impact of globalisation is apparent in certain characteristics of each of these countries, particularly in the context of contributing to major social and cultural changes. As has been highlighted elsewhere in this book, globalisation is also contributing to high levels of interdependence between states, a trend which is generally viewed as being not only inevitable but also welcome. However, as also highlighted, the effects of globalisation have not been universally beneficial. For example, many critics contend that it is a significant contributor to widespread poverty throughout much of the developing world. Indeed, when this is examined in the context of states prone to 'failed-ness' and civil conflict, the impact can be highly destabilising, contributing significantly to increased insecurity and instability. Two features in particular are worth mentioning. First, globalisation has helped to diminish the ability of vulnerable states to retain control of their territory and their sovereign right to a monopoly of legitimate military force. This is because, as the state weakens in the face of conflicts which increasingly spill over from neighbouring countries, insurgency, criminal gangs, ethnic and/or religious groups, 'warlords', mercenaries and other forms of private security organisations, regular armies, human rights groups and the international community in general begin to compete with each other in the space left by the deteriorating state.

## The rise of non-state groups

However, it would not be correct to understand state failures as only due to globalisation. We also need to look at the issue of 'state failure' in order to understand contemporary international relations, including the nature of many post-Cold War conflicts. The way in which the present international system is structured can be explained in the context of the **Peace of Westphalia** (1648), which brought to an end the Thirty Years War, fought for the most part in what is today Germany. The Peace of Westphalia, signed in 1648, led to the emergence and development of the political entities that today we call sovereign states: they were **sovereign** – that is, autonomous or independent – in the sense that they had exclusive right of control over their territory and the population residing within that territory. Indeed, not only did all these states have a genuine right and ability to exercise control over their territory through the enactment of laws and police powers, but also this right was recognised by every other state within the system.

In Chapter 27 we refer to Canada's establishment of the International Commission on Intervention and State Sovereignty (ICISS) in 2001 in response to Kofi Annan's call for an investigation into how to protect civilian lives during times of conflict. The year-long consultation by this Commission concluded that the increase in armed conflicts *within* states was the most prominent feature of organised violence in the post-Cold War period. Nothing has changed since then which might have led the ICISS to change their view. One of the central concerns for the Commission was how to deal with the issue of intervening in what were, largely, the internal affairs of states. The overriding factor here was that the *sovereignty* of states, which had for centuries been regarded as unconditional and absolute (and had been reaffirmed by the United Nations (UN) Charter in 1945) prohibited outside interference in their internal affairs. However, the UN Charter also specified that states had a responsibility to uphold and respect the human rights of their citizens, but, as events since the establishment of the UN have shown, these two principles have not coexisted comfortably. There have been many instances where states have harmed their own citizens – often in brutal and barbaric ways (see Chapter 29).

Religious and/or ethnic differences between protagonists have played a significant role in many recent intra-state conflicts. Chapter 29 refers to instances where ethnic and religious differences have provided a powerful incentive for war. Other examples include increasing tensions between Bulgarians and Turks in Bulgaria, violent clashes between Hungarians and Romanians in Transylvania (Romania) and, in the case of Czechoslovakia, tensions between Czechs and Slovaks led to the disintegration of the state into Czech and Slovak components in 1992. In all these cases ethnic identity has played a major role in the search for security and in some instances that search has become brutal conflict. Elsewhere there have been violent clashes, such as in the former Soviet Union between ethnic Romanians and Russians, Armenians and Azerbaijanis, Meskhets and Uzbeks, and Ossetians and Georgians (Sandole 1992). Note, however, that none of these examples actually led to state failure.

*Source: Getty Images*

**Failed states aren't an 'African problem', and attempts to tackle European cases have proved to be equally problematic.**

The key to a state's ability to control its realm is an effective monopoly of legitimate violence which can be employed as and when the need arises. The period since the end of the Cold War, however, has seen the emergence of many instances where states have lost control over their own territories as well as their populations – and are therefore categorised as having failed in their prime responsibilities to remain independent, stable and protectors of their populations. In addition to this, the government of a failed state is not able to enforce its laws on its citizens, nor is it able to prevent the use of its territory by groups that seek to perpetrate violence for political or commercial purposes. In failed states, legitimate institutions collapse, the law ceases to function and corruption becomes rife. The result is that it is 'every person for themselves' and those with sufficient power and capacity seek to advance their interests by the use of any means deemed necessary. If there is no legitimate central control of government, then a varying number of alternative sources of power and authority emerge to fill the gap once occupied by the state. The new power holders include: militias, guerrilla groups, warlords, mercenaries, and foreign military advisors. In addition, since the state becomes incapable of fulfilling (m)any of its responsibilities – including, citizens' protection and provision of essential goods and services – many people in order to survive turn to crime in a desperate attempt to survive. The links between the remnants of the state and the population become further severed as citizens begin to look for other groups with which to identify, and in this context religious, ethnic and linguistic labels can acquire much greater importance than they used to have. In addition, as the state loses the legitimate ability to control the means of violence, then violence itself becomes privatised with different groups competing against each other for control of territory and resources. The ensuing conflict inevitably causes large numbers of civilian casualties, displacements, emigration and mass refugee movements.

One sad but important observation is that many of the states that are failing – in Africa for example – are actually resource rich, and it is these resources which are further fuelling the conflicts there. Criminal networks, local elites, warlords and even international actors (both legal and illegal) become involved, with some exploiting the environment for their own ends. From the diamond conflicts in the Congo, Angola, Liberia and Sierra Leone to Somali pirates operating in the Indian Ocean, criminal networks become increasingly attracted to regions dominated by failed states. International attention has also been focused on other failed states, including Sudan and former Yugoslavia, countries that are said to 'provide profit and sanctuary to nihilist outlaws' (Mallaby 2002: 2). In the past, when such power vacuums emerged to threaten powerful states' interests, they often had a simple solution: imperialism. But ever since the Second World War, this option has not been viable – even for the sole remaining superpower, the United States of America. Now, in the context of the 'War on Terror', the established principle of 'anti-imperialist restraint is becoming harder to sustain . . . as the disorder in poor countries grows more threatening' (Mallaby 2002: 3). What this suggests is that we are witnessing a possible return to a form of what might be called 'benign imperialism', with powerful countries like the United States sometimes willing to intervene in failed states directly – such as Somalia in the 1990s and Afghanistan and Iraq in the early 2000s – in order to deal with various threats including terrorism and access to resources, such as oil.

In such countries, civil wars are both common and long lasting. Focusing on fifty-two conflicts since 1960, a 2003 World Bank study found that civil wars that started after 1980 on average lasted three times longer than those that had begun in the preceding two decades. The study also noted that when civil wars last longer, the number of countries involved in them grows. In addition, the study suggested that the trend toward violent disorder may prove self-sustaining, because war breeds conditions to make new conflicts more likely. The problem is that when states decline into widespread violence, people understandably focus on how to survive in the prevailing conditions, while longer term issues of state-building are neglected. Under such circumstances, there are clear, and unwelcome, economic results: savings, investment, and wealth creation all decline, while conditions of instability encourage government officials to benefit from their positions by stealing state assets rather than designing policies that might build long-term prosperity. In short, during civil wars, a cycle of poverty, instability, and violence emerges (Mallaby 2002: 2–3). This has been apparent in various countries in recent years, including Somalia and Afghanistan.

Apart from civil wars, other reasons noted for growing violence and social disorder include the consequences of rapid population growth. By 2025, the global population is likely to increase from about six billion to eight billion people. The great majority of these extra people will be born in poor countries, some of which are Muslim societies with powerful currents of anti-Western extremism, including Afghanistan, Algeria, Iraq, and Pakistan. Others will be born in Sub-Saharan Africa, a region with especial demographic challenges, where high birth rates and the AIDS pandemic together threaten some countries with both social disintegration and governmental collapse. These conditions are especially conducive to the growth, organisation and support of both criminal and terrorist groups, contributing to state failure.

In some cases, terrorists will ally themselves with illegal drug producers and suppliers. Much of the global supply of illegal drugs comes from a small number of countries, including Afghanistan and Colombia. In addition, conflict is also conducive to other forms of criminal activity. For example, Sierra Leone's black-market diamonds are said to have benefited various criminals and terrorists, including former President Charles Taylor of Liberia and a Lebanon-based Islamist organisation, Hezbollah. Finally, failed states also pose a challenge to more orderly ones because they increase immigration pressures. Such pressures help to create and sustain the lucrative traffic in illegal workers, a business that can also provide profit for criminals or terrorists. In summary, there is much evidence to sustain the claim that together failed and failing states pose significant threats to regional and international order.

## Political violence and failed states in Africa and Europe

One of the long-established principles of international relations is that governments have sole right and responsibility to deal with their internal political concerns. This has changed in recent years as a consequence of the growing numbers of failed states. As a result, the long-established distinction in international relations between *self-defence* and *humanitarian* intervention is now much harder to maintain. (See Chapters 24–27 for a focus on security issues in international relations.) External military actions in failed states, or pre-emptive attempts to save states from failing, is often judged by both Western countries and 'non-failed' neighbouring states to be sensible and desirable in terms both of self-defence and demands of humanitarianism. Humanitarian concerns are self-evident in situations of civil war or mass killings of civilians, for example, in the 1990s in both Rwanda and Burundi, although in neither case did external interventions actually occur. The likelihood of political violence spilling over into neighbouring countries and regions, as well as the fact that failed states are prime breeding grounds for political extremism and terrorism, may encourage external actions to seek to resolve matters. As the International Relations scholar, Robert Keohane (2002: 39–40) notes, following 9/11 and the subsequent War on Terror, and especially in relation to American interventions in Afghanistan and Iraq, 'sound arguments from self-interest are more persuasive than arguments from responsibility or altruism'.

Next we examine several cases of recent external intervention in failed states in both Africa and Europe. Each was the result of the consequences of civil wars and associated attempts to rebuild state capacities. This reflects the view that if left to their own devices failed states are not conducive to regional stability and peace. As Mozambique's president Joaquim Chissano said, in the context of his efforts to build peace in his own country following a long civil war, 'conflicts, particularly violent conflicts between and within states in other parts of Africa, and in the world in general, are also a danger to our peace and tranquillity. Helping other peoples keep and maintain peace is also a way of defending our own peace' (Harsch 2003: 16).

## African attempts to try to deal with state failures

Following the end of the Cold War over two decades ago, many African countries have been beset by serious political violence, with a proliferation of armed conflicts. This development was facilitated by the fact that at that time, the late 1980s, most African countries had non-democratic governments, and military or unelected one-party regimes were common. Such regimes' stability and 'stickability' – that is, ability to stay in power – was undercut by the end of the Cold War, and associated growth of both pro-democracy movements and outbreaks of often serious ethnic, religious and other social tensions. During the 1990s and 2000s, many African countries – including Somalia, Rwanda, Liberia, Sierra Leone, Côte d'Ivoire, Burundi, Sudan and the Democratic Republic of Congo – witnessed the deaths of hundreds of thousands of people, most of whom were civilian non-combatants. Millions more 'succumbed to war-related epidemics and starvation' (Harsch 2003).

It is suggested that traditional peacekeeping missions – normally created to monitor peace agreements between established armies holding separate territories – are not well suited to dealing with Africa's current conflicts. This is because many of the latter are civil wars or insurgencies with multiple armed factions and grievances rooted in poverty and inequality which are exceptionally hard to deal with by external forces who are often not very knowledgeable about the affected countries' circumstances. Moreover, even when peace accords are successfully negotiated, it is not always the case that all political and military leaders seem able or willing to control their followers. In some countries, such as Sierra Leone and Liberia, local fighters who profited from the chaos of war saw more advantage for a time in continuing to fight rather than laying down their arms immediately (Harsch 2003: 14). In Liberia, claims were made that some Liberians had links with members of Osama bin Laden's al-Qaeda organisation in order to operate an illegal diamond trade. A major American newspaper, *The Washington Post*, published in 2003 an article which focused on alleged al-Qaeda activities in both Liberia and Burkina Faso, presenting evidence that the governments of both countries had hosted two senior al-Qaeda operatives who were said to have bought diamonds worth US$20 million (Farah 2003).

Signs are now emerging that political violence in African countries is being tackled with a renewed determination, to the extent that some regional countries have begun to commit their own resources to conflict prevention, management and resolution. The new sense of resolution coincided with the transformation from the Organisation of African Unity – established in 1963 – into the African Union (AU) in 2002, an intergovernmental organisation expressly modelled on the European Union (EU) (see Chapter 15). In recent years, under the auspices of the AU, regional conflict resolution and security in Africa have taken a higher priority than they used to do. Part of the reason is that unlike the charter of the OAU, the AU's explicitly affords the organisation authority to 'intervene in cases of war crimes, genocide and crimes against humanity' (www.africa-union.org/). Such a situation is characteristic of many contemporary failed states. Among the AU's important institutions in this regard is the fifteen-member Peace and Security Council, which South Africa's

---

 **Box 28.1  State failures contrasted – Sierra Leone and Botswana**

A 2003 World Bank report provided evidence of contrasting examples of what has occurred in one war-torn African country – Sierra Leone – and another – Botswana – that has, in contrast, enjoyed long-term political stability and economic growth. Forty years ago, in the early 1970s, both countries had enjoyed similar per-capita incomes, large diamond resources and potential. Subsequently, Botswana used these resources to become one of the fastest growing economies in the world. Eventually, it became a middle-income country in global terms. Diamond resources in Sierra Leone led to a completely different outcome: collapse into civil war, environmental degradation and for most people, utter poverty. This was primarily because Sierra Leone, unlike Botswana, is very divided ethnically and religiously, making accords harder to reach and maintain. Now, Sierra Leone is at the bottom of the table of national human development and, despite recent improvements, is a state still characterised by significant state failure. In terms of per-capita income, the gap between Botswana and Sierra Leone is now 20 to 1. That is, on average people in Botswana are now twenty times more wealthy than those in Sierra Leone, whereas forty years ago they enjoyed, on average, the same incomes. These examples dramatically demonstrate how much is at stake. For the international community, the challenge consists of shifting the balance to create more examples like Botswana than Sierra Leone.

former president, Thabo Mbeki, identified as 'a collective security and early-warning arrangement to facilitate timely and efficient responses to conflicts and crisis situations in Africa'. In addition, the AU has rolled out a comprehensive new development strategy, the New Partnership for Africa's Development (NEPAD), which includes an 'African Peer Review Mechanism'. Its purpose is to promote good governance within African countries, seen as one of the best ways to prevent domestic political conflicts from leading to coups, insurgency, civil war and failed states (www.nepad.org/). Overall, however, the AU's ability to deal with key issues of security and stability in Africa has been disappointing, leading some to question the viability and capacity of the organisation at a time of increasing problems for the region.

In sum, African efforts to deal with regional failed states aim to deal with endemic regional instability, insecurity and conflicts. In recent times, there has also been helpful intervention by non-African forces, for example, the involvement of British troops was instrumental in ending the civil war in Sierra Leone in 2003. This might be described as a form of pragmatic ad hoc multilateralism, involving partnerships and joint action between various external countries, as well as the United Nations and various African peacekeepers. Each of these actors plays different but complementary roles in trying to resolve conflict in Africa.

## European attempts to deal with civil war and state failure in the Balkans

Failed states are not confined to Africa or other regions of the developing world. Until recently, they were also found in a region on Europe's borders: the Balkans. Many countries in the Balkans were characterised by state failure in the 1990s, the result of the Yugoslav Wars, three separate conflicts which came about following the messy dissolution of the Federal Republic of Yugoslavia in the early 1990s.

The rapid decline in the ability of Yugoslavia to rule itself and the subsequent series of conflicts not only led to state failure but also to external intervention from external forces, including the European Union (EU). The EU's Balkan Stability Pact was an important vehicle for reconstruction that sought to ask states in the Balkans to replace allegiance to a traditional conception of individual sovereignty and to replace it with regional economic, political, and social integration with neighbours. External attempts to rebuild new states in place of the failed Yugoslav state prompted two important questions:

- Which approach is the best one to adopt in aiding post-conflict societies?
- What are the tradeoffs of this approach in terms of securing domestic support and durable reforms?

The key aim of the EU was to establish a liberal peace among the Serbs, Croats and Bosnians, countries in the Balkans, and in particular to deal with three key problems: resolve conflicts, reconstruct societies, and establish functioning market economies. Each was seen to be an important goal in the strategy to avoid future regional wars and increase

## Box 28.2 The Yugoslav Wars of the 1990s

The Yugoslav Wars were a series of violent conflicts which took place within the borders of the former Socialist Federal Republic of Yugoslavia during 1991–1995. The collectively described Yugoslav Wars actually comprised three separate but related wars:

1. War in Slovenia (1991)
2. Croatian War of Independence (1991–1995) and
3. War in Bosnia (1992–1995).

Underlying each of these conflicts were serious tensions that had been growing in Yugoslavia since the early 1980s. In 1990, the potential for war became clear. Already afflicted by serious economic hardship at this time, Yugoslavia was also confronted by rising nationalism among its various ethnic/religious groups. By this time, Yugoslavia had been ruled for over three decades by a series of Communist governments. At the last Communist Party Conference in January 1990, the Serbian-dominated congress voted down Slovenian proposals for an end to the Communist one-party system and for market-orientated economic reforms. The Slovenian and Croatian delegations would not accept this decision and as a result voted with their feet: to leave the congress and eventually to signify the collapse of the Yugoslav Communist Party.

From this time, relationships between Yugoslav's different ethnic/religious groups generally deteriorated. Although the exact causes of the resulting wars were complex, overall they were characterised

interlinked ethnic and religious conflicts involving most of the peoples of Yugoslavia. They primarily involved, on the one hand, Serbs and, on the others, Croats and Bosniaks. But to complicate matters, fighting also took place between Bosniaks and Croats in Bosnia; and there were also separate bouts of violence involving rival Bosniak factions in Bosnia.

Eventually, the wars ended in various stages and in differing ways. What they had in common was the following: 1. international recognition of new sovereign territories, and 2. massive economic disruption to the successor states, which in some cases – for example, Serbia and Bosnia – led to significant state failures (http://www.foreignpolicy.com/articles/2009/06/22/2009_failed_states_index_interactive_map_and_rankings).

The conflicts were widely referred to as 'Europe's deadliest conflicts' since the Second World War. This was partly because of the severity and intensity of the actual fighting and partly because of mass 'ethnic cleansings', which became infamous for the war crimes they were alleged to involve. Certainly, they were the first conflicts since the Second World War formally to be judged as genocidal in character by the international community. Many key individual participants – such as, the former Bosnian Serb leader, Radovan Karadzik – were subsequently charged with war crimes. The International Criminal Tribunal for the Former Yugoslavia was established by the United Nations to prosecute these alleged crimes.

state capacity or, put another way, reduce the likelihood of state failure. The ultimate goal of liberal peace is prosperous stability (Johnson 2005). Moves towards regional integration in the Balkans, as in Western Europe 60 years ago following the Second World War, were widely believed to be the most important way, first, to rebuild failed states in the Balkans and, second, to set them on the road of peace and prosperity. In short, the aim was to (re)build 'the social, political, legal, economic, and security' foundations, in order to provide the necessary room for those in the region to rebuild on the ground (Johnson 2005).

Having begun in 1999, the Balkan Stability Pact was wound up in late 2007, followed by the Regional Cooperation Council, a new body of regional cooperation which came into operation in 2008. Did the Balkan Stability Pact lead to reductions in state failure in the Balkans? To answer this question we need to start by focusing on one of the chief criticisms of EU efforts: a tendency to undermine local authority by retaining significant control over the reform process. The tension that to some extent still exists between the international community and regional states concerning which entity exercises authority over the territory illustrates this struggle. An international relations academic, Rebecca Johnson (2005: 177) points to four significant results of both UN and EU involvement in the area:

- Balkan Stability Pact initiatives attempt to de-emphasise traditional conceptions of sovereignty;
- UN administrative control in both Bosnia and Kosovo serves to prevent local control of the state's authority;
- Such external initiatives serve to wrest control from local decision-makers, while removing local leaders' motivation to reform;
- 'Reform-minded local leaders are forced to try to change their systems of governance knowing they have no discretion and little authority to carry out changes'.

In addition, EU and associated UN attempts to rebuild peace and stability in the Balkans did not manage to address successfully what many see as a major challenge to the task of rebuilding states: al-Qaeda linked terrorism, especially in Bosnia.

Former US president George W. Bush proclaimed that 'the War on Terror' should be 'seamless', that is, Washington expected all countries to assist in fighting the scourge of international terrorism. In return, President Bush promised that the United States would both 'support and reward governments' that, in his words, 'make the right choices'. Regarding two states in the Balkans, Kosovo and the former Yugoslav Republic of Macedonia, President Bush's demand for a 'seamless approach' to deal with the scourge of terrorism appeared in the mid-2000s to be at risk of unraveling. Macedonian government officials claimed that they were not receiving resources that they needed to combat terrorism. The Macedonian government claimed that the Bush administration actually showed little interest in pursuing links they claimed to have uncovered between al-Qaeda and groups allied with Albanian separatists. The latter continued to foment trouble in northern Macedonia, characterised by frequent incursions from neighbouring Kosovo. Macedonian intelligence was in regular contact with both the CIA and the FBI; both organisations were supplied with details of the al-Qaeda relationship with militant Albanian nationalist groups. This was the case both in neighbouring Kosovo, under UN protection, as well as in Macedonia, spared a civil war in 2002–3 following NATO brokering a peace agreement between the majority Macedonians and minority ethnic Albanians. Macedonian officials provided US aides with a 79-page report on al-Qaeda activity in the area. The report, which was compiled by Macedonia's Ministry of the Interior, lists the names of al-Qaeda-linked fighters and outlines the roles of two units, one numbering one hundred and twenty and the other two hundred and fifty, in northern Macedonia (Kurop 2001).

Intertwined Albanian groups in the region, most of them closely aligned with organised-crime syndicates, have as their objective the carving out of what they call 'Greater Albania'. This is envisaged to be an area of some 90,000 square kilometres (36,000 square miles), including Kosovo, Greece, Macedonia, Bosnia, Serbia and Montenegro. Such groups are said to have been disguised under the cover of dozens of 'humanitarian' agencies spread throughout Bosnia, Kosovo and Albania. Funding came from now-defunct banks, including the Albanian-Arab Islamic Bank and from Osama bin Laden's so-called 'Advisory and Reformation Committee', one of his largest Islamist front agencies, first established in London in 1994 (Kurop 2001). According to Kurop (2001) this led to the rise of a 'narco-jihad culture', a reference to the swift increase in heroin trafficking through Kosovo, now said to be the most important Balkan route between South East Asia and Europe after Turkey. It is also said to have funded terrorist activity directly associated with both al-Qaeda and the Iranian Revolutionary Guard. 'Opium poppies, which barely existed in the Balkans before 1995, have become the No. 1 drug cultivated in the Balkans after marijuana. Operatives of two al-Qaeda-sponsored Islamist cells who were arrested in Bosnia on Oct. 23 [2001] were linked to the heroin trade, underscoring the narco-jihad culture of today's post-war Balkans.' (Kurop 2001.)

In sum, as Bodansky (2001) contends, by the early 2000s the Balkans had become the most prominent international area for recruiting and training recruits for Osama bin Laden's al-Qaeda network. Feeding off the region's impoverishment and taking root in the unsettled diplomatic aftermath of the Bosnia and Kosovo conflicts, al-Qaeda, along with Iranian Revolutionary Guard-sponsored terrorists, appeared to be organising and training in Western Europe's backyard.

Bodansky (2001) also claims that since the early 1990s, senior leaders of al-Qaeda have regularly visited the Balkans, including bin Laden himself on three occasions between 1994 and 1996. Bin Laden's second in command, Ayman Al-Zawahiri, the Egyptian surgeon-turned-terrorist leader, was in charge of terrorist training camps, with weapons of mass destruction factories and money-laundering and drug-trading networks throughout many Balkan countries, including Albania, Bosnia, Bulgaria, Kosovo, Macedonia, and Turkey. From further afield, including the Russian republic of Chechnya, many recruits came to join al-Qaeda. In November 2003, a CIA informant disclosed that an Islamist network in Bosnia was sending al-Qaeda fighters to Iraq. In mid-2007, the Muslim leader of Bosnia's tripartite presidency, Haris Silajdzic, was under investigation for international arms smuggling. Police were also said to be investigating former Bosnian Deputy Defence Minister Hasan Cengic, Elfatih Hassanein and a Turkish businessman Nedim Suljak. Hassanein was the head of the Third World Relief Agency (TWRA) and Cengic was closely tied to TWRA. During the Bosnian war in the early 1990s, TWRA was a radical militant charity front providing cover for a massive illegal arms pipeline into Bosnia. Silajdzic was Bosnian foreign minister during the war. Bosnian state prosecutors confirmed that a weapons smuggling investigation into international illegal weapons smuggling had opened but refused to say who was being targeted (Agence France Press, 5 May 2007). However, TWRA has remained active and recent reports suggest that it was still connected to radical militants. In late 2006, it was announced that Hassanein was opening a new charity in Bosnia (http://www.historycommons.org/timeline.jsp?complete_911_timeline_al_qaeda_by_region=balkans&timeline=complete_911_timeline&startpos=100).

## Conclusion

We saw that since September 11 2001 there has been widespread international focus on the phenomenon of failed states because of their link, in many cases, to international terrorist activities. We have also seen that many failed states also feature a high incidence of civil conflicts, meaning that the experience of prolonged conflict within their borders has contributed significantly to their failure. The disappearance of normal state structures that provided citizens with public goods such as health, education and security meant that a variety of actors began to compete with one another in order to fill the lethal vacuum created by the failing state. This was particularly true for failed states, where, in many cases, the disintegration of the state has been accompanied by the criminalisation of society and the privatisation of violence. A multiple range of fighting units were seen to materialise as the state's monopoly on legitimate forms of violence eroded, leading to the emergence of alternative sources of power as groups began to compete with one another – often violently – for the state's resources. Finally, we saw recent attempts in both Africa and the Balkans to deal with state failure. In both cases, there was at least partial success, especially in the latter. On the other hand, it has been shown that repairing states does not necessarily imply a decriminalisation of activities or an elimination of terrorist networks.

## Resource section

## Questions

1. Why do 'failed states' matter for international relations?

2. What can the international community do to prevent state failures?

3. Identify *two* 'failed states', and explain what they have in common and how they are different.

## Recommended reading

Ghani, A. and Lockhart, C. (2008) *Fixing Failed States: A Framework for Rebuilding a Fractured World* (New York: Oxford University Press)
This book addresses one of the central issues of our times: the proliferation of failed states across the world and our apparent inability to stabilise them. According to the authors, there are between forty and sixty failed states, home to around one billion people. The world's worst problems – terrorism, drug and human trafficking, absolute poverty, ethnic conflict, disease, genocide – originate in such states, and the international community has devoted billions upon billions of dollars to solving the problem. Yet by and large, the effort has failed. The authors explain the failure stems in part from an outmoded vision of the state system based on the framers of the post-Second World War order's vision: relatively independent, unified states that control markets and rely on authoritarianism when necessary.

**Hoffman, S. (2006)** *Chaos and Violence: What Globalisation, Failed States, and Terrorism Mean for U.S. Foreign Policy* **(New York: Rowman and Littlefield)**
Hoffmann reflects in this book on the 'proper' place of the United States in a world it has defined almost exclusively by 9/11, the war on terrorism, and the invasion of Iraq. Hoffmann offers an analysis that is uniquely informed by his place as a public intellectual with one foot in Europe, the other in America. He considers the ethics of intervention, the morality of human rights, how to repair the US' relationship with Europe, and the pitfalls of American unilateralism.

## Useful websites

The Failed States Index 2009, http://www.foreignpolicy.com/articles/2009/06/22/the_2009_failed_states_index

# Chapter 29
# New Wars and the Privatisation of Conflict

Establishing connections

The impact of globalisation and the role of Private Military and Security Companies

Security and the private sector

Conclusions

After reading this chapter you will be able to:

- Understand the 'new wars' phenomenon

- Reflect on the connections between 'failed states' and new wars

- Consider the impact of globalisation

- Analyse the impact of the actors involved in the 'new wars' and in particular the phenomenon of the privatisation of conflict and the role played by private security organisations – namely Private Military and Security Companies (PMCs and PSCs)

- Reflect on how these private organisations could be regulated and ultimately used by the international community to stabilise conflict zones

*Source*: Panos Pictures/Chris Stowers

## Introductory box: Civil Wars in Liberia, 1989–1996

The two civil wars in Liberia since the end of the Cold War have been brutal.
The first, between 1989 and 1996, resulted in over 200,000 deaths, with a further
one million people displaced into refugee camps. Samuel Kanyon Doe (a soldier
in the Liberian army) seized power in Liberia in 1980 after successfully overthrowing
the Americo-Liberians (descendents of slaves freed in America and dispatched back
to West Africa) – but despite the hope placed in him, his rule became brutal and
immediately tainted with the blood of his opponents. In 1989, Charles Taylor
(previously a senior member of Doe's government but sacked for corruption in 1983)
used Libyan funds to form the National Patriotic Front of Liberia (NPFL) and launch
an uprising from Côte d'Ivoire. Doe was overthrown and subsequently tortured to
death by Prince Yormie Johnson – a senior commander in Taylor's NPFL and leader
of the Gio tribe. The NPFL later splintered, with Johnson creating the Independent
National Patriotic Front of Liberia (INPFL), and this spilt led to further
fragmentation of Liberia and the emergence of conflict between a number of
different factions, primarily split along ethnic lines. The three-way conflict engulfed
Johnson's Gio tribe, Taylor's larger Mano tribe and Doe's forces, which consisted
mainly of Mandingo and Krahn tribespeople. However, an agreement between
Taylor, Johnson and a number of other relatively powerless warlords resulted in an
uneasy peace and the election of Taylor as President in 1996. Opposition to Taylor
remained, however, in the form of a rebel group, known as the Liberians United for
Reconciliation and Democracy (LURD), supported by Liberia's neighbour Guinea,
and a second war started in the north of the country in 1999. In 2003, the Movement
for Democracy in Liberia (MODEL) emerged in the south and soon Taylor had lost
control of more than two-thirds of Liberia. Taylor stepped down in August 2003 and
subsequently went into exile in Nigeria. He was arrested in March 2006 and put on
trail for war crimes in the Hague in June 2007.

Taylor, a prominent player in Liberia's civil wars, exacerbated his country's
problems by using funds from the sale of Liberia's diamonds to encourage uprisings
and conflicts in the neighbouring states of Côte d'Ivoire, Guinea and Sierra Leone.
In recognition of the premise that the sale of Liberia's diamonds was contributing
to the purchase of arms and fuelling conflicts in the region, the United Nations
imposed sanctions on the industry in 2001 and these were lifted only recently in
April 2007.

## Establishing connections

Since the end of the Cold War, Private Military (PMCs) and Security Companies (PSCs) have played an increasingly visible role in troubled regions of the world. They operate in a wide variety of environments ranging from weak states to states that are on the verge of collapse as well as ones that are in the midst of conflict. Such companies have been used extensively by states such as the US during recent conflicts – such as those in Afghanistan and Iraq. The terrorist attacks on September 11 2001 ushered in an era of global instability and, as a consequence, the demand for PMCs and PSCs has increased significantly. In order to understand the increasing privatisation of conflict, we need to establish a connection between three important features:

1. The 'new wars thesis';
2. Failed states; and
3. The nature of the actors involved in these contemporary conflicts including Private Military and Security Companies.

A prevailing view is that many of the wars in the post-Cold War era share certain characteristics. Most notable among the proponents of the 'new wars' thesis is Mary Kaldor (an academic in International Relations) who has analysed in detail some of the key features. One aspect is the terrible impact that these wars are having, particularly on civilians, not only because of the large number of deaths among non-combatants, but also because of the brutal manner in which many of them are killed, with rape, torture and murder being widely practised (see the Introductory box at the start of the chapter). A second feature is that the combatants are predominantly groups *within* states as opposed to the national armies of states themselves. To use the correct vocabulary, wars in the post-Cold War era have been largely *intra-state* rather than *inter-state*. In addition to this, analysts and governments often group states according to how successful they are at fulfilling the basic functions and responsibilities of a sovereign government. Many of the conflicts in the post-Cold War era have been characterised by a breakdown of political authority in a number of states and the loss of government control over territory. These states are widely referred to as 'failed states' and we have devoted an entire chapter (Chapter 28) to analysing their impact. For our purposes, one important observation is that many contemporary conflicts are occurring in these failed states, a large number of which are based in Africa. The wars in Somalia and Rwanda during the early 1990s, for example, brought about the complete disintegration of central state structures and, even today, Somalia ranks top of the list of states most likely to fail according to the Failed States Index published by the journal *Foreign Policy* (Foreign Policy 2008).

Finally, the forces of globalisation are apparent in certain characteristics of the new wars, particularly in the context of leading to the social and cultural transformation of societies. As has been highlighted elsewhere in this book, globalisation is contributing to high levels of interdependence between states, a trend which is generally viewed not only as being inevitable but also welcome. However, as we have seen, the effects of globalisation have not been universally beneficial, and it is therefore criticised for contributing to widespread poverty throughout the developing world. Indeed, when this is examined in the context of states prone to civil conflict, the impact has been devastating. Two features in particular are worthy of mention: globalisation has diminished the ability of vulnerable states to retain control of their territory and their sovereign right to a monopoly of legitimate military force; also, an analysis of the range and type of actors that step in to fill the vacuum left by the failing state is necessary. As the state weakens in the face of conflict and globalisation, insurgency, criminal and ethnic groups, warlords, mercenaries and other forms of private security organisations, regular armies, human rights groups and the international community in general begin to compete with each other in the space left by the deteriorating state.

Both the Introductory box at the start of the chapter on Liberia and the one on Angola (Box 29.1) highlight the prevalence of the terrible conditions in conflicts where the state has either disintegrated or is engaged in conflict with groups opposed to it. Failed states present a major problem for the international community in that their inability to control their

## Box 29.1 Conflict in the Republic of Angola and its impact on civilians

A number of actors can be identified in the Angolan conflicts, including the Popular Movement for the Liberation of Angola (MPLA), the National Union for the Total Independence of Angola (UNITA) and the National Front for the Liberation of Angola (FNLA). A colony of Portugal since 1576, Angola did not gain independence until 1975, following almost 14 years of rebellion and war against the Portuguese. The Alvor Agreement (15 January 1975) between the MPLA, UNITA, FNLA and the Portuguese government allowed for a transition to independence and eventual elections. The Treaty also called for the armed wings of each of the Angolan factions to be united into the Angolan Defence Forces but deep distrust between the various factions failed to allow the transitional government to solidify and, weeks after it took office clashes between the MPLA and the FNLA led to one of Africa's longest civil wars. It was important enough even for the United States and the Soviet Union to compete with each other by supporting opposing factions and it wasn't until 2002, when over 500,000 people had been killed, that the war formally ended. During the Cold War, the United States supported the anti-Marxist UNITA, while the MPLA was backed by Cuba and the Soviet Union. After the end of the Cold War, however, this support evaporated and although the Angolan conflict was far more complex than the outline given here, since many more smaller factions

and neighboring states had been involved at various stages since 1975, the one specific aspect which we must examine is Angola's resources – diamonds and oil.

Although the FNLA was a spent force by the mid-1980s, UNITA and the MPLA continued to be rivals. Angola's diamond mines and oil reserves became the primary sources of income for the warring factions once support from the Soviet Union and the United States for their respective clients evaporated at the end of the Cold War. MPLA's reliance on oil exports and UNITA's success in mining Angola's diamonds and selling them internationally with the help of private companies such as South Africa's De Beers allowed the war to continue. By 1999 the Angolan government was exporting over $1 billion worth of oil every year, and, since 1990 UNITA had succeeded in selling over $4 billion worth of diamonds despite UN sanctions. Writing in 1999 John Prendergast stated,

This wealth has helped purchase one of the most highly militarized countries on earth, peppered with ten million landmines and up to 100,000 amputees. Angola stands alone at the top of UNICEF's Child Risk Measure, which examines the risk of death, malnutrition, abuse, and development failure for children worldwide.

(Prendergast 1999)

internal environment inevitably creates serious insecurities for states and individuals further afield. Clearly, military challenges to the state are the most significant and it is African states in particular which have proven to be most susceptible to failure in the face of armed opposition groups. Since the Cold War ended, governments in Liberia, Sierra Leone, Somalia, Rwanda, the Ivory Coast and the Congo have, at various stages, lost control of much of their territory and those states, as a consequence, have experienced brutal and protracted civil wars.

## The impact of globalisation and the role of Private Military and Security Companies

Chapter 28 refers to many other examples of failed states such as Somalia and Pakistan and the problems that such states cause for the international community. Here we would like to consider some of the actors that have begun to play a role within such states and the first thing to recognise is that the examples above (and those in Chapter 28) cannot be considered in isolation from the dynamics of the end of the Cold War. This section will reiterate the connections between the end of the Cold War and Mary Kaldor's 'new wars' thesis before moving on to examine how globalisation has impacted upon the types of entities which have emerged to challenge states in the post-Cold War era, and finally considering the private enterprises that have begun to replace state functions of security. Private companies – namely Private Military and Private Security Companies (PMCs and PSCs) – have on the one hand been encouraged by globalisation, but on the other have had a dramatic and unprecedented impact on the conflicts of the post-Cold War era.

### Kaldor's 'new wars', the end of the Cold War and the decline of the state

A number of common factors have been identified in the context of the conflicts of the post-Cold War era. Kaldor's 'new wars' thesis has sought to establish a clear connection between failed states, brutal civil conflict, the diminishing ability of the state to control large swathes of its own territory and the emergence of groups that seek to further destabilise the state. Writing in 2006, Kaldor reaffirmed her belief in the strong connections between failed states and her thesis. The terrible impact on civilians, the factionalised nature of societies, the ethnic basis of the conflicts, the uprooting of people from their homes and communities, 'detention, torture and rape, both as a weapon of war and as a side-effect of war as well as the destruction of historic buildings and symbols', and the criminalisation of the warring groups are all features of the wars we have witnessed in the post-Cold War period (Kaldor 2006: viii).

A further feature of these conflicts appears to be their longevity. As the ability of the state to manage its affairs reduces and as the warring parties begin to search for alternative sources of finance (for instance oil and 'conflict diamonds') it has become almost impossible to distinguish between conflict and post-conflict environments. Many states, including the ones analysed above, become locked in what appears to be protracted conflict interspersed by periods of violent crisis and ceasefire, and Michele Griffen (an academic in International Relations) provides a useful account of why peace cannot prevail in such conflicts:

> Most contemporary conflicts have as their root causes longstanding inequalities between groups [and are] characterized by internecine violence, a proliferation of irregular armed groups, a blurring of distinctions between civilian and combatant and the violent breakdown of political processes and institutions . . . Rarely does the end of hostilities mark a definitive break with previous grievances or patterns of violence; this is especially the case where wars are not played out but terminated by ceasefires and peace agreements.
>
> (Griffen 2000: 423)

Central to this whole thesis, however, is the premise that the state itself is no longer a central actor in the conflicts of the post-Cold War era. This is in contrast to *national* conflicts where the state adopts a central position. During the Cold War, for example, the armed forces of all nations largely resembled each other in that they were, as Kaldor states, 'disciplined, hierarchical, and technology intensive'. She argued that, although there were, of course, guerrilla, terrorist or other groups, they were considered to be marginal, and in this environment the state was assumed to be central (Kaldor 2001a). The cases outlined above, however, have shown that there have been many examples where states have, in the post-Cold War period, lost their ability to retain a monopoly over legitimate violence and have lost control of their own territories. One of the consequences of these civil conflicts is that new types of organised violent groups emerge to supplant the failing state. In addition to the various criminal, ethnic and insurgent groups which emerge from *within*, actors from *outside* the region such as other states, NGOs, international organisations, and even private actors (for example, Private Security and Military Companies) also materialise to fill the vacuum left by the failing state.

## The impact of globalisation

Kaldor has not only encouraged us to think that the state is no longer a prominent actor, but has also highlighted the central role that globalisation has played in diminishing its status. There has traditionally been an assumption that since globalisation is taken to mean an increase in trade and communication flows it leads to the growth of interdependence among states, thereby raising expectations of greater stability in their relations. However, globalisation means far more than this, including the emergence of stateless forces which have resulted in intense economic activity at a local, regional and global level. The essential argument is that the liberal economic forces which have contributed to the phenomenal growth of globalisation have also been instrumental in diminishing the ability of states to provide public goods to their citizens. Public goods can be defined as goods that are in the public domain and therefore available for all citizens to consume – the air we breathe is an example. However, a large number of goods such as education, health care, the postal service, public utilities such as water, gas and electricity, the rule of law, roads and even street lighting, have traditionally been provided by the state. In stable environments, the state continues to be involved in the provision of such goods, even though globalisation has led to the emergence of private actors capable of competing with the state. In Britain, for example, many state-owned public utility companies were privatised over twenty years ago, giving rise to competition in the relevant sectors through the emergence of private companies.

One could argue that *security* is also a public good and, traditionally, its provision has been the sole preserve of the state. In conflict zones, however, where the state has collapsed or is collapsing, traditional state functions such as health provision and education disappear and, as the case studies on Angola and Liberia have shown, the state also fails to provide its citizens with security. In these circumstances, the disintegration of the state is accompanied by the criminalisation of society. Violence itself becomes privatised and this environment is further characterised by the emergence of a multiple range of fighting units, some of which are state-based and others private. This erosion of the state's monopoly of legitimate violence is one of the most prominent features of failed states and with globalisation leading to the diffusion of authority within states, alternative sources of power emerge as groups begin to compete with one another – often violently – for the country's resources.

The liberalisation of the global economy has given rise to many Private Security and Military Companies, and although there is nothing new about private (mercenary) armies, their presence in conflict zones and failed states has increased significantly in the post-Cold War era. Not only have they become a prominent feature, but also they are beginning to provide the whole range of military services, from 'protection' to actual engagement in military action. A number of inter-related questions need to be addressed if we are to understand the connections between the different types of private enterprises and the conflicts of the post-Cold War era. We must start by defining the different types of organisations and clarifying the distinctions between them. We have already analysed the impact of globalisation on the commercialisation of security – but this now needs to be placed in the context of the dramatic events at the end of the Cold War. Finally, we need to address the impact that these entities have had on the security of states – and in particular on failed states and unstable regions.

## Security and the private sector

In reality there are very many people and enterprises (some legitimate and others not) associated with the provision of commercialised security. These can include militias, mercenaries, warlords and other armed groups as well as foreign servicemen enlisted in national armies. For example, the Nepalese Gurkhas have been fighting for the British army for over 200 years, with over 200,000 having fought in the two world wars. Since then, they have served in places such as Hong Kong, Malaysia, Borneo, Cyprus, the Falklands and more recently in Kosovo, Afghanistan and Iraq. Given that there are numerous examples of private fighting forces and individuals it is useful to distinguish between them. To begin with, Article 1 of *The UN Mercenary Convention*, adopted in October 2001, defines a *mercenary* as any person who:

- is specially recruited locally or abroad in order to fight in an armed conflict
- is motivated to take part in the hostilities essentially by the desire for private gain . . .
- is neither a national of a party to the conflict nor a resident of territory controlled by a party to the conflict
- is not a member of the armed forces or a party to the conflict . . .

(UNGA 1989: A/RES/44/34)

Others such as Nathan define mercenaries as 'soldiers hired by a foreign government or rebel movement to contribute to the prosecution of armed conflict – whether directly by engaging in hostilities or indirectly through training, logistics, intelligence or advisory services – and who do so outside the authority of the government and defence force of their own country' (Nathan 1997: 10). A particularly useful definition has been provided by Goddard who described a mercenary as 'an individual or organization financed to act for a foreign entity within a military-style framework, including conduct of military-style operations, without regard for ideals, legal or moral commitment, and domestic and international law' (Goddard 2001: 8). This definition is especially important as it specifies some of the problems associated with private enterprises and individuals offering their security services.

Mercenaries have been used since classical Greece and Rome. The ancient Greeks hired Egyptian mercenaries to fight in their armies; in 401 BC. ten thousand Greek mercenaries were hired by a Persian prince to capture the Persian throne; the Swiss Guard was created in 1506 when one hundred and fifty Swiss mercenaries marched to Rome to serve Pope Julius II; Britain hired Hessian Germans during the eighteenth century to fight against American colonists during the American Revolutionary War; mercenaries were used by Katanga secessionists in the Congo crisis during the early 1960s, and the Americans have also used them in Afghanistan since 2001 and Iraq since 2003. However, they generally have a bad reputation, given that their prime motivation for fighting is financial and they therefore owe little allegiance or loyalty to anyone other than themselves. Despite widespread use, therefore, a moral objection to them has developed stemming from the premise that mercenaries remain outside the control of legitimate authority and fight for personal financial gain rather than elevated ideals such as the common good. To quote from a great political philosopher and ardent critic of mercenaries, Niccolo Machiavelli:

Mercenaries . . . are useless and dangerous. A state based on mercenaries will never be solid or secure. Mercenary forces are not united; they are ambitious, undisciplined, and disloyal. They are careful of friends, villainous with enemies, not fearing God, and faithless among men. Attack and defeat are the same to them. In peacetime, they rob you. In war, the enemy ruins you. The reason is that nothing keeps them in camp except a miserable wage, not enough for them to die for you.

(Machiavelli and Goodwin 2003: 75)

### Box 29.2 Mercenary armies – Israel and the South Lebanese Army

Civil war broke out in Lebanon in 1975 and it was in order to combat the Palestine Liberation Organisation (PLO) – based in Southern Lebanon – that a Lebanese Army Major (Saad Haddad) founded the Free Lebanon Militia (FLM). Given the PLO's opposition to Israeli occupation of Palestinian territories, a large number of the organisation's fighters were stationed in Palestinian refugee camps in Southern Lebanon and regularly launched raids into Israel from there. It was in order to stop these attacks that Israel invaded South Lebanon in March 1978. Since the FLM also opposed the presence of the PLO within Lebanese borders, the Israelis were able to take advantage of this and reach an accord with Haddad. The FLM was subsequently renamed the South Lebanese Army

(SLA) and the Israelis took it upon themselves to provide it with further training. Predominantly made up of mercenaries, its remit was to control an enclave in Southern Lebanon where it systematically carried out torture . . . 'the methods included electric shock, suspension from an electricity pole, dousing with water, painful postures, beating with an electric cable, and sleep deprivation. Amnesty International reports that torture practised by Israel's subcontractor resulted in physical injury and . . . death'.

*Source*: Gordon, N., 'Strategic abuse: outsourcing human rights violations, *Counter Punch*, http://counterpunch.org/gordon09062003.html, accessed 15 June 2009.

The lack of authoritative control over the actions of mercenaries has meant that wherever they have been used, serious allegations of human rights abuses have followed. Due to the nature of what they do, it stands to reason that we find them present in the most unstable regions of the world, which obviously includes failed states. Where law and order have already broken down and the state has failed in its primary responsibility to protect its citizens or provide essential public goods, and where alternative sources of power emerge in the form of militias and other insurgent groups seeking to enhance their own position, mercenaries find themselves being called upon by all sides. What may seem surprising, however, is that even legitimate stable governments outsource security functions to mercenaries – see Box 29.2.

Schreier and Caparini provide an excellent description:

> Traditionally, mercenaries have been defined as non-nationals hired to take direct part in armed conflicts. The primary motivation is said to be monetary gain rather than a nation-state. This is why they are called soldiers of fortune. Mercenaries can also be misguided adventurers, but often they are merely disreputable thugs, ready to enlist for any cause or power ready to pay them . . . These 'dogs of war' are known for their disloyalty and lack of discipline. Many have committed acts of banditry, rape and an array of atrocities in the mutilated host countries.
>
> (Schreier and Caparini 2005: 15)

The freelance nature of mercenaries, therefore, has not only diminished their reputation significantly, but has also led to the international community outlawing mercenary activity. This aversion to mercenaries is most clearly manifest in the Geneva Convention's Additional Protocol I which states that '[a] mercenary shall not have the right to be a combatant or a prisoner of war' (Geneva Protocol 1978). Their unflattering reputation, their lack of accountability, their financial motivation and lack of loyalty other than to themselves have all contributed to the international community viewing mercenaries as a threat.

## Private Military and Private Security Companies

Distinguishing between mercenaries and PMCs and PSCs is not an easy task given that there exists no accepted consensus on the characteristics of each. Indeed, confusion is heightened because the Western media and journalists tend to use the terms interchangeably, so that phrases such as 'corporate mercenaries' are used to refer to PMCs as well as PSCs. This lack of consensus over clear distinctions makes it difficult for us to understand the nature of this industry. Nevertheless, it is possible to identify differences; mercenaries are limited in their capacities, they may lack professionalism and are unable to provide anything beyond direct combat and a limited amount of military training to their employers. Private Security and Private Military Companies, on the other hand, have both had a significant impact on security issues since the end of the Cold War. PSCs are specialised companies that provide security and protection to the personnel, property and industrial equipment of those willing to pay for their services. Similarly, PMCs are private companies that have advanced military skills including intelligence collection and the ability to engage in combat operations and logistics, and they procure and maintain the arms and equipment needed to fight wars. They have the capital, skills and capabilities to provide multilevel services, including advanced combat operations, to their customers.

The essential difference between them is that modern security and military companies have clear objectives, goals and, essentially, corporate structures. In essence they are typical companies. Herein lies the problem, in the sense that, like mercenaries, they too are private actors and, therefore, obviously concerned with the maximisation of profits and minimisation of costs – just like any other corporate enterprise. In other words, they too provide their services in return for monetary reward and, as a consequence of this inescapable fact, serious questions emerge over the value of these entities and their actions in conflict zones. These questions must be addressed since not only are states such as the US and Britain beginning to outsource tasks which would once have been the preserve of their armed forces, but even failing states involved in civil conflict are beginning to employ private security providers.

PMCs and PSCs are a modern manifestation of mercenary armies and have come about due to the conditions prevalent at the end of the Cold War, when Western states became reluctant to commit their own military forces in response to regional conflicts and humanitarian crises. Events such as the loss of eighteen American troops in Somalia in 1993, deployed as part of the failed United Nations Mission to help that unfortunate country, persuaded the then US President, Bill Clinton, to withdraw all American support. This type of withdrawal of commitment on the part of Western states in general has meant that global demand for private security providers has risen sharply in recent years. Another particularly influential factor in the rise of the private security sector has been the rapid downsizing of the large armies of the East and West, in the sense that it provided the companies with a large pool of highly trained military personnel. Such developments have meant that private security providers are here to stay for now, but in order for them to be accepted as legitimate entities they need to make a clear distinction between themselves and mercenaries.

International law has opposed the use of mercenaries largely due to the premise that it is difficult to regulate their behaviour. However, the services of the private security sector have been increasingly in demand since the end of the Cold War. As highlighted, the easing of tensions between the superpowers led to considerable demilitarisation, and this in turn flooded the international markets not only with cheap military equipment but also with many unemployed military personnel. The reduction in tensions between the USA and the Soviet Union allowed the superpowers to retreat from many of their former areas of interest and client states and this withdrawal of support meant that many of the weak ones (not least many African states) grew increasingly incapable of maintaining control of their own territories.

There has been a recognition among the international community that the high levels of interconnectedness brought about by globalisation have meant that ignoring conflicts in unstable regions is no longer an option. Since 11 September 2001, in particular, failed states have begun to be perceived as a serious regional threat. Demilitarisation at the end of the Cold War meant that, not only failing states turned to mercenaries for military support, but also greater powers such as the United States and Britain, who have employed these corporate soldiers with impunity in war zones such as Iraq and Afghanistan. However, rather than referring to these forces as mercenaries, globalisation has given rise to larger entities that closely resemble companies competing for a slice of the market. The end of the Cold War did mean that the threat of nuclear confrontation between East and West had receded, but the 'new wars' of the 1990s and the new millennium have created conditions whereby these companies have been called upon by legitimate nation-state governments in unprecedented ways. They provide security, they fight wars, they safeguard assets, they protect executives of other companies, and they are even called upon to prevent states from failing or indeed hastening their demise. The one common denominator is that Kaldor's 'new wars' have given the green light for these entities to profit from wars. The post-Cold War world is much more complex than the Westphalian world where the nation-state was seen as the corner-stone of international order. The privatisation of conflict is now so widespread around the world that wars from Afghanistan to Somalia, Liberia, Sudan, Iraq, Columbia and Angola (among others) have all seen extensive participation by warlords, mercenaries and other actors willing to profit from conflict.

## Some problems and examples

It is estimated that since the US invasion of Iraq in 2003 there are now some fifty private security companies employing up to 30,000 people. This has led to the conflict there being dubbed the world's first 'privatised war'. Similarly, the US outsourced the task of monitoring the situation in the Balkans to private military companies following the wars in the former Yugoslavia during the 1990s. Other well-publicised examples are failing states that have employed private companies in order to gain an advantage in their conflicts with other segments of their own societies. For example, private security providers have had a long history of involvement in Sierra Leone, largely as protectors of industrial operations. One case is the contract between the government and South African-based Executive Outcomes (EO). In 1995 this company was employed to train its armed forces, lead offensives against, and ultimately secure, the capital Freetown, to bring the Kono diamond mines under government control. In early 1996 the company led a successful armed attack against the Revolutionary United Front (RUF) – a group opposed to the central government. Following this success the RUF agreed to a ceasefire and the relative calm that was achieved allowed elections to be held. Once the contract came to an end in 1997 and the company withdrew, the RUF instigated a coup which brought it to power and led to the exile of the elected government.

The same company also played a significant role in the civil conflict in Angola during the mid-1990s where it was employed by the MPLA dominated government to fight against the UNITA rebels. In 1992 EO was hired by Sonangol (a company owned by the Angolan government) to secure the Soyo oilfield. Backed by Angolan forces, EO succeeded in regaining the field in early 1993, but when it withdrew, UNITA rebels recaptured it. Realising the potential of the company, the Angolan government signed a much more comprehensive contract with it in order to train Angolan troops and lead the war against the rebel forces. The year 1994 was seen as a turning-point in the war between the Angolan government and UNITA rebels, since the government, with the assistance of EO, recaptured diamond and oil fields, thereby significantly reducing the ability of the rebels to fund their operations and forcing UNITA to accept a peace agreement.

A particularly important, well-publicised and recent example of a state's reliance on private security is presented by the United States in Iraq. Although America has relied on private companies elsewhere, such as in Afghanistan and Bosnia, in Iraq's case the use of PSCs has been particularly extensive. These companies have been employed to protect individuals, buildings, politicians and economic assets and they are also closely involved with training Iraq's own police and military forces. Generally, private security contractors have been employed to provide a wide range of services including protecting convoys, individuals, reconstruction sites, government buildings as well as gathering intelligence and assessing threat levels. It is therefore possible to argue that private armies are capable of stabilising conflict zones, supporting faltering states and easing the burden on the armed forces of states such as the US and Britain. Conversely, however, the use of private armed contractors raises serious issues over accountability, transparency, and the lack of widespread information about their costs, performance standards and criteria for hiring of employees. The case study on Blackwater at the end of this chapter further highlights this point.

The media played a leading role in highlighting the excesses of some of these companies. In the case of Blackwater and Triple Canopy employees for instance, *The Washington Post* drew attention to the possibility that their use of force in Iraq was frequent and disproportionate, resulting in significant casualties and destruction of property. Between the period 1 January 2005 and 12 September 2007, there were nearly two hundred instances of firearms discharges by Blackwater operatives. Company employees were fired upon first and therefore had to use force in return in only a handful of cases. In the majority of cases, Blackwater fired first (Jackman 2006). Blackwater employees' lack of cultural sensitivity and sense of impunity led to members of the US Congress, the Media and others raising concerns that the US State Department was failing to investigate killings adequately by these private contractors. The general lack of concern shown by Blackwater and, ultimately, US officials not only undermined US standing in Iraq but also its foreign policy objectives. Steve Fainaru of *The Washington Post* claimed that, by ignoring Iraqi laws and customs, Blackwater placed itself above them and that the hatred felt towards the Americans stemmed largely from the way in which companies such as Blackwater behaved. Iraqis did not know them as Blackwater or other PSCs but only as Americans (Fainaru 2007).

The potential problems posed by private security contractors could indeed be significant, as could their number. PMCs and PSCs are not part of the regular armed forces and, unlike a nation's forces, are concerned with profit and will, therefore, do what they can to save money. This makes their employment immediately problematic in the sense that, since profit dominates their behaviour, they may not be altogether committed to the cause. Similarly, since private contractors operate outside the regular chain of command, their operations are rarely assessed for efficiency. Military command structures are concerned with directing their enormous destructive capabilities towards achieving their objectives, while at the same time ensuring the minimisation of 'collateral damage'. Once again, the dominance of profit as a motive means that the objectives of private contractors are often at variance with those of the regular armed forces. It is in this context that issues such as a lack of care for civilian life and an overly aggressive style become a matter for concern. As the case of Blackwater has shown, even companies employed by the United States and subject to American laws can operate with relative impunity. When it comes to human rights abuses and the deaths of civilians in many of the civil conflicts in Africa, the situation is likely to be much worse, since international law is too weak and ineffectual to have an impact.

When security is outsourced to the private sector the tasks and support to be carried out are subject to a contract. Contracts may be sufficient for simple transactions such as the purchase or sale of a house, but in the case of armed conflict even the most perfectly written contract cannot take into consideration every eventuality that may arise in the event of war. Contracts can place severe limitations on the ability of military commanders to accomplish their objectives, especially if employees of PMCs refuse to take on extra-contractual duties – which is likely to be the case. There is also a premise that it is impossible to determine the effectiveness of PMCs prior to deployment. This is quite different from the way in which the readiness and the operational abilities of armed forces are continuously assessed by commanders and, ultimately, by politicians. In this sense, one could argue that PMCs could even be a threat to the state that employs them. Private contractors may not be subject to the same selection processes and this could lead to states having to employ companies from other countries, thereby raising the possibility that they may not always be loyal to the employer. Defecting from contractual obligations is not the same as desertion and the company is not subject to any real punishment if its employees decide not to fulfil the required duties.

With states such as the USA and Britain making increasing use of PMCs and PSCs in conflict zones to support their own armed forces, it is obvious that such companies are here to stay. However, it is also obvious that there are significant problems associated with the way in which some of them operate in the field. Some of the issues we have highlighted have to do with their overly aggressive style, which often leads to human rights violations. While they are obviously beginning to fulfil a useful role in certain circumstances, the inevitable question is how can the international community prevent some of the industry's excesses. The most obvious answer to this problem is regulation, through the use of national and international law. However, as we identified earlier, there is no clear consensus on the definitions of the various private entities providing security. It is, therefore, difficult for the international community to enact laws that could help to regulate the behaviour of these corporate warriors. Private security providers are often equated with mercenaries, and it is difficult to differentiate between them. Regulating such companies is further hindered by the possibility that the states that employ them are often willing to confer a high degree of immunity from local prosecution. We have already mentioned Blackwater, which was able to act with impunity in Iraq even though it was a US company employed by the USA and therefore subject to US laws. Although it is clear that international law governing their behaviour needs to be strengthened, it is also a matter of enforcement. International law aside, PMCs and PSCs operating in failed states where local institutions, such as courts and other enforcement mechanisms, have collapsed are generally untouchable, and it is in this environment that the abuse of human rights can become a significant cause for concern. It remains the case, however, that the international community's reliance on PMCs and PSCs and the use of them has increased significantly since the invasion of Iraq in 2003 and it is therefore necessary for the mechanisms governing the industry's behaviour to be strengthened.

*Source:* Press Association Images/Karel Prinsloo/AP

Are Private Military Companies a help or a hindrance? In Iraq, Blackwater employees were criticised for their aggressive (and sometimes unlawful) tactics.

## Case study: Blackwater USA

Founded in 1997 and based in North Carolina (USA), Blackwater trains over forty thousand security contractors a year in programmes which include military tactics, intelligence gathering and defensive operations. It even boasts training ranges that can instruct combatants in various environments, including urban warfare, and is so well equipped that police units from around the USA are routinely trained there. Indeed, it has been labelled as one of the most powerful PMCs in the world, directly employing over twenty thousand soldiers and its own air force which includes helicopter gunships. According to Mark Hemingway, the facility contains

- The country's largest tactical driving track . . . for drivers learning how to escape ambushes
- A 1,200 yard long firing range for sniper training
- A 20-acre manmade lake with shipping containers that have been mocked up with ship rails and portholes, floating on pontoons, used to teach how to board a hostile ship
- A K-9 training facility that . . . has 80 dog teams deployed around the world
- A sizeable private armoury
- A formidable armoured vehicle developed by the company itself

*Source*: Mark Hemingway, 'Warriors for hire, Blackwater USA and the rise of private military contractors', *The Weekly Standard*, Vol.012, No.14, 2006.

The protracted wars in Afghanistan and Iraq have provided the company with an even greater presence around the world fulfilling roles as protectors of diplomats, politicians and industrialists among other security functions. It achieved its highest profile role when it was asked to protect US Ambassador Paul Bremer – the highest ranking American civilian in Iraq. Asking a private security contractor to fulfil such a role in the past would have been unthinkable. It came to the attention of the public, particularly in 2004, when four of its employees were captured by an Iraqi mob in Fallujah, killed and hung from lamp posts. This event was a catalyst which persuaded the then US President, George Bush, to authorise an assault against the city.

The relationship between the Iraqis and the company deteriorated further in September 2007 when indiscriminate gunfire from a Blackwater convoy resulted in the deaths of almost twenty Iraqi civilians. One of the complaints made against the private contractors by Iraqi officials had to do with their overly aggressive tactics, and even the US Federal Bureau of Investigation concluded that most of the deaths that occurred on that day were unlawful. The Iraqi government subsequently sought to revoke Blackwater's license to operate in the country, but until then most American private contractors had enjoyed a degree of immunity for their operations. Although the company continued to work after the USA claimed that there was no alternative to protecting high-ranking officials, following a 2008 agreement over the status of foreign forces, Iraqi officials became adamant that the tens of thousands of private contractors would no longer have immunity from prosecution for their actions.

 **Given that PMCs and PSCs are playing an increasing role in conflict zones, how might they be regulated?**

## Conclusions

This chapter has highlighted three issues which are causing increasing concern for the international community, namely some of the characteristics of failed states, the nature of conflicts in the post-Cold War era, and some features surrounding the privatisation of conflict. Finding a connection between these three seemingly separate concerns has been crucial. Mary Kaldor's work on 'new wars' has been particularly influential, as she has attempted to demonstrate that the momentous changes that occurred at the end of the Cold War were likely to impact decisively on the nature of conflicts. Her thesis revolves around the notion that intra-state wars would replace wars between states and that they would be particularly brutal as states turned on themselves, causing civilians to bear the brunt of the brutality. The post-Cold War era has indeed seen the outbreak (and continuation) of numerous civil wars, particularly in Africa, and several examples illustrated this point.

The link to failed states became clear in the context of the intra-state basis of Kaldor's 'new wars' thesis. The high incidence of civil conflicts meant that many of the states experiencing prolonged conflict within their borders were classified as failed in many ways. The disappearance of the normal state structures that provided citizens with public goods such as health, education and security meant that a variety of actors began to compete with one another in order to fill the lethal vacuum created by the failing state. This observation led us to place the analysis of the privatisation of conflict as the third crucial element of this chapter. The link to the emergence of private entities (both legitimate and criminal) was provided by the phenomenon of globalisation which meant much more than simply greater interdependence. Generally, globalisation has led to intense economic activity at a local and regional level as well as globally and, in this sense, it has diminished the ability of states to provide public goods such as security for their citizens. We argued that this was particularly true in the case of failed states, where the disintegration of the state was accompanied by the criminalisation of society and the privatisation of violence. A multiple range of fighting units were seen materialising as the state's monopoly on legitimate forms of violence eroded, leading to the emergence of alternative sources of power as groups began to compete with one another – often violently – for the state's resources.

Finally, an analysis of the private security industry not only highlighted the impact of globalisation, but also showed the extent to which private armies and companies have become a central feature of contemporary intra-state conflicts. Not only have they begun to be used extensively by states such as the US and Britain to 'help' with providing security in a variety of contexts in places such as Afghanistan and Iraq, but also they have begun to play a major role in states which are experiencing civil war. One factor highlighted as being of particular importance was their position as private actors with financial gain as their prime motivation. We argued that their emphasis on profit generally came at the expense of principles, with the consequence that PMCs and PSCs have often violated the human rights of civilians wherever they have been employed, a fact which is clearly demonstrated by examples such as Blackwater in Iraq. However, given that many regions of the world remain prone to conflict and that states such as the US and Britain are increasingly reluctant to commit their own armed forces, these companies are now central players in post-Cold War conflicts and are likely to remain so.

# Resource section

## Questions

1. What impact has the end of the Cold War and globalisation had on the security dilemmas of failed states?

2. What did Mary Kaldor mean by 'new wars'? Do you think this is an accurate way to describe contemporary conflict?

3. What are the essential differences between mercenaries and Private Military Companies?

4. Given that Private Military and Security Companies are predominantly concerned with profit, are they capable of fulfilling a valuable role during time of conflict?

5. Why do you think a disproportionate number of 'failed states' are in Africa?

## Recommended reading

**Kaldor, M. (2006)** *New and Old Wars: Organised Violence in a Global Era* (2nd edn, Oxford: Polity)
This volume is a particularly important one which has fundamentally influenced our way of thinking about contemporary conflict. In distinguishing recent conflicts from those of previous eras, Kaldor has successfully made the all-important link with the phenomenon of globalisation. This second edition is an excellent analysis of the 'new wars' thesis in the context of the post-9/11 era.

**Kinsey, C. (2006)** *Corporate Soldiers and International Security: The Rise of Private Military Companies* (Contemporary Security Studies) (Abingdon: Routledge)
Kinsey presents a very readable summary of the history of private security providers from mercenaries to the recent phenomenon of private security and military companies.

**Münkler, H. (2005)** *The New Wars* (Cambridge: Cambridge University Press)
Originally published in German in 2002 and then translated into English in 2005, Münkler provides an insightful analysis into identifying criteria for the 'new wars' of the post-Cold War era. The view that states no longer have a monopoly on violence justifies his perceptions which set contemporary conflicts apart from past wars.

**Rotberg, R.I. (ed.) (2004)** *When States Fail: Causes and Consequences* (New Jersey: Princeton University Press)
This book presents a useful collection of essays on state failure and is edited by Rotberg who, in the opening chapter, sets out a theory of why states fail. The remainder of the book is split into two sets of chapters which deal with the nature of state failure and the methods of preventing it.

**Uesseler, R. (2008) (translated from the original German by Jefferson Chase),** *Servants of War: Private Military Corporations and the Profit of Conflict* (Berlin, Christoph Links Verlag)
Uesseler's analysis of how private military companies profit from conflict is a timely reminder of the increasing reliance on private contractors by leading states such as the US and Britain. His analysis of the way in which they are able to bypass democratic norms is a reminder of the need to strengthen national and international laws in an attempt to regulate their excesses.

# Chapter 30
# Nuclear Deterrence and Proliferation

**Achieving stability during the Cold War: Mutual Assured Destruction and US strategic doctrine**

**Deterrence and the nuclear non-proliferation regime in the post-Cold War era**

**Where does this leave us?**

Conclusions

After reading this chapter you will be able to:

- Provide an overview of the evolution of US strategic doctrine
- Account for the academic debates regarding whether nuclear weapons enhance stability between protagonists
- Analyse the basis of the NNPT of 1968
- Conduct case studies of the newly proliferating states
- Account for the value of deterrence in the post-Cold War era

## Introductory box: Dropping the bomb on Japan

Sixteen hours ago an American airplane dropped one bomb on Hiroshima, an important Japanese Army base. That bomb had more power than 20,000 tons of TNT. It had more than two thousand times the blast power of the British 'Grand Slam' which is the largest bomb ever yet used in the history of warfare. It is an atomic bomb. It is a harnessing of the basic power of the universe. The force from which the sun draws its power has been loosed against those who brought war to the Far East. We are now prepared to obliterate more rapidly and completely every productive enterprise the Japanese have above ground in any city. We shall destroy their docks, their factories, and their communications. Let there be no mistake; we shall completely destroy Japan's power to make war.

*Source*: www.atomicarchive.com/Docs/Hiroshima/PRHiroshima.shtml, accessed 5 July 2009.

These excerpts from a speech by US President Harry Truman signalled the beginning of a period unique in human history. The bomb on Hiroshima (6 August 1945) was the first ever use of a nuclear weapon by mankind. Three days later on 9 August, Truman authorised the destruction of another Japanese city – Nagasaki.

## Achieving stability during the Cold War: Mutual Assured Destruction and US strategic doctrine

The atomic drops on Japan in 1945 were significant for many reasons. They not only persuaded the Japanese to surrender in the Second World War, but also ushered in an era during which nuclear weapons became the principal means of maintaining international security. Their destructive capability was immense compared to conventional weapons, and that capability increased further as the United States and the Soviet Union began to compete with one another during the Cold War. The history of the Cold War was covered in some detail in Chapter 4 and we recommend you refer back to it while reading this one. The relative stability of this period is often attributed to *mutual deterrence*, a military strategy akin to strategic stalemate whereby both states were able to refrain from attacking each other because of the certainty of fierce retaliation. Better known as Mutual Assured Destruction (MAD), both the USA and Russia remain committed to this strategy even today. The desire to deploy nuclear weapons was not restricted to the superpowers, however, and consequently others sought to develop defence strategies which incorporated them into their arsenals. Alongside the US and the Soviet Union, the Nuclear Non-Proliferation Treaty (NNPT) of 1968 conferred upon China, Britain and France the status of 'nuclear weapon states'. Given that the NNPT was sponsored by these key states there was one additional purpose to the treaty, namely to dissuade other states from acquiring a similar nuclear arsenal.

Herein lies a major contradiction. On the one hand there are those academics such as Kenneth Waltz who take their cue from the Cold War and contend that the spread of nuclear weapons to other states would promote peaceful relations. This view stems from Waltz's own Neo-Realist logic (see Chapter 6) which argues that the best way to achieve stability within the anarchic 'self-help' international system is for states to dissuade others from aggression – i.e. through an effective deterrent, and Waltz saw nuclear weapons as providing just such a deterrent. The question then emerges why, if nuclear weapons were central to the stability of the Cold War, would the established nuclear weapon states seek to prevent their spread and deny the benefit of stability to other states? This key question forms an important basis for any understanding of the issue of nuclear proliferation and to address it, we need to begin by understanding the notion of deterrence.

## Deterrence

**Nuclear deterrence** was the dominant military doctrine during the Cold War. The idea behind the doctrine was that peace between the Cold War superpowers relied on the will power of the two sides to use their nuclear arsenal in the event of a conflict. There was nothing new about nuclear deterrence in that it followed the basic premise of deterrence theory where an opponent's behaviour was changed through the threat of punishment. In the context of the relations between the superpowers this essentially amounted to the creation of peace through a balance of terror based on the weapons themselves. Bernard Brodie is often considered as being central to the development of the ideas behind nuclear deterrence. One of his most inspirational axioms related to what he saw as the difference between the era prior to the Second World War and the following period. In 1946 he stated that 'the chief purpose of our military establishment [had] been to win wars. From now on its chief purpose must be to avert them. It can have almost no other purpose' (Brodie 1946: 76). Brodie recognised the value of these new weapons for his ideas on nuclear deterrence and if we are to understand the role that nuclear weapons are playing in the post-Cold War era we must journey back and look at the impact that these weapons had during the Cold War itself. Furthermore, a consideration of Kenneth Waltz's ideas on Neo-Realism and nuclear weapons will be particularly useful in understanding the connections between the Cold War and nuclear deterrence.

Chapter 6 deals with Neo-Realism in detail, but a brief recap may be useful here. Waltz argued that the international system is characterised by anarchy meaning that there is no formal international and centralised authority. In addition to this, the international system is also composed of *agents* – which we commonly refer to as states – and these states are compelled to act in accordance with the logic of *self-help* because anarchy compels them to do so. At the very least, therefore, states must seek to engage in activities which ensure their survival within the international system, and this usually entails the need to enhance their offensive military capabilities. Heavily influenced by Brodie, Waltz wrote his seminal article 'The spread of nuclear weapons: more may be better' in 1981 after having observed super-power nuclear behaviour during the previous decades. The nuclear arms race between the two superpowers, the enhancements of military preparedness, the constant surveillance of each other's activities, and the various crises during the Cold War all seem to confirm the neo-Realist premise that the international system was indeed anarchic and that it was necessary for states continuously to seek strategies which ensured their survival. The Soviet invasion of Hungary in 1956, its invasion of Czechoslovakia in 1968, the Cuban Missile Crisis of 1962, and the Soviet invasion of Afghanistan in 1979 are just a few examples from the Cold War which highlight the tense nature of the era. There is little doubt that the two superpowers saw each other as economic, ideological and military threats to their own interests in the international system. Despite this intense rivalry, however, the USA and the Soviet Union succeeded in preventing the outbreak of a direct conflict between them, and it is in this context that the Neo-Realist explanation gains significant value. Its insistence on explaining the behaviour of the superpowers on the basis of anarchy explains their reliance on nuclear weapons to enhance security.

One key concept used by Waltz to further explain the stability of the Cold War era was the notion of *polarity* which in this context refers to the way in which power is distributed within the international system. A unipolar system is one in which a single state dominates the others in terms of economic and military strength, whereas in a multi-polar environment more than two states hold largely equal amounts of power. Bipolarity is also significant for Neo-Realists, especially in the context of stability. For Waltz a bipolar world is much more predictable, since the two states keep a constant watch on each other and so the chances for miscalculation are much reduced. Indeed, Waltz placed great emphasis on providing empirical evidence to support his views and referred to a number of features from the Cold War. During this period, two states dominated the anarchic international system – the United States and the Soviet Union. Two alliances further solidified the bipolar nature of the international system. First, the USA and its Western allies formed a defensive alliance, the North Atlantic Treaty Organisation (April 1949), the purpose of which was to provide a mechanism for the mutual defence of member states in the event of an attack by any outside power.

The Soviet Union responded in kind with the establishment of the Warsaw Treaty Organisation (commonly known as the Warsaw Pact) in April 1955. This included Albania, East Germany, Hungary, Poland and Romania, all of whom adhered to a unified military command, and there were Soviet army divisions stationed in most of the other states.

**Box 30.1 NATO in 1949**

The original twelve members of NATO in 1949 were the United States, the United Kingdom, Canada, France, Denmark, Iceland, Italy, Norway, Portugal, Belgium, the Netherlands, and Luxembourg. In 1952, Greece and Turkey joined. West Germany was admitted in 1955 and in 1982 Spain became the sixteenth member. From 1 April 2009 membership stood at twenty-eight states.

The alliance dissolved in 1991 once the Cold War had ended and the Soviet Union itself began to disintegrate. As defensive alliances the purpose of both NATO and the Warsaw Pact was to deter each other and come to the defence of their member states in the event of an attack.

For Neo-Realists, the one crucial mechanism for maintaining stability in this bipolar world was the development and deployment of large numbers of nuclear weapons by both sides. By the late 1960s the total number of nuclear missiles held by both sides amounted to over 40,000, a sufficient number for the two states to destroy each other's industrial and civilian infrastructure. This realisation undoubtedly provided the superpowers with sufficient motive to act with restraint when dealing with each other. By the mid 1960s there was an increasing acceptance that any full-scale nuclear exchange would not produce a victory for either side and that there was no value in risking a direct conflict. Mutual Assured Destruction (or MAD) appeared, therefore, to be reassuringly stable and this balance between the two sides even allowed them to begin exploring ways in which they could improve relations – such as through a number of treaties, beginning with the Limited Test Ban Treaty of 1963. Later in 1968 the Soviet Union and the United States (along with Britain) built upon their improving relations and sponsored the Nuclear Non-Proliferation Treaty. However, we must realise that the relationship between the superpowers cannot be characterised as having been stable throughout the Cold War. Before the two states were able to establish a comparatively stable environment they had to go through many crises, the most notable of which was the Cuban Missile Crisis of 1962. At this stage, having looked at the notion of Cold War stability, we need to turn back the clock once more and explore in some detail the process which ultimately led to the establishment of the balance of power embodied within MAD.

## US Strategic Doctrine: Harry S. Truman and the doctrine of Strategic Bombing (1945–1953)

Chapter 4 dealt with Cold War issues in some detail and you should refer back to it while reading this one. In that chapter you will have read that following the Second World War the two superpowers, despite having been allies during the war, increasingly viewed one another with suspicion. Harry Truman replaced Franklin Roosevelt in the USA as President and immediately adopted a hard stance against the Soviet Union, viewing its takeover of Eastern Europe as little more than aggressive expansionism. One controversial view even claims that America's atomic attacks on Hiroshima and Nagasaki (August 1945) merely one week after the end of the Potsdam Conference intended to achieve more than persuading the Japanese to surrender, and this view that the bombs were designed as a way to impress and intimidate the Soviet Union has gained significant credence in recent years (see Introductory box). An account by Walter Brown (assistant to James Byrnes – Truman's Secretary of State) for instance, reveals that Truman himself agreed with his army generals, Douglas Macarthur and Dwight Eisenhower, that Japan was seeking peace and 'that there was no military need to use the bomb' (Edwards 2005).

*Source: Getty Images/Lambert*

**Despite its name, does the doctrine of Mutual Assured Destruction (MAD) make good strategic sense?**

**Box 30.2  The Hiroshima and Nagasaki bombs – intimidating the Soviet Union**

Many academics now claim that the purpose of the atomic drops on Hiroshima and Nagasaki (6 and 9 August 1945 respectively) was not to force the Japanese to surrender, but to demonstrate to the world, and in particular the Soviet Union, the tremendous military capability of the United States. Academics such as Reg Grant and Jane Claypool have argued that the Japanese were close to defeat in 1945 and that they would have surrendered even without the Atomic drops. Although they acknowledge that dropping the bombs persuaded the Japanese to capitulate more quickly, the Americans were already aware that the Japanese authorities were in favour of surrendering. Such arguments further claim that the competition for the division of Europe and the emerging tensions between the Soviet Union and the United States provided the USA with a perfect excuse to demonstrate its military potency.

*Sources*: Grant, R.G. (1998) *New Perspectives: Hiroshima and Nagasaki*, Austin: Raintree Steck-Vaughn; Claypool, J. (1984). *Turning Points of World War II: Hiroshima and Nagasaki*. Toronto, Grolier.

Ultimately, as Chapter 4 has shown, the ideals of Western capitalism and Soviet communism remained antithetical to one another throughout the Cold War and, in the context of this antagonism, it was inevitable that the military might of both states would remain central to the relationship's development. One of the most important personalities as the Cold War gained momentum was George Kennan, who in his position as an American diplomat in Moscow was well placed to influence the Truman Administration in determining US policy towards the Soviet Union. His famous 1946 'Long Telegram' and subsequent 'Sources of Soviet Conduct' both advised Truman that the Soviet Union was inherently expansionist and that it had to be 'contained'. Though he later criticised Truman for failing to negotiate with the Soviets, there is little doubt that his documents formed a basis for an increasingly aggressive, anti-Soviet and militaristic stance by the USA. It was down to Truman to steer the United States during the final stages of the Second World War; after all, the atomic attack on Japan was initiated by him, as was the so-called *Truman Doctrine* which called for the containment of communism. His proclamation on 12 March 1947 that 'it must be the policy of the United States to support free peoples who are resisting attempted subjugation by armed minorities or outside pressures' not only committed the US to the defence of Europe, but is often taken to mean that the US could not tolerate Soviet gains and influence anywhere in the world (Gaddis 1974). In 1950, for instance, he took the United States to war on the Korean peninsula in an effort to preserve South Korea from the communism that its northern half (North Korea) had succumbed to (see Box 30.3).

It is in this context, therefore, that we must view Truman's role in the evolution of US strategic doctrine, which essentially failed to depart from the longstanding notion of *strategic bombing*. This notion dated back to the 1800s – that wars could only be won through the constant bombardment and destruction of the enemy's society – namely his civilian, industrial and other sectors. The arrival of air power further strengthened the

## Box 30.3 George Kennan and the Long Telegram

The US State Department cabled the US Embassy in Moscow (February 1946) asking for their grasp of Soviet policy vis-à-vis the West and the world in general. George Kennan was an embassy official in Moscow at the time and his reply came in the form of an 8,000 word telegram which was then re-written as an article entitled *The Sources of Soviet Conduct*. His analysis pointed to the overwhelming conclusion that the Soviet Union was determined to advance its relative strength at the expense of the capitalist West and that it was prepared to wage a relentless battle to achieve its objectives of dominating the foreign world. Kennan's Long Telegram was important in that it formed the basis of American policy towards the Soviet Union during the Cold War.

notion of strategic bombing, since the panic generated by the Zeppelin and aircraft raids during the First World War provided a reminder of the need to weaken civilian morale and support for the war effort. The arrival of the atom bomb was a further revolutionary step, and its use against Japan needs to be seen in the context of the conditions prevailing at the time. Whether it was used to force Japan to surrender or to impress the Soviet Union with US military potency, it had a profound impact on the direction of US and Soviet policy. At this stage Truman accepted that the bomb *was* for use in time of war – in other words, it was a legitimate weapon. Just as the arrival of air power magnified the potency of strategic bombardment, the atom bomb revitalised this doctrine by providing it with the ultimate weapon – one which could destroy an entire city.

## Box 30.4 Ballistic missiles and nuclear weapons

A Ballistic Missile is an unmanned self-propelled delivery vehicle that can be used in a surface-to-surface role and which sustains a ballistic trajectory throughout its flight path. Ballistic missiles differ from manned vehicles of war (such as aircraft) in that they are 'fire-and-forget' weapons. They are not piloted by humans, cannot be recalled once fired and at present there is no foolproof means of destroying or diverting them before they hit their target. A ballistic missile is not in itself a weapon, since the technology forms the basis of civilian rocket programmes which are used to launch satellites into space. However, ballistic missiles acquire nuclear weapon status when the payload is converted to one which holds the nuclear material. Furthermore, ballistic missiles differ from one another in terms of the distance they can travel to deliver their payload and include short-, intermediate- and long-range missiles.

Nuclear Weapons have also differed significantly from one another as technology has progressed. The first bombs were those used on Nagasaki and Hiroshima – these were fission (atomic) bombs and worked on the basis that the atomic nucleus split into (usually) two fragments releasing several hundred million volts of energy. A fusion (hydrogen or thermonuclear) bomb, on the other hand, is characterised by the use of a fission explosion to fuse together the nuclei of various lighter nuclei (such as hydrogen isotopes) into heavier ones (such as helium). The result is a much greater explosion than can be produced by a fission bomb. The first hydrogen bomb was exploded by the United States in 1952 and the second was by the USSR in 1953.

In his drive to contain the Soviet Union, Truman provided little guidance on the issue of deterrence, but a number of events conspired to force his administration to initiate a review of military policy. The first ever test by the Soviet Union of its own nuclear weapon in 1949 not only broke the US monopoly, but also created a recognition that Russia would soon develop the ability to deliver its nuclear weapons, thereby rendering the US mainland vulnerable. Distance was no longer a guarantee against attack and this fact, combined with the immense destructive capability of these weapons and the realisation that the Soviet Union would also research and develop ballistic missiles, forced the issue of nuclear planning to a level of significance. It is in this context that Truman's Secretary of State, Dean Acheson, instructed the Policy Planning staff – led by Paul Nitze – to undertake a review of US policy. The result was one of the most influential of Cold War documents – National Security Council document 68 (NSC-68). NSC-68 confirmed Truman's belief that the Soviet Union was a major threat to the US and its allies and advised that the only response to this was a massive buildup of the US military to confront what it referred to as an 'enemy unlike previous aspirants to hegemony . . . animated by a new fanatic faith, antithetical to our own' (NSC-68). Although the document did take note of the Soviet's atomic capability and warned that this capability had greatly increased the threat to the USA, it nevertheless recommended a major increase in America's conventional armed forces and one event, in particular, drove this development – the Korean War (see Box 30.5).

Truman remained committed to his containment policy, since he continued to believe that nothing short of brute force could stop the expansionist sentiments of the Soviet Union. This perception was central to his decisions, which ranged from authorising a massive increase in the defence budget to taking the USA into Korea in 1950 – the first major war of containment. One important element of Kennan's Long Telegram had been 'containment policy' which advised forming a strategy to limit and prevent perceived Soviet expansionism. Beyond this, however, his administration provided little guidance over the issue of nuclear deterrence. The National Security Council, for example, did little to

## Box 30.5  Containing Communism – the Korean War (1950–1953)

Immediately after the Second World War the Korean Peninsula was divided into the North (Democratic People's Republic of Korea) and the South (Republic of Korea). Attempts at reunification failed and on 25 June 1950 North Korea, backed by the communist People's Republic of China, invaded the south. The United Nations, heavily influenced by the United States, intervened on the side of South Korea, and the war continued until North Korea withdrew in May 1953 following an armistice. The Peninsula, however, remains divided to this day and is subject to periodic crises. The Korean War was important for a number of reasons. Each of the two Koreas was supported by opposing Cold War players and, over the three years, up to 1.4 million American soldiers fought against Soviet backed Chinese and North Korean troops. The conflict dramatically raised the tensions of the Cold War, and further strengthened the superpower resolve to militarise their respective armed forces, as well as serving as a precedent for US involvement in Vietnam a decade later.

specify where, and against which targets, nuclear weapons would be used and it was only with the election of Dwight Eisenhower that US Strategic Doctrine began to be elevated to more sophisticated levels.

## Dwight Eisenhower and the doctrine of Massive Retaliation (1953–1961)

Eisenhower appeared better prepared than Truman in that he had both diplomatic as well as military experience – he had after all served as the supreme commander of the Allied Forces in Europe during the Second World War. Therefore, rather than seeing the Soviet Union as a menace that required continuous observation, he saw it as a problem that could be managed. In 1952, the US developed and tested the hydrogen bomb, but this was quickly followed by the Soviet Union testing its own version. This acceleration in the pace of technological breakthroughs, however, gave the impression that there was no stable balance between the two sides, which undoubtedly had an impact on US strategic doctrine. Even towards the end of Truman's presidency, there had been a growing realisation that the vulnerability of both the USA and its NATO allies was increasing due to the advances in nuclear technology and delivery systems, and this perception continued to influence policy under Eisenhower. It was now becoming abundantly obvious that a clear military victory was no longer possible and therefore the most important goal had to be the avoidance of war.

In order to combat this vulnerability, however, Eisenhower believed that there was an important link between the security of the state and its economic strength. Even during his election campaign he had underlined this connection, arguing for savings to be made so that taxes could be reduced. With a huge $60 billion defence budget, it was obvious that he would seek to make significant cuts. This seeming contradiction between maintaining, or indeed enhancing, military strength and making cuts in the budget was achieved by the doctrine of Massive Retaliation (MR). Given that it was much more expensive to maintain labour-intensive conventional forces, Eisenhower sought to enhance the deterrent capabilities of the United States by increasing its nuclear armaments significantly. The easiest way to understand the notion of MR is to reflect on statements by Eisenhower's Secretary of State – John Foster Dulles. Dulles criticised Truman for having lost the initiative in the struggle with the Soviet Union. In an article with *Life* magazine he stated:

> The free world must develop the will and organize the means to retaliate instantly against open aggression by Red armies, so that, if it occurred anywhere, we could and would strike back where it hurts, by means of our own choosing.
>
> (Gaddis 1982: 121)

Dulles was well known for his intensely anti-communist sentiments and he was just as concerned with containing the Soviet Union as the Truman Administration had been. Indeed, Dulles saw Soviet communism as intent on extending its ethos throughout the world, and this would be achieved by overwhelming small states through propaganda and limited war. The basis for this belief came in the form of 'domino theory' which claimed that if one state succumbed to Soviet communism, then the likelihood of neighboring states coming under the same influence was high – giving rise to the so-called 'domino effect'. As Eisenhower stated in 1954:

> Finally, you have broader considerations that might follow what you would call the 'falling domino' principle. You have a row of dominoes set up, you knock over the first one, and what will happen to the last one is the certainty that it will go over very quickly. So you could have the beginning of a disintegration that would have the most profound influences.
>
> (Eisenhower's News Conference, 7 April 1954)

Eventually, the West would be encircled and gradually weakened, so that it had to succumb to communism. He argued, therefore, that the US had to rely on its technological advantage in nuclear weapons to threaten the Soviet Union wherever western security was challenged. Massive Retaliation (MR) was the next stage of the evolution of US strategic doctrine and appeared to signal the extension of US deterrence over the whole territory of NATO. It also gave the impression that the United States was prepared to initiate nuclear war in response to any communist transgression – even if it was not directed at the US. The doctrine came under criticism almost immediately. The over-reliance on nuclear weapons – as embodied within the doctrine of MR – gave the impression that the US was prepared to risk global Armageddon even in the event of a relatively minor infraction by the Soviet Union. However, the Soviet invasion of Hungary in 1956 represented just such an infraction, and yet the US response was muted.

The main criticism levelled against MR was its lack of credibility, and it was partly in response to this that Dulles sought to clarify certain aspects of the doctrine and consequently began to think in terms of limited and attainable objectives. The concept of limited war was not new and had its roots in the philosophy of Captain Basil Liddell Hart (a soldier and leading military historian – 1895–1970), which stressed the premise that, since wars between nations caused so much disruption and destruction, they should be limited. In light of this, Dulles was at pains to deny the premise that the only policy open to the US was massive strategic bombing to deter or counter Soviet aggression. Though this option remained a possibility, he insisted that it was only one of a range of options available as a response to aggression. Despite problems over the definition of MR and confusion over policy, the Eisenhower administration's contribution to the debates on deterrence was immense and one aspect in particular stands out. With both the US and the Soviet rapidly militarising, Eisenhower believed that the Cold War could last for a long time and he therefore sought to avoid the costs associated with mass conventional rearmament. It was largely because of this that nuclear weapons quickly became associated with NATO's defence strategy, as did the view that the West could not match the conventional forces of the Warsaw Pact. The only option for maintaining American security, therefore, appeared to be reliance on a nuclear deterrent.

# President John F. Kennedy, Robert McNamara and Mutual Assured Destruction

President Kennedy sought to distance himself significantly from Eisenhower's doctrine of Massive Retaliation and it was during his era that nuclear deterrence came under sustained analysis and developed to more sophisticated levels. Kennedy's time in office was short-lived, however, since he was assassinated on 22 November 1963. Nevertheless, he presided over some of the most momentous events and developments of the Cold War. Kennedy's goal of stopping the Soviet Union from gaining any strategic advantage found intellectual substance in the ideas of Robert S. McNamara – the Secretary of State for Defense. The President was keen to introduce a wider range of nuclear weapons into the US arsenal, allowing for options other than full-scale war and total destruction. In line with Kennedy's wishes, therefore, McNamara replaced Eisenhower's Massive Retaliation with the doctrine of Flexible Response, encouraging the development of a range of capabilities, both conventional and nuclear, which allowed for a variety of conflicts which would fall short of full-scale nuclear war.

Similarly, Paul Nitze, Assistant Secretary of Defense, supported both Kennedy's vision and McNamara's ideas on flexibility in foreign policy. He believed that for foreign policy to be successful, the USA had to adopt a range of diverse instruments in order to project its force. Nitze had been one of the original drafters of the famous NSC-68, written in 1950 and mentioned earlier. This document advocated a major effort to build up US military strength and Nitze continued to believe this into the 1960s. However, he now proposed a more careful assessment of force projection in a much more dangerous world, one in which the superpowers had thermonuclear weapons (see Box 30.4). As he stated in 1961, 'Even as we must be firm, determined and willing to take risks, we must also avoid the pitfalls of rash actions which could involve the sacrifice of millions of lives, not only in America but elsewhere in the world' (Suri 2005: 19). The strategy of Flexible Response, therefore, was designed to provide the United States with the opportunity to respond to the Soviet Union across the whole spectrum of its behaviour in the international system rather than the all-or-nothing expectations of nuclear war. Its designers saw it as a way of suggesting ways in which nuclear weapons could be used in battle, together with conventional weapons, without resorting to an all out nuclear exchange.

A major criticism of the strategy, however, was that it failed to address the central question of how much force was enough. At first McNamara addressed this by advocating strikes against the Soviet Union's military installations (*counterforce*) as opposed to its civilian centres (*countervalue*). The idea behind this was to preserve as much of the Soviet Union's civilian population and infrastructure as possible in the hope that it would dissuade the Soviets from attacking American cities. Also referred to as the *No-Cities Approach*, McNamara outlined his beliefs in June 1962 during a speech at the University of Michigan in Ann Arbor.

The US has come to the conclusion that . . . basic military strategy in a possible general nuclear war should be approached in much the same way that more conventional military operations had been regarded in the past. That is to say, principal military objectives, in the event of nuclear war stemming from a major attack on the alliance, should be the destruction of the enemy's military forces, not the civilian population.

(McNamara 1963)

Deterrence would continue to operate even while conflict progressed and discrimination between targets necessarily formed the basis of this approach. However, there were problems with the strategy; would the Soviet Union also refrain from attacking American cities and what about the United States? Would the US be able to hold back from attacking Soviet civilian centres if the war began to go against NATO forces? Kennedy himself was to warn the Soviet Union of a 'full retaliatory' strike during one of the most dramatic thirteen days of the Cold War – the Cuban Missile Crisis (see Box 30.6). Furthermore, there was concern that a counter-force strategy might actually undermine deterrence by giving rise to the possibility of a pre-emptive strike in light of the belief that any retaliation would be directed against military sectors.

Given that the Cuban Missile Crisis had brought the world to the brink of nuclear disaster, the superpowers were compelled to explore ways of reducing tensions. In an important speech given at the American University on 10 June 1963, Kennedy stressed that the time had come to begin thinking about curbing the arms race between the two states:

We are both caught up in a vicious and dangerous cycle, with suspicion on one side breeding suspicion on the other, and new weapons begetting counter-weapons. In short, both the United States and its allies, and the Soviet Union and its allies, have a mutually deep interest in a just and genuine peace and in halting the arms race. Agreements to this end are in the interests of the Soviet Union as well as ours.

(www.americanrhetoric.com)

## Box 30.6 The Cuban Missile Crisis (1962)

Dean Rusk was President Kennedy's Secretary of State and played a central role during the Cuban Missile Crisis. Indeed, he is often credited with bringing the United States and the Soviet Union back from the brink of nuclear holocaust. Rusk himself referred to the crisis as 'the most dangerous crisis the world has ever seen', the only time when the nuclear superpowers came 'eyeball to eyeball'. The former Eastern Bloc and communist states refer to it as the 'Caribbean Crisis' whereas in Cuba it is called the 'October Crisis'. Each of the terms, however, refers to a period of thirteen days during October 1962 when, following the discovery of Soviet nuclear weapons in Cuba, Kennedy decided that he would do all he could to force the Soviet Union to withdraw its arsenal. In 1962 the Soviet Union still lagged behind the US in terms of missile technology and as a result Nikita Khrushchev (the Soviet Premier) decided that placing shorter range missiles on the US's doorstep in Cuba would redress the balance and strengthen its deterrent. Once intelligence reconnaissance of Cuba had confirmed that the missiles were being placed, Kennedy formed EXCOM – a group of twelve of Kennedy's closest advisors which included Dean Rusk. Their task was to find a solution to the crisis and after seven days of intense debate, the President took the decision to impose a naval blockade around Cuba. Consequently, Khrushchev ordered his commanders to launch tactical nuclear weapons against the US if Cuba came under US attack, but by 28 October he decided against prolonging what had become a major crisis. Consequently, he decided to withdraw all missiles from Cuba on condition that the US refrain from invading the island.

The goal was now to stress how disastrous a nuclear war would be, and in one of the most important studies on the Cold War, Lawrence Freedman (an International Relations academic) wrote 'The formula chosen to emphasize the disastrous nature of a general nuclear war was that of "Assured Destruction". This term [was] taken to refer to a nuclear strategy based purely and simply on a threat to destroy centers of population with no alternative nuclear options contemplated at all' (Freedman 1989: 245). After advocating city-avoidance *during* nuclear war, McNamara now became single-mindedly concerned with avoiding nuclear war itself, and he argued that the only way of achieving this would be to hold Soviet cities hostage to US nuclear strikes. In addition to the shortcomings of the counterforce strategy, the fact that the Soviet Union had by now significantly increased its own nuclear capabilities also contributed to the emergence of Assured Destruction. The goal was no longer an analysis of what to do once a nuclear war had begun but rather to publicise the dangers.

Assured Destruction was not without its critics, and one complaint was that it did not prevent the Soviet Union from acquiring its own capability. McNamara, however, refused to be concerned about this prospect, indeed he even actively encouraged it since, in his opinion, it strengthened the prospects for deterrence. If the goal now was to avoid nuclear war, what better way to avoid mutual destruction than by establishing a balance? Indeed, by the mid-1960s, the Soviet Union had achieved equality with the US in terms of destructive capabilities (referred to as *nuclear parity*), leading to an unprecedented situation where two states held the potential to erase humanity. Ironically, this prospect created the conditions for stability thereby giving rise to an innovation in the doctrine of Assured Destruction – namely **Mutual Assured Destruction** (MAD), which succeeded in guiding both super-powers towards deterrence. Even after Kennedy's assassination on 22 November 1963 nuclear policy continued to develop along the guidelines laid down by his administration. Not only did Lyndon Johnson (Kennedy's successor) share his beliefs, but McNamara continued to serve as Defense Secretary and saw the doctrine of MAD established as official US policy.

There was an increasing realisation in the US, particularly after the Cuban Missile Crisis, that fighting and winning a nuclear war was not an option. It was imperative, therefore, that the deterrent effect of Mutual Assured Destruction had to work efficiently. The theory itself appeared to offer the prospect of a stable relationship. The doctrine relied on both sides having enough nuclear arsenal to destroy the other and also rested on the principle that if one side was attacked by the other for whatever reason, it could retaliate with greater or at least equal force. The result of this nuclear exchange would be an escalation that led to the total destruction of both sides. Indeed, the impact of the Cuban Missile Crisis went further than encouraging the superpowers to think about ways in which to strengthen their deter-rence against one another. Realising how close they had actually come to a nuclear conflict, the two superpowers intensified their efforts to ease tensions between them and arms control negotiations were one way of strengthening the emerging détente. The Limited Test Ban Treaty, signed in 1963, for instance, prohibited nuclear tests in outer space and under water. In addition to this, the Nuclear Non-Proliferation Treaty in 1968 committed them to working towards preventing the spread of the technology to states other than the recognised nuclear weapons states. They even agreed not to develop anti-ballistic missile systems which could have destabilised the deterrent relationship between them. To this end the Anti-Ballistic Missile Treaty (ABMT) of 1972 was seen by many as a key element of arms control in that it enabled the balance of power to continue unhindered.

The ABM Treaty was negotiated between the USA and the Soviet Union as part of a wider arms control process known as the Strategic Arms Limitation Talks (SALT) which began in Helsinki, Finland in 1970. There were two rounds of talks, beginning with SALT I, which sought to limit the number of ballistic missile launchers to existing levels and allowed for additional submarine launched ballistic missile (SLBM) systems once older equipment had been dismantled. These negotiations culminated with the successful signing of the ABM Treaty. Between 1977 and 1979 President Jimmy Carter of the USA and Leonid Brezhnev (Premier of the Soviet Union) attempted to further the progress which had been made during the SALT I talks. SALT II was the first nuclear arms treaty which attempted to go beyond merely restricting numbers of delivery vehicles to making actual cuts in the number of missiles each state had. Ultimately the treaty was never ratified by the United States, given that the years after 1976 witnessed a worsening of relations between the two superpowers. This resurgence of confrontation is often referred to as the 'Second Cold War' and had its roots in a number of events during the 1970s. Certain actions on the part of the Soviet Union persuaded the USA that it had changed from being a continental to a global power, and from being merely concerned during the 1960s with areas immediately adjacent to it, to dealing with commitments in more distant parts of the world. In 1979, for example, the Soviet Union invaded Afghanistan and this was perceived by the USA as an increasing willingness on the part of the Soviets to use force. In fact, Afghanistan was the culmination of a series of proxy interventions undertaken in a number of Third World countries, namely Soviet support for the MPLA in Angola, for Colonel Mengistu against the Somalis in Ethiopia, their backing for the pro-Soviet South Yemeni attack on North Yemen in 1979, and the joint invasion of Kampuchea with Vietnam in 1977. Therefore, the main reason that Afghanistan caused such alarm in the West was the change in Soviet tactics: Moscow, for the first time, had gone beyond the use of proxies to direct military intervention outside Eastern Europe.

These events occurred alongside a huge increase in the size and capability of the Soviet navy which had, since 1968, developed into a major ocean capable fleet. This was seen as a strong indicator of growing Soviet interests in the global projection of power. Alongside these developments there was a reduction in defence spending in the United States as well as a major decrease in naval ship levels. The increase in Soviet military capabilities, its use of proxies in places like Angola and the invasion of Afghanistan in 1979 persuaded US officials that the Soviet Union was overtaking them in military capabilities. With the election of Ronald Reagan as US President in 1981, tensions increased further. He immediately viewed détente as having eroded American military strength while providing the Soviet Union with an opportunity to match, or even surpass, the USA in many areas. Increasingly, his administration viewed the possibility of a US victory in a nuclear war with the Soviet Union as a key objective and began to develop weapon systems congruent with these goals. One highly controversial step by the Reagan Administration was to initiate research into advanced strategic defence against nuclear attack. Known as the Strategic Defense Initiative (SDI), this was intended to be a highly sophisticated ground and space-based anti-ballistic missile system. Its utilisation of space-based laser technology, subatomic particle beams and computer-guided projectiles led to the label 'Star Wars' being attached to it. The programme ended up costing over $30 billion but was eventually shelved because it contravened the ABM Treaty of 1972 and the concern was that it might ignite a conflict with the Soviet Union.

For its part, the Soviet Union failed to achieve a quick victory in Afghanistan. The costs of this war, combined with increasing economic problems in the Soviet Union and the escalating costs associated with the arms race meant that the Soviet economy began to falter. Mikhail Gorbachev became Soviet General Secretary in 1985 and set about announcing major reforms of the Soviet economic system. Between 1985 and 1989 he persuaded Western states that he was not only committed to reversing the Soviet economic decline but also was determined to force a thaw in the relations between the two sides. Reagan responded by renewing talks on economic issues and reducing nuclear-related tensions. In 1987, the two sides signed the breakthrough Intermediate-Range Nuclear Forces Treaty (INFT) which eliminated all nuclear missiles with a range of between 500 and 5,500 kilometres. The tensions reduced further and soon resulted in the signing of the Strategic Arms Reduction Treaty (START) in 1989. Soviet troops withdrew from Afghanistan in 1988 and a year later the Berlin Wall came down signalling the end of the Cold War.

## Deterrence and the nuclear non-proliferation regime in the post-Cold War era

Having introduced the view that nuclear weapons could in certain circumstances bring about stability between conflicting states and having analysed some key elements of US strategic doctrine during the Cold War, two further questions need to be raised. We have already introduced the first: why, if nuclear weapons do indeed contribute to stability, have the five original members sought to restrict membership of the nuclear club through treaties such as the NPT? Secondly, if deterrence did succeed in preventing global nuclear war between the two superpowers, as indicated by evidence drawn from the Cold War, does it have a role to play in the post-Cold War era?

### The nuclear non-proliferation regime – the twin pillars

There are two essential pillars to the **non-proliferation regime**: the first aims to prevent the proliferation of nuclear weapons to states other than the five original nuclear weapon powers – often referred to as Horizontal Proliferation; the second pillar seeks both to prevent *existing* nuclear weapon states from acquiring new weapons (Vertical Proliferation) and to encourage them to disarm. These objectives have been the subject of a great deal of controversy and the debate over whether or not they have been achieved continues to rage. At the centre of the storm has been the Nuclear Non-Proliferation Treaty of 1968.

This treaty may have conferred nuclear weapon status upon the five original members (USA, Soviet Union, Britain, China and France), but it also sought to encourage all other members of the international community to refrain from acquiring these weapons. The treaty also made the distinction between nuclear weapons technology and the technology required for nuclear energy, specifying that those states which signed up to it *were* entitled to harness the power of the atom to generate energy for their civilian sectors. The primary goal of the treaty, however, was to prevent states from diverting their attention to nuclear weapons production and to a very large extent this has been achieved. Today only four states, India, Pakistan, North Korea and Israel, remain outside the treaty. North Korea acceded to the original treaty but then violated its terms and subsequently withdrew from it in 2003. Both India and Pakistan conducted nuclear tests within days of each other in 1998 and Israel has always maintained a high degree of opacity over its own programme. Other states have also caused concern. The international community suspects that Iran (an NNPT signatory) is at present attempting to develop nuclear weapons and over the past few decades others such as Iraq, Libya, Argentina, Brazil, and South Africa have at one time or another expressed an interest in acquiring nuclear weapons technology. Preventing the proliferation of this technology is central to the foreign policy goals of states such as Britain and the USA.

Despite the attempts by numerous states to acquire nuclear weapons, the NNPT has been relatively successful, largely as a result of the efforts of the major nuclear weapon states in prohibiting the spread of the relevant technology. The regime itself consists of a range of mechanisms, including the treaty of 1968, but also a system of safeguards designed by the International Atomic Energy Agency (IAEA). Under this system, states which had signed up to the NNPT undertook to place all the nuclear material in their territory under the safeguard of the Agency. The purpose of this was to ensure that none of the material was diverted away from peaceful activities to clandestine nuclear weapons programmes. Another element of the non-proliferation regime is the Nuclear Suppliers Group, which consists of a significant number of technologically advanced states that seek to prevent proliferation by establishing a series of guidelines to control the export of material and equipment which could be used to produce nuclear weapons. The group was proposed by the United States in 1974 following a nuclear test by India in the same year, and by 1991 its membership had grown to thirty-four states.

Nuclear Weapons Free Zones (NWFZ) are another mechanism through which states promote non-proliferation. Such zones can be defined as regions within which states decide not to introduce, develop or test nuclear weapons. At present states within Latin America, the South Pacific and South East Asia have declared their regions as NWFZ. More recently in 2006, five Central Asian (CA) states (Kazakhstan, Kyrgyzstan, Tajikistan, Turkmenistan and Uzbekistan) signed the CANWFZ Treaty, but this has not come into force as yet. One additional key element in US non-proliferation strategy has been the provision of nuclear guarantees in support of states that continue to refrain from acquiring their own nuclear weapons. Initiated by China's nuclear tests in 1964, this element in US foreign policy dates back to the mid-1960s and its essence is to provide guarantees to non-nuclear states that they would not be subjected to nuclear blackmail or attack in the event of conflict. These examples demonstrate that the United States (along with the original members of the nuclear club) have remained keen to prevent the spread of nuclear weapons to states other than themselves.

However, the arms control negotiations of the Cold War also suggest that the two super-powers recognised that limiting their own nuclear weapons was central to the security that they both sought. As the analysis of US strategic doctrine has shown, it is not an exaggera-tion to suggest that the Cold War was really all about nuclear weapons. Not only did the Cold War and the nuclear age coincide, but also nuclear weapons significantly influenced the nature of the relationship between the two superpowers. Waltz's faith in the stabilising influence of nuclear weapons notwithstanding and despite the improvement in relations following the Cuban Missile Crisis, the USA and the Soviet Union remained concerned about proliferation by other states but also about the advance of each other's nuclear capabilities. By the mid-1960s it was clear that nuclear weapons were here to stay, and in the context of MAD even had their uses, but the Limited Test Ban Treaty of 1963 demonstrated that the Soviet Union and the USA could find common ground on nuclear issues – as did the NNPT of 1968.

Nevertheless, the numbers of nuclear weapons held by each of the superpowers continued to grow and concern regarding this led to serious attempts at capping their numbers, beginning with the Strategic Arms Limitation Talks (SALT) which produced two agree-ments, SALT I and SALT II. The key word here was 'limitation', because at this time no real thought had been given to their reduction. The SALT I agreement was signed in 1972 and included the ABM Treaty (mentioned earlier) as well as the Interim Agreement which froze the numbers of Intercontinental Ballistic Missiles (ICBMs) and Submarine Launched Ballistic Missiles (SLBMs) at existing levels. This was followed by SALT II, signed in 1979 after seven years of negotiations between the US and the Soviet Union, which was the first nuclear treaty to seek actual reductions in their nuclear arsenals. The SALT rounds were followed by the Intermediate-Range Nuclear Forces Treaty (INF) in 1987 which success-fully eliminated tactical or 'battlefield' nuclear devices from Europe. In addition, the Strategic Arms Reduction Talks I and II, signed in 1991 and 1993 respectively, reduced the numbers of US and Russian long-range missiles and nuclear warheads.

The various treaties mentioned here adequately demonstrate that the superpowers have engaged in arms control measures in order to restrict the inexorable rise in their nuclear arsenals. A major increase in numbers would have been witnessed by the international community and could have influenced other states to seek security through nuclear arms – a prospect which key states such as the US, Britain and the Soviet Union sought to prevent. One of the requirements of the Non-Proliferation Treaty, therefore, was that every five years review conferences should reaffirm its goals of preventing the spread of nuclear weapons, ultimately leading to general and complete disarmament. Although the treaty was

*Source: Getty Images*

**Despite periodic arms reduction agreements, nuclear proliferation is still a serious security problem.**

originally envisaged as lasting for twenty-five years, it was extended indefinitely during the 1995 Review Conference. Despite this, significant obstacles to the treaty's non-proliferation goals remain: first, the failure of nuclear weapon states to disarm and second, the development of nuclear weapons by non-nuclear states.

## The failure to disarm

One of the most significant problems has to do with certain provisions within the NPT itself, most specifically related to Article VI which states that

> Each of the Parties to the Treaty undertakes to pursue negotiations in good faith on effective measures relating to cessation of the nuclear arms race at an early date and to nuclear disarmament, and on a Treaty on general and complete disarmament under strict and effective control.

The preamble to the treaty recalled the success of the superpowers in negotiating the Limited Test Ban Treaty (mentioned earlier) in 1963 and Article VI seeks to build on that by calling upon existing nuclear weapons states to enter into negotiations which will lead to the complete removal of nuclear arsenals. Those that take an optimistic view have pointed to the numerous arms control treaties negotiated since the early 1970s, including SALT I and II, START I and II, the INF Treaty of 1987 (referred to earlier) as well as US statements and many protocols and commitments to general disarmament and non-proliferation (Goldblat 1990: 413–14). These commitments have included the long elusive Comprehensive Test Ban Treaty adopted by the United Nations General Assembly in September 1996. However, as of 2010 this Treaty has not come into force. Conversely, others argue that none of these agreements have led to an effective cessation of the nuclear arms race. Indeed, the original nuclear weapon states continue to retain significant nuclear arsenals.

This failure to disarm has meant that the various NPT Review Conferences have been beset with problems. In 1995, for instance, the Russian wish to sell nuclear reactors to Iran led to such severe criticism from the US that the Review Conference of that year nearly failed to achieve its objectives of extending the NPT indefinitely. Even the most recent conference, in 2005, ended problematically, demonstrating that the non-proliferation regime remains fragile. This conference also failed in its goals of achieving disarmament. The original nuclear weapon states continue to refuse to provide an effective time frame for achieving comprehensive disarmament among themselves. It appears, however, that none of the original five nuclear weapons states is likely to give up nuclear weapons in the near future, and a memorandum from a Pentagon official in 2002 even recommended that the US should resume low-yield nuclear testing in order to help maintain the efficiency of its stockpile. A resumption of testing by any of the nuclear weapon states is likely to persuade the others to restart (Arms Control Association).

The last test by the US was in 1992 and thus far it has held off from conducting any more. Similarly, although China has not signed the Limited Test Ban Treaty (which banned atmospheric testing), it has complied with it since its last test in 1980. Its last underground test was in July 1996 and it has not conducted one since. France invited international environmental and political indignation when former French President Jacques Chirac announced a resumption of testing in June 1995. Its subsequent tests in French Polynesia, particularly in Mururoa Atoll, caused immense geographical degradation to the atoll as well as serious health risks to the inhabitants of the South Pacific. The last test by the Soviet Union took place in October 1990 and the last independent tests by Britain occurred during 1957–1958, with none conducted since. (In fact they were no longer necessary since it had demonstrated an ability to develop nuclear weapons and all its subsequent weapons have been based on US designs.)

## The failure to stem nuclear proliferation

In addition to trying to persuade the nuclear weapon states to disarm, the non-proliferation regime seeks to prevent proliferation to non-nuclear weapon states – namely horizontal proliferation. These efforts have also been seriously hampered in recent years. North Korea has developed nuclear weapons in violation of its Treaty obligations (although it did withdraw from the NPT prior to its tests), and the nuclear posturing between India and Pakistan is very likely to continue, as is Israel's own significant programme. Indeed, the refusal by these three states to sign the NPT ensures that it is not universally applicable. In addition, although Iran is a signatory of the NPT, the international community is concerned that it too is seeking to develop nuclear weapons. Non-proliferation efforts may have been strengthened by the fact that none of the original five nuclear weapon states have conducted tests since 1996, but these efforts have been seriously undermined by India, Pakistan and North Korea. India crossed the threshold and acquired nuclear power status when it tested five underground devices in May 1988, and this prompted its neighbour Pakistan, with whom it has fought three wars since gaining independence in 1947, to conduct its own nuclear tests later the same month. North Korea conducted a test in October 2006 and more recently in May 2009. Israel has always maintained a high degree of ambiguity over its own programme and has never officially admitted to having these weapons, insisting that it will not be the first state to introduce nuclear weapons to the Middle East. Both the IAEA and the USA have concluded, however, that Israel successfully started development of nuclear weapons as far back as 1968, and it is now thought to have produced enough fissile material to stockpile between one and two hundred nuclear weapons.

The non-proliferation regime has clearly experienced problems in fulfilling its twin objectives of disarmament and non-proliferation. One reason for the lack of success is the objectives of states themselves which vary from state to state, with the nuclear weapon states obviously far less bothered about drawing attention to their own failure to disarm. This is, however, of major concern to non-nuclear states which, while keen to ensure the success of non-proliferation efforts, make the logical point that unless the nuclear weapon states disarm and prevent vertical proliferation, it will be impossible to achieve non-proliferation. Even a single state in possession of a nuclear arsenal could act as a stimulus for other states to acquire these weapons. At present almost sixty countries have or are constructing nuclear power or research centres, and forty of these have the capacity to build nuclear weapons should they choose to do so (Hanson 2005: 304). The same concerns are likely to dominate the proceedings of future conferences and there will be many calls for the NPT to be discarded.

## Where does this leave us?

There is one further issue, however, which could further destabilise international efforts at preventing the spread of these weapons. The issue of 'nuclear terrorism' has come to the fore since the attacks on the World Trade Center on 11 September 2001. This dramatic event not only demonstrated the vulnerability of the United States in the face of determined terrorism but also caused destruction and civilian death on an unprecedented scale. The timing of the attack was also significant given that it came soon after the nuclear tests by India and Pakistan. The heightened concern over proliferation intensified following the 9/11 attacks and raised concerns that terrorist groups such as al-Qaeda could well be interested in gaining access to a nuclear device. This concern solidified following the confession by A.Q. Khan, the father of Pakistan's nuclear weapons programme, that he had recently sold nuclear weapons technology to Iran, Libya, North Korea and other states. It wasn't until the year 2000 that his network was finally unearthed and this ultimately led to the seizure, in 2003, of nuclear components on their way to a secret Libyan nuclear weapons programme. Confronted with intense American pressure, Libya agreed to renounce its nuclear programme and at the same time provided enough information to lead to the arrest of Khan and the destruction of his covert network (Albright and Hinderstein 2005: 111).

Khan's revelations have heightened fears that terrorist groups seeking to attack the United States and its allies may be closer to acquiring nuclear weapons than any one had realised. Many observers now believe that nuclear terrorism is a distinct possibility and apart from the fear this has instilled in capitals around the world, it has also forced a rethink over the value of deterrence in the post-9/11 era. As this chapter has shown, Waltzian logic uses the stability of the Cold War as evidence to demonstrate that nuclear weapons can contribute to stabilising the relations between states antagonistic to one another. The doctrine of Mutual Assured Destruction ensured that a nuclear attack by one superpower against the other would result in a full-scale response, causing destruction on a global scale. Consequently, the theory specified that leaders would refrain from using nuclear weapons at all costs. However, since the end of the Cold War the world has witnessed nuclear tests by India, Pakistan and North Korea and has also seen the emergence of non-state actors capable and willing to attack states, both Western and otherwise. The attacks in London on 7 July 2005, in Bali against Western targets on 12 October 2002 and a further attack in October 2005, along with the Madrid train bombing on 11 March 2004, the attacks against the Indian Parliament on 13 December 2001 and the 2008 attacks in Mumbai in which over one hundred and seventy people were killed, are just a handful of a multitude of terrorist incidents since 2001.

It would appear that al-Qaeda and other groups inspired by its ideology do not operate under such constraints; indeed, its members even welcome death in the form of a suicide attack against their targets believing that this is likely to lead to martyrdom. The issue is further complicated by the premise that these groups are known to operate in a number of countries and therefore have no permanent location that can be targeted. The key, therefore, is for the international community to work towards keeping weapons-grade nuclear material out of the hands of terrorists since a failure to do so could lead to an event too terrible to imagine. Given that terrorist groups do not operate on the same principles as states, the implications for deterrence are immense. Deterrence may have worked between the superpowers during the Cold War and it may even continue to operate successfully in the context of stable nuclear weapon states in the post-Cold War era, but rather than the simple East–West balance, the international community now faces a variety of strategic issues, one of which is the threat posed by terrorist groups, against whom deterrence will be ineffectual. Therefore, the stability of nuclear-armed states is of paramount importance. Pakistan, in particular, has been a cause for serious concern in recent years due to the possibility that it could lose control of its nuclear weapons in the face of the Taliban insurgency in the North West Frontier Province (see the Case study).

## Case study: The Indian subcontinent and nuclear weapons

India and Pakistan gained independence from Britain in August 1947 and almost immediately went to war with one another over the disputed state of Kashmir, a situation which ended only when the UN succeeded in brokering a truce in January 1949. The next war over Kashmir came about following a series of skirmishes between April and September of 1965 which developed into a more widespread war and spread along the Indo-Pakistani border into the divided state of Punjab and involved the ground and air forces of both countries. A stalemate persuaded the two to agree to a ceasefire and this lasted until their next war in 1971. The origins of this war were different from the previous conflicts and had their roots in Pakistan's failure to deal with demands for autonomy in East Pakistan, which had begun to call for independence from West Pakistan. With Indian support, the war of 1971 resulted in the creation of the state of Bangladesh. Other conflicts between the two occurred on the 6,000 metre high Siachen Glacier in 1984 and at Kargil in May 1999, both of which are in Kashmir.

India first tested a nuclear explosion on 18 May 1974 and it subsequently declared itself a nuclear weapon state following its tests in 1998 – Operation Shakti. India's tests were quickly followed by Pakistan carrying out its own two weeks later. As this brief summary of the conflicts between India and Pakistan demonstrates, the two states are clearly arch rivals and have entered the new millennium as declared nuclear weapon states. Given their historical animosity and the number of conflicts they have engaged in over the years, the international community has become increasingly concerned at the arms race in which they are now clearly engaged. In line with Waltz's 'more may be better' argument, the question of whether their nuclear tests have contributed to an easing of tensions and greater stability between them is an important one.

Despite their limited conflict in Kargil in 1999, the two states have not been at war with each other since 1971. In addition, proliferation optimists such as Waltz would point to the attack on the Indian Parliament on 13 December 2001 as evidence that a full-scale war between the two was unlikely. On that occasion both sides amassed over a million troops on their border and yet stepped back from an escalation into war. Similarly, the 2008 attack on Mumbai by Pakistani-based terrorist groups did not result in war, even though many Indian politicians called for punitive strikes against Pakistan. Indeed, a joint Indo-Pakistani statement issued as recently as 30 July 2009 specified that war between the two states over Kashmir and terrorism was not a feasible option (+, 30 July 2009). Does this mean, therefore, that we must ask ourselves whether nuclear weapons in both states have contributed to the emergence of a viable deterrent between them?

 **If nuclear proliferation is perceived to be dangerous, why do states such as India and Pakistan seek to acquire these weapons?**

## Conclusions

This chapter has shown that, despite the optimism of Kenneth Waltz's 'more may be better' logic, the international community largely believes that the spread of nuclear weapons is undesirable. This anti-proliferation view has emerged because of a number of protracted challenges to regional and global security. The first is linked to the proliferation of nuclear weapons to states that are hostile to the West, such as Iran and North Korea, and the second concerns the impact on global security if terrorist groups such as al-Qaeda were to access such weapons. These challenges are of major concern to the international community, including the United States, given that they are significantly different from those that existed during the Cold War. Between 1945 and 1989 the United States was in confrontation with another superpower and, despite the hostility between them, an appropriate strategic nuclear doctrine, MAD, had the potential to enhance the prospects of deterrence and, in turn, the stability between them. Today the United States faces Islamic inspired terrorism in many regions of the globe, from North Africa to Pakistan, Afghanistan and India to South East Asia. The use of countless suicide bombing tactics by al-Qaeda has inspired groups across the globe and their declared objective of gaining access to nuclear weapons has raised fears of unprecedented nuclear terrorism. Given that the nuclear non-proliferation regime has proved ineffectual in preventing even states such as India, Pakistan and Israel from developing nuclear weapons, how to prevent terrorist groups from accessing this technology is now a serious issue. If this were to occur, the impact on global stability would be devastating.

## Resource section

## Questions

1. Neo-Realists like Kenneth Waltz believe that nuclear weapons may be a source of stability in the international system. Why do you think this is so?

2. What were the essential differences between President Eisenhower's doctrine of Massive Retaliation and Robert McNamara's Mutual Assured Destruction?

3. Do you think the Nuclear Non-Proliferation Treaty has been relatively successful in preventing proliferation?

4. What is meant by Nuclear Deterrence? Does this still have a role to play in the post-9/11 era?

5. What are the various elements which make up the nuclear non-proliferation regime and what problems are facing this regime?

## Recommended reading

Freedman, L. (1989) *The Evolution of Nuclear Strategy* (2nd edn, Basingstoke: Macmillan)
This remains one of the most comprehensive and well-written accounts of the evolution of strategic doctrine during the Cold War.

Gaddis, J.L. (1982) *Strategies of Containment: A Critical Appraisal of Postwar American National Security Policy* (New York, Oxford University Press)

Goldblat, J. (2007) *Can Nuclear Proliferation be Stopped?* Geneva International Peace Research Institute (GIPRI)
Goldblat provides an excellent overview of the current state of proliferation.

Sagan, S.D. and Waltz, K. (2002) *The Spread of Nuclear Weapons: A Debate Renewed* (2nd edn, New York: W.W. Norton and Co)
This is an excellent summary of the debate between proliferation optimists such as Kenneth Waltz and those who view it as a dangerous development.

*The Bulletin of Atomic Scientists*
This is one of the most respected journals on all topics relating to nuclear weapons and technology. It now publishes many articles on proliferation issues and is available at www.thebulletin.org.

Waltz, K. (1981) 'The spread of nuclear weapons: more may be better', *Adelphi Papers*, No. 171, London, International Institute of Strategic Studies
This is Waltz's original paper on his beliefs that the spread of nuclear weapons would in certain circumstances create stability between antagonists.

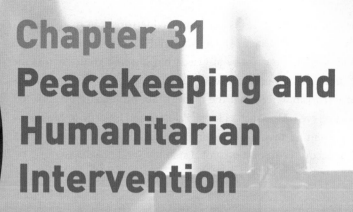

# Chapter 31
# Peacekeeping and Humanitarian Intervention

The original purpose of the United Nations and early peacekeeping

Peacekeeping during the Cold War, 1945–1989

Maintaining international peace and security in the post-Cold War era

Conclusions

After reading this chapter you will be able to:

- Explore the beginnings of the United Nations system

- Use examples to analyse the development of peacekeeping during the Cold War

- Consider the impact of the end of the Cold War on the UN's ability to fulfil its security functions

- Use a number of key post-Cold War crises to reflect on the nature of contemporary peacekeeping

*Source*: Panos Pictures/Chris Stowers

## Introductory box: Conflict in the Persian Gulf (1991)

Kuwait, a tiny Arab Emirate, nestled between Iraq in the north west and Saudi Arabia in the south, may appear an unlikely setting for one of the greatest debates over the role of the United Nations. The seeds were sown, however, when on 2 August 1990 the forces of Saddam Hussein (President of Iraq: 1979–2003) marched across the border and annexed Kuwait. This episode led to a flurry of activity which culminated in the establishment of one of the largest multinational forces assembled since the Second World War. The defining characteristic of the 1991 Gulf War against Iraq was that it had been initiated under the authorisation of the United Nations. The United Nations Security Council (UNSC) adopted numerous resolutions in quick succession, all of which called for the immediate and unconditional withdrawal of Iraq's forces from Kuwait. Throughout the months of diplomacy (2 August 1990–15 January 1991), however, Iraq gave no indication that it would be willing to withdraw. Given Iraq's intransigence, the Security Council adopted Resolution 678 on 29 November 1990. This was significant in that it specified that the coalition assembled against Iraq could use 'all necessary means' to ensure the removal of Iraq from Kuwaiti territory. The aerial bombardment of Iraq began on 15 January 1991, followed by a ground offensive on 23 February which ceased once Kuwait was liberated, a mere one hundred hours after the start of operations.

## The original purpose of the United Nations and early peacekeeping

We must remember the implications of the fact that the Persian Gulf conflict of 1991 occurred after the Cold War had ended. Elsewhere in this book we have characterised the Cold War as an era of intense rivalry between the United States and the Soviet Union, the impact of which was most clearly manifest in the stalemate within the Security Council, the organ tasked with maintaining international peace and security. It consists of fifteen member states including the five veto-wielding permanent members (commonly referred to as the P5), and during the Cold War, this included the Soviet Union, the United States, China, France and Britain. The permanent members used their power of veto regularly during the Cold War and thereby restricted the ability of the UN to act decisively. At the end of the Cold War, however, the perception re-emerged that the UN could once again function as its founding members had envisaged. Iraq's invasion of Kuwait presented the organisation with just such an opportunity and by the end of February 1991, it had demonstrated that, given consensus among the P5 and the political will to ensure the success of the UN, the Organisation could function efficiently.

The original founders of the UN undoubtedly intended the organisation to play a central role in maintaining global and regional security. One only has to read the various sections

Source: Getty Images

**UN peacekeepers play a variety of roles, from observing ceasefires to restoring order. Here, UN soldiers supervise food distribution following a devastating earthquake in Haiti.**

of the UN Charter to realise that the rights and power accorded to the Organisation, and in particular to the Security Council, were significant. This power was embodied within the principle of **Collective Security** defined as a coalition-building strategy where a group of states could come together, agree not to attack one another and also agree to defend each other in case of an attack. Most writings on the UN acknowledge, however, that it has failed in achieving this strategy – largely due to the conflictual dynamics of the Cold War – and as a consequence the members adopted alternative mechanisms to enable the UN to fulfil a semblance of its primary role. **Peacekeeping** emerged in response to the UN's inability to practise collective security, and one of the prime purposes of this chapter is to highlight the essential differences between these two methods of maintaining international peace and security.

There are two broad areas to the UN's efforts to maintain international peace and security that merit our attention. The first relates to the attempts to prevent states from resorting to war against each other and the second involves upholding human rights. In order to understand these positions we must go back in history and consider some of the issues to emerge from the discussions which led to the establishment of the UN. One of the main events was the Dumbarton Oaks Conference which began on 21 August 1944; by 7 October, four states, the United States, the Soviet Union, Britain and the Republic of

China, had negotiated the rubric of what would become the United Nations. The task would not be easy; after all a similar attempt had led to the establishment of the League of Nations twenty years earlier in the wake of the First World War. Much of the discussion at Dumbarton Oaks, therefore, revolved around how to ensure that the United Nations would be a stronger institution than its predecessor. One perceived problem with the League had been that the powerful nations of the world had not played a central role during crucial moments, and it was now stressed that both the Soviet Union and the United States had to be active participants. In addition to this, the new body had to be provided with a great deal of authority, including the right to use armed force if necessary, against a state that had transgressed (Hilderbrand 1990). Ultimately, the proposals that stemmed from this conference established the basis for the UN Charter, the essence of which was the prohibition of the threat or use of force by one member state against another. The founders also agreed on a Security Council which would be given primary responsibility for global security and that would be able to use forceful measures to restore security in the event of a breach of peace.

Chapter I of the proposals established the 'purposes' of the new organisation, which are particularly interesting in that they omit any reference to the protection of human rights. This is an important point because it provides a strong hint at the early nature of the UN. Later in Chapter IX some provision was made, in that the General Assembly was called upon to facilitate 'solutions of international economic, social and other humanitarian problems and promote respect for human rights and fundamental freedoms'. However, the 'power' of the UN was to remain firmly embedded within the Security Council, and it was to remain concerned with maintaining *international* peace and security. The word 'international' is particularly important since it provides a further indication of the essence of the UN: namely, that it was designed to prevent and deal with inter-state disputes and conflicts, and to respect the sovereignty of its members. Consequently, at this stage of the UN's development the founding members agreed that the organisation would refrain from intervening in the internal affairs of its member states and that it was up to each state to respect the basic human rights of its own citizens. Importantly, therefore, the Dumbarton Oaks proposals were heavily geared towards traditional ideas of threats to peace and emphasised the need to use the organisation's collective strength to maintain that international peace. The proposals did not extend, therefore, to the use of military force in response to human rights violations when they occurred within states.

Dumbarton Oaks was followed by the Yalta Conference in February 1945, where the Soviet Union was persuaded by the other founding members to participate actively in the new United Nations. One issue at Yalta was concerned with the right of *veto* that the permanent members of the Security Council gave themselves at Dumbarton Oaks. A 'veto' refers simply to the notion that the party wielding it can exercise the right unilaterally to stop a specific decision from being taken. In the context of the United Nations, the five permanent members of the Security Council have the right to block any resolution and stop any changes from taking place. They have even sought to restrict discussion in the Security Council to issues of which they approved, but have had to give way in the face of determined opposition from other states. As a consequence, the permanent members can exercise their veto power on substantive issues, such as whether or not to approve military action against a state. They cannot, however, exercise this right over procedural issues such as the nature or topic of Council discussions.

## Defining collective security: the essence of the UN

Discussions continued until 26 June 1945, when an initial group of fifty states signed the UN Charter, and today membership stands at 192. The UN Charter is a remarkable document, not least because of the level of power available to the organisation which, on paper, is enormous, and the essence of that power is embodied within the principle of 'collective security'. Traditional international relations, based on Realist principles (see Chapter 6) specifies that states pursue their interests and may resort to the use of force if necessary to safeguard those interests. Increasing connections between states, resulting in greater political and economic interdependence amongst them, however, have led to numerous attempts at avoiding automatic resort to conflict. Included in this mix have been alliances, non-aggression pacts and the inevitable attempt to establish a balance of power among the powerful states of the world. Such mechanisms were prominent prior to the First World War, but they have often been criticised for being too fragile and we can even argue that the onset of war in 1914 was a direct result of their fragility and ultimate collapse.

At the heart of this new method was the assumption that states would be willing to relinquish a significant portion of their sovereignty and interests to an international organisation. In return the organisation would provide a mechanism whereby the combined/collective strength of the member states could be brought to bear upon an aggressor state that decided to cross the threshold from peace to aggression. A body of international law – as embodied in the League's Covenant and now the UN Charter – would be elevated to a level that all member states would be compelled to accept and abide by. The theory behind collective security recognises that military power is a central component of the international system and that the key to encouraging peace between states is to provide a mechanism whereby their relations can be effectively managed. Even though there is a tacit recognition of the continuing centrality of military force, collective security is distinctly anti-Realist in that its advocates oppose important features of Realism, one of which is the balance-of-power mechanism. In theory, a collective security system is far stronger than this Realist method because the capabilities of the collective are deemed to far outweigh the ability of the aggressor.

A second feature of collective security is that it relies heavily on cooperation to create the stability members seek, in contrast to the competitive nature of the anarchic self-help system envisaged by Realists. It is assumed that members of the collective security organisation believe that all other members will come to their aid if they are attacked and, because of this, collective security reduces the amount of hostility and rivalry apparent under conditions of international anarchy. As we have shown elsewhere in this book, the Realist approach to international relations emphasises the centrality of the state and highlights the premise that nation-states are motivated by their national interests. A Realist understanding of the national interest boils down to one basic proposition, namely that, whatever else states seek, they seek to preserve their political autonomy and their territorial integrity. However, collective security requires that states subdue their selfish narrow interests in favour of an indivisible collective interest to which all states contribute (Schachter 1991: 390). In this sense an attack on one is considered as an attack on all. Finally, Innis Claude, as one of the most prolific analysts of collective security, has argued that, all states must trust each other and be confident that all will renounce aggression. This is in contrast to a Realist environment in which states are fearful of each others' motives (Claude 1962).

## Collective security in theory and practice: the UN Charter

Even a cursory glance at the Charter reveals the enormous potential of the United Nations. Its primary purpose is the 'maintenance of international peace and security' and this objective revolves around two frameworks. The first relates to the high standards of conduct expected of the member state (see Box 31.1) and two of the Charter's chapters, VI and VII, are devoted to the second. Both these chapters are highly relevant to us in that they explicitly refer to the UN's role in maintaining peace and security.

Although both Chapters VI and VII of the Charter are devoted to finding solutions to instances of aggression by states, they are significantly different from one another. Whereas Chapter VI provides guidelines for the General Assembly as well as the Security Council to deal with *potential* breaches of the peace, Chapter VII authorises only the Security Council

---

### Box 31.1 The United Nations – principles of international conduct

The Organisation and its Members, in pursuit of the Purposes stated in Article 1, shall act in accordance with the following Principles.

1. The Organisation is based on the principle of the sovereign equality of all its Members.
2. All Members, in order to ensure to all of them the rights and benefits resulting from membership, shall fulfill in good faith the obligations assumed by them in accordance with the present Charter.
3. All Members shall settle their international disputes by peaceful means in such a manner that international peace and security, and justice, are not endangered.
4. All Members shall refrain in their international relations from the threat or use of force against the territorial integrity or political independence of any state, or in any other manner inconsistent with the Purposes of the United Nations.
5. All Members shall give the United Nations every assistance in any action it takes in accordance with the present Charter, and shall refrain from giving assistance to any state against which the United Nations is taking preventive or enforcement action.
6. The Organisation shall ensure that states which are not Members of the United Nations act in accordance with these Principles insofar as may be necessary for the maintenance of international peace and security.
7. Nothing contained in the present Charter shall authorize the United Nations to intervene in matters which are essentially within the domestic jurisdiction of any state or shall require the Members to submit such matters to settlement under the present Charter; but this principle shall not prejudice the application of enforcement measures under Chapter VII.

*Source*: UN Charter

to deal with *actual* breaches. Entitled the 'Pacific Settlement of Disputes', Chapter VI advises conflicting states to resort to peaceful methods to identify solutions to their disagreements. It was in Chapter VII, however, that the Council's most extensive powers were laid down. Entitled 'Action with Respect to Threats to the Peace, Breaches of the Peace, and Acts of Aggression', the provisions in this chapter are quite straightforward. Once the Council determines that a breach of peace or an act of aggression has taken place, it has the right to use any of a number of measures to restore peaceful relations and it is in Article 42 that the Council's ultimate power is to be found.

> Should the Security Council consider that measures provided for in Article 41 would be inadequate or have proved to be inadequate, it may take such action by air, sea, or land forces as may be necessary to maintain or restore international peace and security. Such action may include demonstrations, blockade, and other operations by air, sea, or land forces of Members of the United Nations.
>
> (Article 42)

The two superpowers (the USA and the Soviet Union) were now firmly committed to the new organisation and centrally involved in its creation. Persuading the Soviet Union to remain involved in the process was particularly important given its problems with the League in the past. The Soviet invasion of Finland in 1939 resulted in its expulsion from the League and this soured its relationship with the other members. It was, therefore, important that the Soviet Union should play an active role in the new United Nations. Although

---

### Box 31.2 Defining collective security

1. 'The case for collective security rests on the claim that regulated, institutionalised balancing predicated on the notion of all against one provides more stability than unregulated, self-help balancing predicated on the notion of each for his own. Under collective security, states agree to abide by certain norms and rules to maintain stability and, when necessary, band together to stop aggression.'

   *Source*: Kupchan, C.A. and Kupchan, C.A. (1998) 'The promise of collective security', in M.E. Brown et al. (eds) *Theories of War and Peace: An International Security Reader* (Cambridge, MA: The MIT Press, p.397).

2. 'It reflects a security arrangement whereby a clearly delineated group of nations agrees that if one nation in their membership encroaches upon the sovereignty of another, the rest of the members will take collective action against the aggressive member.'

   *Source*: Lagon, M.P. (1995) 'The Illusions of Collective Security', *The National Interest*.

3. '. . . a system based on the universal obligation of all nations to join forces against an aggressor state as soon as the fact of aggression is determined by established procedure. In such a system, aggression is defined as a wrong in universal terms and an aggressor, as soon as he has been identified, stands condemned. Hence the obligation of all nations to take action against him is conceived as a duty to support right against wrong. It is equally founded upon the practical expectation that the communal solidarity of all nations would from the outset make it clear to every government that 'aggression does not pay'.

   *Source*: Howard, C., Johnson, H.C. and Niemeyer, G. (1954) 'Collective security: the validity of an ideal', *International Organisation*, 8 19–20.

it differed significantly from the League, the new United Nations reflected the same basic premise of collective security. Before it could succeed, however, one additional factor was crucial for its success, namely, willingness on the part of the permanent members to underpin its security functions, and this could only be achieved if there was unanimity within the Council. We have analysed elements of the Cold War elsewhere in this book (Chapter 30 for example) and, as was highlighted, although the Soviet Union and the United States had been allies during the Second World War, this alliance dissolved into enmity once the war ended in 1945. As a consequence, collective security, the premise upon which the UN had been established, failed almost immediately as the Cold War between the two sides rendered the Security Council irrelevant. Given these circumstances, one has to conclude that the failure of the UN at its very inception had less to do with the provisions within the Charter than the lack of agreement amongst the superpowers.

## Peacekeeping during the Cold War, 1945–1989

Even though the UN Charter does not explicitly refer to collective security, its principles are nevertheless strongly implied in the various articles, including the ones we referred to earlier. However, the constant rivalry between the Soviet Union and the United States, particularly manifest in the large number of vetoes they both applied, meant that the Security Council was incapable of functioning in accordance with the principles of collective security and so an alternative had to be found (O'Neil and Rees 2005: 29). This came in the form of **peacekeeping**, and even a superficial examination of this mechanism shows how far removed it is from the notion of collective security. However, we must issue a warning at this stage so that confusion may be avoided later in the chapter. In this section our analysis revolves around peacekeeping as it developed during the Cold War, commonly referred to as traditional peacekeeping. Later we will distinguish between this and the broader post-Cold War type which often has the label second generation peacekeeping attached to it.

The first thing to say about traditional peacekeeping is that there is no provision for it within the UN Charter. Indeed, collective security and peacekeeping are at opposite ends of the spectrum with regard to their fundamental nature. The definitions in Box 31.2 demonstrate that the basis of collective security is *enforcement action*, whereby the full force of the UN (including armed force) may be brought to bear upon the aggressor state. Peacekeeping, as it evolved during the Cold War, incorporates a different set of assumptions at the heart of which are *consent, impartiality* and the *use of force for the purpose of self-defence* only.

These characteristics depict peacekeeping as fundamentally different from what was envisaged in the Charter. Its evolution came to be closely associated with the development of the Cold War itself and was increasingly viewed by the international community

The key characteristics of peacekeeping

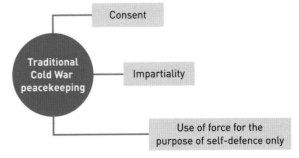

as a mechanism to enable disputing states to minimise the levels of violence between them. Therefore, it came to be seen as a way of reducing violence between states by means other than through the use of enforcement measures. Taken together these three features, outlined in the diagram above, gave UN peacekeeping operations during the Cold War a non-threatening quality, which came to be seen as an essential basis for their success. However, we must not assume that these characteristics were employed in equal measure in all of the sixteen missions during the Cold War (see Table 31.1). There were, in fact, considerable variations in terms of success, size, the degree of consent sought, the use of force employed and the levels of impartiality in the case of the various operations. Despite these variations, however, the essence of Cold War peace operations remained the same in the sense that they were 'activities of a secondary kind' by being reliant in terms of origin and success 'on the wishes and policies of others' (James 1990: 1). Peacekeeping was not to be an authoritative or threatening measure to force disputants to maintain peace. Rather, it was a way for the international community to *help* the warring parties to resolve their differences peacefully.

Peacekeeping is difficult to define but numerous attempts have been made which incorporate some of the characteristics outlined above. One important example was provided by Marrack Goulding who, as head of UN Peacekeeping Operations (1986–1993), was particularly well placed to understand the complexities of the topic. In an article published in 1993 Goulding reaffirmed the importance of consent, impartiality and the use of force only in self-defence. In the case of 'consent', he argued that this principle made peacekeeping appear less threatening and therefore more acceptable to the disputing states. As regards 'impartiality', he specified that it was important that the peacekeepers did not take sides otherwise there was a danger of violating the terms on which the operation itself had been accepted. He further argued that the use of force for self-defence purposes was essential for the continuing success of the operation given that it reinforced the impartiality principle in the hope of continued co-operation on the part of the disputants. Goulding also specified that peacekeeping operations had to be organised by the UN and run under their auspices and finally, given that the UN did not have a standing army of its own, member states would be required to provide personnel and equipment on a voluntary basis.

As already shown, peacekeeping was not foreseen in the UN Charter but emerged as an impromptu response to the failure of the Security Council to function as envisaged. In addition to this, the characteristics associated with peacekeeping also gradually surfaced as the international community began to face various acts of aggression and regional security problems. Far removed from the enforcement basis of collective security, peacekeeping operations during the Cold War included monitoring and observing ceasefire lines, interposing between belligerents, promoting law and order and providing humanitarian aid. It is also possible to argue that the emergence of peacekeeping was closely (though not exclusively) associated with the period of decolonisation, since some of the sixteen operations during the Cold War were established in response to the retreat of European powers from their colonies after the Second World War. Conflicts in Indonesia, Cyprus, Palestine and between India and Pakistan are just some examples of this. Indeed, some of the operations established during the period 1948–1988 continue to the present day – see Table 31.1.

**Table 31.1** UN peacekeeping operations (1948–1991)

| Operation | Duration | Description and Purpose |
|---|---|---|
| UNSCOB | 1947–1951 | **Special Committee for the Balkans.** Observing whether Greek guerrillas were being supplied with equipment by communist states. |
| UNTSO | Since 1948 | **Truce Supervision Organisation.** Monitors ceasefire lines between Israel and its neighbours. |
| UNMOGIP | Since 1949 | **Military Observer Group in India and Pakistan.** Monitors ceasefire lines between India and Pakistan in Kashmir. |
| UNEF I | 1956–1967 | **Emergency Force I.** The first emergency force in the Sinai region to act as a buffer between Israel and Egypt. |
| UNOGIL | 1958 | **Observation Group in Lebanon.** Monitoring troop and arms movement into Lebanon. |
| ONUC | 1960–1964 | **Operation in the Congo.** Providing assistance to the Government of Congo, restoring order and preventing Kataganese secession. |
| UNSF | 1962–1963 | **Security Force** in West New Guinea. |
| UNTEA | 1962–1963 | **Temporary Executive Authority.** Stabilising and providing an administrative mechanism prior to transferring West Irian to Indonesia. |
| UNYOM | 1963–1964 | **Observer Mission in Yemen.** Monitoring troop and arms movements into Yemen from Saudi Arabia. |
| UNFICYP | Since 1964 | **Force in Cyprus.** Preventing Greek and Turkish Cypriots from fighting, maintaining law and order, and monitoring the UN buffer zone created after the Turkish invasion of 1974. |
| UNIPOM | 1965–1966 | **Observer Mission in India/Pakistan.** Monitoring the ceasefire between the two states following the 1965 war. |
| UNEF II | 1974–1979 | **Emergency Force II Sinai.** Acting as a buffer between Egyptian and Israeli forces in the Sinai region. |
| UNDOF | Since 1974 | **Disengagement Observer Force.** Observing the separation between Syrian and Israeli forces on the Golan Heights. |
| UNIFIL | Since 1978 | **Interim Force in Lebanon.** Providing a buffer between Lebanon and Israel. |
| UNGOMAP | 1988–1990 | **Good Offices Mission in Afghanistan and Pakistan.** Monitoring the disengagement of Soviet forces from Afghanistan and assisting in the implementation of various agreements. |
| UNIIMOG | 1988–1991 | **Military Observer Group in Iraq/Iran.** Verifying, confirming and supervising the ceasefire and the withdrawal of all forces to the internationally recognised boundaries. |

As can be seen from the descriptions outlined in Table 31.1, UN peacekeeping operations during the Cold War ranged from observing troop disengagements to monitoring and securing ceasefires and acting as buffers between opponents. These roles were not only unlike the collective security provisions outlined in the UN Charter, but also emerged gradually as the Cold War progressed and the international community began to face various crises. For our purposes Cold War operations can be divided into two broad categories: *observer missions* which consisted of a small group of military observers and *peacekeeping forces*, composed of national armed contingents. Furthermore, separating the Cold War into three time zones provides an effective way to see how peacekeeping became established. You should refer to the descriptions in Table 31.1 while reading the next few sections.

## 1947–1955: The emergence of peacekeeping

This period saw the establishment of three important missions that focused primarily on monitoring, observation and reporting their findings back to the Security Council. UNSCOB was particularly important since it was the first time that observation groups made up of armed personnel were used by the United Nations. German occupation of Greece during the Second World War resulted in the establishment of an underground movement – the National Liberation Front (EAM). Predominantly made up of Communists, the underground movement also consisted of many non-communists and differences between them led to the outbreak of civil war in 1944. Established in 1947, UNSCOB's mandate was to determine to what extent the communist guerrillas were being provided with arms by communist states north of Greece.

UNSCOB was largely successful in fulfilling what was a limited mandate and its success encouraged the UN to establish further missions, UNTSO and UNMOGIP, which continue to operate to this day. In the case of UNTSO, Jewish immigration into Palestine prior to and during the Second World War set the scene for prolonged conflict between the Arabs and the Jews. UNTSO was initially established to monitor a truce between the two sides but when the Jews unilaterally declared the state of Israel in early 1948, this prompted neighbouring Arab states to invade in support of the displaced Palestinians. By the end of 1948, however, the Jews had won the war and were able to force the Arabs to accept a number of Armistice Agreements in 1949. At this stage UNTSO's role shifted to one of supervising the Agreements. UNTSO remains in the region to this day and can be deemed an important mission, since it has remained on the ceasefire lines during and after all the Arab–Israeli conflicts of the Cold War. Similarly, UNMOGIP was established in 1949 in response to the first war between India and Pakistan over the disputed territory of Kashmir and remains in place today. Its mission was similar to that of UNTSO in that it monitored the ceasefire lines, in an attempt to prevent minor incidents escalating into major conflicts.

## 1956–1974: The expansion of peacekeeping

As can be seen from Table 31.1, this period saw a significant expansion of peacekeeping with the establishment of ten further missions, many of which were much larger in scope, ambition and the roles they sought to fulfil. There is insufficient space here to provide detailed descriptions of each of the missions but a few important developments should be mentioned. The nationalisation of the Suez Canal by President Nasser of Egypt in 1956 resulted in the onset of war between Britain, France and Israel on one side and Egypt on the other. However, under intense US and Soviet pressure to withdraw, the Anglo-French goal of capturing the Suez Canal failed, and this resulted in the establishment of UNEF I. There were major differences between this mission and the ones which had preceded it as, in addition to observing and monitoring, the mandate of UNEF I extended to supervising the withdrawal of foreign troops from Egyptian territory, patrolling border areas and preventing military incursions, and securing the ceasefire by acting as a buffer between the disputants (General Assembly A/3354, 1956: 2). Importantly, however, the mission's mandate did not extend to *enforcing* the ceasefire. Nevertheless, this mission was a milestone for UN peacekeeping in that it formalised many of the key characteristics of peacekeeping, namely consent, impartiality and minimal use of force.

In 1960 UN peacekeeping took another step forward with the establishment of ONUC in the Congo as that state gained independence from Belgium – the colonial power. Initially, the mission was established to monitor the withdrawal of Belgian forces and to provide the new government with assistance in maintaining law and order. Subsequent deterioration in security gave rise to the possibility that the state might disintegrate and consequently ONUC's mandate was expanded to include maintenance of the Congo's territorial integrity and political independence. However, in order to achieve this, the operation had to go beyond the essential features of peacekeeping, give up its impartiality and even resort to the use of force outside the confines of self-defence.

Other important missions included UNSF (1962–1963), which maintained law and order in West New Guinea prior to its transfer to Indonesia from Dutch colonial control, and alongside which the UN provided administrative facilities to the territory in the form of UNTEA. Whereas ONUC was of unique importance given its expanded mandate to use force, UNTEA represented the first time that the UN had complete control over a vast territory under the jurisdiction of the Secretary-General. UNFICYP was set up in 1964 to prevent the Greek and Turkish populations of Cyprus from returning to conflict and had the wider goal of preventing conflict between NATO members Greece and Turkey. Its mandate was expanded in 1974 following the Turkish invasion of north Cyprus to include acting as a buffer between the northern (Turkish) part and the southern (Greek) half of the island. Table 31.1 lists other important missions which displayed peacekeeping characteristics.

## 1975–1988: Retrenchment in Cold War peacekeeping

The period between 1956 and 1974 not only saw a significant expansion in peacekeeping operations but also resulted in the formalisation of this method for maintaining international peace and security. As the various missions demonstrated, they employed measures which were significantly removed from the collective security envisaged in the Charter, and yet there were also some notable successes. Despite this, however, after 1975 only one major operation, UNIFIL (1978) was established. This Interim Force in Lebanon was created to confirm Israeli withdrawal from Lebanon and assist the Lebanese Government to restore its authority in areas vacated by the Israelis; however, it demonstrated everything that had gone wrong with peacekeeping. By 1974, the UN had overstretched itself considerably and its problems were exacerbated by the refusal of member states to pay their UN contributions on time, the lack of consent and refusal to co-operate on the part of disputants. Beset with financial problems and a weariness on the part of contributors, therefore, the UN withdrew from peacekeeping. The inability of the Security Council to coerce disputing states to compromise during many Cold War crises has meant that the ultimate goal of achieving security has remained elusive. In many of the regions where UN peacekeepers have been deployed tension, and in some cases, outright conflict and war continue. Since UNIFIL was deployed in 1978 there have been numerous wars between Israel and Lebanon including in 1982 and, most recently, in 2006. Similarly, tensions between India and Pakistan continue to this day over the disputed territory of Kashmir and it is debatable whether the UN operations (UNMOGIP and UNIPOM) have had any discernible influence on the security of the region.

## Maintaining international peace and security in the post-Cold War era

We began this chapter by outlining the UN's role in the war against Iraq in 1991 and we argued that the mandate to use 'all necessary means' to remove Iraqi forces from Kuwait was based upon the enforcement provisions outlined in Chapter VII of the Charter. It is widely accepted that one reason for the UN's new found ability was the end of the Cold War and the easing of tensions between the two superpowers. The optimism generated by this momentous event and the UN's role in the war against Iraq in 1991 reinvigorated the organisation and raised the prospect that the international community would increasingly rely on it to deal with various crises. Often referred to as Second Generation Peacekeeping (2GPK), the post-Cold War period consequently saw a major expansion in UN operations, with over thirty missions established between 1989 and 2004. Although many of these missions incorporated elements of traditional peacekeeping: impartiality, consent and the use of force only in self-defence, the UN was also called upon to carry out a multitude of tasks which went far beyond traditional peacekeeping.

Indeed, the end of the Cold War had a profound impact on the UN in that, suddenly, unprecedented demands were placed upon it. Not only did the Security Council's new-found cooperation result in the establishment of a coalition which succeeded in restoring Kuwait's independence in 1991, but superpower disengagement from numerous regions facilitated the termination of long-standing conflicts and, as a consequence, the UN needed to step in to carry out a wide variety of tasks. In addition to this, however, the focus of UN peacekeeping shifted decisively from dealing with conflicts between states to establishing operations within states which were experiencing some form of civil conflict. This is broadly in line with Mary Kaldor's 'new wars thesis' outlined in Chapter 29, the essence of which is that most of the wars in the post-Cold War era have been intra-state rather than inter-state. Many contemporary civil conflicts share a number of features, including the emergence of militia groups, mercenaries and the decline of state power, with the divisions between warring parties no longer easily definable. Furthermore, the main targets in today's civil conflicts are predominantly civilian populations, who are often deliberately targeted and experience brutal forms of violence, murder, rape, ethnic cleansing, displacement from their homes and other acts of aggression (Mackinlay 2000: 53). The massive changes in global politics and the changing nature of conflict have meant that post-Cold War missions have not only employed traditional peacekeeping methods but have also had to expand to include a range of new tasks which go far beyond Cold War definitions of peacekeeping – tasks such as:

- monitoring elections
- protecting civilians
- providing humanitarian aid and also providing protection for its delivery
- establishing and protecting designated 'safe havens'
- demilitarising combatants
- engaging in the effective administration of territories including states emerging from conflict
- carrying out peace-enforcement activities
- monitoring violations of agreements and international law
- helping to reconstruct state institutions following the end of civil conflict

Since 1990 the essential characteristics of peacekeeping (consent, impartiality and the use of force only in self-defence) have come under increased pressure as the UN has sought to deal with the multidimensional basis of contemporary civil conflicts – namely communal and ethnic rivalries. It was in recognition of these changing circumstances and particularly in response to civil conflicts escalating into brutal wars that the then Secretary-General (Boutros Boutros-Ghali) published *An Agenda for Peace* in June 1992. In this he acknowledged that traditional peacekeeping was not in itself sufficient to ensure lasting peace in conflict areas and consequently began to view the notion of *host state consent* as problematic. He, therefore, introduced a new concept of so-called 'peace-enforcement units' that could be used to bring about a ceasefire between the combatants through the use of force. His proposals were very controversial and divided observers between those who supported his position that the UN had to act more effectively by going beyond traditional peacekeeping and being more forceful, less impartial and less beholden to the need to obtain consent from the parties to the conflict. On the other side were those who pressed for extreme caution when becoming militarily involved in seemingly intractable communal and civil conflicts. Given the optimism during the initial years of the post-Cold War period and the potential for greater cooperation within the Security Council, UN operations expanded significantly. Increasingly the Security Council adopted resolutions with explicit reference to Chapter VII of the UN Charter and without a doubt the UN experienced considerable initial success. Some of the missions since the end of the Cold War are listed in Table 31.2. Below, we provide short descriptions of a few key examples to illustrate some of the problems facing the UN in recent years.

**Cambodia**    As Table 31.2 demonstrates, the UN's role in maintaining international peace and security expanded considerably once the Cold War ended. Following its success in removing Iraq from Kuwait in 1991, the UN established a number of huge missions including Cambodia (UNTAC: 1992–1993) where 22,000 peacekeepers were deployed. The strategic importance of Cambodia meant that, during the Cold War, the French, the Soviet Union and the Chinese had attempted to control the state through a number of puppet regimes. The worst of these regimes was the Khmer Rouge. This was supported by the Chinese and during its period in rule (1975–1979) killed an estimated two million civilians – almost one-fifth of the total population. The invasion by Vietnam in 1979 failed to bring peace, as the Khmer Rouge continued to control pockets of the country. The continued recognition of the Khmer Rouge (as opposed to the government installed by Vietnam in 1979) by Western states meant that it wasn't until the end of the Cold War that the opportunity for peace presented itself. The Paris Peace Accords, signed in October 1991, committed the various Cambodian factions to a ceasefire, an end to their receipt of external military assistance, military demobilisation, electoral registration and the creation of a national army. UNTAC's mandate extended to attempting to attain these goals and it achieved considerable success.

**Former Yugoslavia**    Among the many peace missions established since the end of the Cold War, perhaps the two most important were UNPROFOR in the case of former Yugoslavia and UNOSOM II in Somalia. Both were obvious examples of the rubric of Second Generation Peacekeeping in that they were multidimensional in nature, committed huge amounts of resources, and included peace-enforcement as a significant component. Unlike the UN's mission in Cambodia, success in both of these missions was much more difficult to achieve. The disintegration of Yugoslavia was, broadly speaking, the result of three distinct wars. The first took place in 1991, lasted for only ten days and resulted in Slovenia breaking away from the rest of Yugoslavia. The second war began in Croatia in the spring of 1991 and the third war, in Bosnia–Herzegovina, began in the spring of 1992.

The Serbian wish to preserve the Yugoslav Federation in the post-Cold War era led to increased calls by Slobodan Milosevic, the Serbian President at the time, for greater centralisation. Serbian nationalism, combined with its desire to retain control of the federation, encouraged nationalist reactions among other Yugoslav populations, thus leading to calls for greater autonomy and eventual independence. In Croatia, Franjo Tudjman (the then Croatian leader) sought to emulate Milosevic, with strong anti-communist rhetoric and appeals to Croatian nationalism. Once in power he began to revive symbols of the Croatian nation, effectively removing any references to the Serbs and other nationalities within Croatia. Not willing to be subject to economic and political dominance by the Croatians, the minority Serbs became increasingly assertive, going so far as to demand unification with

**Table 31.2** UN peacekeeping operations (1989–2004)

| Operation | Duration | Description and Purpose |
| --- | --- | --- |
| UNAVEM I | 1988–1991 | Angolan Verification Mission. |
| UNTAG | 1989–1990 | Transitional Assistance Group. |
| ONUCA | 1989–1991 | Observer Group in Central America. |
| UNAVEM II and III | 1991–1995 | Angolan Verification Missions. |
| ONUSAL | 1991–1995 | Observer Mission in El Salvador. |
| UNAMIC | 1991–1992 | Advanced Mission in Cambodia. |
| UNTAC | 1992–1993 | Transitional Authority in Cambodia. |
| UNPROFOR | 1992–1995 | Protection Force in former Yugoslavia. |
| UNOSOM I | 1992–1993 | Operation in Somalia I. |
| UNOSOM II | 1993–1995 | Operation in Somalia II. |
| UNOMUR | 1993–1994 | Observer Mission Uganda/Rwanda. |
| UNMIH | 1993–1996 | Observer Mission in Haiti. |
| UNOMIL | 1993–1997 | Observer Mission in Liberia. |
| UNAMIR | 1993–1996 | Assistance Mission in Rwanda. |
| UNMOT | 1994–2000 | Mission of Observers in Tadjikistan. |
| UNCRO | 1995–1996 | Confidence Restoration Operation in Croatia. |
| UNPREDEP | 1995–1999 | Preventive Deployment Force in the Former Yugoslav Republic of Macedonia. |
| UNTAES | 1996–1998 | Transitional Authority in Eastern Slavonia. |
| UNSMIH | 1996–1997 | Support Mission in Haiti. |
| MINUGUA | 1997 | Guatemala Verification Mission. |
| MONUA | 1997–1999 | Observer Mission in Angola. |
| UNTMIH | 1997 | Transitional Mission in Haiti. |
| MIPONUH | 1997–2000 | Civilian Police Mission in Haiti. |
| UNPSG | 1998 | Civilian Police Mission in Croatia. |
| UNOMSIL | 1998–1999 | Observer Mission in Sierra Leone. |
| MINURCA | 1998–2000 | Mission in the Central African Republic. |
| UNTAET | 1999–2002 | Transitional Authority in East Timor. |
| UNMIBH | 1995–2002 | Mission in Bosnia-Herzegovina. |
| UNMOP | 1996–2002 | Mission in the Croatian Peninsula of Prevlaka. |
| UNIKOM | 1991–2003 | Iraq–Kuwait Observation Mission. |

Serbia. Similar sentiments among the various ethnic groups in Bosnia–Herzegovina, including the Bosnian Muslims, created the conditions for war in that part of the federation. UNPROFOR was initially established (among other roles) to monitor the ceasefire in Croatia, oversee demilitarisation, protect safe areas, deliver humanitarian aid and prevent conflict in other parts of the former Yugoslavia such as Bosnia. Later in 1994, UNPROFOR was reconstructed into three separate operations, which included UNCRO (Confidence Restoration Operation) to stabilise conditions in Croatia leading to a negotiated settlement; UNPREDEP (Preventive Deployment Force), which sought to prevent the spread of conflict into the former Yugoslav Republic of Macedonia and UNPROFOR, which continued operations in Bosnia. The UN's success in former Yugoslavia has been mixed.

**Somalia**    During the early 1990s the UN's mission in Somalia was one of the most important of the post-Cold War era, because it was heavily associated with the UN's Secretary-General and influenced by him. It therefore incorporated all the elements highlighted in *An Agenda for Peace*. Somalia's descent into anarchy at the end of 1991 resulted in the establishment of UNOSOM I, in an attempt to alleviate the starvation of civilians and oversee a ceasefire agreed between the factions. Five hundred Pakistani peacekeeping troops were tasked with securing Mogadishu airport, safeguarding food shipments and escorting aid convoys. UNOSOM I failed, however, because the UN troops were lightly armed and remained severely constrained by traditional rules of peacekeeping, which allowed shooting in self-defence only. Optimistic about the UN's role in peacekeeping following successes in Iraq, Cambodia and elsewhere, the USA agreed to Boutros-Ghali's demand to lead a 37,000 strong United Task Force (UNITAF). This had a Chapter VII mandate Charter to 'use all necessary means to establish as soon as possible a secure environment for humanitarian relief operations' (UNSC Res: 794).

Operation Restore Hope began in early December 1992 and initially had a positive impact on the security situation and on the effective delivery of humanitarian assistance. This apparent success persuaded the Americans to begin to return control to the UN and by the end of March 1993 UNOSOM II was established. However, in reality the efforts made by UNITAF to establish a secure environment were far from complete, and this was manifest in a growing rift between Washington and the UN. The US saw its role as being limited merely to opening supply routes, whereas the Secretary-General sought to use the coalition to disarm forcefully the warring factions. Armed chaos and increasing Somali hostility against the foreign troops gave rise to the impression that UNOSOM II had to be provided with enforcement powers if a secure environment for the provision of humanitarian assistance was to be created. The ambush and killing of twenty-four Pakistani peacekeepers on 5 June 1993 made matters worse, acting as a catalyst which led to a sudden shift from humanitarian intervention to more forceful peace-enforcement. In addition to disarming the factions, the goal of UNOSOM II now extended to identifying the attackers and bringing them to justice. This new objective sucked the UN into an urban war with no prospect of victory. The problem was that the UN forces were required to arrest those who had killed the UN troops and this minimised any chances of a negotiated settlement. The increasing civilian death toll not only turned the Somalis against the UN but also seriously divided the various states contributing to the UN. The Italian contingent refused to get heavy-handed and troops from Islamic countries were equally unhappy with the massive American strikes which were killing fellow Muslims. A fundamental disagreement had emerged with regard to the UN's role in Somalia, with the US seeking to continue the war and others wanting to suspend combat operations and return to the original purpose of protecting humanitarian relief. It is obvious, therefore, that a lack of coordination and agreement between the various contingents and a poor overall command structure contributed to the failure of UNOSOM II; indeed by 1995 the operation had come to an end. Today Somalia remains a failed state in the midst of civil conflict.

**Peacekeeping after Somalia**    The impact of the debacle in Somalia should not be underestimated. Indeed, we would go so far as to argue that the subsequent inaction on the part of the UN and the international community during the Rwandan civil war was largely due to its experiences in Somalia. Over a period of one hundred days during the summer of 1994 almost a million civilians were massacred, with the Assistance Mission for Rwanda (UNAMIR) largely impotent to stop the genocide. A request by the UN for up to 5,000 troops was finally approved at the end of May 1994, but in the face of uncertainty over the right to use force many of the UN member states delayed contributing troops. By the time UNAMIR reached full strength the genocide was already over. By 1995 it had, therefore, become clear that the international community's experiment with multilateralism was under serious threat. However, continuing problems in various parts of the world have meant that the UN has had to remain committed to alleviating some of the worst atrocities.

There is no doubt that the experience in Somalia gave rise to a more realistic understanding of the UN's capabilities. The financial cost of such operations, for example, is immense. Somalia alone has cost over $1 billion per annum. Although the US and some other states could provide the necessary resources, the experience in Somalia led the then US President Bill Clinton to say in 1993, that the 'UN must learn to say no' (Clinton 1993). Apart from financial problems, the UN faces other challenges, not least, the perceived interests of the member states. Sometimes the leading states do not have important interests in a particular region or state and are therefore reluctant to commit their resources or troops and Rwanda was certainly a victim of this.

Furthermore, the UN has been increasingly called upon to provide humanitarian assistance in civil conflicts. The repatriation of refugees; the provision of food and shelter; demobilisation and demilitarisation of former soldiers; the reinstitution of law and order and the restoration of essential supplies have become some of the most important tasks carried out by the UN. But the integration of humanitarian goals with peacekeeping has often been problematic. Attacks by paramilitaries on humanitarian convoys have meant that the UN has been compelled to forego one of the most important bases of peacekeeping – impartiality. This crossover into peace-enforcement has created its own problems, as demonstrated in the case study on Somalia. Indeed, the nature of civil conflicts is such that they are perhaps among the most difficult to resolve. For traditional peacekeeping to succeed there need to be many preconditions, most importantly a firm agreement between the combatants to cease their hostilities and a clear territorial dividing line between the warring parties. These conditions have been largely absent in many of the communal, ethnically based civil conflicts of the post-Cold War era and that has been one of the main sources of difficulty when dealing with these types of conflict.

One major obstacle for the UN is non-interference in what are largely the internal affairs of states. Given that the UN itself upholds the inviolability of the sovereignty of states, interfering in their affairs is not an easy decision to take. Furthermore, there is a great deal of disagreement among states over their particular national interests and whether or not these are affected in the case of many post-Cold War conflicts. States, the public and politicians are generally outraged when faced with horrors such as genocide, mass rape or ethnic cleansing. However, despite this common position, states differ regarding their interests and disagree on the most appropriate way to manage the many crises facing the international community. In addition, the UN suffers from a general reluctance, on the part of its member states, to commit resources, which stems from the premise that recessions or other economic problems make it difficult for states to contribute to the UN coffers. Committing your own troops to solve the humanitarian problems affecting other people is a risky process, especially since military missions in civil conflicts are dangerous for the personnel involved. Many UN troops have been killed in post-Cold War missions, for example in Bosnia and Somalia. Indeed, the death of eighteen US troops in Somalia between 3 and 4 October 1993, when two U-60 Black Hawk helicopters were shot down persuaded President Clinton that the risks to American troops were too great. This event, popularised by Ridley Scott in his movie – *Black Hawk Down* – was a pivotal moment as it led to the withdrawal of American troops from Somalia.

Following the UN's failure in Somalia, the US began to articulate policies that further weakened the organisation both politically and militarily. The results of UN peacekeeping in the post-Cold War era have, consequently, been uneven. While missions have been beneficial in Macedonia, Mozambique, Cambodia, El Salvador and Eastern Slavonia, others, such as that in Somalia, have demonstrated the effects of disastrous policies or, as in the case of Rwanda, the impact of turning a blind eye. After Somalia, the Clinton Administration – under Congressional pressure – became increasingly reluctant to allow the UN to respond to every crisis. This sentiment also had a major impact on US contributions to the UN peacekeeping budget. As the 1990s progressed, Washington gradually withdrew from participating in UN missions – especially when US interests were not affected – and began to encourage regional organisations, and so-called 'coalitions of the willing' as solutions to various crises. Where its interests were under threat, however, the Clinton Administration did deploy forces. In 1994, for example, US troops were deployed to Haiti, and this was later transformed into a UN peace operation. Similarly, in Macedonia, the US agreed to place some of its troops under UN command in the hope that it would prevent the conflict in the former Yugoslavia from spreading. Generally, however, the UN was seen as politically untenable and militarily inefficient and consequently, the US involvement in peace missions declined significantly.

Global instability has continued since the start of the new millennium and so, periodically, the international community has had to turn to the UN to set up peace operations. Indeed, between 1999 and 2004 a number of ambitious missions, sanctioned by the Security Council (including the US) were established. These have included operations in Kosovo, and East Timor as well as a mission to monitor the ceasefire between Ethiopia and Eritrea. Previously established missions in Sierra Leone, the Congo and Lebanon have also been expanded considerably. Despite misgivings regarding the record of the UN, member states continue to rely on it for the maintenance of peace and security, and this has led to considerable debate over how UN structures can be improved to make it more efficient. In 1993, at the height of post-Cold War operations, UN forces numbered in excess of 80,000 troops. A return to this level is unlikely in the foreseeable future, but the costs of UN peacekeeping have once again been rising and this trend is likely to continue. Furthermore, the nature of UN operations in the post-Cold War era remains multidimensional and complex, incorporating elements of peacekeeping as well as peace-enforcement. The international

*Source: Getty Images/Hulton Archive*

**With the rise of countries like India and Brazil, should the UN Security Council open its doors to new permanent members?**

community also continues to be concerned with rebuilding devastated societies and collapsing state structures, but it was this level of overstretch which seriously undermined the UN's reputation in the mid-1990s. The UN, therefore, remains operationally inefficient and there does not appear to be sufficient will on the part of its most powerful members to improve its structures.

## Case study: Schizophrenia over the United Nations

When reading a history of the UN we cannot avoid one overwhelming observation – namely that states have placed an enormous amount of faith in the United Nations, but at the same time have discarded it when it did not suit their interests. Since its creation it has come under intense criticism for failing in its primary purpose of maintaining peace and security and yet between the years 2000 and 2005 almost 90,000 troops served under its command in various regions of the world. This schizophrenia – the tendency both to criticise the UN *and* to demand its assistance – has been disastrous for the organisation. If states such as the US (among others) expect the UN to fulfil its functions, they must do much more to strengthen it. The question, though, is 'how' this can be achieved, and the following list includes a few suggestions which are often discussed.

1. **Reforming the Security Council**  Five permanent members (US, Russia, China, Britain and France) wield all the power of the UN. The question is whether these states are truly representative of the rest of the world. For example, no African or South American state is a permanent member. Ask yourself whether, given their rising power, states such as India, Brazil, Japan, Germany or South Africa should be made permanent members.
2. **Abolishing the Veto**  One reason why the UN has often failed to act in crises around the world is because one or more of the permanent members have exercised their right of veto and prevented the organisation from acting. Would abolishing the veto strengthen the UN?
3. **Establishing a UN rapid reaction force**  At present, when the Security Council passes resolutions in support of UN action in any conflict, member states have to come forward and offer troops and equipment to the UN. This is unsatisfactory since it

takes time for these troops and equipment to arrive. By then the conflict has often worsened with the result that the UN has failed to protect countless lives which might have been saved had it reacted sooner. Would providing the UN with its own rapid reaction force under the command of the Secretary-General enable it to function more efficiently?

4. **Creating a Peacekeeping Commission with adequate intelligence**  Today the UN is a reactive institution rather than a proactive one. In other words it responds to crises rather than acting in a pre-emptive manner in order to prevent states experiencing conflict from deteriorating further. This is particularly important given the large number of failed or failing states. The core functions of such a body would be to identify states experiencing 'stress' and then to act in time to prevent them from collapsing.
5. **Funding**  It is well documented that the UN is inadequately funded. It is common knowledge that even large, economically strong states such as the US have withheld their dues from the UN. How might the UN secure an adequate and steady stream of income?

These are merely a handful of the proposals which have been considered since the end of the Cold War. We have introduced them here for you to discuss in light of the issues raised in this chapter and to encourage you to think of other ways in which the UN could be made more efficient. You may reach the conclusion that in an anarchic world an international organisation such as the UN is only going to be as efficient as the states which comprise it wish it to be.

  **The UN needs to be reformed in order to make it more efficient. How might this be achieved?**

## Conclusions

An important goal achieved in this chapter has been the attempt to distinguish between collective security and peacekeeping. We have showed that Cold War dynamics, manifest in the ideological and arms races between the Soviet Union and the United States, rendered the Security Council incapable of functioning according to the Charter. We have also demonstrated how peacekeeping had to emerge as an ad hoc substitute for the more forceful collective security. Based on the principles of consent, impartiality and the use of force in self-defence only, peacekeeping became the only way that the UN could operate under Cold War conditions. Although the post-Cold War period has been much shorter than the Cold War, the number of missions undertaken by the UN has been far greater than during the Cold War. This not only reflects the increasing potential for co-operation within the Security Council, but is also a sign that the many brutal civil conflicts of this period had to be managed in some way. Consequently, the UN has often had to step beyond the impartial and consensual basis of traditional peacekeeping and adopt mandates which authorise the use of force. The intractable nature of many civil conflicts; the inefficient use of resources; the members' reluctance to contribute equipment and troops; the refusal of key members to maintain their financial contributions and many disastrous decisions during the 1990s have, however, undermined the reputation of the UN considerably and persuaded powerful states such as the US to withdraw unconditional support. These problems have sparked a debate among the academic and policy communities within and outside the UN regarding how the Organisation might be reformed, and some possibilities are offered in the Case study opposite.

## Resource section

## Questions

1. What are the key differences between collective security and peacekeeping?

2. In what ways is Second Generation Peacekeeping different from Traditional Peacekeeping?

3. Given that states are predominantly concerned with fulfilling their own national interests, can an institution such as the UN have any real power?

4. Is the UN the best means of managing conflict in the international system?

5. How successfully has the United Nations maintained international peace and security in the post-Cold War era?

6. What counts as a 'humanitarian' intervention? Illustrate your answer with reference to at least two historical examples.

## Recommended reading

Claude, I.L. (1984) *Swords into Plowshares* (4th edn, New York: Random House)
During his career Inis Claude has been one of the most prolific analysts of the United Nations and this book is one of his most famous.

Durch, W. (ed.) (2006) *Twenty-First-Century Peace Operations* (Washington: USIP Press)
William Durch is another prolific analyst of the United Nations and has written extensively on its history and evolution. This book attempts to consider the challenges facing the UN through a series of important case studies including Kosovo and the Congo.

Isely, E. (ed.) (2010) *United Nations Peacekeeping in the 21st Century* (Nova Science Publishers)
This book begins by acknowledging that the financial and logistical resources needed for the UN to maintain the demands being placed upon it are likely to continue to increase. It then moves on to analyse the threats to the organisation, especially from states unwilling to commit their own resources.

Woodhouse, T. and Ramsbotham, O. (eds) (2000) *Peacekeeping and Conflict Resolution* (London: Frank Cass Publishers)
In this book the authors analyse how peacekeeping may be able to deal more efficiently with the brutal and traumatic impact of the civil wars of the 1990s.

# Chapter 32
# Terrorism and Political Violence

Categorising terrorism

Defining terrorism and the impact of religion

State and sub-state terrorism

Ethno-nationalist terrorism

Conclusion

After reading this chapter you will be able to:

- Understand some of the controversies surrounding the definitions of terrorism

- Use the Arab-Israeli–Palestinian issue to demonstrate the problems of definition

- Make connections between key literature – such as the ideas presented by Samuel Huntington, who talks of impending conflict between the West and the Islamic world – and the terrorist attacks of recent years

- Gain an understanding of non-religious forms of terrorism

*Source*: Panos Pictures/Chris Stowers

## Introductory box: What happened on 11 September 2001?

At 8:46 on the morning of September 11 2001, the United States became a nation transformed. An airliner travelling at hundreds of miles per hour and carrying some 10,000 gallons of jet fuel ploughed into the North Tower of the World Trade Center in Lower Manhattan. At 9:03, a second airliner hit the South Tower. Fire and smoke billowed upward. Steel, glass, ash, and bodies fell below. The Twin Towers, where up to 50,000 people worked each day, both collapsed less than 90 minutes later.

At 9:37 that same morning, a third airliner slammed into the western face of the Pentagon. At 10:03, a fourth airliner crashed in a field in southern Pennsylvania. It had been aimed at the United States Capitol or the White House and was forced down by heroic passengers armed with the knowledge that America was under attack.

More than 26,000 people died at the World Trade Center; 125 died at the Pentagon; 256 died on the four planes. The death toll surpassed that at Pearl Harbor in December 1941.

This immeasurable pain was inflicted by 19 young Arabs acting at the behest of Islamist extremists headquartered in distant Afghanistan. Some had been in the United States for more than a year, mixing with the rest of the population. Though four had training as pilots, most were not well-educated. Most spoke English poorly, some hardly at all. In groups of four or five, carrying with them only small knives, box cutters, and cans of Mace or pepper spray, they had hijacked the four planes and turned them into deadly guided missiles.

*Source*: Excerpt from the National Commission on Terrorist Attacks upon the United States (2004) *The 9/11 Commission Report*. Available at http://govinfo.library.unt.edu/911/report/911Report_Exec.htm [accessed 24 September 2009].

## Categorising terrorism

'**Terrorism**' is undoubtedly one of the most significant political terms in use today. The attacks on the World Trade Center by al-Qaeda terrorists on 11 September 2001 (9/11) propelled terrorism to centre stage in the relations between states. Since then politicians, academics and particularly the media have provided us with a daily appraisal of the threats, detailing further terrorist attacks and the responses to them. The wars in Afghanistan and Iraq, the insurgency in Pakistan, the ongoing bomb attacks in these states and elsewhere, the many civilian deaths at the hands of terrorist bombs as well as the 'collateral damage' caused by NATO forces and the many deaths of American, British and other allied troops, all serve as evidence of the challenges posed by terrorism. This recent concern with terrorism, however, has tended to obscure the fact that this phenomenon emerged as a security issue long before the attacks in September 2001. Indeed, the high level of attention that global

Source: Corbis/Sygma

**The events of September 11 propelled terrorism to centre stage, although they also obscured the fact that the phenomenon emerged as a security issue long before 2001.**

media networks and governments around the globe have given to contemporary terrorism give the impression that it is a new and especially dangerous phenomenon. The defining feature of terrorism since 9/11 appears to be religion, as the West begins to see itself pitted against militant forms of Islam. However, despite the importance placed on religion as a basis for contemporary terrorism, terrorism did not begin with 9/11 and neither is it the exclusive preserve of Islamic militants inspired by al-Qaeda's brand of Islam. The following categories are relevant, although we must stress that they are not entirely distinct from one another and the various events we refer to often fit into more than one category.

- **Religious terrorism.** Since 9/11 the international community has been preoccupied with terrorism which has a predominantly religious character. The wars in Afghanistan and Iraq, the Taliban insurgency in Pakistan, the many terrorist attacks since 11 September 2001 and the ongoing 'War on Terror' give the impression that contemporary religious terrorism has eclipsed all other forms. It is because of the intense emphasis on the religious dimensions of contemporary terrorism that we will devote a considerable part of the chapter to this aspect.

- **State and sub-state terrorism.** In this section we will identify instances where states have turned against their own citizens and also recount examples where individuals and groups have in turn attacked their own state.
- **Ethno-nationalist terrorism.** This sector is characterised by conflicts between groups which are essentially different from one another. These differences can be cultural, religious, ethnic and historical, and the rationale for the violence revolves around the need for one group to prevent its cultural identity becoming diluted. This form of violence between groups is very common and has occurred in many places around the world including Rwanda, Bosnia and Sri Lanka.

## Defining terrorism and the impact of religion

First, however, we must define our central concept, and there are certain attributes of recent terrorism that distinguish it from other historical forms. One of these is the fact that the 9/11 attacks were directed against the homeland of the world's only superpower. This particular attack showed that the immense military and economic might of the United States was insufficient to protect it from one of the most dramatic terrorist attacks in human history. The destruction of the World Trade Center in New York on this fateful day had such an impact on the international system that even today, more than nine years later, the world is still having to deal with its consequences. Subsequent terrorist attacks such as those in London, Madrid and Bali; the wars in Afghanistan and Iraq and the Taliban insurgency in Pakistan are just some of the offshoots of those attacks. A second consequence of 9/11 was that it demonstrated that major cities in the West were vulnerable to attack and gave rise to the nightmare scenario of terrorists using weapons of mass destruction. It appeared, therefore, that the West was now facing a new type of enemy which was motivated, virulently anti-Western, had access to funds and was able to draw upon a large number of followers. Having entered international relations with such force, terrorism is now a constant topic of discussion for the media, academics, politicians and the world's intelligence services.

Any analysis of the impact of terrorism, however, is dependent upon one crucial factor, namely, how to define the term. This is largely because those seeking to provide definitions continue to disagree over the precise meanings, given that their opinions are dependent upon which groups they wish to support or deplore as terrorists. Despite the intense attention being paid to this issue, a survey of the literature dealing with the term demonstrates that an accurate and widely accepted definition remains elusive. Individuals, governments and institutions have tended to adopt their own definitions of terrorism and this lack of consensus is now a central feature of the world of political violence. As long ago as 1988 Alex Schmid, in his academic survey, identified over a hundred different definitions of terrorism (Schmid and Jongman 1988). However, before we can attempt to define the term we must consider the sources of terrorism, and it is in this context that most observers would agree that its basis lies in different forms of extremism. In order to understand terrorism, therefore, we must reflect on the connections between both these terms since all forms of terrorism appear to have their roots in some form of extremist outlook which is strengthened by a deep-seated intolerance of alternative viewpoints. One useful definition is as follows:

> A vague term, which can mean: 1. Taking a political idea to its limits, regardless of 'unfortunate' repercussions, impracticalities, arguments and feelings to the contrary, and with the intention not only to confront, but also to eliminate opposition.
> 2. Intolerance towards all views other than one's own. 3. Adoption of means to political ends which show disregard for the life, liberty, and human rights of others.
>
> (Scruton 1982)

This definition identifies a number of key traits which allow us to make a solid connection between extremism and the terrorist acts the world has witnessed in recent years. Osama bin Laden's followers (al-Qaeda) were responsible for the attacks on 9/11 and this event has led to intense scrutiny of the group's beliefs. Analysts have predominantly sought to explain their virulently anti-Westernism as a function of their preference for Wahhabist ideology. Essentially, Wahhabism advocates a return to the fundamental principles of early Islam in order to reduce the decadence and corruption of modern living. It stresses obedience to the principles laid down in the Qur'an and a rejection of debate and is therefore viewed by many in the West as an extremist version of Islam. The concern with Wahhabism has been so great that it has even featured as the subject of Congressional Hearings in the United States. A recent report defined the term as a 'Sunni Islamic movement that [sought] to purify Islam of any innovations or practices that deviate from the seventh-century teachings of the Prophet Muhammad and his companions' (Blanchard 2008: 1). Another report highlighted the premise that al-Qaeda leaders advocate a violent message rooted in conservative Islamic traditions and goes on to suggest that Wahhabism has promoted hatred and violence, particularly targeting the United States and its allies (Blanchard 2008: 1).

While we must recognise that not all extremists express their views by resorting to violence, terrorism is one such manifestation and, since 9/11, Islamically inspired terrorism has been a central concern. Labelling an act as 'terrorism' implies condemnation of those responsible for it. One important reason why definitions of terrorism are so varied is because they depend upon the ideological bias, cultural background and personal perceptions of those seeking to provide a meaning for the term. Any consensus regarding a definition is therefore difficult to achieve, but all the more necessary given the magnitude of the problems posed by terrorism. Following the attacks on 9/11 the USA, under President George W. Bush, pursued, with single-minded resolve, the goal of establishing a broad antiterrorism coalition. Indeed, this objective has formed the basis of the global War on Terror. The very language used during speeches in the aftermath of the attacks appeared to indicate that the Bush administration sought to distinguish between friends and enemies according to whether or not they supported the USA in its coming War on Terror. In

November 2001 Bush warned the world's nations that standing by was not an option when he stated:

> A coalition partner must do more than just express sympathy; a coalition partner must perform. That means different things for different nations. Some nations don't want to contribute troops and we understand that. Other nations can contribute intelligence sharing. . . . But all nations, if they want to fight terror, must do something . . . Over time it's going to be important for nations to know they will be held accountable for inactivity . . . *You're either with us or against us in the fight against terror.*

(CNN 6 November 2001)

These excerpts from Bush's speech provided a powerful hint at the time that the USA now intended to define its relationship with the world's states according to whether or not they saw terrorism in the same way as the United States did, which has undoubtedly been at odds with the way other states have sought to define terrorism. The Arab-Israeli-Palestinian issue, for instance, is one of the most concrete examples of a difference in opinion over what constitutes terrorist action. This conflict has its roots in centuries of history and although it is not possible to relate every aspect of it here, we will mention a few key issues which will help to explain the differences of opinion regarding the definition of terrorism.

Established by force in 1948, the history of the modern state of Israel has been one of constant antagonism, war, occupation and disagreement between itself and its Arab neighbours. The regions which make up Israel, Syria, Jordan and the Palestinian territories today had been part of the Ottoman Empire since 1516, but with its defeat in the First World War, the mandate for control of these territories passed to the British and the French. The French gained control of Syria and the British gained what subsequently became Israel, Jordan and the Palestinian territories of the West Bank. Numerous sides played a role in the demise of Ottoman control including the Arabs, who were encouraged to revolt by the British in return for a promise of self-rule. However, Britain's foreign secretary, Lord James Balfour, made another promise to the Jews of Europe in 1917, namely support for a Jewish homeland in what was Arab Palestine. This set the scene for decades of conflict, not only between Israel and the Palestinians, but also the wider Arab and Islamic world. The various sides have still not reached an agreement. In addition to the 1947 War of Independence, Israel and its neighbours have gone to war on numerous occasions, including the Sinai Campaign against Egypt in 1956, the Six-Day War in June 1967, the Yom Kippur War in October 1973 and two wars against Lebanon, the most recent being in 2006.

The Israeli-Palestinian conflict is an important example in that it clearly demonstrates the difficulty of reaching a comprehensive definition of terrorism. The disagreements between the Israelis and the Palestinians are based on both sides holding opposing views over the status of Israel. On the one hand, the Arab world is threatened by Israel because the latter has not only occupied Arab/Palestinian lands, but has actively oppressed the population of those territories. Furthermore, by continuing to build Jewish settlements in the West Bank, East Jerusalem and Gaza, Israel is extending its reach deeper into Arab territory.

On the other hand, the beliefs embodied within political **Zionism** have had a major impact on the perceptions held by Jews. These beliefs revolve around the idea that the world's Jews actually constitute a nation and that they have the right to return to what they regard as their ancestral home – namely the land of Israel (Arab Palestine). Consequently, having declared independence in 1948, Israel finds itself surrounded by enemies that are intent on its destruction and is therefore engaged in a struggle for its very survival. It is for the purpose of maintaining its security, therefore, that Israel has justified its continuing occupation of Palestinian areas as well as the heavy-handed tactics employed against the Palestinians themselves.

The events following the Six-Day War (1967) are particularly notable in the context of terrorism in the volatile Middle East. Although regional conflicts in the Middle East have a basis in decades of history, one of the most prominent of Arab leaders – Gamal Abdel Nasser (Egyptian President between 1956 and 1970) – provides a useful starting point. As soon as he came to power he nationalised the strategically important European-owned Suez Canal. This was unacceptable to both the British and French owners, who joined forces with the Israelis and launched an attack on Egypt. Not wishing to see an escalation of the conflict, the United States and the Soviet Union applied immense pressure on the Israelis to withdraw from Egyptian territory and the British and the French also gave up their occupation of the Canal. The United Nations Emergency Force (UNEF) (see Chapter 31), was established by the UN General Assembly with the purpose of securing an end to the Suez Crisis. Nasser was popular not only in Egypt itself but had appeal further afield, and this enabled him to integrate the armies of Egypt and Syria (thus forming the short-lived United Arab Republic), inspire pan-Arab revolutions in Algeria and Iraq and also to play a major role in the establishment of the Palestine Liberation Organisation (PLO) in 1964.

Syrian and Egyptian disdain at the continuing existence of Israel was manifest in repeated guerrilla activities during the 1960s such as the shelling of Israeli settlements from the Golan Heights of Syria. Tensions mounted further in 1964 following Israel's huge irrigation project which involved diverting water from the Jordan River into the Negev Desert. The Syrians began a similar project and, had this succeeded, it would have led to waters on the Israeli side drying up. In order to prevent this, the Israelis launched air strikes against Syrian sites in 1964 and tensions mounted unabated until in 1967, fearful of an all out Arab attack, Israel launched massive pre-emptive strikes against the Syrian, Egyptian and Jordanian air forces. This famous war lasted for only six days (5–10 June 1967) and, at the end of it, Arab air forces had been virtually wiped out and Israel had succeeded in invading and capturing Egypt's Sinai Peninsula, the West Bank of Jordan and the Golan Heights of Syria. Unlike the Suez Crisis, this time the Israelis did not withdraw from captured territory, and they continue to occupy the West Bank and the Golan Heights to this day. The Sinai Peninsula was returned to Egypt in 1979 following a peace treaty between the two enemies, the main purpose of which was to bring to an end the state of war that had existed since 1948.

The Six-Day War is particularly important for two reasons; it resulted in a shift in the balance of power in favour of Israel, given that it had defeated the Arab armies and now

## Box 32.1 Yasser Arafat [1929–2004]

Yasser Arafat's role in resisting Israeli occupation is well documented. During the 1956 Suez War, for instance, he served as a Second Lieutenant in the Egyptian Army, and soon after this conflict he helped in the establishment of Fatah, an organisation determined to see the state of Israel abolished and replaced by a Palestinian state. He spent the following decades fighting against Israel and, while he was seen as a freedom fighter by most of the Arab world, especially the Palestinians, Israel and much of the West saw him as a terrorist. Founded in 1964, the PLO was another group closely associated with Arafat, and like Fatah, this organisation also sought the liberation of Palestine through the use of armed resistance. Arafat became Chairman of the PLO in 1969 and remained so until his death in 2004.

occupied significant Arab land – the Golan Heights and the West Bank. In addition, although the PLO had been established earlier in 1964 under the chairmanship of Yasser Arafat, it was in response to the fiasco of the Six-Day War that it now claimed to be the sole representative of the Palestinian Arabs. Its declared aim was to destroy the state of Israel and reclaim Palestinian land. Since then violence directed against Israel has been reciprocated by regular incursions into Palestinian territories by Israeli troops who are often accused of failing to discriminate between civilians and what are perceived to be Palestinian 'militants'. In addition, the violence directed against Israel has spiralled since the 1960s and today numerous Palestinian groups seek to control the Palestinian territories and continue to commit violent attacks against Israeli targets, which often include civilians. Apart from the PLO, Hamas, the Popular Front for the Liberation of Palestine, the Democratic Front for the Liberation of Palestine, Abu Nidal, Fatah, and the Palestinian Islamic Jihad are some of the groups which have emerged to challenge Israeli occupation.

In reality during the 1970s and 1980s the PLO became an umbrella organisation for a number of Palestinian groups, all of which were opposed to Israeli occupation and used methods which included attacks on civilians as well as guerrilla warfare against Israel. Among the many attacks against civilians, some of the most notable occurred in 1972 when a Fatah group – Black September – hijacked a plane on route to Vienna and forced it to land at Ben Gurion airport in Israel, eventually killing over twenty civilians. Later that year, the same group was responsible for the kidnap and murder of eleven Israeli athletes competing in the Munich Olympic Games. The international condemnation persuaded Arafat to disband Black September and he subsequently ordered the PLO to refrain from attacking Israelis outside the state of Israel and the occupied Palestinian territories of the West Bank and Gaza. Since then, however, various Palestinian groups have carried out countless attacks against Israeli targets, both military and civilian, and many Israeli citizens have been killed over the years. Palestinian groups have also differed as regards their opinion on whether or not to accept the state of Israel. During the early 1990s, for instance, the PLO became heavily committed to achieving peace with Israel, but this was violently opposed by the Islamic Resistance Movement – commonly referred to as Hamas. This group came into existence when the first Palestinian intifada (resistance) broke out in 1987, and since then the movement has carried out a large number of bombings and acts of sabotage. Importantly, it was also during this period that Hamas established Palestinian suicide bombing as a method for terrorising Israeli citizens. Indeed, between 1993 and 2006 Hamas carried out over one hundred and eighty attacks – many of them suicide bombings.

For its part, Israeli occupation of the West Bank and Gaza has come at an equally heavy price in terms of the oppression and deaths of countless Palestinian lives, including civilians. This issue has arisen many times over the years, most recently during Israel's war against Hamas, which began on 27 December 2008 and lasted until 18 January 2009. Israeli action was in response to the ongoing mortar and rocket attacks on Israeli civilian centres by Hamas, with Israel's military operations in the Gaza strip seeking to stop these attacks and to reduce the ability of Hamas to carry out future attacks. The result was twenty-two days of heavy Israeli air bombardment as well as an intense ground offensive, during which Israel was accused of violating the human rights of Palestinian civilians. The intensity of the Israeli action was such that it led the United Nations Human Rights Council to initiate a fact-finding mission on the Gaza conflict. Its report was published on 15 September 2009 and its overwhelming conclusion was that Israel had committed crimes against humanity (see Box 32.2).

This brief account of Israeli-Palestinian history fails to do justice to the complicated nature of the relationship between the two sides. There are some useful books listed in the Recommended reading section at the end of the chapter if you are interested in learning more about this troubled region. This account has been necessary, however, because it clearly shows the difficulty that academics face when defining terrorism. Even a superficial analysis of the Arab-Israeli conflict demonstrates that both sides have been guilty of carrying out acts of violence against each other including, importantly, against civilians. However, there are major discrepancies between those who label the Palestinian groups as

---

 **Box 32.2 Excerpts from the Human Rights Council Report on the Gaza conflict – the Goldstone Commission**

Although the report itself was over five hundred pages long, the following two paragraphs clearly illustrate its overwhelming conclusions.

The conditions of life in Gaza, resulting from deliberate actions of the Israeli forces and the declared policies of the Government of Israel – as they were presented by its authorized and legitimate representatives – with regard to the Gaza Strip before, during and after the military operation, cumulatively indicate the intention to inflict collective punishment on the people of the Gaza Strip in violation of international humanitarian law.

. . . the Mission considered whether the series of acts that deprive Palestinians in the Gaza Strip of their means of sustenance, employment, housing and water, that deny their freedom of movement and their right to leave and enter their own country, that limit their access to a court of law and an effective remedy, could amount to persecution, a crime against humanity. From the facts available to it, the Mission is of the view that some of the actions of the Government of Israel might justify a competent court finding that crimes against humanity have been committed.

*Source*: United Nations General Assembly (2009) 'Human rights in Palestine and other occupied Arab territories', *Report of the United Nations Fact-Finding Mission on the Gaza Conflict, A/HRC/12/48* 25 September.

terrorists and see Israel as the victim and others who view the Israeli occupation and its killings, imprisonment and torture of Palestinians as acts of terrorism. Which of the two sides' actions get labelled as acts of terrorism depends almost entirely on the interests and views of those analysing the dispute. Even though many Western states would like to see the establishment of a Palestinian state, action by Palestinian suicide bombers against Israeli civilians is regarded as abhorrent. On the other hand, most Muslim states largely support Palestinian resistance to the Israeli occupation and view Israel's military occupation of Palestine as illegal.

Any definition of a terrorist is therefore dependent upon the subjective values, background and beliefs of the individual or group defining the term. Those supporting the Palestinians would see them as 'freedom fighters' seeking to resist the aggression of a powerful and illegitimate entity calling itself Israel. On the other hand Israel, as a legitimate state in the eyes of international law, would obviously refute the claim of the Palestinian groups to be freedom fighters and labels them as terrorists. It is in this context, therefore, that states which support Palestinian groups in their fight against Israel – Syria, Libya and Iran for instance – often lobby international fora such as the UN to prevent their protégés being labelled as terrorists. In their opinion such groups are entitled to use all available means to achieve their just goal of a Palestinian homeland. It therefore appears difficult, even on the surface, to determine who is actually a terrorist, but we would like to suggest that, since the international community is engaged in an ongoing War on Terror and, given that states have been invaded and so-called terrorist groups continue to claim the lives of innocent people, it is important that we attempt to simplify this minefield and differentiate between terrorism and other forms of political violence. Given the lack of consensus, any definition of terrorism must be neutral and it must recognise the premise that violence against others is actually used by a large number of groups.

The one overwhelming feature of the attacks on 9/11 was that the majority of those killed were civilians and included nationals of over ninety states. This brings us to the most obvious element in any definition of terrorism, namely, that it is predominantly directed against civilians. In order to clarify this issue further, we can make the case that an objective definition of terrorism can be based upon the provisions set down in international law over what is permissible in times of war between nations. The laws established in the Geneva and Hague Conventions are an excellent starting point given that, although there are differences between them, both represent the international community's efforts to regulate behaviour during times of war. The Hague Conventions are largely concerned with the rights and duties of the combatants themselves, whereas the Geneva Conventions establish a clear distinction between combatants on the one hand and non-combatants on the other. These rulings are deemed to be universal in nature and therefore binding on all states and, for our purposes, the differentiation between soldiers who attack enemy military personnel and those who deliberately target civilians is an important one. Boaz Ganor (an academic) takes a similar approach when defining terrorism in that he distinguishes between guerrilla warfare and terrorism and he also argues that the principle of war relating to states can be extended to conflict between organisations (such as guerrilla and terrorist groups). In this sense therefore, guerrilla warfare is the deliberate use of violence against military and security personnel in order to attain political, ideological and religious goals [whereas] 'Terrorism,' on the other hand, would be defined as the deliberate use or the threat to use violence against civilians in order to attain political, ideological and religious aims.

(Ganor 2002: 288)

This distinction is indeed crucial in the sense that once a group begins to target civilians, it can no longer claim to be fighting for freedom – it has clearly crossed the boundary towards becoming a terrorist organisation. Therefore, even if one agrees with the Palestinians and supports their rights to freedom and self-determination, it is not possible to condone the actions of Palestinian suicide bombers who target Israeli civilians. Conversely, there are many who legitimately condemn heavy-handed Israeli action against the Palestinian territories.

The differences of opinion over definitions were most apparent in April 2002 when the Organisation of the Islamic Conference (OIC) held a particularly important meeting in Kuala Lumpur (Malaysia). This meeting was crucial because it came in the wake of the 9/11 attacks and, given that all of the hijackers were Muslims, a political response to the attacks from the Islamic world was deemed to be necessary. However, the meeting was over-shadowed by increasing levels of violence between the Israelis and the Palestinians, and although the fifty-seven member states of the OIC did approve a declaration which condemned terrorism, they failed in their primary objective – a definition of the term. One of the main differences between the Islamic states present at the conference and the West in general was the attitude to the issue of Palestinian suicide bombers. Regarded as terrorists in the West, these Palestinians are seen in the Islamic world as resisting unlawful occupation of their land by Israel. The OIC, therefore, insisted that it was necessary to make a distinction between acts of terror – such as those perpetrated against the World Trade Center on 9/11 – and the acts of resistance aimed at achieving national liberation and self-determination.

The OIC's position was that Israeli action in the occupied territories stood in the way of any consensus over the definition of terrorism. The USA's well-documented support of Israel and its general refusal to condemn Israeli aggression in the West Bank and the Gaza Strip has led to further entrenchment of the Islamic position. In an explicit reference to Israel, the then Prime Minister of Malaysia opened the Conference by insisting that any definition of terrorism needed to include the targeting of civilians by states. As he stated, 'whether the attackers are acting on their own or on the orders of their government; whether they are regulars or irregulars, if the attack is against civilians then they must be considered terrorists' (ABC News, 1 April 2002). Such differences of opinion have meant that the schism between the West and the Islamic world is wide and any prospect of peace in the Middle East appears, for the moment, to be remote. The relationship between the two camps has been further complicated by numerous other events. Soon after the 9/11 attack, for instance, Islamically inspired terrorists targeted Westerners in Bali, Indonesia on 12 October 2002. The attack was attributed to Jemaah Islamiyah, an Indonesian terrorist group whose goal has been to create an Islamic state made up of Indonesia, Malaysia and parts of the Philippines. Over two hundred civilians, many of them Australian tourists, were killed in the blasts. Since then there have been a large number of additional attacks, not least the rush hour train bombing in Madrid, Spain and the 7 July 2005 bus and underground train bombs in London. What is particularly significant, is that even a cursory analysis of terrorism since 9/11 shows that the largest number of terrorist attacks since 2002 have been carried out by Islamic militants in various parts of the world which include Israel, India, Pakistan, Iraq, and Afghanistan. See, for instance, www.timelineofterrorism.com/ for a detailed list of terrorist incidents.

## The clash between the West and Islam: the Samuel Huntington thesis

It is in the context of the perceived clash between the West and Islam that we must analyse one of the most prominent and controversial ideas to emerge since the end of the Cold War, namely Samuel Huntington's '**clash of civilisations**'. In a highly influential article published in a 1993 issue of the journal *Foreign Affairs*, Huntington argued that the international system was increasingly being dominated by civilisations and that future conflicts would therefore be between these 'civilisations' and that the dominant source of conflict would be cultural (Huntington 1993: 22). He divided the world into seven distinct civilisations, namely Western, Islamic, Confucian, Japanese, Hindu, Latin American and Slavic Orthodox, and he further claimed that conflicts would occur along the cultural fault lines which separated them from one another. His most important views centred on the differences between the presumed civilisations in terms of 'history, language, culture, tradition, and most important, religion'. He saw these differences not only as real but also as the product of centuries of human interaction and he argued that, although differences did not necessarily mean violence, they had in fact 'generated the most prolonged and the most violent conflicts' (Huntington 1993: 23).

Importantly, although he did not explicitly refer to globalisation in this particular article, he did mention one of its consequences – the perception that greater interconnectedness was leading to increased interaction between people of different civilisations. His argument was that this process intensified 'civilization consciousness and awareness of differences between civilizations and commonalities within civilizations', leading ultimately to the entrenchment of the differences as well as increasing animosity between them (Huntington 1993: 24). Perhaps his most powerful claim, however, and one that particularly resonates with us in this chapter on terrorism, relates to his views on cultural characteristics and religious differences. He saw these as areas where it was exceptionally difficult to come to a compromise:

> In the former Soviet Union, communists can become democrats, the rich can become poor and the poor rich, but Russians cannot become Estonians and Azeris cannot become Armenians [and] . . . Even more than ethnicity, religion discriminates sharply and exclusively among people. A person can be half-French and half-Arab and simultaneously even a citizen of two countries. It is more difficult to be half-Catholic and half-Muslim.
>
> (Huntington 1993)

Huntington suggested that the West was at the peak of its power, militarily and economically, and claimed that its attempts to spread its democratic and liberal principles to other regions of the globe would result in 'countering responses from other civilizations', particularly Islam, given the historical animosity between the two sides. The clash of civilisations would occur on the boundaries between them and it is here that Huntington goes further and claims that Islam's problems do not just lie with the West. He states 'violence also occurs between Muslims, on the one hand, and Orthodox Serbs in the Balkans, Jews in Israel, Hindus in India, Buddhists in Burma and Catholics in the Philippines' and he goes on to claim that 'Islam has bloody borders' (Huntington 1996).

The 9/11 attacks appeared to some to confirm Huntington's thesis and had a profound impact, not least on ordinary civilians' sense of safety in the United States and elsewhere in the West. However, the attacks also came at the end of a decade of perceived changes in world politics, the first of which was the end of the Cold War and the reduction in East–West tensions. During the Cold War ideology had a central role in the conflict between the Soviet Union and the United States, with conventional explanations portraying the Soviets as expansionist and driven by a combination of interests and a Marxist-Leninist ideology. The clash thesis, however, stressed that, rather than associating with a particular ideology, states in the post-Cold War era were now likely to identify themselves with a particular culture. Alongside the growth in culture awareness, this view further stressed that there had been a significant resurgence of religion in regions all over the world – but this resurgence had manifest itself particularly within the Islamic world.

Huntington's thesis became a powerful framework upon which academics as well as politicians could base their grasp of global politics, and this has been particularly significant since 9/11. Most importantly, the ideas presented by Huntington formed the basis of George W. Bush's decision to pursue the so-called War on Terror. The Bush administration was successful in exploiting the media to portray the impression that the most obvious symbol of terrorism was the Muslim from the Middle East. Huntington's thesis provided an influential explanation of the attacks – particularly in portraying Arab and Muslim cultures as representing a threat to the values of the United States. Even though Huntington had identified numerous civilisations, it was between the West and Islam that the civilisational clash would occur. His views provided the intellectual background to the War on Terror in that USA foreign policy towards the Middle East was now defined in the context of the relationship between the USA and Islam.

## Are we really in the midst of a clash between the West and Islam?

Huntington's thesis has been criticised in a number of important ways. By seeking to bring about the systematic separation of the world's cultures, Huntington has left no room for any debate on how cultures have interacted with one another over time and the possibility that they may change. Huntington has failed to take into account that leading Western states are themselves already multicultural and becoming more so. By elevating religion to the deciding factor in human life, Huntington has failed to recognise that we as humans have multiple and complex identities where religious affiliation is merely one aspect. The 'clash' thesis makes a serious error when it assumes that Islam, or for that matter all other religious and cultural groupings, are monolithic entities with very few internal divisions. This view fails to recognise the many nuances that exist within each of the civilisations, a situation highlighted by academics such as Dieter Senghaas, who argues that clashes are more likely to occur *within* civilisations rather than between two different ones, largely because, historically, all civilisations have been characterised by huge internal differences (Senghaas 1998). One only has to look at the divisions within Islam to recognise the huge schisms which exist, for instance, between the Sunni and the Shi'ite sects of the religion. Conflicts between these two sects have plagued many Islamic states including Pakistan, where their longstanding rivalry regularly spills over into major incidents of violence (Ali 2008). It would undoubtedly be convenient for the violent militants of Islam to persuade all Muslims that jihad is to be viewed as a war on all infidels. However, one only has to turn to global opinion polls to see how attitudes in the Islamic world have decidedly turned against suicide bombing and support for militancy. The Pew Global Attitudes Project, for instance, encompasses a number of worldwide surveys on various issues, including people's views on current world affairs. According to Pew surveys, support for suicide bombing in Pakistan, for instance, had dropped from 41 per cent in March 2004 to 5 per cent in 2009. Similar findings in Jordan, Indonesia and Egypt have highlighted concern regarding the rise of Islamic extremism in the world (http://pewglobal.org/reports).

Such surveys are important in that they present an alternative to the rigidity of the 'clash' thesis. Indeed, as recently as October 2009 the Pakistani army was compelled to launch a ground offensive against the Taliban in the South Waziristan tribal region bordering Afghanistan. This much-anticipated offensive came at the end of a wave of terrorist attacks against Pakistani state, civilian and international institutions resulting in many deaths. Gauging Pakistani opinions is important, given that the United States has relied heavily on its 'partnership' with Pakistan in its war against terrorism and support does appear to be developing among ordinary Pakistanis to reverse the military and ideological gains made by the Taliban in the hope that this may lead to a reduction in terrorist attacks within the state. It is obviously also very much in the interests of the United States that the Taliban in Pakistan are defeated, given that they themselves are engaged in the war against the Taliban in neighbouring Afghanistan. We could therefore argue that we are seeing some convergence in the interests of both the Americans and the Pakistanis.

Elsewhere other Islamic states have also experienced militant Islam and its brand of violence, namely targeted bombs including suicide bombings. In October 2002, for instance, Jemaah Islamiyah (a violent Islamist group) targeted the Kuta Strip in Bali, an Indonesian tourist haven popular with Australians and other Westerners. Over two hundred people (including one hundred and fifty foreign nationals) were killed. Three men convicted of the bombings were executed by Indonesia in November 2008, signifying the government's counter-terrorism efforts. The Bali bombings had a serious impact on Indonesia's tourism industry and this concern, along with subsequent bombings in the centre of the capital, Jakarta, helped to shift public opinion towards decisive action against militant groups. Detachment 88, Indonesia's counter-terrorism unit, was formed in response to these events and since then has had considerable success in reducing the ability of Indonesian terrorist cells to operate with impunity. By successfully disrupting the activities of Jemaah Islamiyah and by arresting or killing many of its top operatives, the actions of Detachment 88 have persuaded Western governments, including the United States and Australia, to lift travel warnings which had been imposed in response to the 2002 bombings.

These two examples illustrate an important repudiation of Huntington's claim that Islam is clashing wholesale with the West. Both Pakistan and Indonesia are examples of states that have recognised that militant Islam is as much a threat to the cohesion of their own societies as it is to Western states. Indeed, we would go further and argue that poorer states such as Pakistan are under a much greater threat from militants than the stronger liberal democracies of the West. It is therefore unquestionably in the interests of Islamic governments to deal with the threats posed by the militants in their midst. Of course we are not claiming that Pakistan and Indonesia are an adequate representative sample of the entire Islamic world, but it remains important to highlight the inadequacies of the 'clash' thesis wherever possible. Huntington's claims that civilisations are in some way monolithic entities destined to clash with other civilisations is also flawed. Here the Pakistani and Indonesian cases demonstrate very well that civilisations divide and then further sub-divide, with these divided parts often in conflict among themselves.

## State and sub-state terrorism

**State terrorism** *or* **'terrorism from above'** is generally associated with states using their resources either to terrorise their own population or to support proxy groups abroad. In the case of the former, governments have often used the state's military, legal processes and security services to suppress what are perceived to be threats to the legitimacy of the state. The acts carried out by state institutions have ranged from torture, to mass murder and other brutal crimes against humanity. States generally carry out such practices in order to intimidate and even eliminate opposition members. In situations where such states perceive their authority to be under threat, the levels of violence are often extreme. In Chapter 26 (Box 26.1) we outlined instances where individual leaders and states have resorted to intense violence to subjugate their population. Here you will read of Pol Pot's regime in Cambodia (1976–79) enacting policies which resulted in the deaths of up to two million people. Also mentioned is Augusto Pinochet, President of Chile (1974–90) who killed thousands of opponents by employing unusual and particularly brutal forms of torture.

## Box 32.3 Turkey, Iraq and the Kurdish issue

The Kurds are a stateless ethnic group and inhabit parts of Iraq, Turkey, Syria and Iran. Their desire is to establish a state – Kurdistan – but thus far they have failed to do so since the lands claimed by them also form part of the aforementioned states. Turkey for instance incorporated the Kurdish-inhabited regions of eastern Anatolia, and this has long been opposed by Turkey's Kurdish population. Indeed, a long-running separatist conflict has resulted in the loss of thousands of lives particularly during the 1980s and 1990s when Turkey imposed martial law in Kurdish regions in order to control the activities of the separatist Kurdistan Workers Party (PKK), seen by the United States and Turkey as a terrorist organisation. Both sides have carried out executions, torture and destruction of property, though the violence has eased since 1999 when Abdullah Ocalan (the PKK leader) was captured.

A similar pattern emerged in Iraq during Saddam Hussein's era as president, since he periodically enacted policies to intimidate and oppress the indigenous Kurdish population. One such event – known as the al-Anfal Campaign – was carried out in 1982 when up to eight thousand Kurds were arrested and killed. A second component of this plan was carried out in 1988 when the Iraqi army made widespread use of chemical weapons and the destruction of over two thousand Kurdish villages. Estimates of the number killed in this genocide range from fifty thousand to two hundred thousand.

A variation of this form of terrorism is when states act as sponsors of violence elsewhere. In such cases governments encourage and even provide direct assistance to groups in other states to carry out acts of violence against civilians or the other state's institutions. There are many examples of state sponsorship of terrorism, ranging from Pakistan's assistance for anti-Indian militants in Jammu and Kashmir to attempts by the United States to destabilise the Sandinista regime following its overthrow of the USA-supported government of Anastasio Somoza Debayle in Nicaragua. In this case the Sandinistas were a Marxist insurgent group who overthrew Somoza Debayle in 1979. This in turn persuaded the American Central Intelligence Agency to provide funding, equipment and training to the Contras who then, between 1981 and 1983, conducted raids against the Sandinistas. In such cases, therefore, states will participate in terrorist activities and encourage them through the use of proxy groups, even going so far as to provide sanctuary for members of those terrorist groups – such as in the case of Pakistan providing sanctuary to Indian based militants. Another prominent example is that of Hezbollah (Party of God), a paramilitary group situated in Lebanon. The group first emerged in response to Israel's invasion of Lebanon in 1982 and since then its declared objectives have been to resist Israeli occupation of Palestinian territories and to establish Lebanon as an Islamic state. Despite appealing to many Arab and Muslim states, most Western states view Hezbollah as a terrorist organisation. What is of particular importance for our analysis is the support that the organisation receives from both Iran and Syria in the form of funding and weapons.

**Sub-state terrorism** *or* **'terrorism from below'** covers a vast number of events, groups and examples. The central component in this form of terrorism is the violence perpetrated against the state, predominantly carried out by non-state actors. The motivations of these groups are varied and have ranged from wars of national liberation to individuals (or

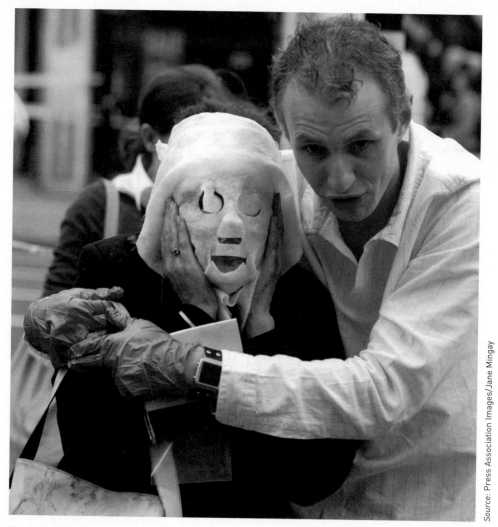

The London bombings of 2005 was an example of sub-state terrorism.

*Source: Press Association Images/Jane Mingay*

groups) who have turned their arsenal against presidents, prime ministers and others who oppose their cause. One of the most visible examples of this form of terrorism was when former United States army sergeant, Timothy McVeigh, bombed the Alfred P. Murrah Federal Building in Oklahoma City on 19 April 1995. McVeigh's bomb killed over one hundred and sixty people and at the time was hailed as the worst terrorist attack on American soil. During his trial he was described as a follower of far-right politics and was portrayed as an anti-government extremist. He was given the death sentence. Indeed, much of 'terrorism from below' is directed against the state and seeks to overthrow existing institutions as a precursor to establishing a new society. Other prominent examples include Euskadi Ta Askatasuna – commonly known as ETA – an armed group that has, since the late 1960s, sought to achieve independence for regions in northern Spain and south west

France that Basque Separatists claim as their own. Similarly, between 1983 and 2009, brutal civil war in Sri Lanka claimed the lives of over eighty thousand people as the Liberation Tigers of Tamil Eelam – also known as the Tamil Tigers – fought as insurgents against the government in an attempt to establish an independent Tamil state in the north of Sri Lanka. The tactics used by the Tamil Tigers (such as suicide bombings) led to the group being labelled a terrorist organisation by Western states. They were defeated by the Sri Lankan army in 2009.

An extreme leftist group was to bring havoc to West Germany during the 1970s and early 1980s. The Red Army Faction – also known as the Baader–Meinhof Gang – bombed department stores, robbed banks and murdered many prominent officials including American soldiers stationed in Germany since the end of the Second World War. Angry at German capitalism and its alliance with the West, the gang hoped that their action would result in fellow Germans rising up, overthrowing the authorities and establishing a Marxist state. A similar leftist group in Italy – the Red Brigade – sought to undermine Italian capitalism and democracy throughout the 1970s and 1980s with terrorist attacks. The police eventually succeeded in dismantling the various cells by the end of the 1980s. These few examples show that sub-state terrorism is the result of a volatile relationship between the state and its society and ultimately all states – irrespective of whether they are rich or poor – can suddenly find themselves targeted.

## Ethno-nationalist terrorism

An ethnic grouping can be seen as a population whose members identify with each other, resulting in a sense of one ethnic group being separate and distinct from others. Common cultural and linguistic practices, a common ancestry and even a common religion are some of the sources of a distinct ethnicity. Nationality on the other hand refers to an individual's relationship to a legal political system and is viewed as a person's membership of a nation and this is traditionally acquired by birth within the territory of a particular state. By extension, nationalism refers to the view that some aspect of nationality should be the only legitimate basis of a nation-state. Ethno-nationalism is the connection between both nationality and ethnicity and is generally viewed as a way of expressing superiority over other groups and the forms of terrorism spawned by this can be particularly dangerous. One only has to refer to the genocide in Rwanda in 1994 when conflict between two ethnically diverse groups resulted in the massacre of over eight hundred thousand people over a period of four months to see the extent of hatred that can exist.

Terrorism in Northern Ireland had a distinctly religious character to it as Catholic nationalists and Protestant unionists began to target each other in 1969 and by 1989 over three thousand people (mostly civilians) had been killed. Both Christian denominations are very different in terms of their political loyalties with the Protestants seeking British support and the Catholics of Northern Ireland wishing to reunify with the rest of Ireland. Wealthy Protestant unionists acquired significant leverage over political processes to the

## Box 32.4  The Brighton hotel bombing

On 12 October 1984, Patrick Magee, a member of the IRA, placed a bomb at the Grand Hotel in Brighton in an attempt to assassinate the then British Prime Minister Margaret Thatcher who was at the hotel (along with her cabinet) for the Conservative Party Conference. The IRA claimed responsibility and issued the following statement:

Mrs Thatcher will now realise that Britain cannot occupy our country and torture our prisoners and shoot our people in their own streets and get away with it. Today we were unlucky, but remember we only have to be lucky once. You will have to be lucky always. Give Ireland peace and there will be no more war.

The explosion did not kill Mrs Thatcher, but five other people lost their lives.

point of encouraging British troops onto Northern Ireland's streets. Such British support for the Protestant minority fuelled anger among the poorer Catholics, resulting in bloody riots in Londonderry and Belfast between 1968 and 1969. Despite attempts by British troops to restore order, the Irish Republican Army (IRA) began a campaign of terrorist action against the Protestant community and the British troops, as well as a bombing campaign against mainland Britain. Protestant paramilitary groups have been equally violent against the Catholic communities. The conflict continued throughout the 1990s and although some progress towards political dialogue was achieved during the mid-1990s, it wasn't until 2005 that the IRA agreed to lay down their arms.

Although there are many more examples of this form of terrorism, we would like to mention one more where different ethnic and religious affiliations have claimed the lives of more than one hundred and twenty-five thousand people during a sixteen-year civil war which began in 1975. In Lebanon, Maronite Christians, Sunni Muslims, Shi'ite Muslims and the Druze all competed violently for political power. To make matters worse, Syrian troops, Iranian infiltrators and Palestinian refugees and fighters also vied for power, thereby leading to a collapse of control by the Lebanese authorities.

## Case study: Ethno-nationalist terrorism and conflict in Sudan

Sudan gained independence from Britain in 1956 but since then has been embroiled in civil conflict between the relatively prosperous and more developed Arab Muslim north and the south, which predominantly comprises Animist and some Christian tribes. The state sits on top of reserves of oil, but ongoing conflict has prevented their exploitation. Ethnic, racial, religious and political differences formed the basis for the conflict as the northern Arabs have sought to unify the state along Islamic traditions at the expense of the non-Muslim population. Attempts to impose Islamic (Shari'a) law on non-Muslims resulted in southern groups launching attacks against the north and since 1983 over 1.2 million people have been killed. Progress towards peace began in 2002 when the Arab government and the southern Sudan People's Liberation Movement/Army (SPLM/A) signed an agreement committing them to a political solution. Steps towards greater autonomy for the south and increased reliance on elections have been subsequently taken.

However, while these historic negotiations continued between the north and south, reports began to emerge in 2003 of increased attacks against predominantly non-Arab civilians in the highly polarised region of Darfur. In response rebel groups representing black African non-Arab Muslims resorted to rebellion and this, in turn, invited government support for local rival tribes and militias, collectively known as the Janjaweed. These rival groups were largely composed of black African Muslims but heavily influenced by Arab traditions and culture. Attacks by the Janjaweed groups on civilians have claimed the lives of more than three hundred thousand people, and have led to more than two million becoming displaced with a large number of refugees fleeing to the neighbouring state of Chad. On 4 March 2009, the International Criminal Court issued an arrest warrant for the President of Sudan (Omar Ahmad Al-Bashir) for inciting genocide and other crimes against humanity. At the start of 2010 the Darfur conflict entered its seventh year, peace remained elusive, and the President had still not been arrested.

 **Why do you think African and Middle Eastern states are so vulnerable to religious terrorism?**

## Conclusion

This chapter has identified a number of key features which need to form the basis of any analysis of terrorism. The first is the issue of definition, where we showed that although there is some consensus among observers, there is no unanimity regarding what actually constitutes terrorism. The Israeli-Palestinian conflict was used to demonstrate the problems associated with defining the term and we showed that the variations are often dependent upon perceptions, individual bias and the opinions of those seeking to provide a definition. Due to the entrenched differences between definitions, we suggested that a degree of simplicity might be introduced into the debate by arguing that, whatever else terrorism may be, it has in recent years appeared to be largely directed against civilian targets.

The 9/11 attacks had a profound impact because they were directed against the world's only superpower and we have therefore devoted a considerable portion of the chapter to considering the role that religion has played in fomenting terrorism. Among the various explanations put forward for the attacks, many observers point to the view that civilisational and religious differences now form the basis of many of the world's conflicts and that cultural differences are now central features of world politics. It is because of the prevailing view that the Islamic world and the West are now locked in conflict, with terrorism as a central feature, that we deemed it necessary to analyse some elements of the broader relationship between the two poles. One view in particular has had a tremendous impact on the debate regarding this relationship and we identified Samuel Huntington as worthy of attention. Huntington put forth his 'Clash of Civilisations' theory in 1993 and since then many academics have sought to either criticise or support his thesis. We further highlighted our belief that there does appear to be a strong link between Huntington's thesis, the 9/11 terrorist attacks and the American response to those attacks. Taken together these elements appear to cement the view that culture and religion are now central features of world politics. This was also apparent in the way in which the Bush administration itself began to define its relationship with the Islamic world. Since it was seen as culturally hostile to the West, it was easy to demonise Islam as a natural enemy to Western values and ideals.

In the final section we referred to the particular dangers of ethno-nationalist terrorism and, as you will have seen from the various examples, religion often forms one element of this brand of terrorism. This shows that there is considerable overlap between the various categories we have dealt with in this chapter. Modern terrorism is likely to continue to feature as a concern for states and regions influencing politicians and diminishing the security of people. The international system is at present in the midst of a long drawn out conflict with groups such as al-Qaeda and an easy solution to the myriad of terrorist threats facing states is unlikely for the foreseeable future.

## Resource section

## Questions

1. To what extent is Samuel Huntington's thesis a valid explanation for the terrorist attacks of recent years?

2. Why is it so difficult to define 'terrorism'?

3. What is the connection between 'extremism' and 'terrorism'?

4. Using examples, explain what is meant by 'state terrorism' and 'sub-state terrorism'.

5. Islamically inspired terrorism is only one example, there are other forms. So why has the international community been so concerned with this particular brand of terrorism?

## Recommended reading

**Huntington, S. (1993) 'The clash of civilizations', *Foreign Affairs*, Summer**

As one of the most influential and controversial articles of recent times, the views presented by Huntington in this particular publication led to much debate among academics as well as politicians over whether cultural conflict had now become a central feature of world politics. The events since its publication, in particular the 9/11 attacks, appear to confirm his thesis that civilisations were now in conflict with one other.

**Huntington, S. (1996) *The Clash of Civilizations and the Remaking of World Order* (London: Simon & Schuster)**

Published three years after the original article, Huntington wrote this book in defence of his thesis and as an attempt to further expand it.

**Lewis, B. (1990) 'The roots of Muslim rage', *The Atlantic*, September (www.theatlantic.com/doc/199009/muslim-rage)**

This is an important article in that Lewis was a historian of the Islamic world and was the first to use the phrase 'the Clash of Civilizations', indicating that he saw conflict between Islam and the West as inevitable.

**Martin, G. (2010) *Understanding Terrorism: Challenges, Perspectives and Issues* (3rd edn, London: Sage)**

A comprehensive, multi-levelled and contemporary treatment of a wide range of issues concerning terrorism.

**Sen, A. (2006) *Identity and Violence: The Illusion of Destiny* (London: Penguin)**

An important and recent critique of Huntington's thesis in which Sen argues that people have multiple identities, religious, occupational and so on. Conflict, according to him, arises when these multiple identities are ignored in favour of a singular affiliation.

# Part 7 The Future

**33 Conclusions: Sovereignty, Globalisation and the Future of International Relations**

*Source*: Getty Images/AFP

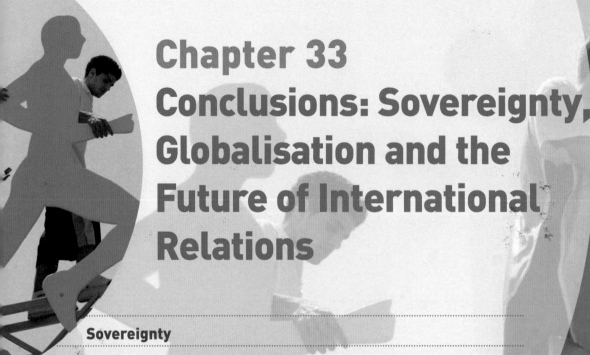

# Chapter 33
# Conclusions: Sovereignty, Globalisation and the Future of International Relations

Sovereignty

Towards global civil society?

Towards global governance?

Conclusion

By the end of this chapter you will be able to:

- Explain the legal and political meaning of sovereignty
- Understand rival perspectives on the significance of sovereignty in the contemporary world
- Appreciate the idea of global civil society
- Critique competing theoretical predictions over whether the future of international relations will continue to be based on interactions between sovereign states or on some alternative form of global governance

*Source*: Getty Images/AFP

## Introductory box: FARClandia

In 1998, as part of a peace deal seeking to end a long running and brutal civil war, the government of Colombia agreed to cede control of a 42,000 km square chunk of territory (roughly the size of Switzerland) to the insurgents of the Revolutionary Armed Forces of Colombia (FARC). Since 1964 FARC, who seek the establishment of a Marxist state, have waged a well-organised military campaign partly funded by criminal activity, against both the Colombian government and irregular right-wing militia within the country. The territory ceded by the government unofficially became known as FARClandia with the guerrillas assuming control of an economy (largely based on cocaine), border crossings, policing, and around one hundred thousand people. Hence, in a sovereign country widely held to be democratic, economically developed and not a 'failed state' (a territory which effectively lacks governance), the government was admitting that it could not govern its own territory.

Although this represents an extreme example, many governments across the world struggle to assert their sovereign control, leading some to speculate that we may soon enter a post-sovereign age in which our conventional image of the political world divided into just under two hundred autonomous states is superseded by a new, more globalised order.

Throughout this book you have explored how the international political system has evolved. You have learned about the persistence of perennial international political issues concerning military and economic interactions between states and also about the impact of 'newer' issues dealing with concerns such as environmental change and human rights. You have also learned about how international organisations have emerged to facilitate dealing with the increased range of issues on the international political agenda and about the evolution of IR theories seeking to conceptualise all of this. Underpinning all of this is sovereignty and contention over whether the significance of this concept is changing, in line with a globalising world. This is explored in this, final chapter.

## Sovereignty

**Sovereignty** is the basis of statehood and, hence, is central to the orthodox understanding of the political world as a system of states. Politically, there are two sides to sovereignty: an *internal* and an *external* dimension.

1. **Internal sovereignty.** Internally, sovereignty refers to exclusive political control. Hence a state's government can be referred to as the *sovereign*, in that it is the ultimate source of legal and political power. The government, be it a monarchy, dictatorship or democratically elected cabinet, is solely responsible for making and upholding the most important laws of the land. The world's sovereign entities, of course, come in many shapes and sizes and many states devolve some powers to regional governors but, even in the most decentralised political systems, certain key responsibilities reside exclusively with the central government and its agencies. Monetary policy and foreign policy are never devolved and sovereigns have an exclusive right to use force to uphold the law, through the enforcement agencies of the police and military forces. Hence the use of force by non-sovereign entities (such as armed secessionist movements) is invariably denounced by the governments affected as illegitimate and 'terrorism'.

2. **External sovereignty.** The exercise of internal sovereignty also has external significance since exclusive legal and political control over a country must also mean that other governments have no right to interfere in that state's affairs. In addition to this right of non-interference, sovereignty also confers upon a country legal equality with other sovereigns including the right to be an entity in diplomacy and international law. Hence non-sovereign entities in international relations are denied a seat and a vote in the United Nations and most other intergovernmental organisations and also the right to have diplomats protected by laws of immunity stationed in other states. Hence while colonies of sovereign states (such as Greenland, a colony of Denmark or Puerto Rico, a colony of the US) and disputed territories (such as North Cyprus or Taiwan) can interact with other countries, they are not able to engage as fully in international relations as they would if they were sovereign.

What, then, distinguishes a sovereign state from any other sort of territory? In **Public International Law** the key reference point is the Montevideo Convention, which arose out of an International Conference of American States in 1933. The Convention sought to clarify which territories of the Americas were entitled to enjoy the privileges of sovereignty and, in doing so, came to be seen by the wider international community as an expression of customary international law (i.e. having applicability the world over as accepted practice) (see Box 33.1).

### Box 33.1 The legal basis of statehood

According to the Montevideo Convention on Rights and Duties of States 1933, a 'state' must have:

a. a permanent population;
b. defined territory;
c. a government capable of maintaining effective control.

Predictably, the third legal criterion for statehood is the most contentious and less easily defined, but the first and second are not without controversy and are enshrined in International Law for a good reason. There are many uninhabited islands and tracts of land in the world which are deemed in International Law to be *terra nullius* or territory of no one. In order to avoid the potential chaos of states scrambling to claim any inhospitable chunks of rock that lie above sea level for purely economic reasons (i.e. to gain exclusive rights for extracting resources or fishing in the surrounding seas) International Law considers such places to be beyond sovereign reach. The most prominent example of this is Antarctica, actually covered by a specific treaty, the 1959 Antarctic Treaty. Antarctica remains *terra nullius* in spite of the teams of scientists who periodically reside on the continent and the sometimes bizarre efforts of governments like Argentina's to assert sovereign control through acts such as flying out couples there to get married and even pregnant women to give birth. Such events are not deemed sufficient in law to constitute a permanent human occupation.

Claims to statehood have also sometimes been made in instances where there is no land but there are people purporting to be citizens of a country. The self-styled Principality of Sealand was founded by UK citizen Paddy Roy Bates (Prince Roy) on an abandoned British Second World War fort in the North Sea, outside of UK territorial jurisdiction (and which, under International Law, should have been disbanded by the British at the close of the war). Although Sealand has no prospect of being accepted as a sovereign state the fact that it is beyond the jurisdictional reach of any country has created some legal headaches. Prince Roy, for example, has profited from allowing internet providers to operate from the fort unrestricted by British, or any other national, laws. Beyond producing such jurisdictional grey areas, some have come to speculate that **cyberstates**, comprising online virtual communities of citizens, could soon come to pose a challenge to the level of control governments have over their country's societies as people's loyalties and interests shift to cyberspace (Smith 2008).

*Source: Rex Features/Peter Lawson*

**The Principality of Sealand, founded on an abandoned Second World War fort in the North Sea, has made one of the more unusual claims to statehood in the modern era.**

The third criterion for statehood (a government capable of maintaining effective control) is more open to interpretation and is triggered by diplomatic recognition; the official acknowledgement of a newcomer among their ranks by the existing members of the sovereign club. This is usually followed by the new state's diplomats being allowed to operate, under the protection of law, in other states and also take up their place in the United Nations (replacing the previous regime of that country if it is a case of a revolution changing the sovereign). Hence becoming a sovereign state is somewhat akin to joining an exclusive golf club in that to get in you need to be an adult and have some clubs but must, crucially, also be judged suitable by the current members.

The traditional practice for judging the suitability of a new sovereign state is, however, supposed to be a value-free determination as to whether the new government is in control or not, rather than a show of support for the newcomer, which may be an emotive issue given that they may well have emerged from a civil war or revolution. This tradition, known in International Law as the **Lauterpacht doctrine** – after Austro-Hungarian born lawyer Hersch Lauterpacht – is still broadly followed but diplomatic recognition became more politicised during the **Cold War** and is today not entirely value-free. The USA heralded a new tendency to withhold recognition of new states it found unpalatable by failing to recognise Communist China after the 1949 revolution. The British, in contrast, followed the Lauterpacht doctrine and recognised the post-revolutionary regime in China despite sharing the same ideological hostility to Communism as their American allies. Thirty years on, however, much of the international community had come to share the USA's laxer interpretation of the Lauterpacht doctrine and when the UK became the first government to recognise the Pol Pot regime in Cambodia they were isolated and widely vilified by their fellow sovereigns for conferring legitimacy on a genocidal dictator. A side-effect of not recognising governments as a statement of disapproval of their human rights record, however, is that in doing so you cede any real prospect of diplomatic leverage over that government. This will make it difficult to undertake foreign policy initiatives to improve human rights and sometimes even to enact diplomatic initiatives for purely self-serving reasons. This became apparent in the aftermath of the 11 September 2001 strikes when neither the USA nor any of their Western allies could wield any effective direct diplomatic pressure over the Taliban regime in Afghanistan to give up al-Qaeda operatives within their territory or secure the release of several hostages. Giving diplomatic recognition to the Taliban would doubtless have been controversial, given their appalling human rights record, but it could also have provided a means of influencing them short of the full-scale war that was quickly resorted to.

Sovereignty became established at the 1648 Treaty of Westphalia, which ended the Wars of the Reformation that pitted Northern Protestant Europe against the Catholic South. The Protestant victory resulted in a peace treaty which asserted that Europe's kingdoms were not answerable to the Pope or any other external authority, thus enshrining the notion of sovereignty in international relations. Hence what is often referred to as the '**Westphalian system**' of sovereign states was inaugurated, a system we still have today over three hundred and fifty years later. In the seventeenth century sovereignty was only considered relevant to

Europe and so did not restrain its great powers from continuing to colonise lands outside of their continent. With the onset of decolonisation in the nineteenth and twentieth centuries, however, the Westphalian system and the notion of sovereignty as underpinning international relations became *globalised*. The independence of Namibia in 1990 – the last colony of Africa – is often considered to mark the completion of this process. By 2010 there were one hundred and ninety-two states in the United Nations covering nearly all the land mass of the world bar Antarctica. The colonies that remain – like Puerto Rico or the UK's Falklands Islands – do so because they are happy to be that way, maintaining the protection of their imperial power while largely running their own internal affairs.

While sovereignty has globalised many contend that globalisation from the mid twentieth century, in a number of ways, has also served to undermine the concept.

## Dominance by superpowers

Sovereign states have, of course, never been equal in power terms and meddling in the affairs of the weak by the strong has always gone on, but this became so pervasive in the Cold War era that it could be said to have rendered any notion of legal equality as meaningless. The dominance of the USA and USSR in this period created asymmetries of power in the state system not seen before which, when added to the ideological zeal that compelled both superpowers to promote their economic model to others, saw the notion of non-interference in the affairs of others go out of the window. The USSR's Warsaw Pact/COMECON allies – Poland, East Germany, Czechoslovakia, Hungary, Bulgaria and Romania – were no more than notionally independent from Moscow and became widely referred to as 'satellite states'. Soviet 'advisors' influenced government meetings and when the Hungarians and Czechs ignored advice and sought to take full control of their affairs in 1956 and 1968 respectively, Moscow sent tanks in instead. In a less explicit fashion several Latin American countries, and most notably Guatemala, Chile and Nicaragua, were subject to American interference in their affairs when they appeared to be moving politically leftwards.

## Economic interdependence

The unprecedented increase in transboundary movements of traded goods and money that characterises contemporary globalisation is seen by many to undermine the notion of even today's most powerful states really being in control of their own affairs. In the contemporary world governments are more than ever at the mercy of global economic forces with financial flows negating their efforts to control the national money supply and the desire not to be uncompetitive leading most to surrender full control of trading policy to the World Trade Organisation and regional trade blocs. In light of this could it be said that legal sovereignty has little practical meaning?

The globalisation of trade and monetary issues due to economic interdependence has also spilled over into other policy areas. Issues once thought of very much as domestic rather than international concerns, like law and order or health, are also increasingly global as well as national concerns. The criminality that undermines the ability of the Colombian government to control its country, referred to in the Introductory box, is inextricably linked to many countries around the world. Colombia is the world leader in coca plant production and the earnings from the illegal trade of the plant's narcotic derivative cocaine to countries like the USA, UK and Spain have funded right-wing and left-wing insurgents as well as internationally operating criminal cartels.

From the fifteenth century when the Black Death plague swept from Asia to Europe and became the single most deadly event in history, it has been apparent that trade and travel can bring disease as well as prosperity. In the contemporary age, while medical progress has given us much greater means to contain the spread of diseases than in the pre-modern age, the scale and rate at which goods and people can cross borders makes implementing such measures increasingly difficult. The 2003 SARS (Severe Acute Respiratory Syndrome) and 2009–10 'Swine Flu' influenza pandemics were the latest in a long line of inter-national diseases that globalised but were distinct in the rapidity in which they were able to move between countries tied together by business interests, tourism and a global food industry. Economic and cultural globalisation also accounts for the internationalisation of non-contagious 'lifestyle illnesses', like lung cancer, diabetes and obesity. Many countries – principally in the Global South – have had to contend with ailments, previously barely known to them, associated with the spread of largely Western habits like smoking and consuming high fat and sugar foods. Western multinational corporations have been keen to exploit new markets for tobacco and fast food with the demand for such products fuelled by their exposure through a globalising media.

## Rise of 'micro-states' and 'failed states'

The economic and political changes unleashed by globalisation have also contributed to the proliferation of sovereign states of a smaller and weaker form than generally seen in earlier eras. Given that economic interdependence has reduced the real autonomy of even powerful countries, the notion that certain small or economically dependent territories should not be deemed sovereign has weakened. Many of the one hundred and ninety-two UN member states could now be said to struggle to meet the third Montevideo Convention criteria. Most new additions to the sovereign club are tiny countries who have earned recognition despite being what would have been thought of in the past as **sub-sovereign** entities such as principalities. Recent members of the UN include territories like Andorra, Monaco, Liechtenstein and San Marino (all previously rejected as League of Nations members) with a long history of making their own laws but dependent on powerful neighbours for defending this autonomy and providing a currency, the two areas of political authority most associated with sovereignty. When in 1998, Lesotho, a tiny state surrounded by South Africa, experienced widespread rioting caused by a disputed election result, they called in their neighbours to sort it out and restore law and order. In such cases it could be concluded that internal sovereign control is not in place and recognition has been given too readily. If a country entirely dependent on another for its internal and external security can be considered a sovereign state does this not render the notion of sovereignty redundant?

In addition to cases where sovereignty is gained more easily than it once was, several established states could be said to have held on to their sovereign status despite it ceasing to have any practical meaning. Chapter 28 explains how the phenomenon of failed states has become more pronounced in recent years. There have always been weak states but rarely in the Westphalian system has there been places like Afghanistan, Somalia and Sudan; existing as coherent political entities in name only. These states have continued to be represented at the UN and have the diplomatic recognition of most sovereign states but these have been privileges conferred on governments demonstrably no longer running the territories they represent. In Afghanistan, for example, recognition of the previous regime persisted in the late 1990s and early 2000s despite the clear fact that it had ceded control to the Taliban. While granting the privilege of sovereignty upon a country is subject to much debate, there is no real precedent for withdrawing recognition for states where sovereignty has vanished.

## Growth of non-state actors

In order to deal with the uncertainties produced by economic and other forms of globalisation governments have increasingly turned to **Intergovernmental Organisations** (IGOs) to simplify their foreign relations and reap mutual rewards from collective action. IGOs have grown in accord with globalisation and have tended to become more significant over time (see Chapter 12). In some cases, such as with some elements of the World Trade Organisation and European Union, governments have formally ceded some sovereignty in order to permit **supranational** decision making in a phenomenon sometimes referred to as 'dual sovereignty'. It is established, for example, that EU law has primacy over the national laws of its member states. Many member states have had to amend laws passed through their own parliaments and approved by their own courts because they were not in accord with the treaties of the European Communities/Union (see Chapter 15). In most IGOs supranational decision-making is not the case and governments retain full legal sovereignty but, even here, the need to do business and get on with others can produce compromises and bargaining in which governments essentially end up doing something other than they would have chosen if acting in isolation.

As is highlighted in Chapter 12 the proliferation of IGOs is not taken by everyone as evidence of a commensurate decline in state sovereignty. Realists posit that since IGOS are, after all, comprised of government representatives they can be used by powerful states to buttress their power vis á vis other sovereigns. Perhaps more pertinent to the future of sovereignty, then, is the proliferation that has also occurred in non-state actors not comprised of states; International Non-governmental Organisations (INGOs). This is analysed in the next section.

## Towards global civil society?

The rise of formal international organisations, in which decisions are taken by government representatives, over the past sixty years has also been accompanied by the growth on the international political stage of a variety of organisations in which governments play no or little part. Elsewhere in this book we can see how some multinational corporations (MNCs) have become wealthier than many sovereign states and influence the decision-making of both governments and IGOs like the World Trade Organisation (see Chapter 17). Equally we can observe that IR has been greatly affected by the rise of armed non-state actors (or 'terrorists') with the world's most powerful state (the US) having been at war with a non-sovereign group (al-Qaeda) for the past decade. It is still, however, possible to contend that terrorists and MNCs are inextricably linked to states and do not, therefore, necessarily represent a diminution of state power in the world. Terrorists are often state-sponsored and fight for particular countries (like Afghanistan) or – in the case of secessionist movements (like Basque seperatists) – are seeking to become new sovereign states. Similarly, MNCs are often used by governments for international political influence as seen in the Cold War when American businesses played a key role in buying influence in strategically important countries in Europe and Asia. Hence the non-state actors which most challenge the logic of a sovereign state system, possibly, are those that explicitly forego governmental influence and, to some extent, exist to challenge the perceived inadequacies of sovereign rule; international pressure groups.

Pressure groups, or not-for profit groups, can be dated as far back as the late nineteenth century. The Sierra Club, for example, was established in 1892 to promote the conservation of nature in the USA and is still influential in environmental politics today. It is from the 1960s, however, when public protest became a regular and systematic feature of political life in Western liberal democracies, that we can see the real emergence of a realm of politics outside the mainstream of government and inter-party parliamentary debate. With industrialisation widespread public protest, in the form of demands for the enfranchisement and social protection of the newly emergent working class, became prominent in the late nineteenth and early twentieth centuries but, by the 1950s, this had largely come to be accommodated by democracy and welfare policies entering the mainstream in most developed countries. Hence political scientists in North America and Western Europe had come to talk of an 'end of ideology' with a consensus having emerged in which people's interests were largely satisfied (Bell 1960). In the 1960s, however, this consensus started to break down and more and more people became attracted to political activism outside of the traditional arena of party politics, giving support to pressure groups and/or taking to the street in protest. Unlike protest in previous ages this has proven to be a structural change and has persisted, grown and internationalised since the 1960s for the following reasons, very much linked to globalisation:

## Technological change

The whole of human history can, in the main, be viewed in terms of technological progress but it was not until the modern era that we can see this as something that empowered those outside of the political and social establishment. Key travel and communications advances, such as the development of aeroplanes and telephones, emerged in the late nineteenth century but from the 1960s these became commonplace and accessible to people outside of the elites. Organising marches and linking together with like-minded activists in other countries hence became more and more of a realistic prospect. With the continued advance of communications technology this phenomenon has evolved with mobile phones, the internet and budget airlines giving larger swathes of societies dissatisfied with the political mainstream the opportunity to voice that dissatisfaction.

## Social change

From a sociological perspective, while a new working class was, by the 1960s, accommodated in mainstream politics in liberal democracies, this era is thought to have spawned new social change in the emergence of a 'new middle class'. This refers to a growing number of people with sufficient wealth to afford to take part in regular political protest and not necessarily supportive of the political status quo in the way normally expected of the relatively well off in society. People able and inclined to take advantage of the technological opportunities offered to them have become a feature of political life and demanded changes from governments in a way which has served to break the consensus of the 1940s and 1950s. Governments in the developed world have become weakened by a 'revolution of rising expectations'. Democratic governments have simultaneously been weakened by economic interdependence and swamped by more and more demands from their citizens. While, for governments, taxes and managing the economy remain central political concerns, albeit ones over which they have less and less control, they have increasingly also had to address issues like human rights and the environment, advanced by pressure groups and wider social movements.

While from the 1960s to the 1990s this phenomenon of regular protest and lobbying was largely confined to democracies in the Global North, this pervasiveness of contemporary information technology (IT) and the globalisation of ideas that this facilitates has increasingly empowered more and more people in undemocratic and previously closed societies. Hence in 2009 a new generation of IT savvy Iranians were able to give voice to their disapproval of apparent electoral fraud by their government to much of the world in the so-called 'Twitter Revolution'.

Pressure groups with international political influence have grown hugely in recent decades from around a thousand at the end of the Second World War to a figure of over sixty thousand in the world today (UIA 2009). Previous chapters have shown how pressure groups have been key players in the emergence and evolution of international politics with regards to the environment, human rights and development. As well as holding governments of their home country to account in the way that has come to be accepted as integral to modern democratic state governance (see Chapter 21) groups like Amnesty International, Greenpeace and Oxfam also influence the conduct of international relations by moulding the international political agenda through advancing issues outside of the obvious interest of governments and helping implement international law. Over two thousand five hundred pressure groups have consultative status with the United Nations which gives them the right to attend and contribute to important conferences. The 1992 UN Conference on the Environment and Development at Rio de Janeiro, the most significant international political event in the history of these two issue areas, was actually organised and managed by pressure groups on behalf of the UN. Groups like Amnesty International have been pivotal in monitoring whether governments who have ratified international human rights conventions actually live up to their word after smiling for the cameras when signing up at the founding treaty. The UN–pressure group relationship is a symbiotic one. The pressure groups benefit from the global exposure that the UN provides. The UN benefits from being able to draw upon the specialist and independent expertise the pressure groups can offer. Most high profile pressure groups can boast a significant budget usually drawn from individual donations which gives them the capacity to hire high-quality professionals and make their presence felt in international political diplomacy without being tainted by association with parochial national interests. Amnesty, Greenpeace, Oxfam and many other groups have memberships in the millions and budgets in the tens of millions (US dollars) which, since they are focused on specific areas, buys them the expertise and means to rival even the wealthiest states. For Liberals this represents the emergence of a global civil society which can check the excesses of governments in international politics in the same way such groups have in Western liberal democracies, acting as what former UN Secretary General Kofi Annan referred to as the 'conscience of the world'. Hence, in this view, pressure groups are central to the achievement of humane global governance in place of traditional practice in international relations dictated by state interests. As with the rise of all non-state actors and the phenomenon of globalisation in general, however, not everyone is convinced that the political world has really changed or is set to do so. Realist Kenneth Waltz, for example, opines that:

> States are not and never have been the only international actors. But then structures are defined not by all the actors that flourish within them but by the major ones.
>
> (Waltz 1979: 93–4)

For Realists, the notion of global civil society has little substance and IR continues fundamentally to be about inter-state politics. This debate is explored further in the next section.

## Towards global governance?

Whether or not the sovereign state is in terminal decline and the **Westphalian system** ready to be succeeded by a new era of international relations, based on global governance, is hotly disputed. In this section the positions of the main IR theories on this question are explored.

# Liberals

The **Liberal** political thought that emerged in the eighteenth century was built on the premise that the state needed to be limited so that it was not allowed to endanger the liberties of the people it was supposed to represent. By the twentieth century, this logic had also come to be applied to international relations. The widespread feeling that the First World War was an avoidable conflict prompted the emergence of **Idealism** (see Chapter 7) which manifested itself in the creation of the League of Nations and the penning of a number of polemical works advocating world government in place of the sovereign system of states. British political activists John Hobson and Leonard Woolf (husband of renowned literary figure Virginia Woolf ), for example, wrote books advocating world government as a means of retreating from endemic conflict and imperialism (Hobson 1915; Woolf 1916). Woolf was a firm advocate of the League of Nations, which emerged after the First World War, whereas Hobson was highly dismissive of this organisation as little more than a victors' club for a nationalistic and pointless conflict. Woolf was more positive, considering the League to be furthering the trend established in nineteenth century international affairs, before the build up to world war, of international organisations like the Universal Postal Union assuming the political stewardship of certain functions not achievable by governments acting independently.

> We are accustomed to regard the world as neatly divided into compartments
> called states. . . . But this vision of the world divided into isolated compartments
> is not a true reflection of facts as they exist in a large portion of the earth today.
>
> (Woolf 1916: 216–7)

Woolf and Hobson were thus pioneers of two differing strands of global governance theory which were further developed after the Second World War. Woolf's work was a source of inspiration for David Mitrany and the **Functionalists**, a branch of Liberalism comprising scholars and activists who favoured a gradualist, bottom-up approach towards world government in which ordinary people would rationally come to switch their loyalties from their states to international non-governmental bodies. In this view, global governance was inevitable as the inadequacies of states, preoccupied with military concerns at the expense of people's real interests of health, welfare and education, became apparent and saw them slowly lose legitimacy and authority (Mitrany 1975).

Hobson's route to world government was more direct and 'top down': the immediate creation of **supranational** federal global agencies assuming control from governments of certain, clearly defined political areas. World Federalism of this sort gained momentum with the failure of the League of Nations and the even greater horrors that unfolded in the second of the century's two world wars. For example, the British and Indian premiers, Churchill and Nehru, both spoke of federation as a recipe for world peace. Advocacy for world Federalism, receded, however, from the 1950s as the Cold War divided the world again and economic recovery convinced even the countries of the emergent European Communities that they need only cooperate rather than federate into a new state.

**Box 33.2 Keohane's tasks requiring global governance**

In Keohane's view the following political aspirations cannot be met by the sovereign state system but are, nonetheless, desirable for those sovereign states:

- a proper functioning system of Collective Security (where all countries together agree to uphold International Law and punish unlawful aggression);

- limiting state recourse to 'negative externalities' (acts favouring one state in the short term but, ultimately, damaging the international community, e.g. polluting the atmosphere);
- common trading standards;
- a global monetary facility;
- human rights.

(Keohane 2002)

World Federalism continues to be advocated by some thinkers and pressure groups, such as the group Federal Union, but this is now very much a minority view unlikely to receive the endorsement of today's prominent international statesmen. Similarly, Functionalism at a global level, even to modern day Idealists, appears too utopian to be a practical international political aspiration. International organisations have proliferated as Mitrany predicted but the most influential ones remain strictly intergovernmental and few people do appear to have switched loyalties and abandoned their states. Consequently, many contemporary Liberals have come to predict and advocate less radical and more pragmatic forms of global governance. Robert Keohane, for example, has reasoned that there is a state utilitarian logic for global governance (i.e. a rationale for states themselves to want to surrender certain powers to global political institutions (see Box 33.2)).

These forms of global governance would be in the interests of ordinary people but also in the interests of most governments since the political tasks concerned cannot be accomplished by states acting in isolation. Hence this Liberal vision is more a case of refining rather than abandoning the concept of sovereignty.

## Social Constructivists

Social Constructivists have added to the pragmatic Liberal perspective that International Relations needs to re-appraise the nature of sovereignty rather than assuming that it is disappearing. A central tenet in Social Constructivist thought that has risen to prominence in IR over the last two decades is the notion that sovereignty is, like all political concepts, a social construction and should not be treated in the same way as a material fact. Alexander Wendt's famous maxim that 'anarchy is what states make of it' neatly captures the idea that some states behave as if they have exclusive control over their own affairs but others choose not to (Wendt 1992). Hence within the European Union France and particularly Germany have embraced European integration and a single currency in the way the UK and Denmark have not. Wendt is not a Liberal and, indeed, is better summed up as a Neo-Realist turned Constructivist since he considers that most countries – but, crucially, not all – are driven by

## Box 33.3 Wendt and the inevitability of a 'world state'

Wendt reasons that the international system has gradually evolved from a condition of anarchy to a more cooperative 'system of states' and then a 'world society', through the self-interest of states seeking to restrain the recourse to international war. In line with this it is posited that further progress towards a 'world state', in which war-making power is fully pooled in a global system of collective security, is both inevitable and in the interests of even the most powerful states.

> (I)f the choice is between a world of growing threats as a result of refusing to recognize others versus a world in which their desires for recognition are satisfied, it seems clear which decision rational Great Powers should take.
>
> (Wendt 2003: 529–30)

a selfish, blinkered pursuit of power. He has, however, come to share much common ground with Keohane in formulating a state-utilitarian case for the inevitability of global governance within the next two centuries.

Social Constructivist ideas on re-defining sovereignty have informed thinking on how many of Europe's long-established sovereign states have come to embrace regional international goverance for utilitarian rather than Idealist or Functionalist reasons. The *Consociationalist* theory of European integration, for example, does not see the European Union's future as a case of taking one of two directions: a federal 'high road' or a strictly intergovernmental 'low road' (with, for example, no majority voting and state vetoes on all issues). Instead, this approach suggests that the states of the European Union will continue to merge economically and politically, not inspired by any holy grail of an idealised United States of Europe but through pragmatic, economic necessity (Taylor 1991). Hence, from this perspective, the launch of a single EU currency did not mark the beginning of the end of sovereign member-states so much as the practical realisation by the governments concerned that this would speed up business and that, German mark apart, the national currencies had, in any way, become largely irrelevant on the global stage. In this frame of thought sovereignty is not being abandoned but pooled in a manner that actually makes rational sense for the governments concerned.

Though principally applied in the context of European integration, Consociationalism could be seen to have global application to the development of the WTO and the numerous international regimes of common rules to which governments increasingly voluntarily commit themselves in order to ease the complications of dealing with modern economic interdependence. In this view, then, sovereignty and regional or global governance should not be understood as opposites but actually complementors. In order for modern governments to exert influence on the world stage they need to come to terms with the limits of their independent power and embrace a more restricted interpretation of their sovereignty.

### Box 33.4 Antonio Negri on contemporary 'Empire'

Negri contends that state sovereignty has already been replaced by the 'empire' of a 'new sovereignty' of global governance based on the interests of a transnational elite. He does, however, view this development as actually offering hope of triggering the global socialist revolution he both predicts and desires.

. . . globalization can be desirable and can correspond, and be part of, a revolutionary process . . . the very possibility of sovereignty can be destroyed by such a regime of desire. . . . [This can] transform the oppressive state of permanent war in which we find ourselves into a liberating war which can eventually lead to an authentic social peace.

(Negri, Hardt and Zolo 2008: 59)

## Marxists

For IR **Marxists** the significance of states and sovereignty has always been overstated in the face of the global economic structures that they feel actually determine the paths states take. Hence, from this perspective, governance has long been global: the imposition of rules and practises that facilitate the accumulation of ever more wealth by the world's economic elite. What is both prescribed and predicted by Marxists, therefore, is a radically different and better form of global governance; a stateless and classless world.

## Realists

For **Realists** talk of sovereignty's demise is much exaggerated and it is too soon to write off the state. Sovereignty continues to be cherished by those who have it and desired by many of those who do not. The number of sovereign states in the world has continued to grow in recent years and this trend looks likely to continue. Some colonies, like Greenland, have edged closer to full independence and many separatist 'stateless nations', like the Chechens, Basques, Kurds and Quebequois, continue to pursue sovereignty. Additionally, the reach of sovereignty is being extended by states looking to expand their territorial claims to include continental shelves hundreds of miles from their coastlines and so erode the notion of *terra nullius*. The scramble that has emerged in recent years to claim large tracts of the Arctic Ocean is a case in point.

Realists also suggest that the growth of global cooperation that has undoubtedly occurred in recent years does not necessarily indicate a decline in state power. International organisations and international treaties have proliferated and, beyond this, less formal rules within **international regimes** in particular areas of common interest have emerged but these can still be seen as arrangements agreed to by sovereign state governments for their mutual interests. Indeed, the more there are of such cooperative arrangements the more there are means for powerful states to exercise hegemonic leverage over other states.

## Box 33.5 Gilpin and the persistence of state power

The renowned neo-Realist IPE specialist Robert Gilpin argues that globalisation has not altered the fundaments of IR and that we still inhabit a state-centric world.

It is certainly true that economic and technological forces are profoundly reshaping international affairs and influencing the behavior of states. However, in a highly integrated global economy, states continue to use their power and to implement policies to channel economic forces in ways favorable to their own national interests and the interests of their citizenry.

(Gilpin 2001: 5)

## Case study: Global crime, sovereignty and global governance

Transnational criminal organisations have thrived under globalisation. The opportunities offered for legitimate business by the shrinking of the world and opening up of many of its borders are there also for the world's growing band of illegitimate businesses.

The sheer volume of goods crossing borders makes it ever easier to smuggle in illegal cargoes and the increased ease of moving money across borders makes it ever easier to launder the profits of such transactions and other criminal ventures. When criminal organisations then learn to break up their operations into different countries, corrupting officials in some and perhaps investing in legitimate business in other countries, it then becomes even less likely that they will be brought to justice. Few now doubt that the robbers are more globalised than the cops. Though Interpol dates back to the 1920s (see Chapter 12) it is still no more than a means for national police forces to exchange information on request and is constrained by sovereignty. Like in the old American movies, the villains have come to learn that if they can cross the borderline the police will have to call off the chase. Interpol is no global police force and its reach and budget is dwarfed by groups like the Russian mafia with tentacles in dozens of countries and strategic alliances with other n'er do wells such as Latin American drug cartels.

States have become almost outmoded organizations: in effect, we are attempting to deal with a twenty-first century phenomenon using structures, mechanisms and instruments that are still rooted in eighteenth- and nineteenth-century concepts and organizational forms.

(Godson and Williams 1998: 324)

Crime has risen on the global political agenda and some robust state responses have been deployed but the problem continues to grow. In 2007, in a neat encapsulation of the impact of globalisation on crime and sovereignty, at the same time as British and American troops were being despatched to Colombia to help its government fight drug barons, the Colombian government were sending ministers to London and Washington to plead for help in curbing the demand for cocaine among their populations which was, ultimately, fuelling the whole phenomenon.

Interpol are unequivocal in recognising their impotence in the face of the globalised criminals:

No one country can effectively fight transnational organized crime within or outside its borders. Therefore, I submit, countries must relinquish some of their procedural or substantive sovereignty in order for the purpose for which sovereignty exists in the first place to remain intact. *Ronald Noble, Secretary General of Interpol 2003.*

(Noble 2003)

**List the political issues – if any – that you think would be better decided at the global rather than sovereign state level. (The fewer there are the more of a Realist you probably are.)**

Realists not only dispute that the sovereign state is in decline but also caution against wishing it away. Sovereign stewardship is still seen as the best means of maintaining order from a power politics perspective. As far back as the 1970s the renowned 'English School' neo-Realist Hedley Bull warned that allowing state sovereignty to erode risked ushering in an era of 'new medievalism' with a retreat to the chaos of pre-Westphalian Europe, when competing jurisdictional claims overlapped and there was no clear understanding of where political authority lay (Bull 1977: 254).

## Conclusion

There seems little doubt that governments have become less and less able fully to control events in their states in the face of globalisation. Whether this signals the end of sovereignty as we know it, a re-definition of the concept, or the need to bolster the state in order to tame globalisation is, however, open to debate.

## Resource section

### Questions

1. Explain what is meant by *sovereignty* and consider whether the significance of this concept has changed over time.

2. Evaluate rival theories of how the international political system is likely to evolve in the future.

3. Are we heading inevitably towards some form of global government?

### Recommended reading

Keohane, R. (2002) *Power and Governance in a Partially Globalized World* (London: Routledge)
The coming together of the thoughts of a man widely held to be the most influential thinker in contemporary IR. Keohane sets out his vision of how the world is transforming and of the form it may evolve to; one of global governance but in which states continue to be significant entities.

Lupel, A. (2009) *Globalization and Popular Sovereignty. Democracy's Transnational Dilemma* (London: Routledge)
Lupel re-evaluates classic historical and contemporary works on both International Relations and democracy, by the likes of Locke, Rousseau, Habermas and Held, in light of the changes being brought about by globalisation. The debate over whether contemporary global change threatens to undermine or enhance the democratic notion of 'rule by the people' is analysed in an authoritative way that bridges Political Theory and International Relations.

## Useful websites

Federal Union, www.federalunion.org.uk/index.shtml

Global Policy Forum, 'What is a State?', www.globalpolicy.org/nations/statindex.htm

# Glossary

**Alter-globalisation:** 'Alter-globalisation' is a view held by 'alter-globalists'. This is a view which does not deny the transformative qualities of globalisation. But its proponents have a wholly pessimistic view of it. And, as the name suggests, they want to 'alter' its outcomes to include better justice and equality for the world's poorest people. They see it as a force for oppression, exploitation and injustice. Unwelcome consequences of globalisation are said to include: restructuring of global trade, production and finance to disadvantage the poor; migratory and refugee movements, especially in the developing world and the former Eastern European communist bloc; increasing international terrorism; burgeoning ethnic and/or religious clashes especially within and between many 'Third World' states; and the recent rise or resurgence of right-wing populists in Western Europe, in, for example, Austria, France, Germany and the Netherlands.

**Americanisation:** is a term used outside the USA to describe the influence of the United States on key areas of international interaction, including: popular culture, technology, business practices, and political techniques or language. The term has been used since the early twentieth century, during which the USA has risen to become a global power with very significant international influence. Critics sometimes give 'Americanisation' a negative connotation. This is because they regard it as both negative and far-reaching, with American influence in many countries leading to the loss or significant undermining of local customs and traditions.

**Anarchy:** Anarchy should not be conflated with chaos or disorder. Within international relations anarchy has become most used as a way of describing a situation in which there is no central government to arbitrate disputes among states; accordingly anarchy becomes central in accounting for state behaviour because states must look out for themselves with no higher authority to appeal to.

**Asian Values:** This refers to the 'East Asian' view of human rights, captured in the concept of 'Asian Values'. It is a view associated with a number of East and South East Asian countries, including Malaysia, Singapore, and China. Regional political leaders, such as former prime ministers Muhammad Mahathir (Malaysia) and Lee Kuan Yew (Singapore) contend that individualistic human rights associated with 'western culture' and its individualistic, self-seeking values are 'culturally alien' to their countries. They claim instead that their countries have different cultures and histories reflecting the importance of the community or the collective, not the individual. These cultural characteristics are said to be embodied in an array of desirable socio-political values: harmony, consensus, unity and community. In Mahathir's view, Malaysia's society is richly imbued with such social and political values. As a result, he claims, human rights regimes are seen by society as legitimate only when they reflect the community's collective values. Consequently, national human rights regimes must necessarily 'fit' local cultural and social values.

**Asylum:** the right to seek sanctuary from political persecution in another country enshrined in the UN Declaration of Human Rights and Geneva Refugee Convention.

**Autarky:** the government policy of pursuing total economic self-reliance by securing all necessary resources without resort to trade.

**Balance of power:** The notion of the balance of power refers to a mechanism whereby states collaborate with each other to maintain their independence against threats from those who would seek systemic dominance, such as Napoleon Bonaparte at the beginning of the nineteenth century. Napoleon's aggression resulted in the formation of a defensive alliance – involving, among others, Britain and Prussia (the forerunner of Germany) – to defeat his bid for control. However, earlier than this, in the early eighteenth century, the states of Europe had collaborated in a war against Louis of France, who was thought to have designs on the creation of a French-dominated super-state involving Spain. Later, during the Second World War (1939–45) the European democracies, and their colonial acquisitions, also joined together to defeat Germany's dreams of systemic domination.

These examples indicate that serious threats to systemic peace trigger defensive coalitions to combat them. But they are temporary alliances that fragment once the threat has been dealt with. In other words, it is a temporary arrangement, a short-lived unity to defeat a common aggressor. It is not intended to prevent *any* conflicts breaking out – it is not a formal mechanism for stability and peace prolongation like the League of Nations or the United Nations.

**Biodiversity:** the variety of living species and their habitats within a given area or the whole Earth (a contraction of *biological diversity*).

**Bipolarity:** During the Cold War (late 1940s–late 1980s), the international order was dominated by two superpowers: the United States of America and the Soviet Union (USSR). Bipolarity refers to a situation of systemic polarisation between two ideologically opposed states.

**Bretton Woods system:** Negotiations were held in 1944 at Bretton Woods (USA). They were held in order to establish a set of regimes, institutions and agreements which would help regulate the global economy. These consisted of an International Bank for Reconstruction and Development (IBRD), the International Monetary Fund (IMF) and later the General Agreement on Tariffs and Trade (GATT) and aimed to facilitate economic growth, development and trade by providing a stable framework for international economic activity. After the Second World War prevailing wisdom suggested its cause had been economic collapse and world recession in the 1930s which created an unstable climate allowing extreme nationalism to flourish. It was believed that when the economic climate was harsh, states took action to protect their own economies. Typically, this involved measures to protect domestic markets, such as increasing tariffs. Knock-on effects of such 'selfish' behaviour were a slow down in world trade and, eventually, international recession. The Bretton Woods system was designed to create a framework in which it would be difficult for states to act in a self-interested way when the going got tough, by, at once, discouraging protectionism and providing a helping hand to countries in temporary economic difficulties.

**Capitalism:** is the core concern of the German sociologist, Max Weber's, famous 'Protestant ethic' thesis. Following a long period of study, Weber arrived at the theory that what was of central importance to the Protestant ethic was its ability to break the hold of tradition. This encouraged people not only to apply themselves rationally to their work but also to feel comfortable in amassing wealth. The possession of wealth was taken to be a sign that you were among God's elect; and this would,

it was believed, encourage poor people to try to acquire wealth. The Protestant ethic made available religious sanctions that encouraged a spirit of rigorous discipline, making it both rational and desirable that individuals would seek to acquire wealth. From this position, Weber believed, capitalism had developed from the seventeenth century in various European countries, including Britain. Over time, capitalism has developed to become the international economic system of choice. Today, very few countries shun the virtues of capitalism for other, alternative systems of economic organisation.

**Cartel:** a group of businesses or governments acting to coordinate the pricing of a particular international commodity that they are prominent exporters of.

**Clash of Civilisations thesis:** The term was originally proposed by historian Bernard Lewis in 1990 and then further developed by Samuel Huntington (a political scientist) in the early post-Cold War period. Drawing on Lewis's argument that Islam and the West had clashed throughout history and were likely to do so again, Huntington suggested that future conflicts were likely to be as a result of cultural and religious identities. He further proposed that nation states were likely to remain the principal actors, but that the conflicts of the future would occur at the points where civilisations came into contact with one another. Although many academics have criticised these views, a significant number contend that the present 'War on Terror' is between the West and Islam – two of the world's major civilisations, the others being Hindu, Latin American, Japanese, Chinese and a possible African one.

**Clinton doctrine:** US foreign policy initiative, while under the Presidency of Bill Clinton (1993–2001), to promote democracy and human rights through diplomacy.

**Cold War:** The collapse of the Soviet Union (USSR) and its communist allies ended the Cold War as a defining feature of international politics. For 40 years until the late 1980s, the Cold War – fought between the USA and the USSR – was the principal issue in international politics. Because both sides had massive quantities of nuclear weapons and could count on other countries as allies then the incipient conflict between them was, it was argued, the most serious global crisis. But all that came to an end – completely and completely as a surprise to many – in 1989. The fall of the Berlin Wall in Germany in 1989, followed by the sudden, unexpected demise of communist systems in the Soviet Union and Eastern Europe in 1990–1, exemplified a fundamental historical change from one epoch to another; these events helped to fuel widespread, albeit transitory, optimism that a 'New World Order' would follow the ideological divisiveness of the Cold War.

**Collective goods problem:** the political problem of how to provide something that benefits all members of a group (such as states) in the long term but imposes such short-term costs on those members that they are tempted not to agree to it. (For example, agreeing to abide by international fishing quotas could prevent the extinction of important fish species, to everyone's benefit, but could also see your country lose out to 'free rider' states who ignore the agreement.)

**Collective Security:** A mechanism whereby a group of states undertake not to attack others within the coalition. Within such a system the states also agree to use their collective military capabilities to come to the aid of a fellow member state if it is attacked. This collective action continues until the aggression has been reversed and the balance of the collective restored. The purpose of a collective security organisation is to maintain peace in a system dominated by sovereign states.

**Communism:** is an ideological system based on the repudiation of capitalism and a key organisational role given to the state and a country's Communist Party, for example in the People's Republic of China or Cuba. In international relations, Communist states, such as the People's Republic of China and, until 1991, the Soviet Union, preside over and rigorously enforce domination of the state and the Communist Party. Such regimes are sometimes referred to as 'anti-religious polities', as some – for example, Albania under the rule of Enver Hoxha (1946–85) – made consistent attempts to 'throttle' religion. In such Communist states, no religious organisations were permitted to be actively engaged with matters of public concern or to play a role in public life.

**Communitarianism/Cosmopolitanism:** Communitarians argue that ethical ideas are rooted in specific communities, and arguments about justice are only convincing within community boundaries. A communitarian argument might therefore be 'Who are we to tell them what they should or shouldn't wear?' or 'In such and such a culture it is OK to eat meat or have multiple spouses and that is as legitimate as situations where these things are not ok.' Cosmopolitan thought characterises liberalism. They extend the notion of community to the entire human race. This is the community of humankind, who possess inalienable human rights by virtue of the universal capacity for reasoned thought. For such thinkers it would be possible to argue that certain things infringe basic human rights and thus cannot be justified because they are considered OK within a particular community. An extreme example might be the idea of human sacrifice; today outlawed by all states but practised in some indigenous communities (for example in Chile) until well into the twentieth century.

**Comparative advantage:** an economic rationale for why free trade produces more trade and more wealth for all states. In a system of unrestricted international trade states can concentrate on what they are good at producing (their 'comparative advantage') rather than trying to do a bit of everything, since they can freely import goods that are produced more efficiently elsewhere. More particularly, comparative advantage ensures that even the relatively disadvantaged countries gain from being able to specialise in what they can produce more efficiently.

**Concert of Europe:** The Concert of Europe was the name given to the balance of power that existed in Europe from the fall of Napoleon in 1815 to the start of the First World War a century later in 1914. The Concert's founding members were Britain, Austria, Russia and Prussia. All had been members of the Sixth Coalition (also known as the Quadruple Alliance) which had been the force that defeated Napoleon. After Napoleon's downfall, France became established as a fifth member of the Concert.

The Concert of Europe was also known as the 'Congress System'. This was because the members used to meet at periodic congresses, opportunities for what we would now call a summit meeting whereby governments could meet face to face to plan a solution by mutual agreement (hence the use of the word 'concert'), whenever a significant problem emerged threatening Europe. Over time, the Concert became a formal institution, although unlike the League of Nations which came into being after the First World War, the Concert never had a permanent meeting place, bureaucracy or budget. During the early years, the Concert met regularly (the Congress of Vienna [1814–1815], Aix-la-Chapelle [1818], Carlsbad [1819], Verona [1822] and London [1830, 1832, and 1838–1839]. However, as time went on and European rivalries developed, for example, in relation to imperialistic acquisitions, meetings of the Concert became less frequent until eventually they ceased altogether.

**Copenhagen School:** This is an important academic tradition within the field of Security Studies, and has its roots in the ideas of Barry Buzan, Ole Wæver and Jaap de Wilde as expressed in their book *Security: A New Framework for Analysis* published in 1998. They reconceptualise the concept of security and offer a broader view beyond the narrow state-centric ideas expressed by realists. The authors advocate a constructivist approach which particularly highlights the social context of the way in which threats are securitised. Security therefore comes to be seen as a 'speech act', whereby the threat being securitised is moved away from ordinary politics by a politician, for instance, and placed into a distinct and separate realm – a realm which ultimately demands more of society's resources and attention.

**Crimes against humanity:** systematic human rights abuses that do not come within existing legally defined categories of abuse, such as genocide or war crimes.

**Critical Security Studies:** Dissatisfaction with the narrow politico-military views expressed by traditional theories such as Realism encouraged academics such as Keith Krause, Michael Williams and Ken Booth to advocate a reconceptualisation of the concept of security. Its rejection of the state-centric mindset of traditionalist ideas has led to intense debate among alternative perspectives such as feminism, constructivism, postmodernism, neo-Marxism and Critical Theory. Some have merely sought to criticise the rigidity of traditionalist ideas, whereas others have advocated a shift away from the state to other referent objects such as the individual. In doing so, they have questioned the nature of the structures and processes which restrict the emancipation of humans.

**Critical Theory:** In IR this covers a number of approaches with a common debt to both the early writings of Marx and to the Frankfurt School, i.e. the Institute of Social Research at Frankfurt University established in 1923 and reconstituted in exile from Nazism in New York as the New School for Social Research after 1934. Critical Theory draws first of all on Marx's insight that philosophers have only sought to interpret the world but the point is to change it. That question of how critical knowledge effectively

understood could contribute directly to radical change is at the heart of all Critical Theory in IR. Critical Theory has become influential in international relations since the mid-1980s, when, even before the end of the Cold War, orthodox Marxism fell out of favour because of its structuralist and economic biases.

**Decolonisation:** Moulded by European imperialism and colonialism, a global states system developed from the sixteenth century. This produced forms of government and states around the world based on western models, including presidential, monarchical and Marxist forms of rule; in most cases in the developing world political regimes came about via European domination. More than 90 per cent of today's developing countries were, at one time or another, colonial possessions of a handful of Western powers, including: Belgium, Britain, France, Germany, Italy, Japan, the Netherlands, Portugal, Spain and the USA. Decolonisation came in two main waves, separated by more than a century. The first occurred in the early nineteenth century, resulting in the independence of 18 Latin American and Caribbean countries. The second occurred between 1945–1975, set in train by the Second World War. During this period, around 90 colonies achieved freedom from foreign rule. Overall, decolonisation was virtually complete by 1990, marked by the independence of Namibia.

**Democratic deficit:** a perceived lack of proper democratic accountability in an intergovernmental organisation generally held to be democratic (such as the European Union).

**Democratic Peace Theory:** Also referred to as the Liberal Peace Thesis, this refers to the belief that Liberal Democracies are not only more peaceful among themselves but also more pacific generally in the international system. Advocates of this viewpoint claim that statistical evidence suggests that Liberal Democracies have established a separate peace among themselves and offer a number of explanations as to why this is so. Among the views put forward is the economic argument that Liberal states tend to be wealthy and that war would be too costly for them. There is also the view that democratically elected leaders are answerable to the voters for the decisions they take, and are therefore obliged to seek alternatives to war. Controversy surrounds this thesis given that the incidence of war between Liberal Democracies and non-democracies is statistically significant. It therefore raises the question whether the former are in fact more peaceful generally.

**Democratisation:** Democracy was originally a form of direct governance by the citizens of a city (*polis*) in ancient Greece. In modern times, democratisation refers to the process of developing a recognisably democratic system of government rooted in representative institutions whose officeholders are chosen by the populace through general elections. Between the mid-1970s and mid-1990s, there was a wave of democratisation, during which dozens of countries in Central and Eastern Europe, Africa, Asia and Latin America made the transition from various forms of non-democratic government to new systems characterised to a significant extent by democratic structures and processes.

**Dependency Theory:** A critique of liberal modernisation theory which argued that poorer countries would pass through various inevitable stages of wealth creation on their way to prosperity. On the basis of detailed historical analysis, dependency theorists argued that patterns of economic growth and development in Latin America and later other developing regions suggested that the region achieved its most impressive performance at times when there was a slow down in world trade and trading links with developed countries were disrupted. They suggested this was because the basic structure of the global economy worked to further the interests of the already rich, developed economies and progressively to impoverish already poor countries. This basic structure of markets and trade was said to make inevitable the development trajectory of individual countries. So, even as large parts of the world emerged from imperialism and colonialism, the former masters continued to dominate, and the former colonies remained economically dependent. From this comes the term dependency, and at international level this mirrors Marx's insight that the prosperity of the few is dependent on the misery of the majority.

**Détente:** Détente occurred during the early 1970s, in the wider context of the Cold War 'fought' between the USA and the Soviet Union (USSR). The Cold War was a more or less permanent relaxation in tensions between these two superpowers. There were two main reasons for détente during the early 1970s, both involving the Vietnam War. First, the Vietnam War, involving the USA and the Communists of North Vietnam, had led to a high level of deaths and destruction and it made many people question the rationality of international conflict. Second, the Vietnam War brought it home to many ordinary people and policy makers that international conflict – especially between the nuclear-weapons possessing superpowers – should be avoided at all costs because of the fear of a nuclear holocaust. This concern grew at this time as a growing number of countries were acquiring nuclear weapons, including the People's Republic of China, the world's most populous country and implacable enemy of both the USA and USSR.

**Development:** 'Development' first emerged as a subject area in the second half of the twentieth century. After the Second World War, scholars and practitioners sought to study the causes of poverty and so-called 'underdevelopment' in a more systematic and sustained way than had previously been the case. These days, the substance of development studies – especially in relation to the developing world – focuses mainly on poverty reduction and improving 'human development' indices. It is a dynamic field whose importance cannot be understated as the gap between rich and poor grows seemingly ever wider.

**Diplomacy:** The balance of power and international law were growing forces for stability and regularisation of interactions between states in the eighteenth century. The third component of the international system progressing at this time was diplomacy. While the concept was not new (such official contact between rulers and governments was known in ancient China, Egypt and India), diplomacy from the seventeenth and eighteenth centuries helped build up and spread the norms and rules of the international system. Initially diplomacy involved the delivery of messages and warnings, the pleading of causes, and the transfer of gifts or tribute. Later, envoys became negotiators, not merely messengers. A permanent system of diplomatic interaction was established during the 1648–1789 period, developing into one of the cornerstones of the international system: a professional diplomatic corps. Diplomats became agents of the state sent abroad for negotiation, reporting and intelligence work. They reported regularly to home government and in the process bureaucratised foreign ministries began to emerge. What this underlined was that governments – all governments – needed regular contact with others and rules to govern such interaction.

**Economic Liberalism:** Economic Liberalism is rooted in an intellectual tradition stretching back particularly to the works of Adam Smith and David Ricardo. Liberalism itself is very broad and covers a wide range of political, economic and moral positions, some of which are quite wary of this position. A strictly economic interpretation of liberalism is concerned with free markets and free trade and less with the economic rights of individuals which might be ensured through welfare. Contemporary 'neo-liberalism' is utilitarian and heavily influenced by classical economic liberalism, believing that markets should be unfettered, and that state intervention to help the less fortunate is undesirable because in the long term it leads to inefficiencies. It should be evident therefore, not only that liberalism can be highly contradictory, but that the application of liberal economics is, in fact, a deeply political facet of world politics. Political liberalism and issues around economic security and ensuring the individual is free to participate in society often lead to arguments which would necessitate sizeable modifications of classical liberal economics to ameliorate its effects on the less fortunate in society.

**Economic nationalism:** is a term used in international relations to describe policies which emphasise national domestic control of a country's economy, labour and capital formation. Economic nationalism may also include such notions as protectionism and import substitution, that is, the banning of external sources of a raw material or finished product and relying on domestic sources of supply instead. Economic nationalist policies may, as in the 1930s, require imposition of tariffs and other restrictions on the international movement of labour, goods and capital. It is in opposition to globalisation as it questions the benefits of unrestricted free trade, a cornerstone of globalisation.

**Economic protectionism:** is an economic policy whose goal is to restrict inter-state trade. Government-imposed methods employed to achieve this end include: placing of tariffs on imported goods, limited quotas allowed of certain imported goods, and a variety of other government regulations which seek overall not only to discourage imports but also to prevent foreign take-overs of domestic markets and companies. This policy is closely linked to anti-globalisation and is the antithesis of free trade, where state-imposed barriers to trade and movement of capital are minimised.

**Emancipation:** In popular usage, to emancipate is to liberate or set free, as in the case of the freeing of slaves. In western philosophy and in critical theory (see above) particularly, emancipation means the achievement of autonomy, the ability to act independently. To be emancipated does not mean that one is free of all constraints and obligations towards others, only those which are deemed oppressive or unnecessarily confining.

**English School:** The term 'English School' denotes a school of thought or collection of works which explore the nature of 'international society' or the 'society of states'. The essence of the English School is encapsulated in the phrase 'anarchical society' made famous by Hedley Bull, oddly an Australian but working in England. The phrase gives a sense both of the lack of a higher formal authority, but nonetheless a set of rules or norms to which states might appeal. Though the English School is sometimes regarded as a variant of Realist thought (both appear to be essentially state-centric) it is not. Its intellectual influences are more varied, drawing upon liberal and rational strands of IR thought and other disciplines like sociology and international law.

**Epistemic community:** transnational group of experts on a given subject.

**Feminism:** A paradigm or meta-narrative within International Relations as well as a socio-political ideology. A feminist perspective employs gender as a central category of analysis regarding gender as a particular kind of power relationship. One of the key facets of this power relationship is the separation, in society, of men, who tend to engage in wage work and politics, and women, who tend to engage in domestic work and childcare. This is what feminists call the public/private division or dichotomy and it is arguably this division which has meant that women have not been considered very often in relation to IR. For feminists, gender is central to our understanding of IR; scholars trace the ways in which ideas about gender are, and have been, central to the functioning of major international institutions and how gender relations might be perpetuated or transformed through policies or laws emanating from international institutions. Overall, feminist IR scholars challenge dominant assumptions about what is significant or insignificant, or what is marginal or central, in the study of IR through the adoption of gender lenses which work to revise or 're-vision' the study (and potentially the practice) of IR.

**Free market economy:** an economy that is largely independent of direct government control.

**Functionalism:** a liberal theory of political integration which prescribes and predicts that sovereign states will gradually be superseded by non-governmental functional international organisations (dedicated to a particular political task) that better meet people's needs. (**Neo-functionalism** is a variant of this theory mostly applied to the European Community/European Union which considers that integration cannot occur by people 'naturally' switching loyalties from their governments to international organisations and needs to be promoted by political elites.

**Fundamentalism:** usually refers to 'religious fundamentalism'. It has been widely employed since the 1970s, especially by the mass media, to describe and account for numerous, apparently diverse, religious and political developments around the globe. While the designation 'religious fundamentalist' was first applied to themselves by conservative evangelicals inside the mainstream Protestant denominations in the early years of the twentieth century, as a generic term, it is now widely applied additionally to a multitude of groups outside the corpus of Christianity, especially, but not exclusively, to Judaist and Islamist entities.

The significance of religious fundamentalism from a political perspective was that it could serve to supply an already restive group with a ready-made manifesto for social change. Religious leaders used religious texts both to challenge secular rulers and to propose a programme for radical reform. Under these circumstances it was often relatively easy for fundamentalist leaders to gain the support of those who felt that in some way the development of society was not proceeding according to God's will or the community's interests. In sum, various manifestations of what might be called religious fundamentalism seem to appeal to different groups for different reasons at different times.

**Global commons:** natural resources outside of any individual state's jurisdiction (such as the atmosphere and the content of seas beyond territorial waters) which are held to be common to all.

**Global governance:** Global governance (or world governance) refers to the efforts of non-state transnational actors to solve problems that affect more than one state or region when there is no existing power, for example, no dominant state, to enforce a desirable outcome. Currently, the issue of global governance is mainly raised in the context of globalisation and how to ensure that its benefits are maximised and disbenefits minimised.

**Global North:** the world's developed and most wealthy states (which are principally in the northern hemisphere).

**Global South:** the *Less Developed Countries* (which are principally in the southern hemisphere).

**Globalisation:** We are now very accustomed to the idea of globalisation. So, it may come as a surprise to learn that 'globalisation' only entered common usage quite recently. In international relations, it only began to be used from the 1980s. It was first used by some economists a few years earlier, when commenting on what they characterised as the emergence of a *global* economy. Now, in the early twenty-first century, the contemporary significance of globalisation is immense, encouraging us to think of it in various ways in relation to international relations. The idea of globalisation focuses our attention on the fact that international relations is experiencing a period of profound change – some might even say, transformation. This suggests various far-reaching processes of change, for example, the upheaval in the global economy (2008–2010), which saw even the most powerful countries, such as the United States, lose ability to influence international economic outcomes.

**Globalisation sceptics:** seek to ascertain what would be a conclusive empirical test of the claims of the globalisation thesis. One way to do this is to seek to compare today's globalisation trends with those noted in the past. For example, is there 'more' globalisation today – with overall greater impact – than there was, say, during what economic historians have averred was the *belle époque* of international interdependence: the late-nineteenth century to the First World War (1914–18). For the globalisation sceptics, such analyses invite the conclusion that what we are witnessing is not globalisation, but a process of 'internationalisation' – more and more significant interactions between what are fundamentally autonomous *national* economies or societies – and 'regionalisation' or 'triadisation', referring to geographically focused, cross-border, economic and social exchanges.

Globalisation sceptics also highlight the importance of 'fragmentation', that is, recent economic, political or cultural 'implosions'. They point to how in recent years empires – for example, that of the Soviet Union, with its former 'imperial' control over vassal states in Central and Eastern Europe – have fragmented into many nation-states, while, on the other hand, growing numbers of poor people in, for example, Africa are excluded from the benefits of economic development. Overall, the sceptic argument highlights the continued salience of territory, borders, place, and national governments in relation to distribution and location of power, production and wealth.

**Green Theory:** This term can be applied to any theory which seeks to understand environmental issues, but is most associated with the idea of 'Deep Ecology'. A deep ecological approach is one which rejects the idea of putting human beings at the centre of analysis. Instead the eco-system is central; nature is viewed as alive and living creatures as deserving of respect. Some deep green thinkers argue that we should assign rights to nature. Green theory may be described as bio- or eco-centric, even though all theory must in a certain sense be human-centred (anthropocentric) as it is only humans who theorise.

**Hegemony (1):** A term coined by Antonio Gramsci (1891–1937) in the early 1920s. His analysis concluded that dominant forms of knowledge and social relationships existed within society which acted as constraints on the abilities of individuals to be aware of the real nature of the world in which they lived and the existing potential to change it for the better. Hegemony in this sense represents the control of common sense knowledge. In large part, Gramsci was trying to explain why the social revolutions that Marx, Engels and other revisionist scholars had anticipated, never took place.

**Hegemony (2):** The concept has been adopted by International Relations in another way (compared with hegemony (1) above) to mean dominant actors in international relations. Thus, state actors such as the United States can be seen as being hegemonic powers possessing leadership/dominance. Charles Kindleberger (1910–2003) used hegemony in this way. His work on economic stability/international regimes helped establish hegemonic stability theory. Kindleberger argued that for the international system to remain stable, a dominant actor must use its power to influence the behaviour of other actors. The hegemon thus either compels or encourages behaviour in a manner which is compatible with international stability. If an actor does not behave in such a manner then that actor is punished by the hegemon.

**Human rights:** principles underlie provisions enshrined in post-Second World War international human rights agreements, including the Universal Declaration of Human Rights, the International Convention on Civil and Political Rights, and the United Nations Resolution on the Elimination of Intolerance Based on Religion or Belief. A central human rights issue is identified in part of Article 2 of the UN 'Resolution on Intolerance': (1) 'No one shall be subject to discrimination by any State . . . on grounds of religion or other beliefs (2) [T]he expression 'intolerance and discrimination based on religion and belief' means any distinction, exclusion, restriction or preference based on religion or belief and having as its purpose or as its effect nullification or impairment of the recognition, enjoyment or exercise of human rights and fundamental freedoms on an equal basis.'

**Human security:** Human security is an approach to security issues which holds as central that many people – especially in the developing world – are experiencing growing global vulnerabilities in relation to poverty, unemployment and environmental degradation. The idea of human security is not in opposition to traditional national security concerns – which centre on the idea that it is the government's job to defend ordinary citizens from external attack by a foreign power. Instead, the human security approach argues that the appropriate focus of security is the individual not the state. In other words, the human security approach takes a people-centred view of security which, proponents claim, is necessary for wider national, regional and global stability. The concept of human security has evolved in the post-Cold War period. It is an approach which draws on a number of disciplinary areas – including, development studies, international relations, strategic studies and human rights.

**Humanitarian intervention:** Humanitarian intervention is premised on a blend of ethics, religion, and law. It is an approach that seeks to deal with a key quandary: what to do when norms of behaviour are flagrantly disregarded leading to mass deaths within countries. It challenges the validity of both Realism and Liberalism as the basis for policy and interpretation in international relations. Since the early 1990s, few foreign policy issues have elicited as much controversy as the use of military force for humanitarian purposes. Humanitarian interventions seek to resolve conflicts among legal norms by identifying ethical principles embedded in the United

Nations Charter and international law and relating them to a pivotal principle of 'unity in diversity'. Seeking to avoid the charge of ethnocentricity, proponents of humanitarian intervention maintain that selected passages from the revered texts of seven world religions may be interpreted as supporting these ethical principles. Connecting law with ethics and religion in this way, the concept of humanitarian intervention is an effort to formulate a normative basis for international law in our multicultural world.

**Idealism:** Idealism is based on assumptions which place primacy on achieving peace and cooperation as the central aim. Norman Angell, for example, argued in the early 1900s that interdependence between states and peoples as well as the inherent good nature of all humans and their desire for peace and prosperity lead to a condition of harmony of interests. When such a condition exists conflict is less likely or even impossible as the interests of actors will not be achieved through taking a course of action which leads to conflict.

One of the core assumptions of idealism is that war and anarchy in the international system are not necessary and are not 'natural' characteristics of the human condition. Instead divisions between people in the form of nationalist identities, state borders, disintegrated markets and non-democratic governance are to blame for conflict and anarchy. For the idealist, these barriers to peaceful interaction can be overcome by actively pursuing certain policies. Included here are the fostering of democratic republics, the creation of IGOs which can act as fora for governments to discuss any disputes rather than wage war over them, and the practice of free marketeering. Early foundations of idealism include works done by Immanuel Kant (1724–1804) including his essay *Perpetual Peace* in which he calls for an international federation of democratic republics.

**Ideology:** During the twentieth century, ideological differences transformed many international relationships. Earlier centuries had been influenced by various kinds of wars: dynastic, national, civil, and imperial. Over time, diplomacy developed to try to advance various goals, including: national security, national expansion or to promote mutual advantages and general peace. During the twentieth century, however, international relations were significantly affected by ideology in various ways, including: how wars were fought, including the Second World War between the forces of fascism

and those of liberal democracy, alliances were made, and treaties were signed. The Cold War was a balance of power between the superpowers that was fundamentally informed by ideological polarisation: the Soviet-dominated Communist bloc confronted the liberal democratic and capitalist West, led by the USA. In addition, after the Second World War, the decolonising developing world demonstrated a nationalist, anti-colonialist ideology in a search for identity and modernity. Over time, the developing world threw off colonial control and the often strident anti-West ideology of earlier decades gave way in most cases to a focused search for improved development.

**Imperialism:** refers to interlinked – political, social and economic – forces, including nationalism and religion, which significantly shaped international relations from the early nineteenth century until after the Second World War. After 1945, there was a swift withdrawal of the European imperial presence from Africa, Asia and the Middle East. Initially regarded by most Europeans as a desirable and acceptable way of spreading their civilisational values and norms, including Christianity, imperialism became increasingly contentious following the publication in 1902 of a book by a British economic historian, John Hobson (*Imperialism: A Study*). Hobson contended that the then current imperial rivalries – which involved the major European powers – was a dangerous source of international friction which would lead inevitably to sustained, serious international conflict. Hobson's view, supported by the Russian Communist theoretician, activist and politician, Vladimir Ilych Lenin, was that imperialism was a key cause of the First World War in 1914. Hobson also argued that the Europeans' competition was not only contoured by competing nationalism but also in the desire for colonial territory, not only to demonstrate national 'greatness' but also to extend pursuit of economic goals to overseas contexts. For example, Britain's imperial activities in India sought both to acquire territory for the sake of British nationalist aggrandisement but also because India provided significant scope for selling goods produced in Britain to a growing number of Indian consumers.

**Intergovernmental organisation (IGO):** an international organisation comprising government representatives of more than one country.

**International law:** The Peace of Westphalia in 1648 coincided with the beginning of the development of the concept of international law. In 1625 the Dutch jurist (student of law) Hugo Grotius had published his famous book, *Law of War and Peace*. This was significant for international relations because Grotius describes how restraints in fighting war are morally justified. In other words, governments *should* follow specific rules of conduct even when fighting a war. The decision to stick to internationally agreed rules of conduct is a highly rational one which has as its goal the maintenance of the international system. Grotius made an analogy between the mutual position and conditions of states in the emerging international system and that of individuals within societies. He noted that while there was international anarchy – no government – there was a variety of bonds and institutions linking states. In short, there was a society of states, a group of similar actors who regulated their mutual relations through broadly comparable domestic institutions – governments – in the areas of diplomacy and trade. Gradually states began to accept that warfare should only be used for purposes of self-defence, righting an injury, or for upholding the fundamental outlines of the states system and its norms and laws (e.g. in a later era the attack by the United Nations against Iraq for transgressions against Kuwait).

**International non-governmental organisation (INGO):** an international organisation comprised of private individuals rather than government representatives.

**International order:** In international relations, a combination of actors, rules, mechanisms and understandings works to manage states' co-existence and interdependence. 'International order' can usefully be thought of as an arrangement or *regime* based on general acceptance of common values, norms – including the body of international law – and institutions that enforce it. In international relations a regime is a set of principles, norms, rules, and decision-making procedures that most important international actors expect to see put into effect in a given area of international relations, including: human rights, human and social development, and democratisation and democracy. There are challenges to current international order in international relations. For example, there are undermining effects on international order from the activities of extremist Islamist organisations, such as al-Qaeda and Lashkar-e-Taiba. There is also the impact of increased international involvement and significance of various countries, including China, which highlight non-Western views of the world,

such as 'Asian values', which appear potentially to highlight different conceptions of international order.

**International Political Economy (IPE):** a sub-discipline of International Relations that arose in parallel with globalisation: the study of the intersection of political and economic issues at the international level.

**International relations (IR):** When we refer to the academic discipline of International Relations we use a capital 'I' and capital 'R'. When we use a small 'i' and a small 'r' (international relations) – we are referring to the totality of significant international interactions involving both states and important non-state actors. Because this is theoretically a limitless endeavour, in practice our emphasis is on states (or governments, the terms are often used interchangeably) and a range of important non-state actors including: multinational corporations (such as, Microsoft, Shell, and Starbucks), international non-governmental organisations (INGOs) (such as, Amnesty International, Greenpeace, and Friends of the Earth), and intergovernmental organisations (IGOs) (such as the UN, the European Union and the Organisation of the Islamic Conference). All such non-state actors play important roles in international relations, and we shall examine them in future chapters.

**International security organisation:** the First World War led to an acknowledgment from the international community that global governance would have to improve considerably if the most extreme forms of violence against humanity were to be outlawed, and the growing interconnectedness and interdependence of nations recognised. The post-war attempt to develop an international security organisation, the League of Nations, however soon foundered as the major countries were without exception unwilling to give up any elements of sovereignty in order to give the League the authority and legitimacy it required. In other words, the subject matter, scope and the very sources of international regulation, particularly the conception of international law, were all called into question after the First World War. After the Second World War a new attempt was made in the form of the United Nations, which has enjoyed modest success over the years in helping to deliver international security.

**International system/society:** The term international system denotes little more than the idea that there are states, they interact and that we can observe regularities in this interaction (trade or wars, for example). The term is useful in so much as it contrasts with reality where the relationships between states are characterised by 'norms' or rules of behaviour. Accordingly, states recognise their responsibilities to each other and – while they pursue their own interests – do not do so at any cost in what is better described as an international society.

**Islamism ('Islamic fundamentalism'):** Islamism (or Islamic fundamentalism) is an ideology and movement that has gained momentum within many Muslim countries in recent decades. It is a set of ideas derived from a conservative religious view, which holds that Islam is not only a religion, but also a political system that should govern the legal, economic and social imperatives of the state. Its goal is to reshape the state and society by implementing its conservative formulation of *Shari'a* (Islamic) law. Much Islamic fundamentalist literature deals not only with other religions, but also with secular political ideologies, such as communism, since it reacts against what it regards as competing political movements. Prior to the rise of Islamic fundamentalist political parties and movements, socialist parties had been widespread throughout much of the Muslim World during the twentieth century, a response to endemic poverty and consequent class tensions. However the collapse of the Soviet Union in 1991 ultimately reduced greatly the influence of this secular ideology. Partly in its place, Islamism emerged as a revolutionary ideology in many Muslim societies throughout the world, acquiring much popular support as a result of increasing anti-Western sentiment due, in part, to control of the West Bank by Israel.

**Less Developed Country (LDC):** a country that is not fully industrialised (i.e. come to have an economy mostly based on manufacturing industries like 'developed' countries) and is consequently considered to be below its economic potential.

**Liberal democracy:** Democracy was originally a form of direct governance by the citizens of a city (*polis*) in ancient Greece. In modern times, democracy refers to governance rooted in representative institutions whose officeholders are chosen by the populace through general elections. Liberal democracy is a common form of representative democracy, with certain key principles: Elections should be free and fair. More generally, the political process should be competitive.

**Liberalism:** A term given to one of the key schools of thought in International Relations. It has a rich

scholarly tradition which dates back to the 1700s and largely focuses on a number of core problems and ways to solve them. Unlike Realists, Liberals believe in the idea of progress, with history as dynamic rather than cyclical. But at the same time liberalism is to some extent ahistorical in that its overall views on international relations and human existence remain constant historically and geographically. Liberalism is also not spatially restricted but universal; while much liberal thought is founded in western experiences and philosophy its analyses and conclusions are focused on all spaces of human existence and so do not vary from one area to another, from one culture to another and so on. This can be seen as one of the reasons why liberalism is perhaps the most dominant perspective on international relations in the contemporary world, but likewise it is one of the reasons why there is also much resistance to it.

**Liberal Peace Thesis:** See Democratic Peace Theory.

**Marxism:** Body of ideas based on the work of Karl Marx. Marxism has informed a variety of approaches to IR theory both within traditional IR and as part of the 'critical turn' from the 1980s; however, Marxism – of itself – is not a theory of IR. Among its key insights to the discipline, Marxism regards classes, not states, as key actors and regards class conflict, not war or economic competition, as the main form of conflict. Later Marxism, which led to these ideas, was predominantly economistic. Earlier Marxism which looked at processes of alienation has influenced more recent critical approaches including postmodernism. The difference between the rhetoric of the dominant liberal ideology and the lived experience of the working classes (and Marx's ideas on these) provides a starting point for looking at the origins of critical theories in IR.

**Mercantilism:** Another way of putting this term is to say 'economic nationalism'. Mercantilism is the idea that judgements about what to do in the economic realm should be based on the effect that any particular course of action will have on the state's position vis-à-vis other states in the international system.

**Most Favoured Nation (MFN):** an undertaking between two governments that, in granting trade concessions to each other (e.g. mutually reducing tariffs on certain goods), they also agree not to grant even greater concessions to another country.

**Multinational corporation (MNC) (includes transnational corporation, TNC):** An MNC is a business that manages production or delivers services in more than one country. MNCs are not new, having first emerged in the nineteenth century or even earlier. Two aspects of economic globalisation have been central to their recent growth in numbers and significance: the internationalisation of production and the internationalisation of financial transactions as a result of freeing of trade barriers and general growth of the global economy.

Nationalists often condemn MNCs as subversive of national cultures and sovereignty. Trade unions regularly criticise them because of their adaptability, and socialists and anti-globalisation activists berate them as amoral instruments of global capitalism. Moving to low-wage economies in pursuit of lower costs, not least to avoid minimum wage legislation, the activities of MNCs can provide an argument for those favouring international organisation. However, when in the early 1990s the European Union tried to control their activities it found it could not realistically prevent them moving from country to country or region to region.

MNCs may organise their production, marketing and/or distribution regionally or globally. Yet, even when they do appear to have clear national interests, it remains the case that their activities are predominantly geared to maximising international competitive position and profitability. Consequently, individual (national) subsidiaries operate in the context of an overall corporate strategy and thus investment and production decisions may not primarily reflect local or national conditions or considerations.

**Mutual Assured Destruction:** During the Cold War, the key attribute – or 'strategic pillar' as it was called – of the nuclear relationship between the USA and the USSR was known as mutual assured destruction (MAD). This was the idea that if either the USA or USSR launched a nuclear strike against the other then the other would retaliate and, despite being damaged by the nuclear strike, would retain sufficient undamaged nuclear weapons to launch their own strike and provoke unacceptable damage against the aggressor. The overall significance of MAD was that for both the USA and USSR it made conquest difficult and expansion futile. For both countries, MAD implied the necessity of developing a relationship which would minimise the likelihood of nuclear conflict between the superpowers. In addition, MAD was important for international security for two more key reasons:

(1) due to the futility of 'overkill', it was possible for the superpowers to reach a weapons parity, and thus equilibrium, bringing stability to the system; and (2) ever fearful of the massive destructive might of nuclear weapons, each superpower had a powerful incentive to constrain its allies: not to do so would – albeit unwillingly – create conditions whereby what is known as a 'proxy war' could break out, with potentially calamitous results. (A proxy war is a war that results when two powers use third parties as substitutes for fighting each other directly.)

**National self-determination:** is the notion that nations should have a free choice in deciding their destiny without external compulsion. In international relations it is the freedom of a people in a given territory or a national grouping spread across several countries to determine their own political status and how they will be governed without undue influence from any other county. There are conflicting definitions and legal criteria for determining which groups may legitimately claim the right to self-determination. The American president, Woodrow Wilson, suggested such a move to the upper house of government in the USA, the Senate, in a speech in January 1917. This was three months before the US entered the war on the allies' side against Germany. Wilson argued that what the world needed was not a 'balance of power, but a community of power, not organized rivalries, but an organized common peace'. A year later, in 1918, Wilson elaborated on this in the announcement of his famous Fourteen Points. Beginning with a commitment to open diplomacy and a disavowal of secret treaties (which had become the norm in the second part of the nineteenth century and the early years of the twentieth), Wilson went on to include the removal of economic barriers ('free trade'), the limitations of armaments procurements ('no more arms races'), the admission of the right of national self-determination (although this was limited to Europe and not meant to include Europe's colonies) and the establishment of a mechanism and structure to ensure all this happened: the League of Nations.

**Neo-Realism:** Comes in various guises, and not all are happy with the prefix 'neo'. Nonetheless, neo-Realism as a 'catch-all' refers to various attempts to defend and update Realism in the light of challenges particularly from Liberalism or Liberal pluralism emerging in the 1970s and 1980s.

**New International Economic Order (NIEO):** By the 1970s, there were few remaining European colonies in the developing world. A key goal of the United Nations was thus achieved: freedom for the developing world from European colonial control. At this time, developing countries began to demand international economic reforms, centring on what was known as a New International Economic Order (NIEO). Calls for a NIEO were based on the idea that the world capitalist economy was structured in order to privilege the wealthy countries and discriminate against the poorer countries in the developing world. To pursue the NIEO, the developing countries sought a thoroughgoing restructuring of the world economy. At this time there was an implicit assumption that nearly all developing countries shared similar economic characteristics and, consequently, were comprehensively and collectively disadvantaged by the prevailing capitalist international economic order. However, the campaign for the NIEO did not succeed; the world economic system stayed as it was. This failure reflected, on the one hand, the collective lack of influence of the developing countries and the collective clout of the much smaller number of rich, capitalist countries that were happy with the way things were. On the other hand, it also demonstrated that, by the 1970s, economic progress among developing countries was variable and that they no longer inevitably shared the same concerns. For example, some, such as the oil-producing countries, including Saudi Arabia, Venezuela and Nigeria, were doing fine out of the old international economic order as a result of rising oil process.

**New World Order:** A term coined by George Bush Snr following the successful expulsion of Iraq from Kuwait in the first Gulf War. For some it captures sincere hopes for a brighter future and the idea that liberal internationalism (which proved impossible without the active role of the USA after the First World War) could now be a real possibility. However sincere such sentiments, like the phrase Brave New World (Huxley), this one quickly aroused criticism/cynicism and within a short while any substance had disappeared behind the idea that New World Order was short-hand for US policy preferences and further American imperialism.

**Non-Aligned Movement:** A bloc of post-colonial developing countries emerged and formed an alliance after the Second World War, known as the Non-Aligned Movement (NAM). Members were non-aligned, that is, they were allies of neither the USA nor the USSR. While, individually, most developing countries played relatively minor roles in international relations during the Cold War, their collective voice focused in the NAM, relatively loud and, at irregular intervals, influential. In recent years, however, the NAM has lost much of its influence due to fragmentation of the bloc of developing countries which now acknowledge a variety of goals in international relations which are not easily captured under the rubric of the NAM.

**Non-state actor:** an organisation with international political significance other than a state. A generic term for both *INGOs* and *IGOs*.

**Nuclear deterrence:** The theory that by possessing nuclear weapons a state will deter other states from attacking it. Connected to the idea of mutually assured destruction (see above) and much studied by strategic studies experts (see below).

**Nuclear non-proliferation regime:** Regime centred on the 1968 Nuclear Non-Proliferation Treaty (NNPT) which seeks to prevent the growth in number and international spread of nuclear weapons. Under the terms of the treaty five declared nuclear weapons states (USA, Russia, China, UK and France) commit themselves not to assist any other states in developing such weapons and the non-nuclear states commit themselves not to become nuclear weapons states (in exchange for peaceful technological assistance from the 'big 5'). The NNPT also commits the nuclear weapons states to work towards reducing their stockpiles of weapons. The regime is implemented by the UN's International Atomic Energy Agency which has the power to carry out inspections of non-nuclear weapons states who are party to the treaty (such as Iran). A key weakness of the regime lies in the fact that, today, countries such as Israel, India and Pakistan have not ratified the NNPT and have hence been free to develop nuclear weapons without any legal restraint while North Korea despite being a party have, nonetheless, still managed illegally to become a nuclear weapons state.

**Patriarchy:** Patriarchal society is a society in which men's dominance over women is institutionalised. Male domination is multi-faceted, and both structural (embodied in institutions like marriage and the family) and ideological through perhaps the celebration of masculine, rather than feminine traits and values.

**Peacekeeping:** Military operations by external parties intended to facilitate the peaceful resolution of a conflict. Though most associated with the United Nations, the word peacekeeping is not defined in the UN Charter but has come to refer to operations more extensive than *mediation* (in which troops are deployed to man a ceasefire line) but less vigorous than *collective security* covered by Chapter 7. Hence UN operations, such as in Somalia and Bosnia-Herzegovina in the 1990s, authorised UN troops to use force to uphold the peace and punish any side considered to be violating the terms of a ceasefire.

**Polluter's dilemma:** a variant of the *collective goods problem* for environmental politics. The dilemma for a government of whether to accept the short-term – economic and political – costs of implementing environmental restrictions on business in order to achieve the longer-term gains of less pollution.

**Positivism:** Positivism suggests that there are 'facts' about the world which can be established by observation and that such observation is neutral/independent or 'value free' i.e. not dependent on the 'position' of the observer as a part of the social world.

**Postmodernism:** Originally coined as a style in architecture from the 1960s, but the idea of going beyond modernism is almost as old as modernism itself. However, the mood in architecture began to influence areas like philosophy and social science where a rejection of both Marxist structuralism and liberalism was seen in some intellectual quarters after the events of 1968. Lyotard defined postmodern thought as a rejection of the stories western thought had told to explain and justify itself over two and a half thousand years from the ideas of Plato, through Christianity, empiricism, rationalism and socialism or Marxist structuralism. In France and continental Europe, these ideas were expressed as post-structuralism because structuralism and related Marxist ideas were the dominant ones in the 1950s, and, for many, liberalism was not a serious intellectual contender. In the anglo-saxon world, postmodernism was more often expressed as a critique of liberalism because liberalism was the hegemonic token which dominated philosophy, education and politics. Postmodern philosophy covers a wide range of ideas and positions, some of which are closer to Marxist writers and some of which share the universal values of human rights and justice which liberals claim to hold.

**Public International Law:** body of law to resolve disputes between states (and also intergovernmental organisations).

**Rationalism/Reflectivism:** Rationalism is characteristic of the inter-paradigm debate in IR, arguing that rational knowledge can be built by testing theories through empirical analysis. Until it was challenged by reflectivism, such ideas (emerging from the behavioural revolution) were seen by most as rigorous and valid means of enquiry. Reflectivism however, argues for a fundamental examination of all kinds of basic assumptions and the need for metaphysical/overarching critique.

**Realism:** In the study of IR, Realism is the label used for a variety of theories which emphasise the importance of power, especially military power, the sovereign state, and the nature of world politics as an unremitting struggle for power, survival and hegemony. Realism is a political view which puts the questioning of power at its heart. Realists do not necessarily say the pursuit of power is a good thing; they argue that it is what there is, whether we like it or not, and whatever difficulties it brings. Realism, they claim, is always pragmatic. Hans Morgenthau's 'Six Principles of International Politics' puts the notion that 'all international politics are power politics' at its heart. Power, for Realists, is primarily material and military, but also based on economic and geopolitical capabilities, on population, and on the strength and coherence of state institutions. Realists also argue that international politics is necessarily a struggle for power to deny other actors the capacity to dominate: this leads them to put the concept of the balance of power at the heart of their account of both the structure and the dynamics of international relations. Unless there is a single global empire, world politics is a struggle between actors who seek domination, but even more seek to prevent others from dominating. (See also Neo-Realism.)

**Realpolitik:** A German word popularised by the policy of Chancellor Otto von Bismarck (1815–1898) and meaning a cold calculation of interests despite the human or moral cost, it is often seen as the essence of Realism. It means Realism about what is possible and a preparedness to use force where necessary. The latter has led to its association with 'lack of principle' or 'ruthlessness'.

**Regime/s:** The term regime has been around in IR theory since the 1970s and several classic definitions have emerged. It is most frequently used to refer to a set of rules, procedures and expectations concerning a given issue area which govern the behaviour of a particular group of actors – who are said to make up the regime which then makes decisions on the basis of this consensus. There are numerous regimes in international relations governing transboundary issues such as the environment or trade.

**Religious fundamentalism:** See Fundamentalism.

**Security Studies:** Concerns itself with a sub-set of the political interactions that make up international relations marked by their particular importance in terms of maintaining the security of the actors. Over time it has become a matter of contention among theorists of International Relations whether Security Studies should maintain its traditional emphasis on military threats to the security of states – which dominated the sub-discipline in the Cold War era – or widen its focus in line with changes brought about by the ending of that conflict and globalisation. Alternative perspectives have argued increasingly that the discipline should either: i) extend its reach to include non-military threats to states, or, ii) go further and bring within its remit the security of all actors in relation to a range of threats, both military and non-military.

**Soft power:** 'Soft power', associated with the American international relations analyst, Joseph Nye, refers to the capability of an entity, usually but not necessarily a state, to influence what others do through persuasion, not force or threats. Soft power attracts or co-opts people; it does not coerce them. Soft power influences people by *appealing* to them, not by *forcing* them to comply. Soft power covers certain attributes – including culture, values, ideas – collectively representing different, but not necessarily lesser, forms of influence compared to 'hard' power. The latter implies more direct, forceful measures typically involving the threat or use of armed force or economic coercion. In short, soft power is neither 'sticks nor carrots' but a 'third way' of achieving objectives. It goes beyond simple influence – that can rest on hard power threats, both military or diplomatic, as well as financial payments – to involve *persuasion* and *encouragement* rooted in shared norms, values and beliefs. To exercise soft power relies on (1) *persuasion*, or the ability to convince by argument, and on (2) ability to *attract*.

**Sovereignty:** status of legal autonomy enjoyed by states so that their government has exclusive authority within its borders and enjoys the rights of membership of the international political community.

**Strategic Studies:** This narrow field of realism, concerned exclusively with military balances, capabilities and intentions was impacted upon (and boosted) by the advent of nuclear weapons. Although technological innovation has always been critical in warfare, nuclear weapons are qualitatively different and their existence has led to other phenomena such as 'proxy wars' characteristic of the Cold War. Strategic studies in the twenty-first century has developed, therefore, into a much broader field of study including ideas on the potential 'first use' of nuclear weapons and the concept of 'mutually assured destruction' (see above).

**Structural Adjustment Programmes (SAPs):** Dozens of countries in the developing world adopted SAPs in the 1980s and 1990s, following pressure from Western governments, the International Monetary Fund and the World Bank. SAPs focused on the rolling out of economic liberalisation and a shrinking of the state's economic role, as conditions for the receipt of significant external economic assistance. SAP-adopting countries abandoned or downgraded national development strategies – that is, those based on state-led programmes and import substitution policies – and rejected nationalisation of foreign-held assets. The overall outcome was to integrate such economies more fully into the global economy. Recent research indicates that under SAPs (1) poverty actually grew, and (2) most economic 'progress' occurred in only a small number of countries (some of them with large populations and unusual appeal for foreign investors), and (3) even in successful cases, many people were actually no better off – and some were poorer than before. In sum, SAPs were externally imposed, yet seriously flawed development strategies that often undermined the already weak developmental position of many poor people. As a result, recent years have seen widespread calls to reform SAPs, tame financial markets, 'upsize' the state, and 'downsize' the single global market.

**Supranational:** political authority above the sovereign state (meaning literally 'over the nation').

**Terrorism:** A common sense notion of the term would concern the deliberate use of violence (by non-state actors) for political ends, especially when this is directed at innocent civilians. What is perhaps most notable, however, is how easily this is stretched for political purposes to include acts of sabotage, corporate negligence and any other number of things depending on one's viewpoint. Many important questions also emerge from such 'common sense', most notably, why should states who kill civilians for political ends not be called terrorists? The idea that 'one person's terrorist is another person's freedom fighter' is one which students of IR are usually introduced to very early on in their studies; historically (without the blur of contemporary events) we can see that very often it is those with power who are able to say who the terrorists are and that history often makes a different judgement as power shifts. In other words, we cannot be sure that today's terrorist will not become tomorrow's freedom fighter.

**Third World:** The term, 'Third World', had two, separate, yet linked, senses during the Cold War. It was used to refer to certain countries: (1) that were economically 'underdeveloped', that is, they had agriculture-based economies and relatively little industrialisation and (2) a relatively unimportant place in international politics. Developmentally, the term sought to capture the notion of a certain type of country: post-colonial and economically weak, compared to the rich countries of the First World. Regarding international relations, a bloc of post-colonial countries emerged and formed an alliance: the Non-Aligned Movement (NAM), whose member countries claimed to be followers of neither the USA nor the USSR. While, individually, most developing countries played relatively minor roles in international relations during the Cold War, their collective voice focused in the NAM, relatively loud and, at irregular intervals, influential. In sum, the term, the 'Third World', had a dual meaning. On the one hand, it referred to a large group of economically underdeveloped, developmentally weak African, Asian, Middle Eastern and Latin American countries. On the other hand, it connoted the proclaimed neutrality of a large bloc of mostly postcolonial, developing countries, organised in the NAM.

**Transnationalism:** Description of a phenomenon in international relations observed particularly by functionalists such as David Mitrany and Liberals/Pluralists such as Robert Keohane. An amalgamation of these arguments noted that as the world got more complex, states were increasingly having to work together on a range of functional areas in order to cope. Cooperation was – in effect – being forced on states, because the costs of not cooperating were too great. At the same time, the complex cobweb of interactions which were transnational was influenced by other

actors such as multinational corporations (MNCs) and international non-governmental organisations (INGOs) and others who interacted with each other and with states in an extremely diverse number of ways.

**Welsh School:** A so called Welsh School of Critical Security Studies was established by Professor Ken Booth with one of its most notable publications being his 'Security and Emancipation' *Review of International Studies*, 17 (4), 1991. Beyond this there is a long standing connection between Wales – particularly Aberystwyth – and the discipline of IR which goes back to 1919.

**Westernisation:** is a process whereby people in a variety of non-Western countries, especially in the developing world and former Communist countries of Central and Eastern Europe, come under the influence of Western, especially American, culture in various areas. These include: technology, law, politics, economics, lifestyle, dress, diet, language, religion, philosophy and values. During the current phase of globalisation and the earlier process of colonisation and imperialism, Westernisation became a pervasive and many would say an accelerating influence in both the developing and former Communist worlds. This is not however to claim that Westernisation is a one-way, imposed process, with the rich and influential Western countries *imposing* their influences, interests and preferences. Often, they are pushing at an open door with many people in the non-Western countries enthusiastically seeking to become part of a more Westernised society, in the hope of attaining Western life or some aspects of it.

**Westphalian system:** The Peace of Westphalia of 1648 was an important point, marking off the mediaeval from the modern period in European development. Like all historical benchmarks, however, the Peace of Westphalia is in some respects a convenient reference point rather than the source of a fully formed new normative system. However, it did create foundations of a new 'Westphalian system' which emerged from the ruins of the political structures and the idealised rationale for them – Christendom – that had earlier existed in Europe for a millennium.

The Peace of Westphalia led to a revolutionary change in the way European states ordered their mutual relations. The Peace created the basis for a decentralised system of sovereign and equal nation states which had never existed before. Henceforward, decentralised, scattered power was regarded as the most legitimate mode of organisation in international relations. But the separateness that replaced the idea of Christendom could only be made legitimate by insisting that the fragmentation of authority now carried with it a new concept: the sovereign equality of states, where rulers have absolute authority within their domains.

**World Systems Theory:** A variant of structuralism that conceptualises world order as being structured into a (rich, developed) core, (poor, underdeveloped) periphery and a number of intermediary or semi-peripheral states.

# Bibliography

## Chapter 1

Anheier, H. and Themudo, N. (2002) 'Organisational forms of global civil society: implications of going global', in M. Glasius, M. Kaldor and H. Anheier (eds), *Global Civil Society 2002*. Oxford: Oxford University Press, pp. 191–216.

Attina, A. (1989) 'The study of international relations in Italy' in H. Dyer and L. Mangasarian (eds), *The Study of International Relations. The State of the Art*. Basingstoke: Macmillan, pp. 344–57.

Beck, U. (2000) *What is Globalization?* Cambridge: Polity.

Clark, I. (1997) *Globalisation and Fragmentation*. Oxford: Oxford University Press.

Cook, C. (2001) 'Globalisation and its critics', *The Economist*, 27 September.

Gillespie, R. and Youngs, R. (eds) (2002) 'The European Union and democracy promotion: the case of North Africa', Special issue of *Democratization*, 9 (1).

Hague, R. and Harrop, M. (2001) *Comparative Government and Politics. An Introduction*. (5th edn), Basingstoke: Palgrave.

Hay, C., Rosamond, B. and Schain, M. (2002) Editors' flyer for *Comparative European Politics*, a quarterly journal first published in March 2003. Details at www.palgrave-journals.com.

Haynes, J. (2005) *Comparative Politics in a Globalizing World*. Cambridge: Polity.

Haynes, J. (2008) *Development Studies*. Cambridge: Polity.

Held, D. and McGrew, A. (2002) *Globalization/Anti-Globalization*. Cambridge: Polity.

Hirst, P. and Thompson. G. (1999) *Globalization in Question. The International Economy and the Possibilities of Governance*. (2nd edn), Cambridge: Polity Press.

Huntington, S. (1996) *The Clash of Civilizations*, New York: Simon & Schuster.

Lipschutz, R. (1992) 'Reconstructing world politics: the emergence of global civil society', *Millennium*, 21 (3): 389–420.

Mittelman, J. (1994) 'The globalisation challenge surviving at the margins', *Third World Quarterly*, 15 (3): 427–41.

Pridham, G. (2000) *The Dynamics of Democratization. A Comparative Approach*. London and New York: Continuum.

Risse, T. and Ropp, S. (1999) 'Conclusions', in T. Risse, S. Ropp, and K. Sikkink, (eds), *The Power of Human Rights. International Norms and Domestic Change*. Cambridge: Cambridge University Press, pp. 234–78.

Sen, A. (2009) 'Capitalism beyond the crisis', *The New York Review of Books*, 56 (5): March. Available at http://www.nybooks.com/articles/22490 (Last accessed January 2010).

Warburg, M. (2001) 'Religious organisations in a global world. A comparative perspective', University of Copenhagen, Denmark. Paper presented at the 2001 international conference, 'The Spiritual Supermarket: Religious Pluralism in the 21st Century', 19–22 April, London School of Economics, Houghton Street, London WC2A 2AE.

Webber, M. and Smith, M. (2002) *Foreign Policy in a Transformed World*. Harlow: Pearson.

Willetts, P. (2001) 'Transnational actors and international organizations in global politics', in J. Baylis and S. Smith (eds), *The Globalization of World Politics. An Introduction to International Relations*. Oxford: Oxford University Press, pp. 356–83.

Willetts, P. (2008) 'Transnational actors and international organizations in global politics', in J. Baylis, S. Smith and P. Owens (eds), *The Globalization of World Politics*. (4th edn), Oxford: Oxford University Press, pp. 330–49.

Woods, N. (2001) *The Political Economy of Globalization*. Basingstoke: Palgrave.

Yilmaz, H. (2002) 'External–internal linkages in democratization: developing an open model of democratic change', *Democratization*, 9 (2): 67–84.

## Chapter 2

Barr, M. (2002) *Cultural Politics and Asian Values*. London: Routledge.

Best, G. (1982) *War and Society in Revolutionary Europe, 1770–1870*. London: Fontana.

Brown, C., with Ainley, K. (2005) *Understanding International Relations*. (3rd edn), Basingstoke, UK: Palgrave Macmillan.

Bull, H. (1977) *The Anarchical Society*. London: Macmillan.

Claes, W. (1995) 'The crisis over UN failures', in *The Guardian*, 3 February.

Dolan, C. (2005) *In War We Trust. The Bush Doctrine and the Pursuit of Just War*. Aldershot, UK: Ashgate.

Fukuyama, F. (1992) *The End of History and the Last Man*. Harmondsworth: Penguin.

Halper, S. and Clarke, J. (2004) *America Alone. The Neo-Conservatives and the Global Order*. Cambridge: Cambridge University Press.

Haynes, J. (2007) *An Introduction to International Relations and Religion*. London: Pearson.

Held, D. and McGrew, A. (2002) *Globalization/Anti-Globalization*. Cambridge: Polity.

King, A. (1993) 'A nonparadigmatic search for democracy in a post-Confucian culture', in L. Diamond (ed.), *Political Culture and Democracy in Developing Countries*, Boulder, CO: Lynne Rienner.

Krasner, S. (1983) *International Regimes I*. Ithaca, New York: Cornell University Press.

Mendelsohn, B. (2005) 'Sovereignty under attack: the international society meets the Al Qaeda network', *Review of International Studies*, 31: 45–68.

Murden, S. (2005) 'Culture in world affairs', in J. Baylis and S. Smith (eds), *The Globalization of World Politics*. (3rd edn), Oxford: Oxford University Press, pp. 45–62.

Ommerborn, W. (n/d, probably 2003) 'The importance of universal principles in Confucianism and the problems connected to Jiang Qing's concept of political Confucianism and his theory of particular principles'. Available at http://www.eko-haus.de/menzius/universal.htm#_ftnref3]%20 (Last accessed 6 January 2010).

Rosenberg, M. (2009) 'A year after Mumbai attack, militants thrive', *The Wall Street Journal*, 24 November. Available at http://online.wsj.com/article/SB125901384192861229.html (Last accessed 5 January 2010).

Sartori, G. (1991) 'Rethinking democracy', *International Social Science Journal*, 129: 437–50.

Tankel, S. (2009) 'Lashkar-e-Taiba: from 9/11 to Mumbai'. Report prepared for the International Centre for the Study of Radicalisation and Political Violence, King's College, London, April/May. Available athttp://www.icsr.info/publications/papers/1240835356ICSRStephenTankelReport.pdf (Last accessed 6 January 2010).

Thomas, S. (2005) *The Global Resurgence of Religion and the Transformation of International Relations: The Struggle for the Soul of the Twenty-First Century*. New York and Basingstoke, UK: Palgrave Macmillan.

## Chapter 3

Engels, D. and Marks, S. (eds) (1994) *Contesting Colonial Hegemony: State and Society in Africa and India*. London: German Historical Institute/British Academic Press.

Furedi, F. (1994) *Colonial Wars and the Politics of Third World Nationalism*. London: I.B. Tauris.

Gellner, E. (1983) *Nations and Nationalism*. New York: Cornell University Press.

Haynes, J. (1993) *Religion in Third World Politics*. Buckingham: Open University Press.

Haynes, J. (1996) *Religion and Politics in Africa*. London: Zed Press.

Hobsbawm, E. (1990) *Nations and Nationalism since 1780*. Cambridge: Cambridge University Press.

Hobson, J. (1902 [2005]) *Imperialism: A Study*. New York: Cosimo Classics.

Khan, M.M.A. (ed.) (2006) *Islamic Democratic Discourse: Theory, Debates and Philosophical Perspectives*. Lanham: Rowman and Littlefield.

Reiffer, B. (2003) 'Religion and nationalism: understanding the consequences of a complex relationship', *Ethnicities* 3 (2): 215–42.

Smith, A.D. (2003) *Chosen Peoples: Sacred Sources of National Identity*. Oxford: Oxford University Press.

## Chapter 4

Arnold, G. (2007) *Historical Dictionary of the Non-Aligned Movement and Third World*. Lanham, MD: Scarecrow.

Brodie, B. (1946) *The Absolute Weapon: Atomic Power and World Order*. New York: Ayer.

Calvocoressi, P. (2008) *World Politics Since 1945*. (9th edn), London: Longman.

Gaddis, J.L. (2007) *The Cold War*. Harmondsworth: Penguin.

Hadjor, K. (1993) *Dictionary of Third World Terms*. Harmondsworth: Penguin.

Halliday, F. (1986) *The Making of the Second Cold War*. (2nd edn), London: Verso.

Haynes, J. (2002) *Politics in the Developing World*. Oxford: Blackwell.

Haynes, J. (2008) *Development Studies*. Cambridge: Polity.

Henig, R. (2010) *League of Nations*. London: Haus Publishing.

Howlett, D. (2008) 'Nuclear proliferation' in J. Baylis, S. Smith and P. Owens (eds), *The Globalization of World Politics*. (4th edn), Oxford: Oxford University Press, pp. 386–401.

Isaacs, J. and Downing, T. (2008) *Cold War: For Forty-five Years the World Held Its Breath*. London: Abacus.

Keylor, W. R. (2006) *The Twentieth Century World and Beyond: An International History since 1900*. Oxford: Oxford University Press.

Taylor, P. and Curtis, D. (2008) 'The United Nations', in J. Baylis, S. Smith and P. Owens (eds), *The Globalization of World Politics*. (4th edn), Oxford: Oxford University Press, pp. 312–29.

# Chapter 5

Clark, I. (1997) *Globalization and Fragmentation. International Relations in the Twentieth Century.* Oxford: Oxford University Press.

Fukuyama, F. (1992) *The End of History and the Last Man.* Harmondsworth: Penguin.

Haynes, J. (2005) *Comparative Politics in a Globalizing World* (website with sample chapter: http://wip.polity.co.uk/haynes/) Cambridge: Polity.

Held, D. and McGrew, A. (eds) (2003) *The Global Transformations Reader: An Introduction to the Globalization Debate.* (2nd edn) Cambridge: Polity.

Held, D. and McGrew, A. (eds) (2007) *Globalization Theory: Approaches and Controversies.* Cambridge: Polity.

Hirst, P. and Thompson, G. (1999) *Globalization in Question. The International Economy and the Possibilities of Governance.* (2nd edn), Oxford: Oxford University Press.

Lechner, F. and Boli, J. (eds) (2007) *The Globalization Reader.* (3rd edn), London: Blackwell.

Ohmae, K. (2008) *The End of the Nation State: The Rise of Regional Economies.* New York: HarperCollins.

Pastusiak, L. (2004) 'We need to build a new world order after the cold war', *International Herald Tribune*, 3 January.

Schirato, T. and Webb, J. (2003) *Understanding Globalization.* London: Sage.

Scholte, J.A. (2005) *Globalization. A Critical Introduction*, (2nd edn), Basingstoke: Palgrave Macmillan.

Schrecker, E. (ed.) (2006) *Cold War Triumphalism: The Misuse of History After the Fall of Communism.* The New Press.

Stiglitz, J. (2006) *Making Globalization Work.* Harmondsworth: Penguin.

Woods, N. (2000) *The Political Economy of Globalization.* Basingstoke: Palgrave Macmillan.


# Chapter 6

Aron, R. (1966) *Peace and War: A Theory of International Relations.* London: Weidenfeld and Nicolson.

Beard, C. (1966) *The Idea of National Interest: An Analytical Study in American Foreign Policy.* Chicago, IL: Quadrangle.

Bull, H. (1977) *The Anarchical Society: A Study of World Order in Politics.* Basingstoke: Macmillan.

Carr, E.H. (1946) *The Twenty Years' Crisis 1919–1939: An Introduction to the Study of International Relations.* London: Macmillan.

Clausewitz, C. Von (1968) *On War* (ed. with introduction by Anatol Rapoport). Harmondsworth: Penguin.

Evans, G. (1975) 'E.H. Carr and International Relations', *British Journal of International Studies*, 1 (2): 77–97.

Gilpin, R. (1987) *Political Economy of International Relations.* Princeton, NJ: Princeton University Press.

Herz, J. (1951) *Political Realism and Political Idealism.* Chicago, IL: University of Chicago Press.

Hobbes, T. (1904) *Leviathan* (ed. A.R. Waller). Cambridge: Cambridge University Press.

Jervis, R. (1988) 'Realism, game theory and cooperation', *World Politics*, XL (3): 317–49.

Kaplan, M. (1966) 'The new great debate: traditionalism vs science in International Relations', *World Politics*, XIX (1): 1–20.

Keohane, R. (1986) *Neorealism and its Critics.* New York: Columbia University Press.

Kindleberger, C. (1973) *The World in Depression, 1929–39.* Berkeley: University of California Press.

Kissinger, H. (1964) 'Coalition diplomacy in a nuclear age', *Foreign Affairs*, 42 (4): 525–45.

Krasner, S. (2001) 'Rethinking the sovereign state model', *Review of International Studies*, 27 (1): 17–42.

Lippman, W. (1943) *US Foreign Policy.* Boston, MA: Little, Brown and Company.

Little, R. (1995) 'Neorealism and the English School: a methodological, ontological and theoretical reassessment', *European Journal of International Relations*, 1 (1): 9–34.

Machiavelli, N. (1988) *The Prince* (ed. by Q. Skinner). Cambridge: Cambridge University Press.

Morgenthau, H. (1964) 'The four paradoxes of nuclear strategy', *The American Political Science Review*, 58 (1): 23–35.

Morgenthau, H. (1973) *Politics Among Nations: The Struggle for Power and Peace.* (5th edn), New York: Knopf.

Morgenthau, H. (1978) *Politics Among Nations: The Struggle for Power and Peace.* New York: Knopf.

Niebuhr, R. (1932) *Moral Man and Immoral Society.* New York: Charles Scribner's Sons.

Niebuhr, R. (1953) *Christian Realism and Political Problems.* New York: Charles Scribner's Sons.

Schelling, T. (1960) *The Strategy of Conflict.* Cambridge, MA: Harvard University Press.

Spykman, N. (1942) *America's Strategy in World Politics: The United States and the Balance of Power.* New York: Harcourt, Brace and Company.

Thucydides (1998) *The Peloponnesian War* (new transl. W. Blanco, ed. W. Blanco and J. Tolbert Roberts). New York: Norton.

Tzu, Sun (2008) *The Art of War.* London: Penguin.

Waltz, K. (1959) *Man, the State and War: A Theoretical Analysis.* New York: Colombia University Press.

Waltz, K. (1979) *Theory of International Politics*. Reading, MA: Addison-Wesley.

Wight, M. (1979) *Power Politics*. Harmondsworth: Pelican.

Williams, M. (1993) 'Neo-realism and the future of strategy', *Review of International Studies*, 19 (2): 103–121.

Wolfers, A. (1962) *Discord and Collaboration: Essays on International Politics*. Baltimore, MD: Johns Hopkins Press.

## Chapter 7

Banks, M. (1985) 'The inter-paradigm debate' in M. Light and A.J.R. Groom (eds), *A Handbook of Current Theory*. London: Francis Pinter.

Brewin, C. (1988) 'Liberal states and international obligations', *Millennium: Journal of International Studies*, 17 (2): 321–38.

Claude, I. (1956) *Swords into Plowshares: The Problems and Progress of International Organisation*. New York: Random House.

Donnelly, J. (2006) *International Human Rights*. (3rd edn), Boulder, CO: Westview Press.

Doyle, M. (1983) 'Kant, liberal legacies and foreign affairs', *Philosophy and Public Affairs*, Summer/Fall.

Doyle, M. (1986) 'Liberalism and world politics', *American Political Science Review*, 80 (4): 1151–69.

Ferguson, Y.H. and Mansbach, R. (1997) 'The past as prelude to the future? Identities and loyalties in global politics', in Y. Lapid, and F. Kratochwil (eds) *The Return of Culture and Identity in IR Theory*. Boulder, CO: Lynne Rienner.

Fukuyama, F. (1992) *The End of History and the Last Man*. New York: Free Press.

Goodwin, B. (1982) *Using Political Ideas*. Chichester: Wiley.

Hawthorn, G. (1999) 'Liberalism since the Cold War: an enemy to itself?', *Review of International Studies*, 25, Special Issue: 145–60.

Hoffman, S. (1995) 'The crisis of liberal internationalism', *Foreign Policy*, 98, Spring: 159–79.

Hurrell, A. (1990) 'Kant and the Kantian paradigm in international relations', *Review of International Studies*, 16 (3): 183–205.

Kant, I. (1991) *Political Writings* (ed. Hans Reiss). Cambridge: Cambridge University Press.

Kegley, C. (ed.) (1995) *Controversies in International Relations*. New York: St Martin's Press.

Keohane, R. (1984) *After Hegemony: Cooperation and Discord in the World Political Economy*. Princeton, NJ: Princeton University Press.

Keohane, R. and Nye, J. (1977) *Power and Interdependence: World Politics in Transition*. Boston, MA: Little Brown.

Kindleberger, C. (2000) *Comparative Political Economy: A Retrospective*. Cambridge, MA; London: MIT Press.

Latham, R. (1993) 'Democracy and war-making: locating the international liberal context', *Millennium: Journal of International Studies*, 23 (2): 139–64.

Luard, E. (ed.) (1992) *Basic Texts in International Relations*. London: Macmillan.

Mitrany, D. (1948) 'The functional approach to world organization', *International Affairs*, 24: 350–63.

Morse, E. (1976) *Modernisation and the Transformation of International Relations*. New York: Free Press.

Ricardo, D. (1971) *The Principles of Political Economy and Taxation*. Harmondsworth: Penguin.

Singer, D. and Small, M. (1972) *The Wages of War: 1816–1865 – A Statistical Handbook*. New York: Wiley.

Smith, A. (1910) *An Inquiry into the Nature and Causes of the Wealth of Nations* (with an introduction by Edwin Seligman). London: J.M. Dent.

## Chapter 8

Amin, S. (1974) *Accumulation on a World Scale: A Critique of the Theory of Underdevelopment (2 Volumes)*. London: Monthly Review Press.

Amin, S. (1990) *Maldevelopment: Anatomy of a Global Failure*. London: Zed Books.

Arrighi, G. and Sliver, B.J. (2001) 'Capitalism and world (dis)order', *Review of International Studies*, 27, Special Issue: 257–79.

Baran, P. (1957) *The Political Economy of Growth*. New York: Monthly Review Press.

Cardoso, F. and Faletto, E. (1979) *Dependency and Development in Latin America*. Berkeley, CA: University of California Press.

Chase-Dunn, C. (1989) *Global Formation: Structures of the World Economy*. Oxford: Blackwell.

Escobar, A. (1995) *Encountering Development: The Making and Unmaking of the Third World*. Princeton, NJ: Princeton University Press.

Galtung, J. (1971) 'A structural theory of imperialism', *The Journal of Peace Research*, 8 (1): 81–117.

Gamble, A. (1999) 'Marxism after communism: beyond realism and historicism', *Review of International Studies*, 25, Special Issue: 127–44.

George, S. (1994) *A Fate Worse Than Debt*. London: Penguin.

Gunder Frank, A. (1979) *Dependent Accumulation and Underdevelopment*. New York: Monthly Review Press.

Harris, N. (1990) *The End of the Third World*. London: Penguin.

Harvey, D. (2003) *The New Imperialism*. Oxford: Oxford University Press.

Kamrava, M. (1993) *Politics and Society in the Third World*. London: Routledge.

Kolko, J. (1988) *Restructuring the World Economy*. London: Random House.

Marx, K. and Engels, F. (1965) *The Communist Manifesto*. New York: Washington Square Press.

McLellan, D. (1977) *Karl Marx: Selected Writings*. Oxford: Oxford University Press.

Mies, M. (1986) *Patriarchy and Accumulation on a World Scale*. London: Zed Books.

Prebisch, R. (1964) *Towards a New Trade Policy for Development*. New York: United Nations.

Rodney, W. (1972) *How Europe Underdeveloped Africa*. London: Bogle l'Ouverture.

Rostow, W.W. (1960) *The Stages of Economic Growth: A Non-Communist Manifesto*. Cambridge: Cambridge University Press.

Said, E. (1993) *Culture and Imperialism*. New York: Knopf.

South Commission (1990) *The Challenge to the South: The Report of the South Commission*. Oxford: Oxford University Press.

Van der Wee, H. (1986) *Prosperity and Upheaval: The World Economy 1945–1980*. London: Viking Books.

Wallerstein, I. (1974, 1980, 1989) *The Modern World-System* (Vols 1–3). San Diego, CA: Academy Press.

Wallerstein, I. (2000) 'From sociology to historical social science: prospects and obstacles', *The British Journal of Sociology*, 51 (1).

Wilber, C. (ed.) (1973) *The Political Economy of Underdevelopment*. New York: Random House.

## Chapter 9

Ashley, R.K. (1981) 'Political realism and human interests', *International Studies Quarterly*, 25 (2): 204–36.

Ashley, R.K. (1986) 'The poverty of neorealism', in R. Keohane (ed.), *Neorealism and its Critics*. New York: Columbia University Press, pp. 255–300.

Barnett, M. (ed.) (1998) *Security Communities*. Cambridge: Cambridge University Press.

Baylis, J. (1997) 'International security in the post-Cold War era', in J. Baylis and S. Smith (eds) (1997) *The Globalization of World Politics: An Introduction to International Relations*. Oxford: Oxford University Press, pp. 193–211.

Brown, C. (1992) *International Relations Theory: New Normative Approaches*. Harlow: Prentice Hall.

Buzan, B., Wæver, O. and de Wilde, J. (1998) *Security: A New Framework for Analysis*. Boulder, CO: Lynne Rienner.

Cox, R.W. (1986) 'Social forces, states and world order', *Millennium: Journal of International Studies*, 10 (2): 126–55; reprinted as 'Social forces, states and world orders: beyond international relations theory',

in R. Keohane (ed.) *Neorealism and its Critics*. New York: Columbia University Press, pp. 204–54.

Cox, R.W. (1987) *Production, Power and World Order: Social Forces in the Making of History*. New York: Columbia University Press.

Croft, S. and Terriff, T. (eds) (2000) *Critical Reflections on Security and Change*. London: Frank Cass.

Dallmayr, F. (2001) 'Conversation across boundaries: political theory and global diversity', *Millennium: Journal of International Studies*, 30 (2): 331–47.

Denzin, N.K. (1995) *The Cinematic Society: The Voyeur's Gaze*. London: Sage.

Devetak, R. (1996) 'Critical theory', in S. Burchill and A. Linklater (eds) *Theories of International Relations*. Basingstoke: Macmillan, pp. 145–78.

Gill, S. (ed.) (1993) *Gramsci, Historical Materialism and International Relations*. Cambridge: Cambridge University Press.

Gill, S. and Law, D. (1988) *The Global Political Economy: Perspectives, Problems and Policies*. Harlow: Prentice Hall.

Gramsci, A. (1971) *Selections from Prison Notebooks*. London: Lawrence and Wishart.

Habermas, J. (1972) *Knowledge and Human Interests*. London: Heinemann.

Held, D. (1990) *Introduction to Critical Theory: Horkheimer to Habermas*. Cambridge: Polity Press.

Hoffman, M. (1987) 'Critical theory and the inter-paradigm debate', *Millennium: Journal of International Studies*, 16 (2): 231–49.

Hoffman, M. (1988) 'Conversations on critical international relations theory', *Millennium: Journal of International Studies*, 17 (1): 91–5.

Horkheimer, M. (1972) *Critical Theory: Selected Essays*. New York: Seabury Press.

Katzenstein, P.J. (ed.) (1996) *The Culture of National Security: Norms and Identity in World Politics*. New York: Columbia University Press.

Krause, K. and Williams, M.C. (eds) (1997) *Critical Security Studies*. Minneapolis, MN: University of Minnesota Press.

Linklater, A. (1988) *The Transformation of Political Community*. Oxford: Polity Press.

Linklater, A. (1990) *Beyond Realism and Marxism: Critical Theory and International Relations*. London: Macmillan.

Linklater, A. (1992) 'The question of the next stage in international relations theory: a critical-theoretical point of view', *Millennium: Journal of International Studies*, 22 (2): 77–98.

Linklater, A. (1996) 'The achievements of critical theory', in K. Booth and M. Zalewski (eds), *International Theory: Positivism and Beyond*. Cambridge: Cambridge University Press, pp. 279–98.

Rengger, N.J. (1988) 'Going critical? A response to Hoffman', *Millennium: Journal of International Studies*, 17 (2): 81–9.

Rengger, N.J. (1990) 'The fearful sphere of international relations', *Review of International Studies*, 16 (4): 361–8.

Rengger, N.J. (2001) 'The boundaries of conversation: a response to Dallmayr', *Millennium: Journal of International Studies*, 30 (2): 357–64.

Rengger, N.J. and Hoffman, M. (1992) 'Modernity, postmodernity and international relations', in J. Doherty, E. Graham and M. Malek (eds) *Post-modernism and the Social Sciences*. London: Macmillan, pp. 127–47.

Rupert, M. (1995) *Producing Hegemony*. Cambridge: Cambridge University Press.

Shultz, R.H. and Pfaltzgraff, Jr, R. (eds) (1997) *Security Studies for the Twenty-first Century*. Washington, DC: Brassey's.

Teriff, T. *et al.* (1999) *Security Studies Today*. Oxford: Polity.

Wyn Jones, R. (1999) *Security, Strategy, and Critical Theory*. Boulder, CO: Lynne Rienner.

## Chapter 10

### *Postmodernism*

Ashley, R.K. (1988) 'Untying the sovereign state: a double reading of the anarchy problematique', *Millennium: Journal of International Studies*, 17 (2): 227–62.

Ashley, R.K. (1989) 'Imposing international purpose: notes on a problematic of governance', in E.-O. Czempiel and J.N. Rosenau (eds), *Global Changes and Theoretical Challenges: Approaches to World Politics for the 1990s*. Lexington, MA: Lexington Books, pp. 251–90.

Ashley, R.K. (1995) 'The power of anarchy: theory, sovereignty, and the domestication of global life', in J. Der Derian (ed.), *International Theory: Critical Investigations*. Manchester: Manchester University Press, pp. 94–128.

Ashley, R.K. (1996) 'The achievements of post-structuralism', in S. Smith, K. Booth and M. Zalewski (eds), *International Theory: Positivism and Beyond*. Cambridge: Cambridge University Press, pp. 240–53.

Ashley, R.K. and Walker, R.B.J. (1990) 'Speaking the language of exile', *International Studies Quarterly*, 34 (3): 259.

Bartelson, J. (1995) *A Genealogy of Sovereignty*. Cambridge: Cambridge University Press.

Baudrillard, J. (1995) *The Gulf War Did Not take Place*. Bloomington, IN: Indiana University Press.

Brown, C. (1992) *International Relations Theory: New Normative Approaches*. Hemel Hempstead: Harvester Wheatsheaf.

Campbell, D. (1993) *Politics without Principle: Sovereignty, Ethics, and the Narratives of the Gulf War*. Boulder, CO: Lynne Rienner.

Campbell, D. (1998a) *National Deconstruction: Violence, Identity, and Justice in Bosnia*. Minneapolis, MN: University of Minnesota Press.

Campbell, D. (1998b) *Writing Security: United States Foreign Policy and the Politics of Identity*. (rev. edn), Manchester: University of Manchester Press.

Connolly, W. (1991) *Identity/Difference: Democratic Negotiations of Political Paradox*. Ithaca, NY: Cornell University Press.

Connolly, W. (1993) *Political Theory and Modernity*. (2nd edn), Ithaca, NY: Cornell University Press.

Der Derian, J. (1989) 'The boundaries of knowledge and power in International Relations', in J. Der Derian and M.J. Shapiro (eds), *International/Intertextual Relations: Postmodern Readings of World Politics*. Lexington, MA: Lexington Books, pp. 3–10.

Der Derian, J. and Shapiro, M. (eds) (1989) *International/Intertextual Relations: Postmodern Readings of World Politics*. Lexington, MA: Lexington Books.

Derrida, J. (1978) *Writing and Difference*. London: Routledge and Kegan Paul.

Derrida, J. (1998) *Of Grammatology*. (rev. edn), Baltimore, MD: John Hopkins University Press.

Devetak, R. (1996) 'Postmodernism', in S. Burchill and A. Linklater (eds) *Theories of International Relations*. London: Macmillan.

Edkins, J. (1999) *Poststructuralism and International Relations: Bringing the Political Back In*. Boulder, CO: Lynne Rienner.

Foucault, M. (1970) *The Order of Things*. London: Tavistock.

Foucault, M. (1979) *Discipline and Punish: The Birth of the Prison*. Harmondsworth: Penguin.

Foucault, M. (1980) *Power/Knowledge: Selected Interviews and Other Writings, 1972–1977* (ed. C. Gordon). Brighton: Harvester Wheatsheaf.

Foucault, M. (1989) *The Archaeology of Knowledge*. London: Routledge.

George, J. (1994a) *Discourses of Global Politics: A Critical (Re)Introduction to International Relations*. Boulder, CO: Lynne Rienner.

George, J. (1994b) 'Thinking beyond international relations: postmodernism – reconceptualizing theory as practice', in J. George (ed.), *Discourses of Global Politics*. Boulder, CO: Lynne Rienner, pp. 191–217.

Hansen, L. (1997) 'A case for seduction? Evaluating the poststructuralist conceptualization of security', *Cooperation and Conflict*, 32 (4): 369–97.

Heidegger, M. (1969) *Identity and Difference*. New York: Harper and Row.

Heidegger, M. (1993) *Basic Concepts*. Bloomington, IN: Indiana University Press.

Neumann, I.B. (1996) 'Self and other in international relations', *European Journal of International Relations*, 2 (2): 139–74.

Nietzsche, F. (1954) *The Portable Nietzsche*. New York: Viking Press.

Nietzsche, F. (1990) *Unmodern Observations*. New Haven, CT: Yale University Press.

Rengger, N. and Hoffman, M. (1992) 'Modernity, postmodernism and international relations', in J. Doherty (eds), *Postmodernism in the Social Sciences*. London: Macmillan, pp. 127–47.

Rosenau, P. (1991) *Postmodernism and the Social Sciences: Insights, Inroads and Intrusions*. Princeton, NJ: Princeton University Press.

Smith, S. (1995) 'The self-images of a discipline: a genealogy of international relations theory', in K. Booth and S. Smith (eds), *International Relations Theory Today*. Oxford: Polity, pp. 1–37.

Smith, S. (1999) 'Is the truth out there? Eight questions about international order', in T.V. Paul and J.A. Hall (eds), *International Order and the Future of World Politics*. Cambridge: Cambridge University Press, pp. 99–119.

Walker, R.B.J. (1987) *One World, Many Worlds: Struggles for a Just World Peace*. London: Zed Books.

Walker, R.B.J. (1993) *Inside/Outside: International Relations as Political Theory*. Cambridge: Cambridge University Press.

Weber, C. (1995) *Simulating Sovereignty: Intervention, the State and Symbolic Exchange*. Cambridge: Cambridge University Press.

### Feminism

Block, D. (2009) *Arming the Spirit: A Woman's Journey Underground and Back*. Edinburgh: AK Press.

Butler, J. (1990) *Gender Trouble: Feminism and the Subversion of Identity*. London: Routledge.

Carver,T., Cochran, M. and Squires, J. (1998) 'Gendering Jones', *Review of International Studies*, 24 (2): 283–98.

Chatterjee, P. (1991) 'Whose imagined communities', *Millennium: Journal of International Studies*, 20 (3): 625–60.

Chinkin, C. (1999) 'Gender, inequality and International Human Rights Law', in A. Hurrell and N. Woods (eds), *Inequality, Globalization and World Politics*. Oxford: Oxford University Press.

Chowdhry, G. and Nair, S. (2002) (eds) *Postcolonialism and International Relations: Race, Gender and Class*. London: Routledge.

Connell, R.W. (1995) *Masculinities*. Cambridge: Cambridge University Press.

Cooke, M. and Woollacott, A. (1993) *Gendering War Talk*. Princeton, NJ: Princeton University Press.

Elshtain, J.B. (1987) *Women and War*. New York: Basic Books.

Enloe, C. (1989) *Bananas, Beaches and Bases; Making Feminist Sense of International Relations*. London: Pandora.

Enloe, C. (1993) *The Morning After: Sexual Politics after the Cold War*. Berkeley, CA: University of California Press.

Enloe, C. (2000) *Maneuvers: The International Politics of Militarizing Women's Lives*. Berkeley, CA: University of California Press.

Freidan, B. (2001) *The Feminine Mystique* (first published 1963). New York: WW Norton.

Fukuyama, F. (1998) 'Women and the evolution of world politics', *Foreign Affairs*, 77 (5): 24–40.

Grant, R. and Newland, K. (1990) *Gender and International Relations*. Milton Keynes: Open University Press.

Harcourt, W. (ed.) (1999) *Women@Internet*. London: Zed Books.

Hoffman, J. (2001) *Gender and Sovereignty*. Basingstoke: Palgrave.

Hooper, C. (2000) 'Hegemonic masculinity in transition: the case of globalization', in M. Marchand and A. Runyan (eds), *Gender and Global Restructuring: Sitings, Sites and Resistances*. London: Routledge.

Hooper, C. (2001) *Masculinities, International Relations and Gender Politics*. New York: Columbia University Press.

Hutchins, K. (2000) 'Towards a feminist international ethics', *Review of International Studies*, 26, Special Issue: 111–30.

Jones, A. (1996) 'Does "gender" make the world go around? Feminist critiques of International Relations', *Review of International Studies*, 22 (4): 405–29.

Jones, A. (1998) 'Engendering debate', *Review of International Studies*, 24 (2): 299–303.

Keohane, R. (1989) 'International Relations theory: contributions of a feminist standpoint', *Millennium: Journal of International Studies*, 18 (2): 245–54.

Keohane, R. (1998) 'Beyond dichotomy: conversations between International Relations and feminist theory', *International Studies Quarterly*, 42 (1): 193–8.

Krause, J. (1995) 'The international dimensions of gender inequality and feminist politics', in J. MacMillan and A. Linklater (eds), *Boundaries in Question: New Directions in International Relations*. London: Pinter, pp. 128–43.

Marchand, M. (1996) 'Reconceptualizing gender and development in an era of globalization', *Millennium: Journal of International Studies*, 25 (3): 577–603.

Marchand, M. and Runyan, A. S. (2000) *Gender and Global Restructuring: Sitings, Sites and Resistances.* London: Routledge.

McGlen, N. and Sarkees, M.R. (1993) *Women in Foreign Policy.* London: Routledge.

Mernisi, F. (1987) *The Veil and the Male Elite: A Feminist Interpretation of Women's Rights in Islam.* New York: Addison Wesley.

Meyer, M. and Prugl, E. (1999) *Gender Issues in Global Governance.* Oxford: Rowman and Littlefield.

Murphy, C. (1996) 'Seeing women, recognizing gender, recasting International Relations', *International Organisation*, 3 (5): 513–38.

Myerson, M. and Northcott, S.(1994) 'The question of gender: an examination of selected textbooks in International Relations', *International Studies Notes*, 19 (1): Winter.

Peterson, V.S. (1990) 'Whose rights? Challenging the discourse', *Alternatives*, 15 (3): 303–44.

Peterson, V.S. (1992a) 'Transgressing boundaries: theories of knowledge, gender and International Relations', *Millennium: Journal of International Studies*, 21 (2): 183–206.

Peterson, V.S. (1992b) (ed.) *Gendered States; Feminist (Re)Visions of International Theory.* Boulder, CO: Lynne Rienner.

Peterson, V.S. and Parisi, L. (1998) 'Are women human? This is not an academic question', in T. Evans (ed.), *Human Rights Fifty Years On: A Reappraisal.* Manchester: Manchester University Press.

Peterson, V.S. and Runyan, A. (1993) *Global Gender Issues.* Boulder, CO: Westview Press.

Pettman, J.J. (1996) *Worlding Women: A Feminist International Politics.* London: Routledge.

Robinson, F. (1999) *Globalizing Care: Ethics, Feminist Theory and International Relations.* Oxford: Westview Press.

Schneir, M. (1972) *Feminism: The Essential Historical Writings.* London: Vintage.

Special Issue: 'Women in International Relations', *Millennium: Journal of International Studies*, 17 (3).

Steans, J. (1998) *Gender and International Relations.* Oxford: Polity Press.

Steans, J. (2003a) 'Conflicting loyalties: women's human rights and the politics of identity', in M. Waller and A. Linklater (eds), *Loyalty and the Post-National State.* London: Routledge.

Steans, J. (2003b) 'Engaging from the margins: feminist encounters with the mainstream of International Relations', *British Journal of Politics and International Relations*, 5 (3): 428–54.

Sylvester, C. (1994a) 'Empathetic cooperation: a feminist method for IR', *Millennium: Journal of International Studies*, 23 (3): 315–34.

Sylvester, C. (1994b) *Feminist Theory and International Relations in a Postmodern Era.* Cambridge: Cambridge University Press.

Tickner, J.A. (1992) *Gender in International Relations: Feminist Perspectives on Achieving Global Security.* New York: Columbia University Press.

Tickner, J.A. (1997) 'You just don't understand: troubled engagements between feminists and IR theorists', *International Studies Quarterly*, 41 (4): 611–32.

Tickner, J.A. (1998) 'Continuing the conversation', *International Studies Quarterly*, 42 (1): 205–10.

Tickner, J.A. (1999) 'Why women can't run the world: international politics according to Francis Fukuyama', *International Studies Review*, 3: 3–12.

Tickner, J.A. (2001) *Gendering World Politics.* New York: Columbia University Press.

True, J. (1996) 'Feminism', in S. Burchill and A. Linklater (eds), *Theories of International Relations.* London: Macmillan.

Walker, R.B.J. (1992) 'Gender and critique in the theory of International Relations', in V.S. Peterson (ed.), *Gendered States: Feminist (Re)Visions of International Relations Theory.* Boulder, CO: Lynne Rienner.

Weber, C. (1994) 'Good girls, bad girls and little girls: male paranoia in Robert Keohane's critique of feminist International Relations', *Millennium: Journal of International Studies*, 23 (2): 337–49.

Weber, C. (2001) *'Gender' in International Relations Theory: A Critical Introduction.* London: Routledge.

Whitworth, S. (1989) 'Gender in the interparadigm debate', *Millennium: Journal of International Studies*, 18 (2): 265–72.

Whitworth, S. (1994a) *Feminism and International Relations: Towards a Political Economy of Gender in Interstate and Non-Governmental Institutions.* Basingstoke: Macmillan.

Whitworth, S. (1994b) 'Theory as exclusion: gender and international political economy', in R. Stubbs and G. Underhill (eds), *Political Economy and the Changing Global Order.* London: Macmillan.

Zalewski, M. (1993a) 'Feminist standpoint meets International Relations theory: a feminist version of David and Goliath', *The Fletcher Forum of World Affairs*, 17 (2): 221–9.

Zalewski, M. (1993b), 'Feminist theory and International Relations', in M. Bowker and R. Brown (eds), *From Cold War to Collapse: Theory and World Politics in the 1980s.* Cambridge: Cambridge University Press.

Zalewski, M. (1994) 'The woman/"women" question in International Relations', *Millennium: Journal of International Studies*, 23 (3): 407–23.

Zalewski, M. (1995) 'Well, what is the feminist perspective on Bosnia?', *International Affairs*, 71(2): 339–56.

Zalewski, M. and Enloe, C. (1995) 'Questions about identity', in K. Booth and S. Smith (eds), *International Relations Theory Today*. Cambridge: Polity Press.

Zalewski, M. and Parpart, J. (1998) *The Man Question in IR*. Oxford: Westview Press.

### Green Theory

Adams, W.M. (1990) *Green Development: Environment and Sustainability in the Third World*. London: Routledge.

Barnett, J. (2001) *The Meaning of Environmental Security: Ecological Politics and Policy in the New Security Era*. London: Zed.

Brundtland, G. (1987) *Our Common Future*. Oxford: Oxford University Press (World Commission on Environment and Development, *The Brundtland Report*).

Carson, R. (1962) *Silent Spring*. Harmondsworth: Penguin.

Conca, K., Alberty, M. and Dabelkoa, G. (eds) (1995) *Green Planet Blues*. Boulder, CO: Westview Press.

Dobson, A. (1995) *Green Political Thought*. (2nd edn), London: Routledge.

Dobson, A. (ed.) (1999) *Fairness and Futurity: Essays on Environmental Sustainability and Social Justice*. Oxford: Oxford University Press.

Eckersley, R. (1992) *Environmentalism and Political Theory: Towards an Ecocentric Approach*. London: UCL Press.

Elliot, J. (1994) *An Introduction to Sustainable Development: The Developing World*. London: Routledge.

Hayward, T. (1994) *Ecological Thought: An Introduction*. Oxford: Polity Press.

Homer-Dixon, T. and Blitt, J. (eds) (1998) *EcoViolence: Links Among Environment, Population and Security*. London: Rowman and Littlefield.

Hurrell, A. and Kingsbury, B. (eds) (1992) *The International Politics of the Environment*. Oxford: Oxford University Press.

Imber, M. (1994) *Environment, Security and UN Reform*. Basingstoke: Macmillan.

Litfin, K. (ed.) (1998) *The Greening of Sovereignty in World Politics*. Cambridge, MA: MIT Press.

Lomborg, B. (2001) *The Skeptical Environmentalist: Measuring the Real State of the World*. Cambridge: Cambridge University Press.

Matthews, F. (1991) *The Ecological Self*. London: Routledge.

McCormick, J. (1989) *Reclaiming Paradise: The Global Environmental Movement*. Bloomington, IN: Indiana University Press.

Meadows, D., Meadows, D.L., Randers, J. and Behrens, W.W. (1972) *The Limits to Growth*. Washington, DC: Potomac Associates.

Mellor, M. (1997) *Feminism and Ecology*. Oxford: Polity Press.

Merchant, C. (1992) *Radical Ecology: The Search for a Liveable World*. London: Routledge.

Paterson, M. (1996a) *Global Warming and Global Politics*. London: Routledge.

Paterson, M. (1996b) 'Green politics', in S. Burchil and A. Linklater (eds), *Theories of International Relations*. Basingstoke: Macmillan, pp. 252–74.

Paterson, M. (2000) *Understanding Global Environmental Politics. Domination, Accumulation, Resistance*. Basingstoke: Macmillan.

Pepper, D. (1996) *Modern Environmentalism: An Introduction*. London: Routledge.

Porritt, J. (1984) *Seeing Green*. Oxford: Blackwell.

Sessions, G. (ed.) (1995) *Deep Ecology for the Twenty-first Century*. London: Shambhala.

Shiva, V. (2002) *Water Wars: Privatization, Pollution, and Profit*. London: Pluto Press.

Susskind, L. (1994) *Environmental Diplomacy: Negotiating More Effective Global Agreements*. Oxford: Oxford University Press.

Thomas, C. (1992) *The Environment in International Relations*. London: Royal Institute of International Affairs.

Vogler, J. and Imber, F. (1996) *The Environment and International Relations*. London: Routledge.

Werksman, J. (ed.) (1996) *The Greening of International Institutions*. London: Earthscan.

Westing, A. (1986) *Global Resources and International Conflict: Environmental Factors in Strategic Policy and Action*. Oxford: Oxford University Press.

## Chapter 11

Adler, E. (1997) 'Seizing the middle ground: constructivism in world politics', *European Journal of International Relations*, 3 (3): 319–63.

Binyon M. (2009) 'How the fall of the wall freed Mandela', *The Times*, November 14.

Bull, H. (1977) *The Anarchical Society: A Study of Order in World Politics*. Basingstoke: Macmillan.

Buzan, B. Wæver, O. & de Wilde, J. (1998) *Security. A New Framework for Analysis*. Boulder, CO: Lynne Reinner.

Christiansen, T., Jørgensen, K.-E. and Wiener, A. (eds) (2001) *The Social Construction of Europe*. London: Sage.

Deutsch, K. (1957) *Political Community and the North Atlantic Area: International Organization in the Light of Historical Experience*. Princeton: Princeton University Press.

Jervis, R. (1998) 'Realism in the study of world politics', *International Organization* 25(4): 971–91.

Kleeman, J (2004) 'What they said about . . . Turkey and the EU', *The Guardian*, 25 September, p. 28.

Onuf, N.G. (1989) *World of Our Making: Rules and Rule in Social Theory and International Relations*. New York: Columbia University Press.

Pettihome, M. (2008) 'Is there a European identity? National attitudes and social identification toward the European Union', *Journal of Identity and Migration Studies*, 2 (1): 15–36.

Risse, T. (1995) 'Democratic peace – warlike democracies? A social constructivist interpretation of the liberal argument', *European Journal of International Relations*, 1 (4): 489–515.

Risse, T., Ropp, S. and Sikkink, K. (eds) (1999) *The Power of Human Rights: International Norms and Domestic Change*. Cambridge: Cambridge University Press.

Ruggie, J. (1998) *Constructing the World Polity. Essays on International Institutionalization*. London and New York: Routledge.

Smith, S. (2000) 'Wendt's World', *Review of International Studies*, 26: 151–63.

Wendt, A. (1992) 'Anarchy is what states make of it: the social construction of power politics', *International Organization*, 46 (spring): 391–425.

Wendt, A. (1999) *Social Theory of International Politics*. Cambridge: Cambridge University Press.

## Chapter 12

Archer, C. (2001) *International Organizations*. (3rd edn), London and New York: Routledge.

Bull, H. (1977) *The Anarchical Society. A Study of Order in World Politics*. London: Macmillan.

Cox, M. (1994) in S. Gill (ed.) *Gramsci, Historical Materialism and International Relations*. Cambridge: Cambridge University Press.

Diehl, P. (ed.) (2005) *The Politics of Global Governance: International Organizations in an Interdependent World*. (3rd edn), Lynne Rienner).

Gilpin, R. (1981) *War and Change in World Politics*. Cambridge: Cambridge University Press.

Keohane, R. and Nye, S. (1971) *Transnational Relations and World Politics*.

Mearsheimer, J. (1994) 'The false promise of international institutions', *International Security*, 19 (3): Winter.

Pease, K.-K. (2009) *International Organizations. Perspectives on Global Governance*. (4th edn), Prentice Hall.

Ruggie, J. (1998) *Constructing the World Polity. Essays on International Institutionalization*. London and New York: Routledge.

United Nations Economic and Social Committee (ECOSOC) (1950) *Resolution 288(X)*, 27 February.

Wallace, M. and Singer, J. (1970) 'Intergovernmental organizations in the global system, 1815–1964: a quantitative analysis', *International Organization*, 24 (2): 239–87.

Waltz, K. (1970) 'The myth of national interdependence', in C.P. Kindleberger (ed.), *The International Corporation*. Cambridge, MA: MIT.

Wendt, A. (2003) 'Why a world state is inevitable', *European Journal of International Relations*, 9 (4): 491–542.

## Chapter 13

Archer, C. (2001) *International Organizations*. (3rd edn), London and New York: Routledge.

Dogan, N. (2005) 'The Organization of the Islamic Conference: an assessment of the role of the OIC in International Relations'. Paper prepared for the Third ECPR General Conference, Budapest, September.

Fassbender, B. (2009) *The United Nations Charter as the Constitution of the International Community*. Leiden: Brill.

Ghorbani, A. (2005) 'The Organization of the Islamic Conference and its contribution to world politics'. Paper prepared for the Third ECPR General Conference, Budapest, September.

Hanhimäki, J. (2008) *The United Nations: A Very Short Introduction*. New York: Oxford University Press.

Hauser, C. (2006) 'Bush says Iran leader's letter fails to address nuclear issue', *New York Times*, 11 May.

Haynes, J. (2007) *An Introduction to International Relations and Religion*. London: Pearson.

Huntington, S. (2002) *The Clash of Civilizations: And the Remaking of World Order*. (2nd edn), New York: Free Press.

Kalin, I. (2006) 'OIC: voice for the Muslim world?', *ISIM Review*, 17, Spring: 36–7. Available at http://www.isim.nl/files/Review_17/Review_17-36.pdf.

Kepel, G. (2004) *The War for Muslim Minds: Islam and the West*. London: Harvard University Press.

Khan, S.S. (2001) *Reasserting International Islam: A Focus on the Organization of the Islamic Conference and Other Islamic Institutions*. Oxford: Oxford University Press.

Marburg, T. (2009) *League of Nations*. Charleston, SC: BiblioBazaar.

Northedge, F.S. (1986) *The League of Nations*. Leicester: Leicester University Press.

Roy, O. (2004) *Globalised Islam: The Search for a New Ummah*. London: Hurst.

Sardar, Z. (1985) *Islamic Futures*. London: Mansell Publishing.

Sheikh, N. (2003) *The New Politics of Islam: Pan-Islamic Foreign Policy in a World of States*. London: Routledge Curzon.

Wendt, A. (2003) 'Why a world state is inevitable', *European Journal of International Relations*, 9 (4): 491–542.

## Chapter 14

Avila, J. (2000) 'Strengthening APEC's institutions', The Philippines Institute for Development Studies, 18, December. Available at http://www3.pids.gov.ph/ris/pdf/pidspn0018.PDF.

Beeson, M. (2008) *Institutions of the Asia Pacific: ASEAN, APEC and Beyond*. London: Routledge.

Christiansen, T. (2001) 'European and regional integration', in J. Baylis and S. Smith (eds), *The Globalization of World Politics. An Introduction to International Relations*. Oxford: Oxford University Press, pp. 495–518.

Delal Baer, M. (2000) 'Lessons of Nafta for U.S. relations with Mexico'. Testimony of Chairman and Senior Fellow, Mexico Project, Center for Strategic and International Studies to the United States Senate Subcommittee on Western Hemisphere, the Peace Corps, Narcotics and Terrorism, April 27. Available at http://www.csis.org/testimony/lessons-nafta-us-relations-mexico.

Hague, R. and Harrop, M. (2001) *Comparative Government and Politics. An Introduction*. (5th edn), Basingstoke: Palgrave.

Heine, J. (1999) 'Latin America. Collective responses to new realities', in L. Fawcett and Y. Sayigh (eds), *The Third World Beyond the Cold War. Continuity and Change*. Oxford: Oxford University Press, pp. 101–117.

Higgott, R. (1998) 'The Pacific and beyond: APEC, ASEM and regional economic management', in G. Thomson (ed.) *Economic Dynamism in the Asia Pacific*. London: Routledge, pp. 335–55.

Hirst, P. and Thompson, G. (1999) *Globalization in Question*, Cambridge: Polity.

Hufbauer, G.C. and Schott, J. (2005) *NAFTA Revisited: Achievements and Challenges*. Washington DC: Institute for International Economics, October.

Kahler, M. (1995) *International Institutions and the Political Economy of Integration*. Washington DC: The Brookings Institution.

Krasner, S. (ed.) (1983) *International Regimes*. Ithaca, NY: Cornell University Press.

Leslie, D. (1997) ' "Governing the economy" within economic unions: Canada, the EU, and the NAFTA', paper presented to *North American Federalism and NAFTA: Three Perspectives*, Canadian Studies Program, April 27–29. Berkeley, CA: University of California.

Lowndes, V. (2002) 'Institutionalism', in D. Marsh and G. Stoker (eds), *Theory and Methods in Political Science*. (2nd edn), Basingstoke: Palgrave, pp. 90–108.

Macdonald, L. and Schwartz, M. (2002) 'Political parties and NGOs in the creation of new trading blocs in the Americas', *International Political Science Review*, 23 (2): 135–58.

Morales, I. (2008) *Post-NAFTA North America: Reshaping the Economic and Political Governance of a Changing Region*. New York and Basingstoke, UK: Palgrave MacMillan.

Morrison, C. and Pedrosa, E. (2007) *An APEC Trade Agenda?: The Political Economy of a Free Trade Area of the Asia-Pacific*. Singapore: Institute of South East Asian Studies.

Oxley, A. (1999) *APEC: The Next Ten Years*. Melbourne: The Australian APEC Centre.

Roy, A.N. (1999) *The Third World in the Age of Globalisation*. London/Delhi: Zed Books/Madhyam Books.

Schirm, S. (2002) *Globalization and the New Regionalism*. Cambridge: Polity.

Schultz, M., Söderbaum, F. and Öjendal, J. (eds) (2001) *Regionalization in a Globalizing World. A Comparative Perspective on Forms, Actors and Processes*. London: Zed Books.

Smith, H. (2000) 'Why is there no international democratic theory?', in H. Smith (ed.), *Democracy and International Relations*. Basingstoke: Macmillan, pp. 1–30.

Smouts, M.-C. (ed.) (2001) *The New International Relations. Theory and Practice*. London: Hurst and Co.

Webber, M. and Smith, M. (2002) *Foreign Policy in a Transformed World*. Harlow: Pearson Education.

## Chapter 15

Adusei, L.A. (2009) 'African Union: is it a failure or success?', ModernGhana.com, 9 February. Available at http://www.modernghana.com/news/201955/1/african-union-is-it-a-failure-or-success.html.

African Union (2002) *Protocol relating to the establishment of the Peace and Security Council*. Available at http://www.africa union. org/root/au/organs/psc/Protocol Peace%20and%20security.pdf.

Annan, K. (2009) 'Africa and the International Court', *New York Times*, 29 June. Available at http://www.nytimes.com/2009/06/30/opinion/30iht-edannan.html.

Ayvaz, T. (2008) 'Turkey to receive 495 million euro pre-accession EU aid', *Turkish Daily News*, 18 July.

Beetham, D. and Lord, C. (1998) *Legitimacy and the European Union*. London: Longman.

Bogdanor, V. (2003) 'Europe needs a rallying cry', *The Guardian*, 28 May.

Christiansen, T. (2001) 'European and regional integration', in J. Baylis and S. Smith (eds), *The Globalization of World Politics. An Introduction to International Relations*. Oxford: Oxford University Press, pp. 495–518.

Etzioni-Halevy, E. (2002) 'Linkage deficits in transnational politics', *International Political Science Review*, 23 (2): 203–22.

Freedom House (2002) 'Freedom in the world 2002. Liberty's expansion in a turbulent world'. Available at http//www.freedomhouse.org/research/survey2002.htm.

Freedom House (2008) 'Freedom in the world – Turkey'. Available at http://www.freedomhouse.org/inc/content/pubs/fiw/inc_country_detail.cfm?year=2008&country=7508&pf.

Hague, R. and Harrop, M. (2001) *Comparative Government and Politics. An Introduction*. (5th edn), Basingstoke: Palgrave.

Harsch, E. (2003) 'Africa builds its own peace forces', *Africa Recovery*, 17 (3): 1, 14–16, 18–20.

Hettne, B. (2001) 'Europe: paradigm and paradox', in M. Schulz, F. Söderbaum and J. Öjendal (eds), *Regionalization in a Globalizing World. A Comparative Perspective on Forms, Actors and Processes*. London: Zed Books, pp. 22–41.

Hill, C. and Smith, M. (eds) (2005) *International Relations and the EU*. Oxford: Oxford University Press.

Hix, S. (2003) *The Political System of the European Union*. (2nd edn), Basingstoke: Macmillan.

Jenkins, G. (2008) *Political Islam in Turkey. Running West, Heading East?* Basingstoke, UK, and New York: Palgrave Macmillan.

Kinzer, S. (2001) *The Crescent and the Star: Turkey Between Two Worlds*. New York: Farrar Straus Giroux.

Makinda, S. and Wafula Okumu, F. (2006) *The African Union: Challenges of Globalization, Security, and Governance*. London: Routledge.

Muthiri, T. (2008) *The African Union and Its Institutions*. New York: Femela.

Osborn, A. (2003) 'EU lifts Turkey's hopes', *The Guardian*, 27 March.

Rosamond, B. (2002) 'Politics and governance above the territorial state', in B. Axford, G. Browning, R. Huggins and B. Rosamond (eds), *An Introduction to Politics*. (2nd edn), London and New York: Routledge, pp. 481–523.

Yilmaz, H. (2002) 'External-internal linkages in democratization: developing an open model of democratic change', *Democratization*, 9 (2): 67–84.

## Chapter 16

Cohen, B. (2003) *The Future of Money*. Princeton, NJ: Princeton University Press.

Gilpin, R. (1987) *The Political Economy of International Relations*. Princeton, NJ: Princeton University Press.

Global Policy Forum (2009) 'Globalization of the economy' Available at http://www.globalpolicy.org/globalization/globalization-of-the-economy-2-1.html.

Josling, T. and Hathaway, D. (2004) 'This far and no farther? Nudging agricultural reform forward' *International Economics Policy Briefs*, Policy Brief 04-1, Peterson Institute for International Economics, March.

O'Brien, R. and Williams, M. (2004) *Global Political Economy: Evolution and Dynamics*, Basingstoke, UK, New York: Palgrave.

Ricardo, D. (1992) *The Principles of Political Economy and Taxation* (first published 1817). London: Everyman's Library.

Ruggiero, R. (1996) Speech to United Nations Conference on Trade and Development, 8 October.

Smith, A. (1983) *The Wealth of Nations* (first published 1776). New York: Penguin.

World Trade Organization (2007) *World Trade Report 2007*. WTO: Geneva.

## Chapter 17

Fortune (2009) *Global 500 Survey*. Available at http://money.cnn.com/magazines/fortune/global500/2009/ (Last accessed 2.3.10).

Hines, C. (2000) *Localization–A Global Manifesto*. London: Earthscan.

Kegley, C. and Raymond, G. (2010) *The Global Future. A Brief Introduction to World Politics*. Boston: Wadsworth.

Rose, A. (2004) 'Do we really know that the WTO increases trade?', *American Economic Review*, 94 (1): 98–114.

Sklair, L. (2002) *Globalization. Capitalism and its Alternatives.* Oxford: Oxford University Press.

UN (2009) *Draft Report of the Commission of Experts of the President of the UN General Assembly on Reforms of the International Monetary and Financial System*, prepared for the UN Conference on the World Financial and Economic Crisis and its Impact on Development (held at New York 24–26 June 2009) .

World Bank (2009) *World Development Indicators 2009.* New York: World Bank Publications.


## Chapter 18

Bauer, P. (1976) *Dissention on Development.* London: Weidenfeld and Nicolson.

Frank, A.G. (1971) *Capitalism and Underdevelopment in Latin America.* Harmondsworth: Penguin.

Galtung, J. (1969) 'Violence, peace and peace research', *Journal of Peace Research* 6 (3): 167– 91.

Goklany, ? (2002) 'The globalization of human well-being', *Policy Analysis*, 477.

ICIDI (1980) *North–South: The Report of the International Commission on International Development Issues.* London: Pan Books.

Payne, A. (2005) *The Politics of Unequal Development.* Basingstoke, UK and New York: Palgrave.

Rahnema, M. (ed.) (1997) *The Post Development Reader.* London: Zed Books.

Ravallion, M. and Chen, S. (2008) 'The developing world is poorer than we thought but no less successful in the fight against poverty', World Bank. Available at http://wwwwds.worldbank.org/external/default/WDS ContentServer/IW3P/IB/2008/08/26/000158349_2008 0826113239/Rendered/PDF/WPS4703.pdf (Last accessed 23.6.09).

Rawls, J. (1971) *A Theory of Justice.* Cambridge, MA: Harvard University Press.

Rostow, W. (1960) *The Stages of Economic Growth*, Cambridge: Cambridge University Press.

Sen, A. (1999) 'Democracy as a universal value', *Journal of Democracy*, 10 (3): 3–17.

Stiglitz, J. (2002) *Globalization and its Discontents.* New York: Norton.

UNDP (1999) *Human Development Report. Globalization with a Human Face.* Oxford: Oxford University Press.

UNDP (2008) *Human Development Report. Fighting Climate Change. Human Solidarity in a Divided World.* Oxford: Oxford University Press.

Wallerstein, I. (1979) *The Capitalist World Economy.* Cambridge: Cambridge University Press.

Watkins, K. (2002) *Rigged Rules and Double Standards: Trade Globalization and the Fight Against Poverty.* Oxford: Oxfam.

World Bank (1991) *World Development Report.* Oxford, Oxford University Press.

World Food Programme (2009) *Hunger.* Available at http://www.wfp.org/hunger/stats (Last accessed 28.6.09).

Ziai, A. (2004) 'The ambivalence of post development: between reactionary populism and radical democracy', *Third World Quarterly*, 25 (6): 1045–1060.


## Chapter 19

Block, D. (2009) *Arming the Spirit: A Woman's Journey Underground and Back.* Edinburgh: AK Press.

Boserup, E. (1970) *Women's Role in Economic Development.* New York: St Martin's Press.

Carver, T. (2003) 'Gender and International Relations', *International Studies Review*, 5 (4): 287–382.

Caldicott, H. (1978), *Nuclear Madness.* CA: Autumn Press.

Enloe, C. (1989) *Bananas, Beaches and Bases: Making Feminist Sense of International Politics.* London: Pandora.

Jha, P., Kumar, R., Vasa, P., Neeraj, D., Thiruchelvan, D. and Mioneddin, R. (2006) 'Low male to female sex ratio of children born in India: National survey of 1.1 million households', *The Lancet*, 248: 211–18 Available at http://pndt.gov.in/writereaddata/mainlinkFile/File114.pdf.

Marchand, M. and Parpart, J. (1995), *Feminism, Postmodernism, Development.* London: Routledge.

Momsen, J.H. (2004) *Gender and Development.* London: Routledge.

Moon, K. (1997) *Sex Among Allies: Military Prostitution in US–Korea Relations.* New York: Columbia University Press.

Moser, C. (1989) 'Gender planning in the Third World: meeting practical and strategic gender needs', *World Development*, 17 (11): 1799–825.

Nash, J. and Fernandez Kelly, M.P. (eds) (1983) *Women, Men and the International Division of Labour.* New York: State University of New York Press.

Parpart, J. and Zalewski, M. (eds) (2008) *Rethinking the Man Question: Sex, Gender and Violence in International Relations.* London: Zed Books.

Peterson, V.S. and Runyan, A.S. (1993) *Global Gender Issues.* Boulder, CO: Westview Press.

Rai, S. (2005) 'Gender and development', in J. Haynes (ed.), *Development Studies.* London: Palgrave Macmillan.

*Refugee Council Report 2009* found at www.refugeecouncil.org.uk/Resources/Refugee%20council/downloads/researchreports.

Sen, A. (2001) 'The many faces of gender inequality', *The New Republic*, 17 September.

Shepherd, L.J. (2008) *Gender, Violence and Security*. London: Zed Books.

Steans, J. (2006) *Gender and International Relations*. Cambridge: Polity Press.

Sylvester, C. (1996) 'The contribution of feminist theory to international relations' in S. Smith, K. Booth and M. Zalewski (eds), *International Theory: Positivism and Beyond*. Cambridge: Cambridge University Press.

Sylvester, C. (2007) 'Whither the International at the end of IR', *Millennium: Journal of International Studies*, 35 (3): 551.

Tickner, J.A. (1992) *Gender in International Relations: Feminist Perspectives on Achieving Global Security*. New York: Columbia University Press.

Tickner, J.A. and Sjoberg, L. (2007) 'Feminism', in T. Dunne, M. Kurki and S. Smith (eds), *International Relations Theories: Discipline and Diversity*. Oxford: Oxford University Press.

UNIFEM (2009) *Progress of the World's Women 2008/2009*. Available at http://www.unifem.org/progress/2008/index.html.

Whitworth, S. (2004) *Men, Militarism and UN Peacekeeping: A Gendered Analysis*. Boulder, CO: Lynne Reinner Publishers.

Zalewski, M. (1993) 'Feminist standpoint theory meets international relations theory: a feminist vision of David and Goliath', *Fletcher Forum of World Affairs*, 17: 13.

Zalewski, M. and Parpart, J. (eds) (1998) *The Man Question in International Relations*. Boulder, CO: Westview Press.

## Chapter 20

Alter, P. (1994) *Nationalism*. London: Hodder Arnold.

Anderson, B. (1991) *Imagined Communities: Reflections on the Origin and Spread of Nationalism*. London: Verso.

Bhabba, H. (1994) *The Location of Culture*. London: Routledge.

Brown, C. and Ainley, K. (2009) *Understanding International Relations*. New York and Basingstoke, UK: Palgrave.

Ferguson, Y. and Mansbach, R. (2007) 'Post-internationalism and IR theory', *Millennium: Journal of International Studies*, 35 (3): 529–49.

Holbrooke, R. (2001) 'Get the message out', *Washington Post*, 28 October.

Huntington, S.P. (1993) 'The Clash of Civilizations?', *Foreign Affairs* 72 (3): 22–49.

Krause, N. and Renwick, J. (eds) (1997) *Identities in International Relations*. London: St Martin's.

Linklater, A. (2007) 'Public spheres and civilizing processes', *Theory, Culture and Society*, 24 (4): 31–7.

Mies, M. (1986) *Patriarchy and Accumulation on the World Stage*. London: Zed.

Russett, B. and Oneal, J. (2001) *Triangulating Peace: Democracy, Interdependence and International Organizations*. New York: Norton.

Travis, A. (2008) 'MI5 report challenges views on terrorism in Britain', *The Guardian*, 20 August.

Wallerstein, I. (1984) *The Politics of the World Economy. The States, the Movements and the Civilizations*. Cambridge: Cambridge University Press.

## Chapter 21

Acemoglu, D. and Robinson, J. (2006) *Economic Origins of Dictatorship and Democracy*. Cambridge: Cambridge University Press.

Carothers, T. (2002) 'The end of the transition paradigm', *Journal of Democracy*, 13 (1): 5–21.

Churchill, W. (1947) Speech at the House of Commons, London, 11 November.

Colomer, J. (2007) *Great Empires, Small Nations. The Uncertain Future of the Sovereign State*. London: Routledge.

Dahl, R. (1971) *Polyarchy: Participation and Opposition*. New Haven: Yale University Press.

Diamond, L. (2008) *The Spirit of Democracy: The Struggle to Build Free Societies Throughout the World*. New York: Times Books.

Dobbins, J., Crane, K. and Jones, S.G. (2007) *The Beginner's Guide to Nation Building*. Santa Monica: RAND Corporation.

Dobbins, J., McGinn, J.G., Crane, K., Jones, S.G., Lal, R., Rathmell, A., Swanger, R.M. and Timilsina, A.R. (2003) *America's Role in Nation-Building: From Germany to Iraq*. Santa Monica: RAND Corporation.

Dunne, T. and Wheeler, N. (eds) (2002) *Human Rights in Global Politics*. Cambridge: Cambridge University Press.

Fukuyama, F. (1992) *The End of History and the Last Man*. London: Hamish Hamilton.

Grugel, J. (2002) *Democratization. A Critical Introduction*. Basingstoke, UK: Palgrave.

Held, D. (1987) *Models of Democracy*. Bloomington, IN: Stanford University Press.

Hill, P. and Sen, K. (2000) 'The internet in Indonesia's new democracy', in P. Ferdinand (ed.), *The Internet, Democracy and Democratization*. Abingdon: Routledge: pp. 119–36.

Huntington, S. (1991) *The Third Wave. Democratization in the Late Twentieth Century*. Norman, Ok: University of Oklahoma Press.

Karl, T. (1995) 'The hybrid regimes of central America', *Journal of Democracy*, 6 (3): 72–86.

Keyman, E. and Icduygu, A. (2003) 'Globalization, civil society and citizenship in Turkey: actors, boundaries and discourses', *Citizenship Studies*, 7 (2): 219–34.

Knaus, G. and Martin, F. (2003) 'Travails of the European Raj', *Journal of Democracy*, 14 (3): 60–74.

Levitsky, S. and Way, L. (2005) 'International linkage and democratization', *Journal of Democracy*, 16 (3): 20–34.

Lipset, S. (1959) 'Some social requisites of democracy. Economic development and political legitimacy', *American Political Science Review*, 53: 69–105.

Pettiford, L. (2004) 'Democratization', in D. McIlver (ed.), *Political Issues in the World Today*. Manchester: Manchester University Press, pp. 33–47.

Przeworski, A., Alvarez, M.E., Cheibub, J.A. and Limongi, F. (2000) *Democracy and Development: Political Institutions and Well-Being in the World 1950–1990*. Cambridge: Cambridge University Press.

Reich, R. (2007) *Supercapitalism: The Transformation of Business, Democracy and Everyday Life*, New York: Alfred Knopf.

Risse, T. (1995) 'Democratic peace – warlike democracies? A social constructivist interpretation of the liberal argument', *European Journal of International Relations*, 1 (4): 489–515.

Rose, R. and Shin, D. (2001) 'Democratization backwards: the problem of third wave democracies', *British Journal of Political Science* 31(2): 331–54.

Russett, B. and Oneal, J. (2001) *Triangulating Peace: Democracy, Interdependence and International Organisations*. New York: Norton.

Russett, B. and Starr, H. (1996) *World Politics. The Menu for Choice*. (5th edn), New York: Freeman.

de Tocqueville, A. (1863) *Democracy in America*. (3rd edn), Cambridge: Sever and Francis.

## Chapter 22

Alderson, K. and Hurrel, A. (eds) (2000) *Hedley Bull on International Society*. Basingstoke, UK: Macmillan.

Benedict, R. (1934) *Patterns of Culture*. Boston: Houghton Mifflin Company.

Donnelly, J. (2007) *International Human Rights*. (3rd edn), Cambridge, MA: Westview.

Harff, B. and Gurr, T. (1988) 'Research note. Toward empirical theory of genocide and politicide: identification and measurement of cases since 1945', *International Studies Quarterly*, 32: 359–71.

Human Rights Watch (2004) *Creating Enemies of the State: Religious Persecution in Uzbekistan*. Available at http://hrw.org/reports/2004/uzbekistan0304/ (Last accessed 25.10.08).

International Federation of University Women (IFUW) (1999) 'International Convention on the Elimination of All Forms of Discrimination Against Women'. Available at http://www.ifuw.org/advocacy/ia_cedaw.htm (Last accessed 5.4.03).

International Lesbian, Gay, Bisexual, Trans and Intersex Association (ILGA) (2009) *Report on State-sponsored Homophobia*. Available at http://ilga.org/ilga/en/article/1251 (Last accessed 5.3.10).

Luttwak, E. (1999) 'Give war a chance', *Foreign Affairs*, 78 (4): 36–44.

Robertson, G. (2000) *Crimes Against Humanity. The Struggle for Global Justice*. London: Penguin.

Schabas, W. (2000) *Genocide in International Law. The Crime of Crimes*. Cambridge: Cambridge University Press.

Schulz, M. (2008) 'UN treasure honours Persian despot', *Spiegel Online International* (15/7/08) Available at http://www.spiegel.de/international/world/0,1518,566027,00.html (Last accessed 30.9.08).

Seng, W.K. (1993) Statement at World Conference on Human Rights, Vienna, 16 June.

Smith, R. (2007) *Textbook on International Human Rights*. (3rd edn), Oxford: Oxford University Press.

UNHCR (2008) *The 1951 Refugee Convention*. Available at http://www.unhcr.org/basics/BASICS/3c0f495f4.pdf.

World Conference on Human Rights (1993) *Vienna Declaration and Programme of Action*. 14–25 June, Vienna.

## Chapter 23

Adams, W. (2004) *Against Extinction: The Story of Conservation*. London: Earthscan.

Carson, R. (1962) *Silent Spring*. Penguin: Harmondsworth.

Graham, J. (2002) 'The role of precaution in risk management'. Remarks prepared for The International Society of Regulatory Toxicology and Pharmacology Precautionary Principle Workshop, Crystal City, VA, 20 June 2002. Office of Information and Regulatory Affairs. Office of Management and Budget Executive Office of the President of the United States. Available at http://www.whitehouse.gov/omb/inforeg/risk_mgmt_speech062002.html (Last accessed 13.3.08).

Haeckel, E. (1866) *Generelle Morphologie der Organismen*. Berlin: Verlag von Georg Reimer.

Hardin, G. (1968) 'The tragedy of the Commons', *Science*, 162: 1243–8.

Hardin, G. (1996) 'Lifeboat ethics: the case against helping the poor', in W. Aitken and H. LaFollette (eds), *World Hunger and Morality*. New Jersey: Prentice Hall.

Humphreys, D. (2006) *Logjam. Deforestation and the Crisis of Global Governance*. London: Earthscan.

Intergovernmental Panel on Climate Change (2007) *Climate Change 2007: The Physical Science Basis. Summary for Policymakers*. Geneva: IPCC.

Lomborg, B. (2001) *The Sceptical Environmentalist*. Cambridge: Cambridge University Press.

Marsh, G.P. (1965) *Man and Nature*. (Reprint), Cambridge, MA: Harvard University Press.

Mazza, P. (1998) 'The invisible hand. Is global warming driving El Nino?', *Sierra Magazine*, 83, May/June.

McMichael, A., Campbell-Lendrum, D. and Kovats, S. (2004) 'Global climate change', in M.J. Ezzati, A. Lopez, A. Rodgers and C. Murray (eds), *Comparative Quantification of Health Risks: Global and Regional Burden of Disease Due to Selected Major Risk Factors*. Geneva: World Health Organization.

Meadows, D.H., Meadows, D.L., Randers, J. and Behrens, W.W. (1972) *The Limits to Growth: A Report for the Club of Rome's Project on the Predicament of Mankind*. London: Earth Island.

Olsen, M. (2003) *Analysis of the Stockholm Convention on Persistent Organic Pollutants*. Dobbs Ferry: Oceana.

Sen, A. (1981) *Poverty and Famines: An Essay on Entitlement and Deprivation*. Oxford: Clarendon Press.

Simon, J. (1981) *The Ultimate Resource*. Princeton, NJ: Princeton University Press.

Simon, J. (1999) *Hoodwinking the Nation*. New Brunswick, USA: Transaction.

Smith, K.R., Corvalán, C.F. and Kjellström, T. (1999) 'How much global ill health is attributable to environmental factors?', *Journal of Epidemiology*, 10 (5): 573–84.

Stern, N. (2006) *The Economics of Climate Change – the Stern Review*. Cambridge: Cambridge University Press.

Sukhdev, P. (2008) *Economics of Ecosystems and Biodiversity (TEEB)*. Germany: Helmholz Association.

Trenberth, K. (1998) 'El Nino and global warming', *Journal of Marine Education*, 15 (2): 12 –18.

Weir, D. and Schapiro, M. (1981) *Circle of Poison*. San Francisco: Institute for Food and Development Policy.

World Meteorological Organization/United Nations Environmental Programme (2006) *UNEP/WMO Scientific Assessment of Ozone Depletion: 2006*. Global Ozone Research and Monitoring Project. Report no. 50.Geneva: WMO.

# Chapter 24

Alkire, S. (2003) *A Conceptual Framework for Human Security*. University of Oxford, Centre for Research on Inequality, Human Security and Ethnicity, Working Paper 2.

Baylis, J., Wirtz, J. Cohen, E. and Gray, C. (eds) (2007) *Strategy in the Contemporary World*. (2nd edn), Oxford: Oxford University Press.

Booth, K. (1991) 'Security and emancipation', *Review of International Studies*, 17 (4): October.

Booth, K. (ed.) (2005) *Critical Security Studies and World Politics*. Boulder, CO: Lynne Rienner.

Booth, K. (2007) *Theory of World Security*. Cambridge: Cambridge University Press.

Burke, A. (2007) *What Security Makes Possible: Some Thoughts on Critical Security Studies*, Department of International Relations, RSPAS, Australian National University, Canberra. Working Paper 2007/1.

Buzan, B. (1987) *An Introduction to Strategic Studies: Military Technologies and International Relations*. London: Macmillan Press Ltd.

Buzan, B. (1991) *People, States and Fear: An Agenda for International Security Studies in the Post-Cold War Era*. (2nd edn), London: Harvester Wheatsheaf.

Buzan, B. (1996) 'The timeless wisdom of realism', in S. Smith et al. (eds), *International Theory: Positivism and Beyond*. Cambridge: Cambridge University Press.

Buzan, B., Wæver, O. and de Wilde, J. (1997) *Security: A New Framework for Analysis*. Boulder, CO: Lynne Rienner Publishers.

Doyle, M. and Ikenberry, J. (1997) 'Introduction' in M. Doyle and J. Ikenberry (eds), *New Thinking in International Relations Theory*. Oxford: Westview Press.

Dunne, T. (2007) 'Realism', in J. Baylis and S. Smith (eds), *The Globalization of World Politics: An Introduction to International Relations*. New York: Oxford University Press.

Enloe, C. (1990) *Bananas, Beaches and Bases: Making Feminist Sense of International Politics*. Berkeley, CA: University of California Press.

Ferrell, R. (1999) 'Reorienting American Foreign Policy', in R. McMahon and T. Paterson (eds), *Problems in American Civilization: The Origins of the Cold War*. (4th edn), Boston: Houghton Mifflin Company.

Foster, G. (2005) 'A new security paradigm', *World Watch*. World Watch Institute: January/February.

Gallie, W. (1956) 'Essentially contested concepts', *Proceedings of the Aristotelian Society*, 56.

Gimbel, J. (1976) *The Origins of the Marshal Plan*. Bloomington, IN: Stanford University Press.

Kennan, G. (1947) *The Sources of Soviet Conduct.* Available at http://www.historyguide.org/europe/kennan.html (Last accessed 14/06/10).

Kennedy-Pipe, C. (2007) 'Gender and security', in A. Collins (ed.), *Contemporary Security Studies.* Oxford, Oxford University Press.

Klein, B. (1994) *Strategic Studies and World Order: The Global Politics of Deterrence.* Cambridge: Cambridge University Press.

Krause, K. and Williams, M. (1997) *Critical Security Studies: Concepts and Cases.* London: UCL Press Ltd.

Liddell Hart, B. (1967) *Strategy: The Indirect Approach.* (4th edn), London: Faber & Faber.

Mahnken, T. and Maiolo, J. (eds) (2008) *Strategic Studies: A Reader.* London: Routledge.

Mathews, J. (1989) 'Redefining security', *Foreign Affairs*, Spring.

Morgenthau, H.J. (1960) *Politics Among Nations. The Struggle for Power and Peace*, (3rd edn), New York: McGraw-Hill.

Mutimer, D. (1999) 'Beyond strategy', in C. Snyder (ed.), *Contemporary Security and Strategy.* London: Macmillan Press Ltd.

Nye, J. and Lynn-Jones, S. (1988) 'International security studies: A report of a conference on the state of the field', *International Security*, 12 (4): Spring.

Sheehan, M. (2005) *International Security: An Analytical Survey.* London: Lynne Rienner Publishers.

Smith, S. (2000) 'Conceptualizing security in the last 20 years', in S. Croft and T. Terriff (eds), *Critical Reflections on Security and Change.* London: Frank Cass.

Smith, S. (2002) 'The contested concept of security', *The Concept of Security Before and After September 11.* Singapore: Institute of Defence and Strategic Studies. Working Paper 23, May.

Spellman, W.M. (2006) *A Concise History of the World since 1945: States and People.* New York: Palgrave Macmillan.

Tarry, S. (1999) 'Deepening and widening: an analysis of security definitions in the 1990s', *Journal of Military and Strategic Studies*, 2 (1): Fall.

Terriff, T., Croft, S., James, L. and Morgan, P. (2001) *Security Studies Today.* Cambridge: Polity Press.

Tickner, A. (1992) *Gender in International Relations: Feminist Perspectives on Achieving Global Security.* New York, Columbia University Press.

Tickner, A. (1995) 'Inadequate providers? A gendered analysis of state and security', in J. Camilleri, A. Jarvis and A. Paolini (eds), *The State in Transition.* Boulder, CO: Lynne Rienner Publishers.

Ullman, R. (1983) 'Redefining security', *International Security*, 8 (1): Summer.

United Nations Development Program (UNDP) (1994) *Human Development Report.* New York: Oxford University Press.

Walt, S. (1991) 'The renaissance of security studies', *International Studies Quarterly*, 35 (2): June.

Wolfers, A. (1952) 'National security as an ambiguous symbol', *Political Science Quarterly*, LXVII (4): December.

## Chapter 25

Babst, D. (1972) 'A force for peace', *Industrial Research*, April.

Brown, C. (2001) *Understanding International Relations.* (2nd edn), New York: Palgrave.

Claude, I. (1984) *Swords into Plowshares.* (4th edn), New York: Random House.

Doyle, M. (1983) 'Kant, liberal legacies, and foreign affairs, part I', *Philosophy and Public Affairs*, 12.

Doyle, M. (2004) 'Liberal internationalism: peace, war and democracy'. Available at http://nobelprize.org/nobel_prizes/peace/articles/doyle/index.html, 22 June 2004. (Last accessed 10 October 2008).

Kegley, C. (1993) 'The neo-idealist moment in international studies? Realist myths and the new international realities', *International Studies Quarterly*, 37.

Knutsen, T. and Moses, J. (1996) 'Democracy and peace: A more skeptical view', *Journal of Peace Research*, 33 (1).

Macmillan, J. (2003) 'Beyond the separate democratic peace', *Journal of Peace Research*, 40 (2).

Morgenthau, H.J. (1960) *Politics Among Nations. The Struggle for Power and Peace*, (3rd edn), New York: McGraw-Hill.

Rummel, R. (1997) *Power Kills: Democracy as a Method of Nonviolence.* New Jersey: Transaction Publishers.

Russett, B. (1993) *Grasping the Democratic Peace: Principles for a Post-Cold War World.* New Jersey: Princeton University Press.

Steigerwald, D. (1994) *Wilsonian Idealism in America.* London: Cornell University Press.

Tucker, R. (2004) 'Woodrow Wilson's new diplomacy', *World Policy Journal*, Summer.

Weart, S. (1998) *Never at War: Why Democracies Will Not Fight One Another.* New Haven: Yale University Press.

Wilson, P. (1995) 'Introduction', in D. Long and P. Wilson (eds), *Thinkers of the Twenty Years' Crisis: Inter-War Idealism Reassessed.* Oxford: Oxford University Press.

## Chapter 26

Ashley, R. (1981) 'Political realist and human interests', *International Studies Quarterly*, 25 (2).

Bayour, E. (2005) 'Occupied territories, resisting women: Palestinian women political prisoners', in J. Sudbury (ed.), *Global Lockdown: Race, Gender and the Prison Industrial Complex*. New York: Routledge.

Booth, K. (1991) 'Security and emancipation', *Review of International Studies*, 17 (4): October.

Boulding, E. (1994) *Building Peace in the Middle East: Challenges for States and Civil Society*. Boulder, CO: Lynne Rienner.

Burke, A. (2007) *What Security Makes Possible: Some Thoughts on Critical Security Studies*. Working Paper 2007/1, Canberra, Department of International Relations, Australian National University.

Conquest, R. (1987) *The Harvest of Sorrow: Soviet Collectivisation and the Terror – Famine*. New York: Oxford University Press.

Cox, R. (1981) 'Social forces, states and world orders: beyond international relations theory', *Millennium: Journal of International Studies*, 10.

Devetak, R. (2005) 'Critical theory', in S. Burchill et al. (eds), *Theories of International Relations*. (3rd edn), Basingstoke: Palgrave Macmillan.

Dutt, M. (1998) 'Reclaiming a human rights culture: feminism of difference and alliance', in E. Shohat (ed.), *Talking Visions*. Cambridge: MIT Press.

Enloe, C. (2004) *The Curious Feminist: Searching for Women in the New Age of Empire*. Ewing, NJ: University of California Press.

Farr, K. (2007) 'Extreme war rape in today's civil-war-torn states', Paper presented at the annual meeting of the American Sociological Association, New York, 11 August 2007. Available at http://www.allacademic.com/meta/p183097_index.html (Last accessed 23 March 2009).

Gilbert, M. (1986) *The Holocaust: A History of the Jews of Europe During the Second World War*. New York: Holt, Rinehart and Winston.

Hansen, L. (2000) 'The Little Mermaid's silent security dilemma and the absence of gender in the Copenhagen School', *Millennium: Journal of International Studies*, 29 (2).

Kaldor, M. (2006) *New and Old Wars: Organised Violence in a Global Era*. (2nd edn), Cambridge: Polity.

Krause, K. and Williams, M. (1997) *Critical Security Studies: Concepts and Strategies*. London: Routledge.

Milmo, C. (2004) 'UN Troops buy sex from teenage refugees in Congo camp', *The Independent*, 25 May.

Ruggie, J. (1998) *Constructing the World Polity: Essays of International Institutionalisation*. London: Routledge.

Steans, J. and Pettiford, L. (2005) *Introduction to International Relations: Perspectives and Themes*. (2nd edn), Harlow: Pearson Education.

Terriff, T., Croft, S., James, L. and Morgan, P. (2001) *Security Studies Today*. Cambridge: Polity Press.

Tickner, A. (1992) *Gender in International Relations: Feminist Perspectives on Achieving Global Security*. New York: Columbia University Press.

Wæver, O. (1995) 'Securitization and desecuritization', in R.D. Lipschutz (ed.), *On Security*. New York: Columbia University Press.

Wendt, A. (1995) 'Constructing international politics', *International Security*, 20 (1): Summer.

Wyn-Jones, R. (1999) *Security, Strategy, and Critical Theory*. London: Lynne Rienner Publishers Inc.

## Chapter 27

Annan, K. (1999), interviewed by Djibril Diallo (Editor-in-Chief), *Choices Magazine*, Publication of the United Nations Development Programme: December.

Buzan, B. (2002) in A. Mack (ed.), 'A report on the feasibility of creating an annual human security report', *Program on Humanitarian Policy and Conflict Research*. Harvard University.

Canadian Peace Alliance (1992) *Transformation Moment: A Canadian Vision of Common Security*. The report of the Citizens' Inquiry into Peace and Security, March.

Clarke, I. (1997) *Globalisation and Fragmentation*. Oxford: Oxford University Press.

Commission on Global Governance (1995) *Our Global Neighbourhood*. Oxford: Oxford University Press.

Hampson, F.O. (2008) 'Human security', in P. Williams (ed.), *Security Studies: An Introduction*. London: Routledge.

Hataley, T.S. and Nossal, K.R. (2004) 'The limits of the human security agenda: the case of Canada's response to the Timor crisis', *Global Change, Peace and Security*, 16 (1): February.

Held, D., McGrew, A., Goldblatt, D. and Perraton, J. (1999) *Global Transformations: Politics, Economics and Culture*. Bloomington, IN: Stanford University Press.

King, G. and Murray, C. (2002) 'Rethinking human security', *Political Science Quarterly*, 116 (4): Winter.

MacFarlane, S.N. and Khong, Y.F. (2006) *Human Security and the UN: A Critical History*. Bloomington, IN: Indiana University Press.

Milanovic, B. (2003) 'The two faces of globalisation: against globalisation as we know it', *World Development*, 31 (4).

Neufeld, M. (2004) 'Pitfalls of emancipation and discourses of security: reflections on Canada's security with a human face', *International Relations*, 18 (1).

Ogata, S. (2001) 'State security – human security', *Fridtjof Nansen Memorial Lecture 2001*. Available at http://www.unu.edu/hq/public-lectures/ogata.pdf.

Ogata, S. (2002) *Globalisation and Human Security*. Weatherhead Policy Forum: Columbia University, 27 March.

Owen, T. (2008) 'The uncertain future of human security in the UN', *International Social Science Journal*, 59 (1).

Paris, R. (2001) 'Human security: paradigm shift or hot air?' *International Security*, 26 (2): Autumn.

Peng Er, L. (2006) 'Japan's human security role in Southeast Asia', *Contemporary Southeast Asia*, 28 (1).

United Nations Development Programme (UNDP) (1994) *New Dimensions of Security*, Human Development Report. Available at http://hdr.undp.org/en/reports/global/hdr1994/chapters (Last accessed 18 February 2009).

United Nations Development Programme (2000) *Human Rights and Human Development*, Human Development Report. Available at http://hdr.undp.org/en/reports/global/hdr2000/.

United Nations General Assembly (2005) 'In larger freedom: towards development, security and human rights for all', *Report of the Secretary-General, A/59/2005*, 21 March.

# Chapter 28

Baldauf, S. (2009) 'Pirates, Inc.: inside the booming Somali business', *Christian Science Monitor*, 31 May. Available at http://www.csmonitor.com/World/Africa/2009/0531/p06s03-woaf.html.

Bodansky, Y. (2001) *Bin Laden: The Man who Declared War on America*. New York: Random House.

Boutros-Ghali, B. (1995) Concluding statement by the United Nations Secretary-General Boutros Boutros-Ghali of the United Nations Congress on Public International Law: 'Towards the twenty-first century: international law as a language for international relations', 13–17 March, New York.

Commission on Post-Conflict Reconstruction (2003) 'Play to win'. Final report of the bi-partisan Commission on Post-Conflict Reconstruction, Washington, DC/Arlington, VA: Center for Strategic and International Studies (CSIS) and the Association of the US Army (AUSA). Available at http://www.csis.org/isp/pcr/playtowin.pdf.

Farah, D. (2003) 'Liberian Is accused of harboring Al Qaeda', *The Washington Post*, 15 May.

Foreign Policy (2009) Available at http://www.foreignpolicy.com/articles/2009/06/22/the_2009_failed_states_index.

Ghani, A. and Lockhart, C. (2008) *Fixing Failed States: A Framework for Rebuilding a Fractured World*. New York: Oxford University Press.

Harsch, E. (2003) 'Africa builds its own peace forces', *Africa Recovery*, 17 (3): 1, 14–16, 18–20.

Hoffman, S. (2006) *Chaos and Violence: What Globalization, Failed States, and Terrorism Mean for U.S. Foreign Policy*. New York: Rowman and Littlefield.

International Crisis Group (2008) 'Somalia: to move beyond the failed state'. Available at http://www.crisisgroup.org/home/index.cfm?id=5836&l=1.

Johnson, R. (2005) 'Reconstructing the Balkans: The effects of a global governance approach', in M. Lederer and P. Müller (eds), *Criticizing Global Governance*. New York: Palgrave Macmillan, pp. 177–94.

Keohane, R. (2002) 'The globalization of informal violence, theories of world politics, and the "liberalism of fear"', *Dialog-IO*, Spring: 29–43.

Kurop, M.C. (2001) 'Al Qaeda's Balkan links', *The Wall Street Journal Europe*, 1 November. Available at http://www.balkanpeace.org/hed/archive/nov01/hed4304.shtml.

Mallaby, S. (2002) 'The reluctant imperialist: terrorism, failed states, and the case for American empire', *Foreign Affairs*, 81 (2): 2–7.

Middleton, R. (2008) 'Somali piracy: a growing issue for Africa and the international community', London: Chatham House. Available at http://www.chathamhouse.org.uk/publications/papers/view/-/id/665/.

National Intelligence Council (2004) *Mapping the Global Future: Report of the National Intelligence Council's 2020 Project*. Washington, December.

Rice, X. (2009) 'Somali pirates "hit jackpot" with seizure of huge oil tanker', *The Guardian*, 1 December.

Rotberg, R.R. (2003) 'The failure and collapse of nation-states. Breakdown, prevention and fear', in R. Rotberg (ed.), *When States Fail: Causes and Consequences*. Princeton, NJ: Princeton University Press, pp. 1–49.

Sandole, D. (1992) 'Conflict resolution in the post-Cold War era: dealing with ethnic violence in the new Europe', Working Paper No.6, Institute for Conflict Analysis and Resolution, George Mason University, October.

Thürer, D. (1999) 'The "Failed State" and international law', *International Review of the Red Cross*, 836: 731–61.

World Bank (2003) *Breaking the Conflict Trap: Civil War and Development Policy*. New York: World Bank.

## Chapter 29

Fainaru, S. (2007) 'Where military rules don't apply; Blackwater's security force in Iraq given wide latitude by state department', *The Washington Post*, 20 September.

Foreign Policy (2008) 'The Failed States Index'. Available at http://www.foreignpolicy.com/story/cms.php?story_id=4350 (Last accessed 5 April 2009).

Fund for Peace (2009) 'Promoting sustainable peace'. Available at http://www.fundforpeace.org/web/index.php (Last accessed 5 April 2009).

Goddard, S. (2001) *The Private Military Company: A Legitimate International Entity Within Modern Conflict* (Thesis). Faculty of the US Army Command and General Staff College, Fort Leavenworth, Kansas.

Griffen, M. (2000) 'Where angels fear to tread: trends in international intervention', *Security Dialogue*, 31.

International Crisis Group (2008) 'Somalia: to move beyond the failed state', *Africa Report No.147*, 23 December.

Jackman, T. (2006) 'US contractor fired on Iraqi vehicles for sport, suit alleges', *The Washington Post*, 17 November.

Kaldor, M. (2001a) *Beyond Militarism, Arms Races and Arms Control*, Social Science Research Council. Available at http://www.ssrc.org/sept11/essays/kaldor.htm (Last accessed 28 April 2009).

Kaldor, M. (2001b) 'Wanted: global politics', *The Nation*, 5 November.

Kaldor, M. (2006) *New and Old Wars: Organised Violence in a Global Era*. (2nd edn), Oxford: Polity.

Machiavelli, N. and Goodwin, R. (2003) *The Prince*. Branden Books.

Nathan, L. (1997) 'Lethal weapons: why Africa needs alternatives to hired guns', *Track Two*, 6 (2): August.

National Intelligence Council (2004) *Mapping the Global Future: Report of the National Intelligence Council's 2020 Project*, Washington, December.

Nevers, R. De (2006) 'The Geneva Conventions and new wars', *Political Science Quarterly*, 121 (3): Fall.

Prendergast, J. (1999) 'Angola's deadly war: dealing with Savimbi's Hell on Earth', *Special Report No.55*, United States Institute of Peace, October. Available at http://www.usip.org/index.html.

Protocol Additional to the Geneva Conventions of 12 August 1949, and Relating to the Protection of Victims of International Armed Conflicts, art. 47, December 7, 1978, 1125 UNTS 3.

Sandole, D. (1992) 'Conflict resolution in the post-Cold War era: dealing with ethnic violence in the new Europe', *Working Paper No.6*. Institute for Conflict Analysis and Resolution, George Mason University, October.

Schreier, F. and Caparini, M. (2005) *Privatising Security: Law. Practice and Governance of Private Military and Security Companies*, Geneva Centre for the Democratic Control of Armed Forces, Occasional Paper, 6: March.

United Nations General Assembly (UNGA) (1989) 'International Convention Against the Recruitment, Use, Financing and Training of Mercenaries', *A/RES/44/34*, 4 December.

## Chapter 30

Albright, D. and Hinderstein, C. (2005) 'Unraveling the A.Q. Khan and future proliferation networks', *Washington Quarterly*, Spring.

Alison, G. (1971) *Essence of Decision: Explaining the Cuban Missile Crisis*. Boston, MA: Little Brown.

Brodie, B. (1946) 'Implications for military policy', in B. Brodie (ed.) *The Absolute Weapon*. New York: Harcourt Brace.

Edwards, R. (2005) 'Hiroshima Bomb may have carried hidden agenda', *New Scientist*, 21: July.

Freedman, L. (1989) *The Evolution of Nuclear Strategy*. (2nd edn), Basingstoke: Macmillan.

Freedman, L. (2007) 'The future of strategic studies', in J. Baylis et al. (eds), *Strategy in the Contemporary World*. (2nd edn), Oxford: Oxford University Press.

Gaddis, J.L. (1974) 'Was the Truman Doctrine a real turning point?', *Foreign Affairs*, January.

Gaddis, J.L. (1982) *Strategies of Containment: A Critical Appraisal of Postwar American National Security Policy*. New York: Oxford University Press.

Goldblat, J. (1990) 'The fourth review of the NPT', *Security Dialogue*, 21 (4).

Hanson, M. (2005) 'The future of the NPT', *Australian Journal of International Affairs*, 59 (3): September.

Kucia, C. (2002) 'Pentagon memo raises possibility of nuclear testing', *Arms Control Association*, December. Available at www.armscontrolassociation.org (Last accessed 10 August 2009).

McNamara, R. (1963) 'McNamara on strategy: a change in policy', *Bulletin of the Atomic Scientists*, April: 36.

Powaski, R.E. (2000) *March to Armageddon: The United States and the Nuclear Arms Race, 1939 to the Present*. Oxford: Oxford University Press.

Suri, J. (2005) *Power and Protest: Global Revolution and the Rise of Détente*. Cambridge, MA: Harvard University Press.

*Time* (1954) 'The nation: the new focus', 29 March.

Waltz, K. (1981) 'The spread of nuclear weapons: more may be better', *Adelphi Papers*, No. 171. London: International Institute of Strategic Studies.

www.americanrhetoric.com/speeches/jfkamericanuniversityaddress.html (Last accessed 3 August 2009).

## Chapter 31

Brown, M.E. Coté, O.R., Lynn-Jones, S.M. and Miller, S.E. (eds) (1998) *Theories of War and Peace: An International Security Reader*. Cambridge, MA: The MIT Press.

Claude, I.L. (1962) *Power and International Relations*. New York: Random House.

Claude, I.L. (2006) 'Collective security as an approach to peace', in D.M. Goldstein, P. Williams and J.M. Shafritz (eds), *Classic Readings and Contemporary Debates in International Relations*. Belmont, CA: Thomson Wadsworth.

Goulding, M. (1993) 'The evolution of United Nations peacekeeping', *International Affairs*, 69 (3).

Hilderbrand, R.C. (1990) *Dumbarton Oaks: The Origins of the United Nations and the Search for Post-War Security*. NC: University of North Carolina Press.

James, A. (1990) *Peacekeeping in International Politics*. London: Macmillan.

Johnson, H.C. and Niemeyer, G. (1954) 'Collective security: the validity of an ideal', *International Organisation*, 8.

Mackinlay, J. (2000) 'Defining warlords', in T. Woodhouse and O. Ramsbotham (eds), *Peacekeeping and Conflict Resolution*. London: Frank Cass Publishers.

May, E.R. and Laios, A.E. (1998) *The Dumbarton Oaks Conversations and the United Nations, 1944–1994*. Cambridge, MA: Harvard University Press.

Mearsheimer, J. (1994/5) 'The false promise of international institutions', *International Security*, 19 (3): Winter.

O'Neil, J.T. and Rees, N. (2005) *United Nations Peacekeeping in the post-Cold War Era*. Abingdon: Routledge.

President Bill Clinton, address to the UN General Assembly, 27 September 1993.

Schachter, O. (1991) *International Law in Theory and Practice*. London: Martinus Nijhoff.

Schweigman, D. (2001) *The Authority of the Security Council under Chapter VII of the UN Charter*. The Hague, the Netherlands: Kluwer Law International.

UN (1956) *Resolution 998 in the Official Records of the General Assembly, First Emergency Special Session, Supplement No.1 (A/3354)*, November 1956.

United Nations Security Council (UNSC) (1992) *UNSC Resolution S/RES/794*, 3 December.

## Chapter 32

ABC News [2002] 'Islamic countries condemn Israel', *ABC News Online,* Monday, 1 April 2002.

Ajami, F. (1993) 'The summoning', *Foreign Affairs*, 72 (4).

Ali, I. (2008) 'Shi'ite-Sunni strife paralyzes life in Pakistan's Kurram tribal agency, *Terrorism Focus*, 5 (17): 30 April.

Blanchard, C. (2008) 'The Islamic traditions of Wahhabism and Salafiyya', *CRS Report for Congress, RS21695*, 24 January.

CNN.com, 'Bush says it is time for action', 6 November 2001. Available at http://archives.cnn.com/2001/US/11/06/ret.bush.coalition/index.html.

Ganor, B. (2002) 'Defining terrorism: is one man's terrorist another man's freedom fighter?', *Police Practice and Research*, 3 (4).

'Growing concerns about extremism, continuing discontent with the US'. Available at http://www.pewglobal.org/reports (Last accessed 13 August 2009).

Huntington, S (1993) 'The clash of civilizations', *Foreign Affairs*, Summer.

Huntington, S. (1996) *The clash of civilizations and the remaking of world order*. London: Simon and Schuster.

Center Conversations, 'Religion, culture, and international conflict after September 11: a conversation with Samuel P. Huntington', *Ethics and Public Policy Center*. Available at http://www.eppc.org/docLib/20030504_CenterConversation14.pdf (Last accessed 11 June 2002).

Laqueur, W. (1987) *The Age of Terrorism*. Boston, Toronto: Little, Brown and Company.

Lewis, B. (1990) 'The roots of muslim rage', *The Atlantic*, September. Available at http://www.theatlantic.com/doc/199009/muslim-rage.

Milton-Edwards, B. (2006) *Contemporary Politics in the Middle East*. (2nd edn), Cambridge: Polity Press.

Rea, T. and Wright, J. (1997) *The Arab-Israeli Conflict*. Oxford: Oxford University Press.

Said, E. and Barsamian, D. (2003) *Culture and Resistance: Conversations with Edward W. Said*. Cambridge, MA: South End Press.

Schmid, A.P. and Jongman, A. (1988) *Political Terrorism, A New Guide to Actors and Authors, Data Bases, and Literature*. New Brunswick: Transaction Publishers.

Scruton, R. (1982) *Dictionary of Political Thought*. New York: Hill and Wang.

Senghaas, D. (1998) *The Clash Within Civilizations: Coming to terms with cultural conflicts*. London: Routledge.

Toft, M.D. (2003) *The Geography of Ethnic Violence: Identity, Interests, and the Indivisibility of Territory.* Princeton, NJ: Princeton University Press.

Welch, D.A. (1997) 'The "Clash of Civilizations" thesis as an argument and as a phenomenon', *Security Studies*, 6 (4).

Wickham, C.R. (2004) 'The path to moderation: strategy and learning in the formation of Egypt's Wasat Party', *Comparative Politics*, 36 (2).

Worth, R. (2007) *Open for Debate: the Arab–Israeli Conflict*. New York: Marshall Cavendish Benchmark.

## Chapter 33

Bell, D. (1960) *The End of Ideology: On the Exhaustion of Political Ideas in the Fifties.* Glencoe, US: Free Press.

Bull, H. (1977) *The Anarchical Society. A Study of Order in World Politics*. London: Macmillan.

Gilpin, R. (2001) *Global Political Economy: Understanding the International Economic Order.* Princeton, NJ: Princeton University Press.

Godson, R. and Williams, P. (1998) 'Strengthening cooperation against transsovereign crime: a new security imperative', *Transnational Organized Crime*, 4 (3&4), Autumn/Winter: 321–55.

Hobson, J. (1915) *Towards International Government.* New York: Macmillan Company.

Keohane, R. (2002) *Power and Governance in a Partially Globalized World*. London: Routledge.

Mitrany, D. (1975) *The Functional Theory of Politics.* London: Robertson.

Negri, A., Hardt, M. and Zolo, D. (2008) *Reflections on Empire* (transl. E. Emery) Cambridge: Polity.

Noble, R. (2003) 'Interpol's way: thinking beyond boundaries and acting across borders through member countries police forces', speech delivered at Tufts University, Boston, 1 March. Available at http://www.interpol.int/public/ICPO/speeches/SG20030301.asp (Last accessed 10.10.09).

Smith, R. (2008) 'Cyberstates and the sovereignty of virtual communities' in E. Kofman and G. Youngs (eds), *Globalization: Theory and Practise.* (3rd edn), London and New York: Continuum.

Taylor P. (1991) 'The European Community and the state: assumptions, theories and propositions', *Review of International Studies*, 17: 109–125.

UIA (2009) *Yearbook of International Organizations 2008-9*. Munich: K.G. Saur.

Waltz, K. (1979) *Theory of International Politics*. Reading, MA: Addison-Wesley.

Wendt, A. (1992) 'Anarchy is what states make of it', *International Organization*, 46 (2): 391–425.

Wendt, A. (2003) 'Why a world state is inevitable', *European Journal of International Relations*, 9 (4): 491–542.

Woolf, L. (1916) *International Government*. New York: Brentano's.

# Index

First World War 7
  Idealism and 134
  imperialism as cause 54–5
  importance 58, 59
  international relations and 58–60
  Liberal Idealism and 517
  Liberal ideas emerging from 120
  Liberalism and 134
  mass killings 520
  Utopian ideas emerging from 120
  Versailles, Treaty of 101
fiscal policies 336
fission bombs 617
fixed exchange rates 140, 337
Flexible Response, USA 621
FLM (Free Lebanon Militia) 600
floating exchange rates 336–7
FLS (Forward Looking Strategies) 391
FNLA (National Front for the Liberation of Angola)
      309, 595
Food and Agriculture Organisation (FAO) 73, 243, 258, 475
force
  democratisation by 433–5
  international concerns on, Cold War and 70
  use in self-defence only 641, 642, 647
forces, UN peacekeeping 644
Foreign Affairs and Security Policy, High Representative
      for, EU 396
foreign direct investment (FDI) 109
foreign investment 368
Foreign Ministers, Council of, OIC 265, 266
foreign policies
  cooperation, regional integration 300
  democratisation 139
  human rights 456–7
  making 7
  United States see United States
foreigners 185, 411, 415
Forest Principles 479
Former Yugoslav Republic of Macedonia see Macedonia
Fortress Europe 280, 282
Forward Looking Strategies (FLS) 391
Foster, Gregory 497
Foster-Lloyd, William 473
Foucault, Michel 193, 417
Fourth World 375
Fox, Vicente 283–4
fragmentation 23, 106–7, 110, 706–7
Framework Convention on Climate Change (FCCC)
      480, 481, 486
France
  Britain and, trade barriers 324
  Concert of Europe 62

constitution 526
Crimean War 59
decolonisation and 82
European integration and 694
European Union and 213
external expansionism 405
external militarism 405
First World War 59
G7/8 membership 350
G20 Group membership 357
hijab, banning wearing of 395
internal authoritarianism 405
international economic system 324
League of Nations and 64, 245
national identity 402, 403
NATO membership 613
nuclear tests 629
nuclear weapons 70, 79
reign of terror 405
Revolution see French Revolution
UN Security Council membership 75, 143, 246, 258
Francophonie 244, 263
Frank, A.G. 368–9
Frankfurt School 173, 176–9, 508, 540–1, 543, 546, 703
Free Lebanon Militia (FLM) 600
free market economy **706**
free-rider problem 471
free trade 61, 140, 163, 328
Free Trade Area of the Americas (FTAA) 284–5, 287
Free Trade Area of the Asia–Pacific (FTAAP) 292
Free Trade Commission, NAFTA 285
Freedman, Lawrence 623
freedom
  of choice 180
  economic 139
  from fear 553, 560–8
  fundamental freedoms, UN Charter 147
  individuals 514
  political 139
  of the seas 476
  from want 553–6, 560–8
freedom fighters 667
Freedom House 302–3
French Revolution 29–30, 50, 56, 157, 445
Frente Nacional de Libertação de Angola (FNLA)
      309, 595
'frontline', women on 388
FSF (Financial Stability Forum) 357
FTAA (Free Trade Area of the Americas) 284–5, 287
FTAAP (Free Trade Area of the Asia–Pacific) 292
Fukuyama, Francis 36, 37, 42, 98, 427, 559
full democracy 423
functional factors, failed states 576